W9-BVT-976

Caribbean Sea

ATLANTIC OCEAN

PACIFIC OCEAN

ATLANTIC OCEAN

CENTRAL AMERICA

Galápagos Islands (Ecuador)

Gulf of Panama

N

VENEZUELA
Maracaibo, Santa Marta, Barranquilla, Cartagena, Coro, Valencia, Caracas, Barquisimeto, Barcelona, Cumaná, Maracay, Maturín, Mérida, Barinas, Ciudad Guayana, Cúcuta, San Cristóbal, Ciudad Bolívar, Bucaramanga, Tunja, Villavicencio, Bogotá, Medellín, Manizales, Pereira, Cali, Neiva, Florencia

GUYANA — Georgetown
SURINAME — Paramaribo
FRENCH GUIANA (France)

COLOMBIA
Boa Vista

ECUADOR Quito, Esmeraldas, Pasto, Ibarra, Ambato, Riobamba, Portoviejo, Guayaquil, Cuenca, Machala, Loja, Piura, Iquitos

Macapá

Negro R.
Amazon R.
Manaus Santarém **Belém** São Luis

Fortaleza
Teresina
Natal
João Pessoa
Recife
Maceió
Aracaju
Salvador

PERU
Chiclayo, Cajamarca, Trujillo, Pucallpa, Chimbote, Huánuco, Cerro de Pasco, Rio Branco, Porto Velho, Huancayo, **Lima**, Ayacucho, Cusco, Ica

Madeira R.
Tapajós R.
Xingu R.
Tocantins R.
São Francisco R.

BRAZIL

Trinidad
BOLIVIA
Juliaca, La Paz, Santa Cruz, Arequipa, Cochabamba, Tacna, Oruro, Sucre, Arica, Potosí, Iquique, Tarija

Cuiabá, **Brasília**, Goiânia, Uberlândia, Campo Grande

Belo Horizonte
Vitória

Paraguay R.

San Salvador de Jujuy, Salta, **PARAGUAY**, Asunción, Pedro Juan Caballero, Campinas, **São Paulo**, **Rio de Janeiro**, Niterói, Santos, Ciudad del Este, San Miguel de Tucumán, Posadas, Encarnación, **Curitiba**, Antofagasta, Copiapó, Resistencia, Corrientes, Florianópolis, Catamarca, Santiago del Estero, La Rioja, Santa Fe, **CHILE**, La Serena, Córdoba, Rivera, **Porto Alegre**

Paraná R.

San Juan, Mendoza, Salto, Paysandú, Valparaíso, Santiago, San Luis, Rosario, **URUGUAY**, Montevideo, Rancagua, Talca, **Buenos Aires**, Río de la Plata, Concepción, Chillán, **ARGENTINA**, Bahía Blanca, Mar del Plata, Temuco, Neuquén

Puerto Montt

Comodoro Rivadavia

Falkland Islands (Islas Malvinas) (U.K.)

Strait of Magellan
Punta Arenas
Ushuaia

South America

Elevation in Feet
15,000
10,000
5,000
2,000
1,000
0
Below sea level

Major Cities
⊛ Capital city
■ Over 5,000,000
● 1,000,000–5,000,000
■ 500,000–999,999
● 250,000–499,999
■ 100,000—249,999
○ Less than 100,000

0 — 250 — 500 mi.
0 — 250 — 500 km

ENCYCLOPEDIA OF

LATIN AMERICAN HISTORY AND CULTURE

EDITORIAL BOARD

ENCYCLOPEDIA OF

LATIN AMERICAN HISTORY AND CULTURE

SECOND EDITION

Volume 6

T–Z

Jay Kinsbruner
EDITOR IN CHIEF

Erick D. Langer
SENIOR EDITOR

CHARLES SCRIBNER'S SONS
A part of Gale, Cengage Learning

Detroit • New York • San Francisco • New Haven, Conn • Waterville, Maine • London

Encyclopedia of Latin American History and Culture

Jay Kinsbruner, Editor in Chief
Erick D. Langer, Senior Editor

For product information and technology assistance, contact us at
Gale Customer Support, 1-800-877-4253.
For permission to use material from this text or product,
submit all requests online at **www.cengage.com/permissions.**
Further permissions questions can be emailed to
permissionrequest@cengage.com

While every effort has been made to ensure the reliability of the information presented in this publication, Gale, a part of Cengage Learning, does not guarantee the accuracy of the data contained herein. Gale accepts no payment for listing; and inclusion in the publication of any organization, agency, institution, publication, service, or individual does not imply endorsement of the editors or publisher. Errors brought to the attention of the publisher and verified to the satisfaction of the publisher will be corrected in future editions.

Library of Congress Cataloging-in-Publication Data

Encyclopedia of Latin American history and culture / Jay Kinsbruner, editor in chief; Erick D. Langer, senior editor. -- 2nd ed.
   p. cm. --
  Includes bibliographical references and index.
   ISBN 978-0-684-31270-5 (set) -- ISBN 978-0-684-31441-9 (vol. 1) -- ISBN 978-0-684-31442-6 (vol. 2) -- ISBN 978-0-684-31443-3 (vol. 3) -- ISBN 978-0-684-31444-0 (vol. 4) -- ISBN 978-0-684-31445-7 (vol. 5) -- ISBN 978-0-684-31598-0 (vol. 6)
   1. Latin America--Encyclopedias. I. Kinsbruner, Jay.

F1406.E53 2008
980.003--dc22   2008003461

Gale
27500 Drake Rd.
Farmington Hills, MI, 48331-3535

978-0-684-31270-5 (set)   0-684-31270-0 (set)
978-0-684-31441-9 (vol. 1)   0-684-31441-X (vol. 1)
978-0-684-31442-6 (vol. 2)   0-684-31442-8 (vol. 2)
978-0-684-31443-3 (vol. 3)   0-684-31443-6 (vol. 3)
978-0-684-31444-0 (vol. 4)   0-684-31444-4 (vol. 4)
978-0-684-31445-7 (vol. 5)   0-684-31445-2 (vol. 5)
978-0-684-31598-0 (vol. 6)   0-684-31598-X (vol. 6)

This title is also available as an e-book.
ISBN-13: 978-0-684-31590-4 ISBN-10: 0-684-31590-4
Contact your Gale, a part of Cengage Learning, sales representative for ordering information.

Printed in the United States of America
1 2 3 4 5 6 7 12 11 10 09 08

CONTENTS

TÁBARA, ENRIQUE (1930–).
Enrique Tábara (*b.* 1930), Ecuadorian artist. Tábara studied painting at the School of Fine Arts in Guayaquil, his native city, and began to paint abstract compositions in 1954. As a young painter, he was influenced by the constructivist movement (founded by Russian artist Vladimir Tatlin in 1913), of which he learned through the work of Uruguayan painter Joaquín Torres García and Ecuadorean painter Manuel Rendón. With the aid of a fellowship from the Ecuadorian House of Culture the following year, he moved to Barcelona, where he studied at the School of Fine Arts and participated in the city's Hispanic-American Biennial (1955). He was influenced by Spanish informalism, from which he derived heavy impastos and textures, applying them to a repertoire of pre–Conquest-inspired themes: Ecuadorian Indian traditions, including rattlesnakes, mirrors, feathers, hieroglyphics, pyramids, and other motifs. During his years in Barcelona, his circle of friends included artists such as André Breton and Joan Miró. He was also connected to the members of the Spanish postwar movement called Dau al Set, which included Antoni Tapies and Manolo Millares. Like the surrealists and dadaists, the work of the Dau al Set artists dialogued with both the conscious and the unconscious human mind.

Returning to Ecuador in 1964, Tábara founded VAN, an Ecuadorian artists' movement against figurative indigenist art (1968). In the early 1970s he turned to a new figuration, often depicting human limbs across his canvases. He won a gold medal at the First Salon of Drawing, Watercolor, and Tempera at the House of Culture in Quito (1970). Throughout his career, his work has been shown at the Museo Rufino Tamayo in Mexico City, the Museum of Modern Art in Paris, and the Modern Art Museum in Bogotá. He has been the recipient of many prestigious awards, including the Swiss Abstract Painting Prize in 1960 and the Gold Brush of Ecuador in 1999. As of 2007, he still lives in Guayaquil, although he frequently visits Barcelona.

See also **Art: The Twentieth Century; Torres García, Joaquín.**

BIBLIOGRAPHY

González, Areán; Carlos Antonio; and Enrique Tábara. *Tábara.* Quito, Ecuador: Doble O Producciones, 1990.

Tábara, Enrique. *Tábara.* Guayaquil, Ecuador: E. Tábara, 1993.

Traba, Marta. *Museum of Modern Art of Latin America: Selections from the Permanent Collection* (1985), pp. 114–115.

MARTA GARSD

TABLADA, JOSÉ JUAN (1871–1945).
José Juan Tablada (*b.* 3 April 1871; *d.* 2 August 1945), Mexican writer. Born in Mexico City, José Juan de Aguilar Acuña Tablada y Osuna first published in *El Universal* in 1892; by the time of his death, more than 10,000 of his poems, essays, chronicles, novels, works of literary criticism, memoirs, and diaries had appeared under more than fifteen pseudonyms. Founder of *La Revista Moderna,* Tablada was strongly influenced by the French poet Charles Baudelaire. A trip to Japan in 1900 led to his introduction of the

Japanese haiku into Spanish, influencing Ezra Pound and the Anglo-American imagist group, as well as poets in his own language. From 1911 to 1912 Tablada lived in Paris. When he returned to Mexico he became a supporter of Victoriano Huerta, for which he was forced into exile in New York in 1914.

Tablada was the first to publish ideographic poems in Spanish; his book *Li-Po y otros poemas: Poemas ideográficos* appeared in 1920, following closely upon Guillaume Apollinaire's *Calligrammes*. Mexican president Venustiano Carranza named Tablada a member of the diplomatic service in Colombia and Venezuela, but Tablada soon resigned and returned to New York in 1920. He went back to Mexico in 1935, but spent his last years in New York, where he died. His inventive, often ingenious imagery, anticipating vanguard tendencies, gave new life to widely varied but common poetic themes, including Mexican landscapes, natural elements, and travel impressions. Tablada's reputation was solidly reestablished in the mid-twentieth century by a new generation of Mexican writers and critics, including Octavio Paz.

See also **Literature: Spanish America.**

BIBLIOGRAPHY

Eduardo Mitre, "Los ideogramas de José Juan Tablada," in *Revista Iberoamericana* 40, no. 89 (October–December 1974): 675–679.

Mark Cramer, "José Juan Tablada and the Haiku Tradition," in *Romance Notes* 16 (1975): 530–535.

Allen W. Phillips, "Cuatro poetas hispanoamericanos entre el modernismo y la vanguardia," in *Revista Iberoamericana* 55, nos. 146–147 (January–June 1989): 427–449.

Additional Bibliography

Lozano Herrera, Rubén. *José Juan Tablada en Nueva York: Búsqueda y hallazgos en la crónica.* México, D.F.: Universidad Iberoamericana, 2000.

Lozano Herrera, Rubén. *Las veras y las burlas de José Juan Tablada.* México, D.F.: Universidad Iberoamericana, 1995.

KEITH MCDUFFIE

TABOADA, ANTONINO (1814–1883).

A military man born in Santiago del Estero, Argentina, Antonino Taboada opposed Juan Manuel de Rosas's administrations (1828–1833 and 1835– 1852) and battled the last federalist *caudillos* in the northern provinces in the 1860s. The child of an affluent and politically prominent family, Taboada was educated in Buenos Aires, where he tightened his links to the anti-Rosas unitarists led by General Juan Galo Lavalle. Persecuted by the Rosas police, in 1839 Taboada fled to Montevideo, Uruguay. Between 1840 and 1841 Taboada led battles in Entre Ríos and Córdoba, where he was captured and sent to prison in Buenos Aires. Taboada escaped and returned to Montevideo. In 1849 he moved to Santiago de Chile and reinforced his political contacts with exiled politicians such as Bartolomé Mitre and Domingo Faustino Sarmiento.

After the fall of the Rosas regime in 1852, Taboada came back to Santiago del Estero. In 1853 Taboada defeated the troops led by General Celedonio Gutierrez, the governor of Tucumán, who had partially occupied Santiago. When Bartolomé Mitre became president of Argentina in 1862, the Taboada family was instrumental in making Santiago del Estero a liberal, pro-Mitre bastion in a mostly anti-Mitre region. Taboada organized the national army in the northwestern provinces and directed successive military campaigns against the *montoneras* (irregular troops) led by the last federalist *caudillos*. Taboada's troops claimed a major victory in April 1867: In Pozo de Vargas, La Rioja, they defeated the troops led by the rebel *caudillo* Felipe Varela. Historians consider that battle a landmark in Argentina's nation-making process.

See also **Argentina: The Nineteenth Century; Lavalle, Juan Galo; Mitre, Bartolomé; Rosas, Juan Manuel de; Sarmiento, Domingo Faustino; Unitario.**

BIBLIOGRAPHY

Primary Source

Los Taboada: Luchas de organización nacional, documentos seleccionados y coordinados, 3. vols. Buenos Aires: Bernabé y Cía., 1937.

Secondary Sources

Bazán, Armando. *Historia del noroeste argentino.* Buenos Aires: Plus Ultra, 1995.

Tenti de Laitán, María Mercedes. *Historia de Santiago del Estero.* Santiago del Estero, Argentina: Copistería Sigma, 2000.

VALERIA MANZANO

TABORGA PIZARRO, MIGUEL DE LOS SANTOS (1833–1906).

Miguel de los Santos Taborga Pizarro was a Bolivian polemicist, historiographer, and cleric. Born on July 5, 1833, into a prominent Creole family, Taborga studied at the San Cristóbal seminary. He was ordained in 1857 and later earned his doctorate in theology at the Universidad San Francisco de Xavier. In 1898 Taborga was named Archbishop of Sucre (La Plata). He was a staunch defender of traditional Catholic doctrines through the newspapers *El Amigo de la Verdad* and *El Cruzado*, arguing against the secularization of Bolivian society. In his essay "El positivismo, sus errores y falsas doctrinas" (Positivism, its errors and false doctrines, 1905), Taborga criticized positivism for its reliance on scientific experimental methods, rather than other forms of knowledge.

Taborga was politically active during the Republican period. He participated in the constituent assembly of 1871, served on a mission to Europe, and was twice elected a senator from Chuquisaca. Taborga involved himself in Bolivia's territorial conflict with Chile. He responded to a Chilean bishop with a memorandum citing historical evidence that the disputed territory belonged to Bolivia. He later wrote the poem "Oración por la Patria."

As a historiographer, Taborga concerned himself with national history, writing several treatises on the subject. He was named a corresponding member of the Royal Spanish Academy. Notable works include: *Crónica de la revolución del 8 de septiembre* (1887), *Documentos inéditos para la historia de Bolivia* (1891), *Un capítulo de la historia de la época colonial* (1905), and the posthumously published *Estudios históricos* (1908). Taborga died on April 30, 1906.

See also **Catholic Church: The Modern Period; Positivism; War of the Pacific.**

BIBLIOGRAPHY

Arze, José Roberto. *Figuras eclesiásticas en Bolivia*. La Paz: Los Amigos del Libro, 1985.

Finot, Enrique. *Historia de la literatura boliviana*, 3rd edition. La Paz: Gisbert, 1964.

Guzmán, Augusto. *El ensayo en Bolivia*. La Paz: Los Amigos del Libro, 1983.

MIGUEL CENTELLAS

TACNA.

Tacna, southernmost department in Peru. Forming part of the country's Pacific littoral, Tacna is bordered by the Peruvian departments of Moquegua and Puno on the north, Bolivia on the east, and Chile on the south. It is divided into two provinces, Tacna and Tarata; the capital city of the department, also called Tacna, had a population of approximately 174,336 according to the 1993 census. Copper mining, cattle raising, and irrigated agriculture, including cotton and alfalfa, are the major economic activities.

Tacna, along with the former Peruvian province of Arica, has a significant position in the history of Latin American international relations. Chile occupied the two provinces during the War of the Pacific (1879–1883), and then, under the provisions of the Treaty of Ancón, was to retain possession of them for ten years, after which a plebiscite would determine whether the inhabitants wished to be citizens of Chile or Peru. The plebiscite was not held, however, and from 1893 to 1929 the Tacna–Arica controversy strained relations between the two countries as Chile continued to occupy the disputed territory. As a last resort, Chile and Peru asked the United States to mediate the dispute. The two nations could never settle on a protocol for the plebiscite, however, and by treaty in 1929 the countries agreed to divide the provinces; Peru reincorporated Tacna, and Chile annexed Arica.

The controversy surrounding the Chilean occupation of Tacna and Arica, and the surrender of Arica to Chile, continues to affect relations between the countries. The city of Tacna has become a powerful national symbol for Peru and is called "the heroic city" to honor the patriotism exhibited by its citizens during the war and throughout the Chilean occupation.

See also **Arica; Peru: Peru Since Independence; Tacna-Arica Dispute.**

BIBLIOGRAPHY

Dennis, William Jefferson. *Tacna and Arica* (1931), is dated but useful. In the *Collección Documental de la Independencia del Perú*, see vol. 23 (1971) for Tacna.

Morris Ayca, María, and Oscar Pantty Neyra. *Espacio y conciencia Geográfica en Tacna*. Peru: Ediciones Tercer Milenio, 1999.

Pinto Huaracha, Miguel. *Geografía del Perú, siglo XIX: Moquegua y Tacna*. Lima,: Seminario de Historia Rural

Andina, Universidad Nacional Mayor de San Marcos, 2002.

Yepes, Ernesto. *Un plebiscito imposible: Tacna y Arica, 1925–1926*. Lima: Ediciones Análisis, 1996.

WILLIAM E. SKUBAN

Novak, Fabián. *Las conversaciones entre Perú y Chile para la ejecución del Tratado de 1929*. San Miguel [Peru]: Pontificia Universidad Católica del Perú, Instituto de Estudios Internacionales, Fondo Editorial, 2000.

WILLIAM F. SATER

TACNA-ARICA DISPUTE. Tacna-Arica Dispute, a diplomatic confrontation between Chile and Peru arising out of the War of the Pacific (1879–1884). The Treaty of Ancón (1883) specified that Chile could occupy the provinces of Tacna and Arica until 1894, when a plebiscite would determine their status. The winner would retain the two provinces; the loser would receive a monetary indemnity. Unfortunately, the treaty did not specify the conditions under which the two nations would conduct the plebiscite. The government in Santiago, hoping to retain sovereignty over the disputed territory, utilized this issue to refuse to hold the election, infuriating Peru, which felt despoiled. Peru repeatedly sought the intervention of others in the Pan-American movement, a strategy Chile successfully defeated. When the Pan-American Union could not force Santiago to cooperate, Peru contemplated using force. Meanwhile, Chile attempted to convert the Peruvian population to its own cause. Failing in its attempt to win over the Peruvians, Chile then tried to populate the disputed territory with Chilean citizens while simultaneously attempting to repress its Peruvian residents. In 1929, during the Carlos Ibáñez administration, Chile and Peru signed the Treaty of Lima and finally settled the dispute: Chile retained Arica, while Peru won Tacna. The resolution of this dispute ended the animus between Santiago and Lima but infuriated Bolivia, which remained without a seacoast.

See also **Arica; Ibáñez del Campo, Carlos; Tacna.**

BIBLIOGRAPHY

William J. Dennis, *Tacna and Arica: An Account of the Chile-Peru Boundary Dispute and the Arbitrations by the United States* (1931).

William F. Sater, *Chile and the United States: Empires in Conflict* (1990), pp. 76–78, 94, 96–97, 101.

Additional Bibliography

Fernández Valdés, Juan José. *Chile y Perú: Historia de sus relaciones diplomáticas entre 1879 y 1929*. Santiago de Chile: ADICA: RIL Editores, 2004.

TACUARÍ, BATTLE OF. Battle of Tacuarí (9 March 1811), a major engagement in the Paraguayan struggle for independence. The January 1811 defeat of a *porteño* invasion force near the town of Paraguarí brought a sense of great pride to the defending Paraguayan militiamen. Led by colonels Juan Manuel Gamarra and Manuel Antanacio Cavañas, these men were normally more accustomed to subsistence farming than to fighting professional soldiers. Once victorious, however, they were more willing to see themselves as masters of their own destiny, even to the point of questioning the instructions of their *peninsular* governor, Bernardo Velazco, as they pursued the *porteños* southward beyond the Río Tebicuary. Despite orders to the contrary from Velazco, they started to fraternize with their *porteño* opponents. General Manuel Belgrano, chief of the invasion force, sent gifts to Cavañas and Gamarra, as well as political missives outlining the goals of the patriots' cause, while his troops took up defensive positions along the shallow Río Tacuarí in the extreme south of Paraguay.

In the end, prodded by Velazco, Cavañas ordered a general assault against the *porteño* position on 9 March 1811, after which Belgrano immediately sued for peace. In turn, he received generous terms from Cavañas and was allowed to depart Paraguay with his army intact. Velazco arrived at the Tacuarí ten days later expecting to preside over Belgrano's surrender and was much abashed to learn of Colonel Cavañas's actions. The majority of Paraguayans, however, knew better. The militia's resistance to Belgrano was less an act of servility to Spanish authority than it was an affirmation of localism. Two months after the victory at Tacuarí, this sentiment was reenacted in a *cuartelazo* (barracks revolt) that brought national independence to Paraguay.

See also **Belgrano, Manuel; Paraguarí, Battle of; Paraguay: The Nineteenth Century.**

BIBLIOGRAPHY

Harris Gaylord Warren, *Paraguay: An Informal History* (1949), pp. 145–147.

John Hoyt Williams, *Rise and Fall of the Paraguayan Republic, 1800–1870* (1979), pp. 24–27.

Additional Bibliography

Ezcurra Medrano, Alberto. *La independencia del Paraguay y otros ensayos.* Buenos Aires: Instituto Nacional de Investigaciones Históricas Juan Manuel de Rosas, 1999.

Giménez, Ovidio. *Vida, época y obra de Manuel Belgrano.* Buenos Aires: Librería "El Ateneo" Editorial, 1993.

THOMAS L. WHIGHAM

TAFT AGREEMENT (1904).

The Taft Agreement (1904) was a concession made by the administration of President Theodore Roosevelt to the republic of Panama. Under the Hay–Bunau-Varilla Treaty (1903), Panama granted the United States the right to "act as if it were sovereign" in the newly created Canal Zone. Roosevelt issued an executive order establishing U.S. custom houses in the Canal Zone. Panamanian businessmen, fearing competition from rival commercial enterprises, protested. Roosevelt dispatched Secretary of War William Howard Taft to Panama to settle the matter. The resulting Taft Agreement provided that the Panama Canal Zone would be permitted to import only those materials deemed necessary for the construction of the canal, the use of its employees, or sale to transiting ships. Canal Zone commissasaries would not be open to the general public, though enforcement of this rule was sometimes lax. The Taft Agreement expired in 1924.

See also **United States-Latin American Relations.**

BIBLIOGRAPHY

Anguizola, Gustave. *The Panama Canal: Isthmian Political Instability.* Washington, DC: University Press of America, 1977.

La Feber, Walter. *The Panama Canal: The Crisis in Historical Perspective.* New York: Oxford University Press, 1989.

Additional Bibliography

Arosemena, Diógenes A. *La Cuestión canalera, de 1903 a 1936.* Panama: [s.n.], 1975.

Woolsey, L. H. "The Sovereignty of the Panama Canal Zone." *American Journal of International Law* 20:1 (January 1926): 117–124.

LESTER D. LANGLEY

TAHUANTINSUYU.

Tahuantinsuyu or Tawantisuyu, the name given by the Incas to their empire. Meaning "Land of the Four Quarters," it derives from the Quechua words for "four" (*tawa*) and "quarter" (*suyu*). The empire of Tahuantinsuyu stretched in the north from the Ancasmayo River, on the modern border between Ecuador and Colombia, to the Maule River in the south, just below the modern city of Santiago, Chile, a distance of 2,500 miles. The *suyus* were the four main administrative units of the empire, and each was named for a province within it: Chinchasuyu, the northwestern quarter; Antisuyu, the northeastern quarter; Contisuyu, the southwestern quarter; and Collasuyu, the southeastern quarter. The *suyus* were originally conceived as four equal units, with the city of Cuzco located at the central point where they all came together. Over time, however, the expansion of the empire increased the territory of the *suyus* unequally.

See also **Incas, The.**

BIBLIOGRAPHY

John H. Rowe, "Inca Culture at the Time of the Spanish Conquest," in *Handbook of South American Indians,* vol. 2 (1946), p. 262.

Additional Bibliography

Rostworowski de Diez Canseco, María. *History of the Inca Realm,* trans. Harry B. Iceland. New York: Cambridge University Press, 1999.

Someda, Hidefuji. *El imperio de los Incas: Imagen del Tahuantinsuyu creada por los cronistas.* Lima: Pontificia Universidad Católica del Perú, Fondo Editorial, 1999.

Villanueva Sotomayor, Julio. *El Tahuantinsuyu: La propiedad privada y el modelo curacal de producción.* Lima: Ediciones Luciérnaga, 1994.

GORDON F. MCEWAN

TAILORS' CONSPIRACY. *See* Inconfidência dos Alfaiates.

TAÍNOS.

Taínos is the name given to a group of people Columbus encountered at first landfall in the Caribbean. Also known as Island Arawak, they are believed to have migrated from South America between 200 BCE and 1200 CE, and shared the islands of the Caribbean with the Ciboney and Carib peoples at the time of the Spanish incursion. Mainly agriculturalists, some aided the Spanish in procuring food and shelter. Their numbers were decimated within a century by illness, malnutrition, overwork, and social collapse precipitated by Spanish colonization of their islands. Knowledge of this group is from the early Spanish chronicles, archaeologists, and linguists. Today, many Caribbean people, in particular inhabitants of Puerto Rico, can claim Taíno ancestry. Interest in Taíno history and culture continues to increase as Taíno descendants organize and seek recognition.

See also **Columbus, Christopher.**

BIBLIOGRAPHY

Louis A. Pérez, *Cuba: Between Reform and Revolution* (1988), esp. pp. 16–20.

Antonio M. Stevens Arroyo, *Cave of the Jagua: The Mythological World of the Taínos* (1988).

Franklin W. Knight, *The Caribbean, the Genesis of a Fragmented Nationalism,* 2d ed. (1990), esp. pp. 7–23.

Samuel M. Wilson, *Hispaniola: Caribbean Chiefdoms in the Age of Columbus* (1990).

Additional Bibliography

Robiou Lamarche, Sebastián. *Taínos y caribes: Las culturas aborígenes antillanas.* San Juan, Puerto Rico: Editorial Punto y Coma, 2003.

Moscoso, Francisco. *Tribu y clases en el Caribe antiguo.* San Pedro de Macorís, República Dominicana: Universidad Central del Este, 1986.

JOYCE E. NAYLON

TAIRONA. Tairona refers to a diverse archaeological complex distributed on the northern and northwestern faces of the Sierra Nevada de Santa Marta, Colombia. The term is also used to refer to an ancient indigenous ethnic group from a territory (*provincia*) located near the upper Don Diego and Buritaca rivers. Tairona also refers to a cultural area (*cultura Tairona*) characterized by a style of pre-Hispanic gold, pottery, and architectural remains dating from 1000 CE until the Spanish conquest.

Three periods of development are recognized for the archaeological complex.

The Early Tairona period is divided into two phases. The first phase dates from 500 BCE to 600 CE and is characterized by small fishing and farming populations that lived in independent hamlets on the coast. An archaeological site example is Puerto Gaira. The second phase dates between 600 CE and 900 CE and is characterized by the development of inland settlements with more emphasis on agricultural production and larger populations that led to the colonization of the Sierra Nevada de Santa Marta. A chiefdom society developed, accompanied by the use of stone in construction of dwellings and pathways connecting the town of the chief with the neighboring hamlets. More variation in the burial practices within and between regions is observed in this period. Burial offerings include gold, pottery, staffs, beads, and other artifacts of stone. Archaeological site examples of this phase are Mamorón, Nahuanjue, and Cinto.

The second period is the Middle, or Classic, Tairona (1000–1501). This period is characterized by the consolidation of the colonized regions, the development of towns, stone road systems, irrigation and agricultural terrace systems, complex chiefdom hierarchies, strong microvertical trade, and an increase in the regional specialization of food and artifact production (pottery, gold, beads, axes, and other lithic artifacts). Examples of urban sites are Ciudad Perdida and Pueblito. The political divisions of these chiefdoms were mainly religious in character, with a chief and/or priest as a head. The principal chiefdoms that controlled relatively large areas during this period were referred to by the Spanish as the Bondas, Posigueicas, Betomas, and Taironas.

The last period is the Conquest (1501–1600). This period is characterized by a decline in population through disease and intensive warfare with the Spanish; collapse of chiefdom societies; abandonment of villages, towns, and road systems; and creation by the survivors of highland refuge areas. A small number of descendants of the chiefdoms that formed the Tairona complex live today in the highlands of the Sierra Nevada and are known as the Kogy (Kogi) or Kaggaba (Kágaba) Indians.

See also **Archaeology.**

BIBLIOGRAPHY

For illustrations of the material culture as well as a general review, see Henning Bischof, "Tairona Archaeology," in *Arte de la Tierra: Taironas* (1991). For a synthesis of the development of Ciudad Perdida and Pueblito, see Jacques Aprile-Gniset, *La ciudad colombiana*, vol. 1, *Prehispánica, de conquista e indiana* (1991). For a perspective on the descendants of the Tairona chiefdoms, see Augusto Oyuela-Caycedo, "Ideology and Structure of Gender Spaces: The Kaggaba Indians," in *The Archaeology of Gender*, edited by D. Walde and N. D. Willows (1991), pp. 327–335.

Additional Bibliography

Bray, Warwick. "Gold, Stone, and Ideology: Symbols of Power in the Tairona Tradition of Northern Colombia," in *Gold and Power in Ancient Costa Rica, Panama, and Colombia: A Symposium at Dumbarton Oaks, 9 and 10 October 1999*, edited by Jeffrey Quilter and John W. Hoopes. Washington, DC: Dumbarton Oaks Research Library and Collections, 2003.

Cardale de Schrimpff, Marianne, and Leonor Herrera, eds. *Caminos precolombinos: Las vías, los ingenieros y los viajeros*. Bogotá: Instituto Colombiano de Antropología e Historia: Ministerio de Cultura, 2000.

Legast, Anne. *El animal en el mundo mítico tairona*. Bogotá: Fundación de Investigaciones Arqueológicas Nacionales, Banco de la República, 1987.

Soto Holguín, Alvaro. *La ciudad perdida de los tayrona: Historia de su hallazgo y descubrimiento*. Colombia: Neotrópico, 1988.

Wilson, David J. *Indigenous South Americans of the Past and Present: An Ecological Perspective*. Boulder, CO: Westview Press, 1999.

AUGUSTO OYUELA- CAYCEDO

TAJES, MÁXIMO (1852–1912).

Máximo Tajes (*b.* 23 November 1852; *d.* 21 November 1912), military leader and president of Uruguay (1886–1890). Tajes began his military career as a distinguished soldier in the army while it was at war with Paraguay. He rose rapidly to the rank of captain (1875) and lieutenant colonel (1880), became minister of war and the navy in 1882, and assumed the presidency in 1886. Tajes pursued the course that had moved Colonel Lorenzo Latorre, who became dictator in 1876, and General Máximo Santos (president, 1882–1886), two men who implanted what has come to be known in Uruguayan history as "militarism." After the resignation of Santos in 1886, however, Tajes followed the advice of Dr. Julio Herrera y Obes and offered himself as constitutionally elected president in order to manage peacefully the transition from militarism to "civilism," a task he fulfilled satisfactorily. His administration took place during the "era of Reus," named after Emilio Reus, a young Spanish financier widely known at the time.

See also **Herrera y Obes, Julio; Latorre, Lorenzo; Uruguay: Before 1900.**

BIBLIOGRAPHY

Enrique Méndez Vives, *El Uruguay de la modernización* (1976).

Washington Reyes Abadie and Andrés Vázquez Romero, *Crónica general del Uruguay*, vol. 3 (1984).

Gonzalo Aguirre Ramírez, *La revolución del Quebracho y la conciliación: De Ellauria a Tajes, 1873–1886* (1989).

Additional Bibliography

Arocena Olivera, Enrique. *La rebeldía de los doctores: El Uruguay del fusionismo al militarismo, 1851–1886*. Montevideo: Librería Linardi y Risso, 1998.

Nahum, Benjamin, and Alberto Nin. *La crisis de 1890*. Montevideo: Ediciones de la Banda Oriental, 1998.

JOSÉ DE TORRES WILSON

TAKALIK ABAJ.

Takalik Abaj, a Preclassic Mesoamerican site on the lower Pacific slope of southwestern Guatemala in the modern department of Retalhuleu, is an early transitional site with precursors of the Olmec influence, pure Olmec, and very early Maya traits. Several hundred pieces of sculpture document the evolution of styles from earliest ground or incised features on otherwise unshaped boulders, through monumental Olmec sculpture such as that of the Veracruz–Tabasco Olmec heartland, to portrait stelae with long-count Maya-like numerals and inscriptions in glyphs that were perhaps ancestral to both central Mexican and Maya glyphs.

The settlement was occupied as early as the third millennium BCE, and after its development consisted of numerous earthen mounds arrayed on wide terraces cut into the sloping hillside. The mounds occasionally have adobe brick or facings of stone cobbles, but no masonry architecture.

The sculptured monuments include many Olmec-style pieces covering the full range of Olmec art, if one includes a possible corner from a large rectangular altar. Some alignments on Str. 7, a large platform, may be for astronomical observation. Monument 23 is a typical Olmec colossal head. Late Preclassic "potbelly" sculpture (Monument 40) ties this area to the northern lowlands. Later, Maya portrait stelae appear without evolved precedents at the site. Their long-count dates, 7.16.0.0.0– 7.16.19.17–19 on Stela 2 and 8.3.2.10.5 and 8.4.5.17.11 (126 CE) from Stela 5 (c. 38–18 BCE) are among the very earliest recorded long counts known. The portrait stelae are possible early evidence of the growing permanence of dynastic rule in the Maya area. Stela 5 shows a personage holding a ceremonial serpent, a motif of ruling power seen on later stelae elsewhere as the two-headed serpent bar.

See also **Archaeology; Maya, The; Olmecs.**

BIBLIOGRAPHY

Graham, John R. "Discoveries at Abaj Takalik, Guatemala." *Archaeology* 30 (1977): 196–197.

Graham, John R., R. F. Heiser, and E. M. Shook. "Abaj Takalik 1976: Exploratory Investigations." In *Studies in Ancient Mesoamerica, III.* University of California Archaeological Research Facility Contribution no. 36 (1978), pp. 85–114.

WALTER R. T. WITSCHEY

TALAMANTES, MELCHOR DE (1765– 1809).

Melchor de Talamantes (*b.* 10 January 1765; *d.* 3 May 1809), Mercedarian friar, precursor of Mexican independence. Born in Lima, Talamantes earned his doctorate in theology at the University of San Marcos. In 1807, Viceroy José de Iturrigaray (1742–1815) charged him with establishing the boundaries of Texas. He gained prestige and influence with important people in the capital. In 1808 he supported the proposal of the *ayuntamiento* (city council) to establish a junta of authorities and submitted a plan to form a national congress. He was imprisoned during the 1808 coup; among his papers was found a plan for independence. He died in San Juan de Ulúa, while on his way to Spain, the victim of yellow fever.

See also **Iturrigaray, José de; Mexico: The Colonial Period; Mexico, Wars and Revolutions: Coup d'État of 1808.**

BIBLIOGRAPHY

Melchor De Talamantes, *Biografía y escritos póstumos* (1909).

José María Miquel I Vergés, *Diccionario de insurgentes* (1969), p. 560; *Diccionario Porrúa de historia, geografía y biografía de México,* vol. 3 (1986), p. 2822.

Additional Bibliography

Hamnett, Brian R. "Process and Pattern: A Re-Examination of the Ibero-American Independence Movements, 1808–1826." *Journal of Latin American Studies* 29:2 (May 1997): 87–120.

VIRGINIA GUEDEA

TALAMBO AFFAIR.

Talambo Affair, a local incident in northern Peru in 1863 that had international repercussions. Because of the strained diplomatic relations between Spain and some of its former colonies, an isolated altercation resulted in an armed confrontation between a Spanish fleet and allied forces of four South American republics (Bolivia, Chile, Ecuador, and Peru) in 1866.

In 1860 the owner of the Talambo estate in Chiclayo had contracted through an agent to hire approximately 175 Basque immigrants to work in the estate's cotton fields. In August 1863 two Basque farmers quarreled with the estate's owner and his men. In the ensuing fight two immigrants were killed and several imprisoned. This incident led to a diplomatic complaint by the Spanish embassy and government.

The commander of the Spanish fleet, allegedly performing a scientific expedition off the Peruvian coast at the time, pressed the Peruvian government of Juan Antonio Pezet to apologize and pay past debts to Spanish nationals. The Spaniards seized the guano-producing islands of Chincha and threatened to bomb the port of Callao in 1865. Pezet tried to find a peaceful solution by supporting the Vivanco-Pareja Treaty. Other military leaders and the public, however, considered Pezet's actions a form of capitulation and ousted him.

See also **Pezet, Juan Antonio.**

BIBLIOGRAPHY

Jorge Basadre, *Historia de la República del Perú,* vol. 3 (1963).

David Werlich, *Peru: A Short History* (1976).

Additional Bibliography

Cerda Catalán, Alfonso. *La Guerra entre España y las repúblicas del Pacífico, 1864–1866: El bombardeo de Valparaíso y el combate naval del Callao*. Providencia, Chile: Editorial Puerto de Palos, 2000.

Novak, Fabián. *Las relaciones entre el Perú y España, 1821–2000*. Lima: Pontificia Universidad Católica del Perú, Instituto de Estudios Internacionales, Fondo Editorial, 2001.

ALFONSO W. QUIROZ

TALAVERA, MANUEL (1875–1950).

Manuel Talavera (*b.* 8 December 1875; *d.* 27 July 1950), Paraguayan politician and businessman. Talavera was a dynamic member of the Colorado Party after the 1947 civil war from which the Colorados emerged victorious. A member of the right-wing *Guion rojo* (Red Banner), Talavera led his faction to victory in the aftermath of the Colorado Party convention in November 1947. The Guionists had actually lost the internal election by two votes, but Talavera's friend and presidential candidate, Natalicio González, also a *Guion rojo*, took control of the Colorado Party by force. After winning the February 1948 elections without opposition, González was sworn in as president on 15 August 1948. In February 1949 a group of dissenters in the party, led by Felipe Molas López, succeeded in overthrowing Gonzalez. Talavera's political career ended after the coup.

See also **Paraguay, Political Parties: Colorado Party.**

BIBLIOGRAPHY

Osvaldo Kallsen, *Asunción y sus calles* (1974).

Paul Lewis, *Paraguay Under Stroessner* (1980).

Additional Bibliography

Prieto Yegros, Leandro. *Natalicio y el "Guión Rojo."* Asunción: Editorial Cuadernos Republicanos, 1997.

MIGUEL A. GATTI

TALAVERA, NATALÍCIO (1839–1867).

Natalicio Talavera (*b.* 1839; *d.* 14 October 1867), Paraguayan poet and journalist. Born in Villarrica, Talavera became independent Paraguay's first published poet. He studied in his native town and in Asunción, where he came to the attention of Ildefonso Bermejo, a Spanish publicist who had been contracted by the Carlos Antonio López government to launch a new state newspaper and other cultural projects. Under Bermejo's tutelage, Talavera became a first-rate writer. He contributed poems and literary essays to Asunción's cultural journal, *La Aurora*, and translated Lamartine's poem *Graciela* from the French.

It was in the field of journalism, however, that Talavera most distinguished himself, regularly producing articles and essays for the state newspaper, *El Semanario de Avisos y Conocimientos Utiles*. More important, after the beginning of the War of the Triple Alliance (1864–1870), Talavera was chosen to edit *Cabichuí*, a satirical newspaper written mostly in the Guaraní Indian language. His own contributions to this periodical included biting accounts of Allied cowardice as well as clever ditties attacking the character of Emperor Dom Pedro II and his consort. Paraguayan soldiers, it was said, set these verses to music and sang them in the trenches to taunt the enemy, who lay just beyond gunshot range.

Talavera wrote a series of chronicles from the battlefield that were serialized in *El Semanario* and much later published as a book, *La guerra del Paraguay*. He himself did not survive the war, becoming ill with what was probably pneumonia as a result of hard campaigning, and died at the Paraguayan army camp of Paso Pucu.

See also **Journalism; Literature: Spanish America; Paraguay: The Nineteenth Century.**

BIBLIOGRAPHY

Natalício Talavera, *La guerra del Paraguay* (1958).

Carlos Zubizarreta, *Cien vidas paraguayas,* 2nd ed. (1985), pp. 179–181.

Additional Bibliography

Kraay, Hendrik, and Thomas Whigham, eds. *I Die with My Country: Perspectives on the Paraguayan War, 1864–1870*. Lincoln: University of Nebraska Press, 2004.

Whigham, Thomas. *The Paraguayan War. Volume 1.* Lincoln: University of Nebraska Press, 2002.

THOMAS L. WHIGHAM

TALLER DE GRÁFICA POPULAR
(TGP). Taller de Gráfica Popular (TGP), Mexican artists' collaborative. Founded in 1937 by Leopoldo Méndez, Luis Arenal, and Pablo O'Higgins, this popular graphics workshop is a center for the collective production of art with sociopolitical content. Sharing the post-Revolutionary idealism of the Mexican muralists, the TGP aimed to reach as broad an audience as possible, primarily through the dissemination of inexpensive wood- and linoleum-block prints. Although still extant in the early 2000s, the collaborative was most prominent in the 1930s and 1940s, an era when populist struggles reached their apogee worldwide. In this period it published over 45,000 prints, including posters, broadsheets, and portfolios; these works became known internationally through exhibitions. The TGP, which attracted such artists as Mexicans Raúl Anguiano, Alberto Beltrán, José Chávez Morado, and Alfredo Zalce, and Americans Elizabeth Catlett and Mariana Yampolsky, became a center for preservation of Mexico's strong tradition in the graphic arts.

See also **Art: The Twentieth Century; O'Higgins, Pablo.**

BIBLIOGRAPHY
Hannes Meyer, ed., *El Taller de Gráfica Popular* (1949).

Judith Keller, *El Taller de Gráfica Popular* (1985).

Museo De Palacio De Bellas Artes, Museo Nacional De La Estampa, and Galería Jose Velasco, *50 años Taller de Gráfica Popular* (1987).

Dawn Ades, "The Taller de Gráfica Popular," in *Art in Latin America: The Modern Era, 1820–1980* (1989).

Additional Bibliography
60 años TGP: Taller de Gráfica Popular. México: Consejo Nacional para la Cultura y las Artes: Instituto Nacional de Bellas Artes, 1997.

Ittman, John W., Innis H. Shoemaker, and others. *Mexico and Modern Printmaking: A Revolution in the Graphic Arts, 1920 to 1950.* Philadelphia: Philadelphia Museum of Art; San Antonio, TX: McNay Art Museum; New Haven, CT: in association with Yale University Press, 2006.

Prignitz-Poda, Helga. *El Taller de Gráfica Popular en México, 1937–1977.* México: Instituto Nacional de Bellas Artes, 1992.

ELIZABETH FERRER

TALLET, JOSÉ ZACARÍAS (1893–1985).
José Zacarías Tallet (*b.* 18 October 1893; *d.* 1985), Cuban journalist. Born in Matanzas, Cuba, Tallet moved to the United States with his family in 1912. He graduated with a bachelor's degree in accounting from the Heffly Institute of Commerce in New York City. Upon his return to Cuba in 1923, he participated in the Protesta de los Trece and the Grupo Minorista, both consisting of disenchanted intellectuals who called for change in Cuban letters and politics in the 1920s. He was instrumental in the formation of several leftist organizations, including the Falange de Acción Cubana, the Movimiento de Veteranos y Patriotas, and the Universidad Popular José Martí, of which he was first president. An ardent Marxist, Tallet expressed his ideas in such journals and newspapers as *Social, Alma Mater, Carteles,* and *Revista de La Habana.* In 1927–1928, he was editor of the journal *Revista de avance,* director of the magazine *El Mundo* from 1928 to 1933, and subdirector of the daily newspaper *Ahora* from 1933 to 1935.

For seventeen years Tallet taught world and Cuban history at the Escuela Profesional de Periodismo "Manuel Márquez Sterling," of which he was director (1959–1960). He is best known for his poetry, in which he treated both the social relevance and the aesthetic contribution of all sectors to Cuban culture. He received the Bonifacio Byrne Prize in Poetry (1944). His first book of poetry was *La semilla estéril* (1951) and his best-known poem is "La rumba."

After 1959 he became an enthusiastic supporter of the Castro revolution. He was a frequent contributor to *Bohemia,* one of Cuba's major journals, until his death.

See also **Cuba: The Republic (1898–1959); Cuba: Cuba Since 1959; Journalism; Literature: Spanish America.**

BIBLIOGRAPHY
Luis E. Aguilar, *Cuba 1933: Prologue to Revolution* (1972).

Harry Swan, "The Nineteen Twenties: A Decade of Intellectual Change in Cuba," in *Revista interamericana* 8, no. 2 (1978).

Instituto De Literatura y Lingüística De La Academia De Ciencias De Cuba, *Diccionario de la literatura cubana,* vol. 2 (1984), pp. 997–998, with extensive bibliography.

Leslie Wilson, "Tallet," in *Dictionary of Twentieth-Century Cuban Literature,* edited by Julio A. Martínez (1990).

Additional Bibliography

López Lemus, Virgilio. *Oro, crítica y Ulises, o, Creer en la poesía: Figuras clave de la poesía cubana del siglo XX.* Santiago de Cuba: Editorial Oriente, 2004.

Whitney, Robert. *State and Revolution in Cuba: Mass Mobilization and Political Change, 1920–1940.* Chapel Hill: University of North Carolina Press, 2001.

DARIÉN DAVIS

TAMANDARÉ, ALMIRANTE. *See* Lisboa, Joaquim Marques.

TAMARÓN Y ROMERAL, PEDRO

(c. 1695–1768). Pedro Tamarón y Romeral (*b.* ca. 1695; *d.* 21 December 1768), bishop in colonial Mexico. Tamarón was born in Villa de la Guardia, in the archdiocese of Toledo, but nothing more is known of him until 1719, when he was in Caracas with Bishop Juan José de Escalona y Calatayud. In 1758 he became bishop of Durango in Mexico. Besides some religious tracts, he wrote a long description of his bishopric (1765), based on firsthand knowledge of practically every settlement of the diocese. Because of the amount of detailed information it contains, it is one of the principal sources for colonial Nueva Vizcaya. Tamarón died in Bamos, Sinaloa, while on the first leg of a general pastoral visit.

See also **Mexico: The Colonial Period.**

BIBLIOGRAPHY

Pedro Tamarón y Romeral, *Demostración del vastísimo obispado de la Nueva Vizcaya* (1765; repr. 1937, 1958).

Additional Bibliography

Rodríguez-Sala, María Luisa. *Los gobernadores de la Nueva Viscaya del siglo XVIII: Análisis histórico-social de fuentes primarias, 1700–1769.* Durango, Mexico: I.I.H., 2000.

CLARA BARGELLINI

TAMAULIPAS. Tamaulipas, a Mexican state

bordering Texas to the north, Nuevo León to the west, the Gulf of Mexico to the east, and the states of San Luis Potosí and Veracruz to the south. It consists of forty-three counties and its state capital is Ciudad Victoria. Tamaulipas covers an area of some 31,800 square miles (just over 4 percent of Mexico's territory) and has 1,924,484 inhabitants (1980) (2.9 percent of the national total).

Evidence of gathering and hunting activities was found at the Cueva del Diablo, the earliest archaeological site in the area at about 8,000 years old. The area was occupied by Olmec, Chichimec, and Huastecan peoples and was conquered by Aztec ruler Motecuhzoma Inhuicamina around 1445–1466.

Amérigo Vespucci might have traveled the area around 1497–1502. By 1517 Francisco Hernández De Córdoba led the Spaniards to the Pánuco River but was defeated by the Huastecas. Francisco de Garay attempted the conquest in 1518, and the next year Juan de Grijalva, Alfonso Álvarez De Pineda, and Diego Camargo repeated the attempt. Finally Hernán Cortés's forces took Chila in 1522.

The area was not easily subdued, and evangelist Fray Andrés de Olmos failed in an attempt to settle the region around mid-century. Franciscan friars founded the missions of Tula, Jaumave, and Palmillas and introduced sheep and cattle in the area, displacing the Indians. By the 1730s Spanish authorities had promoted further colonization north of the Tamaulipas Sierra. In May 1748 the province of Nuevo Santander was founded by José de Escandón.

In 1810 independence sympathizers proclaimed their opposition to the Spanish government and, under the leadership of Albino García, were able to control the area in support of Father Miguel Hidalgo. By mid-1811 loyalists to the Spanish crown, commanded by Joaquín de Arredondo, had taken Aguayo. In 1817 Spanish liberal Francisco Javier Mina y Larrea landed in Soto la Marina, then took Santander and the Bajío area. In 1821 Zenón Fernández, commander of Río Verde, took up arms against the Spanish government in favor of the Plan of Iguala. Antonio Fernández de Córdoba took up the insurgent cause in Aguayo and became governor of the area. After Agustín de Iturbide's empire fell, Felipe de la Garza moved the capital to Padilla, and the area joined the Mexican federation as the new state of Tamaulipas. The capital was moved to Ciudad Victoria. In 1829 the state was invaded by Spaniard Isidro Barradas, who with Spanish support took Tampico. Manuel Mier y Terán and Antonio López de Santa Anna defended the area.

In 1830 local caudillo Francisco Vital Fernández supported the Plan of Jalapa against Vicente Guerrero.

Joining the liberals two years later, he took Matamoros and Ciudad Victoria. During the centralist administration, the area became a department. In 1836 Tamaulipas sent forces against Texas. After Santa Anna's defeat, the area was in dispute between Texas and Mexico. Supporting federalism in 1838, area residents rebelled against President Anastacio Bustamante but were defeated. In 1846 U.S. general Zachary Taylor invaded the area, and after the Mexican-American War (1846–1848) the territory between the Nueces River and the Rio Grande became part of Texas.

In 1854 José de la Garza led the region's liberal rebellion against Santa Anna in support of the Plan of Ayutla. During the Revolution of Ayutla, or the reform, there was little conservative opposition to the liberals. In 1864, however, the conservative forces of Tomás Mejía took Matamoros, and Governor Juan Nepomuceno Cortina supported Maximilian's empire. In 1866 Tamaulipas was captured by liberal general Mariano Escobedo, who took Matamoros and Tampico. In 1876 Porfirio Díaz took Matamoros and proclaimed the Plan of Palo Alto, which modified the Plan of Tuxtepec. During the Porfiriato, Tamaulipas was governed by Servando Canales (1880–1884), Alejandro Prieto (1888–1896), Alejandro Mainero (1896–1901), Pedro Argüelles (1901–1908), and Juan B. Castelló (1908–1911).

During the Mexican Revolution, the state was taken in 1914 by the forces of Pablo Gonzalez, who defeated Carrancist general Lucio Blanco. In 1917 Francisco Gonzalez Villarreal became governor, and in 1920 Emilio Portes Gil was appointed governor by the Obregonist followers of the Plan of Agua Prieta.

See also **Cortés, Hernán; Escandón, José de; Plan of Ayutla.**

BIBLIOGRAPHY

Gabriel Saldívar, *Historia compendiada de Tamaulipas* (1945).

Toribio De La Torre, *Historia general de Tamaulipas,* 2d ed. (1986).

Instituto Nacional De Estadística, Geografía E Informática, *Estructura económica del estado de Tamaulipas: Sistema de cuentas nacionales de Mexico* (1987).

María Del Pilar Sánchez Gómez, *Catálogo de fuentes de la historia de Tamaulipas* (1987).

Gabriel Saldívar, *Historia compendida de Tamaulipas* (1988).

Additional Bibliography

Cartron, Jean-Luc E., and Gerardo Ceballos. *Biodiversity, Ecosystems, and Conservation in Northern Mexico.* New York: Oxford University Press, 2005.

Contreras Islas, Isabel. *Tradición oral, mitas, y leyendas de Tamaulipas.* México, D.F.: Universidad Iberoamericana: Editorial Praxis, 2005.

Herrera Pérez, Octavio. *El norte de Tamaulipas y la conformación de la frontera México-Estados Unidos, 1835-1855.* Ciudad Vitoria: Colegio de Tamaulipas, 2006.

Robles Gil, Patricio. *The Great Tamaulipan Natural Province.* Ciudad Victoria, Tamaulipas: Tamaulipas State Government: Agrupación Sierra Madre, 2006.

CARMEN RAMOS-ESCANDÓN

TAMAYO, FRANZ (1879–1956).

Franz Tamayo, a poet, writer, and politician, is considered the dominant Bolivian intellectual of the first half of the twentieth century. Named Francisco at birth, on February 29, 1879, he later changed his name to Franz. His father was a well-known politician from the Bolivian upper classes, whereas his mother Felicidad Solares was of indigenous descent. Being of mestizo heritage—a difficult condition in the face of Bolivian racism—was the determining factor in his thinking on Bolivia's social and political future. His ideas on education, which he summarized in his *Creación de la pedagogía nacional* (1910; Creation of the National Pedagogy), stressed the importance of Indians for the cultural and social development of the country.

Tamayo's poetry, part of the Bolivian canon, is the last major example of the *modernismo* movement in Bolivian literature. However, his musical verses, infused with German philosophy and, particularly, classical erudition, convey a strong metaphysical scope that goes beyond the definition of Latin American *modernismo*. As evidenced by the titles of some of his books, such as *La Prometheida, o, las Oceánides* (The Prometheia, or The Oceanids) and *Epigramas griegos* (Greek Epigrams), Greco-Roman culture was of great significance for him.

For most of his life, Tamayo actively participated in Bolivian politics. He was a member of the congress (several mandates between 1920 and 1934), the founder of his own political party (Radical Party), a candidate for president of Bolivia (1919 and 1934), and through his newspaper articles, a persistent critic of the governments he opposed, as well as of Bolivian society. Tamayo died on July 29, 1956.

See also **Bolivia, Political Parties: Overview; Literature: Spanish America; Mestizo.**

BIBLIOGRAPHY

Works by Tamayo

Creación de la pedagogía nacional [1944], 3rd edition. La Paz: Biblioteca del Sesquicentenario de la República, 1975.

Epigramas griegos. [1945.] La Paz: Editorial Juventud, 1986.

La Prometheida, o, Las Oceánides: Tragedia Lirica. [1948.] La Paz: Editoria.

Juventud, 1986.

Scopas. [1939.] La Paz: Editorial Juventud, 1987.

Secondary Sources

Albarracín Millán, Juan. *El pensamiento filosófico de Tamayo y el irracionalismo alemán.* La Paz: Akapana, 1981.

Baptista Gumucio, Mariano. *Yo fui el orgullo: Vida y pensamiento de Franz Tamayo.* La Paz: Editorial Los Amigos del Libro, 1978.

Condarco Morales, Ramiro. *Franz Tamayo: El pensador.* La Paz: Edit. e Imp. "San José," 1989.

Díez de Medina, Fernando. *Franz Tamayo: Hechicero del ande—Retrato al modo fantástico.* La Paz: Editorial Puerta del Sol, 1944.

Mitre, Eduardo. "La voz titánica." In *De cuatro constelaciones: Ensayo y antología,* pp. 45–119. La Paz, Bolivia: Fundación BHN, 1994.

Sanjinés C., Javier. "Tamayo, observador: Negociando lo 'letrado' con lo visual." In *Convergencia de tiempos: Estudios subalternos/contextos latinoamericanos estado, cultura, subalternidad,* ed. Ileana Rodríguez, pp. 405–424. Amsterdam and Atlanta, GA: Rodopi, 2001.

LEONARDO GARCÍA-PABÓN

TAMAYO, RUFINO (1899–1991).

Rufino Tamayo (*b.* 26 August 1899; *d.* 24 June 1991), Mexican painter. Tamayo was born in Oaxaca, with its strong pre-Hispanic cultural heritage and Indian population. In 1907 his mother died and the family moved to a different neighborhood, where he began a very intense Catholic and musical education. In 1910–1911, Tamayo lived in Mexico City with his aunt. There he discovered a profound interest in drawing. He earned his living selling fruit. In 1917

he entered the National School of Fine Arts, which he abandoned because of its mediocrity and his lack of interest. Tamayo received almost no formal artistic training, but he acquired a fundamental education from drawing the pre-Hispanic objects and folk art in the Ethnographic Section of the National Museum of Archaeology.

His first solo show took place in 1926 in Mexico City. The twenty paintings and watercolors in that show already displayed his personal use of color and the peculiar images and iconography that characterized his future work. Immediately after, he moved to New York City and became acquainted with and lived near Marcel Duchamp, Stuart Davis, and Reginald Marsh. In October 1926 he opened an exhibition that was well received. In fact, Tamayo was first recognized in the United States and Europe, and only later in his own country. In 1928 he returned to Mexico and began to participate in group shows with Mexican artists. He taught painting at the National School of Fine Arts (1928–1930). Tamayo painted a series of still lifes, although in 1938 his themes centered on portraits and the feminine figure.

The 1930s were important in Tamayo's life. He painted his first mural, *The Music and the Song,* for the National School of Music (1933). In 1936 he again moved to New York, where he lived until 1944. He participated in a New York City project for the Works Progress Administration, which he never completed. At the end of the 1930s his painting began to be acclaimed because of its universal and Mexican meanings. He taught at the Dalton School in New York City and showed his paintings in several galleries. In 1949 he made his first trip to Europe, where he visited France, Spain, Holland, England, and Italy. He lived in Paris for several months. In the later decades of his life, Tamayo worked on his paintings, exploring the richness of the texture of canvas and working with sand, marble powder, and other material.

See also **Art: The Twentieth Century; Hispanics in the United States.**

BIBLIOGRAPHY

Rufino Tamayo: Myth and Magic (1979); *Rufino Tamayo* (1982).

Additional Bibliography

Paz, Octavio. *Rufino Tamayo: Tres ensayos.* México: Colegio Nacional, 1999.

Suckaer, Ingrid. *Rufino Tamayo: Aproximaciones.* México, D.F.: Editorial Praxis, 2000.

BÉLGICA RODRÍGUEZ

TAMBOR DE MINA. Tambor de Mina (or Mina) is a regional variant of the African-Brazilian religion in northern Brazil. Two cult houses founded in the first half of the nineteenth century in São Luís, Maranhão, are still in existence. The Casa das Minas, probably established by members of the royal family of Abomey, who were sold as slaves, is the rare case of a dominant Dahoman tradition in Brazil. Members worship a pantheon of *voduns* (deities) and *tóbôssi* (female child entities) organized in extended families, the most important of which are the Real (Dahoman) or Davice family, the Dambirá family, and the Quevioçô family.

The Casa de Nagô, originally a Yoruban cult house, formed strong ties with the nearby Casa das Minas. Its gods are called *voduns* (not *orishás*), and several *jeje* deities are worshipped. Six Mina cult houses were founded between 1910 and 1920. In the 1990s their number reached about 1,000 in São Luís, and dozens of others were established in the interior of Maranhão, as well as in Pará, Amazônas, and Piauí.

Tambor de Mina is distinguished by the integration of *caboclo* (indigenous) deities, the *fidalgos* (Portuguese kings), and the *gentilheiros* (Turkish warriors), as well as by particular forms of ceremonies, dress, music, ritual language, and spirit possession.

See also **Vodun, Voodoo, Vaudun.**

BIBLIOGRAPHY

Octávio Da Costa Eduardo, *The Negro in Northern Brazil: A Study in Acculturation* (1966).

Manuel Nunes Pereira, *A Casa das Minas: Culto dos voduns jeje no Maranhão,* 2nd ed., enl. (1979).

Sérgio Figueirado Ferretti, *Querbentam de Zomadonu: Etnografia da Casa das Minas* (1985).

Mundicarmo Ferretti, "Rei da Turquia, o Ferrobrás de Alexandria? A importância de um livro na mitologia de Tambor de Mina," in *Meu sinal está no teu corpo: Escritos sobre a religião dos orixás,* edited by Carlos Eugênio Marcondes de Moura (1989), pp. 202–219.

Sérgio Figueirado Ferretti, "Voduns da Casa das Minas," in *Meu sinal está no teu corpo: Escritos sobre a religião dos orixás,* edited by Carlos Eugênio Marcondes da Moura (1989), pp. 176–201.

Additional Bibliography

Ferretti, Mundicarmo Maria Rocha. *Desceu na guma: O caboclo do Tambor de Mina em um terreiro de São Luís, a Casa Fanti-Ashanti.* São Luís: EDUFMA, 2000.

Mann, Kristin, and Edna G. Bay. *Rethinking the African Diaspora: The Making of a Black Atlantic World in the Bight of Benin and Brazil.* London, Portland: F. Cass, 2001.

Moura, Carlos Eugenio Marcondes de, and João Batista dos Santos. *Somávo: O amanha nunca termina: Novos escritos sobre a religião dos voduns e orixás.* São Paulo: Empório de Produção e Comunicação, 2005.

MATTHIAS RÖHRIG ASSUNÇÃO

TAMOIO. Tamoio, Tupi term for "forebear," adopted by the Tupinambá of southern Brazil. In the mid-sixteenth century, when the Portuguese colonists of coastal Brazil began to acquire Tupinambá captives through their Tupinikin and Teminó allies, several Tupinambá groups near Guanabara Bay formed a military alliance which came to be known as the "Tamoio Confederation." While essentially an indigenous movement, the Tamoio revolt gained strength with the arrival of the French in Rio de Janeiro in 1555, who formed an alliance with the Tupinambá. Victimized by a brutal military campaign, especially under Governor Mem de Sá (1557–1572), weakened by the 1563 smallpox pandemic, and stripped of their French allies when those colonists abandoned Brazil, the Rio de Janeiro Tamoio finally succumbed in 1567, though Tamoio groups in Cabo Frio continued to resist until the 1570s. Many survivors of the war were reduced to slavery or placed in Jesuit missions, but others retreated to the interior and reconstructed village society as far away from the Portuguese as possible. By the end of the sixteenth century, the Tamoio had ceased to exist as an independent society, though Tamoio slaves were to be found on farms and plantations throughout Brazil.

See also **Sá, Mem de; Tupinambá.**

BIBLIOGRAPHY

The most complete account in English is John Hemming, *Red Gold* (1978), ch. 6–7. On early Portuguese-Indian relations, see the still-useful work of Alexander N. Marchant, *From Barter to Slavery* (1942). On the French in Rio de Janeiro, Olive P. Dickason, *The Myth of the Savage* (1984), ch. 9.

Additional Bibliography

Magalhães, Domingos José Gonçalves de, and Visconde de Araguaia. *A Confederação dos Tamoios.* 3rd ed. Rio de Janeiro: Estado do Rio de Janeiro, Secretaria de Estado de Cultura, 1994.

Quintiliano, Aylton. *A guerra dos tamoios.* 2nd ed. Rio de Janeiro, Relume Durumá, 2003.

JOHN M. MONTEIRO

TANGA. Tanga, a Portuguese word of African origin; it comes from the Quimbundo term *ntanga,* which means "cloth covering tied to the waist." This clothing was characteristic of Africa. Slaves arrived in Brazil wearing a strip of cloth they called *tanga.* The term is also used in other former Portuguese territories to mean "little skirt." It came to designate a kind of apron used by some indigenous peoples in Brazil to cover the belly and thighs. Used mainly by women to cover their private parts, the tanga can be made of cords or woven with cotton thread and may contain seeds or glass beads. It is triangular and can vary in pattern and decoration.

BIBLIOGRAPHY

Karasch, Mary C. *Slave Life in Rio de Janeiro, 1808–1850.* Princeton, NJ: Princeton University Press, 1987.

Mattoso, Katia M. de Queirós. *To Be a Slave in Brazil, 1550–1888.* Trans. Arthur Goldhammer. New Brunswick, NJ: Rutgers University Press, 1996.

Sweet, James H. *Recreating Africa: Culture, Kinship, and Religion in the African-Portuguese World, 1441–1770.* Chapel Hill: University of North Carolina Press, 2003.

CHARLOTTE EMMERICH

TANGO. Tango, Argentine dance and popular song. The tango first won international notoriety just before World War I. Its origins can be traced to the *arrabales* (poor outskirts) of Buenos Aires, some time around 1880. It was a spontaneous creation that fused the Spanish-Cuban *habanera,* the Argentine Milonga, and the dance tradition of Buenos Aires's declining black communities. The tango's definitely lower-class background meant its immediate repudiation by Argentina's upper and middle classes, but this scarcely affected its rise in popularity. In 1913 ("the tango year," in H. G. Wells's phrase), it became the focus of an intense craze in Western Europe, from where it spread to North America. Its initially rather wild steps were gradually modified into an acceptable form for European and Argentine ballrooms. The version exhibited by Rudolph Valentino in *The Four Horsemen of the Apocalypse* (1921) is singularly inauthentic.

The tango's musical tradition, one of the two or three richest in the Western Hemisphere, took shape between 1890 and 1920. The *bandoneon,* a German-made accordion variant, became the key instrument in the trios and quartets that played the music in the 1900s. The worldwide fame of the tango spelled an end to upper-class disapproval of it in Argentina, where the dance and especially the music entered a genuine golden age from approximately 1920 to 1950, much enhanced by phonograph records, radio programs, and (after 1933) Argentine sound films. The standard tango band, *orquestra típica,* of the 1920s and early 1930s was a sextet of two *bandoneons,* two violins, a piano, and a double bass.

In the early 1920s the tango also became a form of popular song, marvelously perfected by the legendary baritone Carlos Gardel (1890–1935). The dance itself was revived strongly in the late 1930s. Tango bands then reached their fullest size, with upward of a dozen players. Perhaps the most brilliant star of this period was the great *bandoneon* player Aníbal Troilo (1914–1975).

After the early 1950s, tango music lost its supremacy in Argentina, though it retained its share of public affection. Smaller instrumental groups came to replace the magnificent bands of the 1940s, while an "avant-garde" outgrowth of the music developed under the leadership of Astor Piazzolla (1921–1992), who achieved considerable European renown in the 1970s and 1980s.

A musical form rather than a style, the tango should be referred to in English as "the tango," never just as "tango."

See also **Gardel, Carlos; Milonga; Music: Popular Music and Dance.**

BIBLIOGRAPHY

Deborah L. Jakubs, "From Bawdyhouse to Cabaret: The Evolution of the Tango as an Expression of Argentine Popular Culture," in *Journal of Popular Culture* 18 (1984): 133–145.

Simon Collier, *The Life, Music and Times of Carlos Gardel* (1986).

Donald S. Castro, *The Argentine Tango as Social History, 1880–1955* (1990).

Additional Bibliography

Baim, Jo. *Tango: The Creation of a Cultural Icon.* Bloomington: Indiana University Press, 2007.

Collier, Simon, and Ken Haas. *Tango! The Dance, the Song, the Story.* New York: Thames & Hudson, 2005.

Varela, Gustavo. *Mal de tango: Historia y genealogía moral de la música ciudadana.* Buenos Aires: Paídos, 2005.

SIMON COLLIER

he was one of the few leftists to criticize Fidel Castro's government in Cuba in the early 1960s.

See also **Agrarian Reform; Manumission.**

BIBLIOGRAPHY

For Tannenbaum's early career see Helen Delpar, "Frank Tannenbaum: The Making of a Latin Americanist, 1914–1933," in *The Americas* 45 (1988): 153–171. Two of Tannenbaum's many publications are *Peace by Revolution: An Interpretation of Mexico* (1933), and *Ten Keys to Latin America* (1962), which contains his critique of Castro's policies on pp. 201–237.

Additional Bibliography

Hale, Charles Adams. "Frank Tannenbaum and the Mexican Revolution." *Hispanic American Historical Review*, 75:2 (May 1995): 215–246.

Knight, Alan S. "Frank Tannenbaum y la revolución mexicana." *Estudios de Historia Moderna y Contemporánea de México*, 19 (1999): 33–52.

JOHN A. BRITTON

TANNENBAUM, FRANK (1893–1969). Frank Tannenbaum (*b.* 4 March 1893; *d.* 1 June 1969), pioneering Latin Americanist in the United States. The son of Austrian immigrants who arrived in the United States in 1904, Tannenbaum did graduate work at the Brookings Institution, receiving his doctorate there in 1927. Subsequently, he was an internationally recognized historian at Columbia University from 1935 until his death. A versatile scholar in a time of narrow specialization, he wrote on topics ranging from prison reform to international relations to the history of slavery, arguing that Latin American slavery was more benign than slavery in the United States. His chosen area of concentration, however, was the Mexican Revolution and its consequences. His ground-breaking study of land reform, *The Mexican Agrarian Revolution* (1929), established the focus for his research: village Mexico and its struggle to adjust to the modern world.

Tannenbaum was highly skeptical of large organizations—whether governmental or private sector—and wrote provocative critiques of various theories and plans for large-scale industrialization in Latin America. Often in disagreement with other scholars,

TAPAJÓS CHIEFDOM. *See* **Santarém.**

TAPAJÓS RIVER. Tapajós River, a major tributary of the Amazon in central Brazil. About 1,200 miles in length, the Tapajós is 8 to 10 miles wide at its mouth. Only 170 miles of the Tapajós is navigable for steamers due to the large number of cataracts throughout the river. At the mouth of the Tapajós is the city of Santarém, the only major city on the river. In the pre-Columbian period the mouth of the Tapajós was a thriving area, with an estimated population of 86,000. The region is noted for the development of the Santarém civilization, characterized by its high-quality pottery and powerful military, which included the women warriors who are credited with inspiring the myths about the Amazons. The Tapajós region resisted European encroachment until 1639, when it was subjugated by the Portuguese. Throughout most of the colonial period the Tapajós was used as a principal route to the gold-mining regions of Mato Grosso. In 1956 gold was discovered in the

Tapajós region just south of Santarém, an area that remained productive in the early 2000s.

See also **Amazon River; Gold Rushes, Brazil; Santarém.**

BIBLIOGRAPHY

John Hemming, *Red Gold: The Conquest of the Brazilian Indians, 1500–1760* (1978); *Rand McNally Encyclopedia of World Rivers* (1980).

David Cleary, *Anatomy of the Amazon Gold Rush* (1990).

Edward J. Goodman, *The Explorers of South America* (1992).

Additional Bibliography

Gomes, Denise Maria Cavalcvante. *Ceramica arqueólogica da Amazonia: Vasilhas da coleçao tapajonica MAE-USP.* São Paulo: FAPESP: Edusp: Imprensa Oficial SP, 2002.

Goulding, Michael; Ronaldo Barthem; and Efrem Jorge Gondim Ferreira. *The Smithsonian Atlas of the Amazon.* Washington, DC: Smithsonian Books, 2003.

Rodríguez Larreta, Enrique. *"Gold Is Illusion": The Garimpeiros of Tapajos Valley in the Brazilian Amazonia.* Stockholm: Department of Social Anthropology, 2002.

MICHAEL J. BROYLES

TAPERINHA. Taperinha was a culture of the Amazon, circa 5500 to 3000 BCE, known through archaeological findings. The earliest pottery-age site in the Americas, Taperinha was discovered in the 1860s and 1870s by naturalists. The site is a large shell-heap about six yards deep and several acres in area, overlooking the Amazon flood plain just east of the city of Santarém in the Brazilian state of Pará. Archaeologists at first dismissed such early sites, thinking that the craft of pottery-making had come into the Amazon basin from the Andes, some time after 4,000 years ago. The Taperinha culture is dated by fifteen radiocarbon dates from pottery, charcoal, and shells, and two thermoluminescence dates from the carbon-dated pottery, from the site and from a nearby cave. The pots were simple bowls put together with patches of clay. A few had rim decoration of curved incised lines, similar to local Formative pottery roughly 2,000 to 3,000 years old. In that art, the lines are in animal images popular in Amazonian decoration throughout later prehistory. Other artifacts found were shell scrapers and possible shaped bone fasteners. Recent excavations and geophysical surveys at Taperinha and other sites in Amazonia suggest that they were fishing villages with refuse mounds, feasting areas, and human burials. Both fish and shellfish were important foods, but whether the people practiced horticulture is not certain because there were few plant remains. Pollen cores at nearby Prainha show pollen of disturbance species (plants with shallow root systems that cannot prevent soil loss) but not of crops. The isotopic chemistry of the carbon that was dated at Taperinha has the pattern of well-preserved, closed-canopy tropical rainforest.

See also **Archaeology; Precontact History: Amazonia.**

BIBLIOGRAPHY

Roosevelt, Anna Curtenius, et al. "Eighth Millennium Pottery from a Shell Midden in the Brazilian Amazon." *Science* 254, no. 5038 (13 December 1991): 1621–1624.

ANNA CURTENIUS ROOSEVELT

TAPIR. Tapir, mammal related to the horse and rhinoceros. There are three species in the Americas: *Tapirus terrestris* (Brazilian tapir), *Tapir pinchaque* (mountain tapir), and *Tapir Bairdii* (Baird's tapir). The tapir looks like a combination of its two closest relatives and a large pig: it is of short stature, with a heavy body, a thick neck, a prehensile upper lip forming a short, movable trunk, a short tail, and four toes on the front feet and three on the hind feet.

American tapirs, which have dark brown coats, were widely hunted by natives for their highly valued meat and their supposed supernatural healing powers. Their range is from Mexico to South America.

All are threatened with extinction due mainly to destruction of their sole habitat: tropical rain forests. All are legally protected.

BIBLIOGRAPHY

Erwin Patzelt, *Fauna del Ecuador* (1989), pp. 89–91.

Luigi Boitani and Stefania Bartoli, *Simon and Schuster's Guide to Mammals* (1982), p. 345.

Francesco B. Salvatori, *Rare Animals of the World* (1990), pp. 90, 147.

Additional Bibliography

Brooks, Daniel M.; Richard E. Bodmer; and Sharon Matola. *Tapirs: Status Survey and Conservation Action Plan.* Gland, Switzerland: IUCN, 1997.

Royte, Elizabeth. *The Tapir's Morning Bath: Mysteries of the Tropical Rain Forest and the Scientists Who Are Trying to Solve Them.* Boston: Houghton Mifflin, 2001.

RAÚL CUCALÓN

TAPUIA. Tapuia, a generic term used by Europeans in colonial Brazil to designate non-Tupi indigenous societies. In the sixteenth century the term applied mainly to Gê-speaking peoples living near the Atlantic coast, particularly the Aimoré south of Bahia, whose persistent opposition to colonial rule lent the Tapuia archetype negative overtones. Though often portrayed as a rude and barbarous people, Tapuia groups possessed an extraordinarily complex social organization and developed sophisticated political relations with the Europeans, particularly with the Dutch during their occupation of Pernambuco (1630–1654) and with the Portuguese during the Indian wars of the Northeast (1687–1720).

See also **Indigenous Peoples; Pernambuco.**

BIBLIOGRAPHY

John Hemming, *Red Gold* (1978), esp. chaps. 14 and 16, includes detailed discussions of Tapuia-Dutch and Tapuia-Portuguese relations during the seventeenth century. For anthropological treatment of Gê social organization, see David Maybury-Lewis, ed., *Dialectical Societies* (1979).

Manuela Carneiro Da Cunha, ed., *História dos índios no Brasil* (1992).

JOHN M. MONTEIRO

TARAPACÁ. Tarapacá, northernmost region of Chile (1990 population 358,088), located almost completely in a desert environment. Only at isolated points along the coast did the availability of water allow the development of major settlements, such as Arica (1990 population 177,330) and Iquique (1984 population 118,735), dedicated to trade, the shipping of minerals, and fisheries. In some river oases, such as Norte Grande, the production of vegetables, olives, and citrus fruits has flourished. In the past, Iquique was the leading city of Tarapacá for its role as the primary port of export for the nitrate mined in the interior. With the demise of nitrate mining, Arica—only 13 miles from the border with Peru and connected with La Paz, Bolivia, by a narrow-gauge rail—eclipsed Iquique and became even more important in the 1950s and 1960s as a free-trade and duty-free industrial zone. Industry collapsed in the 1970s, but Arica maintained its regional leadership as a trading center with Peru and Bolivia and the site of fish-meal factories.

See also **Arica.**

BIBLIOGRAPHY

Federico Marull Bermúdez, *Historia de la antigua provincia de Tarapacá* (Santiago, 1969).

Sergio Villalobos, *La economía de un desierto: Tarapacá durante la colonia* (Santiago, 1979).

Additional Bibliography

González M., Sergio. *Chilenizando a Tunupa: La escuela pública en el Tarapacá andino, 1880–1990.* Santiago, Chile: Ediciones de la Dirección de Bibliotecas, Archivos y Museos: Centro de Investigaciones Diego Barros Arana, 2002.

González M., Sergio. *El dios cautivo: Las ligas Patrióticas en la chilenización compulsiva de Tarapacá (1910–1922.)* Santiago: LOM Ediciones, 20004.

Podestá Arzubiaga, Juan. *La invención de Tarapacá: Estado y desarrollo regional en Chile.* Iquique, Chile: Universidad Arturo Prat, Ediciones Campus, 2004.

CÉSAR N. CAVIEDES

TARASCANS. Tarascans (now also called Purépecha), the Native American linguistic and cultural group that in pre-Spanish times occupied most of the area of the present Mexican state of Michoacán. The Tarascans dominated an empire that extended into regions of the present states of Guerrero, Guanajuato, and Jalisco but probably did not reach the Pacific coast. The expansionism of the Tarascans and the Aztecs brought them into conflict that cost many lives but did not give either side a decisive victory.

The Tarascan ruler, known as the *cazonci*, had his capital at Tzintzuntzan on Lake Pátzcuaro in central Michoacán. The population of the Lake

Pátzcuaro basin at the time of the Spanish Conquest was about 100,000. Tzintzuntzan was dominated by a platform on which there were five temple structures called *yácatas*. The principal deity was Curicaueri, a god of the sun and fire, to whom perpetual fires were kept burning. A major female deity, Cuerauáperi, was goddess of fertility in humans and the soil. Religious ceremonies included human sacrifice, particularly of war captives.

The first major Spanish expedition entered the region in 1522, under the leadership of Christóbal de Olid, but it withdrew after six months. The last *cazonci*, Tzintzicha Tangaxoan, was executed by Nuño de Guzmán in 1530. Franciscan missionaries arrived in 1525, followed by Augustinians in 1537. The royal judge Vasco de Quiroga, who became first bishop of Michoacán in 1538, is revered as the protector of the Tarascans.

In 1540–1541 one of the Franciscans, probably Jerónimo de Alcalá, wrote *Relación de las ceremonias y ritos y población y gobierno de los indios de la provincia de Michoacán*, the most informative description of the life and culture of the Tarascans. The missionaries also prepared grammars and dictionaries of the language, which is unrelated to other Mesoamerican tongues. The Tarascan grammar published by Maturino Gilberti in 1558 was the first grammar of an American Indian language to be printed.

During the colonial period the Tarascans maintained a mixed cultural identity at the village level, largely centered in their churches, hospitals, and confraternities. They have survived as an identifiable group in Michoacán, where the language is still spoken by over 105,000 people in a number of villages, and they are noted for craftsmanship in copper, wood, lacquer, textiles, and pottery.

See also **Guzmán, Nuño Beltrán de; Indigenous Peoples; Michoacán; Olid, Cristóbal de.**

BIBLIOGRAPHY

Maturino Gilberti, *Arte de la lengua de Michuacán* (1558; 1987).

George M. Foster, *Empire's Children: The People of Tzintzuntzan* (1948).

Jerónimo De Alcalá, *Relación de las ceremonias y ritos y población y gobierno de los indios de la provincia de Michoacán* (1956; 1977).

J. Benedict Warren, *Vasco de Quiroga and His Pueblo-Hospitals of Santa Fe* (1963).

Delfina E. López Sarrelangue, *La nobleza indígena de Pátzcuaro en la época virreinal* (1965).

Jerónimo De Alcalá, *The Chronicles of Michoacán*, translated and edited by Eugene R. Crane and Reginald C. Reindorp (1970), a somewhat faulty translation.

Shirley Gorenstein and Helen Perlstein Pollard, *The Tarascan Civilization: A Late Prehispanic Cultural System* (1983).

J. Benedict Warren, *The Conquest of Michoacán* (1985).

J. BENEDICT WARREN

TARATA (CALLE TARATA). On July 16, 1992, a car bomb exploded on Calle Tarata, a residential street in the upscale Miraflores district of Lima, killing twenty-five civilians and wounding 155 others. The assault was part of a campaign by the radical insurgent movement Sendero Luminoso (Shining Path) to gain control over Lima, the center of economic and political power in Peru. The Tarata bombing became a powerful symbol of Shining Path's use of terrorist methods, and galvanized support among many Lima residents for hard-line measures against the insurgency.

See also **Peru, Revolutionary Movements: Shining Path.**

BIBLIOGRAPHY

"Los asesinatos y lesiones graves producidos en el atentado de la Calle Tarata (1992)." *Informe Final*. Tomo VII, Cap. 2, Sección 2.60. Lima: Comisión de la Verdad y Reconciliación, 2003. Available from www.cverdad.org.pe/ifinal/index.php.

JO-MARIE BURT

TARIJA. Tarija, a temperate, densely populated, subpuna valley in the southern Andean ranges of Bolivia as well as a city. The region was formerly in the Audiencia of Charcas. The "garden city" of Tarija—reminiscent of Seville—was founded in 1574 or 1575 by Luís de Fuentes and named after the first Spanish conqueror to enter the area, Francisco de Tarija. Tarija served as a fortress city against the violent Chiriguano Indians, whose territories bordered the valley and whose hostilities continually threatened the stability of the entire *audiencia*. As a defense zone, Tarija (and other similar settlements) prevented Chiriguano expansion, thus fostering economic growth in the Charcas highlands and valleys.

Apart from defense, Tarija functioned as an important agricultural and livestock supplier to the growing Potosí market, especially after the 1545 silver strike. Tarija became a livestock center soon after Hernando Pizarro established livestock activities there in 1547. The valley also produced maize, wheat, fruits, vegetables, wine, and preserves for the highlands. Tarija, like other areas, was also designated to supply *mita* (draft labor) for the Potosí mines, a considerable burden on local Indians, many of whom, terrified by Chiriguano raids, had fled the area.

Located on the trade route between Tucumán (itself a supplier to the highlands) and Potosí, Tarija was always economically oriented to the highlands. After independence in 1825, Tarija resisted incorporation into Argentina's administrative orbit. Yet, in the 1920s, Bolivia's national railway system excluded Tarija, leaving it to cope with an inadequate transport system to truck products to the highlands. The Chaco War further isolated the region, and the 1952 revolution in Bolivia failed to bring Tarija into the mainstream. Continued economic stagnation has prompted many *tarijeños* to migrate to Argentina as seasonal labor, particularly to the Jujuy, Salta, and Tucumán regions. In 2005 the population of Tarija department was estimated at 459,001, and Tarija city at 183,001. Today, the department of Tarija is the object of several government-sponsored development programs aimed at revitalizing this once-important region.

See also **Chiriguanos; Pizarro, Hernando; Potosí.**

BIBLIOGRAPHY

Klein, Herbert S. *Bolivia: The Evolution of a Multi-Ethnic Society* (1982).

Vázquez Machicado, Humberto; José De Mesa; and Teresa Gisbert, *Manual de historia de Bolivia*, 2nd ed. (1983), p. 126.

Larson, Brooke. *Colonialism and Agrarian Transformation in Bolivia: Cochabamba, 1550–1900* (1988), pp. 60, 70.

Finot, Enrique. *Nueva historia de Bolivia* (1989), p. 98.

Beck, Stephan, and Narel Paniagua. *Historia, ambiente, y sociedad en Tarija, Bolivia*. La Paz: Instituto de Ecología, Universidad Mayor de San Andrés, 2001.

Rojas, Rafael, and Christian Jetté. *Tarija: Pobreza, género, y medio ambiente*. La Paz: Centro de Estudios & Proyectos, Embajada Real de los Países Bajos, 1998.

LOLITA GUTIÉRREZ BROCKINGTON

TARMA. Tarma, province in the central highlands of Peru, department of Junín, and also the name of its provincial capital. The city of Tarma (1990 population 47,472) is situated at an altitude of 10,130 feet above sea level and only 30 miles east of La Oroya, the railway and highway linkage point with Lima, the capital of Peru. The city was founded in 1538 only 4 miles away from the Incan city of Tarmatambo by orders from conquistador Francisco Pizarro. Since precolonial times the area has served as a base for penetrating the eastern jungle. During the colonial period Tarma was a strategic commercial, missionary, and military post. It produced coarse textiles. The millenarianist and anti-Spanish Indian rebellion led by Juan Santos Atahualpa caused social turmoil in the region between 1742 and 1753.

In modern times Tarma has been a gateway to jungle colonization and the development of the coffee-producing areas and the easternmost towns of San Ramón, La Merced, and Satipo. The province has a wide variety of agricultural produce including potatoes, wheat, barley, corn, and quinoa, as well as livestock. In the city of Tarma there are a few factories for producing cement and processing food and fruits. In the early 1950s, Tarma benefited from the regional policy of President Manuel A. Odría, a native of the city of Tarma.

See also **Atahualpa (Juan Santos); Odría, Manuel Apolinario.**

BIBLIOGRAPHY

Florencia Mallon, *The Defense of Community in Peru's Central Highlands: Peasant Struggle and Capitalist Transition, 1860–1940* (1983).

Additional Bibliography

Garayar, Carlos; Walter H. Wust; et. al. *Atlas departmental del Perú: Imagen geográfica, estadística, histórica y cultural*. Lima: PEISA: La República, 2003.

Giarracca, Norma, and Bettina Levy. *Ruralidades latinoamericanas: Identidades y luchas sociales*. Buenos Aires: CLASCO, 2004.

Jahnsen, Freidrich Eduardo, and Ricardo Arroyo Guevara. *El país de las lagunas: Historia y ecología de la Puna de Junín.* Lima: SEDAPAL: Ministerio de la Presidencia, 1999.

Parsons, Jeffrey R.; Charles M. Hastings; and Ramiro Matos Mendieta. *Prehispanic Settlement Patterns in the Upper Mantaro and Tarma Drainages, Junín, Peru.* Ann Arbor: University of Michigan, 2000.

ALFONSO W. QUIROZ

TAUBATÉ CONVENTION.

Taubaté Convention, an agreement reached in 1906 by the Brazilian coffee-producing states of Minas Gerais, São Paulo, and Rio de Janeiro in the Paulista town of Taubaté. Faced with Brazil's largest bumper coffee crop, state officials and planters sought through federal financial aid and state intervention to control the supply of coffee and support coffee prices.

Coffee was Brazil's leading export product during the nineteenth century and production spread from the Paraíba Valley of São Paulo and Rio de Janeiro into the neighboring provinces of Minas Gerais and Espíritu Santo. The initial problems that beset the coffee economy were associated with the capitalist crises in overseas markets in the early 1870s, coupled with local problems related to deforestation, soil depletion, shortage of capital, and planter indebtedness in the initial coffee-producing areas. The emancipation of the slave labor force in 1888 without compensation to slave owners was followed a year later by the fall of the Brazilian monarchy and the onset of the First Republic. In the final decades of slavery and the monarchy, the dynamic center of the coffee economy shifted from Rio de Janeiro to the interior of São Paulo, where pro-monarchist sectors of the Paulista planter class became increasingly disenchanted with the Republican government's ineffective support measures. Between 1901 and 1903 mildly successful efforts were made to form a planters' political party and in 1902, monarchist coffee planters led a protest rebellion to unseat President Campos Sales and the state government that had responded to the coffee crises of overproduction with a decree that prohibited further planting.

The election of Afonso Pena to the presidency in 1906 coincided with the onset of bureaucratic centralization and modernization under the São Paulo state governorship of Jorge Tibiriçá, and,

sympathetic to the plight of Paulista planters, the federal government in 1908 approved the valorization measures outlined in the Taubaté treaty. The treaty called for a £15 million loan with a federal guarantee for the purchase of coffee to hold it off the market and maintain a price above the 1897–1905 international average of thirty-eight francs. All states were to follow São Paulo's example and levy a prohibitive tax on new coffee trees to reduce the supply of coffee. A Coffee Institute was established in São Paulo to regulate the production and commercialization of coffee. A public coffee exchange run by representatives of the planters was to replace the exporters who had been grading coffee, and campaigns to promote Brazilian coffee among foreign consumers were called for. Repayment of the loan would be financed through a three-franc-per-sack export surcharge on coffee and a Caixa de Conversão (Bureau of Exchange) would stabilize the exchange rate.

Many of the treaty's provisions were only implemented partially and some not at all. Financing and storage of coffee continued to be inadequate; the call for a coffee exchange was only fulfilled in 1916; the prohibition on planting new land in São Paulo ended in 1912; and two years later the Caixa de Conversão was terminated. Two additional federal government valorization initiatives rescued coffee producers in ad hoc reactions to crises in the world markets in 1918 and again in 1921.

See also **Coffee, Valorization of (Brazil); Coffee Industry.**

BIBLIOGRAPHY

Stephen C. Topik, *The Political Economy of the Brazilian State, 1889–1930* (1987).

Mauricio A. Font, *Coffee, Contention, and Change in the Making of Modern Brazil* (1990).

Additional Bibliography

Grieg, Maria Dilecta. *Café: Histórico, negócios e elite.* São Paulo, SP: Olho d'Agua, 2000.

Perissinotto, Renato M. *Estado e capital cafeeiro em São Paulo, 1889–1930.* São Paulo: FAPESP: Annablume, 2000.

NANCY PRISCILLA S. NARO

TAUNAY, AFFONSO D'ESCRAGNOLLE (1876–1958).

Affonso d'Escragnolle Taunay (*b.* 11 July 1876; *d.* 20 March 1958), Brazilian historian and educator. Taunay's historical studies centered on his adopted city and state of São Paulo. Taunay wrote extensive multivolume works on the early history of that city, on São Paulo's *bandeirantes* (colonial explorers of Brazil's interior), and on the history of Brazilian coffee. He was the son of Alfredo d'Escragnolle Taunay, the Viscount Taunay, a distinguished novelist, historian, and statesman. Educated in Rio de Janeiro as an engineer, the younger Taunay settled in the city of São Paulo to teach science, but soon gravitated to history. He was the director of the Paulista Museum there from 1917 until his retirement in 1945. In 1934 he was named to the first chair of Brazilian history at the University of São Paulo. In addition to history, Taunay's writings include studies on philology and lexicography, and translations of history and literature. He was extremely prolific, authoring an estimated 1,500 books and articles. He also located and edited numerous descriptive works by foreign travelers on Brazil. Taunay's writing tended to be prolix and short on interpretation, but his research was distinguished by solid archival documentation, much of which he himself discovered and published. He pioneered in the history of the city and state of São Paulo and of coffee and is credited with establishing the exploits of the *bandeirantes* as part of the Brazilian historical consciousness.

See also **Brazil: Since 1889; Taunay, Alfredo d'Escragnolle, Vicomte de; Universidade São Paulo.**

BIBLIOGRAPHY

José Honório Rodrigues, "Afonso d'Escragnolle Taunay, 1876–1958," in *Hispanic American Historical Review* 38, no. 3 (August 1958): 389–393.

Myriam Ellis, *Affonso d'Escragnolle Taunay no Centenário do seu Nascimento* (1977).

Odilon Nogueira De Matos, *Afonso de Taunay, Historiador de São Paulo e do Brasil* (1977).

Additional Bibliography

Brefe, Ana Cláudia Fonseca. *O Museu Paulista: Affonso de Taunay e a memória nacional 1917–1945.*

Oliveira Junior, Paulo Cavalcante de. "Affonso d'E. Taunay e a construção da memória bandeirante." Ph.D. diss. Universidad Federal do Rio de Janeiro, 1994.

EUGENE RIDINGS

TAUNAY, ALFREDO D'ESCRAGNOLLE, VICOMTE DE (1843–1899).

Alfredo d'Escragnolle, Vicomte de Taunay (*b.* 22 February 1843; *d.* 25 January 1899), Brazilian author and politician. Taunay, born in Rio de Janeiro, was the son of Félix Émile de Taunay, a French painter who came to Brazil in 1816 as a member of the French Artistic Mission, with Jean-Baptiste Debret. Taunay enlisted in the army in 1861, graduated from the Military Academy in 1864, and served in the War of the Triple Alliance (1864–1870), in particular at the heroic retreat from Laguna. Soon afterward he wrote an account of the latter, *La retraite de la Lagune* (1871), which was translated into Portuguese a year later by his son, Affonso d'Escragnolle Taunay. He published some seven novels, often under pseudonyms, and several travel books. As a deputy for Goiás (1872–1875) and a senator for Santa Catarina (1886–1889), Taunay was active in politics during the last years of the Brazilian Empire, particularly in the cause of immigration. He remained a monarchist during the first years of the Republic. He died in Rio de Janeiro.

The quality of Taunay's fiction varies. The only novel that has been republished, *Inocência* (1872), his second, is the story of an itinerant doctor who falls in love with the young daughter of a landowner in the distant interior of Mato Grosso and of their tragic death while being pursued by her jealous father. Its most notable quality is its realism: Taunay knew this remote area well, and his descriptions of it are much more authentic than those of his contemporary José Martiniano de Alencar. Two other novels are *A mocidade de Trajano* (1871), his first, which is set in the coffee-growing area of Campinas, São Paulo, and combines romantic plot and realistic setting, and *O encilhamento* (1893), a rather clumsy but interesting roman à clef about the scandal-ridden boom and bust of 1890–1891. His *Memórias*, up to 1870, published (according to his wishes) a century after his birth, in 1943, is one of the few valuable personal reminiscences written in nineteenth-century Brazil.

See also **Brazil: 1808–1889; Literature: Brazil.**

BIBLIOGRAPHY

Antônio Cândido, *Formação da literatura brasileira*, vol. 2, pp. 307–315.

Additional Bibliography

Machado, Irene A. *Roteiro de leitura: Inocência de Visconde de Taunay.* São Paulo: Editora Atica, 1997.

JOHN GLEDSON

TAURIELLO, ANTONIO (1931–).

Antonio Tauriello (*b.* 20 March 1931), Argentine composer, pianist, and conductor. Born in Buenos Aires, he studied composition with Alberto Ginastera at the National Conservatory and piano with Walter Gieseking in Tucumán. A resident conductor with the opera and ballet at the Teatro Colón, he worked extensively in the United States as assistant director and conductor of the New York City Opera, the American Opera Theater at the Juilliard School of Music, and the Chicago Lyric Opera. Tauriello has been a member of the Agrupación Música Viva (AMV) in Buenos Aires, a group founded by Gerardo Gandini, Alcides Lanza, and Armando Krieger. The AMV ensemble presented premieres of his works, and with it Tauriello conducted performances of contemporary music in Argentina and New York. He has also appeared as conductor at the Inter-American Music Festivals in Washington, D.C. In 1968 his Piano Concerto was premiered there, a work in which Tauriello sought to explore freer relationships between the soloist and the orchestra, with the piano part existing as an independent entity. Except for some synchronization cues, the pianist can choose the speed and pacing of musical phrases and the duration of individual notes.

Other works by Antonio Tauriello: *Obertura Sinfónica* (1951); *Ricercari 1 à 6* (1963); *Transparencias* for six orchestral groups (1964); *Música* no. 3 for piano and orchestra (1965); *Canti* for violin and orchestra (1967); and *La mansión de Tlaloc* (1969), which premiered during the Third Festival of Music of the Americas and Spain in Madrid in 1970.

Among his chamber music compositions Tauriello has written *Ilynx* for clarinet, double bass, piano, and percussion (1968); *Diferencias* for flute and piano (1969); *Signos de los tiempos* for flute, violin, clarinet, violoncello, and piano (1969); Serenade no. 2 for eight instruments (1966), written to celebrate Alberto Ginastera's fiftieth birthday and *Diferencias* no. 2 for piano (1969). He has received various honors, including a Guggenheim Fellowship in 1969. He was awarded a Konex Foudnation Merit Diploma for Classical Music twice, in 1989 and in 1999.

See also **Gandini, Gerardo; Ginastera, Alberto Evaristo; Lanza, Alcides; Music: Art Music.**

BIBLIOGRAPHY

Rodolfo Arizaga, *Enciclopedia de la música argentina* (1971), p. 295.

John Vinton, ed., *Dictionary of Contemporary Music* (1974), p. 731.

Gérard Béhague, *Music in Latin America: An Introduction* (1979), p. 338; *New Grove Dictionary of Music and Musicians* (1980).

Additional Bibliography

Ficher, Miguel, Martha Furman Schleifer, and John M. Furman. *Latin American Classical Composers: A Biographical Dictionary.* Lanham, MD: Scarecrow Press, 2002.

Vega, Aurelio De La. "Latin American Composers in the United States." *Latin American Music Review,* 1 (Autumn 1980): 162–175.

ALCIDES LANZA

TÁVARA Y ANDRADE, SANTIAGO

(1790–1874). Santiago Távara y Andrade (*b.* 1790; *d.* 28 January 1874), a major liberal intellectual and politician in the mid-nineteenth century. Távara, a native of Piura, received a degree from the Royal Medical College of San Fernando in 1819. He contributed two widely read works to the formation of a liberal outlook in Peru. *Historia de los partidos políticos* was a series of articles explaining the Peruvian political situation in 1851 that appeared in the Lima newspaper *El Comercio.* The articles were collected and edited in 1951 by Jorge Basadre. Távara also wrote against slavery. His writings formed part of the campaign conducted by a small antislavery movement in Peru. A staunch supporter of Ramón Castilla, Távara penned the only coherent argument for the abolition of black slavery in Peru, *Abolición de la esclavitud en el Perú* (1855), which attacked those who argued that abolition would mean a great increase in crime. He won a seat in the National Convention, serving in 1855–1857, and in the national Chamber of Deputies, which he held from the mid-1860s until his defeat in the hotly contested election of 1868. Távara long had fought electoral corruption, but in this instance both he and his opponent were accused of fraud. After his defeat Távara retired from politics. He died in Piura.

See also **Castilla, Ramón; Slave Trade, Abolition of: Spanish America.**

BIBLIOGRAPHY

Henry F. Dobyns and Paul L. Doughty, *Peru: A Cultural History* (1976).

Peter Blanchard, *Slavery and Abolition in Early Republican Peru* (1992).

Additional Bibliography

Cayo Córdoba, Percy. *Ramón Castilla*. Lima: Editorial Brasa, 1994.

VINCENT PELOSO

See also **Brazil: The Colonial Era, 1500–1808; Guarani Indians; Paulistas, Paulistanos.**

BIBLIOGRAPHY

Richard Morse, ed., *The Bandeirantes* (1965), provides translations of contemporary descriptions of *paulista* raids on the missions and an article on Tavares's 1648 expedition. Charles Ralph Boxer, *Salvador de Sá and the Struggle for Brazil and Angola* (1952), provides an excellent context for Tavares's activities. See also the detailed account in John Hemming, *Red Gold* (1979), chaps. 12–13.

Additional Bibliography

Goes Filho, Synesio Sampaio. *Navegantes, bandeirantes, diplomatas: Um ensaio sobre a formação das fronteiras do Brasil*. São Paulo: Martins Fontes, 1999.

Monteiro, John M. *Negros da terra: Índios y bandeirantes nas origens de São Paulo*. São Paulo: Companhia das Letras, 1994.

JOHN M. MONTEIRO

TAVARES, ANTÔNIO RAPÔSO (1598–1658).

Antônio Rapôso Tavares (*b.* 1598; *d.* 1658), backwoodsman of São Paulo, born in São Miguel de Beja, Portugal. In 1628, Tavares commanded a powerful military force of several hundred *paulistas* (residents of São Paulo) and about 2,000 Indians that crushed the Jesuit reductions of Guairá and transferred at least 30,000 Guaraní slaves to the farms and plantations of São Paulo. Tavares himself set up a wheat farm along the Tietê River with over 100 of the Indian slaves. In search of new captives, he led another large expedition to the Tape missions along the Uruguay River in 1636, again capturing thousands of Guaraní slaves.

In 1648, in his most ambitious adventure, Tavares set out from São Paulo in search of the Serranos (possibly Guaraní) Indians of the Andean foothills. Repelled by Spanish and Jesuit forces in Paraguay and weakened by hunger and disease, the expedition disbanded, with Tavares and a few followers plunging forward through the heart of the Amazon, finally reaching the Portuguese fort of Gurupá in 1651. Though acclaimed subsequently by historians as a great exploratory venture that contributed to the territorial formation of modern Brazil, the expedition was a resounding failure in its time. After wandering aimlessly through the forests of South America for over three years in search of Indian slaves, Tavares returned to São Paulo, where he died a shattered and impoverished man.

TAVARES BASTOS, AURELIANO CÂNDIDO (1839–1875).

Aureliano Cândido Tavares Bastos (*b.* 20 April 1839; *d.* 3 December 1875), Brazilian legislator and publicist. Tavares Bastos was Brazil's leading exponent of the precepts of nineteenth-century liberalism, promoting them in newspaper articles, books, and parliamentary speeches. Intellectually precocious, he received a doctorate in law at the age of twenty from the law school at São Paulo and was elected imperial deputy of his native province of Alagôas the following year. He served the Liberal Party in Parliament from 1861 until 1868. Tavares Bastos ascribed most of the problems of nineteenth-century Brazil to the heritage of Portuguese absolutism, which he said had bequeathed a deficiency of individual liberty and public spirit. His goal was the modernization of Brazil, based on the examples of the United States and Great Britain. He argued for individual liberty, the usefulness of competition, religious freedom, and administrative decentralization. Among the modernizing measures he advocated were the lessening of government restrictions on business enterprise, the lowering of tariffs, the gradual abolition of slavery, the encouragement of immigration (particularly from northern Europe), the reform of education at all levels, and the creation of competent statistical services. He also called for constitutional change in the form of an independent judiciary, direct elections, and a lessening of the power of the emperor. Based on familiarity with British and French liberal thought, Tavares Bastos's proposals for reform were characterized by thorough research and investigation. The most famous of the legislative measures he fostered was Brazil's opening of the Amazon river system to international commerce in 1866. Many other changes he advocated came to fruition after his premature death from pneumonia.

See also **Brazil: 1808–1889.**

BIBLIOGRAPHY

Aureliano Cândido Tavares Bastos, *Cartas do Solitário,* 3d ed. (1938).

Carlos Pontes, *Tavares Bastos (Aureliano Cândido), 1839–1875* (1939).

Evaristo De Moraes Filho, *As Ideias Fundamentais de Tavares Bastos* (1987).

Additional Bibliography

Ferreira, Gabriela Nunes. *Centralização e descentralização no Império: O debate entre Tavares Bastos e visconde de Uruguai.* São Paulo: Departamento de Ciência Política da USP, Editora 34, 1999.

Rego, Walquiria G. Domingues Leão. *A utopia federalista: Estudo sobre o pensamento político de Tavares Bastos.* Maceió, Alagoas, Brazil: EDUFAL, 2002.

Eugene Ridings

TÁVORA, JUÁREZ (1898–1975).

Juárez Távora (*b.* 14 January 1898; *d.* 18 July 1975), Brazilian military officer, *tenente* leader, and 1955 presidential candidate.

Fifteenth son of a politically active family in Ceará, Távora attended school in nearby towns and then went to Rio and Pôrto Alegre with his brothers to complete high school. In 1916 he began army officer training. After commissioning, he met other junior officers and cadets with whom he would later revolt.

After participating in the 1922 *tenente* rebellion, Távora helped capture São Paulo in 1924. Upon abandoning the city, he assumed greater responsibility for leading the rebels and joined forces with Luís Carlos Prestes. He gained a lasting reputation for calm, courageous behavior. Captured in 1925, he was sent to prison and began writing a memoir about the revolt.

Escaping in 1927, Távora fled the country and resumed the conspiracy. Eventually he and most of the others joined the Revolution of 1930, which was organized by Getúlio Vargas's supporters. Távora assumed command of the Northeast and managed to gain control of the entire region within days. Afterward, he was appointed "Viceroy of the North" to oversee security in that region and became active in the Club 3 de Outubro. He formulated vaguely socialist goals for the movement, some of which he pursued in various administrative posts, including minister of agriculture (1932–1934). When his party failed to win a majority in Ceará in 1934, he returned to active duty as a road engineer in the south.

In 1945 Távora joined the National Democratic Union Party to support fellow *tenente* Eduardo Gomes. Throughout the coming years Távora acted as senior statesman of the officer corps concerned with petroleum, electric power, steel, and national defense. Finally he ran for president in 1955 but came in second to Juscelino Kubitschek. Mostly retired, Távora remained on the political sidelines until becoming congressman from Rio de Janeiro. His last post was minister of transport under Humberto de Alencar Castello Branco (1964–1967).

See also **Brazil: Since 1889; Brazil, Political Parties: National Democratic Union of Brazil (UDN); Tenentismo.**

BIBLIOGRAPHY

Neill Macaulay, *The Prestes Column* (1974).

Israel Beloch and Alzira Alves De Abreu, comps., *Dicionário histórico-biográfico brasileiro, 1930–1983* (1984).

Maria Cecília Spina Forjaz, *Tenentismo e forças armadas na revolução de 30* (1989).

Additional Bibliography

Meirelles, Domingos. *As noites das grandes fogueiras: Uma história da Coluna Prestes.* Rio de Janeiro: Editora Record, 1995.

Prestes, Anita Leocádia. *Tenentismo pós-30: Continuidade ou ruptura?* São Paulo: Paz e Terra, 1999.

Michael L. Conniff

TAXATION, SPANISH AMERICA. *See* Public Sector and Taxation.

TAXCO.

Taxco, an important Mexican silver-mining center in the state of Guerrero, especially associated with the eighteenth-century mine owner José de la Borda. Known as Tlachco ("place of the ball court") in pre-Hispanic times, it was a source of copper for the Mexica empire. Along with some iron ore, this copper was being worked by Indians under Spanish direction in the 1520s, soon after the triumph of Hernán Cortés. The first major silver strikes were made in the 1530s, and Taxco (the Spanish corruption of "Tlachco") became one of the more productive silver-mine towns (*reales de minas*) of New Spain. Since it was located in the indigenous heartland, Indian tribute workers could be used to augment slave and wage labor, something that was not possible in northern mining regions. Despite a series of booms and busts, Taxco remained productive into the twentieth century. It is now a popular tourist site and the source of fine silver products.

See also **Mining: Colonial Spanish America.**

BIBLIOGRAPHY

There is no scholarly English-language monograph about Taxco currently available. The standard account in Spanish remains Manuel Toussaint, *Tasco* (1931). Brief, comparative mention of Taxco can be found in Peter J. Bakewell, *Silver Mining and Society in Colonial Mexico: Zacatecas, 1546–1700* (1971).

David A. Brading, *Miners and Merchants in Bourbon Mexico, 1763–1810* (1971). Forced labor in colonial Taxco is discussed in Robert Haskett, "'Our Trouble with the Taxco Tribute': Involuntary Mine Labor and the Indians of Colonial Cuernavaca," in *Hispanic American Historical Review* 71 (August 1991): 447–475.

Additional Bibliography

Enciso Contreras, José. *Taxco en el siglo XVI: Sociedad y normatividad en un real de minas novohispano.* Zacatecas, México: Consejo Nacional para la Cultura y las Artes, 1999.

Mark, Joan T. *The Silver Gringo: William Spratling and Taxco.* Albuquerque: University of New Mexico Press, 2000.

Pérez Rosales, Laura. *Minería y sociedad en Taxco durante el siglo XVIII.* México, D.F.: Universidad Iberoamericana, Departamento de Historia, 1996.

ROBERT HASKETT

TAYASAL.

Tayasal, the last settled outpost of independent Maya to be conquered by the Spanish. It is on the south shore of Lake Petén in the central lake region of the department of Petén, Guatemala. Yucatecan chronicles report that the Itzá Maya fled to the south following the fall of Chichén Itzá and settled at Tayasal. Cortés passed through Tayasal on his cross-peninsular expedition of 1525. Canek, the local Maya ruler, promised Cortés and his twenty soldiers that his people would convert to Christianity. However, this had not occurred by 1618, when two Franciscans, dispatched from Mérida, also failed in efforts to convert them to Christianity. (During their visit to Tayasal they smashed a stone idol of one of Cortes's horses, made by the fearful Maya when the lame original, left behind in 1525, died.) In 1622 a small military expedition from Mérida was slaughtered before it could attain its goal of conquering Tayasal.

Internal divisions among the Maya and the superior military technology of the Spanish contributed to the Tayasal's defeat. Kan Ek', the leader of the Tayasal, actually tried to form an alliance in 1695 with the Spanish, hoping that an outside ally would bolster his leadership. However, these negotiations discredited Kan Ek'. The new leadership that emerged refused to surrender. Consequently, in 1696 and 1697, a 235-man Spanish expeditionary force from Mérida, under the direction of Martín de Ursua, governor of Yucatán, succeeded in reaching the lake. Within a month they built a galley from locally hewn timbers. For twelve days, peaceful efforts to effect the conquest were unsuccessful. Finally, after celebrating a mass at dawn, half the Spanish force rowed toward the town in the galley and defeated the numerous defending Tayasal war canoes with heavy musket fire. The Spaniards seized the town, smashed the Maya idols, and completed the conquest of the Mayas on 13 March 1697. Some survivors escaped and maintained small communities by moving far from Spanish settlements. The Spanish army also relocated some of

---

the remaining Itzá to missions, where they led an unsuccessful rebellion in 1704.

In the course of modern archaeological research, questions have arisen about the endpoint of the Itzá migration from northern Yucatán (some evidence suggests nearby Topoxté rather than Tayasal), although the identification of Tayasal with the final conquest of the Maya is not subject to doubt.

See also **Maya, The.**

BIBLIOGRAPHY

For an account of the conquest of Tayasal, see J. De Villagutierre Soto-Mayor, *Historia de la conquista de la Provincia de el Itzá* (Biblioteca Goathemala, Guatemala, 1933). For information on modern archaeological work in Tayasal, consult Arlen F. Chase, "A Contextual Consideration of the Tayasal-Paxcaman Zone, El Peten, Guatemala" (Ph.D. diss., University of Pennsylvania, 1983), "Con manos arriba: Tayasal and Archaeology," in *American Antiquity* 47, no. 1 (1982): 154–167, and "Archaeology in the Maya Heartland: The Tayasal-Paxcaman Zone, Lake Peten, Guatemala," in *Archaeology* 37, no. 5 (1985).

Danien, Elin C., and Robert J. Sharer. *New Theories on the Ancient Maya.* Salerno, Italy: Edizioni del Paguro, 1999.

Jones, Grant D. *The Conquest of the Last Maya Kingdom.* Stanford, CA: Stanford University Press, 1998.

WALTER R. T. WITSCHEY

TAYLOR, ZACHARY (1784–1850). Zachary Taylor (*b.* 24 November 1784; *d.* 9 July 1850), general during the Mexican War and twelfth president of the United States. Taylor, born in Montebello, Virginia, served in the War of 1812 and in various Indian wars in the Midwest and South. Promoted to brigadier general in the Seminole Wars, he was ordered to Texas in 1844 to provide military support for its annexation by the United States. President James Polk ordered him to the Rio Grande in early 1846 to enforce the U.S. claim to the disputed territory north of that river. On 8 and 9 May 1846, Taylor's troops fought skirmishes with the Mexican army commanded by General Mariano Arista. Polk later claimed that these hostilities were the result of a Mexican invasion of U.S. territory and thus justified a declaration of war.

As commander of the Army of the Rio Grande, Taylor invaded Mexico, and fought and defeated a Mexican army commanded by General Antonio López de Santa Anna at Buena Vista, thus securing northern Mexico for the United States. In 1848 he was nominated and elected president. A member of the Whig Party, he opposed slavery in the newly acquired Mexican territories but supported it in the Old South. He died after a short time in office.

See also **Mexico, Wars and Revolutions: Mexican-American War.**

BIBLIOGRAPHY

Oliver O. Howard, *General Taylor* (1892).

Justin Harvey Smith, *The War with Mexico,* 2 vols. (1919).

Brainerd Dyer, *Zachary Taylor* (1967).

Jack K. Bauer, *Zachary Taylor: Soldier, Planter, Statesman of the Old Southwest* (1985).

Additional Bibliography

Holt, Michael F. *The Rise and Fall of the American Whig Party: Jacksonian Politics and the Onset of the Civil War.* New York: Oxford University Press, 1999.

Taranto, James, and Leonard Leo. *Presidential Leadership: Rating the Best and Worst in the White House.* New York: Wall Street Journal Books, 2004.

RICHARD GRISWOLD DEL CASTILLO

TAZUMAL. Tazumal, the most complex architectural group within the Chalchuapa archaeological zone in western El Salvador, in the present–day department of Santa Ana. It was an important ceremonial and residential center for over a millennium, from the Late Preclassic to the Early Postclassic period (1–1300 CE). The largest Classic center in western El Salvador, Tazumal marks the boundary between the Maya to the west and north, and the non-Maya to the southeast.

The Chalchuapa archaeological zone is located in a broad, fertile basin that is ecologically and physiographically intermediate between the Pacific coastal plain and the Maya highlands. It is composed of a series of ceremonial and residential areas, of which Tazumal is the southernmost.

A massive pyramid temple atop a substructural platform dominates the site. A smaller platform, a ball court, and several house mounds complete the group. Construction of Tazumal probably began around 1 CE. Construction of the pyramid foundation was interrupted about 250 CE, when the Ilopango volcano erupted violently, blanketing the site with ash, which rendered the area uninhabitable. Construction resumed between 450 and 650 CE. Basic construction materials were earthen fill, adobe brick or stone set in adobe, and lime-plaster facing painted white. The style of the pyramid is akin to the neighboring and contemporary Teotihuacán-influenced Kaminaljuyú.

The final, main period of architectural construction at Tazumal lasted from 650 to 1300 CE and witnessed the repeated expansion of the pyramid to its final, massive dimensions—over 23,544 cubic yards in volume. One of the last structures built at Tazumal was the smaller platform, constructed during the Postclassic period (900–1400 CE).

Several stone sculptures have been found at Tazumal, including a stela, known as the "Virgin of Tazumal," in the Late Classic Copán Maya tradition. Of the many freestanding sculptures, two were Chacmools, Mexican sacrificial altars.

The contents of several tombs at Tazumal indicate Honduran and other Central American contact. Polychrome pottery from Copán and the Ulúa Valley, both in western Honduras, was found in tombs at Tazumal. One tomb contained copper-gold figurines from the Nicoya Peninsula of Costa Rica.

As a border area between the Maya and non-Maya, Tazumal never reached a size comparable to its early Classic ally, Kaminaljuyú, or its Late Classic ally, Copán; but neither did it suffer the devastating effects of shifting Classic Maya political fortunes.

Tazumal was probably abandoned during the late Postclassic period, around 1300 CE. By the time of the Spanish conquest, Maya-speaking Pogomam lived in the Chalchuapa zone.

In 2004, heavy rains removed a layer of cement added in the 1950s restoration effort, led by Stanley H. Boggs, that enclosed one of the site's pyramids. A side of the pyramid collapsed, but the event revealed new archaeological findings, including burials, ceramics, and architectural elements, and gave further insight into Tazumal's complex history.

See also **Archaeology.**

BIBLIOGRAPHY

Boggs, Stanley H. "Archaeological Excavations in El Salvador," in *For the Dean,* edited by Erik K. Reed and Dale S. King (1950).

Cobos, Rafael. *Síntesis de la arqueología de El Salvador (1850–1991).* San Salvador, El Salvador: Dirección General de Publicaciones e Impresos, Consejo Nacional para la Cultura y Arte, Dirección General del Patrimonio Cultural, 1994.

Fowler, William R.; photos by Federico Trujillo. *El Salvador: Antiguas civilizaciones.* San Salvador: Banco Agrícola Comercial de El Salvador, 1995.

Lange, Frederick W., ed. *Paths to Central American Prehistory.* Niwot: University Press of Colorado, 1996.

Longyear, John M., III. "Archaeological Investigations in El Salvador," in *Memoirs of the Peabody Museum of Archaeology and Ethnology, Harvard University* 9, no. 2 (1944).

Longyear, John M., III. "Archaeological Survey of El Salvador," in *Handbook of Middle American Indians,* vol. 4, *Archaeological Frontiers and External Connections,* edited by Gordon Ekholm and Gordon Willey (1966).

Sharer, Robert J., ed. *The Prehistory of Chalchuapa, El Salvador,* 3 vols. (1978).

KATHRYN SAMPECK

TEATRO COLÓN. Teatro Colón, Argentina's principal opera house, located in Buenos Aires. The Teatro Colón opened on 25 May 1908 with Verdi's *Aïda* under the baton of Luigi Mancinelli; it succeeded an 1857 house of the same name. Seating approximately four thousand people, the Teatro Colón is the biggest and most prominent opera house in Latin America and one of the major houses of the world. Fifty-eight premieres of Argentine operas have been staged there, among them Héctor Panizza's *Aurora* (1908), Felipe Boero's *El matrero* (1929), Juan José Castro's *Bodas de sangre* (1956) and the first Argentine performance of Castro's *Proserpina y el extranjero* (1960), Alberto Ginastera's *Don Rodrigo* (1964), and Mario Perusso's *La voz del silencio* (1969) and *Escorial* (1989).

The Teatro Colón's repertory included works by Monteverdi and Cavalli, all the traditional Italian, French, and German operatic repertoire as well as contemporary works such as Berg's *Wozzeck* and *Lulu,* Stravinsky's *The Rake's Progress,* Janáček's *Jenufa,* Dallapiccola's *Il prigioniero* and *Volo di notte,*

Pizzetti's *La figlia di Jorio,* Schoenberg's *Erwartung* and *Moses and Aaron,* Milhaud's *Christophe Colomb,* and Poulenc's *Dialogues des Carmélites.* One of the Teatro Colón's most notable events was the world premiere of Ernesto Halffter's completed version of Manuel de Falla's *La Atlántida,* sung in Catalán (1963). Also noteworthy were the South American premieres of Mozart's *Idomeneo* and Berlioz's *Les Troyens* and *Benvenuto Cellini.* A very special event was the production in 1982 of the earliest Spanish opera preserved, *Celos aun del aire matan* (1660), by Juan Hidalgo with a libretto by Pedro Calderón de la Barca. The Teatro Colón also presents symphonic concerts, recitals, and ballet.

See also **Music: Art Music.**

BIBLIOGRAPHY

Roberto Caamaño, *La historia del Teatro Colón* (1969).

Rodolfo Arizaga, *Enciclopedia de la música argentina* (1971); *New Grove Dictionary of Opera,* vol. 1 (1992).

Additional Bibliography

Faillace, Magdalena. *Memoria y presente del Ballet del Teatro Colón, 1925–2005.* Buenos Aires: Teatro Colón, Comision Honoraria de Homenaje por los 80 años de los Cuerpos Estables del Teatro Colón, 2005.

Peña López, Juan Manuel. *El tango en el Teatro Colón.* Buenos Aires: Marcelo Héctor Olivieri Editor, 2006.

Plate, Leonor. *Operas Teatro Colón: Esperando el centenario.* Buenos Aires: Editorial Dunken, 2006.

SUSANA SALGADO

TEATRO SOLÍS. Teatro Solís, Uruguay's principal opera house, located in Montevideo. Opened on 25 August 1856, the Teatro Solís seats twenty-eight hundred people and is the oldest opera house in the Americas. In 1888 Adelina Patti, the great nineteenth-century diva, sang in seven operas there. That same year Verdi's *Otello* was performed with the soprano Romilda Pantaleoni in the role of Desdemona, which she had created for the world premiere at Milan's La Scala the year before. The Solís's golden age began in 1903, when the 285-member opera company of La Scala arrived, led by the conductor Arturo Toscanini and with a roster of singers headed by Enrico Caruso. The Solís presented operatic masterpieces very soon after their world premieres. Puccini's *Madama Butterfly* was performed with both Rosina Storchio and maestro Toscanini, six months after its La Scala premiere. José Oxilia, Victor Damiani, and José Soler were among the world-renowned Uruguayan singers who performed at the Solís. During World War I and the postwar era the Solís hosted famous artists such as Artur Rubinstein and leading orchestras like the Vienna Philharmonic. Vaslav Nijinsky's last stage performance was at the Solís in October 1917. George Gershwin's *Porgy and Bess* was performed for the first time in Montevideo at the Solís in 1955, under the direction of Alexander Smallens, who conducted the Broadway premiere in 1935. The Teatro Solís maintains its commitment to the presentation of local and foreign artists in operatic, orchestral, dance, and dramatic performances.

See also **Music: Art Music.**

BIBLIOGRAPHY

Susana Salgado, *Breve historia de la música culta en el Uruguay,* 2d ed. (1980), and *The Teatro Solís of Montevideo* (forthcoming); *New Grove Dictionary of Opera,* vol. 3 (1992), p. 453.

Additional Bibliography

Bouret, Daniela. *Teatro Solís: 150 años de historias desde el escenario.* Montevideo: Linardi y Risso, 2006.

Bouret, Daniela. *Teatro Solís: Historias y documentos.* Montevideo: Intendencia Municipal de Montevideo, 2004.

Salgado, Susana. *The Teatro Solís: 150 years of Opera, Concert, and Ballet in Montevideo.* Middletown, CT: Wesleyan University Press, 2003.

SUSANA SALGADO

TEBICUARY RIVER. Tebicuary River, stream approximately 300 miles long springing from the Sierra de Caapacú in the south-central highlands of Paraguay and draining the Cordillera of Caaguazú. In a wide but shallow basin around Villarrica, the soil lends itself to cotton and rice cultivation and serves as natural pastures for cattle. In the extended wetlands, ranching is also practiced, and hides are processed in the tanneries of Villarrica or other small settlements along the river, such as Borja, Iturbe, and Villa Florida. The

Tebicuary River joins the Paraguay River 9 miles north of Pilar after draining the Lago Venturoso swamps.

See also **Paraguay River.**

BIBLIOGRAPHY

Hugo G. Ferreira, *Geografía del Paraguay* (Asunción, 1975).

Additional Bibliography

Kleinpenning, J. M. G. *Paraguay: 1515–1870: A Thematic Geography of its Development.* Madrid: Iberoamericana, 2003.

Quiroga, Omar. *Geografía ilustrada del Paraguay.* Asunción: Promociones Culturales, 1997.

Vázquez, Fabricio. *Territorio y población: Nuevas dinámicas regionales en el Paraguay.* Asunción: Fondo de Población de las Naciones Unidas: GTZ: Asociación Paraguaya de Estudios de Población, 2006.

CÉSAR N. CAVIEDES

TECHNOLOGY. Europeans arrived in the New World to find advanced civilizations coexisting with less advanced tribal organizations. The archaeological sites of Machu Picchu, Teotihuacán, and Tikal testify to the remarkable construction and architectural skills of pre-Columbian civilizations. Mayan knowledge of astronomy, the pre-Incan irrigation works (1300–1400 BCE) in northern Peru, and the terraced agricultural system of the Incas are additional evidence of advanced indigenous technology. Indigenous peoples had accomplished stunning advances in breeding and disseminating corn, potatoes, and many other plants. They also developed a method for predicting climate by observing astrological, atmospheric, and oceanic phenomena as well as the behavior of flora and fauna. Other indigenous groups continued to practice more traditional slash-and-burn agriculture and hunting.

Since the European conquest, Latin America has relied heavily on technology from abroad. Despite the steady introduction of new technologies to advanced economic sectors, they have had only a small impact on vast segments of Latin America's population. The importation of new technologies has often failed to produce sustained domestic technological advance. In some cases Latin Americans have made important technological innovations of their own.

MINING, SUGAR, AND HENEQUEN

Indians mined silver, gold, copper, and lead, usually from shallow pits, long before the arrival of the Spaniards. During colonization the Spanish introduced deep-shaft mining techniques that significantly increased the amount of ore that was accessible, and a major technological breakthrough was achieved at the Purísima Grande mine in Pachuca, Mexico, in the mid-1550s when Bartolomé de Medina developed a new amalgamation process for silver, which used large amounts of mercury to extract prodigious amounts of silver from mines in such areas as Zacatecas, Mexico, and Pachuco, Peru. Although the basic technology remained in use for about three centuries, small technological innovations did generate significant increases in productivity. For example, improved furnaces for processing mercury were introduced in Peru in 1633 by Lope de Saavedra, and steam engines were used in mining from the early 1800s.

During the late nineteenth century, sugar from the Pernambuco region was Brazil's leading export. The Pernambuco sugar industry demonstrated an ability to incorporate both superior species of cane and more efficient equipment. In the first part of the 1800s creole sugarcane was replaced by cayenne cane, which was larger, had more extensive branching, contained greater amounts of sugar, and more effectively withstood drought. After 1879 a disease afflicting the cayenne cane motivated the importation of species from Java and Mauritius. In the mid-nineteenth century, sugar producers began shifting from vertical rollers for grinding cane to horizontal rollers that applied greater pressure, faster grinding, and better distribution of the cane on the rollers. In the 1870s vacuum pans were introduced to speed evaporation. Steam engines gradually replaced animals as the major source of power for sugar mills.

The production and export of Yucatán henequen fiber expanded rapidly in the 1880s. Equipment for stripping the fiber was invented in the Yucatán, but interests from the United Kingdom and the United States took over most of the production. By 1880 replacement parts were being produced in the Yucatán, and by 1910 local shops built defibration machines and henequen presses. Innovators in the Yucatán were able to improve on designs and increase operating efficiency, and production reached a peak with World War I.

While the mining, sugar, and henequen industries all enjoyed a period of success and demonstrated an ability to adopt new production techniques, none of these activities launched sustained technological innovations that could spread to other sectors. Cheap land and labor blunted the incentive to modernize production techniques and held the rate of technology adoption far below optimum.

ECONOMIC CHALLENGES

When considered as components of a productive system, imported technologies were not always unequivocally superior. Spanish agricultural methods, for example, did not surpass the *chinampa* agricultural technique used by the Aztecs, and probably the Mayans, which featured raised fields, intensive cultivation, and a variety of crops.

During the first half of the nineteenth century, *saladeros* (beef drying and salting plants) along the Río de la Plata began to operate for an export market. In the 1870s freezing and insulation technologies gave rise to the *frigoríficos* (refrigeration ships) that began to replace the *saladeros*. Further advances in temperature control led to significant exports of beef and mutton to Great Britain beginning around 1900. Although Argentine entrepreneurs recognized a high profit opportunity, virtually all of the *frigoríficos* were operated by foreign interests. The refrigeration technology itself posed no problem for national entrepreneurs, but the main difficulty lay in mastering the complex "soft technologies," which involved the precise timing of receiving beef consignments and loading, unloading, and wholesaling the product, with little room for error. Without these organizational, managerial, and marketing capacities, Argentine entrepreneurs faced high risks.

Between 1944 and 1955 a Mexican monopoly, Syntex Company, gained complete dominance over European competitors in the production of steroid hormones. The firm's success was based on three discoveries. In 1949 barbasco was discovered in Mexico. This plant had much higher yields of steroids and was in greater supply than alternative sources. During the

same year, two researchers at the Mayo Clinic in the United States found that cortisone was helpful in treating the symptoms of arthritis. And in 1951 the Upjohn Company discovered an inexpensive technique for altering the molecular structure of the steroid. This meant an increased demand for barbasco-derived progesterone that could now be used as an intermediate material for the production of cortisone. Syntex thrived during the 1960s, but by the mid-1970s steroid hormone production was once again controlled by foreign enterprises and exports had shrunk from 545 pounds in 1969 to 260 pounds in 1976.

Technological breakthroughs outside the region have occasionally hurt Latin American development. A classic example was the drastic decline in Chile's nitrate exports after introduction of the Haber process, a method of synthesizing ammonia from nitrogen and hydrogen, developed in the early 1900s by the German Fritz Haber.

TECHNOLOGICAL ADVANCES

Mexican research led to the successful development and export of glass manufacturing equipment. It also developed technologies for deep drilling in petroleum extraction and for a method of producing paper from bagasse.

Brazil's production of ethanol from sugarcane and other vegetation is an impressive technological achievement, although it is controversial in terms of economic justification and environmental impact. In 1975 Brazil launched its huge research and development program to produce and substitute ethanol for gasoline. Brazilian researchers were able to upgrade older fermentation methods and achieve necessary technological changes in processing equipment, automobile engines, and sugar production. As of 1990 ethanol accounted for about 15 percent of Brazil's liquid fuel requirements.

The first nuclear power in Latin America was produced at the Atucha I plant in Argentina in 1974, a year during which Brazil and Mexico began to install nuclear power reactors. During the 1970s Colombia, Chile, Peru, and Venezuela had working nuclear centers, while Bolivia, Ecuador, Jamaica, and Uruguay announced intentions to establish their own centers. Cuba signed an agreement with the Soviet Union to install nuclear stations, but after a long series of difficulties, Cuba finally stopped construction in 1992. Chile and Peru have been in the forefront of experimental research to commercialize the extraction of copper through a process of microbial leaching. In Mexico, iron ores are transported by the most advanced, computer-driven pipeline system in the world. Many Latin American manufacturing firms have improved productivity by a constant stream of minor intraplant innovations.

During the late 1960s and early 1970s many of the larger nations of Latin America, including Chile, Colombia, Mexico, Peru, and Venezuela, established or significantly strengthened their national councils for science and technology. During the same period, Argentina, Brazil, Mexico, and the Andean Pact established measures to regulate the importation of technology; this was meant to eliminate imperfections in the transfer of technology that Latin American countries felt put them at a disadvantage. At the same time, there was an increase in the importation of technology along with an emphasis on fostering internal technological capacity. Argentina, Brazil, and Mexico began exporting capital goods, consulting contracts, civil engineering contracts, and turnkey plant facilities, and made some foreign investments that involved technology transfers.

TRENDS SINCE THE 1990S

After the fiscal crises and neoliberal reforms of the 1980s and 1990s, most Latin American states have reduced their investments in technological research and innovation. They have also privatized many state-owned technological enterprises. Private enterprises—both domestic and foreign—have become major forces both for the introduction of new technologies and for fostering domestic technological innovation.

Some Latin American technological enterprises have flourished in the new economic environment. Brazil has developed a thriving small-and medium-size aircraft industry. Based largely on Brazilian design and technical innovations, the industry has been able to adjust rapidly to changing global technological and market conditions. The most successful of these companies is the Brazilian aircraft manufacturer Embraer. The Brazilian government privatized Embraer in 1994. Since then, the company has gradually become a global player in the aircraft industry, specializing in creating a line of short-haul regional jets.

Latin American research institutions have played a significant role in biotechnology. They have propagated potato cultivars through tissue-culture techniques in Argentina, developed a new strain of inocula for soybeans in Brazil, and produced single-cell proteins in Mexico. The boom in biotechnology research in the 1990s is the product of collaborative initiatives between researchers in the public and private sectors. One of these organizations, the Brazilian Organization for Nucleotide Sequencing and Analysis (ONSA), has conducted pioneering genomic research on citrus crops and sugar cane.

A number of countries in Latin America have also embraced the computer revolution. Argentina, Brazil, and Mexico have national policies that promote local production of computers and associated peripheral equipment. In the 1990s local and state governments in Latin America began seeking collaborative relationships with global technology companies. For example, the Brazilian state of Rio Grande do Sul convinced Dell Corporation to establish a computer manufacturing plant to produce computers for the Brazilian and Latin American markets. Significantly, even some of Latin America's smaller countries are participating in these global processes. In 1996 Intel established a center for parts assembly, semiconductor design, and software development in Costa Rica. Other companies have since followed Intel to Costa Rica.

The use of the Internet in Latin America has also grown explosively since the mid-1990s. More than 5 million Latin Americans had access to the Internet in 1999, and the number has continued to grow rapidly. In Latin America the Internet has been used for a wide range of purposes, from e-commerce to education, government, and political protest. Activist organizations from the EZLN in Mexico to indigenous groups in the Amazon have used the Internet to build international political alliances. As with other technological systems, the comparatively high cost of computers and Internet access has meant that Internet users have been predominantly from the upper sectors of society. The proliferation of cybercafes in cities and in some rural areas has, however, broadened access.

Latin American cities have played a globally important role in the innovation of mass transportation. Here, technological innovation has been focused not on developing new technologies but rather on using existing technologies in new ways. Rather than building expensive metro systems, many Latin American cities have instead built relatively inexpensive busways, with dedicated lanes for public transportation. The Brazilian city of Curitiba—now a global model for transportation planners—inaugurated its busways in the mid-1970s. Many cities in Brazil and elsewhere in Latin America have followed suit. Most of these busways, such as Bogotá's TransMilenio, were built through partnerships between public and private enterprise.

These new mass transportation systems are a form of technological innovation that benefits the mass of ordinary Latin Americans. Similarly, cellular telephones have become ubiquitous across Latin America. The impact of technological innovation and industrialization has not, however, been uniformly positive. For example, the opening of the Trans-Ecuadorean oil pipeline has facilitated petroleum exploitation in the Ecuadorean Amazon. While the expanding petroleum industry has generated considerable profits over the short term, oil spills, forest clearances, and road-building associated with the industry have harmed both the region's landscapes and its indigenous groups. The development of maquiladoras, factories along the U.S.-Mexican border, has generated significant pollution problems for the people and landscapes of northern Mexico. The privatization of utilities has also generated popular backlashes. Utilities—such as water, gas, telecommunications, and electricity—are essentially large technological systems for the delivery of basic services. Many Latin Americans fear that the privatization of these utilities will drive up prices, effectively preventing many people from having access to these essential technologies.

Paradoxically, some of the most significant technological innovations in Latin America have involved abandoning the high technologies of the twentieth century. Cuban farmers have embraced organic agriculture on a large scale, forced to do so by economic and political pressures following the collapse of the Soviet bloc. This is not simply a return to older farming practices; organic farming on a large scale requires significant scientific and technological innovation. Organic agriculture is not limited to Cuba. In order to produce certified organic coffee, some coffee farmers in Mexico and Central America are eliminating the high-tech agricultural inputs introduced in the 1970s and 1980s. This technological shift was driven both by a catastrophic collapse in coffee prices in the 1990s and increasing overseas demand for organic produce.

The years since 1980 have been a period of rapid technological innovation and change in Latin America. Partnerships between governments and private enterprise have helped introduce and produce new technologies, many of which are now reaching sectors of Latin American society that had been largely untouched by technological innovations in earlier periods. In some instances, Latin America has even begun to export technologies across the globe. But the benefits of these technological transformations are not equally shared by all Latin Americans. Conversely, their social and ecological costs are frequently borne by the most disadvantaged sectors of Latin American society. The challenge for the future is to ensure that Latin America's technological growth becomes and remains economically, socially, and ecologically sustainable.

See also **Agriculture; Energy; Gasohol Industry; Henequen Industry; Internet; Mining: Modern; Nuclear Industry; Sugar Industry.**

BIBLIOGRAPHY

Baklanoff, Eric N., and Jeffery T. Brannon. "Forward and Backward Linkages in a Plantation Economy: Immigrant Entrepreneurship and Industrial Development in Yucatán, Mexico." *Journal of Developing Areas* 19, no. 1 (1984): 83–94.

Bargalló, Modesto. *La minería y la metalurgía en la América Española durante la época colonial.* Mexico: Fondo de Cultura Económica, 1955.

Bonilla, Marcelo, and Gilles Cliche, eds. *Internet and Society in Latin America and the Caribbean.* Ottawa, ON: International Development Research Council, 2004.

Cole, William E. "Technology, Ceremonies, and Institutional Appropriateness: Historical Origins of Mexico's Agrarian Crisis." In *Progress toward Development in Latin America: From Prebisch to Technological Autonomy,* edited by James L. Dietz and Dilmus D. James. Boulder, CO: Lynne Rienner, 1990.

Collinson, Helen, ed. *Green Guerrillas: Environmental Conflicts and Initiatives in Latin America and the Caribbean.* London: Latin America Bureau, 1996.

Crespi, M. B. A. "La energía nuclear en América Latina: Necesidades y posibilidades." *Interciencia* 4 (1979): 22–29.

Dahlman, Carl J., and Francisco C. Sercovich. "Exports of Technology from Semi-Industrial Economies and Local Technological Development." *Journal of Development Economics* 16 (1984): 63–99.

Eisenberg, Peter L. *The Sugar Industry in Pernambuco: Modernization without Change, 1840–1910*. Berkeley: University of California Press, 1974. See especially pp. 32–62.

Felix, David. "On the Diffusion of Technology in Latin America." In *Technological Progress in Latin America: The Prospects for Overcoming Dependency*, edited by James H. Street and Dilmus D. James. Boulder, CO: Westview Press, 1979.

Gereffi, Gary. *The Pharmaceutical Industry and Dependency in the Third World*. Princeton, NJ: Princeton University Press, 1983. See especially pp. 53–163.

Goldstein, Andrea. "Embraer: From National Champion to Global Player." *CEPAL Review* 77 (August 2002): 97–115.

Gómez, Ricardo. "The Hall of Mirrors: The Internet in Latin America." *Current History* (February 2000): 72–77.

Inter-American Development Bank. *Economic and Social Progress in Latin America, 1988 Report*. Washington, DC: Inter-American Development Bank, 1988. See especially pp. 105–283.

Katz, Jorge M., ed. *Technology Generation in Latin American Manufacturing Industries*. New York: St. Martin's Press, 1987.

Martínez-Torres, Maria Elena. *Organic Coffee: Sustainable Development by Mayan Farmers*. Athens, OH: Ohio University Press, 2006.

Nelson, Roy C. "Harnessing Globalization: Rio Grande do Sul's Successful Effort to Attract Dell Computer Corporation." *Journal of Developing Societies* 19 (2003): 268–307.

Pereira, Armand. *Ethanol, Employment, and Development: Lessons from Brazil*. Geneva: International Labour Office, 1986.

Roberts, J. Timmons, and Nikki Demetria Thanos, eds. *Trouble in Paradise: Globalization and Environmental Crises in Latin America*. New York and London: Routledge, 2003.

Rodríguez-Clare, Andres. "Costa Rica's Development Strategy Based on Human Capital and Technology: How It Got There, the Impact of Intel, and Lessons for Other Countries." *Journal of Human Development* 2 (July 2001): 311–324.

Roper, Christopher, and Jorge Silva, eds. *Science and Technology in Latin America*. London: Longman, 1983.

Rossett, Peter, and Medea Benjamin, eds. *The Greening of the Revolution: Cuba's Experiment with Organic Agriculture*. Melbourne: Ocean Press, 1994.

Wright, Lloyd. "Latin American Busways: Moving People Rather than Cars." *Natural Resources Forum* 25 (May 2001): 121–134.

DILMUS D. JAMES
STUART MCCOOK

TECÚN-UMÁN (?–1524). Tecún-Umán (*d*. 20 February 1524), Native-American leader of resistance to the Spanish Conquest of Guatemala under Pedro de Alvarado y Mesía. Son of the Quiché king Kicab Tanub, and a leader of the Quiché armies, Tecún-Umán has been identified by some writers as the war leader mentioned by Pedro de Alvarado in his first letter of *relación* (recounting) to Hernán Cortés. Alvarado speaks of the warrior as one of the four lords of Utatlán, the Quiché capital, and as general of the region. Alvarado says that Tecún-Umán was killed at the battle of Piñal. (The date is disputed, but many agree on 20 February 1524.)

Since then, especially in the twentieth century, there has been considerable accretion of myth and legend to the name of Tecún-Umán. He was proclaimed the national hero of Guatemala on 22 March 1960.

See also **Spanish Conquest.**

BIBLIOGRAPHY

Busto Rodríguez, Alfonso del. *Muerte heróica de Don Tecún Umán*. Guatemala: s.n., 1995.

Paz Cárcamo, Guillermo. *La mascara de Tekum/Ri uk'oj Tekum*. Guatemala: Editorial Cholsamaj, 2006.

MURDO J. MACLEOD

TEGUCIGALPA. Tegucigalpa, capital of Honduras. Although the site was probably occupied for millennia before the Spanish conquest, the municipality itself was founded upon the discovery of silver mines by Spanish explorers in the 1570s (according to local lore, "Tegucigalpa" means "hill of silver"). When reports of the rich lodes in and around Tegucigalpa reached the Spanish king, he designated the region an *alcaldía mayor*, raising it to municipal status and granting it limited autonomy from Comayagua. The *Real de Minas de San Miguel de Tegucigalpa* was probably formally established on 29 September 1578. By this act, Tegucigalpa became independent of the provincial capital and episcopal see at Comayagua, thus planting a seed of municipal rivalry between the two.

When the most accessible veins of silver played out a few years later, and the lack of adequate labor and transportation facilities, insufficient capital, inappropriate technology, and meager supplies of mercury severely reduced mining activity, the town shrank in size but did not disappear altogether. Cattle ranching, commerce, and political and ecclesiastical administration combined with residual silver mining to sustain Tegucigalpa as the largest and most prosperous town in colonial Honduras. Indeed, there was still sufficient mining activity to prompt Charles III to redesignate Tegucigalpa an official mining district (*real de minas*) in 1762. Although the *alcaldía mayor* was briefly suppressed in the waning days of the Spanish era, it was revived in 1812.

When Central America gained its independence from Spain, Tegucigalpa and Comayagua agreed, on 30 August 1824, at the Constituent Assembly meeting at Cedros that the two towns would take turns serving as the capital of the Province of Honduras. This arrangement was continued informally after the breakup of the United Provinces of Central America after 1838. In 1880, however, President Marco Aurelio Soto moved the seat of government permanently to Tegucigalpa, where it has remained ever since. In 1907, Bishop José María Martínez y Cabañas successfully negotiated the translation of the ecclesiastical see from Comayagua to Tegucigalpa; since then the seat has been raised to archbishopric. For historical and geographical reasons, the country was never able to link its new capital, Tegucigalpa, to a railroad, and, even today, the Pan-American Highway passes some fifty miles to the south of the capital on its way down the isthmus from San Salvador to Managua. Despite both these bottlenecks, Tegucigalpa, with a population of more than 890,000, has experienced a massive influx of campesinos from the hinterland and is undergoing all the typical growing pains of rapid urbanization. Since the 1990s maquiladoras have been established in the Amarateca valley.

On October 30, 1998, Hurricane Mitch destroyed part of the city, and then continued to hover over the region for five days. Deforestation and ground saturation led to flooding and landslides that decimated neighborhoods, bridges, and historic buildings.

See also **Honduras; Mining: Colonial Spanish America.**

BIBLIOGRAPHY

Acosta, Oscar, ed. *Antología elogio de Tegucigalpa* (1978).

Dúron y Gamero, and Rómulo Ernesto. *La provincia de Tegucigalpa bajo el gobierno de Mallol* (1904).

Langley, Lester D. "Down in Tegoose," in his *Central America: The Real Stakes—Understanding Central America Before It's Too Late* (1985).

Martínez B., Juan Ramón. *Honduras, las fuerzas del desacuerdo: Un ensayo histórico sobre las relaciones entre la Iglesia y el Estado (1525–1972)*. Tegucigalpa: Editorial Universitaria, Universidad Nacional Autónoma de Honduras, 1998.

Wells, William V. *Explorations and Adventures in Honduras* (1857).

KENNETH V. FINNEY

TEHUACÁN.

Tehuacán, a city and a valley, about 150 miles south of Mexico City at the southern edge of the state of Puebla. In this valley, corn (*Zea mays*) was first domesticated some 7,000 years ago. Early corncobs, less than an inch long, were uncovered in early levels of two rock shelters, Ajuereado and San Marcos; from the upper levels of these caves and others 26,000 specimens have been gathered that document corn's development from its wild ancestor to the present-day races. Paralleling the record of maize evolution in this stratified cave sequence are data showing the complete cultural development, starting with the early hunters of Ajuereado from 1500 to 900 BCE. In El Riego times (7000–5000 BCE) they became foragers. These foragers then began to cultivate some plants—mixta squash, avocado, gourds, and chili peppers—in the incipient agricultural stage called Coxcatlán (5000–3400 BCE). During the Abejas phase (3400–2300 BCE), the Tehuacán people grew increasing numbers of domesticated plants—moschata squash, black and white zapotes, common and tepary beans—but continued to be incipient agriculturalists, sometimes living in pit house villages.

Sedentary village life, characterized by corn agriculture and crude pottery, occurred in the poorly documented Purrón phase (2300–1500 BCE). Subsequent stages of development were much like those in the rest of Mesoamerica: Formative—Ajalpán (1500–900 BCE) and Santa María (900–200 BCE); Classic—Palo Blanco (200 BCE–700 CE); and Postclassic—Venta Salada (700–1500 CE, the time of the Spanish conquest).

Archaeological investigations in this valley over a twenty-five-year period (1960–1985) have documented one of the few complete and unbroken cultural sequences for Middle America. Even more significant, Tehuacán records not only the domestication of basic New World plants—corn, squash, and beans—but also the development of agriculture itself.

Today Tehuacán is the second-largest city in the state of Puebla, with a 2005 population of 238,229. In the 1990s textile maquiladoras employed about half of the city's workers and resulted in a population boom. When the maquiladoras vacated the city in the late 1990s, its residents were faced with high levels of unemployment and an environmental nightmare.

See also **Archaeology.**

BIBLIOGRAPHY

Byers, Douglas S. *Tehuacán: El primer horizonte de Mesoamérica* (1968): Richard S. Mac Neish, ed., *The Prehistory of the Tehuacán Valley*, 5 vols. (1972).

Lama, Eréndira de la. *Simposium internacional Tehuacán y su entorno: Balance y perspectivas.* Mexico: Instituto Nacional de Antropología e Historia, Consejo Nacional para la Cultura y las Artes, 1997.

RICHARD S. MACNEISH

TEHUANTEPEC, ISTHMUS OF.

Isthmus of Tehuantepec. The Mexican Isthmus of Tehuantepec, 137 miles wide, is located between the Bay of Campeche on the north and the Gulf of Tehuantepec on the south. Described by Miguel Covarrubias as "a bottleneck of jungle and brush," the isthmus is the natural frontier between North and Central America. Its territory is shared almost equally by the states of Oaxaca and Veracruz, and it separates the southern states of Yucatán, Campeche, Tabasco, and Chiapas from the rest of Mexico. Its geography is extremely diverse, ranging from the isolated Chimalapa Mountains to the fertile plains and tropical grasslands on the Gulf coast, and to the arid Pacific lowlands. Its indigenous inhabitants (Nahuas, Popolocas, Mixes, Zoques, Huaves, Chontales, and both valley and isthmus Zapotecs) have maintained a diverse linguistic and cultural heritage despite numerous conquests, colonizations, and intrusions from pre-Columbian to modern times. Despite that diversity, however, the region is known for its matriarchal society and distinctive female costumes and hairstyles, often worn and depicted by Mexican artist Frida Kahlo.

The geography and strategic location of the isthmus made it the favored site of numerous international schemes to construct interoceanic communication between the Gulf and the Pacific. Hernán Cortés first referred to that possibility in his fourth letter to King Charles V, and the first detailed survey was performed in 1771. Between 1842 and 1894 more than nine different foreign promoters were granted concessions and generous subsidies to complete the route, all of which failed.

President Porfirio Díaz inaugurated the Tehuantepec Railroad and the modern port facilities at Coatzcoalcos and Salina Cruz in 1907. The railway was immensely profitable until 1914, when the combination of the Mexican Revolution, World War I, and the inauguration of the Panama Canal severely limited its usefulness. In recent decades, the Mexican government has invested substantially in local infrastructure to support the petroleum and tourism industries, but the area remains underdeveloped.

See also **Kahlo, Frida.**

BIBLIOGRAPHY

Charles Étienne Brasseur De Bourbourg, *Voyage sur l'Isthme de Tehuantepec, dans l'état de Chiapas et de la République de Guatemala* (1861), translated into Spanish by Elisa Ramírez Castañeda as *Viaje al istmo de Tehuantepec* (1981).

Miguel Covarrubias, *Mexico South: The Isthmus of Tehuantepec* (1946).

Edward B. Glick, "The Tehuantepec Railroad: Mexico's White Elephant," in *Pacific Historical Review* 22 (1953): 373–382.

Additional Bibliography

Mecott Francisco, Mario. *Tehuantepec insurgente.* Oaxaca: Instituto Oaxaqueño de las Culturas: CONACULTA: H. Ayuntamiento de Tehuantepec, 2002.

Miano Borruso, Marinella. *Hombre, mujer, y muxé en el Istmo de Tehuantepec.* México, D.F.: Plaza y Valdés: CONACULTA, INAH, 2002.

Schade, Robert C. *Mexico's Tehuantepec Canal Controversy: A Lesson in American Diplomacy.* Méxicali: J. Issachtts Corrales, 1999.

Zeitlin, Judith Francis. *Cultural Politics in Colonial Tehuantepec: Community and State among the Isthmus Zapotec, 1500–1750.* Stanford, CA: Stanford University Press, 2005.

PAUL GARNER

TEHUELCHES.

Tehuelches (or Aonikenks, as they refer to themselves), indigenous inhabitants, also called Patagones, of the Patagonian steppes north of the Strait of Magellan. Anthropologists divide the group into those people who occupied the area from the strait north to the Santa Cruz River—the Tehuelche meridionals—and those who occupied the semiarid region east of the cordillera from the Santa Cruz River north to the Río Negro—the Tehuelche septentrionals. The word *tehuelche* means "people of the south" (*tehuel,* meaning "south," and *che,* "people") in Mapudungun (Mapuche) and came into common usage in the mid-colonial era as intercultural contacts between Mapuches, Creoles, and pampas Indian groups intensified in the aboriginal homelands of the Aonikenks.

The hunt for Guanaco organized the movements of the Tehuelches, who followed the dispersed herds on foot through the arid Patagonian steppes in a seasonal cycle. Tehuelche subsistence on guanaco was supplemented by the rhea (nandu) and roots and seeds gathered seasonally. Known for their endurance in the desertlike environment of the Patagonian region south of the Río Negro, the Tehuelche meridionals maintained a footbound transhumant subsistence cycle well into the eighteenth century.

When neighboring groups to the north and west (Mapuches, Pehuenches, Pampas) acquired the horse in the sixteenth century, they expanded their barter and hunting excursions into the frontiers of the aboriginal territory of the Tehuelches. The northern Tehuelches, however, continued to maintain their traditional subsistence patterns on foot until the beginning of the eighteenth century, when they too adopted the horse, which facilitated a greater range for hunting and intensified interethnic trading. This innovation led finally to a strong commercial exchange with Chilean colonists in Punta Arenas in the nineteenth century, by which time the Tehuelches had replaced the stone and bone tools used for millennia with tools of metal, glass, and other foreign elements.

It was not until the end of the nineteenth and early twentieth centuries that the Tehuelches lost their cultural autonomy, but the end came quickly when Argentine, Chilean, and European colonists effectively curtailed their movements through a combination of military operations, *matanzas* (slaughters), massive deportations, and the intensified exposure to contagious diseases.

See also **Indigenous Peoples.**

BIBLIOGRAPHY

Belloli, Luis Alberto. *Breve diccionario aborígenes patagónicos: Tehuelche, Mapúche, Ona, Yámana y Alakaluf.* El Hoyo, Chubut, Argentina: Author, 2005.

Briones, Claudia, and José Luis Lanata, eds. *Archaeological and Anthropological Perspectives on the Native Peoples of Pampa, Patagonia, and Tierra del Fuego to the Nineteenth Century.* Westport, CT: Bergin and Garvey, 2002.

Briones, Claudia, and José Luis Lanata, eds. *Contemporary Perspectives on the Native Peoples of Pampa, Patagonia, and Tierra del Fuego: Living on the Edge.* Westport, CT: Bergin and Garvey, 2002.

Casamiquela, Rodolfo M. *Rectificaciones y ratificaciones hacia una interpretación definitiva del panorama etnológico de la Patagonia y area septentrional adyacente.* Bahía Blanca, Argentina, Instituto de Humanidades, Universidad Nacional del Sur, 1965.

Fernandez Garay, Ana. *Diccionario Tehuelche-Español/ Índice Español-Tehuelche.* Leiden: CNWS, 2004.

Martinic B., Mateo. *Los Aónikenk, historia y cultura.* Puntas Arenas, Chile: Ediciones de la Universidad de Magallanes, 1995.

Museo Chileno De Arte Precolombino. *Hombres del sur: Aonikenk, Selknam, Yamana, Kaweshkar.* Santiago, Chile: Musters, George Chaworth, 1987.

Nacuzzi, Lidia Rosa. *Identidades Impuestas: Tehuelches, Aucas y Pampas en el norte de Patagonia,* 2nd edition. Buenos Aires: Sociedad Argentina de Antropologia, 2005.

Steward, Julian H., ed. *Handbook of South American Indians,* vol. 1, pp. 17–29. Washington, DC: U.S. Government Printing Office, 1946.

KRISTINE L. JONES

TEIXEIRA, ANISIO ESPINOLA (1900–1971).

Anisio Espinola Teixeira (*b.* 12 June 1900; *d.* 11 March 1971), rector of the University of Brasília (1963–1964) and one of Brazil's most influential educational reformers. In his career as educational administrator he took steps to expand, democratize, and secularize public education. He was born to a landowning family in Caetité, Bahia. After working in Bahia from 1924 to 1927, Teixeira, an admirer of John Dewey and aspects of the North American educational system, earned an M.A. in 1928 from Columbia University's Teachers' College. Moving in 1931 to Rio de Janeiro, Teixeira became a leader of a group known as the Pioneers of New Education. Accused of being a subversive, a populist, and an atheist by various conservative groups, he lost his administrative post in 1935 because of political purges and stayed out of government work, alternately managing a prosperous export business in Bahia and living in Europe, until the end of Getúlio Vargas's Estado Novo in 1945. He then resumed work as a high-level educational administrator, running two national institutes—the Coordination of Training for Advanced Scholars (Coordenação de Aperfeiçoamento de Pessoa de Nivel Superior—CAPES) and the Instituto Nacional de Estudos Pedagógicos (INEP)—and earning the wrath of conservative political groups and the support of intellectuals.

In 1963 Teixeira became rector of the University of Brasília, only to be ousted by the military coup a year later. When the new government threatened to prosecute him for alleged administrative irregularities, a wave of protests from international academic circles came to his defense. Granted special permission to leave Brazil by President Humberto Castelo Branco, Teixeira traveled to the United States, where he accepted university teaching positions. He returned to Brazil in 1966.

See also **Education: Overview.**

BIBLIOGRAPHY

Teixeira's personal archive is held by the Centro de Pesquisa e Documentação de História Contemporánea (CPDOC) of the Fundação Getúlio Vargas. A partial list of his publications includes *Educação para a democracia* (1936); *Educação progressiva* (1950); *Pequena introdução à filosofia da educação, a escola progressiva ou, a transformação da escola,* 7th ed. (1975); and *Educação e o mundo moderno,* 2nd ed. (1977). Works about Teixeira include Fernando De Azevedo, "Anisio Teixeira e a inteligéncia," in *Figuras de meu convívio* (1960); Hermes Lima, *Anisio Teixeira: Estadista da educação* (1978); *Dicionário histórico-biográfico brasileiro, 1930–1983,* vol. 4 (1984).

Additional Bibliography

Mendonça, Ana Waleska P. C. *Anísio Teixeira e a universidade de educação.* Rio de Janeiro: EdUERJ, 2002.

Monarcha, Carlos, and Carlos Guillerme Mota. *Anísio Teixeira: A obra de uma vida.* Rio de Janeiro: DP&A Editora, 2001.

SUEANN CAULFIELD

TEJADA SORZANO, JOSÉ LUIS (1882–1938).

José Luis Tejada Sorzano (*b.* 12 January 1882; *d.* 4 October 1938), president of Bolivia (27 November 1934–17 May 1936). A lawyer by profession, Tejada Sorzano was an expert in banking and a diplomat. He was a legislator from 1914 to 1918 and was minister of finance (Hacienda) during the government of José Gutiérrez Guerra. He was elected vice president in 1931 and assumed the presidency when President Daniel Salamanca was forced to resign.

The Chaco War with Paraguay was the main preoccupation of Tejada Sorzano. There were genuine attempts to secure peace for the beleaguered nation, but Tejada Sorzano had little support and was overthrown by frustrated military officers.

See also **Bolivia: Bolivia Since 1825; Chaco War.**

BIBLIOGRAPHY

Porfirio Díaz Machicao, *Historia de Bolivia: Salamanca, Guerra de Chaco, Tejada Sorzano 1931–1936* (1955).

David H. Zook, Jr., *The Conduct of the Chaco War* (1960).

Additional Bibliography

Farcau, Bruce W. *The Chaco War: Bolivia and Paraguay, 1932–1935*. Westport, CT: Praeger, 1996.

CHARLES W. ARNADE

TEJEDA, LEONOR DE (1574–c. 1640).

Leonor de Tejeda (*b.* 1574; *d.* ca. 1640), educator and nun. Born in Córdoba to a prominent conquistador family, Leonor de Tejeda was married to general Manuel de Fonseca y Contreras when she was twenty years old. While her husband was serving as lieutenant governor of Buenos Aires (1594–1598), Leonor began to see a need for an institution to harbor elite women with a religious vocation. When her husband returned to Córdoba, she began a school for gentlewomen in her home. The childless couple soon petitioned the crown to allow them to undertake the foundation of the first convent in Córdoba. Widowed in 1612, Tejeda continued to use her fortune and her influence with the bishop to press for the convent, which was finally created on the site of her home in 1613. Among the first group of sixteen women who entered the convent of Santa Catalina de Sena was Tejeda, who took the name of Mother Catalina de Sena and served as prioress until 1627. In 1628 she moved to the city's newly founded second convent, that of Santa Teresa de Jesús, where she served as prioress until 1637. She returned to the Sena convent sometime before her death.

See also **Women.**

BIBLIOGRAPHY

Enrique Udaondo, *Diccionario biográfico colonial argentino* (1945), pp. 870–872.

Additional Bibliography

Brown, Jonathan C. *A Brief History of Argentina*. New York: Facts on File, 2003.

Lewis, Daniel K. *The History of Argentina*. Westport, CT: Greenwood Press, 2001.

Rock, David. *Argentina,: 1562–1812: From Spanish Colonization to the Falklands War*. Berkeley: University of California Press, 1985.

SUSAN M. SOCOLOW

TEJEDA OLIVARES, ADALBERTO

(1883–1960). Adalberto Tejeda Olivares (*b.* 28 March 1883; *d.* 8 September 1960), military figure and governor of the state of Veracruz (1920–1924 and 1928–1932). Adalberto Tejeda Olivares was a well-known Mexican statesman of the 1920s who strove to implement the Constitution of 1917 through radical political, economic, social, and anticlerical reforms.

Tejeda grew up in the predominantly Indian canton of Chicontepec, Veracruz, and attended engineering school in Mexico City. With the outbreak of the Mexican Revolution in 1910, he enlisted in the forces of Venustiano Carranza (1859–1920) and rose to the rank of colonel. While serving as state delegate to the Constitutional Convention of 1916–1917, he advocated strong anticlerical measures and stringent limits on foreign ownership of subsoil rights. The two-time governor of Veracruz championed the rights of the urban and rural lower classes by supporting their efforts to organize, strike, obtain land, and enter into politics. President Plutarco E. Calles (1877–1945) appointed him to serve as minister of government from 1925–1928, during which time he pursued an active anticlerical policy against the Catholic rebels, the *cristeros*. In 1934 the ex-governor ran for the presidency as an independent socialist, defying the official revolutionary party. He was subsequently politically ostracized by his assignment to diplomatic posts in France (1935–1937), Spain (1937–1939), and Peru. In 1948 he became a brigadier general. He died in Mexico City.

See also **Calles, Plutarco Elías; Carranza, Venustiano; Mexico, Constitutions: Constitution of 1917; Veracruz (City).**

BIBLIOGRAPHY

Heather Fowler Salamini, *Agrarian Radicalism in Veracruz, 1920–1938* (1978).

Romana Falcón and Soledad García Morales, *La semilla en el surco, Adalberto Tejeda y el radicalismo en Veracruz, 1883–1960* (1986).

Olivia Domínguez Pérez, *Política y movimientos sociales en el tejedismo* (1986).

Additional Bibliography

Ginzberg, Eitan. "Formación de la infraestructura política para una reforma agraria radical: Adalberto Tejeda y la

cuestión municipal en Veracruz, 1928–1932."
Historia Mexicana 49:4 (Apr.–June 2000): 673–727.

Hermida Ruíz, Angel J. *El atentado al gobernador Adalberto Tejeda*. Mexico: s.n., 1994.

HEATHER FOWLER SALAMINI

TEJEDOR, CARLOS (1817–1903).

Carlos Tejedor (*b.* 4 November 1817; *d.* 3 January 1903), Argentine educator, journalist, lawyer, and politician of the national period. Born in Buenos Aires, Tejedor studied law at its university and graduated in 1837. His academic and judicial pursuits included appointments as professor of criminal and mercantile law at his alma mater in 1856 and government counsel two years later. Tejedor also edited the local *El Nacional* (1852). His greatest contribution, however, was in politics. An opponent of Juan Manuel de Rosas, the Federalist caudillo of Buenos Aires, Tejedor returned from Chilean exile after the dictator's overthrow in 1852. He later became a representative to the Buenos Aires provincial legislature (1853). Tejedor was also minister to Brazil (1875) and governor of Buenos Aires Province (1878–1880). As governor, he opposed federalization of the city of Buenos Aires, which was accomplished only after his defeat by General Julio Argentino Roca in the presidential election of 1880 and in the civil war that accompanied it. Tejedor justified his role in that bloody conflict by writing *La defensa de Buenos Aires* (1881). He died in the capital and his statue was erected in Palermo in 1909.

See also **Buenos Aires; Roca, Julio Argentino; Rosas, Juan Manuel de.**

BIBLIOGRAPHY

Juan Silva Riestra, *Carlos Tejedor: Su influencia en la legislación penal argentina* (1935).

Ricardo Piccirilli, et al., eds., *Diccionario histórico argentino*, vol. 6 (1953–1954), pp. 586–587.

José Campobassi, *Mitre y su época* (1980).

Additional Bibliography

Castello, Antonio Emilio. *Corrientes, Tejedor y la revolución de 1880: Liberales y autonomistas enfrentados en lo interior y exterior*. Corrientes, Argentina: Moglia Ediciones, 2001.

Serrano, Mario Arturo. *La capitalización de Buenos Aires y la revolución de Carlos Tejedor*. Buenos Aires: Círculo Militar, 1995.

FIDEL IGLESIAS

TELA RAILROAD.

Tela Railroad, a railroad line built by the United Fruit Company on the north coast of Honduras, radiating inland from Tela. United Fruit acquired the rights from Sam Zemurray, owner of the rival Cuyamel Fruit Company, in 1913. The Tela Railroad Company, a United Fruit subsidiary, constructed an ice plant, a water system, electrical generators, a hospital, and a 1,000-foot wharf at Tela. United also acquired rights to the Trujillo Railroad, which lay to the east of the holdings of Vacarro Brothers, a rival banana firm operating from La Ceiba. By 1921, Tela had moved ahead of La Ceiba as Honduras's chief banana port.

See also **Railroads.**

BIBLIOGRAPHY

Stacy May and Galo Plaza, *The United Fruit Company in Latin America* (1958).

Thomas Karnes, *Tropical Enterprise: The Standard Fruit and Steamship Company in Latin America* (1978).

Additional Bibliography

1913–1988: Ésta es la Tela Railroad Company. La Lima, Honduras: Tela Railroad Company, 1989.

Estudio sobre el regimen concesionario de la Tela Railroad Company. Tegucigalpa, Honduras: Procaduria General de la República, 1975.

Additional Bibliography

Honduras, Procurador General de la República. *Estudio sobre el regimen concesionario de la Tela Railroad Company*. Tegucigalpa, Honduras: Tela Railroad Company, 1975.

LESTER D. LANGLEY

TELENOVELAS.

The most popular form of television in Latin America, telenovelas are serial dramas that tend to run five or six nights per week in prime time for a limited duration of up to eight or nine months. They typically develop a specific main story, along with various subplots involving major and minor characters. The themes usually involve family dramas, romance, villains, urban settings, social mobility, and, increasingly, contemporary social issues. They dominate prime-time viewing hours in almost all of Latin America and tend to receive the highest audience ratings of all programs. Since 2000, however, reality TV shows have begun to encroach upon telenovelas' popularity.

Historically, telenovelas are related to soap operas and serial novels. They are derived from radionovelas, which were first produced in Cuba by Colgate-Palmolive to sell soap to housewives, following North American successes with the soap opera. The genre spread to other countries, often in the form of exported scripts that were reproduced locally. Telenovelas were first produced in Cuba by Colgate-Palmolive in the early 1950s, and again scripts, scriptwriters, directors, and producers flowed to other countries, particularly after the Cuban Revolution in 1959. Many scholars think that telenovelas' roots include French and English serial novels, which were imported and translated throughout Latin America.

The present-day telenovela has changed quite a bit from its roots in soap opera. Most popular culture scholars have come consider it a distinct genre, and its worldwide popularity continues to transform its content and aesthetics. The main differences are more varied themes, increasingly realistic production styles and values, and a very broad audience. Whereas some telenovelas are still oriented toward family dramas and romance, many have more realistic themes. The Brazilian telenovelas *Vale tudo* and *Pantanal* are about economic corruption and ecology respectively. Some telenovelas, particularly Brazilian, Colombian, and Venezuelan, are historically focused. Although Mexico produces more traditional family dramas, it has also created educational telenovelas with themes on health, family planning, and the need for education.

The telenovela has a very strong relationship to its audience. Telenovelas loom large in many Latin American conversations, and popular ones are watched for months by almost everyone with a television set. Many shows are heavily influenced by audience feedback. Plots are changed, and characters are highlighted or dropped over time. Because telenovelas are the most widely viewed productions, they also play a primary commercial role in selling products to the audience. In Brazil, prominently placed commercial products and discussions of products are worked into the visual design and dialogue of telenovelas.

Most of the major Latin American countries produce telenovelas, with Mexico and Brazil as the largest producers and exporters. Colombia, Venezuela, Argentina, Puerto Rico, Chile and Peru and the United States also produce quite a few and often export them. From the late 1970s to the late 1990s, telenovelas occupied a central position in national television productions, displacing imported North American programs from prime time. International telenovela trade took off in the late 1980s, spurring the popularity of telenovelas throughout the United States and Europe. This popularity leveled off in the late 1990s, as European nations produced home-grown versions, grew tired of the genre, and embraced newer media trends. In East and Southeast Asia, particularly Indonesia, Malaysia and the Philippines telenovelas have seen a boom since the late 1990s. With the increasing number of Latino audience in the United States, the U.S. market is prime target for telenovela distributors.

The international popularity of telenovelas has triggered debates over its creative autonomy in the age of global capitalism. To appeal to U.S. markets, Mexican producers incorporate U.S. Latinos and their needs into the script. To better identify with foreign markets, Mexican and Brazilian telenovelas have decreased their on-location footage for more "universal" settings. Telenovela co-productions have become increasingly common. They involve collaboration between producers from various nation-states on a single series. These telenovelas are released to one or several markets, and preserve a mixture of the cultures involved. Some scholars argue that telenovelas have severed strong national ties between Latin Americans and their programs, neutralizing cultural characteristics to reach wider audiences. Others argue that the transformations of telenovelas reflect their aesthetic flexibility in view of economic and cultural processes of media globalization.

See also **Clair, Janete; Radio and Television.**

BIBLIOGRAPHY

Hamburger, Esther. *O Brasil antenado: A sociedade da novela.* São Paulo: Jorge Zahar, 2005.

Havens, Timothy. "Globalization and the Generic Transformation of Telenovelas." In *Thinking Outside the Box: A Contemporary Television Genre Reader*, edited by Gary R. Edgerton and Brian G. Rose, pp. 271–293. Lexington: University Press of Kentucky, 2005.

Kottak, Conrad Philip. *Prime Time Society*. Belmont, CA: Wadsworth, 1989.

Martin-Barbero, Jesús, and Zilkia Janer, "Transformations in the Map: Identities and Culture Industries." *Latin American Perspectives* 27, no. 4 (July 2000): 27–48.

Mattelart, Michèle, and Armand Mattelart. *The Carnival of Images, Brazilian Television Fiction*, trans. David Buxton. New York: Bergin and Harvey, 1991.

Reyes de la Maza, Luis. *México Sentimental: Crónica de la Telenovela*. México City: Clío, 1999.

Vink, Niko. *The Telenovela and Emancipation: A Study on Television and Social Change in Brazil*. Amsterdam: Royal Tropical Institute, 1990.

JOSEPH STRAUBHAAR
SOPHIA KOUTSOYANNIS

TELEVISION. *See* Radio and Television.

TELLER AMENDMENT. Teller Amendment, proposed by Senator Henry M. Teller in 1898 as an amendment to the U.S. declaration of war against Spain in Cuba. It asserted that the United States would make no attempt to establish permanent control over Cuba. The amendment specified that the United States "hereby disclaims any disposition of intention to exercise sovereignty, jurisdiction, or control over said island except for pacification thereof, and asserts its determination, when that is accomplished, to leave the government and control of the island to its people." But though the Teller Amendment restrained the United States from annexing Cuba after the war, when the Spanish forces surrendered in 1898, the United States established military occupation of Cuba, which ended in 1902.

See also Spanish-American War.

BIBLIOGRAPHY

Julius W. Pratt, *Expansionists of 1898: The Acquisition of Hawaii and the Spanish Islands* (1936).

James D. Rudolph, *Cuba: A Country Study* (1985).

Louis A. Pérez, Jr., *Cuba: Between Reform and Revolution* (1988).

Jaime Suchlicki, *Cuba from Columbus to Castro* (1990).

Additional Bibliography

Carrasco García, Antonio. *En guerra con Estados Unidos: Cuba 1898*. Madrid: Almena Ediciones, 1998.

Pérez, Louis A. *The War of 1898: The United States and Cuba in History and Historiography*. Chapel Hill: University of North Carolina Press, 1998.

DAVID CAREY JR.

TELLES, LYGIA FAGUNDES (1923–).
Lygia Fagundes Telles (*b.* 19 April 1923), Brazilian fiction writer. As a law student in São Paulo, Telles published a short story collection, *Praia viva* (Living Beach), in 1944. In 1949 her collection of short stories *O cacto vermelho* (The Red Cactus) received the Brazilian Academy of Letters prize for fiction, marking the beginning of a distinguished literary career that includes four novels, seven short-story collections, and eight prizes. Telles's fiction exhibits both modern literary techniques and knowledge of Brazilian life, with emphasis on the female psyche. Her most celebrated novel, *As meninas* (1973; *The Girl in the Photograph*, 1982), re-creates aspects of the 1964–1984 military regime. Telles's forte is the short story; she is known for her use of the fantastic. Her fiction reflects her era, attracting both readers and critics. Female readers recognize themselves in her strong characterizations of urban women. Her 1990 novel, *As horas nuas* (Naked Hours), follows previous directions in presenting an actress's existential concerns in present-day São Paulo. Politically outspoken, Telles participated in protests against the military regime. In 1985 she became the third woman elected to the Brazilian Academy of Letters. In 1989, her work *As horas nuas* won the Dom Infante Santo Prize from Portugal. In 1994 she was a participant in the Festival of the Book in Frankfurt. In 2001, her book *Invenção e Memória* won the Jabuti Prize for Fiction, and the Grand Prize from the Associação Paulista dos Críticos de Arte. That same year, she was awarded an honorary doctorate from the Universidade de Brasília. In 2005, she won the Camões Prize, the most prestigious prize for literature in the Portuguese language.

See also Literature: Brazil.

BIBLIOGRAPHY

Other works by Telles include *Histórias do desencontro* (1958); *Seminário dos ratos* (1977); *Mistérios* (1981); and *Tigrela and Other Stories* (1986). Critical attention to her fiction includes Richard Burgin, "*Tigrela and Other Stories*," in *New York Times Book Review* (4 May 1986); and John M. Tolman, "New Fiction: Lygia Fagundes Telles," in *Review* no. 30 (1981): 65–70.

Additional Bibliography

Erro-Peralta, Nora, and Caridad Silva. *Beyond the Border: A New Age in Latin American Women's Fiction.* Gainesville: University Press of Florida, 2000.

Rector, Monica. *Brazilian Writers.* Farmington Hills, MI: Thomson Gale, 2005.

Sadlier, Darlene J. *One Hundred Years After Tomorrow: Brazilian Women's Fiction in the 20th Century.* Bloomington: Indiana University Press, 1992.

MARIA ANGÉLICA LOPES

TELLO, JULIO CÉSAR (1880–1947).

Julio César Tello (*b.* 11 April 1880; *d.* 3 June 1947), Peruvian who played a central role in initiating the scientific study of Andean prehistory and establishing the institutional framework for protecting and conserving the Peruvian archaeological patrimony. A native Quechua speaker from Huarochirí, in the highlands east of Lima, Tello brought to his research an indigenous perspective and a passionate commitment to uncovering and elucidating the accomplishments of Andean cultures before the Spanish conquest.

Tello studied science and medicine at the Universidad Nacional Mayor de San Marcos and wrote his doctoral dissertation on the antiquity of syphilis in Peru. With support from the Peruvian government he subsequently attended Harvard, where he studied archaeology and anthropology at the Peabody Museum and completed a master's degree in anthropology. Tello then studied at London University before returning to Peru as that nation's first professional archaeologist. He immediately became the director of archaeology at the Museo Histórico Nacional and launched a series of expeditions that made him world famous.

By 1924 Tello had been appointed director of both archaeological museums in Lima while introducing the teaching of archaeology and anthropology into the Peruvian university system. During a remarkable career that spanned four decades, Tello founded anthropological journals, including *Chaski, Inca,* and *Wira-kocha,* as well as Peru's principal archaeological museum, the Museo Nacional de Antropología y Arqueología.

Concurrent with these academic activities, Tello carried on a political career dedicated to the defense of Peru's indigenous population. In 1917 he was elected as Haurochirí's representative to Congress, where he served for the next eleven years.

Tello's explorations and discoveries covered much of the Peruvian coast and highlands. He identified the Chavín civilization as the matrix out of which later Peruvian cultures developed, and he considered the highland site of Chavín de Huántar as its center. Many of Tello's most important investigations—including those at Paracas on the south coast; Ancón on the central coast; Cerro Sechín, Moxeke, and Cerro Blanco (Nepeña) on the north-central coast; and Kuntur Wasi and Cumbemayo in the northern highlands—demonstrated the existence, temporal priority, and panregional extent of what is now known as the Chavín horizon. By establishing that highland Chavín civilization preceded the better-known coastal cultures such as Moche and Nasea, Tello was able to demonstrate the autochthonous character of Andean civilization and disprove Max Uhle's hypothesis of Mesoamerican and Asian origins of Peruvian high culture. Tello's contention that the roots of Andean civilization lay in still earlier developments within the tropical forest, bolstered by his research at the site of Kotosh, also proved to be influential. His contributions to later Peruvian prehistory include his excavations of the Inca occupation at Pachacamac. Tello's theoretical orientation differed significantly from the approach advocated by his North American colleagues, and in many respects his publications anticipated the ecological and structuralist approaches that became popular many decades later in U.S. and European archaeology.

Tello's publications include "Wira-Kocha," in *Inka,* 1, no. 1 (1923): 94–320, and 1, no. 3 (1923): 583–606; "Discovery of the Chavín Culture in Peru," in *American Antiquity,* 9, no. 1 (1942): 35–66; *Origen y desarrollo de las civilizaciones prehistóricas andinas* (1942); *Arqueología del Valle de Casma* (1956); *Paracas,* 2 vols. (1959–1979); *Chavín, cultura matriz de la civilización andina* (1960); *Páginas escogidas* (1967).

See also **Anthropology; Archaeology.**

BIBLIOGRAPHY

A good source of biographical and bibliographical information is S. K. Lothrop, "Julio C. Tello, 1880–1947," in *American Antiquity,* 14 (July 1948): 50–56.

Additional Bibliography

Amat Olazabal, Hernán, and Luis Guzmán Palomino. *Julio C. Tello: Forjador del Perú autentico.* Lima: Centro de Estudios Históric-Militares del Perú, 1997.

Jaguande D'Anjoy, Alfonso. *El sabio Julio C. Tello.* Lima: A. Jagaunde D'Anjoy, 2001.

                                    RICHARD L. BURGER

TEMPLO MAYOR. *El Templo Mayor*, the Great Temple (*Huey Teocalli*), is the main religious building at Tenochtitlan, the capital city of the Mexica, the dominant people in the cultural area of Mesoamerica during the late Postclassical period (1325–1521). According to sixteenth-century Nahua chronicles, after leaving their mythical place of origin, Aztlan-Chicomostoc, and wandering for a long time, in 1325 the Mexicas found the place that their chief god, Huitzilopochtli, had chosen for them to settle. Stories differ regarding the divine manifestations through which this revelation came. One tells of a double spring of water, one part flowing with blue water and another with red, a clear sign of duality—a principle of Mesoamerican thought by which all things had an opposite and complementary counterpart (sky to earth, water to fire, and so on). Another describes an eagle standing on a cactus, devouring birds with colorful plumage or a serpent (the image on Mexico's present-day coat of arms). In this holy place, the Mexicas founded their most important temple, consisting of a double pyramid-shaped base with four superimposed bodies and twin staircases ascending its main, west-facing façade, leading to two smaller temples on the top. The one on the north was dedicated to Tláloc, the rain god, and the one on the south to Huitzilopochtli, the sun and war god. At the time Tenochtitlan was founded, the Mexicas were a subjugated people who had to pay tribute to the Tepanecs in Azcapotzalco, but they freed themselves from that yoke shortly afterwards and began a series of wars of imperial expansion that would give them control of a territory extending from the Pacific to the Atlantic and from the Huasteca area to the region of Soconusco.

Archeological excavations between 1978 and 1982 brought to light the remains of the Great Temple, as well as another four structures in the sacred precinct of Tenochtitlan, in the heart of present-day Mexico City. It was possible to distinguish seven architectural enlargements of the Great Temple, successively built one on another. The oldest one found is thought to pertain to the reign of one of the first three Mexica governors, between 1375 and 1426, while the more recent one is attributed to Moctezuma II, who reigned from 1502 to 1520, the period when Europeans made contact.

Key archeological findings are the 124 offerings buried in the Great Temple and neighboring buildings, some of which comprise thousands of objects, well illustrating the splendor attained by the Tenochcas in their mere 300 years of imperial conquest. Materials and objects among them have been traced to exotic regions, reaching Tenochtitlan by means of tribute or commercial interchange, pieces manufactured locally and sometimes copying foreign styles, and even antiquities looted from other sites or perhaps conserved as relics. Study of these offerings has revealed that the objects were not randomly placed, but were set in pre-established patterns, to convey specific messages. One of their most important functions was to pay the deities for favors received. Excavations in what was the ritual precinct of Tenochtitlan continue in the early twenty-first century, mainly in the form of archeological rescue operations when public and private works are under construction in Mexico City. Investigation also continues on the archeological remains that have been recovered.

See also **Archaeology; Aztecs; Aztlán; Huitzilopochtli; Mesoamerica; Nahuas; Tenochtitlán; Tlaloc.**

BIBLIOGRAPHY

López Arenas, Gabino. *Rescate arqueológico en la Catedral y el Sagrario metropolitanos: Estudio de ofrendas.* Mexico City: Instituto Nacional de Antropología e Historia, 2003.

López Luján, Leonardo. *The Offerings of the Templo Mayor of Tenochtitlan*, rev. edition, trans. Bernard R. Ortiz de Montellano and Thelma Ortiz de Montellano. Albuquerque: University of New Mexico Press, 2005.

Matos Moctezuma, Eduardo. *The Great Temple of the Aztecs: Treasures of Tenochtitlan*, trans. Doris Heyden. London: Thames and Hudson, 1988.

Velázquez Castro, Adrián. *El simbolismo de los objetos de concha encontrados en las ofrendas del Templo Mayor de Tenochtitlán*. Mexico City: Instituto Nacional de Antropología e Historia, 2000.

ADRIÁN VELÁZQUEZ CASTRO

TEMUCO.

Temuco, city of 210,587 inhabitants (2005) on the northern bank of the Cautín River, the most important urban center of the Araucanía region of Chile (2002 population 869,535). Founded in 1881 by General Gregorio Urrutia after a pacification campaign conducted against the bellicose Araucanian Indians, it became an active colonization center and an outpost to keep the Araucanians at bay. Chilean, Swiss, and German families settled in Temuco, which by 1950 had grown into the fourth-largest urban center of the country. More than an industrial city, Temuco is a service and administrative center for wheat and dairy farmers and for the 185,000 Araucanians who still live in Temuco's environs.

See also **Araucana, La; Chile, Geography.**

BIBLIOGRAPHY

Instituto de Estudios Indígenas. *Tierra, territorio y desarrollo indígena*. Temuco, Chile: Instituto de Estudios Indígenas, Universidad de la Frontera, 1995.

CÉSAR N. CAVIEDES

TENANTS' REVOLT. *See* **Panama, Tenants' Revolt.**

TENENTISMO.

Tenentismo, a 1920s Brazilian politico-military movement that, after joining forces with the 1930 Revolution, exercised great power in the early 1930s. The *tenentes* were young military officers and intellectuals who participated in conspiracies and revolts to protest against political corruption and to force government reforms, especially elimination of the extreme federalism of the period. They first rebelled on 5 July 1922 in Rio de Janeiro against the inauguration of President-elect Artur da Silva Bernardes, who for them symbolized the iniquity of Brazilian politics and social structure. Most troops remained loyal and quickly put down the uprising, but eighteen rebels refused to surrender and

marched down Copacabana beach, where they were fired upon and arrested. Two were martyred and the rest went to prison, among them Antônio de Siqueira Campos and Eduardo Gomes.

During the next two years several more *tenente* revolts erupted, culminating in the July 1924 capture of the city of São Paulo for a month under the leadership of Miguel Costa, of the state police. The brothers Juarez and Joaquim Távora were among the masterminds of this victory. The *tenentes* escaped into the interior, where they joined with other groups, especially one commanded by Luís Carlos Prestes, a captain in the engineering corps.

Led by Prestes and Costa, the revolutionaries (numbering several thousand) set out on a great march (the Prestes Column) through the backlands to publicize their demands for honest elections, political freedoms, amnesty for themselves, and strengthening of the national state. They covered some 15,000 miles in eleven states, mostly in the poor Northeast, using guerrilla tactics to avoid major engagements. Finally, with their ranks thinned and the army dogging their tracks, the *tenentes* crossed into Bolivia in February 1927 and dispersed.

From 1927 until 1930, the *tenentes* remained in exile or underground, hoping for pardons but continuing their criticism of the government and oligarchic society. Those in hiding often met in the Rio clinic of a sympathizer, Dr. Pedro Ernesto Batista. Their ideas ranged from fascist on the right to communist on the left, and no single person spoke for the group. Many took hope when presidential candidate Getúlio Vargas promised them amnesty in the 1930 campaign; and most answered the call when Vargas's managers, Oswaldo Aranha and Góis Monteiro, recruited them for a revolt later in the year. *Tenente* leaders such as João Alberto Lins de Barros, Djalma Dutra, Oswaldo Cordeiro de Farias, and Juracy Magalhães, among the most experienced soldiers in the country, made up the high command of the revolutionary army.

In the months following Vargas's victory, the *tenentes* became convinced that they were being passed over. They wanted army reinstatement at the ranks they would have held, control over a majority of the troops, and influence in government policy. In order to achieve these goals, they formed the Club 3 de Outubro in early 1931 to pressure Vargas. They soon chose their ally Pedro Ernesto as president, partly because he had access to Vargas as the first family's physician.

Within several months Vargas came to depend on the club for political support—his hold on power was extremely tenuous—and in exchange he appointed them as state interventors, promoted them in the army, and consulted them on major decisions. The *tenentes* reached the pinnacle of their power in early 1932, serving as a praetorian guard for Vargas. They compiled an eclectic program of reforms, some socialist, others fascist, to be enacted by a corporatist regime. By mid-1932, however, the club had outlived its usefulness, having provoked a civil war in São Paulo. After his victory, Vargas decided to democratize his government. Some *tenentes* went into civilian politics, while others returned to military life. The club symbols were invoked from time to time, but its leadership had disbanded. Several *tenentes* went on to prominence during the Vargas era and enjoyed heroic images, for example, Távora, Prestes, Gomes, José Américo de Almeida, and Cordeiro de Farias; they did not work together, however, nor forge a common program.

Tenentismo was uniquely Brazilian; nothing like it occurred elsewhere in Latin America, despite frequent military intervention in politics.

See also **Aranha, Oswaldo; Bernardes, Artur da Silva; Brazil, Revolutions: Revolts of 1923-1924; Brazil, Revolutions: Revolution of 1930; Gomes, Eduardo; Prestes, Luís Carlos; Prestes Column; Távora, Juárez; Vargas, Getúlio Dornelles.**

BIBLIOGRAPHY

Jordan Young, *The Brazilian Revolution of 1930 and the Aftermath* (1967).

Boris Fausto, *A revolução de 1930* (1970).

Neill Macaulay, *The Prestes Column* (1974).

Michael L. Conniff, "The Tenentes in Power," in *Journal of Latin American Studies* 10, no. 1 (1977): 61–82.

José Augusto Drummond, *O movimento tenentista* (1986).

Maria Cecília Spina Forjaz, *Tenentismo e forças armadas na revolução de 30* (1989).

Additional Bibliography

Cascardo, Francisco Carlos Pereira. *O tenentismo na Marinha: Os primeiros anos (1922 a 1924.)* São Paulo: Paz e Terra, 2005.

Moraes, João Quartim de. *A esquerda militar no Brasil.* São Paulo: Editora Expressão Popular, 2005.

MICHAEL L. CONNIFF

TENOCHTITLÁN. Tenochtitlán, capital city of Aztec Empire, center of present-day Mexico City. According to native histories, the Mexica founded Tenochtitlán in 1325. They were led by their god Huitzilopochtli to a spot where an eagle perched atop a prickly pear cactus, or *tenochtli;* Tenochtitlán means "By the Prickly Pear Fruits." This divinely ordained site was a marshy island in Lake Texcoco east of Chapultepec. The Mexica developed this marginal property by trading ducks, fish, and other edible lake products for wood and stone from the mainland. As the Mexica gained political power, eventually dominating what is now called the Aztec Empire, they were able to commandeer building supplies and labor and Tenochtitlán grew in size and population. At the time of the Spanish invasion it was the largest city in Mesoamerica, with a probable population of 125,000 or more.

A "Venice of the New World," Tenochtitlán was crisscrossed by canals that served for canoe transportation; moveable wooden bridges allowed for pedestrian passage. The basic layout of the city comprised four sectors, separated by major canals, surrounding the central political-ceremonial precinct (now the *zócalo*), where the rulers had their palaces and the major deities their temples—most notably the Great Temple of Huitzilopochtli and Tlaloc. Within each residential sector lay a variable number of Calpulli, or "big houses," neighborhood units tending toward endogamy and occupational specialization. These served as administrative units for taxation and military draft; each had its own temple and schools. Toward the city's outskirts, raised fields, or chinampas, provided a local source of fresh vegetables and flowers. Causeways to the west and the south linked the city to the mainland; an aqueduct brought fresh water from Chapultepec because the lake water was too saline for drinking. Flood control, another major problem, was partly solved by means of a system of dikes.

Just north of Tenochtitlán lay Tlatelolco, originally an independent Mexica settlement but conquered by Tenochtitlán in 1473. The two islands were separated by a narrow waterway (today the site of the Lagunilla market). Tlatelolco boasted the principal market for the greater urban district. The two islands covered an area of about 3 square miles.

Although Cortés and his Spanish followers marveled at the beauty and orderliness of the island city, they and their native allies leveled most of it during the two-and-a-half month siege that led to Spanish control of the city and its transformation into the capital of New Spain.

See also **Aztecs; Huitzilopochtli; Mesoamerica; Mexico City.**

BIBLIOGRAPHY

Jacques Soustelle, *Daily Life of the Aztecs on the Eve of the Spanish Conquest* (1961).

Diego Durán, *The Aztecs: The History of the Indies of New Spain,* translated by Doris Heyden and Fernando Horcasitas (1964).

Luis González Aparicio, *Plano reconstructivo de la región de Tenochtitlán* (1973).

Frances Berdan, *The Aztecs of Central Mexico: An Imperial Society* (1982).

Johanna Broda, Davíd Carrasco, and Eduardo Matos Moctezuma, *The Great Temple of Tenochtitlán* (1987).

Additional Bibliography

Carrasco Pizana, Pedro. *The Tenochca Empire of Ancient Mexico: The Triple Alliance of Tenochtitlan, Tetzcoco, and Tlacopan.* Norman: University of Oklahoma Press, 1999.

López Luján, Leonardo. *The Offerings of the Templo Mayor of Tenochtitlan.* Trans. Bernard R. Ortiz de Montellano and Thelma Ortiz de Montellano. Niwot: University Press of Colorado, 1994.

Solís Olguín, Felipe R., ed. *The Aztec Empire.* New York: Guggenheim Museum Publications, 2004.

LOUISE M. BURKHART

TEN YEARS' WAR (1868–1878).

Ten Years' War (1868–1878), the first major Cuban struggle for independence. It was also a manifestation of serious social, economic, and political grievances on the island. While it failed to win independence, it did begin the process of slave emancipation in Cuba.

By the 1850s, Cuba had become the world's leading sugar exporter, tied increasingly to the U.S. market. But many agrarian workers had been displaced in the shift from a more diversified agricultural economy to one dominated by slave-produced sugar at the same time that Cuba's population was growing rapidly, as Louis Pérez has asserted. Eastern Cuba was suffering especially in comparison to the newer sugar-producing regions of the west. Abolitionists demanded an end to slavery. Many Creoles wanted political and economic reform and some favored independence or annexation to the United States, which had showed repeated interest in acquiring Cuba. The liberal Spanish government of General Enrique O'Donnell (1858–1863) raised Cuban expectation of reform, but the subsequent conservative government pursued a repressive policy that alienated Cubans of many classes, especially in eastern Cuba.

Political turmoil in Spain, in fact, contributed to the breakdown of order in Cuba. On 18 September 1868 naval officers at Cádiz revolted and ten days later revolutionaries took Madrid, proclaiming a liberal republic. The new government's refusal to grant reforms, however, led an eastern Cuban Creole planter, Carlos Manuel de Céspedes, to proclaim Cuban independence on 10 October 1868 in what came to be known as the Grito De Yara. Calling for independence as well as gradual emancipation of slaves and universal male suffrage, he rallied support against Spain, and began a guerrilla war at Bayamo. On 20 April 1869, a constitutional convention organized a republican government at Guámairo, which supported annexation to the United States. Bitter guerrilla warfare followed, while Spain vacillated between monarchy and republic until the Bourbons were finally restored with the coronation of Alfonso XII in January 1875.

The slavery issue created a deep schism within the revolutionary movement and cost it support of some of the planters of western Cuba. Many of those fighting came from the colored classes, who favored complete and immediate abolition. The military leaders Máximo Gómez and Antonio Maceo represented that view, but the rebel government leaders, dominated by planters, repeatedly refused to allow them to carry the war into the west.

The United States, Britain, and France all were interested in Cuba but none intervened in the devastating conflict. The Virginius Affair, in which Spanish naval forces on 31 October 1873 seized a filibustering ship flying the U.S. flag off Jamaica and executed more than fifty of its officers, crew, and passengers, seriously strained relations with the United States, but U.S. intervention was averted by the diplomatic pressure of England and France.

By 1878 the war had damaged the sugar industry and cost 250,000 lives. At El Zanjón (11 February 1878), the Spanish agreed to some political reform, to freedom for all those slaves who had fought with the rebels, and gradual emancipation for the rest with compensation to the owners. This agreement with the Creole leadership, however, fell far short of giving Cubans autonomy or the social reforms for which many had fought, so that the Pact of Zanjón itself became an issue for continued dissent in Cuba. Immediately after the pact was signed, General Maceo issued the "Protest of Baraguá" and continued to fight on for nearly three more months before finally succumbing to Spanish forces in May.

The war led to a major reorganization of the sugar industry in the 1880s, with major capital investment from the United States. But the Spanish failure to implement the reforms and the continued social and economic problems would contribute to a resumption of the Cuban War for Independence in 1895.

Although it failed to achieve independence, the Ten Years' War spawned a number of important later Cuban leaders, including José Martí, Fernando Figueredo, and Tomás Estrada Palma.

See also **Cuba: The Colonial Era (1492–1898); Estrada Palma, Tomás; Gómez y Báez, Máximo; Grito de Yara; Maceo, Antonio; Martí y Pérez, José Julián; Virginius Affair.**

BIBLIOGRAPHY

Fernando Figueredo, *La revolución de Yara* (1902; repr. 1969).

Hugh Thomas, *Cuba: The Pursuit of Freedom* (1971).

María Cristina Llerena, ed., *Sobre la guerra de los 10 años, 1868–1878* (1973).

Aleida Plasencia, ed., *Bibliografía de la guerra de los diez años* (1968).

Vidal Morales y Morales, *Iniciadores y primeros martires de la revolución cubana*, 3 vols. (1931).

Magdalenta Pando, *Cuba's Freedom Fighter, Antonio Maceo, 1845–1896* (1980).

Philip Foner, *Antonio Maceo: The "Bronze Titan" of Cuba's Struggle for Independence* (1977).

Florencio García Cisneros, *¿Máximo Gómez, caudillo o dictador?* (1986), Ramiro Guerra y Sánchez, *Guerra de los diez años, 1868–1878*, 2 vols. (1972).

Richard H. Bradford, *The "Virginius" Affair* (1980).

James M. Callahan, *Cuba and International Relations* (1899).

Enrique Collazo, *Desde Yara hasta Zanjón* (1893; 1967).

Juan Almeida Bosque, *El general en jefe Máximo Gómez* (1986).

Louis A. Pérez, *Cuba: Between Reform and Revolution* (1988).

Benigno Souza y Rodríguez, *Máximo Gómez, el generalisimo* (1986).

Additional Bibliography

Ferrer, Ada. *Insurgent Cuba: Race, Nation, and Revolution, 1868–1898*. Chapel Hill: University of North Carolina Press, 1999.

Rey, Miguel del. *La Guerra de los 10 años, 1868–1878*. Madrid: Ristre, 2003.

Tone, John Lawrence. *War and Genocide in Cuba, 1868–1898*. Chapel Hill: University of North Carolina Press, 2006.

Ralph Lee Woodward Jr.

TEOTIHUACÁN.

Teotihuacán, the preeminent center of religious, economic, and political power in central Mexico from approximately 100 BCE to 750 CE. The site of this ancient city is about 30 miles northeast of Mexico City, in the Valley of Mexico, a temperate, semiarid region in the central Mexican highlands. At its height (500–600 CE) it was home to at least 125,000 inhabitants and covered 7 to 8 square miles. As the first "true city" in the New World, Teotihuacán represented an unprecedented social transformation and had a significant impact on all subsequent pre-Columbian civilizations in Mexico.

Teotihuacán was above all the seat of a vigorous religion whose most sacred precepts were played out in the construction of a monumental ceremonial center that was the setting for ritual performances and extravaganzas, often including human sacrifice. A wide, north-south thoroughfare, the Street of the Dead, bisected the center and provided the basic orientation (1525' east of north) to which virtually all later ceremonial and residential construction conformed. Three immense pyramid complexes dominate its core: the Pyramid of the Moon, at the north

Protest over Wal-Mart store built near the ancient city of Teotihuacán, Mexico City, 2004. Despite months of protest, Wal-Mart, Mexico's largest retailer, quietly opened a supermarket within view of the Teotihuacán pyramids. The proximity of the store to the once complex urban center generated debate over symbols and nationalism. © ANDREW WINNING/REUTERS/ CORBIS

end of the Street of the Dead; the Pyramid of the Sun, along its east side; and the Ciudadela, the city's administrative center, on the southeast. Directly opposite the Ciudadela is an enormous enclosure that served as the central marketplace. Scores of smaller temple platforms lining the Street of the Dead and elsewhere are built in a style found only in Teotihuacán.

The city's population grew rapidly during the period of major pyramid construction. Its growth involved the massive, planned resettlement of most of the region's rural inhabitants within its limits and the immigration of many foreign residents, probably emissaries and merchants. Problems of housing and administering this diverse agglomeration of people were met through the construction of more than 2,000 stone-walled apartment compounds organized into barrios. Most of these

single-story, windowless structures housed from 60 to 100 people and contained a number of separate apartments consisting of rooms and porticoes arranged around open patios.

At least two-thirds of the urban population were farmers who cultivated land around the city, utilizing the valley's permanent springs for irrigation. Staples such as corn and beans, along with a variety of wild plants, game, and domesticated dog and turkey, constituted the city's food supply. Another large segment of the population were full-time craftsmen involved in ceramic production and the working of obsidian, bone, and feathers. Others were plasterers, painters, warriors, merchants, or bureaucrats. At the apex of this highly stratified society were priest-rulers who governed in the name of the gods.

The Teotihuacán state exercised strong control over its economy, managing (to varying degrees) critical resources, production, and exchange both within the Valley of Mexico and beyond. For example, the distribution of green obsidian for the city's vital obsidian industry was regulated, and many workshops are thought to have been under direct state control. Even some items produced far outside of the city, such as the popular thin orange pottery, appear to have been marketed through the city. Although Teotihuacán's long-distance trade and foreign relations are poorly understood, the impact of the city was felt as far away as the Maya area in Guatemala.

Sometime in the eighth century the ceremonial heart of Teotihuacán was systematically burned and destroyed; the citizens may have been involved. The population fell sharply, its great culture disintegrated, and the city never regained its former eminence.

See also **Archaeology.**

BIBLIOGRAPHY

René Millón, R. Bruce Drewitt, and George L. Cowgill, *Urbanization at Teotihuacán, Mexico.* Vol. 1, *The Teotihuacán Map* (1973), pts. 1 and 2.

William T. Sanders, Jeffrey R. Parsons, and Robert S. Santley, *The Basin of Mexico: Ecological Processes in the Evolution of a Civilization* (1979).

René Millón, "Teotihuacán: City, State, and Civilization," in *Supplement to the Handbook of Middle American Indians.* Vol. 1, *Archaeology,* edited by Victoria R. Bricker and Jeremy A. Sabloff (1981), 198–243.

George L. Cowgill, "Rulership and the Ciudadela: Political Inferences from Teotihuacán Architecture," in *Civilization in the Ancient Americas: Essays in Honor of Gordon R. Willey,* edited by Richard M. Leventhal and Alan L. Kolata (1983), pp. 313–343.

René Millón, "The Last Years of Teotihuacán Dominance," in *The Collapse of Ancient States and Civilizations,* edited by Norman Yoffee and George L. Cowgill (1988), pp. 102–164.

Ruben Cabrera Castro, Saburo Sugiyama, and George L. Cowgill, "The 'Templo de Quetzalcoatl' Project at Teotihuacán," in *Ancient Mesoamerica* 2, no. 1 (1991).

Additional Bibliography

Braswell, Geoffrey E. *The Maya and Teotihuacan: Reinterpreting Early Classic Interaction.* Austin: University of Texas Press, 2003.

Carrasco, David, Lindsay Jones, and Scott Sessions. *Mesoamerica's Classic Heritage: From Teotihuacan to the Aztecs.* Boulder: University Press of Colorado, 1999.

López Austin, Alfredo, and Leonardo López Luján. *Mexico's Indigenous Past.* Trans. Bernard R. Ortiz de Montellano. Norman: University of Oklahoma Press, 2001.

Pasztory, Esther. *Teotihuacan: An Experiment in Living.* Norman: University of Oklahoma Press, 1997.

Sempowski, Martha Lou, and Michael W. Spence. *Mortuary Practices and Skeletal Remains at Teotihuacan,* vol. 3. Salt Lake City: University of Utah Press, 1994.

Sugiyama, Saburo. *Human Sacrifice, Militarism, and Rulership: Materialization of State Ideology at the Feathered Serpent Pyramid, Teotihuacan.* New York: Cambridge University Press, 2005.

MARTHA L. SEMPOWSKI

TEPITO. A traditional, stable, working-class neighborhood, comprising approximately one square kilometer of downtown Mexico City north of the Zócalo, the central square, and roughly bounded by the following four streets: Cinco de Mayo, Lázaro Cárdenas (Eje Central), Rayón, and República de Argentina. Forming part of the historic center of the city, it has been the focus of several revitalization programs over the years. The neighborhood has a strong community spirit as well as a barrio dialect and culture, and has been the place of origin of many of the nation's best-known boxers and *luchadores* (masked wrestlers, practitioners of lucha libre). The "thieves' market" in Tepito in the past had a reputation for smuggled and other goods of dubious origin.

Most of the population rent single rooms in converted and now derelict mansions long since vacated by the elite. Alternatively, they live in other vecindades (courtyard tenements) that were built before 1940s rent control legislation made their construction unprofitable, and contributes to their present dilapidation. The area was badly affected by the 1985 earthquakes, although most of the residents worst affected were rehoused in small apartments built on the same lotsas their original homes. The Casa Blanca vecindad was home to the Sánchez family in American anthropologist Oscar Lewis's classic text *The Children of Sanchez* (1961). The local economy remains one of petty services, sweatshops, and small workshops specializing in low-cost furniture manufacture, shoe production, and similar enterprises.

See also **Mexico, Federal District; Mexico City.**

BIBLIOGRAPHY

Colomb, René. "El Centro Histórico." In *La Ciudad de México en el fin del segundo milenio*, edited by Gustavo Garza. Mexico City: El Colegio de México, Centro de Estudios Demográficos y de Desarrollo Urbano; el Gobierno del Distrito Federal, 2000.

Cross, John C. *Informal Politics: Street Vendors and the State in Mexico City.* Stanford, CA: Stanford University Press, 1998.

Monnet, Jérôme. *Usos e imágenes del centro histórico de la ciudad de México.* Translated by Pastora Rodríguez Aviñoa. Mexico City: Departamento del Distrito Federal, Centro de Estudios Mexicanos y Centramericanos, 1995.

Ziccardi, Alicia. "Delegación Cuautémoc." In *La Ciudad de México en el fin del segundo milenio 2000*, edited by Gustavo Garza. Mexico City: El Colegio de México, Centro de Estudios Demográficos y de Desarrollo Urbano; el Gobierno del Distrito Federal, 2000.

PETER M. WARD

TEQUESTA.

The Tequesta, a native American group in southeast Florida during the colonial period, were encountered in the Miami area by the Juan Ponce de León expedition in 1513. Archaeological evidence indicates the Tequesta and their pre-Columbian ancestors had inhabited the region for at least two thousand years. Their economy was centered on the collection of wild resources, especially fish. Early accounts refer to a chief called Tequesta, who at times was a vassal to the Calusa chief.

In 1566 Pedro Menéndez de Avilés installed a garrison with a Jesuit priest in the main town of Tequesta, but it was withdrawn the following year. In 1568 the Jesuit mission was reestablished, but lasted only to 1570. In 1743 Tequesta was the location of yet another attempt to establish a Jesuit mission and a fort. By then, only remnants of the Tequesta and other south Florida aborigines remained. Disease and warfare had taken their toll, and some Tequesta are thought to have emigrated to Cuba during the eighteenth century.

In 1999 a thirty-eight-foot-wide Tequesta ceremonial stone slab dating from around 100 CE (and dubbed Florida's Stonehenge) was uncovered at a downtown Miami construction site. In 2006 a pair of Tequesta cemeteries were discovered in the downtown area, promising to shed light on Tequesta mortuary practices, disease, and the general health of Tequesta people.

See also **Florida; Indigenous Peoples.**

BIBLIOGRAPHY

Goggin, John M. "The Tekesta Indians of Southern Florida," in *Florida Historical Quarterly* 18 (1940): 274–284.

Zubillaga, Felix, ed. *Monumenta antiquae Floridae (1566–1572)* (1946).

Sturtevant, William C. "The Last of the South Florida Aborigines," in *Tacachale: Essays on the Indians of Florida and Southeast Georgia During the Historic Period*, edited by Jerald T. Milanich and Samuel Proctor (1978).

Milanich, Jerald T., and Charles Fairbanks. *Florida Archaeology* (1980), esp. pp. 232–237.

JERALD T. MILANICH

TERESA CRISTINA

(1822–1889). Teresa Cristina, empress of Brazil, youngest daughter of Francis I, king of Naples, and Maria Isabel, princess of Spain, was born March 14, 1822. In 1843 the young Emperor Pedro II needed a wife and Teresa Cristina, his first cousin, three years his senior, was available. Married at Rio de Janeiro, September 4, 1843, the couple proved ill-matched physically and intellectually. Teresa Cristina's devotion and her sweetness of character captured, for a while, Pedro's affections. She bore four children but her two sons died in infancy. The empress played no part in and exerted no influence on public affairs. Known as *mai dos brasileiros* (Mother of the Brazilians) she conformed to the gender role expected of her, closing her eyes to her husband's infidelities. She devoted herself to her family and to charitable giving. Plagued by sickness (mainly cardiac asthma) from middle age, she could not adjust, after the fall of the empire in November 1889, to a life in exile from Brazil. She died at Pôrto, Portugal, December 30, 1889.

See also **Brazil, The Empire (Second); Pedro II of Brazil.**

BIBLIOGRAPHY

Barman, Roderick J. *Citizen Emperor: Pedro II and the Making of Brazil, 1825–1891.* Stanford, CA: Stanford University Press, 1999.

Barman, Roderick J. *Princess Isabel of Brazil: Gender and Power in the Nineteenth Century.* Wilmington, DE: SR Books, 2002.

Williams, Mary Wilhelmine. *Dom Pedro the Magnanimous, Second Emperor of Brazil.* Chapel Hill: University of North Carolina Press, 1937.

RODERICK J. BARMAN

TERESINA. Teresina (formerly Therezina, or Terezhina), capital of the state of Piauí, Brazil. Teresina, the chief commercial center of the middle of the Parnaíba Valley, has a population of 813,992 (2006 est.). Founded in 1852 as a new state capital, Teresina stands at the confluence of the Parnaíba and Poti rivers and is linked by the former to the Atlantic port city of Parnaíba, 220 miles downstream. It exports livestock, hides, rice, cotton, carnauba wax, palm oil, and other agricultural products of the region. Local industries produce textiles, lumber, soap, sugar, and rum. It is also known as the "Green City" owing to the abundance of mango trees along its streets.

See also **Piauí.**

BIBLIOGRAPHY

Melo, Alcília Afonso de Albuquerque e. *Arquitetura em Teresina: 150 anos: Da origem á contemporaneidade.* Teresina, Brasil: Halley S/A Gráfica e Editoria, 2002.

CARA SHELLY

TERRA, GABRIEL (1873–1942). Gabriel Terra (*b.* 1873; *d.* 1942), president of Uruguay (1931–1938). Terra was a Colorado Party political leader who ostensibly considered himself a Batllist, that is, a follower of the great political leader and two-time Colorado president José Batlle y Ordóñez. By late 1932, Terra had moved ideologically to the right and became increasingly frustrated with the fact that he had to share decision making with a National Council of Administration under the partially collegial executive structure established by the 1918 Constitution. Amid the economic turmoil brought on by the depression, Terra joined forces with the Blanco (National Party) leader, Luis Alberto de Herrera, in a nonviolent coup on 13 March 1933, taking total control of the government. The regime drafted a new constitution that returned Uruguay to a full presidential system and left the Senate in total control of the procoup factions of the Colorados and Blancos. Terra repressed the labor movement and devalued the peso in an attempt to help exporters of livestock. He served a full term under the 1934 Constitution, turning the presidency over to his elected successor, his brother-in-law Alfredo Baldomir.

See also **Herrera, Luis Alberto de; Ordóñez, José; Uruguay, Political Parties: Blanco Party; Uruguay, Political Parties: Colorado Party.**

BIBLIOGRAPHY

Philip B. Taylor, Jr., *Government and Politics of Uruguay* (1960).

Additional Bibliography

Cures, Oribe. *El Uruguay de los años treinta: Enfoques y problemas.* Montevideo: Ediciones de la Banda Oriental, 1994.

Fischer, Diego, and Rosario Cecilio. *Sobremesa presidencial.* Montevideo: Fundación Banco de Boston, 1994.

MARTIN WEINSTEIN

TERRAZAS, LUIS (1829–1923). Luis Terrazas (*b.* 20 July 1829; *d.* 15 June 1923), governor of the state of Chihuahua, Mexico (1860–1873, 1879–1884, 1903–1904). A hero of the wars against the northern Indians and the French Intervention (1861–1867), General Terrazas was the political boss and governor of Chihuahua for much of the period from 1860 to 1910. He and his family came to own more than 10 million acres of land in Chihuahua with a half million head of cattle. He was also one of Mexico's foremost bankers and industrialists.

During the French Intervention, Terrazas stood with President Benito Juárez in Mexico's darkest hours, leading the forces that eventually pushed the French from the state. He maintained his alliance with Juárez, defending him against the revolt of La Noria, led by Porfirio Díaz, in 1872. Terrazas continued to oppose Díaz during the first decade of the latter's dictatorship. Díaz forced him out of power in Chihuahua from 1884 to 1892, but the overwhelming economic resources of the Terrazas family produced a stalemate. A reconciliation was achieved with the return of Terrazas to the governorship in 1903.

Because he and his sons and sons-in-law ran the state as a family fiefdom, occupying nearly all the important government posts, and used their positions to further their economic interests, they became the lightning rod for the discontent that erupted in the Mexican Revolution of 1910. After Terrazas fled to the United States, Pancho Villa confiscated his properties in 1913. The old general returned to Mexico in 1920 and two years later the federal government gave him 13 million pesos as compensation for the loss of his lands.

See also **Chihuahua; Díaz, Porfirio; French Intervention (Mexico); Juárez, Benito.**

BIBLIOGRAPHY

A critical examination of Terrazas's early career is found in Francisco R. Almada, *Juárez y Terrazas: Aclaraciones históricas* (1958). Although commissioned by the Terrazas family, the best biography remains José Fuentes Mares, *...Y México se refugió en el desierto: Luis Terrazas, su historia y destino* (1954). For a complete study of the Terrazas era in Chihuahua, see Mark Wasserman, *Capitalists, Caciques, and Revolution* (1984).

Additional Bibliography

Chávez Barron, Héctor. *Luis Terrazas.* México, D.F.: Clío, 2004.

Márquez Terrazas, Zacarías. *Terrazas y su siglo.* Chihuahua, Mexico: Centro Librero La Prensa, 1998.

MARK WASSERMAN

TERRORISM. A consensus definition of the term *terrorism* does not exist. Actors in conflict generally define the word according to their interests. While a government's definition may be specifically designed to implicate a particular group, the group in question may offer a counter-definition designed to rebut the government's assertion. Groups that have been designated as terrorist organizations will often argue that the government that made the designation is itself a terrorist organization. For the purposes of this article, terrorism will be defined as the deliberate targeting of ordinary people, with violence or the threat of violence, for the pursuit of political goals.

HISTORY

Diverse actors have historically used terrorism in Latin America. States have employed the tactic under military regimes, as in Argentina from 1976 to 1983, Brazil from 1964 to 1985, and Chile from 1973 to 1990. Forced disappearances, torture, and targeted killings have been used by these governments and others to keep internal enemies of the state at bay. Such enemies have included communists, labor unions, and student activists. Drug cartels have planted bombs in shopping malls to erode public confidence in the state, as in the case of Pablo Escobar and the Medellín Cartel in Colombia in the 1980s. Left-wing guerrillas have kidnapped thousands. Right-wing paramilitaries have summarily executed entire villages, claiming that their victims had conspired with guerrillas. In certain cases, individuals thought by some to be "freedom fighters" have been implicated in terrorist acts. Luis Posada Carriles, a Venezuelan national convicted of involvement in blowing up a Cubana airliner in 1976, killing seventy-three people, is one such example (Moghaddam, p. 10).

TERRORISM IN CONTEMPORARY LATIN AMERICA

Terrorism is extremely uncommon in most parts of Latin America in the early twenty-first century. The majority of all terrorist acts in the region takes place in rural parts of Colombia. Cuba remains on the U.S. State Department's list of state sponsors of terrorism, but most people believe this designation to be anachronistic. While Cuba actively supported left-wing revolutionary movements from the 1960s until the 1980s, Fidel Castro asserted in 1992 that his support for insurgents abroad had ended. Analysts generally believe this to be accurate (Sullivan, p. 3). Three terrorism hot spots in the region deserve elaboration: Colombia, Peru, and the Tri-Border area (TBA) of Argentina, Brazil, and Paraguay.

Colombia. Three main groups that could be deemed terrorist organizations operate in Colombia as of 2007. Each of these groups is deeply involved in the international drug trade. The Fuerzas Armadas Revolucionarias de Colombia (FARC; Armed Revolutionary Forces of Colombia) and the Ejército de Liberación Nacional (ELN; National Liberation Army) are left-wing guerrilla movements that began in the early 1960s. Both of these groups claim to fight what they believe is a corrupt government on behalf of Colombia's poor majority. The FARC is by far the larger, stronger, and more dangerous of the two organizations, numbering between 12,000 and 18,000 members. The ELN is also an important challenge for the government of Colombia and a threat to Colombia's rural population, with approximately 3,000 to 4,000 members. Each of these groups is known to have kidnapped, killed, and intimidated Colombian citizens in hopes of consolidating a military presence in the country. Though many Colombians believe these groups no longer retain their decades-old purported ideology of social equality, some believe that they only reluctantly employ terrorist tactics (Brittain and Sacouman, p. 1). Without kidnapping for ransom, for example, these people argue that the groups would lose an important source of revenue used to carry out their hopeful revolutions. Negotiations between these two groups and the government of Colombia have been difficult over the decades. In December 2005 the ELN and the government commenced negotiations in Havana, Cuba, for a ceasefire, but after two years no agreement had yet been reached. Possible negotiations with the FARC are even more difficult, because both sides have stipulated preconditions to talks that have not been met. The third group, the Autodefensas Unidas de Colombia (AUC; United Self-Defense Forces of Colombia), is an umbrella organization of right-wing paramilitary groups that formed in the mid-1990s. This organization is known to have been, and in some cases is still known to be, particularly vicious and violent. According to reports from international nongovernmental organizations (NGOs) such as Human Rights Watch, the vast majority of violations of international humanitarian law in Colombia have been carried out by paramilitaries (Human Rights Watch, p. 112). The Colombian government estimates that, at its strongest, the AUC once numbered as many as 32,000 members. Since then nearly 30,000 have reportedly demobilized and some 16,000 have giv-en up arms (Rangel, p. 1). The negotiation process between the government and the AUC is ongoing.

Peru. The Shining Path is a Maoist guerrilla organization that was founded by a philosophy professor named Abimael Guzmán in Ayacucho, Peru, in 1980. The stated goal of the group is to bring about a peasant-led communist state in which all Peruvians will be equal. From 1980 until 1992 the group waged a brutal war on the people of Peru, targeting elected officials, peasants, activists, and, more generally, the civilian population at large. Having once boasted several thousand members, the group was severely weakened with the capture

of its founder and leader, Guzmán, in Lima in 1992. Convicted on charges of terrorism on October 13, 2006, he began serving a life sentence in Callao. Remnants of the Shining Path remain active in the jungle and Andean region of the country, comprising fewer than 500 members (Hyland, p. 3).

Tri-Border Area (TBA). The area surrounding the intersection of Argentina, Brazil, and Paraguay is not a theater of operations for any terrorist group. However, the TBA is considered an important staging ground for terrorist-related activity. The area has long been known for arms and drug trafficking, contraband smuggling, document and currency fraud, money laundering, and the manufacture and movement of pirated goods (Sullivan, p. 3). The area hosts a relatively large Muslim population, and many analysts believe that the profits gained from illegal activity in the area are destined for organizations associated with Islamic extremism, particularly the Palestinian group Hamas and the Lebanon-based group Hezbollah. In 1992 a bomb exploded at the Israeli Embassy in Buenos Aires, killing twenty-nine people, and in 1994 a bomb exploded at the Argentine-Israeli Mutual Association, also in the Argentine capital, killing eighty-six people. While there is no hard evidence to support the claim, many believe that these bombings were the work of Hezbollah and that the group may have used the TBA for planning. Hezbollah has denied these charges.

See also **Colombia: Since Independence; Guerrilla Movements; Guzmán, Abimael; Peru: Peru Since Independence.**

BIBLIOGRAPHY

Brittain, James J., and R. James Sacouman. "Is the FARC-EP Dependent on Coca?" ANNCOL. March 23, 2006. Available from http://www.peaceobservatory.org/388/is-the-farc-ep-dependent-on-coca.

Human Rights Watch. *War without Quarter: Colombia and International Humanitarian Law.* New York: Human Rights Watch, 1998.

Hyland, Frank. "Peru's Shining Path Gaining Ground?" *Terrorism Focus* 4, no. 28 (September 11, 2007): 3-4.

Moghaddam, Fathali M. *From the Terrorists' Point of View: What They Experience and Why They Come to Destroy.* Westport, CT: Praeger Security International, 2006.

Rangel, Alfredo. "Las elecciones menos violentas en 10 años." Fundación Seguridad y Democracia. October 29, 2007. Available from http://www.seguridadyde

mocracia.org/docs/pdf/conflictoArmado/elecciones MenosViolentas.pdf.

Sullivan, Mark P. "Latin America: Terrorism Issues." CRS Report for Congress RS21049. Updated January 22, 2007. Available from http://fpc.state.gov/documents/organization/81364.pdf.

JOSEPH M. CANTEY JR.

Muñón Chimalpahin Quauhtlehuanitzin. Norman: University of Oklahoma Press, 1997.

Ward, Thomas. "From the 'People' to the 'Nation': An Emerging Notion in Sahagún, Ixtlilxóchitl and Muñoz Camargo." *Estudios de Cultura Náhuatl* 32 (2001): 223–234 and especially 227–229.

ELOISE QUIÑONES KEBER

TETZCOCO. Tetzcoco, the great capital of the Acolhuaque and one of the leading cities in the Basin of Mexico in the late pre-Hispanic period. Located near the eastern edge of Lake Tetzcoco, it was also the head of a powerful confederation of neighboring towns. Founded by the Chichimecs in the twelfth century, it was conquered by the Tepanecs in the early fifteenth century. Following the overthrow of the Tepanec Empire, Mexico Teno-chtitlán, Tetzcoco, and Tlacopán (present-day Tacuba) established the succeeding Empire of the Triple Alliance by 1434. The mestizo chronicler Fernando de Alva Ixtlilxóchitl extolled his native city as the cultural and intellectual center of the basin, led by two outstanding rulers: the warrior, builder, seer, and poet Nezahualcoyotl and his son Nezahualpilli. Remains of Nezahualcoyotl's famed pleasure garden, Tetzcotzinco, survive on a hill outside the present-day city of Texcoco, although there has been little excavation of the ancient capital buried beneath the city.

See also **Alva Ixtlilxóchitl, Fernando; Chichimecs; Nezahualcoyotl; Nezahualpilli.**

BIBLIOGRAPHY

Nigel Davies, *The Aztecs* (1973).

Alva Ixtlilxóchitl, Fernando de. Obras históricas: incluyen el texto completo de las llamadas Relaciones e Historia de la nación chichimeca en una nueva versión establecida con el cotejo de los manuscritos más antiguos que se conocen. Ed. Edmundo O'Gorman & Miguel León Portilla. 2 vols. Reprint of the 3rd edition. México: Instituto Mexiquense de Cultura/Universidad Nacional Autónoma de México, 1997.

Additional Bibliography

Chimalpahin Cuauhtlehuanitzin, Domingo Francisco de San Antón Muñón, et al. *Codex Chimalpahin: Society and Politics in Mexico Tenochtitlan, Tlatelolco, Texcoco, Culhuacan, and Other Nahua Altepetl in Central Mexico: the Nahuatl and Spanish Annals and Accounts Collected and Recorded by Don Domingo De San Antón*

TEXAS. Texas, northeasternmost of the provinces of New Spain, and later of the Republic of Mexico. The name derives from the Spanish term for some of the Caddoan peoples of east Texas. Permanently occupied in 1716, following French incursions in the area, the province remained sparsely settled until after Mexican independence, when an effort was made to attract Anglo-American and European immigrants. In 1845, after having been a separate republic since 1836, Texas annexed itself to the United States.

The Texas coast was first explored by Alonso Álvarez De Pineda in 1519. Parts of the interior were later traversed by Alvar Núñez Cabeza De Vaca and three other survivors of the Pánfilo de Narváez expedition (1528–1536), by the Francisco Vázquez de Coronado expedition (1540–1544), and by Luis Moscoso de Alvarado, successor to Hernando de Soto, and his men (1542). Following these unsuccessful expeditions, the region was ignored until the late seventeenth century.

The establishment of a colony on the Texas coast in 1685 by René Robert Cavelier, Sieur de la Salle, brought a brief Spanish occupation of east Texas (1690–1693). Domingo Ramón led a colonizing expedition northward in 1716, following the arrival of a French trader at a Río Grande outpost, and established missions and a presidio near present-day Robeline, Louisiana. Governor Martín de Alarcón led a reinforcing expedition in 1718 and founded the presidio-mission complex that became San Antonio. With the founding of another presidio-mission complex on Matagorda Bay four years later, the three centers of Euro-American settlement in colonial Texas had been established.

Throughout the colonial period, Texas remained an essentially military province. Along with a base from which to guard against the French (and later the Anglo-Americans) in Louisiana, Texas also provided a buffer against Indian penetration of interior New Spain. Aside from military service, the principal economic activities in the province consisted of maize farming and cattle driving. Smuggling seems also to have been important, particularly in east Texas. The province's population on the eve of the Mexican War of Independence totaled approximately 4,500, not including un-Hispanicized Amerindians.

With the adoption of the Mexican constitution of 1824, Texas was united with the neighboring province of Coahuila to form a single state. Anglo-American settlement, which had begun in 1821 under the auspices of Moses Austin, brought thousands of colonists from the United States but only a few from Mexico. Consequently, according to the conservative estimates of Juan N. Almonte, a Mexican government agent, the Texas population stood at 21,000 in 1834, including 15,000 Anglo-Americans, 2,000 slaves, and 4,000 Mexican Texans. Disputes over land distribution, import tariffs, tax exemptions, and future immigration from the United States combined with political upheavals in Mexico to produce an insurrection and a declaration of independence on 2 March 1836.

Soon after its separation from Mexico, Texas laid claim to all land north of the Río Grande from its source to its mouth, territory that had previously been part of the Mexican states of Tamaulipas, Coahuila, and Chihuahua, and New Mexico Territory. Mexican refusal to acknowledge Texas's annexation to the United States and its territorial claims resulted in the Mexican–American War (1846–1848).

See also **Alamo, Battle of the; Alarcón, Martín de; Álvarez de Pineda, Alonso; Cabeza de Vaca, Alvar Núñez; Coahuila; Texas Revolution.**

BIBLIOGRAPHY

Eugene C. Barker, *The Life of Stephen F. Austin, Founder of Texas, 1793–1836* (repr. 1969); Carlos E. Castañeda, *Our Catholic Heritage in Texas, 1519–1936,* 7 vols. (repr. 1976).

Vito Alessio Robles, *Coahuila y Texas desde la consumación de la Independencia hasta el Tratado de Paz de Guadalupe Hidalgo,* 2 vols., 2d ed. (1979).

Gerald E. Poyo and Gilberto M. Hinojosa, eds., *Tejano Origins in Eighteenth-Century San Antonio* (1991).

Andreas V. Reichstein, *Rise of the Lone Star: The Making of Texas* (1989).

Donald Chipman, *Spanish Texas, 1519–1821* (1992).

Additional Bibliography

Cantrell, Gregg, and Elizabeth Hayes Turner. *Lone Star Pasts: Memory and History in Texas.* College Station: Texas A&M University Press, 2007.

Crouch, Barry A. *The Dance of Freedom: Texas African Americans during Reconstruction.* Edited by Larry Madaras. Austin: University of Texas Press, 2007.

Fradin, Dennis Brindell. *Texas.* Chicago: Childrens Press, 1992.

Frieventh, Benjamín. "Cómo llegamos: Participación hispana en la historia de Houston, Tejas." *Semana* 6, no. 322 (April 1999): 13.

Hine, Robert V., and John Mack Faragher. *The American West: A New Interpretive History.* New Haven, CT: Yale University Press, 2000.

Marquart, James W.; Sheldon Ekland-Olson; and Jonathan R. Sorensen. *The Rope, the Chair, and the Needle: Capital Punishment in Texas, 1923–1990.* Austin: University of Texas Press, 1994.

JESÚS F. DE LA TEJA

TEXAS REVOLUTION. Texas Revolution, series of events and military battles that resulted in the independence of Texas. Unrest began with the Fredonian Rebellion (1826), when some Anglo settlers disputed with Mexican authorities over land claims. In 1832 Anglo-Mexican clashes were exacerbated by the end of the customs exemption (a seven-year dispensation from paying some tariffs or customs taxes on imports and exports to promote economic development of the region), the desire for more local government, and fears that slavery might be abolished as well as by underlying ethnic and cultural differences. Despite creation of new municipalities in Texas, centralization of power in Mexico by President Antonio López de Santa Anna in 1834 and land speculation revived earlier issues and led to renewed conflict in 1835. Opposition to Santa Anna flared in several Mexican states. Texans rejected calls for the arrest of resistance leaders in the summer of 1835. In October they defended a cannon at Gonzales and then captured a small Mexican garrison at Goliad. Under Stephen Fuller Austin, an army of Anglo and Mexican Texans besieged San Antonio later that month. Led by Edward Burleson (1793–1851) and Ben Milam (1788–1835), they captured the town from General Martín Perfecto de Cos in December.

In November, the Texas Consultation government publicly took a federalist stand in favor of the Constitution of 1824, though many Anglo Texans urged independence. Governor Henry Smith (1788–1851) and a general council failed to cooperate or accomplish much during the winter. Meanwhile, Santa Anna gathered an army to put down the revolt. A few Texas troops held San Antonio while volunteers from the United States moved to the Goliad area for an advance on Matamoros. Santa Anna's army surrounded the Texans in San Antonio, commanded by William B. Travis during late February 1836 and stormed the Alamo on March 6, while the Texas Convention of 1836 declared an independent republic on March 2. Later that month, near Goliad, a second Mexican force under José Urrea defeated or captured four groups of Texans, the largest led by James W. Fannin, and executed the prisoners. Sam Houston gathered another Texas army but retreated. The government of President David G. Burnet retreated as well. On April 21 at San Jacinto, Houston defeated a wing of the Mexican army led by Santa Anna. As a prisoner, Santa Anna signed the Velasco treaty, which granted Texas independence and ended the conflict.

See also **Alamo, Battle of the; Austin, Stephen Fuller; Cos, Martín Perfecto de; Santa Anna, Antonio López de; Texas; Urrea, José de.**

BIBLIOGRAPHY

The best summaries of the Texas Revolution are in David J. Weber, *The Mexican Frontier, 1821–1846* (1982); and Paul D. Lack, *The Texas Revolutionary Experience: a Political and Social History, 1835–1836* (1992). Andreas V. Reichstein, *Rise of the Lone Star: The Making of Texas* (1989), emphasizes land issues. An older account of some value is Eugene C. Barker, "Texas Revolution," in *The Handbook of Texas,* edited by Walter Prescott Webb and H. Bailey Carroll, vol. 2 (1952), pp. 757–758.

Additional Bibliography

Brands, H. W. *Lone Star Nation: How a Ragged Army of Volunteers Won the Battle for Texas Independence, and Changed America.* New York: Doubleday, 2004.

Davis, William C. *Lone Star Rising: The Revolutionary Birth of the Texas Republic.* New York: Free Press, 2004.

ALWYN BARR

TEXCOCO. *See* Tetzcoco.

TEXTILE INDUSTRY

This entry includes the following articles:
THE COLONIAL ERA
MODERN TEXTILES

THE COLONIAL ERA

Spanish America satisfied its clothing needs from a combination of household production, a commercialized colonial textile industry, and imports from Europe and Asia. At the time of the Conquest, there was already an appreciable degree of regional specialization in textile manufacturing. Cotton and woolen (vicuña and llama in the Andes) cloth formed an important part of Aztec and Inca imperial tribute. The Spanish endeavored to maintain the flow of tribute in cloth through the *encomienda* system until a drastic decline in Indian population undermined this source of supply. From the 1570s, the *Repartimiento* system of trade through Alcaldes Mayores attempted, but failed (in Mexico at least), to compensate for the decline of tribute in *manta* (ordinary cotton cloth). As a consequence, settlers and Indians were obliged to depend more upon domestic production, to use more leather and less cloth, and to develop a commercialized colonial textile industry. This third course, notably in woolens and silk, was under way within two decades of the conquest of Mexico. Silk enjoyed a brief flurry of growth in Mexico during the mid-sixteenth century until Asian imports and a shrinking Indian population also damaged this labor-intensive industry. Wool proved more successful.

WOOLENS

In response to the high prices of imported cloth, an abundance of wool in the depopulated valleys of central Mexico, and the growth in silver production in the mid-1530s, the Obrajes of Puebla grew to supply fine wool cloth for the entire Mexican *tierradentro* and for the Peruvian market. From the late sixteenth century, Quito's *obrajes* supplied markets to the north in Santa Fe de Bogotá and as far south as Concepción de Chile, Tucumán, Córdoba, and Buenos Aires. By the 1630s, however, the golden age of Puebla's woolen industry had passed, as a result of the prohibition of New Spain's trade with Peru, the enforcement of regulations restricting access to Indian labor, and, above all, Mexico's mining depression. Because of the continued buoyancy of Peruvian silver production, Quito's *obrajes* maintained their prosperity until the early eighteenth century.

During the final century of colonial rule, although the manufacture of fine cloth all but ceased, Spanish America's woolen industry was far from stagnant. In the face of increasing European competition, production shifted from finer to more ordinary and cheaper cloth. Weaving also moved closer to the principal sources of wool supply; Puebla-Tlaxcala yielded to the Bajío and the *tierradentro,* and Quito yielded to Bogotá, Huamanga, Cuzco, La Paz, and Córdoba. Finally, production tended to devolve from the larger *obrajes* to smaller units (containing fewer than ten looms), known as *trapiches* in Mexico and *chorrillos* in the Andes. Where the larger *obrajes* did survive—Mexico City, Tlaxcala, Querétaro, San Miguel el Grande, Huamanga, Quito, Cuzco, La Paz—they tended to be part of larger agricultural enterprises. Salvucci's work on *obraje* woolens rates their potential for transformation as uniformly low. The modernization of woolen spinning technology in Mexico during the 1830s and 1840s sounded the death knell of the *obraje* while granting the domestic weaver and the *trapiche* a new lease on life.

COTTONS

From the later seventeenth century, the resurgence of the Indian population prompted a growth in cotton manufacturing. This took a variety of forms. At first there was a revival of Indian village production in areas that since pre-Hispanic times had specialized in cotton weaving (such as Villa Alta in Oaxaca), through Repartimiento or in response to local and regional market mechanisms, backed by direct mercantile investment (*habilitación*). More significant, however, was the growing specialization of non-Indians—creoles and mestizos—in cotton spinning and weaving in the cities of Mexico's central plateau. The application of the European spinning wheel and the Castilian treadle loom to an industry that still adhered to native technology reversed cotton's decline and set in motion one of the more important (and, until recently, little appreciated) developments in Spanish America's

eighteenth century. Backed by merchants at every stage of production, responding to demographic and ecological pressures, affecting rural as well as ur-ban areas, involving production for extraregional as much as for local markets, and inspiring some notable technological as well as organizational developments, Mexico's new creole-mestizo cotton industry resembled, in most respects, the "protoindustrialization" occurring contemporaneously in Europe.

Again, it was in the Puebla region that these developments first took root, with creoles and mestizos—members of the silk weavers' guild—engaging in cotton weaving from the 1670s. By the second half of the eighteenth century, large groups of non-Indian cotton weavers were in Antigua Guatemala, Puebla, Tlaxcala, Antequera de Oaxaca, Mexico City, Valladolid, Querétaro, and Guadalajara, as well as in numerous smaller towns and villages throughout central and southern Mexico. Similar developments occurred in the Andes, the only difference being that cotton weaving tended to be more of a rural, Indian, and female occupation than in Mesoamerica. Large numbers of cotton weavers could be found in the Socorro region of New Granada, the Cuenca region of Quito, and the Cochabamba region of Upper Peru, transforming cotton grown in Piura, Trujillo, and Arequipa on the Peruvian coast and producing cloth for extraregional markets. Brooke Larson shows that Cochabamba *tocuyo* (the Andean equivalent of the Mexican *manta*) reached the counters of Buenos Aires during the Napoleonic wars.

The potential for the transformation of the cotton industry proved to be considerably greater in Mexico than in the Andes. This was a result of the predominantly urban location of Mexico's cotton weaving, a larger internal market, the greater degree of mercantile involvement, and the more favorable disposition of the postcolonial state toward industrial protection. Against these advantages, Andean cotton weaving could count upon only "the tariff of distance," sufficient to sustain the traditional (unmechanized) industry at modest levels throughout the nineteenth century in parts of Colombia, Ecuador, Peru, and Bolivia.

OTHER TEXTILES

Official attempts in Mexico to encourage the cultivation and manufacture of linen and hemp during the later eighteenth century were unsuccessful. Calico printing experienced a short burst of activity during the Napoleonic Wars. Manufacture of felt and straw hats in households and small workshops (*obradores*) was a dynamic industry during the eighteenth and nineteenth centuries in both Mexico and the Andes. Fibers such as istle, sisal, and palm were used for manufacture of coarse cloth and matting throughout Mesoamerica.

See also **Cotton; Wool Industry.**

BIBLIOGRAPHY

For a review of the literature, see Manuel Miño Grijalva, "La política textil en México y Perú en la Época colonial. Nuevas consideraciones," in *Historia mexicana*, 38 (1988): 283–323; "La circulación de mercancias: Una referencia al caso textil latinoamericano (1750–1810)," in *Empresarios, indios y estado: Perfil de la la economía mexicana (siglo XVIII)* edited by Arij Ouweneel and Cristina Torales Pacheco (1988); and "¿Proto-industria colonial?" in *Historia mexicana*, 38 (1989): 793–818. New Spain's textile industry can now count two important monographs: Richard Salvucci, *Textiles and Capitalism in Mexico: An Economic History of the Obrajes, 1539–1840* (1987); and Manuel Miño Grijalva, *Obrajes y tejedores de Nueva España, 1750–1810* (1990). For Puebla's silk, cotton, and woolen textiles, see Jan Bazant, "Evolución de la industria textil poblana (1544–1845)," in *Historia mexicana,* 1 (1962): 473–516; Guy P. C. Thomson, "The Cotton Textile Industry in Puebla During the Eighteenth and Early Nineteenth Centuries," in *The Economies of Mexico and Peru During the Late Colonial Period, 1760–1810,* edited by Nils Jacobsen and Hans-Jurgen Puhle (1986); and *Puebla de los Angeles: Industry and Society in a Mexican City, 1700–1850* (1989). For Mexican woolen manufactures, see Richard Salvucci, "Entrepreneurial Culture and the Textile Manufactories in Eighteenth-Century Mexico," in *Anuario de estudios americanos,* 39 (1982): 397–419. For late colonial calico printing in Mexico, see Manuel Miño Grijalva, "El camino hacia la fábrica en Nueva España: El caso de la 'Fábrica de Indianillas' de Francisco de Iglesias, 1801–1810," in *Historia méxicana,* 34 (1984): 135–148. For New Granada, see Anthony Mc Farlane, *Colombia Before Independence* (1993). For Quito, see Javier Ortiz De La Tabla, "Obrajes y obrajeros del Quito Colonial," in *Anuario de estudios americanos,* 39 (1982): 341–365; and John Leddy Phelan, *The Kingdom of Quito in the Seventeenth Century* (1967). For Peru, see Fernando Silva Santiesteban, *Los obrajes en el virreinato del Perú* (1964); Miriam Salas De Coloma, "Evolución de la propiedad obrajera en la Huamanga colonial," in *Anuario de estudios americanos,* 39 (1982): 367–395, and *De los obrajes de Canaria y Chincheros a las comunidades de Vilcashuamán, siglo XVI* (1979); Magnus Mörner, *Perfil de la sociedad rural del Cuzco a fines de la colonia* (1978). For Alto Perú and Río de la Plata, see Brooke Larson, "The Cotton Textile Industry of Cochabamba, 1770–1810: The Opportunities and Limits of Growth," in *The Economies of Mexico and Peru During the Late Colonial Period, 1760–1810,* edited by Nils Jacobsen and Hans-Jurgen Puhle (1986); and Carlos Sempat Assadourian, *El sistema de la economía colonial. El mercado interior: Regiones y espacio económico* (1983).

Additional Bibliography

Escandell Tur, Neus. *Producción y comercio de tejidos coloniales: los obrajes y chorrillos del Cusco, 1570-1820.* Cusco: Centro de Estudios Regionales Andinos, Bartolomé de Las Casas, 1997.

Gómez Galvarriato, Aurora. *La industria textil en México.* México, D.F.: Instituto Mora: Colegio de Michoacán : Colegio de México, 1999.

Miño Grijalva, Manuel. *La protoindustria colonial hispanoamericana.* México: El Colegio de México, 1993.

Ramos-Escandón, Carmen. *Industrialización, género y trabajo femenino en el sector textil mexicano: El obraje, la fábrica y la compañía industrial.* México, D.F.: CIESAS, 2004.

Salas de Coloma, Miriam. *Estructura colonial del poder español en el Perú: Huamanga (Ayacucho) a través de sus obrajes: Siglos XVI-XVIII.* Lima: Pontificia Universidad Católica del Perú, Fondo Editorial, 1998.

GUY P. C. THOMSON

MODERN TEXTILES

The first line of manufactures in Latin America to be produced by the factory system was the cotton textile industry. Throughout the nineteenth and early twentieth centuries, cotton textiles made up the greatest part of the industrial output of most Latin American countries. By the 1930s their relative importance had declined as other lines of manufacturing, such as paper, cement, and steel, adopted the factory system.

Cotton and wool goods were being spun and woven prior to the conquest of the Americas, and artisanal production of cloth continued throughout the colonial period. The two centers of colonial production were Puebla, Mexico, and Minas Gerais, Brazil. All production took place in the weaving sheds of independent cottage producers or in rudimentary manufactories that at times used coerced labor. The output of these operations was almost entirely coarse goods for the popular

A worker dyeing fibers at a São Paulo textile factory, c. mid-20th century. Textiles were an important Latin American industry since the colonial period and grew significantly in the nineteenth century. Protection in the mid-twentieth century aided this slowly declining sector that employed a large workforce. © HULTON-DEUTSCH COLLECTION/CORBIS

market, high-quality goods being beyond their technical abilities. Though the data are rough, wool goods were probably more important than cotton goods during this period, with the exception of Brazil, where cotton cloth production dominated.

EARLY FACTORIES

The first factories appeared in the 1830s, when Mexican entrepreneurs in the states of Puebla and México began to mechanize the spinning of cotton yarn. Most of the capital for the construction of these water-powered factories came from merchant activities, though the Mexican government provided some help as well through an industrial development bank, the Banco De Avío, founded in 1830. By the late 1830s, Mexico's textile industrialists had begun to move into mechanized weaving as well. In 1843 Mexico possessed 59 factories operating 125,362 spindles and 2,609 looms in the modern sector of the industry. Almost all of this output was in coarse, gray cloth called *manta,* because high-quality, fine-

weave goods continued to be imported from Europe. By Western European or U.S. standards, Mexico's textile industry was extremely small, but it was the largest in Latin America. This relatively early start allowed Mexico to be the preeminent producer of cotton goods in Latin America until the turn of the century.

By the 1850s the factory system had slowly begun to spread to other countries in the region, and by the 1870s virtually every Latin American country was producing at least some cotton goods by machine. Mexico and Brazil, however, were clearly the two most important producers, because they possessed large markets, good lands for growing cotton, long traditions of artisanal cotton cloth production, and sources of water power near the population centers that consumed the output of their mills. By the early 1880s, the Mexican industry had grown to 99 factories running 249,334 spindles and 8,864 looms with a work force of roughly 11,500. An additional 9,000 spindles, 350 looms, and 700 workers were dedicated to wool production. The annual output of cotton cloth probably ran to 100 million meters. Brazil's industry was approximately one-third the size of Mexico's, with 43 factories running 80,420 spindles and 2,631 looms. Roughly 3,600 workers were employed in these firms, and annual output was in the area of 24 million meters.

EXPANSION

It was not until the 1890s that the textile industry began to grow at a rapid rate. The process of economic growth induced by the export boom of the last decades of the nineteenth century created conditions that were propitious for the industry's expansion. Incomes grew, markets were unified by the building of railroad networks, capital markets matured, and the wealth of the mercantile classes, the most important source of capital for the textile industry, grew rapidly. By 1920 the Mexican cotton goods industry included 120 mills operating 753,837 spindles and 27,301 looms and providing employment for 37,936 workers. Brazil's cotton industry had grown even larger, with 202 mills employing 78,911 workers and running nearly 1.6 million spindles and 52,254 looms. The total production of Brazil's mills was probably close to 500 million meters of cloth. By this point, domestically produced cotton cloth accounted for roughly 80 percent of the market in both countries. Other Latin American countries had viable, but significantly smaller, cotton industries by this time. Chile, for example, had but three mills employing less than 500 workers and running only 5,000 spindles and 400 looms, while Argentina and Colombia had cotton industries that were roughly three times that size.

LARGE FIRMS

What is particularly remarkable about the cotton industries in Brazil and Mexico was the size of the largest firms, which were gigantic even by U.S. standards. Mexico's largest firm, the Compañía Industrial de Orizaba (CIDOSA), founded in 1889, was by 1900 a four-mill operation employing 4,284 workers running 92,708 spindles and 3,899 looms. Had it been in the United States, it would have ranked among the twenty-five largest cotton textile enterprises. Brazil's largest producer, the Companhia América Fabril, was not far behind the CIDOSA operation; it controlled six mills employing 3,100 workers running 85,286 spindles and 2,170 looms.

The predominance of a few large firms in both countries meant that the level of concentration was significantly higher than that which prevailed in the United States; the percentage of the market controlled by the four largest Latin American firms in 1910 was 7.5 percent in the U.S., 16.8 percent in Brazil, and 28.7 percent in Mexico. A similar situation prevailed in the production of wool textiles, where a few firms controlled the lion's share of the market. In Mexico, for example, two firms, the Compañía Industrial de San Ildefonso and La Victoria, S.A., most likely accounted for better than one-third of all the machine-produced wool cloth.

CAPITAL

By the turn of the century, Brazil had overtaken Mexico as the region's premier textile producer, thanks in large part to the capital provided by the Rio de Janeiro stock exchange. Indeed, 28 percent of Brazil's cotton factories, predominantly located in São Paulo, were financed through the sale of equity, compared to just 3 percent in Mexico.

As in the United States and Western Europe, merchants played the most important role in industrial finance throughout Latin America. One reason for their prominence was that only merchants possessed the kind of liquid capital necessary to undertake the sizable investment needed. Another was that merchants had more knowledge of the market than other entrepreneurs and could dovetail their mercantile operations into their manufacturing operations. Indeed, the largest shareholders in the mills often were important cloth merchants who sold to their own wholesaling and retailing operations at a discount.

COMPETITIVENESS

Throughout its history the Latin American textile industry operated behind high tariff barriers and often received both direct and indirect government subsidies. This support was crucial for an industry that could not compete internationally against England and the United States. For this reason almost all of the production of most countries was consumed in the domestic market. Two factors prevented Latin America from developing internationally competitive textile industries. First, start-up costs were higher than those that prevailed in the advanced industrial countries. Lacking the ability to produce their own machinery, Latin American countries imported all of the necessary equipment from abroad and thus needed to set aside funds to cover the costs of transport and insurance in transit. They also needed to pay the salaries of the foreign technical personnel who set up the plant. These added expenses could push up the cost of erecting a mill by as much as 60 percent. Higher start-up costs were compounded by interest rates higher than those in the advanced industrial countries, due in part to a risk premium and less well-integrated financial markets. Second, the productivity of labor in Latin America was a good deal lower than that in the advanced industrial countries. Because workers resisted attempts to instill industrial discipline and routinize work, Latin America's mills typically employed from two to three times the number of workers per machine as did firms in the advanced industrial countries. Output per worker was therefore much lower as well; in 1925 labor productivity in Brazil, Mexico, and Argentina was roughly half that of the U.S. Northeast, one-sixth that of the U.S. South, and one-third that of Japan. Thus, even though wages for Latin American textile workers were from one-third to one-half of those prevailing abroad, these lower wages were offset by lower work intensity.

Women comprised a significant portion of textile workers, particularly after 1900, and their participation had an effect on labor relations throughout Latin America. Employers in Medellín, Colombia, and São Paulo, Brazil, imposed rules to safeguard the morality of their women employees, who sometimes were stigmatized for working outside the traditional sphere of the home. In Mexico, although women worked as millhands, men continued to occupy the highest-paid positions in the Orizaba-Puebla corridor. However, a majority of females have long staffed Mexico's maquiladoras, initially dominated by textile firms. In the 1980s Mexican women formed a seamstresses union, but their struggle for higher wages and job security was defeated by their employers, the government, and male-dominated union leadership. Global competition in the twenty-first century forced most textile factories along the Mexican-U.S. border to close.

WORLD WAR I AND AFTER
Latin America's textile industry did not do well during World War I, since capital goods were hard to purchase and the domestic market was depressed because of the decline in the export sector. The industry did even worse during the Great Depression. It was not until World War II that the industry once again faced the kind of favorable conditions that it had experienced in 1890–1914. By this point, however, the industry was even further behind the rest of the world; though it did begin to produce artificial fibers, decades of protectionism and the lack of new investment meant that most of the installed plant and equipment dated from the years prior to 1914. After 1945 the textile industry persisted, but its economic importance steadily declined.

BIBLIOGRAPHY

Stanley J. Stein, *The Brazilian Cotton Manufacture: Textile Enterprise in an Underdeveloped Area, 1850–1950* (1957).

Warren Dean, *The Industrialization of São Paulo, 1880–1945* (1969).

Dawn Keremitis, *La industria textil mexicana en el siglo XIX* (1973).

Richard J. Salvucci, *Textiles and Capitalism in Mexico: An Economic History of the Obrajes, 1539–1840* (1987).

Stephen H. Haber, *Industry and Underdevelopment: The Industrialization of Mexico, 1890–1940* (1989), and "Industrial Concentration and the Capital Markets: A Comparative Study of Brazil, Mexico, and the United States, 1830–1930," in *Journal of Economic History* 51, no. 3 (1991).

Guy P. C. Thompson, *Puebla de los Angeles: Industry and Society in a Mexican City, 1700–1850* (1989).

Douglas Cole Libby, "Proto-Industrialization in a Slave Society: The Case of Minas Gerais," in *Journal of Latin American Studies* 23 (1991), especially pp. 23–33.

Additional Bibliography

Bittencourt, Luciana Aguiar. *Spinning Lives.* Lanham, MD: University Press of America, 1996.

Cravey, Altha J. *Women and Work in Mexico's Maquiladoras.* Lanham, MD: Rowman and Littlefield, 1998.

Farnsworth-Alvear, Ann. *Dulcinea in the Factory: Myths, Morals, Men, and Women in Colombia's Industrial Experiment, 1905–1960.* Durham, NC: Duke University Press, 2000.

Gutiérrez Alvarez, Coralia. *Experiencias contrastadas: Industrialización y conflictos en los textiles del centro-oriente de México, 1884–1917,* México: El Colegio de México, Centro de Estudios Históricos, 2000.

Ramos-Escandón, Carmen. *Industrialización, género y trabajo femenino en el sector textil mexicano: El obraje, la fábrica y la compañía industrial*. México, D.F.: Centro de Investigaciones y Estudios Superiores en Antropología Social, 2004.

Rodrigues, Jessita Martins. *A mulher operária: Um estudo sobre tecelãs*. São Paulo: Editora Hucitec, 1979.

Winn, Peter. *Weavers of Revolution: The Yarur Workers and Chile's Road to Socialism*. New York: Oxford University Press, 1986.

Wolfe, Joel. *Working Women, Working Men: São Paulo and the Rise of Brazil's Industrial Working Class, 1900–1955*. Durham, NC: Duke University Press, 1993.

STEPHEN H. HABER

TEXTILES, INDIGENOUS.

The tradition of weaving is one of the earliest crafts known to the inhabitants of Latin America. Before the Conquest it was a major expression of culture. Pictorial motifs denoting rank, religion, and politics were a form of visual communication that allowed the weavings to be traded over very large areas, throughout the Andean region and from Mexico to Costa Rica.

Basic to most early cultures were the techniques of twining and, very early on, weaving. Twining, or twisting the fibers together to produce a long continuous rope, was the primary skill needed to provide a satisfactory alternative to vines and reeds, both used by hunters and basket makers. Twined flexible fibers such as grasses, cotton, and hair produced the first weaving threads. Cotton was one of the first cultivated crops in the warm coastal areas of the Americas. Used throughout the weaving cultures of the Americas was a loom based on a group of sticks using the body or stakes to provide tension. The backstrap loom was used by many indigenous groups and a variation of it can be seen in the stake loom of the Andes. These lightweight, wooden looms were economical and easily transported. Common also to the varied societies were the dynamic use of color with availability of an abundance of natural dyes. Although many indigenous groups wove, the craft as an art form was developed by the Maya in Mesoamerica and the Inca in the Andes. A full range of techniques were developed, including gauze, brocading or secondary warp and weft threads, double-cloth, and tapestry weaving.

In Mesoamerica the culture of the early Olmec evolved into the civilization known as the Maya (1500 BCE–CE 1100). In the Mayan religion Ixchel was the goddess of weaving and women were the primary weavers. Despite the decline of the Mayan civilization in the eleventh century, weaving continued. In the Aztec codices of the fifteenth century the tribute lists show the old Mayan area under Aztec control paid tribute in woven goods. The nobles, priests, and warriors wore mantles with brocaded motifs denoting their rank and status. Acid soil conditions have destroyed most of the native textiles and there are few left more than a century old. Motifs on pottery, murals, stelae, and codices depicting ceremonial figures dressed in court attire have been our best early evidence with the exception of textile fragments retrieved from the sacred Canada at the Toltec-Maya site of Chichén Itzá. These were woven in a variety of complex patterns decorated with brocading and open-weave techniques.

In the pre-Conquest Andes the early culture of the Chavín and other regional cultures evolved into the civilization of the Inca. These developing cultures supported and encouraged the weaving craft. And, fortunately, unlike Mesoamerica, the arid Paracas peninsula held its treasure of bodies wrapped in their layers of beautifully woven costumes: color coordinated, with matching motifs brocaded in complimentary hues. There is an abundance of materials sufficient to study the evolution of design elements in these materials, unlike their Mesoamerican counterparts.

Fibers used during the pre-Conquest period in Mesoamerica and eastern South America include a fine white cotton, a short-fiber brown cotton, bast fibers, rabbit hair, spider web, and feathers, all of these plus cameloid hair (llama, alpaca, and vicuña) were used in western South America as well. Dyes and mordants were found in plants, insects, marine creatures, and minerals. The fibers and dyes were found locally or were traded for at markets. Dyes commonly used today in the Andes are soot, leaves from the walnut tree, and cochineal, while indigo is still used in Mesoamerica. Very early fragments show color added by stamping and painting. As the craft developed, additional color was added with designs

An Aymara woman weaving on the edge of Lake Titicaca, Bolivia, 2005. The lightweight, easily transported wooden loom the woman is using dates back to the earliest cultures in the region. AP IMAGES

brocaded into the fabric as it was woven. Appliqué and embroidery were also used. Common to most American weavers was the use of the piece goods as it comes off the loom. Prior to European influence, all clothing was contrived from these straight pieces: skirts, hip wraps, mantles, stoles, and a garment made with a place for the head in the center. Variations on these styles were worn by both men and women. Utilitarian pieces such as men's bags, as well as ceremonial burial robes for their rulers, were made in the same manner. The Andean weavers developed a technique to manipulate the warp and weft threads into shaped pieces. In addition to the backstrap looms, they also developed small string looms for weaving narrow bands that required no wooden parts. Finishes on woven pieces of circular tassels and figures were elaborate.

In the Andean area messages such as astronomical charts were inscribed into textiles. The art of textile interpretation was so detailed that there were specialists—men and perhaps women—called *quilcacamayoc* who interpreted them.

The European treadle loom introduced very shortly after the Conquest brought many changes to the textile tradition. Native men were taught to weave on the new treadle looms and women were excluded from a craft that had been dominated by women. Clothing and household goods and ceremonial items were no longer woven in traditional designs and qualities at home. Bulk yardage needed strong machine-spun threads. Hand-spun yarn gave way to factory produced threads. Wool was introduced and, to a limited degree, silk. Women were employed in households to make lace and embroideries in the European mode. These crafts were taught by the nuns in church schools.

Native dress has changed the least in women's attire. In Guatemala and Chiapas today the native design is seen in the huipil. A woman's top is woven in one, two, or three panels, with an opening for the head in the center and the sides usually sewn below an armhole. The number of panels, length of garment, design, and color are usually determined by the local town, as each is distinct. Huipils seem to be alike, but they vary by ability, arrangement of a common group of motifs and color. Skirts are rectangles but may no longer be dyed with indigo or cochineal. One can still see the Maya wearing huipils, skirts, vests, and carrying bags in the old style especially in areas of strong native church groups. But since 1970 in Guatemala there has been a drastic change in the number of women wearing their village huipil. Many young women favor a lighter commercial huipil or a pattern of their own design for everyday and keep the village huipil for church and celebrations. In the Andes the Aymara still prefer bright colors and motifs from the native flora, while the Quechuas use animal motifs in harmonious patterns. But many of the early influences are more elusive. Natives on the coasts have turned to muslin cut in old styles such as tucked shirt fronts in Honduras or sailor collar shirts in Mexico. Old-style native dress cut from *manta* (muslin) are often embroidered in a running stitch, to look like brocading, or cross-stitched. In Chile a short woolen poncho was adapted by the indigenous horsemen.

New technology and style have also been added to the native textile art. Twentieth-century Cuna in Panama have evolved a women's blouse, *mola*, from body painting. The designs were worked in layers of solid-colored, European cotton fabric in a variety of techniques of layering and appliqué. Over the decades these designs have evolved into a cartoon of Cuna life and religion. Although a form of cross-knit looping was known prior to the Conquest, the indigenous people of Peru and Bolivia have made the craft of multiple-needle knitting into a native art form. Earflap caps, or *ch'ullus,* masks, armwarmers, and leggings have been incorporated into the native costume and ceremonies. Andean knitted products are now sold by commercial designers and alpaca knitting yarn is prized by knitters for its soft hand and lovely colors. In Guatemala the art of *ikat,* tie-dying threads into designs for both the warp and the weft before weaving, are now used in both the backstrap-loomed materials as well as the European-loomed yardage. This patterning was first used in women's skirts and is now produced and traded in such quantities as to be seen throughout the world and copied in India and China.

Major changes have evolved in indigenous textiles in the twentieth century. Air transportation and roads have opened up sheltered cultures to outside influences. Men have worked in factories and positions away from their village and in different climates. Progressive schools and institutions have tried to westernize the natives, diminishing the use of and need for native dress. Native style has been regulated by laws to make it conform to modern decorum. Colors and designs have changed to make textile goods more marketable and pleasing to tourists and wholesalers. Chemical dyes have changed the color from soft or faded natural color to vibrant hues. New fibers such as synthetic silk-like rayon and Orlon have been exchanged for wool and cotton or used as secondary fibers in weaving. In some communities there has been a deliberate attempt to develop new dyes to duplicate the hue of natural dyes and provide a more satisfactory spun thread. Where technology has been used to enhance the native textile culture, everyone has benefited; where it has been used to eliminate the culture by producing a poor, cheap substitute, all societies have suffered.

See also **Cotton; Wool Industry.**

BIBLIOGRAPHY

Lila M. O'Neale, *Textiles of Highland Guatemala* (1945).

Lilly De Jongh Osborne, *Indian Crafts of Guatemala and El Salvador* (1965).

Donald Cordry and Dorothy Cordry, *Mexican Indian Costumes* (1968).

Marjorie Cason and Adele Cahlander, *The Art of Bolivian Highland Weaving* (1976).

Patricia Reiff Anawalt, *Indian Clothing Before Cortez* (1981).

Tammara E. Wasserman and Jonathan S. Hill, *Bolivian Indian Textiles: Traditional Designs and Costumes* (1981).

Laurie Adelson and Arthur Tracht, *Aymara Weavings: Ceremonial Textiles of Colonial and 19th Century Bolivia* (1983).

Adele Cahlander with Suzanne Baizerman, *Double-Woven Treasures from Old Peru* (1985).

Cynthia Gravelle Le Count, *Andean Folk Knitting: Traditions and Techniques from Peru and Bolivia* (1990).

Additional Bibliography

Bruhns, Karen Olsen, and Karen E. Stohert. *Women in Ancient America.* Norman: University of Oklahoma Press, 1999.

Radicati di Primeglio, Carlos. *Estudios sobre los quipus.* Edited by Gary Urton. Lima: Fondo Editorial Universidad Nacional Mayor de San Marcos, 2006.

SUE DAWN MCGRADY

TEZCATLIPOCA. Tezcatlipoca, Aztec deity of rulership, destruction, the night, and the magic arts. The most important deity in Aztec religion, Tezcatlipoca is a complex composite of shifting identities who, like his North American cousin Trickster, defies definition by being himself a principle of disorder. He incited immoral behavior and then punished or pardoned the wrongdoer. He was a shaman, a *nahualli* or shape-changer whose hidden self was the jaguar, though he had many disguises. As the Big Dipper he ruled the night sky, but lost his left foot to the crocodilian Earth monster when the constellation's end star dropped below the horizon. The serpent-footed God K (Tahil) of the Classic Maya is Tezcatlipoca's analogue.

The name Tezcatlipoca, "Smoking Mirror" or "The Mirror's Smoke," alludes to his practice of divination with torch-lit obsidian mirrors. His other names include Yohualli Ehecatl, "The Night, the Wind"; Titlacahuan, "We are His Slaves"; Necoc Yaotl, "Enemy on Both Sides"; Ipalnemohuani, "By Him One Lives"; and Tloque Nahuaque, "Possessor of the Near, Possessor of the Nigh."

Tezcatlipoca was at once one being and four: the Four Tezcatlipocas, lords of the directions, governed the creation and destruction of the Earth and Sun. In the east was the red Tezcatlipoca, Xipe Totec; in the south the blue Huitzilopochtli; white Quetzalcoatl in the west; in the north the Black Tezcatlipoca or Tezcatlipoca proper. He and Quetzalcoatl were paired in a cosmic conflict. Tezcatlipoca humiliated Quetzalcoatl and destroyed the mythic city Tollan (Tula). Placing these events in their historic past, the fatalistic Aztecs saw their own age as controlled by capricious Tezcatlipoca; rulers owed to him their tenuous hold on authority.

Spanish friars saw Tezcatlipoca as particularly demonic, and even identified him as Lucifer; therefore, he may appear more malevolent in colonial sources than he had been before contact.

See also **Aztecs; Huitzilopochtli; Quetzalcoatl.**

BIBLIOGRAPHY

Bernardino De Sahagún, *Florentine Codex,* translated by Arthur J. O. Anderson and Charles Dibble (1952–1983), esp. Books 3, 5, and 6.

Diego Durán, *Book of the Gods and Rites and the Ancient Calendar,* translated and edited by Fernando Horcasitas and Doris Heyden (1971).

Louise M. Burkhart, *The Slippery Earth: Nahua-Christian Moral Dialogue in Sixteenth-Century Mexico* (1989).

Additional Bibliography

Barjau, Luis. *Tezcatlipoca: Elementos de una teología nahua.* México: Universidad Nacional Autónoma de México, 1991.

Carrasco, David, ed. *Aztec Ceremonial Landscapes.* Niwot: University Press of Colorado, 1999.

Olivier, Guilhem. *Mockeries and Metamorphoses of an Aztec God: Tezcatlipoca, "Lord of the Smoking Mirror."* Trans. Michel Besson. Boulder: University Press of Colorado, 2003.

LOUISE M. BURKHART

THAYER OJEDA, TOMÁS (1877–1960). Tomás Thayer Ojeda (June 16, 1877–June 29, 1960) was born in the city of Caldera in northern Chile. He studied in the town of Taltal and finished his secondary education at the Colegio de San Agustín in Santiago, receiving a bachelor's degree in humanities in 1895. Despite severe problems with his eyesight, Thayer Ojeda discovered an early inclination for the study of history. Working at the manuscript division of the Biblioteca Nacional, Thayer Ojeda launched a lifetime career researching the origins of Chilean society, beginning with his *Memoria histórica sobre la familia Alvarez de Toledo en Chile* (1903) and culminating in *Formación de la sociedad chilena* (1939–1941), a three-volume study of the conquest and settlement of Chile between 1540 and 1565.

A rigorous scholar, Thayer Ojeda made substantive use of population data to significantly advance the field of early Chilean colonial history. Besides social and economic history, he also contributed to ecclesiastical history with his impressive *Reseña histórica biográfica de los eclesiásticos en el descubrimiento y conquista de Chile* (1921). Because of his talents in paleography as well as familiarity with colonial manuscripts, he was often called upon by the government to work on judicial and border issues. He also served as director of the Directorate of Libraries, Archives, and Museums.

See also **Chile: The Twentieth Century.**

BIBLIOGRAPHY

Figueroa, Virgilio. *Diccionario histórico, biográfico y bibliográfico de Chile.* 5 vols. Santiago de Chile: Balcells, 1925–1931.

Gazmuri R., Cristián. *La historiografía chilena (1842–1970).* Santiago de Chile: Taurus, 2006.

IVÁN JAKSIĆ

THEATER.   The history of the theater in Latin America is significantly longer than the period of the occupation by the Europeans. Before Columbus's arrival the great civilizations of the New World had developed drama and theatrical forms which satisfied ritual and aesthetic purposes. The Inca Garcilaso de la Vega refers to the comedies and tragedies of the Incas; the Aztecs had developed forms of dance and spectacle in a theatrical mode. Regrettably, none of these survived the Conquest. The only extant pre-Columbian theater piece is the *Rabinal Achí*, a curiously repetitious Maya drama elaborated by the K'iche' (Quiché) of Guatemala. After centuries of oral transmission it was transcribed in 1850 as the *Dance of Tun* and later translated into French by the Abbé Étienne Brasseur de Bourbourg. The play recounts the capture, questioning, and death of the K'iche' warrior. Although the cast is large, there are only five speaking parts and the notable feature is the parallelism that marks the principal interaction between the two warriors.

Theater may have contributed little to the conquest of the Americas, but it was vital to their colonization. The Spanish cleverly adapted indigenous artistic forms to hasten the process of converting the Indians to Catholicism, one of the two major objectives of the Conquest. The earliest recorded theatrical forms in the New World are, in fact, short religious pieces (known as *autos, loas,* or *mojigangas*) developed by the clergy, who at times distorted indigenous concepts in order to convey the tenets of Christianity, primarily for the purpose of catechization. Little evidence remains because of the ephemeral nature of these plays and the severe ecclesiastical censorship of the times. In sixteenth-century Brazil, Padre José de Anchieta wrote *autos sacramentales* incorporating the flora, fauna, and ethnology of the new land, in combinations of Spanish, Portuguese, Latin, and indigenous languages.

In the Spanish-speaking Caribbean, the antecedents for theater can be found in the Corpus Christi festivities of European influence and in the religious festivities of the African slaves. These celebrations originated in the slave barracks at first, then in the meeting places of free blacks where they planned their yearly Three Kings Day celebration (January 6). On that day, the Afro-descendants filled the streets with their *wemileres*, chants, and dances.

By the middle of the sixteenth century, a secular theater responding to the needs of the growing population began to flourish, especially in Lima and other major centers. In Hispaniola, Cristóbal de Llerena (1540–1610) wrote socially critical and comedic *entremeses* as early as 1588, thus becoming the first criollo playwright. In Mexico, Fernán González De Eslava wrote both religious and secular pieces, some in honor of viceregal celebrations and special events. The rapid growth and development in the theater in Spain during the golden age of Lope de Vega, Tirso de Molina, and others, provided impetus for writers in Latin America.

SEVENTEENTH AND EIGHTEENTH CENTURIES

In the seventeenth century the theater of Latin America continued to reflect the literary traditions of Europe, and there was regular interaction between the two continents. The celebrated Spanish playwright Pedro Calderón de la Barca visited the New World, whereas the Mexican-born Juan Ruíz De Alarcón established residency in Spain; his twenty-four plays, although claimed by Mexico as a national legacy, show little evidence of the New World in language or customs. Known as the moralist of his time, he valued human dignity, and his best plays, *Las paredes oyen* (1628) and *La verdad sospechosa,* (1634) are both didactic and entertaining.

The literary genius of the era is the Mexican nun Sor Juana Inés De La Cruz, a prodigy whose superb gift for language combined with a powerful sense of social and sexual equality to produce works with lasting value. *El divino Narciso* (1690) is written as an *auto sacramental*, and *Los empeños de una casa* (1683) represents the American baroque in theater. In 1990 a play attributed to Sor Juana, *La gran comedia de La segunda Celestina*, was discovered in the Mexican archives.

In Brazil the theater of the seventeenth century is marked by a decline of the activities of the Jesuits in presenting drama. In general the representations are linked to religious festivals or to other popular feasts or public occasions. Manuel Botelho de Oliveira is known as one of the first Brazilians to publish his works, but they are Spanish in spirit, technique, themes, and even at times in language.

Throughout the Americas the theater movement reflected the tastes and interests of the privileged classes. The theatrical artists who toured in the New World with Spanish-based productions stimulated local activity, and writers and plays in the Americas tended to echo the themes and styles of European theater.

Just as Spain failed to shine in the eighteenth century after the literary splendor of the baroque had passed, the New World showed little originality with regard to theatrical trends. In Brazil, "O Judeu" (the pen name of Antônio José da Silva) wrote satirical works caricaturing both the nobility and the church, which led to his persecution and burning at the stake. The earliest theater pieces from Argentina are *Siripo* (1789), by Manuel José de Lavardén, and the anonymous *El amor de la estanciera* (ca. 1792), which is recognized as a humble precursor of the gaucho drama. In Mexico, Eusebio de Vela (1688–1737) wrote *comedias* for his Coliseo de Mexico.

NINETEENTH CENTURY

The Wars of Independence that rumbled across Latin America between 1810 and about 1825 did little to break the cultural ties with Spain. Theater fare often consisted of adaptations or translations of European works, and the neoclassical tendencies of the period served didactic purposes, with an emphasis on reason rather than on emotion. In Buenos Aires the Sociedad de Buen Gusto was founded in 1817 to develop an autonomous theater in this fledgling provincial capital, but it survived only two years. As both playwright and actor, Luis Ambrosio Morante (1775–1837) was responsible for its first production, *Cornelia*

Bororquía (1817), one of several plays that dealt with conflicts between civil and religious power. In Mexico the celebrated novelist José Joaquín Fernández de Lizardi (1776–1827) wrote didactic, neoclassical plays. However, an examination of indigenous texts transcribed and published in this century demonstrates that indigenous theater was kept alive through memory and oral tradition and used techniques of subterfuge, linguistic plays, and double entendres to protest colonial rule. An example of this is Nicaragua's *El Güegüense (El macho-ratón)*, a satirical drama considered to be one of Latin America's most distinctive colonial expressions. Written probably in the seventeenth or eighteenth century in a mixture of Spanish and Nahuatl, and performed with music and dance, it was first published in English in 1883 based on Karl Herman Berendt's fusion of two versions owned by Dr. Juan Eligio de la Rocha, Nicaragua's first linguist. The most reliable source available is Carlos Mantica's 2001 edition, transcribed directly from españahuat (a mixture of Spanish and Nahuatl) to contemporary Spanish. UNESCO declared this "play" a Masterpiece of the Oral and Intangible Heritage of Humanity in 2005.

Throughout the colonial period (1500s–1800s), indigenous theater coexisted with other theatrical trends. Late twentieth-century publications in colonial studies have unearthed previously unpublished dramas, revised outdated translations, and worked with new sources and critical tools to provide more reliable transcriptions. These revisionist scholarly works begin to show the literary/artistic qualities of these dramas as well as the ways in which they provide access to the indigenous colonial experience. Moreover, borrowing from performance studies, these publications show how indigenous colonial theater can be used to study the expressive culture of the colonized. As a result, rather than focusing on these performances solely as tools for catechization, they demonstrate how the indigenous lived in a contact, hybrid zone characterized by the negotiation of power and authority between the cultures of the conqueror and the conquered. An excellent example of this work is the four-volume series-in-progress *Nahuatl Theater*, edited by Barry D. Sell and Louise M. Burkhart.

In Brazil, King João VI ordered the construction of the Royal Theater after his flight from the Napoleonic invasion, in order to transplant his favorite Italian operas to Rio de Janeiro. The first play by a Brazilian with a national theme is *Antônio José, ou O Poeta e a Inquisição* (1838) by Domingos José Gonçalves de Magalhães, written as a classical tragedy to express his disgust with the new school of romanticism.

While romanticism was sweeping the European continent, its arrival in Spain and Latin America was arrested by political issues in both sites. In 1833 the Mexican expatriate Manuel Eduardo de Gorostiza (1789–1851) brought his masterpiece, *Contigo pan y cebolla*, back to Mexico as a satirical view of the excessive sentimentalism and idealization of the romantic mode. When the Cuban playwright (born in the Dominican Republic) Francisco Javier Foxá (1816–1865) wrote *Don Pedro de Castilla* in 1836, he became the first Romantic playwright of Latin America. In Lima in 1837, Father Antonio Valdez reportedly "discovered" an ancient Inca text, *Ollantay*, but its European structure led critics to conclude that he had written the text based on ancient themes and legends. From the 1830s to the 1870s the theater was still nourished largely by European themes and techniques. There was a cleavage between exotic and chivalric revivals of European inspiration and incipient efforts to identify customs, deeds, and values of the Americas. The new political and literary freedom of the period generated polemical initiatives to use the stage for propaganda.

The most representative Mexican playwrights of the period reflected both tendencies: Fernando Calderón (1809–1845) generally escaped Mexican boundaries in a search for esoteric European fancies, while his compatriot Ignacio Rodríguez Galván (1816–1842) looked to the traditions and legends of the New World, as in *Muñoz, Visitador de México* (1838). The brutality of the Juan Manuel de Rosas dictatorship in Argentina stifled a free theater development, but while in exile in Bolivia, Pedro Echagüe (1821–1889) staged his version of *Rosas* (1851), full of political invective and recrimination. At home the theater tended to be adulatory or to follow the sentimental, exotic, or satiric-regionalistic models of the romantic period. In Cuba, the most important playwright of the period, Gertrudis Gómez de Avellaneda (1814–1873), is also claimed by Spain given that many of her plays were written and staged to great success there. While influenced by the Romanticism of the period, her works (*Baltazar* and *Saul*, for

example) question and invert the Romantic hero and heroine.

The monarchy in Brazil created an entirely different political climate, and Brazilian works ranged from escapist theater to social commentary, advocating, for instance, the abolition of slavery. The most important was Martins Pena, who with wit and grace developed the comedy of manners, leaving a dramatic legacy that captured the essence of Brazilian customs and values in the mid-nineteenth century.

The disparities in the latter part of the century are even more pronounced throughout the Americas. Just as neoclassic modes survived into the Romantic period, the Romantic modes continued well into the period in which realism characterized the novel and a new psychological base, inspired by Sigmund Freud and Henrik Ibsen, underscored the Spanish theater known as the *alta comedia*, which tried to capture a realistic view of life. The Mexican playwrights José Peón Contreras (1843–1907) and Manuel José Othón (1858–1906) exemplified the period with facile verses and Romantic excesses. In Brazil a new theater modeled on the Gymnase in Paris, where the repertoire of French realism triumphed, enjoyed a brief period of enthusiastic support for its thesis plays on important social issues of the time, but it was superseded by the success of the *revista* (review), a light and comical form popularized by the prolific Artur Azevedo (1855–1908), whose talent for spontaneity, improvisation, and popular psychology ensured success for his farces and satires about Brazilian customs and politics.

The Caribbean saw the apogee of the highly popular *teatro bufo* or *vernáculo* (humorous/vernacular theater) in contrast to the European realistic tradition. This blackface theater started around the 1850s in Havana with Francisco Covarrubias (1755–1850), considered the father of Cuban theater. The plays present stock characters—the learned free black, the Spanish merchant, and the *mulata*—and through the use of *choteo*, or humor and political satire, they aimed to critique the petite bourgeoisie that wanted independence from Spain while maintaining slavery. Puerto Rico also had a popular tradition of comedy and satire with plays presented in open-air *corrales*. Alejandro Tapia y Rivera (1826–1882) became the region's first important playwright. In *La Cuarterona* he started a long tradition of plays dealing with racial difference.

In the latter part of the century, in the Río de la Plata region, there developed the *sainete criollo* (creole burlesque or farce), a theatrical form driven by the moral values, social problems, and ethnic complications of an area rapidly settled by European immigrants, and derived from the indigenous and gaucho traditions. When Eduardo Gutiérrez's novel *Juan Moreira* was adapted for the circus by the Uruguayan clown José Podestá in 1884, the door was opened to a new combination of the Spanish picaresque traditions and local elements full of both life and sadness. Likewise, the Dominican Virginia Elena Ortea (1866–1903) transformed the Spanish zarzuela to advocate equal rights for women in *Las feministas*.

TWENTIETH CENTURY

The foregoing emphasis on Mexico, Brazil, the Caribbean, and the Río de la Plata in no way is meant to suggest a lack of theatrical activity in other countries, all of which have their own rich histories, reflecting the strong influence of European models. It is really in the twentieth century that the theater of Latin America took on a unique and original quality that allowed it to stand with the best of world drama. Latin American theater staged its multidimensionality as it navigated the difficult waters of negotiating aesthetic and political interests. On the one hand, there was a search for and enrichment of a Latin American specificity within this continent's different historical and economic moments. On the other, there was a continuous and sustained process of devouring and transforming the European avant-gardes in order to avoid the divide between the aesthetic and the political.

In much of Latin America the nineteenth-century traditions continued well into the new century. The exception was the Río de la Plata area, where the picturesqueness of the European migration fused with the national atmosphere to provide raw material for the modernized *sainete*, embodied in the plays of the Uruguayan Florencio Sánchez. In such dramas as *La gringa* (1904) and *Barranca abajo* (1905), he mel-ded the concerns of people struggling with their ambience and their own shortcomings into dynamic models that set the standards for his generation. Roberto Payró (1867–1928), Gregorio Laferrère (1867–1913), and Ernesto Herrera (1886–1917) continued the *sainete* tradition.

The impetus for a modernized theater originated in Mexico in 1928 when Salvador Novo and Xavier Villaurrutia, with the patronage of Antonieta Rivas Mercado, launched the Teatro de Ulises, a vanguard theater that brought to Mexico the latest techniques in staging, lighting, and direction. Earlier efforts by the Grupo de los Siete Autores had made some progress, but had not succeeded in breaking the old traditions of the prompter's box or the domination by the primary actor or actress. The new experimental format required a small theater, electric lighting, memorized text, and coordination by the director of all elements of the performance. Other Mexican groups, such as Orientación, quickly followed suit in the effort to establish these universal phenomena in the national aesthetic consciousness.

During the 1930s and into the early 1940s, similar initiatives of modern/national theater projects sprang up throughout the Latin American republics. Theater rejected the outmoded realist tradition that characterized the previous decades of the century. In Argentina the work of Leónidas Barletta with the Teatro del Pueblo had the double objective of modernizing theater craft and delivering a social message. With this group Roberto Arlt, a major playwright long undervalued, staged such plays as *Saverio el cruel* (1936), which incorporates metatheatrical concepts with elements of class conflict.

The renovation occurred in Puerto Rico in 1938 when the Ateneo Puertorriqueño presented three plays selected by Emilio Belaval for their national themes. The national conscience of Puerto Rico was awakened by the desire for social reform for the displaced *jíbaro* (hillbilly) or the immigrant to New York. Belaval's short-lived group, Areyto, was soon followed by others with the same objectives. In Cuba, the staging of Virgilio Piñera's *Electra Garrigó* in 1948 marked the beginning of a modern theatrical trend. His *False Alarm*, published in 1949, predates Ionesco's *The Bald Soprano* and is thus considered the first absurdist play in Latin America.

The Brazilian theater was characterized during these years by revues, farces, operettas, and burlesque, represented by authors continuing the traditions of Artur Azevedo. Although the Semana de Arte Moderna in 1922 revolutionized Brazilian letters, its impact was not felt in the theater. During the 1930s the theater of Joracy Camargo explored sociopolitical theories of class struggle. Change came through

Os Comediantes's brilliant staging of Nelson Rodrigues's multilevel *Vestido de noiva* (1943) by the Polish-emigré director Zbigniew Ziembinski, who had been trained in German Expressionism.

A curious aspect of the Chilean theater movement was that the renaissance occurred through the universities. In 1941 at the University of Chile and in 1943 at the Catholic University of Santiago, semiprofessional theater companies were established to bring to the Chilean stage the principles espoused by Margarita Xirgú with her touring productions of Federico García Lorca's plays.

All of these experimental and independent initiatives, combined with those of other countries, laid the groundwork for the boom in Latin American theater that took form in the 1950s and 1960s. The play by the Argentine Carlos Gorostiza, *El puente*, which premiered in 1949, moved from the experimental stage to the commercial stage in 1950, marking the beginning of a new era. Throughout the Americas, conditions favored an expansion in the theater, and playwrights and directors responded to the challenge with exciting new plays in imaginative stagings. Their numbers were legion. Their objectives, however, were amazingly cohesive: to bring to the Latin American theater a new sense of its own identity, capturing the national and human spirit through believable characters who manifested the social, political, religious, and personal conflicts of individuals in modern societies.

Not all plays, naturally, were masterpieces, but the new generation included those who produced the contemporary canon: Emilio Carballido and Luisa Josefina Hernández (Mexico), Osvaldo de Dragún and Griselda Gambaro (Argentina), Jorge Díaz and Egon Wolff (Chile), René Marqués and Francisco Arriví (Puerto Rico), José Triana, Abelardo Estorino, and Antón Arrufat (Cuba), and a host of others. Their experiments with lights, music, sound, and movement were inspiring to a new generation of directors, including Jorge Lavelli and Jaime Kogan (Argentina), Julio Castillo and Juan Tovar (Mexico), Isaac Chocrón (Venezuela), José Lacomba (Puerto Rico), Orlando Rodríguez (Chile), Zbigniew Ziembinski, Luciano Salce, and José Celso (Brazil), and many others.

This expansion continued virtually unchecked into the 1960s, national differences duly noted, when Latin Americans began to seek inspiration not so much from the traditional European or American sources as from within Latin America itself and to develop the *creación colectiva* (theater developed by the group). The year 1968 marks a critical juncture when theater festivals were organized in Lima, Peru; San José, Costa Rica; Mexico City; and Manizales, Colombia, the latter an event that has continued into the twenty-first century. These festivals developed a sense of solidarity within the Latin American theater community, providing groups with the opportunity to be seen and to see and to draw from the best of their counterparts.

At the same time, in contrast with the "well-made plays" of the 1950s and early 1960s, the theater again became more experimental, reacting against bourgeois standards in favor of a more egalitarian system. Directors assumed a less authoritarian role in order to allow actors to create their own works collectively, especially in those cases where groups felt that plays capable of expressing their sociopolitical aims were not available. Drawing on the models set by the Living Theatre and the Berliner Ensemble, the manifestations of the *creación colectiva* in Latin America are as varied as the groups that represented them, but some are exemplary. In Brazil, Augusto Boal established the Teatro de Arena in 1965 using the *teatro de coringa*, a form that allowed great flexibility in putting actors into direct contact with the staging and the public. Boal, at times in exile, later developed a journalistic theater, an invisible theater, and an image theater under the broad rubric of "theater of the oppressed." Teatro Aleph (Chile), Libre Teatro Libre (Argentina), CLETa (Mexico), Yuyachkani and Cuatrotablas (Peru), and many others experimented with similar politically oriented theatrical forms. The most developed activity was in Colombia, where the TEC (Teatro Experimental de Cali) under the direction of Enrique Buenaventura and La Candelaria (Bogotá) founded by Santiago García, Patricia Ariza, and Carlos José Reyes, developed coherent methodological systems for inverting traditional bourgeois structures.

The Cuban theater followed the typical Latin American patterns until the revolution of 1959 transformed theater not only in Havana but throughout the island. In 1961 the Conjunto Dramático de Oriente was founded. They worked within the tradition of the *teatro de relaciones*, a mode of popular street theater dating back to colonial times. This theater uses tragicomic elements and simple scenery, and it borrows music and dance elements from the carnival as expressive forms. Afro-Cuban playwrights such as Eugenio Hernández Espinosa became active participants in the nascent revolutionary theater scene. His first play, *María Antonia*, gained critical attention in 1967. A tragedy set within the revolution with a marginalized Afro-Cuban woman as a protagonist, the play staged for the first time elements of Afro-Cuban culture previously absent in the theatrical tradition. By the late 1960s, Cuban cultural policies were dictated by the hard-liners, and the revolution began to use the theater as an instrument for social change. Writers such as José Triana and Antón Arrufat fell from favor and were replaced by the collectives such as Teatro Escambray, a group formed in the mountains to address social issues at a popular level within the new government structure. Some playwrights such as Matías Montes Huidobro, Eduardo Manet, and Julio Matas went into exile, while many who remained in Cuba were ostracized until the early 1980s. With major funding for art schools and theater academies throughout the island, the theater movement has flourished in Cuba. In spite of ideological constraints, Cuban theater is extremely reflexive and offers a critical outlook of national problems while it experiments with new forms.

By the mid-1970s, the Southern Cone found itself under authoritarian, military regimes. Dictatorships and their subsequent neoliberal economic policies profoundly transformed theater activity. On the one hand, repression and censorship forced many playwrights into exile and decimated independent theater movements by transforming a number of theater practitioners into "disappeared." On the other, official policies favored and supported a commercial theater that focused primarily on entertainment. Alternative theaters resisted and contested official discourse and fought to keep the memory of the disappeared alive through plays characterized by oblique, indirect language. In Chile, Oscar Castro, one of the few survivors of El Aleph theater group, was able to stage plays in detention camps during the first years of the dictatorship. Later, Juan Radrigán focused on disenfranchised groups through stagings in places outside of the professional theater scene. The theater group ICTUS was able to present plays by Marco Antonio de la Parra, David Benavente, and Isadora Aguirre after 1979. Ramón Griffero founded the group Fin de Siglo after returning from exile in 1983. He staged a number of his plays at El Trolley,

a clandestine space that used to be the union hall for Santiago's trolley workers. In Argentina, the experiment with Teatro Abierto in Buenos Aires in 1981, spearheaded by Oswaldo Dragún, was a collaboration originally among twenty playwrights and twenty directors of different generations and political affiliations who rejected the military regime. They staged Argentina's psychological and sociopolitical reality of the 1980s by recuperating first theatrical spaces that the dictatorship had transformed into commercial theaters and then public spaces with street theater and other popular community art forms, thus giving a new impetus to the Argentine theater. Uruguay's Teatro El galpón returned from exile in 1984.

The politicization of the theater in Latin America throughout the 1970s and 1980s did not replace other forms entirely. While the influence of Bertolt Brecht was ubiquitous, Artaudian strains of total theater were also common, as were occasional remnants of theater of the absurd. Some playwrights experimented with ritual and game-playing, and metatheatrical forms kept pace with a new insistence on documentary-style drama. A new generation of playwrights emerged, including Vicente Leñero, Oscar Liera, and Oscar Villegas (Mexico); José Ignacio Cabrujas and Román Chalbaud (Venezuela); Eduardo Pavlovsky, Ricardo Talesnik, and Diana Raznovich (Argentina); Marco Antonio de la Parra (Chile), Roberto Ramos-Perea (Puerto Rico); Reynaldo Disla (Dominican Republic); Roberto Athayde, Naum Alves de Sousa, and María Adelaide Amaral (Brazil); and many others.

By the early 1990s and into the new millennium, the restoration of democratic governments in most countries relieved some political problems, but the crushing economic issues brought on by inflation and the debt crisis, coupled with overpopulation, inadequate social programs, and the narcotics traffic, produced a paradoxical situation whereby, on the one hand, greater imbalances in Latin America's social spheres were accentuated and, on the other, the cultural sphere tried to be homogenized. Theater as a reflection or abstraction of its surroundings in the early twenty-first century is trying to find a new voice and a place from which to create. Several expressions of "testimonial theater" were produced, such as Uruguay's plays by Marianela Morena that try to reconstruct the lives and keep alive the memory of the disappeared. Chile's Teatro de la Memoria and Argentina's Teatro por la Identidad focused on those who do not know their past because they were taken away from their parents by the military regimes.

Perhaps the most important innovation since the early 1990s has been the encounter of theater with other cultural forms such as film, video, and dance. Whether it is performance, intermediality, image theater, or what many call postdramatic theater, the written word is replaced by the image. Rather than theater being a representation rooted in a dramatic text, these new expressions are based on performativity and on the body's relationship to other spaces. In Argentina, Daniel Veronese, Alejandro Tantanian, and Ricardo Bartis with El Periférico de Objetos transform the stage into a lab in which they work in a border zone where the objects become object texts, object gestures, and object sounds. In Cuba, this break occurred in the late 1980s with Flora Lauten's Teatro Buendía and its emphasis on experimentation as an essential principle of artistic creation. Víctor Varela in 1987 presented in his living room La cuarta pared, a nonverbal piece that marked a radical rupture in Cuban theater and prompted discussions that went beyond aesthetics to ethical and ideological concerns. Incorporating Afro-Caribbean religious elements, Tomás González developed "acting in trance," in which "actors" follow a powerful psychophysical training until they assume or "mount" their "characters" as in a Santería ritual. Fátima Patterson works in the same tradition with Teatro Macubá in Santiago de Cuba, a project that focuses mainly on Caribbean women. In Colombia, Heidi and Rolf Abderhalden's Mapa Teatro uses nonconventional spaces and transforms architecture into the dramatic, thus breaking away from traditional notions of representation. Rosa Luisa Márquez and Antonio Martorell from Puerto Rico also work between theater and the visual arts, transforming materials and audiences through play and creative activities, thereby turning passive viewers into active participants in utopian mini-societies. Tanya Bruguera (Cuba), Diamela Eltit (Chile), Jesusa Rodríguez and Astrid Haddad (Mexico), Elia Arce (Costa Rica–U.S.), Josefina Baez (Dominican Republic–U.S.), and Coco Fuscó and Carmelita Tropicana (Cuba–U.S.) are some artists who use performance to intervene politically as they challenge patriarchy, hetero-normativity and repressive regimes. In all of these instances, the classic actor's role of "as if" is transformed into the performer's "being in" the present; representation gives way to presentness and performativity.

DOCUMENTATION AND WORKSHOPS

Documentation on theater has become increasingly sophisticated in the early twenty-first century as critics and scholars respond to new challenges. A rash of new journals regularly publishes analytical and informational items, including *Conjunto* and *Tablas* (Cuba), *Apuntes* (Chile), *Teatro* (Argentina), *Revista Teatro* (Colombia), *Tramoya* (Mexico), *Latin American Theatre Review*, *Ollantay Theater Magazine*, *Gestos*, and *Diógenes: Anuario Crítico del Teatro Latinoamericano* (United States; now defunct) and *La Escena Latinoamericana* (Canada), not to mention *Primer Acto*, which provides excellent coverage of Latin America. Some of these include Latino theater in the United States. There are also many online journals in such as *Dramateatro Revista Digital*, *Revista Digital de la Escena*, *Teatro en Línea*, *Revista Telón*, and *e-misférica*. Digital theater and performance archives are also being developed. The most important ones are the Hemispheric Institute Digital Video Library (Diana Taylor and New York University), the Cuban/Latino Theater Archive (Lillian Manzor and University of Miami), and the Hugo Salazar del Alcázar Video Theater Collection (Luis Ramos-García and University of Minnesota).

Many of the above artists and critics have led the workshops offered by the Escuela Internacional de Teatro de América Latina y el Caribe (EITALC). Founded in Havana in 1987 by Oswaldo Dragún, it is a Latin American nongovernmental institution with a pedagogical and itinerant nature. Since its first workshop in Machurrucutu, Cuba, in 1989, the school has offered workshops in Argentina, Brazil, Chile, Colombia, Cuba, Ecuador, Mexico, Nicaragua, Uruguay, and Venezuela, as well as Denmark, Germany, Italy, and the United States, thus fostering development and exchange among Latin American theater practitioners. In 1995 the EITALC was recognized as a UNESCO chair in Latin American Theater. The EITALC has been coordinated by Ileana Diéguez from Mexico since Dragún's death in 1999.

See also **Anchieta, José de; Arlt, Roberto; Arriví, Francisco; Arrufat, Antón; Boal, Augusto; Díaz, Jorge; Dragún, Osvaldo; Gambaro, Griselda; Gorostiza, Manuel Eduardo de; Hernández, Luisa**

Josefina; Leñero, Vicente; Literature: Brazil; Literature: Spanish America; Magalhães, Domingos José Gonçalves de; Marqués, René; Novo, Salvador; Oliveira, Manuel Botelho de; Rabinal Achí; Sánchez, Florencio; Triana, José; Villaurrutia, Xavier; Villegas, Oscar; Wolff, Egon.

BIBLIOGRAPHY

The standard works in the field are eight companion volumes titled *Historia del teatro hispanoamericano;* see especially José Juan Arrom, *Época colonial* (1966); and Frank Dauster, *Historia del teatro hispanoamericano (siglos XIX–XX)*, 2nd ed. (1973). Leon F. Lyday and George Woodyard edited a volume of essays on major playwrights, *Dramatists in Revolt: The New Latin American Theater* (1976).

An indispensable four-volume overview of the field was published in Spain by the Centro de Documentación Teatral: Moisés Pérez Coterillo, ed., *Escenarios de dos mundos: Inventario teatral de Iberoamérica* (1988).

The rate of growth in documentation is evident in several excellent publications: Severino João Albuquerque, *Violent Acts: A Study of Contemporary Latin American Theatre* (1991); Ronald D. Burgess, *The New Dramatists of Mexico, 1967–1985* (1991); Gerardo Luzuriaga, *Introducción a las teorías latinoamericanas del teatro* (1990).

Additional Bibliography

Alder, Heidrun, and George Woodyard, eds. *Resistencia y poder: teatro en Chile*. Frankfurt: Vervuert, 2000.

Alder, Heidrun, and Adrián Herr, eds. *Extraños en dos patrias: Teatro latinoamericano del exilio*. Frankfurt: Vervuert, 2003.

Pelletieri, Osvaldo, ed. *Itinerarios del teatro latinoamericano*. Buenos Aires: Galerna, Facultad de Filosofía y Letras, 2000.

Pelletieri, Osvaldo, ed. *Teatro, memoria y ficción* Buenos Aires: Galerna: Fundación Roberto Arlt, 2005.

Rizk, Beatriz J. *Posmodernismo y teatro en América Latina*. Madrid: Iberoamericana, 2001.

Rizk, Beatriz J. *Teatro y diáspora: Testimonios escénicos latinoamericanos*. Irvine, CA: Gestos, 2002.

Rizk, Beatriz J. "Imagining a Continent: Recent Research on Latin American Theater and the Performing Arts." *Latin American Research Review* 42, no. 1 (2007): 196–214.

Rizk, Beatriz J. "The Patriarchy Problem." *Latin American Research Review* 42, no. 2 (2007): 238–252.

Taylor, Diana. *Theatre of Crisis: Drama and Politics in Latin America*. Lexington: University Press of Kentucky, 1991.

Taylor, Diana, and Juan Villegas, eds. *Negotiating Performance: Gender, Sexuality, and Theatricality in Latin/o America*. Durham, NC: Duke University Press, 1995.

Taylor, Diana. *The Archive and the Repertoire: Performing Cultural Memory in the Americas*. Durham, NC: Duke University Press, 2003.

Taylor, Diana, and Sarah J. Townsend, eds. *Stages of Conflict: A Critical Anthology of Latin American Theater and Performance*. Ann Arbor: University of Michigan Press, forthcoming.

Villegas, Juan. *Para la interpretación del teatro como construcción visual*. Irvine, CA: Ediciones de GESTOS, 2000.

Villegas, Juan. *Historia multicultural del teatro y las teatralidades en América Latina*. Buenos Aires: Galerna, 2005.

GEORGE WOODYARD
LILLIAN MANZOR

THIEL, BERNARDO AUGUSTO

(1850–1901). Bernardo Augusto Thiel (*b.* 1 April 1850; *d.* 9 September 1901), bishop of Costa Rica (1880–1901). Thiel was born in Elberfeld, Germany, and was ordained in Paris in 1874. He became a seminary professor in Costa Rica in 1877. He was named to a politically controversial and vacant bishopric by the anticlerical Liberal president Tomás Guardia Gutiérrez as a moderate candidate but was subsequently expelled, along with the Jesuits, by Liberal authorities in 1884. After his return in 1886, Thiel became involved in electoral politics, and in 1889 founded the Catholic Union Party, which campaigned actively against the Liberal regime in 1894. Thiel also made several doctrinal statements on labor's right to organize and to receive "just salaries" in the face of widespread recession during the crisis in world coffee prices, which reduced real wages by 50 percent from 1870 to 1930. He founded a clerical newspaper, *El Mensajero del Clero,* in 1897, and was extremely active in national cultural life. His classic work, "Monografía de la Poblacíon de Costa Rica en el Siglo XIX," in *Revista de Costa Rica en el siglo XIX* (1902), remains a standard source. Thiel died in San José, Costa Rica.

See also **Costa Rica; Guardia Gutiérrez, Tomás.**

BIBLIOGRAPHY

Victor Manuel Sanabria Martínez, *Bernardo Augusto Thiel* (1941).

Octavio Castro Saborío, *Bernardo Augusto Thiel en la historia* (1959).

Constantino Láscaris Comneno, *Desarrollo de las ideas en Costa Rica*, 2d ed. (1975).

James Backer, *La iglesia y el sindicalismo en Costa Rica*, 3d ed. (1978).

Ricardo Blanco Segura, *1884: La iglesia y las reformas liberales* (1984).

Additional Bibliography

Zeledón C., Elías. *Crónicas de los viajes a guatuso, talamanca del obispo Bernardo Augusto Thiel, 1881–1895*. San José, Costa Rica: Editorial de la Universidad de Costa Rica, 2003.

LOWELL GUDMUNDSON

THOMPSON, ERIC (1898–1975). John Eric Sidney Thompson, a British-born eminent scholar of Maya epigraphy, archaeology, ethnohistory, and ethnography, made significant contributions to the understanding of the ancient Maya. Thompson was raised in London, and his pre-academic life included service in World War I and work as a gaucho in Argentina. From 1925 to 1926 he studied anthropology at Cambridge University.

In 1926, on his first of many trips to Mesoamerica, Thompson worked at the archaeological site of Chichén Itzá under the Mayanist Sylvanus Morley. Thompson published extensively on research from this and several other Maya archeological sites (e.g., Caracol, Lubaantun, Pusilha, Cobá, Rio Bec, San Jose, El Palmar, and Benque Viejo) while holding positions at the Chicago Natural History Museum and the Carnegie Institution. He was one of the first investigators to study smaller sites to learn about the lives of nonelites. Thompson also pioneered the use of ethnographic observations of modern Maya in his interpretations of their ancient ancestors.

Thompson's greatest contribution to Maya scholarship was his systematizing epigraphic studies translating ancient Maya hieroglyphs. He worked extensively on correlating the Maya and Gregorian calendars and on deciphering noncalendric hieroglyphs, and his publications on Maya epigraphy remain valuable resources. Thompson's approach to synthesizing archaeological, ethnographic, ethnohistoric, and ethnohistoric evidence in his work set the standard for anthropological research in Mesoamerica. For his scholarly contributions, Thompson was awarded numerous academic and national honors, including a British knighthood.

See also **Archaeology; Chichén Itzá; Maya, The; Mayan Epigraphy; Mayan Ethnohistory; Morley, Sylvanus Griswold.**

BIBLIOGRAPHY

Primary Works

Maya Hieroglyphic Writing: Introduction. Washington, DC: Carnegie Institution of Washington, 1950.

The Rise and Fall of Maya Civilization. Norman: University of Oklahoma Press, 1954.

A Catalog of Maya Hieroglyphs. Norman: University of Oklahoma Press, 1962.

Maya Archaeologist. London: Robert Hale Limited, 1963.

Maya History and Religion. Norman: University of Oklahoma Press, 1970.

Secondary Work

Hammond, Norman. "Sir Eric Thompson, 1898–1975." *American Antiquity* 42 (April 1977): 180–190.

DANIEL M. SEINFELD

THOMPSON, GEORGE (1839–1876). George Thompson (*b.* 1839; *d.* 1876), British military engineer active in Paraguay. Coming to Asunción in 1858 under a contractual agreement with the government of Carlos Antonio López, Thompson helped design and build the Paraguay Central Railroad. He remained in the country after the beginning of the War of the Triple Alliance in 1864, serving the regime of Field Marshal Francisco Solano López as colonel and commander of engineers. His preparation of trenches and defensive earthworks made a critical difference in the early stages of the conflict, particularly at Curupayty (September 1866), where the Brazilians and Argentines were repulsed with extremely heavy losses.

Thompson's spirited defense at Angostura in December 1868 facilitated Solano López's escape northward with what remained of the Paraguayan army. After Lopéz's subsequent surrender to the Brazilians, Thompson was permitted to return to Britain, where he wrote *The War in Paraguay* (1869), a highly detailed account of his experiences that was also highly critical of López. After the war, Thompson returned to Asunción, married into the local elite, and became an important official in the Paraguay Central Railway. He died in Asunción.

See also **López, Carlos Antonio; Paraguay: The Nineteenth Century.**

BIBLIOGRAPHY

Josefina Plá, *The British in Paraguay* (1976).

John Hoyt Williams, "Foreign Técnicos and the Modernization of Paraguay, 1840–1970," in *Journal of Interamerican Studies and World Affairs* 19, no. 2 (1977): 233–257.

Additional Bibliography

Dym, Jordana. "La reconciliación de la historia y la modernidad: George Thompson, Henry Dunn, y Frederick Crowe, tres viajeros británicos en Centroamérica, 1825–1845." *Mesoamérica (USA)* 20, no. 40 (December 2000): 142–181.

THOMAS L. WHIGHAM

THOMSON PORTO MARIÑO, MANUEL TOMÁS

(1839–1880). Manuel Tomás Thomson Porto Mariño (*b.* 1839; *d.* 1880), Chilean military leader. He entered the Chilean navy during the early 1850s. During the war against Spain (1865–1866) he commanded the captured Spanish warship *Covadonga* and served as its captain during the Battle of Abtao (7 February 1866), the only battle between opposing fleets. During the early days of the War of the Pacific (1879–1883), Thomson commanded the *Esmeralda*, *Abtao*, and *Amazonas*. In September 1879 the *Amazonas* was dispatched to the Atlantic to intercept the fast Peruvian transport *Oroya* but failed to find the enemy. On 22 December the *Amazonas* captured the Peruvian torpedo launch *Alay* at Ballenitas in northern Peru. In late January 1880 Thomson was given command of the former Peruvian seagoing monitor *Huáscar*, which had been captured at the battle of Angamos (8 October 1879). The *Huáscar* took part in the attack on Arica on 27 February 1880. While engaging the Peruvian coastal monitor *Manco Capac*, Thomson attempted to maneuver between the *Manco Capac* and the Peruvian shore batteries in order to deprive the enemy of its anchorage. At a critical moment the *Huáscar*'s engine failed, and the ship became an easy target. The *Huáscar* was hit by a large-caliber shell and Thomson was killed instantly.

See also **Chile, War with Spain.**

BIBLIOGRAPHY

Rodrigo Fuenzalida Bade, *Marinos ilustres y destacados del pasado* (1985).

Additional Bibliography

Rodríguez González, Agustín Ramón. *La Armada Española, la campaña del Pacífico, 1862–1871: España frente a Chile y Perú.* Madrid: Agualarga, 1999.

ROBERT SCHEINA

THOUSAND DAYS, WAR OF THE.
See **War of the Thousand Days.**

THREE GUARANTEES, ARMY OF THE.
Army of the Three Guarantees, a military unit based upon the three major planks of Agustín de Iturbide's Plan of Iguala (24 February 1821)—religion, independence, union. Following a decade of war, Iturbide called upon former insurgent and royalist military commanders to join a new army. Given the exhaustion of both sides, the call came at a most propitious moment. The renewal of the Spanish constitution in 1820 permitted Mexican towns and communities to cast off the intolerable burden of wartime taxation and service that had supported district and regional defenses. Realizing that the royalist army was crumbling, officers believed that Iturbide's offer would allow them to retain their positions and powers. Similarly, many insurgent commanders accepted Iturbide's offer of peace and patronage, leaving the few remaining royalist commanders without an effective fighting force. Following triumphant progress with only a few isolated skirmishes fought by the diehard Spaniards, Iturbide led his victorious army to Mexico City and independence. Unfortunately, accelerated promotions within this army helped to create future problems for Mexican governments.

See also **Iturbide, Agustín de; Plan of Iguala.**

BIBLIOGRAPHY

William Spence Robertson, *Iturbide of Mexico* (1968).

Christon I. Archer, "Where Did All the Royalists Go? New Light on the Military Collapse of New Spain, 1810–1822," in *The Mexican and Mexican American*

Experience, edited by Jaime Rodríguez O. (1989), pp. 24–32.

Timothy E. Anna, *The Mexican Republic of Iturbide* (1990).

Additional Bibliography

Archer, Christon I. *The Birth of Modern Mexico, 1780–1824.* Wilmington, DE: Scholarly Resources Inc, 2003.

Herrero Bervera, Carlos. *Revuelta, rebelión y revolución en 1810: Historia social y estudios de caso.* México: Centro de Estudios Históricos Internacionales, 2001.

CHRISTON I. ARCHER

TIAHUANACO. *See* Tiwanaku.

TIANT, LUIS (1940–).

Luis Tiant was one of the most memorable characters and pitchers in the history of major league baseball; he had the most distinctive wind-up of any pitcher. He was born in Marianao, Cuba, the son of a star of the Negro Leagues who was on the New York Cubans when they won the league's World Series in 1947. Tiant played in the Mexican League in 1959 and 1960 before being signed by the Cleveland Indians organization in 1961. He broke into the majors in 1964. A hard-throwing strikeout pitcher in this stage of the career, he had a brilliant season in 1968 with a 21-9 record and a 1.60 earned run average (ERA). He gradually developed a deceptive pitching style that involved extensive physical gyrations and unpredictable hesitations. It was said that wherever you sitting in the stadium he would look straight at you at some point during his delivery. He suffered a stress fracture in his rib cage in May of 1970 with the Minnesota Twins. He joined the Boston Red Sox in the following year. Injury problems continued to plague him, but he reemerged as a crafty pitcher, known for his guile and "heart." He had a sparkling ERA of 1.91 in 1972; he won 20 games in 1973, 22 in 1974 (including seven shutouts), and 21 in 1976. He entered the national spotlight during the 1975 postseason when he pitched a three-hitter in the American League Championship Series sweep of the Oakland Athletics. In the classic 1975 World Series against the Cincinnati Reds, he pitched an opening game shutout against the Big Red Machine. Even though he was not fully in command in the fourth game, he still won another complete-game victory. He was even called on to pitch seven innings in the sixth game, as well. By the time he left the Red Sox, he was second only to Cy Young on the team's all-time strikeout list, with 1,095. Tiant joined the New York Yankees in 1979 and stayed through the 1980 season, but he was no longer the star he had been. He pitched for the Pittsburgh Pirates in 1981 and ended his career with the California Angels in 1982. In nineteen years in the majors, he had a 229–172 record and a 3.30 ERA. Many think that he should be in the Hall of Fame. Since his retirement he has been the baseball coach for the Savannah College of Art and Design. He also has been a pitching coach for Red Sox minor league teams and for the Nicaraguan team in the 1996 Olympics.

See also Sports.

BIBLIOGRAPHY

Berry, Henry, and Harold Berry. *Boston Red Sox: The Complete Record of Red Sox Baseball.* New York: Macmillan Publishers, 1984.

Gammons, Peter. "Luis Tiant." In *Cult Baseball Players: The Greats, The Flakes, The Weird, and the Wonderful,* edited by Donald Perry. New York: Simon & Schuster, 1990.

Honig, Donald. *The Boston Red Sox.* New York: St. Martin's Press, 1984.

Hornig, Doug. *The Boys of October: How the 1975 Boston Red Sox Embodied Baseball's Ideals and Restored Our Spirits.* Chicago: Contemporary Books, 2003.

Preston, Joseph. *Major League Baseball in the 1970s: A Modern Game Emerges.* Jefferson, NC: McFarland & Company, 2004.

Stout, Glenn, and Richard A. Johnson. *Red Sox Century: The Definitive History of Baseball's Most Storied Franchise.* Boston: Houghton Mifflin, 2005.

ANDREW J. KIRKENDALL

TIERRA DEL FUEGO.

Tierra del Fuego is a province in southern Argentina, bordering on the west with Chile, on the north with the Strait of Magellan, on the south with the Beagle Channel, and on the east with the Argentine Sea. Formerly a national territory, Tierra del Fuego became a province in 1992. Its capital is the city of Ushuaia and its population is estimated at 100,000. Before the building of the Panama Canal (1914), the Strait of Magellan was the most important passage between the Pacific and the Atlantic oceans despite its hostile conditions for navigating.

Argentina maintained a lengthy conflict with Chile in the 1970s for control over the Lennox, Picton, and Nueva islands in the southern area of the Beagle Channel. A court of arbitration ruling favoring Chile was rejected by the Argentine dictatorship, and in 1978 the two nations were on the verge of war. Finally, papal mediation allowed Chile to retain sovereignty over the disputed territory.

The main island of the archipelago comprising this province is the island of Tierra del Fuego, separated from the continent by the Strait of Magellan (which connects the Atlantic with the Pacific Ocean). The climate throughout the province is predominantly cold. Its main economic activities are drilling for oil, the home appliance industry, fishing, and tourism. The channels of Tierra del Fuego and the province's national parks are popular tourist attractions, with many cruise ships visiting the area.

See also **Argentina, Geography; Chile, Geography; Magellan, Strait of.**

BIBLIOGRAPHY

Lacoste, Pablo. *La imagen del otro en las relaciones de la Argentina y Chile (1534–2000)*. Buenos Aires: Fondo de Cultura Económica, 2003.

VICENTE PALERMO

TIETÊ RIVER.

Tietê River, a waterway originating in the mountains on the Atlantic coast of Brazil and flowing westerly through the state of São Paulo until joining the Paraná River. Formerly called the Anhembi, the Tietê River's headwaters are the closest to the ocean of all Brazilian rivers. From the many falls and rapids that characterize its course, it got its name "Tietê," meaning "river of many waters."

Through its riparian connections, the Tietê afforded the *bandeirantes* access to the interior of much of Brazil. These explorers used the river to explore for mineral wealth and to capture and enslave the Tupi Indians who lived in the river valley. In the eighteenth century travelers journeyed from the port of Aritaguaba to the mines of Minas Gerais by way of the Tietê. After an 1838 typhoid epidemic decimated most of the boatmen and pilots who knew how to navigate the river, there were fewer water voyages. Eventually railways replaced the Tietê canoe route that had served the Paulistas for two hundred years.

In modern times the Tietê suffers from pollution originating from the city of São Paulo.

See also **Bandeiras; São Paulo (City).**

BIBLIOGRAPHY

Richard M. Morse, ed., *The Bandeirantes* (1965).

E. Bradford Burns, ed., *A Documentary History of Brazil* (1966).

Additional Bibliography

Jorge, Janes. *Tiete, o rio que a cidade perdeu: São Paulo, 1890–1940*. São Paulo: Alameda, 2007.

Kahtouni, Sade. *Cidade das águas*. São Carlos: RiMa, 2004.

Nicolini, Henrique. *Tiete: O rio do esporte*. São Paulo: Phorte Editora, 2001.

SHEILA L. HOOKER

TIGRES DEL NORTE, LOS.

Los Tigres del Norte are a *norteño* band from the state of Sinaloa, Mexico, although they have resided in San Jose, California, since their early days as a group. They were formed in 1968 by lead vocalist and accordionist Jorge Hernández. Other members include his brothers Hernán Hernández, Eduardo Hernández, Luis Hernández and their cousin Oscar Lara. Their binational identity is deeply ingrained in their music, and many of their songs represent the immigrant experience of their legions of fans.

Norteño music combines the Czech and German influences of the accordion and a polka beat with guitar and *bajo sexto* (six-stringed bass), along with a cowboy style of dress. The group is most well-known for their *corridos*, a popular song form that has its origins in Spanish ballads (*romances*), that gained currency in Mexican culture during the Revolution (1910–1920). Corridos serve to tell stories and spread news of importance to the community. *Narcocorridos*, songs that chronicle the pervasiveness of the drug trade in northern Mexican society and culture, are a trademark of the band. "El muro" (The

Wall), from their most recent album, critiques the plan to construct a wall on the U.S.-Mexico border in Spanish, Arabic, French, German and English; the song not only continues their tradition of representing the immigrant/border experience of Mexicans in the United States, but also acknowledges the global scale of the phenomenon.

See also **Borderlands, The; Hispanics in the United States; Music: Popular Music and Dance.**

BIBLIOGRAPHY

Selected Discography

Gracias! América … Sin fronteras (1986); Grammy, Best Mexican-American Performance.

Ídolos del pueblo (1988).

Corridos prohibidos (1989).

Jefe de jefes (1997).

Herencia de familia (1999); Latin Grammy, Best Norteño Performance.

Uniendo fronteras (2001).

Pacto de sangre (2004); Latin Grammy, Best Norteño Album.

Historias que contar (2006); Grammy, Latin Grammy, Best Norteño Album.

Detalles y emociones (2007).

Secondary Sources

Martínez Saldaña, Jesús. "Los Tigres del Norte en Silicon Valley." *Nexos* 16, no. 191 (November 1993): 77–83.

Ramírez-Pimienta, Juan Carlos, and Pimienta, Jorge. "¿Todavía es el corrido la voz de nuestra gente?: Una entrevista con Enrique Franco." *Studies in Latin American Popular Culture* 23 (2004): 43–54.

Villalobos, José Pablo, and Juan Carlos Ramírez Pimienta. "Corridos and la pura verdad: Myths and Realities of the Mexican Ballad." *South Central Review* 21, no. 3 (Fall 2004): 129–149.

CARYN C. CONNELLY

TIKAL. Tikal is a major pre-Hispanic Maya center located in the dense jungles of the northern department of Petén, Guatemala. Tikal is both the largest and the most thoroughly studied Maya site. The site core consists of several large areas of major temple-pyramid complexes on high rocky ground, linked by causeways (*sacbeob*) and surrounded by over twenty square miles of scattered residential remains and distant defensive fortifications. Nearby *bajos* (lowlands) were modified to trap rainwater. Major structures date from the Late Formative to the Late Classic Periods, and dated monuments date from 292 CE on Stela 29 to 869 CE on Stela 11. Tikal sat astride the headwaters of rivers flowing eastward to the Caribbean and westward to the Gulf of Mexico, dominating the cross-peninsular trade routes through two major epochs.

Carved stelae, ceramics, and burial offerings show very close ties between Tikal, Teotihuacán, and Kaminaljuyú in the Early Classic Period (about 378 CE). Stela 31 (dated 435 CE) of ruler Siyaj Chan K'awiil II (Stormy Sky) depicts attendants in Teotihuacán military attire with Teotihuacano weapons. These ties vanish after 354 CE, when a period of reduced construction and activity began. This Middle Classic hiatus, which corresponds to the decline of Teotihuacán, lasted until nearly 700 CE, when renewed activity began the Late Classic Period at Tikal.

Inscriptions also name nearby Maya sites, including Calakmul, Caracol, Uaxactun, and Naranjo, relating either warfare between sites or strategic and marital alliances. The inscriptions tell of more than two dozen rulers spanning 800 years.

Tikal's Great Plaza of Late Classic structures is defined by two east-west facing temple-pyramids, I and II. Temple I, 155 feet high, was the burial pyramid of ruler Jasaw Chan K'awiil, inaugurated in 682 CE. The adjacent north acropolis consists of large temple-pyramids built above tombs of the ruling elite. The burials include skeletons, painted inscriptions, inscribed bones, jade offerings, animal offerings, and ceramic vessels. To the south is a large elite residence or palace. West of the plaza is the largest pyramid at Tikal, Temple IV, 230 feet high, and the probable tomb of Yik'in Chan K'awiil, son of Jasaw Chan K'awiil.

Today Tikal, a UNESCO World Heritage Site and Guatemala National Park of 222 square miles, may be visited via the modern towns of Flores and Santa Elena.

See also **Archaeology; Calakmul; Caracol; Kaminaljuyú; Maya, The; Mesoamerica; Teotihuacán; Uaxactún.**

BIBLIOGRAPHY

Coe, William R. *Tikal: A Handbook of the Ancient Maya Ruins, With a Guide Map.* Philadelphia: University Museum, University of Pennsylvania, 1967.

Shook, Edwin M. *Tikal Reports. Nos. 1–11: Facsimile Reissue of Original Reports Published 1958–1961.* Philadelphia: University Museum, University of Pennsylvania, 1986.

WALTER R. T. WITSCHEY

TIMERMAN, JACOBO (1923–1999). Jacobo Timerman (*b.* 6 January 1923; *d.* 11 November 1999), Argentine journalist, publisher, editor, and writer. Jacobo Timerman was born in Bar, Ukraine (then, the USSR). When he was five years old, his family immigrated to Argentina. His father died when he was only twelve years old, leaving Jacobo and his younger brother with only their mother for support. The family lived in a one-room apartment in the Jewish quarter of Buenos Aires. Timerman soon became involved with local Jewish cultural and political organizations, joining a group called Avuca at fourteen years old. After first studying engineering in school, he began his career in journalism. The post–World War II period was a turbulent time for Argentinean politics with the rise of populist ruler Juan Perón and the resulting turmoil after his overthrow in 1955. It was during this time that Timerman's journalism career took off. He was especially well-known for his reporting in *La Razón*.

Along with friends, Timerman founded the newsweeklies *Primera Plana* (1962) and *Confirmado* (1969) and became a radio and television commentator. He was a political columnist at the Argentine daily *La Razón*, one of the most widely read papers in the nation during the late 1950s and the 1960s. From 1971 to 1977 he was editor and publisher of the influential Argentine daily *La Opinión*, which he helped to found. He fell out of favor with the government and much of the public due to his newspapers' outspoken stance against human rights abuses and his publishing of the names of individuals who had been "disappeared." In 1977 a mob of armed civilians stormed his home and arrested him. This began two years of torture and imprisonment at the hands of the military.

International pressures, as well as internal dissension among the military, gained his freedom. He left Argentina for Israel in 1979, and subsequently lived in Madrid and New York. The story of his imprisonment and torture by the military, *Prisoner Without a Name, Cell Without a Number* (1981), is a forceful account of repression and the violation of human rights in Argentina. The book became an international best-seller. In *The Longest War: Israel in Lebanon* (1982), Timerman expresses his anguish over actions taken by the Israeli armed forces in Lebanon. Upon his return to Argentina in 1984, Timerman became editor-in-chief of *La Razón* for a brief period. His book *Cuba: A Journey* (1990) is based upon a trip that he made to the island in 1987. He has written for the *New Yorker* magazine and in 1987 he published an account of Chile under General Pinochet, *Chile: Death in the South*. He died on November 11, 1999 in Buenos Aires.

See also **Human Rights; Journalism.**

BIBLIOGRAPHY

Ramón Juan Alberto Camps, *Caso Timerman: Punto final* (1982); *Timerman: The News from Argentina* (1984), a video recording available from PBS Video; *Jacobo Timerman: Prisoner Without a Name, Cell Without a Number* (television film, 1990).

Additional Bibliography

Knudson, Jerry W. "Veil of Silence: The Argentine Press and the Dirty War, 1976–1983." *Latin American Perspectives* 24 (November 1997): 93–112.

Mochkofsky, Graciela. *Timerman: El periodista que quiso ser parte del poder (1923–1999).* 2nd ed. Buenos Aires: Editorial Sudamericana, 2003.

Ruíz, Fernando J. *Las palabras son acciones: História política y profesional de La Opinión de Jacobo Timerman (1971–1977).* Buenos Aires: Perfil Libros, 2001.

DANUSIA L. MESON

TIMUCUA. Timucua, a native people and Spanish mission province in north Florida. In the early 1500s the north half of peninsular Florida and the extreme southeast part of Georgia were the home of people who spoke dialects of Timucua. At least twenty-five separate groups, each consisting of from one or two to as many as forty villages, existed. At times chiefs established alliances with one another or one chief established military dominance over others, thereby forming larger political units. The Timucua in north Florida and the lower Saint John's River cultivated corn and other crops. These groups on the coast and in central Florida apparently were not farmers.

The Pánfilo de Narváez (1528) and Hernando de Soto (1539) expeditions traveled through the territories of various of the Timucua groups and severely impacted them. Beginning in the late 1500s and continuing into the seventeenth century, Spanish Franciscan missions, farms, and ranches were established among Timucua peoples. North and north-central Florida became known as Timucua Province. By 1650 disease epidemics had greatly reduced the population of Timucua, and native peoples from Georgia repopulated some of the missions. Only a handful of the Timucua survived past about 1730.

See also **Florida; Indigenous Peoples; Narváez, Pánfilo de; Soto, Hernando de.**

BIBLIOGRAPHY

Jerald T. Milanich and William C. Sturtevant, *Francisco Pareja's 1613 Confessionario: A Documentary Source for Timucuan Ethnography* (1972).

Kathleen A. Deagan, "Cultures in Transition: Fusion and Assimilation Among the Eastern Timucua," and Jerald T. Milanich, "The Western Timucua: Patterns of Acculturation and Change," in *Tacachale: Essays on the Indians of Florida and Southeastern Georgia During the Historic Period,* edited by Jerald T. Milanich and Samuel Proctor (1978).

Additional Bibliography

Worth, John E. *The Timucuan Chiefdoms of Spanish Florida.* Gainesville: University Press of Florida, 1998.

JERALD T. MILANICH

TINAJERO MARTÍNEZ DE ALLEN, EUGENIA

The writer Eugenia Tinajero Martínez de Allen has unjustly been left out of Latin American literary history despite her importance to both the *tradicionista* and *indigenista* movements. Much like Ricardo Palma, Tinajero Martínez deals with many periods and settings in her writing. What sets her apart from other authors is the distinctly Ecuadorian flavor of her legends. If Peruvian legends and *tradiciones* tend to center on Cuzco, for Tinajero Martínez Quito provides a basis for Ecuadorian nationalist literature. Her use of Quito not only counterbalances Peruvian legends but also those of the Incas; some of her stories focus on the Schiris, a pre-Inca group that may or may not have existed but appears frequently in folklore.

See also **Barrera Barrera, Eulalia Beatriz; Cañari; Ingapirca; Matto de Turner, Clorinda; Palma, Ricardo; Quitu.**

BIBLIOGRAPHY

Tinajero Martínez de Allen, Eugenio. *Leyendas indígenas.* Ambato, Ecuador: Impr. de Educación, 1954.

Ward, Thomas. "Perú y Ecuador." In *La narrativa histórica de escritoras latinoamericanas,* edited by Gloria da Cunha, pp. 271–305. Buenos Aires: Ediciones Corregidor, 2004.

THOMAS WARD

TIN INDUSTRY.

The tin industry in Latin America is largely concentrated in Bolivia, which, after Malaysia, has been the largest producer of tin in the world. For over eighty years (1900–1980), tin was Bolivia's largest export. The owners of the tin mines became some of the wealthiest men in the world and extremely powerful within Bolivia. The 1952 revolution of the National Revolutionary Movement (MNR) brought about the nationalization of the most important mines, providing jobs and income for the government. The tin industry also engendered one of the most powerful labor unions in Latin America.

Tin mining became important at the beginning of the twentieth century just as silver mining, the previous economic mainstay of the country, became unprofitable. Nevertheless, the nineteenth-century silver-mining boom was important, for the silver miners built the railroads that connected the highland mining areas with the Pacific coast and made feasible the transportation of a relatively inexpensive product like tin ore. Strikingly, few silver miners were able to make the transition from silver to tin. Only the Aramayo family from southern Potosí, with heavy infusions of European capital, was able to make the switch; they eventually controlled about one-fifth of the country's production. The change from silver to

Women mineworkers in Bolivia sorting tin-ore, c. 1945. Bolivia's tin industry boomed during the first half of the twentieth century and was the country's leading export. The goal of the 1952 revolution to nationalize the mines illustrates the economic and political significance of tin. © HULTON-DEUTSCH COLLECTION/CORBIS

tin also shifted economic power from the Potosí-Sucre axis in the south to La Paz and Oruro in the north. The Federalist War of 1898–1899, which pitted the Conservative government based in the south against the Liberal Party and La Paz Federalists, confirmed the new political and economic configuration of the country. After the Liberals won, La Paz became the permanent seat of the executive and legislative powers and the de facto capital of the country.

Tin mining required a much higher level of capital investment than silver, and for this reason successful tin miners quickly allied themselves with foreign capital. By the early twentieth century three major companies controlled tin mining. In addition to the Aramayo holdings, Mauricio Hochschild, a Bolivian Jew also backed by European companies, held about

20 percent of the market. The most important tin miner, Simón Patiño, a Cochabamba Mestizo who produced about half of Bolivian output, worked with British and later U.S. companies. Despite heavy foreign financial participation, most of the tin industry remained in the hands of Bolivian nationals throughout the twentieth century.

The control the tin barons exerted over Bolivian politics from the early twentieth century to the 1952 revolution was deeply resented by many Bolivians. The Liberal Party and the Republicans were deeply influenced by Patiño and his colleagues. Patiño, however, left Bolivia in the 1920s, never to return. His company, incorporated in Delaware, was run in Bolivia by a series of administrators out of the central office in Paris, France. By this time Patiño's

Bolivian mining holdings formed only a fraction of his business enterprises. His other interests included British and German tin smelteries, agro-industrial enterprises in Bolivia, and tin mines in Malaysia. Thus, although the country's largest tin miner was Bolivian, the mines themselves were run as a small portion of a multinational corporation. The mine owners, their subordinates, and their political allies were called La Rosca, a term that contained many negative connotations.

Despite the attempts at maintaining a paternalistic regime in the mine labor camps, various strikes by miners and their bloody repression by the Bolivian army led to greater labor militancy. The massacre at Uncía in 1923 and especially the Catavi Massacre in 1942 helped create antipathy toward mine owners and made it possible for labor leaders to create alliances with leftist political parties such as the MNR. The alliance with mine labor helped bring about the MNR's opposition to the mine owners and its programmatic commitment to the nationalization of the Big Three's tin operations.

When the MNR finally triumphed in the bloody revolution of 1952, one of the new government's first administrative acts was to nationalize the mines and create the Corporación Minera de Bolivia, or Comibol. In fact, the tin miners were instrumental in the triumph of the revolution. They descended from the mines and helped rout the army and occupied the major Bolivian cities. Thereafter, the largely Trotskyist mine workers remained an important force in national politics and, until the late 1980s, the leaders of the Bolivian labor movement. Although mine owners were later compensated for their losses—the United States insisted on compensation before it would recognize the revolutionary regime—the power of *la rosca* had been broken.

When the military overthrew the MNR in 1964, the new president, René Barrientos Ortuño, attempted to reform Comibol with U.S. advice. To make these reforms possible, Barrientos broke the power of the unions. He sent the army to occupy the mines and arrested labor leaders. This type of repression reoccurred under right-wing military dictators Hugo Banzer in 1971 and Luís García Meza in 1981.

Comibol remained the principal source of cash for the Bolivian government until the 1980s, when declining world tin prices led to the shutting down of most tin mines. The government offered to relocate the unemployed mine workers to the subtropical jungles of Bolivia. Some went to these zones, but poor infrastructure and lack of resources doomed this policy. Other former miners went to work in the coca fields of Cochabamba, and many more moved to the cities, creating a surge of urbanization in cities such as Sucre, Tarija, Cochabamba, and Santa Cruz. The industry remained depressed through the 1990s. In this environment, the government privatized many of its tin mines. However, the increased global demand for commodities in the early twenty-first century, due to the industrialization of China, has boosted tin prices. Foreign investment has increased. Also, in the twenty-first century, Bolivia continues to be the world's largest tin producers.

See also **Banzer Suárez, Hugo; Barrientos Ortuño, René; Bolivia, Political Parties: Nationalist Revolutionary Movement (MNR); Comibol; García Meza, Luis; Hochschild, Mauricio; Mining: Modern; Patiño, Simón Iturri.**

BIBLIOGRAPHY

There is no adequate monograph on the history of the Bolivian tin industry. Partial efforts include Sergio Almaraz Paz, *El poder y la caída: El estaño en la historia de Bolivia* (1967); Juan Albarracín Millán, *El poder minero en la administración liberal* (1972); Walter Gómez, *La minería en el desarrollo económico de Bolivia, 1900–1970* (1976). See also Alfonso Crespo, *Los Aramayo de Chichas: Tres generaciones de mineros bolivianos* (1981). A useful account of Bolivian tin miners is June Nash, *We Eat the Mines and the Mines Eat Us: Dependency and Exploitation in Bolivian Tin Mines* (1979).

Additional Bibliography

Albarracín Millán, Juan. *The London Tin Corporation y el nacionalismo boliviano.* La Paz, Bolivia: Fundación Bartolomé de las Casas, 2002.

Bedregal Gutiérrez, Guillermo. *COMIBOL, una historia épica.* La Paz: Fondo Editorial de los Diputados, 1998.

García Flores, Pedro Pablo. *La minería en Bolivia.* Bolivia: Observador, 2005.

ERICK D. LANGER

TINOCO GRANADOS, FEDERICO

(1870–1931). Federico Tinoco Granados (*b.* 1870; *d.* 1931), the extraconstitutional president of Costa Rica (1917–1919) following the overthrow of

President Alfredo González Flores (1914–1917). As the last military figure to seize power in modern Costa Rica, Tinoco is still a controversial figure. He was minister of war and the navy, commandant of San José, and head of the police at the time of the coup against González. Faced with crushing economic difficulties as a consequence of World War I, González had attempted a series of progressive tax measures in the face of inflationary pressures. Both wealthy and popular interests welcomed his overthrow, but the popularity of the Tinoco regime, led by Federico and his brother José Joaquín, faded quickly. U.S. president Woodrow Wilson chose to make an example of Tinoco and refused to recognize his regime, both on principle and out of a partisan Democratic suspicion that Republican investors such as Minor Keith (United Fruit) and Luis Valentine (Rosario Mining of Honduras) were in league with Tinoco, expecting to conduct oil exploration and to receive investment incentives. Once Costa Rica was isolated internationally, popular living standards suffered even more under Tinoco, and his occasionally bloody repression of would-be rebellions and exile invasions caused his regime's early popularity to evaporate. Just as he was turning power over to his successor, Vice President Juan Bautista Quirós Segura, on 10 August 1919, his brother Joaquín, the war minister, was assassinated in San José. Tinoco left power two days later. Elections were held later that year, and Julio Acosta Garcia was elected president. Tinoco died in Paris.

See also **Acosta García, Julio; Costa Rica; González Flores, Alfredo; Wilson, Woodrow.**

BIBLIOGRAPHY

Federico Tinoco Granados, *Páginas de ayer* (1928).

Carlos Luis Fallas Monge, *Alfredo González Flores* (1976).

Hugo Murillo Jiménez, *Tinoco y los Estados Unidos: Génesis y caída de un régimen* (1981).

Mercedes Muñoz Guillén, *El estado y la abolición del ejercito, 1914–1949* (1990).

Additional Bibliography

Palmer, Steven. *From Popular Medicine to Medical Populism: Doctors, Healers, and Public Power in Costa Rica, 1800–1940.* Durham, NC: Duke University Press, 2003.

LOWELL GUDMUNDSON

TIN-TAN

TIN-TAN (1915–1973). Tin-Tan (Germán Valdés Castillo; *b*. 1915; *d*. 29 June 1973), Mexican comedian and film star. In 1943, Tin-Tan began a radio career in Ciudad Juárez. Turning to comedy, he performed in various border cities of Mexico and the United States. He made his film debut in 1945 with *El hijo desobediente*. He went on to star in thirty-eight films and acted in over 100 more. His unique style incorporated slapstick, satire, musical and dance numbers, and a peculiar manner of speech. Among his classic films are *Calabacitas tiernas* (1948), *El rey del barrio* (1949), *El revoltoso* (1951), and *El campeón ciclista* (1956). Tin-Tan was one of the greatest Mexican film comedians and remains one of the most popular entertainers of all time.

See also **Cinema: From the Silent Film to 1990.**

BIBLIOGRAPHY

Luis Reyes De La Maza, *El cine sonoro en México* (1973).

E. Bradford Burns, *Latin American Cinema: Film and History* (1975).

Carl J. Mora, *Mexican Cinema: Reflections of a Society: 1896–1980* (1982).

John King, *Magical Reels: A History of Cinema in Latin America* (1990).

Additional Bibliography

Muñoz Castillo, Fernando. *Las musas de Tin Tan: Crónicas y recuerdos.* México: Consejo Nacional para la Cultura y las Artes, 1999.

Valdés Julián, Rosalía. *La historia inédita de Tin-Tan.* México: Planeta, 2003.

DAVID MACIEL

TIPITAPA AGREEMENTS

TIPITAPA AGREEMENTS. Tipitapa Agreements, the settlement marking the end of Nicaragua's Constitutionalist War. United States envoy Henry L. Stimson and José María Moncada met on 4 May 1927 in the small town of Tipitapa, a few miles east of Managua, to negotiate an end to the Constitutionalist War in Nicaragua. After Emiliano Chamorro's unsuccessful coup d'état, fellow Conservative Adolfo Díaz regained the presidency in 1926, despite the claims on the office by exiled former vice president Juan Bautista

Sacasa, a Liberal. Under Moncada's protection, Sacasa returned from Mexico and appointed Moncada his minister of war. While Moncada mounted his campaign against the Conservatives, Sacasa set up a "constitutional government" in Puerto Cabezas.

To resolve the crisis, U.S. President Calvin Coolidge sent Stimson as his personal representative. Stimson first held negotiations with the Conservatives, who agreed to the retention of Díaz as president until the 1928 elections and to a general amnesty for all rebels. Once Stimson had secured Conservative support, he then met with Moncada—Sacasa refused to leave Puerto Cabezas. Stimson, realizing that the Liberals would not accept Díaz as president, advised Moncada to accept the terms of the agreement or risk fighting the U.S. In addition to the retention of Díaz as president until the 1928 elections (to be supervised by the U.S., which had given its tacit support to Moncada), the Tipitapa Agreements, as negotiated by Stimson and Moncada, guaranteed the Liberals control of six departments in exchange for an end to hostilities. Finally, they called for the organization of a nonpolitical National Guard under the leadership of U.S. officers.

On 5 May, Moncada told his troops of the agreements; President Díaz declared a general amnesty and appointed a number of Moncada's generals to government positions. All but one of Moncada's generals accepted the Tipitapa Agreements on 12 May 1927 through a signed telegram. The sole exception was Augusto César Sandino, who refused to lay down his arms.

See also **Chamorro Vargas, Emiliano; Díaz, Adolfo; Moncada, José María; Sandino, Augusto César.**

BIBLIOGRAPHY

Richard Millett, *Guardians of the Dynasty* (1977), esp. p. 55.

Neill Macaulay, *The Sandino Affair* (1985), esp. pp. 31–47.

Additional Bibliography

Dodd, Thomas J. *Managing Democracy in Central America, A Case Study: United States Election Supervision in Nicaragua. 1927-33.* Coral Gables, FL: North-South Center: University of Miami, 1992.

Baylen, Joseph O. "Sandino: Patriot or Bandit?" *Hispanic American Historical Review* 31, no. 3. (August 1951): 394-419.

SHANNON BELLAMY

TIRADENTES. *See* **Silva Xavier, Joaquim José da.**

TITHE. *See* **Diezmo.**

TITICACA, LAKE. Lake Titicaca, the highest navigable lake in the world, dominating the highlands of southern Peru and northern Bolivia. At an elevation of 12,467 feet, the lake, actually an inland sea, extends 122 miles in length and 45 miles in width. Its massive surface area of 3,200 square miles moderates the climate of surrounding areas. Several inhabitable islands, including the popular tourist attraction of Taquile, dot the lake.

The lake has had a dominating historical influence on the region. Its waters and shoreline have supported fishing and agricultural practices for millennia. Archaeological investigations reveal the existence of complex societies that long ago benefited from the resources and climatic influence of the lake. Technological changes, especially the advent of steam transportation in the late nineteenth century, contributed to the lake's role as a link between southern Peru and northern Bolivia. With transportation and refrigeration, fish products have recently enhanced the regional economic significance of the lake.

See also **Agriculture.**

BIBLIOGRAPHY

Emilio Romero, *Perú: Una nueva geografía*, 2 vols. (1973).

Additional Bibliography

Escandall Tur, Neus and Alexander Areliano. *Todo Titicaca.* Lima: Terra Firme, 2003.

Salles-Reese, Verónica. *From Viracocha to the Virgin of Copacabana: Representation of the Sacred at Lake Titicaca.* Austin: University of Texas, 1997.

Stanish, Charles. *Ancient Titicaca: The Evolution of Complex Society in Southern Peru and Northern Bolivia.* Berkeley: University of California Press, 2003.

Stanish, Charles, and Amanda B. Cohen. *Advances in Titicaca Basin Archaeology.* Los Angeles: Cotsen Institute of Archaeology at UCLA, 2005.

JOHN C. SUPER

TIWANAKU. Tiwanaku (Tiahuanaco) was a pre-Columbian Andean empire whose most important ceremonial and political center was the city of the same name located on the Altiplano (high plateau) in present-day Bolivia. Although there is some disagreement among scholars as to the exact dates of Tiwanaku culture, it is generally accepted to have been the dominant society in the basin of Lake Titicaca from at least 100 CE to approximately 1200 CE. At its height between 500 and 1000, Tiwanaku's influence reached as far as modern-era Chile and Argentina.

Constructed at the high altitude of 12,600 feet, the ancient city of Tiwanaku comprised a ceremonial-administrative center with monumental stone architecture surrounded by more humble residential areas. Radiocarbon dating indicates that the main temples, courtyards, and stelae were constructed between 100 and 725. Although the public precinct of Tiwanaku is relatively small, excavations by the Bolivian archaeologist Carlos Ponce Sanginés have led him to conclude that the whole city covered about 420 hectares (approximately 1,037 acres) and probably had a population of between 20,000 and 40,000.

Tiwanaku exhibits great technological sophistication and complexity. The unique stone works reveal accurate masonry, flat smooth planes, and 90-degree angles. Inhabitants built boats to ferry immense slabs of rock (320,450 lbs) for their ceremonial buildings. Moreover, Tiwanaku cultures utilized stone tool manufacture and could cast bronze and gold. Using their astronomical knowledge, they mapped the annual solar cycle.

The size of the city and other Tiwanaku urban administrative centers in the Titicaca basin (Lukurmata, Pajchiri, Oje), as well as the material evidence of different social classes found during excavations of city sites, indicate that Tiwanaku society was highly stratified. Scholars believe differentiation was important to state integration. Such social complexity was possible because integration was based on coalitions and alliances, and an economic surplus was produced through the skillful use of the *altiplano* environment for extensive agricultural and herding activities. Near water sources, inhabitants dug canals and constructed raised fields for planting. Doing so enabled them to cultivate potatoes, other root vegetables, and quinoa. They raised alpaca and llamas as pack animals and for wool for clothing. The highland economy was also supplemented with products from other ecological zones that could not be raised on the high plateau. These items, such as the religious and politically important *chicha* (corn beer), as well as maize, coca, and cotton, were acquired through trade or by means of an "archipelago" system in which groups of settlers were sent by the highland state to establish agricultural colonies in the lowlands.

Indeed, rather than governing through central authority, scholars believe that Tiwanaku consisted of a federation of communities and regional centers. Elites resided at the capital ceremonial center and secondary regional centers, which were demarcated with moats. These central areas exhibited greater cultural uniformity than outlying communities. Though the red-slip clay vessels, the hallmark of Tiwanaku ceramics, appear less and less frequently outside the central religious compounds, at the same time, distinct Tiwanaku textile styles have been found in relatively distant San Pedro de Atacama, Chile. Religious rituals and ceremonies, in particular, served to unify the diverse population.

Spread out from the center were corporate kin-based groups known as *ayllus*. Ayllus were bordered by walled compounds, and families lived in smaller housing complexes within. Ancestors were buried locally, seated, often in residential areas. There is no recorded written language of Tiwanaku, and moreover, ayllus pertaining to Tiwanaku were multiethnic and spoke different languages. Residents used headdresses to denote rank and ethnicity. Still, despite the differences, the population shared common religious and ritual identity with the Tiwanaku center, and made pilgrimages to Tiwanaku, which held utmost religious importance. The social diversity of Tiwanaku contributed to its great social complexity, yet it also might have factored in the empire's disintegration. Interestingly, scholars believe that the Tiwanaku and Wari peoples lived peacefully side by side for centuries; there is no evidence of warfare.

After about 375, Tiwanaku material culture spread through wide areas of the Andes, including Bolivian inland valleys and coastal areas of Chile and Peru. In the sixth century another major center of Tiwanaku culture emerged at Huari (Wari) in the central highlands of Peru. The origins of Huari and its connections with Bolivian Tiwanaku are not clear, but the site may have been established through conquest, and then later have operated as an independent imperial capital. Huari culture declined in the ninth century; Tiwanaku itself also waned, but survived until about 1200.

Though the evidence is inconclusive, scholars speculate that drought and warfare may have contributed to the decline of Tiwanaku. Yet the site, culture, and religion continued to hold significant influence throughout the Andean region. Tiwanaku is a sacred place of the Inca, who arrived in the region in the fifteenth or sixteenth century, hundreds of years after the civilization's decline. Indeed, the diety Viracocha, whose image is carved on Tiwanaku's 10-ton granite "Gateway of the Sun," and who is believed to have created the sun and the moon, is also central to Incan religious beliefs. Likewise, Viracocha is important to the Aymara people who populate the area in the present day.

BIBLIOGRAPHY

Albarracín-Jordán, Juan. *Tiwanaku, arqueología regional y dinámica segmentaria.* La Paz: Plural Editores, 1996.

Bermann, Marc. *Lukurmata: Household Archaeology in Prehispanic Bolivia.* Princeton, NJ: Princeton University Press, 1994.

Goldstein, Paul S. *Andean Diaspora: The Tiwanaku Colonies and the Origins of South American Empire.* Gainesville: University Press of Florida, 2005.

Janusek, John Wayne. *Identity and Power in the Ancient Andes Tiwanaku Cities through Time.* New York: Routledge, 2004.

Kolata, Alan L. "The South Andes." In *Ancient South Americans,* edited by Jesse D. Jennings. San Francisco, CA: W. H. Freeman, 1983.

Kolata, Alan L., ed. *La tecnología y organización de la producción agrícola en el estado de Tiwanaku.* La Paz: Instituto Nacional de Arqueología de Bolivia, 1989.

Kolata, Alan L. *The Tiwanaku: Portrait of an Andean Civilization.* Cambridge, U.K.: Blackwell, 1993.

Kolata, Alan L. *Valley of the Spirits: A Journey into the Lost Realm of the Aymara.* New York: Wiley, 1996.

Korpisaari, Antti. *Death in the Bolivian High Plateau: Burials and Tiwanaku Society.* Oxford, U.K.: Archaeopress, 2006.

Lumbreras, Luis G. *The Peoples and Cultures of Ancient Peru.* Washington, DC: Smithsonian Institution Press, 1974.

Molina Rivero, Jorge Emilio. *Conexión aymara y quechua con Tiwanaku.* La Paz: Universidad Pública de El Alto, Departamento de Historia y Cultura Andina, 2002.

Mújica, Elías. "*Altiplano*–Coast Relationships in the South-Central Andes: From Indirect to Direct Complementarity." In *Andean Ecology and Civilization: An Interdisciplinary Perspective on Andean Ecological Complementarity,* edited by Shozo Masuda, Izumi Shimada, and Craig Morris. Tokyo: University of Tokyo Press, 1985.

Ponce Sanginés, Carlos. *Tiwanaku: Espacio, tiempo y cultura: Ensayo de síntesis arqueológica.* 4th ed. La Paz: Editorial Los Amigos del Libro, 1981.

Stanish, Charles. *Ancient Titicaca: The Evolution of Complex Society in Southern Peru and Northern Bolivia.* Berkeley: University of California Press, 2003.

Young-Sánchez, Margaret. *Tiwanaku: Ancestors of the Inca.* Lincoln: University of Nebraska Press, 2004.

ANN ZULAWSKI

TIWINZA. Tiwinza is a twenty-square-kilometer jungle area within territory claimed by Peru in the Cordillera del Cóndor region near the Ecuador-Peru frontier. Occupied by Ecuadorian troops during the 1995 border war, Tiwinza was subject to some of the fiercest fighting in the conflict, during which Peruvian forces were unable to dislodge them. Under the provisions of the October 1998 treaty ratified by both governments, Peru gained sovereignty over the disputed Cordillera del Cóndor territory, but with a provision that one square kilometer of Tiwinza be private property where Ecuador could conduct commemorative ceremonies in perpetuity.

See also **Ecuador-Peru Boundary Disputes.**

BIBLIOGRAPHY

Marcella, Gabriel, and Richard Downes, eds. *Security Cooperation in the Western Hemisphere: Resolving the Ecuador-Peru Conflict.* Coral Gables, FL: North-South Center Press, University of Miami, 1999.

DAVID SCOTT PALMER

TLALOC. Tlaloc (He Who Has Earth), a major god of rain, fertility, and agriculture and one of the most ancient of the Mesoamerican supernaturals. He is easily identified by a distinctive face mask, formed by circular blue rings around his eyes, a moustache-like labial band, and prominent fangs.

The object of widespread veneration, carved and painted images of Tlaloc survive at archaeological sites in central Mexico from Classic period Teotihuacán to Postclassic Mexico Tenochtitlán. Chac of the Maya, Tajin of the Gulf Coast Totonacs, and Cocijo of the Zapotecs and Dzahui of the Mixtecs in Oaxaca are counterparts of Tlaloc in other areas. In Mexico Tenochtitlán one of the twin shrines atop the Templo Mayor (main temple) of the Aztecs was dedicated to him. Five of the eighteen annual *veintena* feasts (Atlcahualo-Cuahuitlehua, Tozoztontli, Etzalcualiztli, Tepeilhuitl, Hueypachtli, and Atemoztli) especially honored Tlaloc and his small assistants, called *tlaloques* (little Tlalocs), who were credited with producing rain, lightning, thunder, and hail. The greatest of all Tlaloc shrines was atop Mount Tlaloc, located between Tetzcoco and Huexotzinco, and elaborate ceremonies were staged there. People who died by drowning and other water-related deaths were believed to dwell in Tlalocán, the paradise of Tlaloc.

See also **Aztecs; Tetzcoco.**

BIBLIOGRAPHY

Mark Miller and Karl Taube, *The Gods and Symbols of Ancient Mexico and the Maya* (1993).

Additional Bibliography

Arnold, Philip P. *Eating Landscape: Aztec and European Occupation of Tlalocan.* Niwot: University Press of Colorado, 1999.

Bonifaz Nuño, Rubén. *Imagen de Tláloc: Hipotesis iconografica y textual.* 2nd ed. México, D.F.: Universidad Nacional Autonoma de México, 1996.

Read, Kay Almere and Jason J. González. *Mesoamerican Mythology.* New York: Oxford University Press, 2002.

ELOISE QUIÑONES KEBER

TLAPACOYA. Tlapacoya, an archaeological site in the eastern Valley of Mexico, on lower slopes of the east edge of a small volcanic hill. These slopes were once the shores of a huge extinct lake, Lago de Chalco, that covered much of what is now eastern Mexico City. The lake's beaches, as well as small caves up the slopes from them, were first occupied by early hunters between 10,000 and 40,000 years ago. Their cultural remains are meagerly documented by crude choppers, scrapers, and knives; a fine prismatic obsidian blade found in the lake deposits was dated by hydration at about 19,000 years old.

Just north of the Paleo-Indian remains, a series of deep trenches establisheda sequence of Archaic occupation. Study of the scarce lithic tools taken from these trenches has allowed us to divide the Archaic sequence into three phases: Playa 1, 5500–4500 BCE; Playa 2, 4500–3500 BCE; and Zohapilco, 3500–2000 BCE. During the first two phases the occupants were probably collectors, while the Paleo-Indians of the third phase were sedentary agriculturists in preceramic times—although a single crude clay figurine was found.

Above these remains, probably not much earlier than 1300 BCE, were a series of strata with abundant ceramics, figurines, and grinding stones of the Formative period (1300–200 BCE), during which people lived in definite villages and practiced agriculture full time. A study of the ceramics and figurines allows this sequence to be divided into a series of phases: Nevada (1300–1200 BCE), Ayotla (1200–1000 BCE), Manantial (1000–800 BCE), Zacatenco (800–400 BCE), and Ticomán (400–200 BCE). The phases document the shift from a time of village agriculture to a period (Ayotla) when the pyramids were constructed and there was influence from the Veracruz coast Olmec (Manantial). During Ticomán, the rise of the state began and laid the foundation for establishment of Teotihuacán.

See also **Archaeology.**

BIBLIOGRAPHY

Paul Tolstoy and Louise I. Paradis, "Early and Middle Preclassic Culture in the Basin of Mexico," in *Science* 167 (1970): 344–351, and "Early and Middle Preclassic Culture in the Basin of Mexico," in *Observations on the Emergence of Civilization in Mesoamerica. Contributions of the University of California Archaeological Research Facility,* edited by Robert F. Heizer and John A. Graham (1971), pp. 7–28.

Christine Niederberger, *Zohapilco, cinco milenios de ocupación humana en un sitio lacustre de la Cuenca de México* (1976).

Paul Tolstoy, Suzanne K. Fish, Martin W. Boksenbaum, Kathryn B. Vaughn, and C. Earle Smith, "Early

Sedentary Communities of the Basin of Mexico," in *Journal of Field Archaeology* 4 (1977): 91–106.

Christine Niederberger, "Early Sedentary Economy in the Basin of Mexico," in *Science* 203 (1979): 131–142.

Pierre Becquelin and Claude F. Baudez, *Toniná, une cité maya du Chiapas (Mexique)*, 3 vols. (1979–1982).

Additional Bibliography

Clark, John E., and Mary E. Pye, eds. *Olmec Art and Archaeology in Mesoamerica.* Washington, DC: National Gallery of Art; New Haven, CT: Distributed by Yale University Press, 2000.

Dixon, E. James. *Bones, Boats & Bison: Archeology and the First Colonization of Western North America.* Albuquerque: University of New Mexico Press, 1999.

Lorenzo, José Luis, and Lorena Mirambell. *Tlapacoya: 35,000 años de historia del Lago de Chalco.* México, D.F.: Instituto Nacional de Antropología e Historia, 1986.

Nárez, Jesús. *Materiales arqueológicos de Tlapacoya.* México, D.F.: Instituto Nacional de Antropología e Historia, 1990.

RICHARD S. MACNEISH

TLATELOLCO.

Tlatelolco, the greatest late pre-Hispanic commercial center of the Basin of Mexico and site of its largest marketplace. The sister city and rival of Mexico Tenochtitlán, Tlatelolco was inhabited by a fiercely independent branch of the Mexica who derived their dynasty from Azcapotzalco. Like the Tenochca, another Mexica branch, they claimed Huitzilopochtli as their patron and their ceremonial precincts were also similarly constructed. Tlatelolco's autonomy ended in 1473 with its defeat by the Tenochca, who thereafter appointed its governors. In 1521 the final, devastating siege of the Spanish conquest took place within its ceremonial precinct. After the Conquest, Tlatelolco became the Indian sector of the colonial city of Mexico, and Franciscan missionaries established the College of Santa Cruz there to educate the sons of Aztec nobility. Tlatelolco's ancient ceremonial precinct is now the location of the Plaza of the Three Cultures, which is marked by the excavated ruins of its Templo Mayor, the adjoining colonial church, and surrounding modern structures. It is also the place and name for the government massacre of students in 1968.

See also **Mesoamerica.**

BIBLIOGRAPHY

Jesús Monjarás-Ruiz, Elena Limón, and María De La Cruz Paillés H., eds., *Obras de Robert H. Barlow*, vol. 2, *Tlatelolco: Fuentes e historia* (1989).

Patricia Galeana De Valadés and Francisco Blanco Figueroa, eds., *Tlatelolco* (1990).

Additional Bibliography

Carrasco, David, ed. *Aztec Ceremonial Landscapes.* Niwot: University Press of Colorado, 1999.

Poniatowska, Elena. *La noche de Tlatelolco: Testimonios de historia oral.* 2nd ed. México, D.F: Ediciones Era, 1998.

ELOISE QUIÑONES KEBER

TLATOANI.

Tlatoani, paramount ruler of the central Mesoamerican Nahua Altepetl (regional state or province). *Tlatoque* (plural) rulership was dynastic, but succession practices varied; the *tlatoani* of Tenochtitlán was "elected" by a small body of elites, with brothers and nephews likely to succeed. The *tlatoani* had broad civil, military, and religious powers, and the *tlatocayotl* (rulership) brought many privileges, including the ability to keep multiple wives and rights to tribute and labor, to private property, and to the best material items available. After the Spanish conquest, *tlatoque* typically became the first governors of the reorganized indigenous communities. Their dominance faded as other elites successfully competed for access to this office.

See also **Aztecs; Nahuas.**

BIBLIOGRAPHY

There is an extensive literature dealing with the *tlatoani.* One of the best primary sources is Bernardino De Sahagún, *Florentine Codex.* Book 8, *Kings and Lords,* translated and edited by Arthur J. O. Anderson and Charles E. Dibble (1954). An excellent study is Susan D. Gillespie, *The Aztec Kings: The Construction of Rulership in Mexican History* (1989). The evolution of *tlatocayotl* in the colonial period is examined in Charles Gibson, *The Aztecs Under Spanish Rule* (1964); Robert Haskett, *Indigenous Rulers: An Ethnohistory of Town Government in Colonial Cuernavaca* (1991); Susan Schroeder, *Chimalpahin and the Kingdons of Chalco* (1991); and James Lockhart, *The Nahuas after the Conquest: A Social and Cultural History of the Indians of Central Mexico, Sixteenth through Eighteenth Centuries* (1992).

ROBERT HASKETT

TLAXCALA. Tlaxcala (full name Tlaxcala de Xicohténcatl; from the Náhuatl *Tlaxcallan*), famous in the Conquest of Mexico as an indigenous city-state in the highlands of Mexico, east of the capital. The 2005 census reported the city's population as 15,777 and that of the surrounding municipality as 83,748. Prior to European contact, Tlaxcala was a vital pocket of independent Nahuatl, Otomí, and Pinome speakers who had resisted absorption into the surrounding Aztec Empire. For about two centuries the Tlaxcalans and the Mexica had enjoyed good relations; the former were important trade partners. But wealth accumulated by Tlaxcalan merchants became the envy of the imperialistic Mexica leaders, and a century of conflict began in the early fifteenth century. Wars between the neighboring rivals became frequent yet indecisive and took on a traditional, ceremonial aspect called *xochiyaoyotl*, literally "Flowery War," a heated contest not originally intended to incur battlefield deaths. Mexica soldiers used this to sharpen battle skills, to obtain honor, and to secure captives to sacrifice later to their gods.

The constant friction with Tlaxcala suited Motecuhzoma, but he did not foresee how it would push the Tlaxcalans into the arms of the Spaniards in their march against Mexico-Tenochtitlán. The Tlaxcalans had become impoverished because of cut trade lines and, constantly facing war, were anxious to throw off their adversaries completely. Still, in 1519 the Tlaxcalans first fought the Spaniards for two weeks, suffering considerable losses, before surrendering and siding with them to fight their traditional enemies. Thereafter, thousands of Tlaxcalans accompanied Spaniards in the battles of conquest all over Mexico and on distant frontiers, many never to return home, either because they died or because they settled with Spaniards, becoming their *naborías* (dependents), or formed model communities for them on the frontier, setting an example for nonsedentary indigenous peoples and helping hold new territorial acquisitions. One example is San Estéban de Nueva, founded next to Saltillo in 1591.

The Tlaxcalans set an example that was followed by other resisters of Aztec rule, but none became so renowned or so well rewarded, partly because of the tireless campaigns by Tlaxcalans to secure privileges as a result of their alliance with the Europeans. Tlaxcalan assistance proved to be a vital factor in tipping the scale in the lopsided battle between the few Spaniards and the large and powerful Aztec empire, and the victors were not allowed to forget their allies. Thus, Tlaxcalans were exempted from the usual pattern of having a Spanish city superimposed over theirs and having their people's labor and tributes divided among Spanish *encomenderos* (*encomienda* grant holders), a departure that makes their colonial history unique.

See also **Motecuhzoma I; Nahuas; Otomí.**

BIBLIOGRAPHY

The best source on pre-Conquest Tlaxcala is Diego Muñoz Camargo, *Historia de Tlaxcala* (1892). Charles Gibson, *Tlaxcala in the Sixteenth Century* (1952), provides good coverage of the Conquest era and after. Rich new sources in Nahuatl have afforded a more detailed description of Tlaxcalan life, clarifying, among other things, the complex four-part division of the province; see James Lockhart, Frances Berdan, and Arthur J. O. Anderson, *The Tlaxcalan Actas: A Compendium of the Records of the Cabildo of Tlaxcala (1545–1627)* (1986). The reference to the Tlaxcalan community of the north comes from Leslie Scott Offutt, "Urban and Rural Society in the Mexican North: Saltillo in the Late Colonial Period" (Ph.D. diss., University of California, Los Angeles, 1982), p. 9.

Additional Bibliography

Cuadriello, Jaime. *Las glorias de la república de Tlaxcala: O la conciencia como imagen sublime.* Mexico: Instituto de Investigaciones Estéticas, UNAM, 2004.

Muñoz Camargo, Diego. *Historia de Tlaxcala: Ms. 210 de la Biblioteca Nacional de París.* Edited by Luis Reyes García and Javier Lira Toledo. Tlaxcala: Gobierno del Estado de Tlaxcala/Centro de Investigaciones y Estudios Superiores en Antropología Social, Universidad Autónoma de Tlaxcala, 1998.

Rendón Garcini, Ricardo. *Breve historia de Tlaxcala.* Serie Breves Historias de los Estados de la República Mexicana, México: El Colegio de México, 1996.

Ward, Thomas. "From the 'People' to the 'Nation': An Emerging Notion in Sahagún, Ixtlilxóchitl and Muñoz Camargo." *Estudios de Cultura Náhuatl* 32 (2001): 223–234 and especially 229–233.

STEPHANIE WOOD

TLAXILACALLI. Tlaxilacalli, a territorial subdivision of the Nahua Altepetl (provincial unit) before and after the Spanish invasion. It was the main holder and distributor of land to its citizens, who paid tribute through *tlaxilacalli* officials. Often grouped in units of four, six, or eight within a single *altepetl*, the *tlaxilacalli* had its own religious structure and marketplace, and was itself subdivided into smaller districts. The term has a very similar meaning to the better-known and more-studied Calpulli, and there seems to have been some regional variation in the application of the terms; a definitive conclusion about their exact relationship and usage awaits further research.

See also **Calpulli; Nahuas.**

BIBLIOGRAPHY

The meaning and structure of *tlaxilacalli* are discussed in several works, among them Pedro Carrasco, "Social Organization of Ancient Mexico," in *Archaeology of Northern Mesoamerica.* Pt. 1, *Handbook of Middle American Indians,* vol. 10, edited by Gordon F. Ekholm and Ignacio Bernal (1971), pp. 363–368; Edward Calnek, "The Internal Structure of Tenochtitlán," in *Ancient Mesoamerica,* edited by John A. Graham (1976), pp. 337–338; Rudolf Van Zantwijk, *The Aztec Arrangement: The Social History of Pre-Spanish Mexico* (1985), pp. 249ff.; Susan Schroeder, *Chimalpahin and the Kingdoms of Chalco* (1991); and James Lockhart, *The Nahuas After the Spanish Conquest: A Social and Cultural History of the Indians of Central Mexico, Sixteenth Through Eighteenth Centuries* (1992).

Additional Bibliography

San Anton Domingo, Francisco de, and Chimalpahin Munon Quauhtlehuanitzin. *Society and Politics in Mexico: Tenochtitlan, Tlatelolco, Texcoco, Culhuacan, and Other Nahua Altepetl in Central Mexico.* Ed. Arthur J. O. Anderson, Susan Schroeder, and Wayne Ruwet. Norman: University of Oklahoma Press, 1997.

Tinajero Morales, José Omar. *Imágenes del silencio: Iconología de Tepetlaoztoc.* México: D.F.: Centro de Estudios del Acolhuacan Santo Domingo Portacoeli, 2002.

ROBERT HASKETT

TOBACCO INDUSTRY.

The tobacco plant (any of the several species belonging to the genus *Nicotiana*, especially *N. tabacum*), is indigenous to the New World, where archaeological evidence indicates that it had been domesticated by 3500 BCE, if not earlier. Many pre-Columbian societies smoked tobacco, often as part of religious ceremonies or in the context of ritual healing—practices that have survived into the present not only among Indian groups but also in African Latin religions such as Candomblé, Umbanda, and Santería. Early European explorers commented on the strange habit of smoking leaves, and carried samples of tobacco back across the Atlantic. The commercial potential of the plant became apparent only from the end of the sixteenth century onward, when snuff and pipe smoking gained widespread popularity in Europe and then in Asia and Africa. Thereafter, tobacco quickly became a major staple in the colonial export trade.

One of the first New World colonies to export tobacco was Brazil, where, in the seventeenth century, the northeastern captaincy of Bahia emerged as the main center of production. Bahian farmers specialized in twist tobacco (tobacco tightly woven into ropelike cords, appropriate for both pipe smoking and chewing). The mixture of molasses and herbs that farmers brushed onto the finished twists gave them a distinctive and much appreciated flavor. There were two main markets for Bahian tobacco: Portugal took the better twists (often for reexport) while tobacco judged lower in quality was shipped to West Africa, where it soon became a highly prized trade good used in bartering for slaves. As the slave trade grew, so too did the volume of exports to West Africa. Tobacco was thus crucial to the development and growth of slave-based agriculture and mining in colonial Brazil.

The years following Brazil's independence (1822) brought a serious decline in the Bahian tobacco trade. Independence by itself weakened established links, through Portugal, to markets in northern and southern Europe. At the same time, British efforts to halt the importation of slaves hampered trade with West Africa. Changing fashions also contributed to the decline. European consumers increasingly preferred cigars (and later cigarettes) to snuff and pipe tobacco. The decline was reversed after 1840, when Bahian growers began to harvest varieties of leaf tobacco that could be used in manufacturing cigars.

A significant export trade in tobacco also developed in colonial Spanish America and most notably in Cuba, where the seventeenth-century surge in European demand encouraged increased production at first near and around Havana and then throughout the island. The real heyday of Cuban tobacco was, however, the nineteenth century, when, paradoxically, sugar had already displaced tobacco as the island's most profitable export. The rapid development of the sugar industry in Cuba, from about 1760 on, had come at the expense of tobacco: in one district after another, *vegas* (tobacco farms) had been replanted with cane. Only in the western and eastern extremes of the island and at a few scattered points in between did tobacco hold its own. Yet from these regions (especially the famous Vuelta de Abajo in western Cuba) came leaf tobacco that was ideally suited for cigars. As early as the 1820s, English consumers eagerly sought out hand-rolled "Havanas." Cigar exports more than doubled between 1840 and 1855. Thereafter, sales of unprocessed leaf quickly outstripped the trade in finished cigars.

At various times, other regions in Latin America have also produced tobacco for export: colonial Venezuela on a small scale, Colombia and Paraguay in the nineteenth century, and, from the end of that century onward, Mexico, Puerto Rico, and the Dominican Republic.

Moreover, tobacco early on became an important commodity in local and regional commerce. By the eighteenth century, one third of the Bahian crop was sold within Brazil. Regional markets absorbed virtually all the tobacco grown in colonial Colombia and Paraguay. In the late eighteenth century, local production as well as imports from Cuba helped meet the enormous demand for tobacco in Mexico, the wealthiest and most populous of Spain's American colonies.

The tobacco sold in domestic and foreign markets frequently came from small and medium-size farms. Tobacco was in many ways an ideal cash crop for the small holder. Although labor intensive, it required neither great amounts of land nor any large outlay of capital. Yet, more often than is commonly acknowledged, tobacco production in Latin America depended on onerous sharecropping arrangements or on coerced labor. Slaves accounted for at least a third of the population in the tobacco districts of colonial and nineteenth-century Bahia, where well-to-do growers typically owned a dozen or more slaves. As late as 1862, more than 17,000 slaves still worked on tobacco farms in Cuba. At the end of the nineteenth century, tobacco growers of Oaxaca, in Mexico, were notorious for relying on a particularly harsh form of debt peonage.

The tobacco trade has long been subject to various restrictions and controls. During the colonial period, many of those restrictions were linked to the creation of Estancos (royal monopolies). The Portuguese *estanco*, established in 1659, handled the sale and distribution of Brazilian tobacco in European markets. On its behalf, colonial authorities enforced numerous laws that governed warehousing, prices, and quality controls. The first Spanish *estanco* lasted only a few years (1717–1724), but a second *estanco*, organized in the 1760s and 1770s, became a major source of revenue for the crown. It monopolized both exports and sales of tobacco within the colonies. To keep prices high, the *estanco* attempted to limit output. The imposition of these controls met with resistance: merchants turned to smuggling, and growers rebelled in Cuba in 1717, 1720, and 1723, and in Colombia in 1781. After Independence, financial necessity led several Spanish American governments to reestablish state tobacco monopolies, which survived until the mid-nineteenth century. In the twentieth century, both Mexico and Cuba granted monopoly privileges to state-owned tobacco companies.

Tobacco also has links to the early history of manufacturing and industry in Latin America. In the 1790s, as many as 8,900 workers—more than half of them women—were employed by the Spanish *estanco* at its cigar and cigarette factory in Mexico City. By the 1850s, both slaves and wage workers manufactured cigars and other tobacco products at numerous workshops and factories in Bahia and Rio de Janeiro. Several hundred workshops competed with larger factories and domestic manufacturing in Cuba's nineteenth-century cigar industry. In the 1860s the Susini firm of Havana pioneered mechanization in the production of cigarettes. By 1900, the tobacco industry in both Cuba and Brazil had already begun to attract foreign investment. However, in 1959, the revolutionary government of Cuba expelled all foreign business. In turn, the United States banned the importation of all Cuban goods, including cigars. Today, large foreign firms dominate the sector in Latin America, where tobacco remains a widely cultivated cash crop.

While smoking continues to be popular in Latin America, there has been increased attention to the negative health effects of tobacco products. For instance, in 2002 Mexico's health secretary announced that the government would ban tobacco advertisements on radio and television.

See also **Agriculture; Bahia; Slavery: Brazil; Tobacco Monopoly.**

BIBLIOGRAPHY

Fernando Ortíz, *Cuban Counterpoint: Tobacco and Sugar* (1947).

Catherine Lugar, "The Portuguese Tobacco Trade and Tobacco Growers of Bahia in the Late Colonial Period," in *Essays Concerning the Socioeconomic History of Brazil and Portuguese India*, edited by Dauril Alden and Warren Dean (1977).

Arturo Obregón M., *Las obreras tabacaleras de la ciudad de México (1764–1925)* (1982).

Jean Stubbs, *Tobacco on the Periphery: A Case Study in Cuban Labour History, 1860–1958* (1985).

Susan Deans-Smith, *Bureaucrats, Planters, and Workers: The Making of the Tobacco Monopoly in Bourbon Mexico* (1992).

Additional Bibliography

Barickman, B. J. *A Bahian Counterpoint: Sugar, Tobacco, Cassava, and Slavery in the Recôncavo, 1780–1860*. Stanford, CA: Stanford University Press, 1998.

Escobar Gamboa, Mauro. *El tabaco en el Perú colonial, 1752–1796*. Lima: Seminario de Historia Rural Andina, Universidad Nacional Mayor de San Marcos, 2004.

González Gómez, Carmen Imelda. *El tabaco virreinal: Monopolio de una costumbre*. Santiago de Querétaro, México: Fondo Editorial de Querétaro, 2002.

B. J. BARICKMAN

TOBACCO MONOPOLY.

Tobacco has traditionally occupied a favored position in state taxation systems because of its popularity and high levels of consumption. Spain monopolized its domestic tobacco trade as early as 1636, and extended a government monopoly over the tobacco trade of its American possessions between 1717 and 1783. The organization and administration of the tobacco monopolies were virtually uniform throughout the empire, although the degree of state regulation varied. In Mexico, the state eventually took over all aspects of the domestic tobacco trade, from the cultivation and purchase of leaf, to manufacture of cigars and cigarettes in state-managed factories, to marketing by government-licensed stores. In comparison, in Cuba and Venezuela the monopoly managed the cultivation and production only of the varieties of raw leaf tobacco that grew in these colonies and were exported to Spain for processing as cigars, cigarettes, and snuff.

The tobacco monopoly proved to be a critical source of government income both in Spain and throughout its empire. Revenues earned from the tobacco monopoly in Spain accounted for almost one-third of total domestic public revenues. Combined, the tobacco monopolies of Spanish America at their peak made significant contributions to crown revenues, representing the second greatest source of revenue after silver and gold. In addition, throughout the eighteenth century monopoly revenues played an increasingly important role in the financial and fiscal affairs of the colonies, which suffered from shortage of specie and lack of formal banks. Historians differ on the economic costs to the colonies of the tobacco monopolies: some argue that they resulted in capital exports and the reduction of capital stock, while others argue that monopoly restrictions redirected resources into other activities. The tobacco monopoly performed better in Mexico than in Peru, where in 1791 the factory system was closed and returned to private control. The Peruvian monopoly still maintained control of actual plant production until the end of Spanish rule.

Recent research suggests that the political and social consequences of Spain's monopolization of the tobacco trade varied, as did the effectiveness of monopoly policy, the variations being explained by the strategies adopted to implement the monopoly, the structure of the local society and economy, and alternative sources of employment. Responses ranged from contraband in tobacco leaf and products, to riot and rebellion by disgruntled farmers and peasants. One of the most extreme examples of opposition to the imposition of a tobacco monopoly is the Comunero Revolt in 1781 in New Granada (Colombia). The social dimensions of the monopoly have recently attracted the attention of historians who emphasize the tobacco monopoly's impact on labor and working conditions, gender roles in the workplace, and the changes engendered in rural society as a result of monopoly policy. Much more research, however, is needed in these areas.

After the colonies declared their political independence from Spain, restructuring of tobacco cultivation, manufacturing, and marketing occurred. Although monopolies were legally abolished, many continued to exist as penurious governments desperately sought revenues. The difficulties of re-creating the colonial-style monopolistic structure manifested itself in the cycles of abolition of a tobacco monopoly, by reestablishment, only to be succeeded by abolition throughout the nineteenth century, although in Colombia, for example, the monopoly facilitated the development and expansion of the tobacco export trade. A major influence on the structure of the tobacco trade and industry in the late nineteenth and twentieth centuries came from monopolies in Europe and the United States, such as the British-American To bacco Company, a consequence of which was the consolidation of, and division of business between, tobacco-exporting and tobacco-manufacturing countries.

See also **Comunero Revolt (New Granada); Tobacco Industry.**

BIBLIOGRAPHY

John B. Harrison, "The Colombian Tobacco Industry from Government Monopoly to Free Trade, 1778–1876" (Ph.D. diss., University of California, Berkeley, 1951).

G. Céspedes Del Castillo, "La renta del tabaco en el virreinato de Perú," in *Revista histórica* 21 (1954).

Agnes Stapff, "La renta del tabaco en Chile de la Época virreinal," in *Anuario de estudios americanos* 18 (1961): 1–63.

José Rivero Muñiz, *Tabaco: Su historia en Cuba*, 2 vols. (1964–1965).

Cam Harlan Wickham, "Venezuela's Royal Tobacco Monopoly, 1799–1810: An Economic Analysis" (Ph.D. diss., University of Oregon, 1975).

Juan Carlos Arias Divito, "Dificultades para establecer la renta de tabaco en Paraguay," in *Anuario de estudios americanos* 33 (1976): 1–17.

John Leddy Phelan, *The People and the King: The Comunero Revolution in Colombia, 1781* (1978).

Jesús Jáuregui Et Al., *Tabamex, un caso de integración vertical de la agricultura* (1980).

Jean Stubbs, *Tobacco on the Periphery: A Case Study in Cuban Labour History, 1860–1958* (1985).

Jesús Antonio Bejarano and Orlando Pulido, *El tabaco en una economía regional: Amablema, siglos XVIII y XIX* (1986).

Christine Hünefeldt, "Etapa final del monopolio en el virreinato del Perú: El tabaco de Chachapoyas," in *The*

Economies of Mexico and Peru, edited by Nils Jacobsen and Hans Jurgen Puhle (1986).

Jerry W. Cooney, "La Dirección General de la Real Renta de Tabacos and the Decline of the Royal Tobacco Monopoly in Paraguay, 1779–1800," in *Colonial Latin American Historical Review* 1, no. 1 (1992).

Susan Deans-Smith, *Bureaucrats, Planters, and Workers: The Making of the Monopoly in Bourbon Mexico* (1992).

Additional Bibliography

Escobar Gamboa, Mauro. *El tabaco en el Perú colonial, 1752–1796.* Lima: Seminario de Historia Rural Andina, Universidad Nacional Mayor de San Marcos, 2004.

González Gómez, Carmen Imelda. *El tabaco virreinal: Monopolio de una costumbre.* Querétaro, Mexico: Fondo Editorial de Querétaro, 2002.

SUSAN DEANS-SMITH

TOBAGO. *See* **Trinidad and Tobago.**

TOBAR DOCTRINE. In a 15 March 1907 letter to the Bolivian consul in Brussels, Carlos R. Tobar, a former Ecuadorian foreign minister, affirmed that "The American republics ... ought to intervene indirectly in the internal dissensions of the republics of the continent. Such intervention might consist, at the least, in the denial of recognition to de factor governments springing from revolution against the constitutional order." In December 1907 representatives of the Central American nations, meeting in Washington, D.C., officially incorporated Tobar's de jure recognition policy into the 1907 Washington Treaties. At the request of Costa Rica more stringent de jure recognition provisions were written into the 1923 Washington Treaties. A succession of isthmian recognition crises, however, convinced many Central Americans that strict adherence to the Tobar Doctrine was not in their best interests. In 1932 Costa Rica and El Salvador, dissatisfied with the existing recognition policy, denounced the 1923 Washington Treaties. Efforts to resurrent the Tobar Doctrine at the 1934 Central American Conference were unsuccessful.

See also **Central America; Washington Treaties of 1907 and 1923.**

BIBLIOGRAPHY

Leónidas García, "La doctrina Tobar," in *Revista de la Sociedad "Jurídico-Literaria"* (Quito) 1 (January–February 1913): 25–71.

Charles L. Stansifer, "Application of the Tobar Doctrine to Central America," in *Americas* 23, no. 3 (1967): 251–272.

Richard V. Salisbury, "Domestic Politics and Foreign Policy: Costa Rica's Stand on Recognition, 1923–1934," in *Hispanic American Historical Review* 54, no. 3 (1974):453–478.

Additional Bibliography

Buchenau, Jürgen. *In the Shadow of the Giant: The Making of Mexico's Central America Policy, 1876–1930.* Tuscaloosa: University of Alabama Press, 1996.

Schoonover, Thomas David. *The United States in Central America, 1860–1911: Episodes of Social Imperialism and Imperial Rivalry in the World System.* Durham, NC: Duke University Press, 1991.

RICHARD V. SALISBURY

TOBAR DONOSO, JULIO (1894–1981).

The Ecuadoran diplomat and historian Julio Tobar Donoso, born January 25, 1894, was one of Ecuador's most distinguished historians of the old guard. Like so many of that country's writers and makers of history, he was a multifaceted intellectual. He studied at the Jesuit Colegio de San Gabriel in his native Quito and took a doctorate in law from the Universidad Central in 1917.

Tobar Donoso was a practicing Catholic and a staunch conservative—his wife was a grandniece of Gabriel García Moreno (president of Ecuador, 1861–1865 and 1869–1875). He was politically active, a journalist, a diplomat, an educator, and a prolific scholar. He was a member of the Asociación Católica de la Juventud Ecuatoriana in his youth and one of the presidents of the Centro Católico de Obrero. He founded the weekly *Acción popular* in 1932. The minister of foreign affairs during the short but devastating 1941 border war with Peru, Tobar Donoso suffered political ignominy for having signed the Protocol of Rio de Janeiro in 1942, that ceded much of the Upper Amazon Basin claimed by Ecuador to Peru. One of the founders of the Pontificia Universidad Católica de Quito in 1948, Tobar Donoso was the dean of its law faculty for twenty-five years and also a professor of political science. Thirty years earlier he had been one of founding members of the Sociedad Ecuatoriana de Estudios Históricos Americanos (1918), the predecessor of the Academia Nacional de Historia del Ecuador (founded 1920). He was also a member of the Société des Américanistes as well as of many other academies and societies, including the Academia Ecuatoriana de la Lengua, of which he became president in 1965.

Especially interested in the national period, his many writings include: *La iglesia ecuatoriana en el siglo XIX* (1934); *Monografías históricas* (1937), which brings together several of his more important articles; *García Moreno y la instrucción pública* (1940); *Derecho territorial ecuatoriano* (1961, 1979, 1982); and the posthumous *El indio en el Ecuador independiente* (1992), all of which are scholarly, sound, mostly pioneering as well as original, and required reading for students of the period. He also shed light on the colonial period. His *Las instituciones del período hispánico, especialmente en la Presidencia de Quito* (1974) is a vade mecum in its own right.

See also **Ecuador-Peru Boundary Disputes; García Moreno, Gabriel.**

BIBLIOGRAPHY

Rueda, Marco Vinicio. *Julio Tobar Donoso, maestro universitario.* Quito: Ediciones de la Universidad Católica, 1982.

Vega y Vega, Wilson C. *Bibliografía del Dr. Julio Tobar Donoso.* Quito: W. C. Vega Vega, 1994.

MICHAEL T. HAMERLY

TOCANTINS.

Tocantins, a Brazilian state created on March 1, 1989, from the portion of the state of Goiás that lay to the north of the thirteenth parallel. It consists of 79 municipalities covering an area of 110,698 square miles and with a population of 1,155,913 (2004 est.). The separation of Tocantins from the rest of the state of Goiás was a vindication for its inhabitants. For a very long time, they had complained that due to the great distances involved, the north received no benefits from the state governments for the development of their area. In 1822, after Brazil had won its independence, the north seceded from the south but was incapable of maintaining its autonomy. In 1956 the Movement for the Creation of the State of Tocantins was formed. The Constitution of 1988 finally made the creation of the state a reality.

Since its establishment, Tocantins has been the fastest-growing Brazilian state, with a thriving economy based on agriculture and agro-industry that attracts immigrants from all over the country. The construction of the long-planned North-South Railway in Brazil will probably boost the state's economic growth even more. Tocantins is also considered one of the best-managed Brazilian states.

See also **Goiás.**

BIBLIOGRAPHY

Celio Costa, *Fundamentos para Criação do Estado de Tocantins* (1982) and *O Estado do Tocantins: Uma geopolítica de desenvolvimento* (1985).

Additional Bibliography

Bognola, I. A., and E. E. de Miranda. "Zoneamento Agro-ecológico do Estado de Tocantins." In *Resumos*, Workshop sobre Agroecologia e Desenvolvimento Sustentáve. Campinas, Brazil: UNICAMP-IB, 1999.

Collicchio, Erich. *Organização estadual de pesquisa agropecuária: Um instrumento de apoio ao desenvolvimento rural sustentável do Tocantis.* Palma Provisão, Brazil, 2006.

LUIS PALACIN

When gold was discovered in the eighteenth century, settlements were established along the tributaries and affluents of the Tocantins. Once the gold was gone, the river became a trade route, despite its cataracts and the great distances it traversed, for towns in the north of Goiás and Pará, with a continuous series of cities: Palma, Porto Real, Pedro Afonso, Carolina, Boa Vista, Imperatriz, Marabá, Tucuruí, and Cametá. Since the 1960s, projects in agriculture, the raising of livestock, and mining have resulted in further settling of the Tocantins valley.

See also **Bandeiras; Brazil, Geography; Goiás; Maranhão; Mato Grosso; Mining: Colonial Brazil; Pará (Grão Pará); Tocantins.**

BIBLIOGRAPHY

Lysias A. Rodrigues, *O Rio dos Tocantins* (1945) and *Roteiro do Tocantins*, 3d ed. (1987).

Francisco Ayres Da Silva, *Caminhos de outrora: Diário de viagens* (1972).

Dalísia Elisabeth Martins Doles, *As comunicações fluviais pelo Tocantins e Araguaia no século XIX* (1973).

Additional Bibliography

Goulding, Michael; Ronaldo Barthem; Efrem Jorge Gondim Ferreira. *The Smithsonian Atlas of the Amazon.* Washington, DC: Smithsonian Books, 2003.

Rocha, Jan. *Brazil.* Oxford: Oxfam, 2000.

Vincent, John S. *Culture and Customs of Brazil.* Westport, CT: Greenwood Press, 2003.

LUIS PALACÍN

TOCANTINS RIVER. Tocantins River, a waterway in Brazil that rises from the central altiplano in the state of Goiás and flows about 1,500 miles north to empty into the bay of Marapatá across from the island of Marajó on the Atlantic coast near Belém. Its basin covers an area of 301,600 square miles in the Federal District and the states of Goiás, Tocantins, Mato Grosso, Maranhão, and Pará. Its entire course was once inhabited by indigenous tribes: Tocoiuna, Tocantin, Pacajá, Guaraju, Tupinambá, Inhaiguara, Bilreiro, Guaiase, Parissó, Apinage, and Cherente. The French explorers La Blanjartier (1610) and La Ravardière (1613) reached it by way of the Maranhão. During the seventeenth century, numerous raids and explorations out of São Paulo and Belém headed toward the Tocantins area in search of Indians to work on the religious settlements and farms.

TOCORNAL, JOAQUÍN (1788–1865). Joaquín Tocornal (*b.* 1788; *d.* 1865), Chilean Conservative politician. Tocornal was the youngest man invited to the *cabildo abierto* (open town meeting) that elected Chile's first national junta on 18 September 1810. He became politically prominent with the Conservative rebellion of 1829–1830, serving as vice president of the Congress of Plenipotentiaries, the body that was chiefly instrumental in establishing the new Conservative regime. During the presidency of Joaquín Prieto (1831–1841), he acted as minister of the interior (1832–1835) and as finance minister (1835–1841). He assumed the interior ministry again (1837–1840) following the murder of Diego Portales (1793–1837).

Tocornal played a key part in ensuring the continuity of government. Despite his ministerial eminence, however, he was unable to win Prieto's approval for his own presidential candidacy in 1841. Prieto preferred the war hero General Manuel Bulnes (1799–1866): Tocornal did not obtain a single vote in the electoral college. He did retain his influence in the Conservative Party, however, and in January 1858 he helped negotiate the formation of the Liberal-Conservative Fusion. His son Manuel Antonio Tocornal (1817–1867) played a prominent part in politics in 1849–1850 and again in the 1860s as a Fusion leader. Had he not died prematurely, he might well have been the Fusion's presidential candidate in 1871.

See also **Bulnes Prieto, Manuel; Chile, Political Parties: Conservative Party; Chile, Political Parties: Liberal-Conservative Fusion (Liberal-Conservadora); Portales Palazuelos, Diego José Pedro Víctor; Prieto Vial, Joaquín.**

BIBLIOGRAPHY

Additional Bibliography

Collier, Simon. *Chile: The Making of a Republic, 1830–1865.* New York: Cambridge University Press, 2003.

SIMON COLLIER

TOLEDO, ALEJANDRO (1946–). The biography of Alejandro Toledo Manrique, Peru's ninety-first president (2001–2006), is a rags-to-riches story. Born on March 28, 1946 to parents of indigenous origins, he grew up in the fishing town of Chimbote, where his father was a bricklayer. As a child he worked as a shoeshine boy, but later—thanks to support from U.S. Peace Corps volunteers—Toledo attended the University of San Francisco on a partial soccer scholarship and eventually earned a doctorate in education from Stanford University in 1992. He founded the political party País Posible (PP; later renamed Perú Posible) in 1994. Toledo ran unsuccessfully for presidency in 1995 and then again in the controversial 2000 election. Opposition to President Fujimori's legally dubious attempt to secure a third term in 2000 helped Toledo obtain 40 percent of the vote in the first electoral round, thus securing him a place in the subsequent runoff. However, he withdrew from the race, accusing the Fujimori regime of conducting a fraudulent election. He then organized with other opposition leaders the Marcha de los Cuatro Suyos, a series of massive rallies to protest Fujimori's second reelection. PP nominated him to run again in 2001. This time, Toledo faced former president Alan García in the runoff, winning with 53 percent of the vote. Inaugurated on July 28, 2001, his performance in office was uneven. He presided over years of substantial economic growth, but his popularity plummeted as people criticized his lack of discipline, his political priorities, and his apparent tolerance for petty corruption and nepotism. Although some congressmen demanded his resignation, Toledo successfully completed his term in 2006.

See also **Fujimori, Alberto Keinya; García Pérez, Alan; Peru: Peru Since Independence.**

BIBLIOGRAPHY

Arévalo, Patricia, and Michelle Salcedo Teullet, eds. *Cinco años: Crecimiento económico sostenido y recuperación democrática: El gobierno de Alejandro Toledo Manrique, 2001–2006.* Lima: Presidencia del Consejo de Ministros, 2006.

Azpur, Javier et al. *Perú hoy: Los mil días de Toledo.* Lima: DESCO, 2004.

Toledo, Alejandro. *Las Cartas sobre la mesa: Testimonio y propuestas para un país posible.* Lima: Instituto de Investigación para el Desarrollo del Perú, 1995.

"Toledo: Shoeshine Boy Turned Economist." *BBC News*, 8 April 2001. Online at http://news.bbc.co.uk/1/hi/world/americas/708450.stm.

"World Briefing/Americas: Peru: Angry President Calls for Unity." *New York Times*, January 20, 2005. Online at http://query.nytimes.com/top/reference/timestopics/people/t/alejandro_toledo/index.htm.

JULIO CARRION

TOLEDO, FRANCISCO (1940–). Francisco Toledo (*b.* 7 July 1940), Mexican artist. Francisco Toledo was born in the Zapotec town of Juchitán, Oaxaca. He first studied in Oaxaca under Mexican painter Arturo García Bustos (1926–). In 1957 Toledo moved to Mexico City to attend the Escuela de Diseño y Artesanía of the Instituto Nacional de Bellas Artes. In 1960 he relocated to Paris, where he studied under printmaker Stanley William Hayter. It was not until 1965 that Toledo finally resettled in Mexico. In 1984, an edition of

Jorge Luis Borges's *Manual de zoológica fantástica* containing his illustrations was published. In 1987, he began accumulating a global art collection, and he established the Instituto de Artes Gráficas de Oaxaca in his former house to display it. He then donated the museum to the state of Oaxaca. From Zapotec folklore his paintings, drawings, prints, sculptures, and ceramics re-create the Zapotec world in which reptiles, amphibians, fish, insects, and human beings exude sexuality.

See also **Art: The Twentieth Century; Borges, Jorge Luis; Oaxaca (State); Zapotecs.**

BIBLIOGRAPHY

Teresa Del Conde, *Francisco Toledo* (1981).

Luis Cardoza y Aragón, *Toledo* (1987).

Andrew Kline, "Francisco Toledo," in *Latin American Art* 3 (1991):35–37.

Additional Bibliography

Colle, Marie-Pierre. *Latin American Artists in Their Studios.* New York: Vendome Press, 1994.

Congdon, Kristin G., and Kara Kelley Hallmark. *Artists from Latin American Cultures: A Biographical Dictionary.* Westport, CT: Greenwood Press, 2002.

Lampert, Catherine. *Francisco Toledo.* London: Trustees of the Whitechapel Art Gallery, 2000.

SHIFRA M. GOLDMAN

TOLEDO Y FIGUEROA, FRANCISCO DE (1515–1582).

Francisco de Toledo y Figueroa (*b.* 10 July 1515; *d.* 21 April 1582), viceroy of Peru (1569–1581). Don Francisco de Toledo, as he signed himself, was born in Oropesa, New Castile, the third son of the third Count of Oropesa. Through his mother he was closely related to the dukes of Alba and distantly to Emperor Charles V. In 1535 he became a member of the Order of Alcántara.

After many years in the crown's military and diplomatic service, Toledo was appointed viceroy of Peru in 1568. The journey to his new post took him from February to September of 1569. He left ship in the extreme north of Peru and traveled by land to Lima, the capital, inspecting settlements on the desert coast as he progressed.

Peru had a thirty-five-year history of interrupted government and rebellion. Toledo immediately showed himself to be suspicious of any group with power on whatever level: the *audiencias* (courts) of Lima and La Plata, the secular and regular clergy, the *encomenderos*, the *cabildos* (town councils), and, of course, the independent Inca state of Vilcabamba. After a critical examination of their actions during his administration, he attacked, and generally managed to reduce, their authority and autonomy.

Among his other duties, Toledo was ordered to make a *Visita General* (general inspection) of his viceroyalty. To visit the entire territory, from New Granada (now Colombia) to Chile, was clearly impossible. But in October 1570 Toledo began a tour of the heartland of his jurisdiction that lasted more than five years and took him through the major administrative, economic, and population centers of the Central Andes: Huamanga, Cuzco, Potosí, La Plata, and Arequipa. No other viceroy in the Spanish Empire ever knew his territory as intimately as Toledo came to know his through this exacting personal inspection.

During the *visita*, Toledo achieved the elimination of Inca resistance at Vilcabamba and the execution of the last independent Inca ruler, Túpac Amaru; the *reducción* (resettlement) of many native people in new towns for more efficient government, evangelization, and extraction of their labor; the final formulation of the *mita* supplying workers to Spanish mercury and silver mines at Huancavelica and Potosí; and full adoption of a silver-refining process utilizing mercury. These last two measures stimulated a vast growth in silver production. Toledo also issued a multitude of regulations on other administrative, economic, and social matters.

Much of what is attributed to Toledo alone, such as the *reducción* program and the mining *mita*, had origins in earlier administrations, but he certainly gave final and legal form to such schemes. Many of his actions seemed, then and later, highly damaging to the native people. For them, he was, and still is, criticized. He was determined that Peru should submit to firm Spanish control and serve Spain's purposes. To those ends, he used whatever means seemed necessary, enforcing the rules with an intolerant and impatient authoritarianism. He enthusiastically praised the efforts of the first inquisitors in Peru, who had traveled with him to Lima. To justify his attacks on Vilcabamba, Túpac Amaru, and other descendants of Inca rulers and nobles, he gathered evidence designed to show that the Incas had been tyrants and that therefore Spaniards had been, and were, fully justified in destroying them.

The rigors of the *Visita General* left Toledo tired and ill. The final five years of his administration were far less active than its first half. Nevertheless, he laid a solid foundation for future Spanish administration of South America. His legislation became a model for governors throughout the empire. He was in a substantial sense the organizer of Spanish Peru, comparable to Viceroy Antonio de Mendoza in Spanish Mexico.

See also **Mendoza, Antonio de; Peru: From the Conquest Through Independence.**

BIBLIOGRAPHY

Roberto Levillier, *Don Francisco de Toledo, supremo organizador del Perú. Su vida, su obra (1515–1582)* (1935).

Arthur Franklin Zimmerman, *Francisco de Toledo: Fifth Viceroy of Peru, 1569–1581* (1938).

Lewis Hanke, *The Spanish Struggle for Justice in the Conquest of America,* (1949: repr. 1965), esp. pp. 135–137, 165–172.

John Hemming, *The Conquest of the Incas* (1970), esp. chaps. 20–23.

Lewis Hanke, ed., *Los virreyes españoles en América durante el gobierno de la casa de Austria: Perú* (1978).

Karen Spalding, *Huarochirí: An Andean Society Under Inca and Spanish Rule* (1984), esp. pp. 156–168, 209–227.

Guillermo Lohmann Villena and María Justina Sarabia Viejo, eds., *Francisco de Toledo: Disposiciones gubernativas para el virreinato del Perú, 1569–1574,* 2 vols. (1986, 1989).

Additional Bibliography

Gómez Rivas, León. *El virrey del Perú don Francisco de Toledo.* [Toledo]: Instituto Provincial de Investigaciones y Estudios Toledanos, Diputación Provincial, 1994.

Merluzzi, Manfredi. *Politica e governo nel Nuovo Mondo: Francisco de Toledo viceré del Perú (1569–1581).* Roma: Carocci, 2003.

PETER BAKEWELL

TOLEDO Y LEYVA, PEDRO DE (1585–1654). Pedro de Toledo y Leyva (Marqués de Mancera; *b.* 1585; *d.* 9 March 1654), viceroy of Peru (1639–1648). Designated the first marqués de Mancera in 1633, former governor of Galicia, and a member of Philip IV's Council of War, Mancera took office as viceroy of Peru in December 1639. He was a vigorous administrator with a mixed reputation. On the one hand he was known for his charity, piety, and Christian fervor. A special friend to the Dominicans, he established a chair of Thomistic theology at the University of San Marcos in Lima exclusively for a Dominican and supported construction of a Dominican church and the school of Santo Tomás. Also in Lima he helped to found a Carmelite nunnery, a hospice and hermitage for the Franciscans, and hospitals for Indians, blacks (San Bartolomé), and the poor. In addition he assisted Franciscan missions in Panataguas with public funds.

On the other hand, Mancera was an efficient but oftentimes arbitrary administrator. On one occasion he ordered the expulsion of all Portuguese Jews living in Peru—6,000 by one estimate—and on another the removal of Lima prostitutes to Valdivia, Chile, to stimulate population growth in that remote region. Imposing a highly unpopular tax on meat and wine to pay the costs, he strengthened fortifications at the port of Callao, where his son Antonio Sebastián was commandant, and built two new galleons for the Pacific fleet (*Armada del Sur*). He also suppressed sixteen holidays, opened new veins at the mercury mine of Huancavelica, and revamped the tribute system. Eager to immortalize himself, Mancera gave his name to the new fort at Valdivia and to the town of Pisco (San Clemente de Mancera). He stepped down as viceroy on 20 September 1648.

See also **Peru: From the Conquest Through Independence.**

BIBLIOGRAPHY

Manuel De Mendiburu, ed., *Diccionario histórico-biográfico del Perú,* vol. 10 (1934).

Robert R. Miller, ed., *Chronicle of Colonial Lima: The Diary of Josephe and Francisco Mugaburu* (1975).

Additional Bibliography

Silverblatt, Irene Marsha. *Modern Inquisitions: Peru and the Colonial Origins of the Civilized World.* Durham, NC: Duke University Press, 2004.

JOHN JAY TePASKE

TOLSÁ, MANUEL (1757–1816).

Manuel Tolsá (*b*. 4 May 1757; *d*. 24 December 1816), sculptor and architect. Tolsá was trained in Valencia and at the Academia de San Fernando in Madrid. In 1791 he arrived in New Spain as director of sculpture at the Academia de San Carlos, bringing with him an important collection of plaster casts of classical works. His activity in New Spain soon included architectural as well as sculptural projects. His best-known work is the equestrian statue of King Charles IV of Spain (1796, cast in bronze in 1803). Popularly known as the "Caballito," it was inspired by the Roman Capitol with its sculpture of Emperor Marcus Aurelius, and was the focal point of the 1796 renovation of the Plaza Mayor of Mexico City. Tolsá also worked on the completion of Mexico City's cathedral, on the baldachin (an ornamental structure over the central altar) of the cathedral of Puebla, on the house of the count of Buenavista (today Museo de San Carlos), and on the Palacio de Minería in Mexico City, as well as on many other projects. Because of his energetic participation in so many endeavors, Tolsá is considered largely responsible for the definitive entry of academic neoclassicism into New Spain.

See also **Architecture: Architecture to 1900; Art: The Colonial Era.**

BIBLIOGRAPHY

Manuel Toussaint, *Colonial Art in Mexico* (1967).

Joaquín Bérchez, "Manuel Tolsá en la arquitectura española de su tiempo," in *Tolsá, Gimeno, Fabregat,* edited by Generalitat Valenciana (1989), pp. 13–64.

Eloísa Uribe, *Tolsá, hombre de la ilustración* (1990).

Additional Bibliography

Pinoncelly, Salvador. *Manuel Tolsá, arquitecto.* México, D.F.: Consejo Nacional para la Cultura y las Artes, 1998.

Salazar Híjar y Haro, Enrique. *Los trotes del Caballito: Una historia para la historia.* México: Editorial Diana, 1999.

CLARA BARGELLINI

TOLTECS.

Toltecs, a people who dominated central Mexico in the years 950–1150/1200 CE and exerted influence over much of the territory of modern Mexico and Central America. Their capital Tula (Nahuatl: Tollan) occupied a ridge overlooking the Tula River in Hidalgo, 40 miles northwest of modern Mexico City. Spanish chroniclers recorded Aztec legends and historical traditions about the Toltecs and Quetzalcoatl, their semi legendary ruler, whose identity and exploits became fused with those of the Feathered Serpent, his deified namesake. Unfortunately, contradictions are so abundant in these accounts that it is difficult to reconstruct a coherent Toltec history. Archaeological investigations at Tula and elsewhere add substantially to the corpus of data, but it is difficult to reconcile much of this information with the ethnohistoric accounts.

Ethnically and linguistically the Toltecs were an amalgam of small migrant groups who entered southern Hidalgo during Teotihuacán's last decades. They included the Nonoalca, refugees from Teotihuacán itself, and the Chichimecs, farmers fleeing south from the increasingly turbulent Mesoamerican frontier zone in north Mexico. There is good reason to believe that Nahuatl was the dominant language in Toltec society, although speakers of Otomí and perhaps other Otomanguean languages were also present in significant numbers.

Agriculture was the basis of Toltec existence, and maize was the staple crop. Beans, squash, cactus fruits and juice, numerous minor plants, and the flesh of dogs, deer, and rabbits all supplemented the diet. Although irrigation was practiced where possible, adequate subsistence was a recurrent problem in this arid region and became a paramount concern as the population grew. The recorded legends suggest that famine, perhaps triggered by decreasing rainfall, led to civil war and, ultimately, Tula's abandonment in the twelfth century.

In addition to farming, the Toltec economy depended upon craft production and commerce. Pottery, stone tools, textiles, personal ornaments, and other products were manufactured in the city and exchanged in markets. Specialized merchants imported fancy pottery, marine shells, green stones, rare animal skins and feathers, cacao, exotic foods, and other luxury goods into Tula while distributing Toltec products far from their homeland.

The evidence suggests the existence of a Toltec empire, but its extent and duration are unknown.

Some archaeologists believe it included Pacific coastal Chiapas and Guatemala, the Yucatán peninsula with its Toltec-Maya center of Chichén Itzá, and much of north and west Mexico, but others challenge this hypothesis.

The Aztecs proudly claimed Toltec ancestry and praised their putative forebears as warriors, master craftsmen, builders, and wise men. They exaggerated, perhaps intentionally, the justifiably impressive accomplishments of the Toltecs while creating a historical fiction designed to validate their own status. The Aztec embellishments notwithstanding, the Toltec legacy in modern Mexico remains considerable.

See also **Archaeology; Chichén Itzá; Mesoamerica; Nahuas; Nahuatl; Nuclear America.**

BIBLIOGRAPHY

Nigel Davies, *The Toltecs Until the Fall of Tula* (1977).

William T. Sanders, Jeffrey R. Parsons, and Robert S. Santley, *The Basin of Mexico: The Ecological Processes in the Evolution of a Civilization* (1979).

Nigel Davies, *The Toltec Heritage* (1980).

Muriel Porter Weaver, *The Aztecs, Maya, and Their Predecessors: Archaeology of Mesoamerica*, 2d ed. (1981).

Richard A. Diehl, *Tula: The Toltec Capital of Ancient Mexico* (1983).

Additional Bibliography

Healan, Dan M. *Tula of the Toltecs: Excavations and Survey.* Iowa City: University of Iowa Press, 1989.

Kirchoff, Paul, Lina Odena Güemes, and Luis Reyes García. *Historia tolteca-chichimeca.* México: CISINAH, INAH, SEP, 1976.

Nicholson, H. B. *Topiltzin Quetzalcoatl: The Once and Future Lord of the Toltecs (Mesoamerican Worlds).* Boulder: University Press of Colorado, 2001.

RICHARD A. DIEHL

TOMEBAMBA. Tomebamba, the principal Inca administrative center for the northern sector of the empire, located in the southern Ecuadorian highlands. The site was founded by Topa Inca Yupanqui during the military campaigns he led against the indigenous Cañari population between A.D. 1460 and A.D. 1470. Huayna Capac, successor to Topa Inca and penultimate ruler of the empire, was born in Tomebamba and resided there for much of his life. Various ethnohistoric sources describe Tomebamba as a "second Cuzco," suggesting that the site was deliberately created in the image of the sacred capital of the Inca Empire. Indeed, certain features of the local landscape are reminiscent of the Cuzco Valley. This resemblance was not lost on the Inca, who sought to magnify the similarities through the imposition of Cuzqueño place-names upon the local topography. Many of these toponyms are still used today.

The site of Tomebamba was first excavated by Max Uhle in the 1920s. Many of the ruins he described now lie beneath the modern city of Cuenca, Ecuador. The architectural remains Uhle encountered were vast in scale and included what he interpreted as religious structures, a central plaza, a palatial residence, guards' quarters, and a convent (*aqllawasi*). Elaborate waterworks, including pools, baths, and canals, as well as terraces and roads, were also recorded. The palatial sector, known as Puma Pungo, is believed to have been the royal residence of Huayna Capac. Substantial quantities of Inca pottery have been recovered from this portion of the site. Tomebamba was devastated by Atahualpa during the Inca civil war that ensued after the death of Huayna Capac in 1527. Though the site lay in ruins by the time the Spanish chronicler Pedro de Cieza De León passed through some twenty years later, it was nonetheless impressive enough for him to describe it as one of the most magnificent Inca sites in all the empire.

See also **Archaeology; Huayna Capac; Incas, The; Yupanqui, Atahualpa.**

BIBLIOGRAPHY

On the archaeology of Tomebamba, see Max Uhle, *Las ruinas de Tomebamba* (1923).

Jaime Idrovo, "Tomebamba: Primera fase de conquista Incasica en los Andes septentrionales," in *La frontera del estado Inca* (1988), Proceedings of the 45th Congreso Internacional de Americanistas, edited by Tom D. Dillehay and Patricia Netherly, BAR International Series, no. 442, pp. 87–104.

John Hyslop, *Inka Settlement Planning* (1990), pp. 140–142, 264–265. For the most detailed ethnohistoric account of the site, see Miguel Cabello De Balboa, *Miscelánea Antártica* (1951; written in 1586), chaps. 21–22.

Additional Bibliography

Idrovo Urigüen, Jaime. *Tomebamba, arqueología e historia de una ciudad imperial.* Quito: Banco Central del Ecuador, Dirección Cultural Regional Cuenca, 2000.

Jamieson, Ross W., and Ion Youman. *De Tomebamba a Cuenca: Arquitectura y arqueología colonial.* Quito, Ecuador: Universidad de Cuenca: Ediciones del Banco Central del Ecuador: Abya Yala, 2003.

Kyle, David. *Transnational Peasants: Migrations, Networks, and Ethnicity in Andean Ecuador.* Baltimore: Johns Hopkins University Press, 2000.

TAMARA L. BRAY

TOMIC, RADOMIRO (1914–1992). Radomiro Tomic, Chilean politician and former ambassador to the United States. Tomic, born May 7, 1914, in the Yugoslav enclave in Antofagasta, helped form the Partido Demócrata Cristiano (PDC). In 1968, after serving as ambassador to the United States, he returned to Chile, where he emerged as one of the leaders of the PDC's progressive wing. Selected as the Christian Democratic candidate for president in 1970, Tomic attempted to hold onto the Christian Democratic faithful while reaching out to the leftist vote by advocating more radical agrarian reform, nationalization of the copper mines, and massive state involvement in economic development. Tomic's tactics failed. Unable to retain the vote of those who had voted for Eduardo Frei six years earlier and often ridiculed for being bombastic, he came in a distant third, winning but 27 percent of the vote.

True to an earlier promise, Tomic endorsed the election of Salvador Allende to the presidency. But the Christian Democrat did not abandon his party and even repudiated those who did leave to join the Movimiento de Acción Popular Unitaria (MAPU) or the Christian Left. Tomic, moreover, became increasingly discontented when it became clear that the Unidad Popular (UP) government would refuse to cooperate with the PDC and that it would not moderate its more radical policies. So much so, apparently, that Tomic, like Frei, supported the 1973 anti-Allende coup. He subsequently fled Chile, later returning to join the anti-Pinochet movement and to act as an elder statesman of the Christian Democratic Party. Tomic supported the national ownership of Chile's mines, and in 1997, CODELCO named a a mine in his honor. He died in Santiago in 1992.

See also **Allende Gossens, Salvador; Chile, Political Parties: Christian Democratic Party (PDC).**

BIBLIOGRAPHY

Radomiro Tomic, *Fundamentos cristianos para una nueva política en Chile* (1945).

Paul E. Sigmund, *The Overthrow of Allende and the Politics of Chile, 1964–1976* (1977), pp. 26, 36, 45, 68, 72, 80, 84, 94–95, 104, 106, 150–151.

Michael Fleet, *The Rise and Fall of Chilean Christian Democracy* (1985), pp. 44, 50, 114–116, 119–123.

Additional Bibliography

Aguilera, Pilar, and Ricardo Fredes, eds. *Chile: El otro 11 de Septiembre.* 2nd ed. New York: Ocean Press, 2006.

Oppenheim, Lois Hecht. *Politics in Chile: Socialism, Authoritarianism, and Market Democracy.* 3rd ed. Boulder, CO: Westview Press, 2007.

Yocelevsky R., Ricardo A. *Chile, partidos políticos, democracia y dictadura, 1970–1990.* Santiago: Fondo de Cultura Económica, 2002.

WILLIAM F. SATER

TOMOCHIC REBELLION. Tomochic Rebellion, an uprising in Mexico's northwestern state of Chihuahua in 1891. Villagers of the mountain pueblo of Tomochic denied allegiance to the government and vowed to obey no one but a teenage folk saint, Teresa Urrea, known as la Santa de Cabora, who, for more than a year, had been preaching social reform in the neighboring state of Sonora. Perhaps half of the 300 villagers did not concur with this millenarian vision and left town, but those who remained began to develop their utopian dream. In September 1892, after failed efforts to negotiate the faithful out of their intransigence, government troops sought to stamp out the movement but were routed by the outmanned, religiously inspired Tomochitecos.

The next month formidable army units from two states besieged the village. For a week the heroic defense held, but with the outcome inevitable, the Tomochitecos released their women and children to federal custody, then fought to the last man. Word of these events spread rapidly throughout the republic; Tomochic became a symbol of steadfast struggle by ordinary Mexicans against the oppressive dictatorship of Porfirio Díaz. Today that resistance is enshrined in literature and *corridos* (ballads) as well as school textbooks.

See also **Chihuahua; Mexico: 1810-1910.**

BIBLIOGRAPHY

Heriberto Frías, *Tomochic* (1989).

Paul J. Vanderwood, "None but the Justice of God," in *Patterns of Contention in Mexican History,* by Jaime E. Rodriguez O. (1992), pp. 227–241.

Additional Bibliography

Frías, Heriberto; Barbara Jamison; and Antonio Saborit. *The Battle of Tomochic: Memoirs of a Second Lieutenant.* Oxford: Oxford University Press, 2006.

Frías, Heriberto. *Tomochic.* Mexico City: Editorial Planeta DeAgostini; Consejo Nacional para la Cultura y las Artes, 2004.

Vanderwood, Paul J. *The Power of God against the Guns of the Government: Religious Upheaval in Mexico at the Turn of the Nineteenth Century.* Stanford, CA: Stanford University Press, 1998.

PAUL J. VANDERWOOD

TONINÁ. Toniná is a large center of the Maya classic period (roughly 200–850 CE), located in the Ocosingo Valley in Mexico surrounded by the peaks of the Chiapas highlands. From the plaza below, the acropolis of Toniná appears as a mountainous step pyramid with temples or palaces at every level. There are sequences of seven terraces carved into a steeply rising hillside that leads to the ceremonial core of the site. One of the few highland sites in full classic tradition, Toniná was closely tied to the cultural heartland and may have been a center of trade between the highlands and lowlands of the Ocosingo Valley.

Toniná may have been a provincial city in the Palenque sphere of influence, or perhaps a capital in the southwest highlands of the Maya region in the state of Chiapas, Mexico. Although the art, architecture, and hieroglyphs of Toniná are similar to those of Palenque, its pottery types resemble those of Chiapa de Corzo, to the north and west. From these pottery types the site occupations can be classified into a series of distinctive cultural phases. Toniná also contains

shards from Oaxaca and Mexico, even farther north, linking the classic period of the Maya with the distinct cultural development of the highlands of Mexico.

Unique to Toniná are its fifteen sculptured stelae (there is also one plain stela). The stelae are relatively short (less than 6 feet) and carved in the round. All depict figures with large headdresses and elaborate clothing. Some of the stelae are crudely made or incomplete; some are of rough sandstone. Also unearthed at Toniná were a jade bead with a hieroglyph date incised, jade plaques with grotesque hands carved on both sides, and jade pendants with relief figures. Toniná also has monuments with distinctive glyphs, but they have been little studied. Toniná's distinction among the many Mayan sites is its possession of the very last long-count date on a Maya monument, defining the end of the classic civilization in 909 CE.

First excavated by Pierre Becquelin and Claude Baudez of the French Archaeological Mission to Mexico (1972–1980), the site is presently being excavated by the Mexican Instituto Nacional de Antropología e Historia, directed by Juan Yadeun.

BIBLIOGRAPHY

Pierre Becquelin, Pierre, and Claude F. Baudez. *Toniná, une cité maya du Chiapas (Mexique)*. 4 vols. Mexico: Mission Arquéologique et Ethnologique Française au Méxique, 1979–1982.

Martin, Simon, and Nikolai Grube. *Chronicle of the Maya Kings and Queens: Deciphering the Dynasties of the Ancient Maya*. London: Thames and Hudson, 2002.

RICHARD S. MACNEISH
KARIN FENN

TONTON MACOUTES. Tonton Macoutes (properly Tonton-Makout or Tontonmakout, sing. and pl.), a Haitian term that describes an old folktale character (Uncle Knapsack) who snatches children into a knapsack or basket (*makout*) and often eats them alive. In the late 1950s, Haitians applied this term to the masked goons working for François Duvalier's secret police, a largely middle-class organization set up to control urban opposition.

Although at first the regime denied the existence of the secret police, in 1962 it presented the Volontaires de la Sécurité Nationale (VSN), a new civil militia composed primarily of peasants, as the official version of the dreaded Tonton Macoutes. In fact, although most VSN leaders were members of the political police, most Tonton Macoutes did not formally join the militia as *milisyen*.

Nevertheless, the regime did its best to merge the identification of the two organizations, already linked by leadership. For more than ten years, the secret police operated away from the public eye, which was constantly distracted by a colorful militia whose main role was symbolic. Throughout the 1960s, unarmed *milisyen* showed their support in government-sponsored parades. Their uniform—blue de-nim shirt and pants, straw hat, and a red sash—evoked the traditional costume of the peasant god Zaka, the colors of the Haitian flag before Duvalier, and peasant armies of the nineteenth century.

The secret police grew behind this symbolic shield. So did the power and training of selected groups of *milisyen* who came to constitute a real counterpart to the traditional power of the Haitian army. The regime of Jean-Claude Duvalier (1971–1986) reinforced the links between the most active branches of the political police, the militia, and selected segments of the army devoted to the Duvalier family: the Leopards anti-insurgency corps, the Presidential Guard, the Port-au-Prince police. By the mid-1980s, the 9,000-strong VSN counted members of these various groups. Even some ministers of government wore the VSN uniform.

By the late 1980s, the name Tonton Macoutes applied to *milisyen*, informers, and torturers alike. After the 1987 overthrow of the dictatorship, the ambiguity of the name protected middle-class members of the secret police who had never worn the VSN uniform: summary justice was applied primarily to lower-class folk, at least some of whom had been *milisyen*.

See also **Duvalier, François; Haiti.**

BIBLIOGRAPHY

Bernard Diederich and Al Burt, *Papa Doc: The Truth About Haiti Today* (1969).

Michel-Rolph Trouillot, *Haiti: State Against Nation. The Origins and Legacy of Duvalierism* (1990).

Additional Bibliography

Jean Jacques, Fritz. *Le régime politique haïtien: Une analyse de l'État oligarchique, 1930–1986.* Montréal: Éditions Oracle, 2003.

Michel-Rolph Trouillot

TOPOXTÉ. Topoxté, a Late Postclassic (1250–1500 CE) ceremonial center located on an island of the same name in the southwestern part of Lake Yaxha, in the northeastern Petén, Guatemala. It is the most important site of a cluster of three contemporaneous island occupations that constitute a large and complex Late Postclassic Maya settlement: adjacent islands are Paxté, with an elite residential and ceremonial settlement, and the larger Cante, with over 100 primarily residential structures.

Topoxté, the eastern and largest island, has elite ceremonial architecture and ceramics. Its temple assemblage—a tall masonry temple, a perpendicular open hall, and two shrines within the plaza that are aligned with the main axis of the temple—stands on the highest point of the island. There are 100 house platforms on the island. The most notable ceramics are effigy censers, ritual pottery, and a red-on-cream decorated type.

This defensive island grouping is part of a network of occupations in the lacustrine environments of the central Petén prior to the Spanish conquest. The architectural data of Topoxté show striking similarities to a center site, Mayapán, in the Yucatán of Mexico; and ceramic censers are similar to contemporaneous pottery from the Yucatán. However, the archaeological culture of the site is also related to the elite culture of regional Petén centers. Topoxté and its neighboring islands form one of several defensive settlements in the lake region of the Petén, suggesting that there were competitive sociopolitical groups in the area prior to the Spanish conquest.

See also **Maya, The; Mesoamerica.**

BIBLIOGRAPHY

William Rotch Bullard, Jr., "Topoxté, a Postclassic Maya Site in Petén, Guatemala," in *Monographs and Papers in Maya Archaeology,* edited by William Rotch Bullard, Jr., Papers of the Peabody Museum of Archaeology and Ethnology, vol. 61 (1970).

Jay K. Johnson, "Postclassic Maya Site Structure at Topoxté, El Petén, Guatemala," in *The Lowland Maya Postclassic,* edited by Arlen F. Chase and Prudence M. Rice (1985), pp. 151–165.

Prudence M. Rice and Don S. Rice, "Topoxté, Manache, and the Central Petén Postclassic," in *The Lowland Maya Postclassic,* edited by Arlen F. Chase and Prudence M. Rice (1985), pp. 166–183.

Additional Bibliography

Evans, Susan Toby. *Ancient Mexico & Central America: Archaeology and Culture History.* London: Thames and Hudson, 2004.

Wurster, Wolfgang W., ed. *El sitio Maya de Topoxté: Investigaciones en una isla del Lago Yaxhá, Petén, Guatemala.* Mainz am Rhein: P. von Zabern: KAVA, 2000.

EUGENIA F. ROBINSON

TOQUI. Toqui, the term applied to Araucanian (Mapuche) military leaders during the warfare that followed the Spanish invasion of Chile in the 1540s. It seems likely that Europeans imposed their own categories of leadership and government on the Araucanian warriors who were most prominent in the wars. In traditional Araucanian society, the *toqui* was less a "generalissimo" or "paramount chief" than a temporary leader chosen by alliances of families to take charge of fighting against other alliances or to supervise communal economic tasks such as pine nut collection or fishing. Lautaro (1535–1557), Caupolicán (*d.* 1558), and Colo Colo (1515–1561), celebrated *toquis* of the sixteenth century, may have had their true status magnified by such poets as Alonso de Ercilla y Zúñiga (1533–1594). To what extent the pressure of the Spanish offensives caused greater concentration of authority among Araucanians is still debated. No centralized state with single leadership ever emerged in Araucania.

See also **Araucanians; Indigenous Peoples; Mapuche.**

BIBLIOGRAPHY

León Echaiz, René. *El toqui Lautaro.* Santiago: Editorial Neupert, 1971.

SIMON COLLIER

TORDESILLAS, TREATY OF (1494). The Treaty of Tordesillas was an agreement between Spain and Portugal that divided administration of their overseas territories. The Papal Donation of Alexander VI in 1493 had conferred to the crown of Castile jurisdiction over newly discovered lands 100 leagues "to the west and south of the so-called Azore and Cape Verde Islands" that were not already under the control of a Christian prince. For reasons still disputed, the Portuguese protested what came to be known as the Line of Demarcation and demanded a meeting to discuss the issue. Negotiators convened at the small town of Tordesillas to the north of Medina del Campo in Spain and reached an agreement that extended Portuguese jurisdiction a full 270 leagues farther west (between 48 and 49 degrees west of Greenwich). The treaty, enacted on 7 June 1494, provided the Portuguese with the legal claim to a large strip of the Brazilian coast, subsequently discovered during the expedition of Pedro Álvares Cabral in 1500.

See also **Cabral, Pedro Álvares.**

BIBLIOGRAPHY

Carvalho, Carlos Delgado de. *História diplomática do Brasil.* Brasília: Senado Federal, 1998.

Davenport, Frances G. *European Treaties Bearing on the History of the United States and Its Dependencies.* Washington, DC: Carnegie Institute of Washington, 1917–1937. Repr. The Lawbook Exchange, 2004. See pp. 2, 84–100.

Harrisse, Henry. *The Diplomatic History of America: Its First Chapter 1452–1493–1494.* London: B.F. Stevens, 1897. See pp. 70–102.

Jornadas Americanistas. *El tratado de Tordesillas y su proyección,* 2 vols. Valladolid: Universidad de Valladolid, Seminario de Historia de América, 1973.

McAlister, Lyle N. *Spain and Portugal in the New World: 1492–1700* Minneapolis: University of Minnesota Press, 1984.

NOBLE DAVID COOK

TORNEL Y MENDÍVIL, JOSÉ MARÍA (1794?–1853). José María Tornel y Mendívil (*b.* 1794?; *d.* 11 September 1853), Mexican politician and general. Born in Orizaba, Veracruz, Tornel joined the insurgency in 1813. Captured and sentenced to death, he survived the War of Independence, becoming private secretary to Antonio López de Santa Anna (1821) and to President Guadalupe Victoria (1824–1829). In his later career, Tornel occupied many other posts, serving as governor of the Federal District (1833–1834) and as minister of war on several occasions. One of Santa Anna's most devoted supporters, Tornel was always closely associated with him and often acted as his spokesman. A man of great energy, he instituted many reforms in the army and was a prolific author on political issues, a translator of Byron, and a playwright. Fervently interested in education, Tornel promoted the Lancasterian system (involving advanced students as monitors) and was director of the Colegio de Minería from 1843 to 1853.

See also **Mexico, Federal District; Mexico, Wars and Revolutions: War of Independence.**

BIBLIOGRAPHY

William Martin Fowler, "José María Tornel: Mexican General/Politician (1794–1853) (Ph.D. diss., University of Bristol, 1994).

Additional Bibliography

Fowler, Will. "Dreams of Stability: Mexican Political Thought During the 'Forgotten Years.' An Analysis of the Beliefs of the Creole Intelligentsia (1821–1853)." *Bulletin of Latin American Research* 14 (September 1993): 287–312.

Fowler, Will. *Tornel and Santa Anna: The Writer and the Caudillo, Mexico, 1795–1853.* Westport, CT: Greenwood Press, 2000.

Vázquez Mantecón, María del Carmen. *La palabra del poder: Vida pública de José Maria Tornel, 1795–1853.* Mexico City: Universidad Nacional Autónoma de México, 1997.

MICHAEL P. COSTELOE

TORNQUIST, ERNESTO (1842–1908). Ernesto Tornquist (*b.* 31 December 1842; *d.* 17 June 1908), founder of one of the first and most important industrial investment banks in Latin America. Tornquist played a major part in the financial development of Argentina in the last quarter of the nineteenth century. Born in Buenos Aires into a mercantile family of Swedish origin, he studied in a German-speaking school and entered the family firm of Altgelt, Ferber, and Co. in 1859. In 1874 he became the senior partner in the firm, which was henceforth called Ernesto Tornquist and Co. The history of the company was marked by steady growth over fifty years, leading the way in Buenos Aires in the fields of international and industrial finance. Tornquist and Co. was the agent for Baring Brothers in Buenos Aires from the 1880s until 1902, as well as representative for prominent Belgian, German, and French banks. Tornquist personally promoted the establishment of the first sugar refinery in Argentina, established in the city of Rosario in 1887; the largest Argentine meat-packing firm, the Sansinena Company; and several of the first metallurgical and chemical firms in the Argentine capital. He was a close financial adviser to the governments of Julio Roca, Carlos Pellegrini, and other conservative leaders at the turn of the century, participating in most of the important monetary and financial reforms of the time. His firm today is a prominent commercial bank in Buenos Aires.

See also **Argentina: The Nineteenth Century; Banking: Overview.**

BIBLIOGRAPHY

Ernesto Tornquist & Co., 1874–1924 (1924).

Additional Bibliography

Gallo, Ezequiel. *Carlos Pellegrini: Orden y reforma.* Buenos Aires: Fondo de Cultura Económica, 1997.

Gilbert, Jorge. *Empresario y empresa en la Argentina moderna: El Grupo Tornquist, 1873–1930.* Victoria, Pcia. de Buenos Aires: Universidad de San Andrés, 2002.

CARLOS MARICHAL

TORO, DAVID (1898–1977). David Toro (*b.* 24 June 1898; *d.* 25 July 1977), president of Bolivia (1936–1937). Born in Sucre, Toro rose from military cadet to chief of staff during the Chaco War. Together with army officer Germán Busch he overthrew the civilian president José Luis Tejada Sorzano in May 1936, and Toro became president. Toro initiated a nationalistic government of "state syndicalism" and "military socialism," which included tax and banking reforms and the establishment of syndicates (unions) that all interest groups were expected to join. The possessions of the Standard Oil Company of New Jersey were nationalized and the Bolivian state oil monopoly (Yacimientos Petroliferos Fiscales

Bolivianos—YPFB), still an important Bolivian agency, was established. Nearly all other social and economic changes were unsuccessful, but a pivotal accomplishment of the Toro period was a decree granting women total equality in all endeavors. The Toro presidency was the very beginning of the great changes that took place in Bolivia after the Chaco War. In July 1937 Busch took over the presidency in a bloodless coup. As ex-president, Toro remained moderately active in government and civic affairs.

See also **Bolivia: Since 1825; Chaco War; Tejada Sorzano, José Luis.**

BIBLIOGRAPHY

Quién es quién en Bolivia (1942).

Porfirio Diaz Machicao, *Toro, Busch, Quintanilla, 1936–1940* (1957).

Carlos D. Mesa Gisbert, *Presidentes de Bolivia: Entre urnas y fusiles* (1990).

Additional Bibliography

Durán S., Juan Carlos. *Germán Busch y los orígenes de la revolución nacional: Fragmentos para una biografía.* La Paz: Honorable Senado Nacional, 1999.

Taboada Terán, Néstor. *Tierra mártir: Del socialismo de David Toro al socialismo de Evo Morales.* Bolivia: s.n., 2006.

CHARLES W. ARNADE

TORO, FERMÍN (1806–1865). Fermín Toro (*b.* 14 June 1806; *d.* 23 December 1865), Venezuelan intellectual, politician, and diplomat. Toro entered public life as a functionary in the ministry of finance in 1828. In 1831 he was a representative in Congress. He was appointed by the regime of José Antonio Páez to preside over the commission charged with bestowing funerary honors on Simón Bolívar's remains when they were repatriated to Caracas. He provided an important synthesis of his economic ideas in his *Reflexiones sobre la ley del 10 de abril de 1834* (1845). He was the secretary of Alejo Fortique, Venezuela's minister plenipotentiary to Great Britain (1839–1846), in London (1839–1841) as well as minister plenipotentiary in New Granada and then in Spain, France, and England in 1846–1847.

During the first years of the José Tadeo Monagas regime, Toro was minister of finance. But as a representative in Congress, he confronted Monagas after the January 1848 assault on Congress. When Monagas was overthrown in 1858, Toro again became politically active, assuming the posts of minister of finance and minister of foreign affairs under President Julián Castro. He was a member of the Valencia Convention in 1858 before retiring from public life and devoting himself to his research in botany, anthropology, and linguistics.

See also **Monagas, José Tadeo; Páez, José Antonio.**

BIBLIOGRAPHY

See Augusto Mijares, *Libertad y justicia social en el pensamiento do Don Fermín Toro* (1947); Virgilio Tosta, *Fermín Toro; Político y sociólogo de la armonía* (1958); José Antonio De Armas Chitty, *Fermín Toro y su época* (1966). A selection of Toro's most important writings are in *Fermín Toro: La doctrina conservadora.*

Additional Bibliography

Arratia, Alejandro. *Etica y democracia en Fermín Toro.* Caracas: Monte Avila Editores, 1993.

Carrillo Batalla, Tomás Enrique. *Historia del pensamiento económico de Fermín Toro.* Caracas: Fuentes para la Historia Republicana de Venezuela, 1998.

Edición homenaje a la memoria de Fermín Toro: Símbolo y ejemplo del diputado de Venezuela. Caracas: Congreso de la República, Ediciones de la Cámara de Diputados, 1996.

INÉS QUINTERO

TORO ZAMBRANO, MATEO DE (1727–1811). Mateo de Toro Zambrano (*b.* 20 September 1727; *d.* 26 February 1811), president of the first national government of Chile (1810–1811). One of the great creole magnates of eighteenth-century Chile, and certainly one of the richest, Toro Zambrano played a full part in the public life of the colony, as militia officer, *alcalde* (mayor) and *corregidor* (municipal magistrate) of Santiago, lieutenant to the governor (1768), and as a member of the committee that disposed of the expropriated properties of the Jesuits after their expulsion in 1767 (he acquired one of the largest Jesuit haciendas). King Charles III conferred on him the title of Conde de la Conquista in 1770.

The crisis of the Spanish empire after 1808 thrust Toro Zambrano into an unexpected role: in July 1810, following the deposition of the Spanish governor Francisco Antonio García Carrasco (1742–1813), To-ro Zambrano became interim governor of the colony. Creole patriots agitating for a national junta persuaded him (partly through his confessor) to agree to a *cabildo abierto* (open town meeting) on 18 September 1810. At this historic assembly a junta was elected with Toro Zambrano as president. He played little part in the work of the new government, and sometimes fell asleep at its meetings. Greatly affected by his wife's death in January 1811, he died soon after.

See also **Charles III of Spain.**

BIBLIOGRAPHY

Jaime Eyzaguirre, *El conde de la Conquista* (1951; 2d ed., 1966).

Additional Bibliography

Gutiérrez Lobos, Víctor. *Los Presidentes de Chile.* Santiago: Zig-Zag, 1993.

Reyno Gutiérrez, Manuel. *Mateo de Toro y Zambrano.* Santiago: La Nación, 1985.

SIMON COLLIER

TORQUEMADA, JUAN DE (c. 1562–1624).

Juan de Torquemada (*b.* c. 1562; *d.* 1 January 1624), Franciscan missionary and historian. Passages in Torquemada's major work, *Monarquía indiana* (Indian Monarchy), lead us to believe that he was born in Spain. He was ordained around 1587 and held several important positions in the Franciscan order. Torquemada was the chronicler of the order, a guardian in Santiago de Tlatelolco and Tlaxcala, and provincial of the Holy Gospel. The *Monarquía indiana* comprises observations on the daily life of the colony and descriptions of Nezahualpilli's and Motecuhzoma's palaces and other archaeological remains, as well as writings on the pre-Hispanic period that built on the work of such Franciscan historians and linguists as Andrés de Olmos, Bernardino de Sahagún, and Jerónimo de Mendieta. Torquemada also consulted Indian codices and maps and the work of the mestizo historians Fernando de Alva Ixtlilxóchitl and Diego Muñoz Camargo; he followed the ethnographic tradition of Olmos and Sahagún of drawing testimonies from Indian informants. This variety of sources has led critics to refer to Torquemada as the "chronicler of chroniclers."

See also **Franciscans; Sahagún, Bernardino de.**

BIBLIOGRAPHY

Howard Francis Cline, *Torquemada and His Franciscan Predecessors: Further Notes on Sources and Usages in the Monarquía Indiana* (1969).

Juan De Torquemada, *Monarquía indiana,* 7 vols. (1975–1983), esp. vol. 7, which is a collection of studies of Torquemada and the *Monarquía indiana.*

Additional Bibliography

Baudot, Georges. *Utopia and History in Mexico: The First Chronicles of Mexican Civilization, 1520–1569.* Niwot: University Press of Colorado, 1995.

Moreno Toscano, Alejandra. *Fray Juan de Torquemada y su Monarquía Indiana.* Xalapa: Universidad Veracruzana, 1963.

JOSÉ RABASA

TORRE, LISANDRO DE LA (1868–1939).

Lisandro de la Torre was an Argentine statesman, political leader, and advocate of popularly elected local government. De la Torre was born on December 6, 1868, in Rosario, Santa Fe, to a landowner father and a mother who descended from one of Argentina's oldest families. He studied law at the University of Buenos Aires during a time of political ferment, graduating in 1886. In 1888 he published a thesis, *El regimen municipal,* comparing models of municipal government in the Western world. He participated in the political demonstration at El Parque in 1889 (Revolución del Parque), organized by students and reform-minded youths. He joined the Civic Union (soon to become the Unión Cívica Radical [UCR]) of Leandro Alem and Aristóbulo Del Valle in the three aborted revolutions of 1890, 1891, and 1893, which aimed to overthrow the conservative oligarchic regime of that time and reform Argentine politics. De la Torre broke with the UCR over political strategy and fought a duel with Hipólito Irigoyen in 1895, after which the two remained lifelong antagonists.

In 1908 de la Torre, a successful cattle breeder in Sante Fe, founded the Liga del Sur (League of the South), an agrarian political party, to reform local government. In 1911 he won a seat in the Sante Fe legislature. In 1914 he founded the Partido demó-crata Progresista (Progressive Democratic Party; PDP) as an alternative to Irigoyen's UCR, which in some provinces was gaining on the entrenched oligarchic governments. As presidential candidate for the PDP in the 1916 first truly national demo-cratic elections, de la Torre tried to unite reform-minded conservatives and progressives against Irigoyen's populist campaign. In a three-way race, de la Torre was abandoned by key conservatives, and Irigoyen won the election by the narrowest of margins. De la Torre served in the chamber of deputies from 1912 to 1916 and from 1922 to 1926, and in the senate from 1932 to 1937. A spellbinding orator, he fought for land reform, sep-aration of church and state, female suffrage, civil divorce, and increased production by domestic industries. He is best remembered for his passionate defense of Argentine meat-packing plants against the famous Roca-Runciman pact of 1933, which gave extraordinary benefits to British meat-packing plants, and for his intense debate with Monseñor Gustavo Franceschi, a conservative defender of tra-ditional Catholicism.

In 1932 de la Torre was defeated in his quest for the presidency as candidate of the Democratic Alliance (PDP and Socialist Party). Defeats suffered in the senate at the hands of conservatives, the assas-sination in the senate chamber of his close political ally, Senator Enzo Bordabehere, while the two were investigating governmental fraud in the meat trade, and the failure of his ranch in the arid western prov-ince of La Rioja led de la Torre to despondency. He resigned his seat in the senate, and on January 5, 1939, he committed suicide in Buenos Aires. His writings are collected *Obras* (1952). De la Torre is remembered as a politician with strong democratic and nationalistic principles who fought against the electoral fraud of the conservative governments that followed the coup of 1930. The PDP still runs for elections in several districts of Argentina as a minor party.

See also **Argentina: The Twentieth Century; Argentina, Political Parties: Progressive Democratic Party;** **Argentina, Political Parties: Radical Party (UCR); Irigoyen, Hipólito; Roca-Runciman Pact (1933).**

BIBLIOGRAPHY

Alonso, Paula. *Between Revolution and the Ballot Box: The Origins of the Argentine Radical Party in the 1890s.* Cambridge, U.K., and New York: Cambridge University Press, 2000.

Amaral, Edgardo L. *Anecdotario de Lisandro de la Torre y Debate sobre el comunismo.* Buenos Aires: Comisión Nacional de Homenaje a Lisandro de la Torre, 1957.

Donghi, Tulio Halperin. *Vida y Muerte de la República Verdadera.* Buenos Aires: Ariel, 1999.

Dorn, Georgette Magassy. *Idealism versus Reality: The Failure of an Argentine Political Leader, Lisandro de la Torre.* Ph.D. diss., Georgetown University, 1981.

Larra, Raúl. *Lisandro de la Torre: Vida y drama del solitario de Pinas.* Buenos Aires: Claridad, 1942.

Vigo, Juan M. *De la Torre contra todos.* Buenos Aires: Nativa, 1974.

Yasky, Samuel. *Lisandro de la Torre de Cerca: Los momentos culminantes de su vida política.* Buenos Aires: Metrópolis, 1969.

GEORGETTE MAGASSY DORN
VICENTE PALERMO

TORRE, MIGUEL DE LA (?–1838).

Miguel de la Torre (*d.* 1838), Spanish general. Torre led Spanish troops against Simón Bolívar and revolutionary armies in the wars for Venezue-lan and Colombian independence. Following a six-month armistice between General Pablo Morillo y Morillo and Bolívar, the Spanish crown gave Torre command of royalist troops. The two sides fought at the Battle of Carabobo, in Venezuela on 24 June 1821. The deaths of between 1,000 and 1,500 Spanish soldiers assured Venezuelan and Colom-bian independence; historians called it the "Colom-bian Waterloo." Torre fled to Puerto Cabello where he surrendered two years later. He was appointed civil and military governor of Puerto Rico in 1823 and named count of Torrepando.

BIBLIOGRAPHY

José Dominique Díaz and Miguel De La Torre, *Mémoires du Général Morillo* (1826).

Irene Nicholson, *The Liberators: A Study of Independence Movements in Spanish America* (1969), pp. 190–193.

Donna Keyse Rudolph, *Historical Dictionary of Venezuela* (1971), p. 111.

Additional Bibliography

Altagracia, Carlos D. "La utopía del territorio perfectamente gobernado: Miedo y poder en la época de Miguel de La Torre, 1823–1837." M.A. thesis, University of Puerto Rico, 1997.

Pérez Tenreiro, Tomás. *Don Miguel de la Torre y Pando.* Valencia: Edición publicada por el Ejecutivo del Estado Carabobo en el Sesquicentenario de la Batalla, 1971.

CHRISTOPHER T. BOWEN

TORREJÓN Y VELASCO, TOMÁS DE

(?–1728). Tomás de Torrejón y Velasco (baptized 23 December 1644; *d.* 23 April 1728), Spanish composer active in Peru. Torrejón y Velasco may have been born in Villarrobledo, Albacete, Spain. He was the son of one of Philip IV's huntsmen and spent his childhood in Fuencarral, becoming a page in the palace of Don Pedro Fernández de Castro, the count of Lemos. Named viceroy of Peru in 1667, the count brought the twenty-three-year-old Torrejón with him to America. From 1667 until 1672 Torrejón worked in Lima's armory as superintendent and later as magistrate and chief justice of Chachapoyas Province. Torrejón's musical career in Lima started on 1 January 1676, when he was named *maestro de capilla* of Lima's cathedral, a position he retained until his death fifty-two years later. Lima was the center of South America's musical life at that time and Torrejón became its leading figure. To celebrate the installation of the second grand organ of the cathedral, eight polychoral *villancicos* composed by Torrejón were performed. His fame spread to Cuzco, Trujillo, and Guatemala, and was enhanced after the premiere of his memorial vespers for Charles II in June 1701. That same year his opera *La púrpura de la rosa*, with a libretto by Pedro Calderón de la Barca, was lavishly premiered at the viceroyal palace on 19 October. It had been commissioned by the new viceroy, the count of Monclova, to celebrate Philip V's eighteenth birthday. As the first operatic work written and produced in the

New World, *La púrpura de la rosa* is of great musicological significance. It has a semimythological plot, based on the story of Venus and Adonis but with popular Spanish characters added. The vast collection of Torrejón's religious music is kept in the archives in Lima, Cuzco, and Guatemala. He died in Lima.

See also **Peru: From the Conquest Through Independence.**

BIBLIOGRAPHY

Robert Stevenson, *The Music of Peru* (1960), and *Torrejón y Velasco: La púrpura de la rosa* (1976).

Gérard Béhague, *Music in Latin America* (1979); *New Grove Dictionary of Music and Musicians,* vol. 19 (1980).

Additional Bibliography

Cardona de Gibert, Angeles, Don William Cruickshank, and Martin D. Cunningham, eds. *La púrpura de la rosa.* Kassel: Reichenberger, 1990.

SUSANA SALGADO

TORRE NILSSON, LEOPOLDO (1924–

1978). Born in Buenos Aires on May 15, 1924, director Leopoldo Torre Nilsson (nickname "Babsy") was renowned as one of the leading participants in the first wave of New Argentine Cinema. The new cinema "movement" emerged in Argentina in the 1950s, sparked in part by the interest of spectators in more socially engaged and internationally aware topics, and in part by the interaction with European postwar vanguard movements (such as Italian neo-realism). These forces inspired the move away from industrial, actor-driven, studio-produced film (particularly the Hollywood model), and toward independently produced cinema with "auteurist" tendencies: films with narrative and aesthetic complexity, and increased technical proficiency.

Nilsson's father was director Leopoldo Torre Ríos, who worked during the classical period (the 1930s and 1940s) of Argentine cinema, giving Torre Nilsson an entrée into the movie industry. In the 1940s he worked as an assistant to his father and also scripted a number of his films, and in the 1950s studied cinema in Europe, thus gaining both practical experience and formal education in film-making. While he did have European training, and in fact was criticized by his New Cinema peers for making films that were bourgeois and European in orientation (as distinct from their own more politically oriented films representing the experience of the Argentine lower classes), Torre Nilsson was committed to developing an authentically Argentinean form of cinematic expression representing specifically Argentine experience.

Torre Nilsson was married to writer Beatriz Guido, and many of his films were based on her novels and short stories, as well as being co-scripted by her. *La casa del ángel* (1957), his ninth film and their first collaboration, was based on one of Guido's novels, and was the first Argentine film to win international acclaim; this was the film that catapulted Torre Nilsson to fame and initiated the period of his most well-known and highly praised work, from 1957 to 1962. Speaking of *La casa del ángel*, the novelist and critic Ernesto Schoo observes, "local spectators soon discovered that a film that spoke of our social myths, of our prejudices and our fears, of the roots of many ancient wrongs could also be made here. Without hypocrisy, without fear, without emphatic moral lessons, without paternalistic speeches" [author translation]. Whereas Guido's stories tend to focus on the loss of innocence and the moral corruption of the privileged classes, Torre Nilsson's films are characterized by innovative camera work and stylistic experimentation.

Torre Nilsson continued making films until his death on September 8, 1978. His subject matter went well beyond the Argentine bourgeoisie and old aristocracy, while still focusing on Argentine culture and experience. A number of his films, particularly from the late 1960s on, were either adaptations of the works of Argentine authors or stories grounded in historical experience. Among them are *Martín Fierro* (1968), a Western based on the nineteenth-century national epic poem; *El Santo de la espada* (1970), adapted from the Ricardo Rojas (1882–1957) novel on José de San Martín, the liberator of Argentina, Chile, and Peru; *Los siete locos* (1973), based on novels by Roberto Arlt; *Boquitas pintadas* (1974) from the novel by Manuel Puig; and the films *La maffia* (1972) and *El pibe cabeza* (1975) about gangsters in 1920s and 1930s Argentina. These films did not receive the acclaim of those he made in the late 1950s and early 1960s. Nevertheless his commitment to independence and originality has had a notable impact on younger generations of Argentine filmmakers.

See also **Cinema: From the Silent Film to 1990; Cinema Novo; Guido, Beatriz.**

BIBLIOGRAPHY

Esplugas, Celia. "Power and Gender: Film Feminism in *Boquitas pintadas.*" *CiberLetras* 3 (August 2000). Available from http://www.lehman.cuny.edu/ciberletras/.

Schoo, Ernesto. "Los magos del gótico criollo." *La Nación* (Buenos Aires), March 13, 2002, Suplemento Cultura. Available from http://www.lanacion.com.ar/220264.

Willcham, Marcelo. "Literatura y cine argentinos: Autoritarismo y testimonio en Beatriz Guido y Leopoldo Torre Nilsson." *Dissertation Abstracts International, Section A: The Humanities and Social Sciences* 58, no. 6 (1997): 2233–2234.

Selected Filmography

La casa del ángel (1957); Palme d'Or nomination, Cannes Film Festival, 1957

La caida (1959); Best Film, Argentinean Film Critics Association, 1960; Golden Bear nomination, Berlin Film Festival, 1959

Fin de fiesta (1960); Golden Bear nomination, Berlin, 1960

La mano en la trampa (1961); Prix de la Critique Internationale/F.I.P.R.E.S.C.I. Prize, Palme d'Or nomination, Cannes, 1961

Setenta veces siete (1962); Palme d'Or nomination, Cannes, 1962

La terraza (1963); Golden Bear nomination, Berlin, 1963

El ojo de la cerradura (1964); Best Film, Argentinean Film Critics Association, 1967

La chica del lunes (1967); Palme d'Or, Cannes, 1967

Martín Fierro (1968); Best Film, Argentinean Film Critics Association, 1969

La maffia (1972); Best Film, Argentinean Film Critics Association, 1973

Los siete locos (1973); Silver Bear, Golden Bear nomination, Berlin, 1973

Boquitas pintadas (1974); Concha de oro, Special Jury Prize, San Sebastián International Film Festival, 1974

CARYN C. CONNELLY

TORREÓN. Torreón, city in southwestern Coahuila, Mexico, on the Nazas and Aguanaval rivers, in the heart of the Comarca Laguna.

In the colonial era, the future site of Torreón was part of the Marquesado of San Miguel de Aguayo, but after Mexican independence the area passed through a number of different owners. In the mid-nineteenth century the area gave rise to a small ranch community, which expanded rapidly with the arrival of the Mexican Central Railroad in 1883. Five years later the International Railroad also passed through Torreón, linking it to Durango and Piedras Negras, and Torreón received villa status in 1893. With the arrival of the Coahuila and Pacific Railroad in 1903, Torreón became the third largest railroad center in Mexico. It was recognized as a city in 1907.

Torreón was strategically important in the Mexican Revolution and formed the geographical core of Francisco Madero's Antireelectionist movement. On 14–15 May 1911, Torreón was the site of one of the bloodiest massacres in the history of the revolution when forces loyal to Madero occupied the city. In the confusion that followed, there erupted a race riot in which over two hundred fifty Chinese were murdered. On 1 October 1913 Francisco Villa took the city after two days of fierce fighting against Victoriano Huerta's Federalist troops. Villa retook the city in early April 1914. Today, Torreón is a large urban and industrial city with a population of 328,086 (1980).

See also **Huerta, Victoriano; Madero, Francisco Indalecio; Mexico, Wars and Revolutions: Mexican Revolution.**

BIBLIOGRAPHY

William K. Meyers, "La Comaraca Lagunera: Work, Protest, and Popular Mobilization in North Central Mexico," in *Other Mexicos: Essays on Regional Mexican History, 1876–1911*, edited by Thomas Benjamin and William McNellie (1984), pp. 243–274.

Alan Knight, *The Mexican Revolution*, vol. 1, *Porfirians, Liberals and Peasants* (1986), esp. pp. 207–210, 278–279, 321–322, 424–426.

Additional Bibliography

Coerver, Don M. *Mexico: An Encyclopedia of Contemporary Culture and History.* Santa Barbara: ABC-CLIO, 2004.

Day-MacLeod, Dierdre, and Roger E. Hernández. *The States of Northern Mexico.* Philadelphia: Mason Crest Publishers, 2003.

Hernández Chávez, Alicia. *Mexico: a Brief History.* Berkeley: University of California Press, 2006.

Pasztor, Suzanne B. *The Spirit of Hidalgo: The Mexican Revolution in Coahuila.* East Lansing: Michigan State University Press, 2002.

AARON PAINE MAHR

TORRES, JUAN JOSÉ (1921–1976). Juan José Torres (*b.* 1921; *d.* 1976), army officer and president of Bolivia (1970–1971). Born in Cochabamba, Torres was a career soldier. He stayed in the armed forces even during the 1952–1964 rule of the Movimiento Nacionalista Revolucionario (MNR) following the Bolivian National Revolution, in spite of the fact that in his youth he had belonged to the Bolivian Socialist Falange (FSB), a fascist-oriented party and bitter enemy of the MNR. Torres was a co-conspirator in the overthrow of MNR leader President Víctor Paz Estenssoro in November 1964, and held important posts in the succeeding military regime. He was in command of the army unit that in 1967 suppressed the guerrilla operation of Ernesto "Che" Guevara.

When General Alfredo Ovando overthrew President Luis Adolfo Siles Salinas in September 1969, General Torres became commander in chief of the armed forces. In that position, he supported the "nationalist" position of Ovando. However, in July 1970 he was forced to resign the post because of pressure from right-wing army leaders. When right-wing officers forced the resignation of President Ovando early in October 1970, General Torres emerged as president, with the support of the leadership of the Central Obrera Boliviana (COB), the national labor confederation. Torres presided over a "nationalist" and "leftist" regime. He cancelled the U.S. Steel concession on the Matilda zinc mine and expelled the Peace Corps from Bolivia.

The COB and leftist parties organized the so-called Popular Assembly, which sought to play the role of the 1917 Russian soviets, but it was not granted any official power by Torres. The COB refused several official invitations from Torres to join his administration. In August 1971, Colonel Hugo

Banzer Suárez, former head of the Military College, led a conspiracy that ousted Torres, who fled to Argentina, where he was assassinated in 1976.

See also **Bolivia, Organizations: Bolivian Workers Central (COB); Bolivia, Political Parties: Bolivian Socialist Falange (FSB); Ovando Candía, Alfredo.**

BIBLIOGRAPHY

Guillermo Lora, *A History of the Brazilian Labor Movement* (1977).

Additional Bibliography

Wagner, Maria Luise. "Reformism in the Bolivian Armed Forces: Juan José Torres, a Case Study." Ph.D. diss., Georgetown University, 1986.

ROBERT J. ALEXANDER

TORRES, LUIS EMETERIO (1844–1935).

Luis Emeterio Torres (*b.* 1844; *d.* 1935), governor and military commander. A veteran of the war against the French intervention and postwar political revolts in Sinaloa, Torres used the ties he cultivated with the notables of Álamos (southern Sonora) and with Porfirio Díaz (while a federal deputy) to secure leadership of a political circle that rose to power in Sonora in the late 1870s and controlled the state until 1911. Though he was elected governor five times (uniquely retaining alternation during the Porfiriato), his principal associates—Ramón Corral and Rafael Izábal—were the administrative and legislative directors. Torres managed political relations within the state and with Mexico City; after 1887 he served as commander of Baja California and then of the entire Northwest military zone. Torres embodied the Porfirista ideal of promoting progress and order: Apache raids were terminated; Yaqui Indian autonomy ended (partly through the use of deportation); economic activity markedly expanded; all political opposition was suppressed.

See also **Corral Verdugo, Ramón; Díaz, Porfirio.**

BIBLIOGRAPHY

Stuart F. Voss, "Towns and Enterprise in Northwestern Mexico: A History of Urban Elites in Sonora and Sinaloa, 1830–1910" (Ph.D. diss., Harvard University, 1972).

Francisco R. Almada, *Diccionario de historia, geografía y biografía de sonorenses* (1983).

Ramón Eduardo Ruiz, *The People of Sonora and Yankee Capitalists* (1988).

Additional Bibliography

Tinker Salas, Miguel. *In the Shadow of the Eagles: Sonora and the Transformation of the Border during the Porfiriato.* Berkeley and Los Angeles: University of California Press, 1997.

STUART F. VOSS

TORRES BELLO, DIEGO DE (1551–1638).

Diego de Torres Bello (*b.* 1551; *d.* 1638), Jesuit founder and first provincial of the Paraguay missions. Born in Villalpando, Castile, Torres joined the Society of Jesus and in 1581 was sent to work in Peru. He served for a few years as superior of the mission in Juli, near Lake Titicaca, then as superior of the Jesuit colleges in Cuzco, Quito, and Potosí. The Juli mission later served as a model for the Paraguay missions. In 1604 Paraguay and Chile were created as a separate Jesuit province, and Torres Bello was designated the first provincial. He set up his residence in Córdoba, Argentina, where he founded the novitiate as well as a seminary, which later became a university. Determined to protect the Indians from the Spaniards, he won approval for his plan to gather the former into mission towns, or "reductions." The first of these missions was founded in 1609; by the eighteenth century there were thirty. Torres Bello laid out the basic norms for the missions in a list of eighteen recommendations. Proficient in Aymara, Quechua, and Guaraní, he personally oversaw the building of the first missions. He finished his term as provincial in 1615, and spent his latter days working in the colleges of Buenos Aires and Chuquisaca, and in the missions among the Indians. He died in Chuquisaca.

See also **Jesuits; Missions: Jesuit Missions (Reducciones).**

BIBLIOGRAPHY

Rubén Vargas Ugarte, *Historia de la Compañía de Jesús en el Perú*, vol. 1 (1963).

Philip Caraman, *The Lost Paradise: The Jesuit Republic in South America*, 2d ed. (1990).

Silvio Palacios and Ena Zoffoli, *Gloria y tragedia de las misiones guaraníes* (1991).

JEFFREY KLAIBER

TORRES BODET, JAIME (1902–1974).

Jaime Torres Bodet (*b.* 17 April 1902; *d.* 15 May 1974), Mexican poet and public figure. Torres Bodet, who published his first book at age sixteen, distinguished himself as a preparatory student and became a protégé of José Vasconcelos at nineteen. He joined the Ateneo de la Juventud in 1918 with other budding intellectual figures, many of whom established the major literary circle known as the "Contemporáneos" in the late 1920s. The prototypical Mexican intellectual of his age, Torres Bodet became a major figure in the public world of international and educational affairs. A professor at the National University, he twice served as secretary of education (1943–1946 and 1958–1964). In foreign affairs, after a long career in the diplomatic service, including posts as ambassador to France and Italy, he became secretary of foreign relations (1946–1948) and secretary general of UNESCO in 1948. Awarded the National Prize for Literature in 1966, he left a monumental four-volume memoir.

See also **Ateneo de la Juventud (Athenaeum of Youth).**

BIBLIOGRAPHY

Jaime Torres Bodet, *Obras Escogidas* (1961).

Emmanuel Carballo, *Jaime Torres Bodet* (1968).

Sonja P. Karsen, *Jaime Torres Bodet* (1971).

Guillermo Sheridan, *Los contemporáneos ayer* (1985).

Additional Bibliography

Curiel, Fernando, ed. *Casi oficios: Cartas cruzadas entre Jaime Torres Bodet y Alfonso Reyes, 1922–1959.* Mexico City: Colegio de México, Centro de Estudios Lingüísticos y Literarios: Colegio Nacional, 1994.

Olea-Franco, Rafael, and Anthony Stanton, editors. *Los contemporáneos en el laberinto de la crítica.* Mexico City: Colegio de México, Centro de Estudios Lingüísticos y Literarios, 1994.

RODERIC AI CAMP

TORRES GARCÍA, JOAQUÍN (1874–1949).

Joaquín Torres García (*b.* 25 July 1874; *d.* 8 August 1949), Uruguayan painter and sculptor. Born in Montevideo, Torres García lived in France, Spain, and New York City from 1892 to 1932. He executed a number of murals and the stained-glass windows of the cathedral of Palma de Mallorca. He was a founding member of both the Cercle et Carré in Paris (1930) and the Asociación de Arte Constructivo in Montevideo (1935). Torres García considered himself a realist. Because of his passion for geometry, order, synthesism, construction, and rhythm, Angel Kalenberg spoke of the linguistic quality of Torres García's art, characterizing his creations as ideograms. His work provides an interesting example of pictorial duality, purely plastic elements being sensitively and skillfully fused with the expression of personal feeling. Among his publications are *Structure* (1935), *The Tradition of Abstract Man* (1938), *The Metaphysics of Indo-American Prehistory* (1940), and *Universal Constructivism* (1944).

See also **Art: The Twentieth Century.**

BIBLIOGRAPHY

Museum of Modern Art of Latin America (1985).

Additional Bibliography

Battegazzore, Miguel A. *J. Torres Garcia: La trama y los signos.* Montevideo: Impr. Gordon, 1999.

Braun, Barbara. *Pre-Columbian Art and the Post-Columbian World: Ancient American Sources of Modern Art.* New York: Harry N. Abrams, 1993.

Fletcher, Valerie J. *Crosscurrents of Modernism: Four Latin American Pioneers: Diego Rivera, Joaquín Torres-García, Wifredo Lam, Matta.* Washington, DC: Hirshhorn Museum and Sculpture Garden in association with the Smithsonian Institution Press, 1992.

Parada Soto, Ana Isabel. *Joaquín Torres García: Un pintor neoplatónica del siglo XX.* Mérida: Universidad de Los Andes, Consejo de Publicaciones, Vicerrectorado Académico, 2004.

AMALIA CORTINA ARAVENA

TORRES RESTREPO, CAMILO (1929–1966).

Camilo Torres Restrepo (*b.* 2 February 1929; *d.* 15 February 1966), Colombian revolutionary priest. From an upper-class (though not particularly wealthy) Bogotá family, Camilo Torres began the study of law at the Universidad Nacional in Bogotá, but in 1947 abruptly changed his career goals and entered the Roman Catholic seminary. His vocation was not grounded in traditional religiosity; rather, he was attracted to the progressive social

Catholicism that was a strong current in postwar Europe and would gain added impetus from the reforms of the Second Vatican Council and from the movement of liberation theology. After his 1954 ordination he studied sociology at Louvain, in Belgium; taught sociology at the Universidad Nacional; served as university chaplain; and worked with Colombia's agrarian reform agency and other social programs. Like many Colombian intellectuals of the 1960s, he was influenced by the Cuban Revolution and felt increasingly alienated from his country's political and socioeconomic establishment.

Torres's social activism and willingness to work with Marxists troubled his ecclesiastical superiors, who ordered him to choose between priestly duties and secular concerns. In response he abandoned the active priesthood and in 1965 launched a new leftist coalition known as Frente Unido (United Front). His acknowledged charisma attracted followers, but he felt frustration over the difficulty of organizing a viable movement with any chance of implementing radical reform by peaceful means. He therefore gave up the legal struggle and joined the Ejército de Liberación Nacional (Army of National Liberation), which of all the guerrilla organizations operating in Colombia was the one most closely associated with the Cuban model.

Torres died in the first military engagement in which he took part. Nevertheless, his memory and his writings continued to exert strong influence on Colombian leftists, for many of whom his personal example legitimated the recourse to violent action.

See also **Colombia, Revolutionary Movements: Army of National Liberation (ELN).**

BIBLIOGRAPHY

Germán Guzmán, *Camilo Torres,* translated by John D. Ring (1969).

Walter J. Broderick, *Camilo Torres: A Biography of the Priest-Guerrillero* (1975).

Additional Bibliography

Pérez Ramírez, Gustavo, Jaime Díaz Castañeda, and Fernando Torres Restrepo. *Camilo Torres Restrepo: Profeta para nuestro tiempo.* Bogotá: Cinep, 1999.

Vargas Velásquez, Alejo, and Eduardo Umaña Luna. *Política y armas: Al inicio del frente nacional.* Bogotá: Universidad Nacional de Colombia, Facultad de Derecho, Ciencias Políticas y Sociales, 1995.

DAVID BUSHNELL

TORRES Y PORTUGAL, FERNANDO DE.

Fernando de Torres y Portugal (sixteenth century), seventh viceroy of Peru. Born in Jaén, Torres y Portugal received the title of conde de Villardompardo in 1576. In 1585 he was appointed viceroy of Peru, where he served until 1589. His rule was marred by conflict with the Inquisition over the activities of his son, don Jerónimo de Torres; nephew, don Diego de Portugal; and secretary, Juan Bello. Torres y Portugal also granted a Peruvian *encomienda* to his grandson, don Francisco de Torres y Portugal. During his rule, Torres y Portugal focused on the silver production of Potosí. After Thomas Cavendish ravaged the coast during his viceregency, Torres y Portugal became concerned with the defenses of the Pacific coast. In an effort to protect the realm he ordered the purchase of five galleons, two smaller ships for coastal service, and two galleys, along with fifty-four pieces of artillery. He returned to Spain in 1592.

See also **Encomienda; Viceroyalty, Viceroy.**

BIBLIOGRAPHY

Manuel De Mendiburu, *Diccionario histórico-biográfico del Perú* (1874–1890).

Additional Bibliography

Burkholder, Mark A. *Politics of a Colonial Career: José Baquijano and the Audiencia of Lima.* Albuquerque: University of New Mexico Press, 1980.

Guibovic Pérez, Pedro. *La inquisición y la censura de libros en el Perú virreinal (1570–1813).* Lima: Fondo Editorial del Congreso del Perú, 2000.

Ponce Lozada, Julio César. *Las comunicaciones en el Virreynato del Perú: Siglos XVI, XVII y XVIII.* Lima: Creaimagen editores, 2004.

Varón Gabai, Rafael. *Francisco Pizarro and His Brothers: The Illusion of Power in Sixteenth-Century Peru.* Norman: University of Oklahoma Press, 1997.

JOHN F. SCHWALLER

TORRE TAGLE Y PORTOCARRERO, JOSÉ BERNARDO DE (1779–1825).

José Bernardo de Torre Tagle y Portocarrero (fourth marqués of Torre Tagle; *b.* 1779; *d.* 1825), president of Peru in 1823. He inherited several royal positions, including a seat on the Lima city council. Elected *alcalde* of Lima (1811–1812), he became a deputy to the Spanish Cortes in 1813. In late 1820, as governor of Trujillo, he announced in favor of José de San Martín, who was advocating a monarchy for independent Peru. When Peru's first president, José de la Riva Agüero, began acting independently of Congress, that body moved to replace him with the very conservative Torre Tagle (1823). Peru was then left with two governments: Riva Agüero's stood for interests in northern Peru, while Torre Tagle's represented Lima. Neither had much support or lasted very long.

Torre Tagle presided over a weak, bankrupt state. When it appeared on the verge of collapse, he committed treason by negotiating secretly with the Spaniards against Simón Bolívar, to whom Torre Tagle had given full control of the army in 1823. Surrendering to the royal army, Torre Tagle presided over the last year of Spanish rule in Peru.

See also **Bolívar, Simón; Wars of Independence, South America.**

BIBLIOGRAPHY

Timothy E. Anna, *The Fall of the Royal Government in Peru* (1979).

Peter Blanchard, *Slavery and Abolition in Early Republican Peru* (1992).

Additional Bibliography

Hunefeldt, Christine. *A Brief History of Peru.* New York: Facts on File, 2004.

Mazzeo, Cristina Ana. *Los comerciantes Limeños a fines del siglo XVIII: Capacidad y cohesión de un elite, 1750–1825.* Lima: PUCP, 2000.

Walker, Charles. *Smoldering Ashes: Cuzco and the Creation of Republican Peru, 1780–1840.* Durham, NC: Duke University Press, 1999.

VINCENT PELOSO

TORRE Y HUERTA, CARLOS DE LA (1858–1950).

Carlos de la Torre y Huerta (*b.* 15 May 1858; *d.* 1950), Cuban naturalist, educator, writer, and public figure. Born in Matanzas, de la Torre was the son of a professor. He began his studies under his father, who instilled in him a love of science and objective methodology. De la Torre earned his baccalaureate from the Instituto de La Habana, and then moved on to study zoology and mineralogy at the university under the famous scientist Felipe Poey. There young Carlos's enthusiasm for mollusks quickly earned him the nickname Carlos Caracol, or Charles the Snail. In 1879 he discovered a new species of mollusk and earned a master's degree. In 1881 de la Torre earned his doctorate from the University of Madrid and moved to Puerto Rico. For several years he was on tenuous terms with the scientific community in Cuba, but he finally returned in 1892 and served as director of two reviews: *La enciclopedia* and *La revista enciclopédica.* During the Cuban War of Independence (1895–1898), de la Torre fled to Paris, where he worked closely with naturalists at the Museum of Natural History and across the Channel at the British Museum. In 1900 he returned to Cuba and cofounded the Cuban National Party, on whose platform he was elected to the Havana City Council. De la Torre continued to write on many subjects, including ethnohistory and anthropology in his later years. He received honorary doctorates from Harvard and Jena universities and was considered a pioneering member of the international community of naturalists.

See also **Cuba, War of Independence.**

BIBLIOGRAPHY

Carlos De La Torre y Huerta, *Clasificación de los animales observados por Colón y los primeros exploradores de Cuba; Distribución geográfica de la fauna malacológica terrestre de Cuba; Historia de Cuba;* and *Geografía de Cuba* (1955).

Carlos Eugenio Chardón, *Los naturalistas en la América Latina* (1949).

Additional Bibliography

Alvarez Conde, José. *Carlos de la Torre, su vida y su obra.* Havana: Siglo XX, 1951.

KAREN RACINE

TORRIJOS HERRERA, OMAR (1929–1981).

Omar Torrijos Herrera (*b.* 13 February 1929; *d.* 31 July 1981), maximum leader and supreme chief of the Panamanian Revolution, chief of state, and commander in chief of the Panamanian National

Guard (1968–1981). Born in Santiago de Veraguas, he entered a military academy in El Salvador after attending public schools in Panama.

A career military man, General Omar Torrijos Herrera rose through the ranks of the Panamanian National Guard, joining several other colonels in leading a coup on 11 October 1968 that removed President Arnulfo Arias Madrid after only ten days in office. Unsuccessful efforts by his colleagues to secure power left Torrijos as the sole leader of the guard.

Torrijos is most remembered for his successful campaign to establish Panamanian control and sovereignty over the canal, a popular cause in Panama, which represented the fulfillment of a longtime national ambition. The general skillfully orchestrated popular sentiment and focused world opinion through a meeting of the U.N. Security Council in March 1993. The Security Council met in the Legislative Palace in Panama City, very close to the frontier separating the Canal Zone from Panama. The Torrijos–Carter Treaty, signed 7 September 1977, established a gradual transition process, assuring U.S. operation of the canal until 31 December 1999 but guaranteeing Panamanian control of the canal on 1 January 2000, thus ending U.S. jurisdiction over Panama's economic resource. The treaty also eliminated the Canal Zone and its special privileges for U.S. citizens three years hence and brought Panama a dramatic increase in canal revenues.

Torrijos's contribution to Panamanian politics, however, was far more significant, for his revolution changed his nation's political institutions and extended political participation to previously excluded and ignored ethnic groups and social classes. A self-made man of the middle class, he focused on ending the dominance of the elite of Spanish ancestry and on opening the political system to the urban masses of laborers and the middle class, which consisted largely of mulattoes and blacks, groups that had previously been denied even citizenship, much less political participation. In this sense, Torrijos permanently changed the nation's politics by opening the system, increasing participation, and ending segregation—an achievement similar to that of neighboring Costa Rica in the 1948 revolution.

The guard represented the main avenue of advance for these classes, and hence led the way to changes placing them in the political mainstream. The Constitution of 1972, which institutionalized

Torrijos's personal control of the state, also expanded the National Assembly to 505 members, theoretically making it more representative of the nation, though all key powers resided in the hands of the maximum leader.

Shifting the nation from import substitution to export-oriented economic growth, Torrijos focused on banking, services, and transportation. The Banking Law of 1970 removed all reserve requirements and all limits on the movement of funds into and out of the country, and allowed establishment of secret accounts while virtually eliminating taxation on bank transactions. These provisions made Panama the "Switzerland of Latin America" overnight, establishing it as an international financial center of convenience and leading to a vast expansion in the banking sector. Construction of new roads, a transisthmian oil pipeline, and a new international airport, as well as new container ports, made the nation a focal point of transportation and transfer that complemented the canal.

Torrijos's reforms included the Labor Code of 1972, which instituted a minimum wage; compulsory arbitration; and the principle of state control of the economy, theoretically establishing the state as the protector of the masses and further weakening the power of the oligarchy. A housing code established the principle of government-subsidized public housing and launched a massive housing and public works construction effort in the cities. Reaching out to the equally neglected peasant masses, he increased government spending for rural access roads and promoted peasant settlements through land acquisitions to increase grain production. Between 1969 and 1973, some 260 farm settlements were formed. Covering 540,000 acres, most were acquired through expropriation in return for long-term bonds or for payment of overdue back taxes.

A fervent nationalist, Torrijos restored pride to his nation by resisting U.S. pressures and joining the nonaligned movement as part of the resistance to the United States. He led the nation in confronting the age-old nemesis, the United Fruit Company, regarding taxes and land ownership; opposed the U.S. blockade of Fidel Castro's Cuba; and allowed the use of Panama as a conduit for Cuban arms supplied to the Sandinista rebels in Nicaragua. Yet he also cooperated with the United States in security matters, accepted compromises regarding the canal, sharing responsibilities for its defense, and provided shelter to the exiled Shah of Iran. His willingness to accept gradual change regarding canal jurisdiction ended an era of violent confrontations and enabled the peaceful settlement of a volatile dispute. Torrijos's death in an unexplained airplane crash cut his tenure and revolution short.

See also **Panama; Panama Canal; United States-Latin American Relations.**

BIBLIOGRAPHY

Walter Lafeber, *The Panama Canal: The Crisis in Historical Perspective* (1979).

George Priestley, *Military Government and Popular Participation in Panama: The Torrijos Regime, 1968–1975* (1986).

Additional Bibliography

Harding, Robert C. *Military Foundations of Panamanian Politics.* New Brunswick: Transaction Publishers, 2001.

León Jiménez, Elda Maúd de. *Torrijos: Un camino por recorrer.* Panama: Fundación Omar Torrijos, 1996.

Vargas, Dalys. *Omar Torrijos Herrera y la patria internacional.* Panama: Fundación Omar Torrijos, 2004.

Velásquez, Osvaldo. *Historia de una dictadura: De Torrijos a Noriega.* Panamá: Litho Editorial Chen, 1993.

KENNETH J. GRIEB

TORTUGA ISLAND. Tortuga Island, a major Caribbean base for French buccaneering from 1630 to 1700. Tortuga Island, just north of the western tip of Hispaniola (present-day Haiti), was an important strategic location in particular for the activities of seventeenth-century French buccaneers. The island had been a rendezvous for rovers of all nations since the time of Francis Drake, and from 1630 on, as tobacco production gave way to sugar growing, it became the headquarters for French freebooting.

Anthony Hilton, aware of its centrality, first settled the island in 1630, helping to provide a strategic location from which freebooters could safely travel. Considering Tortuga a pirate stronghold, the Spanish attacked and captured it in 1634, causing much destruction and killing many people. By 1640, however, the island had been repopulated by numerous English and French, many of whom had migrated there from Caribbean areas suffering from the tobacco depression.

The English initially gained the upper hand in government, oppressing many of the French on the island. Thus, in 1640 the governor of Saint Christopher, L. de Poincy, sent a group composed of Huguenots, under the command of M. Le Vasseur, to Tortuga. In August of that year this group entered the island unhindered and ordered the English to leave. Thereafter the island remained in French hands, although the Spanish unsuccessfully attacked it in 1643 and again in 1654.

Tortuga became an international haunt of buccaneers after the massacre of the Providence Company's settlers in 1634. After attaining power, Le Vasseur fortified Tortuga and established himself as semiofficial governor and leader of robbers. As the century progressed, the island continued to grow in importance as a buccaneer stronghold.

Assuming the governorship of French Hispaniola, and thus Tortuga, in 1665, Bertrand d'Ogéron strongly supported the activities of the buccaneers. While aiding these men on Tortuga, he also tried to establish a more respectable and secure settlement on western Hispaniola. The Tortuga buccaneers played an important role in the Anglo-Dutch War of 1672 to 1678, weakening the Dutch. The seven years from 1678 to 1685 also proved to be very active ones for these buccaneers. The successful buccaneers Captain Nicholas Van Horn and Laurens-Cornille Baldran de Graaf attacked numerous Spanish settlements. But in 1697 the Spanish ceded Saint Domingue (Hispaniola) to France, and the governor of the colony, Jean-Baptiste du Casse, persuaded the remaining buccaneers on Tortuga to settle peacefully on Saint Domingue.

The importance of establishing French control over Tortuga cannot be overestimated, for from this beginning sprang the greatest French colony, Saint Domingue, which became the richest and most highly cultivated of the West Indian islands. Ironically, this area, including Tortuga, now forms one of the poorest countries in the hemisphere, modern-day Haiti.

See also **French West Indies; Piracy.**

BIBLIOGRAPHY

Père P-F-X. Charlevoix, *Histoire de l'Isle Espagnole ou de Saint-Domingue,* 2 vols. (1730–1731).

C. H. Haring, *The Buccaneers in the West Indies in the XVII Century* (1910).

A. P. Newton, *Colonising Activities of the English Puritans* (1914).

N. M. Crouse, *The French Struggle for the West Indies, 1665–1713* (1943).

J. H. Parry, et al., *A Short History of the West Indies,* 4th ed. (1987).

M. A. Peña Batlle, *La isla de Tortuga* (1988).

Additional Bibliography

Barker, David, and Carol Newby. *A Reader in Caribbean Geography.* Kingston: Ian Randle, 1998.

Hornsby, Stephen. *British Atlantic, American Frontier: Spaces of Power in Early Modern British America.* Hanover, NH: University Press of New England, 2005.

Watts, David. *The West Indies: Patterns of Development, Culture, and Environmental Change since 1492.* New York: Cambridge University Press, 1990.

BLAKE D. PATTRIDGE

TOSAR, HÉCTOR ALBERTO (1923–2002). Héctor Alberto Tosar (*b.* 18 July 1923; *d.* 17 January 2002), Uruguayan composer, pianist, and conductor. Born in Montevideo, Tosar began his studies in that city with Wilhelm Kolischer (piano), Tomás Mujica (harmony), and Lamberto Baldi (composition and orchestration). When he was seventeen, his Toccata for orchestra was premiered in Montevideo by maestro Baldi. In 1946 Tosar received a Guggenheim fellowship and went to the United States to study composition with Aaron Copland. With a grant from the French government in 1948 he went to France, where he remained for three years studying under Darius Milhaud, Jean Rivier, and Arthur Honegger (composition), and Eugène Bigot and Jean Fournet (conducting). In 1951 he won the SODRE first composition award for *Oda a Artigas,* a cantata for speaker and orchestra. He also won first prize at the First Inter-American Music Festival (Montevideo) in 1957 for his Divertimento for strings. He composed a Te Deum in 1960 commissioned by the Koussevitsky Foundation.

Tosar was chairman of the composition department at the Puerto Rico Conservatory (1974) and professor (1983–1984) and director of Montevideo's Escuela Universitaria de Música (1985–1987) and Conservatorio Nacional. From 1987 to 1991 he was composer-in-residence at the SODRE. He was also professor of composition and analysis at the Instituto Simón Bolívar in Caracas, and later taught composition at Indiana University (1981–1982). His early works, which combine contrapuntal and harmonic structures in free forms, are dramatic and rarely nationalistic. In his later works Tosar has experimented with jazz rhythms, new forms of instrumentation, as in his aleatoric composition for thirteen instruments, *A-13,* and serial structures. His *Recitativo y variaciones para orquesta* was commissioned by the Fourth Inter-American Music Festival and premiered in Washington, D.C., in 1968. In the 1980s several of his works were premiered in the United States, Mexico, and Venezuela. Tosar has also composed music for the synthesizer. He died in Montevideo.

BIBLIOGRAPHY

Gérard Béhague, *Music in Latin America* (1979); *New Grove Dictionary of Music and Musicians,* vol. 19 (1980).

Susana Salgado, *Breve historia de la música culta en el Uruguay,* 2nd ed. (1980).

Additional Bibliography

Aharonián, Coriún. *Héctor Tosar: compositor uruguayazo.* Montevideo, Uruguay: Ediciones Trilce, 1991.

Aharonián, Coriún. "Héctor Tosar (1923–2002): Muerte de un gran compositor." *Revista musica chilena* 56 (June 2002): 81–84.

Véjar Pérez Rubio, Carlos and Kaarina Véjar Amarillos. *Contrapuntos: Colegio de Compositores Latinoamericanos de Música de Arte, su nacimiento.* Mexico City: Archipiélago, 2000.

SUSANA SALGADO

TOTONACS. Totonacs, a major and historically important ethnic group of east-central Mexico. Inhabiting portions of the high eastern plateau, the rugged Sierra Madre Oriental, and the hilly central coastal plain along the Gulf of Mexico, the Totonacs have successfully adapted to a very wide range of habitats. Their life-styles are accordingly varied but tend to have two basic formats, one that exploits the drier highland environments and the other, the lusher humid lowlands.

The lowland Totonacs were the first indigenous peoples observed closely by the Spaniards when they arrived in 1519 and were induced to join an alliance against their Aztec overlords. The chronicler Bernal Díaz del Castillo goes into detail on how the Tontonac ruler whom he calls "the fat king" was brought into the Spanish fold. The Totonac language is generally classified, along with closely related Tepehua, as a separate and somewhat enigmatic language family called Totonaca, which may be distantly related to Mayan. Dialectical differences, variously put at three or four, are recognized. Recent census figures (2005)—at best only a rough estimate of the present strength of Totonac culture—indicate a total of 230,930 speakers over the age of five for Totonacapan, the traditional area in the states of Veracruz and Puebla. As a result of increasing acculturation, many Totonacs no longer habitually speak their mother tongue, and growing numbers are moving to urban centers as laborers.

Archaeological evidence suggests that the Totonacs may have been relatively late arrivals on the Gulf Coast and that some ancient cities assumed to have been built by them, such as El Tajín and Santa Luisa, were actually associated with earlier peoples. Historically, resource-laden Totonacapan has been coveted by many groups. This is reflected today in the interspersed settlements found in some instances with Nahua, Otomí, Tepehua, or Huastec speakers. When Hernan Cortés arrived at the huge Totonac city of Zempoala (Cempoala), most of Totonacapan had already been subjugated by the Aztecs. After the Spanish Conquest the Totonacs suffered severe population decline and dispersion occasioned by catastrophic epidemics of European-induced diseases as well as by their resistance to evangelization and colonial policies.

The Totonacs remain subsistence agriculturalists with a traditional Mesoamerican emphasis upon maize, beans, and squash. They raise some livestock and, in the lowlands, occasional cash crops such as vanilla. In the highlands the population is concentrated in small towns whereas in the lowlands it is scattered in villages, hamlets, and house compounds near the fields. Compadrazgo, a form of ritual kinship, is an important social bond in both areas. Expansion of the oil industry has led to the destruction of the coastal rain forest, land speculation, and a considerable reduction of traditional Totonac farmland.

Ritual life tends to be more elaborate in the isolated reaches of the mountains. There, some *mayordomías* persist and a greater diversity of dance groups can be found. Among the latter, *huehues, negritos,* and *santiaguerros* are common. Popular in both areas are two physically rigorous dances of pre-Columbian origin: the *guaguas* (*quetzalines*) and the *voladores.* Although these were once pan-Mesoamerican rituals, the Totonacs, particularly of the lowlands, consider them to be very much their own and excel at their presentation. Apart from local patron-saint days, the celebration of All Saints' Day (also called Day of the Dead) with elaborate altars and offerings is particularly important to the Totonacs.

See also **Indigenous Peoples; Volador Dance.**

BIBLIOGRAPHY

The principal ethnographic studies are Isabel Kelly and Angel Palerm, *The Tajín Totonac,* pt. 1 (1952); and Alain Ichon, *La religion des Totonaques de la Sierra* (1969). An important early synthesis is Walter Krickeberg, *Die Totonaken* (1918–1925). Recent data on origins, environment, and historical migration can be found in S. Jeffrey K. Wilkerson, *Ethnogenesis of the Huastecs and Totonacs* (1973); "Eastern Mesoamerica from Prehispanic to Colonial Times: A Model of Cultural Continuance," in *Actes du XLIIᵐᵉ Congrès International des Américanistes,* vol. 8 (1976): 41–55; and "Man's Eighty Centuries in Veracruz," *National Geographic Magazine* 158, no. 2 (August 1980): 202–231.

Additional Bibliography

Chenaut, Victoria, ed. *Procesos rurales e historia regional: Sierra y costa totonacas de Veracruz.* Mexico City: CIESAS, 1996.

Díaz del Castillo, Bernal. *Historia verdadera de la conquista de la Nueva España.* Madrid: Espasa-Calpe, 1968.

S. Jeffrey K. Wilkerson

TOURISM. When people travel from their place of residence for short periods of time for relaxation or exploration, they engage in tourism. Latin American countries, with their indigenous cultures, archaeological sites, beaches, great biological diversity, and rich histories, draw millions of tourists from all over the world every year, mainly from North America and Europe. Tourism is an important source of income for many Latin American countries as well as of foreign currency for the region, and a driving force behind economic development. The tourism sector not only provides a great number of jobs, it is also a recipient of considerable public and private investment. For example, in Mexico and Argentina tourism represents approximately 10 percent of their GDP and in Mexico it is the fourth largest source of foreign exchange.

Development of tourist services varies greatly from region to region. Mexico and Central America (and Costa Rica in particular) receive approximately 50 percent of the tourists visiting Latin America; the Caribbean (Dominican Republic, Puerto Rico, and Cuba) receives another 30 percent; and South America (Brazil, Argentina, and Chile), 20 percent. In 2004 the Latin American countries most visited were Mexico (20 million tourists), Brazil (4 million), and Argentina (3 million). Despite its natural, cultural, and historical attractions, Latin America still receives a small portion of world tourism: Approximately 10 percent of tourists choose the region as a destination. The sector's growth rates since 2000 have been slightly lower than those of Pacific Asia and the Middle East. The main reasons for these differences lie in the relative distances between travelers' home countries and destinations and in the unequal availability of appropriate infrastructure and equipment.

HISTORY OF TOURISM

Modern mass tourism emerged after World War II and has grown at a fast rate since the mid-twentieth century. International tourists numbered 25 million in 1950. The World Tourism Organization (WTO) predicts tourists throughout the world will number about 1 billion by 2010. The determining factors in the rise of mass tourism have been an overall increase in income and free time, the development of the leisure culture, and technological progress in the transportation and communications industries. Technological improvements in transportation shortened traveling distances while the cost of traveling became affordable to a larger percentage of the world population. However, this exponential growth in tourist activity throughout the world has provoked criticism because of harmful effects on the environment, disruption of indigenous communities and their folk traditions, and an excessively commercial bias in the sector's operation. In Latin America these concerns have prompted demands for "responsible tourism" and greater government control.

MEXICO, CENTRAL AMERICA, AND THE CARIBBEAN

Mexico is one of the countries most visited by international tourists; in 2004 it ranked eighth in the world tourism sector. After World War II the Pan-American highway was a significant promoter of tourism in Mexico, facilitating travel from the United States to Acapulco on the Pacific. Other important tourist destinations in Mexico include the Aztec ruins at Teotihuacan and the beach resorts on the Yucatan peninsula (Cancun, Playa del Carmen). The work of the great Mexican muralists Diego Rivera, David Alfaro Siqueiros, and José Clemente Orozco and of the painter Frida Kahlo (1907–1954) and the exceptional National Museum of Anthropology of Mexico are of particular cultural interest. Tourism is also significant in Central America, where visitors seek out the ruins of Copán and the coastal city of La Ceiba in Honduras; the Maya ruins of Tikal and the city of Quetzaltenango in Guatemala; the archaeological site of Tazumal and the beaches of El Salvador; the colonial buildings in the city of Granada and volcanoes in Nicaragua; the rainforests and canal in San José, Costa Rica; and the cultural and musical attractions in Caribbean Panama.

The islands of the Caribbean receive 30 percent of the tourists to the entire region. In the 1970s various governments promoted development of the tourism sector, and in the twenty-first century it represents a significant portion of their gross domestic product. Cuba was one of the pioneering countries in receiving considerable influxes of tourists, mainly from the United States, until the revolution of 1959. In the early twenty-first century the country is visited by tourists from Europe, Latin America, andCanada. Havana (with its unique culture and history) and the beaches of Varadero are its principal attractions. Other frequently visited destinations in the Caribbean are the beaches of Punta Cana, Dominican Republic, and Aruba, an island in the

Lesser Antilles, as well as the beaches of Barbados, Jamaica, and the Bahamas.

SOUTH AMERICA

Tourism in South America has expanded at a relatively slower rate than in other areas of the continent. Nevertheless, the region's governments have realized the importance of international and national tourism to their nations' economic activity. Two of the three most visited countries in Latin America are Argentina and Brazil. The impressive landscapes of Argentine and Chilean Patagonia, with their large winter sports centers operating from July to September; the Perito Moreno glacier in Argentina; and the Iguaçu Falls on the borders of Argentina, Brazil, and Paraguay, are some of the region's attractions. Bogota's Botero Museum, displaying the works of the Colombian painter Fernando Botero (b. 1932), and the Colombian and Venezuelan beaches; Carnival at Rio de Janeiro (one of the biggest in the world); Brazilian beaches and the samba; tango music in Buenos Aires, Argentina; and the indigenous culture and handicrafts of Peru, along with the archaeological ruins of Machu Picchu and the world-famous Inca Trail, are some of the reasons why millions of tourists visit South America each year.

As tourist destinations, the countries of Latin America offer a unique opportunity to experience indigenous cultures, the customs inherited from the colonial era, and Latin charm. Tourists can learn about the Aztec, Maya, and Inca indigenous civilizations (located mainly in Mexico and Peru) by viewing archaeological sites; they can also take in the visual riches of the architecture of the colonial era as well as natural landscapes and beaches, serviced by a modern tourist infrastructure. The lively nightlife of the principal cities of Latin America—Bogota, Buenos Aires, Mexico City, Rio de Janeiro, and Santiago de Chile—is also of great appeal to visitors. The region is currently facing the challenge of reducing social inequality and poverty. Appropriate responses to this challenge will do much to increase domestic as well as foreign tourism. All predictions indicate that the tourist industry will continue to grow.

See also **Archaeology; Art: Pre-Columbian Art of Mesoamerica; Art: Pre-Columbian Art of South America; Art: The Colonial Era; Art: The Nineteenth Century; Art: The Twentieth Century; Art: Folk Art; Travel Literature.**

BIBLIOGRAPHY

Dahles, Heidi, and Lou Keune, eds. *Tourism Development and Local Participation in Latin America.* New York: Cognizant Communication Corporation, 2002.

Getino, Octavio. *Turismo entre el ocio y el negocio: Identidad cultural y desarrollo económico para América Latina y el Mercosur.* Buenos Aires: La Crujía, 2002.

Organización Mundial del Turismo. *Compendium of Tourism Statistics.* Madrid: World Tourism Organization, 2004.

VICENTE PALERMO

TOUSSAINT L'OUVERTURE. *See* **Louverture, Toussaint.**

TRABA, MARTA (1930–1983). Marta Traba (*b.* 25 January 1930; *d.* 27 November 1983), Argentine-Colombian novelist, art critic, and university professor. Traba earned a degree in literature from the Universidad Nacional de Buenos Aires (1948) and took courses with art critic Jorge Romero Brest. In 1949–1950, she studied art history with Pierre Francastel at the Sorbonne and René Huyghe at L'école du Louvre. In Paris she met and married Alberto Zalamea, a Colombian intellectual. She left Europe for Colombia with her family in 1954. In 1958 Traba published her first study on modern art, *El museo vacío.* In 1961 she published an important and pioneering study on Latin American painting, *La pintura nueva en Latinoamérica,* in which she of-fered a critique of the Mexican muralists and Argentine painting, among other topics, that generated considerable controversy. She taught art history at the Universidad de América and the Universidad de los Andes in Bogotá and became a strong advocate for the creation of the Museum of Modern Art in Bogotá, which was constituted in 1962. She was its director from 1964 to 1967. In 1965 Traba moved the museum to the Universidad Nacional de Bogotá, where she joined the faculty. That year she also published her most important study on Latin American art, *Los cuatro monstruos cardinales.* Although Traba published a book of poems in 1952, *Historia natural de la alegría,* it was not until 1966 that her writing of fiction began in earnest. She received the prestigious Cuban Casa de las Américas prize for her first novel, *Las ceremonias del verano* (1966). *Los laberintos insolados,* another novel, was published in 1967. Both novels explore the possibilities of interior growth and exposure to foreign cultures. *Pasó así* (1968), *La jugada del sexto día* (1970), and *Homérica latina* (1979) followed.

Increasingly, Traba's fiction portrayed political turmoil, repression, persecution, and horror in countries under military regimes (Argentina, Uruguay, and Chile). These are the central themes in *Conversación al sur* (1981; *Mothers and Shadows,* 1986) and *En cualquier lugar* (1984). *De la mañana a la noche: Cuentos norteamericanos* (1986) and *Casa sin fin* (1988) were published posthumously. In 1969, after divorcing her first husband, Traba married the Uruguayan critic and writer Angel Rama. They lived in Montevideo, Puerto Rico, Caracas, and Washington, D.C., between 1969 and 1982. Traba and Rama were forced to leave the United States in 1982 when the U.S. Department of State denied them resident visas, a decision that generated heated controversy. They set up residence in Paris, France, where they lived until their death in an airplane crash near Madrid.

See also **Art: The Twentieth Century; Literature: Spanish America; Universities: The Modern Era.**

BIBLIOGRAPHY

Marta Traba, edited by Emma Araújo de Vallejo (Bogotá, 1984); Magdalena García Pinto, *Women Writers of Latin America* (1991).

Additional Bibliography

Pizarro, Ana. *Las grietas del proceso civilizatorio: Marta Traba en los sesenta.* Santiago: LOM Ediciones, 2002.

Verlichak, Victoria. *Marta Traba: Una terquedad furibunda.* Caseros: UNTREF, and Buenos Aires: Fundación Proa, 2001.

MAGDALENA GARCÍA PINTO

TRADE. *See* **Commercial Policy: Colonial Brazil; Commercial Policy: Colonial Spanish America.**

TRADE, COLONIAL BRAZIL. Colonial internal trade in Brazil was circumscribed by geographical, transport, financial, and administrative constraints; it was organized in regional systems focused on important plantation zones and their port cities. The export economy was the focus of both the colonial administration and most of the available merchant capital, and it tended to determine the transport routes. Small vessels carried high-bulk commodities along the coast, but the road network was so poor that overland trade was limited to self-transporting livestock and the relatively high-value, low-bulk goods that could be carried by human porters on mule trains (*tropas*) conducted by *tropeiros.*

Internal trade can be divided into three categories: (1) an extension of the export-import trades in which export commodities were funneled to coastal port cities and imports were distributed from the ports to communities on the coast and in the interior; (2) the internal labor trade in African, Afro-Brazilian, and Amerindian slaves; (3) the trading of commodities and livestock produced in Brazil to supply Brazilian cities and towns, export producers, and mining operations. This discussion will focus on the last category of internal trade. The extent and volume of colonial internal trade can be divided into four periods: pre-1700, 1700–1750, 1750–1808, and 1808–1822.

Before the inception of the mining industry at the end of the seventeenth century, internal exchanges were limited in extent. As the port cities and plantation zones, especially in the Northeast, increasingly experienced shortages of Brazil's staple food of manioc flour (*farinha*), specialized manioc-producing zones emerged within bays and on the coast, for example, at Maragogipe, Jaguaribe, Cairú, and Camamú to supply the Salvador region, and at Una, Porto Calvo, and Alagoas in Pernambuco.

In the Northeast from the 1590s on, livestock ranches were increasingly distanced from their markets in the plantation zones and ports, first along the coast to Paraíba, Rio Grande do Norte, and Sergipe, and then up the São Francisco River valley. Cattle were driven to fair towns on the edge of the plantation districts, to Santo Amaro, for example, which served the region of Salvador. Dried and salted beef (*carne seca*) was also sent from the cattle districts to feed plantation slaves and the urban poor. Similarly, Rio de Janeiro drew its supplies of cattle on the hoof from nearby pastures in its own captaincy. São Paulo, isolated in the first two centuries of colonization, slowly forged trading relationships with other parts of Brazil through commerce in flour, marmalade, and, especially in the first half of the seventeenth century, Amerindian slaves.

Between 1700 and 1750 the discovery of gold and later diamonds in Minas Gerais, Mato Grosso, and Goiás created new transport routes and internal trade networks. Some supplies and livestock intended for the coast were initially diverted to the new mining markets, but during the eighteenth century, cattle ranches extended into the interior near these markets. As the principal export port for gold, the city of Rio de Janeiro took on greater importance and became the focus for the expanded internal trade network of central, southeastern, and southern Brazil.

In order to control contraband, the government forbade the opening of new roads into the interior without permission and set up registers (*registros*) to tax livestock, slaves, and goods by weight as they passed from one captaincy to another. Traffic was further burdened by fees for river crossings (*passagens*). Effective settlement of southern Brazil began in this period, and this region became an important source of mules and cattle on the hoof for other captaincies.

After 1750, gold production began to decline, and coastal export agriculture also experienced a prolonged recession. In the 1790s, however, export production intensified and diversified in traditional plantation zones and expanded into some areas that had previously produced primarily for the internal market. This export resurgence created greater markets for livestock and other commodities, bringing more distant production areas into the internal trade network. As sugarcane replaced cattle in Rio de Janeiro's pastoral areas, southern Minas Gerais became a source of cheese, bacon, and cattle and pigs on the hoof for the Rio market. Beef on the hoof was also drawn from as far away as Rio Grande do Sul and São Paulo (including modern Paraná). A series of droughts in the northeastern interior decimated herds, opening markets for the new *carne seca* industry in Rio Grande do Sul in the late 1780s. Simultaneously, the same captaincy became an important source of wheat for Rio de Janeiro.

Rio also began to draw supplies of *farinha* from distant coastal producers such as Santa Catarina in the south and Porto Seguro to the north. As export producers and city dwellers increasingly relied on the market to supply their wants, dried and salted fish, maize, beans, rice, other foodstuffs, and lumber from small coastal communities also found markets in the major cities and plantation zones.

The 1808 arrival of the Portuguese royal family in Rio de Janeiro brought an influx of population, setting off food price inflation and a construction boom. Salvador and other regional export centers also grew because of the expansion and diversification of export production. The government began to pay more attention to the internal economic development of Brazil, and internal trade began to attract merchant capital to a much greater degree than before. In particular, producers and merchants in southern Minas Gerais and Rio Grande do Sul were able to accumulate capital and develop a positive balance of trade by supplying other regions.

At the close of the colonial period, internal trade remained dependent on the export sector as the dynamic force in the economy, and continued to face daunting obstacles. Among the most important were the limited investment in road improvement and expansion, heavy tax burdens on overland trade, and shortage of capital.

See also **Commercial Policy: Colonial Brazil; Slave Trade.**

BIBLIOGRAPHY

Charles R. Boxer, *The Golden Age of Brazil* (1962).

Maria Thereza Schorer Petrone, *O Barão de Iguape* (1976).

Maria Yedda Leite Linhares, *História do Abastecimento* (1979).

Alcir Lenharo, *As tropas da moderação* (1979).

Stuart B. Schwartz, *Sugar Plantations in the Formation of Brazilian Society* (1985), pp. 89–90, 435–436.

Leslie Bethell, ed., *Colonial Brazil* (1987), pp. 104–110, 113–114, 195–196, 199–200, 303–336.

Additional Bibliography

Baskes, Jeremy. *Indians, Merchants, and Markets: A Reinterpretation of the Repartimiento and Spanish-Indian Economic Relations in Colonial Oaxaca, 1750–1821.* Stanford, CA: Stanford University Press, 2000.

Hill, Ruth. *Hierarchy, Commerce and Fraud in Bourbon Spanish America: A Postal Inspector's Exposé.* Nashville: Vanderbilt University Press, 2005.

Martínez Shaw, Carlos, and José María Oliva Melgar. *Sistema atlántico español: Siglos XVII–XIX.* Madrid: Marcial Pons Historia, 2005.

Mauro, Frédéric. *Portugal, o Brasil e o Atlântico, 1570–1670.* Lisbon: Editorial Estampa, 1997.

Mazzeo, Cristina Ana. *Los comerciantes limeños a fines del siglo XVIII: Capacidad y cohesión de un elite, 1750–1825.* Lima: Pontificia Universidad Católica del Perú, Dirección Académica de Investigación, 2003.

Pedreira, Jorge Miguel Viana. *Estrutura industrial e mercado colonial: Portugal e Brasil (1780–1830).* Lisbon: DIFEL, 1994.

Romano, Ruggiero. *Mecanismo y elementos del sistema económico colonial americano, siglos XVI–XVIII.* México: El Colegio de México, Fideicomiso Historia de las Américas: Fondo de Cultura Económica, 2004.

Stein, Stanley J., and Barbara H. Stein. *Apogee of Empire: Spain and New Spain in the Age of Charles III, 1759–1789.* Baltimore: Johns Hopkins University Press, 2003.

Stein, Stanley J. and Barbara H. Stein. *Silver, Trade, and War: Spain and America in the Making of Early Modern Europe.* Baltimore: Johns Hopkins University Press, 2000.

Topik, Steven, Carlos Marichal, and Zephyr L Frank. *From Silver to Cocaine: Latin American Commodity Chains and the Building of the World Economy, 1500–2000.* Durham: Duke University Press, 2006.

Valle Pavón, Guillermina del. *Mercaderes, comercio y consulados de Nueva España en el siglo XVIII.* Mexico City: Instituto Mo, 2003.

LARISSA V. BROWN

TRADING COMPANIES. *See* Companies, Chartered.

TRADING COMPANIES, PORTUGUESE. In the seventeenth and eighteenth centuries the Portuguese crown established several monopoly trading companies to control and stimulate trade between Portugal and Brazil. They included the Brazil Company (Companhia Geral de Estado do Brasil), created in 1649, transformed into a government agency in 1663, and dissolved in 1720; the Maranhão Company (Companhia de Comércio do Estado do Maranhão), 1682–1685; the Grão-Pará and Maranhão Company (Companhia Geral do Grão-Pará e Maranhão), 1755–1777; and the Pernambuco Company (Companhia Geral de Pernambuco e Paraíba), 1759–1777. The fundamental purpose of the Brazil Company was to protect trade with Brazil, while the three other companies were to supply African slave labor and stimulate production and trade in their respective regions.

THE BRAZIL COMPANY

The Brazil Company was established on the model of the Dutch and English chartered trading companies to protect Brazilian colonial trade from the depredations of Dutch privateers. The company was required to provide thirty-six warships to convoy merchant fleets between the ports of Lisbon and Oporto in Portugal, and Bahia, Rio de Janeiro, and Recife (after recapture from the Dutch in 1654) in Brazil. In return, the company was given a monopoly over all imports of wine, wheat flour, olive oil, and cod into Brazil for sale at prices it could set itself. Moreover, the company collected taxes on the sugar, tobacco, cotton, hides, and other commodities it transported from Brazil to Portugal. Shares in the company were exempted from confiscation by the Inquisition or any other court, and much of the capital was raised (under pressure) from New Christian merchants, descendants of Jews required to convert to Catholicism in 1497.

Although the company was somewhat successful in reducing the capture of ships in the Brazil trade, it came under increasing criticism. Some complaints focused on the protection given to New Christian capital, but smaller Portuguese ports and merchants, who were cut out of the Brazil trade, and Brazilian colonists also criticized its operations. Price increases and inadequate supplies of the monopolized staple foods, along with irregularity of the fleets and consequent spoilage of Brazilian commodities, were the major complaints.

In 1658 the monopolies were abolished and the fleet system modified to require only return sailing from Brazil in one annual convoy. The next year company shares were made vulnerable to confiscation by the Inquisition. Shareholders were compensated and the company was incorporated into the government as a royal council by 1663, continuing to provide convoy services in this form until it was dissolved in 1720.

THE MARANHÃO COMPANY

The short-lived Maranhão Company, organized in 1682 with a twenty-year charter, was intended to stimulate export-crop production in the sparsely settled northern captaincies by providing African slave labor and regular transport to Portuguese markets. Company abuses of its monopoly privileges combined with resentment of Jesuit activities ignited a revolt by colonists that resulted in the dissolution of the company in 1685.

THE EIGHTEENTH-CENTURY COMPANIES

In the eighteenth century, two monopoly trading companies were established as part of the Marques de Pombal's policy to revive and restructure the Portuguese imperial economy. The Grão-Pará and Maranhão Company was designed to stimulate economic development in the still-languishing Brazilian north, while the Pernambuco Company was to revive the economy of that once-prosperous region—in both cases through the introduction of greater supplies of African slave labor, the purchase of traditional and new export crops at good prices, and their transport to Portugal in armed convoys. The companies were also expected to develop colonial markets for Portuguese manufactures. By the 1770s, the Grão-Pará and Maranhão Company was also being used by the crown to expand its military and bureaucratic presence in the Amazon region.

The Maranhão Company was effective in enlarging the supply of African slaves to the north, stimulating greater production of traditional exports, such as cacao, and diversifying export production in Maranhão to include rice and cotton. The Pernambuco Company expanded exports of sugar and hides in Pernambuco, but there was no significant diversification of exports. Both companies provided more regular transport links and funneled large amounts of Portuguese manufactures to colonial markets.

The companies' monopolistic domination of their respective regions' economies produced widespread criticism, especially in Pernambuco. Opponents took advantage of Pombal's fall from power in 1777 to seek the dissolution of the companies that were so associated with his authoritarian rule.

See also **Brazil: The Colonial Era, 1500–1808; Slavery: Brazil.**

BIBLIOGRAPHY

Charles R. Boxer, *The Portuguese Seaborne Empire, 1415–1825* (1969).

Manuel Nunes Dias, *Fomento e mercantilismo: A Companhia Geral do Grão Pará e Maranhão, 1755–1778* (1970).

José Ribeiro Júnior, *Colonização e monopólio no nordeste brasileiro: A Companhia Geral de Pernambuco e Paraíba, 1759–1780* (1976).

Antônio Carreira, *As companhias pombalinas de Grão-Pará e Maranhão e Pernambuco e Paraíba*, 2d ed. (1983).

Leslie Bethell, ed., *Colonial Brazil* (1987), pp. 52–53, 264–269, 305–307.

Bailey W. Diffie, *A History of Colonial Brazil, 1500–1792* (1987), pp. 249–252, 277–280, 403–411.

Additional Bibliography

Costa, Leonor Freire. *Império e grupos mercantis: Entre o Oriente e o Atlântico (século XVII)*. Lisbon: Livros Horizonte, 2002.

Mauro, Frédéric. *Portugal, o Brasil e o Atlântico, 1570–1670*. Lisbon: Editorial Estampa, 1997.

Pedreira, Jorge Miguel Viana. *Estrutura industrial e mercado colonial: Portugal e Brasil (1780–1830)*. Lisbon: DIFEL, 1994.

LARISSA V. BROWN

TRANSAMAZON HIGHWAY.

Transamazon Highway, the red, earthen two–lane road that crosses Brazil from the east to the west. Constructed in the 1970s, the 3,400 mile–long Transamazônica, or BR–320, begins in João Pessoa and skirts the southern edge of the Amazonian plain. Crossing the Belém–Brasília Highway in northern Goiás, it follows the arch of the Amazon in Pará, cutting through Amazonas. With Peru's failure to build a road that would join BR–320 in Acre, officials in Brazil changed the course of the road from Acre to Benjamin Constant, Amazonas.

Although vehicles use ferries or rafts to cross larger rivers, such as the Tapajós, Xingú, or Madeira, log structures cover smaller ones. Some sections of the Transamazon are compacted earth, others are made of plinthite pebbles; the forest constantly re-claims some portions, and other parts flood during the rainy season.

Transamazônica was created as part of a development project initiated by PIN (Programa de Integracão Nacional), which was announced in June 1970 by President Emílio Garrastazú Médici. The scheme called for the building of the Transamazon Highway as a means of transporting immigrants from the poverty-stricken Northeast to the unpopulated and underdeveloped states of Rondônia, Mato Grosso, and Acre. Six different construction companies contracted labor and brought in supplies, while crews began working on 200 mile sections in 1971. The workers left behind the permanent construction camps they built, which contained housing, electricity, schools, health centers, and post offices that served as frontier posts for immigrants. The Brazilian government reserved 6 miles on either side of the Transamazon as settlement sites for those participating in the program. BR-320 was officially opened in December 1973.

See also **Amazon River; Highways; Médici, Emílio Garrastazú.**

BIBLIOGRAPHY

Nigel J. H. Smith, *Rainforest Corridors: The Transamazon Colonization Scheme* (1982).

Thomas E. Skidmore, *The Politics of Military Rule in Brazil, 1964–1985* (1988).

Ben Box, ed., *1990 South American Handbook,* 66th ed. (1990).

Andrew Revkin, *The Burning Season* (1990).

Additional Bibliography

Oates, Wallace E. *The RFF Reader in Environmental and Resource Policy.* Washington, DC: Resources for the Future, 2006.

Smith, Nigel J.H. *The Enchanted Amazon Rainforest.* Gainesville: University Press of Florida, 1996.

Stewart, Douglas Ian. *After the Trees: Living on the Transamazon Highway.* Austin: University of Texas Press, 1994.

CAROLYN JOSTOCK

TRAVELERS, LATIN AMERICAN.

The movement of persons over great distances has been a central feature of Latin American history and culture from pre-Columbian times. Aztec, Inca, and Maya societies developed extensive transportation, communication, and administrative networks that required regular travel to maintain. Similarly, during the Spanish colonial era, hundreds of thousands of conquistadors, missionaries, explorers, and immigrants ventured across the Atlantic Ocean and then fanned out over the continent in search of adventure and a better life. Travel, however, is a self-financed leisure activity associated with the Enlightenment and the emergence of a middle class; it is an activity that is intended both to complete the traveler's education and consolidate his or her social status. Unlike political exile, travel is a voluntary activity characterized by destinations and durations that are self-determined. Although there are hundreds of diaries and travel accounts written by foreigners who came to Latin America in the nineteenth and twentieth centuries, the corpus of works produced by and about Latin Americans abroad is significantly less well developed.

THE COLONIAL PERIOD
During the colonial era, Latin Americans travelers generally chose Europe as their destination in order to display the results of their family's good fortune in America, to seek a higher education, or to take up a place at the royal court. Few ventured beyond Spain or Portugal, although some pious individuals and members of the clergy spent time in Rome. The most famous seventeenth-century Spanish American traveler-resident was Garcilaso de la Vega, who relocated to Spain as a teenager, settled there permanently, and produced great works of literature about his Peruvian homeland and mixed Inca and Spanish heritage. Padre António Vieira did the same for Brazil during the years he spent in Lisbon and Rome.

By the eighteenth century, the United States became an attractive destination for patriotic Latin Americans interested in material conditions closer to home, and in particular the experiment in republican state construction. The Venezuelan precursor to Latin American independence, Francisco de Miranda, made a famous tour of the United States in the eventful years 1783–1784 and left a memoir filled with insightful observations; he also traveled throughout Europe and Russia from 1785 to 1789 and was perhaps the first Latin American to visit Istanbul. After the expulsion of the Jesuits from the Spanish Empire in 1767, large communities of American expatriates congregated in Rome and Leghorn, where they wrote histories of their native lands and their religious order as well as descriptive accounts of American geography and natural history. The wars for independence also displaced thousands of Latin Americans. In London, a large and prominent community gathered which included Francisco Antonio Zea, Servando Teresa de Mier, Agustín de Iturbide, Lucas Alamán, Andrés Bello, Simón Bolívar, Antonio José de Irisarri, Mariano Egaña, Hipolyto José da Costa, Vicente Rocafuerte, José Joaquín de Olmedo, Bernardo O'Higgins, and Bernardino Rivadavia. Others lived and worked in the United States: Manuel Torres, Luis Aury, Vicente Pazos Kanki, Mariano Montilla, Juan Germán Roscio, Pedro Gual, and José Álvarez de Toledo. The Argentine general José de San Martín settled in Belgium in 1823 and traveled with his daughter throughout the continent.

NINETEENTH CENTURY

The phenomenon of travel as a self-conscious, intentional, voluntary endeavor began to expand dramatically in the early decades of the nineteenth century. With the conclusion of the wars for independence and the advent of steam-powered transport, Latin Americans traveled abroad in unprecedented numbers. Some, like the Cuban José Maria Heredia, traveled for adventure and to study other countries and conditions in order to gain useful knowledge; in 1823–1824 he lived in the United States, traveling and keeping detailed notes of his observations and writing his famous ode to Niagara Falls. The Colombian Francisco de Paula Santander left the tense political conditions in his homeland for three years in Europe and the United States, where he toured factories, attended theatrical productions, met with politicians and intellectuals, and kept an extensive diary from 1829 to 1832. Many other prominent Latin Americans undertook tours of the United States or Europe in the middle decades of the nineteenth century, including the Argentine Tomas de Iriarte, the Peruvian scientist Mariano Eduardo Rivero y Ustariz, and the Chilean Benjamín Vicuña Mackenna. The Argentine statesman Domingo Faustino Sarmiento is probably the most famous Latin American traveler of the nineteenth century. Long an admirer of the United States and Europe, he traveled abroad often to study their cultures and institutions, particularly their educational methods. He met the pedagogical theorists Horace and Mary Mann, solicited an honorary degree from the University of Michigan, and kept a detailed travel diary which has been published in English.

Taking the grand tour continued to be an important milestone for Latin Americans of the upper class: Young girls were thought to benefit from exposure to language, fashion, culture, and art; young boys were expected to broaden their intellectual and sexual experiences while gaining exposure to economically useful innovations in science, agriculture, finance, and industry. In the later decades of the nineteenth century, Paris and its delights attracted an increasing number of tourists who wanted to put themselves at the center of new movements in art, literature, music, and dance. At the same time, changing trends in immigration, the growth of a leisure class, the diversification of trade markets, and a growing curiosity about non-European cultural models meant that Latin American travelers also started to venture beyond the traditional destinations. Latin American scientists sent expeditions to China and Japan; some anarchists and radicals visited Russia; abolitionists made pilgrimages to Africa. Travel became an increasingly common way to solidify one's own credentials and affiliations at home, by gaining experience and credibility abroad.

TWENTIETH CENTURY

The connection between travel and identity grew stronger in the twentieth century and was a major factor in the social revolutions in Mexico, Cuba, and Nicaragua. For example, leftist Latin Americans from all countries flocked to the Soviet Union in the 1920s to show their solidarity with the socialist regime and to receive training and credentials that would strengthen their work at home; others traveled to Spain in the 1930s to express their political allegiance to either the Fascists or the Socialists in the Civil War. Travel is also a form of consciousness-raising, a way to step outside the confines of one's own native reality and encounter the problems of others. Latin America's most iconic revolutionary, Ernesto "Che" Guevara, began his intellectual journey as a stereotypical youthful backpacker, who set out to see his continent on a motorbike in 1951–1952 and was profoundly changed by the experience. His transformation from an asthmatic medical student to a socially conscious political activist is well documented in the travel journal he kept, available in English and made into a film called *The Motorcycle Diaries* (2004).

Travel has been an important rite of passage for upper-class Latin Americans for nearly two centuries. In more recent decades, the expansion of affordable transportation options (both domestic and international), a growing tourism infrastructure, and the emergence of a global youth culture have meant that more and different groups of Latin Americans are able to travel.

See also **Alamán, Lucas; Bello, Andrés; Bolívar, Simón; Costa, Hipólito José da; Egaña Fabres, Mariano; Guevara, Ernesto "Che"; Heredia y Heredia, José M; Irisarri, Antonio José de; Iturbide, Agustín de; O'Higgins, Bernardo; Olmedo, José Joaquín de; Rivadavia, Bernardino; Rocafuerte, Vicente; Roscio, Juan Germán; San Martín, José Francisco de; Santander, Francisco de Paula; Sarmiento, Domingo Faustino; Travel Literature.**

BIBLIOGRAPHY

Bunster, Enrique. *Chilenos en California.* 2nd ed. Santiago de Chile: Editorial del Pacífico, 1954.

Carlos, Alberto J. "José María Heredia y su viaje al Niágara." In *La literatura iberoamericana del siglo XIX*, ed. Renato Rosaldo and Robert Anderson, pp. 73–80. Tucson: University of Arizona, 1974.

Cicerchia, Ricardo. *Viajeros: Illustrados y románticos en la imaginación nacional.* Buenos Aires: Ediciones Troquel, 2005.

Fey, Ingrid, and Karen Racine, eds. *Strange Pilgrimages: Travel, Exile, and National Identity in Latin America 1800–1990s.* Wilmington, DE: Scholarly Resources, 2002.

García-Millé, Leonor. "Traces and Perceptions: A Chilean in Europe after the 1848 Revolution." In *The European Revolutions of 1848 and the Americas*, ed. Guy Thomson, pp. 142–158. London: Institute of Latin American Studies, 2002.

Jitrik, Noé, ed. *Los viajeros.* Buenos Aires: Jorge Alvarez, 1969.

Lerner, Victoria. "Dos generaciones de viajeros mexicanos del siglo XIX frente a los Estados Unidos." *Relaciones* 14, no. 55 (1993): 41–72.

Lerner, Victoria. "Espías mexicanos en tierras norteamericanas, 1914–1915." *New Mexico Historical Review* 69, no. 3 (July 1994): 230–247.

Nichols, Madaline. "A United States Tour by Sarmiento in 1847." *Hispanic American Historical Review* 16 (1936): 190–212.

Núñez, Estuardo. *La experiencia europea de José Carlos Mariátegui y otros ensayos.* Lima: Empresa Editora Amauta, 1978.

Núñez, Estuardo. *España vista por viajeros hispanoamericanos.* Madrid: Ediciones Cultura Hispánica, Instituto de Cooperación Iberoamericana, 1985.

Núñez, Estuardo, ed. *Viajeros hispanoamericanos: Temas continentales.* Caracas: Biblioteca Ayacucho, 1989.

Onís, José de. *The United States as Seen by Spanish American Writers, 1776–1890.* New York: Hispanic Institute in the United States, 1952. 2nd ed., New York: Gordon Press, 1975.

Prescott, Laurence. "Journeying through Jim Crow: Spanish American Travelers in the United States during the Age of Segregation." *Latin American Research Review* 42, no. 1 (2007): 3–28.

Salgueiro, Valeria. "Grand Tour: Uma contribução à historia do viajar por prazer e por amor à cultura." *Revista Brasileira de História* 22, no. 44 (December 2002): 289–310.

Sanhueza, Carlos. "From the Southern Hemisphere to the Old World: Travel Accounts of Chileans in Europe and Representations of National Identity in the 19th Century." In *A Fine Line: Explorations in Subjectivity, Borders, and Demarcation*, ed. Richard Weiner and Raúl Galoppe, pp. 47–68. New York: University Press of America, 2005.

Sanhueza, Carlos. *Chilenos en Alemania, y alemanes en Chile: Viaje y nación en el siglo XIX.* Santiago de Chile: DIBAM-LOM, 2006.

Sarmiento, Domingo Faustino. *Travels in the United States in 1847*, trans. Michael Rockland. Princeton, NJ: Princeton University Press, 1970.

Taboada, Hernán. "Un orientalismo periférico: Viajeros latinoamericanos 1786–1920." *Estudios de Asia y Africa* 33, no. 2 (1998): 285–305.

Viñas, David. *De Sarmiento a Dios: Viajeros argentinos a USA.* Buenos Aires: Editorial Sudamericana, 1998.

Zulueta Fernández, Jesús Manuel. *Viajeros hispanoamericanos por la España del fin del siglo 1890–1904.* Cádiz: Universidad de Cádiz, Servicio de Publicaciones, Ayuntamiento de Cádiz, 2002.

KAREN RACINE

TRAVEL LITERATURE. Travel narratives, first-hand accounts of observations made while voyaging, began for Latin America in 1492 with Christopher Columbus, whose composition of letters and logbook carried this European literary genre across the Atlantic. As a region formerly terra incognita developed into various colonial and independent states, and as the era of discovery gave way to business, scientific, and finally leisure travel, the origins and professions of travelogue authors, as well as their narratives' purpose, style, and content, evolved.

Fifteenth-century travel narratives by Europeans primarily related tales of discovery and conquest in the Caribbean and mainland North and South America, prompting European audiences to reconsider their understanding of the world as well as to create governing policies. Columbus's logbooks, the *Five Letters* of Hernán Cortés, and accounts by Bernal Díaz del Castillo, Pedro Pizarro, Jean de Léry, and others provide detailed records of first encounters, exploration, and conquests from Mexico, Peru, and Brazil. Such narratives combined dramatic storytelling, often exaggerated feats of European military prowess, and native savagery. Their themes would become tropes of travel writing about the region: geography, indigenous customs, religions, politics, languages, commerce, agriculture, flora and fauna, and novel consumables such as avocados, tobacco, and cacao. Other accounts, such as conquistador-turned-Dominican friar Bartolomé de las Casas' scathing critique of Spanish treatment of New World residents, *A Brief Account of the Destruction of the Indies* (1542), contributed to Spanish policies meant to mitigate abuses of conquered Americans as well as to the "Black Legend." Missionaries and explorers of the eighteenth century continued to write in this vein about unsettled territories.

When colonies were settled, travel writing became the purview of businessmen, immigrants, royal officials, and the few, mostly European, outsiders who reached Spanish and Portuguese America after monarchs forbade foreigners to travel to or reside there. There is also at least one Middle Eastern account, a manuscript by Elias Al-Musili, a Chaldean priest from Baghdad who visited Spanish America in the late seventeenth century. Spanish views can be found in manuscript letters, court records, official reports, and a few compelling published accounts—including the autobiographical adventures of Catalina de Erauso (1625), known to posterity as "the lieutenant nun" for having escaped a Basque convent and donned men's clothes to pursue a military career in the Americas, and the *Lazarillo de Ciegos* (1773), a tongue-in-cheek narrative in guidebook form published pseudonymously by a Spanish bureaucrat who traveled from Montevideo to Lima evaluating postal services. Foreign sojourners' tales emerge mainly from internal Spanish documents, such as British merchant John Chilton's Inquisition testimony regarding seventeen years as an itinerant merchant in sixteenth-century Mexico and Central America. The few published works were influential, including Thomas Gage's *The English American* (1648), which depicted Spanish America as ripe for invasion and was translated quickly into French, German, and Dutch.

Moreover, because Spain and Portugal never fully controlled the seas, around-the-world voyagers—including privateers William Dampier (1697) and Woodes Rogers (1712)—charted seacoasts from the Caribbean to the Magellan Straits and up to California, and published accounts about their interactions with settlers. Pirates, privateers, and buccaneers recounted natural histories and adventures—two examples are Sir John Hawking's *True Declaration of the Troublesome Voyage* (1569) to Guyana and the West Indies and Alexander Exquemelin's *The Buccaneers of America* (1684). Tales of shipwrecked sailors also made it into print as fact or fiction. Alexander Selkirk, marooned for four years on Chile's Juan Fernández Island and rescued in 1709 by Woodes Rogers, famously inspired Daniel Defoe's *Robinson Crusoe* (1719).

By the mid-eighteenth century, a new breed of explorers emphasized the natural world in travelogues while continuing to write about politics, economics, and society, a trend that continues into the twenty-first century. Frenchman Charles de la Condamine joined forces with Spaniards Jorge Juan and Antonio de Ulloa to determine the length of a degree of latitude in Ecuador, producing scientific texts but also commentary on colonial society. The most famous scientific expedition was the five-year voyage of Baron Alexander von Humboldt, a Prussian naturalist and explorer, with French doctor and botanist Aimé Bonpland. As related in their *Personal Narrative* (1814), the two navigated and mapped the Amazon and Orinoco Rivers, and traveled through Peru, Ecuador, Colombia, Venezuela, Cuba, and Mexico (1799–1804). Humboldt was also an astute observer of politics and society; his "Political Essays" on Mexico (1811) and Cuba (1826) remain important sources of information about Spanish American society on the eve of independence.

In the early nineteenth century, Latin American independence brought new travelers and new styles of travelogue in books and popular journals such as *Harper's*. Britons, French, and Germans, now welcome visitors, promoted economic development with, as Mary Louise Pratt puts it, "imperial eyes"—from exploiting mines to investing in industry to establishing railroads and canals—as well as querying the initial republics' failure to stabilize into "modern" productive societies despite an abundance of natural wealth. Sometimes their reflections, like British views of the Argentine gaucho, contributed, together with those of nationals traveling at home or, like Domingo F. Sarmiento, abroad, to discussions on national identity. North American travelers seeking fame, fortune, and adventure followed, writing accounts such as Anthony King's *Twenty-Four Years in the Argentine Republic* (1846). Women's travel narratives also multiplied: Mariah Graham's *Journal of a Residence in Chile* (1824) appeared soon after independence, followed by Fanny Calderon de la Barca's *Life in Mexico* (1843), and *recuerdos de viaje* (old women's memories) of women visiting their own countries such as Franco-Peruvian Flora Tristan (1838) and Argentine Eduarda Mansilla de García (1882). Scholarly travel narratives took an archaeological and anthropological turn, as John Lloyd Stephens, Gustav von Tempsky, and others reported on ancient ruins and indigenous peoples' customs; leisure travelers visiting for sport, health, and vacation observed the demise of slavery and advent of industrialization; and Protestant agents spread the Gospel in South America and recounted adventures on muleback. After midcentury, with steamship travel contributing to lower prices and shorter travel times, more individuals traveled and wrote up their experiences, resulting in an explosion in mediocre travel narratives.

The genre expanded further in the twentieth century, as transportation by automobile, bus, and airplane put many Latin American cities, mountains, forests, and deserts within relatively easy reach. Travel in twentieth-century Latin America produced focused narratives as compelling as Teddy Roosevelt's *Through the Brazilian Wilderness* (1914) and Zora Neale Hurston's *Tell My Horse* (1938) and more continental approaches, including Ernesto "Che"

Guevara's *Motorcycle Diaries* and Paul Theroux's *The Old Patagonia Express* (1979). Photographs began to replace drawings to illustrate accounts. During the World War II era, texts and film travelogues, such as Donald Duck's virtual travels in *Three Caballeros* (1944), promoted tourism by showing Americans the friendliness and shared values of their southern neighbors, as well as ancient ruins, exotic dances, and relaxing beaches. Travel materials aimed at tourism ignored the vast Latin American wildernesses and metropolises, as well as the region's revolutions and social injustices, which were covered not by travel writers but by journalists such as John Reed in his *Insurgent Mexico* (1914). In the late twentieth century a new travel genre focused on internal personal growth and discovery, as in Mary Morris's *Nothing to Declare* (1988). In the early twenty-first century, individuals seeking to escape the beaten path by, for example, following the Inca trail or diving in the Yucatán's *Cenotes,* post pictures and comments on Web logs even before returning home. Although difficult to codify, this newest genre of travel writing about Latin America returns to familiar themes of discovery, exploration, and conquest—whether of constant external challenges such as mountain peaks and corrupt officials, or more contemporary ones including urban jungles and inner demons.

See also **Black Legend; Bonpland, Aimé Jacques; Calderón de la Barca, Fanny; Carrió de la Bandera, Alonso (Concolorcorvo); Columbus, Christopher; Cortés, Hernán; Díaz del Castillo, Bernal; Gage, Thomas; Gorriti, Juana Manuela; Guevara, Ernesto "Che"; Humboldt, Alexander von; Las Casas, Bartolomé de; Léry, Jean de; Martí y Pérez, José Julián; Roosevelt, Theodore; Sarmiento, Domingo Faustino; Tristan, Flora; Zárate, Agustín de.**

BIBLIOGRAPHY

Compilations

Buchenau, Jürgen. *Mexico Otherwise: Modern Mexico in the Eyes of Foreign Observers*. Albuquerque: University of New Mexico Press, 2005.

Hahner, June E. *Women through Women's Eyes: Latin American Women in Nineteenth-century Travel Accounts*. Wilmington, DE: SR Books, 1998.

Leonard, Irving A., comp., and William C. Bryant, ed. *Colonial Travelers in Latin America*. Newark, DE: Juan de la Cuesta, 1986.

Lockhart, James, and Enrique Otte, eds. and trans. *Letters and People of the Spanish Indies, Sixteenth Century*. Cambridge, U.K., and New York: Cambridge University Press, 1976.

Mayer, William. *Early Travellers in Mexico, 1534–1816.* Mexico, 1961.

Núñez, Estuardo, ed. *Antología de viajeros: Textos fundamentals sobre realidades peruanos.* Lima: Biblioteca Nacional del Peru, 1994.

Szurmuk, Mónica. *Women in Argentina: Early Travel Narratives.* Gainesville: University of Florida Press, 2000.

Accounts

Erauso, Catalina de. *Lieutenant Nun: Memoir of a Basque Transvestite in the New World,* trans. Gabriel Stepto and Michele Stepto. Boston: Beacon Press, 1996.

Farah, Caesar E., ed. and trans. *An Arab's Journey to Colonial Spanish America: The Travels of Elias al-Mûsili in the Seventeenth Century.* Syracuse, NY: Syracuse University Press, 2003.

Gage, Thomas. *Thomas Gage's Travels in the New World,* ed. J. Eric S. Thompson. Westport, CT: Greenwood Press, 1981.

Secondary Sources

Bertrand, Michel, and Laurent Vidal, eds. *A la redécouverte des Amériques: Les voyageurs européens au siècle des indépendances.* Toulouse: Presses universitaires du Mirail, 2002.

Butler, Shannon M. *Travel Narratives in Dialogue: Contesting Representations of Nineteenth-Century Peru.* Ph.D. diss., Ohio State University, 2005.

Monteleone, Jorge. *El relato de viaje: De Sarmiento a Umberto Eco.* Buenos Aires: Librería Editorial El Ateneo, 1998.

Núñez, Estuardo. *Viajes y viajeros extranjeros por el Perú: Apuntes documentales con algunas desarrollos histórico-biográficos.* Lima: Graf P. L. Villanueva, 1989.

Paravisini-Gebert, Lizabeth, and Ivette Romero-Cesareo. *Women at Sea: Travel Writing and the Margins of Caribbean Discourse.* New York: Palgrave, 2001.

Pérez Mejía, Angela. *A Geography of Hard Times: Narratives about Travel to South America, 1789–1849,* trans. Dick Cluster. Albany: State University of New York Press, 2004.

Pratt, Mary Louise. *Imperial Eyes: Travel Writing and Transculturation,* 2nd edition. New York: Routledge, 2008.

Prieto, Adolfo. *Los viajeros ingleses y la emergencia de la literatura argentina, 1820–1850.* Buenos Aires: Editorial Sudamericana, 1996.

JORDANA DYM

TREINTA Y TRES (33) ORIENTALES.

Treinta y tres (33) Orientales, group of patriots of the Banda Oriental (i.e., Uruguay) who in 1825 initiated the final struggle against Brazilian rule. They were led by Juan Antonio Lavalleja, a former collaborator of the Uruguayan independence leader José Gervasio Artigas, who had already led one unsuccessful uprising. Lavalleja took refuge in Argentina, where he gathered other disaffected Uruguayans into a liberation movement and courted Argentine private assistance.

On 19 April 1825 Lavalleja made landing on the Uruguayan coast at La Agraciada, near Colonia. Though his group became known as the "Thirty-three Orientals," several of them were Argentine and one was a French volunteer. They quickly expanded their beachhead, obtaining recruits and supplies. At the end of April, Lavalleja was joined by Fructuoso Rivera, another former lieutenant of Artigas who had lately been serving the Brazilians and had a wide network of followers in the Uruguayan interior. Initial successes, together with the decision of the insurgents to seek incorporation into the United Provinces of the Río De La Plata, led the authorities at Buenos Aires to give them open support. The result was the Argentine-Brazilian war of 1825–1828, into which the struggle of the Treinta y Tres was subsumed.

See also **Brazil, Independence Movements; Uruguay, Congress of 1825; Wars of Independence, South America.**

BIBLIOGRAPHY

John Street, *Artigas and the Emancipation of Uruguay* (1959).

Alfredo Castellanos, *La Cisplatina, la independencia y la república caudillesca* (1974).

Additional Bibliography

Barrios Pintos, Aníbal. *Historia de los pueblos orientales: Sus orígenes, procesos fundacionales, sus primeros años.* Montevideo, Uruguay: Academia Nacional de Letras, 2000.

Golletti Wilkinson, Alberto. *Guerra contra el empresario del Brasil: A la luz de sus protagonistas.* Buenos Aires: Editorial Dunken, 2003.

Narancio, Edmundo M. *La independencia de Uruguay.* Montevideo, Uruguay: Editorial Ayer, 2001.

DAVID BUSHNELL

TREJOS FERNÁNDEZ, JOSÉ JOAQUÍN

(1916–). José Joaquín Trejos Fernández (*b.* 18 April 1916), president of Costa Rica (1966–1970), professor, dean, and vice rector of the University of Costa Rica.

José Joaquín Trejos Fernández came to national prominence only after being nominated as a presidential candidate in 1965 when the former presidents and political adversaries Rafael Ángel Calderón Guardia (1940–1944) and Otilio Ulate Blanco (1949–1953) joined their forces in opposition to the ever more dominant National Liberation Party (PLN). Trejos, although a Calderonist, had little prior political experience but was widely known and respected as a professional of great integrity and rectitude.

After his surprise victory, Trejos's administration distinguished itself in several areas. Among its most notable accomplishments were the sustained growth in the gross national product and the development of the infrastructure on the Atlantic coast with the construction of a highway to Puerto Limon and new wharfage facilities for the port, and the extension of the Tortuguero Canal.

See also **Costa Rica, National Liberation Party.**

BIBLIOGRAPHY

José Joaquín Trejos Fernández, *Reflexiones sobre la educación* (1963).

Charles D. Ameringer, *Don Pepe* (1978).

Harold D. Nelson, ed., *Costa Rica: A Country Study* (1983).

Additional Bibliography

Chincilla Coto, José Carlos and Maynor Antonio Mora. *El sistema de partidos políticos en Costa Rica durante el segundo mitad del siglo XX.* San José: Editorial de la Universidad de Costa Rica, 2005.

Cuevas Molina, Rafael. *Cultura y política en Costa Rica: Entrevistas a protagonistas de la política cultural en la segunda mitad del siglo XX.* San José: Editorial Universidad Estatal a Distancia, 2006.

Ocontrillo García, Eduardo. *Cien años de política Costarricense: 1902–2002; De acensión esquivel a Abel Pacheco.* San José: Editorial de la Universidad de Costa Rica, 2004.

JOHN PATRICK BELL

TRESGUERRAS, FRANCISCO EDUARDO DE

(1759–1833). Francisco Eduardo de Tresguerras (*b.* 13 October 1759; *d.* 3 August 1833), Mexican painter and architect. In contrast to most well-known artists of his time, Tresguerras pursued his career not in Mexico City but in Querétaro, Celaya, and San Luis Potosí. He dedicated himself to painting, music, architecture, engraving, and writing in turn, and can be considered a particularly interesting example of the self-conscious and confident eighteenth-century New World artist. His most famous creation is the church of Nuestra Señora del Carmen in Celaya, with a single tower over the entrance (1802–1807). In painting and drawing his style is rococo, but in architecture he is neoclassical. Although Tresguerras sought recognition from the Academia de San Carlos, he seems never to have been accepted by the Mexico City art establishment.

See also **Architecture: Architecture to 1900; Art: The Colonial Era; Mexico: The Colonial Period.**

BIBLIOGRAPHY

The best source is still Francisco Eduardo Tresguerras, *Ocios literarios,* edited by Francisco de la Maza (1962), his collected works. See also Manuel Toussaint, *Colonial Art in Mexico* (1967).

CLARA BARGELLINI

TRIANA, JOSÉ

(1931–). José Triana, a Cuban playwright from Camagüey, lived in Madrid in the 1950s. With the rise of Fidel Castro in 1959, Triana returned to Cuba, eager to help build a new society. The revolution fostered the arts, primarily as a venue for its leftist ideology. By 1969 the government subsidy for culture was $16 million, a huge investment in the infrastructure of this island nation, much of it fostering theater groups. Triana wrote several plays that were well received; in 1965 he won the coveted Casa de las Américas prize for *La noche de los asesinos,* his most acclaimed work, which ostensibly was a critique of the (Fulgencio) Batista years (1952–1959), but was thought by some to be subversive. After participating in the Nancy Festival of 1957 and marrying a French woman, he returned to Cuba but was ostracized by the regime. In 1980 he fled the island and settled in Paris, where his plays secretly written in Cuba finally became known and appreciated.

See also **Batista y Zaldívar, Fulgencio; Theater.**

BIBLIOGRAPHY

Nigro, Kirsten F., ed. *Parabras más que comunes: Ensayos sobre teatro de José Triana.* Boulder, CO: Society for Spanish and American Studies, 1994.

GEORGE WOODYARD

TRIBUNAL DE CUENTAS.

On 24 August 1605 Philip III ordered establishment of a *tribunal de cuentas* (tribunal of accounts) in Bogotá, Lima, and Mexico City with jurisdiction over New Granada, Peru, and New Spain (Mexico), respectively. Headed by three accountants called *contadores de cuentas* and staffed by a host of lesser bookkeepers and copyists, the *tribunal de cuentas* regulated record-keeping procedures and audited accounts kept by officials of the Real Hacienda (royal treasury) in their jurisdiction. In some regions a *contador de cuentas* was required to inspect treasuries (*cajas*) personally to ensure adherence to proper accounting procedures. At the end of an accounting period, all royal treasury officials submitted their ledgers to the tribunal for auditing. The tribunal, in turn, checked the accounts, challenged discrepancies, and then sent the books to the Contaduría of the Council of Indies in Spain.

Although theoretically the tribunal ensured honest, efficient royal record keeping in the Indies, in fact, the system broke down because *tribunal contadores* simply had too much to do and were virtually drowned in a sea of paper that made it impossible for them to keep up. In fact, in the late eighteenth century, some tribunals were more than twenty years behind in completing their audits.

See also **Mexico: The Colonial Period; Philip III of Spain.**

BIBLIOGRAPHY

Recopilación de leyes de Reynos de las Indias, 4 vols. (1681; repr. 1973), libro VIII, título I and II.

Gaspar De Escalona Agüero, *Gazofilacio real del Perú,* 4th ed. (1941).

Additional Bibliography

Jáuregui, Luis. *The American Finances of the Spanish Empire: Royal Income and Expenditures in Colonial Mexico, Peru, and Bolivia, 1680-1809.* Albuquerque: University of New Mexico Press, 1998.

Klein, Herbert S. *La real hacienda de Nueva España: Su administración en la época de los intendentes, 1786-1821.* México: Universidad Nacional Autónoma de México, Facultad de Economía, 1999.

JOHN JAY TEPASKE

TRINIDAD AND TOBAGO.

Trinidad and Tobago are one state but culturally two distinct islands. They are quite a bit farther apart from each other—twenty miles—than Trinidad is from Venezuela—eight miles. Trinidad's area measures 1,964 square miles, as compared to Tobago's 116 square miles.

Virtually every major European naval power fought over Tobago, which explains why it changed hands more than twenty times. It was finally transferred to Great Britain in 1802 by the Treaty of Amiens. Since the twentieth century, Tobago has developed as a tourist economy and is also sustained by financial transfers, both governmental and private, from Trinidad. It is served by a modern international airport and a ferry service from Trinidad.

Trinidad, on the other hand, remained unchallenged in Spanish hands from the day Columbus sighted it in 1498 until conquered by the British in 1797. The very weak defenses of the island were testimony to its continued insignificance to the Spanish Crown. To the extent that it was developed at all came as a result of the French response to the Royal Cédula de Población of 1783, which enticed many French Catholic colonists (white and colored) with grants of land. At that time Britain, having lost its American colonies, was aggressively seeking to add new ones in the Caribbean. It was from one of Britain's important conquests, French-held Grenada, that many of the migrants to Trinidad came. By the time the British arrived in Trinidad, it would be fair to say that Spain ruled but the French "governed" the island.

Such was the influence of the "old colonists" that the new colonial power was compelled to retain Spanish law (until 1850) and refrain from

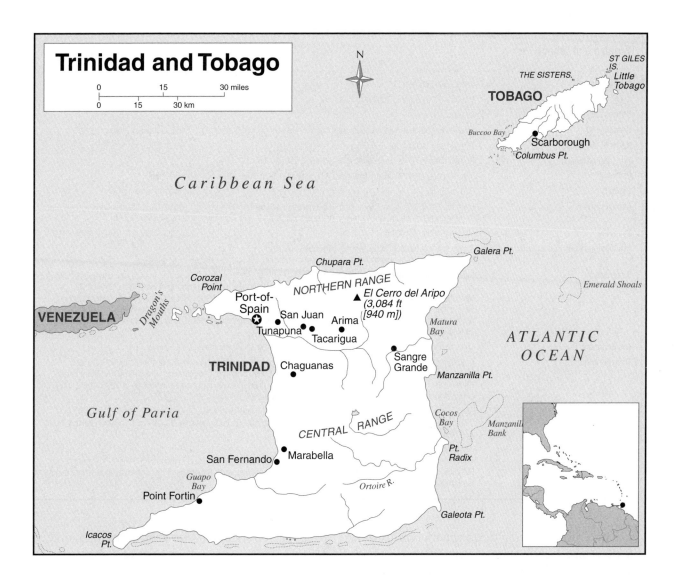

Trinidad and Tobago

0   15   30 miles

0   15   30 km

ST GILES IS.

THE SISTERS.   Little Tobago

TOBAGO

Buccoo Bay   Scarborough

Columbus Pt.

Caribbean Sea

Galera Pt.

Chupara Pt.

Corozal Point

NORTHERN RANGE

El Cerro del Aripo (3,084 ft [940 m])

Emerald Shoals

Port-of-Spain

San Juan   Arima

Tunapuna   Tacarigua

VENEZUELA

Dragon's Mouths

Matura Bay

ATLANTIC OCEAN

TRINIDAD   Chaguanas

Sangre Grande

Manzanilla Pt.

Gulf of Paria

CENTRAL RANGE

Cocos Bay

Manzanilla Bank

San Fernando   Marabella

Pt. Radix

Guapo Bay

Point Fortin

Ortoire R.

Galeota Pt.

Icacos Pt.

making the Anglican Church the "established" church. This was a first in the British Caribbean and explains why Roman Catholicism is the single largest religion on the island. It also explains the persistence of European Catholic festivals such as carnival and of parang, a folk music genre of Christian lyrics sung in Spanish, at Christmas, that originated on the islands. Because the British believed it impossible to govern such "foreigners" with British institutions, as they were doing everywhere else in the Caribbean, they governed Trinidad as a Crown Colony, that is, without an independent house of assembly but rather direct rule from London through an all-powerful governor.

This background and two other historical events go far toward explaining why Trinidad differs so dramatically from the rest of the British West Indies. The first event was the relatively short duration on the island of the slave plantation system. Britain abolished the slave trade in 1808, and Emancipation was proclaimed in 1834. Second, because there was ample vacant land on the island, the black slaves left the plantations and became, first, a small peasantry and, subsequently, urban dwellers. These slaves were replaced by indentured British Indians, a system that lasted from 1854 to 1917. This history determined Trinidad's fundamental demographic and religious characteristics: The rural Indo-Trinidadians (41% of the total) are mostly landowners and small merchants; the urban Afro-Trinidadians (40% of the total) are mostly artisans and workers in the public-sector mining and manufacturing industries. The population is 30 percent Roman Catholic, 25 percent Hindu, 20 percent Protestant, and 8 percent Muslim. English is the common language.

Trinidad and Tobago

Population:	1,056,608 (2007 est.)
Area:	Trinidad: 1,964 sq. mi.; Tobago; 116 sq. mi.
Official language(s):	English
Language(s):	English, English and French patois; Caribbean Hindustani (a dialect of Hindi), French, Spanish, Chinese
National currency:	Trinidad and Tobago dollar (TTD)
Principal religions:	Roman Catholic: 30%; Protestant: 20%; Hindu: 25%; Muslim: 8%
Ethnicity:	Indo Trinidadian: 41%; Afro Trinidadian: 40%; mixed race or other: 19%
Capital:	Port-of-Spain
Annual rainfall:	From 98.4 in to 150 in on Tobago and in the northern and central hill areas of Trinidad. Most hilly sections receive 80 in or more, while in the lowlands the average drops below 65 in and in certain sections below 50 in.
Economy:	*GDP per capita:* $16,700
Principal products and exports:	*Agriculture:* cocoa, rice, citrus, coffee, vegetables; poultry *Industries:* petroleum, chemicals, tourism, food processing, cement, beverages, cotton textiles
Government:	Independence from the United Kingdom, 1962. Constitutional parliamentary democracy. In 2007 the chief of state was President George Maxwell Richards (since 17 March 2003) and the head of government was Prime Minister Patrick Manning (since 24 December 2001). President elected by an electoral college, which consists of the members of the Senate and House of Representatives, for a five-year term (eligible for a second term); the president usually appoints as prime minister the leader of the majority party in the House of Representatives. The next presidential elections were to be held in 2008.
Armed forces:	Trinidad and Tobago Defense Force: 2,700 (2005 est.); Army: 2,000 members; Coast Guard: 700.
Transportation:	In 2002, there were 5,170 mi of roads, of which 2,642 mi were paved. Large sections of Tobago either have poor or undriveable roads. There are no railways. Ports: Port-of-Spain, Brighton, Chaguaramas, Pointe-à-Pierre, Point Fortin, Point Lisas. In 2004, there were six airports and airfields, three of which had paved runways as of 2005. There is one airline, Trinidad and Tobago Airways, owned by the government.
Media:	There were 4 AM and 18 FM radio stations, and 4 television stations in 2004. There were four daily newspapers in 2002: *Trinidad Guardian,* circulation of 46,760; *Trinidad Express,* 51,000; *Newsday,* 25,000; and *Trinidad Evening News,* 33,770.
Literacy and education:	*Total literacy rate:* 98.6% Education is free at primary and secondary levels and compulsory for six years. There are four small, government-run technical colleges, five teachers colleges, and two polytechnic institutes. A campus of the University of the West Indies is located outside of Port-of-Spain.

Two critical events in the twentieth century built on these nineteenth-century foundations to create the industrialized, "middle income" (in World Bank terms, "graduated") state that Trinidad is today. First was the discovery and exploitation of oil starting in the 1920s. Second was the establishment, by the United States during World War II, of two major anti-submarine bases on the island. The Americans introduced an industrial-type labor regime that further prepared the Afro-Trinidadians for the kind of industrial schemes that would be launched after the war. Upon securing independence in 1962, the first prime minister, Eric Williams, pushed to invest the oil and natural gas wealth in a major industrial development in the southern part of the island, Point Lisas, which has become the most important enclave of oil-and natural gas–based industries in the Caribbean. Aside from shipping liquefied natural gas (LNG) to U.S. ports, Point Lisas has steel, ammonia, fertilizer, and plastic industries and is planning an aluminum smelter. The whole complex is served by a modern deep-water port and houses its own technical university, the University of Trinidad and Tobago, established at the beginning of the century. This institution complements the highly regarded faculties of chemistry and petroleum engineering at the University of the West Indies (St. Augustine), which has provided most of the technical staff at Point Lisas.

With a gross domestic product of $18 billion ($16,700 per capita), unemployment down to an all-time low of 5 percent, and a government disposed toward foreign private investments, Trinidad has been one of the fastest-growing economies in the Western hemisphere for the decade 1997 to 2007. Sustaining this growth will depend on the island's successfully confronting two great challenges: managing ethnic pluralism, and controlling subversive violence by minorities. Toward the first goal, Trinidad must maintain peaceful coexistence in a political system evenly divided between the Afro-Trinidadian People's National Movement (PNM) and the Indo-

Trinidadians represented by a succession of parties invariably in opposition to the PNM. These groups both support elections but keep a wary eye on each other at election time. The threat of subversive violence is serious, as some groups have taken advantage of the culturally open and easy-going Trinidadians. In 1970 that threat came from a Black Power uprising and in 1990 from a native Islamic group with arms bought in Florida. Neither succeeded, but both demonstrate the vulnerability of small nations to the menace of conspiratorial movements, whether ideologically driven antidemocratic groups, terrorists, or international criminal organizations.

See also **British-Latin American Relations; Buccaneers and Privateers; Petroleum Industry.**

BIBLIOGRAPHY

Oxaal, Ivar. *Black Intellectuals and the Dilemmas of Race and Class in Trinidad.* Cambridge, MA: Schenkman, 1982.

Williams, Eric. *Inward Hunger: The Education of a Prime Minister.* New edition. Princeton, NJ: M. Wiener, 2006.

Yelvington, Kevin A., ed. *Trinidad Ethnicity.* Knoxville: University of Tennessee Press, 1993.

ANTHONY P. MAINGOT

TRINIDADE ISLAND.

Trinidade Island, a small, uninhabited volcanic island 680 miles off the coast of Espírito Santo. Discovered by Tristão da Cunha for Portugal in the sixteenth century, the island was visited by English astronomer Edmund Halley in 1700 when he explored the South Atlantic as captain of the *Paramour.* The island was reputed to be the site of a fortune in ecclesiastical gold and silver buried by pirates in the nineteenth century. This rumor may have encouraged the 1895 invasion of the island by Great Britain. Britain's justification for its actions was that the island had been unoccupied for more than a century. Upon Brazilian protest and mediation by Dom Carlos I, king of Portugal, Great Britain recognized Brazilian rights to the island in 1896.

See also **Piracy.**

BIBLIOGRAPHY

E. F. Knight, *Cruise of the "Alerte"* (1929).

Additional Bibliography

Azzoni, Carlos Roberto. *Geography and Income Convergence among Brazilian States.* Washington, DC: Inter-American Development Bank, 2000.

Rocha, Jan. *Brazil.* Oxford: Oxfam, 2000.

Vincent, John S. *Culture and Customs of Brazil.* Westport, CT: Greenwood Press, 2003.

SHEILA L. HOOKER

TRINIDAD, PARAGUAY.

Trinidad del Paraná, near the present-day city of Encarnación in southern Paraguay and one of the thirty missions of the Jesuit Province of Paraguay (1607–1767), was a center of missionary effort among the Guarani people. Under Jesuit tutelage the Guarani learned Christianity as well as European agriculture and other skills, and quickly exhibited high artistic talents.

The jewel of Trinidad is its church, begun in 1706. There one is struck by the skill of the Guarani, particularly their holy statuary. Upon the main doors of the church artists carved impressive examples of the native flora. In recent decades archeologists have excavated polychrome statuary that reveals a new dimension to the ability of the native craftsmen and artists.

See also **Guarani Indians; Jesuits; Missions: Spanish America.**

BIBLIOGRAPHY

Ganson, Barbara. *The Guaraní under Spanish Rule in the Río de la Plata.* Stanford, CA: Stanford University Press, 2003.

McNaspy, Clement J., and Jose M. Blanch. *Lost Cities of Paraguay: Art and Architecture of the Jesuit Reductions, 1607–1767.* Chicago: Loyola University Press, 1982.

JERRY W. COONEY

TRINITARIA, LA.

La Trinitaria, Dominican independence movement founded in 1838. La Trinitaria was a secret society organized by Juan Pablo Duarte, Francisco de Rosario Sánchez, and Ramón Mella in 1838 to drive out the Haitian occupation of Santo Domingo (1822–1844). The society was organized into three-man cells with a complex series of codes and passwords. Trinitaria ideals included democracy, representative government, and independence. It attracted widespread support from Dominican patriots and within five years had cells in most major centers. Members signed blood oaths of loyalty to the society and to the independence movement. Its meetings were characterized by rituals using religious symbolism. Its success in mobilizing opposition against the Haitian government led to persecution and repression. After participating in the overthrow of President Jean-Pierre Boyer, the new president, Charles Hérard, exiled the society's leaders.

Once the Haitian occupation ended, Trinitaria leaders were marginalized from the new government by the country's new military leaders. Although it was prevented from attaining power, the ideals and symbol of La Trinitaria remained an inspiration and guiding force for future social movements that wanted to rid the Dominican Republic of repressive domestic governments and foreign intervention.

See also **Democracy; Duarte, Juan Pablo; Mella, Ramón Matías.**

BIBLIOGRAPHY

Selden Rodman, *Quisqueya: A History of the Dominican Republic* (1964).

Howard J. Wiarda, *The Dominican Republic: Nation in Transition* (1969).

Ian Bell, *The Dominican Republic* (1981).

Howard J. Wiarda and M. J. Kryzanek, *The Dominican Republic: A Caribbean Crucible* (1982).

Additional Bibliography

Henríquez Ureña, Max. *La ideal de los trinitarios.* Madrid, Spain: EDISOL, 1951.

Machado Báez, Manuel Arturo. *La Trinitaria.* Trujillo, Peru: Impresa Dominicana, 1956.

HEATHER K. THIESSEN

TRIPLE ALLIANCE. *See* **War of the Triple Alliance.**

TRISTAN, FLORA (1803–1844). Flora Tristan (*b.* 7 April 1803; *d.* 14 November 1844), French social critic and utopian socialist who left

important writings on mid-nineteenth-century Europe and Peru. In 1833–1834, fleeing a disastrous marriage, the Paris-born Tristan sought the support of her deceased father's family in Peru, the aristocratic Tristans. Unable to convince them that she was a legitimate member of the family, she traveled extensively in the midst of a civil war. Her travels culminated in the insightful 1838 travelogue *Pérégrinations d'une paria.* Her subsequent publications in Europe dealt with such major issues as living conditions in London, feminism, and socialism. Her intellectual and political activities continued until her death in Bordeaux. The painter Paul Gauguin was her grandson.

BIBLIOGRAPHY

Flora Tristan, *Peregrinations of a Pariah, 1833–34,* translated by Jean Hawkes (1987).

Mary Louise Pratt, *Imperial Eyes: Travel Writing and Transculturation* (1992), esp. pp. 155–171.

Doris Beik and Paul Beik, eds. and trans., *Flora Tristan, Utopian Feminist: Her Travel Diaries and Personal Crusade* (1993).

Additional Bibliography

Bloch-Dano, Evelyne. *Flora Tristán: Pionera, revolucionaria y aventurera del siglo XIX.* Mexico City: Oceano de México; and Madrid: Maeva, 2003.

Busse, Erika. *El símbolo Flora Tristán en el feminismo peruano.* Lima: Centro de la Mujer Peruana Flora Tristán, 2003.

Cross, Máire. *The Letter in Flora Tristan's Politics, 1835–1844.* Houndmills and New York: Palgrave Macmillan, 2004.

Pérez Mejía, Angela. *La geografía de los tiempos difíciles: Escritura de viajes a Sur América durante los procesos de independencia, 1780–1849.* Medellín: Editorial Universidad de Antioquia, 2002.

Sánchez, Luis Alberto, Marco Martos, and José Jiménez Borja. *Una mujer sola contra el mundo: Flora Tristán.* Lima: Instituto Luis Alberto Sánchez; COFIDE, Corporación Financiera de Desarrollo; and Fondo Editorial, Universidad Nacional Mayor de San Marcos, 2004.

CHARLES F. WALKER

TRONCOSO DE LA CONCHA, MANUEL DE JESÚS (1878–1955). Manuel de Jesús Troncoso de la Concha (*b.* 3 April 1878;

d. 30 May 1955), Dominican lawyer, university professor, and president (1940–1942). A native of Santo Domingo, Troncoso de la Concha received a licentiate in law from the University of Santo Domingo in 1899 and taught civil law there. From 1911 until his death in 1955, he held many important government positions, such as minister of justice, interior and police; development and communication; and war and naval affairs. During the era of Rafael Trujillo (1930–1961), he served as vice president (1938–1942). After the death of Jacinto B. Peynado in 1940, Troncoso de la Concha also became the nominal head of state. (In reality, Trujillo continued to run the Dominican Republic.)

Of his historical works, the most important is *Genesis de la Ocupación Norteamericana de Santo Domingo,* in which he analyzed the political and economic motives for the U.S. occupation of the Dominican Republic. Another one of his important historical writings is *La Ocupación de Santo Domingo por Haití* (1942), in which he made the unorthodox assertion that the Dominican population actually welcomed the Haitian occupation. Among his literary works, the *Narraciones Dominicanas* (1953) occupies a leading position. He died in Santo Domingo.

See also **Santo Domingo; Trujillo Molina, Rafael Leónidas.**

BIBLIOGRAPHY

R. Emilio Jiménez, ed., *Manuel de Jesús Troncoso de la Concha,* 5th ed. (1960).

                                                    KAI P. SCHOENHALS

TROPICAL DISEASES.   *See* Diseases.

TROPICALISMO.   Tropicalismo, a Brazilian arts and music movement also known as *tropicália,* which lasted roughly from 1967 to 1969. Its participants were inspired in part by poet Oswald de Andrade's 1928 "Manifesto antropofágico" (Cannibalistic Manifesto), in which he expressed the idea of artistic cannibalism, defined as the "cultural devouring of imported techniques to reelaborate them with autonomy." By imaginatively and ironically mixing foreign and Brazilian culture, rock and samba, the folkloric and the urban, the erudite and the kitsch, the *tropicalistas* hoped to foster new ideas and perceptions about both Brazilian reality and foreign cultural influences (such as rock and roll) that were becoming part of that environment.

Tropicalismo manifested itself in the theater in productions such as José Celso Martínez Correa's 1967 staging of de Andrade's *O rei da vela,* and in the plastic arts through the work of artists like Hélio Oiticica (whose 1967 ambient artwork "Tropicália" gave the movement its name). The leading proponents of *tropicalismo* in the area of music were Gilberto Gil, Caetano Veloso, Tom Zé, Gal Costa, Nara Leão, Torquato Neto, Os Mutantes, Capinam, and conductors Júlio Medaglia and Rogério Duprat. Together, they released "Tropicália" (1968), an album that was a collective musical manifesto. Seminal *tropicalismo* songs include Gil's "Domingo no parque" (Sunday in the Park), and Gil Neto's "Geléia geral" (General Jelly), and Veloso's "Alegria alegria" (Joy, Joy). Musically, such compositions fused Brazilian folk styles, rock, and modern electronic music, and were credited with greatly expanding experimentation in Brazilian popular music.

See also **Music: Popular Music and Dance.**

BIBLIOGRAPHY

Ana Maria Bahiana, *Nada será como antes* (1980).

Charles Perrone, *Masters of Contemporary Brazilian Song: MPB 1965–1985* (1989).

Chris Mc Gowan and Ricardo Pessanha, *The Brazilian Sound: Samba, Bossa Nova, and the Popular Music of Brazil* (1991).

Additional Bibliography

Castelo, Claudia. *"O modo portugues de estar no mundo": O luso-tropicalismo e a ideologia colonial portuguesa (1933–1961).* Porto: Ediçoes Afrontamento, 1998.

Cyntrão, Sylvia Helena. *A forma da festa: Tropicalismo, a explosão e seus estilhaços.* Brasilia: Editora UnB; São Paulo, SP: Impr. Oficial SP, 2000.

Sanches, Pedro Alexandre. *Tropicalismo: Decadencia bonita do samba.* São Paulo: Boitempo Editoral, 2000.

                                                    CHRIS MCGOWAN

TROPICALISTA SCHOOL OF MEDICINE (BAHIA).

Tropicalista School of Medicine (Bahia), an informal "school" formed by a dozen physicians in Bahia (1860–1890) that made discoveries in parasitology and contributed to ongoing debates on beriberi, leprosy, tuberculosis, dracontiasis, and other tropical disorders. The Tropicalistas started as an outsider movement critiquing the Bahian Medical School for outdated teaching and Brazilian doctors for lack of original investigation into Brazilian disorders. The three founders were foreigners. Otto Wucherer (1820–1875), a German and arguably the most important member, discovered the existence of hookworm (*Ancylostoma*) in Brazil in 1865. He was the first person to describe the embryonic filaria (*Wucheria bancrofti*) in 1866, known today as the cause of filariasis. The Scotsman John L. Paterson (1820–1882) introduced Lister's method of antisepsis to Bahian physicians and organized fortnightly meetings for physicians to discuss their cases and keep abreast of medical advances. The meetings led to the birth of the "school." Paterson also proposed the creation of the journal *Gazeta Médica da Bahia*. The Portuguese founder was José Francisco da Silva Lima (1826–1910), who wrote about beriberi in Bahia, was the first to describe the disorder ainhum (a disease affecting the toes), and provided the perseverance needed to make the *Gazeta Médica da Bahia* one of the most successful medical journals in nineteenth-century Latin America. The Tropicalistas initiated one of the most innovative medical episodes in nineteenth-century Brazil.

See also **Medicine: Colonial Spanish America.**

BIBLIOGRAPHY

Antonio Caldas Coni, *A escola tropicalista bahiana* (1952).

Julyan G. Peard, "The Tropicalista School of Medicine of Bahia, 1860–1889" (Ph.D. diss., Columbia University, 1990), and "Tropical Medicine in Nineteenth-Century Brazil: The Case of the 'Escola Tropicalista Bahiana,' 1860–1890," in *Warm Climates and Western Medicine: The Emergence of Tropical Medicine, 1500–1900*, edited by David Arnold (forthcoming).

Additional Bibliography

Gilberto Hochman, Gilberto, and Diego Armus. *Cuidar, controlar, curar: Ensaios históricos sobre saúde e doença na América Latina e Caribe.* Rio de Janeiro: Editora Fiocruz, 2004.

Peard, Julyan G. *Race, Place and Medicine: The Idea of the Tropics in Nineteenth-century Brazilian Medicine.* Durham, NC: Duke University Press, 1999.

Schwarcz, Lilia Moritz. *The Spectacle of the Races: Scientists, Institutions, and the Race Question in Brazil, 1870–1930.* Trans. Leland Guyer. New York: Hill and Wang, 1999.

Stepan, Nancy. *Picturing Tropical Nature.* Ithaca, NY: Cornell University Press, 2001.

Teixeira, Rodolfo. *Memória histórica da faculdade de medicina do Terreiro de Jesus, 1943–1995.* Salvador: EDUFBA, 1999.

JULYAN G. PEARD

TROTSKY, LEON (1879–1940).

Leon Trotsky (*b.* 26 October 1879; *d.* 21 August 1940), Russian revolutionary. Trotsky, originally named Lev Davidovich Bronstein, was born to a Jewish family in Yanovka, Ukraine. With Vladimir Lenin, he led the Russian Revolution of October 1917; later he guided the Red Army and created the concept of "permanent revolution."

Following Lenin's death, Trotsky's opposition to Stalin resulted in his exile to Turkey, France, and Norway. In January 1937 he came to Mexico at the invitation of President Lázaro Cárdenas and lived for a time at the home of Diego Rivera and Frida Kahlo. Throughout his stay in Mexico, prominent labor leaders such as Valentín Campa and Vicente Lombardo Toledano protested his presence in their country. On 24 May 1940 the famous muralist David Alfaro Siqueiros led an attack on Trotsky's house, but although some 200 shots were fired and one guard was abducted and murdered, Trotsky and his family were unharmed. On 20 August 1940 Ramón Mercader, a Catalan assassin working for the Soviet secret police, attacked Trotsky in his home in Coyoacán. He died the next day.

See also **Cárdenas del Río, Lázaro; Kahlo, Frida; Rivera, Diego.**

BIBLIOGRAPHY

Isaac Deutscher, *The Prophet Outcast* (1963), and Jean Van Heijenoort, *With Trotsky in Exile: From Prinkipo to Coyoacán* (1978).

Additional Bibliography

Dugrand, Alain; James Thomas Farrell; and Pierre Broué. *Trotsky in Mexico.* Manchester: Carcanet, 1992.

Gall, Olivia. *Trotsky en México: Y la vida política en el periodo de Cárdenas, 1937–1940.* Mexico City: Ediciones Era, 1991.

                                    BARBARA A. TENENBAUM

TRUJILLO. Trujillo, a district, province, and department (now called "La Libertad") in Peru, with a capital of the same name. The capital was one of the first European towns (*villas*) established after the Spanish invaded Peru. In 1534, Diego de Almagro laid it out in a fertile coastal river valley, very near the old Chimú capital of Chan Chan. He named the settlement after the Spanish homeland of his partner, Francisco Pizarro. The latter returned to officially found the town in March 1535. Throughout the sixteenth century, the city remained the seat of political and economic power of the Peruvian viceroyalty in the north, being the principal residence of *encomienda*-holding families. It quickly became an important stopover on the overland route south to Lima, the city of the kings. Wheat, sugarcane, and some silver produced in the hinterland provided the basis for a thriving import-export trade.

The city's early predominance did not go unchallenged in the following years. In 1563, another Spanish town, the *villa* of Santiago de Miraflores, was built in the valley of Saña. Despite energetic protests to the central authorities, Trujillo lost some of its most prominent citizens, part of its wide territorial jurisdiction, and a proportion of the Mita (rotating, draft Amerindian laborers), who were reassigned to serve the Spanish founders of the city, which became known as Saña. In 1609 Trujillo became the seat of a bishopric. Its religious hegemony, however, was threatened about a decade later by an earthquake that made the bishop move his headquarters north to Lambayeque. A reluctant bishop was ordered by superiors back to Trujillo and enticed to move with subventions from the government to rebuild his church. Finally, the constant threat of pirates forced the city to enclose itself inside thick defensive walls before the end of the seventeenth century.

Throughout colonial times, Trujillo nonetheless remained an important coastal center of agricultural production and, in the late eighteenth century, of mining. In the 1780s, it became an intendancy, which restored its control over much of its original territorial jurisdiction.

During the nineteenth century, Trujillo was often the scene of political struggles. It was José Bernardo de Torre Tagle y Portocarrero, the intendant of Trujillo, who joined the cause for independence under José de San Martín, giving the movement an important and early boost. Shortly thereafter, in 1823, the city became the scene of rivalry between José Mariano de la Riva Agüero y Osma, Peru's first president, and Torre Tagle, who with the help of General Antonio José de Sucre, established a rival government. Simón Bolívar, the noted Spanish American liberator, used the city as a temporary administrative center for his authoritarian regime in 1824. During these years the Department of Trujillo was renamed the Department of La Libertad, a name it retains. Trujillo was also the locale of a short-lived revolt during the presidential term of José Rufino Echenique, and later it was pillaged by the invading Chileans during the War of the Pacific (1879–1883).

In the twentieth century, Trujillo became famous as the birthplace of Víctor Raúl Haya de la Torre, founder of the political party Alianza Popular Revolucionaria Americana (APRA). It also gained prestige when César Vallejo, the great avant-garde poet, studied at La Libertad University. While there he became acquainted with Trujillo's bohemia, meeting Haya de la Torre, among others.

The consolidation of some sixty-five agricultural estates into three giant agro-industrial complexes after World War I caused massive discontent among the landed class and the city's commercial interests. These segments of society and the organized sugar plantation workers made Trujillo the solid center of APRA. In the 1930s, after Luis M. Sánchez Cerro was elected and then shot by an APRA sympathizer, the rank-and-file Apristas revolted. The military, called in to repress the rebellion, rounded up men with bruises on their trigger fingers and shoulders, indicating that they had fired weapons; marched them to the ruins of Chan Chan; and summarily shot them. This became known as the "Trujillo massacre" and marked the beginning of a legacy of hatred between APRA and the military, which was not finally overcome until Alan García won the presidential elections and was allowed to take office in 1985.

Today, Trujillo is the third largest city of Peru in population with an estimated population of more than 634,000 citizens in 2005. The city fathers have preserved Trujillo's colonial air, evoking tradition, ceremonialism, and conservatism in the architecture of the city center, especially around its central plaza and main commercial street, with their renovated Casonas (great houses), which provide the visitor and Trujillanos alike with reminders of its rich history.

The most important economic center of northern Peru, Trujillo is an inland commercial and transportation center for the surrounding farming areas. Around 1800, the city of Trujillo greatly expanded due to extensive irrigated agriculture, fueled primarily by the sugarcane industry. In 2007 asparagus, rice, and shoes are the area's main products. Among its internationally known products, asparagus is exported to neighboring countries, Europe, and the United States. The areas around Trujillo may be the largest exporters of white asparagus in the world. In 2007 Peru is the world's leading asparagus exporter, followed by China and then Mexico.

See also **Bolívar, Simón; Peru, Political Parties: Peruvian Aprista Party (PAP/APRA).**

BIBLIOGRAPHY

Miguel Feijoo De Sosa, *Relación descriptiva de la ciudad, y provincia de Trujillo del Perú* (1763; repr. 2 vols., 1984).

Frederick B. Pike, *The Modern History of Peru* (1967).

Rubén Vargas Ugarte, *Historia general del Perú* (1971), esp. vols. 1–3, 5–6, 9–10.

Peter F. Klarén, *Modernization, Dislocation, and Aprismo: Origins of the Peruvian Aprista Party, 1870–1932* (1973).

David P. Werlich, *Peru: A Short History* (1978).

Additional Bibliography

Blasco Bazán, Vera. *La revolución de Trujillo: Asalto al cuartel O'Donavan en 1932, primera insurgencia civil del siglo XX.* Trujillo, Peru, 2003.

González Ochoa, José Ma. *Francisco Pizarro (Trujillo, 1478–Lima, 1541).* Madrid: Acento Editorial, 2002.

Instituto Nacional de Estadística e Informática, Perú. Available from http://www.citypopulation.de/Peru-Trujillo. html (2005).

Marmanillo Casapino, Luis Ernesto. *Trujillo monumental: Una revisión del centro histórico.* Trujillo, Peru: Universidad Privada Antenor Orrego, 1996.

Valle Alvarez, Luis. *Aportes para la historia de Chan Chan.* Trujillo, Peru: Ediciones SIAN, 2004.

Zevallos Quiñones, Jorge. *Huacas y huaqueros en Trujillo durante el virreinato, 1535–1835.* Trujillo, Perú: Editora Normas Legales, 1994.

Zevallos Quiñones, Jorge. *Los fundadores y primeros pobladores de Trujillo del Perú.* 2 vols. Trujillo, Peru: Fundación Alfredo Pinillos Goicochea, 1996.

SUSAN E. RAMÍREZ

TRUJILLO, GUILLERMO (1927–).

Guillermo Trujillo (*b.* 1927), Panamanian artist. Trujillo completed a degree in architecture in Panama in 1953 and continued his studies in Spain at the San Fernando Academy, the Moncloa School of Ceramics, and the Escuela Superior de Arquitectura. From 1959 to 1988, he was a professor in the School of Architecture at the University of Panama.

Trujillo is an accomplished painter, sculptor, ceramist, printmaker, and draftsman, with a personal style and iconography rooted in the indigenous cultures and traditions of Panama. Initially he was influenced by Spanish informalism and considered part of the Latin American neofigurative movement, and his paintings cover a wide range, from social satires such as *Los Comisionados* (1964) to landscapes and semiabstractions based on botanical or archaeological themes, like *Paisaje No. 3* (1972).

See also **Art: The Twentieth Century.**

BIBLIOGRAPHY

Mónica Kupfer, *A Panamanian Artist, Guillermo Trujillo: The Formative Years* (M.A. thesis, Tulane University, 1983).

P. Prados, *El Paraíso Perdido de Guillermo Trujillo* (1990); *Guillermo Trujillo: Retrospectiva* (catalogue from the Museo de Arte Contemporáneo, Panama, 1993).

Additional Bibliography

Juan, Adelaida de. "De Trujillo a Matta." *Casa de las Américas* 23 (July–August 1982): 99–100.

Kupfer, Monica E and Edward J. Sullivan. *Crosscurrents: Contemporary Painting from Panama, 1968–1988.* New York: Americas Society Art Gallery, 1998.

Samos, Adrienne and Tania Iglesias. *Panama contemporáneo: 15 artistas panameños.* Panamá: Museo de Arte Contemporáneo, 2001.

MONICA E. KUPFER

TRUJILLO, JULIÁN (1828–1883). Julián Trujillo (*b.* 28 January 1828; *d.* 18 July 1883), president of Colombia (1878–1880). Born into the Popayán gentry, he received his law doctorate in 1849. Trujillo fought in the civil wars of 1854 and 1859–1863 in the army of General Tomás Cipriano de Mosquera, becoming a colonel in 1861 and a general in 1863. He was noted for his courage, and his military prowess in defeating the Antioquian Conservatives in 1877 brought him the presidency. Trujillo's term was marred by a deteriorating economy and deepening dissention among the ruling Liberals. In his quest for an accommodation with the church and the Conservatives, Trujillo was thwarted by the Radical Liberal Congress. His developmental policies were regionally oriented. He contracted for a canal across Panama and negotiated with Francisco Javier Cisneros for a railway from the Pacific to the Cauca Valley. A transitional figure holding moderate Liberal views, Trujillo was caught between the Radicals and Rafael Núñez's Nationalists, toward whom he leaned. He served as general in chief of the army in 1881 and was elected a senator in 1882. He died in Bogotá.

See also **Cisneros Betancourt, Salvador; Parra, Aquileo.**

BIBLIOGRAPHY

Helen Delpar, *Red Against Blue* (1981), pp. 121–123.

Hernán Horna, *Transport Modernization and Entrepreneurship in Nineteenth Century Colombia* (1992), pp. 83–86.

J. LEÓN HELGUERA

TRUJILLO, MANUEL (1846–1945). Manuel Trujillo (*b.* 1846; *d.* 1945), Paraguayan naval officer and memorialist. Born in Asunción, Trujillo entered the armed forces at an early age, joining in the military buildup ordered by President Francisco Solano López in the early 1860s.

He was stationed at the state shipyard and arsenal, working under the direction of British engineers hired by the government to help construct a Paraguayan navy.

During the War of the Triple Alliance (1864–1870), Trujillo fought in half a dozen battles, from the seizure of the port of Corrientes (April 1865) to the fall of Angostura (December 1868). He served aboard several Paraguayan steamers, including the *Yporá* and the *Igurey,* and thus was in a good position to observe naval tactics after the disastrous experience at Riachuelo in June 1865.

Trujillo published a brief account of his war experiences, *Gestas guerreras,* in 1911. Owner of a general store in later life, he was much in demand at veterans' conventions as one of the oldest survivors of the conflict.

See also **Solano, Francisco; War of the Triple Alliance.**

BIBLIOGRAPHY

E. A. M. Laing, "Naval Operations in the War of the Triple Alliance, 1864–70," in *Mariner's Mirror* 54 (1968): 253–280.

Additional Bibliography

Leuchars, Chris. *To the Bitter End: Paraguay and the War of the Triple Alliance.* Westport, CT: Greenwood Press, 2002.

THOMAS L. WHIGHAM

TRUJILLO MOLINA, RAFAEL LEÓNIDAS (1891–1961). Rafael Leónidas Trujillo Molina (*b.* 24 October 1891; *d.* 30 May 1961), military officer and ruler of the Dominican Republic (1930–1961). In 1918 Trujillo, a native of San Cristóbal who had been a telegraph operator and security guard, joined the National Guard that had been established by the U.S. occupation forces in the Dominican Republic. His obedience, discipline, and organizational talents, as well as his enthusiastic participation in the suppression of a guerrilla movement in the eastern part of the country, endeared him to the occupiers, who promoted him rapidly. In 1924, when the National Guard was transformed into the Dominican National Police, Trujillo became its chief officer. When the National Police became the National

Armed Forces in 1928, Trujillo emerged as its commander in chief. By using his power as military chief in the maneuverings of Dominican politics, Trujillo became president by 1930.

THE ESTABLISHMENT OF SUPREME POWER (1930–1940)

During the next decade, Trujillo established the most totalitarian control over his people that any Latin American country had theretofore experienced. All political parties, newspapers, radio stations, trade unions, and private associations that did not agree with him ceased to exist. Persistent opponents were bribed, jailed, murdered, or driven into exile. In order to "whiten" (*blanquear*) his country, Trujillo ordered the massacre of all Haitians in the Dominican Republic. In October 1937, an estimated 25,000 Haitians were slain by his agents. After the completion of this slaughter, the Dominican ruler encouraged the immigration of European Jews and refugees from the Spanish Civil War, as well as Japanese and Hungarians after 1956.

During the first decade of his rule, Trujillo converted much of the Dominican Republic into his private fief by acquiring immense landholdings and monopolies over the export-import trade. Primarily in order to increase his personal fortune (estimated by 1960 to have been U.S.$800 million), Trujillo modernized his country by the introduction of agricultural machinery, new industrial plants, and a paved road system. Impressed by the modernity, cleanliness, and stability of his country, foreign journalists and politicians heaped praise on the Dominican dictator, who launched a campaign of self-glorification. Santo Domingo became Ciudad Trujillo, and Pico Duarte, the highest mountain in the Caribbean (10,500 feet) was renamed Monte Trujillo. The province in which he had been born was named for his father, José Trujillo Valdez, and a western province became known as El Benefactor, a title the dictator had bestowed on himself.

After having himself fraudulently reelected in 1934 for another four years, Trujillo began in 1938 the practice of installing puppet presidents whom he could control from behind the scenes. The first of these presidents was a professor of law, Jacinto B. Peynardo, one of whose first actions was to appoint Trujillo's nine-year-old son, Rafael Trujillo Martínez (Ramfis), brigadier general. Upon Peynado's death in

President Rafael Trujillo (1891–1961), delivering a speech, c. 1950s. Rafael Trujillo ruled the Dominican Republic for more than three decades. By the 1950s, Trujillo was losing his traditional supporters, some of whom conspired in his 1961 assassination. © HULTON-DEUTSCH COLLECTION

1940, Manuel de Jesús Troncoso De La Concha became president of the Dominican Republic.

By means of various austerity measures, Trujillo succeeded in making regular payments on the Dominican Republic's debt to the United States, which pleased U.S. President Franklin D. Roosevelt so much that he invited Trujillo and his family for a White House visit in 1939. One year later, the Trujillo–Hull Treaty went into effect, ending the collection of Dominican customs duties by the United States. Trujillo hailed the closing of this humiliating chapter in Dominican history as his personal triumph and erected a monument commemorating the treaty along Santo Domingo's waterfront, where it still stands.

WORLD WAR II AND THE COLD WAR (1940–1955)

When the United States became involved in World War II, the Dominican Republic was one of the first Latin American countries to declare war on the Axis.

The conflict proved to be a great boon for the export of Dominican coffee, cocoa, tobacco, and sugar. When it became clear by 1944 that the democracies would triumph over the fascist powers, Trujillo thought it wise to create a "political opening" by permitting the organization of a number of opposition parties. The Dominican ruler used the start of the cold war in 1947 to put an end to this experiment by arresting, torturing, and killing the leaders of the opposition that he had allowed to emerge only three years before. Trujillo portrayed himself as the staunchest anticommunist leader of Latin America and in 1955 convoked a Fair of Peace and Brotherhood of the Free World that cost the then astronomical sum of U.S.$50 million. The fair, which was only sparsely attended by foreign dignitaries, represented the apogee of Trujillo's power.

SANCTIONS, DECLINE, AND DEATH (1956–1961)

After the twenty-fifth anniversary of his rule in 1955, Trujillo was beset by both external and internal challenges. The era of dictators in Latin America seemed to draw to a close. In 1955, Juan Perón was toppled in Argentina. Two years later, Gustavo Rojas Pinilla fled Colombia, and in 1958 Marcos Pérez Jiménez was overthrown in Venezuela. By 1959 Trujillo was the unwilling host to Fulgencio Batista, who had fled to Santo Domingo when the triumphant guerrillas of Fidel Castro entered the Cuban capital on 1 January of that year. Venezuela's new president, Rómulo Betancourt, and Fidel Castro of Cuba assisted in the launching of an anti-Trujillo expedition by Dominican exiles on 14 June 1959. The revolutionaries, who returned to their native land by both air drops and coastal landings, were either killed or captured. Although this expedition met with disaster, it inspired some domestic enemies of Trujillo's to form a secret Castroite organization called the Fourteenth of June Movement, which was led by the charismatic lawyer, Manolo Tavarez.

When Trujillo retaliated by bombing Rómulo Betancourt's car, injuring the Venezuelan president and killing a number of his advisers, the Organization of American States imposed severe economic sanctions in 1960 on the Dominican Republic. The administration of Dwight D. Eisenhower, already displeased over Trujillo's 1956 kidnapping and murder of Columbia University instructor Jesús de Galíndez, dealt a crippling blow to the dictator by imposing a special excise tax on Dominican sugar. Domestically, Trujillo aroused a wave of opposition from all segments of society, including the Roman Catholic hierarchy, when it was learned that his secret police had waylaid, raped, and then murdered the three young daughters (Patria, Minerva, and Maria Teresa Mirabel) of a prominent merchant. When a desperate Trujillo dispatched agents to Communist Eastern Europe to seek help against the United States, the CIA sent arms to opposition elements in Santo Domingo; they attacked and killed Trujillo on the night of 30 May 1961. Thus the aging dictator was removed after an iron rule of thirty-one years, but the legacy of his reign loomed over his nation for decades to come.

See also **Fascism; Perón, Juan Domingo; Tronscoso de la Concha, Manuel de Jesús; World War II.**

BIBLIOGRAPHY

Arturo R. Espaillat, *Trujillo: The Last Caesar* (1963).

Robert D. Crassweller, *Trujillo: The Life and Times of a Caribbean Dictator* (1966).

G. Pope Atkins and Larman C. Wilson, *The United States and the Trujillo Regime* (1972).

Jesús De Galíndez, *The Era of Trujillo: Dominican Dictator* (1973).

Bernard Diederich, *Trujillo: The Death of the Goat* (1978).

José Rafael Vargas, *Trujillo: El final de una tiranía* (1985).

Bernardo Vega, *Unos desafectos y otros en desgracia: Sufrimientos bajo la dictadura de Trujillo* (1986), *La vida cotidiana dominicana a través del archivo particular del generalísimo* (1986), *Los Trujillo se escriben* (1987), *Trujillo y Haiti* (1988), *Nazismo, fascismo, y falangismo en la República Dominicana*, 2nd ed. (1989), and *Eisenhower y Trujillo* (1991).

Additional Bibliography

Alvarez López, Luis. *Estado y sociedad durante la dictadura de Trujillo*. Santo Domingo: Editora Cole, 2001.

Capdevila, Lauro. *La dictadura de Trujillo: República Dominicana, 1930–1961*. Trans. Denise Armitano. Santo Domingo: Sociedad Dominicana de Bibliófilos, 2000.

Céspedes, Diógenes, and Juan Bosch. *Los orígenes de la ideología trujillista*. Santo Domingo: Biblioteca Nacional, 2002.

Herrera Rodríguez, and Rafael Darío. *Revueltas y caudillismo: Desiderio Arias frente a Trujillo*. Santo Domingo: Impresos Paulinos, 2002.

Rodríguez de León, Francisco. *Trujillo y Balaguer: Entre la espada y la palabra, 1930–1962.* Santo Domingo: Nostrum; Letra Gráfica, 2004.

Turits, Richard Lee. *Foundations of Despotism: Peasants, the Trujillo Regime, and Modernity in Dominican History.* Stanford, CA: Stanford University Press, 2003.

KAI P. SCHOENHALS

TRUTH COMMISSION. *See* Commissions Regarding 1968 Massacres in Tlaltelolco.

TRUTH COMMISSIONS. Latin America is the home of the truth commission, and has served as an example followed around the world, with truth commissions established in dozens of countries in Europe, Asia, and Africa. "Truth commissions" are official or quasiofficial bodies instituted to investigate and report abuses and crimes committed by fallen authoritarian governments. The theory behind them is that establishing a public record of the facts will give some satisfaction to those seeking justice, discredit any attempted justification of such acts, and provide a common, consensual understanding of history, thereby allowing social reconciliation, underpinning a more democratic politics, and preventing similar acts in the future. To assure that the new political settlements are not undermined by resistance from those who imposed or supported the previous regimes, however, some form of general legal amnesty is usually granted, meaning that the guilty often go unpunished and the new regimes may be constrained to some degree by the need to appease them. The activities of truth commissions in these circumstances may be compromised.

Truth-telling about past violations began with the transitions from dictatorial rule in South America in the mid-1980s, continued in the 1990s with the peace processes in Central America, and has been a feature of the politics of democratization since 2000. There have been three types of truth-telling efforts: executive-sponsored truth commissions, parliamentary investigating commissions, and investigations sponsored by nongovernmental organizations. The impact of such efforts has varied broadly from country to country. Some have produced results recognized as "national" truths marking a strong symbolic break with an authoritarian past; others have received less notice. Some investigating bodies have had broad powers of investigation and have been able to name names, and others not. All, however, testify to the social need to overcome a legacy of suffering and denial by state authorities.

EXECUTIVE-APPOINTED TRUTH COMMISSIONS AND PARLIAMENTARY COMMISSIONS

Argentina (1984), Chile (1990), Honduras (1990–1993), El Salvador (1992–1993), Haiti (1994–1996), and Guatemala (1994–1999) officially established truth commissions that issued public reports. Similar commissions were also established in Ecuador (1996), Uruguay (2000), Peru (2001), Panama (2001), and Paraguay (2003), though well past the period of transition from authoritarian rule. The "Nunca Más" Commission in Argentina was the first such commission, and was followed by the Chilean National Commission for Truth and Reconciliation, which established armed forces responsibility for 2,115 deaths in the period 1973 to 1990. In Honduras the National Ombudsman's office compiled a report in collaboration with local and U.S.-based human rights organizations. In El Salvador the United Nations promoted a truth commission as part of the peace process, and its report was issued in March 1993. In Haiti, a Truth and Justice Commission was appointed by President Jean-Bertrand Aristide to investigate the violations of the Duvalier dictatorship and the military regime that ousted him from power in 1991. In Guatemala a Commission for Historical Clarification produced the report *Memory of Silence*, which established that 130,000 to 200,000 people were killed during the civil conflict and 50,000 were "disappeared." In some countries, notably Bolivia (1982–1983), Paraguay (1992), and Uruguay (1985), there have been parliamentary commissions established to establish and report the truth about past abuses.

THE "NUNCA MÁS" ("NEVER AGAIN") PROJECTS

Nongovernmental organizations, including churches or church-based associations, also undertook investigations in Brazil (1979–1985), Paraguay (1984–1990), Uruguay (1986–1989), Bolivia (1990–1993), and Guatemala (1996), each producing authoritative but unofficial truth reports. The first, in Brazil, was sponsored by the Archbishop of São Paulo with the support of the World Council of Churches; it began its investigation of human rights violations by the military while the country was still under military rule, and published its report *Nunca Mais* on the period 1964–1979 in 1985. In Paraguay the Committee of Churches for Emergency Aid was also supported by the World Council of Churches in its investigation of violations under military rule (1954–1989), publishing the four-volume *Paraguay: Nunca Más* in 1990. In Uruguay the Service for Justice and Peace (SERPAJ) and other NGOs launched a similar project and released *Uruguay: Nunca Más* in 1989. In Bolivia there was a broad civil society committee to investigate violations by the García Meza regime. And in Guatemala the General Archbishopric promoted a truth-telling initiative that culminated in the publication of the *Guatemala: Nunca Más*. A similar exercise was undertaken in Colombia in 1995–2000, which produced the three-volume *Colombia: Nunca Más* on human rights violations between 1965 and 2000.

See also **Argentina, Truth Commissions; Brazil,Truth Commissions; Chile, Truth Commissions; Mexico, Truth Commissions; Peru, Truth Commissions; Uruguay, Truth Commissions.**

BIBLIOGRAPHY

Barahona de Brito, Alexandra. *Human Rights and Democratization in Latin America: Uruguay and Chile.* Oxford: Oxford University Press, 1997.

Baharona de Brito, Alexandra, Carmen González-Enríquez, and Paloma Aguilar, eds. *The Politics of Memory: Transitional Justice in Democratizing Societies.* Oxford: Oxford University Press, 2001.

"Comisiones de la verdad en Latinoamerica/Truth Commissions in Latin America." Alertanet—Portal de derecho y sociedad/Portal on Law & Society. Available from http://alertanet.org/verdad.html.

Freeman, Mark. *Truth Commissions and Procedural Fairness.* Cambridge, U.K., and New York: Cambridge University Press, 2006.

Hayner, Priscilla B. *Unspeakable Truths: Facing the Challenge of Truth Commissions.* New York: Routledge, 2002.

Schabas, William A. and Shane Darcy, eds. *Truth Commissions and Courts: The Tension between Criminal Justice and the Search for Truth.* Dordrecht, Netherlands, and Norwell, MA: Kluwer Academic, 2004.

Theissen, Gunnar. "International Internet Bibliography on Transitional Justice." Available from http://userpage.fu-berlin.de/~theissen/biblio/.

"Truth Commissions." International Center for Transitional Justice. Available from www.ictj.org, search menu.

"Truth Commissions." United States Institute of Peace. Available from http://www.usip.org, search menu.

Weschler, Laurence. *A Miracle, a Universe: Settling Accounts with Torturers.* Chicago: University of Chicago Press, 1998.

ALEXANDRA BAHARONA DE BRITO

TSUCHIYA, TILSA (1932–1984). Tilsa Tsuchiya (*b.* 1932; *d.* 23 September 1984), Peruvian painter. Tsuchiya, a native of Supe, created in her paintings a personal mythology inspired in part by her country's Chavín, Nazca, and Inca cultures. She studied at the National School of the Fine Arts in Lima (1954–1959) and at the workshops of Fernando de Szyszlo, Carlos Quisquez Asin, Manuel Zapata Orihuela, and Ricardo Grau. From 1960 to 1964 she studied painting and engraving at the École des Beaux Arts in Paris. Her artistic training in Peru and France exposed her to diverse styles of painting: muralism, indigenism, abstract expressionism, and surrealism. She represented Peru at the XV Bienal de São Paulo (1979). Her work has been exhibited throughout Europe, Latin America, and the United States. She died in Lima.

See also **Art: The Twentieth Century.**

BIBLIOGRAPHY

Holliday T. Day and Hollister Sturges, *Art of the Fantastic* (1987), Dawn Ades, *Art in Latin America: The Modern Era, 1820–1980* (1989).

Oriana Baddeley and Valerie Fraser, *Drawing the Line: Art and Cultural Identity in Contemporary Latin America* (1989).

Additional Bibliography

Moll, Eduardo. *Tilsa Tsuchiya, 1929–1984.* Lima: Editorial Navarrete, 1991.

Villacorta, Jorge, and Jorge Eduardo Wuffarden. *Tilsa.* Lima: Museo de Arte de Lima, 2000.

MIRIAM BASILIO

TUCUMÁN.

Tucumán is a province in northeastern Argentina. It has a population of 1.3 million and its capital, San Miguel de Tucumán, has a population of 530,000. A small percentage of the province's inhabitants are from the Diaguita Calchaquí indigenous group. According to official estimates, almost half of the province's urban population is lives beneath the poverty line (INDEC, First Semester 2006). Tucumán holds a symbolically prominent place in the history of Argentina. It was there, on 9 July 1816, that representatives from around the country gathered to declare the independence of the United Provinces. Its contemporary history is marked by the tragic events of the guerrilla conflict with the People's Revolutionary Army in the 1970s and their crushing defeat by the military's Operation Independence in 1975.

The province has two geographically differentiated regions: plains in the east and mountains in the west. The climate is subtropical with a dry season. Due to its abundant flora, Tucumán is known as "the garden of the Republic." Its production is relatively diversified. The most industrialized agricultural sectors are sugar and lemons, and there are also extensive soybean and tobacco crops. The manufacturing industry, favored by special tax laws, is also significant. Principal tourist attractions of Tucumán are the Calchaquí valleys, home to the native indigenous ruins of Quilmes, and the El Mollar and Tafí del Valle villas. Tucumán plays an important role in the folk-music culture of northern Argentina. Its capital city still retains much of its colonial architectural heritage.

See also **Argentina, Geography.**

BIBLIOGRAPHY

Baraza de Vargas, Lidia. *Historia de Tucumán*. Buenos Aires: A-Z Editora, 1995.

Instituto Nacional de Estadística y Censos (INDEC). *Series Estadísticas Provinciales, 2006, Primer Semestre*.

Paolasso, Pablo. *Geografía de Tucumán*. San Miguel de Tucumán: La Gaceta, 2004.

VICENTE PALERMO

from the Río de la Plata region were called to meet in the interior city of Tucumán. Convening in March 1816, the congress declared independence on July 9 and elected the first supreme director, Juan Martín de Pueyrredón, in an effort to centralize political authority. Buenos Aires used the occasion to try to assert its control over the territory, but its centralizing ambitions faced the provincial federalist opposition led by José Artigas, and the country degenerated into civil war between centralists and federalists. A Portuguese invasion of Montevideo and the Banda Oriental defeated Artigas; the federalist opposition passed to caudillo leaders of Santa Fe and Entre Ríos. Asserting unilateral control over riverine trade and export-import commerce, Pueyrredón made a final effort to establish control that led to the first, highly centralized constitution of the United Provinces of the Río De La Plata in April 1819. The constitution did not embrace republican ideas and would surely have led to a monarchist state. The combined forces of the provinces forced Pueyrredón to resign in June 1819. The congress dissolved in February 1820.

See also **Artigas, José Gervasio; Pueyrredón, Juan Martín de.**

BIBLIOGRAPHY

David Bushnell, *Reform and Reaction in the Platine Provinces, 1810–1852* (1983), esp. pp. 16–18.

David Rock, *Argentina, 1516–1982: From Spanish Colonization to the Falklands War* (1985; rev. ed. 1987), esp. pp. 92–93.

Additional Bibliography

Esquicentenario del Congreso de Tucumán y de la Declaración de la Independencia: Homenaje de las academias nacionales. Buenos Aires, Ministerio de Educación y Justicia, 1966.

Gianello, Leoncio. *Historia del Congreso de Tucumán*. Buenos Aires: Academia Nacional de la Historia, 1966.

Groussac, Paul. *El Congreso de Tucumán*. Tucumán: Tip. Cárcel penitenciaria, 1916.

JEREMY ADELMAN

TUCUMÁN CONGRESS.

Tucumán Congress, held from 1816 to 1820, was the first assembly to discuss a new constitution. In late 1815, delegates

TÚCUME.

Túcume, also known as El Purgatorio, the largest late pre-Hispanic (c. 1000–1532) site in the Lambayeque Valley on Peru's north coast.

The site is built around and atop a steep hill rising from the coastal plain. A monumental sector composed of eleven large adobe pyramid complexes and associated structures lies on the north and northwest sides of the hill; smaller structures, workshops, and cemeteries are on the other sides.

Because the Peruvian coast is a desert, crops can be grown only through irrigation from the rivers that descend from the highlands. Thus it is Túcume's location on a major pre-Hispanic canal that accounts for much of the site's importance.

Túcume probably began about 1000, as the capital of an independent polity, after the fall of nearby Batán Grande; later, it fell to three successive waves of foreign conquerors. First, around 1350, the Chimú Empire took over the Lambayeque region, moving north from its capital at Chan Chan in the Moche Valley. The Chimú were followed in the 1470s by the Incas, who came from Cuzco, in Peru's southern highlands. Finally, the Spanish conquistadores arrived in 1532 and soon controlled the entire north coast of Peru. Within twenty years, Túcume was in ruins and the surviving population had moved to a nearby village.

The largest and most complex occupation was under the Incas. At this time, structures were built all over the hill, making it look like the largest Huaca (shrine, mound) in the pre-Hispanic world. During the same period the local Túcume people comprised the bulk of the population. As in much of their empire, the Incas apparently used the local elites to help govern conquered provinces.

Scientific research at Túcume began around the turn of the twentieth century, but until recently no large-scale excavations had been carried out at the site. From 1988 to 1994, a major research effort was organized by Thor Heyerdahl, led by Daniel H. Sandweiss and Alfredo Narváez, and funded by the Kon-Tiki Museum in Oslo, Norway, and private donors. In addition to the data on the Inca occupation, emerging results show that Túcume was involved in maritime activities, probably including long-distance exchange.

See also **Conquistadores; Incas, The.**

BIBLIOGRAPHY

A general review of the site and the results of recent research is in Thor Heyerdahl, Daniel H. Sandweiss, and Alfredo Narváez, *The Pyramids of Túcume* (1995). Paul Kosok provides excellent photographs and data on the pre-Hispanic canal systems at Túcume and related sites in *Life, Land, and Water in Ancient Peru* (1965), pp. 147–179. Christopher B. Donnan reviews pottery, chronology, and mythology in late pre-Hispanic Lambayeque in "An Assessment of the Validity of the Naymlap Dynasty," in *The Northern Dynasties: Kingship and Statecraft in Chimor* edited by Michael E. Moseley and Alana Cordy-Collins, (1990), pp. 243–274. In the same volume Izumi Shimada places the Lambayeque region in a deeper chronological framework in his "Cultural Continuities and Discontinuities on the Northern North Coast of Peru, Middle-Late Horizons," pp. 279–392.

Additional Bibliography.

Heyerdahl, Thor. *La navegación marítima en el antiguo Perú con énfasis en Tucume y el Valle de Lambayeque.* Lima: Instituto de Estudios Histórico-Marítimos del Perú, 1996.

Heyerdahl, Thor. *Túcume.* Lima: Banco de Crédito del Perú, 1996.

Moore, Jerry D. *Cultural Landscapes in the Ancient Andes: Archaeologies of Place.* Gainesville: University Press of Florida, 2005.

Moseley, Michael E. *The Incas and their Ancestors: The Archaeology of Peru.* New York: Thames and Hudson, 1992.

Valle Alvarez, Luis. *Desarrollo arqueológico, costa norte del Perú.* 2 v. Urb. Los Pinos: Ediciones SIAN, 2004.

DANIEL H. SANDWEISS

TUGWELL, REXFORD GUY (1891–1979).

Rexford Guy Tugwell (*b.* 10 July 1891; *d.* 21 July 1979), governor of Puerto Rico (1941–1946). In 1932, Tugwell became one of the original members of Franklin Roosevelt's brain trust. He later served as the assistant secretary of agriculture, the director of the Resettlement Administration, chairman of the city planning commission of New York, and chancellor at the University of Puerto Rico. Republicans and big sugar businesses opposed his appointment to the governorship.

Tugwell favored home rule for Puerto Rico and continued economic development through such institutions as the Development Company, the Development Bank, and the Water Resources Authority. He served as the last federally appointed governor of Puerto Rico.

See also **Puerto Rico.**

BIBLIOGRAPHY

Rexford G. Tugwell, *The Stricken Land: The Story of Puerto Rico* (1947).

Enrique Lugo-Silva, *The Tugwell Administration in Puerto Rico, 1941–1946* (1955).

Charles T. Goodsell, *Administration of a Revolution: Executive Reform in Puerto Rico Under Governor Tugwell, 1941–1946* (1965).

Additional Bibliography

Barreto Velázquez, Norberto. *Rexford G. Tugwell el último de los tutores.* San Juan: Ediciones Huracan, 2004.

Namorato, Michael V. *Rexford G. Tugwell: A Biography.* New York: Praeger, 1988.

CHRISTOPHER T. BOWEN

TULA. Tula, the capital of the Toltecs, central Mexico's dominant civilization in the Early Postclassic period (900–1250 CE). The Nahuatl name is Tollan (Place of the Reeds). Aztec legends recorded in the colonial period describe Tula and its builders in glowing terms; archaeologists have verified some of these claims but others are obvious exaggerations.

Located on a ridge overlooking a verdant river valley in Hidalgo, Tula dates back to the eighth century. By 1100 it was a city of at least 35,000 inhabitants, covering almost 6 square miles. Tula Grande, the city's main civic and religious precinct, included temples, ball courts (playing fields), and colonnaded halls surrounding a large open plaza. The buildings were adorned with carved friezes, ornaments, and numerous freestanding stone sculptures, including the famous recumbent Chacmool figures. Pyramid B, known as the Temple of Quetzalcoatl, featured friezes composed of carved and stuccoed panels on all sides, and *atlantes,* gigantic stone sculptures depicting Toltec warriors, supported the temple roof.

Thousands of densely packed but well-constructed houses filled the city. Most had foundation platforms, stone and adobe walls, flat roofs, compacted earth or stucco floors, and subterranean storm drains. They commonly occur in groups of three or four ranged around interior courtyards. Poorer families presumably occupied less substantial wattle and daub houses with thatched roofs.

Some of Tula's inhabitants cultivated lands outside the city, but many worked as artisans. Their products included utilitarian objects consumed by everyone in Toltec society and luxury goods reserved for the elite and for export. Pottery vessels, figurines, textiles, cutting tools and scrapers made from obsidian, and jewelry are just a few of the craft products for which archaeological evidence exists.

The reasons for Tula's demise are not clear. Aztec legends attribute it to drought, famine, and civil unrest, but archaeologists have not been able to verify these accounts. One scholarly view has it that after a century of abandonment, Tula was reoccupied by people of Aztec affiliation who ransacked the ruins in search of sculptures, buried offerings, and other treasures, thereby leaving the site so archaeologically impoverished that a few twentieth-century scholars refused to accept it as the Toltec capital described in the legends. Another view, perhaps more based in mythology, holds that the Aztecs went to Tula to drink from the cultural fountain of *Toltecáyotl* or Toltecness, thereby appropriating the heritage of the great Toltecs.

See also **Archaeology; Mesoamerica; Nahuas; Quetzalcoatl; Toltecs.**

BIBLIOGRAPHY

Richard A. Diehl, *Tula: The Toltec Capital of Ancient Mexico* (1983).

Dan M. Healan, Janet M. Kerley, and George J. Bey III, "Excavation and Preliminary Analysis of an Obsidian Workshop in Tula, Hidalgo, Mexico," in *Journal of Field Archaeology* 10, no. 2 (1983): 127–145.

Alba Guadalupe Mastache, Ana Maria Crespo, Robert H. Cobean, and Dan M. Healan, *Estudios sobre la antigua ciudad de Tula* (1983).

Beatríz De La Fuente, Silvia Trejo, and Nelly Gutiérrez Solana, *Escultura en Piedra de Tula* (1989).

Dan M. Healan, ed., *Tula of the Toltecs: Excavations and Surveys* (1989).

Additional Bibliography

Gómez Serafín, Susana, Enrique Fernández Dávila, and Francisco Javier Sansores González. *Enterramientos humanos de la época prehispánica en Tula, Hidalgo.*

Mexico City: Instituto Nacional de Antropología e Historia, 1994.

Jiménez García, Elizabeth. *Iconografía de Tula: El caso de la escultura.* Mexico City: Instituto Nacional de Antropología e Historia, 1998.

Jones, Lindsay. *Twin City Tales: A Hermeneutical Reassessment of Tula and Chichén Itzá.* Niwot: University Press of Colorado, 1995.

López Austin, Alfredo, and Leonardo López Luján. *Mito y realidad de zuyuá: Serpiente emplumada y las transformaciones mesoamericanas del clásico al posclásico.* Mexico City: Colegio de México, Fideicomiso Historia de las Américas, Fondo de Cultura Económica, 1999.

Mastache, Alba Guadalupe, Robert H. Cobean, and Dan M. Healan. *Ancient Tollan: Tula and the Toltec Heartland.* Boulder: University Press of Colorado, 2002.

Ward, Thomas. "From the 'People' to the 'Nation': An Emerging Notion in Sahagún, Ixtlilxóchitl and Muñoz Camargo." *Estudios de Cultura Náhuatl* 32 (2001), 223–234.

RICHARD A. DIEHL

TULUM. Tulum, a small but significant Late Postclassic (1250–1500 CE) trading and religious center located on the east coast of the Yucatán Peninsula in Quintana Roo, Mexico. It was the most important member of a network of coastal sites, including Tancah, Xelhá, and the island of Cozumel, on a seaborne trade route along the Caribbean coast to Honduras.

The site commands a dramatic setting on a cliff overlooking the Caribbean Sea. It is protected on its three sides by a wall 2,640 feet long and almost seven feet high. The major structures of the site lie in the center of a rectangular enclosure 1,254 feet long. The Castle, the smaller Temple of the Diving God, the Temple of the Initial Series, and the Temple of the Frescoes are the most important buildings. There are also structures in the corners of the walls and along the enclosure. Compared with Classic buildings, the structures at Tulum are small and poorly built.

Polychrome murals and stucco reliefs decorate the interior and exterior walls of the buildings. The paintings are of ritual themes; many are multitiered works showing gods in scenes of ceremonial action. Those of the Temple of the Frescoes and the Temple of the Diving God are the best preserved. The Mixtec style of the paintings is similar to that of the coastal site of Santa Rita Corozal, Belize, which supports the idea that there was cultural contact along the coast. Stucco relief decoration occurs on the corners and niches of buildings. One important motif, a bee god with wings, portrayed in a frontal, diving position, occurs in several locations. The keeping of honey bees is a present-day Yucatán industry, and honey was probably an export in the past.

See also **Mesoamerica; Mixtecs.**

BIBLIOGRAPHY

Samuel Kirland Lothrop, *Tulum: An Archaeological Study of the East Coast of the Yucatán,* Carnegie Institution of Washington Publication 335 (1924).

Donald Robertson, "The Tulum Murals: The International Style of the Late Postclassic," in *Verhandlungen des 38, Internationalen Amerikanistenkongresses,* vol. 2 (1970), pp. 77–88.

Arthur G. Miller, *On the Edge of the Sea: Mural Painting at Tancah-Tulum, Quintana Roo, Mexico* (1982).

Additional Bibliography

Goñi, Guillermo. *De cómo los mayas perdieron Tulum.* Mexico City: Instituto Nacional de Antropología e Historia, 1999.

Shaw, Justine M., and Jennifer P. Mathews, eds. *Quintana Roo Archaeology.* Tucson: University of Arizona Press, 2005.

Vargas Pacheco, Ernesto. *Tulum: Organización político-territorial de la costa oriental de Quintana Roo.* Mexico City: Universidad Nacional Autónoma de México, Instituto de Investigaciones Antropológicas, 1997.

EUGENIA J. ROBINSON

TUMBES. Tumbes, northernmost Peruvian city. Located on the Pacific coast near the Ecuadorian border, at an elevation of 450 feet, Tumbes is an important regional center. It was the site of a significant pre-Columbian fortress, one of the first to be described by Spanish explorers. Its size and beauty suggested to Pedro de Candía and Alonso de Molina, the first European witnesses, the potential wealth of the Inca peoples to the south. The fortress, along with a temple of the sun decorated with gold and silver and a house of the virgins, dominated the site. Agustín de Zárate, who arrived in the early 1540s, reported it was "one of the finest sights in the country until the Indians of Puna Island destroyed it." Diego de Almagro was made "commander" of the fortress of Tumbes, and Hernando de Luque was appointed its first bishop.

At the northernmost part of the Peruvian desert, Tumbes receives sufficient annual rainfall to support scrub vegetation, and the Tumbes River provides irrigation water. In the early seventeenth century, Antonio Vázquez de Espinosa, who traveled the Americas and wrote an extensive geographical treatise, described the area as highly productive. Today, corn is planted for local consumption, and tobacco, rice, and cotton are cultivated. Cattle and goats are raised, and fish are caught. Petroleum was found at nearby Zorritos in 1864, but production levels never matched those of Piura.

See also **Incas, The.**

BIBLIOGRAPHY

Noble David Cook, *Demographic Collapse: Indian Peru, 1520–1620* (1981).

Antonio Vázquez de Espinosa, *Compendio y descripción de las indias occidentales* (1948).

Additional Bibliography

Hocquenghem, Anne-Marie. *Para vencer la muerte: Piura y Tumbes: raíces en el bosque seco y en la selva alta, horizontes en el Pacífico y en la Amazonia.* Paris: CNRS-PICS, 1998.

Zárate, Agustin de. *Historia del descubrimiento y conquista del Perú.* Ed. Franklin Pease G. Y. & Teodoro Hampe Martínez. Lima: Pontificia Universidad Católica del Perú, Fondo Editorial, [1555] 1995.

NOBLE DAVID COOK

TUNGA (1952–). Tunga (*b.* 8 February 1952), Brazilian artist. Born in Palmares, Pernambuco, Antônio José de Barros Carvalho e Mello Mourão received a B.A. in architecture from the Universidade Santa Ursula, Rio de Janeiro, in 1974. He is a leading member of a generation of Brazilian artists, including Waltercio Caldas, Cildo Meireles, and José Resende, who emerged in the early 1970s; they and others founded the journals *Malasartes* in 1975 and *A parte do fogo* in 1980. Inspired by Marcel Duchamp, René Magritte, and the Brazilian neo-concrete artist Lygia

Clark, among others, Tunga creates unsettling installations, sculptures, and films. His installations often feature magnetized objects. Recurring motifs in his work include Siamese twins joined by the hair, lizards consuming each other's heads, and tori—indicative of his interest in topology. By problematizing the concept of binary opposition through the use of magnetism and such motifs, Tunga offers a critique of Western rationalism and the authoritarian institutions it has fostered. He lives in Rio de Janeiro and Paris.

In 2000, Tunga was awarded the Hugo Boss Prize in New York.

See also **Art: The Twentieth Century.**

BIBLIOGRAPHY

Tunga: "Lezarts"/Cildo Meireles: "Through" (1989).

Guy Brett, "Tunga," in his *Transcontinental: Nine Latin American Artists,* edited by Elizabeth A. Macgregor (1990), pp. 48–55.

Paulo Herkenhoff, "The Theme of Crisis in Contemporary Latin American Art," in *Latin American Artists of the Twentieth Century* (1993), pp. 134–143.

Additional Bibliography

Brett, Guy. *Transcontinental: An Investigation of Reality: Nine Latin American Artists.* London and New York: Verso, 1990.

Feinstein, Roni. "Tungás Lost World." *Arts in America,* (1998): 84–88.

JOHN ALAN FARMER

TUNJA. Tunja, a town in northeastern Colombia, 81 miles northeast of Bogotá, 2005 estimated population 152,419. This highland town was founded by the conquistador Gonzalo Suárez Rendón in 1539 on the site of the Chibcha settlement of Hunza, and was declared a city in 1541. During the colonial period, Tunja was a small but important urban center in a largely deurbanized region; by 1610 its population included over seventy *encomienda* holders and was divided into three parishes. Tunja was a relatively minor participant in the Comunero Revolt of 1781 and in the struggle for independence, but one of the key patriot victories of the War of Independence was won at the battle of Boyacá, southeast of the town, on 7 August 1819. The decay of the highland agricultural and artisanal economy over the 1800s plunged Tunja into a long period of stagnation, despite its political role as capital of the department of Boyacá (1821–1832), province of Tunja (1832–1857), state of Boyacá (1858–1885), and department of Boyacá (1886–present). A Conservative Party bastion since the mid-nineteenth century, the town was long the scourge of Liberal publicists for the dominant role of the Catholic church in local affairs. Much of the town's colonial architecture, both civil and religious, is well preserved.

See also **Colombia, Political Parties: Conservative Party.**

BIBLIOGRAPHY

Ramón C. Correa, ed., *Historia de Tunja*, vol. 1 (1944).

Additional Bibliography

Robayo, Juan Manuel. *Iglesia, tierra y crédito en la colonia: Tunja y su provincia en el siglo XVIII.* Tunja, Boyacá, Colombia: Editorial de la Universidad Pedagógica y Tecnológica de Colombia, 1995.

RICHARD J. STOLLER

TÚPAC AMARU (c. 1554–1572).

Túpac Amaru (*b.* c. 1554; *d.* 1572), Inca emperor during early colonial period (1571–1572). Túpac Amaru, the third son of Manco Inca, reigned briefly as emperor of the Inca rump state in the last Inca capital of Vilcabamba, in the *montaña* region of eastern Peru. He was crowned in 1571; the next year the Spanish took the city of Vilcabamba, and Túpac Amaru and his family were captured. Taken to Cuzco, he was condemned to death and executed in the main plaza before a huge crowd of Indians. He was the last of the Inca emperors, and his death extinguished the dynasty. He has remained, nevertheless, a potent symbol of resistance and rebellion in Peru even to the present day. His name has been used by various left-wing guerrilla groups.

See also **Incas, The.**

BIBLIOGRAPHY

Burr Cartwright Brundage, *The Lords of Cuzco: A History and Description of the Inca People in Their Final Days* (1967).

John Hemming, *Conquest of the Incas* (1970).

GORDON F. MCEWAN

TÚPAC AMARU (JOSÉ GABRIEL CONDORCANQUI) (1738–1781).

Túpac Amaru (José Gabriel Condorcanqui) (*b.* March 1738; *d.* 18 May 1781), the most famous leader and martyr of the Great Andean Rebellion of 1780–1783. Born in Surimana, Canas y Canchis (Tinta), José Gabriel was the son of Miguel Condorcanqui and Rosa Noguera and a descendant of Inca Túpac Amaru, executed by Viceroy Francisco de Toledo in 1572. Orphaned in 1750, José Gabriel was raised by an aunt and uncle. As heir to the *cacicazgo* (chieftainship) of Tungasuca, Pampamarca, and Surimana, he attended Cuzco's San Francisco de Borja school. In 1760 he married Micaela Bastidas Puyucahua, and they had three sons: Hipólito, Mariano, and Fernando.

At age twenty-five José Gabriel claimed the *cacicazgo* and also became a successful teamster on the route linking Cuzco to Potosí. His travels made him aware of mounting dissatisfaction with colonial rule. The *repartos* (distributions of merchandise), whereby *corregidores* (provincial governors) forced Indians to purchase costly, unwanted goods, caused great discontent. Indians also resented the abusive *mita* (draft labor) for the mines of Potosí. The government's failure to correct the corruption and abuse of the colonial system proved increasingly galling to José Gabriel. Empowered by other caciques from Tinta, he spent 1777 and part of the following year in Lima, attempting to secure the province's exemption from the *mita*. When Visitador José Antonio de Areche rejected his suit, the cacique considered traveling to Spain to press his case. Meanwhile, he unsuccessfully petitioned the government to recognize him as the marquis of Oropesa, the vacant title that belonged to the heir of the original Incas.

Frustrated at each turn, he returned to Tinta in mid-1778, encouraged by influential friends in Lima to act against the illegality and abuse that the regime allowed to flourish. During the following two years, he conspired and planned. Sporadic local revolts independently erupted throughout the Andes. Areche's policies heightened tensions. He established new customhouses to collect higher taxes and intended to force mestizos to pay tribute. Dissatisfaction extended beyond the Indian population to include many creoles and mestizos.

On 4 November 1780, José Gabriel, taking the name Túpac Amaru, struck, arresting Antonio de

Arriaga, the *corregidor* of Tinta. A convenient target, Arriaga had openly feuded with local clergy and had been excommunicated by the bishop of Cuzco, Juan Manuel Moscoso y Peralta. Túpac Amaru transported Arriaga to Tungasuca, where he tried Arriaga for corruption and abuse of the *repartos* and hanged him on 10 November. As the news spread, both rebels and royalists gathered forces. Many caciques of Tinta joined Túpac Amaru, whose relatives provided most of the movement's leadership. Building support, Túpac Amaru decreed the emancipation of slaves on 16 November. At Sangarara two days later, the rebels defeated a force sent out from Cuzco. Nonetheless, the mounting violence in the wake of Sangarara caused many creoles and mestizos to withdraw their support for the rebellion.

In early December, Túpac Amaru captured Lampa and Azángaro, and his influence threatened both southern and Upper Peru. Viceroy Augustín de Jáuregui and Areche mobilized reinforcements and supplies for the defense of Cuzco. News of their imminent arrival brought Túpac Amaru's forces north from Callao to attack Cuzco. With 40,000 to 60,000 troops, he besieged Cuzco from 2 to 9 January 1781. Aid from royalist caciques helped prevent Cuzco's fall, and Túpac Amaru retreated. Defeated in Tinta, he was betrayed and captured in Langui on 6 April 1781. While the rebellion continued, his captors took him to Cuzco for interrogation and trial. On 18 May he witnessed the torture and execution of his wife and other captive family members and then was pulled apart by four horses.

Although the Great Andean Rebellion comprised more than Túpac Amaru's revolt, other insurgents looked to his leadership. For many Indians his ancestry allowed him to carry the banner of Inca legitimacy, and his violent protest against Spanish colonialism won broad sympathy. Yet his rebellion failed owing to the massive mobilization carried out by the government, his inability to win lasting support from mestizos and creoles, and opposition from many caciques.

See also **Mita; Peru: From the Conquest Through Independence.**

BIBLIOGRAPHY

Daniel Valcarcel, *La rebelión de Túpac Amaru* (1947).

Lillian Estelle Fisher, *The Last Inca Revolt, 1780–1783* (1966).

Boleslao Lewin, *La rebelión de Túpac Amaru y los orígenes de la Independencia Hispanoamérica* (1967).

Alberto Flores Galindo, ed., *Túpac Amaru II—1780* (1976).

Comisión Nacional Del Bicentenario De La Rebelión Emancipadora De Túpac Amaru, *Actas del Coloquio International: "Túpac Amaru y su tiempo"* (1980).

José Antonio Del Busto Duthurburu, *José Gabriel Túpac Amaru antes de su rebelión* (1981).

Scarlett O'Phelan Godoy, *Rebellions and Revolts in Eighteenth-Century Peru and Upper Peru* (1985).

Steve J. Stern, ed., *Resistance, Rebellion, and Consciousness in the Andean Peasant World, 18th to 20th Centuries* (1987), pp. 94–139.

Additional Bibliography

Angles Vargas, Victor. *José Gabriel Túpac Amaru.* Cusco: V. Angles Vargas, 2004.

Cajías de la Vega, Fernando. *Oruro 1781: Sublevación de indios y rebellión criolla.* Lima: IFEA, 2004.

Robins, Nicholas A. *Genocide and Millennialism in Upper Peru: The Great Rebellion of 1780–1782.* Westport, CT: Praeger, 2002.

Stavig, Ward. *The World of Túpac Amaru: Conflict, Community, and Identity in Colonial Peru.* Lincoln: University of Nebraska Press, 1999.

Thomson, Sinclair. *We Alone Will Rule: Native Andean Politics in the Age of Insurgency.* Madison: University of Wisconsin Press, 2002.

Walker, Charles C. *Smoldering Ashes: Cuzco and the Creation of Republican Peru, 1780–1840.* Stanford, CA: Stanford University Press, 1999.

KENDALL W. BROWN

TÚPAC CATARI (JULIÁN APAZA)

(c. 1750–1781). Túpac Catari (Julián Apaza) (*b.* c. 1750; *d.* 14 November 1781), leader of an Aymara insurrection in 1781, which laid siege to La Paz for six months. A commoner born in Ayoayo, Sicasica, Julián Apaza was orphaned at age twelve. He worked in the mines, traded coca leaves and cloth, and married Bartolina Sisa, with whom he had three children. Contemporaries described him as lighter in complexion than most Aymaras and of medium height.

Apaza first came to public notice in early 1781, when insurrection convulsed the provinces of Sicasica, Yungas, and Pacajes. Spanish officials mistakenly blamed the turmoil on Túpac Amaru, who rebelled in November 1780 near Cuzco. Ambitious, charismatic, and messianic, Apaza quickly rose to command the Aymara rebels north of La Paz. Speaking only Aymara, he combined Christian and native rhetoric and claimed to receive messages from God through a small silver box he carried. On some occasions he dressed like the Inca, at others like a Spanish official. He also changed his name to Túpac Catari, associating himself with the great indigenous leaders Túpac Amaru and Tomás Catari. Lacking any traditional claim to leadership, he proclaimed himself viceroy, saying he had received authority from Túpac Amaru.

Túpac Catari's greatest undertaking was the siege of La Paz, which began on 14 March 1781. With an army numbering from 10,000 to 40,000, he controlled access to the city and brutally killed those captured while trying to escape. On 18 July, General Ignacio Flores's army temporarily broke the siege but then had to withdraw. Thereupon Túpac Catari joined his forces with those of Andrés Túpac Amaru and again besieged La Paz. Unable to breach the defenses, they dammed the Choqueyapu River above La Paz to unleash a destructive flood on the city. The approach of another royal column under José de Resequín saved La Paz. Túpac Catari may have lost 5,000 at La Paz, while the besieged suffered two or three times more deaths, many from starvation and disease.

Túpac Catari withdrew toward the north, rejecting offers of pardon. At Peñas on 9 November, Tomás Inga Lipe, a former ally, betrayed him, and he was taken into government hands. Quickly interrogated and condemned, on 14 November he was tied to four horses and cruelly torn apart.

Lack of artillery handicapped Túpac Catari at La Paz, and rivalry between the Aymaras and Quechuas prevented successful integration of the rebel movements, although they occasionally cooperated. Túpac Catari declared his intention of driving the Spanish from Peru, but he also talked of liberating the Aymaras from Inca oppression.

See also **Aymara; Peru: From the Conquest Through Independence; Túpac Amaru.**

BIBLIOGRAPHY

The best study is María Eugenia Del Valle De Siles, *Historia de la rebelión de Túpac Catari, 1781–1782* (1900). Also valuable are M. Rigoberto Paredes, *Túpac Catari:* *Apuntes biográficos* (1897, 1973); Alipio Valencia Vega, *Julián Tupaj Katari, caudillo de la liberación india* (1950); Lillian Estelle Fisher, *The Last Inca Revolt, 1780–1783* (1966); Boleslao Lewin, *La rebelión de Túpac Amaru y los orígenes de la independencia de Hispanoamérica*, 3d ed. (1967), esp. pp. 509–526; Marcelo Grondín, *Tupaj Katari y la rebelión campesina de 1781–1783* (1975); and Jorge Flores Ochoa and Abraham Valencia, *Rebeliones indígenas quechuas y aymaras* (1980).

Additional Bibliography

O'Phelan Godoy, Scarlett. *La gran rebelión en los Andes: De Túpac Amaru a Túpac Catari.* Cuzco: Centro de Estudios Regionales Andinos "Bartolomé de las Casas," 1995.

KENDALL W. BROWN

TUPAMAROS. *See* Uruguay, National Liberation Movement (MLN-T).

TUPI. Tupi, a linguistic trunk composed of seven distinct language branches, among which the Tupi-Guarani family is by far the most widespread. Tupi speakers were the principal indigenous inhabitants of early colonial Brazil, occupying much of the coast between the Río de la Plata and the mouth of the Amazon. While the early literature pointed out the cultural and linguistic unity of these peoples, it also emphasized their fragmented political relations, portraying indigenous Brazil as a patchwork of shifting alliances and animosities. Specific ethnic denominations emerged within this context, and colonial sources divided the coastal Tupi into diverse subgroups, including the Tupinikin, Tupinambá, Tememinó, Tupiná, Amoipira, Caeté, Potiguar, and Tobajara.

Though these larger tribal agglomerations emerged clearly in the context of warfare, the semisedentary agrarian village remained the basic unit of Tupi social and political organization. Composed of four to eight communal *malocas* (lodges), sixteenth-century Tupi villages varied greatly in size and population, ranging from around 100 to over 1,000 inhabitants. Soil exhaustion, growing scarcity of game or fish, political factionalism, or the emergence of a charismatic new leader contributed to the constant fragmentation and subsequent regeneration of villages.

Each village had a headman, often the founder of the community, whose prestige rested on oratorical skills and prowess as a warrior, but whose authority was limited mainly to the military sphere. Shamans also wielded considerable authority in daily life, while the occasional presence of wandering prophets also played an important role in Tupi-Guarani spiritual affairs. Warfare, motivated by constant vendettas between indigenous factions, was a central element in Tupi society and history. The main objective was to obtain prisoners in order to avenge past wrongs, as enemy captives were sacrificed and subsequently eaten in an elaborate ritual ceremony.

During the sixteenth century, the coastal Tupi faced a series of new challenges that ultimately led to their defeat and near extinction. The Portuguese conquest, initially carried out through the intricate mechanism of intertribal relations, eventually found more effective allies in the fatal triad of disease, slavery, and confinement to missions. However, even facing such formidable odds, Tupi peoples reached into their past and developed new forms of resistance. Local groups joined warrior forces to form "confederations," traditional leaders organized violent uprisings against colonists and Jesuit missionaries, and messianic leaders inspired migrations in retreat from areas of Portuguese influence. Nonetheless, the combined effects of colonial oppression, epidemic disease, and migration resulted in the depopulation of the coast by the first half of the seventeenth century. While a few, small groups remain on the coast, several Tupi societies continue to flourish to this day in central Brazil and the Amazon.

In spite of the relatively rapid decline of coastal Tupi populations, their impact on the formation of Brazilian society and culture was great. Peasant populations throughout Brazil, in many cases the result of Tupi-Portuguese miscegenation, preserved indigenous agricultural techniques and crops along with customs and folk beliefs. In the nineteenth century, romantic and naturalist literature and art adopted Tupi symbols, while nationalists such as Couto de Magalhães and Emperor Dom Pedro II actively promoted the use of *nhengatú* (vulgar Tupi) as a national language. In the twentieth century, the modernist generation of 1922 evoked the Tupi past, particularly in the creative use of cannibalism as a metaphor for Brazilian culture.

See also **Indigenous Languages; Indigenous Peoples.**

BIBLIOGRAPHY

On Tupi languages, Aryon Dall'igna Rodrigues, *Línguas brasileiras* (1986), is an excellent starting point. The coastal Tupi are described and analyzed exhaustively in two seminal works of Brazilian anthropology by Florestan Fernandes, *A organização social dos Tupinambá* (1948) and *A função social da guerra na sociedade Tupinambá* (1951). Two recent studies introduce new perspectives on Tupi culture: Manuela Carneiro Da Cunha, ed., *História dos índios no Brasil* (1992); and Eduardo Viveiros De Castro, *From the Enemy's Point of View* (1992). A general account of the conquest may be found in John Hemming, *Red Gold* (1978). Stuart Schwartz, *Sugar Plantations in the Formation of Brazilian Society* (1985), provides an excellent discussion of the decline of native societies in sixteenth-century Bahia. Warren Dean covers the southern coast in "Indigenous Populations of the São Paulo—Rio de Janeiro Coast: Trade, Aldeamento, Slavery, and Extinction," in *Revista de História* 117 (1984). On the Tupi in literature, see David Miller Driver, *The Indian in Brazilian Literature* (1942).

Additional Bibliography

Agüero, Oscar Alfredo. *El milenio en la amazonía: Mito-utopía tupí-cocama, o la subversión del orden simbólico.* Quito: Abya-Yala; Lima: CAAAP, 1994.

Clastres, Hélène. *The Land-without-Evil: Tupí-Guaraní Prophetism.* Urbana: University of Illinois Press, 1995.

Cornwall, Ricardo. *Os Jumas: A continuação da violenta redução dos Tupi.* Madalena: R. Cornwall, 2003.

Giancarlo, Stefani. *Yautí na canoa do tempo: Um estudo de fábulas do jabuti na tradição tupi.* Recife: Fundação Joaquim Nabuco, Editora Massangana, 2000.

Léry, Jean de. *History of a Voyage to the Land of Brazil, Otherwise Called America.* Berkeley: University of California Press, 1990.

Pereira, Moacyr Soares. *Indios Tupi-Guarani na pré-história: Suas invasões do Brasil e do Paraguay, seu destino após o descobrimento.* Maceió: EDUFAL, 2000.

Pompa, Cristina. *Religião como tradução: Missionários, Tupi e Tapuia no Brasil colonial.* Bauru: EDUSC; São Paulo: ANPOCS, 2003.

Rocha, Leandro. *A política indigenista no Brasil, 1930–1967.* Goiânia: Editora UFG, 2003.

Roosevelt, Anna Curtenius. *Amazonian Indians from Prehistory to the Present: Anthropological Perspectives.* Tucson: University of Arizona Press, 1994.

Seki, Lucy. *Gramática do Kamaiurá, lingua Tupi-Guarani do Alto Xingu.* Campinas: Editora da Unicamp, 2000.

Treece, David. *Exiles, Allies, Rebels: Brazil's Indianist Movement, Indigenist Politics, and the Imperial Nation-State.* Westport, CT: Greenwood Press, 2000.

JOHN M. MONTEIRO

TUPI-GUARANI.

Tupi-Guarani, one of the most widespread families of South American Indian languages. It encompasses more than fifty languages spoken in Brazil, Paraguay, Argentina, Bolivia, Peru, French Guiana, Venezuela, and Colombia. According to the classification of Aryon D. Rodrigues, the Tupi-Guarani family is made up of the following languages: Amanaye, Anambe, Apiaka, Arawete, Asurini do Tocantins (Akwáwa), Asurini do Xingu, Ava (Canoeiro), Chiriguano, Emerillon, Guaja, Guajajára, Guarani Antigo, Guarani Paraguaio, Guarawo (Guarayu), Guayaki (Arhe), Hora (Jora), Izoceño (Chane), Kaiwa (Kayova, Pãi), Kamayura, Kayabi, Kokáma, Kokamiga (Cocamilla), Lingua Geral Amazônica (Nheengatu), Lingua Geral Paulista (Tupi Austral), Mbia (Guarani), Nandeva (Txiripa), Omágua, Parakanã, Parintintin, Siriono, Surui (Mujetire), Takunyape, Tapiete, Tapirape, Tembe, Tupi-Kawahib (Tupi do Machado, Pawate, Wiraféd), Tupinamba, Turiwára, Uruba, Wayami, Wayampipuku, and Xeta (Serra dos Dourados).

The most widely spoken Tupi-Guarani language is Paraguayan Tupi, with 3 million speakers, followed by Chiriguano, Ava, and Bolivian Guarani, which is spoken by 50,000 people in Bolivia. Guarani in Paraguay is something of an anomaly, as it is, along with Spanish, an official language of the Paraguayan nation; it is spoken by nearly the entire population of Paraguay. No other indigenous language of the American continents has more nonindigenous speakers than does Guarani. Twenty-one Tupi-Guarani languages are spoken in Brazil by 33,000 Indians. The most popular of them, numbering 7,000 each, are the Tenetehára (Guajajára and Tembe) in the states of Maranhão and Pará, and the Kaiwa in the state of Mato Grosso do Sul. Kaiwa is also spoken by 8,000 people in Paraguay, where it is known as Pãi or Pãi-Tavyterã.

The great geographical diffusion of the Tupi-Guarani languages is proof of earlier migrations, which continued after the beginning of European colonization in Brazil and Spanish America. The Guarani-Mbia continued to migrate, having moved from southwestern Brazil, through northeastern Argentina and eastern Paraguay, until they reached the Atlantic coast. For almost five centuries they migrated up the coast to Brazil's Northeast. They occupied most of the eastern coast of Brazil when the Portuguese colonizers met them in the early sixteenth century. The migrations probably had religious and mythical motivation; according to Guarani-Mbia mythology, the "land without evil" was supposed to be across the big sea. As a consequence of the migrations, Guarani-Mbia is the most geographically widespread of the languages and is spoken in Paraguay, Argentina, and in Brazil from Espiritú Santo to Rio Grande do Sul. In colonial South America two of the languages were extensively documented. Father José de Anchieta made the first grammatical description of Tupinamba, published in 1595, and also produced a number of poems and plays in the language. Around 1625 the missionaries Alonso de Aragona and Antonio Ruiz da Montoya prepared two grammars of Guarani. The latter also published a catechism and two dictionaries.

See also **Guarani Indians; Indian Policy, Brazil; Indigenous Peoples; Tupi.**

BIBLIOGRAPHY

Additional Bibliography

Ruiz de Montoya, Antonio. *Gramática y diccionarios (arte, vocabulario y tesoro) de la lengua Tupi ó Guarani* (1640). Vienna, Faesy y Frick; Paris: Maisonneuve, 1876.

CHARLOTTE EMMERICH

TUPINAMBÁ.

Tupinambá, Tupi-speaking peoples of coastal Brazil. While colonial sources specifically identify the Tupinambá with Rio de Janeiro, Bahia, and Maranhão, modern ethnologists employ the term to designate all the coastal Tupi. Expert warriors, the Tupinambá engaged in constant combat with other Tupi groups, each taking captives who were submitted to lengthy rituals culminating in sacrifice and cannibalism.

Tupinambá warfare, as a fundamental aspect of intervillage relations, in turn provided one of the keys to the European conquest of the coastal region. Initially, local groups forged alliances with Portuguese and French interests in order to gain the upper hand against traditional enemies. But the Europeans were interested mainly in slaves, which distorted the traditional goals of warfare and moved the Tupinambá to resist colonial rule. The Tupinambá's refusal to abandon ritual sacrifice and cannibalism led the Portuguese to launch brutal military campaigns in Bahia and Rio de Janeiro, especially during Mem de Sá's tenure as captain-general (1557–1572). This policy resulted in the enslavement of many and the confinement of others in Jesuit missions (reducões).

Following their military defeat, which was exacerbated by epidemic disease, several Tupinambá groups embarked on long migrations, led by charismatic prophets. The majority settled on the northern coast of Maranhão and in the middle Amazon Valley, while one small contingent reached Spanish Peru. Another prophetic resistance movement, known as the Santidade, flourished closer to Bahia during the second half of the sixteenth century. By the mid-seventeenth century, the coastal Tupinambá no longer existed as an independent indigenous society.

See also **Indigenous Peoples; Slavery: Brazil.**

BIBLIOGRAPHY

Stuart Schwartz provides cogent summaries of Tupinambá society and history, with particular emphasis on Bahia, in *Early Latin America* (1983) and *Sugar Plantations in the Formation of Brazilian Society* (1985). Tupinambá relations with the Europeans receive detailed treatment in John Hemming, *Red Gold* (1978). The classic Brazilian work remains Florestan Fernandes, *Organização social dos Tupinambá* (1948).

Additional Bibliography

Métraux, Alfred. *A religião dos Tupinambás e suas relacções com a das demais tribus tupi-guaranis*. São Paulo: Companhia Editora Nacional, 1950.

JOHN M. MONTEIRO

TURBAY, GABRIEL (1901–1946). Gabriel Turbay (*b.* 28 January 1901; *d.* 17 November 1946), Colombian Liberal leader. Of Syrian-Lebanese descent, he was trained in medicine at the Universidad Nacional in Bogotá, but devoted little time to its practice. He attracted attention during the 1920s as a member of a circle of young socialist intellectuals. After the Liberal Party's return to power in 1930, he occupied a series of responsible government positions, and in 1946 he was the official Liberal candidate for president, opposing the dissident Liberal Jorge Eliécer Gaitán and Conservative Mariano Ospina Pérez. The latter won as a result of the Liberals' division. Turbay then left Colombia for a European tour; he died suddenly in Paris.

See also **Colombia: Since Independence.**

BIBLIOGRAPHY

Agustín Rodríguez Garavito, *Gabriel Turbay, un solitario de la grandeza,* 2d ed. (1966).

Herbert Braun, *The Assassination of Gaitán: Public Life and Urban Violence in Colombia* (1985).

Eduardo Durán Gómez, *Gabriel Turbay, estadista santandereano* (1988).

DAVID BUSHNELL

TURBAY AYALA, JULIO CÉSAR (1916–). Julio César Turbay Ayala (*b.* 18 June 1916), Colombian Liberal Party politician and president (1978–1982). Turbay was born in Bogotá and received a bachelor's degree from the Escuela Nacional de Comercio. Amid growing public dissatisfaction over the Liberal–Conservative power-sharing arrangement known as the Frente Nacional (National Front), then in its twentieth year, he won the presidential election of 1978, in which only 41 percent of the electorate voted. Antigovernment guerrilla groups subsequently intensified their operations, attempting to assassinate the president in 1978, staging an audacious theft of army weapons in 1979, and holding a score of diplomats hostage in the Dominican embassy in 1980. Turbay responded by stepping up military antiguerrilla operations, which soon produced an outcry against numerous arbitrary arrests and the physical abuse of detainees. Colombia was economically stable under Turbay, and government authority was never seriously threatened by the extralegal armed forces. Yet criticism of the political status quo, which Turbay represented, signaled an impending opening of the Colombian political system.

From 1982 Turbay was a senior member of the Liberal Party, leading a group known as the Turbayistas. However, his following was modest at best, owing to the unpopularity of his presidency and to personal shortcomings. In 1990 his daughter, Diana, a journalist, was kidnapped by men working for notorious Colombian druglord Pablo Escobar. She was killed the following year in a botched rescue attempt. In 1991 he was named Colombia's ambassador to Italy. He returned to Colombia in 1993, and that year he was named national director of the Liberal Party. He died in Bogotá on 13 September 2005.

See also **Colombia, Political Parties: Liberal Party; Ospina Pérez, Mariano.**

BIBLIOGRAPHY

Daniel Pécaut, *Crónica de dos décadas de política colombiana, 1968–1988*, 2d ed. (1989).

David Bushnell, *The Making of Modern Colombia, a Nation in Spite of Itself* (1993).

Additional Bibliography

Alcántara Sáez, Manuel, and Juan Manuel Ibeas Miguel, eds. *Colombia ante los retos del siglo XXI: Desarrollo, democracia, y paz.* Salamanca, Spain: Ediciones Universidad de Salamanca, 2001.

Dudley, Steven. *Walking Ghosts: Murder and Guerrilla Politics in Colombia.* New York: Routledge, 2004.

Richani, Nazih. *Systems of Violence: The Political Economy of War and Peace in Colombia.* Albany: State University of New York Press, 2002.

Turbay Ayala, Julio César. *Turbay Ayala, las Fuerzas Armadas y los derechos humanos.* Bogotá, Colombia: Colección Consigna, 1985.

JAMES D. HENDERSON

TURCIOS LIMA, LUIS AGOSTO

(1941–1966). Luis Agosto Turcios Lima (*b.* 1941; *d.* 2 October 1966), Guatemalan guerrilla leader. On 13 November 1960, Turcios Lima led young military officers in rebellion against the corrupt government of Miguel Ydígoras Fuentes (1958–1963). In the aftermath of a coup that lacked ideological direction, Turcios Lima became an advocate of communist revolution through guerrilla warfare and organized the Rebel Armed Forces (FAR) with fellow officer Marco Antonio Yon Sosa in 1962. Although Yon Sosa broke from the Communist Party and the FAR in 1965, Turcios Lima reluctantly accepted its decision to suspend military activity in order to give civilian president Julio César Méndez Montenegro (1966–1970) an opportunity to bring the reactionary military under control. The military, trained and supplied by the United States, rejected Méndez's reformist policies and launched a brutal campaign against the FAR following the accidental death of Turcios Lima. From the devastating losses suffered in the late 1960s, the rebel leaders of the 1970s concluded that there was no democratic alternative to armed revolution.

See also **Guatemala; Ydígoras Fuentes, Miguel.**

BIBLIOGRAPHY

Susanne Jonas and David Tobis, eds., *Guatemala* (1974), esp. pp. 176–203.

Jim Handy, *Gift of the Devil: A History of Guatemala* (1984), esp. pp. 230–234.

Additional Bibliography

Marroquín, Edgar Alberto. *Turcios Lima: Éste sí era comandante.* Japala: Impr. Vásquez, 1998.

PAUL J. DOSAL

TUYUTÍ, BATTLE OF.

Battle of Tuyutí, a major engagement of the War of the Triple Alliance (1864–1870) that took place on 24 May 1866. After the crossing of Argentine and Brazilian forces into Paraguayan territory earlier in the year, the Allied commander, General Bartolomé Mitre, assembled a force of some 35,000 men to drive the Paraguayans from their entrenched positions at the fortress of Humaitá. As these units moved northward through the marshes, the Paraguayans prepared a strong defensive line at Tuyutí, a small area of relatively high ground several miles below the fortress. At the last moment, Marshal Francisco Solano López, the Paraguayan commander, abandoned his defensive strategy in favor of a frontal attack, deploying 22,000 troops, in hopes of catching the Allies off guard. The planned dawn attack never materialized, however, and the Paraguayans were delayed until noon, which gave the Allies time to prepare impressive defenses of their own, especially on their left flank. The resulting carnage was terrible: the Paraguayans lost about 6,000 men and the Allies about 8,000 before the battle subsided at 4 PM.

The inability of the Paraguayan cavalry to achieve an envelopment of the Allied rear decided the contest in favor of the Allies, whose exhausted forces were unable to capitalize on their victory. López managed to continue active operations around Humaitá for another two years.

See also **Mitre, Bartolomé; War of the Triple Alliance.**

BIBLIOGRAPHY

Charles J. Kolinski, *Independence or Death! The Story of the Paraguayan War* (1965).

Leandro Aponte Benítez, *Hombres ... armas ... y batallas de la epopeya de los siglos* (1971), pp. 181–182.

Additional Bibliography

Bethell, Leslie. *The Paraguayan War (1864–1870).* London: Institute of Latin American Studies, 1996.

Leuchars, Chris. *To the Bitter End: Paraguay and the War of the Triple Alliance.* Westport, CT: Greenwood Press, 2002.

Marco, Miguel Angel de. *La Guerra del Paraguay.* Buenos Aires: Planeta, 1995.

Whigham, Thomas. *The Paraguayan War.* Lincoln: University of Nebraska Press, 2002.

THOMAS L. WHIGHAM

TZENDAL REBELLION. Tzendal Rebellion, a major Indian revolt among the Tzeltal, Tzotzil, and Chol Indians of the highlands of Chiapas (1712–1713). Opinions vary as to the causes of the revolt, but most versions agree that the period after 1690, and especially 1700, had been one marked by economic crises, epidemics, and locust plagues in the province. The Indian population was at its demographic nadir, Spanish tribute and labor demands were on the increase, a rapacious generation of civil and clerical leaders was in control in San Cristóbal, the provincial capital, and, under the pressure, divisions began to appear in Indian village society as lesser elites showed discontent not only with their worsened circumstances but also with their own leadership, whom they accused of being unable to defend them.

In the 1690s the *alcaldes mayores* of Chiapas were charged with assessing and collecting the tribute, a task they turned into a monopolistic personal enterprise. To this must be added the activities of Bishop Juan Bauptista Álvarez de Toledo, who set about financing an aggressive program of monumental building in San Cristóbal with a series of money-collecting *visitas* to the countryside.

In 1708 the Chiapan highlands were stirred by the first of a series of Indian cults which the Spanish clergy condemned as heretical. A messianic hermit also disturbed the peace until he was seized and exiled to Mexico. In June 1712 the Virgin Mary appeared to a young girl in Cancuc, and, within weeks, the village had defied attempts to destroy the cult and had summoned over twenty Indian villages to rise up and expel the Spaniards.

Spanish, *pardo,* and loyal Indian militias were unable to contain the revolt, but relief arrived from two sources. From Guatemala came an army led by Governor and Captain-General Toribio de Cossío. Another column led by the local *alcalde mayor* advanced from Campeche.

After a series of battles Cancuc was taken and mopping-up operations pacified the other villages. During their brief independence the Cancuc leaders, helped by Sebastián Gómez de la Gloria, an Indian from San Pedro Chenalhó, attempted to establish legitimacy, set up a government, and ordain a new native clergy. The Spanish authorities were seriously alarmed by this, and the defeat of the revolt was so thorough that it left the province devastated and in deeper poverty.

See also **Chiapas; Indigenous Peoples; Mexico: The Colonial Period.**

BIBLIOGRAPHY

Robert Wasserstrom, "Ethnic Violence and Indigenous Protest: The Tzeltal (Maya) Rebellion of 1712," in *Journal of Latin American Studies* 12 (1980): 1–19.

Victoria R. Bricker, *The Indian Christ, the Indian King: The Historical Substrate of Maya Myth and Ritual* (1981), pp. 55–69.

Kevin M. Gosner, *Soldiers of the Virgin: An Ethnohistorical Analysis of the Tzeltal Revolt of 1712* (1992).

Additional Bibliography

Moscoso Pastraño, Prudencia. *Rebeliones indígenas en los altos de Chiapas.* México: Universidad Nacional Autónoma de México, Centro de Investigaciones Humanísticas de Mesoamérica y del Estado de Chiapas, 1992.

Orozco Zuarth, Marco A. *Chiapas: Geografía, historia, y patrimonio cultural*. Tuxtla Gutiérrez: Ediciones y Sistemas Especiales, 2005.

Viquiera Albán, Juan Pedro. *Maria de la Candelaria, india natural de Cancuc*. México: Fondo de la Cultura Económica, 1993.

MURDO J. MACLEOD

TZ'UTUJIL.

The Tz'utujils (or Zutuhils) are a Maya group living today in the western Guatemalan highlands in an area south, west, and northwest of Lake Atitlán. Tz'utujil, one of the Quichean Maya languages closely related to Kaqchikel, is spoken by approximately 50,000 people today.

In the Late Postclassic period the Tz'utujil capital was at Chiya' (or Chiaa or Chuitinamit), the ruins of which lie across the bay from Santiago Atitlán. During much of the Late Postclassic period the Tz'utujils were subordinate to the K'iche'. They gained independence in the late fifteenth century, but hostilities among the Tz'utujil, K'iche' and Kaqchikel resulted in the loss of Tz'utujil territory to both groups.

The Tz'utujils fell under Spanish control in 1525, and by the mid-sixteenth century a new Tz'utujil capital had been established at Santiago Atitlán. Today Santiago Atitlán is the largest and most important Tz'utujil community.

Like scores of other Guatemalan indigenous communities during the Guatemalan Civil War (1960–1996), the Tz'utujil community of Santiago Atitlán had a volatile relationship with the Guatemalan military. The decade of the 1980s was marked by military aggression and low-intensity warfare, including harassment and disappearances. In December 1990, thirteen Santiago Atitlán residents were murdered and twenty-three were injured at the hands of military personnel in what has been called the Santiago-Atitlán massacre.

Today more than 100,000 Tz'utujil people live near Lake Atitlán, an area much visited by tourists. World-renowned paintings and weavings sold to tourists, and the cultivation of corn and coffee, generate income for the impoverished Tz'utujil. Although the infiltration and influence of the Protestant and Catholic religions is apparent, many Tz'utujil continue to follow traditional religious and cultural practices that have evolved from pre-Columbian times. In 2005 Hurricane Stan claimed hundreds (some say thousands) of Tz'utujil lives; the Tz'utujil communities' recovery from the devastating floods and mudslides continued in the years following the disaster.

See also **Indigenous Languages; Indigenous Peoples; Kaqchikel; K'iche'; Maya, The.**

BIBLIOGRAPHY

Felix W. Mc Bryde, *Cultural and Historical Geography of Southwest Guatemala* (1947).

Sandra Orellana, *The Tz'utujil Mayas* (1984).

Additional Bibliography

Murga-Armas, Jorge. *Santiago Atitlán: Organización comunitaria y seguridad de los habitantes: Un reto para la paz*. San José, Costa Rica: ILANUD/Comisión Europa, 1997.

Stanzione, Vincent James. *Rituals of Sacrifice: Walking the Face of the Earth on the Sacred Path of the Sun: A Journey through the Tz'utujil Maya World of Santiago Atitlán*. Illustrations by Angelika Bauer; photographs by Paul Harbaugh and Brendan Cassidy. Albuquerque: University of New Mexico Press, 2003.

JANINE GASCO

UAXACTUN (WAXACTUN). Uaxactun (Waxactun), a Formative and Classic period Maya site in northern Petén, Guatemala. It is located between Tikal and El Mirador, 25 miles north of Tikal, its largest neighbor. Uaxactun, situated between the watersheds for the Gulf of Mexico and those for the Caribbean, participated in the cross-peninsular trade routes. Investigations during the 1930s by the Carnegie Institution of Washington used the relationships between architecture, ceramics, and carved dated inscriptions to establish the first detailed chronology of the Maya area.

The earliest dated inscription is 8.14.10.13.15 (about 328 CE) from Stela 9; the latest is 10.3.0.0.0 (889 CE) on Stela 12. Uaxactun (eight stone) is a modern name based on the cycle-eight date of Stela 9. Although it may have initially been under the sway of El Mirador, in 358 CE (8.16.1.0.12) Uaxactun first shows the Tikal emblem glyph (on Stela 5), indicating that by this time it was likely under the control of Tikal.

Excavation of Structure E-VII-sub by removal of rubble from a badly destroyed Classic pyramid uncovered a Late Formative truncated pyramid with stairways on four sides and a complete covering of molded stucco, including large masks beside the stairs. This important structure also formed the western element and viewpoint for a plaza with three carefully aligned pyramids along its eastern edge. Sunrise sightings from the eastern stairway of structure E-VII to one of the three structures on the eastern edge of the plaza permitted accurate determination of the solstices and equinoxes. This initial revelation led to further discoveries of astronomically aligned structures throughout the Maya area.

The site consists of major structures along low ridges surrounded by a dense concentration of house mounds. This concentration indicates that farming methods more intensive than slash-and-burn agriculture were practiced in the area.

Uaxactun is accessible by road via Flores and Tikal.

See also **Maya, The.**

BIBLIOGRAPHY

Sylvanus G. Morley and George W. Brainerd, *The Ancient Maya,* 4th ed. (1983), pp. 293–296.

Linda Schele and David Freidel, *A Forest of Kings* (1990), esp. pp. 136–164.

WALTER R. T. WITSCHEY

UBICO Y CASTAÑEDA, JORGE (1878–1946). Jorge Ubico y Castañeda (*b.* 10 November 1878; *d.* 14 June 1946), military figure and president of Guatemala (1931–1944). Born in Guatemala City, Ubico was educated at schools in the United States before entering the military academy in Guatemala (1894), where he remained for three years. He entered the military in 1897, and fought in the border war with El Salvador in 1906, attaining the rank of colonel by the age of twenty-eight.

Ubico served as governor of two states, and, beginning in 1922, as minister of war under President José María Orellana until 1926. The regime of General Ubico remains controversial in spite of considerable economic accomplishments, due to his repressive methods and the popularity of the 1944 revolution that overthrew his regime. Coming to power as president by unanimous election during the turbulent years of the Great Depression, Ubico promoted economic stabilization through frugal policies that restricted government spending while imposing law and order through a restrictive and harsh security apparatus.

Ubico's primary legacy to his nation was the establishment of a systematic infrastructure network, which constituted the basis of the modern Guatemalan economy. By constructing the nation's first highway and telegraph networks, he brought about national unity by linking previously remote parts of the republic with the central core. Ubico considered the Petén highway his greatest accomplishment. Though never quite reaching that distant frontier region, this highway extended the first links from the capital into the northern highlands and the Verapaz region in central Guatemala. The caudillo left the nation with 6,330 miles of road, almost five times the amount that existed when he assumed office. Most were dirt roads constructed by hand.

Ubico's extensive public-works projects included the first paved streets in Guatemala City, the capital, with accompanying sewers, and facilities to house government offices. Construction during his tenure included virtually all the ministry buildings, the National Palace, the Presidential Palace, the legislative building, the Supreme Court building, the post office, and the telegraph office. His efforts extended to a sports stadium, racetrack, public bandstands and parks, public bathhouses, and an aqueduct to bring fresh water to the capital.

Significantly, Ubico's program extended into the nation's smaller cities and remote hamlets. The effort provided virtually all provincial capitals with government buildings, telegraph offices, and military barracks, while extending limited water and electricity service into small towns throughout the nation, following the newly built roads. This marked a clear departure from practices of previous central governments. As a result, the regime and the caudillo enjoyed considerable popularity in the countryside. Construction, however, was done primarily by hand by poorly paid laborers. These efforts promoted economic revival and expansion, while serving to facilitate control from the capital.

Ubico directed a *personalista* regime in which all government actions required his personal approval and all officials took their orders directly from the chief executive. Those in remote regions received authorizations via telegraph. Military officers held key government positions, and his Progressive Party controlled all aspects of government and the legislature, conducting two plebiscites that reelected Ubico without opposition.

Ubico's regime used harsh methods to maintain internal order. Security forces kept a watchful eye on the populace, and political opposition was ruthlessly suppressed. The government controlled the only radio stations and carefully monitored the press. The only facilities to receive external news reports were housed in the National Palace.

Ubico sought to revive agriculture by promoting the cultivation of unused land and to integrate the Indians into the mainstream of the national economy by drawing them from subsistence agriculture into commercial farming. The Vagrancy Law of 1934 abolished debt peonage and substituted a labor obligation to the state, under which all citizens who did not cultivate their own plot of land of a minimum size were considered vagrant unless they were employed for a minimum of 150 days per year. While this constituted the first change in the rural labor system since colonial days, the requirement was long enough to supply labor for the harvesting and planting of export crops. Ubico sought to promote crop diversification, and the highway system enabled an expansion in food production by opening new areas to cultivation and linking once remote regions to the national market.

Ubico sought to promote Guatemalan dominance in Central America, conducting a diplomatic rivalry with his counterpart in El Salvador and seeking to reassert Guatemalan claims to British Honduras (Belize). Ubico maneuvered carefully to influence domestic politics in Nicaragua and Honduras. While his efforts were initially directed toward promoting the rise of the Liberal Party in neighboring nations, he later sought to promote stability in the isthmus through rapprochement with the incumbent regimes of the other Central American countries. Although this was a time-honored policy, it produced rumors of a so-called Dictators League during the late 1930s and early 1940s. The Belize question also resulted in an acrimonious and protracted dispute with Great Britain.

The advent of World War II proved particularly trying, given the importance of the large German community that constituted a significant part of the Guatemalan economy. Until the mid-1930s most Guatemalan coffee was sold on the Hamburg market. Though attracted by German investment and the strong centrist policies of national socialism, Ubico remained a staunch nationalist, rejecting outside influence. Ubico supported the United States as soon as it became involved in World War II, despite his dispute with England regarding Belize, and he supplied agricultural products, such as quinine, to the United States to offset the loss of Asian sources.

The Ubico regime was overthrown in 1944 by a revolt led by students, junior military officers, and disgruntled members of the urban middle class who felt his policies favored the landowners. Ubico went into exile to the United States, where he died.

See also **Debt Peonage; Guatemala; World War II.**

BIBLIOGRAPHY

Kenneth J. Grieb, "The Guatemalan Military and the Revolution of 1944," *The Americas* 32, no. 4 (1976): 524–543.

Kenneth J. Grieb, *Guatemalan Caudillo: The Regime of Jorge Ubico, Guatemala, 1931–1944* (1979).

Chester Lloyd Jones, *Guatemala: Past and Present* (1940).

Carlos Samayoa Chinchilla, *El dictador y yo* (1967).

Additional Bibliography

Dosal, Paul J., and Oscar Guillermo Peláez Almengor. *Jorge Ubico (1931–1944): Dictadura, economía y "La tacita de plata."* Guatemala: Ediciones CEUR-USAC, 1996.

León Aragón, Oscar de. *Caída de un régimen: Jorge Ubico—Federico Ponce: 20 de octubre de 1944.* Guatemala: FLACSO, 1995.

KENNETH J. GRIEB

UGARTE, MANUEL (1878–1951).

Manuel Ugarte (*b.* 1878; *d.* 2 December 1951), Argentine diplomat and writer. Born in Buenos Aires, Ugarte as a young man joined the Socialist Party. A prolific writer, he founded the daily *La Patria* and the review *Vida de Hoy* and became a prominent member of progressive literary and journalistic circles in the capital. A passionate anti-imperialist and pan-Hispanist, Ugarte served during Juan D. Perón's first presidency as Argentine ambassador to Mexico (1946–1948), Nicaragua (1949), and Cuba (1950). He formulated Pan-Hispanism in opposition to U.S.-backed Pan-Americanism. His diplomatic career was cut short by failing health, however. He died in Nice, France, in 1951, and three years later his body was disinterred and buried in La Recoleta cemetery in Buenos Aires. His writings include travel books (*Visiones de España*, 1904), novels (*La venganza del capataz*, 1925), short stories, poems, and political essays (*El porvenir de la América latina*, 1911; *El destino de un continente*, 1923; and *La nación latinoamericana*, 1978).

See also **Journalism; Literature: Spanish America.**

BIBLIOGRAPHY

Benjamín Carrión, *Las creadores de la nueva América... Manuel Ugarte ...* (1928).

María De Las Nieves Pinillos, *Manuel Ugarte: Biografía, selección de textos y bibliografía* (1989).

Norberto Galasso, *Manuel Ugarte*, 2 vols. (1974).

Alberto Guerberof, *Izquierda colonial y socialismo criollo* (1985).

Benito Marianetti, *Manuel Ugarte: Un precursor en la lucha emancipadora de América Latina* (1976).

Ricuarte Soler, *Cuatro ensayos de historia: Sobre Panamá y nuestra América* (1983).

Additional Bibliography

Barela, Liliana. *Vigencia del pensamiento de Manuel Ugarte: Una reflexión sobre la problemática latinoamericana.* Buenos Aires: Editorial Leviatan, 1999.

Galasso, Norberto. *Manuel Ugarte y la lucha por la unidad latinoamericana.* Buenos Aires: Ediciones Corregidor, 2001.

Maíz, Claudio. *Imperialismo y cultura de la resistencia: Los ensayos de Manuel Ugarte.* Córdoba: Ediciones del Corredor Austral: Ferreyra Editor, 2003.

RONALD C. NEWTON

UGARTE, MARCELINO (1860–1929).

Marcelino Ugarte (*b.* 1860; *d.* 1929), Argentine provincial politician, one of the last of the old-regime potentates. A product of the Colegio Nacional and the law faculty of the University of Buenos Aires (from which he did not graduate), Ugarte entered Buenos Aires provincial politics in 1888 and rose to governor in 1902. His administration founded schools, built canals and railroads, opened farmlands in the south of the province, and reduced the public debt. In 1913, in the aftermath of the passage of the Sáenz Peña Law, he became a national senator. His power declined with the growth of Radical strength, however, and he resigned in 1914 to reclaim the provincial governorship. In 1916, balked by political opponents and at odds with President Hipólito Irigoyen, he withdrew to private life—a withdrawal hastened by Irigoyen's intervention in the provincial government.

See also **Sáenz Peña Law.**

BIBLIOGRAPHY

Debenedetti, Edith Carmen. *Marcelino Ugarte: Arquetipo de caudillo conservador.* La Plata: Asociación Amigos del Archivo Histórico de la Provincia de Buenos Aires; Instituto Cultural, Dirección Provincial de Patrimonio Cultural, Archivo Histórico "Dr. Ricardo Levene," 2005.

Zorraquín Becú, Ricardo. *Marcelino Ugarte, 1822–1872: Un jurista en la epoca de la organizacion nacional.* Buenos Aires, 1954.

RONALD C. NEWTON

ULATE BLANCO, OTILIO (1891–1973).

Otilio Ulate Blanco (*b.* 25 August 1891; *d.* 27 October 1973), president of Costa Rica (1949–1953) and founder of the National Union Party (PUN).

Otilio Ulate Blanco came early to an exciting and sometimes turbulent life of journalism and politics when he left high school at age seventeen following his father's premature death. He worked for and invested in a number of daily newspapers until he became the owner and publisher of the premier Costa Rican newspaper *El Diario de Costa Rica.* He was the founder of *La Hora.*

His long involvement in political affairs came to dominate his life from the time he was chosen (1947) as the presidential candidate of the united opposition parties (made up of the National Unification Party, the Democratic Party, and the Social Democratic Party) to oppose the progovernment candidate, former president Rafael Ángel Calderón Guardia (1940–1944). The government's effort to deny Ulate's victory in the 1948 election served as the catalyst for revolution. Ulate was inaugurated in 1949 following eighteen months of de facto government by the Junta Fundadora de la Segunda República headed by José Figueres Ferrer.

Ulate's administration emphasized fiscal restraint and pacification. He ran unsuccessfully in the presidential election of 1962. In 1965 Ulate allied the PUN with Calderón Guardia's National Republican Party to support what was to be the successful candidacy of José Joaquín Trejos Fernández (1966–1970).

See also **Costa Rica; Trejos Fernández, José Joaquín.**

BIBLIOGRAPHY

Charles D. Ameringer's, *Don Pepe* (1978).

John Patrick Bell, *Crisis in Costa Rica* (1971).

Olga Marta Ulate, *A la luz de la moral política* (1976).

Additional Bibliography

Milner, Judy Oliver. "Otilio Ulate and the Traditional Response to Contemporary Political Change in Costa Rica." Ph.D. diss., Louisiana State University, 1977.

Torres Rodríguez, José Luis. *Otilio Ulate, su partido y sus luchas.* San José: Editorial Costa Rica, 1986.

JOHN PATRICK BELL

ULLOA, ANTONIO DE (1716–1795).

Antonio de Ulloa (*b.* 12 January 1716; *d.* 5 July 1795), naval officer, scientist, and royal bureaucrat. Born in Seville, Antonio de Ulloa was educated in his native city and subsequently, like his compatriot Jorge Juan y Santacilia, at the new Spanish naval academy (Guardia Marina) in Cádiz. In 1734, at eighteen, Ulloa was chosen to accompany Juan and the French expedition going to the Indies to measure the exact length of a degree on the equator. Ulloa spent the next ten years (1735–1744) in South America, first assisting Charles Marie de la Condamine at some thirty-five different locations near Quito, then in Lima advising the viceroy on shoring up the coastal defenses of Peru. The two officers finally left for Spain in October 1744 on separate ships, but not before returning to Quito to make new observations with their own instruments. Reunited in Spain in 1746, Ulloa and Juan wrote *Relación histórica del viaje a la America Meridiónal* (Historical Report on the Voyage to America), a four-volume descriptive account of the various places they had visited in the Indies. They also wrote for crown officials a secret report exposing corruption, inefficiency, fraud, and abuses in the Indies that was published later in England in 1826 as an anti-Spanish tract entitled *Noticias secretas de America* (Secret Information on America).

Ulloa remained in the royal service for the next forty-five years. In the early 1750s he traveled about Europe garnering information on road and canal building and dredging harbors, and seeking to attract skilled artisans to migrate to Spain. In 1757 he assumed the governorship of the mercury mine at Huancavelica in Peru. Although he disliked that post intensely, he increased mercury production a bit, reduced the debt of the mine by 200,000 pesos to 77,000 pesos and exposed fraud in the royal treasuries of Peru, which led to a falling out with Viceroy Manuel de Amat y Junient in Lima. Leaving Peru in 1764 to return to Spain, Ulloa found himself sidetracked in Havana by a royal order to go to Spanish Louisiana as governor. His tenure in New Orleans from March 1766 until his forced flight on 1 November 1768 was as stormy as his time in Huancavelica, as he once again proved an unpopular, irascible administrator, especially with the French residents.

Back in Spain, Ulloa returned to Cádiz to teach and do research, his true forté.

Charles III called him back into the royal service—in the 1770s as a naval commander and in the 1780s as chief of Spanish naval operations—but Ulloa was always more content engaged in experiments in science or applied science: astronomy, navigation, bookbinding, metallurgy, printing inks, engraving, electricity and magnetism, surgical techniques, weaving, and agriculture. A representative figure of the Spanish Enlightenment, Ulloa remained intellectually vigorous until his death in 1795, the same year he published the most up-to-date guide in Europe on the latest navigational techniques.

See also **Charles III of Spain; Science.**

BIBLIOGRAPHY

John J. Te Paske, ed. and trans., *Discourse and Political Reflections on the Kingdoms of Peru.* (1978).

Additional Bibliography

Castillo Martos, Manuel. *Creadores de la ciencia moderna en España y América: Ulloa, los Delhuyar y del Río descubren el platino, el wolframio y el vanadio.* Brenes, Spain: Muñoz Moya Editores Extremeños, 2005.

Molina Martínez, Miguel. *Antonio de Ulloa en Huancavelica.* Granada, Spain: Universidad de Granada, 1995.

Orte Lledó, Alberto. *El jefe de escuadra Antonio de Ulloa y la flota de nueva España 1776–1778.* Gijón, Spain: Fundación Alvargonzález, 2006.

Solano, Francisco de. *La pasión de reformar: Antonio de Ulloa, marino y científico, 1716–1795.* Cádiz, Spain: Universidad de Cádiz; and Sevilla: Escuela de Estudios Hispano-Americanos, 1999.

JOHN JAY TEPASKE

UMAÑA BERNAL, JOSÉ (1899–1982).

José Umaña Bernal (*b.* 18 December 1899; *d.* 1 August 1982), Colombian poet and politician. A member of the Los Nuevos generation, Umaña studied with the Jesuits and attended law school at the National University. A multifaceted man, he was a professional reporter, collaborating on newspapers and journals. As a man of the theater, he wrote the prize-winning play *El buen amor* (1927) and directed Bogotá's Municipal Theater in the 1930s. As a politician, he served in parliament, became Colombia's consul to Chile (1927), and traveled throughout Europe, the United States, and Latin America. As a poet, Umaña was rooted in Parnassian and Symbolist esthetics. True to his heritage, he maintained an intellectual approach to poetry, adhering to formal precision, musicality, and purity of language. After he translated Rainer Maria Rilke's works, his own earlier emphasis on love and sadness became tinged with introspection and concern for his own death. His best poetry collections are: *Décimas de luz y yelo* (1942), *Poesía 1918–1945* (1951), and *Diario de Estoril* (1948).

See also **Journalism; Theater.**

BIBLIOGRAPHY

Diccionario de la literatura latinoamericana: Colombia (1959).

Fernando Charry Lara, *Poesía y poetas colombianos* (1985).

Luis María Sánchez López, *Diccionario de escritores colombianos* (1978).

Additional Bibliography

Díaz-Granados, Federico. *Poemas a la patria*. Bogotá: Planeta, 2000–3.

MARÍA A. SALGADO

UMBANDA. Umbanda is a spirit-possession religion practiced by millions of Brazilians, primarily in urban areas. It emerged in the 1920s and 1930s when Brazil was experiencing a measure of political and economic integration at the national level. Umbanda's widespread popularity can be attributed to its focus on helping people deal with a great variety of personal problems and illnesses. Its syncretized cultural elements from Africa, Europe, and precolonial Indo-Brazil also make it attractive.

Umbandists typically hold public spiritist sessions in religious centers located in middle-class and working-class districts twice each week. Inside the Umbanda center are two major areas. Those who have come for spiritual assistance sit in the rear half, with women on one side and men on the other. The front half is devoted to ritual activities and includes an altar covered by a white lace-edged drape. Flowers, a glass of water to draw off evil spiritual fluids from the surroundings, and numerous images of Catholic saints, Old Blacks (spirits of African Brazilians), Caboclos (spirits of Brazilian Indians), and other Brazilian folkloric characters are found on the altar.

The service begins by recognizing Exú, with a special request that this potentially dangerous spirit not disrupt the evening's proceedings. The Umbanda leader, known as "Mother" or "Father," or an assistant, carries a censer filled with burning incense to all parts of the Umbanda center. Individuals use their hands to pull the smoke to their bodies for purification. In the front half of the center, the spirit mediums dressed in white clothing dance in a counterclockwise direction to the polyrhythmic beat of two or three West African drums and other percussion instruments. Using a call-and-response pattern, the leader and mediums acknowledge and praise important deities and spirits of the dead through song. Members of the congregation join in the singing. The leader may offer a brief talk on the importance of charity and of the spiritual works to be performed later that evening. Usually an assistant takes an offering.

Drumming and singing become more intense as spirits of the dead begin to possess the mediums, who by this time are frequently in a light state of trance. As possession occurs, the smiling expression of the mediums is transformed into the stern countenance of the Caboclo spirits or into the face of the aged and calm Old Black spirits. Individuals move forward for a consultation about family or job-related difficulties with one of the possessing spirits. Some say they are feeling nervous, tense, or depressed. Others have headaches. The spirits offer practical advice and recommend magical assistance, such as burning a candle to influence a particular spirit. Before returning to a seat in the rear, an individual may be turned around numerous times. Also, the spirit passes the medium's hands over the client's body. Both of these acts help remove the evil spiritual fluids said to be causing the client's personal problems.

Umbanda's activities apparently serve a variety of functions. Cândido Procópio F. de Camargo argues that Umbanda has a therapeutic function and helps individuals to integrate into urban society. Diana De Groat Brown focuses on Umbanda patron-client relations as part of the larger Brazilian political patronage system and notes that Umbandists have elected state deputies from Rio de Janeiro and Pôrto Alegre. Russell R. Prust regards Umbanda as a place where social networking occurs within a hierarchical social structure in a patron-client relationship. The spirit world is merely an extension of the social hierarchy of the material world and is used to meet one's personal needs. Patricia B. Lerch, taking into account the fact that the majority of Umbanda mediums are women, views Umbanda mediumship as giving women an opportunity to participate with power and authority in the public domain. Superior religious knowledge combined with a medium's personal communication network enables her to distribute material goods, food, and jobs from one client to another according to availability and need.

Roberto da Matta views Umbanda as compensating daily social and political frustrations of the poor by providing opportunities for role reversal, in which a poor individual may act as a spirit medium advising and curing the wealthy. Esther Pressel recognizes the therapeutic and integrative roles of Umbanda and characterizes it as a type of "national folk religion" that helps provide a national identity for some. This identity stems from a mélange of Central African spirits, West African Yoruba deities, Catholic saints, Caboclos, and Old Blacks. Other ethnic and regional characters relating to specific areas of Brazil have been added as Umbanda has spread into more remote parts of the country.

See also **African-Latin American Religions: Brazil; Syncretism.**

BIBLIOGRAPHY

Assunção, Luiz. *O reino dos mestres: A tradição da jurema na umbanda nordestina.* Rio de Janeiro: Pallas, 2006.

Brown, Diana De Groat. *Umbanda: Religion and Politics in Urban Brazil.* Ann Arbor, MI: UMI Research Press, 1986.

Camargo, Cândido Procópio de Ferreira. *Kardecismo e Umbanda: Uma interpretação sociológica.* São Paulo: Livraria Pioneira Editôra, 1961.

Lerch, Patricia B. "Spirit Mediums in Umbanda Evangelizada of Porto Alegre, Brazil: Dimensions of Power and Authority." In *A World of Women,* ed. Erika Bourguignon, pp. 129–159. New York: Praeger, 1980.

Matta, Roberto da. "The Ethnic of Umbanda and the Spirit of Messianism: Reflections on the Brazilian Model." In *Authoritarian Capitalism,* ed. Thomas Bruneau and Philippe Faucher, pp. 239–264. Boulder, CO: Westview Press, 1981.

Pressel, Esther. "Umbanda Trance and Possession in São Paulo, Brazil." In *Trance, Healing, and Hallucination,* ed. Felicitas D. Goodman et al., pp. 113–225. New York: Wiley, 1974.

Prust, Russell R. "Brazilian Umbanda: An Urban Resource Distributional System." PhD diss. University of Wisconsin, Milwaukee, 1985.

Victoriano, Benedicto Anselmo Domingos. *O prestígio religioso na Umbada: Dramatização de poder.* São Paulo: Annablume, 2006.

ESTHER J. PRESSEL

Unanue was born in Arica, Peru. He studied medicine at the University of San Marcos and became a doctor in 1786. In 1789 he won the chair of anatomy at San Marcos, initiating a long and illustrious academic career there.

Unanue first achieved recognition as a principal author for the *Mercurio Peruano,* the voice of enlightened Peruvians in the early 1790s. His international reputation, however, rested on *Observaciones sobre el clima de Lima* (1806; revised 1815), in which he outlined and documented his theory that climate was primarily responsible for disease.

Unanue brought eighteenth-century medicine to Peru. Through his efforts, Lima secured first an anatomical amphitheater (1792) and then the San Fernando College of Medicine and Surgery, which began functioning in 1811.

With the coming of independence, Unanue served briefly as a government minister. He died amid the instability of early Republican Peru, his contributions to Peruvian intellectual life largely forgotten.

See also **Medicine: Colonial Spanish America.**

BIBLIOGRAPHY

John E. Woodham, "Hipólito Unanue and the Enlightenment in Peru" (Ph.D. diss., Duke University, 1964).

John E. Woodham, "The Influence of Hipólito Unanue on Peruvian Medical Science, 1789–1830: A Reappraisal," in *Hispanic American Historical Review* 50, no. 4 (November 1970): 693–714.

Additional Bibliography

Glick, Thomas F. "Science and Independence in Latin America (with Special Reference to New Granada)." *Hispanic American Historical Review* 71, no. 2 (May, 1991): 307–334.

Perazzo, Nicolás. *Sánchez Carrión y Unanue: Ministros del Libertador.* Caracas: Oficina Central de Información, 1975.

MARK A. BURKHOLDER

UNANUE, HIPÓLITO (1755–1833).

Hipólito Unanue (*b.* 13 August 1755; *d.* 15 July 1833), Peruvian physician, academician, and author.

UNGO, GUILLERMO MANUEL (1931–

1991). Guillermo Manuel Ungo (*b.* 1931; *d.* 28 February 1991), leader of the Democratic Revolutionary

Front (FDR) of El Salvador. Son of Guillermo Ungo, the founder of the Christian Democratic Party of El Salvador (PDC), Ungo taught law at the University of Central America (UCA). In 1964 he helped found the National Revolutionary Movement (MNR), which, with the proscription of the left-leaning PAR (Party of Renovating Action) in 1967, became the major social democratic party in the nation. He was chosen by José Napoleón Duarte to be his vice-presidential running mate when the United National Opposition (UNO) coalition was formed to contest the 1972 presidential elections. After the fraudulent defeat of UNO and the exile of Duarte by the military in 1972, Ungo remained in the country as head of the MNR and as a law professor at UCA.

With the overthrow of President Carlos Humberto Romero on 15 October 1979, Ungo became a member of the First Junta of the Revolution. However, when he resigned in January 1980 because of the junta's inability to control the army, the government collapsed. In 1980 Ungo brought the MNR into the newly formed Democratic Revolutionary Front (FDR) and became its president after the murder of its six leaders on 28 November 1980. When the FDR and the guerrilla alliance, the Farabundo Martí National Liberation Front (FMLN), joined forces in October 1980, Ungo and the other members of the Diplomatic-Political Commission (the civilian leadership of the FDR-FMLN, headquartered in Mexico City) were forced to live in exile. Living alternately in Mexico City and Panama City, Ungo became the major spokesman for the democratic forces supporting the guerrilla insurgency.

Ungo took advantage of the political opening afforded by the plan for settling the insurgency wars in Central America proposed by President Oscar Arias Sánchez of Costa Rica in February 1987 (known as the Arias peace plan) and returned to El Salvador in late 1987 to help found the Democratic Convergence, a coalition of the MNR, the Popular Social Christian Movement (MPSC), and the Social Democratic Party (PSD). He ran as its presidential candidate in the elections of 1989, and received a surprisingly low 3.9 percent of the vote.

See also **Arias Sánchez, Oscar; Duarte Fuentes, José Napoleón.**

BIBLIOGRAPHY

Robert Armstrong and Janet Shenk, "El Salvador: A Revolution Brews," in *NACLa Report on the Americas* (July–August 1980).

James Dunkerley, *The Long War: Dictatorship and Revolution in El Salvador* (1982).

Patrick Lacefield, "El Salvador: No Peace in Sight," in *Dissent* (Spring 1990): 154–156.

Hilary Mackenzie, "Q&A: Guillermo Ungo—Return of an Exile," in *MacLean's,* 4 January 1988, 6–8.

Additional Bibliography

Ungo, Guillermo M., and Héctor Oquelí. *El Salvador: Diálogo y negociación.* El Salvador: Movimiento Nacional Revolucionario, 1987.

ROLAND H. EBEL

UNI. *See* **Brazil, Organizations: Union of Indigenous Nations (UNI).**

UNICATO. Unicato, a term that generally refers to Argentine regimes from 1874 to 1916. Specifically, *unicato* denotes the corrupt, one-party system exercised by the Partido Autonomista Nacional with centralized power directed by President Miguel Juárez Celman from 1886 to 1890.

Nicolás Avellaneda had introduced this practice, and Julio Argentino Roca maintained it. Under Juárez Celman, the term came into common use because he made it clear that the president should control the government as well as the party. *Unicato* thus referred to one-man rule during Juárez Celman's authoritarian regime. Juárez Celman established the *unicato* because he relied particularly upon Córdoba land speculators who sought quick results. Mortgage bankers, eager for money but lacking adequate reserves, issued *cédula* land bonds. Juárez Celman encouraged many provinces to set up their own banks and to contract foreign loans. With external credit, the banks enriched *unicato* supporters of provincial governments. During the 1890 congressional sessions, Juárez Celman provided 3.9 million pesos for his provincial allies. He never restored the gold standard after Roca suspended it in 1885. Once new paper money issues tripled after 1886, the depreciation of the currency accelerated against the gold standard. The Bank of Córdoba was the most flagrant offender, securing political favors in exchange for loans that frequently were not paid back.

The term *unicato* also represents the unpopularity of the political system and its loss of legitimacy. The arbitrary techniques used to maintain its supporters in power became increasingly unacceptable when the financial and economic system deteriorated at the end of the 1880s. The *unicato* policy of maintaining the same authorities year after year was one of the causes of the 1890 revolt and the formation of the Union Cívica and its radical offshoot. The *unicato* tradition ended with the enactment of the Roque Sáenz Peña law of 1912, which established new voter rolls and introduced the secret ballot and a new system of voting.

See also **Argentina, Political Parties: National Autonomist Party; Avellaneda, Nicolás.**

BIBLIOGRAPHY

John Henry Williams, *Argentine International Trade Under Inconvertible Paper Money, 1880–1916* (1920).

Efraín Bischoff, *Historia de Córdoba, cuatro siglos* (1977).

Douglas W. Richmond, *Carlos Pellegrini and the Crisis of the Argentine Elites, 1880–1916* (1989).

Additional Bibliography

Botana, Natalio R. and Ezequiel Gallo. *De la república posible a la república verdadera: 1880–1910.* Buenos Aires: Compañía Editora Espasa Calpe Argentina, 1997.

Rock, David. *State Building and Political Movements in Argentina, 1860–1916.* Stanford, CA: Stanford University Press, 2002.

DOUGLAS W. RICHMOND

UNIÓN DE ARMAS.

Unión de Armas, Spain's plan to tax its colonies in the Indies to finance Spain's war in seventeenth-century Europe during the reign of King Philip IV. The most ambitious of several taxation plans, it was championed by the king's *valido* (chief minister), the conde-duque de Olivares, in 1625. According to the plan, each province of the empire would contribute to the support of a common military reserve. Since the Indies could not easily provide manpower for imperial defense, in 1627 the crown assessed Peru 350,000 ducats and Mexico 250,000 ducats, payable annually from the viceregal treasuries for an initial period of fifteen years.

This plan, a thinly disguised attempt to integrate the fiscal institutions of the empire, prompted much opposition in the Indies. In Mexico the *cabildos* (town councils) of the realm debated the matter until 1632 before registering their reluctant approval. Opposition to the unión de armas was even stronger in Peru, where an acceptable compromise plan to raise the revenues— doubling the *alcabala* (sales tax) and the *avería* (fleet tax) and imposing a levy of two reales on each bottle of domestic wine—did not emerge until 1638. In the end, crown revenues from the unión de armas raised substantial sums in the Indies but never approached the 600,000 ducats demanded annually by the crown.

See also **Spanish Empire.**

BIBLIOGRAPHY

The principal work on the *unión de armas* in Spain is J. H. Elliott, *The Count-Duke of Olivares: The Statesman in an Age of Decline* (1986), pp. 244–277. For the Indies, see Fred Bronner, "La unión de armas en el Perú: Aspectos políticos-legales," in *Anuario de Estudios Americanos* 24 (1967): 1133–1176, and Jonathan I. Israel, *Race, Class, and Politics in Colonial Mexico, 1610–1670* (1975), pp. 178–180. For a discussion in the context of seventeenth-century fiscal reform see Kenneth J. Andrien, *Crisis and Decline: The Viceroyalty of Peru in the Seventeenth Century* (1985), pp. 133–164.

Additional Bibliography

Rivarola Paoli, Juan Bautista. *La Real Hacienda: La fiscalidad colonial, siglos XVI al XIX.* Asunción, Paraguay: [s.n.], 2005.

KENNETH J. ANDRIEN

UNITARIO.

Unitario, an Argentine follower of centralist government during the early independence period. From the outset of independence, patriotic creoles split between federalist and centralist factions—the latter known as unitarists. The original centralist Constitution of 1819 failed to win the support of the littoral provinces, led by the caudillos of Santa Fe and Entre Ríos, whose combined forces invaded and occupied Buenos Aires in 1820, leaving the local populace terrified. Unitarists evolved out of the initial centralist factions, and sought to rebuild the country after the anarchy of 1820 and the loss of territory (Paraguay, Bolivia, and the Banda Oriental effectively split permanently from the United Provinces of the Río De La Plata). Their leader was Bernardino Rivadavia, a mulatto follower of the doctrines of the English utilitarian Jeremy Bentham. Rivadavia returned from a diplomatic mission in 1821, and became minister of government and foreign affairs for the Buenos Aires governor, Martín Rodríguez. He immediately set about reforming the administration, culminating in the gathering of a constitutional convention in 1824. A draft of a centralizing constitution was presented in January 1825, and was approved a year later. In its wake, Rivadavia was elected the first president of the Republic. His legislation included land reform, the establishment of the Bank of the Province of Buenos Aires, the revamping of the fiscal machinery (and abolition of the hated Spanish tithes and consumer taxes), and securing diplomatic recognition. It was also an era of flourishing culture, with the proliferation of newspapers, theaters, and, perhaps most important, the creation of the University of Buenos Aires in 1821.

Buenos Aires, however, had clearly centralist ambitions, and some of these reforms were unpalatable to other provinces. The constitution was rejected by the provinces, an action stripping Rivadavia and his followers of claims to legitimacy. He was forced to resign on 7 July 1827, and left the region for good. Rivadavia was replaced as governor of the Province of Buenos Aires by Manuel Dorrego, a leader more attuned to the federalist cause. But the unitarists did not abandon their claims and, led by General Juan Lavalle, sought to retake Buenos Aires by force of arms. They executed Dorrego on 3 December 1828 and renewed the civil war. Order finally came with Juan Manuel de Rosas's seizure of power (1829–1852). Rosas relied on a hybrid administration combining policies of the unitarists and federalists.

See also **Argentina: The Nineteenth Century; Rivadavia, Bernardino.**

BIBLIOGRAPHY

Sergio Bagú, *El plan económico del grupo rivadaviano (1811–1827)* (1966).

David Bushnell, *Reform and Reaction in the Platine Provinces, 1810–1852* (1983), esp. pp. 20–30.

Additional Bibliography

Sabsay, Fernando L. *Rosas: El federalismo argentino.* Buenos Aires: Ciudad Argentina, 1999.

Tau Anzoátegui, Víctor. *Formación del estado federal argentino, 1820–1852: El gobierno de Buenos Aires y los asuntos nacionales.* Buenos Aires: Editorial Perrot, 1996.

JEREMY ADELMAN

UNITED FARM WORKERS UNION.

The organization that would become the United Farm Workers Union (UFW) was founded in 1962 through the efforts of César Chávez, Dolores Huerta, and thousands of agricultural workers in California. Over the years the union has struggled to improve conditions for these workers, who have suffered from discrimination, abusive labor contractors, exploitative farm owners, indiscriminate pesticide use, and low wages. On September 15, 1965, the organization became a full-fledged union and simultaneously gained national prominence by joining the mostly Filipino workers in Delano, California in a strike against the region's grape growers that would last five years.

Chávez, as leader of the UFW, emphasized the importance of nonviolence as a strategy. Over the years he engaged in fasts to emphasize his commitment to this principle. This, combined with his reliance on Protestant and Catholic clergy and lay workers, made the UFW more than a traditional union; it became a social and political movement, with national support from outside the traditional labor movement.

On July 26, 1970, after years of striking, boycotts, marches, meetings, and occasional violent confrontations, the grape growers agreed to sign contracts recognizing the UFW as the bargaining agent for the farm workers. After this the UFW continued organizing farmworkers in other areas.

After violent confrontations with the Teamsters Union, the UFW successfully lobbied the state government to pass the California Agricultural Labor Relations Act in May 1975. This was the first law in the continental United States governing farm labor organizing, insuring farmworkers' rights and an orderly process in union recognition. Over the next few decades the UFW successfully obtained legislation to outlaw the short-handled hoe, indiscriminate use of pesticides, and higher minimum wages.

Chávez died on April 23, 1993. The tremendous outpouring of condolences and support that followed his death was a testimony to his importance as a leader who touched the conscience of America. More than 30,000 people followed his casket for three miles from downtown Delano to the union's old headquarters. Expressions of regret for his passing came from around the world, from international political, labor, and spiritual leaders as well as from thousands of the poor migrant farmworkers to whom he had dedicated his life. As of 2007, the UFW's president is Arturo Rodriguez, who continues to focus the union's efforts on human rights as much as on workers' rights.

See also **Hispanics in the United States.**

BIBLIOGRAPHY

Griswold del Castillo, Richard, and Richard A. Garcia. *César Chávez: A Triumph of Spirit.* Norman: University of Oklahoma Press, 1990.

Levy, Jacques E., and César Chávez. *César Chávez: Autobiography of La Causa.* New York: Norton, 1975.

Weintraub, Daniel. "UFW Tries to End Secret Ballots in Union Elections." *Sacramento Bee*, September 6, 2007.

RICHARD GRISWOLD DEL CASTILLO

UNITED FRUIT COMPANY.

United Fruit Company, one of the first and largest multinational corporations in the Western Hemisphere. As the company has diversified production, the name has been changed to AMK, to United Brands, and, as of the early 1990s, Chiquita, Inc. Often called "The Octopus" by Central Americans, United, through its size and power, personified to many Latin Americans the economic imperialism of the United States.

Three men created United Fruit. Ship captain Lorenzo Dow Baker in 1870 began supplementing his New England trade with bananas from Jamaica. With fruit importer Andrew W. Preston and a number of other partners, he formed the Boston Fruit Company in 1885. The third figure was Minor C. Keith, who in the same period was building a railroad from Costa Rica's central valley to the Caribbean port of Limón. A heroic and deadly venture, the railroad needed cargo, and Keith began growing and marketing bananas on a large scale to provide the traffic. Most of the fruit went to New Orleans; when his agent in that city failed, Keith turned to Preston for financial and sales help. The result, in 1899, was the linking of the three men in a New Jersey corporation they called the United Fruit Company; Preston was president and Keith, vice president.

With the formation of United, a haphazard, boom-or-bust operation was turned into a huge, highly efficient element of world trade. Baker's lone steamer was succeeded by the "Great White Fleet" of more than one hundred ships before 1910; Keith's holdings added more than one hundred miles of rail line to the corporation. A public stock subscription of about $11 million in 1900 permitted the acquisition of hundreds of thousands of acres of land throughout Latin America, only a fraction of which was cultivated at any one time.

United grew so fast that it usually absorbed competitors or helped them survive in order to ensure an adequate crop in times of widespread disease. (United even lent money to help Standard Fruit build a railroad in Honduras.) But the banana grows readily, and soon Sam Zemurray's Cuyamel Fruit Company began to provide real competition. After a bitter land dispute that also involved the Honduras-Guatemala border, Zemurray sold out for $33 million in United stock. When the Great Depression sent the stock plummeting, Zemurray charged mismanagement, took over the Latin American operations, and restored the company's value.

In time the magnitude of the corporation brought serious troubles. It has often been a target for takeovers; one president, Eli M. Black, committed suicide, probably because of revelations concerning company bribes of Honduran officials. The company is perhaps best known among Latin Americans for its part in the overthrow of Guatemalan president Jacobo Árbenz in 1954. Árbenz had pushed through a land reform bill that particularly affected United Fruit because it was the nation's greatest landowner. But with the aid of the U.S. government, a rebel faction overthrew the democratically elected Árbenz, the reforms were wiped out, and United got its land back. After the Conquest, Guatemala also submerged into its darkest period with tens of thousands of peasants disappearing or being killed in broad daylight.

Through the years United lost much of its power. No longer is it a major landowner, because financing local growers and contracting for their fruit crop is much less risky economically and politically; specialists took over the cruise business; diversification has meant less reliance upon Latin America for the company's principal income; antitrust actions forced the sale of the Guatemala division to Del Monte, creating a second strong competitor (besides Standard Fruit) at United's expense; and unwillingness to invest heavily in research in the 1960s pushed United behind Standard in banana sales, even though United is still a much larger corporation overall.

See also **Arbenz Guzmán, Jacobo; Baker, Lorenzo Dow; Banana Industry; Cuyamel Fruit Company; Economic Development; Fruit Industry; Imperialism; Keith, Minor Cooper; Railroads; Standard Fruit and Steamship Company; United States-Latin American Relations; Zemurray, Samuel.**

BIBLIOGRAPHY

Charles D. Kepner, Jr., and Jay H. Soothill, *The Banana Empire* (1935).

Charles Morrow Wilson, *Empire in Green and Gold* (1947).

Stacy May and Galo Plaza, *The United Fruit Company in Latin America* (1958).

Watt Stewart, *Keith and Costa Rica* (1964).

Thomas Mc Cann, *An American Company: The Tragedy of United Fruit* (1976).

Richard H. Immerman, *The CIA in Guatemala* (1982).

Stephen Schlesinger and Stephen Kinzer, *Bitter Fruit: The Story of the American Coup in Guatemala*, exp. ed. (1999).

Paul J. Dosal, *Doing Business with the Dictators: A Political History of United Fruit in Guatemala, 1899–1944* (1994).

Additional Bibliography

Barahona, Marvin, and Julio C. Rivera. *El silencio quedó atrás: Testimonios de la huelga bananera de 1954.* Tegucigalpa: Editorial Guaymuras, 1994.

Bucheli, Marcelo. *Bananas and Business: The United Fruit Company in Colombia, 1899–2000.* New York: New York University Press, 2005.

Chomsky, Aviva. *West Indian Workers and the United Fruit Company in Costa Rica, 1870–1940.* Baton Rouge: Louisiana State University Press, 1996.

Striffler, Steve, and Mark Moberg. *Banana Wars: Power, Production, and History in the Americas.* Durham, NC: Duke University Press, 2003.

Striffler, Steve. *In the Shadows of State and Capital: The United Fruit Company, Popular Struggle, and Agrarian Restructuring in Ecuador, 1900–1995.* Durham, NC: Duke University Press, 2002.

THOMAS L. KARNES

UNITED NATIONS. At the founding conference of the United Nations, which was held in San Francisco in 1945, the Latin American states had two primary concerns: protecting their sovereignty as small powers and protecting the autonomy of their regional system, the Inter-American System. Since 1933, President Franklin D. Roosevelt's Good Neighbor Policy had facilitated the peaceful settlement of disputes in Latin America through its principle of nonintervention. After World War II, the Latin American states sought to ensure their continued autonomy in regional affairs by taking an active role from the outset in the formation and operation of the new world body that became the United Nations.

Proposals for the creation of the United Nations were first discussed at the Dumbarton Oaks Conference in Washington, D.C., in 1944. The Latin American states had resented their exclusion from this conference and distrusted the five major powers meeting there, who were known to favor the primacy of the international organization over regional bodies. Seeking to work out a united front for protecting their interests at the upcoming San Francisco Conference, representatives of the Latin American states met at the Inter-American Conference on Problems of War and Peace in Mexico City in February–March 1945. The resultant Act of Chapultepec put forward a Latin American pro-regional consensus in its provision calling for collective action against aggressors.

At the San Francisco Conference, from April through June 1945, the twenty Latin American states, which constituted two-fifths of the fifty-one attending states, did indeed attain their objective of preserving the autonomy of their regional system. A prime mover in their success was Colombian foreign minister Alberto Lleras Camargo, who chaired the relevant subcommittee. Another important subcommittee member was Senator Arthur Vandenberg, a member of the U.S. Senate Foreign Relations Committee. He was the author of the Vandenberg Amendment, an important provision for Latin America. It became UN Charter article 51, which provided for the "inherent right of individual or collective self-defense" of states. Of special importance to Latin America was chapter 8 of the UN Charter, particularly article 52.1, which states that "nothing in the present Charter precludes the existence of regional arrangements or agencies for dealing with such matters relating to the maintenance of international peace and security as are appropriate for regional action," and article 53.1, providing that a regional "enforcement action" required "the authorization" of the Security Council.

The unity and influence of the Latin American bloc at the San Francisco Conference worked in Latin America's favor with regard to representation in the UN. Two seats were assigned to Latin America among the six nonpermanent seats in the Security Council (the Big Five—England, France, China, the Soviet Union, and the United States—had permanent seats and the veto) and among the fifteen judges of the main judicial body of the United Nations, the International Court of Justice. The Economic and Social Council (ECOSOC), originally an eighteen-member body, had four seats designated for Latin America. Subsequent enlargements of the council resulted in increases for Latin America: in 1973, when membership reached fifty-four, the region garnered ten seats. The first Latin American UN secretary-general, Javier Pérez de Cuéllar of Peru, was selected over three decades after the founding of the organization and served from 1982 to 1991.

During the cold war, the primacy of the Organization of American States (OAS) over the United Nations (via article 52 of the UN Charter) in regional disputes well served the security interests of the United States, which converted the OAS into an anti-Communist alliance against Cuba and the Dominican Republic. When the United States intervened militarily in the Dominican Republic in 1965 and won ex post facto OAS approval of an inter-American peace force to be sent there, some Latin American states turned to the United Nations, seeking its involvement to counter the United States. This event was significant in establishing the legitimacy of the United Nations, in the view of Latin America, as a neutral arbiter in regional disputes.

One of the more important manifestations of the UN's role in Latin America has been the Economic Commission for Latin America and the Caribbean (ECLAC). First established in 1948 as the Economic Commission for Latin America (ECLA, or CEPAL in Spanish), the commission changed its name to include the Caribbean in 1984. It is headquartered in Santiago, Chile. Since the 1950s the ECLAC, a subsidiary of the ECOSOC and one of five UN regional economic commissions, has addressed key issues in the socioeconomic development of the region. The organization's first director, the Argentine economist Raúl Prebisch, mapped Latin America's economic problems in his book *The Economic Development of Latin America and Its Principle Problems*, which was published in 1950 by the UN's Department of Economic Affairs. Along with the German economist Hans Singer, Prebisch theorized that the region's place in the world economy as an exporter of raw materials, or primary products, was the determining factor of underdevelopment. Thus, the ECLA promoted industrialization and protectionism (import-substitution industrialization, or ISI) during the 1950s. The commission encouraged industrial growth during the 1960s; addressed issues of export diversification in the 1970s; grappled with the debt crises of the 1980s; and addressed issues of socioeconomic equity during the 1990s, when neoliberalism was paradigmatic. With the rise of numerous populist, center-left governments in Latin America since the turn of the twenty-first century, there is talk of a new wave of developmentalist economics, or *cepalismo*, in the region.

In the mid-1960s, the Latin American states joined other UN developing states in forming a caucusing group to bargain more effectively with the developed states on economic issues. The Group of 77 (G-77), referring to the number of developing states in the UN at the time, presented a united front before the first meeting of the UN Conference on Trade and Development (UNCTAD I), in Geneva, Switzerland, in 1964. UNCTAD became a permanent organ of the UN General Assembly. In 1974 the G-77 states were successful in passing a General Assembly resolution calling for a New International Economic Order (NIEO) to replace the existing system, which these states believed was dominated by the Western capitalist and former colonial powers. In late 1974 another resolution provided for the Economic Charter on the Rights and Duties of States (CERDS), first proposed by Mexican President Luis Echeverría in 1972.

In April 1982 Argentina attempted to reclaim the Falkland Islands, which the British had controlled since 1833. At the outset of the conflict, most Latin American states were critical of Argentina for violating the nonintervention principle and supported the efforts of the United States, which announced its neutrality, to settle the dispute by serving as a mediator. However, when the United States sided with England, its NATO ally, and maintained that the United Nations, not the OAS, was the proper forum for resolution of the dispute, the Latin American states turned against the United States and supported Argentina in the OAS.

In the 1980s, a major struggle developed between the United States and the Sandinista government of Nicaragua, which came to power after a Sandinista-led popular insurrection overthrew dictator Anastasio Somoza in July 1979. The United States resorted to intervention, first covert and then overt, by aiding the Contras, Nicaraguan exiles operating out of neighboring Honduras. Fearing United States military intervention, four Latin American states—Colombia, Mexico, Panama, and Venezuela—formed the Contadora Group, which became the Contadora Process, an effort to negotiate a settlement. (The states involved in the process expanded to include Argentina, Brazil, Peru, and Uruguay in 1985; the Rio Group in 1987 included the eight states' foreign ministers in addition to the secretaries-general of the OAS and the UN.) In 1984 Nicaragua brought a case against the United States before the International Court of Justice (ICJ), accusing it of intervention. In 1986 the ICJ handed down a decision against the United States.

After negotiating a Central American accord, the Central American presidents requested that the UN oversee the accord's implementation. In 1989 the UN Security Council approved the creation of the UN Observer Group in Central America (ONUCA), which, jointly with an OAS body, disarmed the contras and escorted them from Honduras into Nicaragua. At the request of the Nicaraguan government, the UN created the UN Observer Group for the Verification of Elections in Nicaragua (ONUVEN) to oversee the March 1990 elections. In 1990 the UN Security Council approved the creation of the UN Observer Group for El Salvador (ONUSAL), which negotiated a settlement in the civil war in December 1991. The UN also negotiated a settlement in Guatemala between the government and a guerrilla movement in June 1994.

The role of the UN in Latin America with regard to peacemaking and peacekeeping is significant in that it marks a willingness on the part of the Latin American community to risk its autonomy in regional affairs in favor of international monitoring. Although ONUCA acted jointly with the OAS, ONUSAL acted alone, as did the group that achieved settlement in Guatemala in 1994. Since the 1980s, the UN has also institutionalized its election-observer role in Latin America, one that the region has welcomed. Moreover, Latin American states have been active in UN peacekeeping missions around the world since 1948. Since the late 1990s Latin Americans have been involved in peacekeeping in Angola, the Democratic Republic of the Congo, Ethiopia and Eritrea, East Timor, Liberia, the Ivory Coast, and Sudan, not to mention UN and OAS peacekeeping missions within Latin America, including ongoing peacekeeping operations in Haiti.

In 2003, as the United States and Britain sought a UN Security Council resolution in favor of military action against Iraq, Chile and Mexico drew international attention for their efforts to achieve a diplomatic solution. Chile, on the verge of finalizing a free-trade pact with the United States at the time, was subjected to rather intense diplomatic pressure by the U.S. State Department. The United States ultimately withdrew the resolution before a final vote, abandoning its efforts in light of opposition from permanent members Russia and China.

Since the UN's founding in the wake of world war, its Latin American member states have maintained a strong presence in all areas of the international institution's operation. As economic globalization and regional and global crises unfold over the next decades, Latin American governments will undoubtedly continue to do so.

See also **Economic Development; Falklands/Malvinas War; Nicaragua, Sandinista National Liberation Front (FSLN); United States-Latin American Relations.**

BIBLIOGRAPHY

John A. Houston, *Latin America in the United Nations* (1956), chaps. 1 and 2.

J. Lloyd Mecham, *The United States and Inter-American Security, 1889–1960* (1961), chaps. 9, 10, and 14.

Charles G. Fenwick, *The Organization of American States: The Inter-American Regional System* (1963), chap. 12.

Samuel G. Inman, *Inter-American Conferences, 1826–1954: History and Problems* (1965), chap. 15.

Harold E. Davis and Larman C. Wilson, *Latin American Foreign Policies: An Analysis* (1975), chap. 3.

G. Pope Atkins, *Latin America in the International Political System*, 2d rev. ed. (1989), chaps. 8 and 9.

Jack Child, *The Central American Peace Process, 1983–1991: Sheathing Swords, Building Confidence* (1992).

Additional Bibliography

Santa Cruz, Hernán. "The Creation of the United Nations and ECLAC." *CEPAL Review* 57 (December 1995): 17–33.

United Nations, Economic Commission for Latin America and the Caribbean. *Cincuenta años de pensamiento en la CEPAL: Textos seleccionados.* Santiago, Chile: CEPAL, 1998.

United Nations, Secretary General. *Cooperación entre las Naciones Unidas y la Organización de los Estados Americanos.* New York: United Nations General Assembly, 1996.

LARMAN C. WILSON
PATRICK BARR-MELEJ

UNITED PROVINCES OF CENTRAL AMERICA. *See* **Central America, United Provinces of.**

UNITED PROVINCES OF THE RÍO DE LA PLATA.

United Provinces of the Río de la Plata, an early designation (from 1811 at the latest) for what later became the Argentine Confederation and later still the Argentine Republic. The terminology was suggestive of the United States model and thus of a federative relationship among the provinces that had comprised the Spanish viceroyalty of the same name. In practice, tension between Federalist and Unitarist tendencies thwarted all attempts at formal constitutional organization until 1853, when an enduring Argentine constitution was adopted.

A congress of the United Provinces, meeting at Tucumán, issued Argentina's declaration of independence on 9 July 1816. It did so in the name of the United Provinces of South America, suggesting some doubt as to the precise geographic scope of the union. There were deputies at Tucumán from what is now Bolivia, which had been part of the viceroyalty, though none from Paraguay and Uruguay, which had also belonged to the viceroyalty and whose de facto separation was not yet recognized by Argentine authorities. For most purposes the United Provinces amounted to the territory of present-day Argentina, which alone came under the more or less effective control of the governments that ruled in succession from Buenos Aires following the original May Revolution of 1810.

See also **Argentina, Movements: Federalists; Argentina, Movements: Unitarists.**

BIBLIOGRAPHY

Tulio Halperín-Donghi, *Politics, Economics, and Society in Argentina in the Revolutionary Period* (1975), translated by Richard Southern (1975).

John Lynch, *The Spanish American Revolutions, 1808–1826*, 2d ed. (1986), chap. 2.

Additional Bibliography

Chiaramonte, José Carlos. *Ciudades, provincias, estados: Orígenes de la Nación Argentina, 1800–1846.* Buenos Aires: Compañía Editora Espasa Calpe Argentina/Ariel, 1997.

De la Fuente, Ariel. *Children of Facundo: Caudillo and Gaucho Insurgency during the Argentine State-Formation Process (La Rioja, 1853–1870).* Durham, NC: Duke University Press, 2000.

DAVID BUSHNELL

UNITED STATES AGENCY FOR INTERNATIONAL DEVELOPMENT.

The United States Agency for International Development (USAID) is a government entity responsible for administering official development assistance (ODA) to recipient countries. Created in 1961 to unify previously separate economic assistance activities, the kind of assistance provided has varied over time to reflect changes in U.S. foreign policy interests and concerns, congressional and executive priorities, special-interest-group pressures, and lessons learned about the processes of fostering economic growth, protecting human health, developing agribusiness and marketing, expanding financial access and services, reducing poverty, and enhancing democracy in developing countries.

With headquarters in Washington, D.C., USAID's strength is in its field presence, currently working in one hundred developing countries and in partnership with many other organizations—private voluntary organizations, universities, American businesses and consulting companies, local and indigenous organizations, trade and professional organizations, and other donors. Organizationally USAID is structured into functional and regional bureaus for managing its development activities, one of which is the Bureau for Latin America and the Caribbean (LAC).

An early, major USAID implementation in LAC was the Alliance for Progress, a program stressing economic growth, social change, and democratic political development. Regional economic growth accelerated during the 1960s, and health and education indicators improved significantly. Poverty reduction efforts were not as successful, mostly because political resistance to redistributive measures (through agrarian reform, tax reform, and comprehensive economic planning) was substantial in many countries. Additionally, USAID's programs and projects for enhancing democracy yielded disappointing results.

The U.S. Congress in 1973 passed the New Directions legislation, calling for USAID to give highest priority to programs and projects that directly reduce poverty, improve the lives of the poorest, and expand the poor's capacity to participate in development activities. Some resulting programs were successful, but many were bureaucratically and administratively cumbersome, resulting in unexpectedly high costs per beneficiary.

The LAC-wide economic crisis of the 1980s, and its perceived threats to U.S. interests, resulted in several programs focused on the region, or parts of it, such as the Caribbean Basin Initiative (CBI), and more recently the Central American Free Trade Agreement (CAFTA) initiative. This concern initially produced a sharp expansion of assistance to the region, from $340 million annually in fiscal years (FYs) 1977–1979 to $1.6 billion annually in FYs 1985–1987. This level of support did not hold, however, and began to decline in the 1990s. USAID's economic assistance to LAC in FY 1992 was approximately $1.3 billion, but by FY 1994 it had fallen to about $700 million. The amount has continued to decline, and for FY 2006 the total program funds were $852 million, but this included $216,297,000 for the Andean Counterdrug Initiative, $143,675,000 for Economic Support Funds, and $113,159,000 of PL 480 Title II monies. The Development Assistance (DA) monies are only $223,847,000.

In 2007 USAID has bilateral programs in sixteen countries of LAC, regional programs in each of the three subregions, and a regional program in Washington. In LAC the top strategic priorities seek to advance democracy and human rights, increase economic prosperity and security, combat narcotics trafficking, and address social and environmental issues.

See also **Alliance for Progress; Caribbean Basin Initiative; Economic Development; United States-Latin American Relations.**

BIBLIOGRAPHY

USAID. "USAID History." 2007. Available from www.usaid.gov/about_usaid/usaidhist.html.

USAID. "Latin America and the Caribbean." 2007. Available from www.usaid.gov/policy/budget/cbj2006/lac/.

USAID. "This is USAID." 2007. Available from www.usaid.gov/about_usaid/.

USAID. "USAID Primer: What We Do and How We Do It." 2007. Available from www.usaid.gov/about_usaid/primer.html.

BOB J. WALTER

UNITED STATES–LATIN AMERICAN RELATIONS.

United States–Latin American Relations encompass not only the political relationship between the United States and governments of the continent but also those political, economic, social, and cultural exchanges that often profoundly influence the conduct of diplomacy.

Historically, political, economic, and security concerns have dominated U.S. policy toward Latin America. A parallel development has been the evolution of an inter-American system and its capstone institution, the Organization of American States (OAS, 1948), largely dominated by the United States. In modern times, however, the relationship between the United States and Latin America has become more complicated. Thus, such diverse issues as immigration of Latin Americans into the United States, tourism, the role of U.S. companies in Latin America, and the spread of Protestant evangelicalism among Latin America's indigenous populations have indirectly impacted on the shaping of the "new hemisphere" and its prospects for democracy.

FORMATIVE ERA (1776–1830)

The United States won its independence with Spanish assistance, but relations with Spain were uneasy because of U.S.–Spanish conflict in the trans-Appalachian West and the lower Mississippi Valley. After 1803, when Louisiana became U.S. territory, U.S. pressure on Spanish Florida escalated and set the general pattern of U.S. policy toward the Spanish-American Wars of Independence after 1810.

President Thomas Jefferson (1801–1809) expressed doubts about Haitian independence in 1804, fearing that the antislave revolutionary contagion would spread to the United States. President James Madison (1809–1817) sent agents to several of the new revolutionary camps in 1810. In the War of 1812 (1812–1814) he exploited Spanish defensive weakness by encouraging private Americans to intrude into Spanish Florida. By 1813 U.S. forces had occupied Spanish Florida from the Perdido River to the Mississippi River, and in 1819 the United States acquired the entire Spanish province.

Though many Americans sympathized with the Spanish-American revolutionary struggles, strategic issues dictated a U.S. policy of official neutrality. Also, U.S. leaders, notably Secretary of State John Quincy Adams (1817–1825), expressed concern about Simón Bolívar's 1816 slave emancipation decree and the numbers of colored troops in the patriot armies. Nonetheless, revolutionary agents operated in the United States and procured aid and weapons. After 1821 (when Mexico won its

independence), U.S. policy, in part inspired by changes in British policy after the Napoleonic Wars (1803–1815), moved toward recognition of the new republics. Both perceived a threat of a Spanish reconquest. The United States began extending formal diplomatic recognition to the new republics, and in December 1823 (in response to a British proposal for a joint statement) President James Monroe (1817–1825) announced what became known as the Monroe Doctrine. Its most important principle declared U.S. opposition to further European territorial aggrandizement in Latin America. A second professed the U.S. hope in the future of republican, not monarchical, governments in Latin America (though the United States readily acknowledged the independence of imperial Brazil). The Monroe Doctrine established a unilateral policy. Under the leadership of Simón Bolívar, several of the new republics crafted a defensive hemispheric structure (excluding all save Spain's former colonies) at the Panama Congress of 1826, but only Gran Colombia ratified it.

NINETEENTH CENTURY

In the period 1830–1900 U.S. strategic and economic concerns gave priority to the promotion of commerce (especially in the Caribbean), interest in a transisthmian passage, and the "North Americanization" of the Monroe Doctrine in the 1840s. In the 1840s and 1850s, when dissident Cubans and U.S. slave interests fostered revolution in Spanish Cuba, the U.S. government tried to purchase Cuba. The Texas Revolution (1835–1836) and the annexation of Texas as a state in 1845, U.S. strategic and economic interests in California, and the vigorous U.S. commercial expansionism in the 1840s brought the Mexican War (1846–1848) and diplomatic confrontation with rival Great Britain in Central America. In 1846, in a treaty with New Granada (Colombia), the United States guaranteed transit rights across the Isthmus of Panama. In 1850 the United States and Great Britain signed the Clayton-Bulwer Treaty, providing for a jointly constructed and controlled canal across the Isthmus of Panama. In the 1850s U.S. attention turned to Nicaragua, where filibusters led by William Walker (who had reintroduced slavery in Nicaragua) held power until ousted by Central American armies. Fears of U.S. territorial ambitions in Latin America prompted meetings of

Lithograph of the Battle of Quasimas near Santiago, Cuba, 1898. Of particular interest to the United States since the mid-1800s, Cuba received aid from the United States to defeat the Spanish in 1898, with the expectation the newly independent country would be loyal to its northern neighbor. SNARK/ART RESOURCE, NY

hemispheric states at Lima in 1847 and Santiago de Chile in 1856.

During the U.S. Civil War (1861–1865), the French empire of Napoleon III (supported by Mexican conservatives) imposed the monarch Maximilian in Mexico, precipitating a guerrilla war led by the ousted civilian leader, Benito Juárez. The administration of Abraham Lincoln supported Juárez and after 1864 pressed the French to leave with threats of intervention. Juárez's forces brought down Maximilian's empire in 1867, and U.S. economic interests in Mexico—particularly mining, ranching, and railroading—increased rapidly from the 1870s. Elsewhere, the United States tried to mediate the war between Cubans and Spaniards that raged from 1868 to 1878. Afterward, U.S. business interests

expanded in Cuban sugar. The French commenced to dig a canal across Panama, and in 1885 a revolt in Panama prompted U.S. military intervention. In 1881 U.S. Secretary of State James G. Blaine proposed a Pan-American conference to end the War of the Pacific (1879–1884) between Chile and the allies Bolivia and Peru and to promote closer commercial ties. Blaine's efforts collapsed under Chilean opposition, but when he again became secretary of state (1889), he hosted such a conference in Washington, D.C.

In the 1890s heightened U.S. economic and strategic interests brought confrontation with Chile, a war scare with Great Britain in 1895 during the Venezuela–British Guiana boundary dispute (during which Secretary of State Richard

U.S. Undersecretary of State Sumner Welles cheered by crowd at the Pan-American Conference, Rio de Janeiro, Brazil, 1942. Cooperation and stronger alliances characterize U.S.-Latin American relations in the 1930s and 1940s, the era of the Good Neighbor Policy. © BETTMANN/CORBIS

Olney boasted that the United States was "practically sovereign" in the Western Hemisphere), and culminated in the Spanish-American War (1898). Most Americans believed that U.S. intervention was humanitarian, but it actually stemmed from economic and strategic concerns, to prevent the collapse of the Cuban sugar economy and to fulfill a historic U.S. quest to absorb Cuba as U.S. territory. From a cultural and social perspective, the war served also to illustrate the differences between the "America" defined by Theodore Roosevelt and the continental vision of America articulated by the Cuban revolutionary José Martí.

IMPERIAL ERA (1900–1933)

The U.S. victory over Spain in 1898 commenced a tremendous expansion of U.S. power and influence in Latin America, especially in the Caribbean. In 1902 U.S. forces departed Cuba but left in their wake an independent republic beholden to the United States and, by terms of the Platt Amendment, subject to U.S. intervention. U.S. interests

in a canal across the Isthmus of Panama increased. When the Nicaraguan leader José Santos Zelaya refused to yield sovereign rights over a passage across Nicaragua, President Theodore Roosevelt (1901–1909), who favored the route across Panama, turned his attention to negotiation of a canal treaty with Colombia. The terms ran afoul of Colombian nationalist sentiment, and the U.S. government threw its support to a successful revolutionary movement by Panamanian dissidents and signed a canal treaty with Panama.

In the 1902–1903 Venezuelan debt crisis, in which Germany, Great Britain, and Italy blockaded the Venezuelan coast, Roosevelt voiced concern over European intervention in the hemisphere. He used the Venezuelan debt imbroglio as justification to meddle in the debt-plagued Dominican Republic and announced the Roosevelt Corollary to the Monroe Doctrine, whereby the United States upheld the doctrine by intervening in Latin America to "prevent European intervention." Citing the persistent unrest in Cuba, Roosevelt dispatched an army to the island in October 1906. For three years, Americans ruled Cuba. In Central America, the United States supported the isthmian peace treaties of 1907, and Roosevelt's successor, William Howard Taft (1909–1913), pushed U.S. financial intrusion, known as dollar diplomacy, as the means of avoiding the use of troops. Dollar diplomacy presumably offered the United States yet another means of asserting its own variation of "enlightened" administration over unruly and warring governments. The approach rarely worked, however. In 1912 Taft dispatched a military force to Nicaragua, and a U.S. military presence remained in that country until 1925.

President Woodrow Wilson (1913–1921) condemned "gunboat diplomacy" and dollar diplomacy as imperialism, but his determination to advance U.S. economic interests, preserve U.S. security interests in the face of German operations in the region, and especially to "teach" Latins to "elect good men" transformed him into the biggest interventionist of all U.S. leaders. Though pledging to seek no territorial concessions from Latin American republics, Wilson tried to influence the course of the Mexican Revolution (1910–1917), dispatched an occupying force to Veracruz in April 1914, and, following the raid by the revolutionary Pancho Villa on Columbus, New Mexico, in 1916, sent the Pershing Expedition deep into northern Mexico. In 1915 the Wilson administration launched a nineteen-year de facto military occupation of Haiti and in 1916 established an eight-year military governance of the Dominican Republic.

U.S. involvement in World War I brought an expansion of U.S. political, and especially economic, involvement throughout Latin America. Latin American intellectual and literary figures decried the North American cultural threat to Latin traditions. The United States emerged in the 1920s as the overwhelmingly dominant economic presence in Latin America and, relying on its economic strength, began to dismantle its empire in the Caribbean, send financial advisers to Latin America, and negotiate more positively with Mexico in petroleum disputes brought on by the Mexican constitution of 1917. In late 1926 the United States commenced a large-scale intervention in Nicaragua against the guerrilla army of Augusto César Sandino that lasted until 1933, when U.S. forces had been largely supplanted by the Nicaraguan national guard under Anastasio Somoza García.

GOOD NEIGHBOR POLICY TO THE CUBAN REVOLUTION

In the 1930s President Franklin D. Roosevelt (1933–1945) professed a new policy toward Latin America based on nonintervention, noninterference, and reciprocity. At the inter-American conference at Montevideo, Uruguay, in 1933, the Roosevelt administration pledged nonintervention, though at the time Roosevelt's emissary to revolutionary Cuba, Sumner Welles, was effectively charting Cuba's internal political affairs. Roosevelt signed new economic agreements with Latin American governments in an effort to restore U.S. trade in the hemisphere. After 1935, U.S. concerns over German economic and political influence in Latin America brought efforts to create a hemispheric defense agreement, partially achieved at Lima in 1938. There was a serious crisis with Mexico over that nation's expropriation of foreign petroleum companies in 1938.

From September 1939, when World War II broke out in Europe, the United States intensified its efforts to create an anti-Axis front in Latin America and to subordinate Latin America's economies to the U.S. war effort. Though anti-American sentiment remained strong throughout Latin America, especially in Argentina and Mexico, U.S. policy was largely successful. The United States obtained defense sites, critical in Brazil, and virtually incorporated the Mexican economy into the U.S. war economy. Latin American rural workers, especially in Mexico, Central America, and the Caribbean, migrated to urban factories. Mexicans worked on U.S. farms, ran the railroads, labored in defense plants, and served in the U.S. military. U.S. economic and political pressures on Southern Cone nations, reluctant to jeopardize their neutrality, intensified, and by the end of the war even defiant Argentina had declared war on Germany. At the Chapúltepec meeting of March 1945, Latin America opted for a regional security arrangement, though the United States was already shifting to the global trajectory symbolized by the United Nations. The formal culmination of the regional approach was the Inter-American Treaty of Reciprocal Assistance (1947) and the Organization of American States (1948).

In the postwar era, the United States shifted its political and economic concerns to Europe and Asia and tried to break down hemispheric

Captured men from the Bay of Pigs invasion, Cuba, April 1961. Though the United States recognized Fidel Castro's new government in 1959, bilateral relations soon deteriorated. Continuing tensions stem from Cuba's socialism, its expropriation of U.S. property, and pressure from the Cuban-exile community centered in Miami, Florida. © BETTMANN/CORBIS

economic barriers to U.S. exports and private investments. Latin American leaders pressed for increased U.S. public support and protection of their domestic markets, modeled on the U.S. Marshall Plan for war-torn Europe. After the Korean War erupted, the United States emphasized regional and bilateral security agreements and became increasingly concerned about Communist influence in Latin America. In 1954 the Central Intelligence Agency brought down a non-Communist leftist government in Guatemala; in 1959, following several years of civil strife and a protracted guerrilla struggle, Fidel Castro toppled the government of dictator Fulgencio Batista in Cuba.

CUBAN REVOLUTION TO THE 1989 CHRISTMAS INVASION OF PANAMA

Castro vowed to restructure Cuba along Marxist lines and to de-Americanize the island's political culture. The severity of revolutionary reforms brought a conflict with the United States (where anti-Castro Cubans had fled) culminating in the abortive Bay of Pigs Invasion of April 1961, President John F. Kennedy's (1961–1963) first hemispheric crisis. U.S. opposition to the Cuban Revolution inevitably stunted the purpose of the Alliance for Progress, a vast and ambitious social and economic reform program commenced early in the decade. By the time of Kennedy's death in November 1963, U.S. security concerns were already overriding its commitments to "peaceful revolution" through democratic means in Latin America. When President Lyndon Johnson (1963–1969) dispatched twenty thousand troops to the Dominican Republic in the spring of 1965, on the pretext that the rebellion there would create "another Cuba," Latin Americans were persuaded that Washington's commitment to social justice had dissolved.

But the Alliance for Progress fueled Latin America's economic modernization at the expense of democratic government and social justice for the poor, thus perpetuating the dual society of rich and poor. This was most evident in such countries as Mexico and Brazil, which enjoyed impressive economic growth from the 1950s but where social inequities were severe. By the 1970s, with the U.S. distracted by Vietnam, Latin America appeared to be veering back to authoritarian governments, in Brazil, Argentina, and (with the U.S.-supported coup against the socialist Salvador Allende) Chile. Latin American leaders increasingly supported a hemispheric economic agenda diverging from that of the United States and also backed Panama's call for a new canal treaty. President Jimmy Carter (1977–1981) identified with the "North-South" as opposed to the "East-West" vision of Latin America's place in U.S. foreign policy. He signed a canal treaty with Panama, criticized violations of human rights in Latin America, and initially supported the Sandinista revolution that brought down Anastasio Somoza Debayle in Nicaragua. By the end of his administration many Americans believed that such reformist approaches to Latin America distracted from the real security risks the United States confronted in the region.

Following his resounding victory in the 1980 election, President Ronald Reagan (1981–1989) committed U.S. efforts to toppling the leftist Sandinista government of Nicaragua and supporting the rightist government of El Salvador in its war against Communist guerrillas. After initially following a neutral line, Reagan sided with the British against Argentina in the Falkland Islands conflict of 1982, and in 1983 he dispatched the military to bring down the leftist government in Grenada. Such hard-line policies were accompanied by modest amounts of nonmilitary aid (the most publicized was the Caribbean Basin Initiative of 1983) and expressions of support for democracy and social justice in strife-torn Central America. The 1984 Kissinger Report on the isthmian condition meshed reformist and strategic arguments.

By the late 1980s it was clear that the U.S. efforts to mold Latin America in its own political and economic image had failed. The U.S.-backed Contra rebellion in Nicaragua collapsed under Latin American efforts for a negotiated settlement, and the United States joined Latin America as a debtor nation. Yet, mostly because of internal

Arrest photo of Manuel Noriega, former Panamanian dictator, 1990. Noriega was once considered an ally in U.S. efforts against the spread of communism in Central America. However, deteriorating relations, a coup, domestic concerns, and President George H. W. Bush's "War against Drugs" prompted a U.S. military intervention in Panama in 1989 that ousted Noriega from power. © HANDOUT/REUTERS/CORBIS

pressures, authoritarian governments succumbed to democratic regimes, and Latin America strengthened its economic ties with European and Asian nations. Americans increasingly turned to new "security" concerns, especially in regard to the large numbers of undocumented aliens (many from Latin America), a problem addressed in the 1986 Immigration Reform and Control Act, and the social crisis wrought by narcotics trafficking. President George H. W. Bush (1989–1993) commenced an ambiguous approach to Latin America. With the Christmas 1989 invasion of Panama, aimed at bringing down the dictator Manuel Noriega, he revived charges of U.S. imperialism. His proposal for closer economic ties, especially free trade with Mexico, however, promised a new era in the long and often troubled relationship between the United States and Latin America.

1989 PANAMA INVASION TO THE PRESENT
The approval of the North American Free Trade Agreement (NAFTA) by the United States Congress in 1993, following a debate riddled with warnings about the loss of jobs to Mexico and loss of control on the U.S.–Mexican border, culminated an economic integration that took its basic character in World War II, when the United States tried to incorporate not only Mexico but most of Latin America and the Caribbean into its economic system. In the 1990s the coincidence of several changes in the U.S.–Latin American relationship—the resurgence of democratic governments, the widespread acceptance of neoliberal economic formulas, and the much-heralded Summits of the Americas—signaled the possibility of a more pacific and prosperous era in hemispheric affairs. The optimism reminded some observers of the promise identified with the Alliance for Progress in the 1960s.

Regrettably the euphoria was short lived, as the social and economic inequities some critics identified with the shift to market economies prompted a resurgence of the Left. Relations with Cuba worsened when the U.S. Congress tightened the embargo against the island's government with the Cuban Democracy Act in 1992. Four years later Congress affirmed its growing control over Cuban–U.S. affairs in the Helms-Burton law, which punished those countries trading with both Cuba and the United States. Though the U.S. government heartened at the election of National Action candidate Vicente Fox in Mexico in 2000, the political winds in Latin America continued to shift against professed U.S. wishes, notably with the election of Hugo Chávez in Venezuela in 1998. At the Third Summit of the Americas at Quebec City in April 2001, delegates responded to the growing dissension and pessimism about the social costs of the neoliberal economic agenda—the so-called "Washington consensus"—by reaffirming a determination to create a prosperous and democratic hemisphere.

Early on in his administration, President George W. Bush (2001–2009) declared that his administration would "look south" and that the twenty-first century would be the "century of the Americas." Ironically, the event that might otherwise have been the bellwether for such a prophecy—the signing of

the Inter-American Democratic Charter in Lima, Peru, on September 11, 2001—was for most North Americans tragically overshadowed by terrorist airplane hijackings and their incendiary crashes into the World Trade Center and the Pentagon. In the years following, U.S. relations with other hemispheric governments grew increasingly troubled and, in a few instances, confrontational over the issue of Washington's preoccupation with security concerns. In its 2005 report, the prestigious Inter-American Dialogue noted that, despite impressive economic growth and notable achievement in education, Latin America continued to suffer from widespread social inequities, crime, government corruption, and challenges to the democratic promises of the 1990s. In addition to Cuba, whose government remained estranged from the Organization of American States, the report singled out Haiti, Venezuela, Bolivia, Ecuador, and Nicaragua as countries where anti–United States sentiments had resurfaced. Under President Chávez's administration, oil-rich Venezuela (renamed the Bolivarian Republic of Venezuela) had crafted a hemispheric coalition to challenge the historic political and economic presence of the United States in the hemisphere. One consequence of these dramatic changes was the emergence of a transnational militarism in U.S. relations with the hemisphere. The School of the Americas, long under fire for its role in training Latin American officers in counterinsurgency tactics, was renamed the Western Hemisphere Institute for Security Cooperation. Though in 2004 the school created a human rights protection course, the emphasis in the curriculum remained focused on security issues, particularly the drug trade and the vulnerability of elected governments to the enormous power and influence exercised by the drug cartels, especially in Mexico and Colombia. By March 2007 the deterioration of the U.S. image throughout Latin America had become so serious that President Bush set out on a goodwill tour of five Latin American nations—Brazil, Uruguay, Colombia, Guatemala, and Mexico. As if to roil the hemispheric waters, President Chávez followed with appearances in Argentina and Bolivia, both of them recipients of Venezuelan largesse.

Another, arguably more lasting legacy of the dynamic changes in U.S.–Latin American relations has been the dramatic acceleration of the northward Latin American migration and the growth of the Latino population in the United States.

Protesters strike effigy of U.S. President George W. Bush during Summit of the Americas meetings, Mexico, 2004.
Across Latin America, U.S. economic and foreign policy during the administration of George W. Bush (2000–2008) faced growing resistance from protesters and national leaders, straining relations. © DANIEL AGUILAR/REUTERS/CORBIS

According to a Pew Hispanic Center report, Latinos in the United States numbered almost 42 million in 2005 (60 percent of them native born) out of a total population of 288 million. Of the estimated 35.2 million immigrants to the United States from 1980 to 2005, more than 19 million migrated from Latin America and the Caribbean—11 million from Mexico, 3.23 million from the Caribbean, 2.64 million from Central America, and 2.25 million from South America. Estimates of the number of undocumented aliens in the United States in 2005 ranged from 11 million to 13 million, a third of them from Mexico.

The impact of such rapid growth in the Latino population of the United States has brought about what some observers call the "Latinization" of the nation—a catchall term reflecting everything from a

Latino cultural nationalism and sense of latent political and economic power to widespread apprehension that the long-cherished ideal of assimilation and Americanization is no longer working. Too often overlooked in such assessments is the vibrant cultural exchange among the peoples of the Americas—the Americanization of Latin American cultural tastes and the growth of U.S.-style shopping malls coupled with a parallel rise in U.S. consumption of Latin American food, beverages, music, and literature and use of Spanish. More critically, as U.S. government aid and private investment have subsided, remittances of Latin Americans in the United States to their home countries have risen exponentially since the turn of the century: $54 billion in 2005, more than a third of which goes to Mexico. These are bonds that may prove more durable than any crafted by governments.

See also **Alliance for Progress; Clayton-Bulwer Treaty (1850); Drugs and Drug Trade; Fox Quesada, Vicente; Hispanics in the United States; Migration and Migrations; Monroe Doctrine; North American Free Trade Agreement (NAFTA); Organization of American States (OAS); Panama Canal Treaties of 1977; Platt Amendment; Roosevelt Corollary; World War I; World War II; Dominican Republic.**

BIBLIOGRAPHY

Aguilar Monteverde, Alonzo. *Pan Americanism from Monroe to the Present: A View from the Other Side,* trans. Asa Zatz. Rev. English edition. New York: Monthly Review Press, 1969.

Blasier, Cole. *The Hovering Giant: U.S. Responses to Revolutionary Change in Latin America, 1910–1985,* rev. edition. Pittsburgh: University of Pittsburgh Press, 1985.

Connell-Smith, Gordon. *The United States and Latin America: An Historical Analysis of Inter-American Relations.* New York: Wiley, 1974.

Davis, Harold Eugene, John J. Finian, and F. Taylor Peck. *Latin American Diplomatic History: An Introduction.* Baton Rouge: Louisiana State University Press, 1977.

Langley, Lester D. *America and the Americas: The United States in the Western Hemisphere.* Athens: University of Georgia Press, 1989.

Lowenthal, Abraham F. *Partners in Conflict: The United States and Latin America.* Baltimore: Johns Hopkins University Press, 1987.

McPherson, Alan. *Intimate Ties, Bitter Struggles: The United States and Latin America since 1945.* Washington, DC: Potomac Books, 2006.

Mecham, J. Lloyd. *Survey of United States–Latin American Relations.* Boston: Houghton Mifflin, 1965.

Morse, Richard M. *New World Soundings: Culture and Ideology in the Americas.* Baltimore: Johns Hopkins University Press, 1989.

Shavit, David. *The United States in Latin America: A Historical Dictionary.* New York: Greenwood Press, 1992.

Stuart, Graham, and James L. Tigner. *Latin America and the United States,* 6th edition. Englewood Cliffs, NJ: Prentice-Hall, 1975.

LESTER D. LANGLEY

UNITED STATES–MEXICO BORDER.

The United States–Mexico borderlands constitute the region where the United States and Latin America have interacted most intensely. Over time the nature of that relationship has involved both conflict and interdependence.

THE BOUNDARY AND INTERNATIONAL CONFLICT

International borders are likely to be the scene of conflict because of such basic factors as vague territorial limits, unclear title to natural resources, ethnic rivalries, and restrictions placed on the movement of goods and people across the political line. Where frontier conditions exist, lawlessness is frequently a problem. In remote, sparsely populated areas, the restraints that govern residents of settled regions tend to be weak. Underfinanced local governments struggle to exert their ineffective authority over wide expanses of territory. The international line itself represents a powerful escape valve for fugitives from the law. Bigots and racists tend to take advantage of prejudices that run strong in small communities. In short, at the outer edges of nations, oppressors and transgressors of all shades enjoy shields from punishment not available in the heartland. In the history of the U.S.–Mexico border, these and other problems have complicated the relations between the two countries, making life difficult for the area's residents during periods of heightened animosity.

The Texas rebellion (1836) and the Mexican–American War (1846–1848) exemplified the border-focused conflict in the first half of the nineteenth century. Disorder and bloodshed continued after the demarcation of the new political line following the signing of the Treaty of Guadalupe Hidalgo (1848) and the Gadsden Purchase (1853).

One of the greatest sources of strife in the nineteenth century was the recurring transboundary Indian raids. A provision in the Guadalupe Hidalgo Treaty bound the United States to prevent Indian incursions into Mexico. Unable or unwilling to carry out this provision, the United States abrogated the treaty in 1853 with the completion of the Gadsden Purchase. Nevertheless, an understanding remained that each country assumed responsibility for preventing indigenous tribes from using the respective national territories as springboards for transborder forays. As the depredations into the Mexican borderland settlements continued year after year, Mexico bitterly protested the alleged U.S. indifference to the problem.

Problems with slave hunters, smugglers, robbers, cattle thieves, and desperate characters of all shades further increased the tension between the two countries. The general lawlessness characteristic of many European Americans living along the border led to the violation of Mexico's territorial integrity, including repeated filibustering expeditions into several northern states. Mexican border residents suffered plunder, pillage, and murder at the hands of desperadoes and adventurers. Among the many foreigners who sought to establish empires or colonies on Mexican soil, none is better known than William Walker, whose invasion of Baja California and Sonora in 1853 was short-lived. The U.S. frontier, particularly in Texas, also endured depredations from criminal elements who used the Mexican borderlands as a base of operations. Cattle rustling and smuggling particularly disturbed Texans. Retaliatory raids fomented by European American mistreatment of Mexicans, such as Juan Nepomuceno Cortina's exploits in the Brownsville-Matamoros region in the 1850s, fanned racial hatred even more.

Each country accused the other of failing to suppress such disorders, and by the late 1870s relations became strained almost to the breaking point. With the advent of the railroads in the 1880s and the subsequent influx of more stable elements and influences, however, marauding and raiding activities declined. During the next three decades the frontier experienced relative peace and order.

The Mexican Revolution of 1910 introduced a new era of instability when Mexican bandits and revolutionaries raised havoc in the Texas and New Mexico borderlands. For a time, residents in the U.S. border states lived in fear that extremists from the neighboring country, aided by militant Mexican Americans, would attempt to retake lands lost by Mexico in the nineteenth century. The tensions of the decade occasioned several crossings of U.S. troops into Mexican territory, including the unsuccessful chase of Pancho Villa by General John J. Pershing in 1916–1917. By the middle of the decade, war between the two countries seemed likely; but the crisis abated as the violent phase of the revolution waned and the United States turned its attention to World War I. Thereafter confrontation over borderland violence ceased as a major diplomatic issue between the two nations.

Pinpointing the precise location of the border became a highly volatile problem in the first years of binational contact, and remained a sore point until the 1960s. Disagreement over whether the Rio Grande or the Nueces River constituted the actual boundary between Texas and Mexico became the immediate cause of the U.S.–Mexico War. Acrimony continued over this issue because of the inexact identification of the new line of demarcation in the Treaty of Guadalupe Hidalgo. Errors in surveying caused the Mesilla Valley in present-day New Mexico to become a hotly disputed territory until Antonio López de Santa Anna gave in to U.S. pressure and sold the area as part of the Gadsden Purchase in 1853.

Changes in the course of the unpredictable and often violent Rio Grande have resulted in boundary disputes as well. The best known of such controversies began in El Paso, Texas/Paso del Norte (present-day Ciudad Juarez, Chihuahua) in 1864, when the river suddenly turned southward, resulting in the U.S. annexation of a section of Mexican land known as El Chamizal. Mexicans attempted for decades to regain the lost land through arbitration, escalating their efforts during the era of Porfirio Díaz, but the United States would not accept Mexico's claim to the Chamizal. In 1911 the U.S. government refused to abide by a decision favorable to Mexico rendered by the International Boundary Commission. After decades of stalemate, the two governments finally resolved the issue in 1963 by agreeing to terms essentially worked out in the 1911 arbitration. With the signing in 1970 of a treaty to resolve remaining and future boundary differences, the possibility of serious conflict over border delimitation diminished considerably.

Another problem that has caused bitter controversy pertains to the distribution and use of the water in the rivers that form part of the border region: the Rio Grande, the Colorado River, and the Tijuana River. A century of controversy began in the 1870s when irrigation development reached the U.S. borderlands. Decades of negotiation resulted in two treaties, one in 1906 and one in 1944, that established terms for the division of waters. Yet both treaties contained serious flaws. The 1906 pact divided the water of the upper Rio Grande (from its source to Fort Quitman, Texas) but left the apportionment of the waters of the lower Rio Grande, the Colorado, and the Tijuana unresolved. These omissions triggered a generation of agitation. Matters calmed down somewhat in 1944 with the ratification of the second treaty, but the new pact (covering the waters of the Rio Grande below Fort Quitman and of the Colorado and Tijuana Rivers) not only overestimated stream flow but also contained ambiguous provisions regarding drought and water quality, thus leaving both Mexican and U.S. farmers dissatisfied with the amount and type of water available for their irrigation projects. These and other problems diminished the effectiveness of the treaty. The excessive salt content of the Colorado River water reaching Mexico, which after 1961 began causing serious damage to thousands of acres of Mexican land, became a particularly troublesome issue. The two countries did not resolve this problem until 1973, when a new binational pact provided for the reduction of salinity through the construction by the United States of a desalting plant, the cooperative rehabilitation and improvement of the impaired lands, and the waiver of previous Mexican claims. Although desalination has lessened the problem, saline water has not been totally eliminated. Further, the reduced flow resulting from upstream damming and diversion has practically ruined the once thriving ecosystem of the Colorado River delta.

A prolonged drought from 1992 to 2002 led to severe water shortages and sparked a bitter quarrel between Texas farmers and the Mexican government. The farmers accused Mexico of hoarding water from tributaries that feed into the Rio Grande and pressed the U.S. government to force compliance regarding treaty-mandated water deliveries. With abatement of the drought, Mexico began paying its water debt. By 2005 a binational agreement settled the dispute, although Texans remained bitter over lack of compensation for crop losses.

INTERDEPENDENCE IN THE BORDERLANDS

After the delimitation of the boundary in the mid-nineteenth century, new settlements emerged and existing ones grew as migrants arrived from the interiors of Mexico and the United States. A symbiotic relationship evolved between one side of the border and the other, with the United States assuming the role of dominant partner. One immediate effect of the establishment of the new boundary in 1848 was to convert Mexican frontier settlements at the Rio Grande into satellites of the U.S. economy. The competition provided by U.S. merchants who moved into the region devastated many Mexican businesspeople who had no access to capital and manufactured goods, both of which were more readily available to their counterparts across the line. For ordinary *fronterizos*, the major effect of the new border was a higher cost of living, for after 1848 tariffs had to be paid on foreign commodities. As a result of economic dislocation, scores of Mexicans migrated to the United States, where living conditions were more favorable.

The Mexican government provided some relief to the border communities by allowing a *zona libre* (free zone) to function in certain border areas beginning in the late 1850s. Under the *zona libre*, Mexican border residents could import foreign products without having to pay the normal duties. This helped to stimulate the economy of the border towns, but the external dependence increased. In 1885 the Porfirio Díaz regime recognized the unique conditions at the frontier and extended the *zona libre* along the length of the border. Local trade flourished, ushering in prosperity unseen in previous eras. Yet dependence on the U.S. economy grew deeper because the commercial stimulus was being driven from abroad. Then in 1905, following protests from U.S. merchants hurt by the diversion of commerce to the Mexican side, and pressures from Mexican businesspeople and industrialists in the interior who resented the preferential treatment given to borderlanders, the Mexican government eliminated the *zona libre*. In the decades that followed, borderlanders continuously petitioned for the return of free trade but succeeded only in persuading Mexico City to allow duty-free importation at selected parts of the border.

Meanwhile, U.S. capitalists penetrated the economies of the northern Mexican states, in particular Chihuahua and Sonora. By the 1880s U.S. companies had built railroads along important routes that connected central Mexico with El Norte (The North) and with the United States. As the railroads reached rich mining districts and productive agricultural and ranching areas, they came to symbolize U.S. dominance, for they facilitated the export of precious metals and raw materials to the United States. The railroads also transported Mexican workers to U.S. work sites throughout the borderlands. As owners of Mexican mines, oil fields, farms, ranches, and sundry industries, U.S. citizens exerted disproportionate influence in Mexico, engendering resentment among Mexicans. That resentment played a pivotal role in the turmoil that gripped Mexico in the early years of the twentieth century, an unrest that assumed nationwide proportions by 1910, eventually exploding into a full-scale revolution.

After the revolution, Mexico began the process of political, economic, and social reconstruction, slowly eliminating the conditions that had precipitated internal instability. Modernization and sustained economic growth became strongly institutionalized in the northern states and in the U.S. Southwest. Thus a closer relationship evolved between the two sides of the boundary, shaping the region in ways that differed considerably from earlier periods, when isolation, underdevelopment, and disorder were commonplace.

In 1919 the Volstead Act made it illegal to produce or sell alcohol in the United States, causing the Mexican border cities to become magnets for manufacturers of liquor and operators of bars, nightclubs, casinos, and related establishments. During Prohibition, many U.S. entrepreneurs joined Mexican businesspeople in catering to the demands of a large U.S. clientele eager for alcoholic beverages and entertainment not readily available in the United States. Consequently, cities such as Ciudad Juárez and Tijuana acquired reputations as centers of vice and moral abandon.

The onset of the Great Depression temporarily halted the trend toward institutionalized interdependence along the border. Massive unemployment created strong pressures to rid the United States of foreign workers, with Mexicans targeted as a primary group for deportation and "repatriation." Thus in the 1930s between half a million and one million Mexicans, many of them U.S. citizens, left the United States involuntarily and as repatriates. For the border communities, the returnees presented special challenges because most of them needed basic assistance and transportation to the interior.

The greatest socioeconomic changes in the borderlands have taken place since World War II. At that time the U.S. government began to invest enormous amounts of capital throughout the Southwest in military installations, defense-related industries, and infrastructure projects. The infusion of these external funds stimulated the entire economy, helping to convert the U.S. border region into one of the most dynamic areas in the country. As an extension of the U.S. Southwest, northern Mexico benefited considerably from these trends, as well as from the industrialization policies promoted from Mexico City during the same period. By the late twentieth century El Norte emerged as one of the most modern and prosperous regions within the Mexican republic.

Both sides of the border sported a greatly expanded economy capable of sustaining substantially larger populations. Traditional extractive and agricultural industries were pushed into the background, replaced by manufacturing and high-tech industries that relied heavily on government spending. New forms of industrialization emerged with the establishment of *maquiladoras*, foreign-owned assembly plants situated on the Mexican side of the border. Urban centers throughout the binational borderlands assumed a new look, evolving from isolated, underdeveloped towns into modern, vibrant metropolises. Some cities achieved national prominence within their respective nations. At the border, communities such as Ciudad Juárez–El Paso and Tijuana–San Diego became highly integrated binational centers of great significance for both nation-states.

The post-World War II economic expansion spurred impressive population growth throughout the borderlands. By 2000, 17 million people lived in the Mexican border states, compared with 8 million three decades earlier; north of the boundary, the population of the U.S. border states rose from 34 million to 65 million. Thus by 2000 the combined population of the binational borderlands was 82 million.

DEVELOPMENTS SINCE THE 1990S
Since the 1990s issues related to trade, migration, and drugs have dominated the U.S.-Mexico border relationship. The North American Free Trade Agreement (NAFTA), enacted in 1994, has

significantly increased binational economic interaction, bringing benefits to many consumers and select merchants, industrialists, and workers. However, Mexicans situated in sectors that find it difficult to compete with the U.S. economy have experienced significant setbacks, while U.S. residents that cannot match the cheap-labor industries in Mexico have likewise been hurt. Drug traffickers have capitalized on the NAFTA-driven dramatic rise in truck traffic across the border to smuggle greater amounts of their illegal products into the United States. In addition, NAFTA has worsened migration problems on the border as a result of increased movement to the United States by Mexicans from rural areas in the interior that were devastated by importation of cheap U.S. foodstuffs.

NAFTA's impact on migration is clearly a contributor to the escalation of binational friction over this issue since the 1990s. Yet the troublesome issue of cross-border migration has complex and deep roots that precede NAFTA by many decades. Certain border areas have experienced severe stress as would-be undocumented migrants have been driven from the large border cities by U.S. blockades and forced to cross into the United States by way of remote and dangerous deserts and mountain areas. As a result, more than 3,000 people perished from exposure to the elements between 1993 and 2005. During that period the anti-immigrant sentiment grew substantially in the United States, triggering a wave of anti-immigrant state and local laws as well as pressure on the federal government to pass national restrictive legislation. In 2006 the U.S. Congress engaged in acrimonious debate over the immigration issue, especially in light of concerns that arose after September 11, 2001, about securing the border from foreign terrorists.

Drug trafficking, which also reflects the reality of a porous border and triggers security concerns, has generated many disputes between the two countries. Yet it is the Mexican border communities that have felt the sharpest effects of the drug trade. Cities such as Tijuana, Ciudad Juárez, and Nuevo Laredo have turned into battlegrounds as drug cartels have fought each other as well as law enforcement for the privilege of conducting their nefarious business without obstruction. Protracted violence, crime, and corruption have wreaked havoc on the citizenry. It appears that for years to come the drug problem will remain one of the major challenges confronting the border.

See also **Chamizal Conflict; Díaz, Porfirio; Gadsden Purchase; Guadalupe Hidalgo, Treaty of (1848); Mexico, Wars and Revolutions: Mexican-American War; North American Free Trade Agreement; Pershing Expedition; Santa Anna, Antonio López de; Villa, Francisco "Pancho"; Walker, William.**

BIBLIOGRAPHY

Arreola, Daniel D., and James R. Curtis. *The Mexican Border Cities: Landscape Anatomy and Place Personality.* Tucson: University of Arizona Press, 1993.

Fernández, Raul A. *The United States–Mexico Border: A Politico-Economic Profile.* Notre Dame, IN: University of Notre Dame Press, 1977.

Ganster, Paul, and David E. Lorey. *The U.S.–Mexican Border into the Twenty-First Century.* 2nd ed. New York: Rowman & Littlefield, 2008.

Hall, Linda B., and Don M. Coerver. *Revolution on the Border: The United States and Mexico, 1910–1920.* Albuquerque: University of New Mexico Press, 1988.

Herzog, Lawrence A. *Where North Meets South: Cities, Space, and Politics on the U.S.–Mexico Border.* Austin: Center for Mexican American Studies, University of Texas at Austin, 1990.

Martínez, Oscar J. *Border People: Life and Society in the U.S.–Mexico Borderlands.* Tucson: University of Arizona Press, 1994.

Martínez, Oscar J. *Troublesome Border,* revised edition. Tucson: University of Arizona Press, 2006.

Rippy, J. Fred. *The United States and Mexico.* New York: Knopf, 1926.

OSCAR J. MARTÍNEZ

UNIVERSIDAD AUTÓNOMA DE SANTO DOMINGO. Universidad Autónoma de Santo Domingo, the oldest university in the Americas, founded by papal bull of Paul III in 1538. Originally called la Universidad de Santo Tomás de Aquino, the University was run by the Dominican order until 1801, when it was closed; it reopened as a lay institution in 1815 and was reorganized in 1914. Dictator Rafael Trujillo moved it to University City (the grounds of the unsuccessful World's Fair) in 1955 and later added Autónoma to its name, which was meaningless during his rule.

UASD was a very traditional university in terms of curriculum—mainly law, philosophy, and medicine for a long time—pedagogy, and organization. It was the only university until 1962, when the

Universidad Católica Madre y Maestra was established in Santiago De Los Caballeros. After Trujillo was assassinated in 1961, UASD became a hotbed of opposition to Joaquín Balaguer (then president), who was an alumnus and former rector. Following President Juan Bosch's overthrow by the military in 1963 and the resultant civil war and U.S. intervention in 1965, the UASD students fought for his return and opposed the United States. During the civil war a group of conservative professors and students left UASD and formed their own university, the Universidad Nacional Pedro Henríquez Ureña. Balaguer's election in 1966 was strongly opposed by UASD students; he retaliated against them by cutting UASD's budget.

The student enrollment was around 60,000 in the early 1990s, but began to grow rapidly in the late 1990s and the early 2000s; as of 2005 it had reached approximately 150,000. In 1966 the university established regional university centers. The first were San Pedro de Macorís and Barahona. By 2007, more than ten regional university centers were in operation.

See also **Balaguer, Joaquín; Bosch Gaviño, Juan; Trujillo Molina, Rafael Leónidas; Universities: The Modern Era.**

BIBLIOGRAPHY

Emilio Rodríquez Demorizi, *Cronología de la Real y Pontífica Universidad de Santo Domingo, 1538–1970* (1970).

Frank Moya Pons, *El pasado dominicano* (1986), chap. 8.

Additional Bibliography

García M., José C. *Trujillo y la universidad.* Santo Domingo: Dirección de Publicaciones, Editora Universitaria-UADS, 2002.

Mejía-Ricart G., Tirso. *Historia de la universidad dominicana.* 2nd ed. Santo Domingo: Editoria Universitaria, Universidad Autónoma de Santo Domingo, 1999.

LARMAN C. WILSON

UNIVERSIDAD CATÓLICA MADRE Y MAESTRA.

Universidad Católica Madre y Maestra, a university founded jointly in 1962 by the business community and the Conference of Dominican Bishops in Santiago De Los Caballeros, the second largest city and economic center of the Dominican Republic—85 miles northwest of the capital, Santo Domingo. Along with the conservative but progressive elite, a prime mover in UCMM's creation was the bishop of Santiago, Hugo Eduardo Polanco Brito. Although it is a private and secular university, its rector has always been a priest, starting with Bishop Polanco. The university was established to be insulated from national politics, in contrast to the Universidad Autónoma De Santo Domingo, and to provide instruction and training in the fields that were needed for the development and modernization of the country. It follows the U.S. university model.

UCMM opened on a limited basis in the academic year 1962–1963 with some seventy students in the faculties of education and philosophy. It remained open during the 1965 civil war and steadily increased in enrollment to around 12,000 in the early 1990s. In its early years UCMM received important foreign assistance, including faculty development, from the U.S. government and several universities, the Ford Foundation, and the British government. While President Joaquín Balaguer starved the Universidad Autónoma in the capital during his first term (1966–1970) because of its leftist students, he was generous to UCMM, which was not dependent on government funds.

See also **Balaguer, Joaquín; Dominican Republic.**

BIBLIOGRAPHY

Ian Bell, *The Dominican Republic* (1981).

Agripino Núñez Collado, *La UCMM: Un nuevo estilo universitario en la República Dominicana*, 2 vols. (1982).

Frank Moya Pons, *El pasado dominicano* (1986), chap. 18.

Additional Bibliography

Hernández, Pablo María. *Historia del pensamiento pedagógico en la República Dominicana.* República Dominicana: Editor Impresos Goris, 2001.

Núñez Collado, Agripino. *La Pontificia Universidad Católica Madre y Maestra: En el umbral del siglo XXI.* Santiago de los Caballeros: Pontificia Universidad Católica Madre y Maestra, 2005.

LARMAN C. WILSON

UNIVERSIDAD CENTRAL DE VENEZUELA.

Universidad Central de Venezuela, the leading university of Venezuela, founded by royal decree as the Royal and Pontifical University of Caracas on 22 December 1721. It was the only university in the province of Venezuela during colonial days. A defender of the king's law and privilege and keeper of the purity of the Catholic faith, the university provided courses in theology, law, and medicine.

The university's elite and ecclesiastical orientation was modified after independence, when Simón Bolívar promoted its academic renovation with the help of José María Vargas and José Rafael Revenga. It was named the Central University of Caracas in 1827. The reform was intended to transform the university into a self-supporting scientific and academic center. New courses were created; measures which impeded the entrance of nonwhites were eliminated; costs of the right to a degree were lowered; staff salaries were raised; and courses were taught in Castilian rather than in Latin. Results, however, were mixed: between 1830 and 1899 the university experienced both splendor and decadence both financially and academically.

In the absence of organized political parties during the Juan Vicente Gómez regime, the university became a focus of opposition to the dictator. Gómez responded by shutting down the university from 1912 to 1922, gradually reorganizing each department to his liking. In 1943 the construction of a university city was decreed by President Isaías Medina Angarita, and the process of scientific and academic modernization was resumed. Gradually, new colleges were established and new areas of specialization were added. In the early 1990s, the university consisted of eleven colleges, thirty-five schools, forty-one research institutes, more than 8,000 professors, and about 70,000 students. In the late twentieth century, it considerably broadened its activities, including the development of postgraduate courses in numerous disciplines.

See also **Gómez, Juan Vicente; Venezuela: The Colonial Era.**

BIBLIOGRAPHY

Juan De Dios Méndez y Mendoza, *Historia de la Universidad Central de Venezuela*, 2 vols. (1911, 1924).

Ildefonso Leal, *Historia de la Universidad Central de Venezuela, 1721–1981* (1981).

Additional Bibliography

López, Alexander. *La Universidad Central de Venezuela y el debate político nacional, 1958–1970.* Caracas: Universidad Central de Venezuela, Facultad de Ciencias Jurídicas y Políticas, 1998.

INÉS QUINTERO

UNIVERSIDADE DE CAMPINAS.

Established only four decades ago, the Universidade Estadual de Campinas (UNICAMP) has developed into one of Latin America's leading universities, currently accounting for an estimated 15 percent of the academic and scientific research done in Brazil. One of São Paulo's three state universities, UNICAMP receives most of its funding from a fixed parcel of state tax revenues, with additional resources coming from state, federal, and international agencies. Although financially subordinate to the state government, the university retains a great measure of autonomy in terms of educational policies and priorities. Its origins and early growth were bound closely to the projects and actions of Zeferino Vaz (1908–1981), a charismatic educator whose previous experience included the creation of a medical school in Ribeirão Preto and a controversial stint as intervening rector at the University of Brasília, following the military coup of 1964. After breaking ground for the new campus in a cane field on the outskirts of Campinas in 1966, Vaz led an ambitious campaign to hire more than 200 foreign professors along with many notable Brazilian researchers. With a heavy emphasis on technical research, graduate studies, and cooperation with the private sector, UNICAMP sought to establish an innovative focus from the outset. At the undergraduate level, a common core curriculum, with classrooms strategically located at the hub of the circular campus, also set UNICAMP apart from other Brazilian universities. Over time, however, much of this early distinctiveness faded, in part because of the expansion of graduate programs throughout the country and in part because of the development of strong humanities and social science programs at UNICAMP. In 2006 nearly 47,000 candidates took the standard entrance exam (vestibular), vying for 2,830 spots in fifty-eight undergraduate programs. More than 10,000 students currently are enrolled in sixty-two graduate degree programs (masters and doctorate), including a growing number of foreign students, most of whom are from other Latin American countries.

See also **Education: Overview; Universities: The Modern Era.**

BIBLIOGRAPHY

Gomes, Eustáquio. *O Mandarim: História da infância da Unicamp.* Campinas, Brazil: Editora da Unicamp, 2006.

JOHN M. MONTEIRO

UNIVERSIDADE DE SÃO PAULO.

Brazil's largest and most renowned research university, the Universidade de São Paulo (USP) was founded in 1934. The university grew from the state's Constitutionalist Revolt of 1932 against the national government of Getúlio Vargas. While the uprising failed, it prompted the drafting of a new constitution giving higher priority to public education and, in São Paulo, generated boosterism among affluent coffee planter and industrialist families. This was the environment in which state governor Armando Salles de Oliveira spearheaded the creation of Brazil's first comprehensive university, collaborating with sociologist Fernando de Azevedo and Júlio Mesquita Filho, owner of the *Estado de São Paulo* newspaper. Prior to the creation of USP, Brazilian higher education was fragmented into separate schools offering professional education, so the backbone of the new university was formed by absorbing the state's law school. Reflecting the power of French thought in Brazil, the early USP attracted such scholars as Roger Bastide, Claude Lévi-Strauss and Fernand Braudel. In the 1950s and 1960s, USP begat the so-called "São Paulo School" of research into race relations. Led by Florestan Fernandes, these scholars began to trace racial inequality in Brazil. Fernandes and other members of this movement such as Fernando Henrique Cardoso and Octavio Ianni were purged by the military regime in the 1960s. During the military dictatorship, the campus became a hotbed of student protests. When these were repressed, USP became a recruiting ground for urban guerrilla movements. By 2006 USP had a student body of more than 80,000, of whom 25,000 engaged in post-graduate studies. USP offers doctorates in 289 fields across the sciences, social sciences, humanities, engineering, arts and architecture.

See also **Azevedo, Fernando de; Brazil, Revolutions: Constitutionalist Revolt (São Paulo); Cardoso, Fernando Henrique; Fernandes, Florestan; Ianni, Octavio; Vargas, Getúlio Dornelles.**

BIBLIOGRAPHY

Azevedo, Fernando de. *Brazilian Culture: An Introduction to the Study of Culture in Brazil.* New York: Macmillan, 1950.

Cardoso, Fernando Henrique. *Dependency and Development in Latin America.* Berkeley: University of California Press, 1978.

Fernandes, Florestan. *The Negro in Brazilian Society.* New York: Columbia University Press, 1969.

Lévi-Strauss, Claude. *Tristes Tropiques* [1955]. New York: Penguin Books, 1992.

JERRY DÁVILA

UNIVERSITIES

This entry includes the following articles:
COLONIAL SPANISH AMERICA
THE MODERN ERA

COLONIAL SPANISH AMERICA

Approximately thirty-one universities functioned in Spanish America between the mid-sixteenth century and the winning of independence. Seven universities were founded in the sixteenth century, thirteen in the seventeenth, nine in the eighteenth, and two after 1800. Nine of these institutions were of major importance because of their public character, size, and location; these were Santo Domingo (founded 1538); Mexico and Lima (both founded in 1551); Charcas in Bolivia (1614); Córdova in Argentina (1621); Guatemala (1676); Havana (1721); Caracas (1723), and Santiago, Chile (1738). The primacy, wealth, and population of Lima and Mexico made their universities institutional models for all the others. Together, the colonial universities graduated an estimated 150,000 persons, of whom perhaps 15 to 20 percent received advanced degrees.

The minor universities, generally smaller, poorer, and more isolated, were really college-universities, dependent in government and operation upon a college run by a religious order, almost always the Dominicans or Jesuits. If these institutions were more than two hundred leagues from one of the major universities, they were entitled to confer degrees. The organization of minor institutions followed that of the University of Alcalá, in which a single college was dominant.

The major (public) universities were governed by their faculty and graduates, led by an elected rector within the terms of royal and papal charters. Their statutes were based on those of the University of Salamanca.

All the universities consistently sought, and some secured, the privileges of Salamanca, most notably exemption for graduates from personal taxation and the separate legal jurisdiction for students and faculty called the *fuero académico*. The key feature of major university governance, however, was the Cloister (*Claustro*), an assembly of all graduates holding advanced degrees. This body received and obeyed or protested royal orders, petitioned the crown, managed the money, dealt with the curriculum and the faculty, and conducted ordinary relations with the church and local government. Within the limits set by statutes and enforced royal orders, the Cloister ran the university.

The executive officer of the Cloister was the rector, elected annually by and from its number. The rector called and presided over all Cloister meetings, enforced the statutes and decisions, disciplined faculty and students, inspected pupilages, and presided over examinations and the trial lectures by which professors were chosen. The rector's powers were balanced by those of the *maestrescuela,* who as judge of the schools administered the *fuero académico,* adjudicating disputes or crimes involving students or graduates. He granted degrees in the name of pope and king, presided over the graduation ceremony, and administered the oaths the graduates took.

In contrast, the Alcalá statutes confided governance not to the graduates assembled in cloister, but to the members of a single college, who elected one of their own to serve as rector. This official exercised all the powers of the rector in a large university as well as those of the *maestrescuela*. Management of money and university business was confined to the college; the Cloister had only minor powers over classroom practice and curriculum.

Both the Salamanca- and the Alcalá-style universities had two types of faculty. Junior or temporal chairs were held for four to six years; senior or proprietary posts, once won, were held for life. Both kinds of posts were filled by trial lectures or *oposiciones,* in which contestants, working in isolation, prepared a lesson on a passage from a standard text and then gave and defended it before the students, who selected the winner. From the beginning, these contests were contentious and disorderly and were therefore the subject of progressively more elaborate regulation. Finally, after about 1675, students were excluded from voting; the lessons were heard by juries of experts, and government officials made the final choice.

The *oposición* was only one of the many disputations that were interwoven with classwork. The academic career assumed a knowledge of Latin; the bachelor's degree in arts added to that at least three years' study of logic and natural and moral philosophy. A student could then proceed to one of the major faculties: law, theology, or medicine, all of which required four or five more years of study. In addition to attending classes, students were required to propose and argue increasingly elaborate and difficult theses. The culmination was the licentiate degree, which required three or four years of residence and defense of a number of major "acts" or disputations. Finally, the candidate withstood an examination without limitation of time or number of examiners, followed by a secret vote. The doctorate was entirely ceremonial, expensive, and really only an admission to the corporation of teachers.

The structure of learning that supported the Hispanic worldview at the time most universities were founded was undoubtedly scholastic. But it was a vigorous scholasticism sustained by talented men, suffused by new ideas, and dealing with important questions. Given the limits imposed by their geographic isolation and relative poverty, Hispanic-American universities played a substantial role in the intellectual life of their time.

By the same token, Latin American universities in the eighteenth century shared in the gradually emerging changes in learning. Criticism of the exhausted scholasticism of the eighteenth century gradually spread, as evidenced by, for example, the works of the Spanish philosopher Benito Geronimo Feijóo y Montenegro, but it was to be found also in the Latin texts used in the arts courses.

After the accession of Charles III in 1759, reforms acquired concentration and focus. The proscription of the Jesuits in 1767 removed a powerful institutional rival of many universities, which in many cases inherited Jesuit libraries, buildings, and income. From about 1770 on, new plans of studies were developed in Spain and America that made a larger place for mathematics, Newtonian physics, and modern geography and cosmography. Next, the courses of civil and canon law were changed to emphasize the primacy of the crown over the church and the importance of Spanish rather than Roman and canon law. The theology courses were drastically modified to include critical church history and to strengthen dogmatic rather than speculative scholastic theology. Finally, the education of medical doctors was changed to include modern texts; training in anatomy, chemistry, and botany; and clinical practice.

These changes were, as ever, affected by the precarious and inadequate financing of most institutions. Neither were they achieved without opposition or controversy. Nevertheless, they produced far-reaching changes in the worldview that paralleled those occurring in Spain at the same time.

See also **Enlightenment, The; Fueros.**

BIBLIOGRAPHY

The most useful brief introduction is John Tate Lanning, *Academic Culture in the Spanish Colonies* (1940). His *The University in the Kingdom of Guatemala* (1955) and *The Eighteenth-Century Enlightenment in the University of San Carlos de Guatemala* (1956) constitute the most thorough study of a single university. Agueda María Rodríguez Cruz, O.P., *Historia de las universidades hispanoamericanas,* 2 vols. (1973), is replete with facts and has useful documentary appendices and an extensive bibliography, unfortunately it is not very analytical. Still more documents are in Cándido M. Ajo González De Rapariegos y Sáinz De Zúñiga, *Historia de las universidades hispánicas: Orígines y desarrollo desde su aparación hasta nuestros días,* 8 vols. (1957–1972). On Lima, see Luis Antonio Eguiguren, *La Universidad Nacional Mayor de San Marcos* (1950). On Mexico, see Sergio Méndez Arceo, *La Real y Pontífica Universidad de Mexico* (1952), and Alberto María Carreño, *La Real y Pontífica Universidad de México, 1536–1865* (1961). On scholasticism and reform, see O. Carlos Stoetzer, *The Scholastic Roots of the Spanish American Revolution* (1979).

Additional Bibliography

Menegus Bornemann, Margarita. *Universidad y sociedad en Hispanoamérica: Grupos de poder, siglos XVIII y XIX.* Mexico City: Centro de Estudios sobre la Universidad, Universidad Nacional Autónoma de México: Plaza y Valdés Editores, 2001.

Siebzehner, Batia B. *La Universidad americana y la Ilustración: Autoridad y conocimiento en Nueva España y el Río de la Plata.* Madrid: MAPFRE, 1994.

JOHN C. SUPER

THE MODERN ERA

The Spanish American university, with its main intellectual and administrative origins in the University of Salamanca in thirteenth-century Spain, was one of the most enduring colonial institutions. Late-eighteenth- and early-nineteenth-century intellectual and political influences jarred the university, but did not alter its social, economic, and political functions.

The Wars of Independence and the struggles of early nationhood weakened the universities, but most survived, little changed from their colonial past. They had now become national rather than "royal and pontifical" universities, institutions of the state rather than of crown and church. The University of Buenos Aires was one of the earliest (founded 1821) and most important of the new universities. Some of the new universities, such as the University of the Republic of Uruguay (founded 1849), would remain as the only higher education institution of the country during the nineteenth century. Political and economic difficulties hindered the development of the new and old universities. In Mexico, for example, the Royal and Pontifical University (founded 1551) was modified, closed, and reopened several times between 1810 and 1865. A national university was finally reestablished under the guidance of Justo Sierra with the founding of the National University of Mexico in 1910. For those universities that did function, one supposed prevailing influence was the Napoleonic university, with its emphasis on centralization, the development of distinct faculties, and the training of professionals to meet the demands of emerging nation-states. One of the most famous universities to emerge within this intellectual context was the University of Chile, founded by the Venezuelan intellectual Andrés Bello. Despite the French influence, the university included some moral and humanistic education along with professional training. The University of Chile, in a manner similar to several other new state universities, also had control over primary and secondary education.

For much of Latin America in the nineteenth century, university life was narrowly defined, focusing on jurisprudence and the training of lawyers to promote the interests of the Creole elite that emerged after the Wars of Independence, or medicine and the education of physicians. Faculties of law and medicine dominated the university, acting almost as independent fiefdoms rather than as parts of a larger institution. Conflict in the history of the university in the nineteenth century stemmed from competition between liberal and conservative forces. A central issue was the extent of religious influence in education. The dominant trend was toward secular education, controlled by the state. The scholastic education of the past gave way to the training of the social and political elite of the new nations. *Positivism* provided the philosophical basis for efforts to reorganize the university, emphasizing secular, scientific education to achieve the positivist goals of order and progress. Education under the tutelage of positivism was designed to establish the framework for the orderly economic and social development of society.

Brazil was the exception in university education as it was in so much else. During the colonial period, the University of Coimbra in Portugal served the needs of the empire. In Brazil, Jesuit colleges and seminaries served as centers for advanced studies. With independence, a national educational system was created, but not a university. Technical and vocational institutes satisfied the need for higher education until the creation of the first Brazilian university in the twentieth century. The University of Rio de Janeiro, established in 1920, is usually considered the first Brazilian university, but it was not until 1931 that the first Statute of Brazilian Universities (usually requiring that the university consist of the three faculties of law, medicine, and engineering) was passed. The University of São Paulo (established in 1934) was the first university to fulfill the requirements of the statute.

Law and medicine remained the classic subjects of the university, but were gradually accompanied by a growing emphasis on engineering, mathematics, and the chemical and physical sciences. This was a reflection of the positivist and utilitarian emphasis that affected the university in the late nineteenth century. Education as professional training rather than as the formation of character through humanistic inquiry had become dominant. Yet this education was often inadequate, emphasizing more the title that came with university education than the knowledge. While the university experienced changes in the nineteenth century, it had still not shed its image as an institution of the colonial period (though the nineteenth-century organizational influences were pronounced), serving the interest of a narrow elite rather than the needs of the nation.

This institution, its tradition prompting labels such as "medieval," "monastic," and "anachronistic," came under attack in the early twentieth century. The calls for change culminated in the Córdoba Reforms, initiated in June 1918 at the University of Córdoba in Argentina. The demands of the Córdoba Reforms soon became the Magna Carta of Latin American universities, guiding their development in the twentieth century. Most influential have been the demands for university autonomy, including political, administrative, and financial independence; election of university administrators, with the participation of faculty, students, and alumni; open classrooms and free education; improved teaching and control over faculty; a curriculum appropriate for the current needs of society; and university extension programs, designed to make the university an agent of social reform. University autonomy remained one of the most vocal demands of students and faculty in the twentieth century. Though not often recognized during the turmoil of university politics, autonomy was a tradition that the colonial university had inherited from the University of Salamanca. This included the participation of students in the selection of faculty.

Few of these reforms were enacted in their entirety, but they did signal that the university had become a center of political and social activity, aware of its potential for challenging the past and creating the future. In addition to its traditional teaching and research mission, the university now had a "social mission," broadly defined as the commitment to using the resources of the university to create more equitable and just societies.

This has made the Latin American university a very visible political institution, much more so than in the United States or Europe. The expectation that the university would provide the solution to the social and economic woes of Latin America has been a source of inspiration and frustration since 1918. It represents the core of the dilemmas that confronted the university as it tried to reconcile the different emphases of training versus education, humanism versus scientism, and reformism versus conservation of the established order.

While the Córdoba Reforms faced obstacles that minimized their implementation, they did provide the basis for regional cooperation among Latin American universities. International meetings of faculty and students discussed issues and proposed cooperative programs. This regional effort culminated in the First Congress of Latin American Universities, hosted by Guatemala in 1949. This led to the creation of the Union of Latin American Universities (UDUAL), which expressed its goal "of orienting university education to the full development of the human personality" in the Carta de Guatemala. UDUAL continues to function, publishing *Universidades,* a good source of information on the modern Latin American university.

After World War II, the universities entered a new phase of growth. The physical presence of the university changed with the emergence of the university cities, sprawling modern campuses that did resemble cities. One of the most widely admired new campuses was that of the National Autonomous University of Mexico in Mexico City. The new university city proclaimed the modernity of the university and reinforced the strong centralizing tendency of Latin American politics.

Latin American universities entered a period of unprecedented growth in the 1960s. Increasing social demand for education led to mushrooming enrollments in existing universities and the creation of new ones, public and private.

The percentage of women enrolled has increased faster than general enrollments. In the 1980s women comprised 58 percent of students in Panama (1985), 57 percent in Uruguay (1987) and Cuba (1988), 51 percent in Brazil (1988), 47 percent in Argentina (1987), and 41 percent in Mexico (1988). In addition to increases in university enrollments, there have been jumps in the number of men and women attending non-university institutes of higher education.

The proliferation of higher education institutions included many private universities. A few private universities continued to exist from earlier periods. Notable among them was the Jesuit Pontifical Javerian Catholic University of Bogotá, founded in 1622. Following World War I these were joined by several new Catholic universities. In addition, there were the "popular universities," at times extensions of national universities, at other times independent efforts to take the knowledge and skills of the university to the rural and urban poor. These new institutions did not compensate for the inability of the nation to satisfy the increasing demographic and social pressures for university education. As a result, private higher educational institutions grew more rapidly, and included secular as well as religious education. In 1980, 35 percent of higher-education students attended private institutions. Because private universities differ from public universities in finance, organization, student background, and often in curriculum, it makes it particularly difficult to generalize about recent changes in university education in Latin America.

Student unrest in the 1960s, more common in the public than in the private university, responded to university-related problems and to broader social issues. Lack of access to the university and the increasing distance between university curriculum and professional opportunities contributed to unrest. The traditional programs of law, medicine, and engineering still dominated. Internally, the university faced the old problems of part-time, unprepared faculty; dominance of the traditional organizational structure of the university, particularly the *cátedra,* the chair of professorship so powerful in university affairs; and the lack of adequate support for teaching and research. Finance was a continual problem that often made university autonomy more rhetorical than real. Competition for state funds increased friction between the university and government. Inadequate planning and uncertain revenues in both state and university hampered the development efforts of the university. With the global recession of the 1970s, financial problems became more severe. At the same time, partly as a response to the unrest of the 1960s, new organizations emerged to challenge traditional university life. Staff and faculty unions in particular have exercised their power to demand better salaries and working conditions.

Externally, the university failed to address the social and economic needs of development. Critics went much further, interpreting the university as an instrument of an oppressive international economic order that depended on the economic and social polarization of Latin American society for its well-being. This was reminiscent of the demands of 1918, but was now couched in Marxist terms with clearly stated revolutionary objectives. The university was seen as training an elite that served the needs of national and international capital. In response there was the call for the "popularization" of the university, to use it as a weapon in the fight for social and economic justice. In addition to simply increasing enrollments, the critics called for linking the university to the working classes, forming alliances with them to create a new bloc in the struggle against oppression.

The charged political climate of the late 1960s and early 1970s erupted in violence in Latin America. The most renowned conflict occurred in Mexico City on the eve of the 1968 Olympics as students clashed with army and police at the Plaza de la Tres Culturas. University reform was no longer the only issue. Students demanded sweeping reforms that affected the social, political, and economic life of their countries. The reform efforts often clashed with the repressive military regimes then in power, leading to particularly chilling effects on university life in countries such as Argentina, Brazil, and Chile.

An important development within the university in the 1960s was a new emphasis on extension and social-action programs. They had the responsibility for helping to create a new awareness of the social and economic reality of the oppressive conditions of life rather than simply diffusing the dominant culture of the elite. At the same time, they designed and implemented programs to combat illiteracy, malnutrition, and infant mortality. In a word, extension was to become the bridge between university and society, a network of communication that would overcome the chasm that had traditionally separated the university from the society that it supposedly served.

The neoliberal period in Latin America from the late 1980s through the 1990s also revamped the relationship between the university, society, and economics. At the same time that international financial institutions recommended stricter economic measures and less state intervention, private universities proliferated across the region. U.S.-backed financial assistance packages to higher education peaked as many state institutions were privatized. In fact, the World Bank

and the Inter-American Development Bank set aside approximately 4 to 10 percent of their loans to promote tertiary education in Latin America. During the 1990s, there was also a shift in the educational curriculum. Technical degrees such as engineering, economics and agronomy were privileged. In this sense, the important development within the university in the 1990s was a new renewed interest from the region and from abroad to expand the traditional academic fields and improve the technical degrees and expertise. A clear example of this interest was the creation of private research centers and clusters, which were parallel to the universities. The transformation of the universities as private laboratories of technical experts thus coincided with the increased political and economic interests of the neoliberal decade that favored the formation of a technocratic bureaucracy. Nonetheless, such proliferation of private universities raised new problems in the region. Many had different grading schemes and accreditations. As a result, many students lacked the national accreditation approval that would enable their diplomas to be recognized as official.

In the early twenty-first century the university has demonstrated its power again as locus site of national politics, including the formation of political thought, contestation and legitimacy. In Venezuela, as Hugo Chávez rallied support throughout the country for his third re-election in 2006, the polls indicated clear dissent among the student population in the main universities. This dissent among the universities has matured substantially. In fact, while Chávez planned to hold the referendum in December 2007 on his 69 constitutional amendments, hundreds of students protested against Chávez, the police, and the national guard. The amendments were narrowly defeated.

See also **Education: Overview; National Autonomous University of Mexico (UNAM).**

BIBLIOGRAPHY

For general introductions to the university, see Luis-Alberto Sánchez, *La universidad latinoamericana* (Guatemala: Editorial Universitaria, 1949); Darcy Ribeiro, *La universidad latinoamericana* (Montevideo: Universidad de la República, 1971); Hanns-Albert Steger, *Las universidades en el desarrollo social de la América Latina* (México, D.F.: Fondo de Cultura Económica, 1974); Joseph Maier and Richard W. Weatherhead, eds., *The Latin American University* (Albuquerque: University of New Mexico Press, 1979). Specialized studies include

Daniel C. Levy, *Higher Education and the State in Latin America* (Chicago: University of Chicago Press, 1986), an analysis of the differences between private and public universities; Donald J. Mabry, *Mexican University and the State: Student Conflicts, 1910–1971* (College Station: Texas A&M University Press, 1982), a detailed history of student activism; and Iván Jaksíc, *Academic Rebels in Chile: The Role of Philosophy in Higher Education and Politics* (Albany: State University of New York Press, 1989), a study of the interaction between the history of a discipline, the university, and politics.

Additional Bibliography

Levy, Daniel C. *To Export Progress: The Golden Age of University Assistance in the Americas.* Bloomington: Indiana University Press, 2005.

JOHN C. SUPER
MONICA HERNANDEZ QUIJANO

UNIVERSITY OF THE WEST INDIES.

University of the West Indies, the major university system of the English-speaking Caribbean, formed as the result of a growing need for economic, political, and cultural integration in the region. It has three main campuses, located in Mona, Jamaica; Saint Augustine, Trinidad; and Cave Hill, Barbados. It was established by royal charter in 1948, for 500 to 600 students. Jamaica's main campus serves all of the Caribbean. The Trinidad branch, formally named the Imperial College of Tropical Agriculture, houses the faculties of agriculture and engineering. Until 1962, the university was affiliated with the University of London. Now it is an accredited university offering bachelor's, master's, and doctoral degrees in arts, medicine, natural sciences, and education. By 2007, the student population had grown to approximately 36,000.

See also **Universities: The Modern Era.**

BIBLIOGRAPHY

D. A. Turner, "Science in the 70s: Observations on Science Education in Jamaica," in *Caribbean Quarterly* 20, no. 2 (June 1974): 15–24.

Eric Williams, "The University in the Caribbean," in *Universities for a Changing World: The Role of the University in the Later Twentieth Century,* edited by Michael D. Stephens et al. (1975).

Additional Bibliography

Fraser, Henry, ed. *UWI Cave Hill: Forty Years, A Celebration.* Kingston, Jamaica: University of the West Indies Press, 2003.

Howe, Glenford D., ed. *Higher Education in the Caribbean: Past, Present and Future Directions.* Kingston, Jamaica: University of the West Indies Press, 2000.

DARIÉN DAVIS

URABÁ. Urabá, a gulf in northwestern Colombia and the surrounding region of plains and adjacent hills, lying mainly within the department of Antioquia. The region came under European radar when it was explored in 1501 by Rodrigo de Bastidas and Juan de la Cosa, who were impressed by the amount of gold possessed by the native inhabitants. In 1510 Alonso de Ojeda founded San Sebastián, the first Spanish settlement on the mainland of the New World, near the village of Urabá on the eastern shore of the gulf. Conflict with the local inhabitants led to the early abandonment of San Sebastián, and the surviving Spaniards moved across the gulf, where they founded Santa María de la Antigua.

Urabá languished during the remainder of the colonial period, but in the nineteenth century it was the focal point of Antioquia's effort to build a direct outlet to the Caribbean. It was not until 1954 that a road was completed linking Medellín to Turbo, the largest city on the gulf of Urabá. Afterward the region experienced rapid population growth and became a major producer of bananas and other tropical products. During the 1980s, labor unrest, guerrilla activity, and killings by paramilitary death squads made Urabá one of the most violent areas in Colombia.

See also **Antioquia; Ojeda, Alonso de.**

BIBLIOGRAPHY

James J. Parsons, *Antioquia's Corridor to the Sea: An Historical Geography of the Settlement of Urabá* (1967).

Additional Bibliography

Bucheli, Marcelo. *Bananas and Business: The United Fruit Company in Colombia, 1899–2000.* New York: New York University Press, 2005.

Colombia, Return to Hope: Forcibly Displaced Communities of the Urabá and Medio Atrato Region. New York: Amnesty International USA, 2000.

Martínez Solís, Luis Fernando. Alcides Fernández: Misionero y aviador en Urab: (biografía) 1917–1995. Miami, FL: Palmetto Printing, 2004.

HELEN DELPAR

URBANIZATION. *See* Cities and Urbanization.

URBINA, JOSÉ MARÍA (1808–1891).

José María Urbina (*b.* March 1808; *d.* 4 September 1891), *jefe supremo* (supreme leader) of Ecuador (1851–1852) and president (1852–1856). Born in Ambato, Urbina attended the Naval School at Guayaquil briefly but left early to participate in military actions (siege of Callao, 1824–1826; Malpelo, 1828; defense of Ecuadorian independence, 1830). Rising rapidly through military ranks, he became aide-de-camp to President Juan José Flores. On a diplomatic mission to Bogotá for President Vicente Rocafuerte, he committed a serious indiscretion and was recalled in 1837. Caught plotting against the government, he was banished but returned in 1839 to enter politics under the tutelage of President Flores. For his political loyalty to Flores, Urbina was rewarded with the governorship of Manabí. In 1845 he joined rebels to topple Flores from power. He was promoted to brigadier general and rose to high posts in the provisional government.

President Vicente Ramón Roca (1845–1849) named Urbina chief of the general staff, which enormously increased his political and military power. In 1851, Urbina led a revolt and proclaimed himself *jefe supremo*. He would dominate Ecuadorian politics for the rest of the decade.

As *jefe supremo* Urbina abolished slavery and repelled an armed invasion by Flores from Peru. Under a new constitution he was elected president in 1852 and served a four-year term that was characterized by vigorous executive domination, glib assertions of liberal principles, stern control of the press, and the expulsion of the Jesuits. He severed relations with the Vatican, quarreled with Peru over asylum given to Flores and over Ecuador's southern boundary, and sought unsuccessfully to establish a U.S. protectorate over Ecuador.

From 1856 to 1859, Urbina was the *éminence grise* of the Francisco Robles administration, which collapsed in 1859 after a Peruvian attack at Guayaquil. Urbina fled into exile, plotted in Peru to regain power in Ecuador, but did not return until 1876. He helped place Ignacio Veintemilla in power, but his influence diminished rapidly thereafter. He died in Guayaquil, forgotten by friends and denounced by liberal leaders.

See also **Flores, Juan José; Roca Rodríguez, Vicente Ramón.**

BIBLIOGRAPHY

José Le Gouhir y Rodas, *Historia de la república del Ecuador,* vol. 1 (1920), pp. 401–539.

Luis Robalino Dávila, *La reacción anti-floreana* (1967).

Additional Bibliography

Guerra Cáceres, Alejandro. *Esclavos manumitidos durante el gobierno del Gral. José María Urbina.* Guayaquil, Ecuador: Archivo Histórico del Guayas and Banco Central del Ecuador, 1997.

Macías Núñez, Edison. *El general José María Urbina.* Quito, Ecuador: Presidencia de la República del Ecuador, Comisión Nacional Permanente de Conmemoraciones Cívicas, 1992.

MARK J. VAN AKEN

URBINA, LUIS GONZAGA (1864–1934).

Luis Gonzaga Urbina (*b.* 8 February 1864; *d.* 18 November 1934), Mexican journalist and poet. Born in Mexico City, Urbina studied at the National Preparatory School before launching his career as a journalist. He began composing poetry before the age of sixteen. In 1881 he published some of his verses in *La patria ilustrada*. In 1887 he met his mentor, Justo Sierra Méndez. Thanks to that friendship, Urbina obtained various government positions as well as posts at periodicals, where he wrote theater criticism and some of the first movie reviews in Mexico. Under Sierra's direction and with the cooperation of Pedro Henríquez Ureña and Nicolás Rangel, Urbina compiled the two volumes of Mexican literature, *Antología del centenario* (1910), produced for the centenary celebrations of that year. Although he is considered a poet of the *modernismo* movement, Urbina represents the persistence of romanticism with his *vespertinas,* poems that reflect upon love and melancholy. In 1913 he was appointed director of the National Library, but two years later he left Mexico to live first in Cuba and then in Spain.

See also **Libraries in Latin America; Literature: Spanish America.**

BIBLIOGRAPHY

Angel Miquel, *El nacimiento de una pasion. Luis G. Urbina: Primer cronista mexicano de cine* (1991).

Alfonso Rangel Guerra, "Cartas de Luis G. Urbina a Alfonso Reyes," in *Nueva Revista de Filología Hispánica* 37, no. 2 (1989).

Gerardo Saenz, *Luis G. Urbina: Vida y obra* (1961).

Additional Bibliography

Arístides, César. *El cisne en la sombra: Antología de poesía modernista.* Mexico City: Alfaguarra, 2002.

JOHN WALDRON

URDANETA, ANDRÉS DE (1508–1568).

Andrés de Urdaneta (*b.* 1508; *d.* 3 June 1568), Spanish navigator and explorer. A native of Villafranca de Oria, Guipúzcoa, Urdaneta served as a page on the circumnavigation of García Jofre de Loaysa in 1525. After being shipwrecked in the Moluccas, he returned to Spain in 1536. Urdaneta journeyed to Guatemala in 1538, and in 1541 he went to New Galicia with Pedro de Alvarado. He was *corregidor* of the province of Ávalos in 1543, and visitor of that province until 1545. He became a novice in the Augustinians in 1552 and was named pilot-missionary to the Philippines under Miguel López De Legazpi in 1559. He sailed from Navidad, Jalisco, in November 1564, reached the Philippines in February 1565, and returned to New Spain 8 October 1565. On his return voyage he established the eastbound route, via Japan and California, to Acapulco that was used by the Manila Galleon. Urdaneta retired in 1566 to a monastery in Mexico City, where he died.

See also **Spanish Empire.**

BIBLIOGRAPHY

Enrique Cárdenas De La Peña, *Urdaneta y "el tornaviaje"* (1965).

Mariano Cuevas, *Monje y marino, la vida y los tiempos de Fray Andrés de Urdaneta* (1943).

Additional Bibliography

Cabrero, Leoncio. *Andrés de Urdaneta.* Madrid: Historia 16: Quorum, 1987.

Rodríguez, Isacio R., and Jesús Alvarez Fernández. *Andrés de Urdaneta, Agustino: En carreta sobre el Pacífico.* Valladolid: Estudio Agustiniano, 1992.

W. MICHAEL MATHES

URDANETA, RAFAEL (1788–1845).

Rafael Urdaneta (*b.* 24 October 1788; *d.* 23 August 1845), Venezuelan independence leader and Colombian president. Born in Maracaibo, Venezuela, Rafael Urdaneta studied in Bogotá and at the start of the independence movement joined the patriots of New Granada. He took part in the first civil conflicts (as a federalist) as well as in the struggle against Spain, serving as Bolívar's second in command in the Admirable Campaign (1813). Following the Spanish reconquest of 1815–1816, he was one of those who kept resistance alive in the plains of the Orinoco Basin and later took part in the final liberation of Venezuela.

Urdaneta filled important positions in the government and congress of Gran Colombia. As minister of war in 1828–1829, he was military strongman of Simón Bolívar's final dictatorship. With Bolívar gone, in 1830 he became president-dictator in a last-ditch effort to preserve the power of the Bolivarian party and the unity of Gran Colombia. Forced to step down early in 1831, he returned to Venezuela, where he continued to play a key political role. He was on a diplomatic mission to Spain when he died in Paris.

See also **Wars of Independence, South America.**

BIBLIOGRAPHY

Carlos Arbeláez Urdaneta, *Biografía del General Rafael Urdaneta, último presidente de la Gran Colombia* (1945).

Daniel Florencio O'Leary, *Bolívar and the War of Independence,* edited and translated by Robert F. Mc Nerney, Jr. (1970).

Gerhard Masur, *Simón Bolívar* (1948; rev. ed. 1969).

Additional Bibliography

Párraga Villamarín, Eloy, and Adolfo Romero Luengo. *Venezuela en los años del general Rafael Urdaneta*

(1788–1845). Maracaibo, Venezuela: Universidad Rafael Urdaneta, Comité Ejecutivo de la Junta Organizadora del Bicentenario del Natalicio del General Rafael Urdaneta, 1988.

Pulgar, Juvencio, and Gilberto Mora Muñoz. *Urdaneta vuelve a Colombia.* Caracas: Congreso de la República, 1994.

Yllarramendy, Rogelio. *Homenaje a Urdaneta: Ensayos, artículos e investigación sobre la personalidad y la obra del prócer.* Caracas: Gráficas Franco, 2002.

DAVID BUSHNELL

UREÑA, FELIPE (?–c. 1773).

Felipe Ureña (*d.* after 1773), Mexican sculptor, retablo master. Ureña was largely responsible for the spreading of *estípite* baroque throughout New Spain, in places very distant from Mexico City. His decoration of the sacristy of the Church of San Francisco in Toluca, dedicated in 1729, is the first native work in the style. Ureña had what must have been a sizable workshop in Mexico City, but he also executed retablos and architectural projects in Guanajuato, Aguascalientes, Durango, Oaxaca, and elsewhere. His most famous work, still extant, is the Jesuit church La Compañía in Guanajuato, on which he labored between 1747 and 1765, with interruptions for other projects. Fragments of his wood sculpture exist in Durango.

See also **Architecture.**

BIBLIOGRAPHY

Clara Bargellini, *La arquitectura de la plata* (1991), pp. 138–140.

Additional Bibliography

Halcon, Fátima. "Arquitecutra y retablística novohispana: las obras de Felipe de Ureña en Oaxaca." *Archivo Español de Arte* 274 (1996): 171–182.

Villegas, Víctor Manuel, René Taylor, and Fernando Chueca Goitia. *Churriguera y Felipe de Ureña en Toluca: La Sacristía del Convento Franciscano de la Asunción de Toluca, los churriguera hasta Pedro Ribera y sus obras, la Ermita de Santa María del Puerto de Madrid: La restauración de la sacristyía.* Toluca, Mexico: Gobierno Constitucional del Estado de México and Universidad Autónoma del Estado de México, 1981.

CLARA BARGELLINI

UREÑA DE HENRÍQUEZ, SALOMÉ

(1850–1897). Salomé Ureña de Henríquez (*b.* 21 October 1850; *d.* 6 March 1897), Dominican educator and poet. Ureña de Henríquez was born in Santo Domingo. Her father, Nicolás Ureña de Mendoza, was a distinguished politician, lawyer, and poet who provided her with an excellent education. Together with her husband, Francisco Henríquez y Carvajal, she implemented important education reforms in the Dominican Republic, stressing the significance of women's education. Ureña de Henríquez was the founder of the Instituto de Señoritas. She was profoundly influenced by the Puerto Rican educator Eugenio María de Hostos (1839–1903), who resided in Santo Domingo for over a decade. A fervent liberal, she supported the Blue Party of Gregorio Luperón and opposed presidents Buenaventura Báez and Ulises Heureaux. Beset by frequent illness and faced with the civil wars and dictatorships of one of the most turbulent epochs of Dominican history, she never lost faith in the positivist creed of order and progress.

Ureña de Henríquez was regarded as one of the finest Dominican poets and her writings became known throughout Latin America. Her poetry takes up a variety of themes, such as patriotism ("A Quisqueya," "En defensa de la sociedad," "Anacaona"), sentimentality ("La llegada del invierno," "Tristezas," "Horas de anguistas," "El ave y el nido"), and social and political reform ("Ruinas," which is regarded as one of her best poems). She was the mother of the educator and literary critic Camila Henríquez Ureña; the writer, teacher, and diplomat Max Henríquez Ureña; and the writer, philosopher, and educator Pedro Henríquez Ureña. She died in Santo Domingo.

See also **Dominican Republic; Henríquez Ureña, Max; Henríquez Ureña, Pedro.**

BIBLIOGRAPHY

Enciclopedia dominicana, vol. 7 (1978), pp. 183–185.

Diane E. Martínez, ed., *Spanish American Women Writers* (1990).

Salomé Ureña De Henríquez, *Poesías completas* (1989).

Additional Bibliography

Castro Ventura, Santiago. *Salomé Ureña: Jornada fecunda.* Santo Domingo: Editora de Colores, 1998.

Céspedes, Diógenes. *Salomé Ureña y Hostos.* Santo Domingo: Secretaría de Estado de Cultura and Biblioteca Nacional Pedro Henríquez Ureña, 2002.

Cocco DeFilippis, Daisy, selection and prologue. *Sin otro profeta que su canto: Antología de poesía escrita por dominicanas.* Santo Domingo: Taller, 1988.

KAI P. SCHOENHALS

URETA, ELOY G. (1892–1965).

Eloy G. Ureta (*b.* 1892; *d.* 1965), Peruvian military leader, presidential candidate, and diplomat. Ureta was born in Chiclayo and educated in Chorrillos Military Academy (1909–1913) and the Advanced War School (1922). As brigadier general in 1941, Ureta was in charge of the military operations during the war with Ecuador. He became a popular military figure especially after the victory achieved in the battle of Zarumilla (24 July 1941). He was promoted to division general in 1941. He retired from the army to run unsuccessfully for the presidency in 1945. He was awarded the honorary rank of marshal in 1946. Between 1949 and 1955 he was the Peruvian ambassador to Spain. He died in Madrid.

See also **Zarumilla, Battle of.**

BIBLIOGRAPHY

Daniel Masterson, *Militarism and Politics in Latin America: Peru from Sánchez Cerro to "Sendero Luminoso"* (1991).

ALFONSO W. QUIROZ

URIARTE–BAYARTA AGREEMENT.

The Uriarte–Bayarta Agreement (correctly the Uriarte–Vallarta Agreement), which established the initial boundary arrangement between Guatemala and Mexico, was signed on 7 December 1877, by Ramón Uriarte, the Guatemalan minister to Mexico, and Ignacio Luis Vallarta, the Mexican foreign minister. The boundary dispute reflected imprecise frontiers between colonial jurisdictions. Guatemala inherited claims to Chiapas and Soconusco from the United Provinces of Central America, contending these districts had been part of the Captaincy-General of Central America. Mexico considered these districts to be part of the Captaincy-General of Yucatán, which became part of Mexico.

The agreement provided for demarcation of the boundary from the port of Ocos to Mount Izbul (Ixbul). Although never ratified, despite several time-limit extensions, the agreement provided the basis for the treaty of 27 September 1882, which established this line as the boundary between Mexico and Guatemala.

See also **Boundary Disputes.**

BIBLIOGRAPHY

Ireland, Gordon. *Boundaries, Possessions and Conflicts in Central and North America and the Caribbean.* Cambridge, MA: Harvard University Press, 1941.

Uriarte, Ramón. *La convención de 7 de diciembre de 1877: Apuntes para la historia de la cuestión de límites entre Guatemala y México.* Oaxaca: Impr. de G. Marquez, 1882.

KENNETH J. GRIEB

URIBE, JUAN CAMILO (1941–2005).

Juan Camilo Uribe (*b.* 20 February 1941; *d.* 2005), Colombian artist. Born in Medellín, Uribe is known for his conceptualist and experimental work, which uses popular, religious, and historical icons from Colombian culture. He has participated in group shows since 1968. In 1972 he won first prize at the National Independent Salon, and first prize at the Third Salon of Young Artists in Bogotá, where he had his first solo exhibit three years later at the Galería Oficina. He went to Paris on a grant from the Colombian government in 1977, the same year he represented Colombia at the São Paulo Biennial. His work was shown at the Museum of Contemporary Art in Caracas and at the Primera Bienal del Grabado de América in Maracaibo, Venezuela. Uribe's installation *Arte Telescopio* (1979) featured numerous individual slide viewers hanging from the ceiling throughout the room, documenting bits of his personal life, his exhibits, his friends, and his work. He participated in a traveling exhibition of Latin American art that visited London, Stockholm, and Madrid in 1989. In 1992, his work was shown at the Photo Fest in Houston. He died in Medellín.

See also **Art: The Twentieth Century.**

BIBLIOGRAPHY

Eduardo Serrano, *Cien años de arte colombiano, 1886–1986* (1986).

Additional Bibliography

Herzog, Hans-Michael, and Ospina Nadin. *Cantos cuentos colombianos: Arte colombiano contemporáneo.* Zurich: Diarios Latinoamérica, 2004.

Jaramillo, Carmen Maria. *Otras miradas.* Bogotá: Ministerio de Relaciones Exteriores, 2005.

BÉLGICA RODRÍGUEZ

URIBE HOLGUÍN, GUILLERMO

(1880–1971). Guillermo Uribe Holguín (*b.* 17 March 1880; *d.* 26 June 1971), Colombian composer. Guillermo Uribe Holguín began the study of music in Bogotá, where he was born, and continued his studies in New York and at the Schola Cantorum in Paris. He conducted, taught, served as director of Colombia's Conservatorio Nacional (1910–1935, 1942–1947), and wrote a work on harmony as well as an autobiography. But he is best known as a composer, generally considered Colombia's greatest. His extensive body of works includes eleven symphonies, concerti and chamber music, numerous piano pieces, and songs. In style and technique he was strongly influenced by French impressionism, and for many years he disdained the use of elements from popular Colombian musical culture. Starting with his second symphony (*Del terruño*) in 1924, however, he turned increasingly to national rhythms and melody in his composing, thus giving qualified expression to musical nationalism.

See also **Music: Art Music.**

BIBLIOGRAPHY

Eliana Duque *Guillermo Uribe Holguín y sus "300 trozos en el sentimiento popular"* (1980).

Nicolas Slonimsky, *Music of Latin America* (1945; 1972), pp. 171–172.

Additional Bibliography

Béhague, Gerard. "Music since c. 1920." In *The Cambridge History of Latin America,* volume 10, Leslie Bethell, editor. Cambridge: Cambridge University Press, 1996.

Martina, Aileen. "The Traditional Bambuco in Nineteenth and Twentieth Century Colombian Composition." Mus. M. thesis, University of North Texas, 1993.

DAVID BUSHNELL

URIBE URIBE, RAFAEL (1859–1914).

Rafael Uribe Uribe (*b.* 12 April 1859; *d.* 15 October 1914), Colombian political caudillo, one of the leaders of the Liberal Party between 1880 and his assassination in 1914. Born on an estate in Antioquia, Uribe was the son of a wealthy landowner. He was educated at the Colegio del Estado (the present-day University of Antioquia).

Due to the singular nature of Colombian politics, Uribe was a political leader who had to do double duty as a military leader, like many others of his generation, in the all-too-frequent civil wars between Liberals and Conservatives. He participated in the civil wars of 1876, 1885, 1895, and 1899.

A charismatic caudillo, he never reached the presidency of the nation because he attained political leadership when the Liberal Party had been displaced by a coalition dominated by the Conservative Party; this group established a hegemony over the country until 1930. Uribe and the rest of the Liberal leadership had to labor under political persecution and even exile, a situation that eventually led to the most traumatic of civil wars, the War of the Thousand Days (1899–1902).

As an ideological leader, Uribe is reputed to have been instrumental in a major ideological shift of his party after 1904, when, in the short article "Socialismo de Estado," he exhorted the Liberals to move away from laissez-faire economics and espoused state intervention in economic and social welfare. His platform is reminiscent of the measures then being implemented in Uruguay by President José Batlle y Ordóñez (1903–1907), rather than the socialism his enemies accused him of. However, in the Colombia of the 1900s, it was considered subversive to ask the wealthy to pay taxes.

See also **Caudillismo, Caudillo.**

BIBLIOGRAPHY

Charles W. Bergquist, *Coffee and Conflict in Colombia, 1886–1910* (1978).

Helen Delpar, *Red Against Blue: The Liberal Party in Colombian Politics, 1863–1899* (1979).

Gerardo Molina, *Las ideas liberals en Colombia, 1849–1914* (1970).

Eduardo Santa, *Rafael Uribe Uribe* (1974).

Additional Bibliography

Toro Sánchez, Edgar. *El liderazgo de Rafael Uribe Uribe y la modernización de la nación y el estado.* Bogotá: Teleobjetivo Editores, 2000.

Villalba Bustillo, Carlos. *Las dos repúblicas liberals.* Barranquilla, Colombia: Antillas, 2004.

JOSÉ ESCORCIA

URIBURU, JOSÉ EVARISTO (1831–1914). José Evaristo Uriburu (*b.* 19 November 1831; *d.* 25 October 1914), Argentine statesman, president of Argentina (1895–1898), and senator (1901–1910). Scion of an aristocratic Salta family, Uriburu was part of the so-called Generation of 1880 and one of the most representative figures in the oligarchic politics of the late nineteenth and early twentieth centuries. A leading member of the elite's political machine, the National Autonomist Party (PAN), Uriburu assumed the presidency of the nation after the sudden resignation of Luis Sáenz Peña. Like his predecessor, Uriburu had to deal with the great 1890 depression and he continued Sáenz Peña's policy of consolidating the national and provincial debts. Though brief, his presidency nonetheless produced a number of notable accomplishments. Uriburu's resolution of the ongoing dispute with the British railroad companies over profit guarantees as well as other measures restored investor confidence and led to a return of British capital. In his diplomatic career, Uriburu was one of the principal mediators of the treaty between Chile and Peru that ended the War of the Pacific.

See also **Argentina, Political Parties: National Autonomist Party.**

BIBLIOGRAPHY

Natalio R. Botana, *El orden conservador: la política argentina entre 1880 y 1916* (1977).

Horacio J. M. Guido, *Secuelas del unicato, 1890–1896* (1977).

Additional Bibliography

Instituto de Historia Militar Argentina. *Congreso Nacional de Historia Militar: Buenos Aires, 20, 21 y 22 de noviembre de 1996.* Buenos Aires: Instituto de Historia Militar Argentina, 1999.

JAMES P. BRENNAN

URIBURU, JOSÉ FÉLIX (1868–1932). José Félix Uriburu was a member of the Argentine military and de facto president from September 1930 to February 1932. He was born on July 20, 1868, in Salta and graduated from the Colegio Militar de la Nación. In 1988 he was promoted to lieutenant. He served as director of the Higher School of War beginning in 1907 and was then sent twice to Europe as a military attaché. There he absorbed militarist nationalism, especially the German variety. In 1913 he was elected national deputy for the province of Salta and served until 1914. In 1921 he was promoted to major general. From 1922, having been appointed inspector general of the army, he forged important bonds with the pro-Fascist sectors of the establishment.

With the economic crisis of 1929, the conservative sectors of the ruling class, who had for some time been skeptical of a democracy they had lost control of, closed ranks against President Hipólito Irigoyen—the leader of the Unión Cívica Radical (UCR), or Radical Party, an urban-supported middle class party—claiming he was incapable of maintaining order amid the social instability. General Uriburu, now retired from active military duty and heading this reactionary movement, commanded the September 6, 1930, military-civilian coup that deposed Irigoyen. The supreme court acknowledged him as president, dissolved the congress, and declared a state of siege. Uriburu's regime hounded the opposition and censored the press. Nevertheless, Uriburu's hopes of installing a corporate regime of Fascist-leaning individuals were dashed by the predominance of liberal-conservative sectors. In 1932, in fraudulent elections, General Agustín P. Justo assumed the presidency, which he held until 1938. On April 29 of that year Uriburu died in Paris.

See also **Argentina: The Twentieth Century; Irigoyen, Hipólito; Justo, José Agustín Pedro.**

BIBLIOGRAPHY

Cantón, Darío, José Luis Romero, and Alberto Ciria. *Argentina, la democracia constitucional y su crisis.* Buenos Aires: Paidós, 1972.

Halperín Donghi, Tulio, ed. *Vida y muerte de la República Verdadera, 1910–1930.* Buenos Aires; Ariel, 2000.

Potash, Robert A. *The Army and Politics in Argentina,* vol. 1: *1928–1945, Yrigoyen to Perón.* Stanford, CA: Stanford University Press, 1969.

VICENTE PALERMO

URQUIDI, VÍCTOR (1919–2001).

Víctor Urquidi was a Mexican economist and educator. The son of a diplomat, Urquidi graduated from the London School of Economics in 1940. He joined the Bank of Mexico and worked closely with Raúl Prebisch in the 1950s, directing the Mexican office of the United Nations Economic Commission for Latin America. During the 1940s and 1950s, he directed *El Trimestre Económico*, a leading economic journal, and served as an adviser to Mexican finance minister Antonio Ortiz Mena, before taking over the presidency of the Colegio de México. He produced a generation of top economists, and was inducted into Mexico's prestigious National College in 1960. He became a member of the Club of Rome.

See also **Colegio de México; Economic Commission for Latin America and the Caribbean (ECLAC); Economic Development; Ortiz Mena, Antonio; Prebisch, Raúl.**

BIBLIOGRAPHY

Memorias. Mexico City: Colegio Nacional, 1960.

Silva Herzog, Jesús, with the cooperation of Ana Magdalena Gama Muñoz. *Biografías de amigos y conocidos.* Mexico City: Cuadernos Americanos, 1980.

RODERIC AI CAMP

URQUIZA, JUSTO JOSÉ DE (1801–1870).

Justo José de Urquiza (*b.* 18 October 1801; *d.* 11 April 1870), Argentine soldier and statesman. Urquiza was born in Talar de Arroyo Largo, Entre Ríos, the son of a merchant and landowner. He studied at the Colegio de San Carlos in Buenos Aires and in 1821 became a lieutenant in the militia. In 1826–1827 he served in the Entre Ríos congress, where he argued for democracy, federalism, and educational improvements; he also persuaded the congress to reject the 1826 Constitution. Urquiza expanded his business activities and became a follower of Ricardo López Jordán, who was defeated by a revolution supported by Santa Fe Governor Estanislao López. Urquiza fled to Uruguay, and in 1831 he returned to Entre Ríos to take command of the Army of Observation. In 1837 he was again elected to serve in the provincial congress. In 1838 he was with the Entre Ríos army massed to oppose an attack by Fructuoso Rivera of Uruguay and Berón de Astrada of Corrientes. The attack was repulsed, thanks largely to Urquiza's cavalry. Urquiza continued fighting interprovincial battles. In 1845 he was named governor of Entre Ríos, a province where the dictator and governor of Buenos Aires, Juan Manuel de Rosas, had little influence.

Urquiza established a well-equipped militia composed primarily of landowners, and he financed progressive programs in public education. In 1848 he began building the Palacio San José, his residence, and founded the Colegio del Uruguay. Urquiza was reelected governor in 1849, and in 1851 he announced to the provincial governments and the exiles in Montevideo that he would undertake a campaign against Rosas. To further that goal, he negotiated an alliance with Brazil and Uruguay.

Urquiza opened his campaign by raising the siege of Montevideo by Manuel Oribe. When his forces crossed into Uruguay, many of Oribe's troops and some from Buenos Aires joined them. Meanwhile, Rosas had declared war on Brazil. Urquiza was to command a combined force of Argentine, Brazilian, and Uruguayan troops. Rosas took no defensive measures to stop Urquiza's advance but assembled his army at Santos Lugares. Rosas was defeated at nearby Caseros on 3 February 1852 by a superior cavalry. He fled to Buenos Aires, where he and his daughter sought refuge in the home of the British minister and a few days later sailed for England.

Urquiza appointed Vicente López y Planes as interim governor. In May 1852, at a meeting of provincial governors, at San Nicolás de los Arroyos,

Urquiza was named temporary director of the Argentine Confederation. Buenos Aires disapproved, however, and in September it seceded from the confederation. All the provinces except Buenos Aires approved the constitution in 1853, Paraná became the capital of the confederation, and Urquiza was elected president (1854–1860). The new government lacked adequate resources to create the institutions that would further national integration and economic development. Several military invasions were launched to bring Buenos Aires into the union, and in 1859 Congress authorized Urquiza, governor of Entre Ríos since 1 May 1860, to use military force to subdue the rebellious province. The armies of the confederation under Urquiza clashed with the Buenos Aires army, led by Bartolomé Mitre, at Pavón on 17 September 1861. Urquiza's cavalry won, but the infantry was defeated. Urquiza left the battlefield. Some maintain that he was ill, others that he realized that Buenos Aires could not be defeated, and still others that he was disgusted with the disputes among military and civilian leaders. Urquiza, constitutionally prohibited from succeeding himself, secured the election of José María Dominguez as governor in 1864, and in 1865 he sought—unsuccessfully—to prevent war with Paraguay. Francisco Solano López attacked Corrientes, thus compelling Urquiza to support the unified Argentine government of Mitre.

On 11 April 1870, a group of conspirators assassinated Urquiza at his home. Two of his sons were killed in Concordia, Entre Ríos. Urquiza had amassed a considerable fortune in land, cattle, and meat-salting plants. He and his wife had eleven children, and he legitimized twelve of his natural children.

See also **Argentina: The Nineteenth Century; Rosas, Juan Manuel de.**

BIBLIOGRAPHY

Leslie Bethell, ed., *Argentina Since Independence* (1993), and *Spanish America After Independence, c. 1820–c. 1870* (1987).

Beatriz Bosch, *Urquiza y su tiempo,* 2d ed. (1980).

David Bushnell and Neill Macaulay, *The Emergence of Latin America in the Nineteenth Century,* 2d ed., (1994).

Joseph T. Criscenti, ed., *Sarmiento and His Argentina* (1993).

Vicente Cutolo, "Urquiza, J. J. de," in *Nuevo diccionario biográfico argentino,* vol. 7 (1985), pp. 444–451.

Susana T. P. De Domínguez Soler, *Urquiza: Ascendencia vasca y descendencia en el Río de la Plata* (1992). In English see José Luis Romero, *A History of Argentine Political Thought,* translated by Thomas F. McGann (1963).

John Lynch, *Argentine Dictator: Juan Manuel de Rosas, 1829–1852* (1981).

Alberto J. Masramón, *Urquiza, libertador y fundador* (1982).

Jacinto R. Yaben, "Urquiza, J. J. de," in *Biografías argentinas y sudamericanas,* vol. 5 (1940), pp. 964–975.

Additional Bibliography

Gliemmo, Graciela. *Dolores Costa y Justo José de Urquiza: Alianzas amorosas y políticas entre Buenos Aires y el interior.* Buenos Aires: Planeta, 1999.

Martínez, Carlos María. *Urquiza en el Uruguay, los orientales en Caseros.* Buenos Aires: Instituto Urquiza de Estudios Históricos, 2001.

Pasquali, Patricia. *La instauración liberal: Urquiza, Mitre y un estadista olvidado, Nicasio Oroño.* Buenos Aires: Planeta, 2003.

JOSEPH T. CRISCENTI

URRACÁ (?–1531).

URRACÁ (?–1531). Urracá (*d.* 1531), Panamanian indigenous leader, one of the most romanticized figures in the country, and a symbol of Panamanian patriotism. For nine years he fought the Spaniards Gaspar de Espinosa and Pedrarias Dávila in what is now Veraguas and Natá. Although he was captured once by the Spaniards, he was able to escape. His encounters with the Spaniards are described in Antonio de Herrera y Tordesillas's *Historia general de los hechos de los castellanos en las islas y tierra firme del mar océano* (1549–1625).

See also **Panama.**

BIBLIOGRAPHY

Jorge Conte Porras, *Diccionario biográfico ilustrado de Panamá,* 2d ed. (1986).

Ernesto De Jesús Castillero Reyes, *Historia de Panamá,* 7th ed. (1962).

JUAN MANUEL PÉREZ

URREA, JOSÉ DE   (1797–1849). José de Urrea (*b.* 1797; *d.* August 1849), Mexican general. A fourth-generation frontier military officer, Urrea was born in the presidio of Tucson. He followed in his father's footsteps: commanding frontier garrisons; fighting insurgents; seconding Agustín de Iturbide's plan for independence, but supporting the republicans against the empire. The involvement of both father and son in the rebellion of the Plan of Montaño led to his father's exile and José's dismissal. He reentered the army two years later (1829), rising to the rank of general in 1835 as a protégé of Santa Anna. He distinguished himself in opposing the independence of Texas. As military commander of Sonora and Sinaloa, Urrea launched a series of unsuccessful revolts to reestablish the Federal Constitution of 1824, first in that region in 1837, and then nationally in 1839, 1840, and 1841. With Santa Anna's return to power that latter year, Urrea returned to Sonora as governor and commander general (1842–1844). His aggressive policies against the economic interests and political power of centralist sympathizers, and against the autonomy of the Yaqui and Mayo Indians, provoked a civil war in the state that continued for three years, until a new national government forced him to yield his command. He then fought under Santa Anna in the war with the United States (1846). He died in Durango, of cholera.

See also **Iturbide, Agustín de; Santa Anna, Antonio López de.**

BIBLIOGRAPHY

Francisco R. Almada, *Diccionario de historia, geografía y biografía de sonorenses* (1983), pp. 709–712.

Additional Bibliography

Salmerón, Rubén. "La aventura federalista del General Urrea en el noroeste de México." *Simposio de Historia y Antropología Regionales.* La Paz, Mexico: Universidad Autónoma de Baja California Sur, 1994: 17–26.

STUART F. VOSS

URREA, TERESA   (1873–1906). Teresa Urrea (*b.* 1873; *d.* 1906), popular figure among Mexican revolutionaries. A mestiza born in Ocorini, Sinaloa, Mexico, Teresa Urrea began, around 1890, to claim divine guidance and to preach social reform from her father's rancho at Cabora in the southern part of the state of Sonora. Thousands of Yaqui and Mayo Indians, along with mestizos and whites of various social groups, flocked to hear and revere her as la Santa (saint) de Cabora. In 1892, when armed movements in her name began to wrack the region, the government deported her and her father to Nogales, Arizona, where she continued to inspire armed forays into Mexico. As fame for her healings spread, she traveled from New York to California, performing her "miracles." She died at age thirty-two, in Clifton, Arizona. Throughout her "mission" she denied fomenting revolution, although hundreds of rebels died in her name.

See also **Indigenous Peoples; Mexico: 1810–1910.**

BIBLIOGRAPHY

William Curry Holden, *Teresita* (1978).

Briandon Domecq, *La insólita historia de la Santa de Cabora* (1990).

Paul D. Vanderwood, "Santa Teresa: Mexico's Joan of Arc," in *The Human Tradition in Latin America: The Nineteenth Century,* by William Beezley and Judith Ewell (1989), pp. 215–232.

Additional Bibliography

Vanderwood, Paul J. *The Power of God Against the Guns of Government: Religious Upheaval in Mexico at the Turn of the Nineteenth Century.* Stanford, CA: Stanford University Press, 1998.

Vargas Valdez, Jesús. *Tomóchic: la revolución adelantada: Resistencia y lucha de un pueblo de Chihuahua con el sistema porfirista, 1891–1892.* Ciudad Juárez, Chihuahua, México: Universidad Autónoma de Ciudad Juárez, 1994.

PAUL J. VANDERWOOD

URRIOLAGOITÍA, MAMERTO   (1895–1974). Mamerto Urriolagoitía (*b.* 5 December 1895; *d.* 4 June 1974), president of Bolivia (1949–1951). Born in Sucre, Urriolagoitía became a lawyer and specialized in international law. From 1919 to 1937, he served as Bolivia's Consul General in Great Britain. At the conclusion of his diplomatic career, he returned to Sucre and won election to Bolivia's Senate in the early 1940s. Urriolagoitía became a leading

member of a conservative Republican party coalition (Partido de la Unión Republicana Socialista—PURS). In the election of 1947, the PURS candidate Enrique Hertzog was elected president and Mamerto Urriolagoitía, vice president. Hertzog resigned in May 1949, a few days after the mid-term election resulted in a vote that favored the middle-class reformist Nationalist Revolutionary Movement (MNR). As president Urriolagoitía repeatedly used military intervention to put down worker uprisings in the mining areas and cities. After the MNR won the May 1951 presidential elections, Urriolagoitía resigned on 16 May 1951. He handed over the government to General Hugo Ballivián, who, a few days later, abrogated the elections.

See also **Bolivia, Political Parties: Nationalist Revolutionary Movement (MNR); Bolivia, Political Parties: Republican Party.**

BIBLIOGRAPHY

Herbert S. Klein, *Parties and Political Change in Bolivia, 1880–1952* (1969), pp. 388–400, and *Bolivia: The Evolution of a Multi-Ethnic Society* (1992), pp. 222, 224.

Additional Bibliography

Crespo, Alfonso, and Mario Lara. *Enrique Hertzog: El hidalgo presidente.* Lima: s.n., 1997.

Urriolagoitia Villa, Gastón. *Mamerto Urriolagoitia Harriague: Apuntes sobre una vida.* Buenos Aires: s.n., 1997.

ERWIN P. GRIESHABER

Batista's overthrow. Yet from his first days in office, Urrutia showed little ability in the art of politics practiced amid a volatile revolutionary movement. After attacking growing Communist influence within the government, Urrutia was forced to resign on 17 July 1959, and public sentiment against him was so great that he had to take refuge in the Venezuelan embassy. Urrutia later fled to the United States, where he became a university professor and organizer of an anti-Castro movement. He wrote *Fidel Castro and Co., Inc: Communist Tyranny in Cuba* (1964), his account of the revolution. Urrutia died in Queens, New York.

See also **Castro Ruz, Fidel; Cuba: Cuba Since 1959.**

BIBLIOGRAPHY

Samuel Farber, *Revolution and Reaction in Cuba, 1933–1960* (1976).

Luis A. Pérez, Jr., *Cuba: Between Reform and Revolution* (1988).

Ramón Eduardo Ruiz, *Cuba: The Making of a Revolution* (1970).

Additional Bibliography

Coltman, Leycester, and Julia Sweig. *The Real Fidel Castro.* New Haven, CT: Yale University Press, 2003.

Sweig, Julia. *Inside the Cuban Revolution: Fidel Castro and the Urban Underground.* Cambridge, MA: Harvard University Press, 2002.

MICHAEL POWELSON

URRUTIA LLEÓ, MANUEL (1901–1981).

Manuel Urrutia Lleó (*b.* 1901; *d.* 5 July 1981), Cuban lawyer and judge, appointed president after the Cuban Revolution of 1959 and dismissed six months later by Fidel Castro. Born in Las Villas province, Urrutia received a law degree in 1923 from the University of Havana and was appointed municipal judge of Oriente Province in 1928. He was later named the magistrate of the district of Santiago. Urrutia first gained national recognition in 1957, when he ruled for the dismissal of 100 youths charged with rebellion against the Batista dictatorship for their involvement in Castro's 1953 attack on the Moncada barracks. Castro's decision to appoint Urrutia as president was apparently based on the assumption that Urrutia would be a compromise candidate acceptable to both radicals and moderates who supported

URSÚA, PEDRO DE (c. 1516–1561).

Pedro De Ursúa (*b.* ca. 1511–1516; *d.* 1 January 1561), leader of the search for El Dorado, the "Land of Cinnamon." Born in Navarre, Spain, Ursúa reached Cartagena de Indias on Colombia's coast in 1545. He served as administrator and military leader, pacified the Chitarero and Muso Indians, and founded the cities of Pamplona and Tudela. As *justicia mayor* (municipal deputy) of Santa Marta in the early 1550s, he brought the Tairona Indians under Spanish domination. Subsequently he undertook the task of subduing runaway slaves on the Isthmus of Panama and succeeded in capturing "King" Bayamo, thus ending a threat to intercolonial trade.

The Peruvian viceroy Andrés Hurtado De Mendoza, marqués de Cañete, authorized Ursúa's search for El Dorado, reputed to be in the upper Amazon basin. Ursúa collected about 370 Europeans, from 20 to 30 blacks, and from 600 to 2,000 Indian auxiliaries from several Andean cities in February 1559. They constructed several brigantines, flatboats, rafts, and canoes on the upper Huallaga River, setting forth in September 1560. Pedro de Ursúa faced discontent from the start: some were bothered by the presence of his mestiza mistress, Inés de Atienza; others chafed at the hard work and difficult conditions en route downriver. Lope de Aguirre was at the head of the mutinous group that assassinated Ursúa as he rested in his hammock near the juncture of the Putumayo and Amazon rivers.

The tale of Aguirre's bloody descent to the Atlantic is one of the most tragic in the era of discovery. Over a hundred of his fellow explorers were killed as Aguirre rebelled against all authority, save that of the sword. Survivors sailed out of the Amazon northwestwardly to the island of Margarita, then headed back toward Peru. Aguirre was finally surrounded by a group of royalists in Venezuela and killed on 27 October 1561.

See also **Aguirre, Lope de; El Dorado.**

BIBLIOGRAPHY

José Antonio Del Busto Duthurburu, *La pacificación del Perú* (1984), pp. 142–154.

John Hemming, *Red Gold: The Conquest of the Brazilian Indians* (1978), pp. 195–197.

Additional Bibliography

Amate Blanco, Juan José. "Ursúa en 'El Dorado': 'El Dorado,' móvil o pretexto para la expedición de Ursúa?" *Cuadernos Hispanoamericanos* 547 (Jan. 1996): 111–118.

Minta, Stephen. *Aguirre: The Re-Creation of a Sixteenth-Century Journey Across South America.* New York: H. Holt, 1994.

NOBLE DAVID COOK

URUGUAI, VISCONDE DO (1807–

1866). Visconde do Uruguai (Paulino José Soares de Sousa; *b.* 4 October 1807; *d.* 15 July 1866), Brazilian statesman. Born in Paris, Uruguai was a key spokesman for the early Conservative Party and the driving force in the diplomacy leading to the overthrow of Argentina's dictator, Juan Manuel de Rosas in 1852. Uruguai began his studies at Coimbra and completed them in São Paulo in 1831. His brilliance and character attracted support and early promotion as a magistrate in São Paulo, and then in Rio de Janeiro. His marriage into an established provincial planter clan brought political entrée through his brother-in-law, Joaquim José Rodrigues Tôrres (later Viscount de Itoboraí). In 1834, he was elected to the assembly of Rio de Janeiro Province, which in turn elected him a provincial vice president. In 1836, he was appointed president of the province; that same year the province elected him a national deputy. In the chamber of deputies, with Tôrres and Eusébio de Queirós, Uruguai led the Saquaremas. The latter were the *fluminense* radical reactionaries of the Conservative Party, which had been created in 1837, in an era of reaction, and was directed by Bernardo Pereira de Vasconcelos, Honório Hermeto Carneiro Leão, and Tôrres. Uruguai's role was that of jurist and orator. He and Vasconcelos formulated the positions that halted the Regency's liberal momentum and shored up the authoritarian centralization that was identified with the monarchy. His son and namesake, known as Paulino, maintained this legacy against the reformism of Uruguai's former protégé, the Viscount do Rio Branco, in the 1870s.

Uruguai, increasingly disgusted with politics, was proudest of his role as foreign minister (1849–1853). He earned his title by defending the empire's perennially insecure southern interests from Rosas's Uruguayan ambitions. It was Uruguai, aided in the field by Honório Hermeto Carneiro Leão (later Viscount de Paraná) and Viscount do Rio Branco, who secured Uruguay and the Urquiza alliance that defeated Rosas. Subsequently, Uruguai, after accepting a brief diplomatic mission to Europe, began a retreat from politics. Although meeting responsibilities as a senator (1849) and councillor of state (1853), he gradually sought the solace of study. The *Ensaio sôbre direito administrativo* was published in 1862 and *Estudos práticos sobre a administração das provincias do império* was published in 1865.

See also **Brazil: 1808–1889; Vasconcelos, Bernardo Pereira de.**

BIBLIOGRAPHY

José Antônio Soares De Sousa, *A vida do visconde do Uruguai* (1944).

Thomas Flory, *Judge and Jury in Imperial Brazil* (1981).

João Pandía Calógeras, *A política externa do império*, vol. 3 (1933).

Ilmar Rohloff De Mattos, *O tempo saquarema* (1987).

Additional Bibliography

Ferreira, Gabriela Nunes. *Centralização e descentralização no Império: O debate entre Tavares Bastos e visconde de Uruguai*. São Paulo: Editora 34, 1999.

Needell, Jeffrey D. *The Party of Order: The Conservatives, The State, and Slavery in the Brazilian Monarchy, 1831–1871*. Stanford, CA: Stanford University Press, 2006.

Prado, Maria Emília. *O estado como vocação: Idéias e práticas políticas no Brasil oitocentista*. Rio de Janeiro: Access Editora, 1999.

JEFFREY D. NEEDELL

URUGUAY

This entry includes the following articles:
BEFORE 1900
THE TWENTIETH CENTURY

BEFORE 1900

INDIANS AND SPANIARDS

Before its discovery by Spain in 1516, Uruguay was populated by a few thousand indigenous people. To these peoples the European conqueror gave a variety of names: Charrúas, Minuanes, Bohanes, Guenoas, Yaros, Chanáes, and Guaranis. Their territories spread beyond Uruguay into what later became neighboring Argentina and Brazil. The dominant and numerically most important race, the Charrúas, were advanced hunters, while the Chanáes in addition practiced a primitive agriculture, which had also been developed more fully by the enclaves of Guarani settlement. But all were societies fundamentally based on hunting, canoeing, and fishing. A limited quantity of archaeological remains bears witness to the practice of decorating pottery and working stone.

The arrival of the Europeans, and of the cattle and horses they left behind in Uruguay at the beginning of the seventeenth century, changed the demography, customs, and natural environment of the indigenous peoples. Having become skilled horsemen hunting wild cattle, they ended up decimated by smallpox and by persecution by the white men as their culture was inimical to the forms of labor introduced by the Spaniards. Traditionally, 1831 is identified as the year in which the Charrúas disappeared as a population of any importance, wiped out by the soldiers of the first republican government of independent Uruguay. This annihilation did not diminish the importance of indigenous blood as an element in the composition of the rural population, especially the Guaranís, from territories occupied by the Jesuit Missions.

Nonetheless, the so-called extermination of the Indians at Salsipuedes in 1831 established the myth of a European, white Uruguay, which the dominant classes in the country encouraged, all the more as immigration from outside the continent became the basis for Uruguay's population growth.

The Banda Oriental (literally "Eastern Bank") was the name given by the Spaniards to the territory that became Uruguay. It was a region of late colonization, mainly during the period of Bourbon Spain in the eighteenth century. It was populated for three principal reasons: the quality of its natural grassland and the multiplying numbers of livestock derived from those left by the Spanish discoverers, the advantages of Montevideo as the only natural port on the Río De La Plata, and the fact that it was a frontier territory in permanent dispute between the Spanish and Portuguese crowns. This struggle was often the explanation for the foundation of its cities and towns, as was the case, for example, of the first important European settlement, Colonia del Sacramento, founded by Portugal in 1680, and of Montevideo, established by Spain between 1724 and 1730. The lack of a fixed frontier had its effect on the economy, promoting a contraband trade which made a mockery of Spain's commercial monopoly, as well as on society, encouraging horsemanship and the practice of arms.

Natural grassland, and ownerless cattle and horses running free, gave rise to the *estancia* (ranch), dedicated to cattle production, and to the dominant figure in rural areas, the *estanciero* (ranchowner). Appearing around 1780–1800 were the first Saladeros (meat-salting plants), which converted part

The Cathedral in the Plaza de la Constitucion,
Montevideo, Uruguay, 1880s, (engraving) by French School
(20th century). PRIVATE COLLECTION/ KEN WELSH/ THE
BRIDGEMAN ART LIBRARY

of the beef production into *tasajo,* hard and lean salt beef, consumed at first only by the slaves of Cuba and Brazil. The *saladeros* were part *estancia* and part industry in Montevideo. Although steam power was adopted in 1832 to render the fat, the production of *tasajo* itself required only the dexterity of the gaucho (horseman) to lasso the semiwild cattle, and the skill of the laborers—until 1830 almost all black slaves—who cut the meat in thin strips. The meat was then salted and placed in piles for two or three days, and then laid out in the sun to dry—a process that was, in effect, a manufacture.

Through the port of Montevideo there was a legal trade with Spain and (after 1779) with Buenos Aires as well as an unlawful trade with Portuguese Brazil and with European ships that made "emergency" entries into the harbor. This activity generated sufficient income to maintain the Spanish bureaucracy that governed the Banda Oriental as well as the wealthy traders who formed the municipal body known as the *cabildo,* the imperfect but only

school of self-government to which *criollos* had access. The Banda Oriental formed part of the Viceroyalty of the Río de la Plata following its belated creation in 1776, but Montevideo and a large adjacent area were included in it as a governorship.

The population of the Banda Oriental—about 30,000 in 1800, of whom one-third lived in Montevideo—was divided more clearly perhaps on regional and racial bases than in terms of social classes. Montevideo, as the seat of Spanish authority, was stratified by race and class. Merchants, financiers, absentee *estancieros,* and holders of high office formed an upper class that still kept the flavor of its humble origins in Catalonia, the Canaries, or the Basque country. Traders, storekeepers, the military, less exalted officials, and craftsmen, constituted a middle class in embryo. Below all the rest was the black slave population, one-third of the total.

The interior was a rural world in which social distinctions, though real, tended to be blurred or combined with other cultural and economic aspects in such a way as to become very distinctive. The *estancieros* (known as *latifundistas*) who owned large tracts of land had ejected earlier and less wealthy livestock producers who had lacked the same influence with the Spanish authorities. The majority of these great landowners did not have good title to the lands they held. Many had done no more than begin the process of legal acquisition in Buenos Aires before abandoning it, weary of the slowness of Bourbon bureaucracy as well as its cost, which invariably exceeded the price of the land itself. Others had purchased defined tracts of land from the Spanish crown, but such *estancias* proved to be much greater in size than what had been paid for. As a result the *estancieros* were collectively dependent on the policy of the state, both Spanish at first and independent republican subsequently.

The population of the interior was nomadic and frequently of mixed race. Life was easy, with food consumption consisting almost entirely of meat, which was freely available. Meat production was hugely in excess of a demand limited to the tiny internal market and restricted external markets in Cuba and Brazil. The Banda Oriental, with perhaps 6 million cattle and half a million horses, had the greatest number of both per head of population of any country in the world. The lowest rural laborer—the *gaucho*—was a horseman (even the beggars in

Montevideo were mounted), and had an assured supply of food. When one of the leaders of the 1811 revolution was questioned about how he lived, he replied, "When I needed a shirt I worked; when I needed nothing I did not work." For rural laborers, work was optional, not obligatory. The *latifundistas* regarded with disgust an independent labor force that was only compelled to work when the state from time to time took measures against "vagrants."

The situation was not free of tensions. The Spanish authorities did not allow the *estancieros* to sell cattle hides freely to British and Portuguese merchants, and frequently threatened to make them pay for the lands that they occupied unlawfully. They carried out the threat, for example, in August 1810, just months before the outbreak of the revolution for independence in February 1811. Traders and livestock producers were inconvenienced by subjection to the political, judicial, and commercial authorities (Viceroy, Real Audiencia, and Tribunal del Consulado) located in the neighboring, competing, and envied city of Buenos Aires. The gauchos and Amerindians hated all those measures emanating from the governor of Montevideo, or the *cabildo,* which attempted to limit the volume of contraband trade, or persecute vagrants, or expel small landholders from the territories of the great *estancias.* This last issue had generated enormous resentment. The pioneer settlers had rounded up cattle previously running wild and unclaimed, built ranch houses and cattle pens, and driven off the Portuguese and Amerindians who had invaded their land. And now that the region had been made habitable, they were turned off the land by those owed favors by governors or viceroys, or by wealthy merchants from Buenos Aires or Montevideo who had bought the land and secured expulsion orders against those settled on it. The whole of Uruguay had been settled in four or five successive waves of pioneer settlers, who then found themselves declared "trespassers" by the colonial authority.

CATTLEMEN AND CAUDILLOS, 1810–1850

All of these resentments, both toward local authorities and toward Spain and Buenos Aires, came to a head in 1811, as a result of the earlier French invasion of the Iberian peninsula and the weakening of the constraints of colonial rule. That year the interior rebelled against Spanish authority emanating from Montevideo. The revolution was led by a *criollo* commander of the loyalist (Spanish) army

itself: José Gervasio Artigas. The revolution at first respected the authority of the Junta de Mayo in Buenos Aires, but political, social, and economic differences soon separated *orientales* from *porteños.* In 1813 the April Congress proclaimed the political principles of the revolution: independence from Spain; organization of a single state comprising all the regions of the former Viceroyalty of La Plata, at first as a confederation and subsequently on a federal basis; democracy; and republicanism. Buenos Aires was not to be the capital.

In September 1815 Artigas issued a regulation that distributed the vast wealth of those opposed to the revolution, "bad Europeans and worse Americans," to the least favored in society, especially Amerindians, freed slaves, and poor *criollos.* Each was to receive a modest (by the standards of the time) *estancia,* with the obligation to build a ranch house and two cattle pens, and to round up the cattle. The enforcement of the regulation was in part delayed by the Portuguese invasion in 1816, but the confiscation of the great *estancias* prior to their redistribution contributed to the hatred that the old upper class of the colonial period began to feel toward Artigas and his followers.

Between 1811 and 1814 the *orientales* fought against Spain and eventually succeeded with help from Buenos Aires in occupying Montevideo. Before then, however, in January 1814, Artigas reached the decision that the objective of the revolution could not be to substitute one despotism for another, Buenos Aires in place of Spain, and left the army of Buenos Aires to continue the siege of Montevideo alone. The city fell to the *porteños* in June, after which Artigas made war on Buenos Aires, aided by the littoral provinces of the Uruguay and Paraná rivers, Entre Ríos, Corrientes, and Santa Fe, all of which were attracted by the idea of federalism. The struggle then became one between federalists, who were also republicans, and the forces of Buenos Aires, who were royalist as well as centralist. In 1815, with the victory at Guayabos, Artigas succeeded in displacing the *porteños* and restoring Montevideo to the *orientales,* and established his authority throughout the country.

From 1816 until 1820 Artigas confronted the invasion forces of the Portuguese monarchy now established in Rio de Janeiro. In addition to their traditional desire to occupy the old Banda Oriental, long disputed with Spain, the Portuguese now invaded out of fear that the south of Brazil might otherwise be contaminated with republican and federalist principles. The invasion had the blessing of Buenos Aires, and ended in defeat for Artigas in 1820.

With its trade and livestock industry in ruins following nine years of continuous revolutionary war, the country was in the hands first of Portugal (1820–1822) and then of Brazil (1822–1825). An important element of the upper class collaborated with the invading forces, who, under the command of an able Portuguese general, Carlos F. Lecor, promised to impose order and to restore the property confiscated by Artigas to its former owners. In 1821 a congress of collaborating *orientales* voted for the incorporation of what was now called the Cisplatine Province into the United Kingdom of Portugal, Brazil, and the Algarve.

Eventually, however, the upper class became disillusioned with the Brazilian authorities, and other social sectors found similar frustrations. Anti-Portuguese sentiments, strong in a population of Spanish origin that had been resisting Portuguese encroachments since the seventeenth century, were quickly rekindled. It became evident that the Portuguese were giving preference to their own in the distribution of lands and in commercial concessions. The cost of maintaining the army of occupation was heavy. Lecor's authoritarian rule did not permit even a semblance of self-government, not even following the introduction of the Brazilian Constitution of 1824.

The second stage of the revolution began in April 1825, when thirty-three *orientales*—the number and nationality of whom was in truth somewhat mythical—invaded the country and within a few months had raised a revolt throughout the interior against the Brazilians, who were thus confined to Montevideo. Following the victories at Rincón and Sarandí, the government of Buenos Aires gave its formal backing to the *orientales,* and at the end of 1825 also entered the war against Brazil. The leader of the *orientales* was now Juan Antonio Lavalleja, a rural caudillo, who was soon joined by another, Fructuoso Rivera. Their objectives were more modest than those of Artigas. Whereas the latter sought federalism and social egalitarianism as well as independence from external control, his two former lieutenants were content to free the Banda Oriental from Brazilian rule, while leaving undecided (perhaps deliberately) the nature of future relations with Buenos Aires as well as any solution to the question of landownership. On 25 August 1825 the House of Representatives of the Provincia Oriental declared first the absolute independence of the country, and then its union with the other provinces.

The war with Brazil came to an end with an indecisive victory at Ituzaingó in February 1827. For some months Britain had been attempting to mediate the conflict through its envoy, Lord Ponsonby. The war had seriously disrupted British trade with Argentina because of the Brazilian blockade of the port of Buenos Aires. In addition, though a secondary consideration, Britain had some interest in encouraging the independence of a small state on the Río de la Plata to prevent Argentine control of both sides. The Río de la Plata gave access to the largest system of navigable rivers in South America, and by "internationalizing" it, Britain could ensure that her trade would not be impeded by a strong Argentina. On 4 October 1828 the Brazilian Empire and the Argentine Confederation ratified a preliminary peace agreement declaring the Cisplatine Province separate from Brazil and an independent state. Thus the birth of independent Uruguay was the combined result, in proportions that national historiography has discussed with great fervor, of British self-interest and the Uruguayan desire for autonomy and opposition to the *porteños.*

An elected assembly approved the constitution of the new country, officially designated the Estado Oriental del Uruguay, in 1830. A judicial system based on European and North American models appeared to safeguard internal order. The new state was to be a republic, and individual rights were to be guaranteed through the classic separation of powers. The right to vote was denied to the illiterate, laborers, servants, and vagrants, who collectively constituted the majority of the population. In principle, a minority would elect deputies and senators for three and six years, respectively. They in turn, every four years, would name the president of the republic, who could not serve a second term immediately after the first. This was the constitution that ruled the destiny of Uruguay until 1919.

The reality of the country, however, prevailed over this Europeanized legal framework. Until at least 1876, Uruguayan affairs were dominated by civil wars out of which emerged the two parties, Colorados and

The Battle of Sant'Antonio, in which Garibaldi participated in 1846 (litho). COLECCION BERTARELLI, MILAN, ITALY/ INDEX/ THE BRIDGEMAN ART LIBRARY

Blancos, that eventually modernized and survived into the twentieth century. The first constitutional president, Fructuoso Rivera (1830–1834; 1838–1842), faced three uprisings led by the other main rural caudillo, Lavalleja. His successor, Manuel Oribe (1835–1838), in turn faced two challenges from Rivera. At the battle of Carpintería in 1836, the warring factions for the first time used the devices that would become their traditional forms of identification: white (*blanco*) for the forces of the government, who styled themselves "Defenders of the Law," and at first pale blue (the other main color on the Uruguayan flag) but subsequently red (*colorado*) for Rivera's followers. In his second challenge in 1838, Rivera was successful. This time he was assisted by a squadron of the French, who were anxious to displace Oribe, who had allied himself with Juan Manuel de Rosas, governor of Buenos Aires. Rivera occupied Montevideo and had himself elected president for a second term in 1839. That same year Rivera declared war on Rosas, who continued to regard

Oribe as the legitimate president of Uruguay, and thus began the Guerra Grande. Both the Uruguayan factions now had international support: Rivera was backed by unitarian refugees from Argentina, as well as by the French and British squadrons in the Río de la Plata. The Europeans were fearful that Rosas might annex Uruguay and were also keen to break up his monopoly of shipping on the Paraná River. But with Rosas's support, Oribe now began the siege of Montevideo, which endured for nine years (1843–1851). The conflict was not resolved until the two European nations withdrew their forces and the Brazilian Empire intervened on behalf of a Colorado Montevideo. Oribe (and Rosas) was defeated, but the peace agreement that was signed on 8 October 1851 declared that there were neither victors nor vanquished.

The atmosphere immediately following this conflict was one of reconciliation between the two factions. The destruction of livestock, commerce, and private wealth during the long conflict encouraged unity. But by now factionalism was engrained in the collective memory, and civil conflict soon broke out again. The Blanco president Juan F. Giró (March–October 1852) was overthrown by a mutiny of the mainly Colorado army. The new Colorado leader, the rural caudillo Venancio Flores, governed as president until 1855. In 1856 the spirit of unity and the desire to forget the resentments of the past brought Gabriel A. Pereyra to power (1856–1860). During his presidency a group within the Colorado Party, called the Conservative Party, raised a rebellion, but its leaders were defeated and executed at Quinteros by government troops. During 1860–1864 President Bernardo P. Berro attempted to continue the policy of unity, but the parties reemerged. In April 1863 Flores invaded the country with the support of the Argentine president, Bartolomé Mitre, and with the eventual collaboration of Brazil. Berro looked for assistance to Paraguay to reestablish, as he described it, an equilibrium in the Río de la Plata region. But following Flores's capture of Paysandú in January 1865, one of his generals ordered the principal Blanco leaders to be shot. Thus did each faction acquire its martyrs, and an emotional force that would ensure permanence for both. During Venancio Flores's dictatorship (1865–1868) Uruguay joined Brazil and Argentina in the War of the Triple Alliance against Paraguay. In February 1868 Flores, whose regime had awakened old passions, was assassinated; the same day the former Blanco president, Bernardo Berro, also fell victim to an assassin. New martyrs fed the traditions of the parties.

Flores was the first in the long continuous series of Colorado governments that did not end until 1959. He was succeeded by a constitutional president, Lorenzo Batlle (1868–1872), who faced an uprising under the rural Blanco caudillo Timoteo Aparicio. This was known as the Revolution of the Lances, a sufficient comment on the primitive military technology of the period. Measured in terms of its duration (1870–1872) and destructive effect on livestock, it was second only among Uruguay's civil wars to the Guerra Grande. The factions were reconciled at the so-called Peace of April 1872, as a result of which for the first time the Blancos shared in the government of the country with the Colorados

through the practice of Coparticipación (coparticipation). Nonetheless disorder persisted until 1876, when Colonel Lorenzo Latorre seized power.

It was essentially through the series of struggles, and the various events accompanying them, that Blancos and Colorados acquired some degree of political, social, and even regional significance. The different personalities and social connections of Oribe and Rivera, and the greatest of the wars, the Guerra Grande, gave a new form to the opposition of capital city and interior, which had existed since the colonial period. The Colorados identified with besieged Montevideo, with immigrants, and with unobstructed access for European influence. The Blancos, with their roots in the surrounding countryside, took their identity from the rural environment and the great landowners, and were essentially *criollo*.

Yet these differences do not adequately explain the extent of internal chaos in Uruguay in this period. A fuller understanding of the country, as well as an interpretation of its political character, must take into account its economic, social, and cultural structures, and the technology available to a preindustrial state. The three pillars of conservatism in Latin America, the Catholic church, the army, and landed property, were all weak in Uruguay. Within the church there was no Uruguayan hierarchy in 1830, and not until 1878 was the country granted its first bishopric. The junior clergy was few, often foreign, theologically not well trained, and of uncertain moral character. Lacking major properties of its own, the church's influence was confined to the representation of the majority religion of the country's inhabitants. The army was small, and did not have a monopoly of coercive power. The rural worker used horses, the lasso, and the knife in normal activity, and at the whim of his leader became an active revolutionary and rival to the professional soldiery. Landed property dominated the agrarian structure, but was not firmly established. Those in possession during the years of the revolutionary wars fought against the landowners of the colonial period, whose titles were also often less than perfect. Government had to mediate in these disputes, which often boiled over into battles between Blancos and Colorados. The former in general corresponded to the class of large landowners; the latter more to those who occupied lands, whether large or small, but who lacked legal papers of ownership for them. Hence, instead of the Uruguayan state straightforwardly representing the landowning class, the status of those holding land depended in fact on the political character of the state itself.

Transport and communication facilities remained those of a cattle-raising society. Provided he could change horses en route, a man could ride from Montevideo to San Fructuoso (240 miles) in two days, whereas the regular stagecoach service (which itself only began in 1850) took at least four or five days, even assuming that the rivers and streams were passable and not flooded. Carts carrying hides and wool needed a month for the journey. Cattle were moved to the *saladeros* on the hoof, a task requiring the special skills of the *troperos* (herdsmen). Agriculture, on the other hand, depended entirely on cumbersome and expensive transport by cart, and therefore developed only in the vicinity of the centers of demand. Only the littoral region on the Uruguay River benefited from improved communications, with a three-day steamship service connecting Salto and Montevideo from 1860. Maintaining control of the interior from distant Montevideo with such transport and communication was very difficult. By the time news of a rural uprising reached the capital, the rebellion had taken root. Even the various armies of the government had difficulty in knowing their respective positions and in combining forces, as happened, for example, to the Colorados during the Revolution of the Lances.

THE BIRTH OF MODERN URUGUAY: 1850–1900

The Colorado military governments of Lorenzo Latorre (1876–1880), Francisco Vidal (1880–1882), Máximo Santos (1882–1886) and Máximo Tajes (1886–1890) established centralized power in Uruguay with dominance over the rural caudillos, thus making rural uprisings far more difficult though not yet impossible. There were several reasons why the state and its army could now exercise a monopoly of physical coercion: armaments had become expensive (the Remington repeating rifle and Krupp artillery were now deployed) and required training not available to the gauchos; the introduction of the telegraph and the railway strengthened the power of Montevideo; and developments both in the economy and in society impeded the costly rebellions of the past.

Another factor that contributed to the strengthening of domestic peace was the growth of nationalism, which put an end to the internationalization of the Uruguayan party system based on alliances with Argentine unitarians and federalists and Brazilian factions. The unification of both Argentina and Brazil around Buenos Aires and Rio de Janeiro, respectively, meant that there were fewer appeals from these countries for Uruguayans to take sides in their internal disputes. In this sense, the Revolution of the Lances was the first wholly Uruguayan civil war.

The period of militarism was succeeded by the presidential and authoritarian but civilian governments of Julio Herrera y Obes (1890–1894) and Juan Idiarte Borda (1894–1897). These exclusively Colorado regimes, bolstered by electoral manipulation, were countered by two Blanco rebellions led by the rural caudillo Aparicio Saravia. His rising in March 1897 led to a Colorado government with Blanco acquiescence, that of Juan Lindolfo Cuestas (1897–1903). However, following the election of José Batlle y Ordóñez in 1903, Saravia led the last great rural rebellion in 1904. These two revolts differed from their predecessors in that their political manifestos went beyond mere adherence to party tradition. On both occasions the Blancos defended the modern causes of respect for the popular will in elections and proportional representation for the parties in the legislature.

Internal peace and strong central government in Montevideo were accompanied by changes in the demography, economy, society, and culture of the nation. Uruguay in 1830 had barely 70,000 inhabitants. By 1875 the population was 450,000, and by 1900 it had reached a million. This spectacular increase, by a factor of fourteen in 70 years, was unparalleled elsewhere in the Americas. The high birth rate before 1890 (between 40 and 50 per thousand inhabitants) was combined with relatively low mortality (between 20 and 30 per thousand), but even more crucial in the demographic transformation was European immigration. French, Italians, and Spaniards before 1850, Italians and Spaniards thereafter, arrived in five waves of migration during the nineteenth century. Mass immigration to Uruguay occurred relatively early in comparison with that to Argentina, and was huge in proportion to the very small population of 1830. During the half-century after 1840 the population of Montevideo was between 50 and 60 percent foreign, nearly all of whom were from Europe. The national census of

1860 found that 35 percent of Uruguayans were foreign, a proportion declining to 17 percent in 1908.

The Europeans (especially) and the Brazilians had values that were different from those of the *criollos*. They were more enterprising, and more acquisitive. Their interests were protected during internal wars by their consuls, and any losses were invariably compensated by the Uruguayan state, which was vulnerable to external pressure. By the 1870s they had become the principal wealth-owners in both the capital and the interior, with 56 percent of property in Montevideo and 58 percent of interior land. European immigrants were also pioneers in the manufacture of consumer goods, and in 1889 controlled about 80 percent of such establishments.

The economic structure of the country also changed. Sheep farming was added to cattle production on the *estancias* between 1850 and 1870. According to the census of 1852, the sheep flock was no more than 0.8 million, yielding 14 to 18 ounces of wool per head of a quality fit only for making mattresses. In 1868, however, the flock was estimated at 17 million and now yielded 40 ounces of merino wool per head, as a result of the crossbreeding that had begun with livestock imported from France and Germany. In 1884 wool took the place of hides as Uruguay's most important export commodity, and it retained that position until the great expansion of frozen beef in the second decade of the twentieth century. In addition to the unimproved cattle, whose commercial value largely consisted of the hide, the *estanciero* now produced wool, which was sold at good prices in the European market. Sheep farming was also the foundation of a rural middle class: it made use of lower-quality pastures, needed only one-fifth of the land per animal compared with cattle, and required at first an increased labor input.

By the end of the nineteenth century Uruguay thus had economic characteristics that differentiated it from the rest of Latin America. It produced a foodstuff, meat, and provided for two other basic human needs, leather for footwear and wool for clothing. Its export markets were diversified rather than dependent on a single importer: Brazil and Cuba for *tasajo;* France, Germany, and Belgium for wool; and the United Kingdom and United States for hides. Since Europe was importing commodities that it also produced but at higher cost, Uruguay benefited from a high differential rent. Recent estimates of per capita income in the nineteenth century, based on the assumption that per capita exports represented 15 percent of per capita income, suggest that incomes were high in Uruguay during 1870–1900 (US$317 in 1881–1885, for example), comparable to or higher than those in the United States and much higher than those in Brazil. It should also be noted that Britain's policy of free trade—like that of Europe in general— was an essential part of the economic system within which Uruguay sold commodities in Europe that competed with Europe's own agricultural sector. As long as unrestricted trade lasted, until the international economic crisis at the beginning of the 1930s, Uruguay occupied a secure and profitable position within the European imperial systems.

The arrival of the sheep was followed by the enclosure of the *estancias*. Wire fences were erected between 1870 and 1890, as much to ensure exclusive access for a landowner's livestock to his pasture as to allow crossbreeding of the flocks and herds with European pedigree stock. Fencing destroyed the livelihoods of the laborers who previously guarded the livestock, and gave rise to the previously unknown problem of rural poverty and hunger. It was ironic that this technological unemployment should have been the breeding ground for the last civil wars at the turn of the century, since both sheep and wire fencing implied massive investments, which underlined for the *estancieros* the need for internal order. The landowners who were at the forefront of these changes established in 1871 the Asociación Rural to represent their interests and to seek domestic peace at all costs.

Concurrent with these rural developments was the transformation of urban Uruguay. Beginning in 1860 the first foreign capital began to arrive, especially from Britain. Pioneer investments between 1863 and 1865 included Liebig's Extract of Meat factory, the London and River Plate Bank, and the first London loan to the Uruguayan government. In 1884 the sum of British investments was estimated at £6.5 million; by 1900 the total had reached £40 million. British investment in Uruguay was small compared to its total export of capital to the rest of the world, but was very large relative to domestic urban capital. Uruguay was the fifth most important Latin American recipient of British capital, after Argentina, Mexico, Brazil, and Chile; but on a per capita basis, only Argentina received more. The British built the railways—the first line was opened in 1869 and in 1905 there were 1,200 miles of track—as well as the urban infrastructure of Montevideo (water supply, gas, telephones, trams), while increasing the volume of lending to the government and securing a near-monopoly in the local insurance market.

In the case of the railway companies, the British investors secured important concessions from the Uruguayan government, which urgently needed rail transport at any price provided it could be used to put down rural rebellions. Most of the lines benefited from a government dividend guarantee of 7 percent on a fixed capital sum of £5,000 per kilometer of track. The result was a system characterized by curves and gradients, unnecessarily extended by between 5 percent and 10 percent of its length. The state could only intervene in the fixing of railway tariff rates if profits exceeded 12 percent, which, needless to say, they never did. But the railway was an essential tool if the government was to control the interior. When the Río Negro was spanned by a railway bridge in 1886, the two halves of Uruguay, which invariably had been divided by winter floods, were then united.

Other British companies in Montevideo as well as the railways provoked public hostility with their high tariffs and deficient service. By 1880–1900 the performance of gas, water, railways, and insurance had raised doubts in the minds of the political elite concerning the benefits Uruguay received from foreign investment unsupervised by the state. These sentiments led to the law of 1888, which instituted strict controls on the accounting of the railway companies, and in 1896 to the founding of the first state bank, the Banco de la República Oriental del Uruguay (BROU).

After 1875, population growth and protectionist legislation encouraged the birth of Uruguay's modern manufacturing industry. Small and restricted to the production of consumer goods (foodstuffs, beverages, furniture, textiles, leather), such activities nonetheless gave rise both to capitalists anxious for political stability and to a small proletariat that was hostile to the idea of enlisting in the armies of either the Blancos or the Colorados.

The social structure that resulted from these developments, and at the same time promoted them, was very different from that of the first half of the nineteenth century. Social classes were now more clearly differentiated. Landownership was nonetheless complex since alongside the Latifundio smaller farm units based on the exploitation of sheep had developed. The 1908 census suggests that farms of between 250 and 6,250 acres, roughly equivalent to the estancias of the rural middle class, accounted for 52 percent of total land area, whereas just 1,391 latifundios (in excess of 6,250 acres) occupied 43 percent of the land. This distribution was the result of a long historical process that preserved the position of the large landowners, but required them to coexist with an important rural middle class. The wars of independence and subsequent civil conflicts entailed the destruction and theft of livestock and the general disruption of rural production, but they also had another consequence: property rights changed hands rapidly in the nineteenth century. The latifundio still existed in 1900, but the latifundistas were not the same families as in the colonial period or in the early years of independence. Uruguay's rural upper class had the taint of being nouveau riche, thus diminishing its power and social standing.

At the beginning of the twentieth century the estancieros had two monopolies, of land and of cattle, and the value of both was rising with improvements in the saladero industry but above all with the establishment in 1905 of the first Frigorífico (meat-freezing plant) exporting frozen meat to Europe. Rural workers no longer had the choice of vagrancy or employment on the estancia: they had to work to feed themselves. Those who were unable to work found themselves left to rot in what were called the pueblos de ratas (rat towns), eating food of poor quality in place of their previous meat diet. The modern gaucho was reduced to domestic service or prostitution in the case of the women; general labor, sheepshearing, contraband, or cattle-thieving for the men. It was at this point that internal migration to the cities began. In Montevideo, the idea of a "social question" appeared for the first time. Although upward social mobility was possible, life for workers in industry was hard. A working day of 11 to 15 hours provided the background for anarchist ideology and the foundation of the first trade unions around 1875. The old fear of urban employers of a Blanco uprising was gradually replaced by the new threat of class-based revolution.

There were changes also in the intellectual and cultural environment. The Universidad de la República opened its doors to students of law in 1849, medicine in 1876, and mathematics in 1888. In 1877, the Lorenzo Latorre government acted on the ideas of José Pedro Varela to reform primary education, devoting resources to its development while making it obligatory and free. The rate of illiteracy, previously high, began to fall. The need to increase the population's political involvement, and train it more adequately to fit the changing economic structure, lay behind these developments.

At the same time there was a tendency toward social and cultural secularization. In 1861 the Catholic church began to lose its jurisdiction over cemeteries. In 1879 the state took over the registration of marriages (Registros de Estado Civil), though conceding that the religious ceremony should precede the civil. However, in 1885 civil marriage became obligatory and had to take place before the church ceremony. The first divorce law was approved in 1907. In state schools Catholicism continued to be taught, but the hostility of education officials and of many teachers reduced this to rote learning of the catechism with no explanation. Even this vestige of religious education was suppressed in 1909. More significantly, perhaps, university students adopted an eclectic spiritualism in the third quarter of the century, and subsequently moved to positivism and agnosticism, even to atheism. The Catholic church thus found itself under attack and reacted accordingly, but most of the nation's elite and a good part of the population in general remained hostile to it or regarded it with indifference. According to the 1908 census, among native-born men in Montevideo only 44 percent declared themselves to be Catholics, a few more than the 40 percent who were "liberal." One other sign of modernity was the emergence of a new demographic model. Around 1890 the birth rate began to fall, and the average age of marriage for women rose from twenty to twenty-five. People began to practice artificial birth control even in the face of vigorous denunciation by the clergy. Thus did Uruguay, the first of all Latin American countries to become fully Europeanized, enter the twentieth century.

See also **Banda Oriental; Estancia; Gaucho; Guarani Indians; Orientales; Porteño; Treinta y Tres (33)** Orientales; Uruguay, Political Parties: Blanco Party; Uruguay, Political Parties: Colorado Party.

BIBLIOGRAPHY

J. E. Pivel Devoto and Alcira Ranieri, *Historia de la República Oriental del Uruguay* (Montevideo, 1981).

José Pedro Barrán and B. Nahum, *Historia rural del Uruguay moderno*, 7 vols. (Montevideo, 1967–1978).

J. A. Oddone, *Economía y sociedad en el Uruguay liberal* (Montevideo, 1967).

A. Vázquez Romero and W. Reyes Abadio, *Crónica general del Uruguay*, 3 vols. (Montevideo, 1980–1981).

M. H. J. Finch, *A Political Economy of Uruguay Since 1870* (Hong Kong, 1981).

Gerardo Caetano and J. Rilla, *Historia contemporánea del Uruguay* (Montevideo, 1994).

Additional Bibliography

Arocena Olivera, Enrique. *La rebeldía de los doctores: El Uruguay del fusionismo al militarismo, 1851–1886.* Montevideo: Librería Linardi y Risso, 1998.

Barrán, José Pedro. *La espiritualización de la riqueza: Catolicismo y economía en Uruguay, 1730–1900.* Montevideo: Ediciones de la Banda Oriental, 1998.

Barrios Pintos, Aníbal. *Historia de los pueblos orientales: Sus orígenes, procesos fundacionales, sus primeros años.* 2nd ed. Montevideo: Academia Nacional de Letras, 2000.

Bentancur, Artur Ariel. *El puerto colonial de Montevideo.* 2 v. Montevideo: Universidad de la República, Facultad de Humanidades y Ciencias de la Educación, Departamento de Publicaciones, 1997–1999.

Goldman, Noemí, and Ricardo Donato Salvatore, eds. *Caudillismos rioplatenses: Nuevas miradas a un viejo problema.* Buenos Aires: Eudeba, Facultad de Filosofía y Letras, Universdad de Buenos Aires, 1998.

Kleinpenning, Jan M. G. *Peopling the Purple Land: A Historical Geography of Rural Uruguay, 1500–1915.* Amsterdam: CEDLA, 1995.

López-Alves, Fernando. *State Formation and Democracy in Latin America, 1810–1900.* Durham, NC: Duke University Press, 2000.

Montaño, Oscar D. *Umkhonto: La lanza negra: Historia del aporte negro-africano en la formación del Uruguay.* Montevideo: Rosebud Ediciones, 1997.

Rela, Walter. *Uruguay: Cronología histórica anotada.* 6 v. Montevideo: ALFAR, 1998–.

Verdesio, Gustavo. *La invención del Uruguay: La entrada del territorio y sus habitantes a la cultura occidental.* Montevideo: Editorial Graffiti: Editorial Trazas, 1996.

JOSÉ PEDRO BARRÁN

THE TWENTIETH CENTURY

The history of Uruguay since 1900 contrasts remarkably with the preceding period. Until 1875 civil conflict was the dominant theme. The modernization of Uruguay in the final decades before 1900 involved the creation of a state structure by strong governments capable of suppressing insurrections. The concentration of authority in Montevideo created conditions in which foreign capital could flourish, building an economic infrastructure that further consolidated the new state system. Yet in many respects Uruguay in 1900 still appeared primitive. Economic modernization was still restricted. The division between the main political parties, the Blancos and the Colorados, remained a threat to public order. The electorate was small, and elections were nominal.

By the 1920s, however, Uruguay was transformed. In place of anarchy and conflict, the country developed an institutional structure that was stable,

innovative, and democratic. Social policy was adventurous and characterized by egalitarian and humanitarian influences that had few equals elsewhere in the world. The economic structure was developed by new export trades, an enlarged role for the public sector, and an expanding manufacturing industry promoted by the state. In its cultural life Uruguay enjoyed a diversity and richness extraordinary in so small a country. The image of Uruguay as somewhat exceptional, even utopian, in its middle-class prosperity and stability took shape in the 1920s and was widely shared inside and outside the country for much of the next half-century.

A feature of the nineteenth century that survived to the end of the twentieth was the dominance in politics of the Colorado and Blanco (or National) parties. The appearance of a two-party system, however, should not be mistaken for democratic stability, nor the parties regarded as conventional vehicles for interest aggregation and policy formulation. They originated as armed bands competing for control of the territory of Uruguay in the 1830s, and loyalty to them was entrenched long before any sense of nationhood existed. This fact is crucial to understanding the instinctive loyalty that each party still commands. Adaptation to the age of mass politics was possible only through the development of complex electoral legislation (collectively known as the *ley de lemas*) in the first half of this century and the system of double simultaneous voting (DSV), by which victory goes to the most voted faction of the most voted party. Each party has therefore developed its own liberal, moderate, and conservative factions, which unite under the party banner rather than with those of similar ideological convictions but with different loyalties. As in the nineteenth century, but now by other means, the party struggle is fundamentally to secure control of executive power. Uruguayans elect administrations rather than governments.

The economic and demographic dominance of Montevideo, paradoxical in a country whose economic welfare has always depended on livestock production, is also a legacy of the nineteenth century. Political pressures, exerted by an urban population rising from one-third of the total in 1900 to one-half in the 1990s, have been reflected in the social and economic policy of the twentieth century. The rural sector has provided livestock products for processing and export, while contributing financially to the development of Montevideo and the welfare of its population either by taxation or by urban investment of the rural surplus. The urban-rural tension is particularly significant because, although the high level of exports per capita has endowed Uruguayans with one of the highest standards of living of any Latin American country during this century, the rate of growth of rural output and exports over the long period has been very low. In the late 1950s Uruguay entered a period of secular economic stagnation that focused attention on the causes of poor performance in the livestock sector. For some, the problems of Uruguay in the late decades of the twentieth century are a consequence of a misplaced modernity: state-sponsored welfare prejudicing growth. Others have blamed unenterprising landowners or Uruguay's small size within the international economy. However explained, the deterioration of the economy undermined Uruguay's utopia. By the late decades of the century, the earlier self-confidence was displaced by a debilitating nostalgia for a long-gone golden age.

THE AGE OF BATLLE Y ORDÓÑEZ (1900–1930)

José Batlle y Ordóñez held office twice as president, from 1903 to 1907 and from 1911 to 1915. No other figure in Uruguayan history has had such a decisive influence on the country's development. Indeed, the phrase Batllist Uruguay, which in a strict historical sense refers to his political and social accomplishments, also defines an ideology of state-mediated negotiation and redistribution as a means of resolving social conflict that was dominant through most of the twentieth century. In the belief that it has continued to inspire in the capacity and responsibility of the state to solve the economic and social problems of the citizenry, it has formed a central and enduring part of Uruguay's political culture.

Batlle y Ordóñez himself, a commanding figure who was both a visionary and a politician of great skill, came to the presidency through the ranks of the Colorado Party within a political system that was still oligarchic and largely nonparticipatory. His first major challenge was the uprising in 1903 led by the Blanco caudillo Aparicio Saravia, who made a last attempt to stem the incursions of a unified state and commercial landownership into the traditional Uruguay in the north. With modernization, civil wars were even more costly to the developing livestock sector. The overwhelming military defeat of

Saravia finally freed the sector from that threat, but lasting peace required increased political participation and concessions to the Blanco Party in Montevideo to ensure its supremacy over the caudillo faction of the interior. In 1910 the modern system of double simultaneous voting was introduced to allow a divided party to maintain its cohesiveness by aggregating the votes of its different tendencies.

The background to Batlle's administrations was one of rising prosperity based on the export of rural production. The establishment of the first meat-freezing plant (Frigorífico) in 1904 ushered in a period of rising export values based on the breeding of high-quality cattle capable of producing beef for freezing and chilling. Whatever the inefficiencies and inequities of a rural structure based in *latifundismo*, the political dangers were too great, and the potential gains at a time of economic expansion too limited, to make agrarian reform a priority. Arable production was encouraged, but efforts to diversify the economy were directed mainly toward Montevideo. The tentative protectionism of the 1880s was strengthened and systematized under Batlle. There were also government initiatives promoting the incorporation of new technology in arable farming and manufacturing. Finally, the participation of the public sector in the economy was extended to include banking, insurance, electricity supply, and basic chemicals.

Batlle's social reformism was even more remarkable. Legislation in defense of labor included the eight-hour day in 1915. Provision for retirement pensions, with low age and service prerequisites, was extended from the public sector to areas of the private sector in 1919. Old-age pensions, proposed in 1914, were finally granted in 1919. But if labor and social-security enactments were the central welfare provisions, the range of liberal, secular, and humanitarian legislation implemented at the time conveys the extent of Batlle's radicalism. Separation of church and state, the right of women to initiate divorce, the abolition of capital punishment and of entertainments involving cruelty to animals, full legal rights for children born out of wedlock, and increased provision of education were all achieved before 1920.

Batlle was an exceptional leader who consciously attempted to create in Uruguay a model country. At the same time, his idealism was molded to fit the challenges and tensions that Uruguay confronted, and indeed it is arguable that his radicalism had a conservative aim. Although the antagonism of the two traditional parties had in the past been destructive, Batlle had no intention of allowing such loyalties to be displaced by the more dangerous doctrines of class. The Colorados had to champion the cause of the workers if they were to maintain their dominance in Montevideo, but Batlle was no socialist or class warrior. Batlle preferred to demonstrate that the party was better able to secure workers' objectives than were trade unions or left-wing political groups. The obstacle to reform was not capital as such, and much of Batllism promoted the interests of small domestic producers. It was, rather, the costly, low-quality service provided by British companies in railways and other economic and social structures that gave Batlle a target he could share with all ranks of Uruguayans.

If Batlle's reforms were remarkable mainly for their timing or context, his proposals in 1913 to change the 1830 Constitution were unique. He saw dangers in concentrating executive powers in one person and proposed instead a nine-person collegiate executive (*colegiado*) that would also consolidate Colorado control of government. The 1918 constitution dispersed executive authority between a president and the nine members of the National Council of Administration until its overthrow in 1933. The new constitution, even as modified, represented the high-water mark of Batlle's reforms. To overcome Blanco opposition, the doctrine of *coparticipación* had to be revived, giving both parties the right to nominate the public posts. The split that resulted within the Colorado Party between Batllists and the conservative wing brought to an end the reformist era. At the start of his administration in 1916, President Feliciano Viera announced that there would be no further initiatives.

The 1920s were years of prosperity and relative quietude. After the frantic activity of the Batlle y Ordóñez administrations, political life settled into a pragmatic pattern of alliances and agreements within and between the parties. Although the end of World War I sharply cut the level of demand and prices for livestock products, growing demand in Britain for chilled beef kept the economy buoyant. Landowners increasingly complained of the burden of taxes and of the prices the foreign-owned meat-

Uruguay

Population:	3,460,607 (2007 est.)
Area:	68,039 sq mi
Official language(s):	Spanish
Language(s):	Spanish, Portunol/Brazilero (Portuguese-Spanish mix)
National currency:	Uruguayan peso (UYU)
Principal religions:	Roman Catholic 66%; Protestant 2%; Jewish 1%; none or other 31%
Ethnicity:	European (mostly Spanish and Italian) 88%; mestizo 8%; African 4%; Amerindians almost nonexistent
Capital:	Montevideo (pop. 1,341,000, 2005 est.)
Annual rainfall:	41 in
Principal geographic features:	*Rivers:* Uruguay, Plata *Mountains:* Cuchilla de Haedo; Cuchilla Grande; Cerro Catedral (1,686 ft above sea level)
Economy:	*GDP per capita:* $9,000 (2002 est.)
Principal products and exports:	*Agriculture:* rice, wheat, corn, barley; livestock; fish. *Industries:* food processing, electrical machinery, transportation equipment, petroleum products, textiles, chemicals, beverages
Government:	Republican government, divided into three branches: executive, legislative, and judicial. Executive consists of a president and a vice president, popularly elected for a five-year term, together with a council of ministers. Uruguay has Latin America's oldest two-party system.
Armed forces:	24,000 active personnel in 2005; *Army:* 15,200, organized into four regional divisions; *Navy* (including the naval aviation arm and a naval infantry force): 5,700 members; *Air Force:* 3,100 personnel; 920-member paramilitary guard in two units.
Transportation:	In 2004, railroads: 1,287 mi of track; roadways: 5,446 mi, of which 4,847 mi were paved; 669,700 motor vehicles (2003). Ports: Montevideo, Colonia, Nueva Palmira. Sixty-four airports (2004), of which 9 had paved runways as of 2005.
Media:	As of 2001, Uruguay had 91 AM and 149 FM radio stations and 20 television stations (both private broadcasting companies and the state-run public broadcasting company, SODRE). In 2004 there were at least four major daily newspapers in Montevideo, including *El Diario*, with a circulation of 170,000, *El País*, 110,000; *El Diario Espanol*, 20,000; and *Últimas Noticias*, 19,500.
Literacy and education:	*Total literacy rate:* 98% Education in elementary, secondary, and technical schools and at the University of the Republic in Montevideo is free. Elementary education, which lasts six years, is compulsory. There are five major universities: the University of the Republic, the Catholic University, the University ORT Uruguay, Universidad de la Empresa, and the University of Montevideo.

freezing plants paid for cattle. The greater threat to prosperity, however, was that, though producers continued to improve the quality of their livestock, they showed no inclination to modernize methods of production or to improve their natural pastures and thus increase the animal-supporting capacity of the land. Within the urban economy, the manufacturing industry continued to grow, though largely in the basic consumer industries established before the war; construction activity was also at a high level. During the decade about 200,000 immigrants arrived in Montevideo, with a higher proportion than previously from central Europe, but only a fraction of this number settled.

Late in the 1920s, Batllist reformism resurfaced, with proposals for enlarging the public sector in meat-packing (the Frigorífico Nacional), alcohol and cement production, and the import and refining of oil (Ancap), as well as extensions to the pension program. To secure Blanco support for Ancap, factions of the two parties agreed in 1931 to what came to be called the Pacto del Chinchulín ("pork-barrel agreement"), thereby increasing Blanco participation in state patronage. But by then an era had ended. Batlle y Ordóñez died in 1929, shortly before the full force of the international depression reached the Río de la Plata.

REACTION AND NEO-BATLLISM (1930–1970)

In March 1933 President Gabriel Terra dispensed with the collegiate executive and organized an authoritarian regime based on conservative Colorado and Blanco factions, which had been excluded from the pork barrel. His coup d'etat was presented as a reform of an inefficient constitution, intended to restore probity in public life and halt the growth of the bureaucracy and public sector. The reality was rather different. Although the 1918 constitution did create an executive that was unwieldy, the origins of the coup are easier to find in the opposition of employers (organized in the Committee of Economic Vigilance) to further social reformism, the traditional mistrust of the British public-utility companies toward the Batllists (in addition to the new fears of the oil companies aroused by the Ancap proposal), and the landowners' need to negotiate a trade deal with Britain that would secure a continuing share of the British beef market. The ambitious Terra, already in office as president since 1931, was an ideal instrument with which to implement this agenda. Besides the 1934 constitution, which concentrated executive power in his hands, he had the support of an alliance of his own Colorado followers and those of Luis Alberto de Herrera in the Blanco Party; the independent Blancos and Batllist Colorados were banished to the wilderness.

However, the conservative project of those who backed the coup ran against two obstacles. First, the depression of the export trade, whose value was 40 percent lower in 1932 than in the peak year 1930, was not a consequence of unfavorable policy and therefore reversible. Although the old regime had used trade and exchange controls to limit its impact, any expectation by landowners that controls would be removed and the peso allowed to depreciate ignored the changed circumstances of the 1930s. The curtailed share of the British beef market was permanent; there was no prospect of a significant revival in demand for Uruguay's exports; and manufacturing production for a protected domestic market became increasingly profitable. Relief for the landowners was therefore modest and short-term. Second, many of the characteristics of Batllism, fundamentally the growing dependence of the urban population on state policies and provision, were rooted less in ideology than in the reality of a country whose rural food- and export-producing sector could not employ even the natural increase in the rural population. Hence, in spite of attacks on the fiscal profligacy of the previous regime, public employment grew faster under Terra than it had before 1933. The program of social and labor legislation was interrupted and trade unions severely curbed, but by the late 1930s the urban economy was growing strongly.

By the time Alfredo Baldomir, a relatively liberal Terraist, was elected to succeed Terra in 1938, constitutional change again seemed possible. Terra's regime had been illiberal rather than repressive (a *dictablanda*); but in basing itself exclusively on two-party factions, the new political order could only be provisional. With urban manufacturing now the dynamic sector, the conditions that had earlier made Batllism possible and even necessary were appearing once more. The international context also encouraged liberalization. Official sympathy with Italian fascism was not matched in the streets, whereas the Republican cause in the Spanish Civil War received massive popular support. World War II further isolated the Herrerist Blancos, whose official neutrality masked suspicion of the United States and contrasted with the pro-Allies (and especially pro-U.S.) sentiments of the Colorados. In 1942 the legislature was dissolved in what was termed the *golpe bueno* ("good coup"); under the new constitution of that year all political groups now operated without restriction.

Although the Batllist Colorados did not return to power immediately, they and organized labor were the principal beneficiaries of the new order. The growth of manufacturing in the late 1930s was checked somewhat by wartime shortages, but the national commitment to industrialization was strengthened. By 1945 almost 100,000 workers were employed in the manufacturing industry, and they were increasingly organized in mass-membership trade unions whose ideological orientations (a source of division and weakness in the labor movement before 1933) mattered less than their negotiating function. This revival of trade unionism also revived the issue of class politics as a challenge to the established parties. The issue, and the way it was resolved, was exemplified by growing public concern about working-class living standards. All parties, and at first even urban employers who wished to see their protected market extended, favored higher real wages. The mechanism to effect this, while maintaining state (i.e., party) control over relations between capital and labor, was the introduction in 1943 of tripartite wages councils. The *consejos de salarios* were the outcome of a corporatist tendency that had been developing in the 1930s and a populism (in place of the paternalism of Batlle y Ordóñez) that recognized the political need to harness rather than deny class consciousness.

The presidency of Juan José de Amézaga (1943–1947), the first under the new constitution, was effectively a transitional administration. It was the succession in 1947 of Luis Batlle that signaled the era of neo-Batllism and national self-esteem. Social-security legislation was extended so that by 1954 all occupations were eligible for a retirement pension, and workers' rights were further protected. Although production in the livestock sector of the economy remained stagnant, the high export prices of the wartime and postwar periods fueled the process of economic diversification through import-substituting industrialization. Traditional export activities supported subsidies to the new dynamic industries and arable agriculture through a multiple exchange-rate system and other controls. The sense of national self-sufficiency (and the size of the public sector) was enhanced by state acquisition in 1948 of the railways and other former British public-utility assets. In all these ways the aims of the first Batllist period were accomplished or extended. But it was above all with the constitution of 1952, which entirely replaced the office of president with the collegial National Council of Government (NCG), that neo-Batllism reached its high point. Accepted unenthusiastically by the electorate, the new *colegiado* rested on an agreement between Batllist Colorados and their arch-opponent, Luis Alberto de Herrera. For Herrera, facing the prospect of apparently endless exclusion from office, the *colegiado* offered coparticipation in government: representation for the minority party in the NCG and on the boards of public-sector enterprises, and thus a share in the patronage.

Midcentury marked the high point of Uruguay's achievement as a nation built on prosperity, innovation, and consensus. The 1952 constitution lasted until the indecision and delay that marked its history became insupportable; but it was the ending of economic growth in the late 1950s that undermined the *colegiado*, and the ensuing economic stagnation constituted the dominant theme of Uruguay's history thereafter. Restricted to a market of 2.25 million inhabitants, the manufacturing industry's growth phase was brief. Rural-sector export performance was weak in the 1950s as a result of discriminatory policy, rising domestic demand for beef, and above all the persistent failure to develop and incorporate a technology of pasture improvement appropriate to the country's natural conditions. While populist policy stimulated demand and sought to disguise the resulting distortions, the productive base of the economy was increasingly incapable of responding positively. By the end of the 1950s the annual rate of price increases had reached 40 percent, and there were severe balance-of-payments difficulties. In 1959, following recommendations by an International Monetary Fund (IMF) mission, a stabilization program of exchange and monetary reforms was attempted.

This retreat from interventionism implied a changed political complexion. Luis Batlle was not eligible for a second term as president in 1950, but he was the outstanding figure in the NCG elected in 1954, and the dominance of the Colorado Party continued. In 1958, however, an alliance of traditional Herrerists and the *ruralista* movement of small producers enabled the Blancos to defeat the Colorados for the first time in the twentieth century, and their victory was repeated in 1962. This historic reversal of fortunes for the parties signified little more than disillusion with the Colorados. The invitation to the IMF in 1958 was made more promptly than would have been the case with a Colorado majority, but it proved impossible to maintain the new policy orientation. The other policy initiative of the early 1960s, the creation of the Investment and Economic Development Commission (CIDE) to lay the basis for an economic plan, received general support. In other respects the interval of Blanco dominance implied little change; whichever party held a majority, the effect of the second collegial constitution was to promote the pursuit of short-term political advantage at the expense of long-term policy formulation. The electoral system (DSV and *ley de lemas*), encouraging the division of each party into contending factions, had the same result. As the economic crisis deepened, so the traditional disposition of Uruguayans to seek solutions from the state increased the power of the parties, which alone could open the door to employment in the bureaucracy or accelerate approval of a pension claim. Through the agency of clientelism, the impotence of the parties to halt rising inflation and unemployment had the perverse consequence of strengthening their short-term position.

Although the left-wing parties, with only 9 percent of the total vote in 1962, could make few inroads, political debate outside the institutional structure became increasingly radicalized during the 1960s. The Cuban Revolution and the frustration of CIDE's endeavors were two factors emphasizing that there were choices available to the country that the political process could not articulate. Industrial unrest increased, and in 1964 the trade-union movement achieved for the first time a unified central body, the National Congress of Workers (CNT). But constitutional reform, rather than solutions to the economic crisis, was the main issue in the 1966 elections. They were won by a right-wing faction of the Colorado Party proposing the restoration of the presidency, which (following the death of President Oscar Gestido in late 1967) was occupied until 1972 by Jorge Pacheco Areco.

The four years of Pacheco's rule were a transitional but decisive stage in the downfall of institutional government that culminated in 1973. To the long-term problem of economic decline was added the shock in 1968 of inflation for the first time exceeding 100 percent. Pacheco's response was to increase the representation of private-sector interests in his administration while suppressing dissent through the almost continuous imposition of emergency security measures. A second IMF-sponsored stabilization program was implemented and, in combination with a less orthodox wage and price freeze, was briefly effective in reducing the rate of price increases. Devaluation of the peso increased the incomes of exporters but further reduced the urban real wage. With the legislature incapable of mounting effective opposition, bitter confrontations between workers and students and the government spilled onto the streets.

By 1970, however, the greatest challenge to the authority not merely of the government but of the institutions of the state itself came from a clandestine source, the urban guerrilla National Liberation Movement (MLN-T), or Tupamaros. Although the movement had begun to organize by 1963, it was the oppressive but frequently incompetent practice of state security after 1968 that brought the MLN-T to national and international notice and strengthened its characteristically middle-class membership. Early operations to secure resources, reveal corruption, and release captives demonstrated wit and intelligence, but the incoherence and alien nature of its revolutionary ideology and the descent into personal violence (kidnappings, executions, and random attacks on military personnel) eroded public support. In 1971 the armed forces took command of antisubversive operations, and during the following year the Tupamaros as a guerrilla movement were totally defeated.

From 1971 onward, however, the main competitor of the two traditional parties was the Frente Amplio (Broad Front), an electoral coalition that adhered to the democratic path toward socialism and brought together the seceding left-wing columns of the Blancos (Rodríguez Camusso, Gutiérrez Ruiz) and the Colorados (Zelmar Michelini, Alba Roballo), the Christian Democratic Party, the Frente Izquierda de Liberación (a subcoalition led by the Communist Party), the Socialist Party, and other smaller parties, and also had the support of the main student and workers organizations.

DICTATORSHIP AND DEMOCRACY: SINCE 1973

The demise of the Tupamaros marked the beginning, not the end, of the threat to Uruguay's democratic institutions. The 1971 elections were won by Pacheco's nominee, Juan María Bordaberry, who owed his victory (with 23 percent of the vote) over the Blanco leader Wilson Ferreira Aldunate (26 percent) to the DSV system. Líber Seregni, the candidate of the Frente Amplio coalition, obtained 18 percent of the vote, and the coalition thus succeeded in becoming a third main political contender. By 1972, however, the political initiative lay with the military, which had come to regard the political elite of all parties as financially corrupt or tainted with subversion. The growth of the Frente Amplio (which mirrored Salvador Allende's Unidad Popular in Chile) was of particular concern, not only for the armed forces and the economic powers, but also for neighboring Brazil (then ruled by a dictatorship) and the United States, which sponsored and financed secret activities to prevent that growth from happening.

The military coup of 1973 occurred in stages. In February Bordaberry allowed his presidential authority to be countermanded; in June the legislature was dissolved; and in succeeding months there followed a complete repression not merely of left-wing institutions and their members but indeed of all political and intellectual activity. Pressure groups of all kinds, including those of employers, were silenced. Although the use of torture by the security services was first authoritatively denounced in 1970, the violation of civil and political rights—such as incarceration of political activists, kidnappings and forced disappearances, political assassinations, and appropriation of children born in captivity—now became systematic and coordinated with the dictatorships that ruled in Argentina, Brazil, Chile, and Paraguay (*Plan Condor*). Bordaberry was retained until 1976 as a nominal president in a "civilian-military" regime, but effective authority from early 1973 rested with the commanders-in-chief and the military-controlled Council of National Security

(COSENA). The civilian-military de facto government adopted the ideology of the doctrine of national security—as articulated in the military academies of Brazil and the United States—and the tactics of a "dirty war" that knew no ethical or legal limits. The regime's stated mission was "the defense of the nation, democracy, and Western civilization" against "the Marxist threat."

Bordaberry's own design for a corporatist state, with Blanco and Colorado parties replaced by nominees and "currents of opinion," resulted in his downfall. The military identified the parties as authentic national institutions, whose multiclass allegiance offered the best defense against a politics based on class. The military's plan, announced in 1976–1977, deprived those who had been politically active in the previous decade of their political rights, and it set out a timetable for political reconstruction leading eventually to a controlled democracy. The first stage would be the preparation by the military of a new constitution, to be approved by the people in a referendum in 1980.

The authoritarian regime set out to reorganize the economy (by countering the redistributive policies of earlier democratic governments, lowering workers' salaries and benefits, etc.); in the process, it empowered bureaucrats, advisors (from the World Bank, the IMF, and other organizations), and a group of experts known as the Chicago Boys (followers of the neoliberal economic guru Milton Friedman), inviting their participation in economic governance. An economic plan published by the Colorado government in 1973 spelled out proposals to reshape the economy by promoting market forces and the price mechanism. In modified form the plan was adopted by the military, which shared with economic liberals a lowest common denominator of anti-Marxism; Alejandro Végh Villegas was appointed in 1974 to superintend its implementation from the Ministry of Economy and Finance. Although he resigned in 1976, as architect of the neoliberal economic model in Uruguay Végh had considerable significance. Between 1973 and 1980 the economy grew continuously, with nontraditional exports as the leading sector. Control of inflation (which had reached 100 percent once more in 1973) was a major objective but did not receive priority over a restructuring of the economy that saw real wages almost halved during the course of the regime. The greater openness of the economy and optimism among exporters after decades of protectionism were positive achievements, but at the end of 1978 the emphasis on incentives to exporters was abandoned in favor of a stabilization effort through manipulation of a preannounced but overvalued exchange rate. Cheap dollars encouraged a massive inflow of consumer goods. By the early 1980s the economy was once more in decline; when the experiment with exchange-rate policy was abandoned in 1982, both public and private sectors were burdened by huge external debts. The final years of the military regime were marked by economic decline, inflation, rising debt-service payments, unemployment, and falling real wages, but there were no new initiatives to revitalize the economy.

Although the collapse of the economic model contributed to the downfall of the regime, its political project failed at the first stage. The military's constitution perpetuating its political role was submitted to the electorate in 1980 and was rejected by 57 percent of the electorate. Opposition to the regime, which had until then been private and hazardous, now started to become public and undisguised. In 1982 internal party primaries were held, in which 77 percent of voters supported opposition party factions. Inconclusive talks between military and political leaders on the transfer of power were held in 1983. By the time they resumed in 1984, both parties to the negotiations were anxious that they should succeed, since failure would strengthen the position of the intransigents on either side. The armed forces now seemed less intent on maintaining long-term political influence than on securing a safe passage back to barracks. Their tactics to achieve this centered on weakening the prospects of the radical opposition groups in the elections of November 1984. Hence the Frente Amplio coalition of left-wing parties (but not its leader, Líber Seregni) was rehabilitated, and Ferreira Aldunate, a vociferous critic of the regime, was arrested on his return from exile. As a result, the Blancos were not party to the Naval Club Pact in August, which set the terms of the transfer and reinstated the 1966 constitution, but they agreed to respect the election result. Leaving aside that his two main contenders were prohibited from participating in the election, in March 1985 Julio María Sanguinetti was inaugurated as the first democratically accountable president since 1972.

A feature of the restored political system of 1985 was the extent to which it resembled the system overthrown in 1973. Perhaps because reform might have implied disloyalty to the country's institutions and political traditions, there was no inquest into what had gone wrong before 1973. The 1966 constitution and the voting system were restored intact. The Frente Amplio coalition raised its share of the vote in 1984 to 22 percent, but the traditional parties (and to some extent the old leaderships) continued to dominate. Sanguinetti secured a personal vote of 31 percent, more than Gestido or Bordaberry had received; but this gave him neither a personal mandate nor a majority in the legislature.

Sanguinetti's administration, billed as a government of national unity on the strength of ministries granted to minority factions or distinguished individuals, faced two central challenges: to placate the military and to resurrect the economy. The first issue was sharpened by the immediate release of those Tupamaros still in jail and the political rehabilitation of the MLN-T, which joined the Frente Amplio coalition in 1989. Tension increased over the question of an amnesty for human-rights violations committed by military personnel during the regime. In 1986 a coalition of Colorados and Blancos managed to pass an Amnesty Law (*Ley de caducidad de la pretensión punitiva del estado*) by which the state declined to use its legitimate powers to persecute the armed forces for human rights violations and crimes against humanity. The Amnesty Law, denounced as illegal by international human rights organizations, was challenged in a 1989 referendum (itself the product of a mass mobilization of epic proportions), but was ultimately upheld with 57 percent of votes.

Amid the euphoria of redemocratization, and with widespread calls for expansionist economic policy to revitalize the economy on the basis of domestic demand, Sanguinetti opted instead for an economic strategy that prioritized export-led growth. The

Skyline of downtown Montevideo, capital of Uruguay, late 20th century. Uruguayans for much of the twentieth century enjoyed political stability, and high levels of social spending and standard of living. Though 1973 began a repressive period of military rule, in 1985 the country returned to civilian rule. © BETTMANN/CORBIS

wage and employment benefits were real, if modest, but the gross domestic product grew strongly in 1986–1987. Inflation was curbed but not controlled. The Sanguinetti administration succeeded in consolidating democracy, but by 1988 there was a widespread sense that it had been inadequate to secure overdue change and reform.

The mood of frustration was reflected in the 1989 elections, in which a Blanco candidate was elected president for the first time in that century. Luis Alberto Lacalle, grandson of Herrera, received only 21 percent of the vote, but this was sufficient to defeat his nearest challenger, Jorge Batlle, son of Luis and great-nephew of Batlle y Ordóñez. Less predictably, both leaders, at the head of the largest factions of the two traditional parties, proposed market-oriented economic strategies in which the privatization of state-owned assets and the reform of the social security system were prominent. In 1991 the legislature gave conditional approval to a law permitting the sale of parts of the public sector, but popular opposition forced a referendum in 1992 on the measure, which was rejected by 72 percent of voters. The size of the majority signified a remarkable reaffirmation of faith in the Batllist ideology of state provision. In another major historical turn, in 1989 the socialist Tabaré Vázquez (the Frente Amplio's candidate) was elected mayor of Montevideo, where half the nation's population resides, with 35 percent of the vote. The Frente Amplio has since won four consecutive mayoral elections in the capital: Vázquez in 1989, Mariano Arana in 1994 and 1999, and Ricardo Ehrlich in 2004.

By 1992 two things had become clear: First, the wave of privatization (in response to Washington Consensus and IMF directives) was over, at least for the time being. The referendum had established that almost three-fourths of the population preferred some form of redistributive welfare state, even if it also desired a more efficient and reformed state. Second, the Frente Amplio was ascendant. Indeed, in 1994 former president Sanguinetti was again elected to the presidency based both on his earlier opposition to privatization as well as the alliance he crafted with Hugo Batalla, a former left-leaning Colorado who came to lead the Partido por el Gobierno del Pueblo (the sector of the Frente Amplio receiving the most votes in 1989) and who was now splitting from the leftist coalition and rejoining his old party.

Sanguinetti's second administration aimed at further turning Uruguay into a commercial and financial hub (*plaza financiera*), a provider of services, and a tourist destination. Tax-free havens (*zonas francas*) had been created in 1987 during his first government, intending to attract investors, promote exports, and provide jobs for local labor. By 1999 financial activity, tourism, the public sector, and services had displaced agriculture and industry (both of which fell by half when compared to mid-1980s figures); combined, they represented more than half of the gross domestic product (GDP). In 1994 the traditional parties also succeeded in changing the constitution and establishing a two-round electoral system (*ballotage*), which meant the Left would need to obtain more votes than the Colorado and the Blanco combined—a nearly unthinkable result.

In 1998 the GDP reached its highest point ever, but wealth was unequally distributed and the quality of life of the common folk did not improve as expected. The elections of 1999 gave voters another chance to manifest their discontent. The election of Jorge Batlle—an archrival of Sanguinetti within the Colorado Party—was meant to serve as a punishment for both previous governments. For the first time in history, the Frente Amplio won the most votes of any party (38.5 percent), though, predictably, it lost in the run-off, when it obtained 44 percent of the vote against Batlle's 51 percent. Jorge Batlle's presidency devoted itself to finding markets for commodities (opening the U.S. and Mexican markets to Uruguayan meat and other commodities) and investors (such as the Finnish paper company Botnia). In a gesture toward the leftist segment of the public, he organized a peace commission charged with investigating the fate of the disappeared, but it was not very productive

THE CRASH OF 2002: THE END OF NEOLIBERALISM

Jorge Batlle's administration had to deal with two major crises: an outbreak of mad cow disease affecting the nation's livestock, and the crippling effects of the financial crisis in Argentina of 2001, following the crash of the Brazilian currency and market in 1999. These two events combined resulted in the near total collapse, in 2002, of Uruguay's trade, industry, and financial system. The 2002 crisis was in part a product of financial globalization and speculation, upon which the Uruguayan economy had become dangerously dependent, as well as of its dependence on the Brazilian and Argentine markets. It was also due to the unscrupulous maneuvers of bankers (who emptied out accounts and funneled deposits offshore), coupled with Batlle's attempt to refinance the bankrupt private banks and aid the public banks, where people were rushing to the counters. This resulted in the near exhaustion of national reserves, the loss of personal savings and freezing of accounts, a skyrocketing risk factor, the disruption and destruction of much of the nation's economic activity, the ruin of many industries and businesses, and an unemployment rate that reached 20 percent. It also meant a severe setback in the standard of living of the working and middle classes: 40 percent of the population went into poverty (10 percent into outright indigence), with the rate well above 50 percent among children and youths.

The price of the U.S. dollar doubled, and GDP regressed to early-1990s levels (in 2002, GDP was at US$ 9,000 per year per capita). Social indicators stagnated or fell in terms relative to other countries, as did the Uruguayan ranking in the Index of Human Development (from 31 in the mid-1990s to 43 in 2002). As wealth became further concentrated, Uruguayan society and culture became increasingly unequal, fractured, and polarized. The outgoing migratory flow that had begun in the mid-1960s reached another peak in the aftermath of the 2002 crisis. Out of a population of 3.5 million, nearly half a million Uruguayans were now living abroad. On average, 20,000 persons were leaving every year, mostly young and educated. At the worst point of the banking crisis, the Bush administration lent some quick cash to Batlle, which kept the Uruguayan economy from hitting rock bottom. Nevertheless, time was running out, and the specter of a severe political systemic crisis (like the one facing neighboring Argentina in 2001) appeared on the horizon. The general feeling was that it was about time to give the Left a chance.

THE TWENTY-FIRST CENTURY: REBUILDING THE WELFARE STATE

It came as no surprise when Tabaré Vázquez of Frente Amplio and Rodolfo Nin of Encuentro Progresista, seconded by Danilo Astori as minister of the economy (a figure inspiring trust and geared toward the business community) and the charismatic Tupamaro leader José Mujica (the candidate with the

most votes), swept the elections of 2004, winning 50.5 percent in the first round. A bit more surprising was the triumph of the Frente Amplio in seven of the main departments of the interior (including Canelones, Paysandú, Salto, and Maldonado), historical bastions of the Colorado and Blanco caudillos. Still more surprising was the meager 10 percent obtained by the Colorado party as a whole.

The Vázquez administration's initial goals were to handle and possibly reverse the effects of the prolonged crisis that had only manifested itself more crudely and violently in 2002. Vázquez created a brand new ministry of social development, headed by Marina Arismendi (then secretary general of the Communist Party), to rapidly assess, address, and reduce extreme poverty and poverty (at 30 percent in 2005, and reduced to 20 percent in 2007).

Astori, for his part, managed quickly to chase away fears of economic instability that might be worsened by a dramatic change of rules and course. While honoring the debt (unlike Argentina), Astori succeeded in negotiating better conditions for repaying it while reserving some margin for public spending; paid off parts of the debt (with the IMF); crafted a clearer legal framework; created a decent climate for attracting investors; and succeeded in reinvigorating the public banking system—all of which resulted in an almost immediate growth in economic activity.

Social spending was kept within certain budget limits, but was reorganized, and therefore was far more generous and effective than in previous administrations. Spending took the form of public investments on infrastructure, transfers to public education (now, by law, at 4.5 percent of the budget), the creation of a universal health coverage system (Sistema Nacional Integrado de Salud), and the rise of workers' wages and social benefits. The expansion of the social budget, another political goal, was also made possible by a combination of savings on debt-payments; stricter tax collection; the prosecution of large debtors; the creation of a progressive income tax, which Uruguay till then had lacked; transfers of rent generated by profitable state enterprises; and the effect of the overall expansion of the economy, which grew steadily.

Other changes introduced by the Frente Amplio during the first two years include the revamping of the *consejos de salarios* created in the 1940s, the protection of workers' rights to form and join unions and strike as a last resort (without fearing police action), the approval by the senate of a law on sexual and reproductive health (which includes a new abortion law), the fight to stamp out under-the-table employment, and the shortening of prison sentences and the liberation of many inmates. Still other acts include refinancing or outright pardoning of small farmers' debts, providing credit for worker-run factories and small enterprises, and actively supporting antidiscrimination actions and laws against racism and sexism. For its symbolism, it is also worth pointing out that the ministry of defense and the ministry of the interior are both now headed by women (Azucena Berrutti and Daisy Tourné), as are the ministry of public health (María Julia Muñoz) and the ministry of social development (Marina Arismendi).

For the first time, because of a more active judiciary and a stricter interpretation of the Amnesty Law of 1986, most of the still-living civilians and military officers closely associated with human rights violations committed during the dictatorship have been brought to justice. The list includes former President Bordaberry, former foreign affairs minister Juan C. Blanco, Lieutenant General José Gavazzo, and Colonels Gilberto Vázquez, Jorge Silvera, Ernesto Ramas, Ricardo Arab, Ricardo Medina, Luis Maurente, Sande Lima, among others. Juan Antonio Rod-ríguez Buratti committed suicide when he was about to be detained. Colonel Manuel Cordero, who escaped to Brazil, was incarcerated and faces an extradition request. General Gregorio Álvarez—the last leader during the dictatorship—was also finally imprisoned in December 2007. Furthermore, excavations in military facilities led to the discovery of the corpses of two disappeared political prisoners (union leader Ubagesner Chávez Sosa and law professor Fernando Miranda), thus contradicting prior official accounts that denied their existence.

In the realm of foreign relations, the Vázquez administration reestablished diplomatic relations with Cuba, and closer economic ties and new forms of cooperation were developed with the United States, Chile, Venezuela, and other countries such as India, China, New Zealand, and Thailand. Meanwhile, relations with neighboring Brazil and Argentina, the two powers of the Mercosur, remain cool.

See also **Amézaga, Juan José de; Baldomir, Alfredo; Batlle Berres, Luis Conrado; Batlle y Ordóñez, José; Batllismo; Bordaberry, Juan María; Chicago Boys; Chinchulín, Pact of; Herrera, Luis Alberto de; International Monetary Fund (IMF); Lacalle Herrera, Luis Alberto; Latifundia; Michelini, Zelmar; Neoliberalism; Pacheco Areco, Jorge; Sanguinetti, Julio María; Saravia, Aparicio; Terra, Gabriel; Uruguay, National Liberation Movement (MLN-T); Vazquez, Tabare; Viera, Feliciano.**

BIBLIOGRAPHY

Achugar, Hugo. *La balsa de la medusa: Ensayos sobre identidad, cultura y fin de siglo en Uruguay.* Montevideo: Ediciones Trilce, 1992.

Barrán, José Pedro. *Historia de la sensibilidad en el Uruguay,* vol. 2: *El disciplinamiento (1860–1920).* Montevideo: Ediciones de la Banda Oriental, 1990.

Barrán, José Pedro, and Benjamín Nahum. *Batlle, los Estancieros y el Imperio Británico.* 7 vols. Montevideo: Ediciones de la Banda Oriental, 1979–1987.

Bayley, Miguel Aguirre. *El Frente Amplio: Historia y documentos.* Montevideo: Ediciones de la Banda Oriental, 1985.

Bértola, Luis. *Ensayos de historia económica: Uruguay y la región en la economía mundial, 1870–1990.* Montevideo: Ediciones Trilce, 2000.

Brando, Oscar, and Carlos Abin. *Uruguay Hoy: Paisaje después del 31 de octubre.* Montevideo: Ediciones del Caballo Perdido, 2004.

Caetano, Gerardo, ed. *20 años de democracia: Uruguay 1985–2005: Miradas múltiples.* Montevideo: Taurus, 2005.

Caetano, Gerardo, and José Pedro Rilla. *Breve historia de la dictadura, 1973–1985.* Montevideo: Ediciones de la Banda Oriental, 1987.

Caetano, Gerardo, and Raúl Jacob. *El nacimiento del terrismo, 1930–1933.* 3 vols. Montevideo: Ediciones de la Banda Oriental, 1989–1991.

Chirico, Selva López. *El Estado y las Fuerzas Armadas en el Uruguay del siglo XX.* Montevideo: Ediciones de la Banda Oriental, 1985.

D'elía, Germán. *El Uruguay neo-batllista, 1946–1958.* Montevideo: Ediciones de la Banda Oriental, 1982.

Eloy, Rosa Alonso, and Carlos Demasi. *Uruguay, 1958–1968: Crisis y estancamiento.* Montevideo: Ediciones de la Banda Oriental, 1986.

Finch, M. H. J. *A Political Economy of Uruguay Since 1870.* London: Macmillan, 1981.

Frega, Ana, Mónica Maronna, and Yvette Trochón. *Baldomir y la restauración democrática, 1938–1946.* Montevideo: Ediciones de la Banda Oriental, 1987.

Garcé, Adolfo, and Jaime Yaffé. *La era progresista.* Montevideo: Editorial Fin de Siglo, 2004.

Gillespie, Charles Guy. *Negotiating Democracy: Politicians and Generals in Uruguay.* Cambridge, U.K. and New York: Cambridge University Press, 1991.

Katzman, Ruben, and Fernando Filgueira. *Informe del desarrollo humano en Uruguay.* Montevideo: Programa de Naciones Unidas para el Desarrollo, 2000.

Lindahl, Göran G. *Uruguay's New Path: A Study in Politics During the First Colegiado, 1919–1933.* Stockholm: Göteberg University Library and Institute of Ibero-American Studies, 1962.

Marchesi, Aldo, et al., eds. *El presente de la dictadura: Estudios y reflexiones a 30 años del golpe de Estado en Uruguay.* Montevideo: Ediciones Trilce, 2004.

Mazzei, Enrique, ed. *El Uruguay desde la sociología: Integración, desigualdades sociales, trabajo y educación.* Montevideo: Departamento de Sociología, Facultad de Ciencias Sociales, Universidad de la República, 2003.

Moreira, Constanza. *Final del juego: Del bipartidismo tradicional al triunfo de la izquierda en Uruguay.* Montevideo: Ediciones Trilce, 2004.

Rico, Álvaro, ed. *Uruguay: Cuentas pendientes: Dictadura, memorias y desmemorias.* Montevideo: Ediciones Trilce, 1995.

Taylor, Philip B. *Government and Politics of Uruguay.* New Orleans: Tulane University, 1960.

Trigo, Abril. *Memorias migrantes: Testimonios y ensayos sobre la diáspora uruguaya.* Montevideo: Ediciones Trilce, 2003.

Vanger, Milton I. *José Batlle y Ordóñez of Uruguay: The Creator of His Times, 1902–1907.* Cambridge: Harvard University Press, 1963.

Vanger, Milton I. *The Model Country: José Batlle y Ordóñez of Uruguay, 1907–1915.* Hanover, NH: Published for Brandeis University Press by University Press of New England, 1980.

Villamil, Silvia Rodríguez and Graciela Sapriza. *Mujer, Estado y política en el Uruguay del siglo XX.* Montevideo: Ediciones de la Banda Oriental, 1984.

Weinstein, Martin. *Uruguay: Democracy at the Crossroads.* Boulder, CO: Westview Press, 1988.

Yaffé, Jaime. *Al centro y adentro: La renovación de la izquierda y el triunfo del Frente Amplio en Uruguay.* Montevideo: Linardi y Risso, 2005.

HENRY FINCH
GUSTAVO REMEDI

URUGUAY, COLEGIADO. Colegiado,
a term for the two forms of plural executive system with which Uruguay experimented in the twentieth century. The first *colegiado* (collegial executive) was established with the 1919 Constitution and lasted until the 1933 coup by President Gabriel Terra. The *colegiado* was proposed by President José Batlle y Ordóñez during his second term as president (1911–1915). He thought that the instability and abuse of power so rampant in Latin American politics could be ameliorated by doing away with a presidential system. His proposal produced an uproar even within his own party, where some of his political rivals saw the project as merely a way for him to perpetuate his dominance of national politics. Batlle's original plan called for a *junta de gobierno,* which would consist of nine members, one to be elected each year after an initial election of all nine.

The split within his own party (the Colorados) and opposition from the Blancos (National Party) led to the election in 1916 of a constitutional convention dominated by Batlle's opponents. After over a year of maneuvering, they reached a compromise: The presidency was not eliminated, but the functions of the office were limited to the conduct of foreign affairs and the preservation of international order and external security. A National Council of Administration was created to deal with all other activities of the state. This council consisted of nine members, with six chosen from the majority party and three from the minority party. The expectation was, therefore, that it would include six Colorados and three Blancos. The president and the council would both be elected by popular vote, with the president serving a four-year term and the council members serving for six years, with two members being elected every two years. The 1919 Constitution thus set a bold experiment into motion.

Elections were very close during the 1920s, but the Colorados controlled the presidency. The inefficiencies of the collegial system were masked by the economic well-being Uruguay enjoyed through its trade with Britain. But the depression of the 1930s brought changes. President Terra found the sharing of power with the council totally inadequate for him to deal effectively with the economic and social emergency brought on by the collapsing world economy. Thus, in 1933, with the support of the Blanco leader Luis Alberto de Herrera, Terra closed Congress and abolished the National Council of Administration. The 1934 Constitution, written by Terra and Herrera, restored a presidential system and divided the Senate between the political factions of the two coup leaders. Although a fully constitutional presidential system was restored by the 1942 Constitution, it was not until 1952 that Uruguay would again experiment with a collegial executive.

The second *colegiado* was a purely collegial executive system under which Uruguay was governed from 1952 until 1966. It is called the *Colegiado Integral* because, unlike its predecessor under the 1919 Constitution, there was no office of the president to share executive power with the collegial body.

The second *colegiado* fulfilled Batlle y Ordóñez's old dream of a plural executive for Uruguay. The impetus for its adoption came from his conservative sons, César and Lorenzo, who were increasingly overshadowed within the Colorado Party by their dynamic cousin, Luis Batlle Berres, who served as president from 1947 to 1951. Batlle Berres was an urban populist whose faction had won an overwhelming victory in the 1950 presidential elections. Devastated by the results, Blanco leader Luis Alberto de Herrera reversed his long-standing opposition to a collegial executive and joined with pro-*colegiado* Colorados in the call for constitutional reform. Unable to head off a plebiscite, Luis Batlle Berres supported the reform, which was approved with the adoption of the 1952 Constitution.

Under the new charter the executive, now called the National Council of Government, consisted of nine members, with six seats going to the majority party and three to the party receiving the next highest number of votes. Economic decline and stagnation led to a historic first when the Blancos gained control of the *colegiado* in the 1958 elections, their first control of the executive in the twentieth century. Many changes were expected, but given the almost total coparticipation (power sharing) imposed by the 1952 Constitution and the need to sign an International Monetary Fund agreement, policy shifted very little. With continued economic drift, the Blancos retained control of the executive in the very close 1962 elections. During their second term, pressure built for a more efficient state and executive. Once again, constitutional reform was the mechanism. In the midst of a declining economy, growing inflation, and increased social unrest, Uruguay returned to a presidential system with the adoption of the 1966 Constitution.

The second experiment with a collegial executive succumbed, as did the first, to economic dec-line and the inadequacy of the government's response. On both occasions the *colegiado* was blamed for the problem, but as the mild dictatorship in the 1930s and the increased authoritarianism and descent into military government in the 1970s demonstrated, the problem rested in political leadership, not the *colegiado*.

See also **Batlle Berres, Luis Conrado; Batlle y Ordóñez, José; Terra, Gabriel; Uruguay, Political Parties: Colorado Party.**

BIBLIOGRAPHY

Milton Vanger, "Uruguay Introduces Government by Committee," in *American Political Science Review* 48, no. 2 (June 1954): 500–513.

Philip Taylor, Jr., *Government and Politics of Uruguay* (1960).

Göran Lindahl, *Uruguay's New Path: A Study in Politics During the First Colegiado* (1962).

Martin Weinstein, *Uruguay: The Politics of Failure* (1975).

Additional Bibliography

Costa Bonino, Luis. *La crisis del sistema político uruguayo: Partidos políticos y democracia hasta 1973.* Montevideo, Uruguay: Fundación de Cultura Universitaria, 1995.

MARTIN WEINSTEIN

URUGUAY, CONGRESS OF 1825.

Uruguay Congress of 1825, body convoked by the leaders of Uruguay's rebellion against Brazilian rule. The congress opened on 20 August, just four months and one day after Uruguayan exiles, known as the "Thirty-Three Orientals," crossed over from Argentine territory to begin the expulsion of Brazilian forces. It met at the small town of Florida, slightly north of Montevideo (which was under Brazilian occupation and was not represented). On 25 August it declared null and void the incorporation of Uruguay into the Portuguese and subsequently Brazilian monarchies and proclaimed union with Argentina in the United Provinces of the Río De La Plata. It named Juan Antonio Lavalleja governor and designated Uruguayan representatives to the congress of the United Provinces.

The Uruguayan congress, which eventually moved to the town of San José, created a first set of governmental institutions and enacted a series of reforms, such as a law of free birth, inspired by the same liberal ideology professed by the dominant Unitarist faction at Buenos Aires (which after slight delay accepted Uruguayan annexation and took the province under its protection). The congress closed its sessions in July 1826.

See also **Río de la Plata; Uruguay: Before 1900.**

BIBLIOGRAPHY

John Street, *Artigas and the Emancipation of Uruguay* (1959), chap. 9.

Alfredo Castellanos, *La Cisplatina, la independencia y la república caudillesca (1820–1838)* (1974).

Additional Bibliography

Barrios Pintos, Aníbal. *Historia de los pueblos orientales: Sus orígenes, procesos fundacionales, sus primeros años.* Montevideo, Uruguay: Academia Nacional de Letras, 2000.

DAVID BUSHNELL

URUGUAY, CONSTITUTIONS.

Uruguay has had six constitutions during its existence as a sovereign state: 1830, 1918, 1934, 1942, 1952, and 1966. Nevertheless, its adherence to constitutional democracy—except for eleven and a half years of military rule in the 1970s and 1980s—is remarkable in a region not known for following the norms of elections, civil liberties, and social welfare.

The 1830 Constitution confirmed the independence and juridical sovereignty of Uruguay, officially known as the República Oriental del Uruguay, as established by Brazil and Argentina in a treaty mediated by the English diplomat Lord John Ponsonby. The constitution established a presidential system with the chief executive elected by the General Assembly, or Congress (consisting of the Senate and the Chamber of Deputies) every four years. The president could be reelected after a four-year interim. Comparable to those of his U.S. counterpart, the president's powers included the roles of commander in chief, protector of domestic peace and external security, and architect of the budget. The president governed with a set of ministers, whom he appointed and dismissed at will. Early on, the General Assembly established the right to question (interpellate) the ministers, thus establishing the tradition of a presidential system with an active and influential legislature. The local unit of government was the department, governed by a *jefe político* (executive magistrate), who lived in the principal town of each department and was appointed by the president. During the nineteenth century, the constitution was violated almost as frequently as it was honored. Nevertheless, it remained in force for ninety years, making it the third longest in the history of Latin America.

The 1918 Constitution was the result of a compromise between José Batlle y Ordóñez's vision of a collegial executive and more conservative elements within his own Colorado Party who joined with the Blancos (National Party) in wishing to preserve at least a partially presidential system. This charter was a unique experiment in constitutional law. It created a president who was popularly elected for a four-year term and who would be responsible for foreign affairs and domestic and external security through his control of the armed forces and police. All other executive powers would be in the hands of a National Council of Administration, which consisted of nine members elected by thirds every two years. The 1918 Constitution thus produced a bicephalous executive (*see* Uruguay: Colegiado). The arrangement, coupled with extremely close elections between the Colorado and Blanco parties during the 1920s resulted in a growing stalemate in decision making. With the death of José Batlle in 1929 and the onset of the Great Depression, President Gabriel Terra found himself increasingly frustrated by the partially collegial executive system. He joined forces with the Blanco leader Luis Alberto de Herrera in a 1933 coup that in effect dissolved the bold experiment put in place in 1918.

The 1934 Constitution, in effect written by Terra and Herrera, returned Uruguay to a presidential system by eliminating the dual executive. It gave the two factions led by the coup leaders total control of the Senate, with fifteen seats for each. The president (Terra) would rule with a Council of Ministers. Parliamentary approval of ministers meant that in practice three ministers would be given to the minority party, that is, Herrera's faction. In effect, the coparticipation that had been put in place by the

1918 Constitution was renewed, but it was now restricted to the two coup factions. Under the constitution the boards of directors of all government agencies and Autonomous Entities, which in Uruguay included industrial and commercial corporations, would consist of three to five members who had to be approved by 60 percent of the Senate.

The 1942 Constitution was the product of a "constitutional coup" by President Alfredo Baldomir, who closed the General Assembly on 21 February 1942, just before the scheduled elections. On 29 May he presented his constitutional reform proposal to his newly created Council of State, declaring that the new constitution would go into effect if approved in a plebiscite the following November. There was no doubt that it would be approved since it ended the outdated and unpopular features of the 1934 Constitution. The new charter eliminated the arbitrary division of the Senate between the two 1933 coup factions, calling for senators to be elected by strict proportional representation. Ministers would again be appointed by the entire Congress, and the boards of state corporations would be selected with guaranteed minority participation. Essentially, the 1942 Constitution abolished the exclusion of the Terra-Herrera alliance that was codified in the 1934 Constitution.

The 1952 Constitution gave Uruguay its second *colegiado,* this time in the form of a purely collegial executive system. The constitution was the result of an agreement between Batlle's sons, César and Lorenzo, and the great caudillo of the Blancos, Luis Alberto de Herrera, who gave up his long-standing opposition to the colegiado when he saw how poorly his party did in the 1950 presidential election. Former president Luis Batlle Berres, whose faction dominated the Colorado Party and controlled the presidency, could not oppose such a powerful combination pushing for constitutional reform.

The constitution created a nine-member executive, or *colegiado,* known as the National Council of Government, with six seats going to the majority party and three to the dominant minority party. The division of patronage between the Colorados and Blancos was assured by a constitutional clause mandating that the boards of directors of all state services and industrial enterprises consist of five members, divided three to two between the two major parties. Thus, the long-standing tradition of coparticipation was fully constitutionalized. The healthy Uruguayan economy of the 1940s and 1950s served to mask the inefficiencies of this system.

The 1966 Constitution, which returned Uruguay to a presidential system by eliminating the *colegiado,* was approved in a plebiscite on 27 November 1966. The new charter lengthened the term of all elected officials to five years and reaffirmed the electoral tradition of having all offices contested at the same time, that is, once every five years. The return to the presidential system was a reaction to Uruguay's growing economic crisis and the malaise that had overcome the Colorados and Blancos. The political elite, faced with increased social unrest, rising inflation, and virtually no economic growth, decided to streamline the government by returning to a presidential system. The new constitution created a Central Bank to help control monetary and fiscal policy and a Social Security Bank to try to rationalize the administration of retirement funds. In an attempt to depoliticize the running of state enterprises, the three to two division in their directorships was eliminated. Maintaining the 60 percent requirement for confirmation as director, however, implied that the two traditional parties would continue to split the assignments and the patronage that went with them.

The new constitution also contained several articles on land reform and internal order, which reflected the growing insecurity of the political and economic elites. Article 168 specifically gave the president the power to invoke a state of emergency under the *Medidas Prontas de Seguridad* (Prompt Security Measures). These allowed, in effect, a limited form of a state of siege. This power had existed in the previous constitution but only in cases of invasion or internal rebellion. The provision proved crucial to the government of President Jorge Pacheco Areco (1967–1972), who operated under the *medidas* for all but a few months of his presidency.

In reality, the constitution was suspended under President Juan María Bordaberry in April 1972 and was ignored by the military during its dictatorship from 27 June 1973 until the restoration of civilian rule in 1985. During this period the General Assembly passed a series of institutional acts that the dictatorship used to circumvent the constitution. The military tried to get its own constitution approved, but the project was defeated in a plebiscite in 1980. The 1967 Constitution was fully restored by president Julio María Sanguinetti on 1 March 1985. Since the democratic transition, citizens have used referendums, allowed by the constitution, to shape laws. Referendums have protected water resources, stopped the privatization of public utilities, and safeguarded social security benefits.

See also **Baldomir, Alfredo; Batlle y Ordóñez, José; Bordaberry, Juan María; Herrera, Luis Alberto de; Jefe Político; Sanguinetti, Julio María; Terra, Gabriel; Uruguay, Political Parties: Blanco Party; Uruguay, Political Parties: Colorado Party.**

BIBLIOGRAPHY

Justino Jiménez De Arechaga, *La constitución nacional,* 10 vols. (1949), and *La constitución de 1952,* 4 vols. (1952).

Héctor Gros Espiell, ed., *Las constituciones del Uruguay* (1956).

Alberto Pérez Pérez, *Constitución de la República Oriental del Uruguay,* 2 vols. (1970).

Additional Bibliography

Brito, Alexandra Barahona de. *Human Rights and Democratization in Latin America: Uruguay and Chile.* Oxford: Oxford University Press, 1997.

Gros Espiell, Héctor. *Evolución constitucional del Uruguay.* Montevideo: Fundación de Cultura Universitaria, 2003.

MARTIN WEINSTEIN

URUGUAY, ELECTORAL SYSTEM.

DOUBLE SIMULTANEOUS VOTE

The double simultaneous vote, a crucial element of the Uruguayan electoral and party systems, allows the voter to choose a set of specific candidates within the party of his choice. The practice has been used since 1910, although it has undergone some important constitutional changes. The system is similar to that used in the United States in the primary and general presidential elections, except that the voter simultaneously indicates the party of his preference as well as the candidate of his preference within the party. The candidate with the most votes from the party with the most votes wins. Senators and representatives are elected this way as well.

The practice has contributed to the survival of "catch-all" parties with mixed ideologies and class bases, and it has provided a basic mechanism through which differing factions within parties can cohabit and negotiate. However, the double simultaneous vote has been criticized for promoting intraparty factionalism and transforming parties into mere "vote cooperatives." The Left has called it one of the reasons for the perpetuation of an artificial bipartisan format, which is reinforced by the Ley de Lemas. However, the Left itself uses this electoral mechanism when it embraces the strategy of popular fronts. The double simultaneous vote allows it to present unified electoral fronts while still maintaining original party identities.

LEY DE LEMAS

Ley de Lemas (Law of Party Names), is a key component of the complex Uruguayan electoral process. A complement to the "double simultaneous vote," it regulates the registration and use of party *lemas* (literally "mottoes," it refers to the formal name) and *sublemas* (the names of factions within the parties). A 1925 law defined the notions of *lema* and *sublema,* the criteria for their registration and guidelines for considering them permanent or temporary. This law recognized the traditional political identities of the Blancos and the Colorados and legitimized the practice of the double simultaneous vote for inter- and intraparty competition. A 1934 law stipulated that proprietorship of a party's *lema* belonged to the party *sublema* that had the most legislators, and that this *sublema* could place conditions on or deny the use of the *lema* to others. In 1939 another law was passed that restricted the registration of *lemas* with names similar to existing ones.

The Constitution of 1952 explicitly established a rule that permitted the reunification of the Blanco (National) Party under a single *lema.* The factionalism in this party had resulted in part from the laws of 1934 and 1939. This rule, however, was applicable only to "permanent" *lemas,* thereby preventing different parties on the Left from unifying into popular fronts while still maintaining their original identities. It did not prevent the creation of the Frente Amplio in 1971, although this coalition's members still had to vote under the slogan of only one of its constituent parties, the Christian Democrats. When this party left the Frente Amplio in 1989, the political system decided to recognize the Frente as a permanent *lema*.

See also **Uruguay, Constitutions.**

BIBLIOGRAPHY

Philip B. Taylor, "The Electoral System in Uruguay," in *Journal of Politics* 17 (1955): 19–42.

Alberto Pérez Pérez, *La ley de lemas* (1971).

Aldo Solari, "El sistema de partidos y régimen electoral en el Uruguay," in Rolando Franco, ed., *El sistema electoral uruguayo* (1986).

Luis E. González, *Political Structures and Democracy in Uruguay* (1991).

Additional Bibliography

Costa Bonino, Luis. *La crisis del sistema político uruguayo: Partidos políticos y democracia hasta 1973.* Montevideo, Uruguay: Fundación de Cultura Universitaria, 1995.

Crespo Martínez, Ismael. *Tres décadas de política uruguaya: Crisis, restauración y transformación del sistema de partidos.* Madrid: Centro de Investigaciones Sociológicas, 2002.

FERNANDO FILGUEIRA

URUGUAY, GEOGRAPHY.

Uruguay's official name, the Oriental Republic of Uruguay, reveals that it was once the eastern part of the former United Provinces of the Río De La Plata created in the Viceroyalty of Río de la Plata at the time independence from Spain was declared in 1810. The country stretches between the Uruguay River in the west and the coast of the Atlantic in the east, and from the Cuareím creek, the Cuchilla de Santa Ana, and the Yaguarón River in the north to the shores of the Río De La Plata estuary. With an area of 68,038 square miles, Uruguay is the second-smallest country in South America, after Suriname. The relief features of the country are not greatly defined. The highlands of the country's core are the Plateau of Haedo, with several outreaching ridges (or *cuchillas*), and the Cuchilla Grande, or Central Hills. They never rise above 1,320 feet and divide the country into three distinct plains. To the east extends the low-lying, humid Atlantic coastal plain; to the south the narrower Platine River plains are interrupted by rocky outcrops such as the classic "sighted hill," from which the city of Montevideo took its name; to the west slopes the broad fluvial plain of the Uruguay River, dominated by the valley of the Río Negro, the main watercourse of central Uruguay, fed and maintained by several streams arising in the Haedo Plateau.

The climate is temperate and humid, with higher summer temperatures and precipitation in the northwest due to continental warming in the Uruguay River basin. In the Río de la Plata estuary, cold winds from Argentine Patagonia can bring winter temperatures down to freezing, but along the Atlantic coastal plains the tempering influence of the sea makes for pleasant winters and mild summers. The vegetation reflects the climate and the topographic conditions: forested areas are scarce and restricted to patches along the major watercourses and to the wetlands that border on southern Brazil, where hardwoods alternate with palm stands. Native trees include the *algarobo*, the *nandubay*, and the *quebracho*. In the southern plains and central hills, shrubs and grassland (Pampas) dominate the scenery. These are the regions where most of the cattle ranches and wheat-growing farms are located. Large-scale eucalyptus tree plantations for paper-mill factories cover hundreds of miles in the country's western region and have generated great controversy over their use of fresh water.

The country is organized into nineteen departments, each of them administered by an *intendente* (governor) directly elected by the people every five years. In 2005 Uruguay's population reached 3.4 million. Population imbalances across the country are reflected in the makeup of the departments: the capital, Montevideo, with 1.34 million (2005) inhabitants, contains 40 percent of the Uruguayan populace, whereas the department of Flores (in the southwest) has a mere 25,528 people. Sixty-seven percent of the population lives in a belt that runs along the Río de la Plata from the department of Maldonado to that of Colonia, encompassing the capital. Correspondingly, approximately 80 percent of the manufacturing establishments, 95 percent of the service industries, and 87 percent of the administrative and cultural institutions are also located in this belt. This concentration of resources and population has worked in favor of cultural homogeneity and has created strong demographic conditions in Latin America. Life expectancy is 75.6 years, the daily calorie intake is 2,860 per person, infant mortality is a low 12.02 per thousand, and the birthrate is 14.3 per thousand. In the early twenty-first century the country experienced an economic crisis to the detriment of social indicators.

After its separation from the United Provinces of the Río de la Plata in 1828, Uruguay continued with its traditional colonial ranching activities, as close to three-quarters of the country is grassland, ideal for cattle and sheep raising. But along the Río de la Plata, European immigrants embarked on nontraditional agricultural pursuits, creating a dichotomy in the primary activities of the country that has persisted to the present. In republican times, the quality of the cattle improved through better pasturage, and beef became suitable for export. In the central part of the country, large sheep-raising establishments produced wool as a major export commodity. Land dedicated to the production of wheat and flax expanded in the southwestern area of Uruguay, and forage covered all remaining grazing areas. Thus, the bases of the agrarian export economy were established, and the social and political peace that reigned during the rule of José Batlle y Ordóñez (1903–1907 and 1911–1915) fortified the development of the country. While industries of primary products, such as flour mills, packing plants, textile mills, and leather tanneries, became the pillars of the national economy, many manufactured goods as well as gasoline and natural gas had to be imported. For as long as exports equaled imports, Uruguay functioned as a welfare state and strove for modernization, but when the demand for foreign goods increased and exports of traditional items declined in the 1960s and early 1970s, the country fell into a period that culminated in the collapse of democracy in 1972. Since 1985 Uruguay has enjoyed civilian rule.

See also **Patagonia; Río de la Plata; United Provinces of the Río de la Plata; Uruguay River.**

BIBLIOGRAPHY

The classic historical geography of the country is W. H. Hudson, *The Purple Land* (New York, 1927). Other works include Marvin Alisky, *Uruguay: A Contemporary Survey* (1969); Jorge Chebataroff, *Tierra uruguaya*
(Montevideo, 1954); Ernst Griffin, "Testing the Von Thunen Theory in Uruguay," in *The Geographical Review* 63 (1973): 500–516, and "Causal Factors Influencing Agricultural Land Use Patterns in Uruguay," in *Revista Geográfica* (Mexico), 80 (1974): 13–33; Jaime Klaczko and J. Rial Roade, *Uruguay: El país urbano* (Montevideo, 1981); and J. M. G. Kleinpenning, "Uruguay: The Rise and Fall of a Welfare State Seen Against a Background of Dependency Theory," in *Revista Geográfica* (Mexico), 93 (1981): 101–117.

Additional Bibliography

Azcuy Ameghino, Eduardo. *La otra historia: Economía, estado y sociedad en el Río de la Plata colonial.* Buenos Aires: Imago Mundi, 2002.

Domínguez, Ana, Ruben Gerardo Prieto, and Marcel Achkar, et al., eds. *Perfil ambiental del Uruguay: 2002.* Montevideo: Nordan Comunidad, 2002.

Golin, Tau. *A fronteira.* 2 vols. Porto Alegre, Uruguay: L&PM Editores, 2002.

Kleinpenning, Jan M. G. *Peopling the Purple Land: A Historical Geography of Rural Uruguay, 1500–1915.* Amsterdam: CEDLA, 1995.

Santos, Carlos, et al. *Aguas en movimiento: La resistencia a la privatización del agua en Uruguay.* Montevideo: Ediciones de la Canilla, 2006.

CÉSAR N. CAVIEDES

URUGUAY, MEDIDAS PRONTAS DE SEGURIDAD.

Medidas Prontas de Seguridad, a form of emergency rule granted to the executive under Uruguay's 1966 Constitution (Article 118, Section 17). The Prompt Security Measures are a mild form of a state of siege, which permit the president to suspend some civil liberties. The president must act in concert with the appropriate ministers, and Congress can terminate, or nullify the effect of, any measures taken by the president under this power. President Jorge Pacheco Areco first invoked the *Medidas* on 13 June 1968 while drafting striking bank workers and declaring a freeze on wages and prices. Except for a brief period in 1969, Pacheco used these emergency powers throughout his presidency to deal with strikes and the growing threat from the urban guerrilla movement known as the Tupamaros. As the economic situation deteriorated and social and political tensions rose, the increasingly authoritarian Pacheco found the measures to be his one sure way to take action, and

Congress reluctantly acquiesced. Many feel that the abuses carried out under the measures paved the way for Uruguay's descent into dictatorship in 1973.

See also **Pacheco Areco, Jorge.**

BIBLIOGRAPHY

Martin Weinstein, *Uruguay: The Politics of Failure* (1975).

M. H. J. Finch, *A Political Economy of Uruguay Since 1870* (1981).

Additional Bibliography

Nahum, Benjamín. *El Uruguay del siglo XX*. Montevideo, Uruguay: Ediciones de la Banda Oriental, 2001.

MARTIN WEINSTEIN

URUGUAY, NATIONAL LIBERATION MOVEMENT (MLN-T).

The MLN-T was a guerrilla movement that came out of concealment in 1967 to become a major political force until its decimation by the military in 1972. The Tupamaros, who took their name from Túpac Amaru, a seventeenth-century Inca chieftain who led an unsuccessful rebellion against the Spaniards, were founded in late 1962 by a group of Socialist Party dissidents. Raúl Sendic, a law student who had organized the sugarcane workers in the northeast, is recognized as the originator of the movement. The founding members spent their first few years training, stealing weapons, and organizing clandestine cells. In 1967, in the midst of some spectacular robberies, they announced their existence with a letter to a leftist newspaper stating that they were willing to use violence to raise political consciousness and ultimately change the political and economic structure of the country.

The writings and propaganda of the Tupamaros were clearly nationalist, socialist, and revolutionary but never offered a coherent economic or political plan. The Tupamaros did not see their movement as capable of directly challenging the military or the government for power. Rather, they sought to incite mass action by pointing out the corruption and inefficiency of the government and its security apparatus. By establishing themselves as a parallel power to the government, the Tupamaros hoped to be at the vanguard of a larger revolution.

Recruiting from among the intellectuals, professionals, and unionized workers, the Tupamaros initially developed a Robin Hood image through a series of robberies, exposures of questionable financial transactions by the political elite, and the distribution of food in poor neighborhoods. But this image faded with a series of kidnappings and the assassination of U.S. AID public safety officer Daniel Mitrione. In response to a mass prison escape by more than 100 Tupamaros in 1969, the military was put in charge of antiguerrilla activity. In 1971 the Tupamaros kidnapped British ambassador Geoffrey Jackson and held him as a guarantee that the November 1971 elections would take place. The Tupamaros correctly believed that the leftist coalition known as the Frente Amplio (Broad Front) could not win these elections, but they suspended their activities until after the elections as a show of support.

On 14 April 1972 the Tupamaros ended their truce with a series of assassinations of police and military officials who they claimed were members of death squads. Some eleven people died that day, and the government received parliamentary approval for the declaration of a state of "internal war." The military was given a blank check and, aided by the defection of a top Tupamaro leader, Hector Amadio Pérez, and the massive use of torture, it destroyed the Tupamaros over the next several months.

Many in Uruguay blame the Tupamaros for the descent into military dictatorship in 1973. There is no question that the Tupamaros exacerbated social conflict and helped politicize the armed forces, but the dictatorship was installed after the Tupamaros were destroyed, and it remained in power almost twelve years.

With the resumption of civilian constitutional government in March 1985, all political prisoners, including the Tupamaro leader who had been held under inhumane conditions, were released. The Tupamaros then announced their intention to organize as a peaceful political party. They publish a newspaper and have a radio program, but have little influence in Uruguayan politics. On 29 March, 1988, Raúl Sendic made a public statement affirming that the group would officially become a political party. The Tupamaros formally allied with the Frente Amplio, agreeing to follow their political ideology. Sendic died in 1989, but in that same year the Tupamaros were admitted into the Frente Amplio, which in the first decade of the twenty-first century was known as the Movimiento de Participación Popular, or, popularly, as Espacio 609. This name is an allusion to the large number of diverse groups who participate in the Uruguayan electoral system. In 2004 the Espacio 609 became the most popular section within the Frente Amplio, winning the most votes.

See also **Sendic, Raúl; Uruguay, Political Parties: Broad Front.**

BIBLIOGRAPHY

For an analysis of the Tupamaros' ideology and recruitment patterns, see Arturo C. Porzecanski, *Uruguay's Tupamaros: The Urban Guerrilla* (1973). For an analysis of the theoretical foundations of the movement, see Abraham Guillen, *Philosophy of the Urban Guerrilla: The Revolutionary Writings of Abraham Guillen*, edited by Donald C. Hodges (1973). For a useful set of interviews and documents, see Maria Esther Gilio, *The Tupamaro Guerrillas* (1972).

Additional Bibliography

Actas tupamaras: Una experiencia de guerilla urbana. Madrid: Editorial Revolución, 1982.

Guttiérez, Angel. *Los Tupamaros en la década de los años sesenta.* México: Extemporáneos, 1978.

Tagliaferro, Gerardo. *Fernández Huidobro: De las armas a las urnas.* Montevideo: Editorial Fin del Siglo, 2004.

MARTIN WEINSTEIN

URUGUAY, ORGANIZATIONS

This entry includes the following articles:
AUTONOMOUS ENTITIES
CATHOLIC WORKERS' CIRCLE
NATIONAL WORKERS CONVENTION
RURAL ASSOCIATION
WORKERS' INTERUNION PLENARY NATIONAL WORKERS' ASSEMBLY

AUTONOMOUS ENTITIES

Autonomous Entities (Entes autónomos) is the juridical term for the commercial or industrial state enterprises in Uruguay that are the legacy of the welfare-oriented and state-interventionist ideology of the Colorado Party leader José Batlle y Ordóñez. There are some twenty nationalized industrial and commercial activities run by a board of directors selected by the government. Batlle believed that national sovereignty and the general welfare could be protected only by an interventionist state. Thus, beginning in 1912 with electricity, a wide array of state-owned services were created. Over the decades these grew to include the ports, railroads, an official radio broadcasting service, the national airline (PLUNA), the telephone company (ANTEL), sanitation, water, and oceanographic and fishing activities. The most famous and largest of the entities, the National Association for Fuel, Alcohol, and Cement (ANCAP), was created during the depression and proved to be a huge source of jobs and patronage. ANCAP was given a legal monopoly to refine oil and produce alcoholic beverages and cement. Batlle had wanted these activities in state hands, but he died before his goal was realized. Economic crisis, however, prodded the political elite into action.

While the vision that inspired the autonomous entities may have been noble, in practice many of these state corporations became inefficient makework operations that served as patronage machines for the Blanco and Colorado parties. Control of the entities and of such decentralized services as education, social security, and housing, through such organs as the State Mortgage Bank, Social Security Bank, State Insurance Bank, and the Bank of the Republic, became so important politically that the composition of their boards became the subject of constitutional debate, and formulas were written into several constitutions on how directors were to be assigned.

Louis Lacalle, elected president in 1989, hoped to privatize several of the entities or at least to allow private participation in them. He had a law passed that enabled him to sell the telephone company, but the law was overwhelmingly abrogated in a plebiscite held in 1992. Nevertheless, Lacalle managed to eliminate some of the monopolies currently held by ANCAP and by some of the public banks.

See also **Batlle y Ordóñez, José.**

BIBLIOGRAPHY

Philip B. Taylor, Jr., *Government and Politics of Uruguay* (1960).

Additional Bibliography

Nahum, Benjamín. *El Uruguay del siglo XX.* Montevideo, Uruguay: Ediciones de la Banda Oriental, 2001.

MARTIN WEINSTEIN

CATHOLIC WORKERS' CIRCLE

The Catholic Workers' Circle (Círculo Católico de Obreros de Montevideo) was founded on 21 June 1885, by Juan O'Neill and Luis Pedro Lenguas, who modeled it on those created by the Spanish bishop José María de Urquinaona y Bidot in the Canary Islands and later in Barcelona. The Uruguayan diocese in Montevideo had been established only in 1878. Urquinaona corresponded with O'Neill and Lenguas and explained to them how the circles worked. The Circle of Montevideo, like similar organizations in Spain and Latin America, followed the social teaching of the Catholic Church and later founded regional centers throughout the country. In a relationship sometimes known as Christian Syndicalism, rural labor organizations affiliated with the Catholic Church came to have sizable influence. Having begun with 600 members, the circle increased its membership considerably in later years. The circle was a labor organization designed to protect workers according to the teachings of the church; however, it provided more services than a regular labor organization, among them medical services in its own hospital, a legal aid office, and other charitable services. Its membership included employers and conservative professionals as well as workers; hence, it offered more conservative solutions to social problems than those of radical labor. In fact, it was created, like many other Catholic organizations, to provide an alternative to the radical labor ideas that appeared in the late nineteenth and early twentieth centuries.

See also **Catholic Action; Leo XIII, Pope.**

BIBLIOGRAPHY

Círculo Católico de Obreros de Montevideo (1936).

Additional Bibliography

Pou Ferrari, Ricardo, and Fernando Mañé Garzón. *Luis Pedro Lenguas (1862–1932): Maestro de cirujanos y precursor de la doctrina social católica en Uruguay*. Montevideo: El Toboso, 2005.

Zubillaga, Carlos, and Mario Cayota. *Cristianos y cambio social en el Uruguay de la modernización, 1896–1919*. Montevideo: Centro Latinoamericano de Economía Humana: Ediciones de la Banda Oriental, 1988.

JUAN MANUEL PÉREZ

NATIONAL WORKERS CONVENTION

The National Workers Convention (Convención Nacional de Trabajadores, or CNT) is a trade union umbrella organization that developed between 1964 and 1966, when its structure and program were approved. In terms of membership and years of existence, it has been the most successful Uruguayan trade union organization. Its major predecessors were the anarchist Federación Obrera Regional Uruguayana (Uruguayan Regional Labor Federation—FORU), the anarcho-syndicalist Unión Sindical Uruguaya (Uruguayan Union of Syndicates—USU), the Communist Confederación General del Trabajo del Uruguay (General Labor Confederation of Uruguay—CGTU), and the mostly Communist Unión General de Trabajadores (General Labor Union—UGT).

The CNT was established at a time of deepening social and economic problems and resulting demands for land reform, industrial planning, nationalization of key industries and the banking system, and substantial state intervention in housing, education, and social security. Following the 1973 coup d'état, the CNT was forced underground by President Juan María Bordaberry, but not before it confronted the dictatorship with a general strike that brought about the arrest, imprisonment, and exile of many union leaders.

In 1983 the regime permitted the creation of a coordinating committee, the Plenario Intersindical de Trabajadores (PIT), to prepare for a May Day demonstration. The 1984 congress of the PIT rebaptized the organization as the PIT-CNT, whose main concerns have been the recovery of real wages to predictatorship levels and the legal prosecution of human rights violations. The PIT-CNT has refused to join any of the continental trade union organizations. Its membership in 1992 was estimated at 200,000.

See also **Labor Movements.**

BIBLIOGRAPHY

Héctor Rodríguez, *Nuestros sindicatos, 1865–1965* (1965) and *Unidad sindical y huelga general* (1985).

Germán D'Elía, *El movimiento sindical* (1969).

Alfredo Errandonea and Daniel Costabile, *Sindicato y sociedad en el Uruguay* (1969).

Jorge Luis Lanzaro, *Sindicatos y sistema político: Relaciones corporativas en el Uruguay, 1940–1985* (1986).

Ruth Berins Collier and David Collier, *Shaping the Political Arena* (1991).

Additional Bibliography

Alexander, Robert Jackson, and Eldon M. Parker. *A History of Organized Labor in Uruguay and Paraguay*. Westport, CT: Praeger, 2005.

Giorgi, Alvaro de., Susana Dominzaín, and Lucía Sala de Touron. *Respuestas sindicales en Chile y Uruguay bajo las dictaduras y en los inicios de la democratización*. Montevideo: Centro de Estudios Interdisciplinarios Latinoamericanos, Facultad de Humanidades y Ciencias de la Educación, Universidad de la República, Departamento de Publicaciones, 2000.

Mantero Alvarez, Ricardo. *Historia del movimiento sindical uruguayo*. Montevideo: Fundación de Cultura Universitaria: Asociación de Bancarios del Uruguay, 2003.

Porrini, Rodolfo. *La nueva clase trabajadora uruguaya (1940–1950)*. Montevideo: Universidad de la República, Facultad de Humanidades y Ciencias de la Educación, Departamento de Publicaciones, 2005.

Rodríguez Díaz, Universindo. *El sindicalismo uruguayo: A 40 años del congreso de unificación*.Montevideo: Taurus, 2006.

DIETER SCHONEBOHM
FERNANDO FILGUEIRA

RURAL ASSOCIATION

The guild of Uruguayan landowners was founded in 1871. Although partisan political activity was not inherent in its makeup, it lobbied strongly during the dictatorship of Lorenzo Latorre and has continued to do so. In 1915 the ranchers were confronted by Batllist social reforms, and from the nucleus of the old Rural Association they created the Federación Rural. While the Association had always defined itself as a nonpolitical and nonpartisan organization, the Federation explicitly assumed a political character and adopted a platform in direct opposition to Batllist policies and reforms. The Asociación Rural was an important representative of the interests of wealthy landowners, but it lost its monopoly and hegemony to the Federación Rural, and as the twentieth century progressed, it increasingly came to represent medium and small rural producers.

See also **Batllismo.**

BIBLIOGRAPHY

José Pedro Barrán and Benjamin Nahum, *Historia rural del Uruguay moderno, 1851–1885*, vol. 1 (1967).

Enrique Méndez Vives, *El Uruguay de la modernización*, vol. 5 (1977).

Additional Bibliography

Cancela Vilanova, Walter, Alicia Melgar and Verónica Camacho Durán. *El Uruguay rural cuarenta años de evolución, cambios y permanencias*. Montevideo: CLAEH, 2004.

Moraes, María Inés. *Bella Unión: De la estancia tradicional a la agricultura moderna, 1853–1965*. Montevideo: Centro de Investigaciones Económicas: Ediciones de la Banda Oriental, 1990.

FERNANDO FILGUEIRA

WORKERS' INTERUNION PLENARY-NATIONAL WORKERS' ASSEMBLY

Uruguay's union confederation resulted from the merger of the names of the historical Convención Nacional de Trabajadores and the Plenario Intersindical de Trabajadores. The PIT came to public light through the demonstrations of 1 May 1983, and from then on was a fundamental force in the democratic movement, organizing demonstrations and general strikes that helped legitimize the opposition and erode the military regime. Toward the end of the regime in 1984, the PIT was renamed PIT-CNT, confirming its historical roots in the CNT, which had never been questioned. During the first democratic administration, it adopted a profile less radical than the one it had before 1973. While maintaining its radical rhetoric, it became highly conciliatory in practice.

See also **Labor Movements.**

BIBLIOGRAPHY

Martin Weinstein, *Uruguay: Democracy at the Crossroads* (1988).

Fernando Filgueira, "El movimiento sindical en la encrucijada: Restauración y transformación democrática," in *Revista Uruguaya de Ciencia Política*, no. 4 (1991): 67–82.

Charles Gillespie, *Negotiating Democracy* (1991).

Additional Bibliography

Alexander, Robert Jackson, and Eldon M. Parker. *A History of Organized Labor in Uruguay and Paraguay*. Westport, CT: Praeger, 2005.

Rodríguez, Roger, and Jorge Chagas. *Del PIT al PIT-CNT: Réquiem para el movimiento sindical?* Montevideo: Instituto de Formación e Invetigación Sindical: Centro de Apoyo y Asesoramiento Sindical, 1991.

FERNANDO FILGUEIRA

URUGUAY, PLEBISCITES. There have been four plebiscites (1951, 1966, 1980, 1989) in Uruguay since World War II. The plebiscite of 25 November 1951—the last Sunday in November, which is the traditional date for elections in Uruguay—approved the Constitution of 1952. This Constitution abolished the presidential system and gave Uruguay a collegial executive, known as the Colegiado, consisting of nine members. The 27 November 1966 plebiscite marked the abandonment of Uruguay's experiment with the *colegiado* by approving the 1966 Constitution, which returned Uruguay to a presidential system.

The 30 November 1980 plebiscite was an attempt by Uruguay's military government to "constitutionalize" the armed forces' control of the government. Its proposed constitution called for the creation of a National Security Council (COSENA) that would be dominated by the military and exercise a virtual veto power over executive-branch decisions. An interim president would serve for five years. In addition, the constitutional project called for an automatic majority for the winning party in the legislative.

The traditional parties (Blancos and Colorados) were given little or no opportunity to campaign for a "no" vote, and the Left remained banned. The official and progovernment media campaigned for a "yes" vote, arguing that this was the only way to get the military back to the barracks. The military expected to win, just as Augusto Pinochet had in Chile only a few months earlier, but the proposed constitution was defeated by a 58 to 42 percent vote. This vote was a strategic defeat for the dictatorship. It let average citizens know that they were not alone in the opposition to the seven-year-old dictatorship. The military's defeat in the 1980 plebiscite began a process that led to the November 1984 elections and the restoration of constitutional democracy.

The 16 April 1989 plebiscite was held to determine whether a law granting amnesty to the military would be repealed. The so-called Law on the Expiration of the Punitive Power of the State had been passed in December 1986 to avoid a crisis with the military, which stated that it would not honor subpoenas to testify in civilian trials concerning human-rights abuses during its nearly twelve years in power. Under Uruguay's constitution, any law can be overturned by plebiscite if 25 percent of all eligible voters sign a petition to hold such a referendum. Most observers doubted that the anti-amnesty forces could collect the nearly 550,000 signatures that would be necessary, especially with pleas from the government against the idea and veiled threats from the armed forces. Nevertheless, 635,000 signatures were presented to the Electoral Court, which then took more than a year to verify the signatures, a task that required the last-minute in-person verification of some 20,000 Uruguayans.

During the referendum campaign the Julio María Sanguinetti government and most politicians in the Blanco and Colorado parties supported a vote to uphold the amnesty law. Most of the Left, the labor unions, church and human-rights groups, and a few centrist politicians supported the repeal of the law. In an outstanding example of democracy in action, the Uruguayan people voted on 16 April 1989. The amnesty law was upheld by 57 to 43 percent. The vote to overturn the amnesty carried in Montevideo, where almost half the population lives, but was quite poor in the much more conservative interior of the country. The vote was seen as a victory for the Sanguinetti administration, but the Colorado Party lost some goodwill in the process, which contributed to its defeat in the November elections.

See also **Uruguay, Constitutions.**

BIBLIOGRAPHY

Luis E. González, "Uruguay, 1980–1981: An Unexpected Opening," in *Latin American Research Review* 18, no. 3 (1983): 63–76.

Martin Weinstein, "Consolidating Democracy in Uruguay: The Sea Change of the 1989 Elections" (Bildner Center for Western Hemisphere Studies of the Graduate Center of the City University of New York, Working Paper Series, 1990).

Lawrence Wechsler, *A Miracle, a Universe: Settling Accounts with Torturers* (1990).

Additional Bibliography

Brito, Alexandra Barahona de. *Human Rights and Democratization in Latin America: Uruguay and Chile.* Oxford: Oxford University Press, 1997.

Nahum, Benjamín. *El Uruguay del siglo XX.* Montevideo, Uruguay: Ediciones de la Banda Oriental, 2001.

MARTIN WEINSTEIN

URUGUAY, POLITICAL PARTIES

This entry includes the following articles:
ANTICOLEGIALISTAS
BLANCO PARTY
BROAD FRONT
CHRISTIAN DEMOCRATIC PARTY (PDC)
COLORADO PARTY
COMMUNIST PARTY
SOCIALIST PARTY
UNITY AND REFORM

ANTICOLEGIALISTAS

The anticolegialistas were a group of politicians within the Colorado Party of José Batlle y Ordóñez who were opposed to his 1913 proposal for the creation of a *colegiado* (collegial executive system) to replace the president. Under Batlle's proposal a nine-member council would take over the executive function. More conservative than Batlle and led by his former interior minister, Pedro Manini Ríos, the *anticolegialistas,* who called themselves *riveristas,* formed a splinter party in 1916 known as the Riverista Colorado Party.

Although ostensibly opposed to the *colegiado* because they thought it would make for a cumbersome and inefficient executive, the *anticolegialistas* were opposed to many of the liberal reforms and the progressive social agenda pushed by Batlle. When the *anticolegialistas* received a majority in the elections to the 1916 constitutional convention, Batlle was forced to compromise on his proposal. Thus, the 1919 Constitution created a bicephalous executive, with a president who was responsible for foreign affairs and security matters and a nine-member National Council of Administration that was responsible for all other state activities.

See also **Uruguay, Colegiado.**

BIBLIOGRAPHY

Philip B. Taylor, Jr., *Government and Politics of Uruguay* (1960).

Milton Vanger, *The Model Country: José Batlle y Ordóñez of Uruguay, 1907–1915* (1980).

Additional Bibliography

Caetano, Gerardo. *La república conservadora, 1916–1929.* Uruguay: Editorial Fin de Siglo, 1992.

Devoto, Fernando and Marcela P Ferrari. *La construcción de las democracias rioplatenses: Proyectos institucionales y prácticas políticas, 1900–1930.* Buenos Aires: Editorial Biblos, Universidad Nacional de Mar del Plata, 1994.

MARTIN WEINSTEIN

BLANCO PARTY

The Blanco Party, also known as the Partido Nacional, is one of the two traditional political parties in Uruguay. It came together under Manuel Oribe, the second president of the country (1835–1838), in his struggles against Fructuoso Rivera, the country's first president (1830–1835), who represented the Colorados. The Blanco Party represented the more conservative forces of the country. The nineteenth century was plagued with conflicts between these two political parties, which often led to civil war. The first conflict began in 1836, when Rivera rose against Oribe. An agreement was reached by the two groups after the Blanco revolution of 1897, led by the half-Brazilian gaucho Aparicio Saravia. Under the terms of the agreement, the Blancos were given control of six of the nineteen departments and minority representation in Congress.

When José Batlle y Ordóñez became president in 1903, the country was still divided from the civil war, with the Colorados controlling thirteen departments and the Blancos controlling six, acting mostly on their own, with Montevideo unable to reach them and bring them into line with the rest of the country. Both sides were very distrustful of each other. In January 1904 war broke out once again. The Blancos, led by Saravia, fought for eight months, until Saravia himself was killed in battle. After Saravia's death Blanco resistance collapsed, and an agreement was reached. The Blancos lost control over the six departments. A new electoral law, although endorsing the principle of proportional representation (a major point of the peace agreement after the first Saravia revolution), in fact practically did away with it, leaving the Colorados in complete control of the country.

Following the defeat suffered in the 1904 civil war, the Blanco Party began to reorganize itself into a modern political party and to accentuate its differences with the Colorados. Its main political aims were those of Saravia: the secret ballot and proportional representation. This transformation was accomplished through the leadership of Luis

Alberto de Herrera, who controlled the party from 1920 to 1959. But the party was divided, despite Herrera, between the conservative Herreristas and more progressive forces, such as the Unión Blanca Democrática.

In 1958, for the first time in ninety-three years, the Blancos won the national elections, and they did so again in 1962. The first period of Blanco domination (1959–1963) was controlled by the Herreristas, and the second one (1963–1967) was dominated by the UBD faction. Blanco success was the result of a combination of factors, such as economic problems in the country; urban terrorism; accusations of graft, corruption, and incompetence against the Colorados; and the divisions that plagued the Colorados. After the death of Herrera in 1959, Benito Nardone assumed leadership of the party. He was as vigorous as Herrera. Subsequently, the Blancos fared no better than the Colorados. They had to face the economic situation left by the Colorados and instituted an austerity program. As a result of these policies they antagonized labor. In 1971 the Blanco candidate, Wilson Ferreira Aldunate, received more votes than the Colorado candidate but lost the election because of the complicated *lema* system of voting, which combined primary elections and general elections in one ballot. The military overthrew the elected regime in 1973 and held power until 1984. With the return of democratic governance, the Blancos have continued to be an important electoral competitor. In 1990 the Blanco candidate, Luis Alberto Lacalle Herrera, won the presidency, but lost to the Colorados in 1994. Both the Colorados and the Blancos lost to the leftist coalition called Broad Front, which won the presidency in 2004.

See also **Batlle y Ordóñez, José; Herrera, Luis Alberto de; Nardone, Benito; Oribe, Manuel; Rivera, Fructuoso; Saravia, Aparicio; Uruguay, Political Parties: Colorado Party.**

BIBLIOGRAPHY

Baltasar L. Mezzera, *Blancos y Coloradose* (1952).

Russell H. Fitzgibbon, *Uruguay: Portrait of a Democracy* (1954).

Julio List Clericetti, *Historia politica uruguaya, 1938–1972* (1984).

Gerardo Caetano et al., *De la tradición a la crisis: Pasado y presente de nuestro sistema de partidos* (1985).

Additional Bibliography

Costa Bonino, Luis. *La crisis del sistema político uruguayo: Partidos políticos y democracia hasta 1973.* Montevideo: Fundación de Cultura Universitaria, 1995.

Crespo Martínez, Ismael. *Tres décadas de política uruguaya: Crisis, restauración y transformación del sistema de partidos.* Madrid: Centro de Investigaciones Sociológicas: Siglo Veintinuo de España, 2002.

Pelúas, Daniel. *Coparticipación y coalición: 164 años de acuerdo entre Blancos y Colorados.* Montevideo: Arca: Humus, 2000.

Sosnowski, Saúl, and Louise B. Popkin, eds. *Repression, Exile, and Democracy: Uruguayan Culture.* Durham, NC: Duke University Press, 1993.

JUAN MANUEL PÉREZ

BROAD FRONT

A coalition of the Uruguayan Left that was formed in March 1971, the Broad Front (Frente Amplio) united the country's traditional Left (Communists and Socialists), the Christian Democrats, the new radical Left, and splinters of the traditional parties, such as Alba Roballo and Zelmar Michelini, with his List 99 from the Colorado Party, and Enrique Erro and Francisco Rodríguez Camusso from the Blanco (National) Party. The Frente was the culmination of the strategy of popular fronts that had been embraced by much of the Left in Latin America in the 1970s. In Uruguay, some earlier attempts were the Leftist Freedom Front (Frente Izquierda de Liberación—FIDEL) put forth by the Communist Party and the Popular Union, which united the Socialists and the Blanco splinter group led by Erro. The Frente Amplio arose during a convulsive period in Uruguayan political history that was characterized by crises in the traditional parties, left-wing radicalism in the unions, and the appearance of an urban guerrilla movement. In the elections of 1971, the Frente won 18.3 percent of the vote.

With the coup d'état in 1973, the Frente was outlawed, and its leaders were jailed, persecuted, and sent into exile. Working in secret or from abroad, they developed strategies to oppose the dictatorship, and by the end of the dictatorship the Frente Amplio had become a key negotiator. Legalized once again for the 1984 elections, it won 21.3 percent of the vote. When its more moderate factions—List 99 and the Christian Democrats—were excised, the coalition showed that it had attained its own identity, one that went beyond the groups that composed it.

In 1989 it had its first victory in the capital, electing the Socialist Tabaré Vázquez to the municipal administration of Montevideo, and it demonstrated that it remained a significant force nationally, winning 21.2 percent of the overall vote. In the twenty-first century, Broad Front firmly established its presence winning in 2004 the presidency under Tabaré Vázquez.

See also **Erro, Enrique; Michelini, Zelmar; Vazquez, Tabare.**

BIBLIOGRAPHY

Carlos Real De Azúa, "Política, poder y partidos en el Uruguay de hoy," in Luis Benvenuto et al., *Uruguay Hoy* (1971).

Carlos Zubillaga and Romeo Pérez, "Los partidos políticos, in *El Uruguay de nuestro tiempo* (1983).

Miguel Aguirre, *El Frente Amplio* (1985).

Gerardo Caetano et al., *De la tradición a la crisis: Pasado y presente de nuestro sistema de partidos* (1985).

Luis E. González, *Political Structures and Democracy in Uruguay* (1991).

Additional Bibliography

Lanzaro, Jorge Luis, Daniel Buquet, and Alfonso Castiglia. *La izquierda uruguaya entre la oposición y el gobierno.* Montevideo: Editorial Fin de Siglo, 2004.

Yaffé, Jaime. *Al centro y adentro la renovación de la izquierda y el triunfo del Frente Amplio en Uruguay.* Montevideo: Linardi y Risso, 2005.

FERNANDO FILGUEIRA

CHRISTIAN DEMOCRATIC PARTY (PDC)

The first Catholic organization to act politically in Uruguay appeared in 1910 under the name Catholic Union. In 1919 it won its first parliamentary seat and declared the founding of the Civic Union. Although it carried little weight electorally (3 to 5 percent) through the twentieth century, it did undergo important transformations in the 1950s and 1960s. In 1962, for example, one of its leaders, Juan Pablo Terra, transformed the Civic Union into the Christian Democratic Party, assuming the fundamental theses of progressive Social Christianity and of Christian Democrats internationally. In 1971 the party joined the Frente Amplio (FA), aligning itself with the Uruguayan Left. This caused conservatives in the party to split off and found the Union of Radical Christians. The Christian Democratic Party left the FA following the coup d'état of 1973, but rejoined in 1984. Juan Pablo Terra did not agree with the decision to rejoin the FA and distanced himself from the party. After poor returns in the elections of 1985, the party entered a period of crisis and strategic redefinition. The result was another distancing from the FA in order to present itself in the elections of 1989. The Christian Democrats joined another center-left coalition, the New Space, a social-democratic group. Later the Christian Democratic Party, along with the New Space group, again merged with the FA. In the 2004 elections the FA candidate Tabaré Ramón Vázquez Rosas won the presidency.

See also **Catholic Church: The Modern Period; Uruguay, Political Parties: Broad Front.**

BIBLIOGRAPHY

Carlos Real De Azúa, "Política, poder y partidos en el Uruguay de hoy," in Luis Benvenuto et al., *Uruguay Hoy* (1971).

Gerardo Caetano et al., *De la tradición a la crisis: Pasado y presente de nuestro sistema de partidos* (1985).

Additional Bibliography

Appratto, Carmen. *El Uruguay de la dictadura (1973–1985).* Montevideo: Ediciones de la Banda Oriental, 2004.

Costa Bonino, Luis. *La crisis del sistema político uruguayo: Partidos políticos y democracia hasta 1973.* Montevideo: Fundación de Cultura Universitaria, 1995.

Crespo Martínez, Ismael. *Tres décadas de política uruguaya: Crisis, restauración y transformación del sistema de partidos.* Madrid: Centro de Investigaciones Sociológicas, Siglo Veintinuo de España, 2002.

Narbondo, Pedro, et al., eds. *Uruguay: la reforma del Estado y las políticas públicas en la democracia restaurada, 1985–2000.* Montevideo: Ediciones de la Banda Oriental: Instituto de Ciencia Política, 2002.

Sosnowski, Saúl, and Louise B. Popkin, eds. *Repression, Exile, and Democracy: Uruguayan Culture.* Translated by Louise B. Popkin. Durham, NC: Duke University Press, 1993.

FERNANDO LÓPEZ D'ALESSANDRO

COLORADO PARTY

The Colorado Party is one of the two traditional political parties in Uruguay. It developed around the country's first president, Fructuoso Rivera. The name Colorado, or red, derived from the color of the ribbons the soldiers wore in battle. The Colorado Party found itself in constant struggles with its more conservative opponent, the Blanco Party, for much of the nineteenth century. These struggles often led to civil war.

The Colorado Party has dominated the presidency almost uninterruptedly since independence. Only in the periods 1835–1838 and 1959–1967 were the Colorados not in power. The Colorados have tended to represent the urban middle class, while the conservative Blancos have rural support. And although the Colorados have dominated the presidency, they have had to make occasional concessions to the Blancos in order to govern. The party began to acquire the form of a true political organization under the leadership of José Batlle y Ordóñez, who was elected president in 1903. In his two administrations (1903–1907, 1911–1915), Batlle introduced radical sociopolitical reforms that made Uruguay a model of democracy as well as a model of a welfare state.

The period 1919–1933 was one of high prosperity, and the three Colorado administrations experienced few problems in governing the country, but divisions within the party did appear, particularly over Batlle's reforms. Aside from the Batllistas, which represented the largest faction, others appeared, such as one opposed to the *colegialismo* (a collegial executive for the nation) imposed by Batlle and several following individual leaders. The death of Batlle in 1929 accelerated the divisions within the party. Batlle's reforms did not satisfy everyone. Those on the left thought his reforms had not gone far enough, focusing particularly on his failure to subdivide the great estates for the small farmers. On the other hand, the reforms antagonized the conservatives because they required state intervention in the economy. In 1930, the conservative Colorado Gabriel Terra was elected. He faced strong opposition from within his own party and from the Blancos, but was able to strike a compromise with the Blanco leader Luis Alberto de Herrera. Still, his position was precarious. In 1933, he established dictatorial rule, abolished Batlle's *colegiado* system, and concentrated the executive power in the presidency. In 1938, the *colegiado* was revived by Alfredo Baldomir, and in 1951, during Andrés Martínez Trueba's presidency, a plebiscite approved the *colegiado* as the only executive body.

From the 1940s on, the two main factions within the party have been the Lista 14, representing

colegialistas, and the Lista 15, representing *presidencialistas.* As a consequence of its internal divisions, the party lost control of the national council from 1959 to 1967. After that time, the Colorados regained the presidency once again, but the 1960s were a period of turmoil, exemplified by the terrorist organization the Tupamaros and by economic problems. In 1966, a major reorganization of the political system abolished the *colegiado* system, and a five-year presidency was established. President Juan María Bordaberry, elected in 1971, dissolved Congress in 1973 under pressure from the army, which had been playing an important role in civilian affairs since it began fighting terrorism. The army removed Bordaberry in 1976 and remained in control until 1984, when the country returned to civilian rule. Although dominant during the twentieth century, the Colorados have become much weaker. The party's presidential candidate gained only 10.4 percent of the vote in the 2004 elections.

See also **Baldomir, Alfredo; Batlle y Ordóñez, José; Bordaberry, Juan María; Herrera, Luis Alberto de; Rivera, Fructuoso; Terra, Gabriel; Uruguay, Political Parties: Blanco Party; Uruguay, Political Parties: Broad Front.**

BIBLIOGRAPHY

Baltasar L. Mezzera, *Blancos y Colorados* (1952).

Russelll H. Fitzgibbon, *Uruguay: Portrait of a Democracy* (1954).

Julio Lista Clericetti, *Historia política uruguaya, 1938–1972* (1984).

Gerardo Caetano et al., *De la tradición a la crisis: Pasado y presente de nuestro sistema de partidos* (1985).

Additional Bibliography

Costa Bonino, Luis. *La crisis del sistema político uruguayo: Partidos políticos y democracia hasta 1973.* Montevideo: Fundación de Cultura Universitaria, 1995.

Crespo Martínez, Ismael. *Tres décadas de política uruguaya: Crisis, restauración y transformación del sistema de partidos.* Madrid: Centro de Investigaciones Sociológicas, Siglo Veintinuo de España, 2002.

Mallo, Susana, Rafael Paternain, and Miguel Angel Serna. *Modernidad y poder en el Río de la Plata: Colorados y Radicales.* Montevideo: Editorial Trazas, 1995.

Pelúas, Daniel. *Coparticipación y coalición: 164 años de acuerdo entre Blancos y Colorados.* Montevideo: Arca, Humus, 2000.

Sosnowski, Saúl, and Louise B. Popkin, eds. *Repression, Exile, and Democracy: Uruguayan Culture.* Translated by Louise B. Popkin. Durham, NC: Duke University Press, 1993.

JUAN MANUEL PÉREZ

COMMUNIST PARTY

Founded 18 April 1921, by a majority within the Socialist Party, the Uruguayan Communist Party joined the Communist International in 1922. Its first years were characterized by such extreme radicalism that it had to be disciplined by the International. Toward the end of the 1920s, under the leadership of Eugenio Gómez, the party adopted the views of Stalinism. During this period it occupied, along with the rest of the Left, a marginal position in electoral politics, while making some advances in the area of unionism. As part of the de-Stalinization process, Gómez was expelled from the party in 1955 and replaced as its leader by Rodney Arismendi. With this change of direction, Uruguayan Communists reevaluated the role of democracy and set their sights on the creation of popular fronts. Their first such effort was the Leftist Freedom Front (FIDEL) of the 1960s. By the end of the 1960s, Communism was hegemonic in the Left in both the political and union arenas. During this period an armed wing was created as a contingency against a coup d'état.

In 1971 the party was a founding member of the Frente Amplio, the most important leftist coalition in the history of the country. When the first signs of the impending coup appeared, the Communists supported the military's declarations, which contained shades of progressivism similar to those of Velasco Alvarado in Peru. The conservative and authoritarian nature of the June 1973 coup, however, placed the Communists in opposition to the new military regime. From 1973 until the end of the dictatorship, the Communists suffered systematic persecution by the military government. The party was legalized by the democratic government in 1985 and in 1986 it began adjusting to perestroika in the Soviet Union. In 1989, after the best electoral results in its history (about 10 percent of the vote) and Arismendi's death, the Communist Party entered an internal crisis, finally splitting into two factions: the *renovadores* (renovators), which included all of its legislators, and the *históricos* (traditionalists), which retained the majority in the party and therefore its structure. Despite this internal crisis, the Communist Party has remained active under the leadership of Arismendi's daughter, Ana Marina Arismendi Dubinsky. For the 2004 election, the party joined the Frente Amplio (FA), and Arismendi became minister of social development in the new government.

See also **Arismendi, Rodney; Communism; Gómez, Eugenio.**

BIBLIOGRAPHY

Carlos Real De Azúa, "Política, poder y partidos en el Uruguay de hoy," in Luis Benvenuto et al., *Uruguay Hoy* (1971).

Gerardo Caetano et al., *De la tradición a la crisis: Pasado y presente de nuestro sistema de partidos* (1985).

Fernando López D'alessandro, *Historia de la Izquierda Uruguaya,* vol. 3, *La fundación del Partido Comunista y la división del anarquismo* (1992).

Additional Bibliography

Caetano, Gerardo, Javier Gallardo, and José Pedro Rilla. *La izquierda uruguaya: Tradición, innovación y política.* Montevideo: Trilce, 1995.

Crespo Martínez, Ismael. *Tres décadas de política uruguaya: Crisis, restauración y transformación del sistema de partidos.* Madrid: Centro de Investigaciones Sociológicas, Siglo Veintinuo de España, 2002.

Pérez, Jaime. *El ocaso y la esperanza.* Montevideo: Editorial Fin de Siglo, 1996.

Sosnowski, Saúl, and Louise B. Popkin, eds. *Repression, Exile, and Democracy: Uruguayan Culture.* Translated by Louise B. Popkin. Durham, NC: Duke University Press, 1993.

FERNANDO LÓPEZ D'ALESSANDRO

SOCIALIST PARTY

The first guilds and associations with Marxist orientations appeared in Uruguay at the end of the nineteenth century. In 1901, with some support from progressive Masons, they ran in municipal elections and were defeated. In 1904, Emilio Frugoni attempted to organize the Socialists in support of Batllismo and electoral collaboration, but this plan failed. The Socialist Party was formed on 12 December 1910 with the intention of participating in elections, and a seat was finally won.

Uruguayan socialism arose as a radical response to Batllist social reform. This is in part why the majority of the PS formed the Communist Party in 1921. With this split, the Socialists lost their parliamentary representation until 1928, and they developed a more Western and reformist stance under the direction of Frugoni. In the mid-1950s a new generation of militants encouraged an ideological redefinition that radicalized the PS into a revolutionary and anti-imperialist body. In 1962, with factions that had split from the National Party, the Socialists ran in elections as part of the Popular Union, but the attempt failed roundly. Frugoni distanced himself from the party permanently. At the same time, young militants began to develop a clandestine armed wing, which, after its separation from the party, gave rise to the National Liberation Movement, or Tupamaros.

The Socialist Party was outlawed in 1967, then legalized again in 1971, when it became a founding member of the Frente Amplio and won a parliamentary seat. In 1972 it assumed a Marxist-Leninist ideological stance, which it renounced in 1985. The party was outlawed along with the rest of the Left following the 1973 coup d'état, and it remained so until 1984, when it was formally incorporated into the negotiations for the movement toward democracy. In 1989, the successful Frente Amplio candidate for mayor of Montevideo was the Socialist Tabaré Vázquez. The Socialist Party has continued its relationship with the Frente Amplio. In 2004 the alliance won the presidential campaign, and the leader of the party, Reinaldo Gargano, became minister of foreign relations.

See also **Batllismo; Frugoni, Emilio; Masonic Orders; Uruguay, National Liberation Movement (MLN-T).**

BIBLIOGRAPHY

Carlos Real De Azúa, "Política, poder y partidos en el Uruguay de Hoy," in Luis Benvenuto et al., *Uruguay Hoy* (1971).

Gerardo Caetano et al., *De la tradición a la crisis: Pasado y presente de nuestro sistema de partidos* (1985).

Fernando López D'alessandro, *Historia de la Izquierda Uruguaya*, 3 vols. (1988–1992).

Additional Bibliography

Caetano, Gerardo, Javier Gallardo, and José Pedro Rilla. *La izquierda uruguaya: Tradición, innovación y política.* Montevideo: Trilce, 1995.

Crespo Martínez, Ismael. *Tres décadas de política uruguaya: Crisis, restauración y transformación del sistema de partidos.* Madrid: Centro de Investigaciones Sociológicas, Siglo Veintinuo de España, 2002.

Sosnowski, Saúl, and Louise B. Popkin, eds. *Repression, Exile, and Democracy: Uruguayan Culture.* Translated by Louise B. Popkin. Durham, NC: Duke University Press, 1993.

Vescovi, Rodrigo. *Ecos revolucionarios: Luchadores sociales, Uruguay, 1969–1973.* Barcelona: Nóos Editorial, 2003.

FERNANDO LÓPEZ D'ALESSANDRO

UNITY AND REFORM

The designation Unity and Reform was taken by the old List 15 of the Batllist faction of the Uruguayan Colorado Party, founded by President Luis Batlle Berres between 1952 and 1954. When Batlle Berres died in 1964 his son, Jorge Batlle, assumed the directorship of the faction. But Batlle Berre's death precipitated a crisis over who would lead List 15. During the elections of 1966, List 15 began to designate itself as "Unity and Reform," alluding both to the necessity of overcoming political factionalism and to Batlle's project of reinstating the presidency and doing away with the Colegiado. The Colorado Party won the election, and the referendum reinstating the presidency was approved. Paradoxically, the candidate to triumph within the Colorado Party was not Batlle, but rather General Oscar Gestido. The descendants of List 15 later abandoned the designation Unity and Reform and adopted the term Radical Batllismo.

See also **Batllismo.**

BIBLIOGRAPHY

Angel Cocchi, *Nuestros partidos* (1984).

Martin Weinstein, *Uruguay: Democracy at the Crossroads* (1988).

Additional Bibliography

Costa Bonino, Luis. *La crisis del sistema político uruguayo: Partidos políticos y democracia hasta 1973.* Montevideo: Fundación de Cultura Universitaria, 1995.

Crespo Martínez, Ismael. *Tres décadas de política uruguaya: Crisis, restauración y transformación del sistema de partidos.* Madrid: Centro de Investigaciones Sociológicas: Siglo Veintinuo de España, 2002.

Mallo, Susana, Rafael Paternain and Miguel Angel Serna. *Modernidad y poder en el Río de la Plata: Colorados y Radicales.* Montevideo: Editorial Trazas, 1995.

Pelúas, Daniel. *Coparticipación y coalición: 164 años de acuerdo entre Blancos y Colorados.* Montevideo: Arca: Humus, 2000.

JOSÉ DE TORRES WILSON

URUGUAY RIVER. This important South American river, which supports fishing and tourism, flows through the territories of Brazil, Uruguay, and Argentina before it joins the Río de la Plata. With a length of 1,600 kilometers and a basin measuring 370,000 kilometers, the Uruguay River rises 1,800 meters above sea level in the Serra Peral of Brazil and, along with the Paraná River, flows into the Río de la Plata (Argentina and Uruguay). From its source to the mouth of the Piratini River, the water is not very navigable, but it is possible for mid-draft ships to navigate up to the town of Concepción del Uruguay, Argentina, and for smaller crafts to travel to the town of Concordia, Argentina. There its course is interrupted by a large waterfall, which is the site of the Uruguay-Argentine hydroelectric power plant of Salto Grande, which began operations in 1983.

The Uruguay River is the border between the Brazilian states of Rio Grande do Sul and Santa Catarina, between Argentina and Brazil, between Argentina and Uruguay, and between Brazil and Uruguay. In the first decade of the twentieth century, Uruguay's plans to install two cellulose paste production plants at Fray Bentos, across from the Argentine town of Gualeguaychú, led to a diplomatic conflict between the two nations with an uncertain outcome.

See also **Argentina, Geography; Brazil, Geography; Paraná River; Río de la Plata; Uruguay, Geography.**

BIBLIOGRAPHY

Serrano, Antonio. *Los tributarios del río Uruguay.* Buenos Aires. Imprenta de la Universidad, 1936.

VICENTE PALERMO

URUGUAY, TRUTH COMMISSIONS.
Truth commissions were established in Uruguay after Julio María Sanguinetti was inaugurated in March 1985, ending the military dictatorship that had been in power since 1972. There was no official "truth commission" with the transition from dictatorship, but two parliamentary commissions were held to investigate the fate of those who had disappeared during military rule and that of two legislators who had also vanished. The former commission was held from April to November 1985 and the latter from April 1985 to October 1987. The commissions concluded that the military had been involved in the disappearances and were guilty of crimes against humanity, respectively. However, the findings were never officially announced, provoked no significant public reaction or official response from the military, and were disqualified by the then-president.

In response, the Service for Justice and Peace (SERPAJ) and other NGOs launched the *Nunca Más* project in 1986, releasing a report on 9 March 1989. The report, which detailed the human rights violations committed by the dictatorship, never became the focus of national attention nor elicited an official response, and its launch was overshadowed by the plebiscite to overturn an amnesty law for past human rights violators. Nonetheless, the report became a bestseller in Uruguay.

An official Commission for Peace was finally established on 8 August 2000 under the presidency of Jorge Batlle to establish the fate of the 179 disappeared Uruguayans. The commission members were Archbishop Nicolás Cotugno, José D'Eiía, Luis Pérez Aguirre, José Williman, Gonzalo Fernández and Carlos Ramela. The commission released its report in April 2003, confirming that of some of the disappeared had in fact been killed by the military dictatorship.

See also **Dirty War; Uruguay: The Twentieth Century.**

BIBLIOGRAPHY

Barahona de Brito, Alexandra. *Human Rights and Democratization in Latin America: Uruguay and Chile.* Oxford: Oxford University Press, 1997.

Bergero, Adriana J. and Fernando Reati, eds. *Memoria colectiva y políticas de olvido: Argentina y Uruguay, 1970–1990.* Rosario, Argentina: Viterbo Editora, 1997.

SERPAJ. *Uruguay Nunca Más: Human Rights Violations 1972–1985.* Philadelphia: Temple University Press, 1992.

Sznajder, Mario and Luis Roniger. *The Legacy of Human Rights Violations in the Southern Cone: Argentina, Chile and Uruguay.* Oxford: Oxford University Press, 1999.

Weschler, Laurence. *A Miracle a Universe: Settling Accounts with Past Torturers.* New York: Pantheon Books, 1990.

ALEXANDRA BARAHONA DE BRITO

URVINA JADO, FRANCISCO (?–1926).

Francisco Urvina Jado, from 1902 to 1925 the director of the Banco Comercial y Agrícola, the leading financial institution of Guayaquil—the national commercial center and entrepôt for Ecuador's lucrative cacao bean export trade. Government spending relied heavily on funds borrowed from the Banco Comercial y Agrícola. Critics of this arrangement, such as the sierra (highland) businessman and politician Luis N. Dillon, claimed that the mounting debt gave the bank power to dictate terms to the government. Dillon and others believed that Director Urvina secretly ran Ecuador from behind the scenes. In 1922 Ecuador's monoculture export economy collapsed. The ensuing crisis led to public disclosure of the bank's unsound currency emissions, which had been largely necessitated by government borrowing. Urvina served as a convenient target for popular anger. Following a coup led by young military officers on 9 July 1925, the government seized the assets of the Banco Comercial y Agrícola, arrested Urvina, and sent him into exile. He died of a heart attack in Valparaiso on 20 January 1926.

See also **Alfaro Delgado, José Eloy; Banco Comercial y Agrícola (Ecuador).**

BIBLIOGRAPHY

The best treatment of fiscal and monetary issues is Linda Alexander Rodríguez, *The Search for Public Policy: Regional Politics and Government Finances in Ecuador, 1830–1940* (1985). For the broader political economic context, see Osvaldo Hurtado, *Political Power in Ecuador,* translated by Nick D. Mills, Jr. (1985). Detailed discussion of banking can be found in Julio Estrada Ycaza, *Los bancos del siglo XIX* (1976). The socioeconomic context is analyzed in the pathbreaking study by Lois Crawford De Roberts, *El Ecuador en la época cacaotera* (1980).

Additional Bibliography

Albornoz Peralta, Osvaldo. *Del crimen de El Ejido a la Revolución del 9 de Julio de 1925.* Quito: Subsecretaria de Cultura, Sistema Nacional de Bibliotecas, 1996.

Paz y Miño Cepeda, Juan J. *La Revolución Juliana: Nación, ejército y bancocracia.* Quito: Abya-Yala, 2000.

Pérez Ramírez, Gustavo. *Virgilio Guerrera: Protagonista de la Revolución Juliana, su praxis social.* Quito: Academia Nacional de la Historia, 2003.

RONN F. PINEO

URZAGASTI, JESÚS (1941–).

Jesús Urzagasti (*b.* October 1941), Bolivian poet, writer, and journalist. Urzagasti, one of the most important writers in Bolivia today, was born in Gran Chaco Province, in a small cattle-raising town, and emigrated to La Paz as a young man. Having decided to become a writer, he abandoned plans for a career in geology. He later worked for *Presencia,* a leading Bolivian newspaper.

Urzagasti's first novel, *Tirinea,* was published in 1969; next was *Cuaderno de Lilino* (1972), a book of prose dedicated to a child. *Yerubia* (1978) is his only book of poetry. *En el país del silencio* (1987), Urzagasti's major novel, deals autobiographically with three decades of historical turmoil viewed through the eyes of a narrator who has maintained a sense of solidarity with society and a perception of man's relationship with nature. *De la ventana al parque* (1992), a shorter novel, explores the possibilities of cultural survival and of communication in a country marked by cultural diversity and by verticality of power. In 1994, the University of Arkansas published an English translation of his work *En el país del silencio* under the title *In the Land of Silence.* In the early years of the twenty-first century, he served on the editorial board of the *Bolivian Research Review,* published by the Bolivian Studies Association. As the official national writer of Bolivia in 2004, he led festivities for the International Day of the Book in the capital city of Sucre.

See also **Literature: Spanish America.**

BIBLIOGRAPHY

On Urzagasti's poetry, see Blanca Wiethüchter, "A propósito de las contraliteraturas," in *Hipótesis,* no. 17 (1983), and in "Poesía boliviana contemporánea," in *Tendencias actuales en la literatura boliviana,* edited by Javier Sanjinés C. (1985). On Urzagasti's narrative, see Luis H. Antezana, "Del nomadismo: *Tirinea* de Jesús Urzagasti," in his *Ensayos y lecturas* (1986); Miembros Del Taller Hipótesis, "Dos novelistas contemporáneos: Jesús Urzagasti y Jaime Sáenz," in *Revista iberoamericana,* no. 134 (1986); Mauricio Souza, *"En el país del silencio: Lectura,"* in *El zorro Antonio,* no. 6 (1989).

Additional Bibliography

Prada, Ana Rebeca. *Viaje y narración: Las novelas de Jesús Urzagasti.* La Paz, Bolivia: Instituto de Estudios Bolivianos, Facultad de Humanidades, Universidad Mayor de San Andrés, 2002.

Rivadeneira Prada, Raúl. *Troja literaria*. La Paz, Bolivia: Ediciones Signo, 2002.

Salmón, Josefa, ed. *Construcción y poética del imaginario boliviano*. La Paz, Bolivia: Plural Editores, 2005.

ANA REBECA PRADA

USHUAIA. Ushuaia, town of 64,000 inhabitants (2005) located in a well-protected bay on the northern shore of the Beagle Channel in Argentine Tierra Del Fuego and capital of the homonymous territory. Founded in 1868 by the British missionary Thomas Bridges in his efforts to christianize and protect the Fuegino Indians in their contacts with whalers, seal hunters, and gold prospectors, it was named after the small boat with which Charles Darwin visited the bay in 1832. In 1884 the Argentine government built a village near the mission station, and in 1886 a penal colony was established to supply labor for the exploitation of the adjacent rain forest. Expansion of sheep-raising *estancias* on the flat plains of the island of Tierra del Fuego intensified the functions of Ushuaia as the main Argentine service center of the region. A strong naval detachment was established there in the early 1900s. Ushuaia, the southernmost urban area of Latin America, has been a duty-free port since 1976, enhancing its attraction for tourists who come to enjoy the alpine scenery.

See also **Argentina, Geography.**

BIBLIOGRAPHY

Ernesto J. Fitte, *Crónicas del Atlántico Sur* (Buenos Aires, 1974); Arnoldo Canclini, *Tomas Bridges: Pionero en Ushuaia* (Buenos Aires, 1980); and E. Lucas Bridges, *Uttermost Part of the Earth: Indians of Tierra del Fuego* (1988).

Additional Bibliography

Bertotto, Alejandro H. *La Ciudad de Ushuaia y su ubicación geoestratégica como "puerto de entrada a la Antárdida."* Buenos Aires: Comisión de Geopolítica del Centro de Estudios Estratégicos de la Escuela Superior de Guerra, 2001.

Lupiano, Leonardo L. *Ushuaia: Algunos aspectos del patrimonio arquitecto'nico urbano.* Buenos Aires: Ediciones Dunken, 1997.

CÉSAR N. CAVIEDES

USIGLI, RODOLFO (1905–1979). Rodolfo Usigli (*b.* 17 November 1905; *d.* 18 June 1979), Mexican writer. Born in Mexico City, Usigli was the child of European immigrants. His father died when he was young and his ambitious mother raised four children in the difficult period of the Mexican Revolution. Belonging to the lower-middle-class and suffering from extremely poor vision, Usigli was unable to finish secondary school. In spite of his lack of social status and formal education, however, by the 1940s Usigli emerged as one of the leading innovators in Mexican drama and a major advocate for the establishment of a national theatrical tradition. In his efforts to modernize Mexican dramaturgy, he frequently interpreted the symbols and historical events that contributed to the formation of a Mexican national identity. The plays *El gesticulador* (The Imposter [written 1937, staged 1947]) and *Corona de sombra* (Crown of Shadow [written 1943, staged 1947]) attest to his concern with understanding Mexico's national cultural identity. In addition to his numerous plays, Usigli also published a psychological-detective novel, *Ensayo de un crimen* (Trial Run for a Murder [1944]), which was filmed by Luis Buñuel in 1955. Besides being a dramatist, Usigli also worked as a drama historian, university teacher, and diplomat. He died in Mexico City.

See also **Theater.**

BIBLIOGRAPHY

Ramón Layera, "Rodolfo Usigli," in *Latin American Writers*, edited by Carlos A. Solé and Maria Isabel Abreu, vol. 3 (1989), pp. 1033–1042.

Aurora Ocampo, ed. "Usigli, Rodolfo," in *Diccionario de escritores mexicanos* (1967), pp. 393–395.

Additional Bibliography

Beardsell, Peter. *Teatro para caníbales: Rodolfo Usigli y el teatro mexicano.* México City: Siglo Veintiuno Editores, 2002.

Schmidhuber de la Mora, Guillermo. *Apología de Rodolfo Usigli: las polaridades usiglianas.* Guadalajara, Jalisco, Mexico: Universidad de Guadalajara, 2005.

DANNY J. ANDERSON

USLAR PIETRI, ARTURO (1906–2001). Arturo Uslar Pietri (*b.* 16 May 1906; *d.* 26 February 2001), Venezuelan writer and politician born in

Caracas. Uslar Pietri epitomizes the Latin American writer and intellectual who participates in political life. After obtaining a doctorate in political science (1929), he joined the diplomatic corps and was sent to Paris. He returned to Venezuela in 1934, and taught political economy at the Universidad Central; later he held high positions in several Venezuelan ministries and was a delegate to the League of Nations. After the government fell in 1945, Uslar Pietri went to the United States as an exile and taught at Columbia University. He returned to Venezuela in 1950, reentering political life in 1959 as a senator.

In 1969, Uslar Pietri dedicated himself more to literature and teaching. His essays and fictional works evince his interest in Venezuela's political and economic problems. Currents of democratic thought run through this concern for the national. The first volume of Uslar Pietri's ample and wide-ranging literary output, *Barrabás y otros relatos,* was published in 1928. Written in a modernist prose style, *Barrabás* introduces elements of vanguardism by developing the inner voices of the characters. His novel *Las lanzas coloradas* (1931) brought him fame and was his most important contribution to Spanish American letters. The novel's plot centers on the violence and chaos in the Venezuelan countryside resulting from the military and ideological confusion during the Wars of Independence. This work is a "novel of the land" or a "novel of national interpretation." From 1969 to 1974, he was editor of the Caracas daily newspaper *El Nacional.* From 1975 to 1979, he lived in Paris and served as the Venezuelan ambassador at UNESCO. After returning to Venezuela, he became a television star on the educational show titled *Valores humanos,* which focused on history and the arts. He was ninety-four years old when he died in Caracas on 26 February 2001.

Uslar Pietri's most important short-story collection, *Red* (1936), retains the same vanguardist elements initiated in *Barrabás,* but in this work the author shifts his attention to the vernacular life by using techniques of magical surrealism. Of this collection, "La lluvia" is considered a masterpiece of the genre. Less important works are *El camino de El dorado* (1947), a novel about the conqueror Lope de Aguirre; *El laberinto de fortuna: Un retrato en la geografía* (1962), a political work focusing on the epoch of the Juan Vincente

Gómez dictatorship (1908–1935). Essay collections include *Letras y hombres de Venezuela* (1948), *De una a otra Venezuela* (1950), *Breve historia de la novela hispanoamericana* (1954), *En busca del Nuevo Mundo* (1969), and *Bolívar Hoy* (1983). Uslar Pietri also wrote about theater in *Teatro* (1958), a work in which plays of his appear, and turned his hand to poetry in *El hombre que voy siendo* (1986).

See also **Literature: Spanish America.**

BIBLIOGRAPHY

José Luis Vivas, *La cuentística de Arturo Uslar Pietri* (1963).

Domingo Miliani, *Arturo Uslar Pietri: Renovador del cuento venezolano contemporáneo* (1965).

R. M. R. Dougherty, "The Essays of Arturo Uslar Pietri" (Ph.D. diss., University of Illinois, 1971).

John S. Brushwood, *The Spanish American Novel* (1975), pp. 88–91.

Teresita Josefina Parra, *Visión histórica en la obra de Arturo Uslar Pietri* (1979).

Additional Bibliography

Arráiz Lucca, Rafael. *Arturo Uslar Pietri, o la hipérbole del equilibrio: Biografía.* Caracas: Fundación para la Cultura Urbana, 2005.

Arráiz Lucca, Rafael. *Arturo Uslar Pietri (1906–2001).* Venezuela: Banco del Caribe, 2006.

Febres, Laura, comp. *A los amigos invisibles: Visiones de Arturo Uslar Pietri.* Caracas: Universidad Metropolitana, 2006.

Menton, Seymour. *El cuento hispanoamericano: Antología crítico-histórica.* México: Fondo de Cultura Económica, 1996.

Uslar Pietri, Arturo, and Leonor Giménez de Mendoza. *Arturo Uslar Pietri, 1906–2006.* Caracas: Fundación Polar, 2006.

JUAN CARLOS GALEANO

USPALLATA PASS. Uspallata Pass, passage connecting Mendoza in Argentina with Los Andes and Santiago in Chile. Named for the small village of Uspallata in an intermountainous depression some 140 miles west of Mendoza, the rail and motor route to Chile follows the course of the torrential Mendoza River and passes through the villages of Polvaredas and Punta de Vacas before reaching its culmination at Las

Cuevas (13,170 feet). An international railway tunnel, Cristo Redentor (Christ the Redeemer), leads from there to the Chilean side of the Andes. The Pan-American Highway runs near the pass. The motor road reaches its highest point (13,860 feet) at the foot of the Christ of the Andes monument. Inclement weather shuts down the principal cargo route between the two countries, which is also known as the Paso Libertadores and the Paso de la Cumbre.

See also **Pan-American Highway.**

CÉSAR N. CAVIEDES

USUMACINTA RIVER. Usumacinta River,

a waterway in northwestern Guatemala and southeastern Mexico. Beginning in northern Guatemala, where the Chixoy and La Pasión rivers meet, the Usumacinta flows through a sparsely populated area marking the border between Chiapas, Mexico, and Petén, Guatemala. Surrounded by tropical forest, the river cuts across the rolling limestone plateau of the Petén before entering Tabasco state. In Tabasco the waterway forms an alluvial floodplain and annually inundates large areas, creating numerous lagoons and swamps. Near Frontera, Tabasco, the Usumacinta joins the Grijalva River and flows into the Bay of Campeche. Together, the Usumacinta-Grijalva river system forms Mexico's largest watershed by volume, accounting for nearly half of the country's stream flow.

Historically, the river was a trade artery for the lowland Mayas, yet its modern use has been limited to moving logs and chicle downstream. Efforts to incorporate this peripheral area into modern Mexico have centered upon hydroelectric and flood-control projects. A large dam near Balancán, Tabasco, produces electricity and has enabled the reclamation of agricultural lands and pastures in Tabasco. Further upstream, Mexico and Guatemala have proposed a series of dams along their common border, but the project has been postponed because of costs, the possible flooding of important archaeological sites, and international pressure against developing the largest remaining rain forest in Central America.

See also **Forests; Guatemala.**

BIBLIOGRAPHY

David Barkin and Timothy King, *Regional Economic Development: The River Basin Approach in Mexico* (1970), esp. pp. 102–107.

Nancy M. Farriss, *Maya Society Under Colonial Rule: The Collective Enterprise of Survival* (1984), pp. 152–154.

Larry Rohter, "Dam Project Is Seen as a Threat to Maya Sites," *New York Times,* 26 March 1987, sec. 1, p. 13.

Additional Bibliography

McIntosh, Roderick J., and Joseph A. Tainter. *The Way the Wind Blows: Climate, History, and Human Action.* New York: Columbia University Press, 2000.

Sharer, Robert J., and Loa P. Traxler. *The Ancient Maya.* Stanford, CA: Stanford University Press, 2006.

Usumacinta sites. Albuquerque: Far Horizons, 1998.

MARIE D. PRICE

UTATLAN. Utatlan was the capital of the

Late Postclassic highland Maya K'iche' polity, also known as K'umarcaaj (its K'iche' name). The site is located west of Santa Cruz del Quiché, in the department of Quiché, Guatemala. Utatlan and the related settlements of Chisalin, Ismachi, Resguardo, and Pakaman occupy relatively inaccessible plateaus surrounded by deep ravines. Utatlan proper consists of more than seventy structures centered on a central large plaza, flanked by two temple-pyramids, a large ball court and long platforms usually interpreted as council houses. Surrounding the main plaza, dense settlements occupy all the available land. Residential compounds are disposed around patios and some may include temples and long platforms. Cut-stone masonry with stucco facing is found throughout the site. Some buildings had mural paintings in the Postclassic Mesoamerican style, evidencing the participation of the K'iche' in widespread networks of cultural interaction.

Sixteenth-century documents provide considerable information about Utatlan and its ruling houses, which traced their origins to remote regions and described long migrations passing through the legendary city of Tollan. The historical accuracy of these accounts remains controversial. Archaeological research shows that the K'iche' rose to power after 1300 CE. They established their capital at Utatlan, and grew to become a powerful center, with hegemony over an extensive region in the western highlands and Pacific coastal piedmont of Guatemala. The K'iche' kingdom was organized as a confederacy of several groups, ruled by four lords who were heads of the city's major lineages. The city of Utatlan probably functioned as the court and major military stronghold of these powerful ruling houses. At the time of the Spanish conquest, K'iche' power was rivaled by their former allies the Kaqchikel, who established their own court at the city of Iximche.

A K'iche' warrior, Tecum, the grandson of a K'iche' ruler, led a major battle against the invading Spaniards in 1524 and died in the process. The conquistador Pedro de Alvarado subsequently burned Utatlan; a new town, Santa Cruz, was established for the surviving inhabitants. K'iche' mythical origins and history were recorded in the mid-sixteenth century by members of a noble lineage, using the Spanish alphabet. Known as the *Popol Vuh*, this major literary work is a key source on the religion and mythology of the ancient Maya.

See also **Alvarado y Mesía, Pedro de; Archaeology; Iximché; Kaqchikel; K'iche'; Maya, The; Popol Vuh; Precontact History: Mesoamerica.**

BIBLIOGRAPHY

Carmack, Robert M. *The Quiché Mayas of Utatlan: The Evolution of a Highland Guatemala Kingdom.* Norman: University of Oklahoma Press, 1981.

Popol Vuh: Literal Poetic Version, transcribed and trans. Allen J. Christenson. Winchester, U.K., and New York: O Books, 2004.

Popol Vuh: The Definitive Edition of the Mayan Book of the Dawn of Life and the Glories of Gods and Kings, trans. Dennis Tedlock. New York: Simon and Schuster, 1985.

Smith, Michael E., and Francis F. Berdan, eds. *The Postclassic Mesoamerican World.* Salt Lake City: University of Utah Press, 2003.

JANINE GASCO
OSWALDO CHINCHILLA MAZARIEGOS

UXMAL. Uxmal ("thrice built") is a Maya city located in northwestern Yucatán south of the range of hills known as the Puuc. The site was occupied in the eighth century and reached its maximum florescence between about 850 and 925, shortly after which it, along with many other sites in the Puuc district, was abandoned. Epigraphic research has revealed that Uxmal was governed around 900 by a ruler, "Lord Chac," who took the name of the Yucatecan Maya rain god, and has demonstrated political contacts between Uxmal and Chichén Itzá.

Uxmal's central civic-ceremonial area is defined by a low masonry wall and covers approximately one-half mile north–south by less than one-half mile east–west, with smaller residential structures lying outside. Except for three small Chenes-style buildings, Uxmal's major edifices are superlative examples of Puuc architecture, featuring a construction technology based on lime concrete cores and fine cut-masonry facades. Long, horizontal buildings display complex arrays of precarved stone mosaic elements assembled to form motifs such as step frets, simple and sawtoothed lattices, engaged colonnettes, long-snouted "rain god" masks, and human figures.

Uxmal is known for magnificent edifices such as the Pigeon Group, named for a distinctive openwork roof comb on the structure called the House of Pigeons; the Pyramid of the Magician (or Adivino), a multistage pyramid–temple constructed in five separate campaigns; and the ball court, whose inner platform walls bore feathered serpent sculptures and hieroglyphic rings. Uxmal's most striking architectural monuments are the 328-foot-long range building, or "palace," known as the House of the Governor, perhaps "Lord Chac's" royal residence and administrative center, and the Nunnery Quadrangle, a large compound bordered on four sides by elaborately sculptured, multiroom range buildings set at different levels.

See also **Maya, the; Mesoamerica.**

BIBLIOGRAPHY

Marta Foncerrada De Molina, *La escultura arquitectónica de Uxmal* (1965).

H. E. D. Pollock, *The Puuc: An Architectural Survey of the Hill Country of Yucatán and Northern Campeche, Mexico* (1980).

Jeff Karl Kowalski, *The House of the Governor, a Maya Palace at Uxmal, Yucatán, Mexico* (1987).

Additional Bibliography

Barrera Rubio, Alfredo, and José Huchím Herrera. *Architectural Restoration at Uxmal, 1986–1987 = Restauración arquitectónica en Uxmal, 1986–1987.* Pittsburgh: University of Pittsburgh, Dept. of Anthropology, 1990.

Dunning, N.P. *Lords of the Hills: Ancient Maya Settlement in the Puuc Region, Yucatán, Mexico.* Madison, WI: Prehistory Press, 1992.

Schmidt, Peter J., Mercedes de la Garza, and Enrique Nalda, eds. *Maya.* New York: Rizzoli, 1998.

JEFF KARL KOWALSKI

VACA DE CASTRO, CRISTÓVAL

(c. 1492–1576). Cristóval Vaca de Castro (*b.* ca. 1492; *d.* after 1576), governor of Peru (1541–1544). Born in a small town (Izagre) near León, Spain, Vaca de Castro served as *oidor* (judge) of the Audiencia of Valladolid (1536). Recognizing his administrative abilities, Charles I appointed him (September 1540) for a three-year term to investigate Peru's chaotic political situation. Vaca de Castro reached Panama in January 1541, and because of difficult weather decided to travel overland rather than sail. From coastal Buenaventura in present-day Colombia, he proceeded to Cali, where he recuperated for three months from an illness. In Popayán he learned Francisco Pizarro had been assassinated and Peru was under the control of Diego de Almagro the Younger. Vaca de Castro then moved southward, collecting an army to oust Almagro.

Early in 1542 he left Quito, marched to Piura in northwest Peru, then to Trujillo, back into the highlands, then on to Huamanga. By then Vaca de Castro had the aid of Lima and letters of support from Gonzalo Pizarro in the south. Almagro had been staying in Cuzco and had been negotiating with royalists. The administration of Peru was settled on 16 September 1542 at the battle of Chupas, one of the bloodiest battles of Peru's civil wars. Almagro fled, but was soon captured. He was executed in Cuzco and buried alongside his father.

Vaca de Castro undertook to defuse Peru's turmoil by removing its cause—the large number of discontented soldiers. He supported three major expeditions: In 1543, Captain Juan de Porcel entered the Bracamoros in northwest Peru; Diego de Rojas began the exploration and settlement of the Tucumán region in present-day northwest Argentina; and Captain Juan Pérez de Vergara initiated the conquest of the Moyobamba and Rupa-Rupa in the upper jungle in 1544. A threat of a newly revived Inca state was lessened when the energetic and highly capable leader Manco Inca was assassinated by a group of Spaniards the same year.

The arrival of Peru's first viceroy, Blasco Núñez Vela, brought the end of Vaca de Castro's tenure. The viceroy was welcomed into Lima (15 May 1544) but refused to take advice from the ex-governor. Believing Vaca de Castro to be a member of a conspiracy against him, the new viceroy imprisoned the official and charged him with forcing Indians to work in the mines without salary, authorizing their employment as beasts of burden, and selling *encomiendas*. Before hearings got under way, the viceroy himself was jailed by adherents of Gonzalo Pizarro. Vaca de Castro escaped to Spain, only to face charges there. Caught between the Pizarrist and Almagrist factions at court, he found himself in jail again, in Valladolid, Arévalo, and later Simancas. It was not until 1555 that the court freed and rehabilitated him.

In 1556 he returned to the Council of Castile and in 1559 received back salary. He served on the council until his retirement in 1566. Thereafter, he lived in the convent of San Agustín in Valladolid. After his death, his remains were transferred by order of his second son,

Pedro de Castro, Archbishop of Granada, to the Colegiata del Sacro-Monte of Granada.

See also **Almagro, Diego de; Núñez Vela, Blasco.**

BIBLIOGRAPHY

Manuel De Mendiburu, *Diccionario histórico biográfico del Perú* (1935).

José Antonio Del Busto Duthurburu, *Historia general del Perú: Descubrimiento y conquista* (1978).

Additional Bibliography

García-Gallardo Carcedo, Genoveva. "Cultural Encounters: The Peruvian Artifacts Collected by Cristobal Vaca de Castro." M.A. thesis. Western Michigan University, 2004.

NOBLE DAVID COOK

VACCARO BROTHERS.

Vaccaro brothers (Joseph, Luca, and Felix), three Sicilian Americans who, with a son-in-law, Salvador D'Antoni, engaged in the produce business in New Orleans at the close of the nineteenth century. In 1899 a severe freeze destroyed their orange groves, and of necessity they began the importation of bananas from Honduras. Building railroads, wharves, and Honduras's first bank and hospital, Vaccaro Brothers and Company modernized the banana trade and became Honduras's largest investor and exporter before World War I, and second only to the older United Fruit Company in the international banana trade. The need for capital for research, and expansion to other nations, caused this family company to go public in 1925.

See also **Banana Industry; United Fruit Company.**

BIBLIOGRAPHY

Richard H. Rose, *Utilla: Past and Present* (1904); "The Story of the Standard Fruit and Steamship Company," in *New Orleans Port Record,* October 1947, p. 19.

Thomas L. Karnes, *Tropical Enterprise: The Standard Fruit and Steamship Company in Latin America* (1978).

Additional Bibliography

Díaz Chávez, Filander. *Análisis crítico de las condiciones técnicas de los ferrocarriles de la Standard Fruit Company.* Tegucigalpa, Honduras: Federación de Estudiantes Universitarios de Honduras, 1973.

Levi, Vicki Gold. *Standard Fruit and Steamship Company.* New Orleans: Standard Fruit and Steamship Company, 2003.

Ridgeway, Stan. "Monoculture, Monopoly, and the Mexican Revolution: Tomás Garrido Canabal and the Standard Fruit Company in Tobasco (1920–1935.)" *Mexican Studies* (Winter 2001): 143–169.

THOMAS L. KARNES

VALCÁRCEL ARCE, EDGAR (1932–).

Edgar Valcárcel Arce (*b.* 4 Dec. 1932), Peruvian composer. He was born in Puno and studied in Lima at the National Conservatory with Andrés Sas and at Hunter College in New York City with Donald Lybbert. With a fellowship from the Torcuato Di Tella Institute, Valcárcel studied in Buenos Aires at the Centro Latinoamericano de Altos Estudios Musicales (1963–1964). He studied there with Alberto Ginastera, director of the center, and Olivier Messiaen, Luigi Dallapiccola, Gerardo Gandini, Riccardo Malipiero, and Bruno Maderna. He was in New York City in 1966 with a Guggenheim Foundation fellowship to do graduate work on electronic music under the guidance of Vladimir Ussachevsky and Alcides Lanza. In 1986 he became a professor at the National School of Music in Lima and in 1989 the director of that institution. In 1976 he was a visiting professor of composition at the Faculty of Music, McGill University, Montreal. Valcárcel has received the National Music Prize in 1956 and 1965, the State Choir Prize in 1965, the Composition Prize of the Grand Masonic Lodge in 1971, and the Inocente Carreño Prize, Caracas, in 1981.

His principal works include *Variaciones* for piano (1963); *Espectros* no. 1 for flute, viola, and piano (1964); *Cantata para la noche inmensa* for men's choir and orchestra (1964); *Canto coral a Tupac Amaru* no. 1 for soprano, baritone, chorus, and orchestra (1968); Sonata no. 1 for piano (1965); *Dicotomías* nos. 1 and 2 for piano (1966) and no. 3 for chamber ensemble (1966); *Invención* (1966), electronic sounds; *Fisiones* for chamber ensemble (1967); *Hiwaña uru* for winds, strings, and piano (1967), in memory of Andrés Sas; Piano Concerto (1968); *Canto Coral a Tupac Amaru* no. 2 for chorus and electronic sounds on tape

(1968); *Antaras* for flute and electronic sounds (1968); *Checán* no. 1 for flute, oboe, clarinet, bassoon, horn, and piano (1969), no. 2 for orchestra (1970), and no. 3 for nineteen instruments (1971); Sonata no. 2 for piano (1971); *Karabotasat Cutintapata* for orchestra (1977); *Zampoña sónica* for flute and tape (1976); *Retablo* no. 2 (*Flor de Sancayo*) for piano and electronic sounds (1975); *Antimemorias* no. 2 for orchestra (1980); *Checán* no. 4 for choir (1981); *Homenaje a Stravinsky* for two pianos, flute, French horn and percussion (1982); *Andahuaylillas* for organ (1983); *Concierto para guitarra y orquesta* (1984); and *A Theodoro* for soprano and three French horns (1986). In 2007, he was a judge for the Premio de Compsición Casa de las Americas.

See also **Music: Art Music.**

BIBLIOGRAPHY

Compositores de America 17 (1971):113–120.

John Vinton, ed., *Dictionary of Contemporary Music* (1974), p. 790.

Gérard Béhague, *Music in Latin America: An Introduction* (1979), pp. 313–314; *Octavo festival internacional de música contemporánea* (1992), pp. 29, 83, 119–120.

ALCIDES LANZA

VALDÉS, GABRIEL DE LA CONCEPCIÓN (1809–1844).

Gabriel de la Concepción Valdés (pseud. Plácido; *b.* 18 March 1809; *d.* 26 June 1844), Cuban poet. Plácido, the pseudonym he adopted and through which he became known, was born in Havana, the illegitimate son of a mulatto hairdresser and a Spanish dancer. Shortly after birth he was left at a home for illegitimate childen, but when he was a few months old, he was retrieved by his father's family, who raised him. He received no schooling until the age of ten, and then his education was haphazard, as was his lifelong economic situation (he was occasionally jailed for indebtedness).

Plácido's poetic talent did not earn him money—he worked as a silversmith and a maker of tortoiseshell combs—but it earned him the admiration of the established poets of the day, including José María Heredia. His ability to improvise verse on the spot for various occasions spread his fame and created a great demand for his attendance at all manner of social activities. Eventually his popularity came to be his undoing, however, as the Spanish authorities became suspicious of his active social life and arrested him for conspiracy. Although there was then as later no evidence of his participation in any conspiracy, he was shot by a firing squad in Matanzas. Thus martyred, he became a symbol of the cause of independence.

Plácido's poetry incorporates into traditional Spanish lyrical forms tropical imagery and the romantic themes of intense pathos and the urge for freedom. Although Plácido is not considered a poet of the first rank, many of his poems are recited by heart by Cubans of all ages and have come to form part of popular folklore.

See also **Heredia y Heredia, José M.**

BIBLIOGRAPHY

Frederick S. Stimson, *Cuba's Romantic Poet: The Story of Plácido* (1964).

Additional Bibliography

Batista, José Manuel. "Exposing the Specter of Universality in Early Afro-Hispanic Poetry and the Poetics of its Major "White" Practitioners." Ph.D. diss. University of Georgia, 2003.

Fischer, Sibylle. *Modernity Disavowed: Haiti and the Cultures of Slavery in the Age of Revolution.* Durham, NC: Duke University Press, 2004.

Pérez del Ríío, Luis, and Adis Vilorio Iglesias. *Es falsa la confesión de Plácido?* Santiago, Cuba: Editorial Oriente, 1994.

ROBERTO VALERO

VALDÉS CASTILLO, GERMÁN. *See* Tin-Tan.

VALDÉZ, JUAN.

Juan Valdéz, fictitious Colombian coffee grower, created in 1959 by the National Coffee Growers Federation of Colombia for its advertising campaigns in the United States. Valdéz and his donkey have proven remarkably durable in both print and electronic advertising; a stylized logo was introduced in 1981, and mere invocation of his name is considered sufficient in recent campaigns. Valdéz does not figure in Colombian domestic advertising (where individual brands, rather than the federation, are in control), but his name is familiar to Colombians, who consider him a caricature for foreign consumption, albeit a positive one. While the Valdéz image of a grower lovingly scrutinizing each coffee bean is, to put it mildly, idealized—the western Colombian coffee harvest is a fast-paced affair increasingly reliant upon tens of thousands of migrant wage-laborers—it does suggest the continuing predominance of independent small- and medium-sized producers in Colombia, as opposed to the larger agribusiness-style operations that characterize Brazil. In 2003 Colombian coffee growers banded together under the Colombian Coffee Federation to promote upscale Colombian coffee at home and abroad. They revived the Juan Valdéz logo and opened Juan Valdéz coffee shops throughout Colombia. The stores netted $708,000 in sales in their first year of operation. In 2004 the growers opened Juan Valdéz gourmet coffee shops around the world. These were stocked with coffee and gift items.

See also **Coffee Industry; Colombia, Organizations: National Federation of Coffee Growers.**

BIBLIOGRAPHY

Additional Bibliography

Bergquist, Charles W. *Coffee and Conflict in Colombia, 1886–1910.* Durham, NC: Duke University Press, 1978.

Cuellar Boada, Fidel H. *El crédito cafetero en Colombia: Economía, instituciónes, y política, 1920–2002.* Bogota: Universidad Nacional de Colombia, 2004.

Rincón García, John Jairo. *Trabajo, territorio, y política: Expresiones regionales de la crisis cafetera, 1990–2002.* Medellin, Colombia: La Carreta Editores, 2006.

Roseberry, William, and Lowell Gudmundson, eds. *Coffee, Society, and Power in Latin America.* Baltimore, MD: Johns Hopkins University Press, 1995.

RICHARD J. STOLLER

VALDEZ, LUIS (1940–). Luis Valdez is a playwright and screenwriter born in Delano, California. A central figure in Chicano theater and film, Valdez has brought an awareness of the Chicano struggle to the community itself and to U.S. society as a whole. In 1965 he founded El Teatro Campesino to support César Chávez and the United Farm Workers in the grape strike in California. This theater was the beginning of the development of Chicano theater. In the 1980s Valdez sought to educate mainstream audiences with his play and movie *Zoot Suit* (1981) and the movie *La Bamba* (1987) about the life of rock-and-roll performer Ritchie Valens.

See also **Hispanics in the United States; Theater; United Farm Workers Union.**

BIBLIOGRAPHY

Broyles-Gonzáles, Yolanda. *El Teatro Campesino: Theater in the Chicano Movement.* Austin: University of Texas Press, 1994.

Elam, Harry J., Jr. *Taking It to the Streets: The Social Protest Theater of Luis Valdez and Amiri Baraka.* Ann Arbor: University of Michigan Press, 1997.

Valdez, Luis. *Zoot Suit and Other Plays.* Houston, TX: Arte Público Press, 1992.

Valdez, Luis. *Luis Valdez—Early Works: Actos, Bernabé, and Pensamiento Serpentino.* Houston, TX: Arte Público Press, 1994.

Xavier, Roy Eric. "Politics and Chicano Culture: Luis Valdez and El Teatro Campesino, 1964–1990." In *Chicano Politics and Society in the Late Twentieth Century,* edited by David Montejano. Austin: University of Texas Press, 1999.

MARK A. HERNÁNDEZ

VALDIVIA, LUIS DE (1561–1642). Luis de Valdivia (*b.* 1561; *d.* 5 November 1642), Spanish Jesuit who spent much of his life in Chile defending and protecting the rights of Indians. In 1589, shortly after entering the Society of Jesus, Valdivia was assigned to the province of Peru, where he remained until 1593, when he was assigned to Chile. There he dedicated himself to Christianizing and protecting the Indians against the Spaniards, for which he gained many enemies.

Valdivia believed that waging war on the Indians to subjugate and Christianize them was not morally right. The Indians were free beings and had control over their lives; therefore, they should become Christians or crown subjects of their own free will. At the insistence of the viceroy of Peru, the count of Montesclaros, Valdivia went to Spain in

1609 to inform the crown about the conditions in the region and the efforts to pacify it. He was heard by the Council of the Indies, and after about a year and a half, on 8 December 1610, a royal *cédula* (decree) ordered a change from offensive to defensive methods in the war against the Indians of Chile. In 1611 he went back to Chile, where he gained many more enemies as a result of the new policy. His enemies tried to thwart his efforts by complaining to royal officials and even to the crown. But a *cédula* of 21 November 1615 reiterated the policy. In 1620 Valdivia returned to Spain permanently.

See also **Las Casas, Bartolomé de; Missions: Jesuit Missions (Reducciones).**

BIBLIOGRAPHY

Beatrice Blum, "Luis de Valdivia, Defender of the Araucanians," in *Mid-America: An Historical Review* 24, no. 2 (1942): 109–137.

José Armando De Ramón Folch, *El pensamiento político social del Padre Luis de Valdivia* (1961).

Additional Bibliography

Ablard, Jonathan David. "Luis de Valdivia and Defensive War on the Chilean Frontier." M.A. thesis. University of Virginia, 1994.

Kosel, Ana Carina. "Los sermones de Valdivia: Distribución de lugares, didáctica y poleémica en un testimonio del choque de dos culturas." *Anuario de Estudios Americanos* 54:1 (January–June 1997): 229–244.

JUAN MANUEL PÉREZ

Equestrian statue of Pedro de Valdivia in Plaza de Armas, Santiago, Chile. PHOTOGRAPH BY SUSAN D. ROCK. REPRODUCED BY PERMISSION

VALDIVIA, PEDRO DE (c. 1500–1553). Pedro de Valdivia (*b.* c. 1500; *d.* 1553), Spanish conquistador and founder of Chile. Before undertaking the expedition to Chile, Valdivia had already acquired extensive military experience. He entered the army in 1521, participated in the Spanish campaigns in Flanders and Italy, and fought in the battle of Pavia (24 February 1525). He returned to Spain and married Marina Ortíz de Gaete, a native of Salamanca. The sources available contain conflicting information about this union. Some sources say that he was married before the Italian campaigns, while others say he married after. From 1525, when he was in Milan, to 1535, when he embarked on his voyage to the New World, not much is known about his life.

Valdivia probably sailed for Venezuela in an expedition led by Jerónimo de Alderete. He remained in Venezuela for a year or a year and a half, another period in his life for which there is not too much information. He then went to Peru as a member of an expedition to help Francisco Pizarro suppress an Indian rebellion led by Manco Capac. His experience in the military served him well, and in 1537, Pizarro named him his aide-de-camp. Valdivia gained a reputation as a brave soldier in the war between Pizarro and Diego de Almagro. He and Gonzalo Pizarro led the infantry against the forces of Almagro in the decisive battle of Salinas on 6 April 1538. As a reward for his services, Francisco Pizarro granted Valdivia an *encomienda* in the valley of La Canela.

Valdivia, however, was a man of adventure, and he asked permission from Pizarro to go to Chile, despite the fact that Almagro had gone before and had come back disappointed because he had not found gold. To finance his expedition, Valdivia sold his lands. In the middle of January 1540, he left for Chile from Cuzco accompanied by twelve Spaniards; one woman, Inés de Suárez (who later became the second of four significant women in Valdivia's life); about one thousand Indians; and a few black slaves. Others joined him as he moved on to Chile. Late in 1540, Valdivia reached the Copiapó Valley and called the new land Nueva Extremadura. He moved farther south to Coquimbo and then to the Mapocho Valley, and on 24 February 1541, near the Mapocho River, Valdivia founded Santiago del Nuevo Extremo, present-day Santiago.

The city endured an Indian siege while Valdivia was absent, and the Spaniards suffered many hardships because reinforcements and supplies did not arrive until two years later, in 1543. With more men and supplies, Valdivia continued exploring and in 1544 founded La Serena, halfway between the Copiapó Valley and Santiago. In 1545, he went further south to Quilacura, and at the same time, his lieutenants were exploring other areas.

In 1547, Valdivia left for Peru with the intention of getting more supplies and found himself in the middle of a rebellion led by Gonzalo Pizarro. He sided with the crown's *visitador*, Pedro de Lagasca, and became an important factor in Pizarro's defeat. He returned to Chile on 21 January 1549, after being cleared by Lagasca of accusations leveled against him by his enemies. Once in Chile, Valdivia continued his explorations and founded more cities: Concepción (1550), Valdivia (1552), and Villarica (1552). He died in 1553 in a battle against the Araucanians led by Lautaro.

Valdivia symbolizes the spirit of the conquistadores in his desire for adventure and his drive to explore new lands. He resembles, for example, Alvar Núñez Cabeza De Vaca, Vasco Núñez de Balboa, and Hernando de Soto, men who were driven more by the spirit of adventure than by the hope of finding gold.

See also **Explorers and Exploration: Spanish America.**

BIBLIOGRAPHY

Francisco Esteve Barba, *Descubrimiento y conquista de Chile* (1946).

Jaime Delgado, *Pedro de Valdivia* (1987).

Carmen Pumar Martínez, *Pedro de Valdivia: Fundador de Chile* (1988).

Ida Stevenson Weldon Vernon, *Pedro de Valdivia: Conquistador of Chile* (1946).

Additional Bibliography

Cordero, María de Jesús. *The Transformations of Araucania from Valdivia's Letters to Vivar's Chronicle.* New York: P. Lang, 2001.

Larraín Valdés, Gerardo. *Pedro de Valdivia: Biografía.* Santiago, Chile: Editorial Luxemburgo, 1996.

Nauman, Ann K. *The Career of Doña Inés de Suárez: The First European Woman in Chile.* Lewiston, NY: Edwin Mellen Press, 2000.

JUAN MANUEL PÉREZ

VALDIVIA, CHILE. Valdivia, capital city of the Lake Region in southern Chile (2002 population 127,750), located on the lower Valdivia River. Founded by Pedro de Valdivia in 1552 almost in the middle of Araucanian (mapuche) Indian territory, it was an isolated Spanish enclave in hostile territory during most of the colonial period. In spite of repeated sieges, it was never overrun by the Indians. After independence it was the only part of the Lake Region securely held by the Chileans, and it was chosen as the center of the colonization efforts destined to weaken the southern flank of Araucania. Between 1849 and 1880, numerous German and Swiss families settled in the intermediate depression between the Andes and the Coastal Range, cleared the forests, and started farming and logging enterprises. German colonists established breweries, lumber industries, leather manufactures, and small shipyards that fostered a period of prosperity during the first half of the twentieth century. From Valdivia colonization efforts spread to Osorno, Frutillar, Río Bueno, and Puerto Varas. When industries began to concentrate in Central Chile, Valdivia stagnated, and the powerful earthquake of May 1960 (at 9.5 considered one of world's greatest ever recorded) and the subsequent tsunami inflicted serious damage to the decaying city, changing even the flows of rivers. The presence of cultural establishments such as the University of Valdivia aided in the slow recovery.

See also **Chile, Geography; Earthquakes.**

BIBLIOGRAPHY

Gabriel Guarda, *La toma de Valdivia* (Santiago, 1970).

Additional Bibliography

Cordero, María de Jesús Cordero. *The Transformations of Araucania from Valdivia's Letters to Vivar's Chronicle.* New York: Peter Lang, 2001.

CÉSAR N. CAVIEDES

VALDIVIA CULTURE. Valdivia Culture is the name given to the prehistoric culture that occupied the Pacific coastal lowlands of Ecuador during the Early Formative period (4400–1600 BCE). It was identified at the type site of Valdivia in coastal Guayas province by the Ecuadoran Emilio Estrada, and subsequently investigated by the archaeologists Betty Meggers and Clifford Evans in the late 1950s. Valdivia culture was thought by those scholars to represent an egalitarian, semisedentary littoral adaptation based upon fishing and shellfish gathering, with only rudimentary reliance on horticulture. Its unique ceramic style and "Venus" figurine tradition were originally thought to be the earliest in the New World, and their origins were attributed to diffusionary trans-Pacific voyaging by Neolithic Jomon fishermen from Japan.

More recent research at other important coastal sites such as San Pablo, Real Alto, and Salango, as well as inland sites such as Loma Alta, Colimes, and San Lorenzo del Mate, has promoted considerable rethinking of the nature of Valdivia Culture, its origins, economic base, settlement organization, and cosmological beliefs. The archaeologist Donald Lathrap has forcefully argued that Valdivia represents a "tropical forest culture" having a fundamentally riverine settlement focus, whose ultimate origins can be traced to early population dispersals from the Amazon Basin. Newer subsistence data indicate a mixed economy of flood plain horticultural production (based on maize, beans, manioc, *achira* and other root crops, chili pepper, cotton, and gourds), hunting, fishing, and the gathering of wild plants and shellfish. Certain coastal settlements, such as the type site, are viewed as having specialized in the exploitation of maritime and estuarine resources and traded these products for food crops with inland agricultural communities.

These studies have shed new light on Valdivia chronology and the pace of social change during its 2,000-year time span. An eight-phase ceramic sequence established by Betsy Hill has permitted a more precise delineation of temporal trends in settlement pattern and internal site layout. Large-scale excavations at village sites such as Real Alto and Loma Alta in Guayas province have permitted detailed reconstruction of Valdivia households, community patterning, social organization, burial practices, and ceremonial behavior, all of which underwent significant changes between phases 1 and 8. As a result, it is now clear that Valdivia represents a dynamic, fully sedentary society of village horticulturalists, characterized by progressive demographic growth, household expansion from nuclear to extended family dwellings, and an increasing degree of social ranking and status inequality through time. Beginning as early as Middle Valdivia times, mortuary evidence suggests the establishment of hereditary social status accorded to senior females. Long-distance maritime trade with the complex societies of coastal Peru at this time may have provided an impetus for social change leading to greater complexity in the later Valdivia phases.

There is also evidence of a progressive geographic expansion of Valdivia communities to the north and south out of the Guayas province heartland. Beginning in Middle Valdivia times (phase 3), when settlements appeared on the offshore islands of La Plata and Puná, this outward expansion culminated in Terminal Valdivia times (phase 8), when large inland ceremonial centers with satellite communities appeared in the wetter environments to the north and south. Both the San Isidro site in northern Manabí and the La Emerenciana site in El Oro represent phase 8 ceremonial centers with monumental public architecture of a magnitude not seen in previous Valdivia phases.

See also **Archaeology; Indigenous Peoples; Real Alto; Valdivia, Ecuador.**

BIBLIOGRAPHY

Chandler-Ezell, Karol, Deborah M. Pearsall, and James A. Zeidler. "Root and Tuber Phytoliths and Starch Grains Document Manioc (Manihot esculenta), Arrowroot (Maranta arundinacea), and Llerén (Calathea sp.) at the Real Alto Site, Ecuador." *Economic Botany* 60, no. 2 (2006): 103–120.

Estrada, Emilio. *Valdivia: Un sitio arqueológico formativo en la Provincia del Guayas, Ecuador.* Guayaquil, Ecuador: Museo Víctor Emilio Estrada, 1956.

Hill, Betsy D. "A New Chronology of the Valdivia Ceramic Complex from the Coastal Zone of Guayas Province, Ecuador." *Ñawpa Pacha* 10–12 (1972–1974): 1–32.

Lathrap, Donald W. *Ancient Ecuador: Culture, Clay, and Creativity, 3000–300 B.C.* Chicago: Field Museum of Natural History, 1975.

Lathrap, Donald W., Jorge G. Marcos, and James A. Zeidler. "Real Alto: An Ancient Ceremonial Center." *Archaeology* 30, no. 1 (1977): 2–13.

Marcos, Jorge G. *Real Alto: La historia de un centro ceremonial Valdivia.* 2 vols. Guayaquil, Ecuador: Escuela Politécnica del Litoral, Centro de Estudios Arqueológicos y Antropológicos; Quito, Ecuador: Corporación Editora Nacional, 1988.

Marcos, Jorge G. *Los pueblos navegantes del Ecuador prehispánico.* Quito, Ecuador: Ediciones Abya-Yala, 2005.

Meggers, Betty J. *Ecuador.* New York: Praeger; London: Thames and Hudson, 1966.

Meggers, Betty J., Clifford Evans, and Emilio Estrada. *Early Formative Period of Coastal Ecuador: The Valdivia and Machalilla Phases.* Washington, DC: Smithsonian Institution, 1965.

Pearsall, Deborah M., Karol Chandler-Ezell, and James A. Zeidler. "Maize in Ancient Ecuador: Results of Residue Analysis of Stone Tools from the Real Alto Site." *Journal of Archaeological Science* 31, no. 4 (April 2004): 423–442.

Perry, Linda et al. "Starch Fossils and the Domestication and Dispersal of Chili Peppers (Capsicum spp. L.) in the Americas." *Science* 315, no. 5814 (16 February 2007): 986–988.

Raymond, Scott. "Ceremonialism in the Early Formative of Ecuador." *Senri Ethnological Studies* 37 (1993): 25–43.

Staller, John E. "Late Valdivia Occupation in Southern Coastal El Oro Province, Ecuador: Excavations at the Early Formative Period (3500–1500 BC) Site of La Emerenciana." Ph.D. diss., Southern Methodist University, 1994.

Staller, John E. "Figurinas Valdivia VII–VIII del sitio San Lorenzo del Mate, provincia del Guayas, y la Transición Valdivia-Machalilla." *Miscelánea Antropológica Ecuatoriana* 9 (2000): 99–133.

Zeidler, James A. "Maritime Exchange in the Early Formative Period of Coastal Ecuador: Geopolitical Origins of Uneven Development." *Research in Economic Anthropology* 13 (1991): 247–268.

Zeidler, James A. "Cosmology and Community Plan in Early Formative Ecuador: Some Lessons from Tropical Ethnoastronomy." *Journal of the Steward Anthropological Society* 26, nos. 1–2 (1998): 37–68.

Zeidler, James A. "Gender, Status, and Community in Early Formative Valdivia Society." In *The Archaeology of Communities: A New World Perspective*, edited by Marcello A. Canuto and Jason Yaeger. London and New York: Routledge, 2000.

Zeidler, James A., Peter Stahl, and Marie J. Sutliff. "Shamanistic Elements in a Terminal Valdivia Burial, Northern Manabí, Ecuador: Implications for Mortuary Symbolism and Social Ranking." In *Recent Advances in the Archaeology of the Northern Andes: Essays in Honor of Gerardo Reichel-Dolmatoff*, edited by Augusto Oyuela-Caycedo and J. Scott Raymond. Los Angeles: Cotsen Institute of Archaeology, University of California, Los Angeles, 1998.

JAMES A. ZEIDLER

VALDIVIA, ECUADOR.

VALDIVIA, ECUADOR. Valdivia, archaeological site in coastal Guayas Province, Ecuador. Valdivia is where the Early Formative Valdivia Culture was first defined by Ecuadoran Emilio Estrada in the mid-1950s and subsequently investigated by the Smithsonian archaeologists Clifford Evans and Betty Meggers. The site (G-31) is at the mouth of the Valdivia River valley. Cultural refuse of the Valdivia occupation covers some 4.2 acres on the slope and basal portion of a low spur. The deposits are deepest in the basal sector of the site, where a later Guangala occupation of smaller size overlies the Valdivia deposits. Deep excavations conducted here in 1961 yielded abundant remains of Valdivia pottery, chipped stone artifacts, fire-modified rock, fish and animal bones, and shell. No visible stratigraphy was recognized during excavation, however, and no archaeological features were identified.

The unique ceramic materials and associated radiocarbon dates recovered at Valdivia allowed the investigators to establish a four-phase ceramic sequence (labeled A through D) thought to reflect gradual developmental change through time. At the time, the basal materials were thought to represent the earliest pottery in the New World. Its relative sophistication raised the question of origins and led the investigators to hypothesize a trans-Pacific diffusion of this pottery tradition in the latter half of the third millennium BCE from the Neolithic Jomon culture of Japan, a position that Meggers still strongly defends. This argument was subsequently challenged by a number of scholars on multiple grounds, not least of which was the discovery in the 1970s of very early Valdivia deposits and associated ceramics that predated phase A at Loma Alta, a village site located on alluvial bottomland some 6 miles up the Valdivia Valley as well as at other large village sites such as Real Alto. The latter finds constituted another ceramic "phase" in the emerging eight-phase chronology of Betsy Hill, the chronology that most Valdivia scholars use today.

The littoral location of the site, and its obvious reliance on marine and estuarine subsistence resources, led the investigators to characterize Valdivia culture as a semisedentary maritime adaptation of egalitarian fishermen and shellfish gatherers having only a marginal reliance on horticulture. In reality, this characterization pertains only to smaller beach-front sites, such as G-31, which appear to have specialized in the exploitation of littoral resources. Subsequent archaeological survey of the entire Valdivia valley has revealed that such shoreline settlements formed one component of a more complex regional settlement system that involved the exchange of maritime resources with large inland farming villages such as Loma Alta for horticultural produce and terrestrial game resources.

In spite of their problematic interpretations of Valdivia culture, the pioneering work of Meggers, Evans, and Estrada at site G-31 stands as a landmark in South American archaeology.

See also **Archaeology; Real Alto; Valdivia Culture.**

BIBLIOGRAPHY

Emilio Estrada, *Valdivia: Un sitio arqueológico formativo en la provincia del Guayas, Ecuador* (1956).

Betty J. Meggers, *Ecuador* (1966).

Henning Bischof and Julio Viteri Gamboa, "Pre-Valdivia Occupations on the Southwest Coast of Ecuador," in *American Antiquity* 37, no. 4 (1972): 548–551.

Donald W. Lathrap et al., *Ancient Ecuador: Culture, Clay, and Creativity, 3000–300 B.C.* (1975).

Additional Bibliography

Hill, Betsy D. "A New Chronology of the Valdivia Ceramic Complex from the Coastal Zone of Guayas Province, Ecuador." *Ñawpa Pacha* 10–12 (1972–1974): 1–32.

Marcos, Jorge G. *Los pueblos navegantes del Ecuador prehispánico.* Quito, Ecuador: Abya-Yala, ESPOL, 2005.

Meggers, Betty J., Clifford Evans, and Emilio Estrada. *Early Formative Period of Coastal Ecuador: The Valdivia and Machalilla Phases.* Washington, DC: Smithsonian Institution, 1965.

Meggers, Betty J. "La cerámica temprana en América del Sur: ¿Invención o difusión?" *Revista de Arqueología Americana* 13 (1997): 7–40.

Raymond, J. Scott. "Social Formations in the Western Lowlands of Ecuador during the Early Formative." In *Archaeology of Formative Ecuador*, edited by J. Scott Raymond and Richard L. Burger, 33–67. Washington, DC: Dumbarton Oaks Research Library and Collection, 2003.

James A. Zeidler

VALENCIA, ANTONIO MARÍA (1902–1952). Antonio María Valencia (*b.* 10 November 1902; *d.* 22 July 1952), Colombian composer, pianist, and teacher. Born in Cali, Valencia began his musical studies with his father, cellist and teacher Julio Valencia Belmonte. Later he entered the Bogotá Conservatory (1917–1919) to study piano with Honorio Alarcón. After concert tours in the southern United States, Valencia moved to Paris and enrolled at the Schola Cantorum (1923–1929), where he studied under Vincent d'Indy (composition), Paul Braud (piano), Paul le Flem (counterpoint and fugue), Louis Saint-Requier (harmony and conducting of vocal and instrumental groups), Gabriel Pierné (chamber music) and Manuel de Falla (orchestration). He was offered a professorship, but at the end of his studies he returned to Colombia, where he gave concerts and pursued a career in composition. His early works show an affinity for national music, though his Paris training later led to a concentration on European forms. In his last years, Valencia returned to the melodies and rhythms of his homeland.

Valencia wrote a considerable number of choral religious works demonstrating a solid technique and exceptional use of counterpoint, as, for example, in his *Requiem Mass* (1943). Among his chamber music works are *Duo en forma de sonata* (1926), for piano and violin; *Emociones caucanas* (1938), for violin, piano, and cello; songs on French texts; and many piano pieces. He composed *Chirimía y bambuco sotareño* (1942) for orchestra and wrote orchestrations and arrangements of French music. Valencia founded the Conservatory and School of Fine Arts of Cali (1933), remaining as its director until his death. He was also director of the Bogotá Conservatory (1937–1938). He died in Cali.

See also **Music: Art Music.**

BIBLIOGRAPHY

Composers of the Americas, vol. 4 (1958), pp. 105–110.

Gérard Béhague, *Music in Latin America* (1979); *New Grove Dictionary of Music and Musicians,* vol. 19 (1980).

Additional Bibliography

Senn, Martha, and Pablo Arévalo. *Grandes poetas, grandes compositors, grandes melodies de la canción colombiana.* Bogotá: Fondo Financiero de Proyectos FONADE, 1998.

SUSANA SALGADO

VALENCIA, GUILLERMO LEÓN

(1909–1971). Guillermo León Valencia (*b.* 27 April 1909; *d.* 4 November 1971), president of Colombia (1962–1966). The son of Guillermo Valencia, a celebrated poet and Conservative political leader, Valencia was born in Popayán and studied law at the University of Cauca. Serving in the senate and in the Conservative Party leadership, he became known as a flamboyant orator and impassioned follower of Conservative chieftain Laureano Gómez (president, 1950–1953), who appointed him ambassador to Spain in 1950. Later he moderated his partisanship and distanced himself from Gómez. He was an outspoken critic of President Gustavo Rojas Pinilla (1953–1957). An order (1 May 1957) that Valencia be placed under house arrest sparked a wave of civic unrest that ended the Rojas regime nine days later. Valencia was slated to be the first presidential candidate of the Frente Nacional (National Front), but he was blackballed by Gómez. Instead, he became the National Front nominee in 1962, winning 62.1 percent of the vote.

As president, Valencia continued many of the policies of his predecessor, Alberto Lleras Camargo (1958–1962), though he is usually considered a less competent chief executive. During his administration the armed forces smashed communist-influenced "republics" in central and southern Colombia. In 1964, however, surviving militants founded a southern guerrilla bloc that became the forerunner of the Fuerzas Armadas Revolucionarias Colombianas (Colombian Revolutionary Armed Force—FARC). Valencia also confronted economic difficulties, notably a fall in coffee prices, balance of payments problems, depreciation of the *peso,* and inflation. Opposition to a new sales tax led to a threatened general strike in January 1965, which was averted partly because of government concessions. Criticism of the government by Minister of War General Alberto Ruiz Novoa, who harbored political ambitions, heightened tensions until he was removed in January 1965. After retiring from the presidency in 1966, Valencia again served as ambassador to Spain.

See also **Colombia, Political Parties: Conservative Party; Gómez Castro, Laureano.**

BIBLIOGRAPHY

Jonathan Hartlyn, *The Politics of Coalition Rule in Colombia* (1988), esp. pp. 120–124.

Additional Bibliography

Sáenz Rovner, Eduardo. *Colombia años 50: Industriales, política y diplomacia.* Bogotá: Universidad Nacional de Colombia, Sede Bogotá, 2002.

Téllez, Edgar, and Alvaro Sánchez. *Ruidos de sables.* Bogotá, Colombia: Planeta, 2003.

HELEN DELPAR

VALENTIM, MESTRE. *See* **Fonseca e Silva, Valentim da.**

VALENZUELA, FERNANDO (1960–).

Fernando Anguamea Valenzuela was one of the leading pitchers in major league baseball in the 1980s and was among the most popular players, especially among people of Mexican heritage, of his era.

Born in Navoja, Sonora, Mexico on November 1, 1960, the youngest of seven children, Valenzuela grew up in an impoverished village. He was taught baseball by his older brothers. His talent as an amateur pitcher drew professional scouts and he signed to play in the Mexican Central League in 1978. One year later, the Los Angeles Dodgers bought his contract and assigned him to their minor league system. At the end of the 1980 season he debuted with the big club and pitched 17 2/3 scoreless innings.

In 1981 he startled the baseball world when, after being named the opening day starter, he won eight consecutive games at the start of the season and triggered a cultural euphoria in Los Angeles and elsewhere that the press dubbed "Fernandomania." Following a 13-7 record in that strike-shortened season, he was voted Rookie of the Year and won the National League's Cy Young Award, the first rookie ever to win it. He capped his success with a complete-game World Series victory over the New York Yankees.

Valenzuela, whose polite demeanor and unorthodox windup won him the affection of fans throughout the nation, went on to be on to be one of the leading pitchers of the 1980s. His best season was 1986 when he led the National League with 21 wins and 20 complete games. In 1990 he threw a no-hitter against the St. Louis Cardinals.

Valenzuela retired from the game in 1997. In 2005 he was named by Major League Baseball as a member of the Latino Legends Team.

See also **Sports.**

BIBLIOGRAPHY

Littwin, Mike. *Fernando!* Toronto and New York: Bantam, 1981.

Regalado, Samuel O. *Viva Baseball! Latin Major Leaguers and their Special Hunger.* Urbana: University of Illinois Press, 1998.

Wendel, Tim. *The New Face of Baseball: The One-Hundred-Year Rise and Triumph of Latinos in America's Favorite Sport.* New York: Rayo, 2003.

SAMUEL O. REGALADO

VALENZUELA, LUISA (1938–).

Luisa Valenzuela (*b.* 26 November 1938), Argentine writer. The daughter of Argentine writer Luisa Mercedes Levinson, Valenzuela was born in Buenos Aires and grew up in Corrientes and Buenos Aires, which provided settings for her later fiction. She began her writing career as a journalist for the newspaper *La Nación* and published her first short story at age seventeen. Between 1956 and 1961 she lived in France, where she wrote her first novel, which was published in 1966. But it was with the publication of *Hay que sonreír* (One Has to Smile, 1966) and a collection of short stories, *Los heréticos* (1967), that she was recognized as a promising young writer. In 1969 she won a Fulbright scholarship to participate in the International Writers Workshop at the University of Iowa, where she wrote *El gato eficaz* (1972), a novel in which language rather than characters is the central concern. Later, she traveled throughout Mexico and became interested in Mexican indigenous cultures. She used some of these experiences in writing the stories in *Donde viven las águilas* (Where Eagles Live, 1983). During 1972 Valenzuela lived in Barcelona, where she wrote *Como en la guerra* (1977). This novel also centers on language and surrealistic experiences.

Returning to Argentina, Valenzuela wrote *Aquí pasan cosas raras* (Strange Things Happen Here, 1975). When she felt that the military government threatened her well-being, she moved to New York City. During her sojourn in the United States, some of her works were translated into English. She was featured in popular magazines like *Time* side-by-side with other well-known Latin American writers, and in 1986 the *Review of Contemporary Fiction*, a scholarly journal published in the United States, dedicated an issue to Valenzuela's fiction. *El libro que no muerde* (1980) and *Cambio de armas* (Other Weapons, 1982) were written during this time. The latter is a collection of five lengthy short stories in which Valenzuela's fiction reaches depth and maturity, where female and male sexuality represents the warped and misunderstood relationship between men and women, who are witness to the disintegration of a reality in which they are victims and victimizers.

In 1983 Valenzuela went back to Argentina, where she published a novel on the political manipulations and sorceries of José López Rega, a picturesque and macabre member of the cabinet of the last Peronist regime, titled *Cola de lagartija*. Two subsequent novels also deal with Argentina's reality, *Novela negra con argentinos* (Gothic Novel with Argentines, 1990) and *Realidad nacional desde la cama* (National Reality from the Bed, 1990). In 1991, the Brazilian Academy of Letters awarded her the Machado de Assis medal. In 2001, she published *La traviesa, Peligrosas palabras* and *Los deseos oscuros y los otros. Cuadernos de Nueva York*. A general anthology of her work, *Trilogía de los bajos fondos* appeared in 2004. She has resided in Buenos Aires since 1989.

See also **Levinson, Luisa Mercedes.**

BIBLIOGRAPHY

Sharon Magnarelli, *Reflections/Refractions: Reading Luisa Valenzuela* (1988).

Victoria Guest, *Reweaving the Violated Narrative* (1990).

Juanamaría Cordones-Cook, *Poética de transgresión en la novelística de Luisa Valenzuela* (1991).

Additional Bibliography

Bilbija, Ksenija. *Yo soy trampa: Ensayos sobre la obra de Luisa Valenzuela*. Buenos Aires: Feminaria Editora, 2003.

Craig, Linda. *Juan Carlos Onetti, Manuel Puig and Luisa Valenzuela: Marginality and Gender*. Rochester, NY: Tamesis, 2005.

Medeiros Lichem, María Teresa. *La voz femenina en la narrativa latinoamericana: Una relectura crítica*. Santiago, Chile: Editorial Cuartopropio, 2006.

MAGDALENA GARCÍA PINTO

VALERO, ROBERTO (1955–1994).

Roberto Valero (*b*. 27 May 1955; *d*. 23 September 1994), Cuban writer. Born in the city of Matanzas, Cuba, Valero studied at the University of Havana (1975–1980). In 1980 he joined the approximately 10,800 Cubans who entered the Peruvian Embassy asking for political asylum, and left the island with the Mariel Boatlift. Valero received a Ph.D. in literature from Georgetown University in 1988 and taught both there and at the George Washington University. During his years in Washington he wrote acclaimed books of poetry, such as *Desde un oscuro ángulo* (From a Dark Corner) in 1981 and *En fin, la noche* (At Last the Night) in 1984. At the time of his death, Valero had published extensively, had gained wide recognition for his poetry, and had been honored with several prestigious literary awards. His highly lyrical work is marked by a search for the spiritual and a preoccupation with death and man's relationship to God. In addition to his poetic output, Valero also published a novel, *Este viento de cuaresma* (This Lenten Wind) a finalist for Spain's Nadal Prize in 1989, and a book of literary criticism, *The Forlorn Humor of Reinaldo Arenas* (1991) for which he received the Letras de Oro award in 1989. Valero's other poetic works include *Dharma* (1985), *Venías* (You Came) (1990), and *No estaré en tu camino* (I Will Not Be in Your Way), a finalist for the Adonais Prize in 1991. He was an editor of the art and literature journal *Mariel*. Valero died in Washington, D.C.

See also **Hispanics in the United States; Muriel Boatlift.**

BIBLIOGRAPHY

Reinaldo Arenas, "El Ángulo se ilumina," in Arenas, *Desde un oscuro ángulo* (n.d., ca. 1982), pp. 7–9.

Eduardo Lolo, "Otra vez el día," in *Círculo: Revista de Cultura* 21 (1992): 133–140.

Additional Bibliography

Lauret, Mari. *La odisea del Mariel (un testimonio sobre el éxodo y los sucesos de la embajada de Perú en La Habana*. Madrid: Betania, 2005.

MARÍA BADÍAS GEORGETTE MAGASSY DORN

VALLADARES, ARMANDO (1937–).

Armando Valladares (*b*. 30 May 1937), Cuban poet and prose writer. Valladares was born in Pinar del Río Province. In 1961, while employed by the revolutionary government on the staff of the Cuban postal service, he was arrested and accused of being a counterrevolutionary. After refusing to participate in the government's "rehabilitation" program, he was subjected to severe beatings, torture, forced labor, and twenty-two years of confinement. While in prison he began to write poetry, which he smuggled out of the country in many ingenious ways. His wife, Martha, fought relentlessly to bring international attention to his case, and when his poetry gained recognition outside of Cuba, he became a symbol of the struggle against human rights abuses in that country. When at last Valladares's case was taken up by Amnesty International, which once made him its prisoner of the year, it attracted worldwide attention, dealing a severe blow to the Cuban government's image abroad.

After his release in 1982, Valladares continued to decry the abuses he saw and suffered while in prison in Cuba, and in 1985 he published a memoir of the ordeal, *Contra toda esperanza* (*Against All Hope*), his best-known work, which became a best-seller. Direct and unpretentious, his poetry is permeated by genuine anguish and the desire to end cruelty. Another work by Valladares is *El corazón en que vivo* (*The Heart in which I Live*, 1980). He served for a time as U.S. ambassador for human rights to the United Nations. After the 2001 incident involving seven-year-old Cuban refugee Elian Gonzalez, Valladares updated and re-released his memoir, *Against All Hope*, that year in order to include a commentary on what Elian's future would be like if he were indeed repatriated to Cuba. As of 2007, he was president of the Valladares Project, an international nonprofit organization that protects the rights of children. He was also chairman of the International Council of the Human Rights Foundation, based in New York.

See also **Literature: Spanish America.**

BIBLIOGRAPHY

Britt Arenander, *Fallet Valladares* (1981).

Additional Bibliography

Foss, Clive. *Fidel Castro.* Stroud, U.K.: Sutton, 2006.

Jolis, Alan. "A Cuban Solzenitsyn Cries Out against a Tropical Gulag." *Wall Street Journal,* December 28, 1990.

Latell, Brian. *After Fidel: The Inside Story of Castro's Regime and Cuba's Next Leader.* New York: Palgrave Macmillan, 2005.

ROBERTO VALERO

VALLADARES, JOSÉ ANTÔNIO DO PRADO

(1917–1959). The art critic José Valladares was born in Salvador, Bahia, on May 3, 1917, the son of Antônio do Prado Valladares and Clarice Santos Silva Valladares. At age seventeen he was already working for the newspaper *Diário de Pernambuco* in Recife while attending law school, from which he graduated in 1937.

Returning to Salvador, in 1939 he became the director of museums and monuments of the State of Bahia. He launched the organization of various collections and a line of specialized publications. In 1943 the state government acquired the stately home of the former governor, Góes Calmon, with all its collections, from paintings to furniture and porcelain. The Museu de Arte da Bahia, the creation of José Valladares, was inaugurated in 1946. Art history courses and similar activities established the fine reputation of the museum.

In 1949 Valladares established the Bahia Gallery of Fine Arts (Salão Baiano de Belas Artes), attracting artists from all over the country. Two years later he

was appointed professor of esthetics at the University of Bahia. For years he was the designated art critic for the Bahia periodical *Diário de Notícias* and was the steward for several exhibitions, including the third Bienal de Arte de São Paulo (1955). During the second Congresso Nacional de Museus (1959) he distinguished himself as president of the Fine Arts Department. He died prematurely in a plane crash on December 16, 1959.

See also **Art: The Twentieth Century; Bahia.**

BIBLIOGRAPHY

Leite, José Roberto Teixeira. *Dicionário crítico da pintura no Brasil.* Rio de Janeiro: Artlivre, 1988.

O museu de arte da Bahia. São Paulo: Banco Safra, 1997.

CARMEN LUCIA DE AZEVEDO

VALLADARES, TOMÁS (?–c.1850).

Tomás Valladares (*d.* after 1850), Nicaraguan politician. Active in the confusing era of the breakdown of the United Provinces of Central America, Valladares served as a senator and then president of the Chamber of Deputies in Nicaragua. He was interim chief of state from 1840 to 1841 and subsequently continued to participate in politics. As one of Nicaragua's leading liberals, Valladares served on a junta with Evaristo Rocha, Patricio Rivas, Hilario Ulloa, and Joaquín Caso in the 1840s and was a lieutenant in the wars against José Rafael Carrera, which tore apart the isthmus at mid-century.

See also **Central America, United Provinces of; Junta: Spanish America.**

BIBLIOGRAPHY

Eduardo Cárdenas, *20,000 biografías breves* (1963).

Additional Bibliography

Gudmundson, Lowell, and Héctor Lindo-Fuentes. *Central America, 1821–1871: Liberalism before Liberal Reform.* Tuscaloosa: University of Alabama Press, 1995.

Kinloch Tijerino, Frances. *Nicaragua: Identidad y cultura política (1821–1858).* Managua: Banco Central de Nicaragua, 1999.

KAREN RACINE

VALLADOLID CONSPIRACY (1809).

The Valladolid Conspiracy was a group that gathered in Valladolid, Michoacán, to discuss political issues. It included military men, clergymen, and lawyers. Discontented with the Spanish colonial regime because of the coup d'état of September 1808, which had ended the possibilities of furthering their autonomist interests, they moved from conversation into conspiracy in September 1809. Following the autonomist proposal presented by the Ayuntamiento of Mexico in 1808, they intended to establish a junta or congress in Valladolid in order to prevent the peninsular Spaniards from turning New Spain over to the French. The conspirators counted upon the support of military units and of some Indian communities, who were promised an exemption from paying tribute. The insurrection, which was to occur on 24 December 1809, was revealed on 21 December. The plotters, among them Captain José María García Obeso and Lieutenant José Mariano Michelena, as well as the Franciscan Friar Vicente de Santa María, were arrested. Although their role in the conspiracy was clearly proved by the authorities, they were not severely punished. This leniency was due, in part, to the conciliatory attitude of the viceroy, Archbishop Francisco Javier de Lizana y Beaumont. Several of the plotters took part in the conspiracy of 1810, which gave rise to the insurgent movement.

See also **New Spain, Viceroyalty of.**

BIBLIOGRAPHY

Lucas Alamán, *Historia de Méjio* (1985), vol. 1.

José Mariano Michelena, "Verdadero origen de la revolución de 1809," in *Documentos históricos,* edited by Genaro García, 2nd ed., vol. 1 (1985); and *Diccionario Porrúa de historia, biografía y geografía de México,* 5th ed., vol. 3 (1986), p. 3,070.

Additional Bibliography

Chowning, Margaret. *Wealth and Power in Provincial Mexico: Michoacán from the Late Colony to the Revolution.* Stanford, CA: Stanford University Press, 1999.

Franco Cáceres, Ivan. *La intendencia de Valladolid de Michoacán, 1786-1809: Reforma adminstrativa y exacción fiscal en una región de la Nueva España.* Mexico City: Instituto Michoacano de Cultura: Fondo de Cultura Económica, 2001.

Mejía Zavala, Eugenio. *Antonio María Uraga y Gutiérrez, conspirador de Valladolid en 1809.* Morelia, Michoacán, México: Instituto de Investigaciones Históricas, Universidad Michoacana de San Nicolás de Hidalgo, 2005.

Virginia Guedea

VALLE, ARISTÓBULO DEL (1845–1896).

Aristóbulo del Valle (*b.* 15 March 1845; *d.* 29 January 1896), Argentine politician, journalist, constitutional lawyer, and mentor to reform-minded youth in the 1880s and 1890s. Born in Dolores, Buenos Aires Province, in modest circumstances, he was an early example of the burgeoning Argentine middle class. A veteran of the War of the Triple Alliance, del Valle wrote for the newspapers *El Nacional* and *La Nación,* and served in the Buenos Aires provincial legislature. Elected to the national Congress in 1872, he was a deputy (1872–1876) and later a senator (1877–1895). He distinguished himself as the Senate's most effective orator and defender of the middle class. He played a leading role in the revolutions of the early 1890s, but when they failed, he worked within the oligarchic government to stave off anarchy. He served for short periods as minister of war, navy, interior, and finance under President Luis Sáenz Peña.

Del Valle is credited as one of the early founders, with Leandro Alem, of the Unión Cívica Radical. He established the country's first reformist newspaper, *El Argentino,* and taught constitutional law at the University of Buenos Aires, steering a different course from his conservative predecessor José M. Estrada. Del Valle's major works include: *Nociones de derecho constitucional* (Aspects of Constitutional Law [1897]), *Cuestión de límites interprovinciales* (Interprovincial Boundary Question [1881]), and *La política económica argentina en la década del 80* (Political Economy of Argentina in the 80s [1955]). De Valle's most influential congressional speeches are gathered in *Discursos selectos* (1922) and *Discursos políticos* (1938). His death at the age of fifty deprived the country of one of its leading reformers and most effective public speakers.

See also **Argentina: The Nineteenth Century.**

BIBLIOGRAPHY

Elvira Aldao De Díaz, *Reminiscencias sobre Aristóbulo del Valle* (1928).

Olga N. Bordi De Ragucci, *Aristóbulo del Valle en los orígenes del radicalismo* (1987).

Julio A. Caminos, *Tres figuras del noventa* (1948).

Additional Bibliography

Rock, David. *State Building and Political Movements in Argentina, 1860–1916.* Stanford, CA: Stanford University Press, 2002.

Segovia, Juan Fernando. "Perfil político e ideológico de Aristóbulo del Valle: Idearo de un liberal radical." *Investigaciones y Ensayos* 49 (January–December 1999): 573–614.

GEORGETTE MAGASSY DORN

VALLE, JOSÉ CECILIO DEL (1776–1834).

José Cecilio del Valle (*b.* 22 November 1776; *d.* 2 March 1834), Honduran scholar and statesman. Born in Choluteca, Honduras, Valle moved with his family to newly established Guatemala City in 1789 and matriculated the next year at the University of San Carlos. With the assistance of his teacher, Fray Antonio de Liendo y Goicoechea (1735–1814), and Pedro Juan de Lara, he received a degree in philosophy in 1794 and continued to study civil and canon law until he was admitted to the bar in 1803. Enthused by the Enlightenment philosophies of his teachers, he began a pursuit of knowledge that eventually gained him acknowledgment as an authority in economics and as the most prominent scholar of Central America.

Valle's talents and diligence led him to a life of politics at an early age. For almost twenty years, he faithfully served the captaincy general of Guatemala in hopes of obtaining a high official post in Spain. During the turbulent era prior to independence, Valle advanced rapidly in local politics and became the leader of the moderate conservatives. He served as the mayor of Guatemala City in 1820. Reluctant to support independence from Spain, he nonetheless assumed leadership of the apparently inevitable movement in the fear that social revolution, rather than political freedom, would become the focus of the turmoil. Indeed, he was largely responsible for the writing of the declaration of independence. He was a member of the provisional junta that took control of the government of Central America on 15 September 1821 and annexed the region to Mexico under Agustín de Iturbide, who later became (1822) Emperor Agustín I.

Under the empire, he held several official posts. As the representative from the province of Tegucigalpa (Honduras) to the Constituent Congress of Mexico, he served with distinction and rose to become the vice president of the congress. Although Iturbide imprisoned him on false charges of conspiracy, he was exonerated six months later and made secretary of foreign and domestic affairs. After the fall of Iturbide, Valle was appointed secretary of the department of justice and ecclesiastical affairs by the newly formed Mexican Republic.

When Central America decided to seek its own political destiny, Valle returned to Guatemala in January 1824 and was chosen, along with José Manuel de la Cerda and Tomás O'Horan, to be a member of the provisional junta that governed the isthmus until elections for the United Provinces of Central America were held in 1825. In the presidential elections, Valle won a plurality of the electoral votes, but a technicality prevented him from taking office. The federal congress elected instead Manuel José Arce (1786–1846). Valle responded to the injustice by publishing the *Manifiesto de José del Valle a la nación guatemalteca* (1825), in which he gave an account of the services he had rendered his country and demonstrated the invalidity of Arce's election. During the Arce administration, he represented the department of Guatemala as a deputy to the congress. He ran for the presidency again in 1830 and lost to Francisco Morazán. Finally, Valle was elected president of Central America in 1834, but he became seriously ill on his estate, La Concepción, some 60 miles from Guatemala City, and died en route to his inauguration.

See also **Guatemala City; Iturbide, Agustín de; Philosophy.**

BIBLIOGRAPHY

Louis E. Bumgartner, *José del Valle of Central America* (1963).

Elvia Castañeda De Machado, *Valle en la génesis del panamericanismo* (1977).

José Cecilio Del Valle and Jorge Del Valle Matheu, eds., *Obras de José Cecilio del Valle,* 2 vols. (1929–1930).

José Cecilio Del Valle, *Pensamiento vivo de José Cecilio del Valle... Selección y prólogo de Rafael Heliodoro Valle* (1971).

Pedro Tobar Cruz, *Valle: El hombre, el político, el sabio* (1961).

Rafael Leíva Vivas, *Valle: Precursor del sistema interamericano* (1977).

Franklin Dallas Parker, *José Cecilio del Valle and the Establishment of the Central American Confederation* (1954).

Ramón Rosa, *Biografía de don José Cecilio del Valle* (1882).

Additional Bibliography

Pérez Cadalso, Eliseo. *Valle, apóstol de América.* Tegucigalpa, Honduras: Editorial Universitaria, Universidad Nacional Autónoma de Honduras, 1999.

Sierra Fonseca, Rolanda. *La filosofía de la historia de José Cecilio del Valle.* Obispado de Choluteca, Honduras: Ediciones Subirana, 1998.

MICHAEL F. FRY

VALLE, RAFAEL HELIODORO

(1891–1959). Rafael Heliodoro Valle (*b.* 3 July 1891; *d.* 29 July 1959), Honduran diplomat, professor, journalist, poet, historian, and literary critic. Valle, a descendant of José Cecilio del Valle, was born in Tegucigalpa but received his higher education in Mexico, where he spent much of his adult life. He served the Honduran government in diplomatic posts in Central America, Mexico, and the United States. As Honduran ambassador in Washington, D.C., in the early 1950s, he was especially active in promoting inter-American cultural affairs. He also was a leading journalist in Mexico, where he served as editor of *El Universal* and *Excelsior* (1921–1925). Later, as a professor at the Universidad Nacional Autónoma de Mexico, he wrote prolifically. Among the works he produced were the six-volume *La anexión de Centro América a México* (1921–1927), *Historia de las ideas contemporáneas en Centro América* (1960), and many other historical books and articles dealing especially with Honduras and Mexico. His journalistic and literary writings won him the María Moors Cabot Prize of the Inter-American Press Association in 1940. Valle died in Mexico.

See also **Journalism; Literature: Spanish America.**

BIBLIOGRAPHY

Oscar Acosta, *Rafael Heliodoro Valle, vida y obra,* 3d ed. (1981).

Additional Bibliography

Chapa Bezanilla, María de los Ángeles. *Rafael Heliodoro Valle, humanista de América.* México City: Universidad Nacional Autónoma de México, 2004.

Perdomo T., Claudio Roberto. *El pensamiento de Rafael Heliodoro Valle.* Tegucigalpa, Honduras: Secretaría de Cultura, Artes y Deportes, Dirección General del Libro y El Documento, 1997.

RALPH LEE WOODWARD JR.

VALLEJO, CÉSAR

(1892–1938). César Vallejo (*b.* 16 March 1892; *d.* 15 April 1938), Peruvian poet. Vallejo is Peru's most renowned poet, and his works are remarkable for their striking originality, lexical complexity, and compressed power. They reveal a profound concern for the suffering of others and nostalgia for his Andean childhood. His journalism, dramas, novels, and short stories gloss the major social, political, and cultural movements of the first third of the century and assert the legitimate, if neglected, place of Latin America in contemporary culture and history.

The youngest of eleven children in a middle-class mestizo family, Vallejo entered the University of Trujillo in 1910 to pursue literary studies, but dropped out. He returned in 1913 and received his B.A. in Spanish literature in 1915, at the same time that he began his study of law. He pursued his legal studies until returning to Lima in 1917 as a schoolteacher. After his return, he experienced two ill-fated love affairs, the second one ending shortly before the death of his lover. In 1918 he suffered the loss of his mother, whose memory remained a recurrent theme in his poetry. Falsely accused of participating in political violence in his Andean hometown of Santiago de Chuco in 1920, he was imprisoned for 112 days (6 November 1920–26 February 1921), to which he alluded in his mature poetry as the "gravest moment" of his life.

Seeking wider cultural and intellectual opportunities, Vallejo left Peru for Europe in 1923, spending most of his final fifteen years of life in self-imposed, impoverished exile in France, with periods in Spain and two influential trips to Russia. Expelled from France for leftist political activities in 1931, he joined the Spanish Communist Party in Madrid. He returned to France in 1932. He died in Paris from an unidentified illness.

Vallejo published two books of poetry before leaving Peru: *Los heraldos negros* (1918) and *Trilce* (1922). The first showed signs of an original poetic voice that emerged powerfully in the irrational and hermetic expression of the second work, which shattered all traditions of poetry written in Spanish. *Poemas humanos* (1939) represented the poet at the height of his power to express the plight of the human animal abandoned in an irrational, absurd world where salvation can come only through fraternal self-sacrifice.

Vallejo worked with other writers and intellectuals to further the Republican cause during the Spanish Civil War and visited the war front twice. *España, aparta de mí este cáliz* (1938) was first published by Republican soldiers on the front lines. Although in his last years Vallejo sought to inform Europeans about Peruvian culture, he never returned to Peru.

See also **Literature: Spanish America.**

BIBLIOGRAPHY

Clayton Eshleman and José Rubia Barcia, *César Vallejo: The Complete Posthumous Poetry* (1978).

Jean Franco, *César Vallejo: The Dialectics of Poetry and Silence* (1976).

James Higgins, *César Vallejo: An Anthology of His Poetry* (1970).

James Higgins, *The Poet in Peru* (1982).

James Higgins, *The Black Heralds* translated by Richard Schaaf and Kathleen Ross (1990).

James Higgins, *Trilce* translated by Clayton Eshleman (1992).

Spain, Take This Chalice from Me, is by Clayton Eshleman and José Rubia Barcia, *César Vallejo: The Complete Posthumous Poetry* (1978).

Additional Bibliography

Córdoba V., Juan Domingo. *César Vallejo del Perú profundo y sacrificado.* Lima: J. Campodonico/Editor, 1995.

González Vigil, Ricardo. *César Vallejo.* Lima: Editorial Brasa, 1995.

KEITH MCDUFFIE

VALLEJO, MARIANO GUADALUPE

(1807?–1890). Mariano Guadalupe Vallejo (*b.* 4 July 1807?; *d.* 18 January 1890), military commander in California. Mariano Vallejo was born in Monterey, son of Ignacio Vallejo, an early settler from Jalisco, and María Antonia Lugo. After joining the Monterey military company at age fifteen, he rose to commandant of the San Francisco presidio by age twenty-four. As military commander and director of colonization of the northern frontier during the 1830s, Vallejo evaluated Russian intentions in California, established the Sonoma colony and organized the civilian government of San Francisco, and pacified Indian tribes. Vallejo was appointed *jefe militar* (military chief) of the revolutionary government of 1836, but soon disengaged himself from the rebel group. After central Mexican authority was reestablished, he was appointed military commander of California, whose prime concern was encroaching foreign influence.

Considered a friend of Americans, Vallejo was a force for moderation among leading Mexican citizens of California during the period leading up to the U.S. conquest. Vallejo's personal collection of eleven thousand documents of early California, a major source for Hubert Bancroft's *History of California* (1884–1890), now resides in the Bancroft Library of the University of California.

See also **California.**

BIBLIOGRAPHY

Myrtle M. Mc Kittrick, *Vallejo, Son of California* (1944).

Ralph J. Roske, *Everyman's Eden: A History of California* (1968).

Additional Bibliography

Pérez, Vincent. *Remembering the Hacienda: History and Memory in the Mexican American Southwest.* College Station: Texas A&M University Press, 2006.

Rosenus, Alan. *General M.G. Vallejo and the Advent of the Americans: A Biography.* Albuquerque: University of New Mexico Press, 1995.

E. JEFFREY STANN

VALLENATO. *See* **Cumbia.**

VALLENILLA LANZ, LAUREANO

(1870–1936). Laureano Vallenilla Lanz (*b.* 11 October 1870; *d.* 16 November 1936), Venezuelan politician and intellectual. Vallenilla Lanz traveled to Caracas at a very young age to take up engineering, but he did not finish his studies. After a brief stay in Barcelona, Venezuela, he returned to Caracas and mixed with the intellectual circles in the capital. He was a contributor to *El Cojo Ilustrado,* publishing essays on historical themes, which earned him a reputation, to a degree, as an intellectual. Vallenilla Lanz was named Venezuelan consul in Amsterdam in 1904 and remained in Europe for six years. In Paris he attended the Sorbonne and the College de France, which distinctly influenced his orientation toward the positivist trends of the era.

After his return to Venezuela in 1910, Vallenilla Lanz contributed to important periodicals, met President Juan Vicente Gómez, and became active in politics as a member of the intellectual circle close to the president. He performed important public duties and in 1915 became director of *El Nuevo Diario,* the official government mouthpiece. He conducted an important campaign in defense of the regime and in 1919 published *Cesarismo democrático.* In this work, one of his most important, he used positivist theoretical suppositions as a basis for analyzing the Venezuelan past and concluded by justifying the autocrat as a "Gendarme Necesario," or a natural outgrowth of the collective evolution of Venezuelan society. The work generated contrary opinions. It was translated into several languages and became one of the key works of positivist thought in all of Latin America. Vallenilla Lanz was a member of the Academy of History (1918). In 1931 he was appointed minister of Venezuela in Paris.

See also **Positivism.**

BIBLIOGRAPHY

Federico Brito Figueroa, *La contribución de Laureano Vallenilla Lanz a la comprensión histórica de Venezuela* (1985).

Germán Carrera Damas, *El concepto de la historia en Laureano Vallenilla Lanz* (1966).

Nikita Harwich Vallenilla, ed., *Cesarismo democrático y otros textos* (1991).

Additional Bibliography

Plaza, Elena. *La tragedia de una amarga convicción: Historia y política en el pensamiento de Laureano Vallenilla Lanz, 1870–1936.* Caracas: Universidad Central de Venezuela, 1996.

Inés Quintero

VALLE Y CAVIEDES, JUAN DEL

(1645–1698). Born in Porcuna, Spain, the poet Juan del Valle y Caviedes traveled to the New World at an early age and settled in the Viceroyalty of Peru, where he participated in various mining activities and kept a small shop in the city of Lima. Although he is known mostly for his satirical poetry, he also wrote love and religious poems. His works, which circulated in manuscript form, adhere to thematic and stylistic conventions of the Spanish baroque and reveal a preoccupation with the contradictions of a colonial society that was growing apart from its European origins.

Valle's satire sheds light on local issues of seventeenth-century Peruvian society. His mockery of two important Lima doctors, Francisco Bermejo and Miguel Ossera, reveals when analyzed closely an awareness of the power struggle taking place between economically flourishing Creoles and Spanish peninsular newcomers who benefited from important bureaucratic positions. Similarly, in one of his many misogynist satires concerning prostitution, the poet makes use of humorous wordplay to expose financial corruption amid Peru's mining activities. In various poems, among them a parodic letter to the viceroy, baroque ideas of life as a stage serve to highlight Valle's preoccupation with Peru's colonial subjects as individuals caught between Spanish and nascent New World identities.

See also **Literature: Spanish America.**

BIBLIOGRAPHY

Works by Valle y Caviedes

Valle y Caviedes, Juan del. *Obra completa.* Edited by María Leticia Cáceres, Luis Jaime Cisneros, and Guillermo Lohmann Villena. Lima: Banco de Crédito del Perú, 1990.

Other Sources

Arellano, Ignacio. "Problemas textuales y anotación de la obra poética de Juan del Valle y Caviedes." In *Edición e interpretación de textos andinos: Actas del congreso internacional*, edited by Ignacio Arellano and José Antonio Mazzotti. Madrid: Iberoamericana, 2000.

Lasarte, Pedro. *Lima satirizada (1598–1968): Mateo Rosas de Oquendo y Juan del Valle y Caviedes*. Lima: Pontificia Universidad Católica del Peru, 2006.

Reedy, Daniel. *The Poetic Art of Juan del Valle Caviedes*. Chapel Hill: University of North Carolina Press, 1964.

PEDRO LASARTE

VALPARAÍSO.

Valparaíso, Chile, was arguably the leading Pacific port in the Americas during the nineteenth century, serving as a key financial center and base for British merchants (and the British navy) in the hemisphere. Valparaíso is also noteworthy as the birthplace of Salvador Isabelino Allende Gossens, president of Chile from 1970 to 1973, and as the seat of the Chilean congress since 1990.

Valparaíso, or "vale of paradise," is located seventy-four miles northwest of the capital, Santiago. The city is set on a thin coastal shelf that narrows at points to only five city blocks. A steep escarpment rings the city, with *ascensores* (funicular railways)—Valparaíso's signature feature—providing transportation up and down the hillsides.

The city's founding remains a matter of historical controversy, although most scholars credit Juan de Saavedra (d. 1554), an officer with the Spanish explorer Diego de Almagro, who discovered the site in 1536 and named it after his hometown in Spain. The port grew in importance during the colonial period; Valparaíso was the first good stopping place for ships rounding the tip of South America into the Pacific Ocean. The colonial city also developed a flourishing contraband trade. Valparaíso was repeatedly attacked by pirates in the colonial period, and suffered seven major assaults, including attacks by Francis Drake (c. 1540–1596) in December 1578 and Richard Hawkins (c. 1562–1622) in April 1594.

In the late colonial period Valparaíso's prosperity rose with the opening of trade under the Bourbon Reforms. Following independence in 1818, commerce increased further, with Great Britain becoming the port's leading trading partner. British vessels crowded into the harbor and the English merchant community in Valparaíso grew in size and financial importance. These and other commercially active European immigrants helped to create the distinct cultural blend for which Valparaíso is still known. Disasters, both natural and human-caused, rocked Valparaíso. An earthquake in November 1822 destroyed much of the city. War with Spain brought a naval bombardment of the harbor in March 1866 that laid waste to vast sections of Valparaíso. In August 1906 a devastating earthquake and fire all but destroyed the city.

In the mid-nineteenth century Valparaíso served as the principal port for the export of Chilean wheat. The city's commercial prominence rose again after the completion of a railway to the capital in 1863, a project directed by the U.S. entrepreneur Henry Meiggs (1811–1877). For much of the second half of the nineteenth century Valparaíso was the largest city in Chile. However, the emergence of nitrate exports (a mineral used as a fertilizer and in making gunpowder), mined and shipped from the far north of Chile, diminished Valparaíso's importance in exports in the late nineteenth century. Nevertheless, the city continued as the leading port for Chilean imports, taking in roughly two-thirds of the nation's total, and still handed about one-third of Chile's exports.

The opening of the Panamá Canal 1914 diminished Valparaíso's importance. With the route around Cape Horn no longer necessary, Valparaíso became a port at the end of the world, far from principal trade routes. The slide has continued; Valparaíso is no longer even the largest port in Chile, having been eclipsed by nearby San Antonio.

Valparaíso's population rose steadily from 3,000 in 1700 to 25,000 in 1830, 70,000 in 1865, 120,000 in 1885, and 193,000 in 1930. But given the city's cramped geography, there were limits to its growth. Valparaíso's population reached roughly a quarter of a million in 1960 but has not changed significantly since that time.

Valparaíso recaptured some of its former fame when it became the seat of the Chilean congress, though the new building's design quickly became the subject of considerable criticism. In 2003

Valparaíso was named Chile's "cultural capital" by the congress. In that year Valparaíso's historic quarter was also declared a UNESCO World Heritage Site. Valparaíso continues to serve as the home base for the Chilean navy.

See also **Chile: The Nineteenth Century; Chile: The Twentieth Century; Meiggs, Henry.**

BIBLIOGRAPHY

Calderon, Alfonso, with Marilis Schlotfeldt. *Memorial de Valparaíso en los 450 años de su descubrimiento.* Valparaíso, Chile: Universitarias de Valparaíso, 1986.

Collier, Simon, and William F. Sater. *A History of Chile: 1808–1994.* New York: Cambridge University Press, 1996.

Godoy, Leopoldo Sáez. *Valparaíso 1536–1986: Primera jornada de historia urbana.* Valparaíso, Chile: Ediciones Altazor, 1987.

Godoy, Leopoldo Sáez. *Valparaíso: Lugares, nombres y personajes, siglos XVI–XXI.* Valparaíso, Chile: Ediciones de Playa Ancha, 2001.

Kinsbruner, Jay. *Chile: A Historical Interpretation.* New York: Harper and Row, 1973.

Loveman, Brian. *Chile: The Legacy of Hispanic Capitalism,* 2nd edition. New York: Oxford University Press, 1988.

Pineo, Ronn. "Public Health Care in Valparaíso, Chile." In *Cities of Hope: People, Protests, and Progress in Urbanizing Latin America, 1870–1930,* ed. Ronn Pineo and James A. Baer. Boulder, CO: Westview Press, 1998.

RONN PINEO

VANDOR, AUGUSTO TIMOTEO (1923–1969).

This Argentine union leader and politician was a former officer in the Navy and a worker in the Buenos Aires metallurgical industry, who made a name for himself as a union leader beginning in the 1950s. When Juan Domingo Perón was unseated in 1955, the General Workers Union (*Central General de Trabajadores*) was taken over and Vandor was sent to prison for six months.

Vandor consolidated his position as the principal leader of the powerful Metal Workers Union (*Unión Obrera Metalúrgica—UOM*) during the presidency of Arturo Frondizi (1958–1962) and took part in the Peronist Resistance. But he gradually distanced himself from Perón because he believed that Perón's leadership from exile compromised the unions too much. Vandor tried to make the union movement into a political power that would recognize Perón as its leader while having as much independence as possible. He challenged Perón unsuccessfully in the restricted elections (Peronism was unable to compete entirely freely) during the administration of Arturo Illia (1963–1966) and then openly backed Juan Carlos Onganía's coup d'état in 1966. All this created a crisis within union leadership that resulted in successive divisions of the labor movement. In 1968, the moderate Azopardo CGT (General Labor Confederation), led by Vandor, focused on talks with the military dictatorship without ever abandoning the option of controlled measures of force. Meanwhile, the Argentines' CGT, led by Raimundo Ongaro, adopted a tough, combative stance.

Peronist political and union sectors were already viewing Vandor as a traitor to Peronist precepts and an obstacle to Perón's return to Argentina, and Perón made known his distrust of Vandor. On June 30, 1969, Vandor was assassinated in his union office. The crime was never fully solved, but the perpetrators belonged to some Peronist factions that saw danger in Vandor's actions as a union leader.

See also **Argentina: The Twentieth Century; Frondizi, Arturo; Illia, Arturo Umberto; Onganía, Juan Carlos; Perón, Juan Domingo.**

BIBLIOGRAPHY

Abós, Álvaro. *Cinco balas para Augusto Vandor.* Buenos Aires: Sudamericana, 2005.

Cavarozzi, Marcelo. *Autoritarismo y democracia, 1955–1996. La transición del Estado al mercado en la Argentina.* Buenos Aires: Ariel, 1997.

O'Donnell, Guillermo. *El Estado burocrático autoritario.* Buenos Aires: Editorial de Belgrano, 1982.

VICENTE PALERMO

VANGUARDIA, LA. *See* Coronel Urtecho, José.

VAQUEIROS.

Vaqueiros, cowboys, from the Portuguese word *vaca* (cow). Brazilian cowboys have been important figures in the Northeast, the center-west, and in Rio Grande Do Sul, where they are called Gaúchos. The northeastern Sertão (backlands) is a region of frequent drought and thorny Caatinga (scrub forest). Protectively dressed from head to foot in sturdy leather, including breastplates for their agile horses, *vaqueiros* of the *sertão* have been adept at finding water underground. In times of extreme drought, *vaqueiros* worked as bandits and hired guns or migrated out of the region. The decline of the northeastern ranching industry has made the *vaqueiro* a rare sight today.

In the open tropical savanna of the central states and Roraima, *vaqueiros* dress simply in cotton clothing and straw hats, and in the past rode barefoot, using a toe stirrup. Their horses are resilient, although until the 1930s in the Pantanal of Mato Grosso and on Marajó Island in the Amazon delta, disease regularly decimated mounts, frequently forcing *vaqueiros* to use tame steers as replacements.

From colonial times, *vaqueiros* were instrumental in expanding the Brazilian state into its interior. Cattle drives to distant markets lasted weeks or months, frequently crossing piranha-infested rivers. Salaries on ranches often included one calf in four, permitting some *vaqueiros* to become small ranchers. By the mid-twentieth century the availability of unoccupied land had declined, while the expansion of rail systems and local meat-packing plants modified the ranching economy, forcing the cowboy into wage labor. Nevertheless, modern *vaqueiro* work habits have changed little from the past.

See also **Livestock; Rio Grande do Sul.**

BIBLIOGRAPHY

Edward Larocque Tinker, *Horsemen of the Americas and the Literature They Inspired,* 2nd ed. (1967).

Lúcio De Castro Soares, "Vaqueiro de Marajó," José Veríssimo Da Costa Pereira, "Vaqueiro do Rio Branco," Maria Fagundes De Sousa Doca, "Vaqueiro do Nordeste," and Elza Coelho De Souza, "Boiadeiro," in *Tipos e aspectos do Brasil,* 10th ed. (1975), pp. 65–66, 68–70, 267–268, 457–458.

Richard W. Slatta, *Cowboys of the Americas* (1990), p. 199.

Additional Bibliography

Bell, Stephen. *Campanha Gaúcha: A Brazilian Ranching System, 1850–1920.* Stanford, CA: Stanford University Press, 1998.

Cascudo, Luís da Câmara. *Vaqueiros e cantadores.* São Paulo: Global Editora, 2005.

ROBERT WILCOX

VAQUERÍA.

Vaquería, a wild-cattle hunt. Wild cattle by the millions roamed the Pampa during the colonial era. Although it lacked deposits of precious metals, the Río de la Plata became a wealth-producing region thanks to its huge herds of wild cattle and horses. In *vaquerías,* whether licensed or illegal, gauchos used a hocking blade (*desjarretadera*) to sever the tendon of a cow's hind leg. Then, after crippling hundreds of animals, the riders returned to slaughter and skin them. Once sun-dried, the hides were ready for export. *Vaquerías* gradually depleted the number of animals on the pampa. By the mid-eighteenth century, Estancias began to replace these wild-cattle hunts as the primary means of exploiting livestock.

See also **Livestock; Pampa.**

BIBLIOGRAPHY

Emilio Coni, *Historia de las vaquerías de Río de la Plata* (1930).

Madaline Wallis Nichols, *The Gaucho* (1968), pp. 22–25.

Richard W. Slatta, *Cowboys of the Americas* (1990), pp. 12–14.

Additional Bibliography

Assunção, Fernando O. *Historia del gaucho: El gaucho, ser y quehacer.* Buenos Aires: Editorial Claridad, 1999.

RICHARD W. SLATTA

VAQUERO.

Vaquero, the working cowhand of Mexico, who began his career on frontier missions during the colonial period. Priests used Indian novices to tend the herds of livestock that populated many mission outposts. These vaqueros became excellent riders and ropers who skillfully made much of their own equipment. Idigenous and mestizo vaqueros modified Spanish equipment and riding techniques according to the needs imposed by their local conditions. Vaqueros in Baja California, for example, made extensive use of leather clothing to protect themselves from cacti and other thorny plants. In 1832, vaqueros sailed from Spanish California to Hawaii to train Hawaiians in cattle herding. The Hawaiian cowboy is called *paniolo* (from *español*).

During the nineteenth century, the expansion of the United States into the Southwest led to the Mexican War of 1846, after which some vaqueros went to work on Anglo-American ranches. They taught Anglo cowboys how to handle wild cattle and braid lariats, and imparted much of their folklore and ranching savvy. Vaqueros today, like old-time cowboys, are a vanishing breed.

See also **Charro.**

BIBLIOGRAPHY

David Dary, *Cowboy Culture: A Saga of Five Centuries* (1981).

Richard W. Slatta, *Cowboys of the Americas* (1990).

Additional Bibliography

Garduño, Everardo. *La frontera interpretada: Procesos culturales en la frontera noroeste de México.* Mexicali, Mexico: Universidad Autónoma de Baja California, Centro de Investigaciones Culturales-Museo, 2005.

Wittliff, William D. *Vaquero: Genesis of the Texas Cowboy.* Austin: University of Texas Press, 2004.

RICHARD W. SLATTA

VARAS DE LA BARRA, ANTONIO

(1817–1886). Antonio Varas de la Barra (*b.* 13 June 1817; *d.* 3 June 1886), Chilean politician. An outstanding figure of his period, Varas was the closest political associate of the Conservative president Manuel Montt. Eight times a deputy and twice a senator, he served as minister of the interior from 1850 to 1856, in 1860–1861, and again briefly in 1879. Although he fully supported the authoritarian stance of his intimate friend Montt, Varas was an altogether more attractive character. (In his old age he became quite liberal.) Montt wanted Varas to be his presidential successor in 1861, a prospect that deeply angered the opposition. By accepting the interior ministry again in April 1860, Varas implicitly abandoned all claim to presidential succession. His unselfishness, which won widespread praise, paved the way for the election of the less controversial

José Joaquín Pérez Mascayano. After 1861, Varas headed the National (or, as it was revealingly nicknamed, Montt-Varista) Party in Congress.

See also **Chile, Political Parties: National Party; Pérez Mascayano, José Joaquin.**

BIBLIOGRAPHY

Antonio Varas, *Correspondencia*, 5 vols. (1918–1929).

Additional Bibliography

Bravo Lira, Bernardino. *El Absolutismo ilustrado en Hispanoamérica: Chile (1760–1860) de Carlos III a Portales y Montt.* Santiago, Chile: Editorial Universitaria, 1994.

Collier, Simon. *Chile: The Making of a Republic, 1830–1865.* New York: Cambridge University Press, 2003.

SIMON COLLIER

VARELA, FELIPE

(1821–1870). Felipe Varela (*b.* 1821; *d.* 4 June 1870), Argentine caudillo. Varela was one of the last great regional chieftains of the Argentine interior provinces during the long process of state formation. Born in Huayacama, Catamarca, he moved to La Rioja, where he participated in the civil wars against Buenos Aires. In due course, he became a close ally of Angel Vicente Peñaloza. In 1848 Varela was driven from Argentina to Chile, where he displayed some acumen for business. He became associated with Colonel Tristán Dávila, a local mining magnate, and rose through the ranks of the Chilean military based in Atacama. Ironically, he was promoted to captain in Chile's army for his service in defense of the central government. Varela returned to Argentina in 1855 and became the President Justo Urquiza's loyal follower. He participated in the prolonged federalist resistance of the provinces against Buenos Aires, aligning with Governor Juan Sáa of San Luís in the bloody civil war against Buenos Aires-backed forces. Still a loyal Urquizista, Varela joined the last-ditch alliance against Buenos Aires that led to the 1862 mass insurrection in La Rioja. Varela displayed his military prowess, trouncing Buenos Aires forces repeatedly, but the federalists could not overcome the odds. Following the defeat and execution of Peñaloza (1863), Varela fled again to Chile in 1865. He returned to Argentina in 1866, but his distaste for Buenos Aires's plans for the country led him to revolt for the last time in 1867. He could not, however, defeat the combined forces of Buenos Aires and its allies, led by the Taboadas of Tucumán. After a series of bloody encounters, he fled to Bolivia and then to Chile, where he died at Náutico, sick and impoverished.

See also **Argentina: The Twentieth Century; Urquiza, Justo José de.**

BIBLIOGRAPHY

Beatriz Bosch, *Urquiza y su tiempo* (1980).

David Rock, *Argentina, 1516–1982: From Spanish Colonization to the Falklands War* (1985; rev. ed. 1987), esp. pp. 126–127.

Additional Bibliography

Rojo, Roberto. *Heroes y cobardes en el ocaso federal.* Buenos Aires, Argentina: Ediciones COMFER, 1994.

Torino, Luis Arturo. *La invasión de Felipe Varela y el gobierno de don Sixto Ovejero.* Argentina: s.n., 1995.

JEREMY ADELMAN

VARELA, FLORENCIO (1807–1848).

Florencio Varela (*b.* 23 February 1807; *d.* 20 March 1848), Argentine poet and patriot. Brother of the famous neoclassical, civic poet, Juan Cruz Varela, Florencio wrote his first verses at the age of fifteen in celebration of the decisive battle of Ayacucho during the Wars of Independence. Varela studied law at the University of Buenos Aires, graduating in 1827. Following the Argentine revolution of 1828, he fled to Montevideo. In 1830, he published *El día de Mayo* (May Day), a volume containing five poems dedicated to the Uruguayan people. In exile, Varela became a leader of the Unitarian cause against the dictator Juan Manuel de Rosas. Newspapers supporting Rosas recognized the ardor of Varela's attack, calling him a "savage Unitarian, traitor, and vile slanderer."

In 1841–1842, Varela lived in Río de Janeiro, where he wrote several articles for the *Jornal do Comercio* defending Uruguay against accusations that it had usurped territory from Brazil. While in Río, Varela became friends with Bernardino Rivadavia, who furnished Varela with documentary material for a book he was preparing on Argentine history. In 1843, the Uruguayan government sent Varela on an official mission to France and England.

Tireless in his efforts to overthrow Rosas and use the press as a vehicle for shaping public opinion, Varela founded in October 1845 the *Comercio del Plata,* in whose columns he undermined the political and military structure keeping Rosas in power. Varela was also cofounder of a publishing house that brought out works in Spanish translation as well as books by Hispanic-American writers.

See also **Literature: Spanish America; Varela, Juan Cruz.**

BIBLIOGRAPHY

Rafael Alberto Arrieta, *Historia de la literatura Argentina,* vol. 2 (1958), pp. 149–154, and vol. 6 (1960), pp. 31–32.

Leoncio Gianello, *Florencio Varela* (1948).

Juan Antonio Solari, *Florencio Varela, el decano de los jóvenes* (1948).

Additional Bibliography

Lynch, John. *Argentine Caudillo: Juan Manuel de Rosas.* Wilmington, DE: SR Books, 2001.

Palermo, Pablo Emilio. "Florencio Varela: Vida y muerte de un argentino en el exilio." *Todo Es Historia* 441 (April 2004): 6–19.

MYRON I. LICHTBLAU

VARELA, JOSÉ PEDRO (1845–1879).

José Pedro Varela (*b.* 1845, *d.* 1879), Uruguayan educator. Varela's leadership proved essential in the country's development of free, universal, and secular education. His early contact with educational theory came from his father, who, in 1846, translated from the French the first book on pedagogy to be published in the Plata region. During a trip to the United States in 1867 Varela met Argentine educator and future president Domingo Sarmiento, whose writings on public education he admired. Under the influence of Sarmiento and the Bostonian educator Horace Mann, Varela decided to dedicate his life to Uruguayan educational reform.

In 1868 Varela published the first of many articles in the Montevidean press promoting free and universal elementary schooling. He became a lecturer on educational reform at the National

University that same year. In 1869 he founded Amigos de la Educación Popular, which played a central role in the dissemination of his ideas. Through his newspaper, *La Paz*, he promoted progressive educational ideas and criticized the government of General Lorenzo Batlle. His most influential writings include *La educación del pueblo* (1874) and *La legislación escolar* (1877). In 1865 the first school with a curriculum designed in accordance with Varela's ideas was founded.

Varela's thinking on education centered on his humanistic beliefs: free and obligatory instruction for all citizens, regardless of sex, race, or social class; the development of a rational and scientific curriculum, as opposed to the traditional, scholastic orientation of the Spanish colony; the central role of the state in training teachers and providing for schools; and the intimate link between educating the populace and the emergence of Uruguay as an independent and prosperous country. The idealistic thrust of his ideas, like those of Sarmiento, was premised on the belief that the individual, empowered through education, would become an agent in the modernization of the region's social and political institutions.

In 1876 Varela was named president of the Comisión de Instrucción Pública, which drafted the important *Ley de educación común* (1877). His death at the age of forty-four did not impede the development of one of the most ambitious and successful systems of public education on the continent, which was based on his ideas.

In addition to his books on education, Varela wrote a volume of lyrical poems, *Ecos perdidos* (1985), which rates among the finest Uruguayan lyrical expressions of the period.

See also **Education: Overview.**

BIBLIOGRAPHY

Arturo Ardao, "Prologue," in *Obras pedagógicas: La educación del pueblo* by José Pedro Varela (1964).

Additional Bibliography

González Albistur, Jorge. *José Pedro Varela: El hombre y el mito*. Montevideo, Uruguay: Ediciones de la Plaza, 1997.

Tuni, Rubén Mario. "Los estudios culturales y el fin del siglo XIX." *Confluencia* 16, no. 1 (Fall 2000): 2–10.

WILLIAM H. KATRA

VARELA, JUAN CRUZ (1794–1839).

Juan Cruz Varela (*b.* 23 November 1794; *d.* 23 January 1839), Argentine journalist, politician, poet. In 1810 Varela, a native of Buenos Aires, entered the Montserrat seminary in Córdoba to study for the priesthood; he graduated in 1816 but did not take holy orders. Varela instead turned to love poetry, writing "La Elvira" (1817), "Mi pasión" (1817), and "El enojo" (1819) among others. In 1818 he returned to Buenos Aires, where he staunchly supported liberal politics. He was a friend of Bernardino Rivadavia, becoming his press spokesman and the secretary of the General Congress of 1826. Varela wrote for *El Centinela* and *El Mensajero Argentino* and supported Rivadavia's reforms. He supported the upstart General Juan Galo Lavalle against the legitimate governor of Buenos Aires, Manuel Dorrego, who was executed in 1828 with the encouragement of Varela among others. This act only served to fortify the very forces Lavalle sought to defeat, and by 1829 Varela had to abandon Buenos Aires for exile in Montevideo. In Uruguay he continued to write articles and poetry opposing Juan Manuel de Rosas. Varela lived a spartan life in Montevideo and tried unsuccessfully to return to Buenos Aires. He died in Montevideo.

See also **Rivadavia, Bernardino.**

BIBLIOGRAPHY

Juan María Gutiérrez, *Juan Cruz Varela: Su vida—sus obras—su época* (1918) and *Los poetas de la revolución* (1941).

Additional Bibliography

Chávez, Fermín, Angel Núñez, and Francisco Javier Muñiz. *Historia y antología de la poesía gauchesca*. Buenos Aires, Argentina: Ediciones Margus, 2004.

NICHOLAS P. CUSHNER

VARELA Y MORALES, FÉLIX (1788–1853).

Félix Varela y Morales (*b.* 20 November 1788; *d.* 25 February 1853), Cuban priest, thinker, and patriot. Orphaned at an early age, Varela was still a child when he moved to Saint Augustine, Florida. (The area had been returned to Spain by Britain in 1783 under the Treaty of Paris.) There he was consigned to the care of his maternal grandfather, the commander of the city's Spanish garrison. He became the pupil of Fr. Michael O'Reilly, then the vicar of East Florida, who eventually became his role model. It was Fr. O'Reilly who influenced his decision to enter the priesthood rather than become a soldier, as his family traditions called for. "I wish to be a soldier of Jesus Christ," Varela said at the time. "I do not wish to kill men, but to save their souls."

Varela began attending the San Carlos Seminary in Havana in 1803 and was ordained in 1811. By that time he had already started to teach philosophy at the seminary, which in those days was also open to lay students. He thus became the mentor of many of the most distinguished Cuban intellectuals of the period; later they recognized their debt to him, stating that "he was who first taught us to think."

As an opponent of decadent scholasticism and one of the first who wrote philosophical textbooks in Spanish rather than Latin, Varela enjoyed the support of the bishop of Havana, José Díaz de Espada y Landa. The bishop asked him to teach a new course at the seminary on the constitution framed by the Spanish Cortes in 1812. Such was the reputation of his lectures that he was elected to represent Cuba in the Cortes in 1821. While serving, Varela made several significant contributions, advocating a more benign rule over the colonies and submitting a proposal for the abolition of slavery within fifteen years. Unfortunately, the restoration of Spanish absolutism in 1823 made it impossible for the Cortes to discuss these proposals. Forced into exile by this turn of events, he shortly arrived in the United States.

Varela settled in New York, where he soon stood out as a man of irreproachable life, a learned and devoted parish priest, an able administrator, and a wise educator and director of souls. Above all, he was known for his work with the sick and the poor especially during the great cholera epidemic of 1832, when his charity sometimes reached heroic dimensions. As one contemporary put it, his name was "one of benediction in the city of New York." For this reason Varela was admired and respected by everyone. First in 1829, on a temporary basis, and then without interruption from 1837 onward, he held the office of vicar

general for New York, a post second in importance only to that of bishop. He attended several of the Baltimore Councils as an advisor to American bishops. Varela also played a leading role as a public defender of the Catholic faith in the violent Catholic-Protestant clashes of the period.

Varela's achievements as a priest are as much a part of U.S. ecclesiastical history as they are part of Cuba's history. But although he never made any effort to return to his native land, he always regarded it as his country. Cubans, for their part, rightly regard him as the ideological father of their nationality. When Varela went to Spain as a member of the Cortes, he described himself as "a son of liberty, an American soul." At the time, however, he would have been satisfied with some form of colonial self-government for Cuba. But he soon discovered that most Spanish deputies, including many who enjoyed the reputation of being very liberal, distrusted Spanish Americans and had no faith in their ability to govern themselves. It was then, and most especially after King Ferdinand VII dissolved the Cortes, that he gave up the hope of achieving autonomy for Cuba within the framework of the Spanish monarchy and became the great prophet of Cuban independence.

Varela published his pro-independence articles in the newspaper *El Habanero,* which he founded in the United States. At the time, there were many Cubans who were in favor of Spanish rule, and some of them advocated the annexation of the island to Colombia or Mexico, just as others would support annexation to the United States a few years later. Varela argued against all of these paths. He morally justified rebellion against the oppressive colonial government, saying that it was "inspired by nature and upheld by the sacred laws of self-preservation." As for the idea of Cuba becoming the province of a neighboring state, he wrote: "I am the first to oppose the union of the island to any government. I should wish to see her as much of a political island as she is such in geographical terms."

Ill health eventually led Varela to retire to Saint Augustine, where he died. As a priest, Varela was well ahead of his time; his liberal norms and principles were more in consonance with the orientation of the Second Vatican Council (1962–1965) than with some nineteenth-century Catholic doctrines. As a thinker, he infused new life into philosophical studies in Cuba. As a patriot, he can be justly regarded as the founding father of Cuban nationalism.

See also **Hispanics in the United States; Nationalism.**

BIBLIOGRAPHY

José I. Lasaga, *Cuban Lives: Pages from Cuban History,* translated by Nelson Durán, vol. 1 (1984), pp. 157–180.

Joseph and Helen M. Mc Cadden, *Félix Varela: Torch Bearer from Cuba,* 2nd ed. (1984).

Additional Bibliography

Carnes, Mark C. *Invisible Giants: Fifty Americans Who Shaped the Nation but Missed the History Books.* New York: Oxford University Press, 2002.

Navia, Juan M. *An Apostle for the Immigrants: The Exile Years of Father Felix Varela y Morales, 1823–1853.* Salisbury, MD: Factor Press, 2002.

José M. Hernández

VARGAS, CHAVELA (1919–).

Born Isabel Vargas Lizano in San Joaquín de Flores, Costa Rica on April 17, 1919, Chavela Vargas is a famous singer of Mexican popular music. At the age of 15, she moved to Mexico City and began her career singing in cabarets and cantinas. By the early 1960s, she made headlines for the originality of her interpretative style, winning recognition with the song "Macorina." After a long bout of alcoholism, Vargas returned to the stage in the early nineties, performing in cities across the Americas, France, and Spain. In 2000, she was awarded Spain's highest honor, the Great Cross of Isabel la Católica, by Spanish film director Pedro Almodóvar. Vargas is also an icon for generations of Latin American lesbians. At the age of 82, she published an autobiography, *Y si quieres saber de mi pasado* (And If You Want to Know about My Past, 2001); she released a new album, *Cupaima,* in 2006.

See also **Music: Popular Music and Dance; Sexuality: Gender and Sexuality.**

BIBLIOGRAPHY

Vargas, Chavela, with the collaboration of J. C. Vales. *Y si quieres saber de mi pasado.* Madrid: Aguilar, 2001.

Yarbro-Bejarano, Yvonne. "Crossing the Border with Chabela Vargas: A Chicana Femme's Tribute." In *Sex and Sexuality in Latin America,* edited by Daniel Balderston and Donna J. Guy. New York: New York University Press, 1997.

Sophia Koutsoyannis

VARGAS, DIEGO DE (1643–1704).

Diego de Vargas (*b.* 1643; *d.* 8 April 1704), Spanish governor and recolonizer of New Mexico (1691–1697; 1703–1704). Heir of a proud but indebted noble house in Madrid, Vargas sailed for New Spain in 1673. Appointed by the viceroy, he was commended for his service as Alcalde Mayor of Teutila (Oaxaca) (1673–1679) and Tlalpujahua (Michoacán) (1679–1687). In 1688 he was appointed governor of New Mexico, a colony in exile since the Pueblo Rebellion of 1680, when the Spaniards fled into the El Paso area. Acceding to office in El Paso in 1691, Vargas led a determined, two-stage reconquest. With the aid of Pueblo Indian auxiliaries, he reoccupied the capital at Santa Fe, reimposing Spanish rule and putting down a second revolt in 1696. Confined by his successor in 1697 on charges of misgovernment, Vargas returned to Mexico City, stood trial, and was acquitted. The crown, meanwhile, rewarded him with a noble title of Castile—Marqués de la Nava de Barcinas. Reinstated as governor in 1703, he died the following year at Bernalillo while on a campaign against Apaches.

Although Vargas's final resting place is unknown, a shopping mall, bank, and university dormitory bear his name, and he is the central figure in Santa Fe's annual fiestas.

See also **New Mexico; Spanish Empire.**

BIBLIOGRAPHY

J. Manuel Espinosa, *Crusaders of the Rio Grande: The Story of Don Diego de Vargas and the Reconquest and Refounding of New Mexico* (1942; repr. 1977).

John L. Kessell et al., eds., *Remote Beyond Compare: Letters of Don Diego de Vargas to His Family from New Spain and New Mexico, 1675–1706* (1989).

Additional Bibliography

Kessell, John L., ed. *A Settling of Accounts: The Journals of Don Diego de Vargas, New Mexico, 1700–1704.* Albuquerque: University of New Mexico Press, 2002.

Szasz, Margaret Connell. *Between Indian and White Worlds: The Cultural Broker.* Norman: University of Oklahoma Press, 2001.

JOHN L. KESSELL

VARGAS, GETÚLIO DORNELLES

(1883–1954). Getúlio Dornelles Vargas (*b.* 19 April 1883; *d.* 24 August 1954), president of Brazil (1930–1945 and 1951–1954). Vargas was the dominant political personality of Brazil for nearly a quarter century, and his legacy persisted after his death by suicide. He is widely regarded as the prime mover of the nationalistic social and economic changes that have prompted the modernization of Brazil since the 1930s.

BACKGROUND

Vargas's personal and political prowess stemmed largely from his family heritage and his experience in the authoritarian political system in the border state of Rio Grande do Sul. The third of five sons of a regionally prominent family, Vargas was born at São Borja, a small town in western Rio Grande do Sul on Brazil's frontier with Argentina. His parents, General Manoel do Nascimento Vargas and Candida Dornelles Vargas, were from rival clans that regularly took opposite sides in armed political contests. In this situation, young Getúlio learned the patience, tact, and tolerance that became the hallmark of his political style. Initially intent on pursuing a military career, he resigned from the army after five years to study law in Pôrto Alegre.

EARLY POLITICAL CAREER

Vargas first became involved in state politics while a law student, campaigning for the gubernatorial candidate of the Republican Party. For this service, when he graduated in 1907, he was appointed to the district attorney's office in Pôrto Alegre, where he remained for two years. He then returned to São Borja to practice law and to run successfully for a seat in the state legislature. The only significant function of that body was to approve periodically the governor's budget. Membership in the legislature, however, assured the political future of those who demonstrated unquestioning support of the Republican governor. The Republican Party regime, based loosely on the hierarchical philosophy of positivism, was a veritable dictatorship in which the governor exercised absolute control over the state administration and party. The perennial governor, Borges De Medeiros, ruled by decree in all matters except finance, placed maintaining a balanced budget and treasury surplus above building public works and providing social services, and insisted upon personal loyalty from all party officials. In 1912, Vargas learned that even mild criticism of Borges's rule was unacceptable. For such a mistake he was removed from the state legislature and barred from reelection for five years, until he had displayed appropriate contrition and sworn renewed fealty to his party's boss. When he later became political head of the nation, Vargas was never to demand such obeisance from his followers, but he would share Borges's insistence upon keeping the reins of power in his own hands.

Vargas rose to national prominence in the 1920s, a decade of protest and revolts by young military officers (*tenentes*) and disgruntled civilians against corrupt rule by professional politicians in the service of the rural oligarchy. The *tenentes* were eventually defeated—killed, jailed, or exiled by the government—but they remained heroes to much of the press and the urban population. Vargas made no public statements against the young rebels, even though he held increasingly important posts in the established state and national governments. In 1922 he went to Rio de Janeiro as a newly elected congressman and head of his state's congressional delegation. Four years later he was elevated to the cabinet as finance minister of President Washington Luís Pereira De Sousa, and in 1928, following an uncontested election, Vargas succeeded Borges de Medeiros as governor of Rio Grande do Sul. In contrast to Borges's rigidly conservative fiscal management, Vargas secured federal funds for ambitious development projects of value to farmers and urban businessmen. He also abandoned Borges's strict partisanship, promoting a policy of collaboration with the opposition party. In these ways he united Rio Grande do Sul behind his bid for the presidency of Brazil in the March 1930 elections or, if that failed, by revolution.

THE RISE TO POWER

Vargas had no scruples against the use of force for political ends, but preferred to secure his objectives by nonviolent means, if possible. Because no opposition candidate had ever been elected president in Brazil, he first sought to head the administration ticket, but was rebuffed by President Washington Luís. In these circumstances, Vargas authorized his colleagues to make contingency plans for revolution. At the same time he accepted the nomination of the reformist Liberal Alliance, a coalition formed from Republican Party regimes in three states and opposition parties elsewhere. The Vargas campaign was also supported by the *tenentes* and their civilian followers, who were clamoring for political and social change. Despite his popularity in the cities, he was badly defeated by the entrenched rural-based political machines in seventeen of the twenty states.

While Vargas appeared to accept defeat gracefully, he was in fact patiently waiting for the propitious moment to launch a decisive assault on the federal government. That moment came on 3 October 1930, when the revolution broke out simultaneously in Rio Grande do Sul, Minas Gerais, and Paraíba, the states that had backed his presidential campaign. The troops on both sides were primarily regular army units and militarized state police. After three weeks, by which time the rebels were in control of most of the coastal states, the army high command in Rio de Janeiro staged a coup d'état to halt the intraservice war. The military junta ordered a cease-fire, deposed and exiled President Washington Luís, and agreed to transfer power to the rebel leader when he reached the capital. On 3 November Getúlio Vargas was installed as chief of the provisional government for an unspecified term, with no limitations on his authority.

THE VARGAS ERA

Moving quickly to consolidate his position, Vargas suspended the 1891 Constitution, announced the pending reorganization of the judiciary, dismissed the Congress and all the state legislatures, and replaced elected state governors with interventors responsible only to him. In response to widespread expectations for social reform, he created new cabinet ministries for labor and education, and appointed as their heads civilian reformers with strong ties to state Republican Party leaders. With regard to the armed forces, Vargas granted amnesty to the military rebels of the 1920s, authorized their return to active duty in their respective units, and

appointed regular officers dedicated to the principles of hierarchy and discipline as war and navy ministers. By these actions Vargas eliminated constitutional checks on the executive power, deprived the once-dominant state parties of any legitimate public functions, and, through the interventors, gained control over political activity at all levels throughout the nation. He was now undisputed dictator of Brazil.

There was no protest, because it was widely agreed that a temporary dictatorship was necessary in order to carry out the aims of the revolution. Vargas's heterogeneous following, however, could not agree on the nature and extent of those aims or the length of time required to attain them. Professional politicians and senior military commanders were willing to accept moderate democratic reforms, but they expected the traditional political system to be restored, essentially intact, within a few months. In contrast, most junior officers and civilian radicals saw Vargas as the providential leader who must remain dictator as long as it might take to secure their goals of order, justice, and honest government for the Brazilian people.

Vargas did not publicly reject either interpretation of his role, but most of his actions tended to favor the radicals. He attempted to placate his conservative allies by making repeated vows to respect the de facto autonomy long enjoyed by state governments, and to hold elections to restore constitutional rule as soon as a thorough revision of the electoral laws could be completed. Eventually, however, he so antagonized the conservatives by ignoring states' rights and refusing to call for immediate elections that the establishment political elites in São Paulo and some of his former supporters in other states tried to overthrow him.

The Constitutionalist Revolution of 1932, which raged for three months before collapsing, was far costlier in lives and treasure than the Revolution of 1930. It was limited chiefly to the state of São Paulo, because elsewhere all interventors and the armed forces remained loyal to the dictatorship. Although Vargas's national popularity remained high, the São Paulo rebels claimed a moral victory, for within a year elections were held for the constituent assembly that wrote the Constitution of 1934. This charter incorporated all reforms enacted by the provisional government,

Body of Brazilian President Getúlio Dornelles Vargas, surrounded by mourners, Rio de Janeiro, 1954. Vargas governed Brazil for nearly twenty years (1930–1945, 1951–1954). His presidency marked a watershed in Brazilian nation-building, though the Estado Nôvo period (from 1937 to 1945) was one of authoritarian rule. © BETTMANN/CORBIS

restored full civil rights, and provided for the election of a new congress as well as elected state governors and legislatures. On 17 July 1934, the constituent assembly elected Vargas president of Brazil for a four-year term.

The changes introduced in Brazil under Vargas were expressed in national and often nationalistic terms, but could not fail to reflect the impact of the world economic depression and the struggle between fascism and democracy abroad. The Great Depression cut deeply into Brazil's revenues from agricultural exports and exposed the country's great dependence on foreign sources for industrial products. Vargas dealt pragmatically with these problems, nationalizing much of the nation's rail and sea transportation, setting up advisory councils and official agencies to revive the export economy, and promoting the growth of industry in Brazil by private foreign and domestic firms. These essentially economic policies not only enhanced the

regulatory powers of the central government but also contributed to a great increase in the size and importance of the federal bureaucracy, the middle class, and the urban labor force, which then became permanent features of Brazilian society.

Vargas had no firm ideological convictions: He was motivated by love of power and what he saw as Brazil's national interests. These qualities determined his responses to the increasingly bitter rivalry among fascist and antifascist political systems in the Western world. Abroad, the United States and Nazi Germany were vying openly for Brazil's support. Within Brazil, neofascist, liberal democratic, and Communist organizations clashed and competed for followers, posing a potential threat to Vargas's rule. Thus, in foreign affairs he pursued a flexible policy seeking advantages for Brazil from both camps. At home, following the abortive Communist-led revolt in November 1935, Vargas relied on his congressional majority to suspend civil rights and strengthen his police powers for most of the remainder of his term. A spurious Communist threat was the avowed justification for the coup d'état of 10 November 1937, which Vargas and the armed forces staged to create the allegedly totalitarian Estado Nôvo (New State).

Ostensibly patterned on the European fascist dictatorships, the Estado Nôvo lacked the usual political party, militia, and national police loyal to the dictator. Vargas saw no role for political parties, and he relied upon the army to maintain order. For more than seven years he ruled Brazil without the constraints of Congress or the distractions of parties and elections. His domestic policies continued as before to focus chiefly on the urban population and on the need to strengthen the material and human bases for industrialization. Their fruits were seen in large national electrification and steel manufacturing projects, as well as in the great expansion in public health services and in education at all levels. The major social reforms under the Estado Nôvo were enactment of a minimum wage law and codification of all labor legislation enacted since 1930, which had the effect of bringing urban workers into the political arena as staunch supporters of Vargas.

Despite his apparent identification with fascism and the pro-German bias of some Brazilian military commanders, Vargas finally decided that Brazil's interests would best be served by a close relationship with the United States. In 1942 Brazil entered World War II as one of the Allied powers, and in 1944 Brazil sent a substantial expeditionary force to fight in the Italian campaign.

The incongruity of waging war against dictatorships in Europe while living under a dictator at home was not lost on the Brazilian people, who pressed for an early return to democracy. During 1945 Vargas abolished censorship, released political prisoners, issued a new electoral law authorizing political parties (two of which he himself organized), and called for the election of a new government in December. Fearing that he was planning another coup d'état, the army, led by officers recently returned from Italy, deposed Vargas on 29 October 1945, without recriminations, and installed an interim civilian regime to preside over the December elections.

Although he did not participate in the campaign, Vargas was elected to the Senate, but chose not to serve or to comment publicly on national issues. Rather, he spent the next five years quietly at his home in São Borja. He returned to politics as the candidate of his Brazilian Labor Party in the 1950 presidential elections. He waged a vociferously populist campaign and won with a large plurality. With the grudging acceptance of the armed forces, he was installed in office on 31 January 1951. However, as a democratically elected president obliged to share power with a bitterly divided Congress, Vargas proved unable to cope with the soaring inflation that eroded his labor following, or with the widespread ultranationalism to which his past policies had contributed. In mid-1954 he was overwhelmed by a wave of public revulsion caused by exposure of gross corruption and criminal activities within his official entourage. When the military withdrew its support and demanded his resignation, he complied on 24 August 1954; later that day he committed suicide. Vargas left a political testament in which he presented his death as a sacrifice on behalf of Brazilian workers.

See also **Borges de Medeiros, Antônio Augusto; Brazil, Political Parties: Republican Party (PR); Brazil, Revolutions: Revolution of 1930; Estrada Novo; Luís Pereira de Sousa, Washington; Rio Grande do Sul.**

BIBLIOGRAPHY

José Maria Bello, *A History of Modern Brazil, 1889–1964* (1966).

Paulo Brandi, *Vargas, da vida para a história* (1983).

John W. F. Dulles, *Vargas of Brazil: A Political Biography* (1967).

Stanley E. Hilton, *Brazil and the Great Powers, 1930–1939: The Politics of Trade Rivalry* (1975).

Robert M. Levine, *The Vargas Regime: The Critical Years, 1934–1938* (1970).

Karl Loewenstein, *Brazil Under Vargas* (1942).

Thomas E. Skidmore, *Politics in Brazil, 1930–1964: An Experiment in Democracy* (1967).

Maria Celina Soares D'araujo, *O segundo governo Vargas, 1951–1954: Democracia, partidos e crise política* (1982).

John D. Wirth, *The Politics of Brazilian Development, 1930–1954* (1970).

Alzira Vargas Do Amaral Peixoto, *Getúlio Vargas, meu pai* (1960).

Additional Bibliography

Araújo, Maria Celina Soares de. *As instituições brasileiras da era Vargas*. Rio de Janeiro: EdUERJ, Editora FGV, 1999.

Barros, Edgard Luiz de, *Getúlio!* São Paulo: Nankin Editorial, 2004.

Davis, Darién J., *Avoiding the Dark: Race and the Forging of National Culture in Modern Brazil*. Aldershot, U.K.: Ashgate, 1999.

Levine, Robert M., *Father of the Poor? Vargas and His Era*. New York: Cambridge University Press, 1998.

McCann, Bryan, *Hello, Hello Brazil: Popular Music in the Making of Modern Brazil*. Durham, NC: Duke University Press, 2004.

Williams, Daryle, *Culture Wars in Brazil: The First Vargas Regime, 1930–1945*. Durham, NC: Duke University Press, 2001.

ROLLIE E. POPPINO

VARGAS, JOSÉ MARÍA (1786–1854).

José María Vargas (*b*. 10 March 1786; *d*. 13 July 1854), physician and president of Venezuela (1834–1836). Born in Puerto de la Guaira, Venezuela, Vargas excelled in his studies in philosophy, theology, and medicine at the Royal Pontifical University in Caracas. He continued his medical studies at the University of Caracas (1808). With the fall of the First Republic, he was taken prisoner and then released in 1813. In 1814, he traveled to Edinburgh and London to pursue his medical education, becoming proficient in anatomy, surgery, chemistry, and botany. He returned to Venezuela in 1825 and by 1827 was appointed rector of the Central University by Simón Bolívar. While serving as the university's rector, Vargas founded the faculties of anatomy, surgery, and chemistry.

In 1834, he reluctantly accepted the nomination for the nation's presidency, which he won. Several months after he became president, the military's Las Reformas Revolution broke out (June 1835). Vargas was taken prisoner and expelled from the country. But José Antonio Páez defeated the "reformists," and Vargas was returned to power in August.

Vargas is fondly remembered for continuing to see patients on a medical basis while serving as president. During his short term, Vargas extended education to all youngsters, founded a national library, and promulgated a new legal code. Citing poor health, he resigned in 1836. Returning to academia, he traveled to New York, where in 1853 he unsuccessfully sought a cure for an eye ailment. He died while in New York.

See also **Medicine: The Modern Era.**

BIBLIOGRAPHY

Blas Bruni Celli, *La Hora de Vargas* (1986) and *Imagen y huella de José Vargas* (1987).

Francisco Linares Alcántara, *Vargas: Apoteosis del siglo XIX* (1986).

Augusto Márquez Cañizales, *José María Vargas* (1973).

Additional Bibliography

Agüero Gorrín, Enrique, *Bolívar y Vargas: Bolívar, padre de la legislación médica venezolana: Vargas, padre de la medicina científica venezolana*. Caracas: s.n., 2003.

Caballero, Miguel, and Sheila Salazar, *Diez grandes polémicas en la historia de Venezuela*. Caracas: Fondo Editorial 60 Años, 1999.

ALLAN S. R. SUMNALL INÉS QUINTERO

VARGAS LLOSA, MARIO (1936–).

The Peruvian writer Mario Vargas Llosa was born on March 28, 1936, in the city of Arequipa. Although he has written most of his novels while living in Europe, based primarily in Paris, London, Barcelona, and Madrid, his early experiences and deep attachment to Peru have been his primary creative inspiration. Vargas Llosa has permanent residences in Barranco, a suburb of Lima, and in Madrid (he became a dual citizen of Spain in 1993), but he is an indefatigable traveler, a man of insatiable curiosity.

In the 1960s, when he was a committed socialist, Vargas Llosa became an international literary sensation for his depiction of the corrosive effects of corruption on human hopes and aspirations. *La cuidad y los perros* (*Time of the Hero*, 1963) diagnoses the baseness of the social order through the microcosm of a military academy; *La casa verde* (*The Green House*, 1966) explores the brutality of a corrupt nation at its margins (the Amazonian jungle and the northern coastal area); and *Conversación en La Catedral* (*Conversation in the Cathedral*, 1969) presents a panorama of Peruvian society under a dictatorial regime through a dialogue between Santiago Zavala, a young man who has repudiated his bourgeois family, and Ambrosio, the chauffer and male lover of Santiago's father. Vargas Llosa's early novels were hailed for their political force, but also for their innovations in narrative form. In a literary movement known as the Boom, Vargas Llosa, along with Gabriel García Márquez (Colombia), Julio Cortázar (Argentina), José Donoso (Chile), and Carlos Fuentes (Mexico), contributed to the ascendancy of the Latin American novel to the top ranks of world literature in the 1960s.

In Vargas Llosa's novels a single story can be narrated from various and contradictory points of view. Mystery and intrigue derive not only from the plot but also from the author's intentional vagueness or ambiguity, as well as from his willful withholding of significant information from the reader. Vargas Llosa fuses techniques from the modern novel—the interior monologue of James Joyce, the multiple narrators and dense prose of William Faulkner—with vigorous action and melodramatic plots, some of which recall Latin American popular movies and radio plays. His narratives, while brilliant and engaging, are also in keeping with the French novelist and philosopher Jean-Paul Sartre's recommendation that literature be committed to political causes. By 1968, however, Vargas Llosa began to express public differences with the regimes on which he had pinned his political hopes: He deplored the Soviet invasion of Czechoslovakia and the repression of writers in Cuba. As a result Vargas Llosa was repudiated by cultural organizations of the Cuban Revolution and shunned by former friends and allies on the Left. Nevertheless, his success as a novelist did not diminish. He published *Pantaleón y las visitadoras* (*Captain Pantoja and the Special Service*, 1973), an ironic, humorous take on some of his previous themes. *La tía Julia y el escribidor* (*Aunt Julia and the Scriptwriter*, 1976), an autobiographical fiction, is the first of a series of novels about the compensatory nature of the literary or erotic imagination.

By the 1980s Vargas Llosa had openly abandoned his socialist convictions and became an outspoken advocate of free-market democracy; he has never wavered from his anti-authoritarian outlook or from his defense of human rights. His novels of that decade were concerned with the fragility of societies assailed by fanatics, political opportunists, or well-

intentioned visionaries for whom violence is the most attractive means to make the world a better place. This artistic turn resonated with his growing interest in reconciling the ideas of liberal thinkers such as the Russian-born, British political philosopher Isaiah Berlin and the Austrian-born, British philosopher of science Karl Popper with the views of the French thinker Georges Bataille on eroticism. His masterpiece of this period, *La guerra del fin del mundo* (*The War of the End of the World*, 1981), a historical novel set in nineteenth-century Brazil, explores the human propensity to idealize violence, whether with the visions of the idealists, the intimations of apocalyptic religious leaders, the patriotic fervor of military professionals, or the abstractions of intellectuals who fail to comprehend war for what it is—the most devastating collective experience of all. In this period he wrote *Historia de Mayta* (*The Real Life of Alejandro Mayta*, 1984), on the origins of revolutionary action; *El hablador* (*The Storyteller*, 1986), about a young man fascinated by the indigenous cultures of the Peruvian Amazonian region; and *Elogio de la madrastra* (*In Praise of the Stepmother*, 1989), about the compensations of the erotic imagination as a coping mechanism for the banalities of everyday life.

Vargas Llosa ran for president in the Peruvian elections of 1990, losing to Alberto Fujimori. Since then his writings—fiction and nonfiction alike—have been informed by a less optimistic vision, a growing sense that all struggles to prevail over one's intractable feelings of discomfort are doomed to failure. Hints of the change can be gleaned in *Lituma en los Andes* (*Death in the Andes*, 1993), about the human recourse to irrational violence when law and order cannot be maintained, and *Los cuadernos de don Rigoberto* (*The Notebooks of Don Rigoberto*, 1997), about the inevitable disruptions caused by the impulses to transgress.

Renouncing revolutionary solutions for the problems of sick and corrupt societies, Vargas Llosa has turned to a wistful exploration of the traumas and suffering that can turn some individuals against the world. Set in the Dominican Republic, *Fiesta del Chivo* (*The Feast of the Goat*, 2000) is the first novel about a Latin American dictatorship to explore the process by which a corrupt strongman must undermine the dignity and self-worth of his closest collaborators and associates to remain in power. In *El paraíso en la otra esquina* (*The Way to Paradise*, 2002), Vargas Llosa recreates the lives of the French activist Flora Tristán and her grandson, the painter Paul Gauguin, portraying his fanatical protagonists with indulgence and empathy. Indeed, parallels can be drawn between his fictional account of Tristán's courageous but failed attempt to launch a political movement that would defend the rights of women and workers and his *Pez en el agua* (*A Fish in the Water*, 1993), a memoir of his unsuccessful effort to establish a political party during his presidential campaign of 1990.

Though the male protagonist of *Travesuras de la niña mala* (*The Bad Girl*, 2006), Ricardo Somocurcio, is a translator and not a novelist, his experiences parallel Vargas Llosa's own—living more or less in the same cities at about the same time, and, whether they liked it or not, subject to the vicissitudes of Peruvian history. The novel offers a running commentary on the major political and historical events in Perú from the 1950s until the late 1980s, stopping short of Vargas Llosa's own political campaign for the Peruvian presidency. Somocurcio's attachment to a mysterious woman, the *niña mala* (bad girl) who appears and reappears in his life, is Vargas Llosa's most searching allegory about his own bonds to Peru: a love-hate relationship that has informed the career of one of the world's most celebrated writers and public intellectuals.

See also **Cortázar, Julio; Donoso, José; Fuentes, Carlos; Fujimori, Alberto Keinya; García Márquez, Gabriel; Literature: Spanish America; Peru: Peru Since Independence.**

BIBLIOGRAPHY

Boland, Roy C. *Mario Vargas Llosa: Oedipus and the "Papa" State.* Madrid: Voz, 1988.

Castro-Klarén, Sara. *Understanding Mario Vargas Llosa.* Columbia: University of South Carolina Press, 1990.

Cueto, Alonso. *Mario Vargas Llosa: La vida en movimiento.* Lima: Universidad Peruana de Ciencias Aplicadas, 2003.

Kristal, Efraín. *Temptation of the Word: The Novel of Mario Vargas Llosa.* Nashville and London: Vanderbilt University Press, 1998.

Kristal, Efraín, ed. *The Cambridge Companion to the Latin American Novel.* New York: Cambridge University Press, 2005.

Oviedo, José Miguel. *Mario Vargas Llosa: La invención de una realidad.* Barcelona: Seix Barral, 1982.

Williams, Raymond L. *Vargas Llosa: Otra historia de un deicidio.* Mexico: Taurus, Universidad Nacional Autónoma de México, 2001.

Zapata, Miguel Angel, ed. *Mario Vargas Llosa and the Persistence of Memory.* Hempstead, NY: Hofstra University, and Lima: Universidad Nacional Mayor de San Marcos, 2006.

EFRAÍN KRISTAL

VARNHAGEN, FRANCISCO ADOLFO DE (1816–1878).

Francisco Adolfo de Varnhagen (*b.* 17 February 1816; *d.* 29 June 1878), Brazilian historian and viscount of Porto Seguro (1874). The founder of modern historical writing in Brazil, Varnhagen, however, lived most of his life abroad. The son of a German military officer who had been engaged to supervise the recently created ironworks in Sorocaba (São Paulo), he was raised in Portugal, where his family had been established since Brazilian independence. After first receiving military training to become an engineer, he went on to study paleography and political economy. In 1841, he was granted Brazilian citizenship and, in the following year, he obtained a position in the Brazilian army, where he began his diplomatic career, serving in Portugal (1842–1852), Spain (1852–1858), several Latin-American republics (1859–1868), and Austria (1868–1878). He was a member of the Portuguese Royal Academy of Sciences and of the Brazilian Historical and Geographical Institute.

A product of the intellectual climate of Portuguese romanticism, Varnhagen considered the nation to be the natural framework for historical writing but, at the same time, followed the rules of historical research established by German scholars at the beginning of the century. Probing into the archives of Portugal, Spain, and Brazil, he prepared the work for which he is today chiefly known: the *História geral do Brasil antes da sua separação e independência de Portugal* (1856–1857). He also published a study on the Dutch occupation of Brazil (1871), a second, much altered, edition of the *História geral do Brasil* (1877) and, on his death, left unfinished the *História da independência do Brasil* (1916). His interests also included the history of Brazilian literature and Amerindian cultures and languages. Although deprived of literary craftsmanship and tainted by a very conservative outlook, which marred some of his judgments, his work stands, by virtue of the depth and scope of its scholarship, above all others in nineteenth-century Brazilian historical writing.

See also **Literature: Brazil.**

BIBLIOGRAPHY

J. Capistrano De Abreu, "Necrológio de Francisco Adolfo de Varnhagen, Visconde de Porto Seguro" (1878), in *Ensaios e estudos (crítica e história)*, *I* série (1931), pp. 81–91.

Francisco Adolfo De Varnhagen, *Correspondência ativa*, edited by Clado Ribeiro de Lessa (1961).

José Honório Rodrigues, "Varnhagen: O primeiro mestre da historiografia brasileira (1816–1878)," in *História combatente* (1982), pp. 191–225.

Nilo Odália (org.), *Grandes scientistas sociais*, vol. 9, *Varnhagen: História* (1979).

Additional Bibliography

Odália, Nilo. *As formas do mesmo: Ensaios sobre o pensamento historiográfico de Varnhagen e Oliveira Vianna.* São Paulo: Editora UNESP Fundação, 1997.

Wehling, Arno. *Estado, história, memoória: Varnhagen e a construção da identidade nacional.* Rio de Janeiro: Editora Nova Fronteira, 1999.

GUILHERME PEREIRA DAS NEVES

VARO, REMEDIOS (1908–1963). Remedios Varo (*b.* 16 December 1908; *d.* 8 October 1963), Spanish painter. Born in Anglés, a town in Gerona, Catalonia, Remedios Varo was the daughter of an Andalusian hydraulic engineer and a Basque mother. In 1924 she enrolled at the Academy of San Fernando in Madrid. She moved to Barcelona in 1932 and shared a studio with the Catalan artist Esteban Francés. She participated in the Exposición Logicofobista, organized by ADLAN (Amics de les Arts Nous; Friends of the New Art), in 1936. In Barcelona, Varo met the French surrealist poet Benjamín Péret, with whom she traveled to Paris in 1937, and became involved with the activities of the surrealist circle. Fleeing World War II, Varo immigrated to Mexico in 1942; there she met other exiled artists, including Leonara Carrington, Wolfgang Paalen, José and Kati Horna; with Carrington, Varo established close personal and artistic ties. Most of Varo's works were produced during her stay in Mexico,

where she remained until her death. Her works display a range of fantastic subjects, some of which are based on her interest in alchemy and the occult.

See also **Art: The Twentieth Century.**

BIBLIOGRAPHY

Fundación Banco Exterior (Madrid), *Remedios Varo* (1988).

Lucía García De Carpi, *La pintura surrealista española, 1924–1936* (1986).

Janet A. Kaplan, *Unexpected Journeys: The Art and Life of Remedios Varo* (1988).

Beatriz Varo, *Remedios Varo: En el centro del microcosmos* (1990).

Additional Bibliography

Blanco, Alberto. "El último dibujo de Remedios Varo." *Artes de México* 63, Suppl. (2003): 8–11.

Rivera, Magnolia. *Trampantojos: El círculo en la obra de Remedios Varo.* México City: Siglo Veintiuno Editores, 2005.

ILONA KATZEW

VARONA Y PERA, ENRIQUE JOSÉ (1849–1933). Enrique José Varona y Pera (*b.* 13 April 1849; *d.* 19 November 1933) Cuban philosopher, intellectual, and vice president (1913–1916). A native-born Cuban, Varona earned a Ph.D. from the University of Havana and became a representative from Cuba to the Spanish Cortes, where he strongly supported Cuban autonomy. He called for independence, moved to New York, and joined José Martí's independence movement, editing the revolutionary paper, *La Patria Libre*. After Martí's death, he became Cuba's most influential polemicist. While a member of the cabinet of Governor Leonard Wood during the U.S. occupation, he directed the reopening and reorganization of the University of Havana. Although serving as vice president under General Mario García Menocal, he opposed the president's reelection bid and joined the conservative cause. An opponent of the corruption in post-occupation regimes, he served as a vice president of the National Association of Veterans and Patriots against the government of Alfredo Zayas and led students against faculty improprieties at the University of Havana under Zayas and against the repression of opposition by Gerardo Machado.

Varona led the positivist movement in Cuba, blending the teachings of Auguste Comte with those of other European positivists. A fervent nationalist, he died lonely and unsatisfied. However, his voice and his writings served to lead Cubans during the turbulence of the 1920s and 1930s, and his philosophical and political contributions helped forge the reality of Cuban nationhood.

See also **Marti y Pérez, José Julían; Menocal, Mario Garcia.**

BIBLIOGRAPHY

Miguel Angel Cabonell, *El Varona que yo conocí* (1950).

Elías José Entralgo and Roberto Agramonte, *Enrique José Varona: Su vida, su obra, y su influencia* (1937).

Francisco Romero, "Enrique José Varona," in *Positivism in Latin America, 1850–1900,* edited by Ralph Lee Woodward, Jr. (1971).

Additional Bibliography

Bernal, Beatriz. *Cuba, fundamentos de la democracia: Antología del pensamiento liberal cubano desde fines del siglo XVIII hasta fines del siglo XX.* Madrid: Fundación Liberal José Martí, 1994.

Helg, Aline. *Our Rightful Share: The Afro-Cuban Struggle for Equality, 1886–1912.* Chapel Hill: University of North Carolina Press, 1995.

JACQUELYN BRIGGS KENT

VASCONCELOS, BERNARDO PEREIRA DE
(1795–1850). Bernardo Pereira de Vasconcelos (*b.* 27 August 1795; *d.* 1 August 1850), Brazilian statesman. Born in Ouro Preto, Vasconcelos took his degree in Coimbra (1818) and returned to Brazil in 1820, soon beginning a career as a crown magistrate in São Paulo and Maranhão. He began his political career in the first legislature (1826). He achieved prominence in the conflicts of the Regency period (1831–1840). He helped lead the opposition to the First Reign's absolutist centralism, a struggle that led to Pedro I's abdication in 1831. Vasconcelos, a minister in the Regency's first cabinet, also figured importantly in the triumph of liberal moderates and consequent decentralizing reforms, notably the Additional Act of 1834. Later, ambition, social unrest,

and secessionism thrust him into opposition to moderate Diogo Antônio Feijó, who was then serving as regent. He sought social order and national unity by identifying the crown's central power with the interests of the propertied classes. After Pedro I's death (1834), Vasconcelos allied the more conservative moderates to the first emperor's reactionary supporters. They formed a parliamentary majority that triumphed with the ascension of Regent Pedro de Araújo Lima (later Marqués de Olinda) and the birth of the Conservative Party (1837).

This movement, known as the *Regresso* (reaction), pitted itself against the decentralist liberalism Vasconcelos had once championed. In conservative cabinets (1837 and 1839) and the Senate (after 1838), Vasconcelos, with Paulino José Soares de Sousa (later Viscount do Uruguai), reversed the earlier reforms. They promoted the Interpretation of the Additional Act (1840), reforms of the Criminal Code, and restoration of the Council of State (1841). The Liberal minority attempted to thwart this Conservative reversal by forcing the early majority of Pedro II, who then called them to power (1840). However, the Liberals' cabinet soon imploded, and the Conservative march resumed until the early 1850s, despite brief Liberal administrations and revolts. Vasconcelos, as a senator and councillor of state (1841), remained a preeminent conservative chieftain until his untimely death in 1850.

See also **Brazil: 1808–1889.**

BIBLIOGRAPHY

Roderick Barman, *Brazil: The Forging of a Nation, 1798–1852* (1989).

Thomas Flory, *Judge and Jury in Imperial Brazil* (1981).

Otávia Tarqüinio De Sousa, *Bernardo Pereira de Vasconcelos e seu tempo* (1937).

Additional Bibliography

Carvalho, José Murilho de, ed. *Bernardo Pereira de Vasconcelos.* São Paulo: Editora 34, 1999.

Costa, Emília Viotti da. *The Brazilian Empire: Myths and Histories.* Chapel Hill: University of North Carolina Press, 2000.

JEFFREY D. NEEDELL

VASCONCELOS CALDERÓN, JOSÉ

(1882–1959). José Vasconcelos Calderón (*b.* 28 February 1882; *d.* 30 June 1959), Mexican philosopher and politician. Vasconcelos, a multifaceted intellectual and political figure, had a significant impact on intellectual thought in Latin America and on higher education and political behavior in Mexico. Intellectually, his work on the "cosmic race" (1925), which maintained that the mestizo race combined the best of indigenous and European qualities, was a great contribution to the growing literature of the region. His multivolume autobiography (1935–1939) is a classic in acerbic, intellectual literature. During his tenure as education minister in Mexico in the 1920s, he provided an important refuge for many radical students from South America, exposing them to the dynamic undercurrents of Mexico in the postrevolutionary era. At the same time he also attempted to bring art, music, and classical literature to the Mexican masses, fostering a flowering of the arts most notable for its painting, made world-famous by a generation of muralists that included Diego Rivera, David Alfaro Siqueiros, and José Clemente Orozco. And although he opposed political centralism, Vasconcelos helped to centralize the educational system as it is organized today.

As a moral leader of students and intellectuals, he ran against Pascual Ortiz Rubio, the first official party candidate for the presidency of Mexico, in 1929. His campaign was innovative in that it drew many young female activists into politics. Although he abandoned his supporters in defeat, his essays and articles, written in exile but published in *El Universal,* were among the most widely read in Mexico. He remained in Europe until 1940. While many of his supporters, embittered by the experience, rejected politics altogether after his defeat, others joined the government party, hoping to bring about change from within. These activists, among them Adolfo López Mateos (president 1958–1964), dominated Mexican politics for many years but ignored their original goals.

Vasconcelos was born in Oaxaca, the son of Ignacio Vasconcelos and Carmen Calderón. His grandparents had ties to Porfirio Díaz, whom Vasconcelos later opposed. After completing his education at the National Preparatory School and the National University in 1905, he joined the intellectual circle of the Ateneo de la Juventud. He became interested in political reform when Francisco I. Madero began his anti-reelectionist activity against Porfirio Díaz. He served as Madero's confidential agent in Washington, D.C., and became vice president of the Progressive Constitution Party. Although he never taught a single class, he became rector of the National University (1920–1921) and then secretary of public education (1921–1924). While in exile in Europe from 1924 to 1928, he founded *Antorcha* (1924–1925), an intellectual magazine he used to oppose the Calles regime. In later life, he lost touch with his generation and his disciples, becoming an apologist for fascism.

See also **Mexico: Since 1910; Philosophy: Overview.**

BIBLIOGRAPHY

Gabriella De Beer, *José Vasconcelos and His World* (1966).

John H. Haddox, *Vasconcelos of Mexico* (1967).

José Joaquín Blanco, *Se llamaba Vasconcelos* (1977).

Richard B. Phillips, "José Vasconcelos and the Mexican Revolution of 1910" (diss., Stanford University, 1953).

Hugo Pineda, *José Vasconcelos, político mexicano, 1928–1929* (1975).

John Skirius, *José Vasconcelos y la cruzada de 1929* (1978).

José Vasconcelos, *Memorias,* 2 vols. (1982–1983).

Additional Bibliography

Cárdenas N., Joaquín. *José Vasconcelos: Caudillo cultural.* Oaxaca, Mexico: Universidad José Vasconcelos de Oaxaca, 2002.

Marentes, Luis A., *José Vasconcelos and the Writing of the Mexican Revolution.* New York: Twayne Publishers, 2000.

Mares, Roberto, *José Vasconcelos.* México City: Grupo Editorial Tomo, 2004.

RODERIC AI CAMP

VÁSQUEZ, FRANCISCO DE ASÍS

(1647–1713). Francisco de Asís Vásquez (also Vázquez; *b.* 10 October 1647; *d.* 1713) Guatemalan chronicler of Franciscan colonial church history. Vásquez is best known for writing the carefully detailed, *Crónica de la provincia del santísmo nombre de Jesús de Guatemala* in two volumes, the first appearing in 1714, the second one in 1716, edited and printed by the San Franciscan Monastery in Antigua, Guatemala. He is also the author of *Historia del venerable hermano Pedro de José de Bethancourt* and *Historia lauretana*. The latter narrates the vicissitudes of the Virgin of Loreto, who is venerated in the San Francisco Church in Antigua.

As well as being a renowned professor of philosophy and theology, Vásquez was deputy of the Third Order and superior of the Franciscan monasteries of Guatemala and San Salvador. He became the bishop's representative for the province of Nicaragua and held the titles of examiner of curates and confessors, and censor of the Inquisition. He became the chronicler and custodian of the Franciscan province of Guatemala, a position of supreme prominence in the Franciscan order.

See also **Franciscans.**

BIBLIOGRAPHY

Agustín Mencos Franco, *Literatura guatemalteca en el período de la Colonia* (1967), pp. 33–45.

José A. Mobil, *100 Personajes Historicos de Guatemala* (1979), pp. 67–69.

JANE EDDY SWEZEY

VÁSQUEZ, HORACIO (1860–1936).

Horacio Vásquez (*b*. 1860; *d*. 1936), president of the Dominican Republic (1899, 1902–1903, 1924–1930). Horacio Vásquez came to be recognized as the last president of the Dominican Republic's oligarchic era. He had been very active in plots to overthrow the Dominican dictator Ulises Heureaux during the 1890s and ultimately came to power after Heureaux's assassination in 1899. His supporters came to be known as *Horacistas* and soon grew to become a major political party.

Characterized as inept and chaotic and yet as the most democratic of the period, the Vásquez era government was marked by severe political factionalism and increasing U.S. involvement in Dominican affairs. At the same time, the republic experienced accelerated economic growth and the emergence of a wealthy merchant and planter class. This era was most known, however, for the evolution of U.S.

involvement, from customs collection to controlling national elections, and finally to outright occupation in 1916. Vásquez played a major role during the 1916–1924 occupation as a member of the negotiating committee that effected the withdrawal of the U.S. Marines. Supported by Washington in his 1924 presidential bid, he came to be seen as a puppet of the U.S. government. This perception and economic hardship brought on by the Great Depression resulted in increasing political factionalism, which led to his ouster in 1930 by the army commander Rafael Leónidas Trujillo Molina, who symbolized a new era of dictatorship for the Dominican Republic. Vásquez died in exile in the United States.

See also **Heureaux, Ulises; Trujillo Molina, Rafael Leónidas.**

BIBLIOGRAPHY

Ian Bell, *The Dominican Republic* (1981).

Selden Rodman, *Quisqueya: A History of the Dominican Republic* (1964).

Howard J. Wiarda, *The Dominican Republic: Nation in Transition* (1969).

Howard J. Wiarda and M. J. Kryzanek, *The Dominican Republic: A Caribbean Crucible* (1982).

Additional Bibliography

Domínguez, Jaime de Jesús. *La sociedad dominicana a principios del siglo XX*. Santo Domingo, Dominican Republic: Comisión Oficial para la Celebración del Sesquicentenario de la Independencia Nacional, 1994.

Moya Pons, Frank. *The Dominican Republic: A National History*. Princeton, NJ: Markus Wiener Publishers, 1998.

HEATHER K. THIESSEN

VÁSQUEZ DE ARCE Y CEBALLOS, GREGORIO (1638–1711).

Gregorio Vásquez de Arce y Ceballos (*b*. 9 May 1638; *d*. 1711), Colombia's major colonial painter. Vásquez, a native of Bogotá, studied under Gaspar de Figueroa (1594–1658) and his son Baltasar (1629–1667), both celebrated locally for their canvases. About 1657 Vásquez set up his own studio. With him worked his two children, Feliciana and Bartolomé-Luis, and his brother, Juan Bautista. His patrons were mainly local religious communities. Vásquez's best oeuvre (1680–1705) is religious in theme. Some four hundred paintings are attributed to Vásquez. Many display mediocre composition and perspective and occasional poor figure rendition. These faults have perhaps unfairly been blamed on Vásquez, since there is no agreement regarding the attribution of numerous works.

Vásquez's real forte was drawing. Over one hundred drawings survive, and are truly masterpieces. In 1701, Vásquez was accused of rape and imprisoned for a time. This experience caused him severe economic loss and mental anguish. He died, insane, in Bogotá.

See also **Art: The Colonial Era.**

BIBLIOGRAPHY

Guillermo Hernández De Alba, *Gregorio Vásquez de Arce y Ceballoz* (1966).

Francisco Gil Tovar, *La obra de Gregorio Vásquez* (1980).

Additional Bibliography

Rubiano Caballero, Germán. *El dibujo en Colombia: De Vásquez de Arce y Ceballos a los artistas de hoy.* Bogotá: Planeta Colombiana Editorial, 1997.

J. LEÓN HELGUERA

VASSOURAS. Vassouras (2005 est. pop. 33,206), a city in the highlands Paraíba Valley in Rio de Janeiro State, Brazil, dedicated to cattle raising and mixed farming. In the nineteenth century, this city's coffee production for the foreign market was the highest in the world. The name Vassouras ("broom") derives from a locally grown bush that was used to make brooms. From humble beginnings, Vassouras was settled by migrants from Minas Gerais and by court favorites who were awarded crown grants to settle along the Paraíba River to cultivate coffee. By the time of the census of 1872, the population was over 39,000, half slave and half free.

Vassouras was one of the most prosperous coffee counties in the Paraíba Valley. The neoclassic urban architecture that made its debut in Rio de Janeiro in 1816 was introduced after mid-century in the palatial mansions that successful planter elites constructed on the banks and tributaries of the Paraíba River. Prosperous planter-merchants who diversified their property among rural estates,

slaves, commerce, urban real estate, and investments in budding financial institutions were recipients of prestigious nobility titles (baron and viscount) conferred in the imperial court. Vassouras became a frequently visited and popular highlands cultural center with the advent of railroad communication from Rio de Janeiro in the 1870s.

Crises beset the coffee economy in the 1870s, and planters whose investments were restricted to slaves and land faced reversals of fortune as creditors foreclosed on their property. The urban-based abolition movement that contributed to slave unrest and the departure of ex-slaves from the coffee plantations in the aftermath of the 13 May 1888 emancipation decree shattered the mainstays of the commercial plantation system.

Postemancipation Vassouras never fully recovered from the demise of the slave-based plantation complex. Cattle now graze the hills where coffee trees once flourished. As in other towns in the Paraíba Valley, the barren and eroded hills of Vassouras are grim reminders of the legacy of the coffee boom. Today the city is a tourist destination. Visitors are attracted to its historic buildings, such as the Mansion of the Baron of Vassouras and the old railway station.

See also **Coffee Industry; Slavery: Brazil.**

BIBLIOGRAPHY

Stanley J. Stein, *Vassouras, a Brazilian Coffee County, 1850–1900: The Roles of Planter and Slave in a Plantation Society* (1985).

Nancy Priscilla Smith Naro, "Customary Rightholders and Legal Claimants to Land in Rio de Janeiro, Brazil, 1870–1890," in *The Americas* 48, no. 4 (April 1992): 485–517.

Additional Bibliography

Gomes, Flávio dos Santos. *Histórias de quilombolas: Mocambos e comunidades de senzalas no Rio de Janeiro, século XIX.* Rio de Janeiro: Arquivo Nacional, 1995.

Silva, Rudy Mattos da. *Galeria vassourense.* Vassouras, Rio de Janeiro: EVSA, 1999.

NANCY PRISCILLA SMITH NARO

VATAPA. *See* **Cuisines.**

VAZ FERREIRA, CARLOS (1872–1958).

Carlos Vaz Ferreira (*b.* 15 October 1872; *d.* 3 January 1958); Uruguayan educator, writer, and philosopher. Trained as an attorney, he became a professor of philosophy at the age of twenty-three and later taught legal philosophy at the University of the Republic, where from 1913 until his death he organized and taught seminars. He held directorships in primary-, secondary-, and university-level education. In 1933, during the coup d'état of Gabriel Terra, he was rector of the university. Later, he inspired and founded the College of Humanities and Sciences and served as its first dean.

Vaz Ferreira produced most of his writings between the years 1905 and 1910. He published *Los problemas de la libertad* (1907), *Conocimiento y acción* (1908), *Moral para intelectuales* (1908), *El pragmatismo* (1909), and *Lógica viva* (1910). A good part of these are based on notes from his conferences, and his later work undertaken while at the university basically develops these themes and their pedagogical derivations, which are an essential part of all of his work. With Vaz Ferreira, the sharp polemics of the 1870s and 1880s between different schools of philosophy were brought to a close. He initiated a postpositivist neospiritualism that would characterize Uruguayan thought in the first half of the twentieth century.

See also **Terra, Gabriel.**

BIBLIOGRAPHY

Arturo Ardao, *Introducción a Vaz Ferreira* (1961).

Agustín Álvarez Villablanca, *Carlos Vaz Ferreira* (1938).

Diana Castro, *Pensamiento y acción en Vaz Ferreira* (1969); *Cuadernos de Marcha* 63–64 (July–August 1972).

Pedro Ceruti Crosa, *Crítica de Vaz Ferreira* (1933).

Carlos Mato, *Vaz Ferreira* (1991) and *Pensamiento uruguayo*, vol. 1 (1991).

Sara Vaz Ferreira De Echevarría, *Carlos Vaz Ferreira* (1984).

Jesualdo Sosa, *Vaz Ferreira* (1963).

Additional Bibliography

Andreoli, Miguel, ed. *Ensayos sobre Carlos Vaz Ferreira.* Montevideo, Uruguay: Universidad de la República, 1996.

Mato, Carlos, and Celina Ana Lértora Mendoza. *Pensamiento Uruguayo: La época de Carlos Vaz Ferreira.* Montevideo, Uruguay: Fundación Cultura Universitaria, 1995.

Romero Baro, Jose Ma. *Carlos Vaz Ferreira (1872–1958).* Madrid: Ediciones del Oro, 1998.

JOSÉ DE TORRES WILSON

VÁZQUEZ, TABARÉ (1940–).

Tabaré Vázquez was elected president of Uruguay in 2004, that country's first elected president who was not a member of either the Blanco or the Colorado party. He ran as a member of the Encuentro Progresista-Frente Amplio (Progressive Encounter-Broad Front), which had brought together a wide variety of parties of the left since 1994.

Born on January 17, 1940, Vazquez was the fourth son of a state oil company worker and a housewife and was raised in La Teja, a working-class neighborhood in Montevideo. After graduating from high school, he worked at a number of jobs before entering the Universidad de la República medical school in 1963. Married with children, he graduated in 1969. Having lost both parents and a sister to cancer during the 1960s, he chose to become an oncologist and later continued his studies in France, the United States, Israel, and Japan. Beginning in 1985 he was head of radiotherapy in the oncology department of the Facultad de Medicina. He joined the Socialist Party secretly during the years of military rule (1973–1985), although, unlike a brother who spent time in prison, he did not take part in anti-government activities. From 1979 until 1989 he was the president of the soccer club Progreso, which had been founded by his grandparents.

Vazquez's political activities began in 1987 when he was the treasurer for a campaign organized to oppose amnesty for the military. In November 1989 he was the first socialist elected to the intendancy of Montevideo, Uruguay assuming office in the following February and quickly becoming a national figure. Although unsuccessful in the presidential races of 1994 and 1999, his national support was clearly expanding. A soft-spoken man, he ran on promises of making his country more innovative and democratic and on making the government more transparent. He was elected president in October 2004 with slightly more than 50 percent of the vote, and was inaugurated in March 2005. Although his election was seen as indicative of a general left-wing trend in Latin American politics in the early twenty-first century, in his first year in office he followed orthodox economic policies.

See also **Uruguay, Political Parties: Blanco Party; Uruguay, Political Parties: Broad Front; Uruguay, Political Parties: Colorado Party; Uruguay, Political Parties: Socialist Party.**

BIBLIOGRAPHY

Fernández, Nelson. *Quién es Quién en El Gobierno de la Iquierda?* Montevideo, Uruguay: Editorial Fin de Siglo, 2004.

Lanza, Edison, and Ernesto Tulbovitz. *Tabaré Vázquez: Misterios de un Liderazgo que Cambió La Historia.* Montevideo, Uruguay: Alcierre Ediciones, 2004.

Liscano, Carlos. *Conversaciones con Tabaré Vázquez.* Montevideo, Uruguay: Ediciones del Caballo Perdido, 2003.

Perelli, Carina, Fernanda Figueira, and Silvana Rubino. *Gobierno y Política en Montevideo: La Intendencia Municipal de Montevideo y la Formación de un Nuevo Liderazgo a Comienzos de los Años 90.* Montevideo, Uruguay: PEITHO, 1991.

Vázquez, Tabaré. *El Gobierno del Cambio.* Montevideo, Uruguay: La República, 2004.

ANDREW J. KIRKENDALL

VÁZQUEZ DE AYLLÓN, LUCAS

(c. 1475–1526). Lucas Vázquez de Ayllón (*b.* ca. 1475; *d.* 18 October 1526), judge and leader of an ill-fated colony in La Florida. Vázquez de Ayllón, an official in the Audiencia of Santo Domingo, sponsored two exploratory voyages to the Atlantic coast of La Florida. The earlier one, led by Pedro de Quejo and Francisco Gordillo in 1521, gave rise to the legend of Chicora, a fabled land of riches in the Carolina region.

In 1523 Vázquez de Ayllón was granted a royal charter to establish a colony on the southeast Atlantic coast. Named San Miguel de Gualdape, the colony of six hundred, including African slaves, lasted only for three months in 1526. Many of the colonists, along with Vázquez de Ayllón, lost their lives. It is believed that the African slaves were abandoned when the colony withdrew. The exact location of the colony has not been established.

See also **Santo Domingo, Audiencia of.**

BIBLIOGRAPHY

Henry Harrisse, *Discovery of North America* (1892; repr. 1961), esp. pp. 198–213.

Paul E. Hoffman, *A New Andalucia and a Way to the Orient: The American Southeast During the Sixteenth Century* (1990).

Additional Bibliography

García Icazbalceta, Joaquín. *Biografías, estudios.* México City: Porrúa, 1998.

JERALD T. MILANICH

VÁZQUEZ DE CORONADO, FRANCISCO

(1510–1554). Francisco Vázquez de Coronado (*b.* 1510; *d.* 22 September 1554), Spanish explorer. Vázquez de Coronado was born in Salamanca, second son of nobleman Juan Vázquez de Coronado and Isabel de Lujan. In 1535, he arrived in Mexico with the newly appointed viceroy, Antonio de Mendoza. As the viceroy's protégé, he was appointed a member of the *cabildo* of Mexico City. A short time after his arrival, Vázquez de Coronado had become an important landowner and had married Beatriz de Estrada, daughter of the royal treasurer, Alonso de Estrada. In 1539, he succeeded to the governorship of Nueva Galicia, due to the imprisonment of his predecessor, Nuño de Guzmán. In 1540, Mendoza selected him to lead a massive expedition to explore an unknown area of North America that Fray Marcos de Niza claimed was Cíbola, one of seven cities of untold wealth. The group included over 300 potential conquistadores from Spain, 1,000 Indians, Fray Marcos and five other Franciscans, at least three women, and well over 1,000 pack animals. Vázquez de Coronado's explorers marched from Compostela on the west coast of Mexico through Sonora, eastern Arizona, New Mexico, and the panhandles of Texas and Oklahoma to the Great Bend of the Arkansas River in central Kansas. The expedition was a disaster; it found no wealth, and Vázquez de Coronado and his party destroyed as many as thirteen Pueblo villages in New Mexico while putting down an indigenous uprising against Spanish maltreatment. However, it was responsible for the European discoveries of the Grand Canyon, the Continental Divide, and the Great Plains as well as the people, flora, and fauna of those regions. Its members influenced the cartography of the area and established a written heritage for northwestern Mexico and the southwestern portion of present-day United States. Vázquez de Coronado lived for another twelve years after the expedition's return in 1542. A broken man, he died in Mexico City and was buried in the Church of Santo Domingo.

See also **Cartography: Overview; Explorers and Exploration: Spanish America.**

BIBLIOGRAPHY

Herbert Eugene Bolton, *Coronado on the Turquoise Trail: Knight of Pueblos and Plains,* 4th ed. (1990).

Stewart Udall, *In Coronado's Footsteps* (1991).

David J. Weber, *The Spanish Frontier in North America* (1992).

Additional Bibliography

Flint, Richard, and Shirley Cushing Flint. *The Coronado Expedition: From the Distance of 460 Years.* Albuquerque: University of New Mexico Press, 2003.

Montané Martí, Julio César. *Francisco Vázquez Coronado: sueño y decepción.* Zapopan, Jalisco, Mexico: El Colegio de Jalisco, Fideicomiso Teixidor, 2002.

JOSEPH P. SÁNCHEZ

VEDIA Y MITRE, MARIANO (1881–1958).

Mariano Vedia y Mitre (*b.* 1881; *d.* 19 February 1958) Argentine politician and writer. Born and raised in Buenos Aires, Vedia y Mitre earned a law degree from the University of Buenos Aires. He entered education administration, becoming supervisor of secondary schools (1909–1911) and rector of the Colegio Bernardino Rivadavia (1910–1916). At the same time, from 1908, he was professor of history at the University of Buenos Aires and wrote a series of lesser historical works dealing with nineteenth-century Argentine history. Vedia y Mitre entered municipal politics dramatically in November 1932 when he was made *intendente* (mayor) of Buenos Aires, a position he occupied until February 1938. A controversial administrator, he ran

roughshod over the city council, signed many contracts with foreign transport and public works companies, and ruled in an autocratic style befitting the conservative and fraudulent political spirit of the decade.

Vedia y Mitre made his mark by breaking the political logjam blocking Argentina's transportation system. The Buenos Aires Transport Corporation was set up to regulate all public transportation (subways, buses, tramways, and local railways). He resolved a long-standing dispute with electricity companies over service charges, had major soccer stadiums and a riverside bathing zone and promenade built, and widened the celebrated Avenida Corrientes. He crowned his achievements with a massive obelisk, modeled on that in the Place de la Concorde in Paris, built in the center of a construction project for the city's widest avenue to commemorate the four-hundredth anniversary of the founding of Buenos Aires in 1536. Vedia y Mitre oversaw one of the last major public works and construction waves in Buenos Aires, in an effort to fulfill the Argentine elite's ambitions to inhabit one of the world's great capitals. He died in Montevideo.

See also **Argentina: The Twentieth Century.**

BIBLIOGRAPHY

David Rock, *Argentina, 1516–1982: From Spanish Colonization to the Falklands War* (1985; rev. ed. 1987), chap. 6.

Richard Walter, *Politics and Urban Growth in Buenos Aires: 1910–1942* (1993), esp. chaps. 9–10.

Additional Bibliography

Béjar, María Dolores. *El regimen fraudulento: La política en la provincia de Buenos Aires, 1930–1943.* Buenos Aires: Siglo Veintiuno Editores Argentina, 2005.

Elguera, Alberto, and Carlos Boaglio. "Vedia y Mitre, el intendente del obelisco." *Todo Es Historia* 29, no. 342 (Jan. 1996): 46–66.

JEREMY ADELMAN

VEGA, AURELIO DE LA (1925–).

Aurelio de la Vega (*b.* 28 November 1925). Born in Havana, Vega is one of Cuba's most prominent composers of the twentieth century. He received his bachelor's degree in humanities from De La

Salle College in Havana in 1944, then went on to complete a doctorate in diplomacy at the University of Havana in 1947. His musical training began with private lessons from Frederick Kramer (1942–1946).

In 1947 Vega was appointed cultural attaché to the Cuban consulate in Los Angeles. There he studied composition with Ernest Toch. Upon his return to Cuba in 1949, Vega became editorial secretary of *Conservatorio,* the official publication of the Havana Municipal Conservatory. The following year he composed *Legend of the Creole Ariel* for piano and cello.

From 1953 to 1959 Vega was dean of the music department of the University of Oriente in Santiago. In the latter year he returned to Los Angeles. He became professor of music at San Fernando Valley State College (now California State University at Northridge), and has continued to produce a variety of musical works. In 1966 he received his American citizenship. In 1994 he retired from full time teaching and became a professor emeritus. Four years later, he won the prestigious FACE (Facts About Cuban Exiles) award. In 2001 the spring–summer issue of the *Latin American Music Review* was dedicated to him in honor of his seventy-fifth birthday. In 2004 he received the Herencia award for his accomplishments in teaching and composing.

See also **Music.**

BIBLIOGRAPHY

Compositores de la América/Composers of the Americas 7 (1961): 98.

A. B. Ramsay, "Aurelio de la Vega: His Life and His Works" (Ph.D. diss., San Fernando Valley State College, 1963); *New Grove Dictionary of Music and Musicians* (1980).

Additional Bibliography

Erin, Ronald. "Cuban Elements in the Music of Aurelio de la Vega." *Latin American Music Review* 5 (Spring–Summer 1984): 1–32.

Gonzalez, Sergio. "The Piano Works by Aurelio de la Vega." (Ph.D. diss., University of Miami, 1988).

DARIÉN DAVIS

VEGA, JORGE LUIS DE LA (1930–1971).

Jorge Luis de la Vega (*b.* 27 March 1930; *d.* 26 August 1971), Argentine painter and draftsman. Vega was born in Buenos Aires and studied architecture at the National University. Believing that nonrepresentational art had reached a dead end, he helped to form the New Figuration Group in 1960. In his work Vega depicts violence with a passionate eloquence that stands in marked contrast to the formal refinement of lyrical abstraction and geometrical art. Over the years he had numerous exhibitions in North and South America.

See also **Art: The Twentieth Century.**

BIBLIOGRAPHY

Vicente Gesualdo, Aldo Biglione, and Rodolfo Santos, *Diccionario de artistas plásticos en la Argentina* (1988).

Museum of Modern Art of Latin America (Washington, DC, 1985).

Additional Bibliography

Ramírez, Mari Carmen, Marcelo Eduardo Pacheco, and Andrea Guinta. *Cantos paralelos: La parodia plástica en el arte argentine contemporáneo.* Austin: Jack S. Blanton Museum of Art, University of Texas at Austin, 1999.

AMALIA CORTINA ARAVENA

VEIGA, EVARISTO FERREIRA DA (1799–1837).

Evaristo Ferreira da Veiga (*b.* 8 October 1799; *d.* 12 May 1837), Brazilian journalist and politician. Veiga was a newspaper owner, writer, and congressional deputy elected for three consecutive terms to represent the state of Minas Gerais. As a political propagandist he was influential in promoting the cause of Brazil's independence from Portugal, declared by Pedro I in 1822. Famed for his comment, "We want a constitution, not a revolution," Veiga represented the nationalist interests of Brazil's agro-exporting sector. Once the constitution was promulgated in 1824, Veiga pressed for its execution, arguing that it would be interpreted from a liberal standpoint. Veiga supported independence and the abdication of Pedro I in favor of Pedro's native-born son as measures that would increase the political power of the

Brazilian elite and ensure ready access to international markets. His views were propagated through his newspaper *Aurora Fluminense* (1827–1835). Veiga was also the founder of the Sociedade Defensora da Liberdade e da Independéncia Nacional (Society for the Defense of National Liberty and Independence), one of three major political groups during the regency that followed the abdication of Pedro I in favor of six-year-old Pedro II in 1831. Veiga is held to have been responsible for many of the regents' decisions, most notably the creation of the National Guard as a force that could confront local armies and militias and contain regional unrest.

See also **Journalism; Pedro I of Brazil; Pedro II of Brazil.**

BIBLIOGRAPHY

Lima, Israel Souza. *Biobibliografia dos patronos*. Rio de Janeiro: Academia Brasileira de Letras, 1997–.

SUEANN CAULFIELD

VEIGA VALE, JOSÉ JOAQUIM DA

(1806–1874). José Joaquim da Veiga Vale (*b.* 1806; *d.* 1874), Brazilian sculptor. Veiga Vale spent most of his adult life in the state of Goiás. Lacking formal artistic training, he early began to experiment with woodcarving. Although born in the nineteenth century, his art appears to have remained virtually unaffected by the then popular neoclassical tradition taught at the Imperial Academy of Fine Arts in Rio de Janeiro. Rather, his carvings display an archaic quality that firmly embeds them in the eighteenth-century baroque tradition. His best-known work, the *Santíssima Trindade,* still holds a place of honor in an important religious procession in Vila Boa de Goiás, Veiga Vale's hometown. His series of carved religious figures, housed today in the Museu de Arte Sacra da Boa Morte in Goiás, gained recognition in 1940, when an exhibition of his works took place in Vila Boa de Goiás.

See also **Art: The Nineteenth Century.**

BIBLIOGRAPHY

Eduardo Etzel, *O Barroco no Brasil* (1974); *Arte no Brasil,* vol. 1 (1979), pp. 310–311.

Additional Bibliography

Gomes Júnior, Guilherme Simões. *Palavra peregrina: O Barroco e o pensamento sobre artes e letras no Brasil.* Sao Paulo: Edusp, 1998.

CAREN A. MEGHREBLIAN

VEINTEMILLA, JOSÉ IGNACIO DE

(1828–1908). José Ignacio de Veintemilla (also spelled Veintimilla; *b.* 31 July 1828; *d.* 19 July 1908), president of Ecuador (1878–1883). Born in Quito, Veintemilla studied at the Military College and was commissioned second lieutenant in 1847. He rose rapidly through the ranks, partly through involvement in politics, and became brigadier general in 1866. Under President Jerónimo Carrión (1865–1867) he became minister of war. After narrowly escaping execution by President García Moreno in 1869, he fled into exile.

Veintemilla returned from exile in 1875, ostensibly to support the liberal administration of President Antonio Borrero. However, with support from coastal liberals, he seized power in 1876 and arranged his own election in 1878. His presidency was plagued by great tension and violence between liberals and clerical conservatives, provoked in part by the government's suspension of the ultramontane concordat and by the mysterious poisoning of the archbishop of Quito.

Veintemilla claimed credit for reopening the University of Quito, providing free elementary schools, promoting railroad construction, and maintaining prudent neutrality during the War of the Pacific. He governed arbitrarily and in 1882 sought to perpetuate his rule through dictatorship, but he was forced from office and exiled the next year.

See also **Garcia Moreno, Gabriel; War of the Pacific.**

BIBLIOGRAPHY

Frank Macdonald Spindler, *Nineteenth-Century Ecuador. An Historical Introduction* (1987), esp. pp. 98–129.

Juan Murillo M., *Historia del Ecuador de 1876 a 1888* (1946), esp. pp. 86–286.

Luis Robalino Dávila, *Borrero y Veintemilla,* 2 vols. (1966).

Additional Bibliography

Febres Cordero, Francisco. *De Flores a flores y miel.* Quito, Ecuador: Ojo de Pez, 1996.

MARK J. VAN AKEN

VEINTEMILLA, MARIETTA DE (1858–1907).

Marietta de Veintemilla, born on September 8, 1858, was a controversial and powerful figure and essayist from in the late-nineteenth-century Ecuador. She participated zealously in politics, beginning at the age of eighteen until she was twenty-three years old, when she governed her country and commanded the army in lieu of her uncle, Ignacio de Veintemilla, president and dictator of Ecuador from 1876 to 1883. When her army was defeated, she was taken prisoner and later exiled to Lima, Peru, where she continued exercising her passion for politics as an essayist. She was allowed to return to Ecuador in 1898.

Marietta de Veintemilla should be regarded as one of the founders of Latin American thought for her remarkable and rare ability to blend her main political concerns—nation, progress, fanaticism, education, and women in politics—with more academic interests in history, religion, science, and philosophy. She framed her discussions in the philosophical currents of her time—liberalism, positivism, Krausismo, and Krausopositivism. From positivism she embraced only the support for the dictatorial presidency, considering it the best system of government for achieving progress during her time. The influence of Krausismo is notorious in her works because she assumed the role of philosopher of history, always searching for knowledge in the past to obtain to obtain a harmonious visualization of the present. As with the Puerto Rican essayist Eugenio María de Hostos, her defense of women's education reveals another strong tie to Krausismo, but she never adhered faithfully to any single doctrine, as demonstrated by her leaning toward scientism and spiritualism her later essays. Her major work, *Páginas del Ecuador* (1890), is the only sociopolitical history written by a woman in nineteenth-century Spanish America. In this book she reinterpreted political analysis by previous essayists, providing the most accurate version of the Spanish American politics. Marietta died on March 11, 1907.

See also **Hostos y Bonilla, Eugenio María de; Krausismo; Philosophy: Overview; Positivism; Veintemilla, José Ignacio de.**

BIBLIOGRAPHY

Works by Marietta de Veintemilla

Páginas del Ecuador. Lima: Imprenta Liberal de F. Masías, 1890.

A la memoria del doctor Agustín Leonidas Yerovi. Quito: Imprenta Municipal, 1904.

Goethe y su poema Fausto. Quito: *La Musa Americana,* 1904.

Madame Roland. Quito: *Revista de la Sociedad Jurídico-Literaria,* no. 24, 1904.

Conferencia sobre psicología moderna. Quito: Imprenta de la Universidad Central, 1907.

Secondary Sources

Bossano, Luis. *Perfil de Marietta de Veintemilla.* Quito, Ecuador: Editorial Casa de la Cultura Ecuatoriana, 1956.

da Cunha-Giabbai, Gloria. *Marietta: El pensamiento de Marietta de Veintemilla.* Quito, Ecuador: Banco Central de Ecuador, 1998.

Garcés, Enrique. *Marietta de Veintemilla.* Quito, Ecuador: Casa de la Cultura Ecuatoriana, 1949. This is the best criticism by one of her enemies, justifying her importance.

GLORIA DA CUNHA

VELASCO, JOSÉ MARÍA (1840–1912).

José María Velasco (*b.* 6 July 1840; *d.* 26 August 1912), Mexican painter. Velasco, a major landscape painter, is the foremost Mexican painter of the nineteenth century. He was the favorite pupil of the Italian landscapist Eugenio Landesio, who taught at the Academia de San Carlos between 1855 and 1873. Velasco succeeded him in 1875 and remained on the staff for the rest of his life. In *Excursion in the Environs of Mexico City* (1866), an early work, small figures from different walks of life, against a background of enormous trees and a distant landscape, suggest historical and social commentary. Velasco never ignored the human presence in landscape, but with time that presence became less anecdotal. In 1873 he executed the first of several large canvases titled *Valley of Mexico,* his most famous works.

Although he painted elsewhere in the country (Oaxaca, Veracruz) and produced views of buildings, self-portraits, and portraits, the broad vistas and the clear light of central Mexico were Velasco's favorite subjects. In *The Bridge of Metlac* (1881) he celebrates the modernity of the age of Porfirio Díaz by depicting a train moving through a tropical landscape. *Hacienda of Chimalpa* (1893), a vast, simplified landscape in silvery tonalities, is his most important late work.

Although Velasco traveled to international exhibitions where his paintings received prizes (Philadelphia in 1876, Paris in 1889, and Chicago in 1893), his style was hardly affected by these contacts. Velasco had a strong scientific bent, and he executed many drawings and paintings of plants, animals, and archaeological objects and sites for scientific institutions and publications, as well as meticulous studies of rocks and vegetation.

See also **Art: The Nineteenth Century; Díaz, Porfirio.**

BIBLIOGRAPHY

José María Velasco, 1840–1912, catalog of Philadelphia Museum of Art and Brooklyn Museum exhibition (1944).

Carlos Pellicer, *José María Velasco: Pinturas, dibujos, acuarelas* (1970).

Additional Bibliography

Altamirano Piolle, María Elena. *National Homage, José María Velasco, 1840–1912.* Mexico City: Amigos del Museo Nacional del Arte, 1993.

Moyssén L., Xavier. *José María Velasco: El paisajista.* Mexico City: Círculo de Arte, 1997.

CLARA BARGELLINI

VELASCO, JOSÉ MIGUEL DE (1795–

1859). José Miguel de Velasco (*b.* 29 September 1795; *d.* 13 October 1859), president of Bolivia (1829, 1839–1841, 1848). Velasco was born in Sucre. In 1815 he joined the royalist army. After five years of service and promotion to lieutenant colonel, Velasco defected to the Republican cause. He fought under José de San Martín, Simón Bolívar, and Antonio José de Sucre Alcalá, and participated at the battle of Ayacucho in 1824. After Sucre departed Bolivia in 1828, the new congress elected

Andrés de Santa Cruz president and Velasco vice president. While Santa Cruz was absent from Bolivia, uprisings by other caudillos led to Velasco's ascension to the presidency in January 1829. Six months later, at the request of Congress, Velasco relinquished the presidency to Santa Cruz. During the latter period of the Peru-Bolivian Confederation, Velasco took advantage of the growing unpopularity of Santa Cruz, whose meddling in Peru had become very expensive for Bolivia. Velasco deposed Santa Cruz in 1839, but he in turn was overthrown by another ambitious general, José Ballivián, in 1841. Velasco returned to the presidency in 1848 after the populace of Bolivia became disenchanted with Ballivián. Lacking any coherent program and without widespread support in the army, Velasco was overthrown by Manuel Isidoro Belzú later the same year.

See also **Belzu, Manuel Isidoro; Santa Cruz, Andrés de.**

BIBLIOGRAPHY

Julio Díaz Arguedas, *Los generales de Bolivia (rasgos biográficos) 1825–1925* (1929), pp. 63–66.

Moisés Ascarrunz, *De siglo a siglo, hombres celebres de Bolivia* (1920), pp. 77–79.

Additional Bibliography

Peralta Ruiz, Víctor, and Marta Irurozqui. *Por la concordia, la fusión y el unitarismo: Estado y caudillismo en Bolivia, 1825–1880.* Madrid: Consejo Superior de Investigaciones Científicas, 2000.

ERWIN P. GRIESHABER

VELASCO, JUAN DE (1727–1792). The

eighteenth-century Ecuadorian Jesuit expatriate Juan de Velasco was a historian, linguist, naturalist, and poet. Misinformation abounds regarding Velasco; for example, he did not die in Verona, Italy, in 1819 at the age of ninety-two but in Faenza, Italy, twenty-seven years earlier, on June 29, 1792, at the age of sixty-five.

Velasco is celebrated for his poetry, his contributions to history and philology, and for his proto-nationalism. He was born on January 6, 1727, to Creole parents in Riobamba in what was then the Audiencia of Quito. His father was Sergeant Major Juan de Velasco, after whom he was named, and his mother was María Pérez Petroche. Initially tutored at home, he continued his education with the Jesuits in his native city. Velasco entered the Jesuit novitiate, the Colegio Seminario de San Luis, in San Francisco de Quito, in 1743 and graduated from the Jesuit Universidad de San Gregorio Magno, also in Quito, with a doctorate in theology in 1753, the same year he was ordained a priest. The education he received was second to none in the Americas and nearly on par with that available in Europe inasmuch as the Jesuits in the Audiencia of Quito kept abreast with intellectual developments in the Old World for the most part and are known to have freely imparted these ideas to their students, notwithstanding the *Index of Prohibited Books* and the Inquisition. Velasco made his final vows in 1762. Subsequently Father Velasco was assigned to Cuenca, where he engaged in missionary work among remnants of the Cañari Indians and other ethnic groups, followed by teaching assignments in the Jesuit Colegios in Ibarra and Popayán, then part of the Audiencia and hence the Jesuit Province of Quito. In 1767 Velasco was exiled to Europe along with his fellow Jesuits upon the order's expulsion from Spain's New World dominions. (Velasco never taught in Peru proper and hence was not a member of the faculty of the Universidad de San Marcos in Lima as is sometimes maintained.)

Velasco's most important works were the first history of what is now Ecuador, the three-part *Historia del Reino de Quito en la América Meridional*, and his chronicle of the Jesuit missions in the Upper Amazon Basin, the *Historia moderna del Reyno de Quito y crónica de la Provincia de la Compañía de Jesús del mismo reyno*, both of which were composed while he was in exile in Faenza. Completed in 1789, *Historia del Reino de Quito* would not be published as drafted until 1960. The first nominally complete edition of this work (3 vols., Quito: Imprenta del Gobierno, 1841–1843) was adulterated. Its editor, Agustín Yeroví, not only altered Velasco's wording but expunged entire sections. Nonetheless, Yeroví's version and the reprints thereof should be consulted for their impact on Ecuadorian historiography and letters. The *Historia moderna del Reyno de Quito y crónica de la Provincia de la Compañía de Jesús del mismo reyno* had to wait even longer before beginning to

be published (1941) and as of 2007 has yet to appear in its entirely. Fortunately for ecclesiastical historians, Velasco also devoted considerable space to the Jesuit missions in volume 3 of the *Historia del Reino de Quito*.

Although Velasco was very much a patriot and a proto-nationalist, his "History of the Kingdom of Quito" did not have much of an impact on the ideological underpinnings of the movements for independence in the Audiencia of Quito because it did not circulate in manuscript and did not begin to be published until 1837, initially in Paris and in parts. Part 1, the *Historia natural*, appeared in 1837, and part 2, the *Historia antigua*, with a different editor and a different publisher, was translated into French in 1840. Once the *Historia del Reino de Quito* was published in Quito (1841–1844) in all three parts (i.e., including the *Historia moderna*), however, it began to contribute to the formation of the Ecuadorian state and to mid- and late-nineteenth-century attempts to forge an Ecuadorian nation.

Velasco is less well known as a "natural historian," but his descriptions of the Kingdom of Quito and its inhabitants, provinces, and towns in the *Historia moderna* (part 3 of the *Historia del Reino de Quito*) together with his account of flora and fauna in the *Historia natural* (part 1) constitute one of the two most detailed historical geographic accounts of the eighteenth-century Audiencia of Quito. The other is that of his fellow Jesuit expatriate Mario Cicala, the two-volume *Descripción histórico-topográfica de la Provincia de Quito de la Compañía de Quito* (1771; Quito: Biblioteca Ecuatoriana "Aurelio Espinosa Pólit," 1994–2004).

Velasco was not an important poet but he played a major role in the conservation of the output of many of Ecuador's early poets. The five-volume manuscript in the Biblioteca Nacional del Ecuador (Quito) compiled by him, "Colección de poesías varias, hechas por un ocioso en la Ciudad de Faenza" (1790–1791), is a treasure trove of colonial period poets. Velasco was also a linguist of some importance. His two *Vocabularios* are among the earliest known of northern Quichua, as *runa simi* (language of the people) is known in Ecuador and southern Colombia. Unfortunately, only Velasco's so-called "Vocabulario B" appears to have survived and has been published. See the list of Primary Works below for acceptable editions of Velasco's oeuvre.

See also **Jesuits; Literature: Spanish America; Quito, Audiencia (Presidency) of.**

BIBLIOGRAPHY

Primary Works

Historia moderna del Reyno de Quito y crónica de la Provincia de la Compañía de Jesús del mismo reyno. 1788. Tomo 1: *Años 1550 a 1689.* Quito, Ecuador: Imprenta de la Caja del Seguro, 1941.

Los poetas quiteños de "El ocioso en Faenza." [Historia, crítica, y selección de textos por] Alejandro Carrión, 2 vols. Quito, Ecuador: Casa de la Cultura Ecuatoriana, 1957–1958.

Vocabulario de la lengua indica, introducción, Oswaldo Romero Arteta; versión paleográfica, notas y comentarios de Piedad Peñaherrera de Costales y Alfredo Costales Samaniego. Quito, Ecuador: Instituto Ecuatoriano de Antropología y Geografía; Biblioteca Ecuatoriana "Aurelio Espinosa Pólit," 1964. xxxv, 84 p. (Llacta; no. 20).

Historia del Reino de Quito en la América Meridional. Introducción de Juan Freile Granizo y Galo René Pérez, estudio introductorio de Piedad Costales y Alfredo Costales. Quito, Ecuador: Casa de la Cultura Ecuatoriana, 1977–1979.

Los jesuítas quiteños del extrañamiento. Introducción, selección y traducciones latinas e italianas por Aurelio Espinosa Pólit. Puebla, Mexico: J. M. Cajica Jr., 1960; Quito, Ecuador: Corporación de Estudios y Publicaciones, 1989.

Padre Juan de Velasco, S.I. Introducción por Julio Tobar Donoso, texto establecido por Aurelio Espinosa Pólit. Puebla, Mexico: J. M. Cajica Jr., 1960; Quito, Ecuador: Corporación de Estudios y Publicaciones, 1989.

Cuatro textos coloniales de quichua de la "Provincia de Quito." Quito, Ecuador: Proyecto de Educación Bilingüe Intercultural, 1999.

Secondary Works

Estupiñán Viteri, Tamara. *Tras las huellas de Rumiñahui.* Quito, Ecuador: FONSAL, 2003.

Keeding, Ekkehart. *Das Zeitalter der Aufklärung in der Provinz Quito.* Cologne: Böhlau, 1983. Rev. Spanish version, *Surge la nación: La ilustración en la Audiencia de Quito.* Quito, Ecuador: Banco Central del Ecuador, 2005.

Larrea, Carlos Manuel. *Tres historiadores: Velasco, González Suárez, Jijón y Caamaño.* Quito, Ecuador: Casa de la Cultura Ecuatoriana "Benjamin Carrión," 1988.

Rodríguez Castelo, Hernán. *Literatura en la Audiencia de Quito, siglo XVIII,* 2 vols. Ambato and Quito, Ecuador: Casa de la Cultura Ecuatoriana "Benjamín Carrión," Núcleo de Tungurahua, 2002. See especially vol. 1, pp. 525–606, and vol. 2, pp. 1315–1341.

Roig, Arturo Andrés. *El humanismo ecuatoriano de la segunda mitad del siglo XVIII.* 2 vols. Quito, Ecuador: Banco Central del Ecuador: Corporación Editora Nacional, 1984. See especially vol. 1.

Willingham, Eileen. "Locating Utopia: Promise and Patria in Juan de Velasco's *Historia del Reino de Quito.*" In *El saber de los jesuitas, historia naturales y el Nuevo Mundo,* ed. Luis Millones Figueroa and Domingo Ledezma, pp. 251–277. Frankfurt: Vulvert and Madrid: Iberoamericana, 2005.

MICHAEL T. HAMERLY

VELASCO, LUIS DE (c. 1511–1564).

Luis de Velasco (*b.* ca. 1511; *d.* 1564), second viceroy of Mexico. Velasco was born in Carrión de los Condes, Palencia, in Spain, into the extended family of the constables of Castile. His early career included service in France and Navarre (viceroy, 1547–1548). In 1549 he was appointed the viceroy of Mexico. He served from his arrival in 1550 until his death. Central to his rule was the implementation of the New Laws, which placed restrictions on the *encomienda.* The discovery of silver mines on the northern frontier caused a need for protection from the nomadic Indians. Velasco helped to define the military policy. He also supported expeditions, specifically to Florida under don Tristán de Luna. His son, don Luis de Velasco (the Younger), daughter, and half-brother married into the creole elite. The latter years of his rule were marred by the visitation of Licentiate Jerónimo de Valderrama and by an upsurge of creole animosity toward Spain due to the implementation of the New Laws.

See also **Mexico: The Colonial Period.**

BIBLIOGRAPHY

James S. Olson, ed., *Historical Dictionary of the Spanish Empire, 1402–1975* (1992), p. 624.

Additional Bibliography

Lemon, Jason Edward. "The Encomienda in Early New Spain." Ph.D. diss. Emory University, 2000.

JOHN F. SCHWALLER

VELASCO, LUIS DE ("THE YOUNGER") (1538–1617).

Luis de ("The Younger") Velasco (*b.* 1538; *d.* 1617), viceroy of Mexico and of Peru. Born in Carrión de los Condes, Palencia, in Spain, Velasco first went to Mexico in 1560 to join his father, who was the second viceroy. Earlier he had gone with his brother, don Antonio de Velasco, as a member of the party which accompanied Philip II to England for his marriage to Queen Mary. In Mexico, Velasco married doña María de Ircio, daughter of a conquistador. In 1565 he assisted in the uncovering of the "Cortes Conspiracy." After returning to Spain in 1585, he served as ambassador to Florence. In 1589 he was appointed viceroy of Mexico, where he served until becoming viceroy of Peru in 1595. In 1604 he retired to his estates in Mexico only to be reappointed viceroy of Mexico in 1607 and eventually president of the Council of the Indies in Spain in 1611. He was granted the title of marqués de las Salinas del Río Pisuerga in 1609.

Velasco is credited with the successful pacification of the northern Mexican frontier, reorganization of the textile mills, and the initiation of the drainage of the Valley of Mexico. In Peru he reorganized the system of Indian labor, regulated the textile mills, and reorganized the mercury mines of Huancavelica.

See also **Mexico: The Colonial Period.**

BIBLIOGRAPHY

Manuel De Mendiburu, *Diccionario histórico-biográfico del Perú* (1874–1890).

Vicente Riva Palacio, *México a través de los siglos*, vol. 2 (1939), pp. 447–450, 538–555.

Additional Bibliography

Salazar Andreu, Juan Pablo. *Luis de Velasco.* Mexico City: Planeta DeAgostini, 2002.

JOHN F. SCHWALLER

VELASCO ALVARADO, JUAN (1910–1977).

Juan Velasco Alvarado (*b.* 16 June 1910; *d.* 24 December 1977), military officer and president of Peru (1968–1975), leader of a radical nationalist government that introduced a number of reforms and increased state intervention in economic, social, and political affairs. Velasco was born in Piura and entered the army as a private in 1929. In 1930 he was accepted to the officers' military school, from which he graduated first in his class. After serving as army officer in the Peruvian jungle, he continued his military training in the Advanced War School. In 1959 he was promoted to the rank of brigadier general, and in 1962–1963 he was the military attaché in Paris. In 1963 he was promoted to division general and served in Washington, D.C.

In 1968, Velasco and twelve other army officers plotted to oust President Fernando Belaúnde Terry. They allegedly elaborated the Plan Inca, a blueprint for introducing strategic reforms intended to modernize the country and avoid leftist and social uprisings. Soon after the coup of 3 October 1968, Velasco and his government team initiated a process of nationalization of the petroleum, mining, fishing, and agrarian industries. A vast agrarian reform was implemented, and in 1974 the press was nationalized. With initial popular support, Velasco's popularity had declined considerably by 1975. In 1973 he suffered a stroke that led to the amputation of his left leg. General Francisco Morales Bermúdez Cerruti led a 1975 coup that ousted Velasco and prepared for the return of democracy in 1980. Velasco died in Lima.

See also **Belaúnde Terry, Fernando; Plan Inca.**

BIBLIOGRAPHY

Peter Cleaves and Martin Scurrah, *Agriculture, Bureaucracy, and Military Government in Peru* (1980).

George Philip, *The Rise and Fall of the Peruvian Military Radicals, 1968–1976* (1978).

Juan Velasco Alvarado, *La revolución peruana* (1973).

Additional Bibliography

Franco, Carlos, and Rolando Ames. *El Perú de Velasco.* Lima: Centro de Estudios para el Desarrollo y la Participación, 1986.

Kruijt, Dirk. *Revolution by Decree: Peru, 1968–1975.* Amsterdam: Thela Publishers, 1994.

Lynch, Nicolás. *Política y antipolítica en el Perú.* Lima: DESCO, Centro de Estudios y Promoción del Desarrollo, 2000.

ALFONSO W. QUIROZ

VELASCO IBARRA, JOSÉ MARÍA

(1893–1979). José María Velasco Ibarra (*b.* 19 March 1893; *d.* 30 March 1979), president of Ecuador (1934–1935, 1944–1947, 1952–1956, 1960–1961, 1968–1972). Trained in law at the Central University in Quito, Velasco began his long and remarkable political career at an early age. He was elected to Congress in 1932, became president of the Chamber of Deputies in 1933, and replaced the president of the republic a year later. He attained the presidency five times but was forcibly removed on four occasions. Only his third presidency (1952–1956) was completed in accordance with constitutional provisions.

A spellbinding orator and charismatic figure of the first order, Velasco dominated national politics for nearly five decades. When out of office he was busily planning a return to power, and few prominent public figures were not associated with him at one time or another. A lifelong critic of political parties, Velasco won power through a personal electoral machine, which was dismantled once he left office. Unable to delegate authority, Velasco was a disastrous administrator whose authoritarian proclivities encouraged political unrest.

A widely read intellectual, Velasco had minimal comprehension of economic issues and was inclined toward short-term opportunistic policies. By nature a conservative, Velasco nonetheless put forward a populist image throughout his career. During his 1960 presidential campaign his views were avowedly leftist in character, reflecting the impact of the Cuban Revolution.

Velasco's fifth and final term, after a narrow victory in 1968, was characteristic of his earlier terms in office. The constitution was eventually suspended, and ultimately the military intervened. Velasco went into exile, returning in 1979 to bury his wife; he died a month later. With his demise, the remaining Velasquista forces disintegrated.

See also **Arosemena Monroy, Carlos Julio.**

BIBLIOGRAPHY

George I. Blanksten, *Ecuador: Constitutions and Caudillos* (1951).

Agustín Cueva, *The Process of Political Domination in Ecuador,* translated by Danielle Salti (1982).

Osvaldo Hurtado, *Political Power in Ecuador,* translated by Nick D. Mills, Jr. (1980).

John D. Martz, *Ecuador: Conflicting Political Culture and the Quest for Progress* (1972).

Additional Bibliography

Jaramillo Palacio, José María. *Velasco Ibarra: Presidente idealista: medio siglo de historia en el Ecuador, 1930–1980.* Quito, Ecuador: Delta, 1995.

Norris, Robert E., and Carlos de la Torre. *El gran ausente: Biografía de Velasco Ibarra.* Quito, Ecuador: Ediciones Libri Mundi/Enrique Grosse-Luemern, 2004.

Torre, Carlos de la. *Populist Seduction in Latin America: The Ecuadorian Experience.* Athens: Ohio University Center for International Studies, 2000.

JOHN D. MARTZ

VELÁSQUEZ, DIEGO DE (c. 1465–1524). Diego de Velásquez (*b.* ca. 1465; *d.* 11/12 May 1524) Spanish explorer, conqueror, and first governor of Cuba (1514–1524). Born in the region of Segovia, in Old Castile, Velásquez left few records of his early life. He won early acclaim fighting with the Spanish forces in Italy and his reputation grew when he traveled to the New World on Columbus's second voyage in 1494. For his active role in the conquest of the natives on Hispaniola, he received land and *encomiendas,* amassing great wealth in agriculture. He served as lieutenant governor before being named to lead the expedition to conquer Cuba. Velásquez and three hundred men sailed for Cuba in 1511 and, upon arrival, founded Baracoa, establishing it as the island's first administrative headquarters. The conquest of the island, renowned for its barbarity, lasted three years and decimated the native population.

In 1515, Velásquez moved the capital to Santiago de Cuba. During his government, the center of Spanish activities in the New World shifted to Cuba and the island prospered under his capable leadership. In his latter years, dissension arose over many of his activities, including the use of Indian labor, leading to his dismissal as governor in 1521, though he regained the position in 1523. He died unexpectedly the next year. His wealth diminished with his losses from investments in exploration expeditions, like those of Francisco Hernández

De Córdoba and of Hernán Cortés, yet at his death he was the richest Spaniard in the Americas. He created and organized a profitable and successful colony in Cuba; founded many towns whose names remain today; established a strong Spanish presence in the region, implanting her administration and her culture; and made Cuba a launching point for expeditions throughout the Western Hemisphere.

See also **Explorers and Exploration: Spanish America.**

BIBLIOGRAPHY

Ramiro Guerra y Sánchez et al., *A History of the Cuban Nation*, vol. 1, translated by Emilio Chomat (1959).

Irene Wright, *The Early History of Cuba, 1492–1586* (1916; rep. 1970).

Additional Bibliography

Miranda, Leocésar. *Diego Velázquez de Cuéllar: Colonizador y primer gobernador de la isla de Cuba*. Santiago de Cuba: Ediciones Santiago, 2004.

JACQUELYN BRIGGS KENT

VELÁSQUEZ, JOSÉ ANTONIO

(1906–1983). José Antonio Velásquez (*b*. 8 February 1906; *d*. 14 February 1983), the first and foremost Honduran primitivist painter. Born in Caridad, department of Valle, Velásquez was a barber by profession, without formal artistic training. He began to paint in 1927, and after working at various places throughout Honduras, he moved in 1930 to the village of San Antonio de Oriente, where in addition to being the barber and telegraph operator, he painted scenes of the village. His unique, primitive paintings, reflect the innocence and tranquility of that Honduran village where he spent the next thirty years of his life.

His paintings were discovered in 1943 by Wilson Popenoe, director of the Agricul-ture School at El Zamorano, and his wife. Popenoe hired Velásquez as a barber at his school, but he and his wife encouraged Velásquez to market his paintings in Tegucigalpa. They sold there only at low prices until 1954, when the Popenoes arranged for an exhibition of his work at the Pan American Union in Washington, D.C. This event catapulted Velásquez to international recognition, and in 1955 he was awarded Honduras's most prestigious art award, the Pablo Zelaya Sierra National Prize for Art. Among many other honors, he was elected mayor of San Antonio de Oriente. Now famous, he moved in 1961 to Tegucigalpa and in 1971 was the subject of a movie produced by Shirley Temple Black and filmed in San Antonio de Oriente.

See also **Art: The Twentieth Century.**

BIBLIOGRAPHY

J. Evaristo López and Longino Becerra, *Honduras: 40 pintores* (1989).

Additional Bibliography

Yuscarán, Guillermo. *Velásquez: The Man and His Art*. Tegucigalpa, Honduras: Nuevo Sol Publications, 1994.

RALPH LEE WOODWARD JR.

VELÁZQUEZ CÁRDENAS DE LEÓN, JOAQUÍN

(1732–1786). Joaquín Velázquez Cárdenas de León (*b*. 12 June 1732; *d*. 7 March 1786), Mexican lawyer, mathematician, and miner. Velázquez de León was born near Tizicapán (state of Mexico) where his father and uncle were miners. After his father's death he was tutored in native languages by Manuel Asensio. Later he was placed in the care of his uncle, Carlos Celedonia Velázquez de León, vice-rector of the Colegio Seminario de México, who encouraged his nephew to study science and mathematics. In 1765, Velázquez de León became an instructor at the Real y Pontífica Universidad. From 1765 to 1768, Velázquez de León and Juan Lucas de Lassaga (a Spaniard) studied various aspects of mining and mineralogy, especially smelting methods. In 1766 they presented a plan to the Spanish crown for separating gold from silver. After experimenting for two years, however, the plan proved to be flawed.

In the early 1770s, Velázquez de León visited Europe, where he was already known for his astronomical observations and maps. Upon his return he and Lucas de Lassaga published the *Representación que a nombre de la minería de ésta Nueva España* (1774). It portrayed a deteriorating mining industry that should be reorganized to include a guild and a tribunal to give overall direction, a bank to provide credit and loans, and a mining college to teach modern techniques. Its most important finding was that the industry would benefit from miners supplementing their practical knowledge with scientific knowledge. Some reforms were implemented during the next decade, although the college was not launched until after Velázquez de León's death in 1786. How much the reforms contributed to the acceleration in output of silver remains open to debate. As director general of the Mining Tribunal, Velázquez de León was also in charge of technical education and experimentation. He helped to write the new mining code (1783), which tried to bring mining laws into conformity with mining practices, and he participated in the founding of the tribunal's bank.

See also **Mining: Colonial Spanish America.**

BIBLIOGRAPHY

Walter Howe, *The Mining Guild of New Spain and Its Tribunal General 1770–1821* (1949).

Clement G. Motten, *Mexican Silver and the Enlightenment* (1950, 1972).

Roberto Moreno, "Apuntes biográficos de Joaquín Velázquez de León—1732–1786," in *Historia mexicana* 25 (Julio–Septiembre 1975): 41–75.

Additional Bibliography

Bakewell, Peter J. *Silver Mining and Society in Colonial Mexico: Zacatecas, 1546-1700.* Cambridge, U.K.: Cambridge University Press, 2002.

Couturier, Edith Boorstein. *The Silver King: The Remarkable Life of the Count of Regla in Colonial Mexico.* Albuquerque: University of New Mexico Press, 2003.

Nunis, Doyce Blackman, Chappe d'Auteroche et al. *The 1769 Transit of Venus: The Baja California Observations of Jean Baptiste Chappe d'Auteroche, Vicente de Doz, and Joaquín Velázque Cardenas de León.* Los Angeles: Natural History Museum of Los Angeles County, 1982.

Uribe Salas, José Alfredo, ed. *Historia de la minería en Michoacán.* Morelia: Universidad Michoacana de San Nicolás de Hidalgo, 2002.

RICHARD L. GARNER

VELÁZQUEZ SÁNCHEZ, FIDEL

(1900–1997). Fidel Velázquez Sánchez (*b.* April 14, 1900; *d.* June 21, 1997), Mexican labor leader. Velázquez Sánchez is probably the longest-lived top labor union official in Latin America, having served continuously as secretary general of the Mexican Federation of Labor (CTM) from 1950 to the 1990s. His notoriety came from his long continuity rather than from any dramatic ideological or structural contributions to the Mexican or Latin American labor movement. Velázquez Sánchez's influence stemmed from his reputation for being indispensable to the control of numerous affiliated unions and to their acceptance of their status as a co-opted member of the dominant political coalition in Mexico. Because he had been so successful at this task, no president either wanted to remove him, or had the political courage to do so. This perception of his power gained him a measure of autonomy from Mexico's president, making him the only Mexican official to have enjoyed this advantage for so long. Since the 1970s, it led Velázquez, on occasion, to take stronger, more independent positions for labor vis-à-vis the executive branch, sometimes bringing his vision of politics into conflict with that of the incumbent president. However, because of Mexico's declining economic fortunes during most of the 1970s and 1980s, and the consequent high levels of unemployment, Velázquez was not able to translate his potential power into much political influence. Although the PRI's perpetuation of electoral fraud in the 1990s had made it more dependent on the support of the CTM as the major member of the labor sector, the number of PRI candidates from that sector continues to decline. Velázquez is considered to be representative of the old-style politicians or "dinosaur" faction in contemporary political life.

Velázquez was born in Villa Nicolás, state of México, the son of poor farmers. He completed primary school while working in the fields. It is likely that Velázquez entered the union movement because his father, Gregorio Velázquez Reyna, was killed defending his farm, and Fidel was wounded in the shoulder during the incident. Velázquez began work as a dairyman in the 1920s, and became a labor activist at that time. He assumed his first union post in 1921 and became secretary general of the Milk Industry Workers Union in 1929. Originally a member of the executive committee of the CTM (1936–1940), he became secretary general of the major federation from 1940 to 1946. He, in collaboration with other labor union leaders, succeeded in wresting control away from Vicente Lombardo Toledano. That success eventually led to his domination of the union after 1950. In his capacity as secretary general of the CTM, and dean of Mexico's union leaders, Velázquez served as senator from the Federal District (1946–1952 and 1958–1964) and represented the labor sector on the National Executive Committee of the PRI on several occasions. In 1968 he spoke out against leftist student activists who demonstrated throughout Mexico City in support of communist Cuba and bringing democratic government to Mexico. When many students were wounded or killed by government troops in the infamous Tlatelolco massacre of October 2, 1968, he stood by the government's actions. When Cuauhtémoc Cárdenas founded the Partido de la Revolución Democratico (PRD; Democratic Revolutionary Party) in 1989, Velázquez labeled him a communist and called for his membership in the mainstream PRI party to be revoked. When the Ejército Zapatista de Liberación Nacional (EZLN; Zapatista Army of National Liberation) staged an uprising in the heavily indigenous mountain region of Chiapas, he condemned the rebellion. Although he initially decried NAFTA, the North American Free Trade Agreement with the United States, he eventually supported its passage. In the 1990s, as his health declined, Velazquez's power within the PRI lessened. He died on June 21, 1997.

See also **Mexico, Organizations: Federation of Mexican Labor (CTM).**

BIBLIOGRAPHY

Kevin J. Middlebrook, "The Political Economy of Mexican Organized Labor, 1940–1978" (diss., University of Michigan, 1982).

Virginia López Villegas-Manjárrez, *La CTM vs. las organizaciones obreras* (1983).

Ian Roxborough, *Unions and Politics in Mexico: The Case of the Automobile Industry* (1984).

George Grayson, *The Mexican Labor Machine: Power, Politics, and Patronage* (1989).

Additional Bibliography

González Guerra, José Merced, and Antonio Gutiérrez Castro. *El sindicalismo en México: Historia, crisis, y perspectivas.* México: Plaza y Valdés, 2006.

Rendón Corona, Armando. *Sindicalismo corporativo: La crisis terminal.* México, DF: UNAM, 2005.

Sánchez González, Agustín. *Fidel: Una historia de poder.* México, D.F.: Planeta, 1991.

Sánchez González, Agustín. *Los primeros cien años de Fidel Velázquez.* México, D.F.: Nueva Imagen, 1997.

RODERIC AI CAMP

VÉLEZ, LUPE (1908–1944).

Known as "The Mexican Spitfire" and the "Hot Baby of Hollywood," actress Lupe Vélez came to represent an exotic and generic image of Latin American femininity in Hollywood cinema. Born Maria Guadalupe Villalobos Vélez on 18 July 1908, in the city of San Luis Potosí, Mexico, her first feature-length film was *The Gaucho* (1927) with Douglas Fairbanks. This performance led to a series of costarring roles throughout the 1930s. Her brief love affair with Gary Cooper and five-year marriage to Johnny "Tarzan" Weissmuller were highly publicized in the media, and served to reinforce her tempestuous on-screen image.

Although Vélez started her career as a Latin American temptress, she found her niche in comedy with *Hot Pepper* (1933) and the series of eight *Mexican Spitfire* films (1939–1943). By 1943 her Hollywood career was waning. She starred in the Mexican production *Nana* that year, but it was not the success she had hoped it would be. On 13 December 1944, at the age of thirty-six and five months pregnant, Vélez committed suicide by taking an overdose of sleeping pills at her home in Beverly Hills, California.

See also **Cinema: From the Silent Film to 1990.**

BIBLIOGRAPHY

Agrasánchez, Rogelio, Jr. *Beauties of Mexican Cinema/Bellezas del cine mexicano.* Harlingen, TX: Agrasánchez Film Archive, 2001.

Ramírez, Gabriel. *Lupe Vélez, la mexicana que escupía fuego.* Mexico City: Cineteca Nacional, 1986.

Vázquez Corona, Moisés. *Lupe Vélez, a medio siglo de ausencia.* Mexico City: EDAMEX, 1996.

SOPHIA KOUTSOYANNIS

VÉLEZ DE ESCALANTE, SILVESTRE (c. 1750–1780).

Silvestre Vélez de Escalante (*b.* ca. 1750; *d.* April 1780), Franciscan missionary and explorer. Born in Santander, Spain, Escalante joined the Franciscan order at age seventeen and served among the Pueblo Indians of New Mexico. In 1776 he accompanied Fray Francisco Atanasio Domínguez in an attempt to find a northwesterly route from New Mexico to Monterey. Although the Domínguez-Escalante expedition failed to open a new road to the Pacific coast, it was the earliest known European exploration of the Four Corners area. Escalante's journal provided the earliest written description of this region. Escalante returned to Santa Fe in 1777 and remained in New Mexico for several more years, serving as a missionary and ecclesiastical official.

See also **Explorers and Exploration: Spanish America; Missions: Spanish America.**

BIBLIOGRAPHY

Eleanor B. Adams and Fray Angélico Chávez, eds. and trans., *The Missions of New Mexico, 1776: A Description by Fray Francisco Atanasio Domínguez, with Other Contemporary Documents* (1956).

Herbert Eugene Bolton, *Pageant in the Wilderness: The Story of the Escalante Expedition to the Interior Basin, 1776* (1951).

Fray Angélico Chávez and Ted J. Warner, eds. and trans., *The Domínguez-Escalante Journal* (1976).

Additional Bibliography

Sánchez, Joseph P. *Explorers, Traders, and Slavers: Forging the Old Spanish Trail, 1678–1850.* Salt Lake City: University of Utah Press, 1997.

SUZANNE B. PASZTOR

VÉLEZ SARSFIELD, DALMACIO

(1800–1875). Dalmacio Vélez Sarsfield (*b.* 18 February 1800; *d.* 30 March 1875), perhaps the greatest Argentine jurist of the nineteenth century. Vélez Sarsfield was born in the city of Córdoba and studied law at the law faculty of the university there, graduating in 1823. From 1824 to 1827 he was a deputy in the Constituent Congress in Buenos Aires and was briefly one of the first professors of political economy of the period. During the 1830s he practiced law, wrote important juridical works that included *Instituciones reales de España* and *Prontuario de práctica forense,* and was named president of the Academy of Jurisprudence in 1835. In the 1850s Vélez Sarsfield was deputy and senator in the local legislatures of the province of Buenos Aires and an adviser to the provincial government. In 1863 he was named minister of finance of Argentina by President Bartolomé Mitre, and from 1868 to 1873, was minister of the interior under President Domingo Sarmiento. He is perhaps best known for his work as coauthor, with Eduardo Acevedo, of the Commercial Code of Argentina (1857) and as author of the Civil Code (1864).

See also **Argentina: The Nineteenth Century.**

BIBLIOGRAPHY

Abel Chaneton, *Historia de Vélez Sarsfield* (1969).

Abelardo Levaggi, *Dos estudios sobre Vélez Sarsfield* (1988).

Additional Bibliography

Sánchez Torres y Córdoba, Izquierdo. *Vélez Sársfield: Vida y obra codificadora.* Córdoba, Argentina: Academia Nacional de Derecho y Ciencias Sociales de Córdoba, 2000.

Torres, Félix A. *Dalmacio Vélez Sársfield en la universidad y su correspondencia en Córdoba.* Córdoba, Argentina: Universidad Nacional de Córdoba, 1997.

CARLOS MARICHAL

VELOSO, CAETANO

(1949–). Caetano Veloso (born August 7, 1949) was the principal figure, along with Gilberto Gil, of Tropicalismo, a dada-like late-1960s Brazilian movement of cultural and musical renovation, which included Torquato Neto, Helio Oiticica, José Carlos Capinam, Tom Zé, Gal Costa, and others. As performer, cultural agitator, and composer of numerous songs, including the 1960s classic "Alegria, alegria" (Happiness, happiness, 1967) and Tropicalismo's manifesto "Tropicália" (1968), he and Gil are almost universally credited with redefining the aesthetics of Brazilian popular music by the incorporation of foreign elements such as rock, dismantling existing barriers between popular and "high" culture forms such as concrete poetry, and re-elaborating folk forms.

Veloso was forced into exile by the military government in 1969, probably because he was a prominent proponent of this cultural movement. Since his return to Brazil in 1972, Veloso has continued a prolific career as a singer-songwriter, utilizing genres as diverse as samba, rap, and reggae to produce hybrid compositions with broad popular appeal. "His importance in Brazil," writes the cultural historian Charles Perrone, "can be compared with that of Bob Dylan and John Lennon in the Anglo-American sphere." In 1997 Veloso published his memoirs, which have been translated into several languages. He remains a central figure in Brazilian popular music; his music has received a great deal of attention by scholars worldwide.

See also **Gil, Gilberto; MPB: Música Popular Brasileira; Oiticica, Hélio; Tropicalismo.**

BIBLIOGRAPHY

Campos, Augusto de. *Balanço da Bossa e Outras Bossas,* 3rd edition. São Paulo: Editora Perspectiva, 1978.

Dunn, Christopher. *Brutality Garden: Tropicália and the Emergence of a Brazilian Counterculture.* Chapel Hill: University of North Carolina Press, 2001.

Perrone, Charles A. *Masters of Contemporary Brazilian Song: MPB 1965–1985.* Austin: University of Texas Press, 1989.

Veloso, Caetano. *Tropical Truth: A Story of Music and Revolution in Brazil.* New York: Alfred A. Knopf, 2002.

ROBERT MYERS
ANDREW J. KIRKENDALL

VENEGAS DE SAAVEDRA, FRANCISCO JAVIER (1760–1838).

Francisco Javier Venegas de Saavedra (*b.* 1760, *d.* 1838), viceroy of Mexico (1810–1813). Venegas distinguished himself in 1808 as an officer fighting the French in Spain. Named to govern New Granada (Bogotá) by the Spanish regency (of which his uncle was a member), he was instead diverted to serve in Mexico, where he assumed office as viceroy just two days before the outbreak of Father Miguel Hidalgo's rebellion in September 1810. Venegas responded skillfully to the crisis in the colony, confronting and partially containing the military threat from the rapidly growing insurgency, creating new militia units, imposing a series of wartime revenue measures, instituting an internal security system for the capital and other cities, and abolishing Indian tributes. In attempting to maintain his own authority, Venegas effectively abrogated much of the liberal Spanish Constitution of 1812, though he quarreled with the ultraroyalist faction in the colony. Noted for his personal integrity, Venegas retired in relative poverty to Spain, where he was eventually ennobled (1816). He later served in a series of high political posts.

See also **New Granada, Viceroyalty of.**

BIBLIOGRAPHY

Timothy E. Anna, *The Fall of the Royal Government in Mexico City* (1978).

Hugh M. Hamill, Jr., *The Hidalgo Revolt, Prelude to Mexican Independence* (1966).

Manuel Rivera Cambas, *Los gobernantes de México,* vol. 3 (1964), pp. 287–322.

ERIC VAN YOUNG

VENEZUELA

This entry includes the following articles:
THE COLONIAL ERA
VENEZUELA SINCE 1830

THE COLONIAL ERA

Venezuela's historical development during the colonial period took place in six subregions. During Christopher Columbus's third voyage, when Europeans first set sight on the coast of Venezuela, there was nothing that drew the special attention of the Spanish. None of the areas dominated the others in terms of population or natural resources. During the course of the next three centuries, however, the Coastal Ranges, which stand behind the coast in the central and eastern parts of the country, would come to dominate the others.

Each of the regions has unique characteristics, and in the early sixteenth century there was little to suggest that the area would become a unified country. The Coast Region is a narrow strip along the Caribbean that stretches from Lake Maracaibo in the west to the Orinoco Delta in the east. It is here that foreigners entered the area and attempted to plunder the coastal towns. The Segovia Highlands form a transitional area between the Andes and the Coast Region in the western part of Venezuela. The inhabitants of these highlands, and those of the Andes, which forms a third area, became increasingly dominated by the economic and political elites from the Coastal Ranges.

The other three regions are in the central and eastern parts of the area. There are two Coastal

Petri de Calyce grauſamkeit gegen die Indianer. IIII.

Engraving of Indian captives driven on a forced march by Spanish colonizers from the early Venezuelan city of Cumaná, c. 16th century. Early Spanish colonization of Venezuela was dispersed. In areas of little European interest, indigenous communities enjoyed autonomy. Forced labor for encomienda in the late sixteenth century and missionaries in the seventeenth century brought about greater Spanish hegemony. © CORBIS

Ranges, one immediately inland from the coast in the center of what became Venezuela and the other in the east. During most of the colonial period the Central Coastal Range would be associated with the province of Caracas and the Eastern Coastal Range with Cumaná. The fifth area is the llanos, a vast plain forming the interior heartland of Venezuela. Finally, Guayana, which lies east of the Orinoco River, had the least impact upon the development of the province. During the course of three hundred years one can detect the emergence of the dominance of the Coastal Ranges over the other five areas, and of the Coastal Range near Caracas over the Coastal Range near Cumaná.

THE PEOPLE

There were differences in the various groups of indigenous peoples who populated Venezuela prior to the arrival of the Spanish. There were stable sedentary farmers in the Central Coastal Range and in the Andes, slash-and-burn agriculturalists in the llanos, and hunters and gatherers along the coast and in the major river valleys.

The ability of the indigenous peoples to retain their culture during the colonial period was directly related to the relative power of the Spanish. Not surprisingly, indigenous peoples were able to thrive and resist domination most effectively outside the area dominated by the Europeans. In the Andes, on the llanos, and in Guayana indigenous peoples were able to live more or less on their own terms. The large numbers of whites and blacks entering the Coastal Ranges, however, brought the creation of new cultural traditions in those areas. In the regions that the Spanish avoided, the indigenous people continued to live undisturbed until the twentieth century. Perhaps 15 to 20 percent of the total population in 1800 of approximately 900,000 could be classified as indigenous.

Africans came to Venezuela as slaves from the Caribbean Islands, from Colombia, and some directly from Africa. Most came during the last half of the eighteenth century with the opening of free trade as part of the Bourbon Reforms. Slaves could be found in all parts of Venezuela and were utilized in a wide variety of occupations. At the end of the colonial period approximately 10 percent of the population of colonial Venezuela were African slaves. By the mid-eighteenth century, Africans and their descendents had established Maroon societies in the south, such as Aripao along the Caura River.

The other primary racial group was the Spanish. As in other colonies there was a division into those born in Spain and those born in America. Two other distinct groups were important in the social development of Venezuela. The Canary Islanders, who were associated with agriculture, lived near Valencia and identified themselves as a separate ethnic group. The Basques, who came in large numbers during the monopoly of the Caracas Company in the eighteenth century, were successful in obtaining power and wealth during the late colonial period. All whites, including those born in America and Iberia, represented perhaps 20 percent of the total population at the end of the colonial period.

By the end of the colonial period the majority of the people living in Venezuela were of mixed-race background (pardos). They formed by far the largest ethnic group, perhaps just over one-half of the total population. They dominated the population of the Coastal Ranges at the end of the colonial era and would become an important component of the forces fighting to overthrow the Spanish during the Wars of Independence in the second decade of the nineteenth century.

Venezuela's population was sparse during the colonial period. Although pressures increased at the end of the eighteenth century, for the most part subsistence was not a problem. The majority of the people lived on the agriculture of manioc, maize, and beans, which was supplemented by the abundant supply of meat from the llanos.

THE LABOR SYSTEM

Venezuela's labor system developed in response to, and as a part of, the Caribbean sphere, which was initially the object of gold and slave raids. For a short time in the 1520s pearls were gathered off the coast, but this source of wealth was quickly exhausted. Lacking a great indigenous civilization and significant mineral wealth, Venezuela's labor system would develop much differently than elsewhere on the continent.

Before the arrival of the Spanish, the indigenous population is estimated to have been perhaps fifty thousand along the coast and in the coastal valleys. Others lived in the inland valleys. The Venezuelan indigenous population fell by 50 to 75 percent during the first century after the Conquest.

The Conquest and settlement of Venezuela spread from the extremes in the east and west toward the center. From Cumaná in the east and Coro in the west, the Conquest and settlement converged at Caracas by the last quarter of the sixteenth century. The early search for profits from slave raiding, gold extraction, and pearl fishing gave way to agricultural development. The production of wheat and cacao caused the colonists to turn to the encomienda system. This development proceeded slowly from the central valleys (Caracas, Valencia, and Barquisimeto) to the outlying areas. In the latter, indigenous slavery persisted until the seventeenth century. Encomiendas in Venezuela entailed predominately personal service rather than tribute collecting until the end of the seventeenth century.

In the coastal regions encomienda labor gave way to African slave labor by the third decade of the seventeenth century, especially in the cacao plantation economy. With the exception of the mission areas and the far south, Amerindians in Venezuela maintained the old pattern of subsistence agriculture. Cacao replaced wheat as the principal source of export earnings. The cacao tree was indigenous to Venezuela, and originally the beans were shipped exclusively to Mexico. The market greatly increased when Europeans began to acquire a taste for the product. Caracas emerged as the dominant area of Venezuela because of its role in controlling the production of both wheat and cacao.

CONQUEST AND COLONIZATION

Most of the earliest exploration of what is today Venezuela was a result of the search for slaves to serve the Spanish settlers on Cuba and Hispaniola. This activity did little to establish a permanent Spanish presence in Venezuela. It did, however, provide the Spanish with enough information to cause them to seek other sources of wealth that would provide more permanent settlements.

The Spanish were attracted initially to the islands of Cubagua and Margarita because of the rich pearl beds, which proved to be a source of considerable income for the colonists and the crown in the 1520s and 1530s. The beds quickly played out, although the Spanish had by then established towns on Margarita Island and on the mainland at Cumaná and Barcelona.

The first Hispanic settlement in the vicinity of Caracas was established by settlers from Margarita Island. In 1558 Francisco Fajardo and a few Margariteños settled near the future port of La Guaira. The settlers spent a year trading along the coast, but were driven off by local peoples. Undaunted, Fajardo returned the next year with reinforcements from Margarita Island. This time he divided the indigenous people into encomiendas, the first to be created along the Venezuelan coast. The settlers from Margarita Island had pushed near to the site of what became Caracas. The formal establishment of the town was accomplished by settlers who pushed eastward from the colony's other Hispanic center in Coro.

Serious exploration and settlement of western Venezuela came in 1528, when Charles I granted the Welser banking house the administration of Venezuela in repayment for the bank's support in the religious wars of the sixteenth century. Governor Ambrosio Alfinger and Nicolas Federmann led the early expeditions, which were followed for the next two decades by many others. Driven by their desire to find El Dorado, the German explorers found little else of interest. After two decades the Germans could claim that they had founded Coro and Maracaibo, increased geographic knowledge, and intensified Indian hostility. Nominally the Welser possession lasted until 1556, but the Spanish effectively regained control in the late 1540s.

From the base at Coro, the Spanish established a string of successful settlements. These towns indicated that the colony had matured from the era of simple exploitation under the Welser grant. The establishment of the towns of El Tocuyo (1545), Barquisimeto (1552), Valencia (1556), and Caracas (1567) brought to an end the first phase of the colonial period, which was characterized by the establishment of encomiendas.

The growth of towns during the first two-thirds of the sixteenth century was a very slow process. Prior to the mid-century the Spanish founded four towns, which served as stations for the pearl fisheries and as slaving stations. Two were successful: Cumaná (founded 1520) and Coro (founded 1527). María was abandoned after only a short time and a hurricane struck the fourth, New Cádiz. Fourteen towns were founded during the third quarter of the century. The second wave of community building occurred in the interior valleys as opposed to the earlier development on the coast. These newer sites shared with earlier communities the fact that they were hampered by Indian raids and the lack of an adequate labor base.

Caracas served as a base for the further exploration of the colony, which was not secured, however, until smallpox greatly reduced indigenous resistance in 1580. The indigenous population declined by perhaps two-thirds in the immediate Caracas valley, from perhaps 30,000 to 10,000, because of the epidemic. The elimination of the indigenous peoples as a serious threat to Caracas and the surrounding area allowed the colony to develop in a much more stable climate.

The period from the last quarter of the sixteenth century to the establishment of the captaincy general in the 1770s was an era of slow, almost imperceptible change. The overriding theme of the period was the establishment of Caracas as the dominant economic, social, and political power of the area today known as Venezuela. At the opening of this period Venezuela was a collection of independent geographic regions tied to New Granada, the Caribbean, or Spain. Caracas itself was just one of a number of towns surrounded by a limited geographic area that interacted much more with a distant part of the empire than with another region of what would become Venezuela.

THE COLONIAL ECONOMY

The colonial Venezuelan economy was diversified, producing agricultural products for internal and external markets. In the seventeenth century cacao, wheat, tobacco, and hides dominated external trade. Other products included cotton, indigo, gold, and copper. These products were exported primarily to Mexico and Spain, with the largest volume of trade in the seventeenth century being the cacao and wheat going to Mexico. The funds obtained from external trade went largely to purchase African black slaves and manufactured products from Europe.

There was also a sizable internal trade within the three major economic zones of what would eventually become Venezuela: the central valleys surrounding Caracas, the eastern periphery focusing upon Cumaná and the interior plains, and the western periphery reaching from the Andes to Coro and Maracaibo. At the beginning of the mature colonial period these three areas had little contact with one another. There was a great deal of intraregional trade, but very little interregional trade. There was nothing inevitable about Caracas's eventual domination over the other areas. The Spanish colonial system, which during the eighteenth century called for increasing centralization, was itself responsible for the eventual emergence of Caracas as the dominant city and province.

By the end of the sixteenth century *caraqueños* were selling wheat to Cartagena, where it was used to supply the Spanish fleet, thus bringing the city's residents into the world trading system. In the 1620s Caracas residents discovered that cacao beans could be sold profitably to Nahuas and other peoples in Mexico. In 1622 Mexican imports of Venezuelan cacao were about 6,960 pounds annually, but during the period from 1620 to 1650 they averaged about 133,400 pounds a year, and from 1651 to 1700, 748,200 pounds. This caused an expansion of the area under cultivation from the coastal valleys to the fertile valleys of the Tuy River and its tributary streams. In the 1720s the success of the cacao trade attracted the attention of the Spanish crown, leading to the establishment of the Real Compañía Guipuzcoana de Caracas or Caracas Company.

The Caracas Company was a mercantile enterprise chartered to control trade between Venezuela and Spain from 1728 to 1784. It was formed in Spain in 1728 by José de Patiño. The company was given the exclusive right to control the cacao trade between Venezuela and Spain. In return for this monopoly, the Caracas Company agreed to suppress the contraband trade, defend the Venezuelan coast, stimulate regional production of cacao, and provide slaves to the colony.

The Caracas Company was a mixed success. The first four decades of its existence were marked by expansion and profit. The production and legal exportation of cacao increased significantly during the decades, from 2.5 million pounds per year in the 1720s to over 6 million pounds annually in the early 1760s. This expansion in cacao production and trade, however, did little to enhance the overall condition of the colony. The planters elected to increase production in order to counteract the lower prices paid by the Caracas Company for cacao. This pushed the expansion of the plantation system, a classic case of growth without development. The efforts to halt contraband activities were not totally successful. Finally, the Caracas Company was unable to supply the colony with sufficient numbers of black slaves or European goods. These problems, the Bourbon Reforms, and the wars that disrupted trading patterns caused the company's fortunes to decline, and the crown terminated the Caracas Company's charter in 1784.

The Caracas Company's most enduring legacy was that it ensured the primacy of Caracas over the remainder of the captaincy general. By expanding the economic sphere of the capital, both in terms of area and power, the activities of the Caracas Company preceded the political centralization of the colony later in the century.

MISSIONARY ACTIVITY
The establishment of the Caracas Company was just one example of the crown's increased emphasis on the colony after years of neglect. By the middle of the eighteenth century the crown also moved to increase its control over church and government. The Franciscans, Capuchins, Dominicans, Jesuits, and Augustinians were active in Venezuela during the colonial period. The Franciscans were active from the early years in the colony, eventually establishing themselves in the central area in and around Caracas. In Venezuela the Franciscans are best remembered for their influence on culture and on education. The order contributed substantially to the rise of the dominance of Caracas since it selected the city as the location of its activities in the colony. The location of the center of learning in the colony in Caracas further enhanced the city as the primary settlement in the colony. The separate group of Franciscans were active as missionaries in the Píratu area of eastern Venezuela.

On a much larger scale, the Capuchin order formed part of the Great Mission Arc stretching from Paraguay to the Andes. The two major areas of missionary penetration were in the llanos, established by the Capuchin Franciscans in the last half of the seventeenth century, and in the interior south of Cumaná, established around 1650. The Capuchins were extraordinarily active, founding over 150 towns.

The Dominicans, Augustinians, and Jesuits also contributed to the colony's spiritual development. Each had much less of an influence than the Franciscans and the Capuchins, but nevertheless were part of the missionary activity that enhanced the expansion of European society. By the middle of the eighteenth century the crown moved to control the orders by putting secular clergy in charge of the missions. In 1767 the crown expelled the Jesuits from the colonies and confiscated their property.

THE BOURBON REFORMS

The Caracas Company and the Franciscans are but two examples of institutions that assisted in the dominance of Caracas over the outlying provinces. Perhaps even greater emphasis should be placed on a series of actions taken by the Spanish monarchs known collectively as the Bourbon Reforms, which created the Consulado, the intendancy, the Caracas Battalion, the audiencia, and the captaincy general.

In 1776 the crown ordered the creation of the Intendancy of Venezuela, which placed the six provinces of Venezuela (Caracas, Cumaná, Barinas, Mérida de Maracaibo, Guayana, and Trinidad and Margarita) under a single fiscal administrator in Caracas. In effect this made the intendant's approval necessary for any major project involving royal funds.

Political and military authority were centralized in Caracas with the creation of the Captaincy General of Venezuela. This reform, effected in 1777, was to a large extent mandated by defense interests. Since the creation of the Caracas Battalion in the 1750s, the military forces in Caracas had more influence and power than those in the other provinces. In 1771 a thorough reorganization of the militia created a new command structure that allowed the reform to spread throughout the other provinces. The final bureaucratic centralization occurred in 1786 with the creation of the Audiencia

of Caracas. Prior to this date appeals to a legal tribunal had to go to Santo Domingo or Bogotá. This not only eliminated a great deal of expense and time, but reinforced the dominance of Caracas over the other provinces.

During the last quarter of the eighteenth century these reforms helped create the conditions for an expansion of commerce and production. The intendant became an active participant in economic expansion, a new role for the Spanish monarchy. Trade was liberalized, including the legalization of the trade for many articles formerly available only as contraband. A *consulado* linking merchants and planters from all over Venezuela into a powerful representative group was formed in the 1780s. In 1789 the crown allowed Venezuela at least partial free trade. Expeditions to the Antilles were allowed in order to trade agricultural products for slaves, and the crown even began to approve of trade with allies and neutral nations during the repeated wars with Great Britain.

Other institutional changes added to the prominence of Caracas. In 1725 the Seminary of Caracas was upgraded to the Real y Pontífica Universidad de Caracas. A Colegio de Abogados was established in the 1780s. In 1804 the crown created the Archbishopric of Venezuela, which brought the bishops of Mérida de Maracaibo and Guyana-Cumaná under the power of the Caracas seat.

TOWARD INDEPENDENCE

Venezuela was a beneficiary of the Bourbon economic policies. This was especially true in the export sector, which depended upon slavery and tenancy. Several minor uprisings in the two decades prior to 1810 indicated that there were tensions. In 1795 slaves and free laborers seized a number of plantations in the area near Coro before being ruthlessly suppressed. Two years later royal officials discovered a plot led by local Creole military officers and supported by representatives of all classes. The most dangerous plot may have been that of Francisco de Miranda, who made two unsuccessful efforts to liberate Venezuela in 1806.

On 19 April 1810 the *cabildo* in Caracas deposed the captain-general and the audiencia. The leaders appointed a junta made up of moderate autonomists and revolutionary nationalists. With both groups composed of members of the elite, there was widespread agreement on economic issues. The junta reduced taxes and established free trade. Property qualifications kept most of the population from participating in the political process. Congress convened in March 1811, replaced the junta with a three-person executive, declared independence on 5 July, and wrote a federalist constitution. The two most important leaders were Francisco de Miranda and Simón Bolívar, neither of whom were revolutionaries in the sense of wanting to improve the lot of the majority of the Venezuelan people.

The new republican government was unpopular and was criticized by both radicals and conservatives. The First Republic had a short life. In 1812, after a calamitous earthquake that was taken as an omen by the people, royalist forces persuaded Miranda to capitulate. He did so with the understanding that the lives and property of the republicans would be protected. Bolívar was outraged at Miranda's seemingly treasonous activity and arranged for the latter's arrest by the Spanish. Miranda was sent to Spain, where he died four years later. The stage was set for the long struggle for independence under the leadership of Bolívar.

In 1813 Bolívar returned to fight in Venezuela with a new political philosophy. Instead of democracy and federalism, as represented in the 1811 Constitution, Bolívar called for centralization and a more independent military after the fall of the First Republic. Despite some successes, Bolívar and his republican forces were repeatedly defeated by royalist forces. His most difficult opposition came from José Tomás Boves, a royalist caudillo who had organized the *llaneros* of southern Venezuela into a cavalry.

In 1815 Ferdinand VII sent General Pablo Morillo to northern South America to pacify Venezuela. Morillo, who replaced General Juan Manuel de Cajigal as captain-general, allied himself with the wealthy planter class that had called for the break with Spain in 1811. The lack of efficient bureaucracy forced Morillo to confiscate property to supply his army of pacification. Relying on terror and the military prowess of his experienced corps, Morillo conquered Venezuela and most of New Granada.

The harsh policies of Morillo resulted in a realignment of social forces in the struggle for the expulsion of the royalists. The Creole elites saw clearly that independence from Spain and from tyrants such as Morillo was necessary to maintain their own power and status. Two groups that had formerly fought for the royalists, the *llaneros* and the blacks, joined forces with Bolívar and the elites, creating an alliance between the socially conservative elite and the lower classes. The Venezuelan *llaneros* were led by José Antonio Páez, a brilliant military leader and future Venezuelan president. A national congress meeting in Angostura in 1819 named Bolívar president.

The Congress of Angostura called for the creation of the Republic of Colombia (oftentimes called Gran Colombia), which would unify Venezuela, New Granada, and the still-to-be liberated Ecuador. A constituent assembly met in 1821 to write a new constitution, giving the centralist executive wide-ranging powers. Bolívar, with the title of provisional president of Colombia, began his conquest of northern South America.

It soon became clear that the final chapter in the war between Spain and Venezuela would be settled by force of arms. The patriot victory at the battle of Boyacá in August 1819 caused Morillo to see that the end was at hand. After the liberal rebellion in Spain in 1820, he was ordered to negotiate with the patriots on the basis of the Constitution of 1812. In November 1820 representatives of Bolívar and Morillo signed a six-month armistice.

The Battle of Carabobo is considered to be the final major military engagement of the War for Independence in Venezuela. On the morning of 24 June 1821 the patriots, under the command of Bolívar, faced royalist troops under the leadership of General Miguel de la Torre, who had taken command of the Spanish forces after the departure of Morillo the previous year. Bolívar's forces were joined at Carabobo by the *llaneros* of José Antonio Páez. The patriot force outnumbered the royalists, and half of the royalist force was captured, the rest fleeing to the fort at Puerto Cabello. The patriots also gained important munitions, including artillery pieces and a large amount of ammunition. Bolívar entered Caracas less than a week later. He organized a government at Cúcuta on the border of New Granada and Venezuela, marking the beginning of Venezuelan national reconstruction.

See also **Slavery: Indian Slavery and Forced Labor; Venezuela, Constitutions.**

BIBLIOGRAPHY

Francisco De Pons, *Travels in Parts of South America During the years 1801, 1802, 1803, and 1804* (1806).

James Biggs, *The History of Don Francisco de Miranda's Attempt to Effect a Revolution in South America* (1910).

Alexander Von Humbolt and Aime Boapland, *Personal Narrative of Travels to the Equinoctial Regions of the New Continent, During the Years 1799–1804* (1818).

L. Duarte Level, *Historia patria* (1911).

Bartolomé Tavera Acosta, *Historia de Carúpano* (1930).

Roland D. Hussey, *The Caracas Company, 1780–1784: A Study in the History of Spanish Monopolistic Trade* (1934).

Hector García Chuecos, *Estudios de historia colonial venezolana* (1937–1938).

José Antonio De Sangroniz y Castro, *Familias coloniales de Venezuela* (1943).

Hector García Chuecos, *La capitanía general de Venezuela: Apuntes para una exposición del derecho político colonial venezolano* (1945).

Demetrio Ramos Pérez, *El tratado de limites de 1750 y expedición de Iturriaga el Orinoco* (1946).

Eduardo Arcila Frias, *Economía colonial de Venezuela* (1946).

Enrique Bernardo Núñez, *La ciudad de los techos rojos: Calles y esquinas de Caracas* (1947–1948).

Francisco Javier Yanes, *Historia de la Provincia de Cumaná* (1949).

Castro Fulencio López, *Juan Bautista Picornell y la conspiración de Gaul y España* (1955).

Hector García Chuecos, *Siglo dieciocho venezolano* (1956).

Eduardo Arcila Farias, comp., *El Real Consulado de Caracas* (1957).

Caracciolo Parra Pérez, *Historia de la Primera República de Venezuela* (1959).

Federico Brito Figueroa, *La estructura económica de Venezuela colonial* (1964).

J. A. De Armas Chitty, *Guayana: Su tierra y su historia* (1964).

Graziano Gasparini, *La arquitectura colonial en Venezuela* (1965).

Jerónimo Martínez-Mendoza, *Venezuela colonial* (1965).

Eduardo Arcila Frias, *El régimen de la encomienda en Venezuela* (1966).

Mercedes M. Álvarez, *Temas para la historia del comercio colonial* (1966).

Carlos Itarriza Guillén, *Algunas familia caraqueñas* (1967).

Mercedes M. Álvarez, *El tribunal del Real Consulado de Caracas* (1967).

Raul Tomás López Rivero, *Fortificaciones de Maracaibo: Siglos XVII y XVIII* (1968).

José Sucre Reyes, *La capitanía general de Venezuela* (1969).

Jurt Nagel Von Jess, *Algunas familias maracaiberas* (1969).

Germán Carerra Damas, *La crisis de la sociedad colonial* (1971).

Santiago Gerardo Suárez, *Marina, milicia y ejército en la colonia* (1971).

Jesse A. Noel, *Trinidad, provincia de Venezuela: Historia de la administracion española de Trinidad* (1972).

Carlos Itarriza Guillén, *Algunas familias de Cumaná* (1973).

Robert Semple, "Bosquejo del estado actual de Caracas incluyendo un viaje por La Victoria y Valencia hasta Puerto Cabello, 1810–1811," in *Tres Testigos Europeos de la Primera República* (1974).

John V. Lombardi, *People and Places in Colonial Venezuela* (1976).

J. L. Salcedo Bastardo, *Historia fundamental de Venezuela* (1977).

Allan J. Kuethe, *Military Reform and Society in New Granada, 1773–1808* (1971).

John V. Lombardi, *Venezuela: The Search for Order, the Dream of Progress* (1982).

James Lockhart and Stuart B. Schwartz, *Early Latin America: A History of Colonial Spanish America and Brazil* (1983).

Robert J. Ferry, *The Colonial Elite of Early Caracas* (1989).

Additional Bibliography

Archer, Christon I. *The Wars of Independence in Spanish America*. Wilmington, DE: Scholarly Resources, 2000.

Diaz, Arlene J. *Female Citizens, Patriarchs, and the Law in Venezuela, 1786–1904*. Lincoln: University of Nebraska Press, 2004.

Eastwood, Jonathan. *The Rise of Nationalism in Venezuela*. Gainesville: University Press of Florida, 2006.

Herrera Salas, Jesús María. *El negro Miguel y la primera revolución venezolana: La cultura del poder y el poder de la cultura*. Caracas: Vadell Hermanos Editores, 2003.

Laserna Gaitán, Antonio Ignacio. *Tierra, gobierno local y actividad misionera en la comunidad indígena del Oriente Venezolano: La visita a la provincia de Cumaná de Don Luis de Chávez y Mendoza (1783–1784)*. Caracas: Academia Nacional de la Historia, 1993.

Pollak-Eltz, Angelina. *La esclavitud en Venezuela: Un estudio histórico-cultural*. Caracas: Universidad Católica Andrés Bello, 2000.

Tarver Denova, Hollis Micheal and Julia C. Frederick. *The History of Venezuela*. Westport, CT: Greenwood Press, 2005.

GARY MILLER

VENEZUELA SINCE 1830

Venezuela's insertion into the world economy came through a sequence of events that followed in general design the pattern of all of the Spanish American republics born at the beginning of the nineteenth century. As elsewhere, various uprisings, protests, and incidents throughout the latter years of the eighteenth century and the first few years of the nineteenth marked Venezuela as a society uneasy about its future and dissatisfied with its political, economic, and social relationships. Much can be made of these indications of unrest, from the enthusiasm of young intellectuals for the writings of various French and Spanish Enlightenment authors to the abortive revolution sponsored by Francisco de Miranda during his ill-fated invasion of the Venezuelan coast at Coro in 1806. Slave rebellions and uprisings related to race and class conflict also preoccupied Venezuelans of the period. Although these incidents clearly indicated

a state of unrest, the impetus for major change came, as it always had, from Spain.

THE INDEPENDENCE PERIOD: 1808–1830

In 1808 the Napoleonic invasion of Spain precipitated the abdication of Charles IV in favor of his son Ferdinand VII. Ferdinand fell into the hands of Napoleon's troops, who, holding him captive, placed Joseph Bonaparte on the Spanish throne. These events led to the creation in Spain of a supreme central junta dedicated to the restoration of the legitimate monarch Ferdinand VII and committed to the government of Spain in the name of the captive king. In the face of advancing Napoleonic forces, the junta moved to Seville and then to Cadiz. Finally, in 1809 the Spanish junta dissolved in favor of a regency council.

The news of these events produced a constitutional crisis in Caracas as well as elsewhere in Spanish America. In response, on April 19, 1810, the Caracas *cabildo* held an open session to assert its right to govern the captaincy general of Venezuela. It removed the French-imposed captain-general and organized the Junta Conservadora de los Derechos de Fernando VII. This action formally marks the beginning of the independence movement in Venezuela, although for the participants, the determination of actual independence would not come for more than a decade. In retrospect, this tentative assertion of local control led directly to a full declaration of independence and the successful construction of an independent republic. For those involved in the events of 1810 to 1820, these decades appeared turbulent and uncertain.

Who knew, in 1810, whether Napoleon would send his armies to America to wreak vengeance on the colonials who refused to accept his designated king? Who knew whether Ferdinand VII would return to the throne as an absolutist monarch and send his troops to America to wreak vengeance on those colonials who had ousted his royal officials in favor of a junta or a French pretender? Faced with this uncertain future, the colonials followed the Spanish peninsular model, hoping that the formula of a junta to conserve the rights of Ferdinand VII would protect them from charges of treason should the restoration of the Spanish king come quickly.

Events, of course, often moved faster than the participants could anticipate, and by 1811 the Venezuelan patriots, as those pursuing independence called themselves, succeeded in convening a general congress of the United Provinces of Venezuela that declared the country independent of Spain on July 5, 1811. The congress, recognizing the extensive European military experience of one of its most famous native sons, Francisco de Miranda, placed the country's defense in his hands. Spain, again, intervened, and when the Spanish Cortes of Cadiz approved a liberal constitution in March and restored Ferdinand VII to the throne, the Venezuelan patriots lost ground and Miranda surrendered to the Spanish captain, Domingo Monteverde, in July 1812.

Whatever the events in Spain that reinforced the success of Spanish rule, the Venezuelan experiment in independent self-government proved a dismal failure. Called the *patria boba*, or infant republic, the Venezuelans proved better at the theory than at the practice of government. A weak executive and a timid congress were unable to mobilize the necessary resources. Miranda had better credentials as a European general than as a Latin American military chieftain, and even when he finally received dictatorial powers, he could not rally the masses. Coro, the former capital of Venezuela, along with Maracaibo and Guayana, refused to join Caracas in the independence effort, fragmenting the united American front necessary to liberate Venezuela. Young radicals such as Simón Bolívar had too little experience at the time to provide the local leadership the republic needed. So the first effort at independence failed, and Venezuela remained in the hands of loyal Spanish forces.

Even though defeated in Caracas and elsewhere in Venezuela, the patriots refused to give up, and Bolívar and his colleagues reentered the fight from Colombia by way of Cartagena and then up the Magdalena into the Andes, from where they launched a lightning campaign north along the Andes in what has come to be known as the Campaña Admirable (Admirable Campaign). The Mérida town council recognized the force of this patriot chieftain and awarded Bolívar the title of Liberator in June 1813, a title he kept above all others.

In the rapid advance on Caracas, Bolívar issued a decree of war to the death against Spanish rule. Much discussed by contemporaries and historians, this decree declared everyone in America who had been born in Spain an enemy unless he worked actively for independence, and everyone born in America a friend even if he worked for Spain. Regarded by some as a barbaric example of republican excess, others recognized this decree as a wartime effort to create a national identity for a country as yet unsure of itself. In search of adherents, desperate for recruits and supporters, the decree of war to the death served to polarize the population around the independence-campaign. The Campaña Admirable succeeded quickly, and in August Bolívar entered Caracas, where his title of Liberator was confirmed.

The short-lived triumph collapsed at the hands of the Spanish loyalist commander, a native Venezuelan named José Tomás Boves. Out in the *llanos* (plains) south of Caracas he declared his own war to the death against the patriots and succeeded in mobilizing the plainsmen cavalry against them. Little inclined to fight for the interests of the urban elite represented by the patriots of Bolívar's class, the *llaneros* at Boves's direction fought fiercely on behalf of the king. By mid-July 1814 Bolívar and his colleagues found themselves on the run, and on July 16 Boves entered Caracas triumphant in the name of the king. Bolívar fled Venezuela for Cartagena in September; with the irony of historical fate, Boves, now triumphant, died from wounds received in battle. His royalist cause appeared secure nonetheless, for by 1815 a Spanish army of some ten thousand men under Pablo Morillo, an able Spanish captain, arrived in Venezuela. This marked the end of the Second Republic in the nomenclature of Venezuelan independence historiography.

In the Caribbean, the Venezuelan patriots in exile continued planning and developing their agenda for independence. One of the most celebrated documents of the period, Bolívar's so-called Jamaica Letter, offered a political philosophy for the independence of Venezuela designed to attract the attention of British and other European sympathizers. By 1816 Bolívar had found a strong American supporter in President Alexandre Pétion of Haiti, who sponsored his failed attempt to invade Venezuela in 1815 and then his successful invasion farther east at Barcelona in 1817. From there, Bolívar marched toward Angostura, where he joined forces with other independence caudillos maintaining a successful guerrilla presence in Guayana. He joined Manuel Piar in the successful siege of Angostura (1817). Moving quickly to establish a republican presence and institutionalize the military efforts into a government initiative, Bolívar established a newspaper in 1818, the *Correo de Orinoco,* and

convened the second national congress in 1819 in Angostura, which elected him president of Venezuela.

Drawing on this base of support, Bolívar organized an army and crossed the Andes into New Granada (now Colombia), where, in August 1819, he defeated the royalist army at Boyacá outside of Bogotá. This action effectively liberated New Granada; the congress then created the Republic of Colombia from the provinces of Ecuador, New Granada, and Venezuela and elected Bolívar president. This assertion of authority, of course, required a military campaign to actually liberate central and western Venezuela, still held by the royalists.

Once again, events in Spain influenced the development of Venezuelan affairs. In 1820 the Spanish liberals succeeded in forcing Ferdinand VII to accept their constitution of 1812, a document that curbed his absolutist powers. As part of the liberal success, Pablo Morillo in Venezuela received orders to negotiate with the patriots, leading to an armistice. The patriots, seeing an opportunity, broke the truce after two months, and in January captured Maracaibo. While a congress of Cúcuta continued the task of forming a republic for Colombia, complete with its own liberal constitution, the military effort led by Bolívar and made possible in Venezuela by the armies of Santiago Mariño and José Antonio Páez finally defeated the main royalist army in Venezuela at the second battle of Carabobo (June 1821).

Over the next few years, Bolívar and the Venezuelan and Colombian armies continued to defeat various royalist strongholds. In 1822 the United States recognized the Republic of Colombia, and later in that year Bolívar held a famous Guayaquil meeting with Agustín de San Martín, the liberator of Argentina and Chile. This meeting apparently persuaded San Martín to leave control of Ecuador and Peru to Bolívar's Colombian forces. The patriots captured Puerto Cabello, Venezuela, in November 1823, concluding the military phase of the Venezuelan independence movement.

Between 1824 and 1829 Venezuela and the rest of greater Colombia remained preoccupied with the problems of inventing a country. The notion of Gran Colombia, a brilliant concept drawn from Bolívar's clear recognition of the weakness of individual Spanish American jurisdictions and based

Venezuela

Population:	26,023,528 (2007 est.)
Area:	352,144.48 sq mi
Official language(s):	Spanish
Language(s):	Spanish; indigenous languages
National currency:	bolivar (VEB)
Principal religions:	Roman Catholic 96%, Protestant 2%, other 2%
Ethnicity:	mestizo (mixed race), 68%; European (primarily Spanish, Italian, Portuguese, German), 21%; African, 8–10%; indigenous people, 2%
Capital:	Caracas (pop. 3,226,000, 2005 est.)
Other urban centers:	Valencia, Maracaibo, Maracay, Barquisimeto
Principal geographic features:	*Mountains:* Andes; Pico Bolívar, the highest peak in Venezuela (16,427 ft) *Lakes and rivers:* Lake Maracaibo; Orinoco River *Other:* Guiana Highlands; Angel Falls (3,212 ft high), the highest waterfall in the world
Economy:	*GDP per capita:* $149.9 billion (2006 est.)
Principal products and exports:	*Agricultural:* corn, sorghum, sugarcane, rice, bananas, vegetables, coffee; beef, pork, milk, eggs; fish *Industries:* petroleum, construction materials, food processing, textiles; iron ore mining, steel, aluminum; motor vehicle assembly
Government:	Independence: 1811; constitution: 1999; federal republic; five branches of government; the legislative branch (a unicameral National Assembly), the judiciary, the electoral branch, the citizens' branch, and the presidency. President elected by popular vote for a six-year term. Venezuela has 23 states, the Federal District, and 72 offshore islands grouped under a federal dependency.
Armed forces:	In 2005, 82,300 active personnel in armed forces, in addition to 23,000 members of the *Fuerzas Armados de Cooperacion*, an internal security force. *Army:* 34,000 regulars; *Navy:* 18,300, including an estimated 7,800 Marines, 1,000 Coast Guard members, and 500 naval aviation personnel; *Air Force:* 7,000 personnel.
Transportation:	Cities and towns of the remote regions are linked principally by air transportation. Three hundred sixty-nine airports (2004 est.); 128 had paved runways (2005 est.); 1 heliport. Three main airlines, the government-owned Aerovías Venezolanas S.A. (AVENSA), Línea Aeropostal Venezolana (LAV), and Venezolana Internacional de Aviación, S.A. (VIASA). Nine thousand nine hundred mi of navigable inland waterways; 59,751 mi of highway, of which 20,076 mi were paved. In 2003 there were 1,480,000 passenger cars and 1,157,138 commercial vehicles; railway system totaled 424 mi.
Media:	Estimated 344 commercial radio stations and over 150 FM and AM community radio stations, as well as 31 television channels (2004 est.); 192 radios and 186 television sets for every 1,000 people (2003 est.). Fifteen national newspapers, 77 regional newspapers, and 89 magazines and weekly journals. Leading daily Venezuelan newspapers published in Caracas are: *Ultimas Noticias,* 200,000; *El Universal,* 120,000; *El Nacional,* 100,000; and *Diario 2001,* 100,000 (2004 circulations).
Literacy and education:	*Total literacy rate:* 93% Free public education from kindergarten through university; compulsory education for children ages 5 through 17. Fourteen universities, both national and private, including the University of Venezuela (founded in 1725), Los Andes University (1785), Simón Bolívar University (1970), and the Open University (1977), and the Open University (1977).

on the models of the Spanish colonial period, could not withstand the interests of the local elites. The centrifugal forces splintering Spanish America into independent republics based on the colonial jurisdiction of the *audiencias* overcame even the charismatic leadership of as effective a general and statesman as Simón Bolívar. By 1829 the task of keeping greater Colombia together exceeded Bolívar's capabilities. In Venezuela, José Antonio Páez led the separatists. Building on the resentment against a government as remote and unconnected to Caracas as was Bogotá's, Páez supported a separatist rebellion in 1829 and led Venezuela out of Gran Colombia, marking the state's emergence as a separate and independent republic.

THE CONSERVATIVE OLIGARCHY: 1830–1847

The years from 1830 through the 1870s fall into two major periods named by Venezuelan historiography as the Conservative Oligarchy (1830–1847) and the Liberal Oligarchy (1848–1865). During this time Venezuela passed through the transition required to become a full participant in the expanding world economy, especially the segment dominated by northern Europe (England, Germany, and France), and later on including the United States. Venezuela's economic and political development depended almost entirely on exporting primary agricultural products into this world market.

Although these years saw considerable controversy and various rebellions, changes in the terms of trade and rules of economic life generated the greatest tensions within Venezuela. Driven by world markets for its various commodities, principally coffee and cacao, Venezuelans often found their plans for political and economic development abruptly derailed or substantially diverted by events outside their borders. A bitter controversy over an 1834 law that favored the rights of creditors over the rights of debtors permitted a glimpse into the changes affecting Venezuelan affairs. Formerly, most credit in Venezuela, and especially agricultural credit, came from long-term loans provided by the church with low interest. Independence brought an influx of European capital, delivered in the form of short-term commercial loans with relatively high interest rates.

The April 10, 1834, law made it easier for creditors to foreclose on Venezuelans caught without funds in the short time frames of these loans. When the price of coffee or chocolate declined in Europe, the optimistic estimates of Venezuelan landowners collapsed and they would default on their loans. Used to longer-term relationships, Venezuelan planters found the adjustment to short-term, high-interest-rate loans difficult, and they looked to the political process to protect them. Issues of this nature helped polarize Venezuelan politics between a group calling itself the Conservatives, whose political philosophy appeared to be primarily liberal in its favor of free trade and minimal government restrictions, and a group called the Liberals, which looked to the rural landowners for its support and championed policies that appeared to recall Spanish colonial values.

The ideological and programmatic content of these parties may have had less to do with their cohesion than their personalist ties. Liberals tended to draw on the strength of the military heroes of independence and especially those associated with the Bolivarian faction. The Conservatives tended to cluster around individuals who had rejected Bolívar's Gran Colombia and had either encouraged Venezuelan separatism or had not participated much in the independence epic itself.

The Conservatives had as their champion José Antonio Páez, the hero of independence whose vision for Venezuela never lost its focus in pursuit of grand designs. This great *llanero* warrior turned out to be a careful, canny, and effective caudillo, and as long as his personal strength remained intact, he kept the Conservatives in power. Although labeled Conservative, Páez's regimes had their difficulties with the church until 1832, when the archbishop of Caracas and the bishop of Mérida returned from their exile and swore to uphold the state. In 1833 Congress accepted a solution to the question of patronage and then abolished the tithe. In 1834 Congress granted freedom of worship to all citizens. These changes did not satisfy the church; in 1836 the archbishop of Venezuela, Ramón Ignacio Méndez, refused to recognize civil jurisdiction, and the state exiled him.

Throughout this period, Páez governed either directly or through intermediaries, emerging from retirement to put down this or that rebellion or to guarantee the continuation of policies and individuals that met with his approval. The sequence of administrations began with the first administration of Páez (1831–1835). Then, at the request of the civilians in Congress, Páez ceded power to Venezuela's first civilian president, José María Vargas, an intellectual with no military or significant political experience and no participation in independence wars.

As soon as Vargas took office he found himself at war with the pro-Bolívar separatists from eastern Venezuela led by General Santiago Mariño. This Revolution of the Reforms, as it was called, had a mixed set of objectives, but in addition to resentments over the reduced influence of the independence Bolivarian heroes, the *reformistas* had a separatist agenda that would have set up eastern Venezuela as a republic, perhaps under the leadership of Mariño. Páez, called out of retirement, defeated the rebels but prevented the government from imposing severe penalties for their actions. Vargas, unable to insist on punishment for the rebellion's leaders, resigned in favor of Vice President Andrés Narvarte (1836–1837) and then Vice President Carlos Soublette (1837–1839), who completed his term in close collaboration with Páez.

These years saw continued growth of the economy, with a prospering cacao industry and a boom in the coffee sector, but at the same time Soublette had to suppress various uprisings, notably a popular revolt led by Ezequiel Zamora. In 1847 Páez, thinking his fellow general José Tadeo Monagas suitably loyal to the Conservative cause but nonetheless a representative of the eastern caudillos, allowed him to become president for the 1847–1851 period.

Within a year, however, Monagas had given amnesty to Liberals convicted of treason and conspiracy, and the Conservatives withdrew their support from the government. A subsequent popular revolt in 1848 gave Monagas an opportunity to dissolve the Congress, and a Páez effort to overthrow Monagas and return the country to the Conservatives failed. This marked the beginning of what Venezuelans call the Liberal Oligarchy.

THE LIBERAL OLIGARCHY AND THE FEDERAL WARS

The next national election brought José Gregorio Monagas to the presidency (1851–1855), continuing the policies of his brother. Congress passed the first mining code in 1854, followed by a revision in 1855 that reaffirmed the Spanish rule that subsoil rights belong to the nation and not to private owners of the surface land. Also in 1854 José Gregorio Monagas signed the law abolishing slavery in Venezuela. In 1855 José Tadeo returned to the presidency. His second term saw the beginnings of modernization in Venezuela, with the installation of a telegraph line between Caracas and the port of La Guaira. A new constitution in 1857 strengthened the powers of the presidency at the expense of the powers of the states. A rebellion against Monagas for his abuses of power forced him to resign the presidency in 1858.

The end of the Monagas era of the Liberal Oligarchy signaled the end of the first era of independent government in Venezuela. The country had succeeded in defining its national territory, establishing a functioning government that could handle the task of linking Venezuela into the Atlantic export economy, and enhancing its colonial agricultural structures sufficiently to continue to provide increased quantities of coffee and stable amounts of cacao to that market. Venezuela did not resolve the question of legitimate political power, failing to find a mechanism that could manage and transfer power. Unable to rely on constitutional legitimacy, the country continued to depend on caudillos backed by force to maintain the authority of its governments.

Although effective for short periods in times of prosperity, this system had too little popular support to survive hardship or contentious disputes over the disposition of the benefits of power. The resulting political and military instability, enhanced by considerable social instability, led to a sequence of uprisings that eventually ended the Páez era and plunged the country into a five-year destructive cycle of rebellion and civil war called the Federal Wars (1859–1863).

Ostensibly fought over the question of central versus state authority and power, the Federal Wars represented a dispute over the management of the country's foreign commerce and trade. A provisional government of General Julián Castro sponsored a constitutional convention in Valencia that produced the constitution of 1858, designed to reconcile federalist and centralist ideas about the relative authority of states and the central government. The Federalists, unwilling to accept this compromise, went to war in 1859 under the leadership of General Ezequiel Zamora against the administration of Dr. Manuel Felipe Tovar, who had been named president for the 1859–1861 period.

Zamora won a major victory in this war in 1859, but in 1860 an assassin killed him and the government's troops defeated the Federalist forces at Coplé, ending this period of Federalist rebellion. Tovar's administration gave way to the administration of Dr. Pedro Gual in 1861; Gual had presided for less than a year when General José Antonio Páez returned once again to lead the Centralists. The Caracas merchants supported Páez's presidency, hoping for stability, but by 1863 the Centralists lost the Federalist Wars, and the Treaty of Coche signified the end of the Páez era.

In time-honored fashion, a new constituent assembly met from late 1863 to mid-1864 to establish the priorities of the triumphant Federalist forces and draft a new constitution. This group elected General Juan C. Falcón, the victorious leader of the Federalists, as provisional president, with General Antonio Guzmán Blanco as vice president.

THE FEDERALISTS AND THE REGIMES OF ANTONIO GUZMÁN BLANCO AND CIPRIANO CASTRO: 1864–1908

Between 1864 and 1870 Venezuela experimented with the governmental structure established in the 1864 constitution. A newly federalized Caracas welcomed the leadership of General Falcón, first as provisional president from 1863 to 1865 and then as president from 1865 to 1868. The Federalists suffered economic difficulties and constant political and military disturbances in the various states. Finally, Liberals and Conservatives joined together in a coalition to overthrow the Federalist government. General José Tadeo Monagas returned to lead this revolution, and Falcón resigned into exile in 1868. For two years the coalition of Liberals and Conservatives tried to control the states from the central government within the boundaries of the constitution of 1864, but this effort generally failed. General Antonio Guzmán Blanco, a Federalist vice president under Falcón, organized a Liberal Union opposition to the coalition, and in 1870, supported by elements of all parties, Guzmán Blanco occupied the capital, ending the experiment with a decentralized federalist government.

Between 1870 and 1908 Venezuela experienced considerable economic and political progress with a more or less strong, stable central government. Much of the transportation and communications infrastructure was modernized. Similar to the positivist movements in Mexico, Argentina, and elsewhere in Spanish America, the Venezuelans in this Guzmanato, as it was called, placed a strong emphasis on positivist values of effective hard work, conservative social values, strong support for order and progress, and little concern for the underclasses. Committed to the pursuit of a Venezuela tightly coupled to Europe and to a lesser extent North America, these leaders organized their country to be responsive to the economic, social, and intellectual interests of the leading overseas countries of France, England, Germany, and the United States.

Guzmán Blanco, the first Venezuelan strongman with no ties to the independence generation, displayed a ruthless effectiveness. His administrations, textbook liberal regimes, made education free and obligatory and reduced the power and prerogatives of the church to the extent that he exiled Archbishop Silvestre Güevara y Lira in 1870, closed the seminaries, and gave the university jurisdiction over religious studies. He later established civil marriages and a civil registry of births and deaths (1873) and closed convents and other religious communities. A rebellion in 1872 against his government not only resulted in the defeat of the rebels but the unprecedented execution of the rebel leaders. A final uprising against Guzmán Blanco in 1874–1875 involving General León Colina and General José Ignacio Pulido also failed, marking the end of major resistance until Guzmán Blanco chose to leave power near the end of the nineteenth century.

Even though Antonio Guzmán Blanco remained the most powerful force behind the government during this generation, he often acted through presidential surrogates. From 1877 to 1878 General Francisco Linares Alcántara served as his hand-picked successor. Linares Alcántara turned against Guzmán Blanco, but a counterrevolution in 1879 led by General Gregorio Cedeño and General Joaquín Crespo restored Guzmán Blanco to power as the Supreme Director of the Republic.

Guzmán Blanco's second major period of direct government, 1879 to 1884, known in Venezuelan historiography as the Quinquenio, represented a period of economic change and prosperity with considerable railroad and telegraph construction and a renovation of public works in Caracas and other major cities. As did other Spanish American states at the time, Venezuela modernized at least the surface elements of its society to more closely match European models. It invested heavily in infrastructure to make the colonial export economy compete effectively in world markets with such commodities as coffee. Guzmán Blanco consolidated political and economic power in the central government in Caracas with a reduction in the number of states and the assignment of presidential elections to a federal council (constitution of 1881).

In the 1884–1886 period, Guzmán Blanco turned over the presidency to General Joaquín Crespo, whose two-year term ended with the reelection of Guzmán Blanco for a third administration, known as the Aclamación. This period proved to be the least successful of the Guzmán Blanco presidencies, either because changing circumstances no longer matched his style or, more likely, because the accumulated resentments against his repressive political tactics made it impossible for him to govern.

Guzmán Blanco's success in negotiating large foreign loans for Venezuela had made him rich, and in his later years he became virtually an expatriate. He spent such a large portion of his time in Europe that he clearly lost the personal commitment to local Venezuelan affairs so necessary for the control of a fractious and still highly personalist government apparatus. He was elected president again in 1886, but faced with substantial opposition, he turned over the government to General Hermógenes López, president of the federal council, and returned to Europe for good (1888).

Elected as the first civilian president since 1834, Dr. Juan Pablo Rójas Paúl disassociated himself from Guzmán Blanco, but his short term (1888–1890) provided only a transition to the administration of Raimundo Andueza Palacio (1890–1892). Andueza tried to hold onto the presidency for a second term by dismissing the congress and calling a constituent assembly in 1892, but General Joaquín Crespo led what he called the Legalist Revolution and took control of the government for a second time (1892–1898).

Crespo continued the constitutional reform movement, and a national assembly returned the country to a constitution similar to that of 1864. The Crespo administration also revived the Guayana boundary dispute with Great Britain that led to an arbitration demanded by U.S. president Grover Cleveland.

A serious economic crisis in 1895 paralyzed commerce and produced a mass action of Caracas workers and artisans protesting the lack of jobs. As happened elsewhere in Spanish America, the economic difficulties encouraged European-inspired workers' parties. Venezuela's Popular Party appeared in these years, dedicated to improving the education of workers and the creation of cooperatives.

General Ignacio Andrade's short administration (1898–1899) continued with additional constitutional reforms that reestablished the states as they were in the 1864 constitution and gave the president the right to name provisional presidents of each state. Venezuela lost the arbitration hearing with Great Britain over the Guayana boundary dispute, and President Andrade's administration fell to the so-called Liberating Revolution, which brought General Cipriano Castro into power.

Cipriano Castro's tenure (1899–1908) marks the transition from Guzmán Blanco's nineteenth-century administration to the modern bureaucratic authoritarian regimes of twentieth-century Venezuela. His ascendancy also asserted the strength of the Andean region in Venezuelan political life. Recognizing that Caracas and its sophisticated bureaucratic apparatus had the skills and the knowledge required to connect Venezuela into the Atlantic trading world, the Andean ascendancy showed that the Caraqueño elites did not have the political tools needed to manage a poorly integrated national governing system that barely organized the country sufficiently to produce the goods Venezuela traded.

So the transaction between Caracas and its hinterland used the Andinos' authority of force to manage the countryside and used the Caraqueño elites' technical sophistication to manage world markets, credit, trade, and diplomacy. This bargain began with Cipriano Castro but did not reach its full development until the subsequent regime of Juan Vicente Gómez.

The two presidencies of Cipriano Castro (1899–1905, 1905–1909) were dominated by internal dissension, international conflict, and a growing recognition that hydrocarbon deposits would become an ever larger part of the Venezuelan export business. A revolution led by General Manuel Antonio Matos between 1901 and 1903, supported by international interests, attempted to oust Castro but failed. Castro then refused to pay European creditors, which resulted in a blockade of the Venezuelan coast by English, German, and Italian ships. This crisis, resolved in 1903 by the Washington Protocol, required Venezuela to allocate 30 percent of its customs receipts to pay the European claims and represented a considerable loss of prestige for Venezuela. The growing importance of hydrocarbons in the Venezuelan economy led to a 1904 mining code and then a 1905 law that permitted hydrocarbon concessions for periods of up to fifty years. A regulation the subsequent year reaffirmed the right of the president to grant and administer these hydrocarbon concessions without intervention by the congress.

Cipriano Castro proved to be a poor national leader and a petty tyrant. As his support declined along with his health, he relied more and more on his vice president, General Juan Vicente Gómez, an Andean colleague who had accompanied him on the campaigns of prior years. Gómez, recognizing the declining health and effectiveness of Castro, encouraged him to go to Europe for a cure. Once Castro was safely out of the way, Gómez deposed him at the end of 1908 and took over the presidency.

FROM JUAN VICENTE GÓMEZ TO MARCOS PÉREZ JIMÉNEZ: 1908–1958

The era of Juan Vicente Gómez inaugurated the contemporary history of Venezuela. During the generation of his control (1908–1935), Venezuela became one of the world's foremost exporters of petroleum products. Based on the substantial revenues generated from this export, Gómez modernized and controlled Venezuela, transforming it from an agricultural into a petroleum export economy. He also transformed the political process. Gómez took advantage of improvements in transportation and communications, seen first during the years of Cipriano Castro but institutionalized during the Gómez regime. With a telegraph in every hamlet and village in Venezuela, the central government knew within minutes or hours about any hostile political activities. With the improvements in roads and railroads, the central government moved troops around the republic with much more efficiency.

No longer could a rural caudillo gather his friends and neighbors, issue a call to arms, and begin a march on Caracas. At the first sign of such activity, reported in detail to the capital on the telegraph run by the state, Gómez mobilized his local supporters and federal troops to quash the incipient revolution. The means of violence, guns and ammunition, became something of a government monopoly. Where earlier caudillos could count on the household armament of every Venezuelan to provide at least the basic military matériel for an uprising, by the end of the nineteenth century, the growing sophistication and expense of rifles, cannon, Gatling guns, and other armaments made them largely inaccessible to individuals. Revolution became a process of subverting government military detachments or of seeking foreign support to launch a rebellion. All of this Gómez used to his advantage to keep his regime free from serious challenge for most of his years in office.

The Gómez period began with a provisional presidency (1908–1910) and a new constitution that led to his first official presidency (1910–1914). When his term concluded, he provoked a political crisis over his intention to seek another term, suspended constitutional guarantees, and imprisoned his opposition. Using loyal place holders to run the details of government, Gómez granted presidential powers to José Gil Fortoul in 1913 and to Victorino Márquez Bustillos in 1914. In 1915 a compliant congress reelected Gómez for the 1915–1922 period, but Gómez retained Márquez Bustillos as provisional president for the entire period.

These early decades of the Gómez era saw the beginning of the petroleum boom that was to remake the political and economic destiny of the country. A subsidiary of the Royal Dutch Shell company (Caribbean Petroleum Company) began commercial operations in Venezuela with the Zumaque-I oil well in the Mene Grande field of the Lake Maracaibo Basin, beginning the full-scale exploitation of petroleum. Petroleum exploration expanded with the construction of pipelines from the Mene Grande field to Venezuela's first oil refinery in San Lorenzo and with the first significant exports of petroleum into the world market.

Throughout this early period, Gómez's regime contended with a variety of plots and attempted revolts, but his government suppressed them all and imprisoned, tortured, or killed various conspirators. Venezuela continued to revise its laws on hydrocarbons, reaffirming its ownership of the subsoil rights as well as the government's right to concede concessions for exploration and exploitation of petroleum. Venezuela passed its first hydrocarbons law in 1920, and in 1921 Gómez permitted foreign oil companies to participate in the drafting of new legislation even more favorable to them.

In 1922 the ever-agreeable congress reelected Gómez for the period 1922 to 1929. Continuous changes in the hydrocarbons law in 1922 improved conditions for foreign oil companies. This law, with provisions for (largely unenforced) benefits for workers, remained mostly in force for more than two decades, with minor alterations in 1925 and 1928. Gómez also created the Venezuelan Petroleum Company (CVP) to serve as the government's vehicle for awarding concessions. American oil companies began buying these concessions from the CVP in 1924. The accelerating pace of oil expansion produced not only great wealth for Venezuela and selected Venezuelans, but it also generated a labor movement and the first labor protest against the high cost of living in 1925 in the Bolívar fields. Government troops suppressed the strike. Although the government approved the first labor law permitting unions and recognizing accident compensation, death benefits, and a nine-hour work day, this law did not take effect until the end of the Gómez era in 1935. By 1926 Venezuela had completed its transformation into an oil export economy, with the value of petroleum exceeding coffee.

Not all Venezuelans approved of the caudillo's dictatorial regime or the selectivity of petroleum prosperity. A student protest in 1928 led to the arrest of student leaders, sympathy strikes, and riots.

Student leaders joined with young military officers in a failed effort to provoke a barracks revolt. Gómez retaliated by closing the Central University and the Military Academy. Many among these early revolutionaries later became the principal leaders of the post-Gómez democratic regimes and regarded the 1928 strike as a formative experience.

In 1929, making what was true in practice true in law, congress appointed Gómez chief of the army and appointed Juan Bautista Pérez president of the republic. Gómez, living in Maracay as had become his tradition, continued to run the government. The Juan Bautista Pérez administration (1929–1931) suppressed various antigovernment revolts while the country's petroleum exports grew until Venezuela became the world's largest oil exporter in 1929. Dissatisfied with Pérez, congress in 1931 asked for his resignation, reformed the constitution once again, and then reelected Gómez as president.

In this term (1931–1935), Gómez had his minister of foreign relations, Itriago Chacín, occupy the presidency. Reflecting the influence of international politics on domestic affairs, Venezuelans founded a Communist Party in 1931, although the government refused to make it legal. In December 1935, Juan Vicente Gómez died of natural causes, ending his regime and unleashing a difficult two-decade transition from caudillo government to democratic reforms.

General Eleázar López Contreras (minister of war and marine) had the task of containing the forces unleashed by the death of Gómez. Elected president for the period 1936 to 1941, López encountered a host of new political parties that immediately joined in opposition to the government. A widespread strike in 1936 failed to force the government to adopt democratic reforms, and a variety of leftist parties, including the precursor to Democratic Action, joined together in the National Democratic Party (PDN). The government refused to recognize this party because of its leftist orientation.

Continued turmoil produced an oil workers' strike in 1936–1937, supported by the PDN, that forced López to grant a wage increase, although he dissolved the union and exiled its political leaders. A new hydrocarbons law for the first time appeared to give more control of the petroleum resources to the state, and the government chartered the Venezuelan Central Bank in 1939. Lopez also enacted a social security law.

General Isaías Medina Angarita (1941–1945) served as López's hand-picked successor. Democratic Action (AD), Venezuela's dominant political party after 1958, was formed and gained government recognition under Medina. In 1942, continuing the modernization of Venezuela's social and economic legislation, the government passed the country's first income tax law. A 1943 hydrocarbons law established the first nationalistic petroleum legislation that placed the country's interests first. To counter the growing strength of AD, the government supported the creation of the Venezuelan Democratic Party (PDV). Increased political freedom and discussion spawned other organizations, including a politically powerful and enduring Federation of Chambers of Commerce and Industry (Fedecámaras).

In 1945 this political reformism produced a constitutional change that retained an indirect system for the election of the president, instituted the direct election of congressional deputies, and ended restrictions on communist activities. An agrarian reform law, a popular and contentious issue in many other Spanish American countries at about the same period, promised to distribute government land to peasants. These reforms and the gradual opening of the political process, including the grant of legal status to the Communist Party (PCV), failed to forestall revolt, and in October 1945, AD and the Patriotic Military Union (a group of young military officers) succeeded in overthrowing the government of Medina.

Although the period 1945–1948, known as the *trienio* junta, offered a dramatic promise for democratic reform, the leaders of the civilian-military council could not maintain their reform movement. The seven-man council led by Rómulo Betancourt recognized two major parties, the Democratic Republican Union (URD) in 1945 and the Committee for Political Organization and Independent Election (COPEI), or Social Christian Party, in 1946; these groups played a major role in the subsequent development of Venezuela's democratic tradition. URD came from the perspective of left-of-center reformism and COPEI from a solidly Christian Democratic tradition.

The council approved a new oil company earnings tax designed to gain a true fifty-fifty split between government and private companies in oil profits, and approved a new election law that allowed direct election of the president and of delegates to a national constituent assembly. Along with other reform activities, the oil workers founded a union in 1946 (Fedepetrol), and in the elections for the National Constituent Assembly, Betancourt's party, AD, won a majority. This assembly took over the government from the council and succeeded in suppressing an army revolt. The subsequent elections brought Rómulo Gallegos, the famous Venezuelan author, to office as the first popularly elected civilian president in Venezuelan history.

Gallegos entered office in 1948 with high intellectual and cultural prestige, and his administration moved quickly to implement a variety of radical reform measures, including an agrarian reform law that would expropriate private property with compensation and an income tax on companies guaranteeing the government 50 percent of the profit on petroleum exports. Military officers, concerned with the radical nature of these reforms, met with Gallegos in November 1948; soon thereafter a military coup deposed him, ending the democratic experiment.

For the next decade Venezuela operated under the control of various military officers or coalitions of officers. For the 1948–1952 period, a junta headed by three officers, Carlos Delgado Chalbaud, Marcos Pérez Jiménez, and Luis Felipe Llovera Páez, managed the country. They exiled Gallegos, dissolved Democratic Action, suppressed strikes, disbanded the AD-dominated Confederation of Venezuelan Workers (CTV), outlawed the Communist Party, and suspended classes at the Central University of Venezuela. Dissension in the ranks of the military produced the assassination of junta president Delgado Chalbaud in 1950.

Conservative forces organized the Independent Electoral Front (FEI) to support the candidacy of Pérez Jiménez for president. When the elections of 1952 gave the victory to the URD party, Pérez Jiménez voided the results, sent URD leaders into exile, and had the armed forces designate him provisional president. Between 1952 and 1958 Pérez Jiménez served as president, naming his brand of authoritarian rule the New National Ideal. This ideal relied, as did many similar Spanish American authoritarian regimes at that time, on extensive public works to generate employment and heavy doses of political repression to maintain the authority of the government and resist radical or reformist initiatives.

The National Constituent Assembly, recognizing the inevitable, named Pérez Jiménez president officially for the 1953–1958 term and approved a new constitution. Two new universities appeared, in part to supplant the radical traditions of the closed Central University of Venezuela. The Universidad Católica Andrés Bello and the Universidad Santa María were to have high academic standards and no political activity. In 1956 the Pérez Jiménez government, responding to its foreign supporters, granted new oil concessions after a lapse of just over a decade. The repressive nature of the Pérez Jiménez regime became so extreme that the archbishop of Caracas, Monsignor Rafael Arias Blanco, issued a pastoral letter in 1957 criticizing labor conditions, and a clandestine Movement for National Liberation (MLN) appeared under the leadership of military officers plotting to overthrow the dictator. Pérez Jiménez, turning to a classic tactic of authoritarian rulers, staged a plebiscite on his presidency for the 1958–1963 period. In response, on January 23, 1958, the air force led a rebellion against the dictator supported by popular uprisings and a general strike. Pérez Jiménez left the country for exile in Miami.

THE DEMOCRATIC GOVERNMENTS OF AD AND COPEI: 1958–1994

The fall of Pérez Jiménez in 1958 ended the cycle of authoritarian, military regimes begun with Juan Vicente Gómez in 1908. The fifty years of military-sponsored rule left unresolved the issue of legitimacy in Venezuelan political life. No government since independence had survived economic difficulty or political stress without the support of military force, and many of the changes in political power had come only when the military could be persuaded to intervene. Venezuela's democratic era, which began in 1958, marked a radical departure from its political traditions, less because the military ceased to be important than because the civilian leadership found ways to keep the military focused on the maintenance of civilian government rather than the assumption of political power. This change came only at the cost of a difficult struggle, and though in retrospect it is evident that the democratic tradition owes its founding to the ouster of Pérez Jiménez, the stability of this tradition appeared much in doubt during the early years.

In January 1958 a junta of military officers and civilian leaders led by Rear Admiral Wolfgang Larrazábal assumed control of the country, and Venezuela's political exiles returned to begin reconstituting the political parties that had operated in exile or clandestinely in the country. In the turbulent months of 1958, the principal political parties, AD, COPEI, and URD, agreed in the Pact of Punto Fijo to support the winner of the presidential election and, whatever the electoral outcome, to support a coalition government. In the November election, AD and its candidate Rómulo Betancourt won the presidency with a 49 percent plurality. Before Betancourt took office, the government increased its share of petroleum profits to more than 60 percent.

The 1959–1964 administration of Rómulo Betancourt produced a dramatic sequence of events that challenged the stability and viability of democratic government and generated a series of social and political reforms that continue to shape Venezuela. Juan Pablo Pérez Alfonso, named minister of mines and hydrocarbons, became the Venezuelan government's chief architect of an international petroleum policy through OPEC in collaboration with other world producers. The government passed a new and more effective agrarian reform law in 1960.

Throughout the Betancourt regime, many factions on the left and right attempted to overthrow the government or eliminate the president. An assassination attempt in June 1960 failed, although Betancourt was wounded and the government charged the Dominican Republic's dictator, General Rafael Trujillo, with the attempt and sought sanctions from the Organization of American States (OAS). From the left, the government was challenged by the Movement of the Revolutionary Left (MIR), the first of several fragments from the AD party. The coalition government lost URD's support in November 1960 and the MIR and the Communist Party of Venezuela (PCV) began a campaign against the government.

Within this turmoil, the government moved quickly to push an activist economic agenda with the construction of Ciudad Guayana, a center in eastern Venezuela along the Orinoco River designed by an urban planning team made up of United States educators. OPEC met in Caracas, further establishing Venezuela's leading role in this organization. In 1961 Congress took control of the granting of oil concessions away from the presidency.

By 1962 the moderate reformist tendencies of AD appeared too timid to many, and dissidents from various factions moved into opposition, resulting in several armed rebellions, some involving the military. The government suspended the activities of the PCV and the MIR, and splinter groups, principal among them the Armed Forces of National Liberation (FALN), began a guerrilla war against the government to disrupt the 1963 elections. These groups operated in a manner similar to other revolutionary groups in Spanish America, many inspired by the example of the Cuban Revolution and all sharing a radical ideology, the rhetoric of which was international but the programs of which addressed local concerns and issues.

Venezuela broke relations with Cuba in 1963 when an arms cache that proved to have originated there was found on a deserted beach. The Venezuelans sought OAS sanctions. In spite of threats of major violence, the 1963 elections took place on schedule, and Raúl Leoni, AD's candidate, became president with 32 percent of the vote.

The Leoni presidency (1964–1969) continued the programs established by the Betancourt regime, although Leoni maintained a somewhat lower political profile. His government struggled to construct a working majority and various coalitions failed to endure throughout his rule. The government succeeded in gaining OAS sanctions against Cuba for its sponsorship of revolution in Venezuela. Continued guerrilla activity led to suspensions of constitutional guarantees, but none of the efforts to overthrow the government succeeded. Venezuela became more active in hemispheric affairs with its participation in the Latin American Free Trade Association (LAFTA), and was successful in getting an accord with Great Britain that recognized its position on the Guayana boundary dispute (1965). It participated in the Punta del Este conference on Latin American economic integration in 1967, and agreed in the same year to form a regional Andean Common Market with Colombia, Chile, Ecuador, and Peru.

Indicative of the growing effectiveness of national institutions, in 1968 the supreme court of justice convicted the former dictator Marcos Pérez Jiménez of corruption in office. The Leoni years, less violent than his predecessors but still turbulent, ended with the transfer of power to the opposition Christian Democratic Party (COPEI) with the election of Dr. Rafael Caldera for the 1969–1974 period with 27 percent of the vote.

Caldera, with a weak mandate, had difficulty with his program in the legislature as AD refused to participate in a coalition, creating a stalemate. Caldera lifted the ban on the Communist Party but eliminated the autonomy of the university. OPEC met again in Caracas, and a new income tax law continued increasing the Venezuelan share of oil company profits. Splinter political parties continued to form, including the Movement to Socialism (MAS), which emerged out of the PCV in 1971. Expanding the growing government control of Venezuelan oil, congress passed a Hydrocarbons Reversion Law in 1971 that prepared for government control of existing concessions when their terms expired. The government nationalized the natural gas industry in the same year. In 1973 Venezuela formally joined the Andean Pact, bringing its economy into closer collaboration with others in its region.

Carlos Andrés Pérez, AD's candidate, won the election of 1973 with a 49 percent share, reversing the decline in winning pluralities and representing another peaceful transition of power from one party to another in Venezuela's new democratic tradition. The first Pérez administration (1974–1979) saw a great increase in government intervention in the economy and an increase in economic prosperity, based mostly on the growth of petroleum revenues. Pérez's government nationalized the iron industry in 1974 and the steel and petroleum industries in 1975. This ambitious program of change produced its detractors, and in the 1978 elections Luis Herrera Campíns, the COPEI candidate, won the presidency with 46 percent of the vote, in yet another peaceful change of governing parties.

Herrera Campíns (1979–1984) struggled with economic difficulties as the oil boom and the extravagant expansion of Venezuela based on the revenues derived from petroleum appeared to come to an end. Although COPEI had strong political support at the beginning of this period, the economic decline of Venezuela brought about by the decline in the world price for petroleum and the general

crisis of international debt provided the most serious challenges. Venezuela worked with OPEC to try to freeze the price of petroleum in 1981, but this effort failed and the government found itself with an inflation rate of 8 percent (high for Venezuela) and an unemployment rate of at least 8 percent. The Venezuela oil company became part of a controversy over its management, and the government, in search of new sources of revenue in 1982, launched a program to develop the tar sand belt north of the Orinoco, a long-term project that would require high oil prices to be profitable.

Faced with rumors of an imminent devaluation of the bolívar, Venezuela's reserves declined because of large amounts of capital flight from the country, and the government took control of dollar accounts of state businesses. Inflation in 1982 reached 8.3 percent, and about $5 billion apparently fled the country as a result of speculation against the bolívar. By 1983 about 70 percent of the exterior debt of Venezuela, calculated at about $30 billion, came due, and in February the government introduced a new system of controls on foreign exchange to stop capital flight, froze prices for sixty days, and stopped paying interest on the national debt.

While the economic news during the Herrera Campíns period went from bad to worse, diplomatic and political activity continued apace. Congress declared former president Pérez responsible for the inflated price of a refrigerator ship that exceeded its cost by some $10 million, and this conviction served as a symbol of the widespread corruption and profiteering that characterized the Venezuelan boom of the late 1970s. Venezuela lost one of its most prominent founders of the democratic era when Rómulo Betancourt died in 1981 at the age of seventy-three. On the diplomatic scene, the dispute between Venezuela and Guyana revived when the truce between the two countries ended in 1982. Elsewhere in the hemisphere, Venezuela sided, diplomatically and verbally, with Argentina in the Falklands/Malvinas War with Great Britain.

Clearly, the increased economic uncertainty and Venezuela's unaccustomed inflation and currency instability contributed greatly to the defeat of COPEI and the election of Jaime Lusinchi of AD as president for the 1984–1989 period with a large

A man herding cattle on the plains of the Los Llanos region, Venezuela, late 20th century. Land reform and government subsidies support Venezuela's agricultural sector, once central to the economy. In the twenty-first century, oil and the petrochemical industry dominate. KEVIN SCHAFER/CORBIS

margin of 57 percent and control of congress. The Lusinchi regime continued to cope with economic difficulties derived from the decline in the world price of oil and the general international economic difficulties of world trade. It introduced a variety of austerity measures with the hope that growth would restore the country to its traditional stability and prosperity. However, inflation continued to rise and reached an unprecedented 20 percent in the Lusinchi period. The government made an agreement with its principal international bankers on a refinancing plan and resisted the approach of the International Monetary Fund involving major changes in the country's economic structure.

In search of a prosperous past, Venezuelans turned once again to Carlos Andrés Pérez (1990–1994) to help them resolve the Venezuelan version of the Latin American economic readjustment crisis. In his first incarnation, Pérez had spent freely and nationalized liberally, but with the changing times, his policies changed also. Imposing strong austerity measures, his regime promptly triggered a violent street riot for four days beginning on February 27, 1989, that almost toppled his presidency and left many dead and much property destroyed. Even the fury of the populace could not deter the necessary readjustments demanded by the world market and especially by the continued low price of oil. Pérez continued carefully but systematically to privatize the economy (returning as much of the public sector as possible into private hands), opened up Venezuelan opportunities to foreign investment, and reduced the high subsidies paid for a wide range of consumer goods.

Although this policy produced considerable improvement in economic statistics (inflation at 80 percent in 1989 fell to around 30 percent by 1994 and the country's growth rate in the early

1990s exceeded most other Latin American countries), too many Venezuelans found themselves worse off than a decade earlier, with more than 40 percent of the population living in poverty, perhaps half of these, by some calculations, in extreme poverty. The continued drumbeat of inflation and unemployment, accompanied by rising resentment against suspected profiteering in high places, including the presidency, led Congress to bring corruption charges against the president. In May, Carlos Andrés Pérez stepped down to answer the charges, and Congress appointed the noted historian Ramón J. Velásquez to serve out the rest of the term (1993–1994).

THE POST-PETROLEUM ECONOMY, FROM VELÁSQUEZ TO CALDERA

Velásquez, relieved of at least the controversy over corruption, proceeded with the privatization plans, the economic reforms, and especially with the imposition of a value-added tax to address a growing government deficit. Implemented against great public protest and with much controversy and speculation, the tax continued to dominate political and popular discourse throughout the period of the presidential campaigns. With the economy stagnating at an expected growth rate of only 2 or 3 percent, the country struggling with continued capital flight, and inflation sticking stubbornly to around 30 percent, the December 1993 electoral battle focused on issues of the economy but turned on the personal qualities of the candidates. The old political parties of AD and COPEI, both seriously weakened by internal strife and splintering factions, and in AD's case by the fall from grace of former president Carlos Andrés Pérez, ran weaker campaigns against upstart parties and coalitions.

The winning party, led by disaffected COPEI founder and former president Dr. Rafael Caldera, combined a heterogeneous group of left-of-center, Christian Democrats and conservative or reformist splinter groups into a coalition called the Convergencia. Trading on the magic of Caldera's name, his reputation for personal honesty, and the echoes of the prosperous and dynamic period of his previous presidency, the Convergencia argued for a new approach, different from the Pérez austerity, more just in its distribution of the pain of economic readjustment, and free from the corruption of past regimes. Caldera's coalition won the election with about 30 percent of the vote, with about 40 percent of the electorate abstaining (a new high), ending the

era of two-party government that had prevailed from 1959 to 1994.

The Caldera presidency (1994–1999) served to mark the transition between the era of two-party government and the emergence of a new, populist political regime. At the same time, it marked another shift in the nation's approach to the exploitation of Venezuela's petroleum resources and the distribution of the benefits of oil exports. Although the character of this shift did not appear immediately during the second Caldera presidency, in retrospect the gradual disintegration of the governing elite, the growing disparity between middle and upper class on one side of the income divide and the relatively disenfranchised urban poor on the other, and the fundamental economic difficulties caused by low international oil prices all combined to undermine the remaining authority of the traditional party system and the political, economic, and governing infrastructure that supported it.

Caldera, in search of political peace, pardoned the participants in the previous (1992) coup attempt, allowing some to return to the country from political exile abroad and others to exit the prison system. Reentering political life, these leaders began a populist mobilization effort that soon saw the emergence of former coup leader Lieutenant Colonel Hugo Chávez Frías as spokesman and eventually caudillo leader of the movement. The message of these populist groups, focused on the economic difficulties of the country, the growing poverty and shrinking opportunities for the urban poor, the high levels of visible government corruption especially in the pre-Caldera era, and the general dissatisfaction with ineffective government bureaucracies found a sympathetic audience.

THE ERA OF HUGO CHÁVEZ

In the elections of 1998, Hugo Chávez Frías and his Movement of the Fifth Republic (MVR) party won against a weak and fragmented opposition, inaugurating a new era in Venezuelan political history. The subsequent Chávez regimes have been characterized by multiple challenges, in particular an aggressive opposition movement that provoked exceptionally contentious political mobilizations among supporters and opponents of the government. Each cycle of crisis concluded with some form of electoral contest in which the Chávez coalition of supporters and the opposition parties attempted to use the electoral process to determine which group would control the country. Since 1998 the Chávez parties have continuously revised and reformed the formal rules of government through constitutional change (approving a new constitution in 1999) and legislation, each cycle increasing the control of the government and the president over economic, social, and political structures, enterprises, and policies. Although an attempted coup in 2002 almost succeeded, after a brief interlude Chávez loyalists in the military returned the caudillo to power. By the close of 2006, the Chávez regime had captured all of the legislative seats in the national congress, virtually all of the state and local political positions, and almost all of the significant appointments in the judiciary and other significant government agencies.

The key aspects of this early twenty-first-century transformation of Venezuela included a redistribution of government revenue toward the poor, especially in the main urban centers, through an extensive network of social, educational, health, and nutrition programs, each designed to provide opportunities or subsidies to the less economically self-sufficient sectors of the population. Although much controversy surrounded the effectiveness of these programs, they succeeded in demonstrating the commitment and engagement of the Chávez government with the popular classes and distributed a variety of tangible benefits to a significant proportion of the less privileged sector of the population. At the same time, as has been characteristic of earlier Venezuelan regime changes, the new Chávez government removed much of the top level of middle-class technocrats, bureaucrats, and political appointees and replaced them with Chávez loyalists, thereby creating a new group within the highly prosperous upper-middle class. In addition, the Chávez administration favored those economic enterprises (public or private) that supported the regime and its objectives and punished the less supportive. The Chávez government also focused on control of all significant sectors of the economy through the nationalization of previously privatized enterprises such as the national telephone company (CANTV) and Caracas' privately held electric utility (Electricidad de Caracas). In addition, international companies operating in Venezuela have found regulations and various forms of profit sharing increasingly burdensome. In the case of international petroleum companies, the participation of the Venezuelan government in the ownership and profits of the enterprises grew dramatically.

Opposition actions such as the work stoppages in December 2001, an attempted coup in April 2002, and another work stoppage focused on PDVSA (the state oil monopoly), though effective for short periods, succeeded mostly in damaging the economy and creating an opportunity for the Chávez regime to take control of key economic institutions. A recall referendum in August 2004 designed to remove Chávez from office failed in spite of strong mobilization by anti-Chávez forces, as Chávez achieved a 59 percent endorsement in the voting. However, the controversy over voting irregularities and possible reprisals against those signing the petition in favor of a referendum further divided the population between pro- and anti-Chávez forces. In the elections of December 2006, Chávez won about 60 percent of the vote over a strong candidate with consolidated support from the main opposition parties. As each of the cycles of challenge and response to the Chávez regime has played out, the victorious Chávez forces have followed their victories with continued expansion of controls over most aspects of Venezuelan political and economic life, including the media, labor, education, universities, agriculture, and both domestic and international business enterprise. At the end of January 2007, the Chávez-controlled legislature authorized the president to rule by decree for eighteen months. The Chávez regime soon took control of the political process, the courts, most of the media, the central bank, foreign trade and commerce, and the national oil company. Many observers commented on the authoritarian style of governance; nonetheless, the Chávez regime preserved all the forms, if little of the substance, of democratic government.

The transformations in Venezuela initiated by the Chávez regimes in the early twenty-first century built on two primary elements: The first resulted from the country's extreme dissatisfaction with the exceptionally weak administrations in the latter years of the twentieth century, as the coalition of political parties and economic interests that had sustained the democratic system established in 1958 fragmented. The second relied on the rapid rise in oil prices during the first years of the twenty-first century, which created windfall revenue to support the wide-ranging program of nationalizations, subsidy programs for the poor, reorganization of government agencies, extensive public works, and an aggressive nationalist foreign policy built primarily around anti-Americanism and hostility to the free-trade globalization agenda promoted by the United States. The ambitious international policies pursued by the Venezuela government during these years often involved substantial investments in subsidized oil sales to ideologically aligned partners in Latin American and Cuba, as well as an aggressive anti-American campaign to realign Venezuela with countries in the Middle East hostile to the United States, U.S. trading rivals such as the Soviet Union and China, and Latin American coalitions opposed to U.S. free trade initiatives. These efforts, though garnering some sympathy from those nations benefiting from Venezuelan oil subsidies and other commercial transactions, did not create the international leadership position the Chávez regime sought. Although the Chávez revolution appeared well established by early 2007, its long-term success remained in question as the dramatic program initiatives and major reorganization of the economy remained somewhat ad hoc, relying on the continued availability of large surplus revenue from historically high international petroleum prices. This remarkable inflow of revenue gave Venezuela strong financial reserves, but at the same time created a rapid consumer boom, significant and persistent inflation, a need for price and currency controls, a decline in international investment, and concerns about the sustainability of the many initiatives and programs launched by the Chávez regimes.

See also **Andueza Palacio, Raimundo; Betancourt, Rómulo; Bolívar, Simón; Boves, José Tomás; Cabildo, Cabildo Abierto; Caldera Rodríguez, Rafael; Caudillismo, Caudillo; Chávez, Hugo; Crespo, Joaquín; Delgado Chalbaud, Carlos; Federal War (Venezuela 1859-1863); Ferdinand VII of Spain; Gallegos, Rómulo; Gil Fortoul, José; Gómez, Juan Vicente; Gran Colombia; Guyana; Guzmán Blanco, Antonio Leocadio; Herrera Campins, Luis; Larrazábal Ugueto, Wolfgang; Latin American Free Trade Association (LAFTA); Leoni, Raúl; Liberalism; Llanos (Venezuela); López Contreras, Eleázar; Lusinchi, Jaime; Medina Angarita, Isaías; Miranda, Francisco de; Monagas, José Gregorio; Monagas, José Tadeo; Páez, José Antonio; Pérez, Carlos Andrés; Pérez Jiménez, Marcos; Soublette, Carlos; Spain; Universidad Central de Venezuela; Vargas, José María.**

BIBLIOGRAPHY

Alexander, Robert J. *Rómulo Betancourt and the Transformation of Venezuela.* New Brunswick, NJ: Transaction Books, 1982.

Allen, Robert Loring. *Venezuelan Economic Development: A Politico-Economic Analysis.* Greenwich, CT: Jai Press, 1977.

Baloyra, Enrique A., and John D. Martz. *Political Attitudes in Venezuela: Societal Cleavages and Political Opinion.* Austin: University of Texas Press, 1979.

Burggraaff, Winfield J. *The Venezuelan Armed Forces in Politics, 1935–1959.* Columbia: University of Missouri Press, 1972.

Ellner, Steve. *Organized Labor in Venezuela, 1958–1991.* Wilmington, DE: SR Books, 1993.

Ellner, Steve, and Daniel Hellinger, eds. *Venezuelan Politics in the Chávez Era: Class, Polarization and Conflict.* Boulder, CO: L. Rienner, 2003.

Ellner, Steve, and Miguel Tinker Salas, eds. *Venezuela: Hugo Chávez and the Decline of an "Exceptional Democracy."* Lanham, MD: Rowman and Littlefield, 2007.

Ewell, Judith. *Venezuela: A Century of Change.* Stanford, CA: Stanford University Press, 1984.

Ferry, Robert J. *The Colonial Elite of Early Caracas: Formation and Crisis, 1567–1767.* Berkeley: University of California Press, 1989.

Gilmore, Robert L. *Caudillism and Militarism in Venezuela, 1810–1910.* Athens: Ohio University Press, 1964.

Herman, Donald L. *Christian Democracy in Venezuela.* Chapel Hill: University of North Carolina Press, 1980.

Levine, Daniel H. *Conflict and Political Change in Venezuela.* Princeton, NJ: Princeton University Press, 1973.

Lombardi, John V. *Venezuela: The Search for Order, the Dream of Progress.* New York: Oxford University Press, 1982.

Lombardi, John V., et al. *Venezuelan History: A Comprehensive Working Bibliography.* Boston: G. K. Hall, 1977.

Martínez, Aníbal R. *Venezuelan Oil: Development and Chronology.* New York: Elsevier, 1989

Martz, John D., and David J. Myers, eds. *Venezuela: The Democratic Experience,* revised edition. New York: Praeger, 1986.

McCoy, Jennifer, and David J. Myers, eds. *The Unraveling of Representative Democracy in Venezuela.* Baltimore, MD: Johns Hopkins University Press, 2004.

Mijares, Augusto. *The Liberator,* trans. John Fisher. Caracas: North American Association of Venezuela, 1983.

Powell, John Duncan. *The Political Mobilization of the Venezuelan Peasant.* Cambridge, MA: Harvard University Press, 1971.

Randall, Laura. *The Political Economy of Venezuelan Oil*. New York: Praeger, 1987.

Tugwell, Franklin. *The Politics of Oil in Venezuela*. Stanford, CA: Stanford University Press, 1975.

Vila, Manuel Pérez, ed. *Diccionario de historia de Venezuela*. Caracas: Fundacíon Polar, 1988. CD-ROM format, Caracas: Fundacíon Polar, 2000.

JOHN V. LOMBARDI

VENEZUELA, ARMED FORCES OF NATIONAL LIBERATION (FALN).

The FALN was a pro-Cuban Marxist-Leninist guerrilla army that began operations in Venezuela in 1962. Its membership included groups opposed to the government of President Rómulo Betancourt: dissident military officers, radical members of the Venezuelan Communist Party, and leaders of the Movement of the Revolutionary Left (Movimiento de Izquierda Revolucionaria—MIR), a breakaway splinter faction of Betancourt's ruling Democratic Action Party (Acción Democrática—AD).

Following his election in 1958, Betancourt faced bitter opposition from several factions. By 1960, some leftists had organized the MIR. Two years later, radicals from the Communist Party, such as Douglas Bravo and Teodoro Petkoff, set up the FALN to undertake a Cuban-inspired struggle against the legitimate Venezuelan government. At that time, the leaders of the newly founded FALN advocated a long, campesino war against the government rather than a coup. They were joined in 1962 by Américo Martín and by the reactionary Lieutenant Colonel Juan de Díos Moncada Vidal, who became one of the FALN's guerrilla commanders.

During 1962, the FALN launched an urban and rural guerrilla war. The following year, it tried to disrupt the elections to force a military coup. But it did not succeed, and some 90 percent of the electorate went to the polls.

On assuming office in 1964, Raúl Leoni declared a state of emergency. He invoked censorship, closed schools, arrested demonstrators, lifted congressional immunity, and suspended the writ of habeas corpus. He rounded up leaders of the Communist Party, including members of the National Congress, and isolated the FALN from its urban supporters. A strong military campaign further reduced guerrilla forces. Leoni also used the police to eliminate FALN sympathizers.

Forced to the countryside, the FALN fought in isolated districts. It never mounted a popular war there, however; as one woman later wrote of her life as a guerrilla, "nothing has occurred here." Without popular support the FALN faltered. Even continued assistance and encouragement from Cuba could not keep the FALN struggle alive.

During its existence, the FALN attracted women to its ranks. One, Arelia Laya, served as a commander in Lara. Students also joined the FALN as "weekend warriors," but their sporadic involvement proved ineffectual and their participation steadily declined.

By 1967, the Communist Party withdrew its support of the FALN. In 1968, newly elected President Rafael Caldera offered amnesty to any guerrilla who voluntarily surrendered. Most of the FALN leaders accepted this offer and, like Martín and Petkoff, turned their attention to legitimate political movements. Bravo and some MIR factions continued the struggle for a few more years.

See also **Guerrilla Movements.**

BIBLIOGRAPHY

Richard Gott, *Guerrilla Movements in Latin America* (1971).

Angela Zago, *Aquí no ha pasado nada* (1972).

David Blank, *Politics in Venezuela* (1973).

Teodoro Petkoff, *Razón pasión del socialismo: El tema socialista en Venezuela* (1973).

Raymond Estep, *Guerrilla Warfare in Latin America, 1963–1975* (1975).

Alfredo Peña, *Conversaciones con Américo Martín* (1978) and *Conversaciones con Douglas Bravo* (1978).

Judith Ewell, *Venezuela: A Century of Change* (1984).

Additional Bibliography

Art, Robert J. and Louise Richardson. *Democracy and Counterterrorism: Lessons from the Past*. Washington, DC: United States Institute of Peace Press, 2007.

Corro, Alejandro del, ed. *Venezuela: La violencia*. Cuernavaca, Mexico: Centro Intercultural de Documentación, 1968.

Tarver Denova, Hollis Micheal, and Julia C. Frederick. *The History of Venezuela*. Westport, CT: Greenwood Press, 2005.

WINTHROP R. WRIGHT

VENEZUELA, CONGRESSES OF 1811, 1830, AND 1864.

The congresses in which the principal political transformations of nineteenth-century Venezuela occurred. Venezuela's first Constituent Congress, convened in 1811, declared independence on 5 July and went on to ratify the first constitution of a Latin American republic. The Congress was comprised of representatives from the seven provinces that adhered to the 19 April 1810 pronouncement of the *cabildo* of Caracas, which marked the beginning of Venezuela's independence movement. These representatives set up the chief governing authority of the republic. They elected men to the executive and judiciary; they also normalized and organized all the judicial, political, fiscal, and economic operating mechanisms of the newly established republic. The Congress was the scene of the most important debates of the era. Because of the devastating March 1812 earthquake, and the social crisis it provoked, the Congress approved the concession of extraordinary powers to the executive and effectively suspended its own activities. The fall of the republic and the flare-up of war prevented any further sessions from taking place.

The Constituent Congress of Venezuela convened in Valencia from 6 May to 14 October 1830 to sanction the dissolution of Gran Colombia and the establishment of Venezuela as an independent republic. Its members ratified a constitution organizing the republic under a central-federal system that lasted twenty-seven years. Under the electoral system they established, eligibility for office was limited and the right to vote was based on economic factors such as landownership and income level. Elections were held on 25 March 1831, and José Antonio Páez was proclaimed president. The new republic's chief executive began to fix the bases of the nation along liberal lines.

After the Federal War (1859–1863), a Constituent Congress met from December 1863 to April 1864. It ratified the 1864 Constitution, which established a federal system that it technically maintained into the 1990s. The Congress of 1864 also approved an electoral system of universal male suffrage, administrative decentralization, and provincial autonomy. The name "Republic of Venezuela" was replaced by the name "United States of Venezuela."

See also **Venezuela, Constitutions.**

BIBLIOGRAPHY

Pablo Ruggeri Parra, *Historia política y constitucional de Venezuela*, 2 vols. (1949).

José Gil Fortoul, *Historia constitucional de Venezuela*, 4th ed., 3 vols. (1953–1954).

Congreso Constituyente 1930, Venezuela, *Actas del Congreso Constituyente de 1830*, 3 vols. (1979–1982).

Manuel Pérez Vila, ed., *Actas de los congresos del ciclo Bolivariano: Congreso Constituyente de 1811–1812*, 2 vols. (1983).

Additional Bibliography

Zahler, Reuben. "Honor, Corruption, and Legitimacy: Liberal Projects in the Early Venezualan Republic, 1821–50." Ph.D. diss., University of Chicago, 2005.

INÉS QUINTERO

VENEZUELA, CONSTITUTIONS.

Venezuela has had twenty-seven constitutions since 1811, the most recent of which was promulgated in 1999. Why this apparent surfeit of constitutions for a country that was dominated by *caudillos* and military elites throughout much of its independent history? Owing to chronic instability, virtually every new regime sought to declare its independence from predecessor regimes by writing a new constitution. In the Spanish American tradition, instead of adding amendments or changing specific provisions, an entirely new constitution was enacted, even if very little of substance was actually changed. In the nineteenth century two of the main changes dealt with the balance between centralism and federalism, and expansion or retraction of the suffrage. One feature of Venezuela's constitutional history has remained constant, however: Venezuelan government is essentially presidentialist. Even the most recent and most democratic constitution—that of 1999—provides for a powerful chief executive who can assume extraordinary powers.

The first constitution of the new Republic of Gran Colombia, written in 1811, was inspired by the U.S. Constitution and the French Declaration of the Rights of Man and clearly reflects the thinking of an educated oligarchy. It provided for a weak central government and placed literacy requirements on suffrage and property-holding requirements on officeholding. The Angostura Constitution of 1819, reacting against excessive federalism, strengthened the power of the executive and central authority. In 1830, after breaking away from Gran Colombia, Venezuela promulgated its own constitution, which reflected a compromise between unitary and federalist government. Between 1830 and 1900 eight constitutions were written, effecting slight changes in the balance of power between the federal government and the states.

Venezuela's symbolic reverence for federalism is seen most strikingly in the 1864 Constitution, which expressed an extreme form of regionalism and localism. This exaggerated federalism was counteracted in 1881, when a constitution enacted by the dictator Antonio Guzmán Blanco (1829–1899) reduced the number of states from twenty to nine in order to shrink the number of powerful state *caudillos* who aspired to national power. It also replaced direct suffrage with indirect suffrage. In 1909 the twenty states were restored, and they exist to this day.

Under the dictatorship of General Juan Vicente Gómez (1908–1935) seven constitutions were written, and like so many previous constitutions, they were honored more in the breach than in the observance. One interesting aspect of Gómez's later constitutions—after oil was discovered—was a move from economic liberalism toward the limitation of the right to private property in order to conserve natural resources.

The overthrow of General Gómez led to a politically more liberal regime, which was reflected in the Constitution of 1936. It shortened the presidential term from seven to five years, guaranteed certain individual rights, and made cabinet ministers responsible to Congress. However, it left intact the indirect election of the president and outlawed communism. The 1947 Constitution, which was in effect only briefly, was drafted by a constituent assembly controlled by the social democratic Democratic Action (Acción Democrática). The most politically and socially liberal constitution in Venezuela's history up to that time, it provided for the direct and secret vote in presidential and congressional elections, and explicitly guaranteed the rights of workers and peasants.

After ten years of military dictatorship (1948–1958) the architects of the new democratic system framed a constitution that called for a strong central government but expressed due concern for individual liberties and social justice. The Constitution of 1961, promulgated during the presidential term of Rómulo Betancourt (1945–1948), was designed not only to ensure popular democratic government but also to create a modern welfare state that would seek a more equitable distribution of the national wealth. These principles are reflected in lengthy sections that enumerate a host of political, economic, and social rights. The Constitution of 1961 provides for twenty states, two federal territories, and a federal district. All governors are appointed by the president, an indication that a country that still pays lip service to federalism is in reality a centralist republic. Although it specifies three independent and equal branches of government, numerous provisions underscore the powerful role of the president and the executive branch. They authorize the president to declare a state of emergency and to suspend or curtail certain constitutional guarantees in the wake of internal disorder or external conflict. The president, however, cannot succeed himself, and cannot run as a candidate for ten years after he leaves office. The document provides for a bicameral Congress and a Supreme Court whose justices are elected by Congress for nine-year terms.

In practice, the 1961 Constitution—the longest-lived of any Venezuelan constitution—generally worked well for many years. But the deterioration in the functioning of the post-1958 democratic system during the 1980s and early 1990s led to calls for constitutional reform. Indeed, the two-party system broke down in 1998 when the population elected President Hugo Chávez (b. 1954), a socialist former colonel. Advocating a more equal society, Chávez proposed many sweeping constitutional changes. In 1999 Chavez's reworking of the constitution was approved by a popular referendum. Many of the changes strengthened the executive branch by allowing the president to run for two terms. Furthermore, the new constitution changed the bicameral legislature to a unicameral body. In 2007 Chávez tried to pass more constitutional reforms that would have ended presidential term limitations and given the chief executive greater authority to declare emergency rule. Even though Chávez has remained popular, the electorate narrowly voted down these changes in a popular referendum in December.

However, Chávez has suggested that he will continue to pursue these constitutional changes.

See also **Venezuela.**

BIBLIOGRAPHY

American University, Foreign Areas Study Division. *Area Handbook of Venezuela.* Washington, DC: Author, 1964.

Ellner, Steve, and Miguel Tinker Salas, eds. *Venezuela Hugo Chávez and the Decline of an "Exceptional Democracy".* Lanham, MD: Rowman and Littlefield, 2007.

Fitzgerald, Gerald E., ed., *The Constitutions of Latin America.* Chicago: Henry Regnery, 1968.

Fitzgibbon, Russell H., ed. *The Constitutions of the Americas.* Chicago: University of Chicago Press, 1948.

Fortoul, José Gil. *Historia constitucional de Venezuela,* 3 vols. 5th ed. Caracas: Ministerio de Educación, 1967.

Kelley, R. Lynn. "Venezuelan Constitutional Forms and Realities." In *Venezuela: The Democratic Experience,* edited by John D. Martz and David J. Myers. New York: Praeger, 1977.

Sánchez García, Antonio. *Dictadura o democracia Venezuela en la encrucijada.* Caracas: Editorial Altazor, 2003.

WINFIELD J. BURGGRAAFF

VENEZUELA, IMMIGRATION. Upon establishing an independent nation in 1830, Venezuelans instituted a policy of populating their nation with European immigrants. Immigration laws of 1831, 1837, and 1840 authorized the national government to subsidize the relocation of European agricultural workers to Venezuela. But despite efforts to recruit immigrants throughout Europe, few came. Between 1832 and 1845, only 12,610 persons immigrated to Venezuela. The majority of these came from the Canary Islands, a traditional source of Venezuelan immigrants.

During the second half of the nineteenth century, Venezuelan governments continued to try, without success, to attract white European immigrants. In part, they desired laborers for the rural areas, but increasingly they sought immigrants to "whiten" the multiracial populace. The desire to whiten the population not only led to an increased demand for European immigrants but also contributed to legislation that excluded nonwhites from immigrating to Venezuela. In 1855, the National Congress defeated a proposal to pay contractors to bring Chinese workers to Venezuela. On 20 July 1891, a new immigration code prohibited the immigration of blacks and Asians.

The new code failed to achieve its desired results for two reasons. First, whites did not flock to Venezuela. Second, blacks from the Antilles did come, either illegally or by obtaining temporary work permits. By 1898, some 5,000 to 7,000 blacks had entered the Guayana and Orinoco regions from nearby Trinidad and British Guiana. East Indians fled to eastern Venezuela to escape from indentured servitude in nearby Trinidad.

During the administration of Juan Vicente Gómez (1908–1935), attempts to encourage massive immigration from Europe met with little success. Corruption and poor economic conditions in Venezuela before the petroleum boom meant that the opportunities for social mobility found in other countries, such as the United States, Argentina, and Brazil, did not exist. Gómez further complicated matters by his distrust of foreigners, especially non-Catholic, non–Spanish–speaking individuals, whose culture and intentions he did not understand. His xenophobia, and that of his followers, offset any immigration his administration sponsored.

On 15 September 1938, a presidential decree established the Technical Institute of Immigration and Colonization as a department of the Ministry of Agriculture and Livestock. Its primary objectives included implementation of a rural development program, the settlement of immigrants in rural districts, and the "ethnic improvement of the country's population."

A large influx of immigrants began only after World War II. Between 1941 and 1961, immigration increased markedly; the foreign-born population grew from 49,928 to 526,188. Since the 1940s, Colombians accounted for the largest percentage of foreign population, although between 1950 and 1961 Spaniards and Italians made up the largest portion of immigrants. The latter two groups moved mostly to urban centers, where they had considerable success as merchants, contractors, and business leaders.

In 1966 the restrictions on nonwhite immigration ended, but by that time whites dominated the economy. As in other parts of Latin America, Spanish and Italian immigrants and their descendants controlled important sectors of the economy, especially the construction industries, export–import enterprises, and small businesses.

European immigration has slowed since the 1960s. However, population movements from Chile, Peru, and Ecuador, as well as from Santo Domingo and Colombia, have increased.

See also **Gómez, Juan Vicente; Race and Ethnicity.**

BIBLIOGRAPHY

Elizabeth Yabour De Caldera, *La población de Venezuela: Un análisis demográfico* (1967).

Chen-Yi Chen and Michel Picouet, *Dinámica de la población: Caso de Venezuela* (1979).

Susan Berglund–Thompson, "The 'Musiues' in Venezuela: Immigration Goals and Reality, 1936–1961" (Ph.D. diss., University of Massachusetts, 1980).

Ermila Troconis De Veracoechea, *El proceso de la inmigración en Venezuela* (1986).

Juan Almecija B., "El crecimiento demográfico venezolano, 1936–1971," in *Boletín de la Academia Nacional de la Historia* 71, no. 281 (1988): 131–148.

Add.Bibliography

Pellegrino, Adela. *Historia de la inmigración en Venezuela siglos XIX y XX*. Caracas: Academia Nacional de Ciencias Económicas, 1989.

Sequera Tamayo, Isbelia, and Rafael J Crazut. *La inmigración en Venezuela*. Caracas: Academia Nacional de Ciencias Económicas, 1992.

WINTHROP R. WRIGHT

VENEZUELA, LAS REFORMAS REVOLUTION.

Venezuela: Las Reformas Revolution, a Venezuelan militarist movement in 1835 against the government of Dr. José María Vargas (1835–1836). The consensus attained with the creation of the republic in 1830 began to disintegrate as a result of political tensions dividing the ruling elite. With the privileges they had won during the years of the War for Independence progressively waning, the members of the military viewed the candidacy of Santiago Mariño in the elections of 1834 with the hope of regaining their power. Mariño's defeat at the polls and the victory of Vargas caused further political disintegration, which resulted in the armed uprising

of an important group of military men. All active members of the Liberating Army, these included Santiago Mariño, Pedro Briceño Méndez, Diego Ibarra, and Pedro Carujo, among many others.

The revolution broke out in Maracaibo and Caracas in June and July 1835. The revolutionaries drove Vargas from power in July and proposed the return to military rule, the establishment of a federal system, the installation of Catholicism as the state religion, and the taking over of public offices by men who had made independence possible. However, the movement was suffocated militarily by José Antonio Páez, and its instigators were expelled from the country. Vargas returned as president in August 1835.

See also **Vargas, José María.**

BIBLIOGRAPHY

Caracciolo Parra-Pérez, *Mariño y las guerras civiles*, 3 vols. (1958–1960).

Robert L. Gilmore, *Caudillism and Militarism in Venezuela, 1810–1910* (1964).

Catalina Banko, *Poder político y conflictos sociales en la República Oligárquica, 1830–1848* (1986).

Manuel Pérez Vila, *La Revolución de las Reformas* (1984).

Additional Bibliography

Briceño Vasquez, Carlos. *La miopía del "Tiempo de caudillos."* Caracas: s.n., 1994.

Castellanos, Rafaél Ramón, and José Ignacio Lares. *Caudillismo y nacionalismo: De Guzmán Blanco a Gómez: Vida y acción de José Ignacio Lares*. Caracas: s.n., 1994.

Vetencourt, Roberto. *Tiempo de caudillos*. Caracas: s.n., 2004.

INÉS QUINTERO

VENEZUELA, ORGANIZATIONS

This entry includes the following articles:
ECONOMIC SOCIETY OF THE FRIENDS OF THE COUNTRY
FEDERATION OF STUDENTS OF VENEZUELA (FEV)
PATRIOTIC SOCIETY OF CARACAS

ECONOMIC SOCIETY OF THE FRIENDS OF THE COUNTRY

The Economic Society of the Friends of the Country was an institution to promote the economic and educational progress of Venezuelan society. The society was inspired by similar organizations that arose in Europe in the middle of the eighteenth century. It was created by the Organic Law of Public Education of 18 March 1826 and was finally organized in 1829. It consisted of a representative group of notables from diverse professions and of various political orientations. Their object was to diagnose Venezuelan society and take steps that would promote progress in the recently formed republic.

The society's primary areas of concern were agriculture, commerce, the arts and crafts, and public instruction. It created a commission to examine each of these areas. The society put out documents expressing views about the organization of the state, judicial codes, and economic liberalism. It designed various studies gauging the problems and deficiencies in Venezuela and often laid out the solutions that its members felt should be implemented. The society engaged in intensive activities from its beginnings in 1829, and many of them are recorded in the periodical published by the institution itself, *Memorias de la Sociedad Económica de Amigos del País*. From the outbreak of Las Reformas Revolution in 1835, it was in a partially dismantled state until its final extinction in 1847.

BIBLIOGRAPHY

Ramón Hernández Ron, *La Sociedad Económica de Amigos del País* (1943).

Sociedad Económica De Amigos Del País, Caracas, *Memorias y estudios, 1829–1839,* 2 vols. (1958).

Additional Bibliography

Parra Pérez, Caracciolo, Cristóbal L Mendoza and Rafael Angel Rivas Dugarte. *Historia de la primera República de Venezuela*. Caracas: Biblioteca Ayacucho, 1992.

INÉS QUINTERO

FEDERATION OF STUDENTS OF VENEZUELA (FEV)

The Federation of Students of Venezuela (Federacíon de Estudiantes, or FEV) was a Venezuelan student organization opposed to the government of Juan Vicente Gómez (1908–1929, 1931–1935). The General Association of Students was established in 1909, and on various occasions it participated in protests against the government. As a result the university was closed several times and the unity among its academicians destroyed. When the university reopened in 1925, the General Association of Students was reborn with the new name Federation of Students of Venezuela.

In 1928, FEV sponsored the week of the student, a festival that turned into an antigovernment demonstration. As a result FEV organizers were imprisoned or exiled but their actions had gained great popularity and became Venezuela's first urban mass movement. Exiled FEV leaders formed several political parties, two of which had lasting significance—the Partido Revolucionario Venezolano (PRV) and the Agrupación Revolucionaria de Izquierda (ARDI). The FEV was dissolved until 1935, but with the death of Gómez in that year, it reappeared as one of the organizations leading the protests of 1936.

See also **Universities: The Modern Era.**

BIBLIOGRAPHY

E. López Contreras, *Proceso político social, 1928–1936* (1955).

María De Lourdes Acedo De Sucre and Carmen Margarita Nones Mendoza, *La generación venezolana de 1928* (1967).

Joaquín Gabaldón Márquez, *Memoria y cuento de la generación del vientiocho* (1978).

Arturo Sosa and Eloi Legrand, *Del garibaldismo estudiantil a la izquierda criolla: Los orígenes marxistas del proyecto de A.D. (1928–1935)* (1981).

Additional Bibliography

Caballero, Manuel. *Las crisis de la Venezuela contemporánea 1903–1992*. Caracas, Venezuela: Monte Avila Editores Latinoamericana, 1998.

INÉS QUINTERO

PATRIOTIC SOCIETY OF CARACAS

The Patriotic Society of Caracas was a Venezuelan pro–independence organization. After the *cabildo* of Caracas ousted the Spanish governor on 19 April 1810 and later formed the Junta Conservadora de los Derechos de Fernando VII, the Patriotic Society was formed in Caracas the following August with the purpose of propagandizing on behalf of the emancipation process. The society was inspired by similar clubs in revolutionary France. Francisco de Miranda and Simón Bolívar took the lead in organizing and promoting it. Antonio Muñoz Tebar, Vicente Salias, Francisco Espejo, Miguel Peña, and others also participated. Its fundamental objective was to achieve independence and the establishment of a democratic republic in Venezuela. Its voice was the periodical *El Patriota Venezolano.*

The society attained a high degree of popularity in the first half of 1811 due to the radical positions its members expressed in favor of declaring independence once and for all in Venezuela. Branches were formed in Valencia, Puerto Cabello, Barcelona, and Barinas. With the fall of the First Republic in 1812, the society dissolved and was never re–formed.

See also **Bolívar, Simón; Miranda, Francisco de; Venezuela: The Colonial Era.**

BIBLIOGRAPHY

Andrés F. Ponte, *La Revolución de Caracas y sus próceres* (1960).

P. Michael Mc Kinley, *Pre-Revolutionary Caracas: Politics, Economy, and Society, 1777–1811* (1985).

Additional Bibliography

Armas Chitty, José Antonio de. *La independencia de Venezuela.* Madrid, Spain: Editorial MAPFRE, 1992.

Racine, Karen. *Francisco de Miranda, A Transatlantic Life in the Age of Revolution.* Wilmington, DE: Scholarly Resources, 2003.

INÉS QUINTERO

VENEZUELA, POLITICAL PARTIES

This entry includes the following articles:
COMMUNIST PARTY
CONSERVATIVE PARTY
COORDINADORA DEMOCRÁTICA
DEMOCRATIC ACTION (AD)
LIBERAL PARTY
MOVEMENT FOR THE FIFTH REPUBLIC
MOVEMENT TO SOCIALISM (MAS)
NATIONAL CONVERGENCE
SOCIAL CHRISTIAN COPEI PARTY

COMMUNIST PARTY

Communist ideas began to be heard in Venezuela during the administration of Juan Vicente Gómez. In 1926 a group from the opposition, including Gustavo Machado and Salvador de la Plaza, organized in Mexico the Communist-oriented Venezuelan Revolutionary Party. Later, revolutionary ideas gained popularity among those sent to prison as a result of the antigovernment student activity of 1928. It was not until 1 May 1931, however, that the first manifesto of the Communist Party was circulated, and that year is believed to be the year the Venezuelan section of the Communist International was founded. Despite disagreements and internal factionalism, it survived as an illegal party until 1941, when the government of Isaías Medina Angarita legalized it. After the revolution of 18 October 1945, the party participated in Venezuelan elections, winning 3.6 percent of the vote for a constituent assembly in 1946. It was outlawed again by the military government of Marcos Pérez Jiménez in 1950 but was legalized once again in 1958, when democracy was reinstated.

Inspired by the guerrilla movements developing in Latin America during the 1960s, the party promoted armed struggle against the government of Rómulo Betancourt. With the guerrillas defeated, the party resumed legal operations and went through various splits, the most important of these involving the rise of the Movement to Socialism in 1973. Twenty years later it remained a small minority party, winning about 1 percent of the vote. Its program supported the installation of a socialist system based on the principles of Marxism and the class struggle. Since 1998, the party has backed the government of populist Hugo Chávez, a former colonel who has attracted international attention for his anti-American rhetoric and his praise for Cuba's communist leader Fidel Castro.

See also **Communism.**

BIBLIOGRAPHY

Juan Bautista Fuenmayor, *1928–1948: Veinte años de política* (1968).

Robert J. Alexander, *The Communist Party of Venezuela* (1969).

Fernando Key Sánchez, *Fundación de Partido Comunista de Venezuela*, 2nd ed. (1984).

Manuel Caballero, *Entre Gómez y Stalin: La sección venezolana de la Internacional Comunista*, 2nd ed. (1989).

Additional Bibliography

Ellner, Steve, and Daniel Hellinger, eds. *Venezuelan Politics in the Chávez Era: Class, Polarization, and Conflict.* Boulder, CO: L. Rienner, 2003.

Pla, Alberto J. *La Internacional comunista y América Latina: Sindicatos y política en Venezuela (1924–1950).*

Rosario, Argentina: Ediciones Homo Sapiens, Centro Estudios de Historia Obrera, UNR, 1996.

INÉS QUINTERO

CONSERVATIVE PARTY

The Conservative Party was founded in the 1840s as the pro-government party during the administration of José Antonio Páez. With the establishment of the republic in 1830, the elite forged a consensus concerning the political system to be adopted for Venezuela. Nevertheless, during the next five years disagreements arose, resulting in a split into two opposing political factions competing for power.

The group in power and centered around Páez came to be called the Conservative Party by the rival faction, the Liberals, and this is the name that has been used in Venezuelan historiography. Its composition was diverse, consisting of businessmen, landowners, and intellectuals, but the party's economic policies tended primarily to favor the business sector. The Conservatives remained dominant until 1847, when they were displaced as a result of the political turnabout undertaken by President José Tadeo Monagas. They took part in his overthrow in 1858 and confronted the Liberals during the Federal War (1859–1863). The Conservatives subsequently lost political influence, however, and the period of Liberal dominance began. The Conservative Party never returned to office.

See also **Páez, José Antonio.**

BIBLIOGRAPHY

Robert L. Gilmore, *Caudillism and Militarism in Venezuela, 1810–1910* (1964).

Catalina Banko, *Poder político y conflictos sociales en la República Oligárquica, 1830–1848* (1986).

Elías Pino Iturrieta, *El pensamiento conservador venezolano del siglo XIX: Antología* (1992).

Additional Bibliography

Pino Iturrieta, Elías. *Ideas y mentalidades de Venezuela.* Caracas: Academia Nacional de la Historia, 1998.

INÉS QUINTERO

COORDINADORA DEMOCRÁTICA

The Coordinadora Democrática (CD) was a coalition of political parties and civil organizations created to oppose the government of President Hugo Chávez. It was founded in 2002, and among its constituents were most of the political parties that had held power in Venezuela during the Punto Fijo era. Some of the major parties represented in the CD were Acción Democrática (AD), Comité de Organización Política Electoral Independiente (CO-PEI), La Causa R, Movimiento al Socialismo (MAS), Primero Justicia, and Convergencia. This coalition did not have a consolidated political identity, since some of the parties were rightist (e.g., Convergencia) and some came from the left tradition (e.g., MAS).

The CD was directly involved in several direct actions to diminish the legitimacy of and popular support for the Chávez government. The first action was a national strike that began on 2 December 2002, and lasted two months, seriously affecting both the economy and the oil industry. The second action took place in 2004 when the CD lead a revocatory referendum against President Chávez, using the constitutional rules created in 1999. Shortly after the president was confirmed in the referendum with 59 percent of the vote, the CD was dissolved.

See also **Chávez, Hugo; Venezuela, Constitutions.**

BIBLIOGRAPHY

"Acuerdo entre la representación del gobierno de la República Bolivariana de Venezuela y los factores políticos y sociales que lo apoyan y la Coordinadora Democrática y las organizaciones políticas de la sociedad civil que la conforman." Caracas, May 23, 2003. Available from http://www.embavenez-us.org/news.spanish/acuerdo_23mayo2003.htm.

Arriagada Herrera, Genaro. "Zavalita ¿Cuándo se Jodió Venezuela? ¿Antes de Chávez? ¿Con Chávez? (II)." AsuntoPublicos.org, Informe No. 426. Oct. 25, 2004. Available from http://www.asuntospublicos. org/detalle.php?id=2054.

Consejo Nacional Electoral, Venezuela. Available from http://www.cne.gov.ve/.

Hawkins, Kirk. "Populism in Venezuela: The Rise of Chavismo." *Third World Quarterly* 24, no. 6 (2003): 1137–1160.

PATRICIO ENRIQUE ZAMORANO

DEMOCRATIC ACTION (AD)

Democratic Action is one of Venezuela's two major political parties and an important force in building and strengthening the modern democratic system. Its origins date back to the so-called Generation of

'28, when a group of university students organized massive protests against the long-standing dictatorship of Juan Vicente Gómez. Driven into exile, these young activists returned in 1936 following Gómez's death and founded the Venezuelan Organization (ORVE). They continued the struggle for democratic pluralism and on 13 September 1941 officially established AD. The new party gradually built grassroots support while fighting for direct elections.

Faced with official barriers to competitive elections, AD, together with junior military officers, launched a successful uprising on 18 October 1945. During the next three years AD introduced far-reaching reforms, first under the provisional presidency of Rómulo Betancourt and then under the elected administration of Rómulo Gallegos, an eminent writer and educator. Gallegos was toppled by the military in late 1948. For the next decade AD was harassed and persecuted by the dictatorship of Marcos Pérez Jiménez. In 1958, following an uprising that ousted the dictatorship, AD collaborated with rival parties to create the democracy that has endured ever since.

Rómulo Betancourt was elected to a five-year term and survived despite assassination attempts from the Right and the guerrilla insurgency of Castroites. He was succeeded in 1964 by his fellow *adeco* (member of Acción Democrática) Raúl Leoni. Five years later AD lost the presidency to Rafael Caldera of the Social Christian COPEI Party as a result of a debilitating party division. In 1974, AD recaptured power with the victory of Carlos Andrés Pérez, a onetime protégé of Betancourt. The party lost to COPEI in 1979, regained the presidency with Jaime Lusinchi in 1984, and retained it in 1989 in the person of Pérez. He was the first modern president to win a second term after the constitutionally mandated two terms out of office.

Through the 1990s, COPEI and AD dominated national politics and maintained an extensive organizational structure. Ideologically it is a member of the Socialist International and is regarded as the most influential Latin American member. Yet, by the end of the 1990s, both parties had lost considerable credibility and were widely seen as corrupt. This disenchantment allowed Hugo Chávez, a former colonel who staged a coup in 1992, to become president in 2000. Since Chávez's election and reelection in 2006, the AD has lost

political power. In 2005 the AD boycotted the legislative election and therefore does not hold any seats in the National Assembly.

See also **Betancourt, Rómulo; Gallegos, Rómulo; Leoni, Raúl; Pérez, Carlos Andrés.**

BIBLIOGRAPHY

Robert J. Alexander, *The Venezuelan Democratic Revolution* (1964).

John D. Martz, *Acción Democrática: Evolution of a Modern Political Party in Venezuela* (1966).

Rómulo Betancourt, *Venezuela: Oil and Politics,* translated by Everett Baumann (1979).

Robert J. Alexander, *Rómulo Betancourt and the Transformation of Venezuela* (1982).

David J. Myers, "The Venezuelan Party System: Regime Maintenance Under Stress," in *Venezuela: The Democratic Experience,* edited by John D. Martz and David J. Myers, rev. ed. (1986).

John D. Martz, "Venezuela," in *Latin America and Caribbean Contemporary Record,* vol. 6, edited by Abraham F. Lowenthal (1989).

Additional Bibliography

Ellner, Steve, and Daniel Hellinger, eds. *Venezuelan Politics in the Chávez Era: Class, Polarization, and Conflict.* Boulder, CO: L. Rienner, 2003.

Hernández, Carlos Raúl, and Luis Emilio Rondón. *La democracia traicionada: Grandeza y miseria del Pacto de Punto Fijo (Venezuela 1958–2003).* Caracas, Venezuela: Rayuela, Taller de Ediciones, 2005.

Sosa A., Arturo. *Rómulo Betancourt y el Partido del Pueblo, 1937–1941.* Caracas: Editorial Fundación Rómulo Betancourt, 1995.

JOHN D. MARTZ

LIBERAL PARTY

The Liberal Party arose in Venezuela in 1840 to oppose the government of José Antonio Páez. Its formation resulted from the breakup of the consensus among the ruling elite that had been the foundation for the republic's establishment in 1830.

In the pages of *El Venezolano,* the Liberal Party's mouthpiece, an intense campaign was waged in defense of political pluralism, freedom of the press, and the existence of parties as a mechanism for settling political differences. In the area of economics, party members expressed fierce opposition to the Conservative government's measures because they favored the business sector. Like the Conservative Party, the Liberal Party was composed of groups with diverse orientations and interests; however, its stress was upon promoting agriculture and defending the interests of landowners.

The Liberals initially backed the first government of José Tadeo Monagas, then later participated in the March Revolution of 1858, in which they allied with the Conservatives in removing Monagas from power. Seeing their political participation limited under the government that arose out of this revolution, the Liberals distanced themselves from the regime. They mounted a new revolution which quickly spread throughout the country and initiated the Federal War (1859–1863).

During the period of great political instability after the war, the Liberals came to power. Finally in 1870, with the triumph of the April Revolution led by Antonio Guzmán Blanco, the period of Liberal Party dominance, which would last until the end of the century, began. By the end of Cipriano Castro's regime in 1908, however, the party was virtually defunct.

See also **Páez, José Antonio.**

BIBLIOGRAPHY

Elías Pino Iturrieta, *Las ideas de los primeros venezolanos* (1987).

Inés Quintero, *Pensamiento liberal del siglo XIX: Antología* (1992).

Additional Bibliography

Raynero, Lucía. *La noción de libertad en los políticos venezolanos del siglo XIX, 1830–1848.* Caracas: Universidad Católica Andrés Bello, 2002.

Vaamonde, Gustavo Adolfo. *Oscuridad y confusión: El pueblo y la política venezolana del siglo XIX en las ideas de Antonio Guzmán Blanco.* Caracas: Universidad Católica Andrés Bello: Fundación Polar, 2004.

Zahler, Reuben. "Honor, Corruption, and Legitimacy: Liberal Projects in the Early Venezualan Republic, 1821–50." Ph.D. diss., University of Chicago, 2002.

INÉS QUINTERO

MOVEMENT FOR THE FIFTH REPUBLIC

The Movement for the Fifth Republic (MVR) is a Venezuelan leftist political party founded in 1997 by then-presidential candidate Hugo Chávez. The party's ideology is based on the creation of a socialist Venezuelan state, a project Chávez has dubbed the Bolivarian Revolution. Upon Chávez's release from prison following a failed coup attempt in 1992, the Bolivarian Revolutionary Movement (MBR-200) set its sights on victory in the December 1998 elections. In July 1997 the Movement for the Fifth Republic was created as the political organization of the MBR-200.

As the MVR presidential candidate, Hugo Chávez pledged to dismantle *puntofijismo*, a dual-party system created by the main political parties in 1958 under Marcos Pérez Jiménez's military regime. This promise of expanded political access, as part of a broader antipoverty and anticorruption platform, which also included constitutional re-form, attracted other alternative parties, including Movement to Socialism (MAS) and Homeland for All (PPT). When these parties opted to support Chávez, the Polo Patriotico (Patriotic Pole) alliance was created. This alliance secured Chávez a decisive victory on 6 December 1998. Chávez won the largest percentage of the popular vote (56.2%) in four decades. After a national referendum approved a new constitution in 1999, Chávez was reelected to a second six-year term. Boycotting by the political opposition during the 2005 parliamentary elections allowed the Movement for the Fifth Republic and its allies to win all 167 seats in the national assembly, consolidating power.

The name "Movement for the Fifth Republic" emphasizes the party's goal of reformulating the Venezuelan state. The Confederation of the States of Venezuela was created upon independence in 1811; although the Second Republic of Venezuela was quickly crushed, the country was liberated by Simón Bolívar in 1821 and incorporated into Gran Colombia. José Antonio Páez's rebellion in 1830 created the third Republic of Venezuela. In 1864 the country was renamed the United States of Venezuela, but in 1953, under Pérez Jiménez, it reverted to the Republic of Venezuela. Chávez created the fifth republic by renaming the country the Bolivarian Republic of Venezuela in 1999.

The Movement for the Fifth Republic has transformed Venezuela into a socialist state through large-scale nationalization and the expansion of social projects, utilizing oil revenues to bankroll state grocery stores and medical programs as well as extensive foreign aid to other Latin American countries. The party has used nationalism and its antipoverty platform to consolidate popular support yet has been unable to stem political and social polarization in Venezuela.

Following his reelection in the December 2006 elections, Chávez proposed the dissolution of the MVR and the creation of the United Socialist Party of Venezuela (PSUV), which was to incorporate all twenty-three of the parties that form his support base. Although half of these parties did not join the PSUV, the MVR officially joined in March 2007. A national referendum proposing constitutional reforms that would have allowed Chávez to run for reelection failed at the polls in December 2007. The fears of Chávez's opposition, that the reforms would have allowed him to become president for life, did not come to pass. In the wake of the referendum's failure, the future of the PSUV is unclear.

See also **Chávez, Hugo; Pérez Jiménez, Marcos; Venezuela, Constitutions; Venezuela, Political Parties: Movement to Socialism (MAS).**

BIBLIOGRAPHY

Ellner, Steve and Daniel Hellinger, eds. *Venezuelan politics in the Chávez Era: Class, Polarization, and Conflict.* Boulder, CO: L. Rienner, 2003.

Gott, Richard. *Hugo Chávez and the Bolivarian Revolution.* New York and London: Verso, 2005.

Medina, Medófilo, and Margarita López Maya. *Venezuela: Confrontación Social y Polarización Política.* Bogota: Ediciones Aurora, 2003.

Romero, Aníbal. *Venezuela: Historia y Política (Venezuela: History and Politics.* Caracas: Editorial Panapo, 2002.

KATY BERGLUND SCHLESINGER

MOVEMENT TO SOCIALISM (MAS)

At a session of the central committee of the Venezuelan Communist Party in 1969, there arose a series of differences that led in 1970 to the split of twenty-two of its members who left to form the MAS on 19 January 1971. The dissidents sought to promote a nondogmatic Marxism. They did not desire unconditional alignment with the Soviet Union, especially after the 1968 Soviet invasion of Czechoslovakia. They also rejected the idea that socialism could be imported mechanically from one country to another, since each country has its own experiences and reality. The MAS criticized the bureaucratization, excessive centralism, and monolithic nature of the Communist Party, which they felt impeded debate and the exercise of democracy. The program of the MAS postulated the construction of a democracy that was socialist, pluralist, participatory, and self-managing. It called for the elimination of state or political monopolies, a substantial improvement in the living conditions of Venezuelans, and reforms of the education and electoral systems, all under the slogan of attaining "Venezuelan socialism."

The creation of the MAS represented an important attempt at renovating Venezuelan political thought. Since its foundation, it has participated in all electoral processes, establishing itself as the third strongest political force in the country. Nevertheless, its electoral representation has never surpassed 10 percent. It has managed to maintain significant representation in the national Cong-ress municipal councils, and state legislatures, but does not appear to be a viable contender for power. In 2000 Venezuelan politics was fundamentally changed when populist Hugo Chávez, a former colonel, won the presidency in 2000. The more traditional parties were considerably weakened. Initially, MAS support Chávez, but later decided to join opposition parties.

See also **Chapare; Chávez, Hugo; Venezuela, Political Parties: Communist Party.**

BIBLIOGRAPHY

No work detailing the political course of the MAS has been published. The following books, written by participants in the process, provide information on the creation and evolution of the party. Teodoro Petkoff, *¿Socialismo para Venezuela?* (1970); Eleazar Díaz Rangel, *¿Cómo se dividió el PCV?* (1971); Teodoro Petkoff, *Proceso a la izquierda* (1976); Moisés Moleiro, *La izquierda y su proceso* (1977); Pompeyo Márquez, *Una polémica necesaria* (1978); José Vicente Rangel, *Venezuela y Socialismo* (1978). See also Steve Ellner, *Venezuela's* Movimiento al Socialismo: *From Guerrilla Defeat to Innovative Politics* (1988).

Additional Bibliography

Casanova, Richard A. *Un partido para el futuro: Reflexiones para el debate.* Caracas: Ediciones Polémica, 2001.

Ellner, Steve, and Daniel Hellinger, eds. *Venezuelan Politics in the Chávez Era: Class, Polarization, and Conflict.* Boulder, CO: L. Rienner, 2003.

INÉS QUINTERO

NATIONAL CONVERGENCE

National Convergence (CN) is a Christian democratic political party in Venezuela, officially founded on 5 June 1993, by former President Rafael Caldera. Caldera, who was also a founding member of the COPEI party, broke off from COPEI before his second run for the presidency (his first presidential term came with COPEI, from 1969–1974). Convergencia, as it is known in Venezuela, co-opted some small left-wing parties, as well as some center-right parties. The party's platform was shaped in part to bring the military into the fold in the wake of a failed military coup in 1992, and in part to address the concerns of the business community regarding Venezuela's poor macroeconomic standing. Six months after CN emerged, Caldera was propelled to a narrow victory with just over 30 percent of the vote. The rise of CN also marked the crippling of many of Venezuela's traditional political parties, including Democratic Action, which had dominated the political scene from the 1950s through the 1980s.

CN's vitality was largely a product of the 1990s. Under the direction of Caldera, the party suffered the backlash of a worsening economy, and an onset of chilly relations with Colombia. Caldera's policy responses probably only exacerbated the eroding popularity of CN. He instituted austerity measures, privatization, and pardoned Hugo Chávez for his failed coup attempt. Chávez's political rise correlated with the decline of CN. In the parliamentary elections of 2000, CN managed to win only one seat out of 165. CN remains a party in Venezuela, though it has been largely marginalized by Chávez.

See also **Caldera Rodríguez, Rafael; Chávez, Hugo; Venezuela: Venezuela since 1830.**

BIBLIOGRAPHY

McCoy, Jennifer, and William Smith. "Democratic Disequilibria in Venezuela." *Journal of Inter-American Studies and World Affairs.* 37, no. 2 (Summer 1995): 113–179.

SEAN H. GOFORTH

SOCIAL CHRISTIAN COPEI PARTY

The Committee for the Organization of Independent Electoral Politics (Comité de Organización Política Electoral Independiente—COPEI) was established after World War II as a Christian Democratic political party. Founded in 1946, COPEI, together with Democratic Action (AD), was one of the two principal political parties in Venezuela in the second half of the twentieth century.

In the late nineteenth century, the Vatican began to recognize the problems of poverty and the mistreatment of labor. Although Catholics were not taking direct orders from the Vatican, this new stance helped push them into electoral politics. In 1934 the Christian Democratic movement was established internationally at the Congress of Catholic Youth in Rome. The young Venezuelan Rafael Caldera Rodríguez, one of COPEI's founders, participated in this event. Back home, he and other Catholic young people later founded the National Student Union (UNE) in 1936, separating themselves from the Federation of Venezuelan Students, a more radical organization, which defended the process of educational secularization. Later, the UNE founded the Electoral Action organization in order to participate in the municipal elections of 1938. In 1942 this organization merged with the Nationalist Action Movement and called itself Acción Nacional (National Action), finally taking the name by which it is still known, COPEI, in 1946. In terms of political orientation, COPEI tended to be moderate reformers seeking to provide the humane social and economic standards for the poor and working classes advocated by the Vatican.

Over the next half century, the party participated in every national electoral process in Venezuela and achieved steady growth. After the overthrow of the Marcos Pérez Jiménez regime in 1958, the party formed an alliance with the Democratic Action Party and the Democratic Republican Union in order to bring about a government of national unity that would guarantee the preservation of democracy. At that time it had about 15 percent of the vote. In 1968 Caldera Rodríguez, the party's principal national figure, won the presidential elections and COPEI achieved power for the first time, significantly increasing its share of the vote. In 1978 the party scored another victory with the election of its candidate, Dr. Luis Herrera Campins, as president of the republic. In the mid-1990s COPEI remained the second national party. The party had some triumphs in regional elections; several state governors were elected from its ranks; and in the mid-1990s it was represented significantly—although it was not the majority party—in Congress. Like many of the older political parties in Venezuela, COPEI lost support in the 1990s as the electorate began to see the party system as corrupt and inefficient. Caldera split from COPEI and returned to the presidency in 1994 with a new party called Convergencia. In the 2000 elections, in which Hugo Chávez, a former colonel, won the presidency, COPEI won only 5 of 165 seats in the National Assembly. Protesting the government of Chávez, COPEI did not participate in the 2005 elections and no longer has representation in the legislature.

With a Christian socialist orientation, the party's basic doctrines follow the general principles of the Christian Democratic International, to which it belonged. Its members defended the democratic system, civil and political liberties, a program of social benefits, individual freedoms, and the incentive of private property.

See also **Brazil, Organizations: National Students Union (UNE); Caldera Rodríguez, Rafael; Venezuela, Political Parties: Democratic Action (AD).**

BIBLIOGRAPHY

Rafael Caldera, *Especificidad de la democracia cristiana Rafael Caldera*, 2nd ed. (1973).

José Elías Riera Oviedo, *Los socialcristianos en Venezuela* (1977).

Donald Herman, *Christian Democracy in Venezuela* (1980).

Guillermo Luque, *De la Acción Católica al Partido Copei, 1933–1946* (1986).

Additional Bibliography

Carnevali de Toro, Dinorah. *Araguatos, avanzados y astronautas: COPEI, conflicto ideológico y crisis política en los años 60.* Caracas: Editorial Panapo, 1992.

Ellner, Steve, and Daniel Hellinger, eds. *Venezuelan Politics in the Chávez Era: Class, Polarization, and Conflict.* Boulder, CO: L. Rienner, 2003.

Mainwaring, Scott, and Timothy Scully. *Christian Democracy in Latin America: Electoral Competition and Regime Conflicts.* Stanford, CA: Stanford University Press, 2005.

Molina, José Enrique, and Angel Eduardo Alvarez Díaz, eds. *Los partidos políticos venezolanos en el siglo XXI.* Caracas: Vadell Hnos., 2004.

INÉS QUINTERO

VENTA DE INDIOS MAYAS A CUBA.

The sale of Maya Indians to Cuba began with the Caste War (1847-1901) on the Yucatán peninsula. The Yucatán governor Miguel Barbachano (1807-1959) decreed on November 6, 1848, that every rebel Indian captured would be exiled from the region for ten years.

This decision by the Yucatán authorities favored the Cuban hacienda owners and governors, who were experiencing a scarcity of black slaves and were interested in Mayan immigration. The deportation of Indians was made official in 1849. Barbachano offered soldiers 5 pesos for each rebel captured; the Yucatán government was receiving from the Spanish commercial houses 25 pesos for each rebel. From 1849 to 1861 the Yucatán governors deported 700 to 2,000 Indians to Cuba, as well as many peaceful Maya and mestizo people.

Despite pressure from England and from some officials in the Mexican government, the elite whites of Yucatán continued with the trafficking, arguing that their actions were based on "philanthropy and humanity"—that it was an alternative to killing the rebels, and that the Indians' living conditions were better in Cuba. They also supported the sales with alleged labor contracts that provided for the return of the Indians in five to ten years. The trafficking ended when Mexican president Benito Juárez stopped the activity in 1861 by establishing the death penalty for anyone who continued it.

See also **Cuba: The Colonial Era (1492–1898); Juárez, Benito; Mexico, Wars and Revolutions: Mexican-American War; Yucatán.**

BIBLIOGRAPHY

Falcón, Romana. *Las rasgaduras de la descolonización. Españoles y mexicanos a mediados del siglo XIX.* México: Centro de Estudios Históricos-El Colegio de México, 1996.

La guerra de Castas. Testimonios de Justo Sierra O'Reilly y Juan Suárez y Navarro. México: Consejo Nacional para la Cultura y las Artes, 2002.

Rodríguez Piña, Javier. *Guerra de Castas: La venta de indios mayas a Cuba, 1848–1861.* México: Consejo Nacional para la Cultura y las Artes, 1990.

JUSTO MIGUEL FLORES ESCALANTE

VERA CRUZ, ALONSO DE LA (c. 1507–1584).

Alonso de la Vera Cruz (also Veracruz or Gutiérrez de Veracruz; *b.* ca. 1507; *d.* 1584), Augustinian friar and distinguished philosopher, theologian, and educator in early colonial Mexico. Born in Caspueñas, Toledo, Spain, he studied grammar, literature, and rhetoric at the University of Alcalá. Afterward he pursued philosophy and theology at the University of Salamanca, where he was a pupil of the famous Dominican Francisco de Vitoria. He traveled to Mexico in 1536 at the invitation of Francisco de la Cruz and took the Augustinian habit in 1537. The long, varied list of Vera Cruz's accomplishments includes serving as missionary to the Tarasacan Indians, whose language he mastered; teaching in the Augustinian *colegio* in Michoacán, where he established one of the earliest New World libraries; founding the monasteries of Cuitzeo, Yuririapúndaro, Cupándaro, and Charo in Michoacán; and founding the College of San Pablo in Mexico City in 1575 and endowing it with a fine collection of books that he had transported from Spain in sixty boxes. In 1553, Vera Cruz was appointed first rector and professor of Scripture and Thomistic theology at the newly established University of Mexico. A preeminent orator and classic writer in the Spanish language, Vera Cruz was an eloquent voice of Scholastic theology in Mexico and has been called the "father of Mexican philosophy." He died in Mexico City.

See also **Missions: Spanish America; Philosophy: Overview.**

BIBLIOGRAPHY

Ernest J. Burrus, ed., *The Writings of Alonso de la Vera Cruz,* 5 vols. (1967–1975).

Arthur Ennis, *Fray Alonso de la Vera Cruz, O.S.A. (1507–1584): A Study of His Life and His Contribution to the Religious and Intellectual Affairs of Early Mexico* (1957).

O. Carlos Stoetzer, *The Scholastic Roots of the Spanish American Revolution* (1979).

Additional Bibliography

Beuchot, Mauricio, and Bernabé Navarro. *Dos homenajes: Alonso de la Veracruz y Francisco Xavier Clavigero.* Mexico City: Universidad Nacional Autónoma de México, 1992.

Castro, Sarai. "Alonso de la Veracruz as an Aristotelian Natural Philosopher." In *Method and Order in Renaissance*

Philosophy of Nature: The Aristotle Commentary Tradition, edited by Daniel A. Di Liscia, Eckhard Kessler, and Charlotte Methuen. Brookfield, VT: Ashgate, 1997.

Torre Rangel, Jesús Antonio de la. *Alonso de la Veracruz, amparo de los indios: Su teoría y práctica juridica.* Aguascalientes, Mexico: Universidad Autónoma de Aguascalientes, 1998.

J. DAVID DRESSING

VERACRUZ, CITY OF.

The principal seaport of Mexico is located 265 miles southeast of Mexico City on the Gulf Coast. This city has been Mexico's major center of foreign commerce and primary source of commercial revenue since the Spanish conquest.

On Good Friday, 22 April 1519, Hernán Cortés landed his Spanish expedition on the small island of San Juan De Ulúa, near the present city of Veracruz, and established the first base of operations for his conquest of the Aztec civilization. The Spaniards found the coastal plain inhabited by Totonac Indians, who had established their administrative center at Zempoala, 25 miles to the north. The first settlement, which Cortés named Villa Rica de la Vera Cruz, was established several miles to the north, where ships could anchor more easily. The Spanish conquistador immediately appointed town councilmen, who in turn named him captain of the expedition with full military authority. Veracruz thus became the first municipality in the Spanish colony of New Spain (Mexico).

In 1599 the Spanish viceroy ordered the settlement of Veracruz to be moved next to the port itself so the storehouses and treasury would be adjacent to the ships. During the colonial period Veracruz flourished as the only official Gulf port of New Spain and the major link between the colony and Cádiz (Spain). Its customhouses provided the primary source of revenue for colonial government. Needless to say, its wealth attracted numerous foreign privateers. John Hawkins and Sir Francis Drake plundered the town in 1568, while the French corsairs left the town, with its 6,000 inhabitants, in ruins in 1683. These foreign incursions prompted the Spaniards to build massive fortifications, which culminated with the erection of the Fortress of Santiago and the island fortress San Juan de Ulúa to protect the harbor.

Throughout the nineteenth century, the city of Veracruz continued to remain Mexico's window to the world and the "treasury of the republic," but these attributes took on new meaning as rival political factions battled for control of its revenues. Although Veracruz and its environs could boast a population of only 14,340 at the time of independence in 1821, its commercial importance was second only to that of Mexico City. By mid-century at least three-quarters of Mexico's exports and imports passed through the port. Every major British, French, and German commercial house in Mexico City maintained a branch office in Veracruz. Travelers described the city's population as dominated by Africans and mulattoes. Despite the frightening reports of yellow fever epidemics, ravaging hurricanes (*nortes*), and the lack of potable drinking water, Veracruz was still considered a tempting financial prize to Europeans. The French ordered the occupation of the port in 1838 to secure the repayment of defaulted French loans. In 1847 the U.S. forces under General Winfield Scott opted for an amphibious landing to the south of the city so as to launch a devastating bombardment of the city from the rear. When the French intervened again in 1861, they seized Veracruz's customhouses to cover Mexico's outstanding debts.

Liberal as well as Conservative rebel leaders were no less eager to fill their coffers with Veracruz revenues and to launch their revolts from a port that provided a perfect escape should their rebellions fail. *Veracruzano* Antonio López de Santa Anna announ-ced his rebellion against Emperor Agustín Iturbide there in 1823. Liberal leader Benito Juárez found refuge from the merciless attacks of the Conservative armies long enough to establish his capital there between 1858 to 1860.

Veracruz was decimated by these continual occupations and sieges, but it underwent an astounding revival in the late nineteenth century. President Porfirio Díaz set about to increase foreign trade by encouraging foreign investors to modernize docks, dikes, and wharves and construct a potable water system. The completion of two railroad lines to the capital vastly improved living conditions and contributed to a dramatic rise in its population from 16,000 in 1877 to 53,000 in 1910.

During the Revolution of 1910, Veracruz once again played a critical role as a major source of income for the central government as well as for rival revolutionary factions. The United States likewise recognized its strategic importance when it seized the customhouses in April 1914 to cripple the government of Victoriano Huerta. Venustiano Carranza's forces took possession of the port immediately after the U.S. occupation and made it their capital from November 1914 until August 1915, while repelling the armies of Francisco "Pancho" Villa and Emiliano Zapata. During his stay in Veracruz, Carranza issued important decrees concerning agrarian and labor reforms which won him the much-needed support of the Mexican lower classes. The city emerged as a key center of organized labor during the Revolution as longshoremen, railroad workers, tradesmen, and tenants formed militant anarchist and anarcho-syndicalist unions.

Veracruz port facilities have undergone several rehabilitation programs since 1940 to improve unloading equipment and warehouse facilities and to reconstruct the waterfront. By 2005 the city and metropolitan area had grown into a prosperous commercial and industrial center with over 700,000 inhabitants. Its shipments include such items as petroleum, fruits, molasses, rum, coffee, tobacco, and chicle. As a manufacturing center, it produces chemicals, cement, flour, tobacco products, soap, candles, liquor, tiles, footwear, and chocolate. Despite its hot, muggy climate, its slow pace of life attracts tourists for its picturesque colonial Plaza of the Constitution, abundant seafood, and vivacious *jarocho* (Veracrucian) music. The song "La Bamba" has probably brought more fame to this city than its beaches. The city hosts an annual Afro-Caribbean festival in July, which spotlights the city's links with Caribbean culture. Its inhabitants also take pride in its renowned Carnaval celebration, the largest in Mexico.

See also **Carranza, Venustiano; Cortés, Hernán.**

BIBLIOGRAPHY

Manuel B. Trens, *Historia de la H. Ciudad de Veracruz y de su ayuntamiento* (1955).

Robert Quirk, *An Affair of Honor* (1962).

Carmen Blázquez Domínguez, *Veracruz liberal, 1858–1860* (1986).

Berta Ulloa, *Veracruz, capital de la nación, 1914–1915* (1986).

Alfred H. Siemens, *Between the Summit and the Sea* (1990).

Michael C. Meyer and William L. Sherman, *The Course of Mexican History*, 4th ed. (1991).

Additional Bibliography

Antuñano Maurer, Alejandro de. *Veracruz: Primer puerto del continente*. México: ICA, 1996.

Contreras Cruz, Carlos, and Claudia Patricia Pardo Hernández. *De Veracruz a Puebla: Un itinerario histórico entre la colonia y el porfiriato*. San Juan Mixcoac, México: Instituto Mora, 1999.

HEATHER FOWLER-SALAMINI

VERACRUZ, OCCUPATION OF.

Occupation of Veracruz, the April 1914 seizure of Veracruz, Mexico, by U.S. troops to prevent delivery of a shipment of arms to the regime of General Victoriano Huerta, whose government President Woodrow Wilson had declined to recognize. Although the landing on 21 April was justified as a response to the Tampico incident a week earlier, when Mexican soldiers arrested a group of U.S. sailors, the selection of Veracruz rather than Tampico as the site of the landing was due to the arms shipment.

U.S. Marines and Navy personnel sought to seize only the customs house and dock area, but resistance by Mexican troops and the local populace, which shocked public opinion and policy makers in the United States, resulted in the occupation of the entire city. The military operation was undertaken on short notice, with little planning and a small force. Had Mexican federal troops offered more organized resistance, the landing would have proven very costly. The Revolutionaries condemned the occupation but refused Huerta's request to join forces against the U.S. invaders. While many expected U.S. troops to launch a full-scale military intervention, they occupied only Veracruz.

Veracruz remained occupied for seven months, a factor that contributed to the fall of the Huerta regime but did not fully deny him access to arms shipments from abroad. Efforts to mediate through the Niagara Falls Conference proved unsuccessful. The episode produced considerable strain between the Wilson administration and the Revolutionaries because of Venustiano Carranza's refusal to negotiate with the United States or to offer any guarantees for the citizens of Veracruz. His stance delayed the evacuation of the port by several months.

U.S. troops withdrew in November 1914, in effect turning the port and vast quantities of war material over to Carranza in time to support his efforts in a new conflict with General Francisco ("Pancho") Villa.

See also **Huerta, Victoriano; Villa, Francisco "Pancho".**

BIBLIOGRAPHY

Robert E. Quirk, *An Affair of Honor: Woodrow Wilson and the Occupation of Veracruz* (1962).

Kenneth J. Grieb, *The United States and Huerta* (1969).

John M. Hart, *Revolutionary Mexico* (1987).

Additional Bibliography

Eisenhower, John S. D. *Intervention! The United States and the Mexican Revolution, 1913–1917*. New York: W.W. Norton, 1993.

Koth, Karl B. *Waking the Dictator: Veracruz, the Struggle for Federalism and the Mexican Revolution, 1870–1927*. Calgary: University of Calgary Press, 2002.

Palomares, Justino N. *La invasión yanqui en 1914*. Mexico City: n.p., 1940.

KENNETH J. GRIEB

VERACRUZ, STATE OF.

The eleventh largest Mexican state (28,114 sq. mi.) and the third most populous (6,940,544 inhabitants in 1990 and 7,110,214 in 2005), Veracruz stretches for some 400 miles along the Gulf of Mexico and comprises three broad physiographical and cultural regions.

Northern Veracruz stretches from the Río Tamesí in the north to the Sierra de Chiconquiaco in the south, and rises from sea level to elevations as high as 9,000 feet in the Sierra Madre Oriental. Most of the region is lowland, with a climate ranging from hot and humid to hot and subhumid, with a summer wet season. During the pre-Hispanic period, Olmec influence at such places as Santa Luisa (c. 1150) gave way to interaction with highland cultures and a refocusing of settlement at the centers of El Tajín (c. 400–900) and Castillo de Teayo (founded c. 850). Cattle ranches spread throughout the lowlands during the colonial period, after warfare and disease had virtually exterminated the native population, a pattern persisting until the twentieth-century development of petroleum resources stimulated immigration. The foothills around Papantla harbor most of the state's remaining native peoples.

Central Veracruz stretches south from the Sierra de Chiconquiaco to the Río Blanco, and rises from sea level to peaks as high as 18,405 feet in the neovolcanic axis, resulting in a dramatic altitudinal zonation of vegetation from savanna to pine-oak forest. The climate ranges from hot and subhumid with an intense winter dry season in the lowlands to temperate and humid at higher elevations, and permits a wide range of crops. During the pre-Hispanic period, Remojadas (c. 300–900) and Cempoala (founded c. 1200) were major centers.

In 1519 the Spaniards under Hernán Cortés landed here and allied themselves with the Totonacs before going on to conquer the Aztecs. By 1600 the crown had established Veracruz at its present location as the official port of New Spain. Jalapa, now the state capital, hosted the annual merchant fair. The region had become a vital transportation corridor between Spain and New Spain. The rapid demise of the Indian population stimulated the establishment of livestock in the lowlands and sugarcane on the more humid slopes around Jalapa and Orizaba, where African slaves resisted and established refuge communities. Control of the region continued to play a key role in the struggle for power in Republican Mexico: by Antonio López de Santa Anna (1833–1855), by the United States (1847–1848, 1914), by Benito Juárez's Liberals (1858–1861), and by the French (1862–1867). Turn-of-the-century migration to the growing textile mills of Orizaba provided a proletarian base for the subsequent popular revolution.

Southern Veracruz stretches from the Río Blanco in the north to the Río Tonalá in the south, and rises from sea level to elevations as high as 5,413 feet in the Sierra de los Tuxtlas. Much of the region is tropical lowland with a hot, humid climate. During the pre-Hispanic period it was the heartland of the prototypical Olmec, established at such centers as San Lorenzo (c. 1200–900) and La Venta (c. 900–400), just south of the Río Tonalá in Tabasco. Subsequently the region became a resource hinterland for highland cultures, a pattern the Spaniards continued by establishing livestock ranches and sugar plantations. Only with the control of lowland diseases, the discovery of petroleum, and the construction of drainage and irrigation projects in the twentieth century has the region's population increased dramatically.

See also **Veracruz, Occupation of.**

BIBLIOGRAPHY

Manuel B. Trens, *Historia de Veracruz*, 6 vols. (1947–1950).

Thomas T. Poleman, *The Papaloapan Project* (1964).

José García Payón, "Archaeology of Central Veracruz," in *Handbook of Middle American Indians*, vol. 11, edited by Gordon F. Ekholm and Ignacio Bernal (1971).

Peter Gerhard, *A Guide to the Historical Geography of New Spain* (1972).

Arturo Gómez-Pompa, "Ecology of the Vegetation of Veracruz," in *Vegetation and Vegetational History of Northern Latin America,* edited by Alan Graham (1973).

Heather Fowler Salamini, *Agrarian Radicalism in Veracruz, 1920–38* (1978).

Michael D. Coe and Richard A. Diehl, *In the Land of the Olmec*, 2 vols. (1980).

Jorge L. Tamayo, *Geografía moderna de México*, 9th ed., rev. (1987).

Alfred H. Siemens, *Between the Summit and the Sea* (1990).

Patrick J. Carroll, *Blacks in Colonial Veracruz* (1991).

Additional Bibliography

Amezcua Cardiel, Héctor. *Veracruz: Sociedad, economía, política y cultura.* México, D.F.: Centro de Investigaciones Interdisciplinarias en Humanidades, 1990.

Blázquez Domínguez, Carmen. *Breve historia de Veracruz.* México: Colegio de México, Fideicomiso Historia de las Américas, 2000.

García Díaz, Bernardo; Lourdes, Alonso, and Adalberto Ríos Salía. *El Estado de Veracruz.* México: Grupo Azabache, 1993.

ANDREW SLUYTER

VERAPAZ. Verapaz, a mountainous district in central Guatemala, divided since 1877 into two departments, Alta Verapaz and Baja Verapaz.

Alta Verapaz covers 3,354 square miles. The population was 958,417 in 2004, an increase of 22.5 percent from 1999; its chief agricultural products are coffee and cardamom. The capital is

Cobán. Baja Verapaz covers 1,206 square miles and has a population of 150,000 (1985); its chief agricultural products are corn, beans, sugarcane, and citrus. The capital is Salamá. Ethnically, the population of Verapaz is mainly Kekchí and Pokonchí Indian.

Sharply folded mountains have isolated the Verapaz from cultural, religious, and political changes to the north and south. The inhabitants of the region, which the Kekchí called Tezulutlán, repulsed conquest with such ferocity in 1530 that the Spaniards named it the "Land of War." But Fray Bartolomé de Las Casas saw in this area an opportunity to put into practice his precept of a peaceful conquest and conversion of the Indians. Around 1542, Dominicans entered the region and began missionary work by establishing *reducciones,* with Cobán as the principal mission center. The crown declared the area the exclusive domain of the Dominican order and forbade Spanish settlement there. By the end of the decade, most of the area, now renamed Verapaz (Land of True Peace), was under Dominican control and nominally Christian.

Dominican control continued, albeit somewhat diminished, until the early part of the nineteenth century. In defiance of royal orders, Ladinos (Guatemalans of European heritage) settled in the Baja Verapaz in the colonial period, and their influx accelerated after independence. Difficulty of communication kept the Alta Verapaz isolated until mid-century.

About 1860, Ladino and foreign merchants, especially Germans, moved into the Verapaz. In the Alta Verapaz, settlers appropriated communal lands which they turned into large estates. The inhabitants of those communities were transformed into servile laborers. The new owners transformed the Verapaz into a leading coffee department.

The commercialization of the coffee industry came about largely through the efforts of a small group of Germans who controlled production, processing, and distribution. They provided capital resources, marketing connections, entrepreneurial skills, and a capitalist approach to investment and profit. Germans initiated transportation improvements and built a railroad to connect with a water route to the Caribbean port of Livingston, which reinforced the department's economic separation from the rest of Guatemala. German hegemony continued until World War II, when the Guatemalan government expropriated and then nationalized most German-owned properties.

The construction of a paved highway between Cobán and Guatemala City in the early 1970s linked the Verapaz more closely to the rest of the country and brought economic and social changes. The opening of roads, however primitive, into areas previously accessible only by muleback, stimulated commerce and attracted immigrants from other parts of Guatemala. This influx of non-Kekchí/Pokonchí will doubtless alter the character of the Indian population.

Evangelical groups have been active throughout the area, and a significant minority of the population now belongs to various Protestant sects. The Verapaz was the scene of considerable guerrilla activity in the early 1980s, which resulted, in part, in an increased national military presence in the area.

See also **Guatemala; Las Casas, Bartolomé de; Missions: Jesuit Missions (Reducciones).**

BIBLIOGRAPHY

José Victor Mejía, *Geografía descriptiva de la República de Guatemala* (1922).

Guillermo Náñez Falcón, "German Contributions to the Economic Development of the Alta Vera Paz" (M.A. thesis, Tulane University, 1961).

Arden R. King, *Cobán and the Verapaz* (1974).

Francis Gall, comp., *Diccionario geográfico de Guatemala,* 4 vols. (1976).

Karl Theodor Sapper, *The Verapaz in the Sixteenth and Seventeenth Centuries,* translated by Theodore E. Gutman (1985).

Additional Bibliography

Biederman, Guy. *Alta Verapaz.* San Francisco, CA: San Francisco State University, 1990.

Danien, Elin C. *Maya Folktales from the Alta Verapaz.* Philadelphia: University of Pennsylvania, Museum of Archaeology and Anthropology, 2005.

GUILLERMO NÁÑEZ FALCÓN

VERGARA, MARTA (1898–1948). Marta Vergara (*b.* 1898; *d.* after 1948), leader of the Chilean women's movement, founding member of the Comité Pro Derecho de las Mujeres (1933) and, with other members of the Asociación de

Mujeres Universitarias, of the Movimiento Pro Emancipación de la Mujer Chilena (MEMCH) (1935). Vergara edited the MEMCH journal, *La Mujer Nueva*. Her political sympathies were with the Chilean left and the Chilean Communist Party, though she was not a party member. Vergara lived and traveled abroad much of her life and was connected to the international diplomatic and intellectual communities. From 1941 to 1948, she lived in Washington, D.C., where she served as Chilean representative to the Inter-American Commission of Women.

See also **Feminism and Feminist Organizations.**

BIBLIOGRAPHY

Marta Vergara, *Memorias de una mujer irreverente* (1961).

Additional Bibliography

Lavrin, Asunción. *Women, Feminism, and Social Change in Argentina, Chile, and Uruguay, 1890–1940*. Lincoln: University of Nebraska Press, 1995.

CORINNE ANTEZANA-PERNET

VERGARA ECHEVEREZ, JOSÉ FRANCISCO (1833–1889).

José Francisco Vergara Echeverez (*b.* 10 October 1833; *d.* 15 February 1889), late nineteenth-century Chilean statesman. A prominent politician, Vergara, the son of an army officer, was educated as an engineer. While holding public office, including a ministerial portfolio, he was particularly recognized for his service during the War of the Pacific. Beginning his career as a nursemaid for an indecisive and perhaps senescent general, Vergara, a colonel of a National Guard cavalry unit, first served in the Tarapacá campaign. Landing with the troops at Pisagua, he fought at San Francisco and participated in the ill-fated attack on Tarapacá.

Although Vergara resigned from active military service, he continued to advise the army's general staff, often suggesting well-conceived plans which, unfortunately, the military commander rejected. Vergara subsequently held the post of minister of the interior in the Domingo Santa María government. Although he was a brilliant and dedicated administrator, he failed to win the Conservative Party's nomination for the 1886 presidential campaign. Upon retiring to his farm in what is now Viña del Mar, he unexpectedly died.

See also **War of the Pacific.**

BIBLIOGRAPHY

William F. Sater, *Chile and the War of the Pacific* (1986), pp. 21, 23, 27, 32–34, 37–38, 47–51, 54–56, 182–185.

José Francisco Vergara, "Memorias," in *Guerra del Pacífico: Memorias de José F. Vergara y diario de campaña de Diego Dublé Almeida*, edited by Francisco Ruz Trujillo (1979).

WILLIAM F. SATER

VERÍSSIMO, ÉRICO (1905–1975).

Érico Veríssimo (*b.* 17 December 1905; *d.* 1975), Brazilian novelist. Born in Cruz Alta, Rio Grande do Sul, Veríssimo belonged nonetheless to the later modernist novelists of Brazil, who at first preferred the *novela*, a short novel emphasizing one character and limited space and time. One of his first such fictional efforts, *Clarissa*, was an immediate success. The youthful Veríssimo was fascinated by the plastic arts, but he left painting with colors for painting with words. Counterpoint, flashbacks, montage, simultaneity, telescoping, diary, and documentary are only a few of the devices he used in his broad, cosmopolitan view of the world. Veríssimo wrote in the first person and expressed details so convincingly that the reader readily becomes absorbed in the characters; yet psychological development and philosophy are subordinate to the story.

Veríssimo's humanistic and ideological themes were often conveyed by symbols and portrayed in characters. Music is often found in his works as allusions and symphonic structures, for instance, in *Música ao longe* (1935). Dialogue, used sparingly in his early novels, becomes increasingly important in his great multivolume work, *O tempo e o vento*.

Veríssimo quickly developed the novel as his preferred genre. He was the first in Brazil to make effective use of the point-counterpoint novel. He focused on urban life and immediately became a best-selling novelist, the first writer in Brazil to live by the pen. Other novels, *Caminhos cruzados* (1935), *Um lugar ao sol* (1936), *Olhai os lírios do campo* (1938), and *O resto é silêncio* (1943), followed in rapid succession, each a result of Veríssimo's continuing experimentation in his medium.

In *O tempo e o vento,* Veríssimo gives his broad, penetrating view of the history of his home state. On a wide panoramic screen developed in three volumes (the third of which has three parts), Veríssimo chronicles the vicissitudes of two families. He presents in human and symbolic terms the rise of Rio Grande do Sul from the mythical past and its history from the founding of its society in the middle of the eighteenth century to the dictatorship of Getúlio Vargas in the first half of the twentieth. The principal subject of this great work is the evolution of the urban middle class, along with all the inherent issues, both in the state and in the nation. Volume 1, *O continente,* appeared in 1949 and volume 2, *O retrato,* in 1951; the first two books of volume 3, *O arquipélago,* were published in 1961, and the third, the following year.

See also **Literature: Brazil.**

BIBLIOGRAPHY

Guilhermino César, "O romance social de Érico Veríssimo," in *O contador de histórias: Quarenta anos da vida literária de Érico Veríssimo,* compiled by Flávio Loureiro Chaves (1972).

Regina Zilberman, *A Literatura no Rio Grande do Sul* (1982).

Additional Bibliography

Aguiar, Flávio, and Ligia Chiappini Moraes Leite. *Civilização e exclusão: Visões do Brasil em Erico Veríssimo, Euclides da Cunha, Claude Lévi-Strauss e Darcy Ribeiro.* São Paulo: FAPESP: Boitempo Editorial, 2001.

Bordini, Maria da Glória, and Regina Zilberman. *O tempo e o vento: História, invenção e metamorfose.* Porto Alegre, Brazil: EDIPUCRS, 2004.

Silva, Maria das Graças Gomes Villa da. *O Horror antigo e o horror moderno em: O tempo e o vento e Noite de Érico Verissimo.* Araraquara, Brazil: Laboratório Editorial da FCL; and São Paulo: Cultura Acadêmico Editora, 2004.

Young, Theodore Robert. *O questionamento da história em O tempo e o vento de Erico Verissimo.* Lajeado, Brazil: FATES Editora, 1997.

RICHARD A. MAZZARA

VERNET, LOUIS (1792–1871). Louis Vernet (*b.* 1792; *d.* 1871), first governor of the Islas Malvinas (Falkland Islands) under the authority of Buenos Aires (1829–1831). Vernet was a central figure in the incidents that led to the establishment of continuous British possession of the islands. He was born in France but he had lived in Hamburg and the United States before coming to Buenos Aires in 1817. In 1826 he set up a cattle business on the islands that provisioned passing ships with fresh and salted beef before they rounded Cape Horn. His presence and activities were challenged by seal hunters (mainly from the United States), so in 1829 the Buenos Aires government appointed him governor and gave him exclusive control of fishing and hunting in the area, an act that was protested by the British. In 1831, after several warnings against unlawful hunting, Vernet seized the *Harriet,* a U.S. sealing vessel, and took it to Buenos Aires. George W. Slacum, the U.S. consul in Buenos Aires, reacted strongly, called Vernet a pirate, and demanded payment for damages. The U.S. Navy corvette *Lexington* was in the Río de la Plata at the time, and at Slacum's instigation its captain, Silas Duncan, sailed to the islands in late 1831, destroyed Vernet's settlement, and declared the islands *res nullis* (property of no one). A little over a year later the British expelled the remaining Argentines and began their century and a half of continuous occupation of the islands.

See also **Falklands/Malvinas War.**

BIBLIOGRAPHY

Mary Cawkell, *The Falkland Story 1592–1982* (1983).

Lowell S. Gustafson, *The Sovereignty Dispute over the Falkland (Malvinas) Islands* (1988).

Eugenio A. L. Ravenal, *Las Islas de la Discordia, el asunto de las Malvinas* (1983).

Additional Bibliography

Balmaceda, Rodolfo. *La Argentina indefensa: Desmalvinización y desmalvinizadores.* Buenos Aires: Editorial Los Nacionales, 2004.

JACK CHILD

VERRUGA. *See* **Diseases.**

VÉRTIZ Y SALCEDO, JUAN JOSÉ DE (1719–1799). Juan José de Vértiz y Salcedo (*b.* 11 July 1719; *d.* 1799), governor of Buenos Aires (1770–1777), viceroy of Río de la Plata

(1778–1784). Born in Mérida, Yucatán, while his father was serving as governor, Vértiz was trained as a military man in Spain and later participated in the Italian campaigns. He arrived in Río de la Plata as governor in 1770. Although he was forced to step aside during the brief viceroyalty in Cevallos, he soon succeeded him. As second viceroy of Río de la Plata, Vértiz was the true architect of viceregal government in the Río de la Plata. While governor and later viceroy, Vértiz was a very successful leader: he implemented a series of far-reaching reforms, including the creation of the intendency system; free trade; improvement of public services, education, and welfare; geographical exploration; construction of forts; and agricultural experimentation. Vértiz returned to Spain in 1784.

See also **Río de la Plata, Viceroyalty of.**

BIBLIOGRAPHY

José Torre Revello, *Juan José de Vértiz y Salcedo: Gobernador y virrey de Buenos Aires* (1932).

Enrique Udaondo, *Diccionario biográfico colonial argentino* (1945), pp. 937–939.

Additional Bibliography

Lesser, Ricardo. *Los orígenes de la Argentina: Historias del Reino del Río de la Plata*. Buenos Aires: Editorial Biblos, 2003.

SUSAN M. SOCOLOW

VESCO, ROBERT LEE (1935–).

Robert Lee Vesco, a U.S. financial manipulator and white-collar criminal, was born 4 December 1935, to immigrant parents in a lower-class Detroit neighborhood. Having quickly achieved wealth, he became the subject of an investigation by the U.S. Securities and Exchange Commission in the early 1970s. After his questionable financial activities were revealed, Vesco fled to the Bahamas and then to Costa Rica, where a close relationship with President José Figueres helped him evade U.S. extradition attempts. Seeking again to evade U.S. extradition, he returned to the Bahamas, where he is alleged to have been the money launderer for drug cartels. Under intense U.S. pressure, the Bahamas refused him political asylum, and in 1981 Vesco found refuge in Antigua. In 1982, however, again under U.S. pressure, Vesco fled to Nicaragua. He later turned up in Cuba, where he led a shadowy existence. In 1996 the Cuban government sentenced him to thirteen years in prison on charges of attempting to steal and export Cuban pharmaceutical patents.

See also **Drugs and Drug Trade.**

BIBLIOGRAPHY

Herzog, Anthony. *Vesco: From Wall Street to Castro's Cuba: The Rise, Fall, and Exile of the King of White Collar Crime*. New York: Doubleday, 1987.

ANTHONY P. MAINGOT

VESPUCCI, AMERIGO (1454–1512).

The Florentine navigator and cosmographer Amerigo Vespucci was the first to reveal to Europe the existence of a previously unknown continental landmass south of the equinox, and also to state that the empirical knowledge attained in the exploration of this new land could change long-held ideas in the cosmographical tradition. He was born on March 9, 1454, into an extended family that enjoyed relative economic success and played a prominent role in Florentine political and cultural life. In 1478 an uncle, Guido Antonio, went to the court of Louis XI in France on a diplomatic mission on behalf of Lorenzo de' Medici, bringing Amerigo as his secretary. Amerigo returned to Florence in 1482, this time to work as Lorenzo di Pierfrancesco de' Medici's head steward, a position he retained until 1491.

Vespucci's involvement in overseas exploration began in Seville, where between 1492 and 1496 he looked after Lorenzo's commercial interests and worked with Giannotto Berardi, outfitting fleets to America. Vespucci's participation in three overseas voyages can be documented, all involving the exploration of South America. His two first voyages covered most of the northern and eastern continental coasts; a third voyage under Fernão de Noronha (1503), exploring only between Bahía and San Vicente, seems to have been inconsequential. He returned to Seville in 1504 to begin working in the Casa de Contratación in 1507 and the following year became pilot major, the officer in charge of licensing pilots, inspecting navigational instruments, and keeping up-to-date navigational charts, an occupation in which he would remain until his death on February 12, 1512.

Vespucci's first voyage was a defining moment in his realization that new information acquired in exploration could be used to correct and expand the theories previously stated by philosophers and geographers. He departed from Cádiz as a pilot in Alonso de Hojeda's expedition (May 18, 1499–June 1500) and explored from present-day Surinam to Lake Maracaibo. In his letter to Lorenzo di Pierfrancesco of July 18, 1500, he says he was attempting to round the Cape of Cattigara near the Sinus Magnus, the easternmost part of the Indian Ocean in Asia. His main concern, however, was not so much to describe territories uncharted on European maps, because unknown islands and stretches of land had always been supposed to exist. He rather "longed to be the author who would designate the other polar star of the firmament" (1992, p. 6). He was convinced that navigation could change cosmographic history, that is, radically challenge accepted ideas of the world and cartographic practice. Designating the southern star closest to the *firmament* (the one that moved the least) not only satisfied a navigational need for a point of reference in the sky but also served to connect the poles and the skies symmetrically through an imaginary axis (an essential conceptual device in mapping). He further sought to become a cosmographical authority by putting forth two more major propositions: a detailed explanation of his method for calculating longitude; and a confutation of the theory of the inhabitability of the Torrid Zone. Thus his main goal was to break the boundaries of learned geographical discourse and set new standards for cosmographical knowledge.

It was after his second voyage that he put forth the claim that the countries he had explored should be considered a *New World*. He had left from Lisbon, this time at the service of the Portuguese king Manuel I, in the expedition commanded by Gonzalo Coelho (May 13, 1501–July 22, 1502). They landed near Cape San Roque on the northern coast of Brazil and explored the coast to the south as far as Patagonia. His observations during this voyage revolved around three main themes that further developed and expanded his observations of his first voyage: the existence of a continent previously unknown, whose diversity and novelty surpassed the world known to antiquity; the habitability of the equinoctial region; and the designation of the Southern Cross to determine the southern pole.

These statements were first published in the *Mundus Novus* (1503), a letter addressed to Lorenzo di Pierfrancesco and later included in Francanzano Montalboddo's *Paesi*, a collection of exploration narratives. It was, however, the *Lettera* addressed to Piero Soderini, a collection of four spurious voyage accounts attributed to Vespucci, that brought him fame. Martin Wadseemuller included Vespucci's letter as an appendix to his *Cosmographia introductio*, where he presented an updated world map. Here the name "America" was given to the portion of the South American continent explored by Vespucci. The Soderini letter was thus canonized as the authoritative source on Vespucci's voyages, and it continued to reappear in important collections such as the *Novus Orbis* and Giovanni Battista Ramusio's *Navigationi*.

See also **America; Explorers and Exploration: Spanish America; Manuel I of Portugal; Noronha, Fernão de.**

BIBLIOGRAPHY

Primary Works

Alberic[us] Vespucci[us] Laure[n]tio Petri Francisci de Medicis Salutem Plurima[m] Dicit. París: Felix Baligault y Jehan Lambert, 1503.

Lettera di Amerigo Vespucci delle isole nuouamente trovate in quattro suoi viaggi. Florence: A. Tubini & A. Ghirlandi, 1505.

Secondary Works

Caraci, Ilaria Luzzana. *Navegantes italianos*. Madrid: Mapfre, 1992.

O'Gorman, Edmundo. *La invención de América*. Mexico: Fondo de Cultura Económica, 1977.

Pohl, Frederick J. *Amerigo Vespucci, Pilot Major*. New York: Columbia University Press, 1944.

Rivera Novo, Belén, and Luisa Martín-Merás. *Cuatro siglos de cartografía en América*. Madrid: Mapfre, 1992.

Roa-de-la-Carrera, Cristián. "El Nuevo Mundo como problema de conocimiento: Américo Vespucio y el discurso geográfico del siglo XVI." *Hispanic Review* 70, no. 4 (2002): 557–580.

Varela, Consuelo. *Amerigo Vespucci*. Madrid: Anaya, 1988.

Wolff, Hans. *America: Early Maps of the New World*. Munich: Prestel, 1992.

CRISTIÁN ROA-DE-LA-CARRERA

VIAL, PEDRO (c. 1746–1814). Pedro Vial (*b.* ca. 1746; *d.* 1814), explorer and pathfinder of the Spanish Southwest. A native of Lyons, France, Vial spent his first years in the New World on the Missouri River, working as a gunsmith for various southwestern tribes. As part of the Spanish attempt to protect and strengthen the northern frontier, he was recruited to open three new roads connecting Santa Fe with Spanish outposts to the east. Commissioned by the Spanish governor of Texas, Vial established an overland communication route between San Antonio and Santa Fe in 1787. Under the auspices of the governor of New Mexico, he opened a second road from Santa Fe to Natchitoches, Louisiana, in 1788. From 1792 to 1793 Vial blazed a third trail from Santa Fe to Saint Louis, traveling what later became the Santa Fe Trail. After these trailblazing excursions, Vial continued to work for the Spanish crown. He was enlisted to help protect Spain's claims to Texas and New Mexico against Anglo-American encroachment, and he led an unsuccessful attempt to intercept the Lewis and Clark expedition of 1804–1806. With his extensive knowledge of the Southwest, including its native tribes and languages, Vial was also a valuable guide and interpreter, serving in this capacity until his death in Santa Fe.

See also **Santa Fe, New Mexico.**

BIBLIOGRAPHY

Carlos E. Castañeda, *Our Catholic Heritage in Texas,* vol. 5 (1942), pp. 150–170.

Noel M. Loomis and Abraham P. Nasatir, *Pedro Vial and the Roads to Santa Fe* (1967).

Additional Bibliography

John, Elizabeth A. H. Translated by Adán Benavides. "Inside the Comanchería, 1785: The Diary of Pedro Vial and Francisco Xavier Chaves." *Southwestern Historical Quarterly* 98, no. 1 (July 1994): 27–56.

Pace, Robert F., and Donald S. Frazier. *Frontier Texas: History of a Borderland to 1880.* Abilene, TX: State House Press, 2004.

Suzanne B. Pasztor

VIAMONTE, JUAN JOSÉ (1774–1843). Juan José Viamonte (*b.* 9 February 1774; *d.* 31 March 1843), Argentine military officer and governor of Buenos Aires. Born in Buenos Aires, Viamonte began a professional military career in the late colonial period. He opposed the British Invasions of 1806–1807, and after the May Revolution of 1810 he joined the first disastrous expedition of the Argentine patriots to Upper Peru. He later took part in the struggle against Federalist dissidents of the littoral provinces and their Uruguayan protector, José Gervasio Artigas.

Viamonte retired from the military in 1822 but remained active in public life, serving as acting governor of Buenos Aires in 1829, just before the first governorship of Juan Manuel de Rosas. He became governor again in 1833, but his essential moderation and evenhanded treatment of Rosas's enemies infuriated the latter's supporters, who unleashed a campaign of terrorism. In 1834 Viamonte resigned, paving the way for Rosas to return to office. Increasingly disaffected, he moved in 1840 to Uruguay, where he died in Montevideo.

See also **Argentina: The Colonial Period.**

BIBLIOGRAPHY

Armando Alonso Piñeiro, *Historia del general Viamonte y su época* (1959); *Vidas de grandes argentinos,* vol. 3 (1963), pp. 305–312.

David Bushnell

VIANA, FRANCISCO JOSÉ DE OLIVEIRA (1883–1951). Francisco José de Oliveira Viana (*b.* 20 June 1883; *d.* 28 March 1951), Brazilian social theorist. Born in Saquarema, Viana was a major figure in the alienated first generation of the Old Republic (1889–1930). Viana was a publicist and jurist whose legacies are the tradition of authoritarian nationalism and the Estado Novo's *trabalhista* (corporativist sindicalist) legislation. Viana, trained at the Faculty of Law in Rio de Janeiro, was influenced by Serzedelo Correia and Sílvio Romero. A disciple of Alberto Tôrres in the 1910s, he first gained prestige writing critical essays, which were an established genre in the era's journalism. His greatest work, *Populações meridionais do Brasil* (1920), was followed by other studies on Brazilian society, history, and politics, the best of which were written before 1940.

With the Revolution of 1930, analysis began to give way to application, as Viana served President

Getúlio Vargas as consultant, jurist, and minister. His most notable impact was on constitutional law and corporativist legislation that successfully helped contain and co-opt the political potential of the emerging urban proletariat. His direct influence on the intellectual milieu of the 1920s and 1930s was enormous, especially his analysis of Brazil's social, racial, and political evolution. He asserted that Brazil, hindered by mass degradation, racial inferiority, and tendencies toward disaggregation and clientelism, was historically predisposed toward enlightened, centralized, authoritarian government and endangered by liberalism. Although his ideas derived from European positivist and corporativist theorists from the 1880s to the 1920s, he remains indirectly influential today. He died in Niterói.

See also **Brazil, Revolutions: Revolution of 1930; Vargas, Getúlio Dornelles.**

BIBLIOGRAPHY

João Batista De Vasconcelos Torres, *Oliveira Viana* (1956).

Jarbas Medeiros, *Ideologia autoritária no Brasil* (1978).

Jeffrey D. Needell, "History, Race, and the State in the Thought of Oliveira Viana," in *Hispanic American Historical Review* 75, no. 1 (February 1995): 1–31.

Thomas E. Skidmore, *Black into White* (1974).

Evaldo Vieira, *Autoritarianismo e corporativismo no Brasil* (1981).

Additional Bibliography

Bresciani, Maria Stella Martins. *O charme da ciência e a sedução da objetividade: Oliveira Vianna entre intérpretes do Brasil.* São Paulo: Editora UNESP, 2005.

Moraes, João Quartim de, and Elide Rugai Bastos. *O Pensamento de Oliveira Vianna.* Campinas, Brazil: Editora da Unicamp, 1993.

Piva, Luiz Guilherme. *Ladrilhadores e semeadores: A modernização brasileira no pensamento político de Oliveira Vianna, Sérgio Buarque de Holanda, Azevedo Amaral e Nestor Duarte (1920–1940).* São Paulo: Departamento de Ciência Política da USP: Editora 34, 2000.

JEFFREY D. NEEDELL

law office was Andrés Quintana Roo (1787–1851), with whom she was betrothed. After Quintana Roo joined the movement in 1812, she decided to help the insurgents. Affiliated with the secret society, Los Guadalupes, she received and distributed insurgent correspondence. She also sent the insurgents money, arms, and weapons, and helped several individuals to join them. She fled in March 1813, when she was discovered in San Antonio Huixquiluean on her way to Tlalpujahua. Her uncle convinced her to return, and she was detained in the College of Belén. Although the authorities prosecuted her, she did not inform on the conspirators. When she was rescued and taken to Oaxaca by the insurgents in April 1813, the authorities confiscated her property. The insurgent Congress granted her a pension that same year. She married Quintana Roo, whom she followed in his travels as deputy of the Congress. They were discovered in 1817 and she was captured in the sierra of Tlatlaya; both accepted amnesty from the royalists. Her remains rest in the Column of Independence.

See also **Guadalupes, Los.**

BIBLIOGRAPHY

Genaro García, *Leona Vicario, heroína insurgente* (1910).

José María Miquel I Vergés, *Diccionario de insurgentes* (1969), pp. 597–598; *Diccionario Porrúa de historia, biografía y geografía de México,* vol. 3 (1986), p. 3120.

Additional Bibliography

Adams, Jerome R. *Notable Latin American Women: Twenty-nine Leaders, Rebels, Poets, Battlers, and Spies, 1500–1900.* Jefferson, NC: McFarland & Co., 1995.

Aguirre, Eugenio. *Leona Vicario, la insurgente.* Mexico City: Editorial Alhambra Mexicana, 1990.

Castellanos, Francisco. *Leona Vicario: Heroina de la independencia.* Mexico City: Editorial Diana, 1997.

Staples, Anne. *Leona Vicario.* Mexico City: Departamento Editorial, Secretária de la Presidencia, 1990.

VIRGINIA GUEDEA

VICARIO FERNÁNDEZ, [MARÍA] LEONA (1789–1842). [María] Leona Vicario Fernández (*b.* 10 April 1789; *d.* 21 August 1842), Mexican insurgent heroine. A rich heiress, Vicario Fernández lived under the care of her uncle, Agustín Fernández de San Salvador. Working in her uncle's

VICEROYALTY, VICEROY. Viceroyalty, the largest territorial unit in the Spanish colonies, and viceroy, its chief executive. The failure of the first audiencias to provide stable rule in the New World and the desire to gain control over the new

colonies resulted in the Spanish crown's naming viceroys for the newly created viceroyalties (regions) of New Spain (1535) and Peru (1543). The viceroyalty of New Spain encompassed land from the northern boundary of the province of Panama to what is now the United States and included the Caribbean islands and part of the province of Venezuela. The Philippine Islands ultimately fell under its jurisdiction as well. The viceroyalty of Peru included Panama and all Spanish possessions in South America, with the exception of a coastal strip of Venezuela. When the crown created the viceroyalties of New Granada in northern South America and of the Río De La Plata (roughly present-day Argentina, Uruguay, Paraguay, and Bolivia) in 1739 and 1776, respectively, it reduced the viceroyalty of Peru to Peru, Charcas, and Chile.

Viceroys were to serve as the monarch's alter ego and, as such, lived in palaces surrounded by retainers. As the chief executive, a viceroy presided over the *audiencia* located in his capital; had ultimate responsibility for the receipt, expenditure, and remission to Spain of tax revenues; served as commander in chief of the military; exercised royal patronage over the church; was charged with the settlement and economic development of his territory; and was responsible for the humane treatment of the native population.

From 1535 to 1808, the crown gave regular appointments to ninety-two men for the posts of viceroy. In the beginning, it named men of impeccable social standing and demonstrated ability. Many viceroys had titles of nobility, claimed military qualifications, and belonged to military orders. When the extension of European conflicts to the New World led the crown to emphasize military ability, especially in the eighteenth century, the social background of viceroys declined. In general, the greater weight given to ability over birth resulted in viceroys who, as a group, served satisfactorily in their posts.

Viceroys were named for a limited tenure, in contrast with *audiencia* ministers. The average tenure in office of seventeenth- and eighteenth-century viceroys in New Spain and Peru was between six and seven years. With only a few exceptions, viceroys were men born and reared in Spain.

The title "viceroy" was also used in Brazil beginning in 1720, but the authority of the office was normally limited to a captaincy-general. Rio de Janeiro replaced Bahia as the viceregal capital in 1763.

See also **Spanish Empire.**

BIBLIOGRAPHY

Clarence H. Haring, *Spanish Empire in America* (1947).

Dauril Alden, *Royal Government in Colonial Brazil* (1968).

Mark A. Burkholder, "Bureaucrats," in *Cities and Society in Colonial Latin America*, edited by Louisa Schell Hoberman and Susan Migden Socolow (1986).

Additional Bibliography

Barrios, Feliciano. *El gobierno de un mundo: Virreinatos y audiencias en la América hispánica.* Cuenca, Ecuador: Ediciones de la Universidad de Castilla-La Mancha, 2004.

Cañeque, Alejandro. *The King's Living Image: The Culture and Politics of Viceregal Power in Colonial Mexico.* New York: Routledge, 2004.

Zimmerman, Arthur Franklin. *Francisco de Toledo: Fifth Viceroy of Peru, 1569–1581.* New York: Greenwood Press, 1968, especially chapters IV, V, VI, VII, VIII.

MARK A. BURKHOLDER

VICOS PROJECT. Vicos Project, a controversial experiment in applied anthropology in the 1950s and the 1960s in the department of Ancash, in the north–central Andes of Peru. In 1951, Cornell University–based scholars, under an agreement with Peruvian authorities, rented the publicly owned hacienda of Vicos with the intention of improving the lives of the peasants and conducting research. Storerooms, a school, and a clinic were built; basic medical care was provided; and modern agriculture and marketing techniques were taught. In 1962, the estate was sold to the peasants. Some scholars have questioned the objectives and/or results of the Cornell–Peru Project. The Vicos experiment influenced the 1969 agrarian reform.

See also **Anthropology.**

BIBLIOGRAPHY

Henry F. Dobyns, Paul L. Doughty, and Harold D. Lasswell, eds., *Peasants, Power, and Applied Social Change* (1971).

Barbara D. Lynch, *The Vicos Experiment: A Study of the Impacts of the Cornell-Peru Project in a Highland Community* (1982).

William W. Stein, "Reflexiones críticas sobre el Proyecto Peru–Cornell," in *Revista del Museo Nacional* (Lima), 48 (1986–1987): 287–316.

Additional Bibliography

Stein, William W. *Deconstructing Development Discourse in Peru: A Meta-ethnography of the Modernity Project at Vicos.* Lanham, MD: University Press of America, 2003.

CHARLES F. WALKER

VICTORIA, GUADALUPE (1785–1842).

Guadalupe Victoria (*b.* 29 September 1785; *d.* 21 March 1842), Mexican revolutionary leader and president (1824–1829). Born in Tamazula, Durango, under the name Miguel Fernández y Félix, he studied law at the College of San Ildefonso but abandoned his studies in 1811 to join Morelos's forces, changing his name to Guadalupe Victoria in honor of the Mexican Virgin and for victory. He emerged as one of the major insurgent leaders after Morelos was killed.

Accepting the Plan of Iguala in 1821, Victoria was soon jailed for his opposition to Emperor Iturbide. In 1824 he became Mexico's first president. Although he attempted to consolidate the new government by avoiding excesses and refusing to side with either the *Escoceses* (Scottish rite Masons) or the *Yorkinos* (York rite Masons), he proved unable to transfer his office peacefully to Manuel Gómez Pedraza in 1829. Victoria's administration suffered from lack of funds and an inability to control the radical mass politics that divided the nation. Thereafter, he retired from public life because of chronic illness.

See also **Plan of Iguala.**

BIBLIOGRAPHY

Romeo Flores Caballero, *Counterrevolution: The Role of the Spaniards in the Independence of Mexico* (1974), pp. 47–124.

Michael P. Costeloe, *La Primera República Federal de México, 1824–1835* (1975), pp. 11–216.

Stanley C. Green, *The Mexican Republic: The First Decade, 1823–1832* (1987), pp. 41–161.

Elmer W. Flacus, "Guadalupe Victoria: Mexican Patriot and First President" (diss., University of Texas, 1951).

Jaime E. Rodríguez O., "Mexico's First Foreign Loans," in his *The Independence of Mexico and the Creation of the New Nation* (1989), pp. 215–235.

Additional Bibliography

Briseño Senosiain, Lillian, María Laura Solares Robles, and Laura Suárez de la Torre. *Guadalupe Victoria, primer presidente de México, 1786-1843.* Mexico City: Secretaría de Educación Pública: Instituto de Investigaciones Dr. José María Luis Mora, 1986.

Campa Mendoza, Víctor. *Homenaje al general Guadalupe Victoria: Primer presidente constitucional de los Estados Unidos Mexicanos.* Durango, Mexico: Instituto Tecnológico de Durango, 2004.

JAIME E. RODRÍGUEZ O.

VICTORIA, MANUEL (?–1832).

Manuel Victoria (*d.* after 1832), governor of Baja California (1829–1831) and Alta California (1831–1832). Lieute-nant Colonel Victoria was very unpopular during his brief administration for seeking to abolish the *ayuntamientos* (town councils) in Alta California and to replace the local politicians with military rule. Victoria was overthrown in a revolt of his own troops and immediately recalled to Mexico. His overthrow led to greater autonomy in Alta California.

See also **Baja California.**

BIBLIOGRAPHY

David J. Weber, *The Mexican Frontier, 1821–1846: The American Southwest Under Mexico* (1982).

ROBERT H. JACKSON

VICUÑA. *See* Llama.

VICUÑA LARRAÍN, FRANCISCO RAMÓN (c. 1775–1849).

Francisco Ramón Vicuña Larraín (*b.* c. 1775; *d.* 13 January 1849), Chilean Liberal politician. A prominent personality in the congresses and governments of the 1820s, Vicuña Larraín was president of the Senate in 1829 and in that capacity was the first to become acting president of the republic while President Francisco

Antonio Pinto (1775–1858) recuperated from an illness (July 1829). In September 1829 an irregularity in the election of the vice president by congress (which selected a Liberal in spite of the fact that a Conservative had won a plurality of votes) provoked the successful Conservative rebellion that over the next few months destroyed the Liberal regime and inaugurated a long period of Conservative hegemony (1830–1857). Vicuña Larraín, who continued as acting president following Pinto's final withdrawal from office, was powerless to stem the tide: on 7 November 1829 a public tumult in Santiago forced him to hand power over to a junta headed by General Ramón Freire (1787–1851). With the presidential sash hidden in a hat, Vicuña Larraín withdrew to Valparaíso and from there to Coquimbo, where he was captured when the province fell into Conservative hands. He was the brother of Manuel Vicuña Larraín (1777?–1843), first archbishop of Santiago; father of the Liberal politician Pedro Félix Vicuña Aguirre (1806–1874); and grandfather of the brilliant writer-politician Benjamín Vicuña Mackenna (1831–1886).

See also **Chile: The Nineteenth Century.**

BIBLIOGRAPHY

Diego Barras Arana, *Historia general de Chile* (1884–1902), vol. 15.

Additional Bibliography

Vicuña, Carlos. *Biografía de don Francisco Ramón de Vicuña y Larraín: Conferencia leída en la Sociedad Chilena de Historia y Geografía.* Santiago de Chile: Imp. Universitaria, 1913.

SIMON COLLIER

VICUÑA MACKENNA, BENJAMIN

(1831–1886). Benjamin Vicuña Mackenna (*b.* 25 August 1831; *d.* 25 January 1886), Chilean lawyer, politician, and historian. The son of an eccentric intellectual father, Vicuña Mackenna was educated at the University of Chile. He became involved in politics while still a student, achieving the distinction of being jailed by the Manuel Montt administration for participating in the 1851 revolution. Following that abortive struggle, Vicuña Mackenna traveled abroad, then returned to Chile, only to be exiled a second time. Following the 1861 conclusion

of Montt's administration, Vicuña Mackenna successfully ran for the legislature, where he served as both a deputy and a senator.

During Chile's ill-fated war against Spain in the mid-1860s, Vicuña Mackenna traveled to the United States, where he attempted to purchase weapons. In the early 1870s, as the provincial governor of Santiago, he instituted various programs to beautify the city. After Federico Errázuriz prevented him from receiving the Liberal Party's 1876 nomination for president, Vicuña Mackenna ran as a candidate of the Liberal Democratic Party, an organization he created. Although he campaigned throughout the country, it became clear that the Liberal political machine had rigged the election in favor of Aníbal Pinto. Consequently, Vicuña Mackenna withdrew his nomination, although he continued to serve in the Senate.

An avowed nationalist, Vicuña Mackenna had many firm opinions, which he never hesitated to share, either in the press or the halls of Congress. In addition to his political career, he proved to be an extremely prolific writer. He wrote for numerous newspapers as well as authored dozens of books, many of them valuable monographs, on a variety of economic and historical topics.

See also **Chile, Political Parties: Liberal Party; Montt Torres, Manuel.**

BIBLIOGRAPHY

Luis Galdames, *A History of Chile* (1941), pp. 166, 315, 320, 353–354, 426.

Eugenio Orrego Vicuña, *Vicuña Mackenna, vida y trabajos,* 3d. ed. (1951).

Additional Bibliography

Gazmuri Riveros, Cristián. *Tres hombres tres obras.* Santiago de Chile: Editorial Sudamericana: Centro de Investigaciones Diego Barros Arana, 2004.

Gazmuri Riveros, Cristián, Manuel Loyola, and Sergio Grez Toso. *Los proyectos nacionales en el pensamiento político y social chileno del siglo XIX.* Santiago de Chile: Ediciones UCSH, 2002.

Vicuña Urrutia, Manuel. *El País americano: La oligarquía chilena como actor urbano en el siglo XIX* Santiago: Universidad Finis Terrae: Museo Histórico Nacional, 1996.

WILLIAM F. SATER

VICÚS. The Vicús culture inhabited the upper Piura Valley on the far north coast of Peru. It is believed that the Vicús culture began at about 100 CE and continued until between 500 and 700 CE. Until the late 1980s, most archaeological materials of this culture were ceramics excavated by grave robbers in search of gold. Early scientific work was restricted to the study of a small number of tombs. The Upper Piura Archaeological Project (1987–1990) worked the area between Cerro Vicús and Loma Negra, excavating public and domestic architecture. A large ceremonial site dating to the Vicús culture was found at Cerro Vicús. This complex features a large trapezoidal structure that has a central ramp and four terrace levels that ascend the central structure.

The public architecture is composed of wooden posts set in rows at about sixteen-inch intervals. They are joined by braided cord and a framework of cane on both sides of the logs. This frame is filled with clay mortar that was pushed into it, leaving finger and cloth impressions in the mud. Vicús domestic architecture is rectangular in shape and is built of logs and perhaps wattle and daub.

Vicús ceramics exhibit influences from the Ecuadorian coast, southern Colombia, and the contemporaneous Gallinazo and Moche cultures of the north coast of Peru. They are best known for their negative, or resist, painted and burnished surfaces as well as vessels of white paint on red clay. A three-phase sequence has been proposed for the Vicús style. White paint on red clay is present throughout the sequence, negative painting is absent during the first phase, and it appears in very scarce quantities during the second phase of the Vicús sequence. The second phase also marks the introduction of modeling techniques that exhibit close ties to the Gallinazo style. A marked presence of Gallinazo-related negative painting and Moche-style artifacts are only present in the last phase.

The relationship between the Vicús, Gallinazo, and Moche cultures is one of the most pressing areas of archaeological inquiry on the far north coast of Peru. This is because Gallinazo- and Moche-related materials are mixed in the same artifact assemblages, and because it is very difficult to assign the Moche-related materials to a specific temporal phase.

See also **Archaeology; Gallinazo; Moche.**

BIBLIOGRAPHY

Burger, Richard L. "Current Research: Andean South America." *American Antiquity* 54, no. 1 (1989): 187–194.

Burger, Richard L. "Current Research: Andean South America." *American Antiquity* 55, no. 1 (1990): 172–179.

Kaulicke, Peter. "El periodo intermedio temprano en el Alto Piura: Avances del proyecto arqueologico 'Alto Piura' (1987–1990)." *Bulletin de l'Institut Français d'Études Andines* 20, no. 2 (1991): 381–422.

HEIDY P. FOGEL

VIDAURRI, SANTIAGO (1808–1867). Santiago Vidaurri (*b*. 25 July 1808; *d*. 8 July 1867), governor of the state of Nuevo León–Coahuila, Mexico (1855–1865). Born in Lampazos (Nuevo León) near the United States border, Vidaurri was one of the most outstanding leaders of northern Mexico. While secretary of the Nuevo León government in 1855, he rebelled against President Antonio López de Santa Anna and became one of the stalwarts of liberalism in the northeast. On 23 May 1855 he occupied Monterrey, the capital of Nuevo León. Two days later he revealed the Plan Restaurador de la Libertad (Plan for the Restoration of Freedom), which announced his support for the republican cause. On orders from the Northern Army, he took possession of Saltillo, the capital of Coahuila, on 23 July 1855. From then until his dismissal by President Benito Juárez, he governed both states, which he formally united on 19 February 1856. His military and political hegemony extended to Tamaulipas, where the border and maritime customhouses proved to be strategic. During his administration, he furnished customhouses on the Río Bravo, instituted the so-called Vidaurri tariff, and maintained strong liberal trade policies. This program won him the support of merchants from Monterrey, other areas of the northeast, and from Texas, and helped him amass substantial resources for supporting armed forces under his control, which he used to defend liberalism and maintain his own regional power.

The Vidaurri era, which coincided with the Civil War in the United States, laid the foundation for the future economic and industrial development of Monterrey. Vidaurri's autocratic behavior and harsh exploitation of the customhouses provoked a crisis with Juárez, which exploded in the beginning of 1864. In order to subdue Vidaurri, Juárez decreed the separation of Nuevo León and Coahuila on 16 February and imposed martial law. In March, Vidaurri abdicated and left the country. Some time later he joined the empire of Maximilian. He was named *consejero* (adviser), *ministro de hacienda* (chancellor of the exchequer), and commander of one of Maximilian's brigades. Vidaurri was captured in Mexico City when the French forces were defeated. Porfirio Díaz ordered his execution by firing squad.

See also **Díaz, Porfirio; Nuevo Léon.**

BIBLIOGRAPHY

Israel Cavazos Garza, *Diccionario biográfico de Nuevo León* (1984).

Mario Cerutti, *Economía de guerra y poder regional en el siglo XIX: Gastos militares, aduanas y commerciantes en años de Vidaurri (1855–1864)* (1983).

Additional Bibliography

Berrueto Ramón, Federico. *Tres vidas.* Saltillo, Mexico: Universidad Autónoma de Coahuila, 2003.

Gálvez Medrano, Arturo. *Santiago Vidaurri: Exaltación del regionalismo nuevoleonés.* Monterrey, Mexico: Edición Facsimilar, 2000.

Gálvez Medrano, Arturo. *Regionalismo y gobierno general: El caso de Nuevo León y Coahuila, 1855–1864.* Monterrey, Mexico: Gobierno del Estado de Nuevo León, Secretaría General, AGENL, 1993.

Tyler, Ronnie C. *Santiago Vidaurri y la confederación sureña.* Monterrey, Mexico: AGENL, 2002.

MARIO CERUTTI

VIDELA, JORGE RAFAEL (1925–).

Jorge Rafael Videla (*b.* 2 August 1925), military leader and president of Argentina (1976–1981). Born in Mercedes, province of Buenos Aires, he graduated from the Military Academy (Colegio Militar) in 1944. During his early career he was rewarded with assignments of significant responsibility and educational opportunity. In 1954 he graduated from the Senior War College, and he became the director of the Military Academy in 1971. Two years later Videla was promoted to chief of the General Staff, the number two position in the army. In 1975, General Videla was elevated to commander in chief of the Argentine Army.

These were trying times for Argentina. Juan Perón died on 1 July 1974 and his wife, María Estela Martínez de Perón, a political novice, succeeded him. Urban guerrilla violence increased significantly; kidnappings, assassinations, and car bombings were common. Also, the country was staggering under triple-digit inflation. On 24 March 1976 the Argentine armed forces seized control of the government. General Videla emerged as its leader and was declared president of the republic.

Videla carried out an aggressive war against the guerrillas. He retired in 1981, turning the government over to his handpicked successor, General Roberto Viola. Videla and other members of the military juntas that ruled between 1976 and 1982 were tried for excesses committed during what became known as the Dirty War. The defendants were charged with imprisonment without charge, torture, and executions. On 9 December 1985 Videla was convicted and sentenced to life in prison. In December 1990 he was released under a general amnesty. In 1998 his amnesty was revoked, and he spent thirty-eight days imprisoned in the old Caseros Prison, convicted of kidnapping minors during the Dirty War. His sentence was later changed to house arrest due to his poor health. Ever since the 2003 election of President Néstor Kirchner, the Argentinean government has sought to prove that Videla was not a legal president of the country. In September 2006 a federal judge decided that the pardon which had been granted to him in 1990 was unconstitutional. On 25 April 2007 he was reconvicted of human rights abuses.

See also **Dirty War; Kirchner, Nestor; Viola, Roberto Eduardo.**

BIBLIOGRAPHY

Susan Calvert and Peter Calvert, *Argentina: Political Culture of Instability* (1989).

Martin Edwin Andersen, *Dossier Secreto* (1993).

Additional Bibliography

Gasparini, Juan. *Mujeres de dictadores: Perfiles de Fidel Castro, Augusto Pinochet, Ferdinand Marcos, Alberto Fujimori, Jorge Rafael Videla i Slobodan Milosevic a través de los retratos de sus mujeres.* Barcelona, Spain: Península Ediciones, 2002.

Seoane, María, and Vicente Muleiro. *El dictador: La historia secreta y pública de Jorge Rafael Videla.* Buenos Aires: Editorial Sudamericana, 2001.

Túrolo, Carlos M. *De Isabel a Videla: Los pliegues del poder.* Buenos Aires: Editorial Sudamericana, 1996.

Verbitsky, Horacio. *Doble juego: Al Argentina católica y militar.* Buenos Aires: Editorial Sudamericana, 2006.

ROBERT SCHEINA

VIEIRA, ANTÔNIO (1608–1697).

Antônio Vieira (February 6, 1608–July 18, 1697) was a Jesuit missionary, preacher, writer, and diplomat. Born in Lisbon and taken as a child to Bahia, Brazil, Vieira went to live in that city's Jesuit college at the age of fifteen. It was during his novitiate that Vieira embraced the missionary vocation that would guide him throughout his life. He learned Tupi-Guaraní and spent most of the 1630s as a missionary in Bahia. The earliest of Vieira's published sermons was preached in 1633 to an audience of black slaves at a Bahia sugar mill. Vieira reluctantly accepted the "necessity" of replacing Indian slaves with African slaves in Brazil, arguing that Indians were unable to withstand the backbreaking labor to which the Portuguese subjected them. Vieira criticized the abuses committed by owners of African slaves, but he never developed a comprehensive condemnation of African slavery like the one he produced in his sermons and letters on Indian slavery.

In 1641 Vieira was sent to Lisbon by the viceroy in Bahia to express the support of the Brazilian colony for King João IV following the Portuguese Restoration. He soon became the favorite preacher at court and a confidant of the king, who dispatched him on a series of diplomatic missions to Amsterdam and Rome. During the 1640s Vieira put forward a series of controversial proposals designed to limit the power of the Inquisition, to encourage New Christian merchants to invest in Portuguese commercial enterprises, and to cede Pernambuco to the Dutch. For the latter initiative Vieira was vilified as "the Judas of Brazil."

Vieira returned to Brazil in 1653 as superior of the Jesuit missions in the Amazon. Relations between the Jesuits and settlers there were strained by the missionaries' control over the distribution of Indian workers to Europeans. João IV gave Vieira the additional task of curbing the notorious slaving expeditions the Portuguese were conducting in the Amazon. From his base in São Luís do Maranhão, Vieira worked to improve relations between the Jesuits and the settlers while leading a series of highly successful missionary expeditions in the backlands of the Amazon. Seeking to enforce crown legislation protecting the Indians from enslavement, Vieira preached in a 1653 sermon to the settlers in São Luís:

> Do you know, Christians . . . what fast God desires from you this Lent? That you loose the bonds of injustice, and that you let those whom you hold captive and oppressed go free. These are the sins of Maranhão. These are the sins that God sends me to announce to you: "Announce to my people their rebellion" (Isaiah 58:1). Christians, God sends me to undeceive you, and I undeceive you on the part of God. You are all in a state of mortal sin. You all live and die in a state of damnation and go directly to hell. Already many [settlers] are there, and you too will soon be with them unless you change your lives." (*Sermões*, 12:327)

Unable to prevent the enslavement of the Indians, Vieira returned briefly to Portugal in 1655 to present his case against the settlers at court. Soon after his arrival in Lisbon, Vieira preached his most famous sermon, the "Sermão da Sexagésima," from the pulpit of the royal chapel. In it he attacked the homiletic conventions of the day and the idleness of the clergy in Portugal, particularly that of the Jesuits' rivals, the Dominicans. Sounding one of the central themes of his writings, Vieira argued that work in the overseas missions was the highest service a priest could render to the Church.

Tensions with the settlers persisted after Vieira's return to Maranhão. In what proved to be the turning point of his missionary career, rebellious settlers expelled Vieira and his fellow Jesuits from the Amazon in 1661 and sent them back to Lisbon. Vieira gradually abandoned his effort to promote the peaceful incorporation of the Indians into colonial society. During the latter part of his career Vieira worked to protect the Indians by separating them from the settler communities as completely as possible.

While in the Amazon, Vieira wrote *Esperanças de Portugal* (1659), a privately circulated prophetic treatise that was to provide the pretext for his arrest in 1663 by the Inquisition. Vieira for many years criticized the Inquisition on both religious and socioeconomic grounds. He was an equally vigorous critic of the Church hierarchy, and with the death of João IV in 1656 he was no longer protected from retribution. Drawing on traditional Jewish messianism and apocalyptic folk beliefs then current in Portugal, Vieira developed—in *Esperanças* and his subsequent defense before the tribunal, as well as in later writings such as *História do futuro*—a millenarian interpretation of Portuguese history that placed ever greater emphasis on the crown and the Jesuits as agents of divine providence. Vieira spent five years in prison or under house arrest. Following his release by the Inquisition in 1668, he had a successful sojourn as a preacher in Rome before returning to Brazil in 1681. During the last years of his life he served again as a Jesuit administrator, edited his sermons for publication, and wrote *Clavis Prophetarum*, a treatise left unfinished at his death. Vieira continues to be considered one of the greatest writers in the Portuguese language and a central figure in the religious and political history of the Luso-Brazilian world.

See also **Bahía; Inquisition: Brazil; Jesuits; João IV of Portugal; Tupi-Guarani.**

BIBLIOGRAPHY

Works by Vieira

Cartas do Padre Antônio Vieira, 3 vols, ed. João Lúcio d'Azevedo. Coimbra, Portugal: Imprensa da Universidade, 1925–1928.

Sermões, 16 vols, ed. Augusto Magne, S.J. São Paulo: Editora Anchieta, 1943–1945.

Obras Escolhidas, 12 vols, ed. Hernani Cidade and Antônio Sérgio. Lisbon: Livraria Sá da Costa Editora, 1951–1954.

Defesa Perante o Tribunal do Santo Ofício, 2 vols, ed. Hernani Cidade. Salvador, Bahia, Brazil: Publicações da Universidade da Bahia, 1957.

Livro Anteprimeiro da História do Futuro, 2 vols, ed. José van den Besselaar. Münster, Germany: Aschendorffsche Verlagsbuchhandlung, 1976.

Apologia das coisas profetizadas, ed. Adma Muhana. Edições Cotovia, 1994.

Os autos do processo de Vieira na Inquisição, ed. Adma Muhana. São Paulo: Editora da Universidade Estadual Paulista; Salvador, Bahia: Fundação Cultural do Estado da Bahia, 1995.

Clavis Prophetarum. Book III (Bilingual Latin and Portuguese), trans. Arnoldo de Espírito Santo. Lisbon: Biblioteca Nacional, 2000.

"Two Slaveries: The Sermons of Padre Antúnio Vieira, Salvador, Bahia (ca.1633) and So Luis do Maranho (1653)" [in English]. In *Colonial Latin America: A Documentary History*, ed. Kenneth Mills, William B. Taylor, and Sandra Lauderdale Graham. Wilmington, DE: Scholarly Resources, 2002.

Secondary Sources

Boxer, Charles R. *A Great Luso-Brazilian Figure: Padre Antônio Vieira*. London: Hispanic and Luso-Brazilian Councils, 1957.

Cohen, Thomas M. *The Fire of Tongues: António Vieira and the Missionary Church in Brazil and Portugal*. Stanford, CA: Stanford University Press, 1998.

D'Azevedo, João Lúcio. *História de Antônio Vieira*. 2 vols. Lisbon: Livraria Clássica Editora, 1918–1920.

THOMAS M. COHEN

VIEIRA, JOSÉ CARLOS DO AMARAL

(1952–). José Carlos do Amaral Vieira (*b.* 2 March 1952), Brazilian composer and pianist. Amaral Vieira was better known as a pianist until 1984, when an Amaral Vieira Festival featuring an amazing diversity of musical works by the young composer was held in São Paulo. The festival included fourteen concerts during which 157 works by Vieira were performed. When Vieira later announced his intention to record the complete piano works and transcriptions of Franz Liszt, a project that would require seventy compact discs to complete, and it became obvious that no commercial company would undertake this vast project, Vieira established Scorpio, his own recording label. New musical works and vast projects appear to blossom forth from his fertile mind and nimble fingers with incredible rapidity. In a nation in which Heitor Villa-Lobos established a tradition of explosive creativity with more than one thousand musical works, Vieira is attempting to surpass his predecessors. Vieira's compositional style in works such as *Elegy, Nocturne and Toccata* (for piano [1980]), and *Variações Fausto* (a set of variations in fantasia form on a theme of Franz Liszt's *Faust Symphony* [1985]) shows his ability to write brilliantly for the piano and his intense involvement with the compositional style of Franz Liszt. From 1993 to 1995 and from 1998 to 2002 he was president of the Brazilian Contemporary Music Society. In 2000, he became a member of the Brazilian Academy of Music. In 2001, he became president of the Drama and Music Conservatory Foundation of São Paulo.

See also **Music: Art Music.**

BIBLIOGRAPHY

Additional Bibliography

Chase, Robert. *A Guide to Contemporary Memorial Music.* Lanham, MD: Scarecrow Press, 2007.

Sher, Chuck, ed. *The Latin Real Book: The Best Contemporary and Classic Salsa, Brazilian Music, Latin Jazz.* Petaluma, CA: Sher Music Co., 1997.

DAVID P. APPLEBY

VIEQUES PROTESTS.

The Vieques protests took place from 1999 through 2003 on the Puerto Rican island of Vieques, thirteen miles east of the main island. Since the early 1940s, the United States Navy and Marine Corps had maintained a base on Vieques for the testing of bombs and practicing bombing techniques. Locals began to protest activities at the base after the accidental death of a Vieques civilian, David Sanes, on 19 April 1999. The Vieques bombings became a flash point for those who opposed Puerto Rico's status as a commonwealth of the United States.

Locals began to engage in acts of civil disobedience on the testing grounds, eventually building encampments in the hopes of impeding naval bombing. Their cause gained international support from such well-known figures as the environmental lawyer Robert F. Kennedy Jr., the civil rights activist Jesse Jackson, and Guatemalan Nobel Prize Prize winner Rigoberta Menchú. On 4 May 2000, U.S. Marines forcibly evacuated the encampments in order to put an end to the protests, but five days later hundreds of demonstrators returned to the site and refused to leave until the United States announced it would vacate Vieques. In May 2003 the U.S. Navy withdrew; much of the island was designated a wildlife reserve and placed under the control of the U.S. Fish and Wildlife Service.

See also **Puerto Rico, Geography; United States-Latin American Relations.**

BIBLIOGRAPHY

Grosfoguel, Ramón. *Colonial Subjects: Puerto Ricans in a Global Perspective.* Berkeley: University of California Press, 2003.

McCaffrey, Katherine T. *Military Power and Popular Protest: The U.S. Navy in Vieques, Puerto Rico.* New Brunswick, NJ: Rutgers University Press, 2002.

Pérez Viera, Edgardo. *Victoria de un pueblo: Crónica del grito de Vieques.* San Juan, P.R.: Editorial Cultural, 2002.

EMILY BERQUIST

VIERA, FELICIANO (1872–1927).

Feliciano Viera (*b.* 8 November 1872; *d.* 13 November 1927), president of Uruguay (1915–1919). Viera was the son of a veteran colonel of the Colorados who fought in the internal wars of Uruguay. At first a proponent of Batllismo, he separated from the main body of this group and gave rise to a splinter faction known as Vierismo. More conservative than José Batlle and his reformist followers, Viera maintained a popular and charismatic style. After the failure of the Batllist constitutional project at the polls in 1916, Viera became the main force behind a movement to halt the social reforms that had characterized previous periods. In this way, Viera obtained a vote of confidence from the conservatives, which he in fact never betrayed. The political faction his actions had generated lost relevance with his death.

See also **Batllismo.**

BIBLIOGRAPHY

Milton Vanger, *The Model Country: Batlle of Uruguay* (1980).

José P. Barrán and Benjamín Nahum, *La derrota del batllismo, 1916* (1987).

FERNANDO FILGUEIRA

VIEYTES, HIPÓLITO (1762–1815).

Hipólito Vieytes (*b.* 12 August 1762; *d.* 5 October 1815), journalist and political figure of Argentine independence. Born in San Antonio de Areco, Buenos Aires Province, Vieytes attended the well-known Real Colegio de San Carlos, where he studied law and philosophy. Committed to physiocratic doctrines and to the promotion of useful works, he spread his views by establishing various newspapers, including the *Semanario de Agricul-tura, Industria y Comercio* in 1802, and collaborated with Manuel

Belgrano on *El Correo de Comercio* in 1810. Many scholars credit Vieytes with the inception of modern journalism in his country. Vieytes served in the capital as police superintendent and representative to the General Constituent Assembly in 1813. Though he is regarded as one of the intellectual authors of the Argentine independence movement, he eventually succumbed to the political instabilities of the time. Vieytes was arrested and exiled in 1815 after the overthrow of Supreme Director Carlos María de Alvear. He died in San Fernando shortly thereafter.

See also **Journalism.**

BIBLIOGRAPHY

Alberto Reyna Almandos, *Claros orígenes de la democracia argentina* (1957).

Arturo Capdevila, *Vidas de grandes argentinos,* vol. 3 (1966), pp. 313–317.

Additional Bibliography

Cordero, Héctor Adolfo. *Juan Hipólito Vieytes en la historia de la lucha por la independencia argentina.* Buenos Aires: Instituto de Estudios Históricos de San Fernando de Buena Vista, 1997.

FIDEL IGLESIAS

VIGIL, DONACIANO (1802–1877).

Donaciano Vigil (*b.* 6 September 1802; *d.* 11 August 1877), governor of New Mexico (1847–1848). Vigil was a popular and well-educated native New Mexican. In New Mexico's Revolution of 1837, Vigil was captured at La Cañada by the revolutionists and appointed secretary for the rebel government. While questions were raised about his loyalty, he was later cleared of any misconduct. In the 1830s and 1840s, Vigil served as a member of the departmental assembly, editor of a Spanish newspaper in New Mexico, and military secretary under governor Manuel Armijo. When the United States occupied New Mexico in 1846, General Stephen W. Kearny appointed him secretary of the territory and upon the assassination of Charles Bent (*d.* 1847) in Taos, Vigil became governor. An antimilitarist, Vigil proclaimed the first elections in the territory under U.S. rule. Later, he served in the territorial legislature.

See also **New Mexico.**

BIBLIOGRAPHY

Stanley Crocchiola, *Giant in Lilliput: The Story of Donaciano Vigil* (1963).

Ralph Emerson Twitchell, *The History of the Military Occupation of the Territory of New Mexico from 1846 to 1851* (1909), pp. 207–228.

Janet Lecompte, *Rebellion in Rio Arriba, 1837* (1985), esp. pp. 13–16, 40–61.

Additional Bibliography

Salazar, J. Richard. *The Military Career of Donaciano Vigil.* Guadalupita, NM: Center for Land Grant Studies, 1994.

Vigil, Donaciano, and David J. Weber. *Arms, Indians, and the Mismanagement of New Mexico.* El Paso: Texas Western Press, University of Texas at El Paso, 1986.

AARON PAINE MAHR

VIGIL, FRANCISCO DE PAULA GONZÁLEZ (1792–1875).

Francisco de Paula González Vigil (*b.* 13 September 1792; *d.* 9 June 1875), Peruvian priest, liberal politician, and author. Vigil rose to prominence in the early post-Independence era for his 1832 attack on presidential usurpation of constitutional authority. In 1834 he presided over the liberal National Convention, and in 1836 he helped prevent Bolivian annexation of his native Tacna. From 1845, Vigil served as director of Peru's National Library, writing voluminously on church-state relations and national reform. Influenced by Enlightenment thought, Vigil extolled the virtues of reason, freedom of conscience, republicanism, education, and work. His religious dissertations provoked condemnation by the church for their assertion of the authority of national churches over the Roman Curia.

See also **Anticlericalism; Libraries in Latin America.**

BIBLIOGRAPHY

Jorge Basadre, "Homenaje: Francisco de Paula González Vigil," in *Textual* 10 (October 1975): 13–23.

Jeffrey L. Klaiber, *Religion and Revolution in Peru, 1824–1976* (1977).

Additional Bibliography

Broadhurst, John Christian. "Francisco de Paula González Vigil: Peruvian pensador." Ph.D. diss., University of Virginia, 1974.

MATTHEW J. O' MEAGHER

VILA. Vila, incorporated township of the Portuguese Empire. The first *vila* in Brazil was established in São Vicente in 1532. By 1650, only thirty-seven more *vilas* and cities had been founded, seven by the crown and the remainder by local initiative. The *vila* incorporated both secular and ecclesiastical power as the site of the town council and church. Town councils (*câmaras municipais; Senados Da Câmara*) consisted of elected councilmen, justices of the peace, and the procurator; appointed auxiliary employees. After 1696, a crown magistrate (*juiz de fora*) was added. Town councils exercised broad local powers including taxation, price setting, market supervision, hygiene standards, law enforcement, and public works. During the colonial period, councils overstepped their formal boundaries and even overruled viceroys and governors. Their political and judicial powers were curtailed under the empire in 1828.

See also **Cities and Urbanization; Portuguese Empire.**

BIBLIOGRAPHY

Charles R. Boxer, *Portuguese Society in the Tropics: The Municipal Councils of Goa, Macao, Bahia, and Luanda, 1510–1800* (1965).

A. J. R. Russell-Wood, "Local Government in Portuguese America: A Study in Cultural Divergence," in *Comparative Studies in Society and History* 16 (March 1974): 187–231.

Richard M. Morse, "Brazil's Urban Development: Colony and Empire," in *From Colony to Nation: Essays on the Independence of Brazil,* edited by A. J. R. Russell-Wood (1975).

Additional Bibliography

Centurião, Luiz Ricardo Michaelsen. *A cidade colonial no Brasil.* Porto Alegre, Brazil: EDIPUCRS, 1999.

JUDY BIEBER FREITAS

VILAR, MANUEL (1812–1860). Manuel Vilar (*b.* 15 November 1812; *d.* 25 November 1860), sculptor. Trained in his native Barcelona and Rome, Vilar was chosen as director of sculpture when the Academia de San Carlos in Mexico City was reestablished. He arrived in 1846. Vilar had studied with Pietro Tenerani and was sympathetic to the ideals of the Nazarenes (a group of German painters who sought to revitalize Christian art). He brought to Mexico an important collection of plaster casts acquired in Rome, and worked with the energy of a believer in the redemptive value of art to revive monumental sculpture in Mexico. He produced work with themes that were classical, religious, and secular, as well as portraits. Probably his most ambitious work was a full-size bronze statue of a pre-Columbian hero, *Tlahuicole* (1851). Autographed manuscripts and many documents provide information about his life and career.

See also **Art: The Nineteenth Century.**

BIBLIOGRAPHY

Salvador Moreno, *El escultor Manuel Vilar* (1969).

CLARA BARGELLINI

VILA RICA. *See* **Ouro Prêto.**

VILARIÑO, IDEA (1920–). Idea Vilariño (*b.* 1920), Uruguayan poet and critic. She taught literature in the high school system of Montevideo, where she was born, as did many other women of her generation. She began teaching in 1984 as a humanities faculty member at the University of the Republic in Montevideo. She has written critical studies of the poetry of the Spaniard Antonio Machado, *Grupos simétricos en poesía de Antonio Machado* (1951), and the Uruguayan Julio Herrera y Reissig, *Julio Herrera y Reissig* (1950), as well as many articles on other Spanish poets. She published a thorough study on tango lyrics in *Las letras de tango* (1965). Her critical essays have appeared in *Clinamen, Asir, Hiperión, Marcha, Puente, Carte Segrete, Texto Crítico, La Opinión, Revista del Sur,* and *Brecha.* She is also an accomplished translator of Shakespeare into Spanish.

Vilariño's poetic expression is concise, with minimal utilization of rhetorical devices, and expresses a dark world, where the vital elements fail to survive. In form, her poetry is also brief, without much artifice. She has published *La suplicante* (1945), *Cielo, cielo* (1947), *Paraíso perdido* (1949), *Nocturnos* (1955), *Poemas de amor* (1957), *Pobre mundo*

(1966), *Treinta poemas* (1967), *Poesía* (1970), and *Segunda antología* and *No* (1980). She has received many prestigious awards, including the 1987 Premio a la labor intelectual José Enrique Rodó, awarded by the municipal government of Montevideo. In 1993, she was awarded a month of fellowship for the Complutense University in Madrid. In 2004, she won a Konex Award for literature.

See also **Literature: Spanish America.**

BIBLIOGRAPHY

Juan Parra Del Riego, *Nocturnos, y otros poemas* (1965).

Susana Crelis Secco, *Idea Vilariño: Poesía e identidad* (1990).

Additional Bibliography

Berry-Bravo, Judy. *Idea Vilariño: Poesía y crítica*. Montevideo, Uruguay: Ediciones de la Banda Oriental, 1999.

Berry-Bravo, Judy. *Texts and Contexts of Idea Vilariño's Poetry*. New York: Spanish Literature Publications Co., 1994.

Crelis Secco, Susana. *Idea Vilariño: Poesía e identidad*. México: UNAM, 1990.

MAGDALENA GARCÍA PINTO

Picchu had been Vilcabamba. In 1964 the American explorer Gene Savoy convincingly demonstrated that Bingham's original identification of Espiritu Pampa as the lost city of Vilcabamba was correct. Subsequent archaeological excavations have provided further confirmation.

See also **Bingham, Hiram; Incas, The; Túpac Amaru.**

BIBLIOGRAPHY

Guillén Guillén, Edmundo. "Documentos ineditos para la historia de los Incas de Vilcabamba: La capitulación del gobierno español con Titu Cusi Yupanqui." *Historia y Cultura* (Peru) 10 (1976–1977): 47–93.

Guillén Guillén, Edmundo. "Titu Cusi Yupanqui y su tiempo: El estado imperial Inka y su tragico final, 1572." *Historia y Cultura* (Peru) 13–14 (1981): 61–82.

Hemming, John. *The Conquest of the Incas: The Search for the Lost Cities of the Amazon*. New York: Harcourt, Brace, Jovanovich, 1970.

Savoy, Gene. *Antisuyo: The Search for the Lost Cities of the Amazon*. New York: Simon and Schuster, 1970.

GORDON F. MCEWAN
SUZANNE AUSTIN

VILCABAMBA.

Vilcabamba, a region in the southern highlands of Peru, also lends its name to a chain of mountains located in that area. After the Spanish conquest of Peru, Vilcabamba became the site of the last capital of the Inca state. Located in a remote area about 100 miles west of Cuzco, the city was founded by Manco Inca in 1539. During the next three decades the city served as a staging area for raids against Spanish military forces sent to capture the Inca stronghold. Following the assassination of Manco Inca in 1544, Vilcabamba was ruled by his successors, Syri Tupac, Titu Cusi Yupanqui, and finally Tupac Amaru.

After the invasion and capture of the city by the Spanish in 1572, Tupac Amaru was executed and the city abandoned, its location eventually forgotten. In the twentieth century the search for Vilcabamba was a principal preoccupation of explorers and archaeologists. Yale University professor Hiram Bingham identified the ruins at Espiritu Pampa (Quechua for Spirit Plain or Ghost Plain) as Vilcabamba in 1911. He later changed his mind and insisted that Machu

VILLA, FRANCISCO "PANCHO"

(1878–1923). Francisco "Pancho" Villa (*b.* 5 June 1878; *d.* 20 July 1923), Mexican revolutionary, general, governor of Chihuahua (1913–1915). Christened Doroteo Arango, one-time bandit and muleteer, Villa became one of the most important and controversial leaders of the Mexican Revolution (1910–1920).

The history of Villa's youth is masked in legend. He was by occupation a hacienda peon, miner, bandit, and merchant. There is a colorful story of his killing a *hacendado* who had raped his sister and his subsequent escape to banditry. Most certainly, according to biographer Friedrich Katz, he was a cattle rustler, which far from branding him an outlaw brought him a degree of popular renown. Villa eventually settled in San Andrés, Chihuahua, a village in the throes of violent protest against taxes imposed by the Chihuahua state government controlled by the Terrazas family.

In 1910 Villa joined the revolution led by Francisco I. Madero in Chihuahua. After Madero's victory in May of 1911, Villa retired to Chihuahua City, using his mustering-out money to begin a meat-packing business. He returned to military duty in 1912 to fight against the counterrevolution of Pascual Orozco, Jr. His commander, General Victoriano Huerta, ordered him executed for insubordination, but Madero intervened, sending him to prison, from which he escaped shortly thereafter. Following a few months in exile in the United States, Villa returned to avenge the overthrow and assassination of Madero by Huerta in February 1913. In March 1913 Villa crossed the Rio Grande from Texas with a handful of men. His key lieutenants came from the northern villages that had once been military colonies in the Indian wars of the eighteenth and nineteenth centuries. Toribio Ortega and Porfirio Talamantes, for example, had led their Chihuahuan villages, Cuchillo Parado and Janos, respectively, in protests against land expropriations. With his peasant-worker army, Villa conquered Chihuahua in the name of the Constitutionalist movement in 1913.

In control of Chihuahua from late 1913 through 1915, Villa expropriated the estates of the landed oligarchy and used the revenues they produced to finance his army and government. His rule in Chihuahua was an ingenious compromise between the need to satisfy the demands of the revolutionary masses for land reform and the immediate necessity of obtaining funds to win the war first against Huerta and then against his despised rival, Venustiano Carranza. He promised to distribute the confiscated properties after the triumph of the Revolution. In the meantime, these estates, some managed by his generals and others by a state agency, supported the widows and orphans of veterans and the starving unemployed of the mining and timber regions of Chihuahua, and provided the necessary funds for supplying the Villista army.

His Division of the North, led by an elite corps, the *dorados,* paved the way to Huerta's defeat. Along the way south from his initial victories in Chihuahua, Villa fought bloody battles, first at Torreón in April and then at Zacatecas in June 1914. His split with Carranza widened, however, and Villa withdrew from the campaign.

It was during the fight against Huerta that Villa first manifested his hatred for Spaniards. In Torreón he rounded them up and shipped them across the U.S. border, in the meantime confiscating their property. Later he would commit additional atrocities against them.

The Constitutionalists defeated Huerta in 1914 but almost immediately split into two factions, one led by Villa and the other by Carranza. One of the crucial issues between the two leaders was Carranza's intention to return the landed estates confiscated by the Villistas to their owners. This would have undercut much of Villa's support by depriving him of the main symbol of reform and the main source of his funds.

When a revolutionary convention met in Aguascalientes in the fall of 1914, Villa, allied with Emiliano Zapata, the peasant leader from the state of Morelos, demanded that Carranza abdicate as leader of the Revolution. When Carranza refused, Villa and Zapata declared themselves to be in armed opposition under the provisions of the convention. In November 1914 the Conventionist armies of Villa and Zapata occupied Mexico City. The Constitutionalists were in apparent disarray. The Conventionist alliance between Villa and Zapata dissipated, however, because neither of their regionally based, popular movements could sustain long-term military or political success outside its home area.

In a series of brutal battles in the center of the country in 1915 (Celaya, 6–7 April and 13–16 April; León, throughout May; Aguascalientes, 10 July), however, Villa suffered major defeats at the hands of the Carrancista general Alvaro Obregón Salido. Villa's tactics of unrelenting attack were disastrous in the face of Obregón's entrenched troops. Villa's once mighty army disintegrated. The crucial battle took place at León (also called Trinidad), where over thirty-eight days at least five thousand men died.

Villa, though badly defeated and eliminated as a major military force, stayed in the field. His prestige was irretrievably damaged and his allies rapidly defected. In late 1915 he made a desperate effort to establish a foothold in Sonora but failed when Obregón dispatched troops through the United States to reinforce Constitutionalist troops in Agua Prieta. A series of defeats followed, sending Villa back across the Sierra Madre to Chihuahua.

Villa was forced once again to adopt guerrilla tactics. Many of his aides, especially the more respectable former Maderistas, went into exile in the United States. Villa stayed and tormented the national and state governments for four years. This "second wind" of Villismo brought it back to its roots as a local, popular movement based in the sierras of Chihuahua.

In 1916 Villa responded to U.S. recognition of and cooperation with Carranza by viewing Americans with increasing hostility. One of his lieutenants murdered seventeen American engineers at Santa Isabel, Chihuahua, in January. On 8–9 March several hundred Villista raiders crossed the border into Columbus, New Mexico. Although his motives for the attack are much debated, there is some evidence Villa sought to precipitate a military intervention by the United States in order to prevent an agreement with Carranza that would have rendered Mexico a virtual protectorate of the United States.

A force led by U.S. general John J. Pershing futilely chased Villa from mid-March 1916 until early February 1917, nearly a year. After Pershing's withdrawal, for the next two years Villa periodically occupied Chihuahua's major cities, Ciudad Juárez and Hidalgo de Parral. He was able to raise armies of from one thousand to two thousand men.

Shortly after the 1920 overthrow and murder of Carranza by his own army, led by Alvaro Obregón, the interim president of Mexico, Adolfo De La Huerta, negotiated Villa's amnesty and retirement. As part of the bargain, the general obtained a large hacienda in northern Durango, Canutillo, and a substantial subsidy for himself and a retinue of his troops. In 1923 Villa was assassinated in Hidalgo de Parra, perhaps because the national regime feared he would join de la Huerta, who would rebel some months later.

See also **Chihuahua; Madero, Francisco Indalecio; Mexico, Wars and Revolutions: Mexican Revolution; Orozco, Pascual, Jr.; Zapata, Emiliano.**

BIBLIOGRAPHY

Francisco R. Almada, *Gobernadores del Estado de Chihuahua* (1980), provides the basic biographical data. See also Martín Luis Guzmán, *Memoirs of Pancho Villa*, translated by Virginia H. Taylor (1965).

Friedrich Katz, *The Secret War in Mexico* (1981), "Pancho Villa, Peasant Movements, and Agrarian Reform in Northern Mexico," in *Caudillo and Peasant in the Mexican Revolution*, edited by D. A. Brading (1980), and "Pancho Villa: Reform Governor of Chihuahua," in *Essays on the Mexican Revolution: Revisionist View of the Leaders*, edited by George W. Wolfskill (1979).

Silvestré Terrazas, *El verdadero Pancho Villa* (1984).

Additional Bibliography

Alba, Víctor. *Pancho Villa y Zapata: Águila y sol de la Revolución Mexicana*. Barcelona: Planeta, 1994.

Katz, Friedrich. *The Life and Times of Pancho Villa*. Stanford, CA: Stanford University Press, 1998.

McLynn, Frank. *Villa and Zapata: A History of the Mexican Revolution*. New York: Carroll & Graf Publishers, 2001.

Taibo, Paco Ignacio. *Pancho Villa: Una biografía narrativa*. Mexico City: Planeta, 2006.

MARK WASSERMAN

VILLACORTA CALDERÓN, JOSÉ ANTONIO (1879–1964).

José Antonio Villacorta Calderón (*b.* 1879; *d.* 22 April 1964), Guatemalan historian, anthropologist, and bibliographer. Villacorta Calderón is particularly noted for his general histories of Guatemala and his important editorial work. Significantly, he edited the Maya sacred book *Anales de los Cakchiqueles* (1937). He also compiled in his *Bibliografía guatemalteca* (1944) a complete listing of bibliographic information for all the volumes exhibited at a national exposition in honor of the anniversary of printing in Guatemala in 1939. His most famous and widely read work, *Historia de la República de Guatemala* (1960), is a detailed survey of Guatemala, from political independence from Spain to 1885, based on extensive research in secondary and archival sources. Often used as a textbook in schools, the book has been influential in shaping the historical views of countless Guatemalans. Villacorta Calderón was one of the most significant and prestigious of the shapers of academic life in twentieth-century Guatemala.

See also **Guatemala.**

BIBLIOGRAPHY

José Antonio Villacorta Calderón, *Monografía del departamento de Guatemala* (1926); *Bibliografía guatemalteca* (1944); *J. Antonio Villacorta C. en las ciencias y letras americanistas, juzgado por sus contemporáneos* (1949); and *Historia de la República de Guatemala, 1821–1921* (1960).

MICHAEL F. FRY

VILLA EL SALVADOR.

An urban residential district on the outskirts of Lima, Villa El Salvador (VES) has become an international symbol of community-based development and citizen participation. VES began in 1971 as a land invasion in the flat, sandy dunes of southern Lima to meet the needs of homeless families from Lima's slums and newly arrived migrants from the countryside. Initially a pet project of the reformist military government of Juan Velasco Alvarado, VES later became a center of left-wing organizing. From its early years, residents have mobilized to address local problems, from hunger to crime, and to demand public services such as water, electricity, and schools. VES was established as a municipal district in 1983 and in the early twenty-first century is a vast city of 380,000 residents.

See also **Cities and Urbanization; Moyano, Maria Elena.**

BIBLIOGRAPHY

Blondet, Cecilia. *Las mujeres y el poder: Una historia de Villa El Salvador*. Lima: Instituto de Estudios Peruanos, 1991.

Burt, Jo-Marie, and César Espejo. "The Struggles of a Self-Built Community in Peru." *NACLA Report on the Americas* 28, no. 4 (1995).

Zapata Velasco, Antonio. *Sociedad y Poder Local, la comunidad de Villa El Salvador 1971–1996*. Lima: DESCO, 1996.

JO-MARIE BURT

VILLAGRA, FRANCISCO DE

(c. 1512–1563). Francisco de Villagra (Villagrán; *b.* 1512?; *d.* 22 June 1563), Spanish conquistador. A soldier with experience in North Africa, Villagra went to America in 1537, and accompanied Pedro de Valdivia (1500–1553) on his expedition to Chile in 1540. During Valdivia's absence from the new colony in 1547–1548, he acted as interim governor, and in that capacity ordered the execution of Pedro Sancho De Hoz, who had plotted to seize control. In 1549 Valdivia sent him to fetch reinforcements from Peru, a mission he eventually completed after many adventures. Early in 1552, again on Valdivia's instructions, he attempted an overland expedition to the Strait of Magellan by way of the eastern side of the Andes, only to turn back at the Río Negro.

After Valdivia's death (December 1553), Villagra unsuccessfully claimed the governorship of Chile: his forcible seizure of the government was firmly resisted by the *cabildo* (municipal council) of Santiago. He remained an active leader in the warfare against the Araucanians, bringing about the defeat of the *toqui* (chief) Lautaro in 1557. It was not until the departure of governor García Hurtado De Mendoza (1535–1609) that Villagra finally secured the governorship (1561–1563). On his death it passed to his cousin Pedro de Villagra (1563–1565), a brilliant tactician, who was eventually dismissed by the viceroy of Peru.

See also **Conquistadores; Valdivia, Pedro de.**

BIBLIOGRAPHY

Reyno Gutiérrez, Manuel. *Francisco de Villagra*. Santiago, Chile: La Nación, 1984.

SIMON COLLIER

VILLAGRÁ, GASPAR PÉREZ DE

(1555–1620). Gaspar Pérez de Villagrá (*b.* 1555; *d.* 1620), soldier and chronicler. Born in New Spain, Villagrá was one of the few early creoles to study at the University of Salamanca. After his return to New Spain he was appointed *procurador general* (solicitor general) and captain in Juan de Oñate's 1596 conquest and colonization expedition to New Mexico, where Villagrá participated in many operations, including the battle of Ácoma (1599). After a visit to Spain, Villagrá published his epic poem *Historia de la Nueva México* (1610), which related the history of the Oñate expedition. Although sometimes marked by hyperbole and heroic vision, Villagrá's *Historia* remains valuable today as an eyewitness account of the conquest of New Mexico.

His literary achievement notwithstanding, shortly afterward he was found guilty of executing two deserters in New Mexico and forcibly bringing dozens of Ácoman women to convents in Spain, for which he was banished from the province for six years and from Mexico City for two years. In 1620, en route from Spain to fill a bureaucratic position in Guatemala, Villagrá died at sea.

See also **New Spain, Viceroyalty of.**

BIBLIOGRAPHY

Ralph Emerson Twitchell, *Captain Don Gaspar de Villagrá: Author of the First History of the Conquest of New Mexico by the Adelantado Don Juan de Oñate* (1924).

Gaspar Pérez De Villagrá *History of New Mexico,* translated and edited by Gilberto Espinosa (1933).

Additional Bibliography

Weber, David J., Jerry R. Craddock, John Herman Richard Polt, Gaspar Pérez de Villagrá, and Vicente de Zaldívar. *Zaldívar and the Cattle of Cíbola: Vicente de Zaldívar's Report of His Expedition to the Buffalo Plains in 1598: A Bilingual Edition.* Dallas, TX: William P. Clements Center for Southwest Studies, Southern Methodist University, 1999.

AARON PAINE MAHR

BIBLIOGRAPHY

Alejandro Villaseñor y Villaseñor, *Biografías de los héroes y caudillos de la independencia* (1962), vol. 1, pp. 110–118.

Christon I. Archer, "Banditry and Revolution in New Spain," *Bibliotheca Americana* 1, no. 2 (1982): 59–89.

Brian R. Hamnett, *Roots of Insurgency: Mexican Regions, 1750–1824* (1986).

Additional Bibliography

Broseta, Salvador. *Las ciudades y la guerra, 1750-1898.* Castelló de la Plana, Spain: Centro de Investigación de América Latina, Universitat Jaume I, 2002.

Rodríguez O., Jaime E. *El proceso de la independencia de México.* México City: Instituto Mora, 1992.

Van Young, Eric. *The Other Rebellion: Popular Violence, Ideology, and the Mexican Struggle for Independence, 1810-1821.* Stanford, CA: Stanford University Press, 2001.

Wobeser, Gisela von. *Dominación colonial: La consolidación de vales reales en Nueva España, 1804–1812.* México City: UNAM, 2003.

ERIC VAN YOUNG

VILLAGRÁN, JULIÁN AND JOSÉ MARÍA "EL CHITO".

Julián and José María ("El Chito") Villagrán, Mexican insurgents. Julián Villagrán (*b.* 1760; *d.* 21 June 1813), his son Chito (*b.* ca. 1780; *d.* 14 May 1813), and their kinsmen, clients, and allies were in many ways typical of the great creole clans of lower and middling economic position who led the insurgency in the Mexican provinces in the period 1810–1821. Julián was a muleteer, minor landowner, and sometime militia officer; Chito, a delinquent and estate foreman in their native town of Huichapán in central Mexico. Chito joined the rebellion to escape legal charges against him for the murder of a local landowner and town official with whose wife he had been amorously involved; Julián, to protect his son and to pursue vague political and economic goals. Their forces attacked or occupied a number of important provincial towns from late 1810 through mid-1813, including Huichapán, Ixmiquilpán, Zimapán, and Tulancingo. Both refused to acknowledge any higher insurgent authority in their spheres of influence; both rejected royalist pardons; and both were captured and executed in 1813.

See also **Mexico, Wars and Revolutions: War of Independence.**

VILLAGRÁN KRAMER, FRANCISCO

(1922–). Francisco Villagrán Kramer (*b.* 5 April 1922), vice president of Guatemala (1977–1980). Born in Guatemala City into a Protestant family, Francisco Villagrán earned his law degree at the University of San Carlos in 1951. Active in the October Revolution (1944), he served both Juan José Arévalo (1945–1951) and Jacobo Arbenz (1950–1954) at international conferences. He helped Mario Méndez Montenegro (1912–1965) found the Partido Revolucionario (PR) in 1957, but broke with the PR to organize the more leftist Revolutionary Unity Party (URD) in 1958.

Considered a radical, he was exiled by the Enrique Peralta Azurdia military regime (1963–1966) in 1965. The new constitution drafted that year raised the minimum age for the presidency from thirty-five to forty to specifically bar him from the 1966 elections.

Concerned about growing political polarization and violence, Villagrán returned to the PR in 1978 to become General Romeo Lucas García's (1978–1982) running mate in order to, in his words to a *Washington Post* reporter, "avoid a Custer's last stand in Guatemala." Failing to moderate the repressive character of the regime, he helped organize the Democratic Front Against Repression in 1979. He resigned as vice president in September 1980. He subsequently became a leader in the Christian Democratic Party (DCG), and also worked for the World Bank. After that, he served on the Inter-American Juridical Committee of the Organization of American States (OAS), as well as on the United Nation's International Law Commission. In 1994 he won election to the Guatemalan Congress, and he headed its committee on human rights. In 1997 he was nominated for a seat on the Inter-American Commission on Human Rights, an arm of the OAS. His nomination was controversial due to the death squads that operated in Guatemala while he served as vice president. His own son was one of those who spoke out against him, doing so in a 1997 letter to the editor of the *New York Times*.

See also **Guatemala.**

BIBLIOGRAPHY

Henry Wells, ed., *Guatemala: Election Factbook* (1966).

Carlos C. Haeussler Yela, *Diccionario General de Guatemala*, vol. 3. (1983).

Francisco Villlagrán Kramer, *Biografía política de Guatemala: Los pactos políticos de 1944 a 1970* (1993).

Additional Bibliography

Comisión para el Esclarecimiento Histórico. *Guatemala: Causas y orígenes del enfrentamiento armado interno.* Guatemala: F&G Editores, 2006.

García, Prudencio. *El genocidio de Guatemala: A la luz de la sociología militar.* Madrid: Sepha Edición y Diseño, 2005.

Grandin, Greg. *The Last Colonial Massacre: Latin America in the Cold War.* Chicago: University of Chicago Press, 2004.

Villagrán Kramer, Francisco. *Biografía política de Guatemala.* Vol. 2, *Años de guerra y años de paz.* Guatemala: Editorial de Ciencias Sociales, 2004.

ROLAND H. EBEL

VILLALBA, JÓVITO (1908–1989). Jóvito Villalba (*b.* 23 March 1908; *d.* 8 July 1989), Venezuelan political leader. A native of Nueva Esparta State, Villalba attended the Central University of Venezuela, where he became one of the most prominent members of the student Generation of 1928 as leader of the Venezuelan Students Federation. His eloquent oratory in opposition to the dictatorship of Juan Vicente Gómez resulted in his imprisonment from 1928 to 1934. After 1935 the young lawyer was a founder and leader of influential political organizations. In 1946 he joined a new political party, the Republican Democratic Union (Unión Republicana Democrática—URD), and quickly rose to be its secretary-general, a post he held for decades. In 1952 he ran for president in a military-sponsored election, but his apparent victory over the official candidate was nullified by the military authorities, who promptly deported him. After his return from exile in the United States in 1958, Villalba became a principal architect of the new democratic political system. He headed the URD, served in Congress, and ran unsuccessfully as his party's presidential candidate in 1963 and 1973.

See also **Universidad Central de Venezuela.**

BIBLIOGRAPHY

Iván Claudio, *Breve historia de URD* (1968).

Manuel Vicente Magallanes, *Los partidos políticos en la evolución histórica venezolana* (1973).

Robert J. Alexander, ed., *Biographical Dictionary of Latin American and Caribbean Political Leaders* (1988).

Additional Bibliography

Croce, Arturo. *Jóvito Villalba en la historia política de Venezuela.* Caracas: Edición Homenaje, 1990.

Valero, Jorge. *La diplomacia internacional y el Golpe de 1945.* Caracas: Monte Avila Editores Latinoamericana, 2001.

Velázquez, Ramón J., et. al. *Presencia de Jóvito Villalba en la historia de la democracia venezolana.* Caracas: Ediciones Centuaro, 1986.

WINFIELD J. BURGGRAFF

VILLA-LOBOS, HEITOR (1887–1959). Heitor Villa-Lobos (*b.* 5 March 1887; *d.* 17 November 1959), Latin America's most famous twentieth-century composer. Born in Rio de Janeiro, Heitor Villa-Lobos was the son of a minor library official and amateur musician, Raul Villa-Lobos, and Noemia Villa-Lobos. The composer's earliest childhood recollections were of Saturday evenings when friends came to the household for music making. Villa-Lobos's first musical instruction was from his father, who taught him to play the cello and provided him with ear training. When Villa-Lobos was asked if he considered himself to be self-taught, he often replied that he received such a complete musical foundation from his father that further instruction was unnecessary.

In 1899 Raul Villa-Lobos died during a small-pox epidemic, leaving the family in desperate financial circumstances. Noemia Villa-Lobos attempted to provide for the needs of the family by taking in laundry. Although she enrolled Tuhú, as she called young Heitor, in classes that would prepare him for a medical career, he was much more interested in all-night music-making sessions with young improvisers of popular music, the *chorões*. He frequently missed school, and when his mother tearfully objected, he ran away from home to live with an aunt who was more sympathetic to his musical interests and who played Bach preludes and fugues in a manner that never ceased to amaze him.

At eighteen Villa-Lobos traveled in the northern and northeastern parts of Brazil, an area rich in folk traditions. After selling some rare books that had belonged to his father, Villa-Lobos embarked on a journey through Brazil that lasted several years. He was gone such a long time that his mother assumed, not unreasonably, that he had been killed. Although Villa-Lobos frequently cited the period of his travels as one of collecting folk melodies which he subsequently used in his major works, there is little evidence that he made a systematic effort to collect folk materials firsthand. However, he did acquire an extensive knowledge of his native country—its folk traditions, customs, and various kinds of musical styles.

Back in Rio de Janeiro by 1911, he began to establish himself as a musician and composer. In 1913 he married Lucilia Guimarães, a pianist and teacher at the National Institute of Music. Limited financial resources necessitated their moving into the small house of the Guimarães family. Villa-Lobos kept the family awake most of the night as he composed, usually beginning after the evening meal and working at the piano throughout the night. By 1915 he had collected a portfolio of works and arranged several concerts, the first of which was held in Nova Friburgo, a town in the state of Rio de Janeiro. By November of the same year he was ready

Brazilian composer Heitor Villa-Lobos, 1957. Though lacking a traditional formal education in music, Villa-Lobos combined his interests in Brazilian folk music and folklore to create a prolific composing career that earned him international acclaim. BREITENBACH/PIX INC./TIME LIFE PICTURES/GETTY IMAGES

for a complete program of his works in the the capital city of Rio de Janeiro.

The first review of Villa-Lobos's works were mixed. While recognizing a significant original talent, all the critics noted his lack of traditional training and disregard of conventional harmonic and formal principles of writing. In his attempt to find more acceptable expression for some of his musical ideas, Villa-Lobos was supported by his friend Darius Milhaud, who joined the staff of the French embassy in Rio in 1917. Milhaud encouraged Villa-Lobos to find his own way rather than imitate European models. With a recommendation from Arthur Rubinstein, Villa-Lobos secured funds in 1923 for a short trip to Europe, where he presented a few concerts of his music. In 1927 he obtained assistance for a longer stay, and with the help of Rubinstein and several Brazilian musicians in Paris, he performed several works at the Salle Gaveau, in Paris, on 24

October and 5 December 1927. With these performances Heitor Villa-Lobos established himself as a talented and original composer, and soon thereafter received invitations to present his music and conduct orchestras in London, Amsterdam, Vienna, Berlin, Brussels, Madrid, Liège, Lyon, and other European cities.

Villa-Lobos remained in Europe until 1930. With the country in a state of intense political disruption, Villa-Lobos decided to return to Europe to resume his career shortly after his arrival. In the meantime, however, he wrote a memorandum to the state government in São Paulo, expressing his distress at the condition of musical training and proposing a program of universal music education. He was summoned to appear at the governor's palace to defend his proposal. The next years were the busiest of Villa-Lobos's life. He postponed his plans to return to Europe and remained in São Paulo, and later Rio de Janeiro, as organizer and director of a program of choral singing, music education, and mass choral performances intended to instill patriotism. All of these programs were supported by the Getúlio Vargas government. In 1944 Villa-Lobos visited the United States for the first time and during the final years of his life, he spent several months each year in Paris and New York.

Villa-Lobos wrote a torrent of musical works, variously estimated at two or three thousand, including arrangements and adaptations. Although he is recognized for his incredible fecundity and facility of musical writing, most of his music is unknown and has not been performed internationally, despite worldwide performances during the Villa-Lobos Centennial Celebrations in 1987 and 1988, which gave a broader representation of his life work. His sixteen *Choros* are a microcosm of the riches of Brazilian rhythmic invention and the diversity of its folk music. His *Nonetos,* although frequently referred to as chamber music, call for a gigantic percussion section. His late string quartets, written when the composer was near death, represent some of his finest writing. Individual works such as *Uirapurú* (The Magic Bird) draw their inspiration from various Brazilian myths and show the composer's mastery of orchestration. The best-known work of Villa-Lobos is the aria from *Bachianas brasileiras* no. 5, written in 1938. Because of his use of national and regional materials, he is regarded as a crucial figure in the development of Brazilian musical nationalism. Capturing, and building on, the urban salon music tradition of Ernesto Nazareth, Villa-Lobos molded diverse elements into a musical language that has been internationally recognized as an expression of both individual genius and the spirit of Brazilian music.

See also **Music: Art Music.**

BIBLIOGRAPHY

David P. Appleby, *The Music of Brazil* (1983).

Vasco Mariz, *Heitor Villa-Lobos: Compositor brasileiro,* 11th ed. (1989).

Stanley Sadie, ed., *The New Grove Dictionary of Music and Musicians* (1980).

Additional Bibliography

Appleby, David P. *Heitor Villa-Lobos: A Life (1887–1959).* Lanham, MD: Scarecrow Press, 2002.

Béhague, Gerard. *Heitor Villa-Lobos: The Search for Brazil's Musical Soul.* Austin: Institute of Latin American Studies, University of Texas at Austin, 1994.

Guérios, Paulo Renato. *Heitor Villa-Lobos: O caminho sinuoso da predestinação.* Rio de Janeiro: Editora FGV, 2003.

Paz, Ermelinda Azevedo. *Villa-Lobos e a música popular brasileira: Uma visaão sem preconceito.* Rio de Janeiro: Eletrobrás, 2004.

DAVID P. APPLEBY

VILLALONGA, JORGE (c.1665–?). Jorge Villalonga (Conde de la Cueva; *b.* c. 1665; active late seventeenth and early eighteenth centuries), viceroy of the New Kingdom of Granada (1719–1724). Philip V named Villalonga the first viceroy of the newly established Viceroyalty of New Granada in June 1717. Promoted from his position as governor of the Callao presidio, Villalonga was to effect the political reform program established by Antonio de la Pedrosa y Guerrero at the king's behest (1718–1719). Specifically, metropolitan officials expected Villalonga to solidify the Caribbean defenses of New Granada, curb smuggling, quell political infighting, promote economic development and so increase crown revenues, and project royal authority. From his very arrival in Santa Fe in November 1719 with demands for pomp, however, Villalonga provoked much internal opposition to his policies and demeanor. While Villalonga's *residencia* (end-of-tenure review) generally praised him, the king and his ministers judged his rule to be ineffective at best, for in late 1723 they decided to extinguish the viceroyalty and return the colony to *audiencia* rule. Villalonga returned to Spain in 1724 and became minister of war.

See also **Audiencia; Viceroyalty, Viceroy.**

BIBLIOGRAPHY

The best surveys of Villalonga's rule and the first attempt to establish the Viceroyalty of New Granada are in Spanish and include María Teresa Garrido Conde, *La primera creación del virreinato de Nueva Granada (1717–1723)* (1965); and Sergio Elías Ortiz, *Nuevo Reino de Granada: El virreynato, 1719–1753*, in *Historia extensa de Colombia*, vol. 4 (1970), pp. 29–58.

Additional Bibliography

Fisher, John Robert and Allan J. Keuthe. *Reform and Insurrection in Bourbon New Granada and Peru.* Baton Rouge: Louisiana State University Press, 1990.

McFarlane, Anthony. *Colombia before Independence: Economy, Society, and Politics under Bourbon Rule.* Cambridge: Cambridge University Press, 2002.

Silva, Renán. *Saber, cultura, y sociedad en el Nuevo Reino de Granada, siglos XVII y XVIII.* Medellín, Colombia: La Carreta Editores, 2004.

LANCE R. GRAHN

VILLALPANDO, CRISTÓBAL DE

(c. 1650–1714). Cristóbal de Villalpando (*b.* c. 1650; *d.* 20 August 1714), painter. Villalpando is responsible for the most agitated of Mexican colonial baroque paintings; he was also for many years an official of the painters' guild of Mexico City. There is considerable discussion about his training. Suggestions include study with José Juárez, Antonio Rodríguez, and his father-in-law, Diego Mendoza of Puebla. Much is also made of the influence on his work of Baltasar de Echave Rioja. His works are found throughout Mexico and many are of enormous size, decorating vaults and entire walls. His earliest known paintings were for a retablo at Huaquechula, Puebla, signed and dated in 1675. Between 1684 and 1686 he executed four huge

canvases for the sacristy of the cathedral of Mexico City, and in 1688 he painted the dome of the Capilla de los Reyes of Pueblo Cathedral. Often inventive in their iconography, his compositions recall Peter Paul Rubens and Juan de Valdés Leal. His brilliant coloring is sometimes shrill, and he makes generous use of shadow for dramatic effects. His production is uneven.

See also **Art: The Colonial Era.**

BIBLIOGRAPHY

Francisco De La Maza, *El pintor Cristóbal de Villalpando* (1964).

Additional Bibliography

Gutiérrez Haces, Juana. "The Mexican Painter Cristóbal de Villalpando: His Life and Legacy." In *Exploring New World Imagery: Spanish Colonial Papers from the 2002 Mayer Center Symposium*, edited by Donna Pierce. Denver, CO: Frederick and Jan Mayer Center for Pre-Columbian and Spanish Colonial Art, Denver Art Museum, 2005.

Gutiérrez Haces, Juana. *Cristobal de Villalpando: Catálogo razonado, 1549–1714.* Mexico City: Fomento Cultural BANAMEX, 1997.

CLARA BARGELLINI

VILLANUEVA, CARLOS RAÚL (1900–

1975). Carlos Raúl Villanueva, born in England on May 30, 1900, was the premier Venezuelan architect of the twentieth century. He was educated in Paris at the Lycée Condorcet and the school of architecture of the École Nationale des Beaux-Arts, where he studied with Gabriel Héraud. Villanueva's projects were numerous and demonstrated a long-term vision devoted to recreating the landscape of Caracas. In addition to acting as an architectural consultant to the Worker's Bank of Venezuela, he was a pioneer of urban renewal, planning El Silencio, a complex of apartments and shops, in Caracas and the low-cost General Rafael Urdaneta housing developments in Maracaibo during the 1940s. Between 1944 and 1957 he designed several buildings for the University of Caracas, among them the library and the medical school. Villanueva is known for his design of "floating structures," which include his crowning achievements: the university's Olympic Stadium (1950) and the Olympic swimming pool (1957). Villanueva was the founder and first president of the Venezuelan Society of Architects; he was also a professor of architecture at the Central University of Venezuela. He died in Caracas on August 16, 1975.

See also **Architecture: Modern Architecture.**

BIBLIOGRAPHY

Moholy-Nagy, Sibyl. *Carlos Raúl Villanueva and the Architecture of Venezuela*. New York: Praeger, 1964. Spanish edition: *Carlos Raúl Villanueva y la arquitectura de Venezuela*, trans. Clara Diament de Sujo. Caracas: Instituto del Patrimonio Cultural, 1999.

Páez, Rafael. *Los hombres que han hecho Venezuela*. Caracas: Editorial Biosfera/Petare: Distribuidora Escolar, 1983.

Villanueva, Paulina, and Maciá Pintó. *Carlos Raúl Villanueva*. Photographs by Paolo Gasparini. Sevilla: Tanais Ediciones, 2000. English edition: *Carlos Raúl Villanueva*. New York: Princeton Architectural Press, 2000.

MICHAEL A. POLUSHIN

VILLARÁN, MANUEL VICENTE (1873–1958).

Manuel Vicente Villarán (*b.* 11 October 1873; *d.* 21 February 1958), a leading authority on constitutional issues in early-twentieth-century Peru. Villarán was born in Lima. At the age of twenty-three, having received a degree in law, he joined the department of sociology at the University of San Marcos. In 1904 he led the progressive Civilista faction that supported José Pardo y Barreda for president. He argued passionately for education, saying that Peru needed well-educated middle and working classes to forge a modern nation. But he also agreed with Javier Prado y Ugarteche that the laziness and mental inertia of the indigenous people were the cause of the country's low level of development. He was minister of justice, religion, and instruction during Augusto Leguía's first government (1908–1910) and helped to bring the first U.S. educators to Peru. In 1918 he wrote a newspaper essay, "Costumbres electorales," decrying the sorry state of political maturity of the Peruvian masses in the nineteenth century. In 1922 he became the rector of San Marcos and held that post until early 1924. Subsequently, he taught law and advised various governments during the 1920s and 1930s. After World War II he lived in virtual obscurity. Villarán's books include *El arbitraje de Washington en la cuestión peruanochilena* (1925), *Bosquejo histórico de la constitución inglesa*, 2nd ed. (1935), and *La Universidad de San Marcos de Lima: Los orígenes, 1548–1577* (1938).

See also **Peru, Political Parties: Civilista Party.**

BIBLIOGRAPHY

Jesús Chavarría, *José Carlos Mariátegui and the Rise of Modern Peru, 1890–1930* (1979).

Steve Stein, *Populism in Peru: The Emergence of the Masses and the Politics of Social Control* (1980).

Additional Bibliography

Roel, Virgilio. *De Manuel Vicente Villarán a la revolución científica y tecnológica y la nueva reforma universitaria*. Lima: G. Herrera Editores, 1996.

VINCENT PELOSO

VILLARRICA.

Villarrica, capital city of the department of Guairá in south-central Paraguay (not far from the Tebicuary River), with 40,300 inhabitants (2004). Founded in 1570, the small Spanish enclave suffered continued attacks by Paulista raiders from Brazil during colonial times until it was established as a permanent settlement in 1682. It is the center of the Yerba Maté industry of Paraguay and an important processor of orange concentrates. After World War I, German colonists moved into the uplands north of Villarrica and formed the agrarian bases of the region with tanning establishments, flour mills, sugar mills, and cotton-threading mills.

See also **Paraguay, Geography; Tebicuary River.**

BIBLIOGRAPHY

Hugo G. Ferreira, *Geografía del Paraguay* (Asunción, 1975).

Add.Bibliography

Salas, José Luis. *Villarrica y los franciscanos: Memoria de cuatro siglos caminando juntos*. Asunción, Paraguay: s.n., 2003.

CÉSAR N. CAVIEDES

VILLARROEL, GASPAR DE (1587?–1665).

Considered by many to be the first major contributor to Ecuadoran letters, Gaspar de

Villarroel is a complicated figure from the colonial period who resists strict definitions and categories.

Villarroel was an important presence in the colonial church. His fame as a preacher and his extensive publications led to appointments as bishop of Chile (1637) and Arequipa (1651), and ultimately, as archbishop of Charcas (1660). His first work, *Comentario sobre el Cantar de los Cantares*, was lost before it could be published. Between 1631 and 1633, Villarroel published his first theological treatise, *Comentarios, dificultades y discursos literales y místicos sobre los Evangelios de la Cuaresma*. In 1636, a year before his elevation to the bishopric, he published *Comentarios al libro de los Jueces*. Between 1656 and 1657 he published his most important work, a reconciliation of monarchical and pontifical authority titled *Gobierno Eclesiástico-Pacífico y Unión de los Dos Cuchillos Pontificio y Regio*. Villarroel returned to theology in his last two works, *Historias Sagradas y Eclesiásticas Morales, con Quince Misterios de nuestra fe* (1660) and *Primera parte de los comentarios, dificultades, y discursos literales, morales y místicos, sobre los Evangelios de los Domingos de Adviento, y de los todo el año* (1661).

A subtle narrator who said of himself, "writing has been a temptation for me from a very early age" (Zaldumbide, p. 27), Villarroel, like many of his peers, pays little attention to indigenous peoples and concerns. His work does, however, provide important insights into the seventeenth-century religious, historical and political mind.

See also **Catholic Church: The Colonial Period; Literature: Spanish America.**

BIBLIOGRAPHY

González Echevarría, Roberto, ed. *The Oxford Book of Latin American Short Stories.* New York: Oxford University Press, 1997.

Guerra Bravo, Samuel. "Gaspar de Villarroel." In *Historia de las literaturas del Ecuador.* Vol. 1. Edited by Juan Valdano. Quito, Ecuador: Universidad Andina Simón Bolívar, Sede Ecuador; Corporación Editora Nacional, 2002.

Rodríguez Castelo, Hernán. *Literatura en la Audiencia de Quito, siglo XVII.* Quito, Ecuador: Banco Central del Ecuador, 1980.

Zaldumbide, Gonzalo. *Fray Gaspar de Villarroel, siglo XVII.* Puebla, Mexico: J. M. Cajica, Jr., 1959.

V. DANIEL ROGERS

VILLARROEL LÓPEZ, GUALBERTO

(1908–1946). Gualberto Villarroel López (*b.* 1908; *d.* 21 July 1946), president of Bolivia (1943–1946). Villarroel was a virtually unknown military officer when he came to power in a coup against the administration of General Enrique Peñaranda. An instructor in the reformist military college and a key figure in the secret nationalist military lodge Razón de Patria (the Nation's Right, known as RADEPA), Villarroel allied himself with the leftist-fascist Nationalist Revolutionary Movement (Movimiento Nacionalista Revolucionario—MNR) during the coup.

Under his government, largely dependent upon the MNR for popular support, important mine labor legislation was passed. In 1945 the government organized the First National Indian Congress, during which a thousand Indian leaders met. As a result, *pongueaje*, or free-labor services to the hacienda owners, was abolished, and other reforms were advanced, though the legislation was never enacted.

Despite its attempt at reform, the Villarroel regime brutally suppressed the opposition, executing various opposition leaders after a failed coup in 1944. Villarroel himself went to his death in 1946, when a teacher's strike turned violent. A mob stormed the presidential palace and hanged the president from a lamppost in the adjoining plaza.

The Villarroel regime is noted for its attempts at social reform and for the participation of the MNR, which in 1952 would lead Latin America's second social revolution.

See also **Bolivia, Political Parties: Nationalist Revolutionary Movement (MNR).**

BIBLIOGRAPHY

Augusto Céspedes, *El presidente colgado (Historia boliviana)* (1966).

Herbert S. Klein, *Parties and Political Change in Bolivia, 1880–1952* (1969), pp. 369–382.

Luis Peñaloza C., *Historia del Movimiento Nacionalista Revolucionario, 1941–1952* (1963), pp. 55–94.

Additional Bibliography

Bello, Francisco R. *Memorias sobre Bolivia: La revolución de Villarroel.* Buenos Aires: Repertorio Latinoamericano, 2001.

Guzmán Rojas, Alberto, compiler. *Chuspipata, la montaña maldita: el gobierno y la caída de Gualberto Villarroel: los fusilamientos de noviembre de 1944: Los sangrientos sucesos del 13 de junio y 21 de julio de 1946: testimonio documental del juicio de responsabilidades instaurado por el H. Congreso Nacional.* Bolivia, 1996.

Murillo Cárdenas, Eliodoro, and Gustavo Larrea Bedregal. *Razón de Patria, Villarroel y nacionalismo revolucionario.* La Paz: Editorial e Impr. Metodista, 1988.

ERICK D. LANGER

VILLAS BÔAS BROTHERS.

Villas Bôas brothers, rights activists who became internationally known during the 1960s and 1970s for their defense of Brazilian Indians. Orlando (1914–2002), Cláudio (1916–1998), and Leonardo (1918–1961) Villas Bôas opposed the policy of the Brazilian government, which at that time favored rapid integration of Indians into the national society and economy. They argued strongly that reservations should be protected from outside influences for an indefinite period to protect Indian cultures and ways of life.

The brothers were members of the Roncador-Xingu expedition of 1943 sent to survey unexplored regions of central Brazil. Their experience with unacculturated Indians of the Upper Xingu River Basin convinced them to remain there and devote their lives to the welfare and protection of Indians. In 1954, when a devastating measles epidemic struck the Upper Xingu tribes, the Villas Bôas brothers mobilized the support of the Medical School of São Paulo, which set up a model program of medical assistance for the Indians.

In 1961 the Villas Bôas brothers were instrumental in persuading the Brazilian government to set aside most of the Upper Xingu region (8,800 square miles) as a national park for protection of the Indians and wildlife preservation. The two surviving brothers, Orlando and Cláudio, became the administrators of the Xingu National Park. Anthropologists, journalists, and other visitors were impressed with the well-being and peace in which the Indians of the park lived. In 1967 the Villas Bôas brothers received the Founders' Gold Medal of the Royal Geographical Society and in 1971 they were nominated for the Nobel Peace Prize.

Some supporters of Indian self-determination have criticized the Villas Bôases' administration of the Xingu Park as overly protective and paternalistic. It has also been pointed out that idyllic images of the park disseminated in Brazil and abroad tend to mask the much less favorable conditions under which many Indians in other parts of the country live. Nevertheless, by 1994, six thousand Indians lived within the park in eighteen different tribal groups. Claudio Villas Boas died at eighty-one years of age on 1 March 1998. When Orlando died in 2002, the Xingu Indians celebrated a traditional funeral festival called a Kaurup in his honor, even though this ceremony was not usually held for outsiders.

See also **Indian Policy, Brazil; Xingu Reserve.**

BIBLIOGRAPHY

Robin Hanbury-Tenison, *A Question of Survival for the Indians of Brazil* (1973).

Orlando Villas Bôas, *Xingu: The Indians, Their Myths* (1973).

Shelton H. Davis, *Victims of the Miracle: Development and the Indians of Brazil* (1977).

Adrian Cowell, *The Decade of Destruction: The Crusade to Save the Amazon Rain Forest* (1990).

Orlando Villas Bôas and Cláudio Villas Bôas, *A marcha paro o oeste* (1994).

Additional Bibliography

Garfield, Seth. *Indigenous Struggle at the Heart of Brazil: State Policy, Frontier Expansion, and the Xavante Indians, 1937–1988.* Durham, NC: Duke University Press, 2001.

Hemming, John. *Amazon Frontier: The Defeat of the Brazilian Indians.* Cambridge, MA: Harvard University Press, 1987.

Ramos, Alcida Rita. *The Predicament of Brazil's Pluralism.* Brasília: Universidade de Brasília, 2001.

Rocha, Leandro Mendes. *A política indigenista no Brasil, 1930–1967.* Goiânia, Brazil: Editora UFG, 2003.

NANCY M. FLOWERS

VILLAURRUTIA, JACOBO DE (1757–1833).

Jacobo de Villaurrutia (*b.* May 1757; *d.* 23 August 1833), judge and journalist in Central America and Mexico. Jacobo de Villaurrutia López Osorio was born in the city of Santo Domingo on the island of Hispaniola. His father was Antonio

Villaurrutia, a native of Mexico; his mother was María Antonieta López de Osorio. In his youth, he moved to Spain, where, as part of the family, he was a page for Francisco Lorenzana, archbishop of Mexico and later cardinal and archbishop of Toledo. Under Lorenzana's protection, Villaurrutia began his studies, completing the equivalent of a master's degree on 14 May 1781, and a doctorate in law four days later from the University of Toledo.

Villaurrutia began a successful career in public administration. On 2 November 1782 he was appointed magistrate and chief justice for Alcalá de Henares, a post he held for five years. In May 1792 he was named judge of the Audiencia of Guatemala, and later became a founder of the Sociedad Económica de Amigos del País (Economic Society of Friends of the Country). The purpose of this organization and similar ones in the Spanish dominions was to promote industry and the arts. They also promulgated the ideas of Spanish intellectuals through journalism.

Villaurrutia's innovative ideas led to his removal from his post in 1808 and transfer as a criminal court magistrate to Mexico City, where he continued his work in journalism, aided by Carlos María de Bustamante. His periodical was finally suppressed by Viceroy José de Iturrigaray. When problems arose as a result of Napoleon's invasion of Spain, Villaurrutia played an important role in opposing the Spanish authorities in Mexico, for which he was expelled from Mexico in 1814. Upon returning to Spain, he was appointed judge in Barcelona and became dean and internal regent. When Mexican independence was declared in 1821, he resigned and returned to Mexico, where he was appointed regent of the *audiencia* in 1822 and president of the Supreme Court of Justice in 1824. In 1827 he was circuit judge for the Federal District, the state of Mexico, and the territory of Tlaxcala. In November of the same year he was elected minister of the Supreme Court, and in 1831 he became its president. He died of cholera in Mexico City.

See also **Guatemala, Economic Society of.**

BIBLIOGRAPHY

Manuel Berganzo, *Diccionario de historia y geografía* (1853–1856), and "Biografía de don Jacobo de Villaurrutia," in *Anales de la Sociedad de geografía e historia de Guatemala* 25 (December 1951): 388–396.

OSCAR G. PELÁEZ ALMENGOR

VILLAURRUTIA, XAVIER (1903–1950). Xavier Villaurrutia (*b.* 27 March 1903; *d.* 25 December 1950), Mexican poet, critic, and playwright. Villaurrutia was born and died in Mexico City. He belonged to the generation known as the Contemporaries. With Salvador Novo, he participated in the review and theatrical group Ulises. He studied drama at Yale (1935–1936) and was one of the first professional writers of his country. He wrote an avant-garde novel (*Dama de corazones*, 1928) and the plays *Parece mentira* (1934), *¿En qué piensas?* (1938), and *La hiedra* (1941). His screenplays include *Vámonos con Pancho Villa* (1934) and *Distinto amanecer* (1943). He translated William Blake, André Gide, and many others and was a critic of literature, film, and the fine arts (*Textos y pretextos*, 1940). The most notable of his work, however, is his brief and rigorous poetry: *Reflejos* (1926), *Nocturnos* (1933), *Décima muerte* (1941), *Canto a la primavera* (1948), and especially *Nostalgia de la muerte* (Buenos Aires, 1938), in which the verbal creativity of the avant-garde is united with classic Spanish lyricism and a reflection on mortality reminiscent of Nahuatl poetry. His works were collected by Alí Chumacero, Luis Mario Schneider, and Miguel Capistrán (*Obras*, 2d ed. 1966). Eliot Weinenberg has translated *Nostalgia for Death* (1992), which includes an essay by Octavio Paz.

See also **Literature: Spanish America; Paz, Octavio.**

BIBLIOGRAPHY

Merlin H. Forster, *Fire and Ice: The Poetry of Xavier Villaurrutia* (1967).

Eugene Moretta, *The Poetic Achievement of Xavier Villaurrutia* (Cuernavaca, Mexico, 1971).

Octavio Paz, *Xavier Villaurrutia en persona y en obra* (1978).

Additional Bibliography

Hernández Rodríguez, Rafael. *Una poética de la despreocupación: Modernidad e identidad en cuatro poetas latinoamericanos.* Santiago: Editorial Cuarto Propio, 2003.

Oropesa, Salvador A. *The Contemporáneos Group: Rewriting Mexico in the Thirties and Forties.* Austin: University of Texas Press, 2003.

Salmerón Tellechea, Cecilia. "Décima muerte de Xavier Villaurrutia o la simultaneidad de lo disímil." In *Poéticas mexicanas del siglo XX*, edited by Samuel Gordon.

Mexico City: Ediciones y Gráficos Eón: Universidad Iberoamericana, 2004.

Sefamí, Jacobo. *El destierro apacible y otros ensayos: Xavier Villaurrutia, Alí Chumacero, Fernando Pessoa, Francisco Cervantes, Haroldo de Campos.* Tlahuapan, Mexico: Premiá, 1987.

Ulacia, Manuel. *Xavier Villaurrutia, cincuenta años después de su muerte.* Mexico City: Ediciones Sin Nombre: Conaculta, 2001.

J. E. PACHECO

VILLAVERDE, CIRILO (1812–1894).

Cirilo Villaverde (*b.* 28 October 1812; *d.* 20 October 1894), Cuban writer. Villaverde was born on a sugar plantation and, as a young writer and lawyer in Havana, he wrote romantic stories and accounts of his travels in his home province, Pinar del Río. Dedicated to freeing Cuba from Spanish control, Villaverde favored annexation by the United States and, to that end, worked as a secretary for General Narciso López. Because of his conspiratorial activities, Villaverde was imprisoned by the Spaniards in 1848. One year later, he escaped to the United States, where he worked as a teacher, married fellow Cuban Emilia Casanova, and continued contributing to Spanish-speaking publications.

Villaverde resided in the United States until 1858, and then again from 1861 until his death. In 1882 he published *Cecilia Valdés,* a novel about Spanish colonialism and slavery in early-nineteenth-century Cuba. It shows how the Cuban oligarchy's push toward modernization of the sugar industry had dramatic consequences for the slaves, symbolized by the book's eponymous female protagonist. With this novel of manners, more than with any other work, Villaverde secured his place in Cuban literary history.

See also **Hispanics in the United States; Literature: Spanish America.**

BIBLIOGRAPHY

Imeldo Alvarez, ed., *Acerca de Cirilo Villaverde* (1982).

Reynaldo González, *Contradanzas y latigazos* (1983).

William Luis, *Literary Bondage* (1990).

Additional Bibliography

Artalejo, Lucretia. *La máscara y el marañón: La identidad nacional cubana.* Miami: Ediciones Universal, 1991.

Casanova-Marengo, Ilia. *El intersticio de la colonia: Ruptura y mediación en la narrativa antiesclavista cubana.* Madrid: Iberoamericana; and Frankfurt am Main: Vervuert, 2002.

Molina, Sintia. *El naturalismo en la novela cubana.* Lanham, MD: University Press of America, 2001.

INEKE PHAF

VILLAVICENCIO.

Villavicencio, Colombian city. The capital of Meta Department, located on the left bank of the Guatiquía River, east of the Cordillera Oriental. It is 1,542 feet above sea level and 76 miles from Bogotá. Villavicencio, which was earlier called Gramalote, was formally established in 1842. Called the "Gateway to the Llanos," it is, with approximately 361,058 inhabitants, the main urban center of the plains region and a distribution and shipment center for cattle and other plains foodstuffs. Villavicencio has a university known for its program in tropical zoology. The city is served by an airport and is a highway hub. It also is the main public health center for the region.

See also **Llanos (Colombia).**

BIBLIOGRAPHY

Enrique Ortega Ricaurte, comp., *Villavicencio, 1842–1942* (1943).

Instituto Geográfico Agustín Codazzi, *Diccionario geográfico de Colombia,* vol. 2 (1980), pp. 1778–1779.

Additional Bibliography

Espinel Riveros, Nancy. *Villavicencio, dos siglos de historia comunera, 1740-1940.* Villavicencio: s.n., 1997.

J. LEÓN HELGUERA

VILLAZÓN, ELIODORO (1848–1940).

Eliodoro Villazón (*b.* 22 January 1848; *d.* 14 September 1940), president of Bolivia (1909–1913). Born in Sacaba in the department of Cochabamba, Villazón was trained as a lawyer. He entered politics and became deputy from Cochabamba to the Assembly of 1871 when he was only twenty-three years old. At the

National Convention of 1880 he caught the attention of Narciso Campero, the recently installed president (1880–1884). Under Campero, Villazón was appointed minister of finance and later financial agent in Europe. After returning from abroad, Villazón joined the Liberal Party and became one of its most loyal members. When the Liberals came to power after the Federal War of 1898, Villazón became minister of foreign affairs. In 1909 the leader of the Liberals, Ismael Montes, who had been president from 1904 to 1908, selected Villazón to be the party's presidential candidate in a special election made necessary by the death of Montes's successor. Elected overwhelmingly, Villazón, as caretaker for Montes, continued government support for railroad construction and successfully negotiated loans with Europeans that led to the formation of the Banco de la Nación.

See also **Campero, Narciso; Montes, Ishmael.**

BIBLIOGRAPHY

William Belmont Parker, *Bolivians of Today,* 2nd ed. (1922), pp. 317–320.

Herbert S. Klein, *Parties and Political Change in Bolivia, 1880–1952* (1969), pp. 43–44.

ERWIN P. GRIESHABER

VILLEDA MORALES, RAMÓN (1908–1971).

Ramón Villeda Morales (*b.* 1908; *d.* 8 October 1971), Honduran president (1957–1963). Villeda Morales studied medicine in Europe and Honduras. Called the "Little Bird" for his small stature and oratorical prowess, he was also known for his cosmopolitan polish, rare in Honduran politicians. He dominated the Liberal Party as chairman and founded the party newspaper, *El Pueblo.* Although he won a plurality in the 1954 presidential election, a subsequent coup deprived him of office.

In 1957 Villeda Morales came to power after a military coup overthrew Julio Lozano Días. Between the coup and his inauguration, Villeda Morales seems to have participated in a pact of the Blue Water (named after the United Fruit Company villa where the clandestine pact was apparently devised). He agreed to conform radical agrarian and labor reforms to Alliance for Progress ideology in return

for ample U.S. aid and Honduran military support. The 1958 labor code brought realistic worker benefits. The 1962 Agrarian Reform Law nationalized, with compensation, undeveloped land for peasants. In response to the 1954 United Fruit strike, peasant organizations were legalized. However, Villeda Morales's close relationship with Serafino Re-mauldi, a Central Intelligence Agency (CIA) operative and labor representative, assured that an AFL-CIO alliance of peasant and labor organizations dominated labor.

The limited reforms of Villeda Morales nonetheless brought conservative opposition and charges of Communist infiltration. Afraid that the 1963 Liberal presidential candidate would make good on Villeda Morales's "second republic" rhetoric, military chief Oswaldo López Arellano staged a successful coup two months before the election.

Several factors point to CIA involvement in the Arellano coup. Villeda Morales, who had CIA links through Remauldi, piqued the agency by pushing for a more radical successor. This apparently prompted CIA endorsement of Arellano's coup. Also, CIA backing is indicated by the quick commendation of the coup by the U.S. ambassador and the Voice of America, although this support was repudiated by the U.S. State Department.

Arriving in New York in 1971 as Honduran ambassador to the United Nations, Villeda Morales suffered a fatal heart attack. The Honduran Liberal Party continues to invoke the memory of Villeda Morales as a Kennedyesque figure.

See also **Central Intelligence Agency (CIA); Lozano Díaz, Julio; United Fruit Company.**

BIBLIOGRAPHY

Philip Agee, *Inside the Company: A CIA Diary* (1975).

Robert Mac Cameron, *Bananas, Labor, and Politics in Honduras, 1954–1963* (1983).

James Rudolph, ed., *Honduras: A Country Study* (1983).

Additional Bibliography

Natalini de Castro, Stefanía. *Significado histórico del gobierno del Dr. Ramón Villeda Morales.* Tegucigalpa, Honduras: Universidad Nacional Autónoma de Honduras, Editorial Universitaria, 1985.

EDMOND KONRAD

VILLEGAIGNON, NICOLAS DURAND DE

(1510–1572). Nicolas Durand de Ville-gaignon (*b.* 1510; *d.* 29 January 1572), French colonizer in Brazil. Born in Provins, Villegaignon was a knight of Malta and nephew of the Grand Master. He served under Emperor Charles V at Algiers and fought the Turks in Hungary and at Tripoli. An experienced seaman, Villegaignon defied the English fleet by escorting Mary Stuart (later called Mary Queen of Scots) to France to marry the dauphin. Villegaignon, a warrior and humanist, anguished over spiritual matters and at one point embraced Calvinism.

As vice-admiral of Brittany, he interested Admiral Gaspard de Coligny in using Brazil, a land already visited by Normans and Bretons, as a sanctuary for Protestant refugees. In November 1555, with three boats manned by Catholics and Protestants, Ville-gaignon arrived at Guanabara Bay. He fortified a small island as a base for further exploration, naming the colony La France Antarctique. Encouraged by the reformer John Calvin, three hundred Protestants arrived in March 1557. Villegaignon, noted for his generous treatment of the native peoples, was less forgiving to the Protestants, whom he punished harshly for even slight transgressions. He returned to France in 1559, leaving his nephew in charge.

The newly arrived French colonists encountered resistance from the established Portuguese settlers in Brazil. Deemed heretics by the Portuguese, they supported the indigenous peoples against their colonial overlords. With only seventy-four men, the French held out for twenty days until the Portuguese (led by Mem de Sá) took the island and razed the fort. Survivors fled to the mainland to live among the native people. Villegaignon finally conceded the colonial rights to Portugal, and he remained in France until his death.

See also **French Colonization in Brazil.**

BIBLIOGRAPHY

Charles André Julien, *Les français en Amérique* (1946).

Charles André Julien, *Les débuts de l'expansion et de la colonisation françaises* (1947).

Brasil, Servico De Documentação Geral Da Mariuha, *Historia naval brasileira*, vol. 1 (1975).

Philippe Bonnichon, *Los navegantes franceses y el descubrimiento de America* (1992).

Frank Lestringant, *Le Huguenot el le sauvage* (1990).

Michel Mollat and Jacques Habert, *Giovanni et Girolamo Verrazano, navigateurs de François 1er* (1982).

Samuel Eliot Morison, *The European Discovery of America,* vol. 2 (1974).

Additional Bibliography

Elmalan, Serge. *Nicolas Durand de Villegagnon ou l'utopie tropicale.* Lausanne, Switzerland: Favre, 2002.

Mariz, Vasco, and Lucien Provençal. *Villegagnon e a França Antártica: Uma reavaliação.* Rio de Janeiro: Biblioteca do Exército Editora: Editora Nova Fronteira, 2000.

PHILIPPE BONNICHON

VILLEGAS, MICAELA. *See* **Perricholi, La.**

VILLEGAS, OSCAR

(1943–). Oscar Villegas (*b.* 18 March 1943), Mexican playwright. Villegas, a native of Ciudad del Maíz and a graduate of the directing program of the National Institute of Fine Arts, is generally considered to be the most talented playwright of his generation. His inveterate experimentation produces plays rich in interesting techniques, including one, *El señor y la señora* (1969), in which the speeches are not identified by character. His themes are contemporary and sometimes shocking: youth, love, sex, myths, values, and traditions, presented most often in one-act plays. Villegas's two major plays are *Atlántida* (1976), which takes place in a declining society without values, and *Mucho gusto en conocerlo* (1985), which also paints the hypocrisy and perversions that assault human sensibilities. Difficult economic and theatrical conditions in Mexico have hindered productions of Villegas's works; by occupation he is a ceramicist.

See also **Theater.**

BIBLIOGRAPHY

George Woodyard, "El teatro de Oscar Villegas: Experimentación con la forma," in *Texto Crítico* 4, no. 10 (May–August 1978): 32–41.

Ronald D. Burgess, "The Early Years: Villegas and López," in *The New Dramatists of Mexico (1967–1985)* (1991), pp. 14–29.

Additional Bibliography

Adler, Heidrun. *Un viaje sin fin: teatro mexicano hoy.* Madrid: Iberoamericana, 2004.

Burgess, Ronald D. *The New Dramatists of Mexico, 1967–1985.* Lexington: University Press of Kentucky, 1991.

Leñero Franco, Estela. *Voces de teatro en México a fin de milenio.* Mexico City: Conaculta, 2004.

Schmidhuber de la Mora, Guillermo. *El advenimiento del teatro mexicano: Años de esperanza y curiosidad.* San Luis Potosí, Mexico: Arriaga, 1999.

GEORGE WOODYARD

VILLORO, LUIS (1922–). Born on 3 November 1922, in Barcelona, Spain, to Mexican parents, Luis Villoro is considered one of the most important philosophers in the Spanish language. Villoro has written many works analyzing concepts of belief, truth, and ethics, and the relationships among these variables. He has also extensively explored Mexican intellectual history, including indigenous ideas during the Revolutionary period. His work earned him the National Award for Social Science, History, and Philosophy in 1986 and a Research in the Humanities award at the Universidad Nacional Autónoma de México in 1989. While serving as a professor there and at the Universidad Autónoma Metropolitana, he was part of the influential group Hiperión, which was formed to encourage discussion, analysis, and philosophy of Mexican culture. Villoro has been a member of El Colegio Nacional since 1978 and served as a UNESCO ambassador for Mexico from 1983 to 1987. He has published numerous books and articles and was a founder of the journal *Crítica: Revista Hispanoamericana de Filosofía.*

See also **Philosophy: Overview.**

BIBLIOGRAPHY

Works by Villoro

En México, entre libros: Pensadores del siglo XX. Mexico: El Colegio Nacional: Fondo de Cultura Económica, 1995.

Creer, Saber, Conocer, 9th edition. Mexico: Siglo Veintiuno, 1996.

El poder y el valor: Fundamentos de una ética política. Mexico: El Colegio Nacional: Fondo de Cultura Económica, 1997.

AMANDA LAIS GRAY

VIÑA DEL MAR. On Chile's central coast, Viña del Mar, or "Vineyard of the Sea," is among the most popular resort cities in Latin America. With a population of approximately 330,000 (est. 2007), it boasts more than a dozen beaches, many cultural activities and attractions, picturesque views, a renowned casino, and fine dining. Spanish settlers arrived in the area—called Peuco by its indigenous inhabitants—in the sixteenth century, establishing two haciendas (agricultural estates) where the city is today: the Hacienda Viña del Mar and the Hacienda Las Siete Hermanas. The area, which was under the civil authority of the neighboring port city of Valparaíso, remained largely rural and agricultural until the nineteenth century, when an important rail line was constructed linking the central coast and Santiago, the capital. Economic growth followed, and in 1878 Viña del Mar became an independent municipality. It became a center of industry as the turn of the century approached, hosting a number of important foreign-owned and operated companies. It was not until the 1930s that Viña del Mar emerged as a top tourist destination with the opening of the famed Municipal Casino, the O'Higgins Hotel, and a presidential retreat in the hills overlooking the Pacific Ocean. Viña del Mar's weather is strikingly similar to that of California's central and northern coasts. It is not surprising, then, that one of Viña del Mar's sister cities is Sausalito, California, near San Francisco. Viña del Mar is also known as the "Garden City" and each February plays host to one of the hemisphere's largest music festivals.

BIBLIOGRAPHY

Larraín de Castro, Carlos J. *Viña del Mar.* Santiago: Editorial Nascimento, 1946.

Vicuña Mackenna, Benjamín. *Crónicas viñamarinas.* Valparaíso: Talleres Gráficos Salesianos, 1931.

PATRICK BARR-MELEJ

VINCENT, STÉNIO JOSEPH (1874–1959). Sténio Joseph Vincent (*b.* 1874; *d.* 1959), president of Haiti (1930–1941). A member of the mulatto elite, Vincent was a lawyer, diplomat, and politician. He served as the mayor of Port-au-Prince and went on several diplomatic missions to Paris, Berlin, and the Hague. Vincent headed both the anti-interventionist Nationalist Party and the Patriotic Union and gained the presidency on the basis of his opposition to the U.S. occupation. Vincent was elected president by the National Assembly in November 1930. Although he entered office committed to the principle of parliamentary government, he based his power on officially controlled plebiscites.

As president, Vincent was widely regarded as partial toward mulattoes. He was particularly suspicious of the *Garde d'Haiti,* a predominantly black national guard organized by the U.S. Marines. As such he built up his own special presidential guard, which kept its weapons in the National Palace. In 1934 Vincent visited the United States and convinced President Franklin D. Roosevelt to withdraw the U.S. Marines. Thereafter, Vincent's fervent nationalism abated somewhat. In 1935 Vincent extended his tenure in office by five years. In addition, he declared the Senate "in rebellion to the will of the people" and expelled its members from the chamber. He then made several overtures to improve U.S.-Haitian relations and to attract U.S. tourists, such as offering to amend a law that would have facilitated casino gambling.

Vincent's popularity waned, however, because of his antipathy toward blacks and his weak reaction to the Dominican massacre of Haitians in 1937. In 1941 Vincent decided against having his term in office extended again and instead retired peaceably. He died in Port-au-Prince.

See also **United States-Latin American Relations.**

BIBLIOGRAPHY

Robert J. Alexander, ed., *Biographical Dictionary of Latin America and Caribbean Leaders* (1988).

Roland I. Perusse, *Historical Dictionary of Haiti* (1977).

Brenda Gayle Plummer, *Haiti and the United States: The Psychological Moment* (1992), esp. pp. 133, 141–144, and 154–157.

Additional Bibliography

Nicholls, David. *From Dessalines to Duvalier: Race, Colour, and National Independence in Haiti.* New Brunswick, NJ: Rutgers University Press, 1996.

Schmidt, Hans. *The United States Occupation of Haiti, 1915–1934.* New Brunswick, NJ: Rutgers University Press, 1995.

DOUGLAS R. KEBERLEIN

VIÑES Y MARTORELL, BENITO (1837–1893).

Benito Viñes y Martorell (*b.* 19 September 1837; *d.* 23 July 1893), pioneer of hurricane forecasting. A Jesuit priest born in Catalonia, Spain, Viñes was sent to Havana to take charge of the Belén Observatory (Belén was a Jesuit preparatory school), where he carried out his scientific work for the rest of his life. He was well acquainted with all that was then known about hurricanes, which amounted to very little as far as the signs announcing their coming or their passing were concerned. He devoted his life to finding a way to detect these signs.

Viñes began by studying the movements of the clouds that he called "featherlike cirrostratus." He then combined the data he gathered with information about the relationship between changes in barometric pressure and the paths of hurricanes that had blown through at the same time in previous years. After a while, he found it possible to predict, within certain limits, the path that a hurricane would follow. On 11 September 1875 he was able to make the first accurate hurricane forecast in history. A year later, again in September, the only sea captain who did not heed his warning lost his ship in the Straits of Florida.

In time Viñes was able to establish a network of information sources in the Caribbean. But he never had at his disposal the sophisticated observing tools that are available today, and thus his "laws of the hurricanes" (which also explained the structure of these tropical storms) have been superseded by researchers. This does not mean, however, that the essential validity of his observations has been proved erroneous. On the contrary, according to Dr. Neil L. Frank, director of the U.S. National Hurricane Center, they have been rediscovered and confirmed. Viñes's work is a historical landmark in the field of hurricane forecasting. Viñes died in Havana.

See also **Hurricanes.**

BIBLIOGRAPHY

José I. Lasaga, *Cuban Lives: Pages from Cuban History* (1988), vol. 2.

José Fernández Partagás, ed., *Memoir of the Homage to Rev. Father Benito Viñes, S.J. in the Centennial of the First Hurricane Forecast* (1975).

Additional Bibliography

Ramos Guadalupe, Luis Enrique. *Benito Viñes S.J.: Estudio biográfico*. Havana: Editorial Academia, 1996.

JOSÉ M. HERNÁNDEZ

VIOLA, PAULINHO DA (1942–).

Brazilian musician and composer Paulinho da Viola (born Paulo César Batista de Faria on November 12, 1942) was raised in an environment dominated by samba and choro, the popular music of the day. His father, guitarist César Ramos Faria, was a member of the group Época de Ouro, and played with some of the most important popular musicians of the day. The young musician started composing at an early age, and by his teens was busy playing cavaquinho and guitar (in Portuguese the viola, hence his nickname). He composed his first Carnaval samba in 1962, and later was active with several samba schools.

Known as a performer as well as a composer, da Viola's music embraces the two traditions in which he was raised. He recorded and performed samba and choro extensively through the 1960s and 1970s; by the 1980s he was one of the most popular samba singers in the country. In the 1990s his work demonstrated sophistication uncommon in samba, combining various popular music traditions. His 1996 album *Bebadosamba*, which sold more than 100,000 copies, is exemplary of his work, bridging the gap between traditional and progressive. He has stated that "I do not live in the past, the past lives in me."

See also **Music: Popular Music and Dance; Samba; Samba Schools.**

BIBLIOGRAPHY

Dunn, Christopher. *Brutality Garden: Tropicália and the Emergence of Brazilian Counterculture*. Chapel Hill: University of North Carolina Press, 2001.

McGowan, Chris, and Ricardo Pessanha. *The Brazilian Sound: Samba, Bossa Nova, and the Popular Music of Brazil*. Philadelphia: Temple University Press, 1998.

Perrone, Charles A. *Masters of Contemporary Brazilian Song: MPB 1965–1985*. Austin: University of Texas Press, 1989.

THOMAS GEORGE CARACAS GARCIA

VIOLA, ROBERTO EDUARDO (1924–1994).

Roberto Eduardo Viola (October 13, 1924–September 30, 1994) served as military leader and *de facto* president of Argentina from March 29 to December 11 of 1981. Born in Buenos Aires, he graduated from the Military Academy (Colegio Militar) in 1944. While a colonel, Viola served as an Argentine representative to the Inter-American Defense Board in Washington, D.C. (1967–1968). In 1975 he was promoted to chief of the general staff.

He was deeply involved in the Dirty War (1976–1982). In 1981 he succeeded General Jorge Videla as the president of the republic. Viola, who represented a "moderate" branch of the harsh military regime, tried a timid liberalization of political activity but was incapable of dealing with Argentina's faltering economy. by the end of the year General Leopoldo Galtieri politically outmaneuvered Viola and by December 22 had seized the presidency. A democratic government took power in 1983, and in 1985 Viola was sentenced to prison for his participation in state terrorism. In December 1990 he was released under a general amnesty decreed by President Carlos Saúl Menem.

See also **Argentina: The Twentieth Century; Dirty War; Galtieri, Leopoldo Fortunato; Menem, Carlos Saúl; Videla, Jorge Rafael.**

BIBLIOGRAPHY

Cardoso, Oscar Raúl, Ricardo Kirschbaum, and Eduardo van der Kooy. *Malvinas, la trama secreta*. Buenos Aires: Planeta, 1992.

Novaro, Marcos, and Vicente Palermo. *La dictadura militar*. Buenos Aires: Paidós, 2003.

Munck, Gerardo. *Authoritarianism and Democratization: Soldiers and Workers in Argentina, 1976–1983*. University Park: Pennsylvania State University Press, 1998.

VICENTE PALERMO

VIOLENCIA, LA.

Between the mid-1940s and the early 1960s Colombia was convulsed by political violence, which according to various estimates claimed between 100,000 and 250,000 lives. This period is known simply as "the Violence," a designation suggesting the inadequacy of any single explanation for the phenomenon; the name also suggests, as the historian Gonzalo Sánchez has noted, the hurricane-like force that made the phenomenon so incomprehensible to its countless victims. While the idiom of the *Violencia* was political—a struggle between affiliates of Colombia's two dominant parties, Liberal and Conservative—in its regional variations and in its consequences, the *Violencia* cannot be understood apart from its social and economic grounding.

Colombia's postindependence history had been characterized by frequent episodes of political violence, but these were clearly bounded and usually elite-led conflicts whose social repercussions were limited. The Liberal election victory of 1930, however, triggered a new modality of endemic partisan violence, centered in the countryside and rarely organized (though sometimes manipulated) by political elites. This violence flared anew with the Conservatives' return to power in 1946, first in "backward" regions like Nariño and Boyacá, then throughout much of the interior. This violence both fed, and was fed by, the growing estrangement between party leaders at the national level, which culminated in late 1949 in the dictatorship of Mariano Ospina Pérez. Ospina's use of viciously sectarian Conservative police (nicknamed *chulavitas*, after the rural subdivision that provided many of them), and the response of lightly organized Liberal guerrillas, raised the level of violence to unprecedented levels by 1949–1950. The uprisings in Bogotá, Cali, Barrancabermeja, and other cities following the assassination of populist Liberal leader Jorge Eliécer Gaitán in April 1948 also brought the *Violencia* to urban centers, albeit fleetingly.

By 1950–1953 most of rural Colombia, with the notable exception of the Atlantic Coast, was engulfed by the *Violencia*, but its characteristics varied widely. On the vast eastern plains, or llanos, Liberal resistance took on an increasingly redistributive, revolutionary character under Guadalupe Salcedo; this was also true of the movement of Rafael Rangel in the Magdalena River valley of Santander, a region with a long radical tradition. In southern Tolima, Liberal and Communist forces fought the Conservative regime, and not infrequently each other. But throughout much of the country—Boyacá and the Santanders in the northeast, and the coffee-producing regions of northern Tolima, Antioquia, and Caldas—the *Violencia* defied easy social or ideological characterization: Liberal and Conservative smallholders, sharecroppers, and laborers fought each other with unbridled ferocity, with no more explicit "program" than their respective party affiliations.

The overthrow of the Conservative dictatorship by the military under General Gustavo Rojas Pinilla in June 1953 slowed the *Violencia* in some regions, particularly on the llanos, but violence in much of Colombia continued unabated. The military itself was responsible for some of the more grotesque episodes of the mid-1950s, including mass executions and aerial bombardments in Tolima. In 1957 the leaders of the two parties reached an agreement, eventually known as the National Front, which permitted a return to civilian rule in 1958 under a rigid scheme of Liberal-Conservative parity at all levels. This agreement, with its corresponding legitimation of the state's role in "pacification" through both socioeconomic and military strategies, made possible the gradual diminution of the *Violencia* by the early 1960s; just as important, the agreement permitted the effective redefinition of continuing violence as simple delinquency (in the case of *bandolerismo*, the banditry that plagued the western coffee zones until the late 1960s), or as subversion (in the case of the leftist guerrilla groups whose origins lay in the Liberal/Communist split of the early 1950s).

The cumulative effects of the *Violencia* by the early 1960s were enormous, not only in the number of lives lost and properties destroyed. The face of Colombia was transformed as the cities filled with hundreds of thousands of rural migrants: new urban markets and a new urban work force propelled Colombian industrialization as peaceful development never could. Rural property was also transformed, as smallholders were displaced by agribusiness (in Cesar and Valle del Cauca), or by town-dwelling merchants (in Caldas); even where smallholder neighbor fought neighbor, the lack of "structural" change masked profound dislocation, which official policies (such as a Supreme Court decision restoring the properties of those who lost them by force or threat) could not reverse.

The historiography of the *Violencia* has until recently been divided between the empirical and the analytical, each lacking the necessary element of the other, as several writers have noted. Although an understanding of the Manichaean logic of Colombia's political system is accepted as a key element in any understanding of the *Violencia*, secularly political explanations are no longer considered sufficient;

however, ambitious socioeconomic explanations that privilege the structural imperatives of industrialization of agrarian capitalism have also lost favor. Instead, analysis has focused on regional and local cases, revealing a diversity of causal factors rooted in, among other things, class structure and political culture. Of attempts at innovative synthesis, those of Daniel Pécaut and Charles Bergquist are particularly noteworthy: the former emphasizes the "hegemonic crisis" of the state as the violently "prepolitical" invades the political realm, while the latter argues for the Hobbesian logic of nominally political violence between socially indistinguishable smallholders.

See also **Class Structure in Modern Latin America; Colombia, Political Parties: Conservative Party; Colombia, Political Parties: Liberal Party; Gómez Castro, Laureano; Lleras Camargo, Alberto.**

BIBLIOGRAPHY

Paul H. Oquist, *Violence, Conflict, and Politics in Colombia* (1980).

Daniel Pécaut, *Orden y violencia*, 2 vols. (1987).

Gonzalo Sánchez Gómez, " 'La Violencia' in Colombia: New Research, New Questions," translated by Peter Bakewell, in *Hispanic American Historical Review* 65, no. 4 (November 1985): 789–807.

Charles Bergquist, Ricardo Peñaranda, and Gonzalo Sánchez, eds., *Violence in Colombia: The Contemporary Crisis in Historical Perspective* (1992).

Additional Bibliography

Acevedo C, Darío. *La mentalidad de las élites sobre la violencia en Colombia, 1936–1949*. Bogotá, Colombia: Instituto de Estudios Políticos y Relaciones Internacionales: El Ancora Editores, 1995.

Ayala Diago, César Augusto. *Resistencia y oposición al establecimiento del Frente Nacional: Los orígenes de la Alianza Nacional Popular, ANAPO: Colombia, 1953–1964*. Bogotá, Colombia: Universidad Nacional de Colombia, Facultad de Ciencias Humanas, Departamento de Historia, 1996.

Bolívar, Ingrid Johanna. *Violencia política y formación del Estado: Ensayo historiográfico sobre la dinámica regional de la violencia de los cincuenta en Colombia*. Gainesville: University Press of Florida, 2003.

Green, W John. *Gaitanismo, Left Liberalism, and Popular Mobilization in Colombia*. Gainesville: University Press of Florida, 2003.

Roldán, Mary. *Blood and Fire: La Violencia in Antioquia, Colombia, 1946–1953*. Durham, NC: Duke University Press, 2002.

RICHARD J. STOLLER

VIRACOCHA. Viracocha, the greatest of the Inca gods. Viracocha created all the other gods, as well as men and animals, and so ruled them all. The deity had no name but only a series of titles most commonly given as Ilya-Tiqsi Viracocha Pachayacachiq, which in Quechua means "Ancient Foundation, Lord, Instructor of the World." The Spanish most commonly referred to him as Viracocha, using one of his titles as a name. Viracocha was usually represented as a man, and the Spanish reported seeing a solid gold standing figure about the size of a ten-year-old boy.

Viracocha was believed to have traveled through the Andes after the creation, performing miracles and teaching people how to live. He finally set off across the Pacific Ocean from a place near Manta in Ecuador, walking on the water. Viracocha was believed to have turned over the administration of his creation to the deities of the Inca pantheon and to the Huacas (natural spirits).

The term *Viracocha* also came to be applied to Europeans by the natives of the Andes. It is still used today as the common Quechua name for Caucasian foreigners.

See also **Incas, The.**

BIBLIOGRAPHY

John H. Rowe, "Inca Culture at the Time of the Spanish Conquest," in *Handbook of South American Indians*, vol. 2 (1946), pp. 183–330.

Burr Cartwright Brundage, *The Empire of the Inca* (1963) and *The Lords of Cuzco: A History and Description of the Inca People in Their Final Days* (1967).

Arthur A. Demarest, *Viracocha: The Nature and Antiquity of the Andean High God* (1981).

Geoffrey W. Conrad and Arthur A. Demarest, *Religion and Empire: The Dynamics of Aztec and Inca Expansionism* (1984).

Additional Bibliography

Cotterell, Maurice. *The Lost Tomb of Viracocha: Unlocking the Secrets of the Peruvian Pyramids*. London: Headline, 2001.

D'Altroy, Terence N. *The Incas*. Malden, MA: Blackwell, 2002.

Johnson, Carlos A. *Valverde por qué desprecias a mis serpientes, Yaku Mama y Sacha Mama? Cuentos incas*. New York: Ediciones, Español, Ya, 2000.

Salles-Reese, Verónica. *From Viracocha to the Virgin of Copacobana: Representation of the Sacred at Lake Titicaca*. Austin: University of Texas Press, 1997.

Urton, Gary. *Inca Myths.* Austin: University of Texas Press, 1999.

GORDON F. MCEWAN

VIRGIN ISLANDS. Virgin Islands, an archipelago of small islands and reefs between Puerto Rico and the Leeward Islands. The British Virgin Islands are a crown colony, while the American Virgin Islands—Saint Thomas, Saint Croix, and Saint John—have shared a common Danish history since the seventeenth century. In 1917, the United States acquired the islands to protect the Panama Canal. However, American and West Indian cultures conflict, adding to problems of race, local independence, rivalry between Saint Thomas and Saint Croix, and the tourist economy, a continuation of the Danish free port tradition.

Christopher Columbus discovered the Virgin Islands in 1493, and named them after Saint Ursula and her 10,000 fellow virgin martyrs. Despite Saint

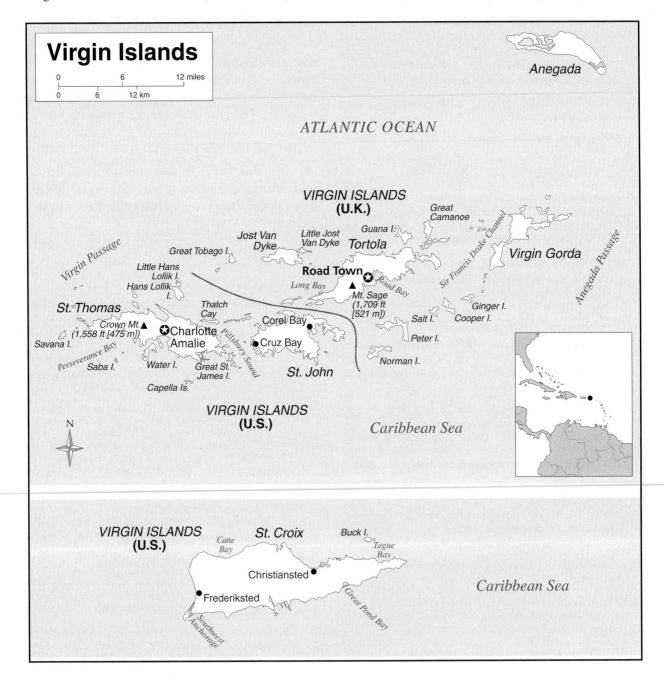

U.S. Virgin Islands

Population:	108,448 (2007 est.)
Area:	737 sq. mi
Languages:	English; Spanish; Spanish Creole; French; French Creole
National currency:	U.S. dollar
Principal religions:	Baptist 42%; Roman Catholic 34%; Episcopalian 17%; other 7%
Ethnicity:	Black 76%; white 13%; Asian 1%; other 6%; mixed-race 4%
Capital:	Charlotte Amalie
Annual rainfall:	Varies from 45–55 in on the northern coast and interior to 25–35 in in the south, southeastern, and coastal areas
Economy:	*GDP per capita:* US$14,500 (2004)

Thomas's harbor midway in the Caribbean, possible attack from Spaniards and Caribs discouraged colonization. Nevertheless, the Danish West India Company established a permanent settlement in 1672.

Since the Danes were interested only in slave trading and customs receipts, the original Dutch trading and culture dominated. Capitalism broke down national barriers, and a mixed planter and merchant class developed that was hostile to the Danish metropole. Continuous Danish neutrality made Charlotte Amalie, the port of Saint Thomas, wealthy from auctioning war prizes and selling stores to buccaneers.

After U.S. purchase, the Supreme Court dashed islanders' citizenship hopes by defining the islands as an "unincorporated territory." Both the Navy Department and succeeding civilian governors failed to solve problems of race, local government, and a dependent economy even though the islands were a "laboratory of the New Deal."

During World War II, alien labor and economic dependency on government increased, and blacks and mulattoes filled local bureaucracies. After the war the Virgin Islands became dependent on permanent military facilities. Tourism started in the 1960s, becoming the latest in a string of boom/bust economies related to the islands' strategic location. A government and private-sector partnership built a tourism image for cruise ships and "shopping bag" tourism. In spite of labor inflow and low unemployment (0.23 percent), extensive moonlighting indicated a low-pay/inflation economy. As of 2007, tourism accounted for 80 percent of economic activity.

The three main islands have different geographies and societies. Saint John, once having one hundred sugar plantations, degenerated rapidly after a ferocious slave rebellion in 1733, and has a small population and little influence. Saint Thomas's commercial and cosmopolitan tradition has been augmented by consecutive immigrants: "Cha-Chas" from nearby Saint Barthélemy, laborers from Puerto Rico and the other Antilles, and U.S. "Continentals." Saint Croix, bought from France in 1733, has been dominated by Danish sugar planters. By 1954, 40 percent of the island was still owned by twelve families and one foreign corporation. The rivalry between the commercial and planter oligarchies of Saint Thomas and Saint Croix carried over into the relations with the new black middle-class elite.

See also **Caribbean Antilles; United States-Latin American Relations.**

BIBLIOGRAPHY

Hendrik De Leeuw, *Crossroads of the Buccaneers* (1937).

Gordon K. Lewis, *The Virgin Islands: A Caribbean Lilliput* (1972).

Additional Bibliography

Dookhan, Isaac. *A History of the Virgin Islands of the United States.* Kingston, Jamaica: Canoe Press, 1994.

EDMOND KONRAD

VIRGINIUS AFFAIR. Virginius Affair, a confrontation that resulted in the summary execution in 1873 of 53 Americans at the hands of Spanish authorities in Cuba. The *Virginius,* a Cuban-owned vessel traveling under the American flag, regularly carried arms to revolutionaries in Cuba. While it was on such a mission in October 1873, a

Spanish cruiser captured the *Virginius* and took it to Santiago, where the executions took place. Subsequent negotiations between Washington and Madrid resulted in an $80,000 reparation award to the families of those executed, but the Spanish commander responsible was not punished; he was instead promoted to a higher rank.

See also **Cuba: The Colonial Era (1492–1898).**

BIBLIOGRAPHY

Charles E. Chapman, *A History of the Cuban Republic: A Study in Hispanic-American Politics* (1927).

Philip S. Foner, *A History of Cuba and Its Relations with the United States,* vol. 1 (1962).

Ramiro Guerra y Sánchez, *Guerra de los diez años, 1868–1878,* 2 vols. (1972).

Additional Bibliography

Allendesalazar, José Manuel. *Apuntes sobre la relación diplómatica hispano-norteamericana, 1763–1895.* Madrid: Ministerio de Asuntos Exteriores, 1996.

Botero, Rodrigo. *Ambivalent Embrace: America's Troubled Relations with Spain from the Revolutionary War to the Cold War.* Westport, CT: Greenwood Press, 2001.

Bradford, Richard H. *The Virginius Affair.* Boulder: Colorado Associated University Press, 1980.

THOMAS M. LEONARD

VISCARDO Y GUZMÁN, JUAN PABLO

(1748–1798). Juan Pablo Viscardo y Guzmán (*b.* 20 June 1748; *d.* February 1798), Peruvian Jesuit. Viscardo was born in Pampacolca (region of Arequipa) into a long-established creole family. He entered the Society of Jesus in 1761 and, although still a novice, was affected by the expulsion of the Jesuits ordered by Charles III in 1767. Early the following year Viscardo went to Cádiz, a trip which marked the beginning of an exile that took him to Italy, France, and England, where he died.

Viscardo is best known for his inflammatory "Letter to Spanish Americans," published in French in 1799 and in a Spanish translation in London in 1801. In it, Viscardo cataloged the alleged tyranny of colonial Spanish rule for three centuries and forcefully outlined why the colonies should be independent. Some historians consider him the "first and most important ideological precursor of Hispanic American independence." It has yet to be demonstrated, however, that his "Letter" was a significant stimulus for independence.

See also **Anticlericalism; Charles III of Spain; Jesuits.**

BIBLIOGRAPHY

D. A. Brading, *The First America: The Spanish Monarchy, Creole Patriots, and the Liberal State 1492–1867* (1991), pp. 535–540.

Rubén Vargas Ugarte, S.J., *La carta a los españoles americanos de Don Juan Pablo Viscardo y Guzmán,* 2nd ed. (1964).

Additional Bibliography

Bacacorzo, Jorge, Gustavo Bacacorzo, and Xavier Bacacorzo. *Los hermanos Viscardo y Guzmán: Pensamiento y acción americanistas.* Lima: Universidad Ricardo Palma, 2000.

Belaunde Ruiz de Somocurcio, Javier de. *Juan Pablo Viscardo y Guzmán, ideólogo y promotor de la independencia hispanoamericana.* Lima: Fondo Editorial del Congresso del Perú, 2002.

Valera, Luis. *Juan Pablo Viscardo y Guzmán, 1748–1798: El hombre y su tiempo.* Lima: Fondo Editorial del Congreso del Perú: Consorcio de Universidades, 1999.

MARK A. BURKHOLDER

VISCONTI, ELISEU D'ANGELO

(1866–1944). Eliseu d'Angelo Visconti (*b.* 1866; *d.* 1944) Brazilian painter. Born in Italy, Visconti came to Brazil as an infant with his family. Although he studied music during his youth, he chose painting over the violin. He took his first art classes at the Liceu de Artes e Ofícios (School of Arts and Crafts) in Rio de Janeiro. Then in 1885 he enrolled in Brazil's Imperial Academy of Fine Arts, where his talents were quickly recognized. During the first artistic competition of the republic, Visconti won a travel award that allowed him to study in Europe. While there, he won prizes and recognition as a student at the École des Beaux Arts in Paris and took classes at the School Guérin, where he studied decorative art under the tutelage of Eugène Grasset.

He returned to Brazil in 1897 and by 1901 had his first individual exhibition, showing eighty-eight works. In 1905, while in Paris, he received a governmental commission from Brazil, the first of many, to execute a panel painting destined for the entrance of the Municipal Theater in Rio de Janeiro. For the foyer, ceiling, and proscenium of the theater, he also did paintings celebrating the arts through allegorical themes.

In 1946 Brazil's National Museum of Fine Arts organized a retrospective of his works that included 285 oil paintings as well as watercolors, drawings, and decorative pieces. Visconti's work is stylistically eclectic with influences drawn from impressionism and realism. He once referred to himself as a "presentist" who produces an art that is constantly changing and modifying.

See also **Art: The Twentieth Century.**

BIBLIOGRAPHY

Arte no Brasil, vol. 2 (1979), pp. 578–587.

Additional Bibliography

Cavalcanti, Ana Maria Tavares. "Entre a alegoria e o deleite visual: as pinturas decorativas de Eliseu Visconti para o theatro municipal do Rio de Janeiro." *Arte & Ensaio* 9, no. 9 (2002): 46–57.

Morai, Frederico. "Eliseu Visconti e a crítica de arte no Brasil." In *Aspectos da arte brasileira*, Wladimir Alves de Souza, editor. Rio de Janeiro: Edição FUNARTE, 1980.

CAREN A. MEGHREBLIAN

VISITA, VISITADOR.

Visitador Visita, a special investigation undertaken in the Spanish colonies in response to perceived mismanagement or an emergency.

Visitas were of two types. A specific visita focused on a single official or lesser jurisdiction such as a village or *corregimiento*. A general visita, in contrast, focused on an entire audiencia district or viceroyalty. In a general visita, a *visitador-general* was sent from Spain to undertake a detailed and often lengthy examination of government and church officials' actions and of conditions within a specified region. Since a *visitador-general* could interrogate anyone he chose and was often sent because of concerns over a viceroy's behavior, relations between him and the viceroy were rarely cordial. While general visitas invariably disrupted the viceroyalty where they took place, few, if any, were clear successes.

First seriously used in the New World in the 1540s, general visitas proved to be very expensive and, consequently, few were undertaken. The best-known late colonial visita was that of New Spain by José de Gálvez from 1765 to 1771. Gálvez took a series of steps to bolster royal revenues, notably by establishing a royal tobacco monopoly that won him acclaim at court. When he subsequently became minister of the Indies in 1776, he sent *visitadores-generales* to New Granada and Peru. Their actions contributed to uprisings against the government in both locations.

See also **Gálvez, José de; New Spain, Viceroyalty of.**

BIBLIOGRAPHY

Clarence H. Haring, *The Spanish Empire in America* (1947), pp. 153–156.

Additional Bibliography

Guamán Poma de Ayala, Felipe. *Nueva crónica y buen gobierno*. 3 vols. Ed. John Murra, Rolena Adorno & Jorge L. Urioste. Madrid: Historia 16, 1987, folios 676[690]–691[705].

Mongrovejo, Santo Toribio. *Libro de visitas de Santo Toribio Mogrovejo*. Ed. José Antonio Benito. Lima: Pontificia Universidad Católica del Perú, 2006.

Río, Ignacio del. *La aplicación regional de las reformas borbónicas en Nueva España: Sonora y Sinaloa, 1768–1787*. México: Universidad Nacional Autónoma de México, Instituto de Investigaciones Históricas, 1994.

Taylor, William B. *Magistrates of the Sacred: Priests and Parishioners in Eighteenth-century Mexico*. Stanford, CA: Stanford University Press, 1996.

Zimmerman, Arthur Franklin. *Francisco de Toledo: Fifth Viceroy of Peru, 1569–1581*. New York: Greenwood Press, 1968, especially chapters IV, V, VI, VII, VIII.

MARK A. BURKHOLDER

VITALINO PEREIRA DOS SANTOS, MESTRE

(1909–1963). Mestre Vitalino Pereira dos Santos (*b.* 1909; *d.* 1963), Brazilian sculptor. Mestre Vitalino's work was virtually unknown until 1947 when the Pernambucan painter and illustrator Augusto Rodrigues saw his art and recognized that his miniature clay figurines represented a new popular ceramic tradition for Brazil. The sculptures recount daily life among the inhabitants and their animals in the backlands of Vitalino's home state of Pernambuco. Unlike other popular ceramicists of his time, Vitalino sculpted them with a softness of line and curve, and imbued them with wit and subtle irony.

His work was included in the 1948 Exposicão de Arte Popular in Rio de Janeiro. Prior to 1953 Vitalino grouped together and painted his subjects. Later, his compositions focused on single figures, which he left unpainted. He influenced the popular artists Nó Caboclo and Zé Rodriguez. Vitalino's sons continued the tradition popularized by their father.

See also **Art: The Twentieth Century.**

BIBLIOGRAPHY

Arte no Brasil, vol. 2 (1979), esp. pp. 830–831.

Additional Bibliography

Frota, Lélia Coelho. *Mestre Vitalino.* Recife: Fundação Joaquim Nabuco, Editora Massangana, 1986.

Mello, Paulino Cabral de. *Vitalino, sem barro: O homem: 80 anos de arte popular.* Rio de Janeiro: Ministério da Cultura; Brasília: Fundação Asssis Chateaubriand, 1995.

CAREN A. MEGHREBLIAN

VITERI Y UNGO, JORGE (1802–1853).

Jorge Viteri y Ungo (*b.* 23 April 1802; *d.* 25 July 1853), bishop of El Salvador and Nicaragua. Born in San Salvador of Spanish parents and educated in Guatemala, Viteri was active in the politics of Central America following the collapse of the federation. A noted orator and a leading adviser to Rafael Carrera, who was close to the Guatemalan conservative elite, he became a member of the Guatemalan Council of State in 1840. In 1842 he visited the Vatican, where he secured establishment of a separate diocese of El Salvador, to which Pope Gregory XVI named him the first bishop. Viteri also arranged for appointment of Francisco de Paula García Peláez as archbishop of Guatemala.

Viteri was an active force in Salvadoran politics in alliance with General Francisco Malespín, but when Malespín ordered the execution of a priest, Pedro Crespín, in 1845, Viteri excommunicated Malespín. Opposition to Viteri's meddling in politics forced him out of El Salvador in 1846. He went to Nicaragua, where the Vatican formally named him bishop of Nicaragua and Costa Rica on 5 November 1849. He was active in the politics of Nicaragua until his death.

See also **Carrera, José Rafael; García Peláez, Francisco de Paula.**

BIBLIOGRAPHY

E. Aguilar, *El…los documentos que comprueban la complicidad que el Sr. Obispo Viteri ha tenido en… [el trastorno del] orden de este estado el 1 de noviembre último* (1846).

Ramón López Jiménez, *Mitras salvadoreñas* (1960), pp. 47–71.

Arturo Taracena, "Biografías sintéticas," in *Revista de la Academia guatemalteca de estudios genealógicos, heráldicos e históricos* 7 (1979): 552.

Santiago R. Vilanova Meléndez, "Doctor y maestro don Jorge Viteri y Ungo, primero obispo de la diócesis de San Salvador," in *San Salvador y sus hombres* (1967), pp. 109–122.

Ralph Lee Woodward, Jr., *Rafael Carrera and the Emergence of the Republic of Guatemala, 1821–1871* (1993).

RALPH LEE WOODWARD JR.

VITIER, CINTIO (1921–).

Cintio Vitier (*b.* 25 September 1921), Cuban essayist, poet, and literary critic. The son of prominent Cuban educator Medardo Vitier, Cintio Vitier was born in Key West and spent most of his childhood in Matanzas, Cuba. In 1935 he moved to Havana, where from 1942 to 1947 he was editor of the literary journal *Clavileño.* Although he received a law degree from the University of Havana, he never entered the profession. During his student years he became part of the literary group that revolved around the magazine *Orígenes,* through which he befriended the founder, José Lezama Lima, as well as the poets Eliseo Diego and Fina García Marruz, whom he married in 1947. Between 1947 and 1961 he taught French and compiled key anthologies of Cuban poetry, including *Diez poetas cubanos, 1937–1947* (1948), *Cincuenta años de poesía cubana, 1902–1952* (1952), and *Los grandes románticos cubanos* (1960).

Vitier is best known for his literary analysis. One of his books on this subject, *Lo cubano en la poesía* (1957, repr. 1970), is still considered an authoritative work defining the Cuban poetic sensibility.

Vitier has edited critical editions of the complete works of José Martí and, along with Fina García Marruz, is the recognized authority on Martí within the island. (He was director of the José Martí wing of the National Library from 1968 to 1973 and a researcher at the Centro Martiano from 1987 to

1988.) He has edited several literary publications, including *La Nueva Revista Cubana, Anuario Martiano,* and *Revista de la Biblioteca Nacional "José Martí."* Since 1959 he has represented Cuba at numerous international cultural activities. As of the mid-1990s, he was retired and living in Cuba. In 2002, he won the title of Official of Arts and Letters from France, and the medal of the Cuban Academy of Sciences.

See also **Literature: Spanish America.**

BIBLIOGRAPHY

Benigno Sánchez-Eppler, *Habits of Poetry, Habits of Resurrection* (1986), deals with the influence of the Spanish Nobel laureate Juan Ramón Jiménez on the work of Eugenio Florit, José Lezama Lima, and Cintio Vitier. See also Arcadio Díaz Quinones, *Cintio Vitier: La memoria integradora* (1987).

Additional Bibliography

Labrada Aguilera, Agustín. *Un paseo por el paraíso: Doce entrevistas con escritores de México y Cuba (1995–2005).* México, D.F.: Poder Legislativo del Estado de Quintana Roo, 2006.

Ruiz Bencomo, Ruby. *Dedicado a Cintio Vitier.* Havana: Instituto Cubano del Libro, 2005.

Salgado, Maria Antonia. *Modern Spanish American Poets: First Series.* Detroit, MI: Gale Group, 2003.

ROBERTO VALERO

VITÓRIA.

Vitória, capital of the Brazilian state of Espírito Santo since 1823. A port city (2005 population 313,300) Vitória is located on the island of Vitória in the bay of Espírito Santo. Founded in 1535 by Vasco Fernandes Coutinho, the city was originally named Vila de Nossa Senhora da Vitória. On the periphery of the city is Tubarão, Brazil's principal port for iron ore exports. Railways connect Vitória to the mines of Minas Gerais and the city of Rio de Janeiro.

See also **Espírito Santo; Mining: Colonial Brazil; Mining: Modern.**

BIBLIOGRAPHY

Additional Bibliography

Leme, Maria Cristina da Silva, and Ana Fernandes. *Urbanismo no Brasil, 1895–1965.* São Paulo: FUPAM, 1999.

SHEILA L. HOOKER

VITORIA, FRANCISCO DE (1486–1546).

Francisco de Vitoria (*b.* 1486; *d.* 12 August 1546), one of the founders of international law. Francisco de Vitoria, a Dominican friar, was the *prima* (senior) professor of theology at the University of Salamanca (1526–1546). His published works include *De Indis I* (1537/ 1538) and *De Indis II* or *Dure jure belli* (1538/1539), collections of lectures published posthumously. Vitoria outlined the rights of Spaniards in the New World and wrestled with the moral questions raised when a government founded on Christian principles imposes its will on pagans. Subscribing to the Thomistic theory that all men (including pagans) are rational beings who belong to a worldwide community based on natural law and a law of nations (*jus gentium*), Vitoria argued that Spaniards should respect the political sovereignty and property rights of the native peoples they found in the Indies. Thus, Spaniards did not have any inherent rights over subjects in the New World based on jurisdiction. War was justified only if natives prevented Spaniards from trading and living with them in peace, practiced cannibalism, refused to allow missionaries to preach, or discouraged conversion to Christianity.

See also **Catholic Church: The Colonial Period; Dominicans.**

BIBLIOGRAPHY

J. A. Fernández-Santamaría, *The State, War, and Peace: Spanish Political Thought in the Renaissance, 1516–1559* (1977), esp. pp. 58–119.

Bernice Hamilton, *Political Thought in Sixteenth-Century Spain* (1963), esp. pp. 119–134 and 171–176.

Additional Bibliography

Barrientos García, José. *Un siglo de moral económica en Salamanca, 1526–1629.* Salamanca, Spain: Ediciones Universidad de Salamanca, 1985.

Castilla Urbano, Francisco. *El pensamiento de Francisco de Vitoria: Filosofía política e indio americano.* Barcelona: Anthropos, Editorial del Hombre; Iztapalapa, Mexico: Universidad Autónoma Metropolitana, Unidad Iztapalapa, 1992.

Hernández Martín, Ramón. *Francisco de Vitoria y su Reलेción sobre los indios: Los derechos de los hombres y de los pueblos.* Madrid: Edibesa, 1998.

Goti Ordeñana, Juan. *Del Tratado de Tordesillas a la doctrina de los derechos fundamentales en Francisco de Vitoria.*

Valladolid, Spain: Secretariado de Publicaciones e Intercambio Científico, Universidad de Valladolid, 1999.

Ramos Pérez, Demetrio. *La Etica en la conquista de America: Francisco de Vitoria y la Escuela de Salamanca.* Madrid: Consejo Superior de Investigaciones Científicas, 1984.

Rovira, María del Carmen. *Francisco de Vitoria: España y America el poder y el hombre.* Mexico City: Miguel Angel Porrúa, 2004.

SUZANNE HILES BURKHOLDER

VIVANCO, MANUEL IGNACIO (1806–1873).

Manuel Ignacio Vivanco (*b.* 1806; *d.* 1873), conservative Peruvian military caudillo. Born in Lima, the son of a Spanish merchant, Vivanco was educated in the traditional San Carlos school. He joined the independence forces to fight the decisive battles of Junín and Ayacucho. After Independence Vivanco sided with several military leaders, including Pedro Bermúdez, the conservative Felipe Santiago Salaverry, and Agustín Gamarra, who opposed the Peru-Bolivia Confederation. In 1841, Vivanco campaigned on behalf of his own "regenerating" movement with the undemocratic intent of strong government to end the caudillo struggle.

Especially strong in the southern provinces of Arequipa, Vivanco was able to control power during the multiple military uprisings of the early 1840s. However, in 1844, his archenemy, General Ramón Castilla, was able to defeat Vivanco's forces and initiate a gradual reorganization of the Peruvian state. Vivanco continued to oppose Castilla. In the elections of 1850 he ran against Castilla's official candidate, José R. Echenique. In 1856 he started a revolution against Castilla in Arequipa. During the beleaguered regime of Juan Antonio Pezet, Vivanco was the Peruvian representative who in 1865 signed the popularly repudiated Vivanco-Pareja Treaty that led to the ousting of Pezet and the decline of Vivanco's popularity. He died in Valparaíso, Chile.

See also **Peru: Peru Since Independence.**

BIBLIOGRAPHY

Jorge Basadre, *Historia de la República del Perú*, vol. 3 (1963), pp. 697–707.

Celia Wu, *Generals and Diplomats: Great Britain and Peru, 1820–40* (1991).

Additional Bibliography

Chirinos Soto, Enrique. *Vidas paralelas: Vivanco y Piérola.* Lima: Talleres Gráficos Villanueva, 1966.

ALFONSO W. QUIROZ

VIZCAÍNO, SEBASTIÁN (1548–1623).

Sebastián Vizcaíno (*b.* 1548; *d.* 1623), Spanish explorer and cartographer of the Californias. A native of Estremadura, Vizcaíno was a cavalry commander in the invasion of Portugal in 1580. He went to New Spain in 1583 and became merchant-militia commander at Manila in 1586. He conducted explorations in connection with his pearl-fishing monopoly, in the Gulf of California, from June to November 1596, founding La Paz on 13 September. Vizcaíno was general of an expedition that charted and mapped the Pacific coast of the Californias from 5 May 1602 to 21 February 1603; it also gave placenames from Cabo San Lucas to Cabo Blanco (in present-day Oregon). He was chief magistrate of Tehuantépec in 1604 and opened a supply route from Coatzocoalcos to the Pacific in 1606. After being granted an *encomienda* in the province of Ávalos in 1607, Vizcaíno served as the first European ambassador and cartographer in Japan (March 1611-January 1614). In October-November 1615 Vizcaíno repelled Dutch corsairs led by Joris von Spilbergen in Colima. After serving as chief magistrate of Acapulco (1616), he retired in 1619 to Mexico City, where he died.

See also **Explorers and Exploration: Spanish America.**

BIBLIOGRAPHY

W. Michael Mathes, ed., *Californians I: Documentos para la historia de la demarcación comercial de California, 1583–1632* (1965).

W. Michael Mathes, *Sebastián Vizcaíno and Spanish Expansion in the Pacific Ocean, 1580–1630* (1968).

Additional Bibliography

Cabezas, Antonio. *El siglo ibérico del Japón: La presencia hispano-portuguesa en Japón (1543–1643).* Valladolid: Instituto de Estudios Japoneses, Universidad de Valladolid: Secretariado de Publicaciones, Universidad de Valladolid, 1995.

Camino, Mercedes Maroto. *Producing the Pacific: Maps and Narratives of Spanish Exploration (1567–1606).* Amsterdam: Rodopi, 2005.

Martínez Shaw, Carlos. *Spanish Pacific from Magellan to Malaspina*. Madrid: Ministerio de Asuntos Exteriores, Secretaría de Estado para la Cooperación Internacional y para Iberoamérica, Dirección General de Relaciones Culturales, 1988.

O'Donnell y Duque de Estrada, Hugo. *España en el descubrimiento, conquista y defensa del Mar del Sur*. Madrid: Editorial MAPFRE, 1992.

Padrón, Ricardo. *The Spacious Word: Cartography, Literature, and Empire in Early Modern Spain*. Chicago: University of Chicago Press, 2004.

Torre Villar, Ernesto de la. *La expansión hispanoamericana en Asia: Siglos XVI y XVII*. México City: Fondo de Cultura Económica, 1980.

W. Michael Mathes

VODUN, VOODOO, VAUDUN.

Vodun is a syncretic religion with a history estimated by some anthropologists to date back more than 10,000 years. Having its philosophical and cosmological roots in ancient African rural societies established in Egypt, Asia Minor, East Africa, and Ionia, Vodun developed into one of the major African religions of the ancient world. After the conquest of the African societies that had built theocratic empires in these regions, practitioners of Vodun migrated to West Africa, where more than thirty ethnic groups continued to contribute to its development. From West Africa, specifically from Benin (ancient Dahomey), Vodun followers were traded as slaves to the New World. Consequently, Vodun is currently practiced not only in Benin, where it is the official religion, but also in the Caribbean, Latin America, the United States, and throughout the African diaspora. Since its ancient beginnings, Vodun has demonstrated a vigorous capacity for adapting itself to changing geographical, cultural, and political environments, including sustained and brutal governmental campaigns (especially in Haiti) aimed at its demise.

Derived from the Dahomean word *vudu*, which means "spirit," the term *Vodun* condenses a highly complex worldview predicated on the belief that human beings are influenced by divine spirits or "laos," who manifest the will of the one supreme God when they "possess" individuals during specific ritualistic rites, ceremonies, and consultations. The term also encompasses the notion that a metaphysical interrelationship exists between matter and spirit, the quality of life being dependent on the maintenance of harmony between the two and between human beings and spirits. According to this worldview, the spirits are intermediaries between individuals and God, who is immutable, inconceivable, and unapproachable; the universe is an indivisible, interrelated whole; and there is a sacred, organic interaction between the living and the dead (the ancestors), who are themselves spirits and who serve perpetually to ground the practitioners in their own history and tradition. The influence of spirits may be helpful or harmful to the lives of the folk. Accordingly, these spirits must be honored and consulted in meticulously structured ceremonies, where they are offered carefully chosen food and drink, the essence of which they consume during the act of possession.

European colonists used the term Voodun both as a reference to the African dances performed by devotees of the religion and also as a decidedly pejorative label for the religion's beliefs, values, practices, and ceremonies. Thus Vodun came to be widely regarded as evil, barbaric superstition and witchcraft, a perspective that is illustrated in many Western films and supported by definitions of the term in standard English dictionaries. Beginning in the 1950s, however, the Catholic Church in Haiti, after more than two centuries of attempting to obliterate Vodun, adopted a policy of accommodation. In the 1990s Pope John Paul II apologized for the Catholic Church's role in maligning African religions and invited Western institutions to be more tolerant of them. In 2003 Vodun's status as a religion was officially sanctioned by the Haitian government.

When documenting this religion's syncretic nature, Western scholars generally associate Vodun primarily with the Africans who were enslaved in Haiti and their descendants. These scholars emphasize the Christian influences—some spirits of Vodun, for example, are equated with specific angels or saints—that continue to testify to Vodun's syncretic aspect, its ability to modify itself to New World conditions. They tend to regard Haitian Vodun as a New World religion born out of the meshing of African and Christian worldviews. However, scholars who are themselves practitioners of this religion underscore that Haitian Vodun and the other African syncretic religions in the West—Santería in Cuba, Candomble in Brazil, and Obeah in the English-speaking Caribbean—derive from neighboring sects of the same religion and that, despite changes and differences in pantheon and rituals, they have retained their African cosmological essence. Generally speaking, scholars of Caribbean and Latin American religion are united in their findings that Vodun continues to play a major role in the shaping and perpetuation of folk culture and social mores, especially in Haiti, where it is absorbed into the national identity and interwoven into the fabric of Haitian literature, art, film, music, and folklore. It is estimated that, worldwide, there are more than 30 million adherents of Vodun.

See also **Lwa; Santería.**

BIBLIOGRAPHY

Courlander, Harold. *The Drum and the Hoe: Life and Lore of the Haitian People.* Berkeley: University of California Press, 1986.

Herskovits, Melville J. *Life in a Haitian Valley.* New York: Knopf, 1937. Repr., Princeton, NJ: Markus Wiener Publishers, 2007.

Hunter-Hindrew, Mamaissii Vivian. *Mami Wata: Africa's Ancient God/dess Unveiled,* 2nd edition. New York: MWHS, 2005.

Jahn, Janheinz. *Muntu: An Outline of the New African Culture.* Translated by Marjorie Grene. New York: Grove Press, 1961. Revised edition: *Muntu: African Culture and the Western World.* Translated by Marjorie Grene. New York: Grove Weidenfeld, 1990.

Thompson, Robert Farris. *Flash of the Spirit: African and Afro-American Art and Philosophy.* New York: Vintage Books, 1984.

MELVIN B. RAHMING

VOLADOR DANCE. Volador Dance, a unique and athletic ritual dance of pre-Columbian origin utilizing a high pole. Once practiced by many peoples throughout ancient Mexico and Central America, the dance today is primarily observed by the Totonacs, and occasionally by neighboring groups, in the Mexican states of Veracruz and Puebla. Its precise origins and significance are obscure, but it apparently reached its apogee with other solar rituals just before the Spanish Conquest. The dance retains many of its ancient characteristics, including steps, action sequence, orientation to the four cardinal points, and flute and drum accompaniment.

There are four, and at times six, dancers, called *voladores* (fliers), plus the musician. Having climbed the pole, as high as 137 feet, the dancers fall off a rotating platform with ropes tied to their waists. As the cords unwrap from the staff, they swirl around it for several minutes before reaching the ground. Except for tourist purposes, the dance is normally performed on local feast days.

See also **Totonacs.**

BIBLIOGRAPHY

Descriptions of the dance as traditionally practiced by the highland Totonacs can be found in Alain Ichon, *La religion des Totonaques de la Sierra* (1969); and for the lowland Totonacs in Salomón Pérez Diego D'poza, *Danza de los voladores* (1968). The nature of the dance today is examined in S. Jeffrey K. Wilkerson, "The Flute Calls, Totonac Voladores: Ritual Fliers of Mexico," *The World and I* 6, no. 6 (June 1991): 638–651.

S. JEFFREY K. WILKERSON

VOLCANOES. Volcanoes, integral part of the geologic makeup of Mexico, Central America, the Antilles, and the Andean nations of Latin America. In historic times, normally with little variation, about fifty volcanoes are active in any given year in the world. Compared with other natural hazards, volcanic eruptions are less frequent, result in relatively fewer human casualties, and ordinarily produce less economic loss. Nevertheless, several eruptions in Latin American history were remarkable for loss of life. Deadly eruptions after 1600 include Cotopaxi in Ecuador (1741: 2,000 lives lost; 1877: 1,000), Nevado del Ruiz in Colombia (1845: 1,000; 1985: ca. 25,000), Soufrière on Saint Vincent (1902: 1,560), Pelée on Martinique (1902–1905: 29,000), Santa María in Guatemala (1902: 6,000), and El Chichón in Mexico (1982: ca. 2,000). The three 1902 disasters, together with that of 1985, account for 75 percent of all twentieth-century deaths from volcanic activity worldwide.

Latin American historical documents record numerous additional eruptions. Mexico has a volcanic chain along the nineteenth parallel. There, for example, Colima had eruptions of various magnitude in 1576, 1590, 1611–1613, 1749, 1770, 1795, 1806–1808, 1818, 1869, 1885–1886, 1892, 1909, and 1913. Popocatépetl erupted with moderate to large force in 1720; Orizaba, in 1545, 1566, 1569, 1630, and 1687; San Martín, in 1664 and 1793–1794. Only two volcanoes have been born in historic times in North America, both in Mexico: Jorullo in 1759 and Paricutín in 1943.

In Central America, all but Honduras have volcanoes. Moderate to large eruptions include Arenal (Costa Rica, 1500s and 1968–1969), Momotombo (Nicaragua, 1560 and 1609), Pacaya (Guatemala, 1565, 1664, and 1965), Santa Ana (El Salvador, 1576 and 1880), San Miguel (El Salvador, 1586), Masaya (Nicaragua, 1670), San Salvador (El Salvador, 1671), Atitlán (Guatemala, 1827), Turrialba (Costa Rica, 1866), Momotombo (Ni-caragua, 1905), Irazú (Costa Rica, 1918 and 1963–1965), Acatenango (Guatemala, 1925), Izalco (El Salvador, 1955 and 1957), Poas (Costa Rica, 1961), Cerro Negro (Nicaragua, 1962, 1968, and 1971), and Rincón de la Vieja (Costa Rica, 1967). The 1835 eruption of Cosigüina in Nicaragua was one of the major volcanic events in recorded history. In addition to that of 1902, Santa María in Guatemala had sizable eruptions in 1922, 1956, and 1976. Guatemala's Fuego is the Central American volcano with the greatest number of moderate to large eruptions, a dozen from the 1580s to the 1970s. El Salvador's Ilopango, which erupted in 1875, also erupted in pre-Columbian times, probably causing shifts in settlement patterns.

In the Antilles, volcanic activity began at much studied Pelée about 13,500 years ago. Notable eruptions occurred in 1851 and 1929–1932, in addition to the 1902–1905 episode. Soufrière (Saint Vincent) erupted in 1718, 1812, 1902–1903, 1971–1972, and 1979. There has been volcanic activity in historic times on Guadeloupe, Saint Kitts, and Dominica as well.

Volcanic activity is fairly common in the Andean nations. In Colombia, Nevado del Ruiz has had twelve eruptive stages in the last 11,000 years, notably in 1595, 1845, and 1985. Galeras erupted with moderate to large force in 1535, 1590, 1616, 1717, 1834, 1869, and 1924. Puracé erupted in 1849 and 1885; Doña Juana, in 1899. Ecuador has some of the largest volcanoes in the world. Cotopaxi has had a dozen moderate to large eruptions in historic times, notably those of 1744, 1768, and 1877. Reventador has been just as active, with larger twentieth-century eruptions in 1929, 1936, 1944, 1958, and 1960. Guagua Pichincha (near Quito) erupted in 1566,

1587, 1660, and 1831; Tungurahua, in 1886 and 1918—all with moderate to large explosions. Sangay has been regularly active, especially in the 1730s, 1840s, and 1930s. Ecuador's territory includes the Galápagos with Fernandina, Cerro Azul, and Sierra Negra volcanoes.

Peru's volcanic activity has had moderate force, aside from Huayna Putina's large eruption in 1600. El Misti, Peru's most famous volcano, erupted in 1677, 1784, and 1787; Tutupaca, in 1780 and 1802. Ubinas has erupted with the greatest frequency, a dozen times between 1677 and 1969. Among Latin nations, Chile has the greatest number of active volcanoes, mainly in the less-populated south. In colonial days, Peteroa (1660 and 1762) and Nevados de Chillán (around 1750) erupted. Twentieth-century eruptions have included Puyehue (1921 and 1960), Cerro Azul (also called Quizapu, 1907, 1914, and 1932), and Llaima (1946–1947 and 1957).

Latin America's historic eruptions provide examples of diverse physical hazards: (1) Pyroclastic flows of hot rock fragments mixed with hot gases move rapidly from the volcano, as at El Chichón (1982) and Pelée (1902). (2) Lahars, or mudflows, result from ice/snowmelts or released water impoundments mixed with debris. These submerge adjacent farmland and villages, as at Cotopaxi (1877), Santa María (1902), Irazú (1964–1965), and Nevado del Ruiz (1985). (3) Tephra, or ash falls, make breathing difficult, cover vegetation, and can collapse or bury structures. Eruptions notable for the distance tephra traveled are Cosigüina (1835: 672 miles), Soufrière (1902: 792 miles), and Cerro Azul (1932: 1,776 miles). Some evidence indicates that weathered volcanic soil is especially fertile; research supports the conclusion that volcanic dust contributes to global cooling by blocking sunlight. (4) Lava, or molten rock, erupts relatively nonexplosively and moves slowly. Nevertheless, it can engulf whole villages, as at Parícutin (1943). (5) Sometimes explosions send forth solid projectiles, as at Arenal (1968). (6) Toxic gases can be health hazards (Masaya, 1946). Before the twentieth century, disease and starvation were more significant longer-term results of eruptions.

See also **Environment and Climate; Latin America; Science.**

BIBLIOGRAPHY

Russell J. Blong, *Volcanic Hazards* (1984).

Centro Regional De Sismología Para América Del Sur, *Riesgo volcánico: Evaluación y mitigación en América Latina* (1989).

David T. Lescinsky, "Nevado del Ruiz Volcano, Colombia: A Comprehensive Bibliography," in *Journal of Volcanology and Geothermal Research* 42, no. 1–2 (1990): 211–224.

Payson D. Sheets and Donald K. Grayson, eds., *Volcanic Activity and Human Ecology* (1979).

Tom Simkin et al., *Volcanoes of the World* (1981).

Robert Tilling, ed., *Volcanic Hazards* (1989).

Volcano News (1979–1986).

Volcano Quarterly (1992).

Additional Bibliography

Martí, Joan, and Gerald Ernst. *Volcanoes and the Environment.* Cambridge and New York: Cambridge University Press, 2005.

ROBERT H. CLAXTON

VOLIO JIMÉNEZ, JORGE (1882–1955).

Jorge Volio Jiménez (*b.* 26 August 1882; *d.* 20 October 1955), Costa Rican politician. Volio Jiménez was born in Cartago, Costa Rica, to a bourgeois family. From a young age, he held Christian and reformist ideas, in pursuit of which he formed study groups and in 1902 created the daily *La Justicia Social.* In 1903 he went to the University of Louvain in Belgium to study for the priesthood. He was ordained in 1909, at which time he also received a master's degree in philosophy. He then took his Christian-socialist ideas back to his country and worked as priest and professor. In 1911, his fighting spirit took him to Nicaragua, where he participated in the resistance against the U.S. intervention. In 1915, he left the priesthood in order to work as a journalist and professor. Between 1917 and 1919 he fought against the dictatorship of General Federico Tinoco in Costa Rica, whose defeat in the battle of El Jobo led to the reestablishment of a liberal democracy. In 1920 Volio Jiménez received the rank of major general. In 1922 he was elected to Congress and in 1923 he formed the Reformist Party, of which he was a candidate for president.

During the 1920s, Volio Jiménez outlined a reformist ideology that questioned the liberal system and the dominant oligarchy and advocated reforms favoring the working class. His program called for state intervention to obtain agrarian reform, civil rights, tax reform, political democracy, a public university, and protection of the nation's resources. He played an important role in awakening the workers, peasants, and middle class to political participation, and several of his ideas were later put into practice, especially during the 1940s. Owing to his alliance with the liberals, he served as vice president of the republic from 1924 to 1926. In 1932 he participated in a failed coup d'état and later retired from politics. Between 1940 and 1948, he was dean of Philosophy and Letters at the University of Costa Rica. From 1954 until his death in San José, Costa Rica, he served in Congress.

See also **Tinoco Granados, Federico; Volio Jiménez, Jorge.**

BIBLIOGRAPHY

Carlos Araya Pochet, *Historia de los partidos politicos: Liberación nacional* (1968).

Additional Bibliography

Chávez Méndez, Rodolfo, and Arnoldo Mora. *Un acercamiento al pensamiento teológico de Jorge Volio.* San José, Costa Rica: Ministerio de Cultura, Juventud y Deportes, Editorial de la Dirección de Publicaciones, 1998.

Ramírez A., Victoria. *Jorge Volio y la revolución viviente.* San Pedro de Montes de Oca, Costa Rica: Ediciones Guayacán, 1989.

Solís, Javier. *El benemeritazgo del general Volio.* San José, Costa Rica: Editorial Universidad Estatal a Distancia, 1990.

JORGE MARIO SALAZAR

VOLTA REDONDA. A town in the Paraíba Valley of the state of Rio de Janeiro, Volta Redonda is the home of Brazil's first steel mill, founded in 1941. Getúlio Vargas, visionary president of Brazil (1930–1945 and 1950–1954), brought the country out of the agrarian age into economic modernity by constructing a host of industrial projects, among which was the Companhia Siderúrgica Nacional (CSN). The premier integrated steelmaker, it has played a vital role in the industrialization of the country for six decades.

Deftly playing off the United States against Nazi Germany, Vargas was able to secure a more favorable deal from Washington, which included a credit of $20 million towards the transfer of technology and purchase of equipment, although the Brazilian military openly favored a closer association with Germany, the then rising continental military power. With technology and advice from the United States, the country's first steel rolled off the line in 1946.

Today, CSN produces about six million metric tons, or a little over fifth of all Brazilian annual steel production (28 million tons in 2005). The company has focused on three areas: steelmaking, mining (iron ore, dolomite, limestone), and transport and electricity infrastructure. CSN owns five mills, three in Brazil and two overseas, Heartland Steel, in the United States and Lososider, in Portugal. It has narrowly lost a bid to India's Tata to acquire the Anglo-Dutch Corus Steel in early 2007, but its internationalization push remains strong. Rather than pursue an abrupt, all-or-nothing privatization of the company, the government of Brazil began to sell off its shares in CSN as early as in 1993. Today, 95 percent of the company's shares are in private hands—the Vicunha Siderúrgica holds 45.2 percent. With China's demand for steel increasing between 10 and 13 percent per year since 2003, CSN is well-positioned to emerge as a global integrated steelmaker with its control of one of the world's largest iron mines, Casa de Pedra in the state of Minas Gerais, Brazil.

See also **Globalization; Iron and Steel Industry; Vargas, Getúlio Dornelles.**

BIBLIOGRAPHY

Baer, Werner. *The Development of the Brazilian Steel Industry*. Nashville, TN: Vanderbilt University Press, 1969.

Companhia Siderúrgia Nacional, corporate website. Available from www.csn.com.br.

Wirth, John D. *The Politics of Brazilian Development 1930–1954*. Stanford, CA: Stanford University Press, 1970.

EUL-SOO PANG

VON VACANO, ARTURO (1938–).

Arturo Von Vacano (*b.* 1938), Bolivian writer and journalist born in La Paz. Except for *El apocalipsis de Antón* (1972), an allegorical novel dealing with the violence and contradictions of a drastically stratified society in a setting marked by native cultural sacredness, the narrative of Von Vacano is highly autobiographical. *Sombra de exilio* (1970) concerns the reaching of adulthood during the Revolution of 1952 and the following years. *Morder el silencio* (1980) continues the experience of the man in *Sombra de exilio* and sets forth the impossibility of a literary vocation in a social context paralyzed by military dictatorship, violence, and the predominance of utilitarian values. All of Von Vacano's narrative strongly criticizes power and is characterized by a sense of blocked social redemption. *Morder el silencio* has been published in English as *Biting Silence* (1987), with the translation by Von Vacano himself. Von Vacano has published short pieces in Bolivian literary magazines and newspapers. Fleeing Bolivia in 1980, he lived as an exile in the United States, working as a writer, editor, and translator for United Press International in New York and Washington, D.C. In 2004, he published *Hombre masa, o, la solución de todo: novela de ideas*.

See also **Literature: Spanish America.**

BIBLIOGRAPHY

For a general view of Bolivian contemporary narrative and Von Vacano's place in it, see Luis H. Antezana, "La novela en el Último cuarto de siglo," in *Tendencias actuales en la literatura boliviana*, edited by Javier Sanjinés C. (1985). See also Ana Rebeca Prada, "Sobre *Morder el silencio* de Arturo Von Vacano," *Revista iberoamericana*, no. 134 (1986): 255–264. For interviews with Von Vacano, see Alfonso Gumucio Dagrón in his *Provocaciones* (1977), and *Hipótesis*, no. 7 (1978).

Additional Bibliography

Barnadas, Josep M. *Arturo von Vacaro: Sombra del exilio: Esquema metodológico de aproximación a la narrativa boliviana*. Cochabamba, Bolivia: Editorial los Amigos del Libro, 1977.

Castañón Barrientos, Carlos. *Literatura de Bolivia*. La Paz, Bolivia: Librería Editorial 'Juventud,' 2001.

Whitehutcher, Blanca, and Alba María Paz-Soldán. *Hacia una historia crítica de la literatura en Bolivia*. La Paz, Bolivia: PIEB, 2002.

ANA REBECA PRADA

VOODOO. *See* **Vodun, Voodoo, Vaudun.**

W

WAGLEY, CHARLES WALTER (1913–1991).

Charles Walter Wagley (*b.* 9 November 1913; *d.* 25 November 1991), American anthropologist. Born in Clarksville, Texas, and a graduate of Columbia University (B.A., 1936; Ph.D., 1941), Wagley was a leading scholar of Latin American studies and one of the most prominent anthropologists of his time. He directed Columbia's Institute of Latin American Studies from 1961 to 1969 and was the Franz Boas Professor of Anthropology from 1965 to 1971 at the same institution. In 1971 Wagley moved to the University of Florida at Gainesville, where he became graduate research professor of anthropology and Latin American studies. Wagley is best known for three field studies he carried out in Brazil between 1939 and 1950. His 1939–1940 study among the Amazonian Tapirapé Indians culminated in several articles and the book *Welcome of Tears: The Tapirapé Indians of Central Brazil* (1977), which was published in Portuguese in 1988. Collaborative work among the Tenetehara, carried out in 1941–1942 with his friend and colleague Eduardo Galvão, led to the book *The Tenetehara Indians of Brazil* (1949). The most widely known of Wagley's works, *Amazon Town: A Study of Man in the Tropics* (1953), is based upon fieldwork carried out first in 1948 among farmers and rubber collectors in the town of Itá (a pseudonym) on the banks of the Amazon.

In later years Wagley dedicated himself to writing works on race and class in Brazil, including *Minorities in the New World: Six Case Studies* (1958), with Marvin Harris; *The Latin American Tradition: Essays on the Unity and the Diversity of Latin American Culture* (1968); and *Race and Class in Rural Brazil* (1952), an edited volume based upon the Bahia State–Columbia University Community Study Project directed by Wagley in collaboration with the Brazilian anthropologist Thales de Azevedo.

See also **Anthropology; Race and Ethnicity.**

BIBLIOGRAPHY

Maxine L. Margolis and William E. Carter, eds., *Brazil, Anthropological Perspectives: Essays in Honor of Charles Wagley* (1979).

Additional Bibliography

Wagley, Charles. *Looking through the Kaleidescope: Essays in Honor of Charles Wagley.* Gainesville: Dept. of Anthropology, University of Florida, 1990.

JANET M. CHERNELA

WALCOTT, DEREK (1930–).

Derek Walcott (b. January 23, 1930) is a West Indian poet, playwright, and painter from St. Lucia in the Lesser Antilles. Walcott's poetic expression of the Caribbean experience earned him the Nobel Prize in Literature for 1992. The Swedish Academy cited Walcott, the first Caribbean writer to win this prestigious award, for the historical vision of his Homeric endeavor, *Omeros* (1990). The Odyssey-inspired sixty-four-chapter poem retells the epic, casting Creole-speaking characters in a Caribbean landscape. Walcott's artistic efforts question the place of history and the role of the artist in postcolonial society. His creolization of Eurocentric themes and forms make him a self-proclaimed "mulatto of style" and, possibly, the English language's greatest living poet.

Walcott was born in Castries, St. Lucia, and his ancestry reflects the ethnic and cultural inheritance of his island. He claims Dutch, French, and African blood and speaks English, French, and Creole. His father, a civil servant and watercolorist, died when Walcott and his twin brother were toddlers. The boys were raised, along with a sister, by their mother, a Methodist schoolteacher. Walcott spent his childhood among artistically inclined, intellectual people and acknowledges the influence of this community on his development.

Whereas other Caribbean intellectuals and artists sought education, inspiration, and opportunity in England, Walcott spent his formative years in the Caribbean—an experience that undoubtedly solidified his lifelong artistic and personal commitment to the region. He attended St. Mary's College in St. Lucia and in 1953 graduated from the University of the West Indies in Jamaica. During this time he began what he considers an artistic apprenticeship—experimenting with form in poetry and language in drama and imitating great visual artists in painting. His first works, *25 Poems* (1948), *Epitaph for the Young* (1949), and *Poems* (1951), were locally published as booklets. Even this early work reflects the breadth of Walcott's cultural references and his claims to the great traditions to which his ancestry and upbringing entitled him.

In 1950 he started the St. Lucia Arts Guild, which debuted his early plays, including *Henri-Christophe* (1950). He founded the repertory company named Little Carib Theatre Workshop in Trinidad in 1961. It became the Trinidad Theatre Workshop in 1966 and enjoyed moderate success performing in the Caribbean and North America. His early dramatic works, such as *Ti-Jean and His Brothers* (1958) and *Dream on Monkey Mountain* (1967), animate the local landscape and its folk culture to portray a culturally decolonized Caribbean.

The publication of *In a Green Night* (1962) brought Walcott recognition as a poet. The expansive and successful poetic oeuvre that followed developed his romance with Caribbean landscapes and seascapes while invoking history and its great men. He situates his own West Indian subjectivity among such figures as a New World Adam, Robinson Crusoe, Toussaint L'Ouverture, and the Old Master painters. Walcott's extensive travels outside the region increasingly informed his poetry, as suggested by *The Fortunate Traveller* (1981) and *Midsummer* (1984). Walcott's work earned him acclaim in international literary circles; however, his dramatic and poetic posturing as the inheritor of all great traditions was unfashionable among the decidedly anti-colonial impulses of his Caribbean contemporaries.

From the early 1980s, Walcott taught poetry, creative writing, and drama at Boston University while dividing his time between Trinidad and the United States. His most recent and self-stated final book, *The Prodigal* (2004), is a culmination of the themes, images, and art that have characterized his career.

See also **Literature: Spanish America.**

BIBLIOGRAPHY

Poetry Collections by Walcott

In a Green Night: Poems 1948–60. London: Cape, 1962.

The Castaway and Other Poems. London: Cape, 1965.

The Gulf and Other Poems. London: Cape, 1969.

Another Life. New York: Farrar, Straus, Giroux; London, Cape, 1973.

Sea Grapes. New York: Farrar, Straus, Giroux; London, Cape, 1976.

The Star-Apple Kingdom. New York: Farrar, Straus, Giroux 1979.

Omeros. New York: Farrar, Straus, Giroux, 1990.

The Bounty. New York: Farrar, Strauss, Giroux, 1997.

Tiepolo's Hound. New York: Farrar, Strauss, Giroux, 2000.

The Prodigal. New York: Farrar, Strauss, Giroux, 2004.

Plays by Walcott

Dream on Monkey Mountain and Other Plays. New York: Farrar, Straus, Giroux, 1970. Also contains *The Sea at Dauphin; Ti-Jean and His Brothers; Malcochon, or The Six in the Rain.*

The Joker of Seville & O Babylon! New York: Farrar, Straus, Giroux, 1978.

The Haitian Trilogy. New York: Farrar, Straus, Giroux, 2002. Contains: *Henri Christophe; The Haitian Earth; Drums and Colours.*

The Antilles: Fragments of Epic Memory: The Nobel Lecture. New York: Farrar, Straus, Giroux, 1993.

What the Twilight Says: Essays. New York: Farrar, Straus, Giroux, 1998.

Secondary Sources

Baugh, Edward, *Derek Walcott.* Cambridge and New York: Cambridge University Press, 2006.

Bobb, June D. *Beating a Restless Drum: The Poetics of Kamau Brathwaite and Derek Walcott.* Trenton, NJ: Africa World Press, 1998.

Brown, Stewart, ed. *The Art of Derek Walcott.* Bridgend, UK: Seren Books, 1991.

Burnett, Paula. *Derek Walcott: Politics and Poetics.* Gainesville: University Press of Florida, 2001.

Hamner, Robert D. *Derek Walcott,* rev. edition. New York: Twayne, 1993.

Handley, George B. *New World Poetics: Nature and the Adamic Imagination of Whitman, Neruda, and Walcott.* Athens: University of Georgia Press, 2007.

King, Bruce, *Derek Walcott and West Indian Drama.* Oxford: Clarendon Press, 1995.

Nobelprize.org. "Derek Walcott." Available from http://nobelprize.org/nobel_prizes/literature/laureates/1992/walcott-bio.html.

LARA CAHILL

WALKER, WILLIAM (1824–1860).

William Walker (*b.* 8 May 1824; *d.* 12 September 1860). The most famous American filibuster, Walker conquered Nicaragua in 1855–1856. His various expeditions to Mexico and Central America from 1853 to 1860 fostered anti-Americanism in the region. In particular his impact upon Nicaragua, which suffered extensive property destruction and much loss of life because of his involvement there, was especially profound and lingers to this day. Walker's expeditions interrupted normal transit across Nicaragua's isthmus and embroiled the United States in disputes with Mexico, the countries of Central America, Colombia, and Great Britain.

EARLY LIFE

Walker was born in Nashville, Tennessee, and graduated from the University of Nashville in 1838. He received an M.D. degree from the University of Pennsylvania in 1843 and furthered his medical education in Europe, after which he spent several years in law, journalism, and politics in New Orleans and California. Perhaps curiously, given his later military escapades, surviving documents describe the slightly built Walker as a shy, somewhat effeminate youth. Several scholars have argued that the death in 1849 of Ellen Galt Martin, a deaf mute with whom he had fallen in love, radically transformed Walker's personality and paved the way for his filibustering career.

EXPEDITION TO MEXICO

The self-proclaimed "Colonel" Walker's filibusters began on October 1853, when, aboard the schooner *Caroline,* he departed San Francisco with forty-five followers bound for Mexico's Baja (Lower) California but actually intending the eventual conquest of the Mexican state of Sonora. Walker captured La Paz on 3 November, raised a flag with two stars signifying Lower California and Sonora, proclaimed the creation of the Republic of Lower California, and soon announced himself president. Mexican resistance forced Walker to flee to Ensenada, which he proclaimed his capital. Reinforcements from California arrived there, but Walker experienced supply deficiencies and made the mistake of provoking resistance from Antonio María Melendrez by attacking the ranch of Melendrez's father.

On 18 January 1854, Walker proclaimed the formation of the Republic of Sonora, consisting of the states of Sonora and Lower California. In March, Walker and about one hundred filibusters set out for Sonora. He crossed the Colorado River into Sonora on 4 April but soon returned to Lower California. Harassed by Mexican guerrillas, Walker retreated northward, crossing the U.S. border with his thirty-three remaining followers on 8 May and surrendered to U.S. military authorities. In October, a jury in San Francisco acquitted Walker of violating American neutrality laws. By threatening Mexico with uncompensated territorial losses, however, Walker's expedition may have helped persuade Mexico to cede, in a treaty signed on 30 December 1853, the territory which became known as the Gadsden Purchase.

EXPEDITIONS TO CENTRAL AMERICA

Though Walker became one of the most despised figures in Central American history, he initially entered Nicaragua's affairs by invitation. Locked in conflict with the Legitimist, or Conservative, ruling party in Nicaragua, that country's Democrats, or Liberals, contracted in 1854 for Walker to bring three hundred filibusters (described as colonists, to avoid flagrantly violating U.S. neutrality statutes) to Nicaragua and occupy 52,000 acres of land. Walker and fifty-seven men calling themselves the Immortals departed San Francisco on 4 May 1855 and arrived in Nicaragua in June. As colonel of *La Falange Americana* (the American phalanx), Walker captured Granada, the Legitimist capital, on 13 October.

In a subsequently negotiated agreement, Walker became commander in chief of the Nicaraguan army under a coalition government. When he came into possession of letters by Minister of War Ponciano Corral, the former Legitimist Army commander, soliciting intervention from other Central American states to oust Walker, he had an excuse to eliminate his most formidable rival by having him executed for treason. From November 1855 to June 1856, Walker ruled Nicaragua through a figurehead, President Patricio Rivas. Walker received reinforcements, assisted by the Accessory Transit Company, an American enterprise holding a monopoly over isthmian transit across Nicaragua. The weekly English- and Spanish-language publication *El Nicaragüense* testified to Walker's Americanization of the country. To encourage native support, the paper dubbed Walker the Gray-eyed Man, after a Mosquito Indian legend.

In May 1856, the United States recognized Rivas's government. Following Rivas's break with Walker that June, the filibuster was elected president on June 29 in a controlled election. Inaugurated on 12 July, Walker entertained visions of one day ruling all Central America. However, the loss of U.S. recognition, growing U.S. interference with his supply of reinforcements, armed interventions by other Central American states receiving support from Great Britain, the opposition of shipping magnate Cornelius Vanderbilt, and epidemic disease combined to undermine Walker's cause. His reestablishment of slavery in a 22 September decree won him increased favor in the slave states of the American Union, but this move could not save his regime. Forced to evacuate Granada, Walker had the city destroyed.

On 1 May 1857, Walker surrendered to U.S. naval captain Charles H. Davis and subsequently returned to the United States. Still claiming the presidency of Nicaragua, Walker devoted the rest of his life to filibustering schemes.

In 1860, landing at Trujillo, Honduras, by way of Ruatán and Cozumel, Walker eventually surrendered to British naval commander Norvell Salmon, who in turn handed him over to Honduran authorities. He was executed at Trujillo by a local firing squad on 12 September 1860.

See also **Filibustering; United States–Latin American Relations.**

BIBLIOGRAPHY

Charles H. Brown, *Agents of Manifest Destiny: The Lives and Times of the Filibusters* (1980).

Albert Z. Carr, *The World and William Walker* (1963).

Frederic Rosengarten, Jr., *Freebooters Must Die! The Life and Death of William Walker, the Most Notorious Filibuster of the Nineteenth Century* (1976).

William O. Scroggs, *Filibusters and Financiers: The Story of William Walker and His Associates* (1916).

William Walker, *The War in Nicaragua* (1860; repr. 1985).

Additional Bibliography

Bolaños Geyer, Alejandro. *William Walker, the Gray-eyed Man of Destiny.* Lake Saint Louis: A. Bolaños-Geyer, 1988–1991.

Harrison, Brady. *Agent of Empire: William Walker and the Imperial Self in American Literature.* Athens: University of Georgia Press, 2004.

May, Robert E. *Manifest Destiny's Underworld: Filibustering in Antebellum America.* Chapel Hill: University of North Carolina Press, 2002.

Montúfar, Lorenzo, and Raúl Aguilar Piedra. *Walker En Centroamérica.* Alajuela: Museo Histórico Cultural Juan Santamaría, 2000.

ROBERT E. MAY

WALLACE, PETER Peter Wallace (*fl.* 1630s), Scottish buccaneer. According to popular legend, Captain Peter Wallace (Willis) was the first European to harbor inside the barrier reef along the coast of present-day Belize. His base of operations was said to be founded in 1638 near the mouth of the Belize River. Wallace captained the *Swallow*, out of Tortuga Island, and Swallow Cay off the coast of Belize City is said to have been named after his ship. His name in Spanish became "Wallix" and later "Valis" or "Ballese" and was used as the name for the settlement at the mouth of the Belize River. Emory King, president of the Belize Historical Society, favors this thesis and notes that documents discovered from the Bay Islands refer to the area as "Wallix" or "Wallis."

Other theories suggest that Belize may be of Maya origin from the word *belix,* meaning "muddy water" or *belakin,* meaning "land that looks toward the sea." It is also possible that the name Belize is derived from the Spanish term *baliza* or the French term *balise,* meaning "lighthouse" or other sea marker indicating dangerous conditions, the mouth of an important river, or the site of previous wrecks. In the eighteenth century, for example, the Spanish referred to a small settlement at the mouth of the Mississippi River as the *belize.*

See also **Buccaneers and Freebooters.**

BIBLIOGRAPHY

Narda Dobson, *A History of Belize* (1973), esp. pp. 47–52.

Emory King, *I Spent It All in Belize* (1986), esp. pp. 9–10.

Tom Barry, *Belize: A Country Guide* (1989), p. 1.

Additional Bibliography

Garber, James F. *The Ancient Maya of the Belize Valley: Half a Century of Archaeological Research.* Gainesville: University Press of Florida, 2004.

Leslie, Robert. *A History of Belize: Nation in the Making.* Benque Viejo del Carmen, Belize: Cubola Productions, 2002.

Thomson, Peter. *Belize: A Concise History.* Oxford: Macmillan Caribbean, 2004.

                                        BRIAN E. COUTTS

WARD, HENRY GEORGE (1797–1860).
Henry George Ward (*b.* 27 February 1797; *d.* 2 August 1860), British diplomat in Mexico. Son of Robert Plumer Ward, a British member of Parliament, Henry Ward entered the diplomatic service immediately after finishing his education at Harrow. Although only twenty-six when British Foreign Secretary Lord Canning appointed him second commissioner to Mexico in 1823, Ward had previously been appointed attaché at the British legation in Stockholm in 1816, at The Hague in 1818, and at Madrid in 1819. His mission was to evaluate the political stability of Mexico's new government. Together with Lionel Hervey and Charles O'Gorman,

he negotiated a trade, friendship, and navigation agreement between Mexico and Britain. In May 1825 he was officially appointed chargé d'affaires and finally succeeded in obtaining ratification by Mexico of a Treaty of Friendship, Commerce, and Navigation between Mexico and Great Britain on 15 March 1826, well before U.S. envoy Joel R. Poinsett, who promoted U.S. interests in Guadalupe Victoria's cabinet, could negotiate a similar treaty. Ward intervened in Mexican politics in favor of the conservative Scottish Rite Masons (Escoseses) and against the liberal York Rite Masons. He was influential in the naming of Manuel Mier y Terán as the director of the commission to establish the boundary between Mexico and the United States.

In February 1827 Canning recalled him from Mexico, in part because of his lavish expenditures. He returned to Britain in July 1827 and the following year published his two-volume work *Mexico in 1827,* written to evaluate mining possibilities and to stress the economic advantages of Britain's processing of Mexican raw materials. He went on to become a member of parliament and governor of Ceylon and Madras.

See also **Canning, George; Victoria, Guadalupe.**

BIBLIOGRAPHY

Henry Mc Kenzie Johnston, *Mission to Mexico* (1992).

J. Fred Rippy, *Rivalry of the U.S. and Great Britain over Latin America (1808–1830)* (1929).

Additional Bibliography

Villegas Revueltas, Silvestre. *Deuda y diplomacia: la relación México-Gran Bretaña, 1824–1884.* Mexico City: Universidad Nacional Autónoma de México, 2005.

                                 CARMEN RAMOS-ESCANDÓN

WAR OF FOUR DAYS.
War of Four Days, a struggle beginning 29 August 1932 in Quito that resulted from the congressional disqualification of president-elect Neptalí Bonifaz Ascasubi. Bonifaz, previously the first president of the Banco Central, in 1931 won Ecuador's first free election in nearly forty years. In the inevitable post election maneuvering, Congress voted to disqualify Bonifaz on the grounds that he had been born on foreign soil. The son of a Peruvian diplomat and Ecuadorian

mother, he was born at the Peruvian Embassy in Quito, technically foreign territory. More to the point, however, Bonifaz had until age forty-six listed his citizenship as Peruvian. A bitter military clash over the presidency erupted, with fighting in and around Quito. Four battalions from the Quito garrison supported Bonifaz, defending against attacks from General Ángel Isaac Chiriboga Navarro and Colonel Carlos Salazar. Quito suffered four days and nights of fierce combat during which the city went without light, water, and food. Fighting raged from house to house, with sharp exchanges of artillery fire in residential neighborhoods. The anti-Bonifaz provincial units prevailed by 1 September 1932, but only after at least 200 people had been killed.

See also **Bonifaz Ascasubi, Neptalí.**

BIBLIOGRAPHY

David W. Schodt, *Ecuador: An Andean Enigma* (1987), provides a summary treatment of Ecuadorian political economy. Osvaldo Hurtado's *Political Power in Ecuador,* translated by Nick D. Mills, Jr. (1985), offers an interpretive analysis. John D. Martz, *Ecuador: Conflicting Political Culture and the Quest for Progress* (1972), and George I. Blanksten, *Ecuador: Constitutions and Caudillos* (1964), provide accounts of the political context.

Additional Bibliography

Sampedro Villafuerte, Arturo. *De Flores a Mahuah: 170 años de pobre democracia.* Ecuador: Editorial J. Cárdenas G., 2000.

RONN F. PINEO

WAR OF INDEPENDENCE. *See* **Wars of Independence, South America.**

WAR OF JENKINS'S EAR (1739–1748).

War of Jenkins's Ear (1739–1748), war between Spain and England over transatlantic trade in the West Indies. The war resulted from the failure of England and Spain to negotiate disputes arising from issues addressed at the Peace of Utrecht (1713–1714), which granted England and, in particular, the South Sea Company, the *asiento* and the right to send a shipload of merchandise to Spanish America every year. In 1738 Captain Robert Jenkins appeared before the House of Commons and claimed that personnel on *guarda costas,* ships commissioned by local governors to search for contraband on English ships, boarded his vessel; in an ensuing dispute, his ear was cut off. After the English capture and destruction of fortifications at Portobelo, Panama, American trade was revitalized through the transition from the fleet system to the use of single ships licensed by the crown, the *registros,* which, through more rapid and frequent service, provided a greater volume of trade between Spain and its colonies. The war ended with the Treaty of Aix-la-Chapelle.

See also **Foreign Trade.**

BIBLIOGRAPHY

John Horace Parry, Philip Sherlock, and Anthony Maingot, *A Short History of the West Indies* (1987).

John Lynch, *Bourbon Spain, 1700–1808* (1989).

Additional Bibliography

Woodfine, Philip. *Britannia's Glories: The Walpole Ministry and the 1739 War with Spain.* Woodbridge, Suffolk, UK: Royal Historical Society/Boydell Press, 1998.

SUZANNE HILES BURKHOLDER

WAR OF THE MASCATES.

War of the Mascates, a battle between native Brazilian planters and Portuguese immigrant merchants in 1709–1711. The onset of Brazil's so-called Golden Age led to the swarming of Portuguese to the littoral and interior of Brazil. Their arrival triggered anti-Portuguese nativist sentiment in several parts of Portugal's most vital colony. One center of such sentiment was the northeastern sugar-producing captaincy of Pernambuco, where persistent bitter feelings existed between the indebted sugar-planting self-proclaimed aristocrats who controlled the political life of the capital, Olinda, and the merchants and clerks who lived in the port town of Recife. The planters considered the merchants, whom they termed *mascates* (peddlers), their social inferiors and blamed them for their indebtedness. The merchants and their allies resented the pretensions of the planters and their opposition to the incorporation of Recife as an independent town.

A series of clashes between the two groups led to the flight of two governors, a prolonged but ineffective siege of Recife, a surprise uprising by Recife's garrison, an early call for regional independence, and a severe repression undertaken by newly arrived governor Felix José Machado de Mendonça (1711–1715). Although there were surprisingly few casualties, the Pernambucan disturbances produced enduring resentments that would find expression in later revolts, especially those of 1817 and 1824.

See also **Pernambuco; Recife.**

BIBLIOGRAPHY

C. R. Boxer, *The Golden Age of Brazil, 1695–1750: Growing Pains of a Colonial Society* (1962), chap. 5 and sources cited therein.

Additional Bibliography

Mello, Evaldo Cabral de. *A fronda dos mazombos: nobres contra mascates, Pernambuco, 1666-1715.* São Paulo: Companhia das Letras, 1995.

DAURIL ALDEN

WAR OF THE PACIFIC.

War of the Pacific (1879–1884), an important conflict arising from a long-standing border dispute which pitted Chile against Bolivia and Peru. For years Bolivia and Chile had both claimed portions of the Atacama Desert. Then, in 1874, after years of bitter argument that threatened to precipitate a war, La Paz and Santiago settled the issue by having Chile relinquish its claims to the southern portion of the desert, in return for which La Paz promised not to increase the taxes on any Chilean corporation operating in the once-disputed territory.

In late 1878, the Bolivian dictator Hilarión Daza raised the export tax on a Chilean company mining nitrates in the Atacama. When La Paz refused to abrogate this impost, Chile, arguing that the Bolivian tax nullified the 1874 treaty, reoccupied the area it had once claimed. Daza responded by declaring war on Chile, but Santiago did not respond immediately. In April 1879, Chile officially learned that Peru had secretly signed an alliance promising to aid Bolivia if it went to war with Chile. When Peru stated that it would honor this obligation, Chile declared war on Peru and Bolivia.

Daza apparently adopted his truculent policy because his nation needed money and he believed that Santiago, already embroiled in a boundary dispute with Argentina, would not dare risk a two-front war. The Bolivian leader, however, miscalculated. Chile's president, Aníbal Pinto, although initially willing to negotiate, had little choice: domestic political and economic interests demanded that he act or be deposed.

Chile's declaration of war seemed foolhardy, since the combined Peruvian and Bolivian divisions outnumbered Chile's by two to one and Peru's fleet possessed four ironclads—including two top-heavy, and therefore unseaworthy, monitors—to Chile's two. In truth, because they all lacked a skilled officer corps, adequate weapons, and a technical infrastructure, none of the belligerents seemed prepared for war.

In order to attack their adversary and supply their troops once they went on the offensive, the two principals, Chile and Peru, first had to win control of the sea-lanes. Although the Chilean navy seemed better prepared, its commander, Admiral Juan Williams Rebolledo, adopted a passive strategy. Instead of attacking the Peruvian fleet at its home base of Callao, Williams blockaded the nitrate port of Iquique. Because this tactic deprived Peru of nitrate revenues, he believed that it would force the Peruvian fleet to attack him. Instead of complying, however, the Peruvian commander, Admiral Miguel Grau, reinforced Lima's southern garrisons and harried Chilean coastal shipping. Finally, stung into action by an angry public, Williams ventured north to attack Callao. When he arrived, he discovered that the Peruvian navy had gone south to Iquique, where it attacked the Chilean wooden ships, the *Esmeralda* and the *Covadonga,* that were blockading Iquique. During the unequal struggle, the Peruvians sank the *Esmeralda* but in the process ran one of their two ironclads, the *Independencia,* aground, leaving Admiral Grau with but one seaworthy ironclad, the *Huascar.* Thus, the battle off Iquique on 21 May 1879 altered the naval balance of power and the course of the war.

Grau, outnumbered, continued to attack Chile's coast. He even sent a vessel south to Punta Arenas to capture ships as they passed through the Strait of Magellan carrying war matériel to Chile. Williams did not respond until Peru's navy seized the Chilean troop transport the *Rimac.* Wounded by the ensuing

The Naval Battle of Iquique, fought between the Chilean *Esmeralda* and the *Huascar* on the 21st of May 1879 (engraving).
PRIVATE COLLECTION/ INDEX/ THE BRIDGEMAN ART LIBRARY

public outrage, Williams quit. His replacement, Admiral Galvarino Rivera, working in conjunction with civilian officials to refurbish the Chilean fleet, then launched an offensive designed to destroy the *Huascar*. On 8 October 1879, off Point Angamos, Chile's two ironclads, the *Blanco Encalada* and the *Cochrane*, cornered the *Huascar*. Although outnumbered, Grau refused to strike his colors. Within minutes the Chilean gunner straddled the *Huascar* and killed most of its crew, including Grau. The surviving sailors attempted to scuttle the ship, but a Chilean boarding party captured the *Huascar* before it could sink.

Although the Chileans now controlled the sea-lanes, they did not know whether to strike at the Peruvian heartland, as they had in the 1836 war of the Peru-Bolivia Confederation, or to nibble away at the edges of their enemies' territory. Given the Chilean government's lack of confidence in its military, it decided to attack the southernmost Peruvian province of Tarapacá. In October 1879 the Chileans landed at Pisagua and Junín. Although Santiago's troops had to make a seaborne assault and scale well-defended bluffs, they subdued the enemy garrisons. After establishing a beachhead, Chilean commander General Erasmo Escala planned to advance inland, severing Iquique's supply lines to the interior of Peru. This tactic, in conjunction with a naval blockade, was designed to effect a Chilean takeover of the nitrate-rich province of Tarapacá.

Neither Peru nor Bolivia had remained passive while the Chileans were marshaling their forces. General Daza had ponderously marched his improvised, hastily raised army from the *altiplano* to Arica. The plans called for Daza to march his men south to a point where they would link up with a Peruvian army led by General Juan Buendía, who would advance from the south. Once united, the allied force would then supposedly drive the Chileans back into the sea from which they had so ungraciously arrived.

This grandiose operation never occurred as planned. The inept Daza led his ill-prepared and poorly equipped men into the desert, where they quickly succumbed to the heat and lack of supplies. Rather than persevere (not one of Daza's strong points), the Bolivian simply returned to Arica, without informing Buendía of his changed plans. Meanwhile, the Chileans penetrated the interior, capturing the oasis of Dolores.

Fortunately for Chile's Escala, an advance party from his force sighted Buendía's troops as they marched north. Thus aware of the Peruvian advance, the Chileans threw up hasty positions on a small mountain overlooking the coveted water supply. The combined Bolivian-Peruvian force launched their attack late in the afternoon of 19 November 1879. Their futile assaults in the face of determined Chilean opposition collapsed. The allied army fled to the interior.

Before the Chileans captured the province of Tarapacá, one more battle remained. One of Escala's subordinates, who believed the Peruvians to be demoralized, launched an attack on the city of Tarapacá. This audacious plan collapsed because of faulty intelligence and an unexpectedly quick Peruvian response. Although the Chileans lost heavily in that engagement, the remaining Peruvians retreated and within a matter of days Chile had occupied Iquique.

The Chilean military's poor performance in the Tarapacá campaign forced President Aníbal Pinto to act cautiously. He ordered his men to land in the province of Tacna, a strategy which he hoped would force the Peruvians to counterattack. When they did not, Pinto ordered an assault on Moquegua. The Chilean commander, Manuel Baquedano, easily captured the city but had to launch a brutal frontal assault to dislodge the Peruvians from the high ground. Regrettably from the Chilean point of view, this action did not inspire Peruvian commander Admiral Lizardo Montero to counterattack. Thus, Baquedano ordered his men to cross the desert and capture the city of Tacna.

This trek began on 8 April 1880. By early May the Chileans had advanced to within 23 miles of their objective. The allied army had dug in on a promontory commanding the road to Tacna. As before, Baquedano simply overpowered his outmanned enemy. While successful, this tactic proved costly in terms of men; some Chilean units suffered 30 percent casualties. Still, the assault carried Tacna and permitted the Chileans to take the port of Arica in a daring predawn assault. By June, Chile controlled Tacna.

Following an abortive peace conference, the Chileans planned to move on Lima. After the Chilean civilians raised an army of 20,000, Baquedano ordered General José Villagrán to secure a bridgehead at Chilca while Baquedano brought up the main portion of the army by sea. With some mid-campaign personnel changes the attack went as planned, so that by early December 1880 the Chilean army stood poised to attack Lima.

The Peruvian defenses consisted of two lines of hastily built fortifications anchored on low mountains and reinforced by the fleet's remaining monitor. Rather than flanking Lima's defense line, which would have allowed the Chileans to envelop their objective, Baquedano as always ordered a frontal assault. On 13 January 1881 the Chileans forded the Lurín River and, after bloody fighting, broke the enemy's line. Chilean discipline, however, collapsed: rather than pursuing the enemy, many troops looted the city of Chorrillos, allowing the enemy's army to flee to Lima. When an attempt to negotiate the surrender of the Peruvian capital collapsed, the Chileans again attacked, easily vanquishing the remaining defenders dug in along the Surco River. By 17 January, the Chileans had taken Lima.

Regrettably for Chile, peace did not follow. A newly formed Peruvian government proved hesitant to cede Tarapacá as well as Tacna to Chile. Moreover, the remnants of the Peruvian army continued to resist. Facing the possibility of a protracted war, in 1881 and 1882 the Chileans launched punitive expeditions to eradicate Peruvian reistance. The struggle dragged on, however, consuming Chilean treasure and blood. Only in 1883, when the Chilean army had vanquished the forces of Andrés Cáceres at Huamachaca, did Peru capitulate and sign a peace treaty ceding Tarapacá to Chile and allowing it to occupy Tacna and Arica for ten years. When faced with the possibility of an invasion, Bolivia, which had withdrawn into the *altiplano,* accepted an armistice that gave the Atacama to Chile. By 1884, Chile had increased its size, acquired a monopoly of the world's supply of nitrates, and dominated the Southern Hemisphere's Pacific Coast.

See also **Atacama Desert; Daza, Hilarión; La Paz; Pinto Garmendia, Aníbal; Williams Rebolledo, Juan.**

BIBLIOGRAPHY

Robert N. Boyd, *Chili: Sketches of Chili and the Chilians During the War 1879–1880* (1881).

Mariano Felipe Paz-Soldán, *Narración histórica de la guerra de Chile contra Perú y Bolivia* (1884).

Gonzalo Bulnes, *La guerra del Pacífico* (1919).

Carlos Dellepiane, *Historia militar del Perú*, vol. 2 (1941).

Roberto Querejazu Calvo, *Guano, salitre, sangre* (1979); *Historia del ejército de Chile*, vols. 5 and 6 (1981).

Augusto Pinochet, *La guerra del Pacífico* (1984).

William F. Sater, *Chile and the War of the Pacific* (1986).

Additional Bibliography

Larraín Mira, Paz. *Presencia de la mujer chilena en la Guerra del Pacífico.* Santiago de Chile: Universidad Gabriela Mistral, 2002.

Méndez Notari, Carlos. *Héroes del silencio: los veteranos de la Guerra del Pacífico, 1884–1924.* Santiago: Ediciones Centro de Estudios Bicentenario, 2004.

WILLIAM F. SATER

WAR OF THE PERU–BOLIVIA CONFEDERATION.

War of the Peru-Bolivia Confederation (1836–1839), a conflict between Chile and an alliance of Peru and Bolivia. In 1836, the Bolivian leader Andrés Santa Cruz created a confederation consisting of his country and Peru. The government in Santiago, displeased by the creation of a more powerful neighbor to the north, soon had reason to fear the confederation when the Santa Cruz government nullified an 1835 treaty that had given Chileans preferential tariff treatment. Peru, anxious to develop its port of Callao, also imposed a special tax on goods entering the nation via the Chilean port of Valparaíso. Both measures jeopardized Santiago's economy. Angered by these steps and the fact that a political enemy, General Ramón Freire, had used a Peruvian port to launch an expedition hoping to depose the Joaquín Prieto government, Chile's leader, Diego Portales, ordered his fleet to attack Callao, where it seized three Peruvian vessels. Infuriated, Santa Cruz arrested Chile's envoy but almost immediately released him with an apology. Portales seized upon the occasion of this diplomatic gaffe to demand that Santa Cruz apologize for the arrest; pay Chile money it had lent Peru; offer compensation for the abortive Freire expedition; and, finally, not only limit Peruvian naval strength but dissolve the confederation. When Santa Cruz refused, Portales declared war.

Initially, Chile did not fare well. Santa Cruz's troops vanquished the first Chilean expeditionary force soon after it landed in Peru. Santa Cruz's peace terms proved generous: Chile had only to return the three boats it had captured earlier and tacitly recognize the confederation. In return, the confederation would pay part of its debt to Chile and would permit Santiago's army to return home. However, once the Chileans reached home, their government repudiated the agreement and sent another army, under General Manuel Bulnes, against the confederation. In early 1839, Bulnes defeated the forces of Santa Cruz, first at the battle of Buin, then on 20 January 1839 at Yungay. The Bolivian leader fled and the confederation collapsed, allowing Chile to control the Pacific Coast for decades.

See also **Peru-Bolivia Confederation.**

BIBLIOGRAPHY

Robert N. Burr, *By Reason or Force: Chile and the Balancing of Power in South America*, 1830–1905 (1965), pp. 33–57; *Historia del ejército de Chile* (1981), pp. 189–240.

Additional Bibliography

Fajardo Sainz, Humberto. *Andrés de Santa Cruz y la Unión Latino Americana.* Santa Cruz de la Sierra, Bolivia: H. Fajardo Sainz, 2003.

Maquito Colque, Tania Micaela. *La sociedad arequipeña y la Confederación Perú-Boliviana, 1836–1839.* Arequipa, Peru: DREMSUR Editores, 2003.

WILLIAM F. SATER

WAR OF THE SPANISH SUCCESSION.

War of the Spanish Succession (1701–1713), a conflict between France and Austria (Bourbons and Hapsburgs) for the Spanish throne. After the death of the childless Hapsburg monarch Charles II, the principal candidates for the Spanish throne were the Austrian archduke Charles and Philip of Anjou, the grandson of the French monarch Louis XIV. Both were direct descendants of Philip IV of Spain through the marriages of his daughters. On his deathbed, Charles II left the throne to Philip of Anjou, but the inheritance was disputable since Philip's grandmother, María Teresa, had renounced her rights to the Spanish throne when she married Louis XIV.

In May 1702, an Austrian, British, and Dutch alliance declared war on France and Spain. With a shortage of troops, arms, and supplies, Spain depended on France to support Philip's claim. Thus, the war on Spanish soil was fought chiefly by foreign troops. The war began with an unsuccessful allied attempt to seize Cádiz in August 1702. This was quickly followed by the destruction of the Franco-Spanish silver fleet in Vigo Bay, resulting in Spain's increased reliance on French shipping for the protection of the fleet system. Although trade between France and the Spanish colonies was officially prohibited, interloping trade thrived under the mask of French protection and during the war France benefited more from Spain's colonies than Spain did.

In 1703 Portugal joined the allies, thus giving England a strategic base for operations. Aided by rebels and insurgents, the allies took Valencia and Catalonia in 1705 and entered Madrid in 1706. However, a decisive Franco-Spanish victory at Almansa in 1707 marked an important turning point in the war. The Treaty of Utrecht (1713) acknowledged Philip V as king of Spain and the Indies, gave Charles (now emperor) the Spanish Netherlands and possessions in Italy (thereby dissolving the Burgundian-Hapsburg empire), and made important trading concessions to England (the Asiento, or slave trade).

See also **Asiento.**

BIBLIOGRAPHY

Pedro Voltes Bou, *El Archiduque Carlos de Austria, rey de los Catalanes* (1953).

Juan Mercader Riba, *El capitans generals* (1957) and *Felipe V y Catalunya* (1968).

Henry Kamen, *The War of Succession in Spain, 1700–1715* (1969).

Alan David Francis, *The First Peninsular War, 1702–1713* (1975).

Additional Bibliography

Bernardo Arés, José M de. *La sucesión de la monarquía hispánica, 1665–1725: Lucha política en las Cortes y fragilidad económica-fiscal en los reinos.* Córdoba, Spain: Universidad de Córdoba, Servicio de Publicaciones: CajaSur Publicaciones, 2006.

SUZANNE HILES BURKHOLDER

WAR OF THE SUPREMES.   War of the Supremes (1839–1842), a series of regional rebellions in Colombia, during the regime of José Ignacio de Márquez. The origins of the rebellions varied, but all shared a resentment of centralist control by Bogotá, and all were led by self-styled *jefes supremos* (supreme chiefs), usually of military extraction. The first revolt, in the southwestern province of Pasto in June 1839, started as a protest against the closure of several small convents; but by mid-1840, under the caudillo José María Obando, its goal was the ouster of Márquez, and a federal reorganization. Separate rebellions in the northeastern provinces, Antioquia, and the Atlantic coast (September–October 1840) also sought a vaguely defined "federalism"; rebels in Panama (November 1840) sought outright independence. By late 1840 the government's position seemed hopeless—a top official admitted as much in a famous circular—but crucial victories in October 1840–April 1841 turned the tide, and a combination of mass amnesties and occasional executions pacified the country by early 1842. The war produced a conservative, centralist reaction as seen in the Constitution of 1843; it also accelerated the political polarization that would give rise to the Liberal and Conservative parties by the end of the decade.

See also **Herrán, Pedro Alcántara; Mosquera, Tomás Cipriano de; Márquez, José Ignacio de.**

BIBLIOGRAPHY

Gustavo Arboleda, *Historia contemporánea de Colombia,* vol. 1 (1918).

Roberto M. Tisnés Jiménez, *María Martínez de Nisser y la Revolución de los Supremos* (1983).

Additional Bibliography

Botero Herrera, Fernando. *Estado, nación y provincia de Antioquia: Guerras civiles e invención de la región 1829-1863.* Medellín, Colombia: Hombre Nuevo Editores, 2003.

RICHARD J. STOLLER

WAR OF THE THOUSAND DAYS.
War of the Thousand Days (1899–1902), the last and greatest of Colombia's nineteenth-century civil wars. On 18 October 1899, Liberals in the northeastern

department of Santander rose in revolt against the Conservative regime in power since 1886, and warfare soon spread throughout much of the country. The Liberals failed to capitalize on their early victory at Peralonso (15–16 December 1899), permitting the government to retain the initiative throughout the war. At Palonegro (11–25 May 1900), near Bucaramanga, the government routed the Liberals in the largest battle in modern South American history. During the next two years the focus shifted to the central departments of Cundinamarca and Tolima, and conventional warfare gave way to a guerrilla struggle, both sides frequently acting without control from above. By late 1902 the warring factions, and the country, were exhausted; but the Liberals' position was far more desperate, after their failure to win support from Liberal regimes in neighboring countries. In October–November 1902 the largest Liberal armies, in Panama and on the Atlantic coast, capitulated in return for amnesty and limited political reforms; Liberal guerrilla holdouts in the interior were then crushed by the government. As many as 100,000 may have died in the conflict, from disease more than from combat wounds; the war also produced, albeit indirectly, Panama's separation from Colombia (under United States auspices) in 1903.

See also **Panama.**

BIBLIOGRAPHY

Charles W. Bergquist, *Coffee and Conflict in Colombia, 1886–1910* (1978).

Additional Bibliography

Galindo H., Julio Roberto. *Benjamín Herrera, Jorge Eliécer Gaitán: grandes caudillos liberales, gestores de la Universidad Libre.* Santafé de Bogotá, Colombia: Corporación Universidad Libre, 1998.

Parra Ramírez, Esther, and Eduardo Guevara Cobos. *Periódicos santandereanos de oposición a la regeneración, 1889–1899.* Santander, Colombia: Universidad Autónoma de Bucaramanga, 2000.

RICHARD J. STOLLER

WAR OF THE TRIPLE ALLIANCE.

War of the Triple Alliance (Great War, Paraguayan War), the protracted conflict (November 1864–March 1870) in which Paraguay fought to preserve its sovereignty from Argentina, Brazil, and Uruguay.

CAUSES OF THE WAR

Brazil precipitated the conflict by invading Uruguay and interfering in its domestic affairs. In response Paraguayan dictator Francisco Solano López closed the Paraguay River to Brazilian traffic, seized a Brazilian steamer, invaded the Brazilian province of Mato Grosso, and ignored Argentina's denial of permission to cross the Misiones region to attack the province of Rio Grande do Sul in Brazil. The victory of the Colorados, the liberal party in Uruguay, which Brazil supported, along with Argentine anger over Paraguay's invasion of its territory, concern over the growing power of Paraguay, and military attacks on Brazil led to an alliance of Argentina, Brazil, and Uruguay, which declared war against Paraguay on 1 May 1865.

The Paraguayan army carried the war into the Brazilian provinces of Mato Grosso and Rio Grande Do Sul, but Paraguay's success was short-lived. At the battle of Riachuelo on 11 June 1865, the Brazilian navy severely damaged the Paraguayan fleet on the Paraná River south of Corrientes, limiting it to defensive actions. The Paraguayan armies that had invaded the provinces of Corrientes, Argentina, and Rio Grande do Sul also were soundly defeated. Within six months the allies halted the Paraguayan offensive and thereafter kept the war confined to Paraguay. By January 1866, allied ships had blockaded Paraguay, and in April allied armies crossed the frontier. A Paraguayan victory at Curupaití in September 1866 discouraged further allied offensives, and Paraguayan defenders confined the allied forces of Bartolomé Mitre to the southwest border region.

Paraguayans regard the May 1866 and November 1867 battles of Tuyutí in the Humaitá region as victories, since they slowed allied actions. But the war turned against Paraguay in 1868. In January, Brazilian General Luis Alves de Lima e Silva, who later become the duke of Caxias, took command of the allied armies and one month later a Brazilian naval vessel passed the well-fortified complex of Humaitá, ascended the Paraguay River, and bombarded Asunción. The fall of Humaitá left Asunción indefensible, so López shifted the capital first to Luque and then to Piribebuy. The Lomas Valentinas campaigns, which occurred in the Valentine Hills some 20 miles south of Asunción in December 1868, foreshadowed the defeat of Paraguay.

The allies took Asunción and looted it but did not establish a provisional government until 15 August 1869, when both Caacupé, the new site of the Paraguayan arsenal, and Piribebuy had been captured. Brazilian troops under the Conde d'Eu, Gaston Luis Felipe d'Orleans, destroyed the Paraguayan army at Piribebuy in a bloody campaign, after which López fled north with the remnants of his army. The Acosta-ñu confrontation between Brazilian troops and Paraguayan adolescent soldiers on 16 August 1869 led to many more deaths. López continued to wage guerrilla warfare until Brazilian cavalry surprised and killed him on 1 March 1870 at Cerro Corá.

From the opening of the war López directed his own armies and then, after the first disasters, assumed field command. His use of brutal measures to continue the war, including the drafting of young boys, his intolerance of disagreement, and the execution, imprisonment, and torture of officers, government officials, and their family members during the last year of the war revealed him to be a desperate, cruel dictator. Yet his fight to defend Paraguay against overwhelming odds made him national hero.

On 20 June 1870, Brazil, Argentina, and Paraguay signed a preliminary accord that ended the war, promised elections within three months, guaranteed nonintervention in Paraguayan politics, and assured free navigation of the Paraná and Paraguay rivers. The last Brazilian troops evacuated Paraguay six years later, but Argentina continued to administer Villa Occidental until 1878, when the arbitration of U.S. President Rutherford B. Hayes resulted in its recognition as Paraguayan territory.

The causes of the war are disputed. Blame has been attributed to Francisco Solano López, Bartolomé Mitre, Dom Pedro II of Brazil, Uruguayan internal political disturbances, Brazilian national interests, and British intrigue. Most historians today believe the war developed from the efforts of Brazil, Argentina, Uruguay, and Paraguay to preserve political stability and a balance of power in the region.

The war lasted six years, in part because the allies did not marshal sufficient military power. By threatening to dismember Paraguay, they encouraged desperate Paraguayan resistance and López's stubborn persistence. According to allied agreements, Argentina was to contribute 25,000 men, Uruguay 5,000, and Brazil 40,000, but by the beginning of 1865 Brazil and Uruguay were each 20 percent under force, and Argentina sent less than half the promised troops. In August 1867 the allied army had 43,500 troops, of which 36,000 were Brazilians, 6,000 Argentines, and 1,500 Uruguayans. To defend Paraguay, López had 35,305 soldiers and 3,306 officers in 1864 and successfully recruited replacements during the war.

RESULTS OF THE WAR

Despite its defeat Paraguay remained independent, serving as a buffer between Argentina and Brazil, but it paid a high price. The war destroyed a half century of economic development, ended social experimentation that had favored the campesinos, and destroyed a system of modernization based on the country's own resources. Paraguay lost between 8.7 and 18.5 percent of its prewar population—not 50 percent, as is often claimed—38 percent of its prewar territory, including the loss to Argentina of an economically valuable 17,568 square miles in the Misiones area, and all of its heavy and most of its light industry. Foreign influences and dependence on Argentina and Brazil replaced the self-sufficient, nationally directed economy of earlier decades, and a new political instability was reflected in the thirty-two presidents who administered Paraguay between 1870 and 1932.

The war also affected Brazil and Argentina. In Brazil the war created respect for the professional officers associated with the rising urban middle classes. It delayed consideration of internal issues such as slave emancipation. And although the war squandered lives and funds abroad, it increased the size of Brazil's territory. Argentina, the chief beneficiary, obtained territory and destroyed Paraguay's rival power. Argentina invested less capital and fewer lives in the war than the other allies, while its cattle ranchers, farmers, and merchants benefited from the Brazilian military's purchases of Argentine food and supplies. And President Mitre used the war to subdue the interior and increase the power of centralized authority.

See also **López, Francisco Solano; Mato Grosso; Rio Grande do Sul.**

BIBLIOGRAPHY

A great deal of literature about Paraguay has focused on the causes of the war. Pelham Horton Box, *The Origins of the Paraguayan War* (1930, repr. 1967), blames Francisco Solano López for the war, while F. J. Mc Lynn,

"The Causes of the War of Triple Alliance: An Interpretation," in *Inter-American Economic Affairs* 33 (Autumn 1979):21–43, faults the policies of Argentina, specifically its president, Bartolomé Mitre; Juan José Cresto, *La correspondencia que engendró una guerra: Nuevos estudios sobre los orígenes de la guerra con el Paraguay* (1953, repr. 1974) holds the internal political conflicts of Uruguay responsible, and Carlos Pereyra, *Francisco Solano López y la guerra del Paraguay* (1953), attributes the war to Brazil. José Alfredo Fornós Peñalba, "Draft Dodgers, War Resisters, and Turbulent Gauchos: The War of the Triple Alliance Against Paraguay," in *The Americas* 38 (April 1982):463–479, believes foreign interests, particularly those of the British, to be more responsible, whereas Efraím Cardozo, *Vísperas de la guerra del Paraguay* (1954), argues that efforts to maintain a balance of power in the Río de la Plata region were responsible for the war. Diego Abente, "The War of the Triple Alliance: Three Explanatory Models," in *Latin American Research Review* 22, no. 2 (1987):47–69, reexamines the evidence with mathematical models and concludes that a modified power transition best explains the origin of the war.

The major revisionist work on the demographics of Paraguay was contributed by Vera Blinn Reber, "The Demographics of Paraguay: A Reinterpretation of the Great War, 1864–1870," in *Hispanic American Historical Review* 68 (May 1988): 289–319. The most complete descriptions of the war are found in Juan Beverina, *La guerra del Paraguay,* 5 vols. (1921), and Efraím Cardozo, *Hace cien años: Crónicas de la guerra de 1864–1870,* 6 vols. (1866–1872). John Hoyt Williams, *The Rise and Fall of the Paraguayan Republic, 1800–1870* (1979): 206–226, gives a description of the campaigns and effects of the war, as do two primary sources, George Thompson, *The War in Paraguay* (1869), and Andrew James Kennedy, *La Plata, Brazil, and Paraguay During the Present War* (1869). The results of the war are well covered in Harris Gaylord Warren, *Paraguay and the Triple Alliance: The Postwar Decade, 1869–1878* (1978).

Additional Bibliography

Bethell, Leslie. *The Paraguayan War (1864–1870).* London: Institute of Latin American Studies, 1996.

Leuchars, Chris. *To the Bitter End: Paraguay and the War of the Triple Alliance.* Westport, CT: Greenwood Press, 2002.

Marco, Miguel Angel de. *La guerra del Paraguay.* Buenos Aires: Planeta, 1995.

Whigham, Thomas. *The Paraguayan War.* Lincoln: University of Nebraska Press, 2002.

VERA BLINN REBER

WARS OF INDEPENDENCE, SOUTH AMERICA.

By the end of the eighteenth century, there were increased complaints in colonial South America against Spanish rule: the restrictions on direct trade outside the empire, the discrimination against American natives in appointment to high office, and other grievances real and imaginary. The dynamic economies of Caracas and Buenos Aires were more inconvenienced by Spanish commercial policy than were silver-mining Peru and Upper Peru (modern Bolivia), where economic growth was slower. Likewise, there was awareness of the American Revolution and, among the educated, familiarity with the liberal and democratic political ideas emanating from France and the Anglo-Saxon world. But in the two Perus, for example, the dominant Hispanic minority, its fears of the Indian majority heightened by memory of the Túpac Amaru revolt of 1780–1781, was hesitant to set in motion a process of change that it might not be able to control.

Prior to the Napoleonic invasion of Spain and the deposition of the Spanish royal family in 1808, there was little interest in outright independence; indeed there was widespread support for the Spanish Central Junta formed to lead resistance against the French.

Some of the colonists would have preferred to set up autonomous juntas to rule in the king's absence. But the first efforts to create such juntas were thwarted by colonial officials who remained loyal to the Spanish junta. Indeed, the first junta actually set up in America, at Montevideo in September 1808, was an ultraloyalist body whose leaders doubted the fealty to Spain of the French-born acting viceroy of the Río de la Plata, Santiago de Liniers y Bremond.

By contrast, juntas in La Paz in July and Quito in August 1809 were the work of colonists who were determined to take control into their own hands, even though still professing allegiance to Ferdinand VII. In Quito, such professions were perfectly sincere. There the junta was led by members of the local nobility who wished to preserve existing social structures yet were convinced of their own right to a greater voice in political affairs. To exercise regional power in the name of a distant monarch seemed a perfect formula for achieving these objectives. It was not acceptable, however, to the viceroy of Peru, José Fernando Abascal, who dispatched forces to Quito as well as to La Paz to suppress the juntas.

REVOLUTIONARY AGITATION

In the first half of 1810 the continuing decline of Spanish fortunes in the war against Napoleon inspired colonial activists to try again. On 19 April leading Creoles in Caracas established a junta to take the place of the Spanish captain-general of Venezuela, and on 25 May a similar junta emerged in Buenos Aires. Santa Fe de Bogotá followed on 20 July with a junta that initially included the viceroy of New Granada but soon dismissed his services. Santiago de Chile obtained its junta on 18 September, while Quito set up another of its own on 22 September. Peru conspicuously held aloof, but in Upper Peru by the end of the year a revolutionary army sent from Buenos Aires had introduced a new political order.

All the new governments initially pledged allegiance to the captive Ferdinand VII, but they lost no time in asserting their own powers. They dismissed officials suspected of disloyalty and suppressed outright opposition by force. They opened ports to neutral trade, decreed changes in the tax system, and enacted other miscellaneous reforms. At Caracas the new leadership moved quickly to abolish the slave trade, though not to disturb the institution of slavery itself.

The more radical supporters of the new governments, such as Mariano Moreno, one of the secretaries of the Buenos Aires junta, used the press and political agitation to prepare Spanish Americans for more sweeping changes, publishing the first Latin American edition of Jean-Jacques Rousseau's *Social Contract*. In Caracas Francisco de Miranda joined Simón Bolívar and other revolutionary activists in founding the Sociedad Patriótica to promote public improvements and gain support for independence. The campaign succeeded when on 5 July 1811 Venezuela became the first of the Spanish colonies to declare outright separation from the mother country.

LOYALIST RESISTANCE

Well before the Venezuelan declaration, it had become clear that not everyone was prepared to accept the creation even of juntas ostensibly loyal to Ferdinand. The Buenos Aires junta had to cope with a counterrevolutionary conspiracy only weeks after it seized power, and its forces also met resistance—at first easily overcome—in their occupation of Upper Peru. Nor did Paraguay and Uruguay, both integral parts of the same Viceroyalty of Río de la Plata, accept its claim to rule.

Likewise, outlying Venezuelan provinces such as Maracaibo and Guayana refused to accept the leadership of Caracas and its junta, which proceeded to use force in a not very successful attempt to win their obedience. Guayaquil and Cuenca (in what is now Ecuador) rejected the establishment of the second Quito junta, exactly as they had rejected the first in 1809. The junta of Santa Fe de Bogotá faced the defiance of local juntas in places such as Cartagena that insisted they had as much right as anyone in the colonial capital to exercise the power of deposed royal officials, as well as the defiance of certain areas that wanted to maintain as far as possible the colonial status quo. Peru, moreover, continued to stand apart, despite miscellaneous plotting and a minor uprising (quickly suppressed) in June 1811 at the southern town of Tacna, inspired in part by the presence of Buenos Aires forces nearby in Upper Peru.

One source of opposition to the unfolding new order was the peninsular Spaniards, who included most top colonial bureaucrats and churchmen as well as many of the wealthiest merchants. These by and large opposed any alteration in the formal relationship between America and Spain, preferring to obey whatever rump government continued to hold sway in some part of Spain. However, the Spanish element was nowhere numerous enough to control events unaided, particularly as creole officers and other Spaniards already integrated by marriage and other ties were heavily represented in the military command structure.

Among the creoles some remained distrustful of change. Others were alarmed by the efforts of the Buenos Aires forces invading Upper Peru to enlist support, for tactical reasons, of the Upper Peruvian Indian majority. The Indians, however, distrusted the intentions of the newcomers from the south and generally avoided entanglement. Black slaves and *pardos* (free blacks) in Venezuela looked askance at a revolution led by slave-owning, race-conscious creoles and were often susceptible to the appeals of loyalist opponents—even though the new government had outlawed the slave trade and in its December 1811 republican constitution outlawed discrimination on racial grounds.

The best predictor of alignments for and against the revolution was regional rivalry. It was no accident that Maracaibo and Guayana, whose political subordination to Caracas dated only from 1777 and were still not wholly reconciled to it, refused to follow the orders of the Caracas junta; nor that distant Paraguay, whose mostly mestizo population spoke more Guaraní than Spanish and felt few cultural or other ties with Buenos Aires, failed to accept the revolutionary authorities in the port city as successors to the viceroy. Guayaquil in Ecuador resented the domination of Quito and felt greater attraction, economically and otherwise, to Lima; it therefore collaborated with Peru's loyalist Viceroy Abascal.

Similar divisions of sentiment on regional lines could be seen in Peru itself. Still mindful of past Indian revolts, even reform-minded creoles in Lima generally continued looking for change to come within the imperial system. Yet in the Peruvian highlands resentment of Lima's hegemony was sufficiently intense for groups of disaffected creoles and mestizos to throw support to sporadic Indian uprisings over concrete local abuses, as at Huánuco in 1812. Two years later, creoles and mestizos in Cuzco who resented Lima and chafed under the rule of the local audiencia launched an uprising and enlisted the support of the Indian leader Mateo García Pumacahua (*see* Pumacahua Rebellion), until then a staunch loyalist. The more successful he was in recruiting other Indians, however, the more the original supporters of the rebellion had second thoughts. In the end, all highland uprisings were put down.

The resources at the disposal of the Peruvian viceroy not only proved capable of quelling outbreaks in Lima's Andean hinterland but (as in 1809) effectively defended the legitimist cause in neighboring colonies. Quito autonomists were again bested by forces from Lima—though not until 1812, by which time they had got around to a half-hearted declaration of independence. Peruvian armies supplemented by local levies similarly rolled back, in 1811, the Buenos Aires forces that had occupied Upper Peru the year before; and they repelled new invasions from the same direction in 1813 and 1815. Finally, the viceroy's forces restored Spanish authority in Chile in a campaign of 1813–1814 whose successful conclusion led to an exodus of Chilean patriots seeking refuge on the eastern side of the Andes.

CONFLICT IN THE RÍO DE LA PLATA

Revolutionary authorities in what is now Argentina went through a series of transformations from junta to junta, from first to second triumvirate, and finally a succession of "supreme dictators," in the course of which they enacted measures to limit the power of the church, expand individual liberties, and promote ties with northern Europe, but not formally declaring independence until 1816. They managed to hold the northwestern provinces against counterattacking loyalists from Upper Peru, who in 1812 penetrated as far as Tucumán. Yet after an unsuccessful campaign early in 1811 to bring Paraguay into obedience, they watched as Paraguayans in May 1811 set up their own junta, in practice independent of both Spain and Buenos Aires.

Argentine forces became bogged down in Uruguay in a confusing contest among pro-Spanish loyalists, local Uruguayan patriots, adherents of Buenos Aires, and Portuguese troops sent from neighboring Brazil in the hope of winning a foothold for Portugal in the Río de la Plata. In the short term the victor was the Uruguayan leader José Gervasio Artigas, to whom Buenos Aires forces turned over the city of Montevideo in February 1815, a year after they had wrested it from the Spanish. In 1816 superior forces from Brazil made a clean sweep and annexed the entire area.

WAR IN THE NORTH

Fortunately for those loyal to Spain, Venezuela was closer than the Río de la Plata not just to Spain itself but, more important, to Cuba and Puerto Rico, where colonial rule was not yet seriously challenged. With reinforcements from Puerto Rico as well as Venezuelan recruits, the Spanish commander Domingo de Monteverde in March 1812 launched an offensive against Venezuela's republican government and almost immediately received the fortuitous help of a major earthquake that wreaked havoc on Caracas and other patriot-held centers. Republican morale as well as material resources suffered, but the new regime was already weakened by internal dissension. Appointment of Francisco de Miranda as dictator in April could not stave off defeat. Soon after the patriots' loss of the strategic coastal fortress of Puerto Cabello, Miranda capitulated, on 25 July 1812. Taken prisoner in violation of the surrender terms (when a group of former associates prevented his escape), Miranda was shipped to a Spanish prison, where he died in 1816.

This loss was by no means the end of the fighting in Venezuela. Early in 1813 a group of patriots led by Santiago Mariño, who had early taken refuge in Trinidad, began carving out a base of operations in the east, and later in the year Bolívar, who had fled first to Curaçao and then to Cartagena, crossed into Venezuela from the west, with backing from an independent government established in New Granada. After a successful whirlwind campaign, Bolívar reentered Caracas on 6 August; however, he did not restore the 1811 Venezuelan constitution but ruled in effect as military dictator.

Earlier on his way to Caracas Bolívar had issued his decree of "War To the Death" that promised execution for any Spaniard not actively supporting independence. This measure did not initiate but rather formalized the increasing brutality of the war in Venezuela. It was never uniformly applied in practice. However, the harshest phase of the struggle was about to come, as royalist guerrilla leaders exploited not just regional but ethnic and social tensions to build up irregular forces of devastating effectiveness. Especially damaging to the patriot cause were the *llaneros* (plainsmen) of the Orinoco Basin, skilled horsemen of generally mixed race and recently threatened in their way of life by the attempt of creole landowners (for the most part now patriots) to convert the previously open range of the region into large private estates. Recruited by the royalists, they helped chase Bolívar and other revolutionary leaders into exile or hiding once more by the end of 1814.

Bolívar again made his way to New Granada, where since 1810 the revolutionists had contained royalist forces in certain regional enclaves but became enmeshed in their own internecine disputes. The most important of these quarrels pitted Santa Fe de Bogotá, which under the leadership of Antonio Nariño aspired to bring together all New Granada under a centralist form of government, against other provinces that wanted a loose federation. Lacking any effective general organization, the provinces of New Granada declared independence in piecemeal fashion—Cartagena as early as 1811 and Santa Fe two years later. But the patriots proved unable to maintain their independence. Nariño was taken captive in mid-1814 while on a campaign against one of the royalist enclaves and shipped to prison in Spain like the Venezuelan Miranda.

The return of Bolívar later that year did not save the situation. Weakened by their disunity, New Granada's patriots were no match for the veteran troops that Spain was able to send to America following the final defeat of Napoleon and the restoration of Ferdinand VII. An expeditionary force led by Pablo Morillo reached Venezuela in early 1815, after the patriot regime there had collapsed, and proceeded later that year to New Granada. Morillo took Cartagena after a bitter siege in December; a column dispatched to the interior entered Santa Fe in 1816.

THE REVIVAL OF PATRIOT FORTUNES

By mid-1816, the one part of Spanish South America where the revolutionists clearly had the upper hand was present-day Argentina, where formal independence was at last declared on 9 July 1816. Moreover, the first indication of a definitive turning of the tide was the successful crossing of the Andes early in 1817 by a joint army of Argentines and displaced Chilean patriots under the command of Argentina's José de San Martín. Coming out into the Central Valley of Chile, San Martín defeated the royalists in the battle of Chacabuco on 12 February. San Martín suffered one serious defeat before his second major triumph in the battle of Maipú on 5 April 1818. Meanwhile, however, he set up a revolutionary government in Chile, which he entrusted to his Chilean collaborator Bernardo O'Higgins, and that government finally issued Chile's declaration of independence in February 1818.

A few royalist enclaves remained after Maipú, but San Martín could now start preparing for an expedition northward to Peru, which had all along been his ultimate objective. He landed in Peru in September 1820 and consolidated a coastal foothold while hoping for either a general uprising in his favor or a negotiated peace with the Spaniards. Neither one occurred, but the royalists did withdraw their forces to the highlands, allowing San Martín to occupy Lima, where he proclaimed Peruvian independence on 28 July 1821. He organized a government and decreed various liberal reforms but was still avoiding a frontal assault on the royalist armies massed in the Andes when in July 1822 he traveled to Guayaquil to confer with his Venezuelan counterpart, Bolívar.

In the north the fortunes of war had changed even more radically. Bolívar had left New Granada slightly before Morillo restored it to royalist control, spending time in the West Indies. In 1816 he returned to Venezuela, ultimately joining forces with José Páez and other *llaneros*. Bolívar failed to dislodge the royalists from the Venezuelan highlands, but with Páez's help he created a patriot stronghold in the Llanos and in the east, organizing a government at Angostura on the lower Orinoco River.

In mid-1819 Bolívar scored his greatest military triumph by turning westward from the *llanos* to the heart of New Granada, where the royalists faced mounting discontent and a rise in patriot guerrilla activity. Bolívar's army climbed the Andes and on 7 August 1819 won a crucial victory in the battle of Boyacá. After that, resistance quickly collapsed in the central core of the colony, including Santa Fe de Bogotá which Bolívar entered three days after Boyacá.

It took three more years to expel the royalists from all outlying areas of New Granada, but meanwhile Bolívar and Páez liberated Andean Venezuela, where the definitive engagement was fought at Carabobo in June 1821. Panama fell into Bolívar's hands later the same year through a local uprising. Another spontaneous revolt had earlier deposed the royalist authorities at Guayaquil, and Bolívar commissioned his trusted lieutenant Antonio José de Sucre to proceed there to organize a campaign against Quito. Sucre's efforts culminated in victory at Pichincha, 24 May 1822, on the very outskirts of Quito, which sealed the liberation of the Ecuadorian highlands.

In July 1822 Bolívar pressured Guayaquil into joining the Republic of Colombia—formally established by the Congress of Cúcuta of 1821 to comprise all the former Viceroyalty of New Granada. He also conferred with San Martín on what still remained to be done. The details of their discussions remain a matter of controversy, but the upshot is known: San Martín resigned his command in Peru, clearing the way for Bolívar in 1823 to accept a Peruvian invitation to come and take command. Bolívar had the difficult task of combining his Colombian forces with the Chileans and Argentines left behind by San Martín and local recruits; and the Peruvian patriot leader proved fickle. The royalist armies still holding the Peruvian Andes were larger than any he had faced before. Eventually, however, Bolívar mounted a campaign that resulted in Sucre's victory at Ayacucho on 9 December 1824. It was the last major engagement of

the war in South America. Royalist resistance in Upper Peru crumbled soon afterward, and the last Spanish fortress in South America, at the Peruvian port of Callao, surrendered in January 1826.

THE IMPACT OF THE INDEPENDENCE STRUGGLE

The Wars of Independence had uneven effects. Venezuela, where population may even have declined slightly, was hardest hit, while Paraguay was affected hardly at all. Agriculture was frequently disrupted and livestock herds decimated by passing armies, but in most cases the recovery of grazing and crop farming needed little more than time and good weather. Mine owners, however, suffered widespread destruction of shafts and equipment, and merchants had seen their working capital diverted to military expenses on both sides of the struggle.

The conflict left the newly independent governments with a burden of domestic and foreign debt, as well as a class of military officers, many of humble background, who were often unwilling to accept a subordinate peacetime role. Others who backed the losing side suffered loss of positions or confiscation of assets, but there was little change in basic social structures. One of the few exceptions was a sharp decline in slavery due to (among other factors) the drafting of slaves for military service in exchange for freedom.

Additional changes flowed not from the nature of the fighting but from the breakdown of imperial controls resulting in expanded contacts with the non-Spanish world and elimination of barriers to trade with countries outside the empire. Foreign ideas and customs likewise found penetration easier, mainly among the educated and more affluent upper social sectors.

See also **Bogotá, Santa Fe de; Nariño, Antonio; Quito; Río de la Plata; Sucre Alcalá, Antonio José de.**

BIBLIOGRAPHY

The best overview in any language is that contained in the pertinent chapters of John Lynch, *The Spanish-American Revolutions, 1808–1826,* 2d ed. (1986). Valuable monographs on specific regions include Tulio Halperin Donghi, *Politics, Economics, and Society in Argentina in the Revolutionary Period* (1975); Simon Collier, *Ideas and Politics of Chilean Independence, 1808–1833* (1967); Timothy Anna, *The Fall of the Royal Government in Peru* (1979); Stephen K. Stoan, *Pablo Morillo and Venezuela, 1815–1820* (1970); Charles W.

Arnade, *The Emergence of the Republic of Bolivia* (1957); and John Street, *Artigas and the Emancipation of Uruguay* (1959).

Additional Bibliography

Archer, Christon. *The Wars of Independence in Spanish America*. Wilmington, DE: Scholarly Resources, 2000.

Guerra, François-Xavier. *Las revoluciones hispánicas: Independencias americanas y liberalismo español*. Madrid: Editorial Complutense, 1995.

Rodríguez O, Jaime E. *The Independence of Spanish America*. Cambridge: Cambridge University Press, 1998.

Terán, Marta and José Antonio Serrano Ortega. *Las guerras de independencia en la América española*. Zamora, Mexico: Colegio de Michoacán, 2002.

DAVID BUSHNELL

"WAR TO THE DEATH."

"War to the Death," the name given to a speech by Simón Bolívar during the Venezuelan War of Independence. After the fall of the First Republic, the failure of Spanish navy captain Domingo Monteverde to observe the capitulation of 25 July 1812 caused the struggle for independence to take on a progressively more violent nature. Many denunciations were made against cruelties and excesses committed by the royalist troops, as well as against provocations by the republicans. When Bolívar entered Venezuela on 15 June 1813, he delivered in Trujillo what came to be known as his "War to the Death" speech, which ended with the sentence: "Spaniards and Canarios, depend upon it, you will die, even if you are simply neutral, unless you actively espouse the liberation of America. Americans, you will be spared, even when you are culpable" (from Lynch, *The Spanish American Revolutions,* p. 203). The speech is significant in that it spared the Venezuelans who may have supported the royalists. It was Bolívar's aim then to go beyond royalist and republican categories and to make this a war between nations—Spain and America. In this sense, the speech was an affirmation of Americanism.

The war progressed, and prisoners continued to be executed on both sides until 1820. That year brought the signing of the War Regularization Treaty between Bolívar and Pablo Morillo, commander of the opposing Spanish forces, ending the period of "war to the death."

See also **Bolívar, Simón; Morillo, Pablo.**

BIBLIOGRAPHY

See Cristóbal Mendoza, *Guerra a muerte* (1951), and Lino Iribarren Celis, *Glosas para una nueva interpretación de la historia militar de Venezuela durante la Guerra a Muerte, 1814* (1964). On the War of Independence in general, see John Lynch, *The Spanish American Revolutions, 1808–1826* (1973).

Additional Bibliography

Lynch, John. *Simón Bolívar: A Life*. New Haven, CT: Yale University Press, 2006.

INÉS QUINTERO

WASHBURN, CHARLES AMES (1822–1889).

Charles Ames Washburn (*b.* 1822; *d.* 1889), U.S. diplomat and minister to Paraguay during the War of the Triple Alliance (1864–1870). A political appointee of Abraham Lincoln (and brother of Elihu Washburne, an important Republican politician), Washburn arrived in Asunción in November 1861. At first he was on good terms with Paraguay's president, Francisco Solano López, but their relationship deteriorated after the war began. In 1867, Washburn offered his services as mediator between Paraguay and the Allies, but his pompous, uncompromising personal style hardly made him the best diplomat for the task.

Rebuffed on all sides, Washburn then publicly took up the role of protector of all foreign residents in Asunción, despite the fact that López had branded many of them as probable spies. These suspicions soon focused on Washburn himself, who was accused of being the ringleader of a massive conspiracy against the government. Although nothing was ever proved, López had scores of people tortured and quite a few executed in an effort to demonstrate the U.S. minister's guilt. Instead of labeling the charge a monstrous fabrication, however, Washburn fed the suspicion by replying in detail to the accusations. He only barely escaped from Paraguay thanks to the timely arrival, in 1868, of a U.S. warship sent to remove him from the country. He later defended his actions at a Senate investigation into Paraguayan affairs and in a vituperative two-volume memoir, *The History of Paraguay* (1871).

See also **López, Francisco Solano; War of the Triple Alliance.**

BIBLIOGRAPHY

Harris Gaylord Warren, *Paraguay: An Informal History* (1949).

Additional Bibliography

Webb, Theodore A. *Impassioned Brothers: Ministers Resident to France and Paraguay.* Lanham, MD: University Press of America, 2002.

THOMAS L. WHIGHAM

WASHINGTON CONFERENCE (1889).

See **Pan-American Conferences: Washington Conference (1889).**

WASHINGTON TREATIES OF 1907 AND 1923.

In 1907 and again in 1922–1923, Washington, D.C., was the site for a Central American international conference. On both occasions the prospect of escalating isthmian conflict prompted interested powers—the United States and Mexico in 1907 and the United States alone in 1922—to bring the Central American nations together in an effort to resolve their outstanding problems. Building on the institutional machinery developed at the 1906 Marblehead and San José conferences, the isthmian delegates at the 1907 Washington Conference produced a series of treaties and conventions designed to promote isthmian peace and stability. The 1907 treaties featured a permanent Central American Court of Justice with mandatory jurisdiction and a recognition policy—the Tobar Doctrine—that called for the nonrecognition of Central American governments that came to power by revolutionary means. A subsequent dispute over the Central American Court's ruling on the Bryan-Chamorro Treaty led Nicaragua to denounce the treaties in 1917.

Uncertainty over the continuing status of the agreements and renewed international tension in Central America induced the United States to convene another Central American conference in December 1922. The resultant treaties included a more stringent de jure recognition policy, a Central American Tribunal with nonmandatory jurisdiction, and an arms limitation agreement. Dissatisfaction with the new recognition policy, however,

led to the 1932 denunciation of the Washington Treaties by Costa Rica and El Salvador.

See also **Bryan-Chamorro Treaty (1914); Central America; Central American Court of Justice; Tobar Doctrine.**

BIBLIOGRAPHY

Dana G. Munro, *Intervention and Dollar Diplomacy in the Caribbean, 1900–1921* (1964), esp. pp. 151–155, and *The United States and the Caribbean Republics, 1921–1933* (1974), esp. pp. 123–126.

Richard V. Salisbury, "Domestic Politics and Foreign Policy: Costa Rica's Stand on Recognition, 1923–1934," in *Hispanic American Historical Review* 54, no. 3 (1974): 453–478.

Thomas M. Leonard, *U.S. Policy and Arms Limitation in Central America: The Washington Conference of 1923* (1982).

Additional Bibliography

Salisbury, Richard V. *Anti-Imperialism and International Competition in Central America, 1920–1929.* Wilmington, DE: SR Books, 1989.

RICHARD V. SALISBURY

WATERMELON RIOT (PANAMA RIOT).

Watermelon Riot (Panama Riot), an incident in Colón, on the isthmus of Panama, the part of New Granada (later Colombia) on 15 April 1856. Under the Bidlack Treaty of 1846, New Granada granted the United States the "right of way or transit" across Panama in return for a U.S. pledge to guarantee the "perfect neutrality" of the isthmus and maintain uninterrupted transit. With the discovery of gold in California, U.S. investors completed a transisthmian railroad in 1855, increasing the number of travelers passing through Panama.

In the spring of 1856, the refusal of a U.S. citizen to pay a Colón street vendor for a piece of watermelon resulted in an altercation in which a shot was fired. An outraged mob of 600 local residents attacked U.S. citizens wherever they found them, and shots fired by both sides resulted in eighteen North American and two Panamanian deaths and sixteen North American and thirteen Panamanian wounded.

The incident, the first known anti-American riot in Panama, led to a U.S. decision to permanently station warships off the coast. This response, in turn, led to the first U.S. armed intervention in Panama when 160 marines landed at Colón on 19 September 1856 to protect U.S. citizens and preserve order, thereby preventing the outbreak of civil war. A subsequent claims commission awarded U.S. citizens $160,000 in damages for losses resulting from a dispute over a piece of watermelon worth ten cents.

See also **New Granada, United Provinces.**

BIBLIOGRAPHY

E. Taylor Parks, *Colombia and the United States: 1765–1934* (1935).

Graham H. Stuart and James L. Tigner, *Latin America and the United States* (1975).

J. Fred Rippy, *The Capitalists and Colombia* (1976).

Additional Bibliography

Arosemena, Pablo. *El incidente de la Tajada de Sandía: El motín del 15 de abril de 1856.* Panamá: Editorial Portobelo, 1997.

Lindsay-Poland, John. *Emperors in the Jungle: the Hidden History of the U.S. in Panama.* Durham, NC: Duke University, 2004.

Shields, Charles J. *Panama.* Philadelphia: Mason Crest Publishers, 2003.

KENNETH J. GRIEB

WATER WITCH INCIDENT.

While surveying the Paraná River in February 1855, the USS *Water Witch* was fired upon from the Paraguayan fort Itapirú, killing the helmsman and injuring others. The American warship had been sent to survey the Río de la Plata system, a regular undertaking by warships of the major naval powers. A year earlier, the *Water Witch's* commanding officer, Lieutenant Thomas Jefferson Page, had been involved in a dispute between Paraguayan president Carlos Antonio López and a U.S. business concern. As a result, Paraguay closed its waterways to foreign warships, but the United States considered the Paraná River an international waterway. In 1858 the United States dispatched a squadron of warships, which included the *Water Witch,* to resolve the issue. While the majority of the squadron remained downriver at Corrientes, Argentina, the *Water Witch* and the *Fulton* proceeded to Asunción, arriving in January 1859. The U.S. commissioner, James B. Rowlin, negotiated an apology, a $10,000 indemnity for the family of the slain helmsman, and a new commercial treaty between Paraguay and the United States.

See also **Paraná River.**

BIBLIOGRAPHY

Thomas J. Page, *La Plata, the Argentine Confederation, and Paraguay* (1859).

Pablo Max Ynsfrán, *La expedición norteamericana contra el Paraguay, 1858–1859,* 2 vols. (1954–1958).

Additional Bibliography

Mora, Frank and Jerry W Cooney. *Paraguay and the United States: Distant Allies.* Athens: University of Georgia Press, 2007.

ROBERT SCHEINA

WEAPONS INDUSTRY.

The manufacture of armaments is a relatively recent phenomenon in Latin America that has enabled the hemisphere's countries to reduce their dependence on external markets. Latin America's major arms makers are Argentina, Brazil, and Chile. Under military rule, each of these countries built up its own self-sufficient weapons industries to make handguns, rifles, machine guns, hand grenades, armored personnel carriers, combat aircraft, tanks, submarines, patrol boats, missiles, rockets, and sophisticated communications gear. During the cold war the United States and the Soviet Union specialized in high-technology systems, leaving low-tech weaponry to advanced developing countries such as Argentina, Brazil, and Chile. The world was never short of regional wars and authoritarian regimes, particularly in Africa, Latin America, the Middle East, and Asia, which offered expanding markets.

In the early 1980s the world arms market surpassed $50 billion annually. The U.S. Arms Control and Disarmament Agency has estimated that Latin America's share of the world arms market at that time was less than 10 percent. Brazil alone accounted for between 6 and 8 percent of the world's total, or more than 90 percent of Latin America's exports. Brazil, as the most diversified exporter, annually sold as much as $2 billion worth of aircraft, armored cars, missiles, rocket launchers, and communications equipment. The Middle East was its major buyer. In 1985, Iraq alone spent more than $1 billion to import various systems of Brazilian armament. As of 2007 Argentina sells rockets, missiles, and low-flying reconnaissance aircraft. Chile's main exports are explosives such as mines, cluster bombs, and aircraft bombs. In Argentina armament manufacturing was a state-owned military enterprise, whereas in Chile and Brazil private firms predominated in the arms business.

The rise of the arms industry in Latin America resulted from a number of factors: sanctions and embargoes imposed by the United States for political and ideological reasons, a desire to attain self-sufficiency, and as a natural outgrowth of successful industrial economies. Argentina began the General Directorate of Military Factories (Fabricaciones Militares), its chief arms maker, during World War II as a way to substitute domestic arms for imports. U.S.–Brazilian fallout during the administration of Jimmy Carter (1977–1981), Brazil's industrial capabilities, and growing demands from overseas markets all fueled the arms industry boom. When the United States and Europe refused to sell arms to Chile's Pinochet regime (1973–1990), Chile developed a self-sufficient domestic weapons industry. The military regimes of the Southern Cone countries were able to meet their own internal security needs.

The Brazilian arms industry was built around 1,000 private firms and 400 producers of components. In its heyday it was producing an aircraft every twenty hours, an armed personnel carrier every eighteen hours, and 1,000 weapons systems per week. Embraer, the air force's aircraft manufacturer, alone had more than 500 component suppliers. The country's twenty shipyards produced submarines, patrol boats, and tankers, working through some 400 suppliers. After the late 1980s, however, Latin America's arms industry fell on hard times as the cold war and the Iraq-Iran (1980–1988) ended, and newly installed civilian regimes in the developing world cut back on military spending.

In 2005 the top fifteen countries with the most generous military expenditures spent $1.16 trillion. For Latin America, the military budget increased by 31 percent from 1996 to 2005. In dollar terms, South America spent $15.7 billion in armament in 1996 and $20.6 billion in 2005. Brazil's military budget, which stood at 1.7 percent of its gross domestic product (GDP) in 2000, is the continent's biggest. In this respect it is far behind Jordan and Israel, which respectively spent 8.87 percent and 8.39 percent of their GDPs. The United States spent 3.07 percent.

Embraer of Brazil is the only Latin arms manufacturer among the world's 100 largest weapons makers. It sold $390 million worth of arms in 2005, accounting for 10 percent of the company's sales, and ranked fifty-fifth in the world in 2005. U.S. and European firms together claimed 93.9 percent of the global arms sales (63.3 percent and 30.6 percent, respectively); Brazil's share is a minuscule 0.1 percent.

Dual use of civilian technology in information technology has made countries such as Singapore, Korea, Taiwan, and Malaysia rising players in global arms manufacturing, but no country in Latin America can claim that role. As the result, major Latin American countries have opted to import.

Venezuela, Peru, Argentina, Cuba, and even Mexico have imported arms from Russia: Sukhoi jets, Antonov transports, Mi-17 and Mi-25 attack helicopters, tanks, armored vehicles, and AK rifles have become staple imports. Russia's exports to Latin America rose from U.S.$300 million to $600 million between 1998 and 2005, according a U.S. congressional report. Venezuela's purchase of 100,000 Kalishnikov assault rifles, fifty attack helicopters, and twenty-four SU-30 (Sukhoi) jet fighters in 2006 brought Moscow $3 billion but rattled its other nations, including the United States (Sánchez 2007b). The Russians are also building an AK automatic rifle factory in Maracay that will make Venezuela the first Latin American country to be self-sufficient in the firearms (Sánchez 2007b). Mexico, too, bought Antonov transports, Ural heavy-duty trucks, and Mi-17 and Mi-25 helicopters from Russia (Sánchez 2007b). Generally, it is less expensive to buy weapons from Russia than from the United States or Europe.

Chile has bought arms from the United States and European nations. Its purchase of a fleet of F-16s from the United States drew the ire of Peru, Bolivia, and Argentina, their traditional foes and rivals. Under the Chilean law, 10 percent of the profits from the state-owned copper mining company (CODELCO) is earmarked to the armed forces (Sánchez 2007a). With the high price of copper ($3.00 per pound at the end of 2006), the Chilean military spending spree has modernized its arsenal: The navy received eight frigates—four from the Netherlands and four from Britain—as well as two submarines from a Franco-Spanish consortium; the army received 118 Leopard IIA4 tanks from Germany at the cost of $100 million; and in addition to the ten F-16s from the United States, the air force also acquired eighteen secondhand aircraft from the Netherlands (Sánchez 2007a).

Fueled by profits from high oil, gold, and base-metal prices, Latin America has begun to spend money to acquire information-age weaponry. In addition to this, Brazil is capable of producing nuclear arms, although in public it has adhered to the terms of the Nuclear Nonproliferation Treaty, the Tlatelolco Treaty (Latin America's treaty to keep the continent free from nuclear weapons), and the agreement of the Nuclear Suppliers Group. The Brazilian air force reportedly has built at least two atomic bomb devices (between 20 to 30 kilotons); its navy has perfected indigenous techniques of enriching uranium, and the army has continued to play a role in civilian nuclear research (Feldman 2006). As late as 2006, Brazil resisted the International Atomic Energy Agency's inspection of its centrifuges at Resende (Feldman 2006). After the early 1990s, due to the "lost decade" of economic recession, the return of civilian democratic governments, the end of the cold war, and the lack of advanced information technology and chemical technologies, Latin America's arms industry fell on hard times.

See also **Armed Forces; Carter, Jimmy; Nuclear Industry; Pinochet Ugarte, Augusto.**

BIBLIOGRAPHY

Ball, Nicole. *Security and Economy in the Third World.* Princeton, NJ: Princeton University Press, 1988.

Clare, Joseph F. "Whither the Third World Arms Producers." In *World Military Expenditures and Arms Transfers*, ed. Daniel Gallick. Washington, DC: U.S. Arms Control and Disarmament Agency, 1988.

Feldman, Yana. "Country Profile 11: Brazil." FirstWatch International and Stockholm International Peace Research Institute. July 2006. Available from http://www.sipri.org/contents/expcon/cnsc1bra.html.

Franko-Jones, Patrice. *The Brazilian Defense Industry.* Boulder, CO: Westview Press, 1992.

Miller, Morton S. "Conventional Arms Trade in the Developing World, 1978–1986: Reflections on a Decade." In *World Military Expenditures and Arms Transfers 1987*, ed. Daniel Gallick. Washington, DC: U.S. Arms Control and Disarmament Agency, 1988.

Sánchez, Alex. "Chile's Aggressive Military Arm Purchase Are Ruffling the Region, Alarming in Particular Bolivia, Peru and Argentina." Council on Hemispheric Affairs, August 7, 2007 (2007a). Available from http://www.coha.org/2007/08/07/chile%e2%80%99s-aggressive-military-arm-purchases-is-ruffling-the-region-alarming-in-particular-bolivia-peru-and-argentina/.

Sánchez, Alex. "The Russian Arms Merchant Raps on Latin America's Door." Council on Hemispheric Affairs, March 20, 2007 (2007b). Available from http://www.coha.org/2007/03/20/the-russian-arm%e2%80%99s-merchant-raps-on-latin-america%e2%80%99s-door/.

Stockholm International Peace Research Institute. "Nuclear Suppliers Group–Plenary Meeting 2002." Prague, May 17, 2002. Available from http://www.sipri.org/contents/expcon/nsg_plenary02.html.

Stockholm International Peace Research Institute. "Brazil: Past Nuclear Policies." March 2006. Available from http://www.sipri.org/contents/expcon/cnsc2bra.html.

Stockholm International Peace Research Institute. "Trends in Arms Production." Arms Production Project, 2007. Available from http://www.sipri.org/contents/milap/milex/aprod/trends.html.

Tuomi, Helena, and Raimo Vayrynen, *Transnational Corporations, Armaments, and Development* (1982).

Varas, Augusto. *Militarization and the International Arms Race in Latin America.* Boulder, CO: Westview Press, 1985.

Varas, Augusto. *La política de las armas en América Latina.* Santiago: Falcultad Latinoamericana de Ciencias Sociales Collocazione, 1988.

EUL-SOO PANG

WEFFORT, FRANCISCO CORREIA

(1937–). Francisco Correia Weffort is one of Brazil's leading political scientists, known for his probing analysis of populism, syndicalism, and the role of leftist and labor-based political movements in the consolidation of democracy in Brazil and other Latin American nations with a history of authoritarian and corporatist regimes. A 1962 graduate of the University of São Paulo, Weffort has taught in Brazil and abroad. He is a faculty member of the Political Science Department of the University of São Paulo and a founding member of the Center for the Study of Contemporary Culture. In 1984, he published *Por Que Democracia?*, an important statement of the Brazilian left's renewed commitment to democracy after decades of military rule. Weffort was one of the original founders of the Workers Party (PT), serving as its secretary general in the early 1980s. In 1995, however, he became minister of culture under Party of Brazilian Social Democracy (PSDB) President Fernando Henrique Cardoso, with whom he had a long personal association. As minister, he tried to promote the wider availability of libraries and culture in general while at the same encouraging a move away from a state-centered vision of culture and cultural promotion and toward more private sources of funding.

See also **Brazil, Political Parties: Party of Brazilian Social Democracy (PSDB); Brazil, Political Parties: Workers Party (PT); Cardoso, Fernando Henrique; Universidade São Paulo.**

BIBLIOGRAPHY

French, John D. *The Brazilian Workers' ABC: Class Conflict and Alliances in Modern São Paulo.* Chapel Hill: University of North Carolina Press, 1992.

Gianini, Adhemar and Francisco C. Weffort. *PT, um projeto para o Brasil.* São Paulo: Editora Brasiliense, 1989.

Weffort, Francisco Correia. *O Populismo na Política Brasileira.* Rio de Janeiro: Paz e Terra, 1980.

Weffort, Francisco Correia. *Por Que Democracia?* São Paulo: Editora Brasiliense, 1984.

Weffort, Francisco Correia. *Qual Democracia?* São Paulo: Companhia das Letras, 1992.

ANDREW J. KIRKENDALL

WEINGÄRTNER, PEDRO (1853–1929).

Pedro Weingärtner (*b.* 1853; *d.* 1929), Brazilian painter. Born in Pôrto Alegre, Weingärtner did not take up painting until he went to Germany in 1879. After four years in Hamburg and Karlsruhe, he moved to Paris, where he studied under the painters Tony Robert-Fleury and Adolphe Bouguereau. In 1885 he received a travel award from the personal coffers of the Brazilian emperor Dom Pedro II that allowed him to continue his artistic training in Italy. Before leaving for Rome, however, he had his first exhibition. The ten paintings he showed were received favorably, and one critic was so impressed with Weingärtner's drawing abilities that he declared him "Brazil's first painter." While in Rome, he executed genre paintings and paintings with themes drawn from classical subject matter. Examples include *Bad Harvest, Jealousies, Bacanal,* and *Cock Fights.* The French press criticized *Cock Fights* when it was shown at the Paris Salon because it was a copy of Jean-Léon Gérôme's painting of the same title. Weingärtner's first gaucho paintings were exhibited in 1892. Paintings such as *Late Arrival* and *Tangled Threads* affirmed his talent.

Throughout his later life, Weingärtner spent many years living and painting in Rome. In spite of the winds of modernism, he remained devoted to themes of daily life, classical subject matter, and life among the gauchos in Pôrto Alegre.

See also **Art: The Nineteenth Century.**

BIBLIOGRAPHY

Arte no Brasil, vol. 2 (1979), pp. 569–570.

Additional Bibliography

Coelho Netto, J. Teixeira. *500 años de pintura no Brasil.* São Paulo: Lemos Editorial, 2000.

CAREN A. MEGHREBLIAN

WELLES, SUMNER (1892–1961).

Sumner Welles was a career diplomat from the United States who became assistant secretary of state (1933–1937), undersecretary of state (1937–1943), and a principal adviser on Latin American affairs to President Franklin D. Roosevelt. After several minor assignments, in 1922 Welles went on a special mission to the Dominican Republic, where he negotiated the withdrawal of U.S. Marines from the country. In *Naboth's Vineyard* (1928), Welles argued that the Dominican Republic could govern itself despite traditional U.S. assumptions about Dominican "immaturity" or the influence of foreign powers. He sharply criticized the Taft administration's policy of Dollar Diplomacy and U.S. interference in Dominican elections. He argued that U.S. military occupation generated resistance rather than pro-U.S. sentiment or economic development, and he bemoaned U.S. officials' ignorance of local customs and wishes.

On a mission to Cuba in 1933, Welles veered back toward interventionism when, following the ouster of President Gerardo Machado y Morales, he advised against recognition of the revolutionary government and called for the stationing of U.S. warships in Cuban waters. His actions made him persona non grata in Cuba and led to his recall in December 1933. Aside from the Cuban episode, Welles remained one of the main architects of the Good Neighbor Policy.

Earlier U.S. administrations had sought diplomatic solutions to crises in Mexico and Nicaragua, but the Roosevelt administration went farther in seeking to abstain from direct intervention in Latin American affairs in any form. Welles persuaded Roosevelt to remove the last U.S. forces from Haiti and the Dominican Republic and abrogate the Platt Amendment, which permitted U.S. intervention in Cuba. The withdrawal of the U.S. military was easier because pro-U.S. dictators enforced order with their own forces, but the Good Neighbor Policy was not merely rhetorical. When Mexico nationalized U.S. oil installations in 1938, Roosevelt neither dispatched troops nor backed the oil companies, forcing them to settle with Mexico.

Welles also helped make Washington officials more amenable to a series of inter-American agreements during the 1930s that enshrined the principle of nonintervention in formal declarations. Welles led a small group of State Department diplomats who had years of experience in Latin America, sophisticated understanding of inter-American affairs, respect for the sovereignty of Latin American nations, and a tendency to emphasize local conditions and actors when analyzing the causes of political developments. Welles's friendship with Roosevelt, and the president's respect for his intelligence and decisiveness, gave him easy access to the White House. Following his resignation in 1943 over policy disputes with Secretary of State Cordell Hull (and under the cloud of a sex scandal), Welles criticized U.S. interference in the election of Juan Perón in Argentina in 1945. Many Latin American diplomats shared the view of Colombian president Carlos Lleras Restrepo, who remarked in 1983: "Of all the North American public officials of this century, none has known Latin America better and wished to serve her with such sincerity as Sumner Welles" (p. 291).

See also **Good Neighbor Policy; Perón, Juan Domingo; Platt Amendment; Roosevelt, Franklin Delano; United States-Latin American Relations.**

BIBLIOGRAPHY

Primary Work

Naboth's Vineyard: The Dominican Republic, 1844–1924. 2 vols. New York: Payson and Clarke, 1928.

Secondary Works

Gellman, Irwin F. *Good Neighbor Diplomacy: United States Policies in Latin America, 1933–1945.* Baltimore: Johns Hopkins University Press, 1979.

Lleras Restrepo, Carlos. *Crónica de mi propia vida.* Vol. 2. Bogotá, Colombia: Stamato Editores, 1983.

Woods, Randall Bennett. *The Roosevelt Foreign-Policy Establishment and the "Good Neighbor": The United States and Argentina, 1941–1945.* Lawrence: Regents Press of Kansas, 1979.

THOMAS M. LEONARD
MAX PAUL FRIEDMAN

WELSER, HOUSE OF.

House of Welser, wealthy and influential German banking and commerce house based in Augsburg, which leased from the Spanish crown a large part of western Venezuela from 1528 until 1545. The lease was extended as partial payment of a considerable debt contracted by Charles V with the house of Welser. The agreement granted the Germans administration of that region (then largely unexplored and unsettled) and the right to explore, colonize, and extract whatever wealth they could. In exchange, the Welsers' obligations included the foundation of two towns of 300 *vecinos* each, the construction of three fortifications, and the importation of 50 German miners to the island of La Española (Hispaniola). The representatives of the Welsers mounted numerous expeditions into the Venezuelan interior to extract a return on their investment. Their search for gold and their pillaging alienated both Spaniards and Indians, and eventually convinced the Spanish crown to deny renewal of the lease in 1545 and to completely sever German ties with Venezuela by 1556.

See also **Banking: Overview.**

BIBLIOGRAPHY

Juan Friede, *Los Welser en la conquista de Venezuela* (1961).

Jules Humbert, *La ocupación alemana de Venezuela en el siglo XVI Periódo llamado de los Welser, 1528–1556* (1983).

Additional Bibliography

Häberlein, Mark and Johannes Burkhardt. *Die Welser: neue Forschungen zur Geschichte und Kultur des oberdeutschen Handelshauses.* Berlin: Akademie Verlag, 2002.

Walter, Rolf. *Los alemanes en Venezuela: Desde Colón hasta Guzmán Blanco.* Caracas, Venezuela: Asociación Cultural Humboldt, 1985.

J. DAVID DRESSING

WEST INDIES FEDERATION. During the long history of British colonialism there were numerous attempts at federating several or all of the English-speaking Caribbean islands. The plans invariably came from a colonial office bent on cutting administrative costs. Local residents were seldom consulted, but when they were, they tended to be quite opposed to such schemes. In 1876 there were serious riots in Barbados when "Bajans" learned that the colonial office planned to integrate them into a Windward Islands federation. Antifederalist sentiment was especially strong in the larger islands, such as Jamaica and Trinidad, and in the mainland territories of British Guiana and British Honduras. In 1926 the Wood Commission (a fact-gathering group of people led by Major E. F. L. Wood, sent by the British government to acquire knowledge of the issues involved) reported that hostility against proposals for a federation was so intense that no realization could be foreseen. A similar finding was rendered by a 1936 commission about a proposed federation linking Trinidad with the Windward and Leeward Islands.

The colonial office revived federation ideas with even greater vigor after World War II. The war represented a major watershed in West Indian life, a change that appeared to make such a federation a logical and realistic proposition. The most important changes were those that affected the colonial relationship. With its back against the wall, Great Britain ceded the defense of its Caribbean islands to the United States when it traded fourteen islands for forty U.S. destroyers. Additionally, the ability of German U-boats to cut the commercial and navigational lines with the region meant that the United States replaced Great Britain as the area's most important commercial partner.

The war also wrought internal political and social changes. Labor disturbances that spread throughout the region in 1936–1938 spawned powerful trade union movements and political parties based on them. Because these parties uniformly favored decolonization, it was assumed that they would favor it in any particular package the British were willing to offer. This sentiment led to the first conference on a British West Indian Federation in Montego Bay, Jamaica, in 1947. The meeting was successful in setting up a Standing Closer Association Committee, which drafted a federal constitution. The committee presented its report to a conference in London in 1953. Except for British Guiana and British Honduras, the governments of the ten other territories accepted the committee's proposals on federation.

In 1956 a third, and final, conference was held in London. All that remained was the selection of a site for the federal capital. This decision turned out to be more difficult than expected, a clear indication that the federation would not be free of conflict. After much acrimonious inter-island bickering, the conference selected the one island that all the others had originally opposed, Trinidad. Twelve hundred miles of sea now separated Jamaica from its ostensible capital city. In the 1958 federal elections, the federalist party won a slim majority, carried mostly by the vote of the smaller islands. In both Trinidad and Jamaica, the sitting government that supported federation lost. Because local politics was also very much a part of the election, it is difficult to determine where anti-incumbent sentiment left off and antifederation feelings began. Regardless, the vote did not bode well for the future of the federation, as majorities in the two islands that comprised more than 80 percent of the land area, 77 percent of the population, and three-quarters of the wealth, had voted against it.

Barbados's Sir Grantly Adams was selected as the first federal prime minister. He presided over a federal government with little power and even less funds. With no power to raise its own taxes, it depended on contributions from the members, assessed in terms of national income. The government also received and distributed the grants that still came from the Colonial Development and Welfare Acts. In short, it had just enough to keep up appearances and fund the University of the West Indies and the West India Regiment. This was not a federal government that could overcome the intense insularity of islands so distant geographically and politically from each other. By 1961 that insularity was particularly intense in Jamaica, where Alexander Bustamante and his Jamaican Labour Party forced a referendum on the island's continuance in the federation. Their main complaint was that, with the removal of British grants to the smaller islands, the larger islands would have to pick up the tab.

Despite a valiant effort by Norman Manley and his People's National Party to save the federation, the secessionist sentiment won. Following this decision, Trinidad's Eric Williams communicated his intention of following Jamaica's example with the celebrated statement that "nine minus one leaves zero." By 1962 the West Indies Federation was dead. All that is left of the effort are the University of the West Indies and the sentiment that forming an economic union is a more realistic first step toward an eventual political union. In the early twenty-first century, the region is still struggling to make that first step a firm and convincing one.

See also **Adams, Grantley Herbert; Barbados; British-Latin American Relations; Caribbean Sea, Commonwealth States; Guyana; Jamaica; Leeward Islands; Manley, Norman Washington; Trinidad and Tobago; Windward Islands.**

BIBLIOGRAPHY

Knight, Franklin W. *The Caribbean: The Genesis of a Fragmented Nationalism*, 2nd edition. New York: Oxford University Press, 1990.

Lowenthal, David, ed. *The West Indies Federation*. New York: Columbia University Press, 1961. Repr., Westport, CT: Greenwood Press, 1976.

ANTHONY P. MAINGOT

WEYLER Y NICOLAU, VALERIANO

(1838–1930). Valeriano Weyler y Nicolau (*b.* 17 September 1838 *d.* 20 October 1930), captain-general of Cuba (1896–1898) who supervised the Spanish war effort to subdue the independence movement on that island. His mission was twofold: to end the Cuban conflict by military means and to restore colonial consensus through political methods. He instituted what would become the model by which colonial powers responded in their colonies: the reconcentration policy.

The reconcentration policy divided Cuba into war zones. In these zones the entire population was ordered into concentration camps located in the major cities. The Spanish Army then assumed that all those found in these areas were rebels and dealt with them accordingly. The concentration camps were not meant to punish their residents, but Spanish and local officials were not prepared to care for the displaced peasants. Inadequate food supplies and sanitary facilities led to the spread of disease and the death of tens of thousands of the 300,000 inhabitants.

Under General Weyler the royalist army inflicted widespread destruction of life and property. In addition to the reconcentration policy and the attacks on the rebels, the army burned entire villages, homes, fields, and food reserves. They also slaughtered the livestock. Vast stretches of the countryside were reduced to wasteland. The new offensive led by Weyler succeeded in containing the revolutionaries but was unable to defeat them. Weyler's tactics proved to be counterproductive, as the atrocities resulted in more Cubans supporting the revolution and caused a public outcry in the United States and even in Spain. In January 1898 Weyler was replaced and a more conciliatory Spanish policy was adopted.

See also **Cuba, War of Independence.**

BIBLIOGRAPHY

Enciclopedia universal illustrada, vol. 70 (1958), pp. 153–156.

Frank Freidel, *The Splendid Little War* (1958).

Louis A. Pérez, Jr., *Cuba: Between Reform and Revolution* (1958).

Hugh Thomas, *Cuba; or, the Pursuit of Freedom* (1971).

Additional Bibliography

Ferrer, Ada. *Insurgent Cuba: Race, Nation, and Revolution, 1868–1898*. Chapel Hill: University of North Carolina Press, 1999.

Izquierdo Canosa, Raúl. *La reconcentración, 1896–1897.* Ciudad de La Habana, Cuba: Ediciones Verde Olivo, 1998.

Tone, John Lawrence. *War and Genocide in Cuba, 1895–1898.* Chapel Hill: University of North Carolina Press, 2006.

DAVID CAREY JR.

WHALING. Sixteenth-century accounts of Brazil contain numerous references to whales, although whaling was apparently never undertaken during the century. Several species, including gray, blue, humpback, and sperm whales, migrated to protected points along the Brazilian coast from June to August for breeding purposes, and their presence soon attracted mercantile interest. Around 1602 Biscayan fishermen introduced whaling to the Bay of All Saints at Salvador, Bahia. Simultaneously, the Portuguese crown declared the capture of whales and the preparation of derivatives a royal monopoly. During the rest of the seventeenth century, whaling stations spread from Bahia north to Pernambuco and Paraíba and south to Rio de Janeiro, São Paulo, and Santa Catarina on the basis of regionalized royal grants. In 1743, however, the grants pertaining to operations from Rio de Janeiro to Santa Catarina were incorporated into a single privilege, and by 1765 Pombaline policy dictated the consolidation of all Brazilian whaling activity into one exclusive grant. This consolidated privilege prevailed until 1801, when the royal monopoly was terminated.

Contrary to the designs of liberal crown policy, rather than attracting fresh entrepreneurial energy to whaling, the suspension of exclusive privilege marked the beginning of a process of stagnation and decline of a once prosperous industry. Few investors were willing to risk their capital in whaling, given that two centuries of particularly predatory practices had greatly depleted the whale populations (females, for example, were lured to whalers by way of the capture of suckling offspring). Likewise, routine refining and preparatory processes had rendered Brazilian whale oil, meat, baleen, and spermaceti inferior in quality and high in price when compared with foreign products. By the mid-nineteenth century, Brazilian whaling had succumbed to European and U.S. competition, although sporadic activity continued into the twentieth century. However, the Brazilian government officially ended whaling in 1985, and in 2000, then President Fernando Henrique Cardoso approved the nation's first whale sanctuary.

See also **Fishing Industry.**

BIBLIOGRAPHY

An authoritative history of Brazilian whaling is Myriam Ellis, *A baleia no Brasil colonial* (1969). See also Caio Prado Júnior, *The Colonial Background of Modern Brazil*, translated by Suzette Macedo (1967), pp. 217–218; Andrée Mansuy-Diniz Silva, "Imperial Reorganization, 1750–1808," in *Colonial Brazil*, edited by Leslie Bethell (1987), pp. 261–269.

Additional Bibliography

Souza, Miguel Augusto Gonçalves de. *O descobrimento e a colonização portuguesa no Brasil.* Belo Horizonte, Brazil: Editora Itatiaia, 2000.

Douglas Cole Libby

WHEAT. Wheat, widely cultivated crop important to Latin America's large-scale agribusiness as well as to small-scale peasant cultivation. Christopher Columbus introduced wheat to the New World in 1493, and the following year the first crops were reaped. The early settlers planted typical Spanish wheats of the day, such as *Triticum vulgare*. Eventually, however, hardier varieties of common wheat (*Triticum aestivum*), used in making bread and pastry, and durum wheat (*Triticum turgidum*), used in making pastas, replaced the original species. Although wheat was grown primarily for domestic use throughout the region, wheat-flour consumption tends to be highest where European influences have predominated, as in Chile and Argentina, whereas in areas where indigenous and African cultures have persevered, maize, rice, and manioc remain the principal sources of starch.

In the late nineteenth and early twentieth centuries, wheat became commercially important in a few Latin American countries. In the 1880s, for example, Argentina started to produce a large enough surplus to become a leading wheat-exporting nation. Seeking farmers to raise alfalfa as cattle feed, the cattle barons of the Argentine pampas attracted European peasants by offering them sharecropping arrangements. To prepare the land for alfalfa, the immigrants grew wheat, which proved a successful crop in its own right. Other major producer nations include Brazil, Chile, Mexico, and Uruguay, but none produces surpluses rivaling Argentina's.

Originally domesticated in the Near East, wheat is not naturally suited to Latin America's tropical climate. It grows best where temperatures are mild and rainfall moderate. This explains the success of wheat cultivation in temperate subtropical regions like the belt of the grassland extending from Rio Grande do Sul in Brazil southwest through Uruguay to Buenos Aires province in Argentina. Depending on seasonal climatic conditions, wheat also does well at high altitudes, such as in the central plateau of Mexico and the highland valleys of Ecuador.

The development of high-yield, rust-resistant wheat varieties has been the focus of considerable scientific investigation in Latin America. Experimental farms established in Argentina and Uruguay before World War I eventually bred durable grains that were well adapted to local climates and mechanical harvesting. In Mexico, a green revolution study initiated in 1943 with Rockefeller Foundation participation yielded a stout, semi-dwarf hybrid that withstood the weight of fertilizers without falling over. These discoveries helped wheat growers around the world.

Despite the fact that the improved varieties and the machines made to harvest them generally were available only to large-scale agribusiness, small-scale peasant agriculture contributed greatly to wheat production in many Latin American countries. Studies conducted in the 1970s showed that peasants produced nearly one-third of the wheat consumed in Mexico and 70 percent in Colombia. In sharp contrast to farming wheat from the air-conditioned cab of a modern combine, these peasant farmers often planted, tended, and harvested by hand. Improving their productivity and conditions continued to be a compelling problem in Latin America, for the region as a whole remained dependent on wheat imports: more than 8.2 million short tons were imported in 1989 alone. Critics of the agribusiness blame this situation on the few powerful brokers that control most of the world wheat trade. However, Argentina has become a major exporter of wheat since the 1990s, when the Argentine government eliminated the tax on wheat that had held back production. Also, in 1994 the Southern Common Market (Mercosur) trading pact lowered the tariffs on wheat between Brazil and Argentina. This change helped Argentina become Brazil's principal wheat supplier and aided its return as a major exporter in the world market.

See also **Mercosur.**

BIBLIOGRAPHY

James R. Scobie, *Revolution on the Pampas: A Social History of Argentine Wheat, 1860–1910* (1964).

Rudolph F. Peterson, *Wheat: Botany, Cultivation, and Utilization* (1965).

Roger Burbach and Patricia Flynn, *Agribusiness in the Americas* (1980).

Emiliano Ortega, "Peasant Agriculture in Latin America," in *CEPAL Review* 16 (April 1982): 75–111.

Charles B. Heiser, Jr., *Seed to Cultivation: The Story of Food*, new ed. (1990), pp. 67–79.

Additional Bibliography

Adelman, Jeremy. *Frontier Development: Land, Labour, and Capital on the Wheatlands of Argentina and Canada, 1890–1914.* Oxford: Clarendon Press, 1994.

Gelman, Jorge. *Campesinos y estancieros.* Buenos Aires: Editorial Los Libros del Riel, 1998.

CLIFF WELCH

WHEELOCK ROMÁN, JAIME (1947–1994).

Jaime Wheelock Román (*b.* 30 May 1947), Nicaraguan leader and member of the Sandinista National Directorate. Jaime Wheelock was born in Managua. His family owned a large coffee farm in the fertile region of Carazo, near the town of Jinotepe. Wheelock gained firsthand knowledge of large agro-export operations that would influence his politics later in life. He attended the best schools in Managua and traveled abroad frequently.

Wheelock met several Sandinista leaders in the 1960s but did not join the movement until 1969. In 1970 he was accused of killing a National Guardsman and fled to Chile, where he studied politics, sociology, and agricultural law. Considered brilliant by his professors, he has been described by both friends and enemies as vain, materialistic, and intellectually arrogant. During his studies in Germany in 1972 and 1973, Wheelock applied Marxist-Leninist thought to Nicaraguan politics and society. This resulted in his *Imperialismo y dictadura* (1975), a historical survey of coffee farming and agro-export industrialization since the nineteenth century.

Wheelock published the book in Nicaragua and injected his ideological and theoretical perspective into the Sandinista debate over tactics and strategy. A clash between Wheelock's "Proletarian Tendency" and the prevailing doctrine of prolonged popular war was inevitable. The Proletarians considered the Maoist, voluntarist approach of Carlos Fonseca, Henry Ruíz, and Tomás Borge to be a waste of time. The internecine struggle of the Sandinista leadership reached a pinnacle with bitter exchanges. Borge threatened Wheelock with physical harm, which caused him to take refuge in the house of a priest. The Proletarians were purged from the guerrilla organization in October 1975.

However, Wheelock pressed forward with his notion of how revolution would come about in Nicaragua. He organized labor strikes among poor barrio dwellers as the national crisis worsened in 1977 and 1978. Wheelock, Luis Carrión, and Carlos Núñez focused their attention on the vast settlements on the outskirts of Managua, where they gained a substantial following. This contributed to the reunification of the Proletarians with the Sandinista directorate in March 1979.

Wheelock became minister of agriculture and agrarian reform after the insurrection. He directed the redistribution of land confiscated from Somoza and his associates to peasants. However, Wheelock was an exponent of pragmatic, gradualist policies that were reflected in the 1981 agrarian reform law.

By 1983 the Sandinista agrarian program was threatened by the influence of counterrevolutionary forces in rural areas. Many peasants in the northeast had not benefited from the government's strategy, and they began to join the contras. Wheelock therefore decided to increase the pace of land distribution. He oversaw the creation of an extensive cooperative system known as the Area of People's Property, which gave more control over planting and harvesting to individual farmers. A new agrarian reform law was passed in January 1986. Wheelock used some of its provisions to expropriate the property of several large exporters of coffee and cotton, accusing them of sending bank credit out of the country instead of using it for production. The objective was to demonstrate Sandinista resolve to support small private farmers and peasant cooperatives. Nevertheless, the general failure of agrarian reform was one of the contributing factors to the electoral defeat of the regime in February 1990. The Nicaragua Opposition Union and Violeta Barrios De Chamorro received majorities in most rural areas. Wheelock has written several articles in the postelection period justifying the actions of the Ministry of Agriculture. He blames aggression from the Reagan administration and decapitalization of the banking system by "unpatriotic" producers for the Sandinistas' inability to secure property rights and, thus, the loyalty of peasants.

At the party congress in July 1991, the debate over agrarian reform intensified and Wheelock was the target of much criticism. Several social scientists and political figures opened a public dialogue about the plight of the peasant in the Nicaraguan revolution. Wheelock responded in the newspaper *Barricada*, explaining his views about agricultural policy in the 1980s. He also denied the rumor that he controls several properties confiscated from Somocistas.

See also **Barrios de Chamorro, Violeta; Borge, Tomás; Fonseca Amador, Carlos; Nicaragua, Organizations: Sandinista Defense Committees; Nicaragua, Sandinista National Liberation Front (FSLN); Ruíz, Henry.**

BIBLIOGRAPHY

Jamie Wheelock Román, *Imperialismo y dictadura*, 5th ed. (1980).

Forrest Colburn, *Post-Revolutionary Nicaragua* (1986).

Gabriele Invernizzi et al., *Sandinistas: Entrevistas a Humberto Ortega Saavedra, Jaime Wheelock Román y Bayardo Arce Castaño* (1986).

Rose Spalding, ed., *The Political Economy of Revolutionary Nicaragua* (1987).

Dennis Gilbert, *Sandinistas* (1988).

Jaime Wheelock, "La verdad sobre la reform agraria," in *Barricada*, 28–30 August 1991.

Additional Bibliography

Domínguez, Jorge I., and Marc Lindenberg, eds. *Democratic Transitions in Central America*. Gainesville: University Press of Florida, 1997.

MARK EVERINGHAM

WHEELWRIGHT, WILLIAM (1798–

1873). William Wheelwright, a transportation entrepreneur, was born on March 16, 1798, in Massachusetts. A merchant mariner stranded in Buenos Aires in 1822, Wheelwright arrived in 1824 in Chile, where he established himself as the operator of a merchant vessel sailing between there and Panama. Following a short stay in Ecuador, he returned to Chile, where he founded another maritime company, which operated out of the nation's most important port, Valparaíso. In 1835 the Chilean government awarded Wheelwright a monopoly to operate a steamship line in

Chilean waters. Wheelwright established the Pacific Steam Navigation Company in Britain, and had two steamships built there, the *Chile* and the *Peru*. They arrived in Chilean waters in 1840 and instituted the first regular steamship service along the Pacific Coast of South America, serving especially the northern mining ports of Caldera, Huasco, and Coquimbo, Chile, as well as Callo, the port for Lima, Peru.

Wheelwright is often credited with constructing a railroad between Santiago and Valparaíso, but the Chilean government never granted him a contract to construct the line. He later shifted his emphasis in the transportation industry by helping to build the first rail lines connecting the northern port of Caldera with the mining center of Copiapó. He also helped establish telegraph service connecting the capital with Valparaíso. He subsequently left Chile for Argentina, where he again became involved in railroading. Wheelwright died on September 26, 1873.

See also **Railroads.**

BIBLIOGRAPHY

Duncan, Roland E. "William Wheelwright and Early Steam Navigation in the Pacific, 1820–1840." *The Americas* 32, no. 2 (1975): 257–281.

Kinsbruner, Jay. "The Business Activities of William Wheelwright in Chile, 1829–1860." Ph.D. diss. New York University, 1964.

Kinsbruner, Jay. "Water for Valparaíso: A Case of Entrepreneurial Frustration." *Journal of Interamerican Studies and World Affairs* 10 (1968): 653–661.

WILLIAM F. SATER

WHITE Y LAFITTA, JOSÉ (1835–1918).

José White y Lafitta (*b.* 31 December 1835; *d.* 15 March 1918), Cuban violinist and composer. A world-famous black musician, White was born in Matanzas, Cuba. There he met the renowned American composer Louis M. Gottschalk, who in 1855 persuaded White's family to send him to study at the Paris Conservatory. There he worked under the master violinist Jean-Delphin Alard, whom he temporarily replaced at the Conservatory when Alard was away.

White was highly praised by the critics and musicians of his time. He traveled throughout the world, playing for royalty and receiving standing ovations from the most sophisticated audiences. He may have

been the first black musician to appear with an American orchestra. At home he sympathized with the Cuban insurgents in the Ten Years' War (1868–1878) against Spain. He composed a popular piece for violin and orchestra titled "La bella cubana," for which he was expelled from Cuba in 1875 when his playing it in a Havana theater caused a patriotic disturbance. Most of his works, however, are classic compositions. His Violin Concerto was played for the first time in the United States in New York City in 1974.

See also **Music: Art Music; Ten Years' War.**

BIBLIOGRAPHY

José I. Lasaga, *Cuban Lives: Pages from Cuban History* (1881; repr. 1968), vol. 2.

James M. Trotter, *Music and Some Highly Musical People* (1878).

Additional Bibliography

Sublette, Ned. *Cuba and Its Music: From the First Drums to the Mambo.* Chicago: Chicago Press Review, 2004.

JOSÉ M. HERNÁNDEZ

WHYTEHEAD, WILLIAM KELD (c. 1810–

1865). William Keld Whytehead (*b.* c. 1810; *d.* July 1865), British engineer active in Paraguay. When Paraguayan president Carlos Antonio López decided to launch a major modernization program for his country in the mid-1850s, he turned to British experts—a natural choice, considering that he had already cemented good relations with Britain thanks to the 1853–1854 visit of his son, Francisco Solano López. Thus, the younger López applied to the firm of John and Alfred Blyth of Limehouse, who agreed to supply Paraguay with more than a hundred trained machinists and engineers. To act as engineer in chief, the Blyth brothers selected their most talented man, a Scot named William Keld Whytehead.

Though only in his early thirties, Whytehead had proved himself as an arms designer and arsenal operator in France. He even held several patents for improvements in the steam engine. When he arrived in Asunción in January 1855, Whytehead was given a measure of power unheard of for a foreigner: he directed hundreds of Paraguayan laborers as well as all of his European colleagues. Over the course of a decade in rustic Paraguay, he supervised the construction of a modern arsenal, an iron foundry and industrial smithy, a railroad, new port facilities and government buildings, and a shipyard that, during Whytehead's time, produced a half-dozen steamships. Such tremendous changes in such a short time were rightly regarded as a marvel.

While paying close attention to these projects, Whytehead also had to mediate disputes between the various engineers and the Paraguayan government. For all of this, he received the handsome salary of 600 pounds annually (a sum second only to that of the president) along with many other perquisites. His myriad responsibilities notwithstanding, he still found time to maintain a voluminous correspondence in several languages (including Swedish) and to contribute articles to European technical journals.

The coming of the War of the Triple Alliance (1864–1870) placed new burdens on Whytehead. He received orders to place all of the state projects on a war footing. Not surprisingly, he began to feel the pressure of overwork. A bachelor, he had no opportunity to find solace in family life, and in the end homesickness, physical exhaustion, and repeated bouts of illness drove him to a state of depression and ultimately suicide.

See also **Industrialization; War of the Triple Alliance.**

BIBLIOGRAPHY

Josefina Plá, *The British in Paraguay, 1850–1870* (1976).

John Hoyt Williams, *The Rise and Fall of the Paraguayan Republic, 1800–1870* (1979), pp. 180–190.

THOMAS L. WHIGHAM

WIESSE, MARÍA (1892–1964).

WIESSE, MARÍA (1892–1964). María Wiesse de Sabogal was a Peruvian writer. She joined the indigenist movement around 1919 and in 1922 married the noted painter José Sabogal. She was an active member of the group led by the socialist activist José Carlos Mariátegui, about whom she wrote a biography, *José Carlos Mariátegui: Etapas de su vida* (1945). Wiesse was a born storyteller, yet her style is more didactic than literary. Among her numerous books in various genres are the biographical studies *Santa Rosa de Lima* (1922; Saint Rose of Lima) and *José Sabogal, el artista y el hombre*

(1957; José Sabogal, the Artist and the Man); the novels *La huachafita* (1927) and *Diario sin fechas* (1948; Newspaper without Dates); and the short story collections *Nueve relatos* (1933; Nine Stories), *Aves nocturnas* (1941; Nocturnal Birds), *Pequeñas historias* (1951; The Small Histories), *Linterna mágica* (1954: Magic Lantern), and *El pez de oro y otras historias absurdas* (1958; The Gold Fish and Other Absurd Histories).

See also **Literature: Spanish America; Mariátegui, José Carlos; Sabogal, José.**

BIBLIOGRAPHY

Unruh, Vicky. *Performing Women and Modern Literary Culture in Latin America: Invervening Acts.* Austin: University of Texas Press, 2006. See chapter 7.

GIOVANNA MINARDI

WILDE, EDUARDO (1844–1913).

WILDE, EDUARDO (1844–1913). Eduardo Wilde (*b.* 15 June 1844; *d.* 5 September 1913), Argentine statesman, diplomat, and writer. Wilde, born in Tupiza, Bolivia, became a symbol of the liberal "Generación del Ochenta" (Generation of 1880) that came to power with President Julio Argentino Roca in 1880. Wilde graduated from the Medical School of the University of Buenos Aires in 1870 and made an outstanding contribution during the yellow fever epidemic that scourged that city in 1871. In 1875 he was appointed professor of forensic medicine and toxicology at the University of Buenos Aires and professor of anatomy at the Colegio Nacional. He became interested in issues of public health and in 1878 published his *Curso de higiene pública*. He served in Congress as a national deputy for Buenos Aires (1874–1876, 1876–1880). President Roca chose him as his minister of justice and education, and it was in that post that Wilde made his mark. In the early 1880s, a series of laws gave the national government jurisdiction over primary education and the Civil Register of Births and Marriages (Office of Vital Statistics), which had been in the hands of the Catholic church. After successfully defending the secularizing laws, Wilde remained at the forefront in the ensuing confrontations with militant Catholics, which continued during his service as minister of the interior under

President Miguel Juárez Celman (1886–1889). During this period he returned to his concern with public health, pushing forward a project for the construction of a drainage and sewage system for the city of Buenos Aires that would produce a dramatic improvement in sanitary conditions. In 1898 he was appointed president of the National Department of Health and was later chosen to represent his country in Madrid and Brussels. He published several collections of articles and short stories, such as *Tiempo perdido* (1878) and *La lluvia* (1880).

See also **Medicine: The Modern Era.**

BIBLIOGRAPHY

Néstor T. Auza, *Católicos y liberales en la generación del ochenta* (1975).

Enrique Pezzoni, "Eduardo Wilde: Lo natural como distancia," in *La Argentina del ochenta al centenario*, edited by G. Ferrari and E. Gallo (1980).

Héctor Recalde, *La higiene y el trabajo*, 2 vols. (1988).

Additional Bibliography

Acerbi, Norberto. *Vida y obra del Dr. Eduardo Wilde: La construcción del estado nacional roquista.* Buenos Aires: Original & Copia, 1995.

EDUARDO A. ZIMMERMANN

WILLIAMS, ALBERTO (1862–1952).
Alberto Williams (*b.* 23 November 1862; *d.* 17 June 1952), Argentine composer, conductor, pianist, and teacher. Born in Buenos Aires into a family of musicians, Williams's first teacher was Pedro Beck (piano). Later he studied with Nicolás Bassi (harmony) and Luis Bernasconi (piano) at the Escuela de Música in Buenos Aires. While very young he gave piano recitals at the Teatro Colón. Williams published his first piece, the mazurka *Ensueño de juventud*, in 1881. At age twenty he received a government scholarship and went to Paris, where he enrolled at the National Conservatory and studied under Georges Mathias (piano), Auguste Durand (harmony), and Benjamin Godard (counterpoint). He was also a pupil of César Franck's and Charles de Bériot's in composition. After publishing a number of piano pieces in Paris, he returned in 1889 to Argentina, where he gave recitals and began incorporating into his works tunes, rhythms, and

forms derived from native folklore. In Argentina, he became a pioneer of the nationalist style, which began with his *El rancho abandonado* (1890), a piano work. From 1892 on, he promoted nationalism in music, founding performance series such as the Concerts of the Athenaeum, National Library Concerts, Popular Concerts, and the Buenos Aires Conservatory Concerts. He was also active in the field of music education, where he could apply the modern methods he'd learned in Paris. In 1893 he founded the Buenos Aires Conservatory of Music, later renamed the Conservatorio Williams, which he directed until 1941. He conducted in Buenos Aires and Europe, where, in performances of his own work, he led the Berlin Philharmonic in 1900 and gave three concerts in Paris during the 1930 season.

Williams's works can be divided into three periods: the first, marked by a European influence, runs through 1890; the second, for which he is known as the progenitor of Argentine nationalism, covers 1890–1910; and the third, which dates from the publication of his Symphony no. 2 (1910), was nationalist but with an international character. Williams wrote nine symphonies and other orchestral works, chamber music, choral and vocal works, and several piano pieces, as well as several pedagogical and technical books. He died in Buenos Aires.

See also **Music: Art Music.**

BIBLIOGRAPHY

Rodolfo Arizaga, *Enciclopedia de la música argentina* (1971).

Gérard Béhague, *Music in Latin America* (1979); *New Grove Dictionary of Music and Musicians,* vol. 20 (1980).

Composers of the Americas, vol. 2 (1956).

Additional Bibliography

Benarós, León. "Los primeros intentos por historiar la actividad musical académica en la Argentina." *Todo Es Historia* 455 (June 2005): 18.

Veniard, Juan María. "Los primeros intentos por historiar la actividad musical académica en la Argentina." *Inves-tiga-ciones y Ensayos* 78, no. 773 (January–December 2002): 383–402.

SUSANA SALGADO

WILLIAMS CALDERÓN, ABRAHAM
(1896–1986). Abraham Williams Calderón (*b.* 16 March 1896; *d.* 24 March 1986), Honduran

military figure and politician. In 1954, Honduras suffered directly the political results of the coup d'état in Guatemala in the form of a large strike against the United Fruit Company in the North Coast region. The strike was due in part to the perception of the company as dominating Central American politics. Political unrest, exacerbated by the strike, culminated in a split within the National Party (PNH) when it became clear that the party would nominate former President Tiburcio Carías Andino (president 1933–1949), who owed his political career to United Fruit. Former vice president Williams Calderón is known primarily for leading the newly organized National Reformist Movement (MNR) splinter group in the 10 October 1954 presidential election. He lost to Ramón Villeda Morales, who obtained 121,213 votes. The aging Carías Andino received 77,041 votes, and Williams Calderón received 53,041. Despite his poor showing in the polls, Williams Calderón and the MNR continued to play an active political role. However, with the National Party splintered, the Liberal Party (PLH) won the 1957 elections as well.

See also **Honduras; United Fruit Company.**

BIBLIOGRAPHY

Luis Mariñas Otero, 2d ed., *Honduras* (1983).

James A. Morris, *Honduras: Caudillo Politics and Military Rulers* (1984).

Additional Bibliography

Euraque, Darío A. *Reinterpreting the Banana Republic: Region and State in Honduras, 1870–1972.* Chapel Hill: University of North Carolina Press, 1996.

Funes, Matías. *Los deliberantes: El poder militar en Honduras.* Tegucigalpa, Honduras: Editorial Guaymuras, 1995.

                                    JEFFREY D. SAMUELS

Madrid's vessels, the *Covadonga*. Williams again served as commander of the Chilean flotilla during the War of the Pacific. By then an old man and perhaps ill, Williams seemed incapable of waging as aggressive a war as he had decades earlier. Obsessed with the idea of winning the Conservative Party's nomination for the 1881 presidential campaign, Williams acted cautiously to avoid any disasters which might wreck his political career. His failure to blockade Callao and his overall incompetence, which resulted in the capture of the *Rimac,* as well as his refusal to cooperate with the Aníbal Pinto government eventually led to his dismissal. As a pro-Balmaceda officer he refused to join his naval colleagues in launching the 1891 revolution. Williams also worked as a hydrographer, fixing the borders between Chile and Bolivia, and served as the maritime governor of Atacama.

See also **War of the Pacific.**

BIBLIOGRAPHY

William F. Sater, *The Heroic Image in Chile* (1973), pp. 40–42, 46, 49, 65–68, 171–172, and *Chile and the War of the Pacific* (1986), pp. 19–20, 39–41, 59–60, 184.

Additional Bibliography

Cavieres Figueroa, Eduardo. *Chile-Perú, la historia y la escuela: Conflictos nacionales, percepciones sociales.* Valparaíso, Chile: Ediciones Universitarias de Valparaíso, 2006.

Larraín Mira, Paz and Ángel Soto. *Anécdotas del Guerra del Pacífico.* Santiago, Chile: Centro de Estudios Bicentenario, Universidad Gabriela Mistral, 2006.

Leciñana Falconí, Carolina. *La Guerra del Pacífico, 120 años después: Diplomacia y negociación.* Lima: s.n., 2004.

Sater, William. *Andean Tragedy: Fighting the War of the Pacific, 1879–1884.* Lincoln: University of Nebraska Press, 2007.

                                    WILLIAM F. SATER

WILLIAMS REBOLLEDO, JUAN (1826–1910). Juan Williams Rebolledo (*b.* 1826; *d.* 1910), Chilean naval officer who commanded his country's fleet in 1865 during its difficult struggle against the Spanish navy. The son of an English officer who had helped Chile win its independence and a resourceful officer himself, Williams not only attempted to hold off the Spanish—an impossible task, given the small size of Chile's fleet—but managed to capture one of

WILLIMAN, CLAUDIO (1863–1934). Claudio Williman (*b.* 2 September 1863; *d.* 9 February 1934), president of Uruguay (1907–1911). After graduating with a degree in law in 1888, Williman taught courses in mathematics and physics at the University of the Republic. From 1902 to 1924 he served as rector of the university. He was one of the founders of the College of Mathematics and the School of Commerce, today called the College of

Economic Sciences. Between 1904 and 1907, he served as minister of government in the administration of President José Batlle y Ordóñez. After this term, Williman was nominated as a candidate for the presidency by the Colorado Party. He won the election and served from 1907 to 1911.

Williman's administration was characterized by meticulousness and strict control over public spending, and is often considered conservative when compared to that of Batlle y Ordóñez. Throughout the Williman administration, Batlle stayed in Europe with his family, but in 1910 he returned to Uruguay to take up the role of chief of the Colorado Party, and in 1911 he succeeded Williman as president.

See also **Batlle y Ordóñez, José; Uruguay, Political Parties: Colorado Party.**

BIBLIOGRAPHY

Benjamin Nahum, *La época batllista* (1984).

Washington Reyes Abadie and Andrés Vázquez Romero, *Crónica general del Uruguay,* vol. 4 (1984).

Additional Bibliography

Giménez Rodríguez, Alejandro. *El libro de los presidentes uruguayos: de Fructuoso Rivera a Jorge Batlle (1830–2004)*. Montevideo, Uruguay: Linardi y Risso, 2004.

Nahum, Benjamín. *El Uruguay del siglo XX*. Montevideo, Uruguay: Ediciones de la Banda Oriental: Instituto de Economía: Instituto de Cienca Política, 2001.

JOSÉ DE TORRES WILSON

WILLKA. *See* **Zárate Willka, Pablo.**

WILSON, HENRY LANE (1857–1932). Henry Lane Wilson (*b.* 3 November 1857; *d.* 22 December 1932), U.S. ambassador to Mexico (5 March 1910–17 July 1913). Born in Crawfordsville, Indiana, Wilson attended public school and studied at Wabash College in Crawfordsville, graduating in 1879. He practiced law in Indiana and Seattle, Washington, until 1897, when he was chosen to represent the United States as minister to Chile and Belgium before serving as ambassador to Mexico (1909–1913). At that time only the U.S. representative in Mexico held the rank of ambassador. Wilson became one of the most controversial envoys to serve in Mexico.

Wilson intensely disliked and was highly critical of President Francisco I. Madero, who assumed office in November 1911 as the result of a revolution that overthrew the government of General Porfirio Díaz. The ambassador disagreed with the aims and conduct of the regime, repeatedly recommending military intervention to restore stability. Wilson also disagreed with the objectives of U.S. President Woodrow Wilson, who took office shortly after Madero's fall and death.

Henry Lane Wilson is best known for his role in the Pact of the Embassy, which resulted in charges in Mexico that he colluded with General Victoriano Huerta to overthrow the Madero government and failed to protect the life of Madero. The ambassador felt that his actions were required to end the combat in the capital and protect the lives of American and other foreign residents. He advocated U.S. recognition of the Huerta regime, which he believed offered the best prospect for the restoration of stability in Mexico. President Woodrow Wilson ignored the ambassador in conducting subsequent relations with the Huerta regime, though Ambassador Wilson was not recalled until July 1913. Victoriano Huerta continued as president of Mexico in the face of opposition by President Wilson and a revolution in the north, until he relinquished office on 15 July 1914.

See also **Madero, Francisco Indalecio; Wilson, Woodrow.**

BIBLIOGRAPHY

Kenneth J. Grieb, *The United States and Huerta* (1969).

Michael C. Meyer, *Huerta: A Political Portrait* (1972).

Stanley R. Ross, *Francisco I. Madero: Apostle of Mexican Democracy* (1955).

Henry Lane Wilson, *Diplomatic Episodes in Mexico, Belgium, and Chile* (1927).

Additional Bibliography

Barrón, Luis. *Historias de la Revolución mexicana*. Mexico City: Centro de Investigación y Docencia Económicas; Fondo de Cultura Económica, 2004.

Eisenhower, John S. D. *Intervention! The United States and the Mexican Revolution, 1913–1917*. New York: W.W. Norton, 1993.

Meyer, Jean A., and G. Héctor Pérez-Rincón. *La revolución mexicana*. Mexico City: Tusquets Editores, 2004.

KENNETH J. GRIEB

WILSON, WOODROW (1856–1924).
Woodrow Wilson (*b*. 28 December 1856; *d*. 3 February 1924), president of the United States from 1913 to 1921. An academic-turned-politician who frequently spoke in terms of idealism, Wilson encountered frustrations in the implementation of his policies in Latin America. He disparaged the meddlesome dollar diplomacy of the previous administration of William Howard Taft and expressed confidence in the Latin American nations' capacity for self-government. In response to a mixture of concerns about hemispheric security and political stability, however, Wilson ordered several armed interventions in the region. In 1916, for example, U.S. forces moved into the Dominican Republic, occupied the capital of Santo Domingo, and became embroiled in a frustrating guerrilla war. Wilson also ordered interventions in Cuba and Haiti.

Mexico's unpredictable social revolution posed the greatest hemispheric challenge to Wilson's policies. He attempted to influence events in Mexico with two interventions: the first in the port of Veracruz in 1914 to place pressure on the dictatorial government of Victoriano Huerta (1913–1914), and the second in northern Mexico in 1916, in pursuit of rebel leader Francisco "Pancho" Villa, who had raided the border town of Columbus, New Mexico. Neither intervention brought the stable government or hemispheric security Wilson intended. His idealism combined with his use of armed intervention left a legacy of misunderstanding and bad feelings in U.S. relations with Latin America.

See also **United States–Latin American Relations.**

BIBLIOGRAPHY

Bruce J. Calder, *The Impact of Intervention: The Dominican Republic During the U.S. Occupation of 1916–1924* (1984).

Robert Freeman Smith, *The United States and Revolutionary Nationalism in Mexico* (1976).

Mark Gilderhus, *Diplomacy and Revolution* (1977) and *Pan-American Visions: Woodrow Wilson in the Western Hemisphere* (1986).

Additional Bibliography

Barrón, Luis. *Historias de la Revolución mexicana*. Mexico City: Centro de Investigación y Docencia Económicas; Fondo de Cultura Económica, 2004.

Eisenhower, John S. D. *Intervention! The United States and the Mexican Revolution, 1913–1917*. New York: W.W. Norton, 1993.

Meyer, Jean A., and G. Héctor Pérez-Rincón. *La revolución mexicana*. México: Tusquets Editores, 2004.

Ninkovich, Frank A. *The Wilsonian Century: U.S. Foreign Policy since 1900*. Chicago: University of Chicago Press, 1999.

JOHN A. BRITTON

WILSON PLAN.
Wilson Plan (1914), a diplomatic proposal by the Woodrow Wilson administration for a peaceful solution to the civil conflict between political factions in the Dominican Republic and Haiti. Under its provisions, the warring factions would lay down their arms, choose a provisional president (if they could not agree, the U.S. president would select one), and hold a constitutional convention and a peaceful election. Despite the holding of an election for a new president in the Dominican Republic, the political situation in the country further deteriorated, and in 1916 the United States military commenced an eight-year military occupation. In Haiti, the Wilson Plan was virtually unworkable because the president was chosen by the national assembly.

See also **United States-Latin American Relations.**

BIBLIOGRAPHY

Lester D. Langley, *The Banana Wars: United States Intervention in the Caribbean, 1898–1934* (1983).

David Healy, *Drive to Hegemony: The United States in the Caribbean, 1898–1917* (1988).

Additional Bibliography

Atkins, G. Pope and Larman C. Wilson. *The Dominican Republic and the United States: From Imperialism to Transnationalism*. Athens: University of Georgia Press, 1998.

Fernandez, Ronald. *Cruising the Caribbean: U.S. Influence and Intervention in the Twentieth Century*. Monroe, ME: Common Courage Press, 1994.

LESTER D. LANGLEY

WINDWARD ISLANDS. In contemporary political terms, "the Windward Islands" generally designates the ex-British colony comprising St. Lucia, St. Vincent, Grenada, and Dominica, now all independent states. Geographically and topographically, the Windwards include all the islands that stretch south from Dominica to Grenada and the Grenadines (not including Trinidad, Tobago, and Barbados). They are part of a volcanic chain and also exposed to periodic hurricanes that form off Africa in the Atlantic. The table provides information about the size, population, and gross domestic product of the formerly British islands.

For some time after Columbus's exploration of the islands, the Windwards were largely ignored by Europeans and left to the indigenous Caribs. In the early seventeenth century, the British and French undertook colonization, and so began the long struggle, an extension of long-standing Anglo-

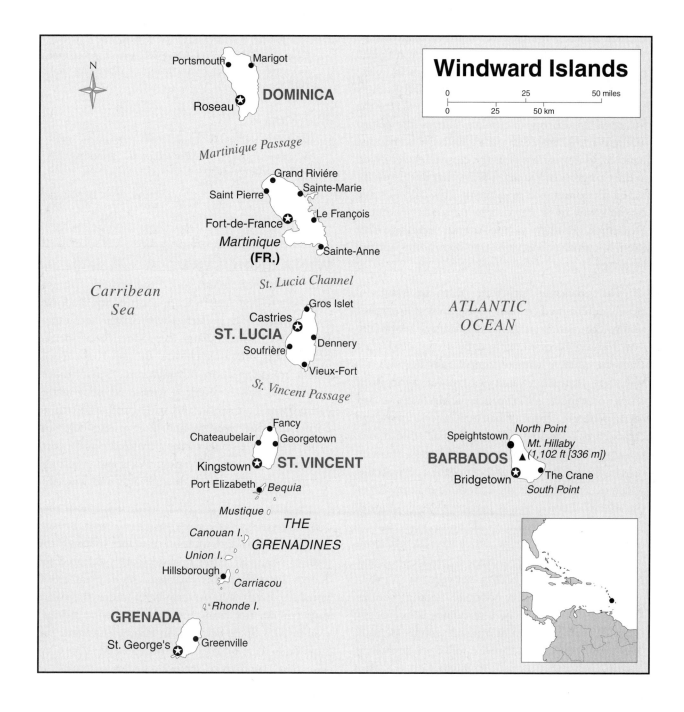

	Size (km²)	Population (in thousands)	GDP (per capita, in U.S. dollars)[a]
Dominica	750	90	3,500
St. Lucia	620	155	4,000
St. Vincent and N. Grenadines	390	130	3,000
Grenada and S. Grenadines	340	110	3,500

[a]Estimates, 2007

Table 1

French conflict, for control of these islands. The Windwards were the scene of several important naval battles. In 1782, off St. Lucia, the French Admiral de Grasse was defeated by England's Admiral Rodney in a battle that had much wider implications for the future of this European conflict. During the Napoleonic Wars (1799–1815), the islands often changed hands, and it was only after the close of the conflict, at the Congress of Vienna (1815), that Britain established its dominance over them. This colonial past explains why in St. Lucia, and to a lesser extent in Dominica, English is the official language but French patois (dialect) is the commonly spoken language.

The economic structure of these islands is largely determined by their topography. Of volcanic origin, the islands are generally rugged, mountainous, and well forested, with many streams and lakes. With an equable climate, ample rainfall, and rich soil, they produce a variety of tropical agricultural crops for export, all of which—including the formerly profitable crops of bananas, spices, limes, and cacao—are in decline. Although small-scale manufacturing has gained importance, the most substantial change has been the growth of the tourist trade, which now constitutes the economic mainstay of all the islands. Ecotourism is particularly important in Dominica, while sailing and more conventional tourism dominates in the other islands. Mustique in the St. Vincent Grenadines is privately owned, but the other small islands between St. Vincent and Grenada are very popular sailing venues. Carriacou in the Grenada Grenadines is one of the spots favored by sailors staying for longer periods. The deep sheltered harbors of Fort-de-France, Martinique, and Castries, St. Lucia, are the chief

cities in the inter-island trade of the more northern islands of St. Lucia and Dominica. Port-of-Spain, Trinidad, serves mainly the southern islands of St. Vincent and Grenada, but its oil and gas wealth is converting it into one of the main investors in the whole eastern Caribbean. All these independent islands belong to the Organization of Eastern Caribbean States (OECS) and to the Single Market and Economy plan of the Caribbean Community (CARICOM). They are also members of the United Nations and the Organization of American States.

See also **British-Latin American Relations; Caribbean Common Market (CARIFTA and CARICOM); Leeward Islands; Organization of American States (OAS).**

BIBLIOGRAPHY

Economist Intelligence Unit (EIU). *Country Profile: Windward and Leeward Islands.* London: EIU, 1997– . Annual survey.

ANTHONY P. MAINGOT

WINE INDUSTRY. An appetite for the fruit of the vine accompanied the Spanish flag and the cross to the Americas. Spanish conquistadores, settlers, and friars preferred wine to the fermented beverages of Amerindians. Reproduction of Iberian secular and religious culture in the New World meant transplantation of viticulture. Sanctification of religious rituals required wine, and missionaries carried vine cultivation and wine production to all corners of the Spanish and Portuguese colonies. Wine was also a staple of the "civilized class" (*gente decente*), which ensured wine imports and eventually the establishment of private vineyards and wineries.

NEW SPAIN

Cultivation and fermentation of grapes followed the path of conquest. After Hernán Cortés defeated the Aztecs, he ordered his *encomenderos* to plant 1,000 vines for every 100 Amerindians under their care each year for five years. Vineyards and wine production in New Spain centered in Parras, Durango, San Luis de la Paz, and Celaya, north of Mexico City. The first commercial wineries began operation in

Parras no later than 1623. By 1779 Franciscan missionaries had carried vine cultivation (*Vitis vinifera*) into California at Mission San Juan Capistrano. Grape cultivation spread throughout the California mission system, and at Mission San Gabriel it grew into a successful business. Under the guidance of Father José Zalvidea, the annual yield at San Gabriel increased between 1806 and 1827, when production reached 400 to 600 barrels of wine and 200 barrels of brandy. These early vineyards produced the Mission grape, known in other regions of the empire as the Criolla or Pais grape.

SOUTH AMERICA

In South America, Spanish settlers had introduced vine cultivation into the heartland of the Inca Empire by the 1540s. Bartolomeu de Terrazas pioneered viticulture in the Cuzco area, and grapes planted on the eastern slopes of the Andes and near Charcas supported the manufacture of aguardiente. Neither of these efforts was as successful as the vines introduced by Francisco de Carabantes in the more hospitable desert coastal zone. Vineyards soon blossomed around Lima, Trujillo, and Arequipa. Jesuit estates in the southern coastal region controlled some of the largest and most productive vineyards. Carabantes carried vines to Chile when he was sent by Pedro de Valdivia's expedition in 1548. The vineyard of Diego García de Cáceres produced the first Chilean sacramental wine in 1555. Francisco de Aguirre planted vines in the north near Copiapó, Chile, and his son-in-law, Juan Jufré, expanded cultivation and carried vines across the Andes to the Cuyo region of Argentina before 1570. Catholic missionaries carried vines into the more remote regions of South America to ensure a steady supply of sacramental wine.

Vines on the east coast of South America came directly from Europe. An expedition by Martim Afonso de Sousa, captain-general of São Vicente, transported the first vines to Brazil around 1532. Older settlements in Paraguay provided the Jesuit priest Pablo Cedrón with vines for missions in Santiago del Estero in 1557 and later in Córdoba. A Jesuit missionary, Roque González De La Cruz, brought vines to the mission of Santa Cruz do Sul in the Portuguese territory of Rio Grande do Sul in 1626.

LIMITS ON PRODUCTION

Cultivation of the vine and production of wine became so successful in the Spanish colonies that wine producers in Spain convinced King Philip II to restrict American production. In 1595 the Council of the Indies imposed limits on wine production and vine cultivation. Philip II's successors repeated the restrictions in 1620, 1628, and 1631. In 1654 the imperial government prohibited new plantations and levied a tax on established vineyards. Despite the crown's attempts to restrict grapevines in its American colonies, *Vitis vinifera* and the Muscat of Alexandria prospered there. Locally produced wine remained an important item in regional trading networks throughout the empire.

Although crown efforts failed to eliminate the colonial wine industry, other factors inhibited its growth. Restricted by regional markets, limited capital, and primitive technology, colonial vintagers operated on a small scale. Vine stocks deteriorated; primitive wine presses, labor-intensive methods of expressing juice, and inadequate storage facilities and temperature controls impeded expansion. When trade restrictions were lifted at the end of the colonial period, European wines—French, Italian, and Spanish—flooded the Latin American market.

LARGE-SCALE ENTERPRISES

Not until the mid-nineteenth century did grape growing and wine production become organized as large-scale commercial enterprises in Latin America. Entrepreneurs introduced new capital and technology and revitalized the aging vine stock with new varieties. The wine industry became more standardized, centralized, and lucrative. Private production replaced mission wines and in some areas all but eliminated foreign competitors.

California. The Mexican territory of California attracted the first innovators. The change began as the Mexican government started secularizing the missions after 1833. Joseph Chapman and Jean Louis Vignes introduced new vine varieties in the 1830s, but the acknowledged pioneer of the California wine industry was Agoston Haraszthy de Mokesa, who arrived in 1849.

Chile and Argentina. The wine industries of Chile and Argentina profited most from the introduction of new capital, techniques, and varieties of vine. In Chile, Silvestre Ochagavia Errázuriz revitalized wine production by importing new vines and equipment from Europe in 1851, thereby inspiring other growers to modernize their operations. The pioneers of this period included Luis Cousiño, Domingo Concha y Toro, and Manuel Antonio Tocornal Grez. Modern wine production in Argentina started in the western province of Mendoza. Tiburcio Benegas, Emilio Civit, and other prominent landowners used provincial resources and lobbied the national government for aid in modernizing production. New grape varieties and technicians to run a viticulture school were brought from France and Italy. These changes promoted the development of a market for domestic wine.

Government involvement in and regulation of the wine industry increased in Chile and Argentina in the twentieth century. Both countries taxed wine production and supported technical schools to improve yield. In the 1930s the Chilean national government, influenced by prohibitionists, slowed the spread of vineyards by holding maximum production to 60 liters per capita. The military government lifted these restrictions in 1974. The Argentine government drafted comprehensive wine regulatory legislation in 1932 and in 1959 established the National Institute of Vitiviniculture (INV) in Mendoza. The INV oversees all aspects of the industry. In Chile a private organization of exporters and bottlers fills that role. Wine production increased in Chile from 84 million gallons in 1952 to 160 million gallons in the mid-1980s, when there were 270,000 acres in vines. In 1993 Argentina had 500,000 acres planted in vines, and wine is its third largest industry. Argentina is one of the top ten largest wine producers in the world.

The wine industry in Latin America has undergone a revolution since the 1980s. More areas are producing wine and the industry's focus has shifted from mass production or quantity of wine to boutique or quality production. Although in most countries the per capita consumption of wine has increased, it has steadily decreased in Argentina. Offsetting this decrease is an increase in the price of wines consumed. Argentine and Chilean producers have moved toward developing wines of higher quality for export, and in both areas, an influx of foreign capital has facilitated the production quality wines for domestic consumption and export.

Mexico and Brazil. Every country in Latin America makes wine, with the exception of the Central American states. Two areas besides Chile and Argentina deserve special mention. Mexico successfully revitalized its industry after the Revolution by increasing tariffs and importation restrictions on foreign wines. This encouraged foreign and local investment in vineyards and wineries. In Brazil, the state of Rio Grande do Sul has become the most important area of production.

Overall improvements in wine production in Latin America have increased consumption at home and abroad. Argentine and Chilean wines have earned international recognition. Higher quality and lower prices have liberated wine from religious and class restrictions. In the early twenty-first century, wine appears on many Latin American tables.

See also **Alcoholic Beverages.**

BIBLIOGRAPHY

Adams, Leon D. *The Wines of America*, 2nd edition. New York: McGraw-Hill, 1978.

Bustos Herrera, Oscar. *El vino chileno: Producción y características.* Santiago de Chile: Editorial Universitaria, 1985.

Côrte Real, Mauro. *Os bons vinhos do Sul.* Porto Alegre, Brazil: Editora Sulina, 1981.

Cushner, Nicholas P. *Lords of the Land: Sugar, Wine, and Jesuit Estates of Coastal Peru, 1600–1767.* Albany: State University of New York Press, 1980.

De Blij, Harm Jan. *Wine Regions of the Southern Hemisphere.* Totowa, NJ: Rowman & Allanheld, 1985.

Footer, Kevin Carrel. "Vinos finos de alta montaña." *Ameritas* (February 2003): 49–53.

Foster, William, and Alberto Valdés. "South America." In *The World's Wine Markets: Globalization at Work*, ed. Kym Anderson. Cheltenham, UK; Northampton, MA: Edward Elgar, 2004.

Pinney, Thomas. *A History of Wine in America: From the Beginnings to Prohibition.* Berkeley: University of California Press, 1989.

Pozo, José del. *Historia del vino Chileno.* Santiago de Chile: Editorial Universitario, 1998.

Queyrat. Enrique. *Los buenos vinos argentinos.* Buenos Aires: Librería Hachette, 1974.

Supplee, Joan E. "Provincial Elites and the Economic Transformation of Mendoza, Argentina, 1880–1914." PhD diss., University of Texas, 1988.

JOAN E. SUPPLEE

Additional Bibliography

Amaral, Raúl. *Los presidentes del Paraguay (1844–1954): crónica política.* Asunción, Paraguay: Centro Paraguayo de Estudios Sociológicos, 1994.

Lewis, Paul H. *Political Parties and Generations in Paraguay's Liberal Era, 1869–1940.* Chapel Hill: University of North Carolina Press, 1993.

THOMAS L. WHIGHAM

WISNER VON MORGENSTERN, FRANZ (1800–1878).

Franz Wisner von Morgenstern (*b.* 1800; *d.* 1878), Hungarian military officer active in Paraguay. Coming to South America in 1845 after minor service in the Austrian army, Wisner was contacted by Paraguayan president Carlos Antonio López, who wished to train his rustic battalions in modern European military techniques. For a time, Wisner commanded the tiny state flotilla stationed on the Paraguay River. He later headed an expeditionary force that intervened in the Argentine province of Corrientes in 1849. During the 1850s, Wisner gained a trusted position within the Paraguayan hierarchy and played a key role in obtaining the services of British military engineers who supervised the modernizing of the national army, which later effectively resisted the Brazilians and Argentines for six years during the War of the Triple Alliance (1864–1870).

Wisner, meanwhile, wrote an official biography of the Paraguayan dictator José Gaspar Rodríguez de Francia. He also accepted a commission as chief military engineer on the state railway project, and later at the fortress of Humaitá. Captured at the 1868 battle of Lomas Valentinas (also called Pikysyry), Wisner returned to Paraguay after the war to prepare a major cartographical survey of the country; published in Vienna in 1873, it was easily the best complete map of Paraguay to appear up to that time. In his later years, Wisner, now the patriarch of a large Asunción family, was head of Paraguay's national railroad, and of the Immigration Office.

See also **López, Carlos Antonio.**

BIBLIOGRAPHY

Harris Gaylord Warren, *Paraguay and the Triple Alliance: The Postwar Decade, 1869–1878* (1978).

Carlos Zubizarreta, *Cien vidas paraguayas,* 2d ed. (1985).

WOLFF, EGON (1926–).

Egon Wolff (*b.* 13 April 1926), Chilean playwright. Wolff is the most staged—both in his own country and abroad—award-honored, and translated of Chilean dramatists; his plays have been performed in thirty countries, translated into twenty languages, and produced as films in Mexico and England. The son of German immigrants, Wolff pursued a parallel career as an engineer, in the manufacture and sale of chemical products. Unlike many artists and intellectuals of his generation, he steered clear of self-serving political posturing. Similarly, his plays are largely devoid of partisan didacticism. He focused instead on the social issues at work in the rapidly changing Chilean society of his day. In terms of form he preferred the fourth-wall theater (in which the proscenium arch represents a "fourth wall" to the audience) and complied with the classical Aristotelian dramatic unities. Stylistically, he favored social and psychological realism, with doses of poetry and humor.

His plays *Mansión de lechuzas* (*Mansion of Owls,* 1958), *Discípulos del miedo* (*Disciples of Fear,* 1958), *Niñamadre* (*A Touch of Blue,* 1960), and his most discussed work *Los invasores* (*The Invaders,* 1963) exemplify his characteristic probing into snobbery, prejudice, and the clash between social classes. He portrays the tension between traditional values—dictated by a crumbling ruling class—and those of the emerging middle class, including the heritage of postwar non-Spanish European immigrants. *El signo de Caín* (*The Sign of Cain,* 1969), *Flores de papel* (*Paper Flowers,* 1970), and *Kindergarten* (1977) explore the concepts of freedom and commitment on an individualistic level. In *Espejismos* (*Mirages,* 1978), *El sobre azul* (*The Blue Envelope,* 1978), *José* (1980), *Álamos en la azotea* (*Poplars on the Roof Terrace,* 1981), *La balsa de la Medusa* (*Medusa's Barge,* 1984), and *Háblame de Laura* (*Tell Me About Laura,* 1986), Wolff deftly and poetically plumbs the depths of personal relationships. After his wife died in a tragic accident in 1995, he stopped working for about five years. In 2000, he published two new works, *Encrucijada* and *Tras una puerta cerrada.*

See also **Theater.**

BIBLIOGRAPHY

Juan Andrés Piña, "Evolución e involución en las obras de Egon Wolff," in *Mensaje,* no. 269 (1978).

Klaus Portl, "Wolff's Theater der Angst," in *Revista Iberoamericana,* no. 3 (1979).

Jacqueline Eyring Bixler, "Language in/as Action in Egon Wolff's *Háblame de Laura,*" in *Latin American Theatre Review* 23 (fall 1989): 49–62.

Elena Castedo-Ellerman, "Egon Wolff," in *Latin American Writers,* edited by Carlos A. Solé and Maria Isabel Abreu, vol. 3 (1989), pp. 1311–1315.

Additional Bibliography

Bravo-Elizondo, Pedro. *La dramaturgia de Egon Wolff: interpretaciones críticas (1971–1981).* Santiago, Chile: Editorial Nascimiento, 1985.

Oyarzún, Carola. *Wolff.* Santiago, Chile: Ediciones Universidad Católica de Chile, 2006.

ELENA CASTEDO

WOLFSKILL, WILLIAM (1798–1866). William Wolfskill (*b.* 20 March 1798; *d.* 3 October 1866), mountain man and California pioneer. Wolfskill was born in Kentucky and moved with his family to Missouri in 1809 under Daniel Boone's (1734–1820) leadership. Wolfskill accompanied William Becknell's (*ca.* 1790–*ca.*1832) second expedition to Santa Fe in 1822 and opened a trading post at Taos, New Mexico. After several years of trapping beaver, he opened the Old Spanish Trail to California in 1831 and settled in Los Angeles. Wolfskill became a pioneer in the cattle, citrus, and wine industries in southern California. He acquired several ranches and became active in community affairs during the Mexican and early American periods. Wolfskill married María Magdalena Lugo in 1841, reared six children, and died in Los Angeles.

See also **California.**

BIBLIOGRAPHY

Leroy R. Hafen and Ann W. Hafen, *The Old Spanish Trail* (1954).

Iris Higbie Wilson Engstrand, *William Wolfskill, 1798–1866: Frontier Trapper to California Ranchero* (1965).

Additional Bibliography

Dary, David. *The Santa Fe Trail: Its History, Legends, and Lore.* New York: A.A. Knopf, 2000.

Sánchez, Joseph P. *Explorers, Traders, and Slavers: Forging the Old Spanish Trail, 1678–1850.* Salt Lake City: University of Utah Press, 1997.

IRIS H. W. ENGSTRAND

WOMEN. Women have long played significant roles in the history of Latin America. Awareness of their participation and experiences offers a useful lens through which to understand the vast region that lies between the Rio Grande and Tierra del Fuego. There is no one Latin American woman, but women from diverse cultures, ethnicities, classes, racialized categories, professions, ages, and sexual orientations, among others. Whether we are speaking of a woman from Mexico, Peru, Brazil, Haiti, or Guyana, these factors merit consideration. These women might not be able to speak to one another since their respective national languages are Spanish, Portuguese, French, and English. Moreover, it is not unlikely that a Guatemalan woman's first language is Maya-K'iche', not Spanish, that a woman of the Andes speaks only Quechua and that a woman of the Amazon speaks only a Tupi dialect. Despite the many differences in life experiences, women's diverse experiences in Latin America often share common themes.

CONQUEST/CONTACT

Only a very small number of Spanish, Portuguese, French, and enslaved African women were present in the Spanish Conquest, as such a dangerous voyage was not considered appropriate for women. Rather, the women who did come were most often poor and their status did not preclude them from undertaking such a trip and struggling for survival in unknown lands. Indigenous women, consequently, figure logistically and symbolically in the Iberian conquest of the Americas. Spanish and Portuguese colonization was a deeply gendered process. Colonizers depicted America as a feminized space or the colonized, native population as emasculated. Indigenous women mediated between these different cultures, serving as interpreters, negotiators, trophies, and sexual partners. Though some Europeans raped and kept native women as concubines, they relied upon indigenous women for food preparation and child rearing.

This ambivalent positioning of native women in the colonial order later became a focus of debate among Spanish American and Brazilian intellectuals, who became historians of national identity and origins. Many of the post-independence nationalists, described how seafaring European males encountered the indigenous women of Middle, Central, and South America and produced a "new race." with the best qualities from both "races". The story of La Malinche/Doña Marina/Malintzín (1504?–1528), an Aztec woman given in tribute by a Tabascan ruler to conquistador Hernán Cortés, is representative of this allegory. Her knowledge of languages played a pivotal role in the Spanish overthrow of the Aztec regime in central Mexico. La Malinche became a founding myth of modern Mexico, symbolizing indigenous women as mothers of Mexico's *mestizo* culture. Yet La Malinche is also regarded as a traitor, further illustrating the long association of women with weakness and deceit.

Not only in Mexico but throughout the Americas indigenous women are similarly at the center of national origin myths and mestizaje. Often, as in the case of Brazil, African and Afro-Brazilian women are also considered symbolic mothers of the national "race."

In addition to these early groups and native inhabitants, slaves and immigrants contributed greatly to the diverse population of Latin America. Between 1513 and 1850, more than 5 million Africans were brought as slaves to the region. Moreover, since the late nineteenth century the large Latin American nations have received successive waves of immigrants from Europe and Asia. Spaniards, Portuguese, Italians, and Germans settled in significant numbers in Mexico, Argentina, Uruguay, Chile, and southern Brazil. Koreans, Chinese, and Southeast Asians have also immigrated to the Latin American nations; outside of Japan, Brazil has the largest population of citizens of Japanese descent. Immigrants from India, Pakistan, Syria, Lebanon, Iran, and Iraq have made their way to South America. Although in some cases the first generation settled in rural areas, the daughters and granddaughters of these European, African,

Asian, and Middle Eastern immigrants now live in Latin American cities as well.

COLONIAL PERIOD

As scholar Susan Socolow argues, women in the colonial period "were defined first and foremost by their sex and only secondarily by their race or social class." This statement illustrates the role patriarchy—a social system where men are regarded as the authority in family and society—played in shaping the life possibilities of colonial women. Yet Socolow and others emphasize the importance of colonial racial, caste, ethnic, and class hierarchies, and how demography, life cycle, time, regional variations, and local economies impacted women's experiences.

The colonial church provides a telling example of the ways in which women worked within and sometimes exceeded standard social and legal restrictions. The church largely determined social mores and reinforced the strictures that propertied families placed upon their daughters, for whom marriage or a religious vocation as a nun were the respectable choices. Convents acquired wealth and served as important sources of credit for elite society. Consequently, despite the images of cloistered women, these religious communities tell more complicated stories of social hierarchies and illustrate women acting independently and having strong influence in the colonial economy. Yet, convents cloistered women and reproduced social hierarchies - criollas and Spaniards in the Santa Clara convent of Cuzco, Peru, could wear the coveted black veil; while mestizas and Andean women were only allowed to wear the white veil – but did not disconnect the sisters from the outside world.

Elite women also fought for their rights in the larger public sphere. Women's economic influence was not limited to convents, for they also ran large estates and oversaw the complex business affairs of their families. In Mexico, the Marquesa de San Francisco served as the executor of her father's estate until her brother returned from Spain and resumed family leadership. By choice, and at the expense of leaving the elite culture in the capital, the Marquesa regained her autonomy by moving to oversee family land in the Bajío. Scholarship challenges the idea of the secluded, elite colonial woman further still by exploring cultural categories like honor and illegitimacy. For instance, numerous women of privileged status engaged in sexual relations outside of marriage or became pregnant out of wedlock. For a woman, public honor was crucial. However, pregnant elite women could preserve their public honor, if they married or kept the pregnancy and birth secret except from select family members and friends.

Lower class and indigenous women also became crucial actors in both the public and private sphere of colonial Latin American society. Indigenous women were widely involved in small-scale trade, such as in the sale of chicha, or corn beer, in the Andes and pulque in New Spain. Throughout the Americas, women owned taverns, chicherias and pulperias. Women in colonial Potosí and Spanish, mestiza, and native women elsewhere made loans, creating vibrant petty credit systems throughout the Americas. The large degree to which rich, poor, and the middling sectors of colonial women resorted to the courts to defend their honor and claim social status illustrates the significance of these distinctions in their everyday lives.

Slavery, like colonialism, was profoundly gendered. Because of their strength, more enslaved African men than women were sent to the Americas, though women of African descent were soon present in every region, from Mexico City to Buenos Aires. Many slave women worked at field labor on the sugar, tobacco, cotton, and coffee plantations of the Caribbean and mainland Latin America. They were concubines and petty marketers during the gold mining boom in colonial Minas Gerais, Brazil. Female slaves were found in larger concentrations in urban areas, working in households or earning money for their owners as market women, street vendors, wet nurses, or prostitutes. To the extent that their particular situations allowed them to do so, they recreated their African religious and cultural practices and deeply influenced the formative national cultures in Brazil, the Caribbean, Colombia, and Venezuela.

WOMEN AND NATIONAL FORMATION
Female patriots were vital to the success of the independence movements and played a wide range of roles in the struggles. In addition to the biographies of these women used to rouse patriotic fervor, women were outspoken activists, nurses, and resistance fighters. In later years, Latin American women pointed to the loyalty of their predecessors in the effort to gain rights and citizenship for women.

In the transition from colonialism to nation-state formation, scholars continue to explore and debate the legacy of gender relations. Some argue that women emerged from independence with improved legal, political, and social status. Others maintain that governments in the new republics guaranteed expanded rights to men of all classes, but left women in a position more marginal than they occupied under colonial rule. This research calls into question broader teleological narratives of women's progress under liberal states providing a more complex picture. While continuity in patriarchal control continued from the colonial era, women from all sectors of society contested such authority.

While an ideology of domesticity in the nineteenth century reaffirmed women's traditional roles as mothers and caretakers, it also opened new arenas of public participation, particularly for elite women. As wives and mothers, women became involved outside the home, championing moral reform, founding publications, and engaging in debates over education throughout Latin America. Teresa González de Fanning in Peru called for educating women in order to improve the lives of future generations. In the struggle between secular liberal values and religious corporatist politics that marked the nineteenth century, the question of who would educate young women was played out among Catholic female teaching orders, independent dames' schools, and the new public schools. Though they might have been excluded from formal politics, it is not to say that Latin American women were not politically active.

Slavery persisted into the late-nineteenth century throughout Latin America, affecting the lives of African and Afro-Latin American women and their descendents. Though difficult, enslaved women were sometimes able to save enough money from their earnings to purchase their freedom. A woman's status as slave or free was critical because it directly affected the status of her children. Perhaps because they generally lived in greater intimacy with their masters as domestic servants, manumission of women outnumbered that of men in Salvador and Rio de Janeiro, Brazil.

Women participated in the social and class conflicts occurring from the 1890s through the 1920s. Several examples can be cited. In the long guerrilla wars that led to Cuban independence from Spain in 1898, female soldiers known as *mambisas* distinguished themselves in battles against the Spanish troops and became part of the formative myth of the Cuban nation; they were viewed as warriors, patriots, revolutionaries, and the moral center of national sovereignty. Female schoolteachers and factory workers played a crucial role in the politics that led to the Mexican Revolution of 1910. Women were at the heart of the great Río Blanco textile workers' strike of 1907. Soldaderas, women who fought with the revolutionary troops, became folk heroines. Such organizations as the Hijas de Cuáuhtemoc demanded the resignation of President Porfirio Díaz and staged public protests against the regime. In contrast, Carmen Romero Rubio y Castelló, the president's wife, symbolized the alliance of the regime with the conservative hierarchy of the Catholic Church.

WOMEN'S WORK AND WORKING WOMEN

The history of women in paid occupations in Latin America underwent extensive change during the twentieth century. On the one hand, there was the emergence of the middle-sector working woman—skilled factory workers, teachers, government clerks. While great differences in the social and economic statuses of these women existed, their pay scales, benefits, and relative job security distinguished them on the other hand as a group from women in the unregulated, informal sectors of the economy, which included domestics, market women, vendors, laundresses, prostitutes, and rural laborers.

Women were the preferred labor force in the textile and tobacco industries after 1900, prized for their smaller hands and lower pay. Yet female laborers often faced social stigmas because working outside the home and in an industrial setting particularly were not considered a woman's proper place. Social reformers argued that such work would destroy a woman's innocence and cause moral degradation. Men opposed women's industrial work because it threatened their masculinity and their higher wages. To counter these claims, a number of responses were constructed. For example, textile mill factory owners in Medellín, Colombia, successfully ameliorated concerns by promoting an ideal of sexual chastity among their female labor force, demanding employees remain single and not become pregnant during their tenure.

Women did not prove to be the docile labor force their employers anticipated, as they engineered strikes and slow-downs to improve their livelihoods. However, as women, they faced greater difficulty in organizing to improve their working conditions: the hostility of employers and officials, lack of support from their male coworkers, long working hours, and family demands left scant energy for union work. Not only work, but also struggling for better job conditions was viewed as transgressing women's idealized domestic role.

Although women had begun entering new fields in urban areas, in 1930 the great majority of them still lived in the country. Rural women's work was immensely varied: women carried out mining-related tasks in Potosí; worked communal agricultural plots and ran trade networks in the Peruvian sierra; hulled and sorted spices in the Caribbean; worked the sugar, rubber, and banana plantations of Brazil, Haiti, and Cuba; harvested the wheat and grapes of Chile and Argentina; and did domestic labor on ranches, estates, and plantations. And everywhere women prepared daily meals, cared for children, and maintained their own households in addition to whatever other work they might perform. Yet life in rural areas saw change as well. Chile's Agrarian Reform between 1964 and 1973, for instance, expanded women's paid agricultural employment in the fruit and vegetable sector, while at the same time promoted women's domesticity, which differed from previously held *campesina* notions.

CHANGES IN LEGAL AND CIVIL STATUS

Prior to the twentieth century, women's civil status was governed by a complex body of statutes rooted in Iberian and ecclesiastical law; in practice, the legal status of most women was determined by their relationship to the male heads of household. Indigenous women living within their traditional communities (Maya, Guajira, Aymara, Guarani) conformed to the customs of each community. Although elaborate sets of laws governing slave women had evolved by the nineteenth century, individual slave women had little

Periods of enactment of female suffrage in Latin America	
Pre-World War II	
Ecuador	1929
Brazil	1932
Uruguay	1932
Cuba	1934
World War II	
El Salvador	1939
Dominican Republic	1942
Panama	1945
Guatemala	1945
Post-World War II	
Argentina	1947
Venezuela	1947
Chile	1949
Costa Rica	1949
Haiti	1950
Bolivia	1952
Mexico	1953
Honduras	1955
Nicaragua	1955
Peru	1955
Colombia	1957
Paraguay	1961

Table 1

true legal recourse. In all cases, full citizenship was limited to men of property.

Female suffrage in Latin America came about after years of continued struggle. The history of female suffrage offers an illustration of the politics involved in seeking redress through legal change. The struggle for suffrage grew out of women and feminist movements pursuing reforms linked to family and motherhood and developed into demands for women's equality. Effective universal suffrage, male or female, did not exist in any Latin American nation until after World War II. Requirements concerning property, employment, and residence largely restricted the vote to elite sectors. Moreover, irregular transitions of power and the suspension of civil liberties, including elections, characterized the political environment in many Latin American nations between 1929, when female suffrage became law in Ecuador, and 1961, when women obtained the vote in Paraguay. Three periods of enactment may be distinguished (see table 1).

Examination of the list of the first group of states to enact suffrage for women points to the variety of motives that prompted governments to bring women into the national polity. In Mexico,

Argentina, Brazil, Colombia, Venezuela, Chile, and Cuba, suffrage resulted from long-fought campaigns on the part of thousands of women and their male allies. In contrast, in Ecuador, the political coalition that promulgated the female vote was deeply conservative; it viewed women as loyal to the Catholic Church and politically malleable and believed that the female vote would buttress the conservatives' political base vis-à-vis challenge from the Socialist Party. Members of the political left largely concurred with the conservative assessment. Argentine women had waged a half-century-long campaign for the vote; woman suffrage laws had been passed in many other nations of the Western Hemisphere; and commitment to equal political rights was part of the charter of the United Nations, to which Argentina was a signatory. Finally in 1947 Eva Perón delivered the new female vote for the Peronist Party.

Despite the passage of woman suffrage in every Latin American country by 1961, voting continued to be limited by language and literacy requirements. Rural women were often excluded. In some countries, such as Guatemala, male suffrage was universal, but female suffrage was restricted to women who could read and speak Spanish; thereby significantly reducing women's participation in Brazil, Guatemala, Bolivia, and Ecuador. In Peru, Quechua-speaking Peruvians did not receive the franchise until 1980, a restriction affecting the women who stayed in the sierra and maintained the home community more than the men who migrated out to work or fulfill military service.

THE PERIOD 1959–1989

The Cuban Revolution in 1959 raised new questions about social hierarchy, race, and class throughout the hemisphere. Symbolic of the shift in public consciousness is the 1960 publication in Brazil of Carolina Maria de Jesus's *Cuarto de Despejo* (Child of the Dark). Carolina, who lived in a São Paulo favela, described in her book the daily ordeals she faced collecting and selling rags and paper in order to provide for her three children. Shedding light on Brazil's urban poor and women of color, the book sold 90,000 copies in six months.

Women joined the emerging revolutionary movements of the 1960s and 1970s in response to authoritarian rule throughout region. Young women made up almost half of the "soldiers"—those who carried out bank robberies and kidnappings—of the Tupamaro movement in Montevideo, Uruguay. In rural guerrilla groups, women were more apt to be seen as *compañeras,* companions of the male revolutionaries. Haydée Tamara Bunke Bider (1937–1967), known as "Tania," was an exception; she was key to Che Guevara's effort to establish a revolutionary front in Bolivia and became a martyr to a generation of young women after her death under fire.

Liberation theology, which emerged from the Latin American Catholic Church in the wake of the Second Vatican Council (1965) and the Second Latin American Bishops' Conference (1968) in Medellín, Colombia, did not address the specific needs of women; but women of the church—laywomen, nuns, congregants, and participants in Base Communities—were deeply involved in the church's commitment to "the poorest of the poor." Women were also active in defending conservative politics. In Brazil in 1964 and in Chile in 1973, upper- and middle-class women organized street demonstrations, such as El Poder Femenino in Chile to protest the erosion of homemakers' buying power, the spectre of communism, and the threat to the family, and to call for military intervention to "restore order."

In the 1970s, ideas of the international feminist movement spread throughout the region. The Latin American feminist movement emerged during the somber climate of the 1970s. Many early feminists came from leftist opposition movements whose male leadership was sometimes sexist. Moreover, members of these groups, both men and women, often viewed feminism as an imperial or elite concern and its issues secondary to larger revolutionary goals. Likewise, the gender ideology of military regime dictatorships promoted a conservative view of women as mothers and wives, and thus, feminism was considered subversive. Early feminist groups in Chile, Argentina, and elsewhere functioned inconspicuously, and though they denounced patriarchy, principally they joined in solidarity with the many multi-class movements denouncing social, economic, and political oppression brought on by the authoritarian military regimes. For many women, it was not feminist ideology but the widespread political mobilization against reactionary social and political policies in the late 1970s in Chile, Argentina, Brazil, and

Uruguay and against economic austerity in the 1980s that marked a watershed in women's political activism and made possible lasting legacies. In 1981 in Bogotá, Colombia, feminists organized the first Feminist Encuentro, a space for dialogue and collective action among women from Latin America and the Caribbean, and conferences were held every two or three years after. It must be noted, however, that class and ethnicity often divided early second wave feminists.

In the nations of Brazil, Uruguay, Paraguay, Argentina, and Chile, the 1970s and early 1980s were marked by the suppression of civil liberties, the ascension of bureaucratic authoritarian military regimes, and a politics of terrorism, including mass arrests, the disappearing of political activists, torture, imprisonment, and death squad assassinations. A similar politics of terrorism prevailed in Guatemala and El Salvador and reverberated in the civil war in Nicaragua. Like their male counterparts, women were visible throughout the political spectrum: as victims of political oppression, supporters of incumbent regimes, perpetrators of torture, members of the armed resistance, and pro-regime supporters. *Las madres,* the mothers of those who had disappeared in the government's war against terrorism emerged from this era. On April 30, 1977, in Buenos Aires, seven of these women—*las madres*—went to the Plaza de Mayo, the historic center of Argentine government, and staged a silent demonstration on behalf of their disappeared loved ones; four years later, on 1 May 1981, over six thousand Argentines joined them to protest the continued violation of human rights by the military regime. *Las madres* became a metaphor for the thousands of Latin Americans who dared protest through nonviolent means the practice of state terrorism against the populace. In the wake of the military regimes' crumbling in the mid-1980s, women were successful in bringing women's issues—health care, divorce, domestic violence, political access—into debates surrounding the redemocratization process in which they had played an important part.

THE 1990S AND THE TWENTY-FIRST CENTURY

By 1990 evidence indicating dramatic change in the traditional patterns of life for Latin American women converged. First, contemporary Latin American women were overwhelmingly urban. Rural to urban migration between 1930 and 1970 spurred rapid urbanization. More than 75 percent of all Latin Americans live in urban areas. In 1980, only 2 percent of the female labor force in Argentina was described as rural; in Mexico, only 12 percent; in Brazil, which has the highest number of rural women of any major Latin American nation, the figure is 20 percent. Second, the visible entry of middle-class women into the paid labor force—an 83 percent increase between 1970 and 1990 in all areas of Latin America except the Caribbean—closely resembled the work participation profiles of women in the industrialized West. Driven partly by the harsh inflationary conditions of the 1980s, women's employment outside the home, combined with higher levels of education and greater access to birth control information in urban areas resulted in a significant drop in the birthrate. In Mexico, in 1950, each woman bore an average of six children but by 1990, the number was halved. In 2007, it fell slightly further to just over two children. Birth rates in Cuba, Argentina, Uruguay, and Costa Rica also fell. In countries and regions where women are primarily rural and where female literacy remains low, such as Guatemala and Ecuador, birthrates and infant mortality rates are moderately higher. Further, there was greater continuity in women's careers, meaning that they remain employed during their child-bearing years and do not quit their jobs to bring up children. In urban areas, women represent 40 percent of the economically active population in the twenty-first century.

The pattern of greater female involvement in the formal labor force has occurred concurrently with the growth in concrete numbers of women whose economic status is precarious. In the twenty-first century, millions of poor women and their families live in and around the megacities of Latin America—São Paulo, Rio de Janeiro, Buenos Aires, Lima-Callao, Santiago, Bogotá and Mexico City—and attempt to eke out a daily living in the informal economy. In 1994, 36 percent of the working poor were women but by 2002 the proportion had increased to 43 percent. In addition, the percentage of poor households headed by women has also grown.

Women are overrepresented in the urban and rural informal sector. Between 1990 and 1996 in urban zones, women's participation increased from an estimated 59 to 65 percent. While poor and working-class women have long-held informal jobs selling food and in domestic service, previously middle-class women joined the ranks owing to the privatization of formerly state-run industries, layoffs in government bureaucracies, and cuts in social spending during the 1990s.

Representative of this phenomenon is the social movement of unemployed workers in Argentina known as the *piqueteros,* or picketers. Women comprise a majority of the piquetero movement, which has spread throughout the country since 1997 in the Jujuy province and is known best for its strategies. Nationally, piqueteros have a wide range of demands and protests, though many have organized at a neighborhood level where residents devise creative strategies to cope with economic depression, particularly in the form of soup kitchens, bakeries, and barter.

Poverty tends to be higher in rural areas, and due to economic decline in this sector, an increasing number of women have sought paid employment. Women in the twenty-first century make up the majority of the workforce in Colombia's cut flower industry, Mexico's strawberry production, and Chile's fruit and vegetable sector. What these women share in common is their jobs' temporary status; their work is without benefits and either without a contract or with one that only officially employs them for a short period of time.

Tax incentives and low labor costs have encouraged multinational corporations to establish manufacturing facilities throughout the region, and women comprise the majority of the labor force. Begun in the 1960s along Mexico's border with the United States, "export processing zones" expanded especially during the 1990s especially to the Caribbean and Central America. In Puerto Rico and the Dominican Republic, female employment in the export processing zones grew largely in response to economic crisis and the need to supplement declining male wages. The unsolved murders of more than 700 women in Ciudad Juárez, Mexico, many of them maquiladora workers, has brought attention to women's increasing participation.

In the Caribbean, coastal Mexico, Belize, Guatemala, and Costa Rica, the international tourism industry is a primary and fast-growing employer of female hotel clerks, tourist guides, maids, waitresses, and cooks. Similarly, the picking and packing of agricultural goods for the global market, largely the work of women, puts money directly into the hands of female workers, a practice that is visibly altering traditional male-female and generational relationships in many communities. Increased integration into the global economy is also visible in changing social mores. Latin American women are still largely culturally Catholic, but in practice society is increasingly secular.

Linked with women's increased participation in the labor force is migration. Latin America was the first region to reach parity in the numbers of men and women migrants. In the past, women principally traveled from rural to urban areas in the company of partners. Today, migrant women are young, single mothers who are the main economic providers for their families. Though rural to urban migration remains important in countries with higher rural populations, such as Paraguay, international migration between urban areas has increased significantly. Women account for more than half of all international migrants. In 2000, the South American countries that absorbed the most migrants were Argentina (35 percent) and Venezuela (26 percent). There were considerable flows of Colombian women to Venezuela and Ecuador, Nicaraguan women to Costa Rica, and Peruvian women to Chile.

The results of over two decades of women's political activism were visible with more women in political office, new legislation that expanded women's rights in divorce and marriage, in the creation of all-female police stations, and in increased attention to domestic violence against women. Liberalization of family laws in Chile following the return to democracy in 1990 improved women's rights. Yet it was only in 2004 that Chile finally legalized divorce, the last country in the region to do so. The divorce law was important for women because until its implementation, husbands were considered the legal head of the family, oftentimes leaving women beholden to their husbands for financial decisions. In 2007, legislators in Mexico's Federal District voted 46 to 19 to legalize abortion during the first 12 weeks of pregnancy, joining Cuba, Guyana, and Puerto Rico.

The dynamics of the women's movement mobilized international support for a focus on women. Individuals and local groups of women were increasingly interconnected through global and regional networks. Since the Fourth World Conference on Women in Beijing in 1995, Argentina, Brazil, Chile, Ecuador, Mexico, and Central American nations have created councils, commissions, and institutes tasked with women's advancement.

In Argentina in 1991, women's advocates succeeded in passing the Ley de Cupos, which set a quota requiring that one-third of all candidates be female. The law increased women's participation from 4 percent to 34 percent, placing Argentina among the top ten countries in the world with regards to women in national parliaments. While in 1993, 30 women were elected to the House, in 2005, 120 women were in the Upper and Lower House. Additionally, since 1999, 22 of 24 Argentine provinces had adopted quota rules for state and local posts. Thirteen more countries in the region have since implemented similar national laws. Besides national representation, female politicians succeeded in creating new laws that increased women's participation within political parties. Such measures, undertaken in Argentina, Bolivia, Costa Rica, Chile, and Mexico, for instance, have increased female involvement significantly. Moreover, in Mexico, women have served as presidents of the Partido Revolucionario Institucional (PRI) and the left-leaning Democratic Revolution Party (PRD), both major parties. Finally, women in Latin America have attained the highest political office. In Nicaragua, Violetta Barrios De Chamorro was elected president in the closely monitored elections of 1990. Rosalia Arteaga briefly acted as president of Ecuador in 1997, and voters elected Michelle Bachelet, Chile's first woman president, in 2006. Cristina Fernández de Kirchner, wife of Argentine president Néstor Kirchner announced her candidacy for the presidency in 2007.

While gains in formal political settings and on paper are impressive, barriers to entry, discrimination, and setbacks persist. In 2001, Colombia's high court ruled the 1999 quota law for women unconstitutional in 2001. Elsewhere, many women have argued that provisions for women, especially within political parties are only weakly enforced. In Mexico's 2000 election, though both the PRI and PRD complied with the 30 percent candidate quotas, most women candidates were placed in difficult districts or were listed as substitutes for male candidates. Moreover, formal political gains have been outpaced by the rise of women in informal politics. Women lead and comprise the majority of non-governmental organizations (NGOs) and social movements in Latin America. Representative of this is the K'iche' Indian Rigoberta Menchú (*b.* 1960) who was awarded the Nobel Peace Prize in 1992 for her work on behalf of human rights, notably among the indigenous people of her homeland in northwestern Guatemala. Menchú remains a prominent advocate for the rights of indigenous people everywhere.

Significant challenges to women's rights persist in the areas of domestic violence, sexual rights, and reproductive health. In many countries, domestic violence is only classified as a misdemeanor rather than a felony. Outside of the home, pregnancy-based discrimination and sexual harassment confront the greater numbers of women in the formal workforce.

In the new millennium, women are more highly educated, more urban, and more engaged in activities outside the household (economic, political, and social) than ever before. Women have won important institutional spaces—university women's studies programs, NGOs, and governmental positions. Modern communications systems, technology, globalization, radio and television, patterns of migration, and access to transportation have all contributed to an expanded worldview. Throughout Latin America deep political and economic instabilities that threaten efforts to revise gender-based social and cultural attitudes persist. The ostensible gains—political citizenship for women, a focus on the double burden of poor women, racial discrimination, greater access to schooling for girls, labor regulations that take women's work into account—are under constant threat of erosion. Women are not coincidental but vital to democracy if it is to prove viable, and they are central to overcoming seemingly implacable social and economic problems. In this effort the importance of collective memory, of bearing witness, of knowing the history of women cannot be underestimated.

See also **Bachelet, Michelle; Feminism and Feminist Organizations; Feminist Congresses, First and Second, 1916, Yucatan; Liberation Theology; Malinche; Marriage and Divorce; Menchú Tum, Rigoberta; Migration and Migrations; Piqueteros;** **Pulperos; Río Blanco Strike; Soldaderas; Women in Paraguay.**

BIBLIOGRAPHY

June Hahner, *Women in Latin American History* (1976).

Asunción Lavrin, *Latin American Women: Historical Perspectives* (1978).

Silvia Marina Arrom, *The Women of Mexico City, 1790–1857* (1985).

Marifran Carlson, *FEMINISMO! The Woman's Movement in Argentina from Its Beginning to Eva Perón* (1988).

Patricia Seed, *To Love, Honor and Obey in Colonial Mexico: Conflicts over Marriage Choice, 1574–1821* (1988).

Elsa Chaney and Mary García Castro, *Muchachas No More: Household Workers in Latin America and the Caribbean* (1989).

Asunción Lavrin, ed., *Sexuality and Marriage in Colonial Latin America* (1989).

Marietta Morrissey, *Slave Women in the New World: Gender Stratification in the Caribbean* (1989).

K. Lynn Stoner, *From the House to the Streets: The Cuban Woman's Movement for Legal Reform, 1898–1940* (1989), and *Latinas of the Americas: A Source Book* (1989).

Elsa Tamez, *Through Her Eyes: Women's Theology from Latin America* (1989).

June Hahner, *Emancipating the Female Sex: The Struggle for Women's Rights in Brazil, 1850–1940* (1990).

Susan Hill Gross and Mary Hill Rojas, *Contemporary Issues for Women in Latin America* (1991).

Donna Guy, *Sex and Danger in Buenos Aires* (1991).

Francesca Miller, *Latin American Women and the Search for Social Justice* (1991).

Teresa Valdes and Enrique Gomariz, eds., *Mujeres latinoamericanas en cifras: Chile* (1993).

Additional Bibliography

Bruhns, Karen Olsen, and Karen E. Stothert. *Women in Ancient America.* Norman: University of Oklahoma Press, 1999.

Burns, Kathryn. *Colonial Habits: Convents and the Spiritual Economy of Cuzco, Peru.* Durham, NC: Duke University Press, 1999.

Caufield, Sueann. *In Defense of Honor: Sexual Morality, Modernity, and Nation in Early Twentieth-century Brazil.* Durham, NC: Duke University Press, 2000.

Chambers, Sarah C. *From Subjects to Citizens: Honor, Gender, and Politics in Arequipa, Peru, 1780–1854.* University Park: Pennsylvania State University Press, 1999.

Dias, Maria Odila Leite da. *Power and Everyday Life: The Lives of Working Women in Nineteenth-century Brazil.* Trans. Ann Frost. New Brunswick, NJ: Rutgers University Press, 1995.

Dore, Elizabeth, and Maxine Molyneux, eds. *Hidden Histories of Gender and the State in Latin America.* Durham, NC: Duke University Press, 2000.

Farnsworth-Alvear, Ann. *Dulcinea in the Factory: Myths, Morals, Men, and Women in Colombia's Industrial Experiment, 1905–1960.* Durham, NC: Duke University Press, 2000.

French, John, and Daniel James, eds. *The Gendered Worlds of Latin American Women Workers: From Household and Factory to the Union Hall and Ballot Box.* Durham, NC: Duke University Press, 1997.

Graham, Sandra Lauderdale. *Caetana Says No: Women's Stories from a Brazilian Slave Society.* New York: Cambridge University Press, 2002.

Higgens, Kathleen J. *"Licentious Liberty" in a Brazilian Gold-Mining Region: Slavery, Gender, and Social Control in Eighteenth-Century Sabaráa, Minas Gerais.* University Park: Pennsylvania State University Press, 1999.

Hutchinson, Elizabeth Quay. *Labors Appropriate to Their Sex: Gender, Labor, and Politics in Urban Chile, 1900–1930.* Durham, NC: Duke University Press, 2001.

James, Daniel. *Doña Maria's Story: Life History, Memory, and Political Identity.* Durham, NC: Duke University Press, 2000.

Klubock, Thomas M. *Contested Communities: Class, Gender, and Politics in Chile's El Teniente Copper Mine, 1904–1951.* Durham, NC: Duke University Press, 1998.

Lavrin, Asuncion. *Women, Feminism, and Social Change in Argentina, Chile, and Uruguay, 1890–1940.* Lincoln: University of Nebraska Press, 1998.

Lewin, Linda. *Surprise Heirs I: Illegitimacy, Patrimonial Rights, and Legal Nationalism in Luso-Brazilian Inheritance, 1750–1821.* Stanford, CA: Stanford University Press, 2003.

Lewin, Linda. *Surprise Heirs II: Illegitimacy, Inheritance Rights, and Public Power in the Formation of Imperial Brazil, 1822–1889.* Stanford, CA: Stanford University Press, 2003.

Lewis, Laura. *Hall of Mirrors: Power, Witchcraft, and Caste in Colonial Mexico.* Durham, NC: Duke University Press, 2003.

Navarro, Marysa, and Virginia Sánchez Korrol, eds. *Women in Latin America and the Caribbean.* Bloomington: Indiana University Press, 1999.

Rodríguez, Victoria E. *Women in Contemporary Mexican Politics.* Austin: University of Texas Press, 2003.

Rosemblatt, Karin Alejandra. *Gendered Compromises: Political Cultures and the State in Chile, 1920–1950.* Chapel Hill: University Of North Carolina Press, 2000.

Socolow, Susan M. *The Women of Colonial Latin America.* Cambridge, UK: Cambridge University Press, 2000.

Tinsman, Heidi. *Partners in Conflict: The Politics of Gender, Sexuality, and Labor in the Chilean Agrarian Reform, 1950–1973.* Durham, NC: Duke University Press, 2002.

Twinam, Ann. *Public Lives, Private Secrets: Gender, Honor, Sexuality, and Illegitimacy in Colonial Spanish America.* Stanford, CA: Stanford University Press, 1999.

FRANCESCA MILLER
MEREDITH GLUECK

WOMEN IN PARAGUAY.

According to traditional thought, women have played a more critical role in the history of Paraguay than in other Latin American states—so much so, in fact, that women have assumed the status of patriotic icons. School textbooks portray women as the principal defenders of the nation, as the bravest of the brave in repulsing those who would see Paraguay dismembered and broken. While this image constitutes a historiographical oddity, in reality women have shaped the course of events in Paraguay in some unusual ways.

The Guaraní, the dominant ethnic group in the Paraguayan region during the pre-Columbian era, set the basic pattern. Semisedentary agriculturalists, they reserved the bulk of labor in the fields for female members of various clans. While men dedicated themselves to hunting and fishing, Guaraní women cultivated maize, beans, manioc root, tobacco, squashes, peanuts, and cotton (also weaving the latter into clothing). They were largely responsible for child-rearing as well.

The arrival of the Spaniards in 1537 did not much affect the lives of Paraguay's women. The Spaniards, seeking a quick route to the silver of Peru, had ascended the Paraguay River carrying only the bare necessities, and no European women accompanied them. Stranded among the Guaraní, they soon took up with Indian women. Regarding the newcomers as members of their extended kin group, the women labored for them just as they had labored for their own men. They bore mestizo children, taught them Guaraní, and helped them forge a colonial order that was only partly Spanish. The first governor, Domingo Martínez de Irala, took several Guaraní wives and legitimized their offspring.

Very few immigrants entered Paraguay during the colonial period. This fact alone assured that the early pattern of indigenous-white relations would retain its influence into the late 1700s. Women still did most of the farm work, though now the earlier Guaraní-based kinship structures had been supplanted by the encomienda. The women still raised children who were monolingual in the Guaraní tongue and who also thought more like Guaraní than like Spaniards, whatever their surnames might happen to be. This socialization process later provided the basis for a fervent nationalism among many Paraguayans, who viewed themselves as being decidedly different from other Latin Americans. National independence, which came in 1811, thus reflected not just political realities but also cultural factors.

Paraguayan women, having prepared the social environment for a sense of cultural separateness, now helped shape the new nation. The dictator Dr. José Gaspar Rodríguez de Francia (1814–1840) forbade marriages between Paraguayans and Spaniards. This reinforced traditional structures governing the role of women while, at the same time, undercutting the influence of such formal, Spanish-based institutions as legally sanctioned marriage and the church. Informal liaisons remained the rule, as did long hours in the field for women. Those hours likely increased during the 1850s and 1860s, when the governments of Carlos Antonio López (1841–1862) and Francisco Solano López (1862–1870) expanded the state military establishment, drafted thousands of men, and left women and children to produce a good portion of the foodstuffs.

Paraguayan women played a significant role in the War of the Triple Alliance (1864–1870). The Paraguayan War added still further burdens. With all of the men at the front, Paraguayan women, though especially rural women of the lower classes, supported almost the entire war economy. They donated their jewelry and cash. They worked in hospitals. As in the past, women provided most of the agricultural labor, yet they took on new tasks like harnessing oxen and butchering cattle. As the war turned against Paraguay, women volunteered for military service. It is unclear if many actually fought, though observers at the 1869 battle of Acosta Ñu reported that the Paraguayan defenders included a considerable number. In that same year, Solano López evacuated the central district and retreated to the northeast, taking with him his now meager army, his Irish mistress, and a multitude of poor women who, malnourished and diseased, nonetheless followed López to the end. Despite their critical role in the survival of Paraguay during the War of the Triple Alliance, the status of women did not change significantly. However, for many women, the experience of war engendered a broad-based sense of nationalism and citizenship.

The Paraguayan defeat in 1870 brought new challenges. Brazilian troops occupied Paraguay for six years. With perhaps half the country's population having perished in the conflict, women were said to outnumber men four or five to one. It took a generation to reestablish an even ratio between the sexes. Throughout this time women struggled as never before to eke out a living on the land and in the towns. Foreign visitors witnessed the toils of female porters, carters, street sweepers, and farm workers. Later writers claimed that this era brought a matriarchal order to Paraguayan society, though this has never been proven conclusively.

The same period did bring some significant changes. In 1869, the first national school for girls was founded in Asunción. Educational opportunities in the capital and elsewhere afforded women career possibilities undreamt of previously. The full ramifications of this change became clear only in the 1900s, when women joined the ranks of recognized educators, poets, and artists.

In the twentieth century, women often chose migration as a strategy to find better livelihoods. In the first half of the century, emigrants followed agricultural cycles, arriving at yerba-maté plantations on the eastern frontier for harvest. Later, migration followed rural-to-urban and urban-to-urban patterns. Instead of eking out an existence in agriculture or crafts, many women have sought contract and salaried positions in the capital, Asunción. Others still find domestic work abroad, especially in Buenos Aires. Although this employment has created opportunities, some women find themselves vulnerable to exploitation.

The twentieth century has not, however, seen a progressive expansion of political influence for Paraguayan women. The various dictatorial regimes as well as the Chaco War with Bolivia (1932–1935) and the 1947 Civil War have tended to infuse the political culture of the country with a military spirit that manifestly has limited the participation of women. Women might be scholars, doctors, lawyers, and administrators, but political offices were usually beyond their reach. Only in 1961 did women receive the right to vote, and although some female deputies were elected in the 1960s and 1970s, a full thirty years passed before a Paraguayan president named a woman as minister. Various women's groups and feminist organizations came into being in the 1980s, but overall, as compared with all of its neighbors, Paraguay still has far to go in advancing the interests of its women.

See also **War of the Triple Alliance; Women.**

BIBLIOGRAPHY

Elman R. Service, *Spanish-Guaraní Relations in Early Colonial Paraguay* (1954).

Olinda Massare De Kostianovsky, *La mujer paraguaya: Su participación en la Guerra Grande* (1970).

Domingo M. Rivarola, "Apuntes para el estudio de la familia en el Paraguay," *Revista Paraguaya de Sociología* 8, no. 21 (1971): 84–104.

Grazziela Corvalán and Mabel Centurión, *Bibliografía sobre estudios de la mujer en el Paraguay* (1986).

Barbara Potthast-Jutkeit, "The Ass of a Mare and Other Scandals: Marriage and Extramarital Relations in Nineteenth-Century Paraguay," *Journal of Family History* 16, no. 3 (1991): 215–239.

Additional Bibliography

Asociación Interdisciplinario. *Violencia doméstica, sanción o impunidad? Usos y costumbres en denuncias de violencia doméstica sobre mujeres, niñas y niños en Argentina, Paraguay y Uruguay.* Montevideo: Editorial Psicolibros, 2005.

Bareiro, Line, Clyde Soto, and Mary Monte. *Alquimistas: Documentos para otra historia de las mujeres.* Asunción: Centro de Documentación y Estudios, 1993.

Caballero Aquino, Olga, and Gloria Giménez Guanes. *Madres en la paz y en la guerra: Testimonios de mujeres paraguayas, 1930–2004.* Asunción: SERVILIBRO, 2004.

Cooney, Jerry W., and Thomas L. Whigham, eds. *El Paraguay bajo los López: Algunos ensayos de historia social y política.* Asunción: Centro Paraguayo de Estudios Sociológicos, 1994.

Cortés, Rosalía, and Lilyan Mires. *Mujeres, pobreza y mercado de trabajo: Argentina y Paraguay.* Santiago: Oficina Regional de la OIT para América Latina y el Caribe, 2003.

Gorriti, Juana Manuela. *Peregrinaciones de una alma triste.* Edited by Mary G. Berg. Buenos Aires: Stockcero, 2006.

Küppers, Gabriele, ed. *Compañeras: Voices from the Latin American Women's Movement.* London: Latin American Bureau, 1994.

Potthast-Jutkeit, Barbara. *"Paraíso de Mahoma," o, "País de las mujeres"? El rol de la familia en la sociedad paraguaya del siglo XIX.* Translated by Carmen Livieres de Maynzhausen. Asunción: Instituto Cultural Paraguayo-Alemán, 1996.

Sosa Portillo, Zulma C. *La migración interna femenina en el Paraguay.* Asunción: Presidencia de la República, Secretaría Técnicade Planificación, Dirección General de Estadística, Encuestas y Censos, 1996.

MARTA FERNÁNDEZ WHIGHAM

WOOD. *See* **Lumber Industry.**

WOOD, LEONARD (1860–1927). Leonard Wood (*b.* 9 October 1860; *d.* 7 August 1927), commander of the First United States Volunteer Cavalry (the "Rough Riders") and U.S. military governor of Cuba (December 1899–May 1902). Born in Winchester, New Hampshire, and an 1884 graduate of Harvard Medical School, Wood became President McKinley's physician in 1895 and established close ties with Theodore Roosevelt. Wood was appointed military commander of both the city and province of Santiago before succeeding John Brooke as governor of Cuba. In 1910 Wood served briefly as a special ambassador to the Argentine Republic. Though Chief of Staff of the Army from 1910 to 1914, he was passed over by Woodrow Wilson to lead the American Expeditionary Force in France in favor of John J. Pershing. Wood was the principal challenger to Warren Harding for the Republican presidential nomination in 1920 and served as governor-general of the Philippines (1921–1927). He died in Boston.

See also **Philippines; Roosevelt, Theodore.**

BIBLIOGRAPHY

Hermann Hagedorn, *Leonard Wood: A Biography*, 2 vols. (1931), is the authorized treatment.

Jack C. Lane, *Armed Progressive: General Leonard Wood* (1978). See also David F. Healy, *The United States in Cuba, 1898–1902: Generals, Politicians, and the Search for Policy* (1963).

Additional Bibliography

McCallum, Jack Edward. *Leonard Wood: Rough Rider, Surgeon, Architect of American Imperialism.* New York: New York University Press, 1996.

LINDA K. SALVUCCI

WOOL INDUSTRY. As with other commodity-driven Latin American economies based on a single primary sector, Argentine and Uruguayan export-led growth from 1830 to 1900, and the diversification of those nations' economies, was founded on the burgeoning wool industry.

Explorers and traders first brought sheep to the Southern Cone in the sixteenth century. During the colonial period, however, there was no significant wool industry. In the seventeenth and eighteenth centuries, small numbers of the Spanish Merino breed were brought from Spain to Chile and Argentina, but they had little impact on the local sheep stocks. In Argentina the Pampa sheep (descended from the Spanish Churra) and the smaller Criolla produced coarse wool and a finer red wool, respectively. By 1757 the sheep population of Montevideo had reached 71,000, with tens of thousands more in the Río de la Plata region. But it was only after 1810, following a trend in Europe, that Southern Cone ranchers began to take an interest in herd improvement and the quality of wool shorn. Ranchers imported purebred sheep from Germany, Spain, France, the United States, and Australia. They introduced breeding programs and developed fine-wool flocks.

Workers at the Cooperativa Lavalan wool factory, Buenos Aires, Argentina, 2002. Argentina's wool industry has enjoyed a resurgence in the early twenty-first century, despite the nation's otherwise troubled economy. ALI BURAFI/AFP/ GETTY IMAGES

In Argentina, civil war impeded sheep breeding and the emergence of a wool industry until the mid-nineteenth century. In 1822 wool represented only 0.94 percent of total exports from the province of Buenos Aires. By 1851 that figure had risen modestly to over 10 percent. Ranchers bred the Argentine Merino as a larger animal producing medium- to fine-quality wool for export. By 1855 Argentina was exporting 10,000 tons of wool annually, mostly for textile mills in Europe and the United States. In an effort to stimulate wool production, Chile's Sociedad Nacional de Agricultura encouraged the introduction of new methods in animal husbandry. Late nineteenth-century Uruguayan flocks were similar to the European Merinos but produced a high-quality "Montevideo wool type" that enhanced the reputation of the Río de la Plata region's wool exports.

During the mid-1800s, wool production in Argentina and Uruguay determined the integration of the region into the world market. Wool exports grew quickly after 1840 and spurred Argentine and Uruguayan export-led growth. In 1840 Argentina exported less than 2,000 tons of wool. By 1870, 237,000 tons had been shipped overseas (55,000 tons in 1870 alone). From 1875 to 1900, a rapid expansion in the sheep population signaled the emergence of Argentina and Uruguay as world leaders in wool sales. Chile's production lagged behind, while Paraguayan exports were negligible. In Argentina, sheep raising was concentrated chiefly in the provinces of Buenos Aires, Entre Ríos, Corrientes, Santa Fé, and Córdoba (though in the twentieth century, the wool industry expanded to other regions, most notably Patagonia).

Like many Latin American commodity values, wool prices fluctuated quickly. In one case that characterized the relation between wool production on the pampa and world markets, production in Argentina and Uruguay rose with a price increment attributable to the Crimean War and the consequent withdrawal of Russian exports to the European market. But in 1857–1858, with the return of Russian production, prices for Argentine and Uruguayan wool dropped promptly. This pattern of rapid price fluctuations characterized cycles of strong and moderate growth in the wool industry during the late nineteenth century. For the most part, wool-industry profits were high for the *estancieros* (ranchers),

the middlemen, and the shipping houses in Buenos Aires and other littoral ports.

Many factors shaped the wool industry during the late-nineteenth-century expansion. At times, labor and land shortages limited expansion. By contrast, the growth of local credit availability in Buenos Aires and the building of rail lines through many provinces enhanced export opportunities. The export sector was further stimulated by the rise in the international demand for wool as Germany, France, and Belgium followed the British lead into textile industrialization. By 1880 wool represented half the value of Argentine exports; in 1895 the sheep population in Buenos Aires Province alone reached 84 million, reflecting the leading role wool played in the provincial economy. In the final years of the nineteenth century, however, cereals and meat overtook wool in relative importance to Argentine and Uruguayan sales abroad. Wool did not regain its position of primacy in the Río de la Plata region economy but remained a vital sector of production in the twentieth century.

After 1900 Argentina and Uruguay continued to lead the region in wool production. Chilean exports during the twentieth century were moderate, while Paraguay produced little wool. Between 1934 and 1954, Argentina's share of world wool exports ranged from 10 percent to 14 percent. During this period Argentina began large-scale production of wool textiles but, as it had earlier in the century, continued to import large quantities of finished wool goods. In 1937 Argentina imported 2,027 tons of woolen and worsted piece goods, principally from the United Kingdom and Italy. In 1938 the 151,877 tons of wool exported accounted for 11 percent of Argentine exports by value. During the 1930s the principal importers of wool from Argentina were the United Kingdom, Germany, France, the United States, Belgium, and Italy.

By mid-century Argentina's sheep population was the third largest in the world after Australia's and the Soviet Union's. A 1952 census placed the Argentine number at 54 million. The annual consumption of wool by a substantial domestic spinning and weaving industry stood at 60,000 tons. During the 1950s Argentina ranked as the world's fourth largest raw-wool producer, exporting an average 330 million pounds of wool and sheepskins. Chile exported 50 million pounds of wool annually over the same decade, while Paraguay's overseas shipments were negligible. Uruguay ranked fifth in wool exports, with annual shipments of 115 million pounds. After the 1960s, despite sometimes heavy annual fluctuations, wool exports remained steady over the long term. Producers were unable to eliminate foot-and-mouth disease from herds and contended that the industry was limited in the late twentieth century by a lack of credit and government marketing supports. Between the 1970s and the 1990s, wool production dropped to half its post-World War II levels. In the twenty-first century, however, Argentina's wool industry has rebounded. A currency devaluation made imported wool expensive enough that domestic production increased dramatically, and simultaneously made Argentina's wool very competitive on the international market. Also, Argentina reduced export taxes on wool exports, an additional stimulant to production.

See also **Textile Industry: The Colonial Era; Textile Industry: Modern Textiles.**

BIBLIOGRAPHY

Barclays Bank, *Wool* (1960).

Werner Von Bergen, *Wool Handbook* (1963).

Commonwealth Economic Committee, *World Trade in Wool and Wool Textiles, 1952–1963* (1965).

Banco Ganadero Argentino, *Temas de economía Argentina: Mercados y precios de la lana* (1969).

Carlos F. Díaz Alejandro, *Essays on the Economic History of the Argentine Republic* (1970); *An Illustrated World History of the Sheep and Wool Industry* (1970).

Aníbal Barrios Pintos, *História de la ganadería en el Uruguay* (1973).

Manuel E. Macchi, *El ovino en la Argentina* (1974).

Jonathan C. Brown, *A Socioeconomic History of Argentina, 1776–1860* (1979).

Vera Blinn Reber, *British Mercantile Houses in Buenos Aires, 1810–1880* (1979).

M. L. Ryder, *Sheep and Man* (1983).

Hilda Sabato, *Agrarian Capitalism and the World Market: Buenos Aires in the Pastoral Age, 1840–1890* (1990).

Additional Bibliography

Barsky, Osvaldo, and Jorge Gelman. *Historia del agro argentino: Desde la conquista hasta fines del siglo XX.* Buenos Aires: Grijalbo Mondadori, 2001.

DAVID M. K. SHEININ

WOOSTER, CHARLES WHITING (1780–1848). Charles Whiting Wooster (*b.* 1780; *d.* 1848), officer in the Chilean navy. Born in New Haven, Connecticut, he was the nephew of David Wooster, hero of the Battle of Danbury during the American Revolution. Wooster went to sea at an early age. During the War of 1812 he served on board the U.S. privateer *Saratoga*. Having earned substantial prize money and gained significant influence, he was named captain of the Port of New York after the war. With the death of his young wife he chose to join the fight for independence in Chile.

Investing his entire fortune, Wooster purchased the brigantine *Columbus*, which he outfitted with sixteen guns. He carried a cargo of rifles to Chile, arriving 25 April 1818. Wooster was commissioned into the Chilean navy as a commander and put in charge of the frigate *Lautaro*. The *Lautaro* along with the *San Martín* intercepted a Spanish squadron on 25 October at Talcahuano and captured the frigate *Reina María Isabel*, which was escorting reinforcements for the royalist army in Peru. The following day the Chilean squadron captured the transports one by one. This was a significant victory for the patriots.

When Thomas A. Cochrane was hired by the Chileans to command their fleet, Wooster resigned rather than serve under the British officer, a former enemy. Between 1818 and 1822 Wooster engaged in commercial pursuits, including whaling. When Cochrane resigned from the Chilean navy, Wooster was recommissioned with the rank of captain and again took command of the *Lautaro*. Between 1822 and 1826 he campaigned against the royalists in Chiloé and southern Peru. In 1829 he was promoted to rear admiral.

Following the capture of Chiloé, the Chilean navy, except for the *Aquiles*, was sold off. In 1829, while Wooster was ashore, the crew mutinied against the selection of Joaquín Vicuña as vice president. At the direction of the Chilean government, Wooster boarded the British frigate *Thesis*, which captured the *Aquiles* and returned it to Chilean control. However, on 8 December Vicuña was driven from the capital and took refuge on the *Aquiles*. The forts at Valparaíso, also in the hands of the rebels, drove the ship out of port. Wooster sailed to Coquimbo, where Vicuña surrendered. These events ended Wooster's career in the navy. Wooster settled in California, where he had become one of the most powerful property owners in San Francisco.

See also **Wars of Independence: South America.**

BIBLIOGRAPHY

Claudio Collados Nuñez, ed., *El poder naval chileno*, 2 vols. (1985).

Rodrigo Fuenzalida Bade, *Marinos ilustres y destacados del pasado* (1985).

Additional Bibliography

Arancibia Clavel, Patricia, Isabel Jara Hinojosa, and Andrea Novoa Mackenna. *La marina en la historia de Chile.* Santiago de Chile: Sudamericana, 2005.

ROBERT SCHEINA

WORLD BANK. The World Bank is the world's largest multilateral development institution. Each year the bank extends almost $20 billion in financial and technical assistance to countries throughout the developing world. The World Bank plays an especially important role in the social and economic progress of Latin American nations. Its loans and grants to governments and businesses throughout the region have contributed to economic growth, poverty reduction, the preservation of natural environments, and public sector reform.

FOUNDING AND PURPOSE

The idea of a World Bank was initially proposed at the July 1944 United Nations Monetary and Financial Conference in Bretton Woods, New Hampshire. The bank, which was formally established in 1945 and began operations in 1946, is headquartered in Washington, D.C., and has offices in more than one hundred countries throughout the world. Although technically a specialized agency of the United Nations, the World Bank has its own governing structure, membership, revenue sources, and administrative practices. Its operations are thus largely autonomous of United Nations control. While the World Bank's initial loans were designed to help rebuild the war-torn economies of western Europe, it soon shifted its focus to the developing nations in Latin America, Africa, and Asia.

World Bank loans are allocated almost exclusively to the governments of member states and must have an explicitly developmental purpose. At the same time, a small number of loans are also extended to private investors under government guarantees. The cumulative total of World Bank lending since its inception had surpassed $500 billion by 2007. The bank also offers technical and advisory services to member countries and training programs for local government officials.

STRUCTURE AND RESOURCES

The highest policy-making body of the World Bank is its Board of Governors. Each member nation of the bank is allowed to appoint one governor and one alternate. The Board of Governors meets annually to consider applications for new membership, review the overall policy orientation of the bank, and establish its lending strategies. The World Bank also has a twenty-four-member Board of Executive Directors who are responsible for day-to-day operations. The executive directors meet twice weekly to approve new loan applications and oversee the design and implementation of bank-sponsored activities. The president of the World Bank, who serves as chairman of the executive board, is responsible for the general management of the bank and oversees a staff of ten thousand. The president is nominated for a renewable five-year term by the member nation holding the largest shares in the bank (which has always been the United States) and is confirmed by the executive board.

The World Bank is organized into six regional bureaus: Latin America and the Caribbean, Africa, the Middle East and North Africa, South Asia, East Asia and the Pacific, and Europe and Central Asia. Each regional bureau is headed by a vice president. Within each region, the bank operates offices in most member countries. The country offices work with local governments to devise development plans, called Country Assistance Strategies, and assist in the implementation of bank-supported development projects.

Resources of the World Bank derive from a number of different sources. Member countries are assessed an annual subscription or quota, which is calculated to reflect each nation's relative economic strength. Voting power within the bank is based on these capital subscriptions. The larger industrialized countries hold the most subscriptions and thus exercise the greatest influence over general lending policies and decisions on specific loan applications. The World Bank also receives repayment of principal on previously extended loans and generates earnings through various investments. The largest source of revenue, however, comes from private capital markets. The World Bank sells medium- and long-term bonds on global financial markets.

AFFILIATED INSTITUTIONS

The World Bank has a number of affiliated institutions, which together are referred to as the World Bank Group. The oldest institution, established in 1945, is the International Bank for Reconstruction and Development (IBRD). Comprising 184 member countries, the IBRD remains the largest and most influential component of the World Bank Group. IBRD loans are extended at near-market interest rates and generally have a ten-to-twenty-year maturity period. Loans are allocated for projects that are designed to develop a nation's productive facilities and can be expected to generate sufficient funds for repayment. The IBRD also offers a small number of grants, risk management products, and advisory services.

In 1960 the World Bank established the International Development Association (IDA) to provide concessional loans to its poorest member states. IDA loans are interest-free, have longer maturity periods (usually thirty-five to forty years with a ten-year grace period), and carry a small service charge. Its resources come from the initial subscriptions of its members, periodic replenishments from its principal donors, and net income transfers from the IBRD. The IDA also provides more grants than the IBRD. The IDA, which currently has 165 member countries, also works to mobilize and coordinate economic assistance from donor countries and other international organizations.

The International Finance Corporation (IFC), which was established in 1956 and currently has 178 member countries, is the private sector affiliate of the World Bank. It provides loans and loan guarantees to businesses seeking to invest in the developing world. Loans from the IFC are typically at near-market interest rates with seven-to-twelve-year maturity periods. The IFC also makes equity investments in projects, usually investing in the early phase of a project and then selling off shares

once the project becomes profitable. The IFC works to increase flows of private investment by bringing foreign and domestic partners together for joint ventures.

The Multilateral Investment Guarantee Agency (MIGA), which was formed in 1988 and has 167 member countries, provides insurance for foreign investors in the developing world against noncommercial losses. Its insurance products typically provide protection from expropriation of property, breech of contractual commitments, currency restrictions, or political violence. MIGA also provides technical and advisory services to improve the investment climate in the developing world and help member countries attract and retain foreign investment.

Lastly, the International Center for the Settlement of Investment Disputes (ICSID) was created in 1966 to help mediate conflicts between host governments and private foreign investors. ICSID, which has 143 member countries, provides facilities and procedures for the arbitration of investment disputes. Its central purpose is to attract greater foreign investment to the developing world by fostering an atmosphere of mutual confidence between states and foreign investors.

LENDING PROGRAMS TO LATIN AMERICA

The World Bank has traditionally played an important role in the economic and social development of Latin America. Roughly 25 percent of all World Bank loans since the mid-1950s have been allocated to nations in this region. Almost $6 billion in loans, grants, and credits are currently disbursed to Latin American nations each year. The bank's Regional Bureau for Latin America and the Caribbean currently manages bank-supported projects and programs in thirty-four member countries.

The World Bank's lending policies in Latin America have evolved considerably over time. During the 1950s and 1960s most loans were allocated for the development of the region's physical infrastructure. Bank officials argued that poor physical infrastructure was an impediment to attracting the private capital investment necessary for industrialization and economic growth. The World Bank sponsored large-scale projects in public utilities (hydroelectric dams, electrical power plants, water and sewage facilities), transportation (roads, railways, airports, and maritime ports), and communications (telephone services).

During the 1970s the World Bank's lending strategy in Latin America was revised to place greater emphasis on meeting the basic needs of poor communities. Although infrastructural investments had contributed to economic growth, critics charged that the benefits of growth accrued to a relatively narrow elite and largely bypassed the region's poor. In response to these concerns, the World Bank refocused its lending on smaller-scale projects in nutrition, preventative health care, primary education, public housing, and rural development. Whereas infrastructural projects continued to be supported, social investments became a larger part of the bank's lending portfolio in the region.

POLICY-BASED LENDING

The World Bank's strategy in Latin America was again altered in the 1980s. During this period many nations in the region were experiencing severe economic difficulties, including substantial current accounts deficits, deteriorating foreign reserves, and the accumulation of large external debts. The bank argued that any gains realized from individual development projects were quickly eroded by the region's generalized economic downturn. Working closely with its sister institution, the International Monetary Fund (IMF), the bank assumed a leading role in helping shape the domestic and foreign economic policies of the region.

The most significant innovation was the introduction of policy-based lending. The bank worked with Latin American governments to enact macroeconomic reforms designed restore fiscal health and economic stability. "Structural adjustment" loans were granted to governments willing to cut public sector spending, lessen regulatory constraints on the private sector, reform tax structures, privatize state-owned industries, and integrate their economies in global markets through the promotion of exports and removal of barriers to foreign investment.

SOCIAL INVESTMENTS

Policy-based lending has been a controversial component of the World Bank's work in Latin America. Supporters contend that these reforms have helped balance government accounts, increase foreign exchange earnings, and lower inflation rates. For

critics, structural adjustment has only intensified the region's already severe inequalities. The poor and working classes, they argue, are most adversely affected by cutbacks in government social programs, removal of price controls on basic necessities, and the loss of public sector employment.

In the mid-1990s the World Bank again revised its policies in Latin America. The bank's Heavily-Indebted Poor Countries Initiative, first launched in 1996, has granted debt relief to some of the region's poorest countries, including Bolivia, Guyana, Honduras, and Nicaragua. The World Bank has also altered its lending strategies. Although structural adjustment lending continues to be part of the bank's portfolio, it has sought to offset the social costs of economic reform through new investments in basic services. Support for nutrition, primary health care, education, employment training, and rural development projects is explicitly designed to compensate those groups most adversely affected by economic reform.

The provision of basic health care has been especially prioritized by the World Bank. The bank supported projects in maternal and child health in Argentina, Brazil, Guatemala, and Paraguay, the extension of health care to remote rural communities in El Salvador and Mexico, and an immunization project in Bolivia. The bank has also allocated considerable resources to prevent the spread of HIV/AIDS in Brazil and the Caribbean. Improvements in education have also been prioritized. The World Bank has supported education reform projects in Brazil, Guatemala, and Uruguay. Basic education projects in El Salvador, Grenada, and Paraguay helped reduce repetition rates in primary and secondary schools, and primary education projects in Argentina and Mexico helped increase completion rates in elementary education in some of these nations' poorest regions.

The World Bank has also directed more of its resources toward meeting the particular needs of women and ethnic minorities. The bank has supported efforts to combat gender-based discrimination and enhance women's participation in economic development. Nutrition, health care, and education programs that specifically meet the needs of girls and women have been supported in Brazil, Mexico, Central America, and the Andean region. The World Bank has also targeted its loans toward indigenous and Afro-Latino communities in the region. The bank has supported projects in Central America and the Andean region that are designed to enhance economic opportunities for indigenous groups. The bank has also supported education and job-training programs for people of African descent in Brazil, Colombia, Guyana, Panama, Venezuela, and most Caribbean nations.

NATURAL ENVIRONMENTS

The World Bank is working to preserve natural environments in Latin America. Although environmental needs were not a priority in the early decades of its operations, and projects were sometimes faulted for damaging the environment, the bank has now become more committed to sustainable development. It has supported a range of environmental initiatives in the region. The bank has funded projects to protect the region's water resources, including coastal and marine systems, dams and reservoirs, groundwater, river basins, and watersheds. In addition, it has supported programs to conserve the Amazon rainforest. In Mexico and Costa Rica bank-supported projects have helped indigenous communities improve the management and conservation of their forest resources. The bank is cooperating with Mexico and six Central American countries to protect the Mesoamerican Biological Corridor. It has funded biodiversity protection projects in Brazil, Bolivia, and Ecuador. The bank's Clean Air Initiative for Latin American Cities focuses on improving urban air quality in Bogota, Buenos Aires, Caracas, Lima, Mexico City, Santiago, and São Paulo. Bank officials have also worked with local officials throughout the region to establish regulatory and institutional frameworks for sustainable environmental management.

PUBLIC SECTOR REFORM

The World Bank has become heavily involved in the promotion of public sector reform in Latin America. This is another area in which the bank was faulted in the past. World Bank loans, critics charged, supported authoritarian governments in the region. By strengthening these regimes, assistance from the bank only reinforced repressive political structures and economic inequalities. World Bank officials have acknowledged that project failure was often caused by political and administrative weaknesses in recipient countries.

Thus the World Bank has placed public sector reform and "good governance" near the top of its regional agenda. Bank officials now argue that the success of development assistance largely depends on the quality of governance in recipient countries. Social and economic progress is not possible without impartial, effective, and reliable public sector institutions. The World Bank placed particular emphasis on enhanced public sector management. It has supported projects to strengthen civil services, reform public enterprises, and upgrade financial management systems. An Institutional Reform Project in Bolivia, for example, established performance-based incentives for the civil service. In Argentina, the bank supported ministerial reorganization that strengthened administrative capabilities and improved the management of information systems. The World Bank has also worked to reform judicial institutions in the region. Technical assistance was provided to reform courtroom management systems in Argentina, Ecuador, and El Salvador, increase administrative efficiency in Bolivia, Guatemala, and Honduras, streamline judicial procedures in Colombia and Venezuela, and train judges and court personnel in Peru. The World Bank has also worked to enhance public sector accountability and transparency. It has supported a number of projects to improve auditing, budgeting, accounting, and internal oversight procedures. The bank has worked to improve access to information about government expenditures and ensure open bidding processes for all public contracts. This includes projects to modernize public auditing systems in Bolivia, enhance procurement and debt management in Guatemala, and establish integrated financial management systems in Argentina, Chile, Ecuador, and Honduras.

CONCLUSION

The World Bank has long played a significant role in the economic and social progress of Latin America. While the bank's early emphasis on infrastructural projects and private enterprise development remains an important component of its lending strategy, its agenda has expanded to include a much wider range of economic, social, and environmental programs. Expansion of the bank's lending portfolio reflects both in-house learning from past experience and a response to outside criticism. It is placing greater emphasis on meeting the basic needs of poor communities, enhancing gender and ethnic equality, preserving natural environments, and reforming public administration. Given the bank's rapidly expanding development agenda for Latin America, and the considerable resources at its disposal, it will continue to play a major role in the region's social and economic development well into the twenty-first century.

See also **Economic Development; International Monetary Fund (IMF); United Nations.**

BIBLIOGRAPHY

Arias Robles, Marta, and José María Vera Villacian. *Banco Mundial y Fondo Monetario Internacional: ¿Una ayuda para los países pobres?* Barcelona: Cristianisme i Justícia, 2002.

Baum, Warren C. *La inversión en desarrollo: Lecciones de la experiencia del Banco Mundial.* Madrid: Tecnos, 1985.

Caufield, Catherine. *Masters of Illusion: The World Bank and the Poverty of Nations.* New York: Henry Holt, 1996.

Gilbert, Christopher L., and David Vines, eds. *The World Bank: Structure and Policies.* Cambridge, U.K.: Cambridge University Press, 2000.

Kapur, Devesh, John P. Lewis, and Richard Webb. *The World Bank: Its First Half Century,* 2 vols. Washington, DC: Brookings Institution Press, 1997.

Mosley, Paul, Jane Harrigan, and John Toye. *Aid and Power: The World Bank and Policy-Based Lending.* London: Routledge, 1991.

Pincus, Jonathan R., and Jeffrey A. Winters, eds. *Reinventing the World Bank.* Ithaca, NY: Cornell University Press, 2002.

Sanahuja, José Antonio. *Altruismo, mercado y poder: El Banco Mundial y la lucha contra la pobreza.* Barcelona: Intermón Oxfam, 2001.

FRANCIS ADAMS

WORLD WAR I.

World War I, a conflict that presented the nations of Latin America with some difficult choices, as they balanced their need for German investment with distrust of Great Britain and their friendship for the United States. Germany had emerged during the early part of the century as an important new source of investment, offering new capital and alternatives to the traditional reliance on England and France. Most of the nations followed the lead of the U.S. government, however, though there were exceptions. During the period of neutrality, the first Pan-American Financial Conference was held in 1915 to cushion the economic impact of the war.

When the United States entered the conflict during 1917, many Latin American nations followed despite their heightened sensitivities to recent U.S. expansion and hemispheric hegemony. Eight nations declared war on Germany: Brazil, Cuba, Costa Rica, Guatemala, Haiti, Honduras, Nicaragua, and Panama. Five others broke diplomatic relations (Bolivia, the Dominican Republic, Ecuador, Peru, and Uruguay), several of which openly announced that they were "neutral in favor of the United States," thus risking retaliation by German submarines. Even nations in the midst of disputes with the United States, such as Mexico, resisted the temptation to support the Germans, despite open proposals such as the Zimmermann Telegram. There were, however, multilateral security arrangements during the neutrality period or during the conflict.

The war and the accompanying Allied blockade of Germany disrupted long-standing trade patterns by impeding commerce with much of Europe, especially when combined with the shift of the European economies to a wartime basis. Latin Americans found themselves cut off from trading partners and sources of investment and capital. The result was increased economic and financial reliance on the United States, refocusing trade northward as well as increasing the importance of interchange with neighboring nations. There were some exceptions, such as raw materials production, which now became more important to the United States. The Chilean nitrate industry boomed during the prewar and war years. These changes in trade patterns laid the basis for stronger financial and economic ties with the United States that persisted after the war. Argentina, Chile, and Mexico remained fully neutral, reflecting ties to Germany, dislike for England, and disputes with the United States.

Eleven Latin American nations participated in the Versailles Conference, with ten signing the treaty and thereby becoming charter members of the League of Nations. Six other Latin American nations adhered to the League Covenant, and ultimately all the nations of Latin America became League members, though some later withdrew. Latin America played a significant role in the League and in the establishment of the International Court of Justice and by so doing gained considerable prestige in international diplomacy. Brazil served almost continuously on the League Council during its years of membership, and the court included two justices from the region.

See also **Chile, Organizations: Chilean Nitrate Company (COSACH); Zimmermann Telegram.**

BIBLIOGRAPHY

Percy A. Martin, *Latin America and the War* (1925), offers the classic study. See also Joseph S. Tulchin, *The Aftermath of War: World War I and U.S. Policy Toward Latin America* (1971).

Mark T. Gilderhus, *Pan-American Visions: Woodrow Wilson in the Western Hemisphere, 1913–1921* (1986). Many individual country studies also treat the wartime era.

Additional Bibliography

Albert, Bill and Paul Henderson. *South America and the First World War: The Impact of the War on Brazil, Argentina, Peru, and Chile.* Cambridge, UK: Cambridge University Press, 2002.

Schoonover, Thomas David. *Germany in Central America: Competitive Imperialism, 1821–1929.* Tuscaloosa: University of Alabama Press, 1998.

Segura, Jorge Rhenán. *La sociedad de las naciones y la política centroamericana: 1919–1939.* San José, Costa Rica: Euroamericana de Ediciones, 1993.

KENNETH J. GRIEB

WORLD WAR II.

World War II, an international conflict that, with the exception of Argentina, brought about a sense of inter-American solidarity unknown before. But the Latin American nations did not quickly commit themselves to the Allied cause. Their leaders did not share the concern of the United States with the developing hostilities in Europe and Asia between 1935 and 1938. Rather, they appeared more concerned with reaffirming President Franklin D. Roosevelt's Good Neighbor Policy that had been initiated in 1933. Given these diverse views, Washington found it difficult to obtain Latin America's cooperation on hemispheric defense before 1940. At the Inter-American Conference for the Maintenance of Peace held in Buenos Aires in 1936, Roosevelt and Secretary of State Cordell Hull asked for trade and credit embargoes against the European warring factions. Instead, they received only an innocuous agreement to meet when an emergency arose that affected their common defense. By the time of the Eighth Inter-American Conference of American

States in Lima, Peru, in 1938, Austria and Czechoslovakia had fallen to Nazi Germany and China had engaged Japan in a test of survival. Fearing the Western Hemisphere to be in greater danger than in 1936, the U.S. delegation went to Lima seeking a mutual defense pact, but the Latin Americans were not prepared to formulate a plan of action against the Axis powers.

The first collective action to meet the dangers of World War II came at a meeting of foreign ministers in Panama in 1939 following the German invasion of Poland and the outbreak of the European War. The Declaration of Panama proclaimed a safety belt around the Western Hemisphere, extending from 300 to 1,000 miles from the eastern and western coastlines, within which, at least in theory, no belligerent act was to be allowed. After the fall of France in June 1940, the foreign ministers convened a month later in Havana. The subsequent Declaration of Havana decreed that the European colonies in the Western Hemisphere were off limits to the Axis powers and could be occupied by a hemispheric nation pending final settlement of the territory's disposition. Furthermore, any attack upon one hemispheric nation was to be considered an act of aggression against all. By the time of the Havana conference, the United States also had determined its hemispheric military defense policy. A line was drawn at Brazil in order to secure the Caribbean sea routes and the Panama Canal. The Latin American armies would not be raised to the status of a fighting ally, but would act only to meet an external attack until U.S. forces could arrive. Toward that end, agreements placed U.S. military missions in all but Bolivia, to which no mission was ever sent. Subsequently, the Lend-Lease Act of 1941 provided for $400 million in military assistance to Latin America over a three-year period, the bulk of it scheduled to be disbursed in 1943 and later.

Following the Japanese attack on Pearl Harbor on 7 December 1941, Costa Rica, Cuba, the Dominican Republic, El Salvador, Guatemala, Haiti, Honduras, Nicaragua, and Panama immediately declared war on the Axis powers. Meeting at Rio de Janeiro in January 1942, the foreign ministers of all of the Latin American republics recommended that their governments sever diplomatic relations with the Axis nations. Ultimately, Mexico and all of the South American nations did so. Mexico and Brazil declared

Anti-aircraft searchlights over the Panama Canal, 1939. A declaration of a safety zone around the Panama Canal was one of the first actions of the Inter-American Conference of American States after the outbreak of World War II. © BETTMANN/CORBIS

war on the Axis powers in 1942; Bolivia and Colombia did so in 1943. The ministers at Rio also committed their governments to institute measures to eliminate possible Axis subversion. The most notable measure was the internment and deportation of German, Japanese, and Italian nationals and their descendants to either their homelands or camps in the United States. Unfortunately, many innocent people and political opponents fell victim to the program, and many had their properties confiscated. The Caribbean was the area of the most significant military action. Until late 1942, German U-boats played havoc with Allied shipping in the region. Subsequently, Brazil and Mexico sent troops to the war zones. Throughout the war, Nelson A. Rockefeller's Office of Inter-American Affairs coordinated economic policies. Few Latin American countries benefited from the war because of the loss of European markets. The unimportance of coffee, sugar, and tropical fruits caused severe economic hardship on the Caribbean islands and in Central America. Conversely, the need for Bolivian tin, Chilean copper, and Venezuelan oil brought a measure of prosperity

to those nations. Brazil and Mexico also benefited when the United States financed steel mills in those nations. However, no plans for postwar conversion were made, and with Europe in shambles, the Latin Americans did not recover their traditional trading partners after 1945. Allied wartime propaganda also contributed to the demands of the generation of rising expectations. If the Allies were fighting to eliminate tyranny in Asia and Europe, why not put an end to Latin American dictatorships? Political protests along these lines were most evident in Central America near the end of the war.

As postwar planning for the United Nations began to take shape, Washington warned the Latin American states that only those who had declared war on the Axis nations would be eligible for membership in the international organization. The threat prompted Ecuador, Peru, Venezuela, Uruguay, Paraguay, and Chile to declare war in early 1945. Argentina remained reluctant. Argentina's traditional resistance to Washington's dominance of hemispheric affairs was now complicated by its pro-fascist military, which had extended its influence in

Argentinian foreign minister Hipólito Jesú Paz (seated) signs the Japanese Peace Treaty, 1951. J. R. EYERMAN/TIME LIFE PICTURES/GETTY IMAGES

politics until 1943, when a coup gave it complete control of the government. A large German and Italian immigrant population resided in the nation. Throughout the war, the United States increased the pressure on Argentina. Washington publicly denounced the government for having deserted the Allied cause, froze Argentine gold stocks and tightened shipping regulations, and withheld recognition of President Edelmiro Farrell from March 1944 to April 1945. When the diplomats convened in Mexico City in early 1945 for the Inter-American Conference on Problems of War and Peace, only Argentina was absent. The gathering's major objective was to strengthen Pan-American solidarity for the upcoming meeting of the United Nations in San Francisco. The resultant Act of Chapultepec contained a proviso stating that the Monroe Doctrine secured the American republics against even an American aggressor, a statement that satisfied Argentina and contributed to its declaration of war against Germany and Japan on 27 March 1945.

See also **Pan-American Conferences: Mexico City Conference (1945).**

BIBLIOGRAPHY

Harley Notter, *Postwar Foreign Policy Preparation, 1939–1945* (1949).

John A. Houston, *Latin America in the United Nations* (1956).

Stetson Conn and Byron Fairchild, *Framework of Hemispheric Defense* (1960).

Stetson Conn, Rose C. Engleman, and Byron Fairchild, *Guarding the United States and Its Outposts* (1964).

Alton Frye, *Nazi Germany and the American Hemisphere, 1933–1941* (1967).

J. M. Espinosa, *Inter-American Beginnings of U.S. Cultural Diplomacy, 1936–1948* (1976).

Michael J. Francis, *The Limits of Hegemony: United States Relations with Argentina and Chile during World War II* (1977).

Gerald K. Haines, "Under the Eagle's Wing: The Franklin D. Roosevelt Administration Forges an American Hemisphere," *Diplomatic History* 1 (1977): 373–388.

R. A. Humphreys, *Latin America and the Second World War,* 2 vols. (1981–1982).

David G. Haglund, *Latin America and the Transformation of U.S. Strategic Thought, 1936–1940* (1984).

Additional Bibliography

Endries, Carrie Anne. "Exiled in the Tropics: Nazi Protesters and the Getúlio Vargas Regime in Brazil, 1933–1945." Ph.D. diss. Harvard University, 2005.

Friedman, Max Paul. *Nazis and Good Neighbors: The United States Campaign against the Germans of Latin America in World War II*. Cambridge, UK: Cambridge University Press, 2003.

Leonard, Thomas and John F. Bratzel. *Latin America during World War II*. Lanham, MD: Rowman & Littlefield, 2007.

Peredo Castro, Francisco. *Cine y propaganda para Latinoamérica: México y Estados Unidos en la encrucijada de los años cuarenta*. Mexico City: Universidad Nacional Autónoma de México, Centro de Investigaciones sobre América del Norte: Centro Coordinador y Difusor de Estudios Latinoamericanos, 2004.

THOMAS M. LEONARD

WYKE-AYCINENA TREATY (1859).

Wyke-Aycinena Treaty (1859), an agreement confirming British rights to Belize. The treaty was signed 30 April 1859 by Pedro de Aycinena, Guatemalan foreign minister, and Charles Lennox Wyke, British chargé d'affaires and plenipotentiary to Guatemala. The treaty has long been controversial. Article 7, added by the negotiators, ambiguously called for Guatemala and Great Britain to cooperate in erecting a transit way from Guatemala City to the Atlantic coast "near the settlement of Belize." Disputes over each government's expected contribution prevented the article's fulfillment. An additional convention of 1863 attempted to clarify Article 7, but lapsed because of Guatemala's failure to ratify it. Beyond the road issue, the treaty itself was subject to more fundamental disagreement. Guatemala held that it was a "disguised cession" of territory, possibly violating the Clayton-Bulwer Treaty of 1850, for which the road was compensation. British governments saw it as a simple boundary agreement, defining the limits of previously held territory. Guatemala continued to contest the validity of the treaty, and thus British rights to Belize, into the late twentieth century.

See also **Aycinena, Pedro de; Clayton-Bulwer Treaty (1850).**

BIBLIOGRAPHY

R. A. Humphreys, *The Diplomatic History of British Honduras, 1638–1901* (1961).

Wayne M. Clegern, *British Honduras: Colonial Dead End, 1859–1900* (1967).

Additional Bibliography

Brown, Richmond F. "Charles Lennox Wyke and the Clayton-Bulwer Formula in Central America, 1852–1860." *The Americas* 47, no. 4 (April 1991): 411–445.

Brown, Richmond F. *Juan Fermin De Aycinena: Central American Colonial Entrepreneur, 1729–1796*. Norman: University of Oklahoma Press, 1997.

RICHMOND F. BROWN

WYLD OSPINA, CARLOS (1891–1956).

Carlos Wyld Ospina (*b.* 19 June 1891; *d.* 17 June 1956), Guatemalan writer and journalist, member of the influential Generation of 1920. Wyld was born in Antigua to wealthy parents, Guillermo Wyld and Soledad Ospina. Largely self-taught, he began to write romantic poetry at an early age. As a novelist he is regarded as a chief exponent of *criollismo*, a literary movement devoted to denouncing social evils and to promoting national regeneration. Among his most notable works in this vein are *El solar de los Gonzaga* (1924; Ancestral Home) and *La gringa* (1935). In his short stories, such as "La tierra de las Nahuyacas" (1933; "The Land of the Nahuyacas"), he was among the first to depict realistically the wretched condition of the Indian majority, thus becoming a precursor of the Indigenista movement.

It was in Mexico that Wyld established himself as a journalist of note, becoming the editor of the paper *El Independiente* (1913–1914). Upon his return to Guatemala, he settled in Quetzaltenango, where he taught literature and worked as the editor of *Diario de Los Altos*. In 1920 he founded, in association with the writer Alberto Vásquez, *El Pueblo*, the organ of the Unionist Party in which he bitterly criticized the Guatemalan dictator Manuel Estrada Cabrera. He also founded the cultural magazines *Estudio* (1922) and *Semana* (1939), and from 1922 to 1925 worked as the editor of the prominent newspaper *El Imparcial*. He married Amalia Cheves, a noted poet from Cobán. From 1937 to 1942, he served as deputy in the National

Assembly. He died in Quetzaltenango while serving as director of the Bank of the West.

See also **Literature: Spanish America.**

BIBLIOGRAPHY

Francisco Albizúrez Palma and Catalina Barrios y Barrios, *Historia de la literatura guatemalteca,* vol. 2 (1981), pp. 97–108.

Carlos C. Haeussler Yela, *Diccionario general de Guatemala,* vol. 3 (1983).

Additional Bibliography

Arias, Arturo. *La identidad de la palabra: Narrativa guatemalteca del siglo veinte.* Guatemala: Artemis & Edinter, 1998.

JORGE H. GONZÁLEZ

XAVIER, FRANCISCO CÂNDIDO (CHICO) (1910–2002).

Chico Xavier, born 2 April 1910 in Minas Gerais, was a Spiritist medium, widely credited for inspiring the mainstream acceptance of Spiritism in Brazil. An occult religion encompassing a belief in Jesus Christ and reincarnation, based on the writings of the nineteenth-century French researcher Allan Kardec, Spiritism claims an estimated twenty million Brazilian adherents in the early twenty-first century. Chico completed more than 400 published "psychographic" works, despite his elementary-level education and his multiple chronic health problems late in life. He donated all proceeds to charity.

Chico claimed to have been in contact with numerous spirits, to whom he credited all his books. Emmanuel, identified as a reincarnation of a Roman senator, Publius Lentulus, authored a five-volume series offering a first-hand account of the birth of Christianity and the early history of the Catholic Church. André Luiz, pseudonym of a spirit incarnated as a doctor in Rio de Janeiro during the 1930s, wrote another popular series that illustrated his post-mortem life in the spiritual world.

In 1959 Chico moved to Uberaba, in Minas Gerais, where he provided free spiritualist sessions to thousands of individuals, including celebrities, religious leaders, and Brazilian presidents. During this period he also made numerous television appearances, and was promoted by his supporters for the Nobel Peace Prize. Adding to his legacy, Chico died on the same day, 30 June 2002, that Brazil won the World Cup.

See also **Spiritism.**

BIBLIOGRAPHY

Bellos, Alex. "Chico Xavier: Brazil's Leading Medium; His Many Books Were Dictated by the Dead." *The Guardian*, July 11, 2002. Available from http://books.guardian.co.uk/obituaries/story/0,,753357,00.html.

Souto Maior, Marcel. *As Vidas de Chico Xavier*, 2nd edition. São Paulo: Editora Planeta do Brasil, 2003.

Stoll, Sandra Jacqueline. *Espiritimo á Brasil*. São Paulo: EDUSP, 2003.

Xavier, Francisco C. *Nosso Lar: A Spiritual Home*. Phoenix, AZ: Allen Kardec Educational Society, 2000.

Xavier, Francisco C., Andre Luiz, and Andrea Dessen. *The Messengers*. Phoenix, AZ: Allen Kardec Educational Society, 2005.

LANCE MURCHISON

XICA DA SILVA. *See* **Silva, Xica da.**

XIMÉNEZ, FRANCISCO (1666–1730).

Francisco Ximénez (*b*. 28 November 1666; *d*. between 11 May 1729 and mid-1730), a Dominican priest who translated the *Popol Vuh*, the Maya–K'iche' story of creation.

Born in Écija, Andalusia, Ximénez joined the Dominican order in 1688 and was sent to Guatemala to continue his religious studies. He was ordained in 1690. His facility for learning the Indian languages soon became evident, and he was assigned as parish priest in San Juan Sacatepéquez to learn the Kaqchikel language. Under the guidance of another friar who knew Kakchikel, he prepared a grammar in that language and went on to master the K'iche' and Tz'utujil languages.

While serving in Chichicastenango from 1701 to 1703, Ximénez found a manuscript of the ancient book of the K'iche' people, the *Popol Vuh*. He translated into Spanish its story of creation and the history of the K'iche' nation. The *Popol Vuh* is now considered the national book of Guatemala.

Later Ximénez founded a hospital for Indians in Rabinal and developed a treatment for rabies. During his stay at Rabinal he also began a careful study of bees. Ximénez became interested in the flora and fauna of Guatemala. His work as a naturalist was recorded in *Historia natural del Reino de Guatemala*. About 1715 he began writing the history of the Dominican order in Guatemala, *Historia de la provincia de San Vicente de Chiapa y Guatemala de la Orden de Predicadores*. His writings were often critical of the Spaniards. He died in the convent of Santo Domingo in Santiago de Guatemala.

See also **Indigenous Peoples.**

BIBLIOGRAPHY

Juan Rodríguez Cabal, *Apuntes para la vida del... Francisco Ximénez* (1935).

Francisco Ximénez, *Historia natural* (1967) and *Historia de la provincia de San Vicente de Chiapa y Guatemala de la Orden de Predicadores* (1971).

Additional Bibliography

Quiroa, Nestor I. "Francisco Ximénez and the 'Popol Vuh': Text, Structure, and Ideology in the Prologue to the Second Treatise." *Colonial Latin American Historical Review* 11, no. 3 (Summer 2002): 279–300.

DAVID L. JICKLING

XIMENO Y PLANES, RAFAEL. *See* Jimeno y Planes, Rafael.

XINGU RESERVE. Xingu Reserve (National Indian Park), a reserve for multiethnic indigenous peoples and national park is located in northern Mato Grosso along the Xingu River. The reserve was established in 1961 with two goals in mind: the preservation of flora and fauna for the distant future and the protection of endangered peoples more immediately. It was created by the Brazilian government on the advice of the Villas Bôas brothers. Within the reserve, non-indigeneous settlement, tourism, missionary activity, and commercial enterprise are illegal. The population in 1979 was estimated at 1,800 individuals, representing four language groups: Arawak, Carib, Gê, and Tupi. At establishment, the reserve encompassed 13,200 square miles. However, in 1971, after completion of the Transamazon Highway (BR 080), the reserve's boundaries were changed. Approximately 35 percent of the park was detached for commercial development. At the same time, new territory along the Ronuro, Batovi, and Culiseiu rivers increased the total area of the reserve to 18,000 square miles. This new land is poor-quality *campo* (a relatively dry savanna), partially occupied by cattle ranchers and unsuitable for habitation owing to a lack of game. While the operation of the reserve has received world acclaim (the Villas Boâs brothers were nominated for the Nobel Peace Prize), the living conditions of the people within the reserve have engendered controversy even though they are acknowledged to be better than those of Brazil's indigenous in general. The international attention that the Xingu Reserve receives should not obscure endemic Brazilian problems regarding its original inhabitants pejoratively called "Indians."

See also **Brazil, Geography; Indian Policy, Brazil.**

BIBLIOGRAPHY

Orlando Villas Boas, *Xingu: The Indians, Their Myths* (1973).

Robin Hanbury–Tenison, *A Question of Survival for the Indians of Brazil* (1973).

Carmen Junqueira, *The Brazilian Indigenous Problem and Policy* (1973).

Shelton H. Davis, *Victims of the Miracle* (1977).

MICHAEL J. BROYLES

XINGU RIVER.

XINGU RIVER. Xingu River, a large southern tributary of the Amazon in north-central Brazil; it rises in Mato Grosso, flows north into Pará, then enters the Amazon west of the island of Marajó. The Xingu's total length approaches 1,230 miles, but it is navigable only for the lower 96 miles. Its chief tributary is the Iriri, whose branches flow through Xingu National Park, in northeast Mato Grosso.

In lieu of more efficient alternatives, the Xingu River provided essential access to Brazil's interior for the earliest Catholic missionaries, as well as for Brazilian frontiersmen, traders, and slave raiders. In 1961 the Xingu National Park was created by Orlando and Claudio Villas Bôas to protect the Amerindians from extermination. The park was enlarged from 8,800 to about 10,400 square miles in 1968, and now includes the Tupi, Carib, Arawak, and Gê linguistic groups. In 1979 the Villas Bôas brothers estimated the park's population at 1,800. Non-Indian settlement, missionary activity, commercial exploitation, and tourism are prohibited within the park, but pressure from property developers continues. The controversial Transamazon Highway passes through the north section of the park, threatening the Indians' autonomy and isolation, and effectively reducing the park territory by 50 percent. Plans for a Xingu hydroelectric complex threaten more than 9,000 people along the Xingu with resettlement.

See also **Amazon Region; Marajó Island; Mato Grosso; Pará (Grão Pará); Transamazon Highway; Villas Bôas Brothers.**

BIBLIOGRAPHY

Adrian Cowell, *The Heart of the Forest* (1961).

Orlando Villas Bôas and Claudio Villas Bôas, "Saving Brazil's Stone Age Tribes from Extinction," in *National Geographic* 134, no. 3 (1968): 424–444, *Xingu: The Indians, Their Myths* (1973), and *Xingu: Tribal Territory* (1979).

Additional Bibliography

Goulding, Michael, Ronaldo Barthem, and Efrem Jorge Gondim Ferreira. *The Smithsonian Atlas of the Amazon.* Washington, DC: Smithsonian Books, 2003.

Heckenberger, Michael. *The Ecology of Power: Culture, Place, and Personhood in the Southern Amazon, A.D. 1000–2000.* New York: Routledge, 2005.

Santos, Leinad Ayer O. and Lúcia M. M. de Andrade. *Hydroelectric Dams on Brazil's Xingu River and Indigenous Peoples.* Cambridge, MA: Cultural Survival, 1990.

CAROLYN E. VIEIRA

XOCHICALCO.

XOCHICALCO. Xochicalco is an archaeological site in the modern state of Morelos, in central Mexico. The ancient city rose to power around 650 CE and was an important political and religious center until 900 CE. At the time of the Spanish Conquest, Xochicalco was part of the Aztec tribute province of Cuauhnahuac and was recognized as an important place in native historic traditions.

Xochicalco developed during a period of cultural upheaval and rapid sociopolitical change in central Mexico. The period between 650 and 900 was characterized by the decline of the powerful center of Teotihuacán, the breakup of its pan-Mesoamerican empire, an increase in militarism, and the emergence of independent, competing city-states within Teotihuacán's former political domain. Xochicalco is representative of all these features. During its maximum development the site covered an area of approximately 1.5 square miles and supported a population of between 10,000 and 15,000 people. Xochicalco is the earliest known fortified city in central Mexico. The site was constructed over a series of low hills, and seven defensive precincts have been identified that were fortified using ramparts, dry moats, and concentric terracing.

Most of western Morelos was under Xochicalco's direct political control between 650 and 900. Political power is evident in the scale of monumental architecture, including the construction of central Mexico's first and only paved road system, which linked Xochicalco with outlying sites in the region. Xochicalco engaged in long-distance trade with many areas of Mesoamerica, including the Gulf Coast, Oaxaca, and the Maya region. The site's many sculpted monuments identify the three earliest named rulers in central Mexico, and the Pyramid of the Plumed Serpents was venerated as a sacred place at the time of the Conquest.

Xochicalco society represents an early expression of the Aztec cultural pattern. This pattern is characterized by military conquest, the formation of tribute empires, internal social stratification based on participation in warfare, and the practice of human sacrifice, which was linked to the religious practice of nourishing the gods through sacrificial ritual.

See also **Archaeology; Aztecs; Precontact History: Mesoamerica; Teotihuacán.**

BIBLIOGRAPHY

Hirth, Kenneth. "Xochicalco: Urban Growth and State Formation in Central Mexico." *Science* 225 (1984): 579–586.

Hirth, Kenneth. "Militarism and Social Organization at Xochicalco, Morelos." In *Mesoamerica after the Decline of Teotihuacán, A.D. 700–900*, ed. Richard A. Diehl and Janet Catherine Berlo. Washington, DC: Dumbarton Oaks Research Library and Collection, 1989.

Hirth, Kenneth. *Ancient Urbanism at Xochicalco.* Salt Lake City: University of Utah Press, 2000.

Litvak King, Jaime. "Xochicalco en la caída del Clásico, una hipótesis." *Anales de Antropología* 8 (1970): 102–124.

Piña Chán, Román. *Xochicalco: El mítico Tamoanchán.* Mexico City: Instituto Nacional de Antropología e Historia, 1989.

KENNETH HIRTH

XOCHIMILCO. Xochimilco in the early twenty-first century is one of the sixteen *delagaciones* (political subdivisions) of Mexico's Federal District, but in the twelfth and thirteenth centuries CE it was the capital of a large and powerful city-state that dominated the freshwater part of the Valley of Mexico. The name "Xochimilco" is derived from the Nahuatl *xochitl* and *milli*, meaning "where the flowers grow," and referring to the rich agricultural productivity and abundance of flowers that have typified the area since pre-Columbian times. The Aztec defeat of Xochimilco in 1430 pushed back its territorial bounds to the southern shore of Lake Xochimilco. It was surrounded by canals and *chinampas* (fields reclaimed from the lake marshes), and at the time of the Spanish Conquest, Hernán Cortés described it as "a pleasant city … built on the freshwater lake." Its fertile lands produced quantities of food that were sent to the Aztec capital as tribute and trade goods during the pre-Columbian and early colonial periods. After the Conquest, Xochimilco was assigned to

Pedro de Alvarado as an *encomienda* (a trusteeship labor system), and was designated one of only four colonial *ciudades* in the Valley of Mexico in 1559.

Agricultural products from Xochimilco continued to be carried into Mexico City by canoe during the early twentieth century. It remained a small suburban city located ten to fifteen miles south of Mexico City's main plaza and was connected to it mainly by electric streetcar. Even in the twenty-first century, about two thirds of the delegacion's area remains in agriculture and forest, with landscapes and agricultural practices little changed from those of pre-Columbian times. Farmers use small canoes to navigate the network of canals that connect the "floating gardens." *Trajineras*—brightly colored, flower–bedecked special boats whose names are spelled out in cut flowers of many hues—are poled through the canals, carrying thousands of residents and visitors, especially on weekends and holidays. Despite the beauty of the area, however, the stagnant water in the canals has contributed to a serious deterioration of its environmental quality.

See also **Cortés, Hernán; Mexico, Federal District.**

BIBLIOGRAPHY

Garza, Gustavo, and la Programa de Intercambio Científico y Capacitación Técnica, eds. *Atlas de la Ciudad de México.* Mexico City: Colegio de México, 1987.

Hodge, Mary G. *Aztec City-States.* Ann Arbor: Museum of Anthropology, University of Michigan, 1984.

Parsons, Jeffrey R. et al. *Prehispanic Settlement Patterns in the Southern Valley of Mexico: The Chalco-Xochimilco Region.* Ann Arbor: Museum of Anthropology, University of Michigan, 1982.

JOHN J. WINBERRY

XUL SOLAR, (1888–1963). Xul Solar (Oscar Agustín Alejandro Schulz Solari; *b.* 14 December 1888; *d.* 10 April 1963). Argentine painter and illustrator who also made musical instruments and toys. Xul Solar was born in San Fernando, Buenos Aires Province. He studied engineering and architecture at the University of Buenos Aires. He left school and traveled to Paris, where he studied drawing and painting with Emilio Pettorutti in 1908. His first artistic attempts, in 1917, related to art nouveau forms. The art of Xul Solar possesses an esoteric flavor of deep religious and metaphysical suggestion. In an imaginary space, Xul Solar combines faces, magical elements, and fragmentary objects, treating his material in a schematic, planimetric way with dynamic action and an exceptional refinement of color.

See also **Art: The Twentieth Century.**

BIBLIOGRAPHY

Vicente Gesualdo, Aldo Biglione, and Rodolfo Santos, *Diccionario de artistas plásticos en la Argentina* (1988).

Mario H. Gradowczyk, ed., *Xul Solar* (Buenos Aires, 1990).

Additional Bibliography

Abós, Alvaro. *Xul Solar: Pintor del misterio.* Buenos Aires: Sudamericana, 2004.

AMALIA CORTINA ARAVENA

XUXA (1963–). Xuxa is a Brazilian model, actress, singer, and children's television show host. Born Maria da Graça Meneghel on March 23, 1963, in Santa Rosa, Rio Grande do Sul, Brazil, Xuxa (pronounced "shoo-sha") was the highest-paid Brazilian performer even before her children's show *Xou da Xuxa* was picked up by the Fox Network in 1992 for broadcast in the United States. Xuxa first came to public attention in Brazil in 1978 as a model for the national photo magazine *Manchete* (Headline), in which she, a tall blonde, was a striking contrast to most Brazilian models. In 1980 she made further headlines as the girlfriend of soccer star Pelé and by appearing nude in the Brazilian edition of *Playboy* and in films such as *Amor Estranho Amor* by Walter Khoury (1982), which features Xuxa in a sex scene with a young boy. At about this time, the Brazilian press began comparing her with Marilyn Monroe. In 1983 she hosted a children's television show called *Clube da Criança* (Children's Club) for the Manchete Television

Network, in which she was presented as a sex symbol, wearing miniskirts and short shorts. As a television personality, she is known for her ingenuousness, spontaneity, and what critics call a permissive approach to children's entertainment. She moved to Brazil's TV Globo in 1986 to obtain broader exposure on a much more widely watched network. The *Xou da Xuxa* show became slicker, and certain trademarks, like Xuxa blowing kisses (*beijinhos*) to the audience increased. As with other Globo stars, her records, concerts, and movies were cross-marketed by Globo television and radio stations. She also began merchandizing a wide variety of products under her name and image. In 1990 production of her show moved to Argentina for the Latin American and Hispanic U.S. markets. Then in 1992, her show was packaged for syndication in English in the United States and was picked up by the Fox Network for early-morning daily broadcast in 1993. She has also starred in a number of commercially successful movies, including *Xuxa Requebra* (1999) and *Xuxa Popstar* (2000). Xuxa won the Latin Grammy for Best Latin Children's Album two years in a row for *Xuxa Só Para Baixinhos* volume 2 (2002) and volume 3 (2003). For many critics, Xuxa symbolizes a Brazilian ethnic and sexual identity contradiction between a blond ideal and a brown reality.

See also **Radio and Television.**

BIBLIOGRAPHY

Amelia Simpson, *Xuxa: The Mega-Marketing of Gender, Race, and Modernity* (1993).

Additional Bibliography

Fragata, Cássia, and Ana Lúcia Neiva. *Xuxa.* São Paulo: Artemeios, 2001.

Kinder, Marsha, ed. *Kids' Media Culture.* Durham, NC: Duke University Press, 1999.

Valdivia, Angharad N. *A Latina in the Land of Hollywood and Other Essays on Media Culture.* Tucson: University of Arizona Press, 2000.

JOSEPH D. STRAUBHAAR

YAGUL. Yagul, an archaeological site located 23 miles from Oaxaca City and 2 miles from the market town of Tlacolula in the Valley of Oaxaca, Mexico. Yagul was excavated by Ignacio Bernal, Lorenzo Gamio, and John Paddock during the 1950s and 1960s. Although the site shows evidence of more ancient occupations, most of the excavated and consolidated remains date from the Post-Classic period (ca. A.D. 900–1521). The site was occupied at the time of the Spanish conquest, and the people of present-day Tlacolula refer to it as the *pueblo viejo* (old town).

Yagul sits atop a mountainous spur whose peak supports an ancient fortress. On the flanks of the spur was the administrative and ritual center of the ancient city, and on the lands at its base were the houses of common people. Excavations in the center of the city uncovered the Palace of the Six Patios, a large residence with a floor plan similar to those of the nearby palaces of Mitla. A narrow street ran between the palace and the council hall, whose walls were decorated with *grecas* (mosaics) similar to those of Mitla. A ball court similar to one at Monte Albán lies near the palace. Also near the palace is Patio 4, a plaza with four mounds around it and an altar at its center. Mound 4E, on the east side, is a temple. In front of it is a large boulder sculpted to resemble a jaguar or frog. More than thirty tombs have been excavated at Yagul. Tomb 30 in Patio 4 had panels of false *grecas* decorating it and contained fine Mixteca polychrome pottery vessels. The Yagul excavations served to define the period (ca. A.D. 900–1521) that followed the collapse and general abandonment of Monte Albán and generated a lively controversy concerning proposed Mixtec conquests of Zapotecs in the Valley of Oaxaca during this time.

See also **Archaeology; Art: Pre-Columbian Art of Mesoamerica.**

BIBLIOGRAPHY

Ignacio Bernal, "The Mixtecs in the Archeology of the Valley of Oaxaca," in *Ancient Oaxaca,* edited by John Paddock (1966), pp. 345–366.

Charles Wicke, "Tomb 30 at Yagul and the Zaachila Tombs," in *Ancient Oaxaca,* edited by John Paddock (1966), pp. 336–344.

Ignacio Bernal and Lorenzo Gamio, *Yagul: El palacio de los seis patios* (1974).

Marcus Winter, *Oaxaca: The Archaeological Record* (1989), pp. 119–121.

Michael D. Lind

YAMANA. Yamana (also called Yaghanes), maritime inhabitants of the Strait of Magellan and Cape Horn, the so-called nomads of the seas. Their society is thought to have consisted of about 3,500 individuals who lived in a simple social organization recognizing no chiefs or superior authorities. The Yamana believed in Watauinéiwa, a supreme god, invisible and omnipotent, who was accompanied by secondary deities. The Yamana hunted sea mammals, fished, and collected mollusks. They lived in huts made with boughs and tree branches, which they regularly abandoned in search of better hunting.

Related prehistorically and linguistically to the Alakaluf (Kawashkar) to the north, the Yamana occupied the coasts of the Beagle Channel and the islands that extend south to Cape Horn. As with the Alakaluf, some argue that the maritime peoples first appeared in these southern waters 5,200 to 6,400 years ago, although others claim a Paleolithic (11,000 B.C.) past.

The material culture, including bone implements, harpoons, and canoes made of tree bark for hunting sea mammals, as well as remains of coastal sites with abundant shell deposits, contrasts with the nearly exclusively terrestrial orientation in the material culture of the Selk'nam (ona) to the north and east of the Yamana. Like their neighbors the Alakaluf, the Yamana survived sporadic encounters with European expeditioners in southern waters but were quickly decimated as a result of more intensive encounters with nineteenth-century whalers and early twentieth-century colonists. Today the few Yamana who survive continue to fish but also cultivate small gardens and live in prefabricated houses in the small community of Ukika, near Port Williams, on the north coast of Navarino Island on the southern tip of Chile.

BIBLIOGRAPHY

Julian H. Steward, ed., *Handbook of South American Indians,* vol. 1 (1946), pp. 17–24.

Richard Shutler, Jr., ed., *South America: Early Man in the New World* (1983), pp. 37–146.

Museo Chileno De Arte Precolombino, *Hombres del sur: Aonikenk, Selknam, Yamana, Kaweshkar* (1987).

KRISTINE L. JONES
JOSÉ ANTONIO PÉREZ GOLLÁN

YAN. *See* **Prado, João Fernando de Almeida.**

YANACONAS. Yanaconas, in the broadest sense of the word, a colonial-era term for indigenous people and their descendants who were separated from their ancestral communities. The specific circumstances under which that separation had occurred and the precise meaning of the term varied considerably throughout the viceroyalty of Peru, but virtually every usage of the term refers to Amerindians who had been removed—physically, culturally, and economically—from their traditional communities. The Spanish term *yanacona* is thought to derive from the Inca term *yana,* personal servant or retainer whose special duties and altered relationship with other community members had, in turn, altered the *yana's* own relationship with his or her *ayllus* (kin groups). Consistent with their practice of adapting indigenous terms to describe colonial structures that had only a superficial resemblance to traditional practices, the Spaniards first used the term *yanaconas* to describe servants from any Andean ethnic group, for the Spanish tended not to observe such differences.

When Francisco de Toledo y Figueroa reorganized Peru's indigenous communities in the 1570s, he differentiated between *yanaconas de españoles* (of Spaniards), who were in private service to Spaniards, and *yanaconas del rey* (of the king), who, according to Toledo's reasoning, owed allegiance—and therefore taxes and labor service—only to the crown, which could allocate that labor as it saw fit. Toledo conducted a careful census of the *yanacona* population, limiting the number of individuals who could claim either type of *yanacona* status for themselves and their descendants. In the following years, an increasing number of people either sought *yanacona* status or had it conferred upon them by employers who secured *licencias de yanaconas* (roughly, *yanacona* permits) from colonial authorities. *Yanaconas* enjoyed certain advantages, including reduced taxes and, most important, protection from the Mita (the state forced-labor system), but *yanaconas,* who participated in a wide range of labor relationships, such as sharecropping, wage labor, and debt peonage, could be brutally exploited by their employers. Although they could not legally be sold into slavery, *yanaconas* were legally tied to the land they worked, and property transfers often included the services of *yanaconas.*

Throughout the colonial period, the increasing number of menial laborers having—or claiming—*yanacona* status was a constant drain on the state labor system. By the eighteenth century, in some areas of the viceroyalty the number of indigenous people who were living apart from their home communities—voluntarily or involuntarily, through *yanacona* status or migration or flight—exceeded the number of indigenous people still living in those communities and trying to fulfill their tax and labor obligations. Various viceroys tried to incorporate the *yanacona* sector into the state labor system, but powerful interests kept most *yanaconas* in the private labor sector. Although the end of colonial rule altered the legal definition of and regulations governing *yanacona* status, the term continued to be applied to non-European laborers.

See also **Forasteros; Incas, The; Repartimiento; Slavery: Spanish America.**

BIBLIOGRAPHY

Arthur Franklin Zimmerman, *Francisco De Toledo; Fifth Viceroy of Peru, 1569–1581*. New York: Greenwood Press, 1968.

Steve J. Stern, *Peru's Indian Peoples and the Challenge of Spanish Conquest: Huamanga to 1640*. Madison: University of Wisconsin Press, 1982.

Karen Spalding, *Huarochirí: An Andean Society Under Inca and Spanish Rule*. Stanford, CA: Stanford University Press, 1984, esp. pp. 85–88.

Brooke Larson, *Colonialism and Agrarian Transformation in Bolivia: Cochabamba, 1550–1900*. Princeton, NJ: Princeton University Press, 1988, esp. pp. 82–87.

Ann M. Wightman, *Indigenous Migration and Social Change: The Forasteros of Cuzco, 1570–1720*. Durham, NC: Duke University Press, 1990; esp. pp. 83–85.

ANN M. WIGHTMAN

YANES, FRANCISCO JAVIER (1776–1842).

Francisco Javier Yanes (*b.* 12 May 1776; *d.* 17 June 1842), political activist and historian of the Venezuelan independence movement. Yanes was born in Cuba but moved to Venezuela at a very young age. He studied law at the University of Caracas. He was connected with the independence movement from its start. Yanes was a member of the Sociedad Patriótica de Caracas and of the Constituent Congress of 1811; he was also a censor at *El Publicista*, the official publication of the Congress. He left the country at the fall of the First Republic in 1812, returning in 1813. The Congress of Angostura designated him a member of the Supreme Court of Justice of Venezuela in 1819 and in 1820 as president of the Court of Almirantazgo.

With the creation of Gran Colombia, Yanes was appointed a member of the Superior Court of Justice of Venezuela (1821), which was subordinate to the government in Bogotá. He worked on the publication of the periodical *El Observador Caraqueño* (1824–1825) with Cristóbal Mendoza, historian, journalist, and first president of Venezuela (1811), with whom he also collaborated on an important collection of twenty-two volumes of documents concerning Venezuela's emancipation [Francisco Javier Yanes and Cristóbal Mendoza, *Colección de documentos relativos a la vida pública del Libertador de Colombia y del Perú, Simón Bolívar*, 22 vols. (1983)]. Yanes was a member of the Sociedad Económica de Amigos del País (1829) and of the Constituent Congress of 1830. After 1830 he devoted himself to judicial activities and to his private life. His personal archive can be found in the National Academy of History in Caracas.

See also **Venezuela, Congresses of 1811, 1830, and 1864; Venezuela, Organizations: Economic Society of the Friends of the Country.**

BIBLIOGRAPHY

No biography of Yanes exists, nor is there any work concerning his intellectual career. However, several renditions of his own works include valuable biographical information: Francisco Javier Yanes, *Relación documentada de los principales sucesos ocurridos en Venezuela desade que se declaró estado independiente hasta el año de 1821*, 2 vols. (1943); *Compendio de la historia de Venezuela, desde su descubrimiento y conquista hasta que se declaró estado independiente* (1944); and *Manual político del venezolano* (1959).

Additional Bibliography

Cañizales Verde, Francisco. *Francisco Javier Yanes: Teniente Justicia Mayor*. Barquisimeto, Venezuela: Editorial Textos, 1997.

INÉS QUINTERO

YÁÑEZ COSSÍO, ALICIA (1929–).

Alicia Yáñez Cossío, born on September 10, 1929, in Quito, is a writer and member of the Ecuadorian Academy of Language. Yáñez's poetic motifs echo the themes of her fiction: Anti-establishment and anticolonial, she is concerned with social exploitation and justice in the developing world and the evolution of nationalism. Her work also addresses women's conditions, their contributions to society and difficulties in the face of discrimination; her female characters struggle for a decent and independent existence. She took up the lyrical genre with the poetry collections *Luciolas* (1949), *De la sangre y el tiempo* (1964), and *Poesía* (1973). Her first novel, *Bruna, soroche y los tíos* (*Bruna and Her Sisters in the Sleeping City*, 1972), which brought her critical acclaim and the prize for best novel of the year awarded by the *El Universal* newspaper, displays characteristics of the Latin American literary "boom." Her innovative formal techniques, such as corrosive irony, playfulness, and light humor, come into play in the short story collections *Más allá de las islas* (1980), *Cuentos cubanos* (1992), and *El viaje de la abuela* (1996); and in her other novels, *La cofradía del mullo del vestido de la Virgen Pipona* (*The Potbellied Virgin*, 1985), *La casa del sano placer* (1989), *El Cristo Feo* (1995; winner of the Sor Juana Inés de la Cruz prize in Paris), *Aprendiendo a morir* (1997), *Y amarle pude . . .* (2000), and *Concierto de sombras* (2004). Her works broke new ground in Ecuadorian fiction, earning her a place of importance in Hispanic letters.

See also **Literature: Spanish America.**

BIBLIOGRAPHY

Works by Yánez Cossío in English Translation

Bruna and Her Sisters in the Sleeping City, trans. Kenneth J. A. Wishnia. Evanston, IL: Northwestern University Press, 1999.

The Potbellied Virgin, trans. Amalia Gladhart. Austin: University of Texas Press, 2006.

Works on Yánez Cossío

Angulo, María Elena. "La narrativa de Alicia Yánez Cossío: Hacia la recuperación de un espacio social para la mujer latinoamericana." *Letras Femeninas* 21 (1995): 21–28.

Carullo, Sylvia Graciela. "*La Casa del Sano Placer* de Yánez Cossío: Aproximaciones a Lysistrata." *Centro de Estudios la Mujer en la Historia de América Latina* (CEMHAL) 6, no. 64 (2005).

Menton, Seymour. "Transformaciones: *El Cristo feo* (1995) de Alicia Yánez Cossío." In *Caminata por la narrativa latinoamericana*. Mexico: Fondo de Cultura Económica, 2005.

Rojas-Trempe, Lady. "Alicia Yánez Cossío." In *Narradoras ecuatorianas de hoy: Una antología crítica*, ed. Adelaida López de Martínez and Gloria Da Cunha-Giabbai, pp. 31–71. San Juan: Editorial de la Universidad de Puerto Rico, 2000.

Saine, Ute Margaret. "Female Representation and Feminine Mystique in Alicia Yánez Cossío's 'La mujer es un mito.'" *Letras Femeninas* 26 (2000): 63–80.

LADY ROJAS BENAVENTE

YÁÑEZ SANTOS DELGADILLO, AGUSTÍN (1904–1980).

Agustín Yánez Santos Delgadillo (*b.* 4 May 1904; *d.* 17 January 1980), Mexican novelist and public figure. Of the many novels and literary studies Agustín Yánez produced, he is best remembered for his focus on the regional qualities of his native culture in the small, rural towns of Jalisco, in western Mexico. *Al filo del agua* (*On the Edge of the Storm*), his best-known work in this genre, was first published in 1947 and is considered an outstanding example of a historical novel depicting, in the words of critic John Brushwood, "the reality of Mexico on the edge of the Revolution." Brushwood considers it a turning point in Mexican literature.

Yánez was born in Guadalajara, Jalisco, the child of modest, extremely religious parents. A law school graduate, he quickly joined the intellectual scene, after first involving himself with the Cristero Rebellion, a religious uprising against the government. He moved to Mexico City, where he taught at the National University and served at a number of administrative posts. After holding several minor posts in the federal government, he became governor of his home state (1953–1959). He became a speech writer for President Adolfo López Mateos, who appointed him assistant secretary of the presidency (1962–1964). In 1964, he became secretary of public education. Unlike many intellectuals, Yánez did not surround himself with disciples, although he gave his time to intellectual institutions as president of the Seminar of Mexican Culture (1949–1952) and the Mexican Academy of Language (1973–1977).

See also **Cristero Rebellion; Literature: Spanish America.**

BIBLIOGRAPHY

John S. Brushwood, *Mexico in Its Novel* (1966).

Agustín Yánez, *Obras escogidas* (1968).

Barbara Graham, "Social and Stylistic Realities in the Fiction of Agustín Yánez" (Ph.D. diss., University of Miami, 1969).

Alfonso Rangel Guerra, *Agustín Yánez* (1969); *Mester* 12 (1983), entire issue.

Additional Bibliography

Arias Urrutia, Angel. *Entre la cruz y la sospecha: los cristeros de Revueltas, Yánez y Rulfo*. Madrid: Iberoamericana, 2005.

Harris, Christopher. *The Novels of Agustín Yáñez: A Critical Portrait of Mexico in the 20th Century.* Lewiston, NY: E. Mellen Press, 2000.

Marquet, Antonio. *Archipiélago dorado: el despegue creador en la obra narrativa de Agustín Yáñez.* Mexico City: Universidad Autonoma Metropolitana, 1997.

RODERIC AI CAMP

YANOMAMI.

The Yanomami are the largest group of unassimilated indigenous people in the South American rainforest. Their name, also written as Yanoama or Yanomamö, is derived from their word meaning human being. The Yanomami number around 33,000 and occupy an area covering some 74,000 square miles on both sides of the border between Brazil and Venezuela. They are skilled hunter-gatherers and swidden farmers, who live in villages composed of a single large communal roundhouse or a few smaller houses. Social and political relations are based on kinship and marriage ties. Their family of languages distinguishes them from the Carib- and Arawak-affiliated peoples that surround them. The heart of the Yanomami homeland is the isolated, mountainous Parima section of the Guiana Highlands. The boundary separating Brazil and Venezuela passes directly through their territory, but very few Yanomami have adopted the language or national culture of either of these two modern states.

During the colonial period, Spanish and Portuguese expeditions encountered only a few small outlying Yanomami groups, who usually fought them off. Traditional material culture is perishable in the humid tropical environment; tangible evidence of their past, including stone tools and clay vessels, is extremely rare. The Yanomami are probably the same people that have been referred to since the eighteenth century as Waika, Shamatari, Shirishana, or Guajaribo. The first sustained contact with the Yanomami was not achieved by outsiders until 1947. Since the 1980s, many Yanomami have suffered greatly from encroachments into their territory by mineral prospectors, especially gold miners (*garimpeiros*). In 1991 and 1992 both Venezuela and Brazil legally set aside large portions of Yanomami territory: a protected ecological zone of about 32,000 square miles in Venezuela, and a federally recognized

indigenous reserve of about 37,300 square miles in Brazil.

See also **Guiana Highlands; Indigenous Peoples.**

BIBLIOGRAPHY

Borofsky, Robert. *Yanomami: The Fierce Controversy and What We Can Learn from It.* Berkeley: University of California Press, 2005.

Milliken, William, and Bruce Albert, with Gale Goodwin Gomez. *Yanomami: A Forest People.* London: Royal Botanical Gardens, Kew, 1999.

Tierney, Patrick. *Darkness in El Dorado: How Scientists and Journalists Devastated the Amazon.* New York: Norton, 2000.

WILLIAM J. SMOLE
GALE GOODWIN GOMEZ

YAQUI INDIANS.

The Yaquis (also called Yoemem) are a "cross-border" indigenous nation of northwestern Mexico (Sonora) and the southwestern United States (Arizona) that has stood out for its long and successful resistance to acculturation and assimilation into Mexican society. Since their "discovery" by Europeans in 1533, the Yaquis have insisted on retaining their own distinctive identity as a separate people and culture, and they have waged numerous wars to prevent the loss of their communities, land, water, and way of life in the Yaqui River Valley. They have steadfastly maintained some form of internal organization and government for more than four hundred years, including the exile barrios outside the Yaqui River Valley in both Sonora and Arizona.

On the Mexican side of the border, the Yaqui people do not identify themselves as Mexicans; instead they use the term *Yoemem* (people, humans). At times, the Mexican government has worked in favor of the Yaqui Nation. In 1916 then constitutional governor Adolfo de la Huerta (himself one-quarter Yaqui) made attempts to restore Yaqui land, and in 1934 President Lázaro Cardenas granted official recognition and land title to Yaqui peoples. On the U.S. side of the border, the Pascua Yaqui tribe of Arizona was given title to 202 acres of desert land in 1964 and was federally recognized in 1978.

An indigenous people with identity rooted in a land base, the Yaquis were primarily agricultural. During long periods of resistance in the nineteenth and twentieth centuries, however, they were prevented from deriving much of their subsistence from the soil in their contested homeland; thus, many became temporary wage laborers in the haciendas, mines, and railroads of Sonora and Arizona. Nevertheless, unlike other frontier Indian communities, Yaqui participation in the larger economy did not result in their permanent assimilation into the larger society. For, even as they worked for wages, they struggled to preserve their autonomous communities—physically, politically, and culturally. For example, pre-contact Yaqui religious practices, such as the deer-dance, have evolved and melded with Catholicism, forming a prominent feature of yearly Easter celebrations. The dual characteristic of separatism and partial integration is the source of Yaqui strength and key to their survival as a distinct people and culture up to the present day.

See also de la Huerta, Adolfo; Indigenous Peoples; Yaqui Rebellion, 1885–1898.

BIBLIOGRAPHY

For an interpretive study of Yaqui culture, see Edward Spicer, *The Yaquis: A Cultural History* (1980). For a narrative history of Yaqui contact and struggle with the outside world, see Evelyn Hu-de Hart, *Missionaries, Miners, and Indians: Spanish Contact with the Yaqui Nation of Northwestern New Spain, 1533–1820* (1981) and *Yaqui Resistance and Survival: The Struggle for Land and Autonomy, 1821–1910* (1984).

Additional Bibliography

Fabila, Alfonso. *Las tribus yaquis de Sonora: Su cultura y anhelada autodeterminación*. Mexico: Departamento de asuntos indígenas, 1940. Repr., Mexico: Instituto Nacional Indigenista, 1978.

EVELYN HU-DEHART

YAQUI REBELLION, 1885–1898.

Yaquis resisted Porfirian rule throughout the dictatorship. In 1875, led by José María Leyva Cajeme, they built and maintained a state-within-a-state until 1886. In 1887 the invading Mexican army crushed the defensive system of fortifications erected under Chief Cajeme. Rejecting the government's offer to settle down as colonists on their own land, most Yaquis fanned out to work in mines, railroads, and haciendas on both sides of the Sonora-Arizona border, constituting the critical weapons conduit and social base of support for highly effective guerrilla warfare waged by small bands of warriors under the rebel leader Juan Maldonado Tetabiate.

For the next decade, the governor and general Luis Torres struggled without much success to distinguish between Yaqui *broncos* (warriors) and *pacíficos*, prized workers whose employers refused to cooperate with the authorities for fear of losing their irreplaceable labor. In 1897 Tetabiate and Torres signed the Peace of Ortiz to facilitate the repatriation of thousands of war-weary families back to their homeland, but peace lasted only three short years. Realizing the futility of distinguishing between warriors and workers, the Diaz regime embarked on the final solution: the deportation of thousands of Yaqui men, women and children out of Sonora to the henequen plantations of the Yucatán.

See also Yaqui Indians.

BIBLIOGRAPHY

Hu-DeHart, Evelyn. *Missionaries, Miners, and Indians: History of Spanish Contact with the Yaqui Indians of Northwestern New Spain, 1533–1820*. Tucson: University of Arizona Press, 1981.

Hu-DeHart, Evelyn. *Yaqui Resistance and Survival: Struggle for Land and Autonomy, 1821–1910*. Madison: University of Wisconsin Press, 1984.

Hu-DeHart, Evelyn. *Adaptación y resistencia en el Yaquimí: los Yaquis durante la colonia*. Mexico City: CIESAS, 1995.

EVELYN HU-DEHART

YATAITY CORÃ, CONFERENCE OF.

Conference of Yataity Corã, an abortive peace conference that took place on 12 September 1866 during the War of the Triple Alliance (1864–1870). The Paraguayan army, led by President Francisco Solano López, had experienced a series of reverses in 1866, notably its defeat at the battle of Tuyutí in May. López was therefore anxious to end the war on honorable terms or, at the very least, to gain time to prepare further defenses. Arrangements were made for a personal interview in the land between the Paraguayan and Brazilian lines. There, López met with the Argentine commander, Bartolomé Mitre.

COLONIALISM, NATIONHOOD, AND ETHNICITY

Celebrating the Haitian bicentennial, 2004. A Haitian man raises shackles above his head to symbolize Haiti's independence from France and the subsequent abolition of slavery in Haiti two hundred years earlier. AP IMAGES

Venezuelans drag a statue of Christopher Columbus through the streets of Caracas, 2004. Columbus Day is commemorated as Indigenous Resistance Day in Venezuela. Columbus is viewed as a symbol of oppression in countries throughout Latin America and the Caribbean, where Columbus Day is used as an opportunity to remember the people who were already living in the region when Columbus arrived. AP IMAGES

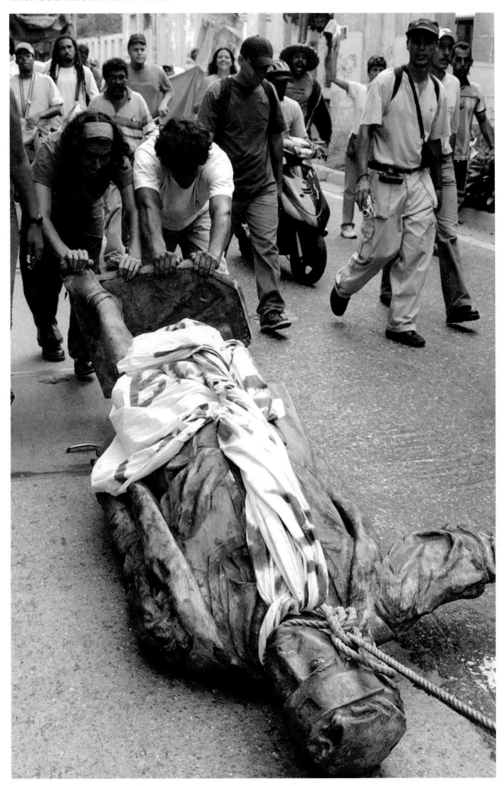

RIGHT: Poster calling for Puerto Rican independence, Cuba, 1990s. The Castro regime has espoused the cause of Puerto Rican independence due to the linked history of the two islands. Throughout much of the nineteenth century Cuba and Puerto Rico were the last Spanish colonies in the New World; Puerto Rico was ceded to the United States in 1898. Cuba technically achieved independence but remained under the U.S. sphere of influence until 1959. © Richard Bickel/Corbis

BELOW: *Juárez, Symbol of the Republic against the French Intervention,* 1972. Fresco by Antonio González Orozco. Juárez, who was president at the time of the French intervention in Mexico and who successfully overthrew the French-installed emperor, remains today a symbol of liberal ideals and Mexican independence. Giraudon/Art Resource, NY.

ABOVE: **Argentines of Spanish descent line up outside the Spanish consulate in hopes of obtaining Spanish citizenship, 2003.** A new Spanish law extending citizenship to Latin Americans of Spanish descent, combined with economic crises in a number of Latin American countries, have led to a reverse migration of Latin Americans to Spain in the early twenty-first century. AP IMAGES

RIGHT: **French president Jacques Chirac visits Martinique and Guadeloupe, 2000.** A banner reading "Welcome to our president" greets President Chirac on an official visit to Martinique and Guadeloupe. The islands are both overseas departments of France; residents are French citizens and are able to vote in French national elections. © RUET STEPHANE/CORBIS SYGMA.

Brazilian soccer fans celebrate Portugal's defeat of the Netherlands in a semifinal match. Colonial ties prove strong as Brazilian fans treat a Portuguese victory as their own at the European Nations championship in Lisbon, 2004. JAVIER SORIANO/ AFP/GETTY IMAGES

ABOVE: Delegates from indigenous groups at the World Social Forum, 2003. Delegates in traditional Amazonian dress confront very modern problems, such as Third World Debt and the proposed Free Trade Area of the Americas, at this antiglobalization forum in Porto Alegro, Brazil. Andre Felipe/Getty Images

LEFT: Demonstrators march against ChevronTexaco in Ecuador, 2003. Indigenous communities continue to press Chevron to clean up the contamination left behind by their drilling operations in the Amazonian rainforest. The signs these protestors hold reads "Texaco never again!" © Lou Dematteis/Reuters/Corbis

OPPOSITE: A Zapatista holds a painting depicting Zapatista leader Subcomandante Marco with national heroes Emiliano Zapata and Pancho Villa. The Zapatista movement's platform combines championing the rights of indigenous peoples with antiglobalization and other populist concerns. Wesley Boxce/Liaison/Getty Images

ABOVE: **Bolivian president Evo Morales, his vice president, and the commander of the army wear traditional red ponchos on a visit to the village of Achacachi, 2007.** Morales, Bolivia's first indigenous president, incorporates many traditional elements of Andean culture into his duties as president, sharply distinguishing himself from the elites of European descent that had ruled Bolivia until his election. AP IMAGES

RIGHT: **Supporters of Venezuelan president Hugo Chavez carry a portrait of Simón Bolívar, 2007.** The South American independence hero Bolívar has been claimed by Chavez and his followers as a symbol for his political program, which he calls the Bolivarian Revolution. AP IMAGES

The meeting was a study in contrasts between the splendor of López's uniform and the rough informality of Mitre's attire. Although their conversation was evidently amicable, López was disappointed to find that the Argentines and their Brazilian allies had no intention of giving up the fight while López remained in power in Paraguay. Their efforts frustrated, the two men departed and the war began anew, leading ten days later to a horrendous defeat for the Allies at Curupayty and four more years of fighting.

See also **López, Francisco Solano; Mitre, Bartolomé; War of the Triple Alliance.**

BIBLIOGRAPHY

Adolfo I. Báez, *Yatayty-Corá: Una conferencia histórica (recuerdo de la guerra del Paraguay)* (1929).

Charles J. Kolinski, *Independence or Death! The Story of the Paraguayan War* (1965).

Additional Bibliography

Bethell, Leslie. *The Paraguayan War (1864–1870).* London: Institute of Latin American Studies, 1996.

Leuchars, Chris. *To the Bitter End: Paraguay and the War of the Triple Alliance.* Westport, CT: Greenwood Press, 2002.

Marco, Miguel Angel de. *La Guerra del Paraguay.* Buenos Aires: Planeta, 1995.

Whigham, Thomas. *The Paraguayan War.* Lincoln: University of Nebraska Press, 2002.

THOMAS L. WHIGHAM

YAXCHILÁN. Yaxchilán, Maya archaeological site located in Chiapas, Mexico. Renowned for its numerous well-preserved stone monuments beautifully carved with scenes of human figures accompanied by long hieroglyphic texts, Yaxchilán has provided epigraphers with crucial information concerning the history and organization of Classic Maya society. The city's monuments were placed in front of and inside many small temples built atop ridges and terraces that overlook a great U-shaped bend midway along the Usumacinta River, which is now the international border between Mexico and Guatemala.

First brought to public attention in the 1880s through the photographs of two European explorer-archaeologists, Alfred P. Maudslay and Teobert Maler, the Yaxchilán texts have proved critical in deciphering Maya history as told from the point of view of kings. During a period of almost five centuries (320–808 CE), the Yaxchilán polity was ruled from its capital by a sequence of *ahaw*, or lords, each of whom oversaw one or more *sahal*, or provincial lords, who governed communities subordinate to the king. While the names of at least fifteen kings are recorded in the texts, the most important of these were Shield Jaguar I (647–742 CE) and Bird Jaguar IV (709–c. 770 CE), rulers responsible for building most of Yaxchilán's temples and monuments. The predominant themes of the Yaxchilán inscriptions are warfare and bloodletting, both central activities in the ritual lives of kings. Also recorded in the texts are details of marital and military alliances, ritual practices and religious ideas, and terms for kinship and political office, information that enables archaeologists to reconstruct important aspects of Maya social, political, and religious organization.

A broad historical context for the glyphic information is provided by the excavations of the Mexican archaeologist Robert García Moll, whose preliminary results indicate that Yaxchilán was occupied from the Late Preclassic through the Terminal Classic periods.

See also **Archaeology; Maya, The.**

BIBLIOGRAPHY

Alfred P. Maudslay, *Biologia Centrali-Americana: Archaeology,* 5 vols. (1889–1902).

Ian Graham, *Corpus of Maya Hieroglyphic Inscriptions: Yaxchilán,* vol. 3, parts 1–3 (1977–1988).

Linda Schele and David Freidel, *A Forest of Kings* (1990), pp. 262–305.

Carolyn E. Tate, *Yaxchilán: The Design of a Maya Ceremonial City* (1992).

Additional Bibliography.

Brokmann, Carlos. *Tipología y análisis de la obsidiana de Yaxchilán, Chiapas.* Mexico City: Instituto Nacional de Antropología e Historia, 2000.

García Moll, Roberto. *La arquitectura de Yaxchilan.* Mexico City: Plaza y Valdés; Instituto Nacional de Antropología e Historia, 2003.

García Moll, Roberto, and Daniel Juárez Cossio, eds. *Yaxchilán: antología de su descubrimiento y estudios.* Mexico City: Instituto Nacional de Antropología e Historia, 1986.

Kaneko, Akira. *Artefactos líticos de Yaxchilán*. Mexico City: Instituto Nacional de Antropología e Historia, 2003.

Martin, Simon, and Nikolai Grube. *Chronicle of the Maya Kings and Queens: Deciphering the Dynasties of the Ancient Maya*. New York: Thames & Hudson, 2000.

Mathews, Peter. *La escultura de Yaxchilán*. Trans. Antonio Saborit. Mexico City: Instituto Nacional de Antropología e Historia, 1997.

Miller, Mary Ellen, and Simon Martin, eds. *Courtly Art of the Ancient Maya*. San Francisco: Fine Arts Museums of San Francisco; New York: Thames & Hudson, 2004.

KEVIN JOHNSTON

YBYCUÍ. Ybycuí, site of a major foundry and industrial smithy in mid-nineteenth-century Paraguay. Established by President Carlos Antonio López in 1850, as part of a major program of military and state economic expansion, the foundry of Ybycuí (or La Rosada) was well situated to take advantage of local iron deposits and sources of water. It was the only government-sponsored ironworks in South America at the time, and has since become the subject of much scholarly inquiry as a possible example of internally generated industrialization.

Work at the foundry was directed by foreign engineers contracted by López. The labor force was made up of convicts, slaves, some free workers, and, after the beginning of the War of the Triple Alliance (1864–1870), by prisoners of war. Operations at the foundry were often hampered by technical difficulties. Nonetheless, it did produce a substantial quantity of iron, much of which was for military use (especially for cannonballs and artillery pieces). This made Ybycuí a prime target during the fighting. In May 1869, it was raided by a roving Uruguayan cavalry unit, and a month afterward, Brazilian demolition teams dynamited what was left of the foundry. It was partially restored in the 1960s and now serves as a historical museum.

See also **Iron and Steel Industry; Weapons Industry.**

BIBLIOGRAPHY

Josefina Plá, *The British in Paraguay, 1850–1870* (1976).

Thomas Lyle Whigham, "The Iron Works of Ybycuí: Paraguayan Industrial Development in the Mid-Nineteenth Century," in *The Americas* 35 (October 1978): 201–218.

Additional Bibliography

Cooney, Jerry W. and Thomas Whigham. *El Paraguay bajo los López: algunos ensayos de historia social y política*. Asunción, Paraguay: Centro Paraguayo de Estudios Sociológicos, 1994.

THOMAS L. WHIGHAM

YDÍGORAS FUENTES, MIGUEL (1895–1982). Miguel Ydígoras Fuentes (*b.* 17 October 1895; *d.* 6 October 1982), president of Guatemala (1958–1963). Born in Pueblo Nuevo, Retalhuleu, to a family of Basque ancestry, Ydígoras pursued a military career, rising to the rank of general. He served as a departmental governor and as the head of the department of highways during the dictatorship of General Jorge Ubico (1931–1944), when he developed a reputation in the countryside as a tough but fair administrator. As a reward for supporting the new junta of the October Revolution (1944), he was named ambassador to Great Britain, where he became impressed by British parliamentary democracy.

In 1950 he ran for the presidency of Guatemala against Jacobo Arbenz (1950–1954), but was forced into hiding during much of the campaign. Exiled to El Salvador, he helped organize the U.S.–backed insurrection that toppled Arbenz in 1954.

After the assassination of President Carlos Castillo Armas in July 1957, Ydígoras reorganized his political party, Reconciliación Democrática Nacional, and campaigned for the presidency against Miguel Ortiz Passarelli, the official candidate. When the government declared Ortiz the winner in a disputed election, Ydígoras launched the massive street demonstrations that succeeded in overturning the election. In January 1958 he defeated Colonel José Luis Cruz Salazar in what was considered to be a fair and free election.

The Ydígoras Fuentes regime was a peculiar mixture of populism, economic conservatism, and nationalism. Thus, he strongly supported the creation of the Central American Common Market and pushed through an industrial incentives law, a law protecting foreign investment, a limited agrarian reform law, and an income-tax law. Ydígoras also permitted substantial personal liberty.

Faced with the threat of Castroite subversion and the need for support from the United States, Ydígoras secretly provided a base for the Bay of Pigs Invasion. Reaction by nationalist officers led to a military uprising in November 1960 that was put down by loyal army units with U.S. assistance. In 1961 several of the rebellious officers launched the guerrilla movement that has continued into the 1990s.

In March 1962 charges of electoral manipulation, administrative incompetence, and corruption precipitated a student-led protest movement that forced Ydígoras to install a military cabinet in order to retain power. But the military turned against him when he permitted their old nemesis (and also that of the United States), former president Juan José Arévalo (1945–1951), to return to Guatemala to contest the 1963 elections. Ydígoras was overthrown on 30 March 1963 in a coup led by his defense minister, General Enrique Peralta Azurdia (1963–1966).

Ydígoras lived in exile in Nicaragua, Costa Rica, and El Salvador until the early 1970s, when he returned to Guatemala under an amnesty offered to all ex-presidents living abroad by President Carlos Arana Osorio (1970–1974). He commented extensively in the press on Guatemalan affairs. In 1980 he traveled to the Vatican to see fulfilled a goal for which he had worked many years—the beatification of Hermano Pedro de Bethancourt.

See also **Arana Osorio, Carlos; Castillo Armas, Carlos.**

BIBLIOGRAPHY

Miguel Ydígoras Fuentes, *My War with Communism* (1963).

Thomas Melville and Margorie Melville, *Guatemala—Another Vietnam?* (1971).

Stephen Schlesinger and Stephen Kinzer, *Bitter Fruit: The Untold Story of the American Coup in Guatemala* (1982, repr. 1983).

James Dunkerley, *Power in the Isthmus: A Political History of Modern Central America* (1988), Fransico Villagrán Kramer, *Biografía política de Guatemala: Los pactos políticos de 1944 a 1970* (1993).

Additional Bibliography

Ebel, Roland H. *Misunderstood Caudillo: Miguel Ydígoras Fuentes and the Failure of Democracy in Guatemala.* Lanham, MD: Tulane Studies in Political Science and University Press of America, 1998.

ROLAND H. EBEL

YEGROS, FULGENCIO (1780–1821).

Fulgencio Yegros (*b.* 1780; *d.* 17 July 1821), Paraguayan militiaman and political figure. Born into a well-established and wealthy creole family, Yegros chose a career with the colonial militia at an early age. During the first decade of the nineteenth century, he commanded troops against the Portuguese and their Indian allies. His chief claim to military fame, however, came in 1811, when his cavalry defeated a *porteño* expeditionary force at the battles of Paraguarí and Tacuarí. The vanquished *porteño* commander, Manuel Belgrano, invited Yegros to a parley after the conclusion of the fighting, and convinced him to join the patriot cause. Soon thereafter, Yegros joined with other militia leaders in a *cuartelazo* (barracks revolt) against the colonial governor, which led to independence shortly thereafter.

Though ill at ease in the political realm, Yegros joined the junta together with fellow officer Pedro Juan Caballero, cleric Francisco Xavier Bogarín, businessman Fernando de la Mora, and a distant relative, José Gaspar de Francia. The latter quickly eclipsed the other members of the junta and began formulating Paraguayan policy without much consulting of his associates. In October 1813 an extraordinary congress assembled in Asunción and replaced the junta with a two-man consular government led by Francia and Yegros. It was clear from the beginning that Francia held all the real power. Yegros's tenure was brief; within a year, Francia abolished the consulate and founded a "supreme dictatorship" that lasted until his death in 1840.

Yegros, who had hoped to retire peacefully to his ranch at Quyquyó, found himself implicated in an antigovernment conspiracy in 1820. Fearing that this might signal the beginning of a revolt, Francia had his old associate arrested, tortured, and finally shot, less than 100 yards from the government house.

See also **Belgrano, Manuel; Francia, José Gaspar Rodríguez de.**

BIBLIOGRAPHY

Luis G. Benítez, *Historia de la cultura en el Paraguay* (1976), p. 97.

Carlos Zubizarreta, *Cien vidas paraguayas,* 2d ed. (1985), pp. 87–92.

Additional Bibliography

Garay, Blas, and Gregorio Benítes. *La revolución de la independencia del Paraguay.* Asunción, Paraguay: El Lector, 1996.

Thomas L. Whigham

YELLOW FEVER.   *See* Diseases.

YERBA MATÉ.   Yerba Maté, *Ilex paraguariensis,* tea made from the maté plant, a hollylike bush. Pre-Columbian peoples in South America developed a liking for the tea. The gaucho and other inhabitants of the Río de la Plata adopted the beverage, which remains very popular. The plant is now cultivated in Paraguay and the northern riverine provinces of Argentina. The highly caffeinic beverage is traditionally served in a pear-shaped gourd (also called a maté). Tea leaves are placed in the gourd and hot water is poured over them. The gourd is passed from person to person, and each sips the hot drink through a metal straw called a *bombilla.* More hot water and leaves are added as needed.

Many folk beliefs and rituals have grown up around the drink. According to a traditional poem, maté served with milk means respect. Sweetened maté indicates friendship; flavored with balm mint, it communicates displeasure. The beverage is most often consumed "straight," with nothing added.

See also Food and Cookery; Gauchos.

BIBLIOGRAPHY

Richard W. Slatta, *Gauchos and the Vanishing Frontier* (1983), pp. 78–79.

Amaro Villanueva, *El maté: Arte de cebar* (1960).

Additional Bibliography

Whigham, Thomas. *La yerba mate del Paraguay, 1780–1870.* Asunción, Paraguay: Centro Paraguayo de Estudios Sociológicos, 1991.

Richard W. Slatta

YERBA MATE INDUSTRY.   The yerba maté economy has been limited to the Southern Cone of South America since the seventeenth century, with no significant involvement of external capital. It is an integrated industry: Argentina is the main producer, followed by Brazil and Paraguay. Uruguay and Chile are importers. According to recent estimates, approximately 500,000 tons of yerba are prepared worldwide each year (260,000 in Argentina, 180,000 in Brazil and 30,000 in Paraguay). World trade involves fourteen percent of this production (70,000 tons).

The product has spread beyond its region of traditional consumers to Syria and Lebanon (12,000 tons per year), with lesser imports by Israel, Saudi Arabia, and some African nations. Expansion of yerba mate production has been limited by a small growth of demand. (Demand for yerba mate is rigid; the product has no near substitutes and is considered an inferior good, with a negative income elasticity.)

The Jesuits (1608–1767) were the ones to begin cultivating yerba mate (a perennial plant native to South America that is dried and ground and then made into an infusion) and they became the leading suppliers of colonial markets. Its cultivation was abandoned during the nineteenth century and wild herbs from Paraguay, Brazil, and the Argentine province of Misiones were used. The crop was worked by unpaid laborers (*mensúes*) under the debt-based compulsory labor system.

In the mid-nineteenth century, the yerba mate industry expanded with the introduction of steam-driven mills, leaf classification practices, and control of the blend for consumption. The yerba mate market of the time is believed to have been almost entirely comprised of the populations of Argentina, Paraguay, Uruguay, and Chile, half of the population of Bolivia, one third of Brazil, and one quarter of Peru.

During the Paraguayan War (1865–1870), Argentina imported yerba mate from Brazil and several Argentine companies installed mills in that country. The Compañía Mate Laranjeira firm, backed by Argentine, Brazilian, and British capital, obtained the concession to exploit the wild herbs on two million hectares of the southern Mato Grosso.

Annual volumes of yerba mate producing countries (in thousands of tons), 1996

	Argentina	Brazil	Paraguay
Production	260,000	180,000	30,000
Domestic consumption	200,000	174,000	40,000
Exports	43,000	26,000	—
Imports	—	20,000	5,000

Table 1

Argentina is the world's leading producer of yerba mate. Ninety percent of production comes from the Misiones province and the remaining ten percent from northeast Corrientes province. In Misiones in the early twentieth century, the Argentine government encouraged its cultivation through colonist farmers. Immigrants would receive 25-hectare plots with the obligation to plant yerba mate. As a result, the herb is now produced mainly on family farms, while the preparation and marketing are more concentrated and represent the more capitalized sector of the industry.

In Brazil, the yerba mate industry did not develop until the second half of the twentieth century, when its cultivation was promoted. The southern Brazilian states of Paraná, Santa Catarina, and Rio Grande do Sul are the leading producers. Paraguay's yerba mate production is located in the east (Itapúa, Canindeyú, Amambay and Alto Paraná) and is insufficient to meet domestic demand.

The creation of the MERCOSUR southern common market in 1992 and the elimination of harvest and planting quotas in Argentina in 1991 boosted exports to Brazil and Paraguay, countries to which Argentina had historically imported yerba mate. MERCOSUR, and Brazil in particular, became the leading destination of Argentine exports. Table 1 summarizes information on production, consumption, and foreign sales of yerba mate

The inelastic nature of the demand creates periodic crises of overproduction and the price of the product is highly dependent on regulation of trade between the southern nations of South America. The government regulated this activity in Argentina from 1935 to 1991. Deregulation favored the industrial part of the business (yerba mate mills) and negatively affected the 17,000 small farmers who grow the raw material, as the price of the leaf fell by almost sixty percent. Recent protests from farmers re-established government control in the form of the newly created National Yerba Mate Institute.

The yerba mate industry in southern Brazil is fragmented, however, characterized by small companies and no market leaders.

See also **Yerba Maté.**

BIBLIOGRAPHY

Barsky, Osvaldo, and Jorge Gelman. *Historia del agro argentino. Desde la conquista hasta fines del siglo XX.* Buenos Aires: Grijalbo—Mondadori, 2001.

Bartolomé, Leopoldo. "Colonos, plantadores y agroindustrias. La explotación agrícola familiar en el sudeste de Misiones." *Desarrollo Económico.* Vol. 15, n. 58, 240–264. Buenos Aires: Ides, 1975.

Bolsi, Alfredo. "Misiones (una aproximación geográfica al problema de la yerba mate y sus efectos en la ocupación del espacio y el poblamiento)." *Folia Histórica del Nordeste.* n. 7., Resistencia: Universidad Nacional del Nordeste, 1986.

Echeverria, Mirta. "Formas de reclutamiento y fijación de la fuerza de trabajo en los yerbatales misioneros en la primera mitad del siglo." *Revista Paraguaya de Sociología.* Vol. 23, n. 66, 29–37. Asunción: CPES, 1986.

Gortari, Javier. "El Mercosur y la economía yerbatera. Una aproximación al impacto en la pequeña producción regional." *Realidad económica.* n. 154, 98–117, 1998.

Linhares, Temístocles. *História Econômica do Mate.* Rio de Janeiro: José Olympio, 1969.

Morner, Magnus. *Actividades políticas y económicas de los jesuitas en el Río de la Plata.* Buenos Aires: Paidós, 1968.

Rau, Víctor. "La génesis del proletariado rural altoparanaense." *Estudios Regionales.* 5–17. Posadas: Universidad Nacional de Misiones, 2006.

Schiavoni, Gabriela. *Colonos y ocupantes. Parentesco, reciprocidad diferenciación social en la frontera agraria de Misiones.* Posadas: Editorial Universitaria, 1995.

GABRIELA SCHIAVONI

YERMO, GABRIEL DE (1757–1813).

Gabriel de Yermo (*b.* 1757; *d.* 1813), leader of the Mexican coup d'état of 1808. The Sodupe-born Yermo was a rich Spanish merchant and landowner who became the enemy of Viceroy José de Iturrigaray (1742–1815) because of financial matters, specifically, the taxes levied on products Yermo imported. Backed by the Audiencia of Mexico, Yermo and 300 armed men apprehended the viceroy and his family on the night of 15 September 1808. By so doing, they successfully prevented the establishment of the governing junta that the *ayuntamiento* (city council) proposed and that Iturrigaray appeared to support. Also detained were several members of the *ayuntamiento* and Fray Melchor de Talamantes (1765–1809).

See also **Mexico, Wars and Revolutions: Coup d'État of 1808.**

BIBLIOGRAPHY

Enrique Lafuente Ferrari, *El virrey Iturrigaray y los orígenes de la independencia de Méjico* (1940); *Diccionario Porrúa de historia, biografía y geografía de México,* vol. 3 (1986), p. 3188.

Additional Bibliography

Archer, Christon I. *The Birth of Modern Mexico, 1780–1824.* Wilmington, DE: Scholarly Resources Inc., 2003.

VIRGINIA GUEDEA

YNSFRÁN, EDGAR L. (1920–1991).

Edgar L. Ynsfrán (*b.* 1920; *d.* 1991), Paraguayan politician. When General Alfredo Stroessner seized power in 1954, he needed competent allies to give his regime a veneer of legitimacy and respectability. In this effort it was natural that he would turn to Edgar L. Ynsfrán, a talented young intellectual who had made a name for himself in Colorado Party circles ever since the 1947 civil war. A protégé of the right-wing former president Juan Natalicio González, Ynsfrán was a lawyer by training. He had already served as a Colorado deputy, police official, and member of the Junta de Gobierno. He was also a much read essayist, an indefatigable worker, and a shrewd party organizer. Most important of all, he was willing to act as Stroessner's agent in political matters.

The general made Ynsfrán his interior minister in the mid-1950s at precisely the time when the democratic opposition—as well as the left-leaning guerrilla groups—were actively seeking the dictator's ouster. Ynsfrán took energetically to combating these threats. Though he gave the impression of being a tranquil, austere scholar, in fact he filled Paraguay's jails with hundreds of political prisoners, many of whom were tortured.

By the mid-1960s, Ynsfrán's repressive apparatus had destroyed nearly all of Stroessner's enemies in the country. The very success of his campaign, however, gave Ynsfrán a measure of power uncomfortably close to that of the president himself. Not wishing to place too much temptation before his minister's eyes, Stroessner abruptly dropped Ynsfrán from the cabinet in 1966. Thereafter the former interior minister devoted himself to business matters and to the building of a magnificent library of Paraguayan books, documents, and memorabilia, much of which was donated to the nation just before his death. In the last two years of his life, he attempted a political comeback, but his unsavory past prevented him from making much headway, even within his own Colorado Party.

See also **Paraguay, Political Parties: Colorado Party; Stroessner, Alfredo.**

BIBLIOGRAPHY

Edgar Ynsfrán, *Tres discursos* (1956), *passim;* Paul H. Lewis, *Paraguay Under Stroessner* (1980), pp. 79–99, 116–134.

Riordan Roett and Richard S. Sacks, *Paraguay: The Personalist Legacy* (1991), pp. 55–57.

Additional Bibliography

Lachi, Marcello, and Roberto Céspedes Ruffinelli. *Insurgentes: La resistencia armada a la dictadura de Stroessner.* Asunción, Paraguay: Uninorte, 2004.

Paredes, Roberto. *Stroessner y el stronismo.* Asunción, Paraguay: Servilibro, 2004.

THOMAS L. WHIGHAM

YNSFRÁN, PABLO MAX (1894–1972).

Pablo Max Ynsfrán (*b.* 30 June 1894; *d.* 2 May 1972), Paraguayan educator and historian. Born in Asunción, Ynsfrán received formal training as a diplomat during the 1920s and 1930s, but early on expressed as much interest in the study of history as in the practical application of politics. From 1923 to 1928 he taught philosophy and Roman history at the Colegio Nacional de la Capital (Asunción) at the same time as he served as a congressional deputy.

The Chaco War of 1932–1935 found Ynsfrán in Washington, D.C., as Paraguay's chargé d'affaires.

There he participated in the 1938 Chaco peace conference and was subsequently chosen to be public works minister by President José Félix Estigarribia.

With the start of the Higínio Morínigo dictatorship in 1940, Ynsfrán went into exile in the United States. He became a professor of Latin American history at the University of Texas at Austin, where he remained until his death.

Ynsfrán wrote two finely detailed studies, *The Epic of the Chaco: Marshal Estigarribia's Memoirs of the Chaco War, 1932–1935* (1950), and *La expedición norteamericana contra el Paraguay, 1858–1859* (1954), as well as many articles and polemical pieces.

See also **Chaco War; Estigarribia, José Félix.**

BIBLIOGRAPHY

Charles J. Kolinski, *Historical Dictionary of Paraguay* (1973), pp. 266–267.

Jack Ray Thomas, *Biographical Dictionary of Latin American Historians and Historiography* (1984), pp. 353–354.

MARTA FERNÁNDEZ WHIGHAM

YON SOSA, MARCO ANTONIO

(1932–1970). Marco Antonio Yon Sosa (*b.* 1932; *d.* June 1970), Guatemalan guerrilla leader. On 13 November 1960, Yon Sosa led a revolt of nationalist army officers against the corrupt government of Miguel Ydígoras Fuentes (1958–1963). After a brief exile, he returned to eastern Guatemala as a proponent of radical revolution through guerrilla warfare, and organized the Rebel Armed Forces (FAR) with Luis Turcios Lima and the Communist Party. Yon Sosa broke from the FAR in 1965 over ideological issues, but he continued the guerrilla struggle as leader of the Revolutionary Movement of November 13 (MR-13). An advocate of immediate socialist revolution through general insurrection, Yon Sosa rejected the electoral strategies of the FAR, although the two guerrilla movements forged a tenuous alliance during the devastating counterinsurgency program supported by the United States in the late 1960s. After a confrontation with the army, he fled Mexico, where he was killed by Mexican authorities. The FAR and MR-13 provided the training ground for the rebel leaders of the 1970s.

See also **Ydígoras Fuentes, Miguel.**

BIBLIOGRAPHY

Susanne Jonas and David Tobis, eds., *Guatemala* (1974), esp. pp. 176–203.

Jim Handy, *Gift of the Devil: A History of Guatemala* (1984), esp. pp. 230–234.

Additional Bibliography

Landau, Saul. *The Guerrilla Wars of Central America: Nicaragua, El Salvador, and Guatemala.* London: Weidenfeld and Nicolson, 1993.

Pinto Soria, Julio César. *El estado y la violencia en Guatemala (1944–1970).* Guatemala: Universidad de San Carlos de Guatemala, Centro de Estudios Urbanos y Regional, 2004.

PAUL J. DOSAL

YORKINOS.

Yorkinos, the York rite Masonic lodges. As Mexican national politics became increasingly polarized in 1825, leading figures such as José Miguel Ramos Arizpe, Ignacio Esteva, Manuel Gómez Pedraza, Vicente Guerrero, and Lorenzo de Zavala formed Masonic lodges independent of the Scottish Escoceses. The U.S. minister Joel R. Poinsett agreed to obtain formal charters from the Grand Masonic Temple in New York, thus formally establishing the York rite lodges or *yorkinos*. Although the *yorkinos* eventually became the "populist" party, initially, the group included many moderates. Within a short time, radicals took control of the lodges, which spread rapidly throughout the nation. In 1827, the discovery of a conspiracy by the Franciscan Joaquín Arenas to return Spain to power resulted in the passage of laws expelling the Spaniards and to state and national electoral victories by radical *yorkinos*. This, in turn, led to an unsuccessful revolt by the *escoceses* and to riots in December 1828 which forced president-elect Gómez Pedraza to flee the country and elevated Guerrero to the presidency. After 1828 the lodges were banned; Mexican Masonry reorganized in 1830 as the *Rito Nacional Mexicano,* but intervened in politics less directly.

See also **Masonic Orders.**

BIBLIOGRAPHY

Luis J. Zalce y Rodríguez, *Apuntes para la historia de la masonería en México,* 2 vols. (1950).

Virginia Guedea, "Las sociedades secretas durante el movimiento de independencia," in *The Independence of Mexico and the Creation of the New Nation,* edited by Jaime E. Rodríguez O. (1989), pp 45–62.

Additional Bibliography

Anna, Timothy E. *Forging Mexico: 1821–1835.* Lincoln: University of Nebraska Press, 1998.

Solares Robles, Ma Laura. *Una revolución pacífica: Biografía política de Manuel Gómez Pedraza, 1789–1851.* Mexico City: Instituto de Investigaciones Dr. José María Luis Mora: Acervo Diplomático de la Secretaría de Relaciones Exteriores, 1996.

Solís, Ruth and Carlos María de Bustamante. *Las sociedades secretas en el primer gobierno republicano, 1824–1828: según el Diario Histórico de C.M. de Bustamante.* Mexico City: ASBE, 1997.

JAIME E. RODRÍGUEZ O.

YORUBA. The Yoruba are a West African people who inhabit southwest Nigeria, the southern Benin Republic (formerly Dahomey), and southern Togo. Known in the Americas by subethnic names such as Yaraba, Oyo, Aku, Nago, Lucumi, Ijesha, Egba, and Ijebu, transatlantic Yoruba-speaking communities and customs reestablished themselves following dispersal by the slave trade. Yoruba slave exports began in the late 1700s, but the collapse of the Yoruba imperial capital at Oyo circa 1837 and attendant civil wars augmented their slave numbers. This volume was maintained until the abolition of the slave trade in Brazil in 1850. In the British Caribbean, where the slave trade became illegal after 1807, captured Africans were imported as indentured laborers until the 1860s.

Yorubaland's late role as a slave reservoir accounts for the persistence of Yoruba culture in Brazil, Cuba, Trinidad, and Grenada. Cultural manifestations include language use restricted largely to ritual, food preparations and names, folktales and legends, divination methods and accompanying poetry, sacred and secular songs, drum types, and drum rhythms. The most overt cultural domain is religion, centered on natural forces called orishas (Orixás) meaning "saints," or "powers." Each orisha is identified by specific colors, paraphernalia, and chants. Ceremonies are conducted by the self- or family-appointed male or female leader of a religious community, as the religion possesses no overall regulatory body. Yoruba-derived ceremonies are most elaborately articulated in Shango in Recife, Candomblé in Bahia, and Santería of Cuba. Trinidad and Grenada maintain analogous rituals, called Shango or Orisha. Ancestor veneration is a subsidiary aspect of the religion, but is separately enacted in the Saraka in Trinidad and Carriacou (the Grenadines), Etu in Jamaica, and Oku in Guyana. Overall, the cultural distinctiveness of the Yoruba in different nations reveals the ways in which culture can be creatively adapted to local environments and survive. Also, local governments have come to accept at least parts of the Yoruba culture. For instance, in Bahia, Brazil, local Candomblé ceremonies are now promoted for tourism purposes.

See also **African-Latin American Religions: Overview; Slavery: Spanish America.**

BIBLIOGRAPHY

William Bascom, *The Yoruba of Southwestern Nigeria* (1969), and *Shango in the New World* (1972).

George Simpson, *Black Religions in the New World* (1978).

Sheila Walker, "Everyday and Esoteric Reality in the Afro-Brazilian Candomblé," in *History of Religions* 30, no. 2 (1990): 103–128.

José Jorge De Carvalho and Rita Laura Segato, *Shango Cult in Recife, Brazil* (1992).

Additional Bibliography

Falola, Toyin, and Matt D. Childs, eds. *The Yoruba Diaspora in the Atlantic World.* Bloomington: Indiana University Press, 2004.

MAUREEN WARNER LEWIS

YRENDAGÚE, BATTLE OF. Battle of Yrendagúe, a conflict that took place at a small fort in Paraguay near the border with Bolivia during the Chaco War (1932–1935). The fighting occurred on 8 December 1934 and secured Paraguay's victory against Bolivia, its landlocked neighbor. Paraguayan General José Félix Estigarribia ordered Colonel Eugenio Garay to occupy Yrendagúe with support from his Eighth Division. The numerically inferior Paraguayan forces marched on foot for about fifty miles to the fort. Once they captured Yrendagüe, the Bolivians lost access to all of the water wells in the area. Water was extremely scarce in that region of the Chaco, and, as a result, 4,000 Bolivian cavalry troops were forced to surrender and perhaps twice that number died of thirst.

See also **Chaco War.**

BIBLIOGRAPHY

Pablo Max Ynsfrán, *The Epics of the Chaco War: Memoirs of General Estigarribia* (1950).

David H. Zook, *The Conduct of the Chaco War* (1960).

Additional Bibliography

Cuadros Sánchez, Augusto. *Los orígenes de la revolución nacional: La guerra del Chaco y sus seculas, 1932–1943: relato de un cambatiente y "estratega" de la clase tropa*. La Paz: Editorial "Los Amigos del Libro," 2003.

Farcau, Bruce W. *The Chaco War: Bolivia and Paraguay, 1932–1935*. Westport, CT: Praeger, 1996.

MIGUEL A. GATTI

YRIGOYEN, HIPÓLITO. *See* Irigoyen, Hipólito.

YUCATÁN. Yucatán, a peninsula in southeastern Mexico, including the Mexican states of Yucatán, Campeche, and Quintana Roo, northern Tabasco, northeastern Chiapas, and the northern parts of the modern republics of Guatemala and Belize. The region has been occupied for millennia, most notably by the Maya, who built their civilization in the area some time after 300 B.C. Europeans arrived on the peninsula during the first decade of the sixteenth century and the Spanish conquistadors conquered the Mayas in 1542, the year in which the Spaniards founded the city of Mérida, the capital of the colonial province and of the modern state of Yucatán. One unfortunate result of contact with Europeans for the Mayas was a substantial demographic decline caused by the wars of conquest, forced labor, and by the introduction of Old World diseases. The Maya population, which had numbered at least 500,000 and perhaps as high as 800,000 in the early sixteenth century, declined to only about 100,000 by the late seventeenth century.

The colonial regime was at first based almost entirely on Maya peasant community labor, which produced food and exportable goods, especially cotton textiles, for the Spanish colonists. Spaniards limited their own activities to stock raising on ranches (*estancias*), although in Campeche (the western part of the peninsula) the colonists also organized production of salt and dyewood and established a shipbuilding industry. Politically, the province of Yucatán was ruled by a governor captain-general (*gobernador capitán general*) appointed by the Spanish crown.

In the eighteenth century the Maya population began a demographic recovery, while at the same time the number of non-Indians—Spaniards, mestizos, and mulattoes—also increased substantially. By 1800 the population of the province was over 400,000. Demographic growth resulted in an increased demand for food and other goods, thus leading to the expansion of the landed estates, which produced not only cattle but also maize, sugarcane, rice, and cotton. The economy was also stimulated by commercial and political reforms, including the establishment of the intendancy (chief administrator), which resulted in increased trade with Cuba and the abolition of the Repartimiento (a peonage system that coerced the Maya into producing cotton textiles).

Yucatán did not participate in the Mexican struggle for independence, but once Mexico became independent in 1821, Yucatán adhered to the rules of the new nation. Disagreements with the Mexican government, however, led Yucatán's rulers on several occasions to declare the state a sovereign nation. In the decades after independence from Spain those rulers also carried out a program of decolonization and modernization, which, in effect, ended up further depriving Maya communities of their traditional lands. As a result, in 1847 the Mayas of the eastern and central parts of the state rose in rebellion and attempted to drive the non-Indians from the peninsula. This Caste War of Yucatán lasted several decades (although most of the violence ended in 1855) and resulted in death and destruction on a massive scale.

In the late nineteenth century, Yucatán—which had been separated from the state of Campeche in

1858—began a recovery based on the export of sisal, or Henequen fiber. Eventually, enormous profits were earned by the large landowners, and Yucatán became the most prosperous state in Mexico. This recovery was accomplished, however, by instituting a rigorous system of debt peonage to force the Mayas to work on the plantations, and, consequently, little of the wealth trickled down to the peasants, who made up the majority of the population.

The conservative regime was so well entrenched that it survived the early years of the Mexican Revolution. In 1915, however, the Carranza government, after putting down one last Yucatecan separatist movement, imposed a reformist governor, Salvador Alvarado (1879–1924), who abolished peonage and permitted labor to organize. By 1918 the socialists, led by Felipe Carrillo Puerto (1872–1924), had become the leading political party, and they took power in 1920. Two years later Carrillo Puerto was elected governor. The socialists attempted radical reforms, but their government was overthrown by reactionaries in late 1923; Carrillo Puerto and several of his supporters were executed by firing squad in early 1924. As a result, the Mexican government came to control politics in Yucatán, working through the socialists, who became the basis for the ruling party in the state.

In the 1930s, President Lázaro Cárdenas (1895–1970) destroyed the landowning aristocracy in Yucatán by carrying out an agrarian reform. At the same time, however, the henequen industry, which almost ceased to exist by 1990, had begun its long-term decline. Yucatán's economy came to be based mostly on commerce and tourism, with only a minor amount of industry.

See also **Cárdenas del Río, Lázaro; Carrillo Puerto, Felipe; Caste War of Yucatán; Conquistadores; Diseases; Estancia; Gobernador; Henequen Industry; Maya, The; Mérida; Repartimiento; Textile Industry: The Colonial Era.**

BIBLIOGRAPHY

Eligio Ancona, *Historia de Yucatán*, 5 vols. (1878–1880).

Juan Francisco Molina Solís, *Historia de Yucatán durante la dominación española*, 3 vols. (1904–1913).

Gilbert M. Joseph, *Revolution from Without: Yucatán, Mexico, and the United States, 1880–1924* (1982).

Nancy M. Farriss, *Maya Society Under Colonial Rule* (1984).

Allen Wells, *Yucatán's Gilded Age: Haciendas, Henequen, and International Harvester, 1860–1915* (1985).

Inga Clendinnen, *Ambivalent Conquests: Maya and Spaniard in Yucatán, 1517–1570* (1987).

Robert W. Patch, *Maya and Spaniard in Yucatán, 1648–1812* (1993).

Additional Bibliography

Bracamonte y Sosa, Pedro. *La memoria enclaustrada: Historia indígena de Yucatán, 1750–1915.* México, D.F.: CIESAS: INI, 1994.

Coerver, Don M; Pasztor, Suzanne B, and Buffington, Robert. *Mexico: An Encyclopedia of Contemporary Culture and History.* Santa Barbara, CA: 2004.

Joyce, Kelly. *An Archaeological Guide to Mexico's Yucatán Peninsula.* Norman: University of Oklahoma Press, 1993.

Patch, Robert. *Maya and Spaniard in Yucatan, 1648–1812.* Stanford, CA: Stanford University Press, 1993.

Quezada, Sergio. *Breve historia de Yucatán* . México: Colegio de México, Fideicomiso Historia de las Américas, 2004.

Reed, Nelson A. *The Caste War of Yucatán.* Stanford, CA: Stanford University Press, 2001.

Sierra O'Reilly, Justo. *Los indios de Yucatán.* Mérida, Yucatán, México: Universidad Autónoma de Yucatán, 1994.

ROBERT W. PATCH

YUNGAS. Yungas, tropical river valleys of Bolivia that spread northeast to southeast beyond the temperate valleys of the eastern Andean slopes. Here, Amazon winds maintained the humidity necessary for the cultivation of crops not available in the highlands. The pre-Inca Aymara empire sustained its highland centers by sending Mitmaes (colonists) down to the *yungas* to cultivate fruits, maize, and, for highland elite consumption, the stimulant coca. In return, the highlands sent items not produced in the tropical zones, such as meat, potatoes, quinoa, and wool, thus fulfilling their obligations in this Andean system of reciprocity.

With the Spanish conquest and subsequent discovery of silver, coca use changed dramatically and was no longer confined to the native elite. Coca consumption now enabled Andeans to endure harsh mining activities for protracted periods of time. Production in Cuzco could not meet the increased demand, and the *yungas* of La Paz became a major coca zone. Not only did Aymara agricultural migrants continue to replace the nomadic peoples of the region, merchants imported African slaves, who by the early nineteenth century had become a viable Aymara-speaking subgroup in this region. La Paz and its neighboring *yungas* now thrived while other regions experienced economic decline.

Other less accessible *yungas* existed in the provinces of Cochabamba and Santa Cruz. The Chaparé region, northeast of Cochabamba, formerly controlled by the Yuracarés, today produces prodigious amounts of coca. In the colonial period, La Paz merchants intervened and prevented Chaparé competition. The *yungas* of Pocona, which was first settled in 1538 and incorporated into the jurisdiction of Mizque before the end of the century, were mass-producing coca by 1557.

Even today, the fertile *yungas* and Oriente regions remain largely underdeveloped despite their year-round growing season. Poor infrastructure, disease (human and plant), pests, floods, and soil erosion discourage serious agricultural activity.

See also **Andes; Incas, The; Mining: Colonial Spanish America; Yungas.**

BIBLIOGRAPHY

Josep M. Barnadas, *Charcas: Orígenes históricos de una sociedad colonial* (1973), pp. 35, 427.

Alberto Crespo R., *Esclavos negros en Bolivia* (1977), pp. 143–146.

Herbert S. Klein, *Bolivia: The Evolution of a Multi-Ethnic Society* (1982).

Morris D. Whitaker and E. Boyd Wennergren, "Bolivia's Agriculture Since 1960: An Assessment and Prognosis," in *Modern-Day Bolivia: Legacy of a Revolution and Prospects for the Future*, edited by Jerry R. Ladman (1982), pp. 238–239.

Brooke Larson, *Colonialism and Agrarian Transformation in Bolivia: Cochabamba, 1550–1900* (1988), p. 47.

Additional Bibliography

Lagos, Maria L. *Autonomy and Power: The Dynamics of Class and Culture in Rural Bolivia.* Philadelphia: University of Pennsylvania Press, 1994.

Klein, Herbert S. *Haciendas and Ayllus: Rural Society in the Bolivian Andes in the Eighteenth and Nineteenth Centuries.* Stanford, CA: Stanford University Press, 1993.

Kuznar, Lawrence A. *Ethnoarchaeology of Andean South America: Contributions to Archaeological Method and Theory.* Ann Arbor, MI: International Monographs in Prehistory, 2001.

Léons, Madeline Barbara and Harry Sanabria. *Coca, Cocaine, and the Bolivian Reality.* Albany: State University of New York Press, 1997.

Meruvia Balderrama, Fanor. *Historia de la coca: los Yungas de Pocona y Totora (1550–1900).* La Paz: Plural Editores: CERES, 2000.

Sanabria, Harry. *The Coca Boom and Rural Social Change in Bolivia.* Ann Arbor: University of Michigan Press, 1998.

Spedding, Alison. *Kawsachun coca: economía campesina cocalera en los Yungas y el Chapare.* La Paz: PIEB, Programa de Investigación Estratégica en Bolivia, 2004.

LOLITA GUTIÉRREZ BROCKINGTON

YUNGAY, BATTLE OF.

Battle of Yungay, a military action in 1839 that resulted in the destruction of the Peru-Bolivia Confederation, which was headed by Grand Marshal Andrés de Santa Cruz and opposed by the Chilean government and a group of Peruvian military leaders. Two military expeditions were sent from Chile to fight the confederation. The first, led by Admiral Manuel Blanco Encalada, was unsuccessful despite the Chilean naval superiority achieved by the end of 1836. However, the second expedition, with a combined force of six thousand men led by General Manuel Bulnes and with the participation of Peruvian leaders Agustín Gamarra, Antonio Gutiérrez de la Fuente, and Ramón Castilla, managed to defeat Santa Cruz's forces in the decisive battle of Yungay in the highlands north of Lima. Gamarra's subsequent attempt in 1841 to invade Bolivia led to his defeat and death in the battle of Ingaví.

See also **War of the Peru-Bolivia Confederation.**

BIBLIOGRAPHY

Jorge Basadre, *Historia de la República del Peru,* vol. 1 (1963).

Additional Bibliography

Fajardo Sainz, Humberto. *Andrés de Santa Cruz y la Unión Latino Americana.* Santa Cruz de la Sierra, Bolivia: H. Fajardo Sainz, 2003.

Maquito Colque, Tania Micaela. *La sociedad arequipeña y la Confederación Perú-Boliviana, 1836–1839.* Arequipa, Peru: DREMSUR Editores, 2003.

ALFONSO W. QUIROZ

YUPANQUI, ATAHUALPA (1908–1992).

A seminal figure in the twentieth-century history of Argentine folk music, Atahualpa Yupanqui influenced generations of musicians, folklorists, and poets throughout the Americas and Europe. Born Héctor Roberto Chavero on January 31, 1908, in Pergamino, he adopted the Quechua pseudonym Atahualpa Yupanqui while still a youth, a reference to the last Inca ruler and a portent of his lifelong promotion of indigenous and working-class peoples and issues. He spent much of his early life traveling the rural areas of Argentina, learning and collecting the music of *payadores* (itinerant poets) and other folk music styles. Yupanqui's first song, "Caminito del Indio," written in 1926, introduced the evocative "Indianist" and protest themes as well as the difficult finger-picking guitar style that would define much of his later work. The politicized nature of his songwriting and his public affiliation with the Communist Party in the 1940s and early 1950s frequently put him at odds with the Argentine government, and he was arrested and briefly imprisoned on several occasions.

Yupanqui's international career was launched after a tour of Eastern bloc countries in 1949–1950, when he was introduced to Edith Piaf in Paris, who in turn promoted and performed with him in a number of Left Bank clubs. He was invited to record his first LP, *Minero Soy* (I Am a Miner), for the Chant du Monde label in 1950, which was awarded the *gran prix* for best folklore disk given by the Academia Charles Cros, the first of many such prizes he would garner in his long career. Though popular in his home country and a revered figure in the emergent *nueva canción* movement throughout South America in the 1960s, Yupanqui moved his permanent residence to Paris in 1967 due to ongoing problems with the military regime in Argentina. He continued to tour and perform internationally until his death on May 23, 1992, and he remains a popular and influential figure in France and much of Latin America in the early twenty-first century. An excellent retrospective of his work is contained on *30 Ans de Chansons* (Chant du Monde, 1996).

See also **Music: Popular Music and Dance; Payador.**

BIBLIOGRAPHY

Primary Works

El canto del viento. Buenos Aires: Honegger, 1965.

El payador perseguido. Buenos Aires: Companía General Fabril Editora, 1972.

Secondary Works

Boasso, Fernando. *Tierra que anda: Atahualpa Yupanqui, historia de un trovador.* Buenos Aires: Corrigedor, 2006.

Luna, Félix. *Atahualpa Yupanqui.* Madrid: Ediciones Júcar, 1974.

JONATHAN RITTER

ZAACHILA.

ZAACHILA. Zaachila, an archaeological site located 9 miles south of Oaxaca City, within the present-day village of Zaachila in Oaxaca, Mexico. Zaachila was excavated by Roberto Gallegos in the 1960s. It includes ten visible mounds, one of which, Mound A, was the locus of excavations. Although evidence of older occupations exists at Zaachila, the excavated remains date from the Postclassic period (c. A.D. 900–1521). Excavations atop Mound A revealed a large residence with rooms arranged around a central patio. Beneath the patio floor were two elaborate tombs with offerings of Mixteca polychrome pottery, onyx vessels, turquoise masks, carved jade, engraved bone, and delicate gold jewelry. The Mixteca polychrome vessels are among the finest ever discovered, and the delicate goldwork rivals that of Monte Albán Tomb 7. Most remarkable, however, are the stucco reliefs on the walls of Tomb 1. Two owls decorate opposite walls of the antechamber. On the east wall of the main chamber, the stucco figure of a god of death beckons an individual who is identified by the calendrical name Nine Flower. On the west wall, another god of death with a hummingbird above him beckons an individual named Five Flower. Alfonso Caso has identified Five Flower in the painted manuscripts, or Codices, that detail the genealogies of Mixtec rulers. He has shown that Five Flower, related to the rulers of the Mixteca Alta center of Yanhuitlán, ruled Zaachila about A.D. 1280. Tomb 1, then, with its rich offering was most likely the final resting place of Five Flower. He and his ancestors and descendants had in all likelihood occupied the residence of Mound A and were among the twenty-three individuals buried in the two tombs beneath its patio floor.

See also **Archaeology; Oaxaca (City).**

BIBLIOGRAPHY

Roberto Gallegos, "Zaachila: The First Season's Work," *Archaeology* 16, no. 4 (1963): 226–233.

Alfonso Caso, "The Lords of Yanhuitlán," in *Ancient Oaxaca,* edited by John Paddock (1966), pp. 313–335.

Roberto Gallegos, *El Señor 9 Flor en Zaachila* (1978).

John Paddock, *Lord Five Flower's Family: Rulers of Zaachila and Cuilapán* (1983).

Marcus Winter, *Oaxaca: The Archaeological Record* (1989), pp. 123–124.

Additional Bibliography

Anders, Ferdinand, Maarten E. R. G. N. Jansen, and Gabina Aurora Pérez Jiménez. *Crónica Mixteca: el rey 8 Venado, Garra de Jaguar, y la dinastía de Teozacualco-Zaachila: libro explicativo del llamado Códice Zouche-Nuttall, Ms. 39671 British Museum, Londres.* Mexico City: Fondo de Cultura Económica; Graz: Akademische Druck- und Verlagsanstalt, 1992.

Byland, Bruce E., and John M. D. Pohl. *In the Realm of 8 Deer: The Archaeology of the Mixtec Codices.* Norman: University of Oklahoma Press, 1994.

Jansen, Maarten E. R. G. N., Michel R. Oudijk, and Peter Kröfges. *The Shadow of Monte Alban: Politics and Historiography in Postclassic Oaxaca, Mexico.* Leiden: Research School CNWS, School of Asian, African and Amerindian Studies, 1998.

Melchor Calvo, Gerardo. *Historia de un pueblo: relatos y costumbres de Zaachila.* Oaxaca, Mexico: Instituto Oaxaqueño de las Culturas: Fondo Estatal para la Cultura y las Artes, 1996.

MICHAEL D. LIND

ZABLUDOVSKY, ABRAHAM (1956–).

Mexican journalist Abraham Zabludovsky Nerubay is the son of Jacobo Zabludovsky. He worked as a television news anchor on *24 Horas de la Tarde* (1986–1988) and on Abraham Zabludovsky en Televisa (1998–2000). In 1991 he founded the weekly *Época*, which he edited until 1998. In 1999 he started the news program *De la A a la Z on Radio 13*, which he anchors in a critical and incisive style. Zabludovsky earned a licentiate's degree in political science from Trinity University of San Antonio, Texas. In 1997 he received the National Journalism Prize.

See also **Journalism in Mexico; Radio and Television; Zabludovski, Jacobo.**

RAUL TREJO

ZABLUDOVSKY, JACOBO (1928–).

Journalist Jacobo Zabludovsky Kraveski was born in Mexico City and anchored *24 Horas* (1970–1997), the television news program with the largest viewing audience in Mexico. He was the country's most influential journalist at a time when private television was subordinate to the Mexican government. He created the international news channel *Eco* in 1988 and in 1998 resigned from Televisa because of criticism of his alleged bias toward the authoritarian government. In 2001 he started the radio news program *De Una a Tres*. He was the attorney for the National Autonomous University of Mexico and taught journalism there as well. He authored *La conquista del espacio* (1962), *Charlas con pintores*, (1966) and other books, and received various prizes, including the King of Spain International Journalism Award. In his own words, he is first and foremost a reporter.

See also **Journalism in Mexico; Radio and Television; Zabludovski, Abraham.**

BIBLIOGRAPHY

Conger, Lucy. "The State Loses Its Grip on News." *U.S. News & World Report* 124, no. 4 (February 2, 1998): 44.

Quinones, Sam. "Televisa's Top Anchor Ends Era." *Media* 17, no. 6 (February 2, 1998): 8–9.

RAUL TREJO

ZACATECAS.

Zacatecas, a city and a state in north-central Mexico. The name comes from the Zacateco Indians, thought to have built fortifications during the classic period in what is today southern Zacatecas and Aguascalientes to defend central Mexico from the Chichimecs. The city of Nuestra Señora de los Remedios de Zacatecas was founded by Spaniards in 1548. With the discovery of silver at Fresnillo, Sombrerete, and other places, miners, soldiers, merchants, cattle ranchers, missionaries, and royal officials flocked to Zacatecas, which became an important mining region and a major center for expeditions that explored and settled northern New Spain. The province of Zacatecas was part of the Kingdom of Nueva Galicia until it became the Intendancy of Zacatecas toward the end of the eighteenth century.

Hidalgo's revolt led large numbers of the wealthiest inhabitants, and even government officials, to abandon Zacatecas. When Hidalgo and his followers passed through Zacatecas in January 1811, after his defeat at Puente de Calderón, he attracted arms and supporters. Battles continued in various parts of Zacatecas throughout 1812 and 1813, and control of the city changed hands several times. With independence and the fall of Iturbide, Francisco García Salinas and Valentín Gómez Farías were elected as representatives to the national Congress. In October 1823 the local representatives declared the province the Free and Federated State of Zacatecas. Mining was revived, attracting English capital.

The state and its representatives were important national proponents of liberalism and federalism until the militia of Zacatecas was defeated by national armies under Anastasio Bustamante in 1832 and Antonio López de Santa Anna in 1835. Attacks by Apaches and Comanches increased in the 1840s and remained a serious problem for decades. Victoriano Zamora led the liberals supporting the Plan of Ayutla to power in Zacatecas, and Jesús González Ortega, leading Zacatecan troops, ended the War of the reform by defeating the conservatives at San Miguel Calpulalpán (1860). Although French forces occupied Zacatecas in 1864, armed resistance continued throughout the reign of Maximilian.

Trinidad García de la Cadena led an unsuccessful revolt against President Benito Juárez in 1869 and against President Porfirio Díaz in 1886. Despite the growth of mining, agriculture, and technological improvements, the Díaz regime was not popular in Zacatecas. Armed rebellion broke out there in December 1910 with the attempt to arrest supporters of Francisco Madero. In June 1914, insurgent forces led by Francisco Villa defeated federal forces holding Zacatecas and destroyed the last of Victoriano Huerta's army. Violent rebellions associated with the Cristero rebellion broke out in 1926 in various parts of the state.

The city of Zacatecas is the largest in the state, with a 2005 population of 122,889. Mining no longer plays a primary role in the local economy and the city has become a popular tourist destination due to its rich colonial architecture. UNESCO delcared the historic center of the city a World Heritage Site in 1993. Today, Zacatecas is one of the safest, yet poorest, states in Mexico.

See also **Chichimecs; Hidalgo y Costilla, Miguel.**

BIBLIOGRAPHY

Elías Amador, *Bosquejo histórico de Zacatecas* (1943).

Philip Wayne Powell, *Soldiers, Indians, and Silver: The Northward Advance of New Spain, 1550–1600* (1952).

Peter J. Bakewell, *Silver Mining and Society in Colonial Mexico: Zacatecas, 1546–1700* (1971); *Diccionario Porrúa de historia, biografía y geografía de México*, 5th ed. (1986).

Additional Bibliography

Flores Olague, Jesús. *Breve historia de Zacatecas*. México: El Colegio de México, 1996.

García González, Francisco. *Familia y sociedad en Zacatecas: La vida de un microcosmos minero novohispano, 1750–1830*. México: El Colegio de México, Centro de Estudios Historícos, 2000.

D. F. STEVENS

ZACHRISSON, JULIO (1930–). Julio Zachrisson (*b.* 1930), Panama's foremost printmaker. Zachrisson studied in Panama under Juan Manuel Cedeño at the Instituto Nacional de Bellas Artes in Mexico (1953–1959), at the Vanucci Academy in Perugia (1959–1960), and at the San Fernando Academy in Madrid.

Zachrisson's prints, which include etchings, drypoints, woodcuts, and lithographs, are characterized by a unique sense of satire and sociopolitical commentary. The grotesque characters in his fantastic world are drawn from urban Panamanian folklore, Spanish literature, classical mythology, and personal experience. Since the 1970s, he has also painted these subjects in oil on wood or canvas. As of 2008 he lives in Spain.

See also **Art: The Twentieth Century.**

BIBLIOGRAPHY

Marta Traba, *Dos décadas vulnerables en las artes plásticas latinoamericanas, 1950–1970* (1973).

Antonio Gallego, *Historia del grabado en España* (1979); *Zachrisson: obra calcográfica* (catalogue from the Museo Municipal de Bellas Artes, Spain, 1981).

Additional Bibliography

Zachrisson, Julio, and Isabel Biscarri. *Zachrisson*. Zaragoza, Spain: Gobierno de Aragón, Departamento de Educación y Cultura, 1996.

MONICA E. KUPFER

ZACULEU. Zaculeu, or Saqulew, meaning "white land" in K'iche', an archaeological site located in the Huehuetenango Valley of the western Guatemalan highlands, occupied from the Early Classic (ca. A.D. 300) until the arrival of the Spaniards. During the Late Postclassic period, Zaculeu served as the capital of the Mam (Maya) ethnolinguistic group. It sits on an easily defended plateau, protected on three sides by steep cliffs, and may have once had a wall on its fourth side.

Zaculeu was an important center in the Classic period (ca. 300–900). Caches and burials discovered by archaeologists have contained numerous well-crafted goods, such as pyrite plaques and jade carvings.

Many of the structures at Zaculeu were either built or modified during the Late Postclassic period, a period when the population of the settlement is thought to have been substantial. Much of the original residential area presumably lies beneath the modern town of Huehuetenango, 5 kilometers away, so more precise population figures cannot be determined.

The architectural style of the Late Postclassic structures is similar to those at K'iche' and Kaqchikel centers to the east, bearing influence from

Central Mexico rather than Maya. The arrangement of buildings on the landscape differs, however, presumably reflecting earlier patterns. Temple pyramids with altars, palaces, plazas, residential complexes, and a ballcourt comprise the site. Zaculeu does not contain hieroglyphics or carved monuments. In the 1940s, the United Fruit Company sponsored archeological excavations and restorations, the latter, unusually, involving the layering of walls and surfaces in thick white plaster.

Zaculeu and the area it controlled were conquered by the K'iche' sometime between 1425 and 1475, and the K'iche' continued to dominate the area until the arrival of the Spaniards. In 1525 Gonzalo de Alvarado led Spanish forces that conquered the center.

See also **Archaeology; K'iche'.**

BIBLIOGRAPHY

Richard B. Woodbury and Aubrey S. Trik, *The Ruins of Zaculeu, Guatemala,* 2 vols. (1953).

John W. Fox, *Quiché Conquest* (1978), esp. pp. 143–150.

Additional Bibliography

Ferguson, William M., and Richard E. W. Adams. *Mesoamerica's Ancient Cities: Aerial Views of Pre-Columbian Ruins in Mexico, Guatemala, Belize, and Honduras.* Rev. ed. Albuquerque: University of New Mexico Press, 2001.

VanKirk, Jacques, and Parney Bassett-VanKirk. *Remarkable Remains of the Ancient Peoples of Guatemala.* Norman: University of Oklahoma Press, 1996.

JANINE GASCO

ZAID, GABRIEL

ZAID, GABRIEL (1934–). Gabriel Zaid, born on October 14, 1934, is a Mexican poet and essayist. Although an engineer by training, Zaid has become one of the Mexican literary establishment's most active members, recognized as a poet, essayist, literary critic, translator, editor, and researcher. He is a member of El Colegio Nacional and the Mexican Language Academy. Zaid won the Xavier Villaurrutia Prize (1972) and the Magda Donato Prize (1986) for his poetry, which has been described as meticulously structured, refined, concise, and as the antithesis of the confessional and exuberant poetry of Jaime Sabines, his contemporary. His literary criticism has concentrated on poetic theory and practice. Besides editing the work of renowned poets, Zaid has promoted the work of young writers in several anthologies. In *Asamblea de poetas jóvenes de México* (1980), he identified a new generation of poets among the ever-increasing numbers who published in small presses and/or literary journals and supplements in the 1970s. As a cultural critic, his books, such as *La economía presidencial, De los libros al poder,* and *Adiós al PRI,* and his articles, appearing regularly in *Vuelta,* engage the current political debates.

See also **Literature: Spanish America.**

BIBLIOGRAPHY

José Joaquín Blanco, "Gabriel Zaid," in his *Crónica de la poesía mexicana* (1983), pp. 249–255.

Julián Meza, "Autoritarismo presidencial y peticionarismo ciudadano," in *Cuadernos Hispanoamericanos* 448 (1987): 160–164.

Julio Ortega, "Una nota sobre *Práctica Mortal* de Gabriel Zaid," in *Lugar de Encuentro,* edited by Norma Klahn and Jesse Fernández (1989), pp. 153–156.

Additional Bibliography

González Torres, Armando, and Magali Lara. *Zaid a debate.* Mexico: Jus, 2005.

Zaid, Gabriel. *Antología general,* edited by Eduardo Mejía and Rogelio Carvajal Dávila. Mexico: Océano, 2004.

NORMA KLAHN

ZALDÚA, FRANCISCO JAVIER (1821–1882). Francisco Javier Zaldúa (*b.* 3 December 1821; *d.* 21 December 1882), Colombian president. Born in Bogotá, Francisco Javier Zaldúa was a distinguished professor of law and an active member of the Liberal Party. He served frequently in Congress and in other positions, and presided over the constituent convention of Ríonegro in 1863. In the subsequent division of the party between the more doctrinaire Radicals and the Independents who followed Rafael Núñez, Zaldúa initially aligned himself with the latter, even though he was essentially a moderate. Thus both factions accepted him as their presidential candidate in 1881. Despite that consensus, however, his term was marked by bitter wrangling with Congress, cut short by his death after less than a year as president.

See also **Núñez Moledo, Rafael.**

BIBLIOGRAPHY

James William Park, *Rafael Núñez and the Politics of Colombian Regionalism, 1863–1886* (1985), pp. 226–235.

Ignacio Arizmendi Posada, *Presidentes de Colombia 1810–1990* (1989), pp. 163–166.

Additional Bibliography

Delpar, Helen. *Rojos contra azules: el Partido Liberal en la política colombiana, 1863–1899*. Santafe de Bogotá, Colombia: Procultura, 1994.

DAVID BUSHNELL

ZAMBO. Zambo, the lowest of a series of derogatory names by which Spaniards referred to members of the racially mixed groups called *castas* (castes). While the so-called *castas* could refer to any person of racially mixed origin, Spaniards reserved their most derogatory terms, some of which were zoological, such as "wolf" and "coyote," for those of mixed Indian and black ancestry. These terms originated in the eighteenth century and became best known through a series of paintings that depicted the various racial mixtures in a variety of settings, showing their dress, food, and family lives. In these paintings *zambo* is the label for the lowest form of racially mixed person. These derogatory terms were rarely used on official records of either a religious or governmental nature but were usually used as epithets; they are found most frequently in criminal records, which reveal that their use triggered brawls, and in records of civil suits over matters of social status.

See also **Caste and Class Structure in Colonial Spanish America; Race and Ethnicity.**

BIBLIOGRAPHY

Nicolás León, *Last castas del México colonial* (1924).

Lyle Mc Alister, "Social Structure and Social Change in New Spain," in *Hispanic American Historical Review* 43, no. 3 (1963): 349–370.

Magnus Mörner, *Race Mixture in the History of Latin America* (1967).

John K. Chance, *Race and Class in Colonial Oaxaca* (1978).

Patricia Seed, "Social Dimensions of Race: Mexico City, 1753," in *Hispanic American Historical Review* 62, no. 4 (1982): 569–606.

Patricia Seed and Philip Rust, "Estate and Class in Colonial Oaxaca Revisited," in *Comparative Studies in Society and History* 25 (1983): 703–709, 721–724.

Rodney Anderson, "Race and Social Stratification: A Comparison of Working Class Spaniards, Indians, and Castas in Guadalajara, Mexico, in 1821," in *Hispanic American Historical Review* 68, no. 2 (1988): 209–243.

Douglas Cope, *Limits of Racial Domination* (1993).

Additional Bibliography

Carrera, Magali M. *Imagining Identity in New Spain: Race, Lineage, and the Colonial Body in Portraiture and Casta Paintings*. Austin: University of Texas Press, 2003.

Katzew, Ilona. *Casta Painting: Images of Race in Eighteenth-century Mexico*. New Haven, CT: Yale University Press, 2004.

Katzew, Ilona, ed. *New World Orders: Casta Painting and Colonial Latin America*. New York: Americas Society, 1996.

Stephens, Thomas M. *Dictionary of Latin American Racial and Ethnic Terminology*. Gainesville: University of Florida Press, 1989.

PATRICIA SEED

ZAMORA, RUBÉN (1942–). Rubén Zamora is a Salvadoran political leader. Born on November 9, 1942, in Cojutepeque, Zamora received his law degree from the University of El Salvador in 1968; at about the same time, he joined the Christian Democratic Party (PDC). In 1969 he moved to England to pursue graduate studies in political science at the University of Essex. He returned to El Salvador after an army-led reformist coup d'état overthrew the repressive government of General Carlos Humberto Romero on October 15, 1979. Zamora was appointed secretary of the presidency (chief of staff) to the newly created civilian-military junta. When conservative army officers blocked political and economic reforms that the junta intended to implement, Zamora and most members of the junta and cabinet resigned on December 31, 1979. The PDC made a pact with the military and joined it in a second junta. Zamora's older brother, Mario, the attorney general for the poor, was assassinated by a death squad in late February 1980. Appalled by the increasing human rights violations and the PDC's insistence on continuing its coalition with the military, Zamora and several other leading Christian

Democrats resigned from the party on March 9. Zamora and his family went into exile in Nicaragua.

In April 1980 Zamora helped found the Democratic Revolutionary Front (FDR), a coalition of political parties, unions, and mass organizations. Together with an influential group of former PDC members, he founded the Popular Social Christian Movement (MPSC) in May 1980, and was its secretary-general until 1993. From January 1981 to December 1986 Zamora served as an MPSC member of the Political-Diplomatic Commission of the FDR and Farabundo Martí Front for National Liberation (FMLN). In October and November 1984 he returned to El Salvador as a member of the FDR-FMLN negotiating team for the first two meetings between the government and revolutionary organizations.

In November 1987 Zamora returned to El Salvador to help build the MPSC. With Guillermo Manuel Ungo and Enrique Roldán, the leaders of the two social democratic parties, Zamora organized the Democratic Convergence on November 27, 1987, which began to participate in national elections with the 1989 presidential elections. Publicly threatened with death on armed forces radio during the 1989 FMLN offensive, Zamora remained in El Salvador. In 1993 he became the coalition candidate for president of the republic of the Democratic Convergence and the FMLN, which had become a legal political party following the 1992 Salvadoran peace accords that ended the eleven-year civil war. He lost the April 1994 election to ARENA candidate Armando Calderon Sol in a run-off. He served as a deputy in the legislative assembly (1997–2000) and ran for president in 2000, coming in third behind the ARENA and FMLN-USC candidates. Zamora has published numerous works on politics and government in El Salvador, including *El Salvador, heridas que no cierran: Los partidos políticos en la post-guerra* (1998) and *La izquierda partidaria salvadoreña: Entre la identidad y el poder* (2003). As of 2007 Zamora continues to live in El Salvador and owns a consulting firm. He has consistently described himself politically as a social Christian. In practice, this has meant embracing socioeconomic policies that are close to the Social Democrats but are informed by progressive, Roman Catholic theology.

See also **El Salvador, Political Parties: Farabundo Martí National Liberation Front (FMLN).**

BIBLIOGRAPHY

Joseph S. Tulchin and Gary Bland, eds., *Is There a Transition to Democracy in El Salvador?* (1992).

Tommie Sue Montgomery, "El Salvador," in *Political Parties of the Americas, 1980s to 1990s*, edited by Charles Ameringer (1992); "Armed Struggle and Popular Resistance in El Salvador: The Struggle for Peace," in *The Latin American Left: From the Fall of Allende to Perestroika* (1993); and *Revolution in El Salvador: From Civil Strife to Civil Peace*, 2d ed. (1995).

Richard Stahler-Sholk, "El Salvador's Negotiated Transition: From Low-Intensity Conflict to Low-Intensity Democracy," in *Journal of Interamerican Studies and World Affairs* 36 (Winter 1994): 1–59.

Additional Bibliography

Byrne, Hugh. *El Salvador's Civil War: A Study of Revolution*. Boulder, CO: Lynne Rienner, 1996.

Peterson, Anna L. *Martyrdom and the Politics of Religion: Progressive Catholicism in El Salvador's Civil War*. Albany: State University of New York Press, 1997.

TOMMIE SUE MONTGOMERY

ZAMORANO, AGUSTÍN JUAN VICENTE

(1798–1842). Agustín Juan Vicente Zamorano (*b.* 1798; *d.* 1842), Spanish military officer in California and printer. A native of Saint Augustine, Florida, Zamorano served as a royalist cadet in the Mexican Wars of Independence. As a lieutenant of engineers, he went to California with Governor José María Escheandía in February 1825. While commandant of the presidio at Monterey (1831–1836), Zamorano ordered (from Boston) the first printing press in California in 1834; the first work printed on it, in the same year, was a set of regulations. Zamorano surveyed the Santa Rosa settlement for Governor José Figueroa in 1834, and the following year he printed Figueroa's *Manifesto a la República mejicana*, which concerned colonization. He served as commandant of Loreto in 1839–1840 and was named inspector of Alta California in 1842. He died shortly after his arrival in San Diego.

See also **Figueroa Alcorta, José.**

BIBLIOGRAPHY

George L. Harding, *Don Agustín V. Zamorano: Statesman, Soldier, Craftsman, and California's First Printer* (1934).

Cecil Alan Hutchinson, *Frontier Settlement in Mexican California* (1969).

W. MICHAEL MATHES

ZANJÓN, PACT OF.

ZANJÓN, PACT OF. Pact of Zanjón, the armistice that ended the Ten Years' War, the first Cuban War of Independence, in 1878. It was made possible by the exhaustion of the Cuban rebels, their failure to expand the struggle to the western half of the island, and the astute policies of the Spanish general Arsenio Martínez Campos. The peace did not provide for the independence of Cuba nor for the abolition of slavery, but it did allow a measure of self-government, the liberation of slaves who had joined the rebel army, and freedom for all rebel leaders who agreed to leave Cuba. Many Cubans criticized and refused to accept these terms, among them the mulatto general Antonio Maceo, who staged the celebrated though futile "Protest of Baraguá" for several months. But even Maceo himself had to leave Cuba eventually, and peace returned to the island for a while.

In spite of the disappointment of Zanjón, Cubans did not give up. The Ten Years' War succeeded in creating a strong nationalistic spirit that very soon manifested itself in further attempts at rebellion against Spain.

See also **Cuba, War of Independence; Maceo, Antonio.**

BIBLIOGRAPHY

Hugh Thomas, *Cuba; or The Pursuit of Freedom* (1971), chap. 22.

Additional Bibliography

Ferrer, Ada. *Insurgent Cuba: Race, Nation, and Revolution, 1868–1898.* Chapel Hill: University of North Carolina Press, 1999.

JOSÉ M. HERNÁNDEZ

ZAPATA, EMILIANO

ZAPATA, EMILIANO (1879–1919). Emiliano Zapata, the Mexican revolutionary, was born August 8, 1879, and raised in his native village of Anenecuilco in the small south-central state of Morelos. In 1911 Zapata took up arms against the regime of long-time president Porfirio Díaz, and quickly became one of the most prominent leaders of the Mexican Revolution (1910–1920). He is most often remembered for voicing rural demands for land and local liberties.

Zapata was the ninth of ten children of a *campesino* (peasant) family. He received little schooling, though he did learn to read and write. During his early years, the centuries-long struggle between Morelian villages and haciendas for land and water was becoming increasingly tense as the haciendas sought to expand. Like other young men raised in this environment, Zapata had trouble with the law from an early age: In 1897 he fled Morelos to avoid arrest for a minor infraction at a fiesta. By 1906 he was helping to defend Anenecuilco's land in the courts, and in 1909 he was elected president of the village council.

Meanwhile, national politics were becoming unsettled. In 1910, after an aborted campaign for the presidency, Francisco Madero called for a revolution against the dictatorship of Porfirio Díaz. In March 1911 Zapata responded by helping form a small guerrilla band. He soon attained leadership of this group, which grew large enough by May to capture the regional center of Cuautla, Morelos. The taking of Cuautla, only about fifty miles south of Mexico City, was an important factor in forcing Díaz from power.

Zapata soon discovered, however, that the new national leadership was more dedicated to democracy than to land reform. The large landowners of Morelos immediately maneuvered to preserve their power in the state, and it gradually became clear that Madero, a hacienda owner himself, identified with them. Zapata was attacked by the conservative Mexico City press, which began calling him the "Attila of the South" for the real and imagined atrocities committed by his followers. Under these circumstances he was reluctant to disarm his forces. After weeks of negotiations, in August 1911 troops were sent against him under the command of General Victoriano Huerta. Zapata returned to the mountains, now to fight an ostensibly revolutionary regime.

To explain their cause to the nation, Zapata and a local schoolmaster named Otilio Montaño composed the Plan of Ayala in November. This document was a remarkable expression of the goals of many of Mexico's peasant rebels. It clarified

General Emiliano Zapata seated, center, with his staff, 1912. From humble origins, Emiliano Zapata became an important leader in central Mexico during the Mexican Revolution. This revered national hero inspired the Zapatista revolutionary movement in Chiapas that emerged in 1994. © CORBIS

Zapata's demands for land, calling not only for the return of lands the haciendas had stolen, but for the expropriation of one third of all hacienda holdings for villages without land titles, and the confiscation of the property of those who opposed Zapata's rebellion. It also insisted on the rule of law and the right of the people to choose their own leaders. These proposals were among the most radical social and economic ideas advocated by leading figures of the 1910 Revolution.

The struggle against Madero lasted until Huerta deposed and assassinated him in a February 1913 coup. Huerta sought to make peace with Zapata, but Zapata did not trust his promises, and the fighting continued. *Zapatismo* grew as peasants from Morelos, Mexico State, the Federal District, Puebla, Guerrero, and farther afield joined Zapata against the new and in some ways more oppressive regime. As the movement expanded it became more heterogeneous, and it was Zapata's task to discipline it enough to make it a force on the national scene. One measure of his success was that by the summer of 1914 he controlled Morelos and large parts of neighboring states, and threatened Mexico City.

In July 1914 Huerta followed Díaz into exile, and Zapata's forces soon came into contact with the troops of two northern revolutionaries who had also opposed Huerta: Venustiano Carranza and Francisco "Pancho" Villa. Zapata was now confronted with a crucial decision about what kind of alliances, if any, would be most useful to the pursuit of his agenda. Consulting closely with Manuel Palafox, his most prominent intellectual adviser at the time, he eventually sided with the popular Chihuahuan rebel Villa against Carranza, a hacienda owner like Madero who gave little indication that he favored land reform.

By November 1914 the war started again. On December 4 Zapata and Villa met at Xochimilco in the Federal District to firm up their alliance. Two days later they made their official entry into Mexico City, which the Zapatistas had actually occupied in late November. When Zapata captured Puebla on December 16, it looked as though he and Villa would quickly defeat Carranza, but a series of assassinations in the capital strained relations between the two leaders. Moreover, there was conflict among the urban intellectuals they had put in charge of their national government.

Just before Christmas, Zapata returned to Morelos. With the aid of Palafox, who was minister of agriculture in the new government, he began to carry out the land reform he had promised. In some respects 1915 was a utopian period in Morelos, a time in which Zapata helped the campesinos act on their hopes for change in a way that they have seldom been able to do in Mexican history. But internal tensions limited what Zapata could accomplish. Neighboring villages often fought over land and other resources, and differences between Zapatista guerrillas and the civilian population were becoming more evident.

In mid-1915 Villa lost the biggest battles of the revolution to Carrancista general Álvaro Obregón. In early August Zapata's army was driven out of Mexico City, and in the spring of 1916 Carranza's troops invaded Morelos. There was no longer any realistic hope that Zapata might defeat the forces arrayed against him. Some historians contend that this failure was inevitable given the nature of the various revolutionary factions; others have argued that Zapata might have better supported Villa's military effort or that he might have negotiated a more successful national alliance. In any event, Zapatismo now entered a long decline.

Still Zapata did not give up. With the help of a new chief adviser, Gildardo Magaña, he began to seek alliances with anyone who might help him fight Carranza. But conflict within Zapatismo now reached its highest level, and several prominent leaders defected. The most striking case was that of Otilio Montaño, coauthor of the Plan of Ayala, who was implicated in an uprising against Zapata in May 1917. Zapata ordered Montaño executed to send a message to other would-be traitors, but there was no way to counter the centrifugal forces at work. Zapata's efforts to lure supporters from other revolutionary camps thus became increasingly desperate. Finally, he invited a supposedly disaffected Carrancista colonel named Jesús Guajardo to join him. After exchanging a few letters, on April 10, 1919, Guajardo and Zapata met at a place called Chinameca. With a handful of men Zapata rode through the gate of the hacienda there and Guajardo's troops, assembled as if to give him military honors, shot him dead.

Zapata left a deep mark on Mexican life. Some in Morelos still claim that he is not dead, that a man who looked like him took his place at Chinameca and Zapata is hiding in the mountains until the people need him again. Meanwhile, for both the government and many of those who opposed that government prior to 2000, the figure of Zapata has become an enduring symbol of rural Mexico's struggle for justice. The most notable contemporary example of his symbolic influence was the guerrilla rebellion in the heart of Chiapas in January, 1994. Know as the Zapatista Army of National Liberation (EZLN), or more commonly, the Zapatistas, these largely indigenous rural peasants led a movement against the government of Carlos Salinas (president 1988–1994), who had instituted an agrarian reform that dispensed with the long-standing ejido program, which granted land and use rights to individual villages, but not legal ownership to the villagers. An advocate of economic neoliberalism and a regional economic treaty with the United States and Canada, Salinas hoped to improve rural development through market capitalism. The rise of the Zapatistas, although readily oppressed by government forces, contributed significantly to the decline of the Institutional Revolutionary Party's control. Thus to this day Zapata continues to symbolize, for many Mexicans, a figure who did not compromise on his principles.

See also **Carranza, Venustiano; Colombia, Political Parties: Liberal Party; Díaz, Porfirio; Huerta, Victoriano; Madero, Francisco Indalecio; Mexico, Political Parties: Institutional Revolutionary Party (PRI); Mexico, Wars and Revolutions: Mexican Revolution; Mexico, Zapatista Army of National Liberation; Mosquera, Tomás Cipriano de; Neoliberalism; Obregón Salido, Álvaro; Plan of Ayala; Salinas de Gortari, Carlos; Villa, Francisco "Pancho".**

BIBLIOGRAPHY

Avila Espinosa, Felipe Arturo. *Los orígenes de zapatismo.* Mexico: El Colegio de México, Centro de Estudios Históricos, 2001.

Brunk, Samuel. *Emiliano Zapata: Revolution and Betrayal in Mexico*. Albuquerque: University of New Mexico Press, 1995.

Espejel, Laura, Alicia Olivera, and Salvador Rueda, eds. *Emiliano Zapata: Antología*. Mexico City: Instituto Nacional de Estudios Históricos de la Revolución Mexicana, 1988.

Hernández, Alicia. *Anenecuilco: Memoria y vida de un pueblo*, 2nd edition. Mexico City: Colegio de México, Fideicomiso Historia de las Américas, Fondo de Cultura Económica, 1993.

McLynn, Frank. *Villa and Zapata: A Biography of the Mexican Revolution*. London: Jonathan Cape, 2000.

Millon, Robert P. *Zapata: The Ideology of a Peasant Revolutionary*, 2nd edition.. New York: International Publishers, 1995.

Sotelo Inclan, Jesús. *Raíz y razón de Zapata*. 2nd edition. Mexico: Editorial CFE, 1970.

Warman, Arturo. *"We Come to Object": The Peasants of Morelos and the National State*. Translated by Stephen K. Ault. Baltimore, MD: Johns Hopkins University Press, 1980.

Womack, Jr., John. *Zapata and the Mexican Revolution*. New York: Knopf, 1968.

RODERIC AI CAMP
SAMUEL BRUNK

ZAPATA, FELIPE

ZAPATA, FELIPE (1838–1902). Felipe Zapata (*b.* 24 May 1838; *d.* 28 July 1902), Colombian Liberal journalist and politician. He was born in Bogotá to a family of the Santander elite and attended the Colegio de Piedecuesta in his home region. He was imprisoned after the Liberals' defeat at Oratorio (1860). As a delegate to the Rionegro Convention (1863), Zapata resisted the extreme federalists and the anticlericals among his colleagues. He was a leading opponent of General Tomás Cipriano de Mosquera's increasing authoritarianism, a position revealed in articles published in *La Unión* (March–June 1866) and *El Mensajero* (November 1866–March 1867). In both these Bogotá newspapers, Zapata chipped away at his opponent with calm logic. He later served in several Liberal governments in ministerial roles and was minister plenipotentiary to Great Britain and France in 1874. Zapata did not hesitate to criticize the foibles of his fellow Liberals. He opposed Rafael Núñez but condemned the Liberal revolutionaries in 1885. He moved to London in that year, becoming a liaison with Francisco Javier Cisneros and British financiers. He died in London.

See also **War of the Thousand Days.**

BIBLIOGRAPHY

Ramón Zapata, *De los hombres que hicieron historia. Felipe Zapata* (*El Vidente*) (1971).

Helen Delpar, *Red Against Blue* (1981), pp. 141–142 and passim.

Additional Bibliography

Delpar, Helen. *Rojos contra azules: el Partido Liberal en la política colombiana, 1863–1899*. Santafe de Bogotá, Colombia: Procultura, 1994.

J. LEÓN HELGUERA

ZAPATISTA ARMY OF NATIONAL LIBERATION. *See* **Mexico, Zapatista Army of National Liberation.**

ZAPOTECS. Zapotecs, a linguistically related population of indigenous people in the southern Mexican state of Oaxaca, of whom there were some 300,000 in the 1990s. Zapotecs have occupied the Oaxaca area since at least 1500 B.C.

The Zapotecs call themselves *bene zaa*, which means either "the native people" or "the cloud people." The term "Zapotec" derives from the Nahuatl *Tzapotecatl*, meaning "people of the *zapote* tree." It was first applied to native inhabitants in Oaxaca by the Aztecs in the fifteenth century.

Present-day Zapotecs are generally divided into four major groups: the Valley Zapotecs, who occupy the fertile Valley of Oaxaca in the center of the state; the sierra or Mountain Zapotecs, occupying the districts of Ixtlán, Villa Alta, and Choapán; the Isthmus Zapotecs, who live on the tropical Isthmus of Tehuantepec; and the Southern Zapotecs of the sierra Miahuatlán region. This distribution corresponds roughly to their location at the time of the Spanish conquest in 1521.

The Zapotec languages (Zapotec and Chatino) belong to Otomanguean, a large linguistic stock that is one of the oldest in Mesoamerica. It includes a number of other language groups, such as Mixtec, Cuicatec, and Mazatec in Oaxaca, Otomí in the states of Mexico and Hidalgo, and Mangue in Central America, none of which is related to the Mayan or Uto-Aztecan stocks.

Zapotec is a language family or group rather than a single language. The languages within it differ from one another as much as do the modern Romance languages. Scholars disagree about the number of Zapotec languages, some recognizing as few as five while others postulate as many as forty-five.

In pre-Spanish times the Valley Zapotecs had developed one of the earliest writing systems in Mesoamerica (ca. 500 B.C.). Hieroglyphic inscriptions are found in abundance at the ancient Zapotec city of Monte Albán, now a famous Mexican archaeological site. This metropolis rivaled other Classic Period (ca. 100–900) Mesoamerican cities such as Teotihuacán in central Mexico, and was built earlier than those in the Maya area. After the fall of Monte Albán around 800, the Zapotecs continued to maintain a distinctive and complex stratified culture at such sites as Zaachila, Mitla, and Yagul in the Valley of Oaxaca and Guiengola near Tehuantepec. The power of Zapotec elites, however, was considerably undermined by invading Mixtecs and Aztecs before the Spanish conquest.

During the Spanish colonial period, Zapotecs were reduced to tribute-paying peasants and today are still predominantly villagers and farmer–artisans. Thus modern Zapotec culture is largely a village culture since Zapotec is, for the most part, spoken only in the home and the village. Modern Zapotec culture is very similar to that of many other parts of rural Mexico and is a complex amalgam of modern Mexican, Spanish colonial, and pre-Hispanic characteristics.

Since the 1970s, many Zapotecs seeking work have migrated to cities in Mexico and to the United States. During this same period, some Valley Zapotec villages, such as Teotitlán del Valle, have specialized in the production of crafts for which they have become nationally and internationally famous. The success of the Teotitlán weavers has brought to the village a renewed pride in its Zapotec heritage that is manifest in the development of programs to preserve Zapotec language and customs. Another town that has shown a particular interest in preserving its Zapotec heritage is Juchitán in the Isthmus region.

The most famous Zapotec is Benito Juárez, born in the sierra village of Guelatao, who was president of Mexico from 1858 to 1872. In recent times, each president of Mexico has made an annual pilgrimage to Oaxaca to celebrate Juárez's birthday, a national holiday. Today, Isthmus Zapotec poets such as Victor de la Cruz, Victor Terán, Natalia Toledo Paz, and Sierra Zapotec Mario Molina Cruz are some of the most prolific and respected indigenous writers in Mexico, leading the way in the renaissance of Mexican indigenous literary production.

See also **Indigenous Peoples; Juárez, Benito; Mesoamerica; Monte Albán.**

BIBLIOGRAPHY

A general overview of the Zapotecs from earliest times to the present is Joseph W. Whitecotton, *The Zapotecs* (1984). For the pre-Hispanic period, see Kent V. Flannery and Joyce Marcus, eds., *The Cloud People* (1983). Good ethnographies of modern Zapotec villages are Lynn Stephen, *Zapotec Women* (1991), and Laura Nader, *Harmony Ideology: Justice and Control in a Zapotec Mountain Village* (1990).

Additional Bibliography

Chiñas, Beverly Newbold de. *Mujeres de San Juan: La mujer zapoteca del Istmo en la economía.* Translated by Antonieta Sánchez Mejorada. Mexico City: Secretaría de Educación Pública, 1975.

García Antonio, Epifanio. *Imagen de un pueblo indígena a fines del siglo XX.* Mexico City: INI, 2001.

JOSEPH W. WHITECOTTON

ZARACONDEGUI, JULIÁN DE (?–1873).

Julián de Zaracondegui (*d.* 1873), Peruvian merchant. Heavily involved in lending activities in Lima in the 1850s, Zaracondegui had excellent political connections. By 1860 he had established himself in a variety of enterprises. Owner of a major export-import business in Lima, he was also a member of the Tribunal del Consulado (the merchant regulatory board), a guano consignee, a general director of the Banco de Lima, and an officer of the welfare agency called Beneficiencia Pública de Lima. He also served a term in the Chamber of Deputies. In the 1850s Zaracondegui founded a marketing firm to sell Peruvian cotton in Europe, and in 1859 he formed a partnership with the Aspíllaga Family to purchase a cotton plantation in the Saña Valley of the north coast. He put up the necessary cash—the equivalent of $120,000—and the Aspíllagas managed production on the plantation. Soon the cotton failed and the owners turned to sugar, thereafter the main crop in that region.

Zaracondegui's fortunes began to deteriorate after 1870. When one of his partners, Manuel de Argumániz, scandalized Lima by accusing him of undermining the cotton merchandising operation, difficulties befell his other enterprises. The financial crisis of 1873 blindsided many entrepreneurs, Zaracondegui among them, and he committed suicide.

See also **Banking: Overview; Cotton.**

BIBLIOGRAPHY

Michael Gonzales, *Plantation Agriculture and Social Control in Northern Peru, 1875–1933* (1985).

Paul Gootenberg, *Imagining Development: Economic Ideas in Peru's "Fictitious Prosperity" of Guano, 1840–1880* (1993).

Additional Bibliography

Zegarra, Luis F. *Institutions, Economic Development and Early Banking in Latin America, 1850–1930.* Ph.D. diss. University of California, Los Angeles, 2002.

VINCENT PELOSO

ZARAGOZA, IGNACIO (1829–1862).

Ignacio Zaragoza (*b.* 1829; *d.* 8 September 1862), Mexican military officer and hero of the battle of Puebla (5 May 1862). Born in Bahía de Espíritu Santo, in the Mexican province of Texas, and educated in Matamoros and Monterrey, Zaragoza hoped to pursue a career in business but found his opportunities limited by the devastated condition of the Mexican economy and his status as a mestizo. Zaragoza turned to a traditional occupation in his family—the military. He first joined the militia as a sergeant, and later was accepted into the regular army as a captain in 1853.

Zaragoza supported the Plan of Ayutla in 1854 and spent the rest of his life fighting on the side of the liberals. He fought against Santa Anna's army at Saltillo and in defense of Monterrey. When President Ignacio Comonfort supported the Plan of Tacubaya, Zaragoza organized riflemen in the capital against the conservative forces and in defense of the Constitution of 1857. With Leandro Valle, he led the liberal forces that took Guadalajara from Severo del Castillo and defeated Leonardo Márquez. Zaragoza served as quartermaster under Jesús González Ortega during the battle of Calpulalpán, where the liberal victory over the conservatives ended the War of the Reform.

In April 1861 President Benito Juárez named Zaragoza his minister of war, replacing González Ortega, who had resigned in protest of Juárez's policies. Zaragoza held this post until December, when he resigned to take command of the Army of the East, confronting the forces of England, France, and Spain, which had landed in Veracruz that month to force payment of Mexico's foreign debt. After the English and Spanish forces withdrew and the French began their march on Mexico City, Zaragoza lost a battle at Azcultzingo and was forced to retreat. He quickly ordered fortifications built on the small hills of Loreto and Guadalupe that overlooked the city of Puebla. Mexican troops, armed with muskets the British had captured from Napoleon I at Waterloo and had sold to the Mexican government in the 1820s, faced roughly equal numbers of better-equipped and professionally trained French soldiers commanded by General Charles Fernand Latrille, Count of Lorencez. On 5 May 1862, the French made repeated assaults up the slopes of the Cerro de Guadalupe but were beaten back by Zaragoza's army. French casualties numbered roughly one thousand of a force of six thousand. The French retreated to Orizaba to await reinforcements, delaying their invasion of central Mexico for a year and giving Juárez's government time to organize resistance.

The moral and political effects of the victory far outweighed its importance in military terms. Zaragoza's victory over the French at Puebla became a powerful symbol of Mexico's national defiance of foreign interference and the occasion of one of Mexico's most important national holidays, Cinco de Mayo. Zaragoza died a few months later of typhoid in Puebla.

See also **French Intervention (Mexico); Plan of Ayutla.**

BIBLIOGRAPHY

Walter V. Scholes, *Mexican Politics During the Juárez Regime, 1855–1872* (1957), pp. 70–71, 87–88, 90.

Guillermo Colin Sánchez, *Ignacio Zaragoza: Evocación de un héroe* (1963).

Justo Sierra, *Political Evolution of the Mexican People*, translated by Charles Ramsdell (repr. 1969), pp. 293–295, 311–314.

Richard N. Sinkin, *The Mexican Reform, 1855–1876: A Study in Liberal Nation-Building* (1979), pp. 50, 158, 177; *Diccionario Porrúa de historia, biografía y geografía de México*, 5th ed. (1986).

Additional Bibliography

Morán, Paola. *Ignacio Zaragoza.* Mexico City: Planeta Mexicana, 2005.

D. F. STEVENS

ZÁRATE, AGUSTÍN DE (c. 1508–1514–after 1578).

Agustín de Zárate, an important early chronicler of Peruvian history, was born sometime between 1508 and 1514. He was still alive in 1578, although his exact date of birth and death still eludes researchers. It is known that he was named secretary to the Real Consejo de Castilla in 1528 and that in 1543 he was named accountant general of Peru, possibly at the early age of twenty-eight. His *Historia del descubrimiento y conquista del Perú* is of consequence for a number of reasons: it serves as a source for other, better-known chroniclers, including Inca Garcilaso de la Vega and Felipe Guaman Poma de Ayala; it attempts a primitive ethnology (a few chapters); and it indicates the role the author played in the Pizarro–Almagro civil wars. Nevertheless, posterity has not remembered Zárate. This may be because his work represents a philologist's nightmare, not only because the 1577 version suppresses certain chapters from the 1555 first edition (as discussed by Dorothy McMahon and Marcel Bataillon), but also because, as Paul Roche has discovered, there exist different printings of the first edition—partisan, pirate tomes produced as a result of the Pizarro-Almagro intrigues.

See also **Cieza de León, Pedro de; Garcilaso de la Vega, El Inca; Guaman Poma de Ayala, Felipe; Peru: From the Conquest Through Independence.**

BIBLIOGRAPHY

Works by Zárate

Historia del descubrimiento y conquista del Perú. Anvers (Antwerp): Martin Nucio, 1555.

Historia del descubrimiento y conquista del Perú. Sevilla: Alonso Escribano, 1577.

Secondary Sources

Bataillon, Marcel. "Zárate ou Lozano? Pages retrouvées sur la religión péruvienne." *Caravelle: Cahiers du Monde Hispanique et Luso-Brésilien* 1 (1963): 11–28.

Hampe Martínez, Teodoro. "La misión financiera de Agustín de Zárate, contador general del Peru y tierra firme (1543–1546)." *Historia y Cultura* 17 (1984): 91–124.

Leonard, Irving A. "On the Lima Book Trade." *Hispanic American Historical Review* 33, no. 4 (1953): 511–525.

Lostaunau Ulloa, Alejandro. "El cronista Agustín de Zárate." *Boletín del instituto Riva-Agüero* 9 (1972–1974): 172–181.

McMahon, Dorothy. "Variations in the Text of Zárate's Historia del Descubrimiento y Conquista del Peru." *Hispanic American Historical Review* 33, no. 4 (1953): 572–586.

Roche, Paul. "Les corrections almagristes dans l'edition princeps de *l'Histoire du Perou* d'Agustín de Zárate." *Caravelle: Cahiers du Monde Hispanique et Luso-Brésilien* 31 (1978): 5–16.

Roche, Paul. *Agustin de Zarate: Temoin et acteur de la rebellion pizarriste.* Nantes, France: Université de Nantes (Acta Hispanica 1), 1985.

Ross, Kathleen. "Historians of the Conquest and Colonization of the New World: 1550–1620." In *The Cambridge History of Latin American Literature*, ed. Roberto González Echevarría and Enrique Pupo-Walker, pp. 101–142, and esp. 118–122. Cambridge, U.K., and New York: Cambridge University Press, 1996.

THOMAS WARD

ZÁRATE WILLKA, PABLO (?–1903).

Pablo Zárate Willka (*d.* 1903), an Aymara Indian from the Bolivian Altiplano who led an Indian uprising that grew out of the Bolivian Civil War (1899). *Willka* is an archaic Aymara word, meaning "greatness" or "eminence," that had previously been used by Indian protest leaders, including Luciano Willka in 1870–1871. We now know that the more important Willka of 1899 was Pablo Zárate, born on an unknown date in Imillaimilla, between Sicasica, La Paz, and Eucaliptus, Oruro.

Zárate, assuming the name *Willka*, originally joined the federalist cause led by José Manuel Pando, later president of Bolivia, whose main preoccupation was to move the capital from Sucre to La Paz. But Zárate Willka and his Indian contingents soon demanded social changes, including the return of Indian communal lands lost several decades earlier. The uprising turned violent and became extensive. After Zárate Willka's capture in April 1899, the revolt collapsed. He died either while escaping from jail or being transported to another location. However, other versions of his death have some currency.

See also **Pando, José Manuel.**

BIBLIOGRAPHY

Ramiro Condarco Morales, *Zarate, El "Temible" Willka*, 2d enl. ed. (1983), includes lengthy bibliography, pp. 493–504.

Additional Bibliography

Antezana Salvatierra, Alejandro Vladimir. *Los liberales y el problema agrario de Bolivia, 1899–1920.* La Paz, Bolivia: Plural Editores: Centro de Información para el Desarrollo, 1996.

CHARLES W. ARNADE

ZARCO, FRANCISCO (1829–1869).

Francisco Zarco (*b.* 1829; *d.* 1869), Mexican journalist and politician. Born in Durango's capital, where his father was a minor bureaucrat in the state government and a colonel in the military, Zarco was largely self-educated because his family could not pay for his education. Luis de la Rosa named Zarco to a post in his foreign relations ministry in 1847. Zarco soon turned to journalism, writing political, literary, and biographical articles, some of which earned him the antipathy of President Mariano Arista, who had Zarco jailed, and of President Antonio López de Santa Anna, who forced him into exile. With the triumph of the Revolution of Ayutla, Zarco was able to return to Mexico and in 1855 was named editor of *El Siglo XIX*, a journal in which he continued to publish until shortly before his death. Representing Durango at the Constituent Congress of 1856–1857, Zarco was elected secretary by acclamation. His history of the congressional debates is a classic work on Mexico's political history. Zarco served as floor manager for the provisions of Constitution, known as the Ley Lerdo, that would force the church to sell its real estate. He defended the law as a prudent measure that would save the government from bankruptcy and benefit the clergy as well as the government. Later events pushed Zarco to recommend the confiscation of clerical property on the grounds that the clergy, by supporting the Rebellion of the Polkos in 1847 and the French Intervention after 1861, had proven to be disloyal to the nation and an "enemy of the people."

At the beginning of the War of the Reform in 1858, Zarco was arrested by the conservative government but managed to escape. In hiding, he continued to publish for two years, until he was discovered and jailed again. The liberal victory brought his release in December 1860, and the following month, President Benito Juárez asked Zarco to serve as his minister of government and minister of foreign relations. Zarco negotiated a settlement of French claims but resigned when the Mexican congress rejected the proposed treaty.

Zarco remained a supporter of Juárez in congress and his adviser. He continued publishing in Mexico City until May 1863, when the French forces approached, then moved north to San Luis Potosí and later to the United States, where he kept the international community informed about Mexico's struggle for national sovereignty and resistance to monarchy and aristocracy. After the defeat of the Empire, Zarco returned to Mexico and was again elected to the national legislature.

See also **Anticlericalism; Arista, Mariano; French Intervention (Mexico).**

BIBLIOGRAPHY

Francisco Zarco, *Historia del Congreso extraordinario constituyente de 1856–1857,* 5 vols. (1898–1901; repr. 1956).

Walter V. Scholes, *Mexican Politics During the Juárez Regime, 1855–1872* (1957), pp. 6, 60, 69, 92–97, 130–131.

Raymond Curtis Wheat, *Francisco Zarco, el portavoz liberal de la Reforma,* translated by Antonio Castro Leal (1957).

Richard N. Sinkin, *The Mexican Reform, 1855–1876: A Study in Liberal Nation-Building* (1979), pp. 49, 121, 134, 150–151; *Diccionario Porrúa de historia, biografía y geografía de México,* 5th ed. (1986).

Additional Bibliography

Rodríguez O, Jaime E. *The Divine Charter: Constitutionalism and Liberalism in Nineteenth-century Mexico.* Lanham, MD: Rowman & Littlefield Publishers, 2005.

Villegas Revueltas, Silvestre. *El liberalismo moderado en México, 1852–1864.* Mexico City: Universidad Nacional Autónoma de México, 1997.

Woldenberg, José. *Francisco Zarco.* Mexico City: Cal y Arena, 1996.

D. F. STEVENS

ZARUMILLA, BATTLE OF.

Battle of Zarumilla (also known as the battle of Zarumilla-Chacras), 25 July 1941, was fought between Ecuadorian and invading Peruvian troops over disputed border territory in the Ecuadorian coastal province of El Oro. Border skirmishes flared up in 1941 and rapidly escalated into a serious engagement. Ecuadorian President Carlos Alberto Arroyo Del Río nevertheless kept the nation's better units of troops stationed in Quito, choosing to guard his beleaguered presidency against internal enemies. Peru's attack overwhelmed Ecuador's meager defenses. Ecuador suffered some 500 killed; Peru, 80 to 100. Peru seized El Oro and began to move on the important port city of Guayaquil. As Peru advanced and bombed coastal towns, troops in Guayaquil mutinied. In January 1942 the two nations agreed to the Rio Protocol, whereby Ecuador yielded to demands for 80,000 square miles in exchange for Peru's withdrawal from El Oro. In August 1960 populist Ecuadorian president José María Velasco Ibarra declared the treaty null and void.

See also **Yelasco Ibarra, José María.**

BIBLIOGRAPHY

For the most evenhanded treatment of competing boundary claims, see David Hartzler Zook, Jr., *Zarumilla–Marañón: The Ecuador–Peru Dispute* (1964). A brief overview can be found in John D. Martz, *Ecuador: Conflicting Political Culture and the Quest for Progress* (1972).

George I. Blanksten, *Ecuador: Constitutions and Caudillos* (1964).

Additional Bibliography

Gándara Enríquez, Marcos. *El Ecuador del año 1941 y el Protocolo de Río: antecedentes, hechos subsiguientes: Arroyo y su tiempo.* Quito, Ecuador: Centro de Estudios Históricos del Ejército, 2000.

Yepes, Ernesto. *Tres días de guerra, ciento ochenta de negociaciones: Perú, Ecuador 1941–1942.* Lima: Universidad Nacional Agraria La Molina; Universidad del Pacífico, Centro de Investigación, 1996.

RONN F. PINEO

ZAVALA, JOAQUÍN (1835–1906).

Joaquín Zavala (*b.* 30 November 1835; *d.* 30 November 1906), president of Nicaragua (1879–1883, 1893). Zavala, a native of Managua, continued work on the Pacific Railroad, extended telegraph lines to Las Segovias, favored public education, founded the National Library, and continued the process of secularization by decreasing church influence in both government and education. In addition, he maintained peace in the country.

Zavala, a Conservative, was reelected to the presidency in 1893 when acting President Salvador Machado stepped down in the face of a rebellion led by the Genuines, a splinter group of the Conservative Party, and by Liberals commanded by José Santos Zelaya. Zavala, however, was an ally and friend of Zelaya's and thought Zelaya could bring modernity to Nicaragua. Nonetheless, Zavala and Zelaya engaged in two battles to determine their country's future. Zavala lost both of these crucial battles, and his administration quickly fled Managua, leaving the government to Zelaya.

See also **Zelaya, José Santos.**

BIBLIOGRAPHY

Sara Luisa Barquero, *Gobernantes de Nicaragua, 1825–1947* (1945), esp. pp. 139–141.

Benjamin I. Teplitz, "The Political and Economic Foundations of Modernization in Nicaragua: The Administration of José Santos Zelaya, 1893–1909" (Ph.D. diss., Howard University, 1973), esp. pp. 9, 26–30.

Additional Bibliography

Cruz S., Arturo J. *Nicaragua's Conservative Republic, 1858–93.* New York: Palgrave, 2002.

SHANNON BELLAMY

ZAVALA, JOSÉ VÍCTOR (1815–1886).

José Víctor Zavala (*b.* 1815; *d.* 1886), Guatemalan military leader. As a young corregidor, Zavala provided aid that was crucial to José Rafael Carrera's

1848 return to power. By 1854 Zavala was a core member of Carrera's new government, which also included Zavala in-laws José Najera, Manuel Francisco Pavón Ayciena, and Luís Batres Juarros.

Zavala continued his military climb with the successful 1854 siege of Omoa and with the command of Guatemalan troops during the National War (1856–1857) against William Walker. Zavala returned to Guatemala as a national hero and proven Carrera ally. His general popularity as a moderate progressive led to public outrage over his loss in the 1869 presidential election. Zavala climaxed his career as commander in chief of the army of Liberal Justo Rufino Barrios, who attempted to unify Central America.

See also **Corregidor; Walker, William.**

BIBLIOGRAPHY

Joaquín Zavala Urtecho, "Huellas de una familia vasco-Centroamericana en cinco siglos," in *Revista de pensamiento conservador de Centroamerica* 24, no. 1 (1970): 140–190.

Ralph Lee Woodward, *Rafael Carrera and the Emergence of the Republic of Guatemala, 1821–1871* (1993).

Additional Bibliography

Clegern, Wayne M. *Origins of Liberal Dictatorship in Central America: Guatemala, 1865–1873.* Niwot: University Press of Colorado, 1994.

Pompejano, Daniele. *La crisis del antiguo régimen en Guatemala (1839–1871).* Guatemala: Editorial Universitaria, Universidad de San Carlos de Guatemala, 1997.

EDMOND KONRAD

ZAVALA, LORENZO DE (1788–1836).

Lorenzo de Zavala (*b.* 3 October 1788; *d.* 15 November 1836), Mexican politician and writer. Born in Mérida, Yucatán, Zavala distinguished himself as a liberal member of the San Juan group in Mérida during the first constitutional period (1810–1814). Incarcerated in 1814, he spent three years in prison. Elected deputy to the restored Spanish Cortes in 1820, Zavala joined other American deputies in favoring home rule. He returned to Mexico in 1822 and was elected to the First Constituent Congress. He sided with Mexico's emperor, Agustín de Iturbide, when he dissolved the congress.

After the fall of the monarchy, Zavala was elected to Congress once again, this time as a federalist. He joined the *yorkinos* (York Rite Masons) in 1825, becoming a leading radical. In 1827, Zavala was elected governor of the state of Mexico, where he introduced legislation to disentail church property and to break up village lands to encourage private ownership. The following year he joined the revolt of Acordada, eventually becoming minister of the treasury in the Vicente Guerrero administration. In that capacity he had the temerity to levy new taxes in a vain attempt to restore sound fiscal policy. Driven out of office in 1829, Zavala traveled to the United States and Europe, where he wrote *Ensayo histórico de las revoluciones de Mégico.* He returned to Mexico and to politics in 1832; the following year he was elected to Congress once again. Shortly thereafter, he accepted the post of minister to France, where he remained until 1835.

With the collapse of federalism, Zavala returned to Texas, where he owned vast properties as a result of many years of land speculation. When Texas declared independence, he joined the separatists, becoming the first vice president of that republic. Suffering from poor health, he died in 1836, apparently from pneumonia.

See also **Iturbide, Agustin de; Texas Revolution.**

BIBLIOGRAPHY

Raymond Estep, *Lorenzo de Zavala: Profeta del liberalismo mexicano* (1952) and "Lorenzo de Zavala and the Texas Revolution," in *Southwestern Historical Quarterly* 57 (January 1954): 332–335.

Charles Macune, *El estado de México y la federación mexicana* (1978).

Barbara A. Tenenbaum, *The Politics of Penury: Debts and Taxes in Mexico, 1821–1856* (1986).

Additional Bibliography

Henson, Margaret Swett. *Lorenzo de Zavala: The Pragmatic Idealist.* Fort Worth: Texas Christian University Press, 1996.

JAIME E. RODRÍGUEZ O.

ZAVALA, SILVIO (1909–).

Silvio Zavala (*b.* 7 February 1909), Mexican historian known for his work on the economic history of sixteenth-century Mexico, the political philosophy of the

Spanish Conquest, and the nature of colonial economic institutions. Born in Mérida, Yucatán, he received a doctorate in law from the Universidad Central de Madrid in 1931. Zavala founded and served as director of the *Revista de historia de América* (1938–1965). He was also director of the National History Museum (1946–1954) and president of the Historical Commission of the Pan-American Institute of Geography and History (1947–1965). Zavala founded and was director of the Centro de Estudios Históricos at El Colegio de México (1940–1956) and was president of the college from 1963 to 1966. On the diplomatic front, he represented Mexico as permanent delegate to the United Nations for Education, Science and Culture (1956–1963) and as ambassador to France (1966–1975).

Zavala's scholarly work includes a pioneering study on the nature of the colonial labor systems, *La encomienda indiana* (1935), and one on colonial law, *Las instituciones jurídicas en la conquista de América* (1935). He published eight volumes of documents on labor, *Fuentes para la historia del trabajo en Nueva España* (1939–1946). His work is wide-ranging and includes *Francisco del Paso y Troncoso: Su misión en Europa, 1892–1916* (1938) and other substantial contributions to the study of colonial institutions in Spanish America.

See also **Pan-American Institute of Geography and History; United Nations.**

BIBLIOGRAPHY

François Chevalier, "Silvio Zavala, primer historiador de la América hispano indígena, el caso del trabajo de la tierra," in *Historia Mexicana* 39, no. 153 (1989): 21–32.

Silvio Zavala, "Apreciación sobre el historiador frente a la historia," in *El historiador frente a la historia*, by Horacio Crespo et al. (1992), pp. 47–56.

Additional Bibliography

Colegio de Sinaloa. *2 historiadores dos: Silvio Zavala, Miguel León-Portilla: homenaje de El Colegio de Sinaloa.* Culiacán, Sinaloa, Mexico: El Colegio de Sinaloa, 2005.

Colegio Nacional (Mexico). *Biobibliografía de Silvio Zavala.* Mexico City: El Colegio Nacional, 1999.

CARMEN RAMOS-ESCANDÓN

ZAYAS Y ALFONSO, ALFREDO (1861–1934).

Alfredo Zayas y Alfonso (*b.* 21 September 1861; *d.* 11 April 1934), president of Cuba (1921–1925). An urban leader of the struggle against Spanish domination, Zayas held many offices after independence: president of the Senate (1905), revolutionary leader (1906), and adviser to the occupation authorities during the second U.S. intervention in Cuba (1906–1909). In 1909–1913 he was vice president and in 1921 finally succeeded in ascending to the presidency.

Historians usually focus on the nepotism, graft, and corruption that characterized Zayas's administration and tend to underemphasize his achievements. Nevertheless, despite his mismanagement, Zayas reestablished Cuba's international credit, which had been suffering from a sugar crisis. He succeeded in keeping within certain bounds the interference of U.S. envoy General Enoch Crowder. And he secured title to the Isle of Pines in 1925 after twenty years of U.S. procrastination. Above all, Zayas recognized that Cuba was undergoing a period of transition and that new social and political forces were emerging in the country. While in office, he had to face increasing student turbulence at the University of Havana, numerous bitter strikes, and even an uprising organized by the Veterans' and Patriots' Association. But Zayas preferred compromise to violence and managed to keep the peace. He always respected the right to dissent. In 1925, unable to secure his own reelection, he ceded the presidency to General Gerardo Machado y Morales and retired to private life.

See also **Crowder, Enoch Herbert; Cuba, Revolutions: Cuban Revolution.**

BIBLIOGRAPHY

A good study on Zayas by Nestor T. Carbonell appears in the Patronato Ramon Guiteras Intercultural Center's *Presidentes de Cuba* (1987), pp. 139–179.

Additional Bibliography

Whitney, Robert. *State and Revolution in Cuba: Mass Mobilization and Political Change, 1920–1940.* Chapel Hill: University of North Carolina Press, 2001.

JOSÉ M. HERNÁNDEZ

ZEA AGUILAR, LEOPOLDO (1912–2004).

Leopoldo Zea Aguilar (*b.* 30 June 1912, *d.* 8 June 2004), Mexican philosopher and scholar. One of the leading intellectual historians and philosophers in Latin America, Zea obtained undergraduate and graduate degrees from the National Autonomous University of Mexico (UNAM). His distinguished career included important administrative positions, an impressive publication record, and the mentorship of generations of Latin American students. Among his most celebrated books are: *El apogeo y decadencia del positivismo en Mexico* (1944), *Dos etapas del pensamiento hispanoamericano* (1949), *América en la historia* (1957), and *Filosofía de la historia de América* (1976). He received numerous academic awards from all over the world and was instrumental in the development of Latin American intellectual centers and scholarship throughout Latin America.

See also **Philosophy: Overview.**

BIBLIOGRAPHY

Additional Bibliography

Federación Internacional de Estudios sobre América Latina. *Leopoldo Zea y la cultura.* Mexico City: UNAM, Centro Coordinador y Difusor de Estudios Latinoamericanos, 2005.

Zea Aguilar, Leopoldo. *Impulsemos la integración y la unidad de nuestros pueblos.* Mexico City: Asociación por la Unidad de Nuestra América-México, 2003.

DAVID MACIEL

ZEBALLOS, ESTANISLAO (1854–1923).

Estanislao Zeballos (*b.* 22 July 1854; *d.* 4 October 1923), Argentine statesman and intellectual. As minister of foreign affairs under presidents Miguel Juárez Celman (1888–1890), Carlos Pellegrini (1891–1892), and José Figueroa Alcorta (1906–1908), and minister to the U.S. government between 1893 and 1896, Zeballos played a key role in determining Argentine foreign policy during the liberal-conservative era.

Zeballos began his political career as a provincial deputy in Buenos Aires in 1879; he was elected in 1880 and again in 1884 to the National Congress. During his periods as minister of foreign affairs, Zeballos continued the line adopted by the Argentine delegation to the 1889 Pan-American Conference in Washington, D.C.: a rejection of any hemispheric economic agreement that could jeopardize Argentine connections with European markets. Also of great consequence for Latin American international relations at the turn of the century was Zeballos's personal feud with José Maria da Silva Paranhos, Barão de Rio Branco, a Brazilian diplomat. After 1906, as President Figueroa Alcorta's foreign minister, Zeballos embarked upon an arms race with Brazil which—although Zeballos resigned in 1908—continued until 1914. In 1910, Zeballos became one of the delegates to the fourth Pan-American Conference in Buenos Aires. He was reelected to Congress for the 1912–1916 period and continued to influence public life through his writings on international relations. He wrote frequently for the press, mainly *El Nacional*, which he founded, and *La Prensa*. He also founded and directed a prestigious academic journal, *Revista de Derecho, Historia y Letras*. Professor of international law, he was appointed dean of the University of Buenos Aires Law School in 1910 and 1918. Zeballos was also a founder of the Sociedad Científica Argentina and president of the Sociedad Rural Argentina.

See also **Figueroa Alcorta, José; Juárez Celman, Miguel; Pellegrini, Carlos.**

BIBLIOGRAPHY

On Zeballos and Argentine foreign policy, see Thomas F. Mc Gann, *Argentina, the United States, and the Inter-American System, 1880–1914* (1957); Harold F. Peterson, *Argentina and the United States* (1964); and Alberto Conil Paz, "Zeballos y Drago," and Gustavo Ferrari, "La Argentina y sus vecinos," both in *La Argentina del ochenta al centenario,* edited by G. Ferrari and E. Gallo (1980).

Additional Bibliography

Rodríguez, Fermín. *Estanislao S. Zeballos: un desierto para la nación.* Buenos Aires. Facultad de Filosofía y Letras, Universidad de Buenos Aires, 2000.

Shaw, Enrique E. *Zeballos y la imaginación de Argentina, 1898–1906.* Córdoba, Argentina: Universidad Nacional de Córdoba. Centro de Estudios Avanzados, 2003.

EDUARDO A. ZIMMERMANN

ZEDILLO PONCE DE LEÓN, ERNESTO (1951–).

Ernesto Zedillo was president of Mexico from 1994 to 2000, and may be viewed as a significant contributor to Mexican democracy, having introduced a number of important institutional changes that encouraged greater political participation.

Zedillo was born into modest circumstances on December 27, 1951, in Mexico City, but spent most of his childhood in Mexicali, where he attended public schools. He began his preparatory studies at the National Polytechnic Institute (IPN) Vocational School No. 5, completing an economics degree from IPN in only three years in 1972. In 1971 he became an economic researcher in the office of the president of Mexico, where he came under the mentorship of Leopoldo Solís, one of Mexico's leading economists. In 1974, he received a government scholarship to attend Yale University, completing an MA and PhD in economics from 1974 to 1978. After his return to Mexico, he worked in the Bank of Mexico, and was in charge of the Exchange Risk Trust Fund. In 1987, he was appointed assistant secretary of Planning and Budgeting, and a year later, President Carlos Salinas de Gortari (president 1988–1994) chose him to lead the Secretariat of Planning and Budgeting. That agency was incorporated into the Treasury in 1992, and Zedillo became secretary of public education. He resigned the following year to serve as Luis Donaldo Colosio's campaign manager in the 1994 presidential election. When Colosio was assassinated mid-campaign, Salinas selected him as the candidate of the Institutional Revolutionary Party (PRI). He took office December 1, 1994, something of an accidental president.

Zedillo essentially was an academic and economic technocrat before being appointed to a series of high-level public positions. As a presidential candidate, he campaigned on the issue of continuing Salinas' neoliberal economic policies, including the further integration of Mexico into the system of capitalist globalization furthered by NAFTA, the free trade agreement with the United States and Canada. His opponents from the other two major parties, Cuauhtémoc Cárdenas of the PRD and Diego Fernández de Cevallos of the PAN, hotly contested the 1994 presidential election. Colosio's assassination (the first time a presidential candidate had been assassinated since 1929), and the uprising of the Zapatista guerrillas in Chiapas in January 1994, created a highly unstable political situation, leading many Mexicans to expect grave consequences. Zedillo campaigned on a platform of political reforms, most notably the rule of law and increasing political participation. In addition, he proposed to increase education, reduce poverty, and expand employment.

Voter interest in the 1994 presidential race increased significantly as the Catholic Church and civic organizations encouraged citizens to participate. Ultimately, Zedillo won the election with approximately half of the ballots cast, followed by 26 percent for the PAN candidate and only 17 percent for the PRD candidate. Most remarkable was the voter turnout of 78 percent, the highest ever recorded in a presidential election. Shortly after Zedillo took office, he faced a major economic crisis after his administration devalued the peso against the U.S. dollar, allowing it to float free. This produced a run on the peso, the withdrawal of foreign investment and domestic capital, an annual inflation rate of 50 percent, a huge interest rate increase, and a loss of between 250,000 to a million jobs. By 1997 the president was able to stabilize the economy and to increase economic growth significantly. He increased social expenditures over those of all his predecessors since 1946, by 53 percent, but was not able to reduce the unequal distribution of income. Mexico's top 20 percent of income earners garnered 54.1 percent of the income, compared to just 4.2 percent shared among the lowest 20 percent. By the end of his administration, the United Nations estimated that approximately 57 percent of the population still lived in poverty.

The most dramatic changes during the Zedillo administration were political. His philosophy differed substantially from his predecessor's both in tone and substance. Despite strong opposition from within his own party, he persisted in moving Mexico away from its semi-authoritarian political model toward increased electoral competition, and more importantly, toward reducing executive branch power.

Zedillo set in motion four fundamental changes that improved conditions for electoral democracy and which made possible the electoral victory of the opposition in the 2000 presidential election, ousting his party after seven decades in office. The first of these changes involved decentralizing presidential authority. Unlike his predecessor, he rarely intervened in political disputes, increasing local autonomy and encouraging the development of institutional solutions. An excellent example of this was his introduction of an open PRI primary process to select its 2000 presidential candidate, allowing any registered voter, regardless of party affiliation, to participate. He broke with the prior pattern of designating his own successor.

Second, he increased the autonomy of state governors, thereby encouraging greater federalism, a concept contained in the 1917 Constitution. His administration increased state authorities' control over fiscal resources. It may well be that increased local and state authority contributed most significantly to the rise of political competition and participation, and to increased level of democratization in 2000.

Third, and extremely significant to the process of electoral democracy, he passed the 1996 electoral reforms, which among other changes implemented public financing of parties in presidential campaigns, thus equalizing the playing field among the leading parties and alliances. In short, he eliminated the incumbent party's financial linkage to the state.

Finally, he strengthened governmental institutions, laying the groundwork for a stronger judiciary at the level of the supreme court, and a stronger legislative branch. He specifically encouraged voter participation by guaranteeing the independence of the supreme institution in charge of the electoral process, the Federal Electoral Institute.

See also **Cárdenas Solorzano, Cuauhtémoc; Colosio Murrieta, Luis Donaldo; Globalization; Mexico, Political Parties: Democratic Revolutionary Party (PRD); Mexico, Political Parties: Institutional Revolutionary Party (PRI); Mexico, Political Parties: National Action Party (PAN); Mexico, Zapatista Army of National Liberation; Neoliberalism; North American Free Trade Agreement (NAFTA); Salinas de Gortari, Carlos.**

BIBLIOGRAPHY

Favela, Alejandro, et al. *El combate a la pobreza en el sexenio de Zedillo.* Mexico City: Plaza y Valdés, 2003.

Levy, Daniel C., and Kathleen Bruhn, with Emilio Zebadúa. *Mexico: The Struggle for Democratic Development.* Berkeley: University of California Press, 2001.

Purcell, Susan Kaufman, and Luis Rubio, eds. *Mexico under Zedillo.* Boulder, CO: Lynne Rienner, 1998.

Ward, Peter, and Victoria Rodríguez, with Enrique Cabrero Mendoza. *New Federalism and State Government in Mexico: Bringing the States Back In.* Austin: Lyndon B. Johnson School of Public Affairs, University of Texas, 1999.

RODERIC AI CAMP

ZELAYA, JOSÉ SANTOS (1853–1919).

José Santos Zelaya (*b.* 31 October 1853; *d.* 17 May 1919), president of Nicaragua (1893–1909). Zelaya came to the presidency of Nicaragua in September 1893 by means of a revolution. His presidency was important to Nicaragua from several points of view. Politically, Zelaya's presidency constitutes the only substantial interval of rule by the Liberal Party in Nicaragua's history until the 1930s and the arrival of the Somozas. Liberal rule resulted in several important measures to secularize and modernize Nicaraguan society. Economically, Zelaya presided over a commercial expansion that had considerable effect on Nicaragua's citizens. Internationally, his administration coincided with the period of Nicaragua's greatest influence on its Central American neighbors.

Although critics often make light of the ideological commitments of Central American political figures, there is no doubt that Zelaya was committed to Liberal reforms. The Constitution of 1893 strengthened municipal government, separated church and state, prohibited convents and monasteries, guaranteed lay education, established a unicameral legislature, and abolished the death penalty. Like other positivist Latin American leaders, Zelaya was dedicated to bringing economic progress to his country, even by authoritarian methods. He undertook measures to promote export agriculture and granted concessions for the purpose of exploiting natural resources. Railway construction and the building of steamships for use on lakes Managua and Nicaragua received particular attention. Zelaya's zeal for reform, his commitment to economic progress and education, and his youthful cabinet contributed to making Managua an important headquarters for Liberals from northern South America and Central America during his presidency.

Despite democratic procedures outlined in the Constitution of 1893, Zelaya managed elections and ruled as a dictator. He faced approximately fifteen serious efforts by Conservatives to overthrow him. Having modernized and strengthened the Nicaraguan army, Zelaya had little difficulty suppressing his opponents. Unsuccessful rebels were jailed, received amnesty, and often fought again. He was not unusually repressive compared with other Central American presidents of the time.

It was in the field of international affairs that Zelaya made his most significant mark. Sympathetic to the alluring idea of restoring the Central American confederation, he lent his support in 1895 to the creation of the República Mayor, a union of Nicaragua, El Salvador, and Honduras. Although he was an admirer of Justo Rufino Barrios, the Guatemalan president who attempted to restore the confederation by force in 1885, Zelaya took no military measures to preserve the union of the three states. When a coup in El Salvador threatened the union, Zelaya counseled nonintervention, and the union collapsed. During the period 1902–1905, he promoted numerous international peace conferences among the Central American states.

Nicaraguan relations with Honduras and Costa Rica, Nicaragua's immediate neighbors, were primarily peaceful in the early years of Zelaya's presidency, although they deteriorated in 1907–1909. Zelaya initiated negotiations resulting in the signing of a treaty that, when it was finally accepted long after Zelaya's presidency, ended a border dispute between Honduras and Nicaragua. The border with Costa Rica, which had been determined by treaty in 1858 but was not marked, also occupied Zelaya's attention. Negotiations with Costa Rica led to the marking of the border in 1898.

Problems with Great Britain and the United States were not so easily resolved. In his first year in office Zelaya determined to recapture Nicaraguan sovereignty over the Miskito Coast, which had been yielded formally by Great Britain over thirty years earlier but which was still subject to British influence over the Miskito Indians. Zelaya sent troops to Bluefields, headquarters for the Miskitos, and expelled the British consul, provoking British wrath and a brief British blockade of the port of Corinto. In the end Zelaya prevailed. A treaty accepting full Nicaraguan sovereignty was signed by Great Britain in 1904. The Miskito Coast was appropriately named the Department of Zelaya in recognition of his bold action.

The United States sided with Nicaragua on the issue of Miskito sovereignty, but other problems steered Nicaraguan relations with the United States on a perilous course. In the late 1890s, when it appeared that engineers preferred a Nicaraguan route for the proposed isthmian canal, negotiations stalled over Zelaya's resistance to Washington's demand for extraterritorial jurisdiction over the canal zone. When canal construction began in 1904 in Panama, the United States closely watched Zelaya, who was rumored to be courting other nations for possible construction of a rival canal. In 1907, when rivalry between Nicaragua and Guatemala spilled over into Honduras and El Salvador, threatening the stability of the Central American isthmus, Washington began to consider Zelaya a meddler and a threat to peace. An incident in 1909 involving the execution of two U.S. mercenaries led to a decision by Washington to support a rebellion against Zelaya. Recognizing that he could not stay in office against the opposition of the United States, Zelaya resigned and went into exile in December 1909.

See also **Nicaragua, Constitutions; Panama Canal.**

BIBLIOGRAPHY

Charles L. Stansifer, "José Santos Zelaya: A New Look at Nicaragua's 'Liberal' Dictator" in *Revista/Review Interamericana* 7, no. 3 (1977): 468–485, is the principal English-language source on Zelaya. Dana G. Munro, *Intervention and Dollar Diplomacy in the Caribbean, 1900–1921* (1964), tracks the relations of the Zelaya administration with the United States, but always taking the point of view of the United States. A dissertation by John E. Findling, "The United States and Zelaya: A Study in the Diplomacy of Expediency" (University of Texas, 1971), provides more detail on the relations between the United States and Nicaragua in the Zelaya era than is available in Munro. Neither Munro nor Findling has much to say about domestic issues. Of the Spanish-language sources, José Dolores Gámez, *Remembranza histórica del General J. Santos Zelaya* (1941), and Enrique Aquino, *La personalidad política del General José Santos Zelaya* (1945) are the best.

Additional Bibliography

Baracco, Luciano. *Nicaragua, Imagining the Nation: A History of Nationalist Politics in Nicaragua from 19th Century Liberals to 20th Century Sandinistas.* New York: Algora Pub., 2005.

Gobat, Michel. *Confronting the American Dream: Nicaragua under U.S. Imperial Rule.* Durham, NC: Duke University Press, 2005.

Gutiérrez, Harim B. *Una alianza fallida: México y Nicaragua contra Estados Unidos, 1909–1910.* Mexico City: Instituto Mora, 2000.

Paredes, Melvin Javier. *Zelaya y el protestantismo: Génesis de los evangélicos en el Pacífico de Nicaragua.* Managua: CIEETS-Editorial: UPOLI: Sirviendo a la comunidad Visión Mundial Nicaragua, 1995.

CHARLES L. STANSIFER

ZELAYA SIERRA, PABLO (1896–1933).

Pablo Zelaya Sierra (*b.* 1896; *d.* 1933), twentieth-century Honduran painter. Zelaya studied at the Academy of Fine Arts of Costa Rica and subsequently at the San Fernando Academy in Madrid, where he came under the strong influence of Daniel Vásquez Díaz before returning to Honduras. His painting of *Las Monjas* was especially praised and was representative of his paintings while at San Fernando Academy. Although he died young, his neorealist painting made a strong impression in Honduras. His formal style exhibited strong technical perfection, but he often emphasized the figurative rather than the literal. He is credited with applying the Spanish style of Vásquez Díaz to Honduran motifs. His paintings *La muchacha del huacal* and *Dos campesinas* are especially fine examples of this.

See also Art: The Twentieth Century.

BIBLIOGRAPHY

J. Evaristo López and Longino Becerra, *Honduras: 40 pintores* (1989).

Additional Bibliography

López R., J. Evaristo, Pablo Zelaya Sierra, and Longino Becerra. *Pablo Zelaya Sierra: vida y trayectoria artística.* Tegucigalpa, Honduras: Baktún Editorial, 1991.

RALPH LEE WOODWARD JR.

ZELEDÓN, BENJAMÍN FRANCISCO (1879–1912).

Benjamín Francisco Zeledón (*b.* 4 October 1879; *d.* 4 October 1912), Nicaraguan Liberal general. The Liberal–Conservative coalition formed in the wake of the overthrow of dictator José Santos Zelaya (1909) proved to be extremely unstable. In July 1912, Minister of War Luis Mena revolted against Conservative President Adolfo Díaz. Mena's chief lieutenant, Benjamín Zeledón, followed suit, to protect the coffee interests. Zeledón quickly seized Managua, Granada, and Masaya. Díaz grew increasingly concerned and requested military assistance from U.S. President William Howard Taft, who dispatched a Marine contingent on 4 August 1912. The marines soon numbered 2,700. Mena, outnumbered and overwhelmed, fled the country, leaving the struggle to Zeledón. Both marines and Nicaraguan troops loyal to Díaz pursued Zeledón, who was killed at El Arroyo while attempting to break out of a U.S. encirclement. The victors paraded Zeledón's body on horseback in order to discourage further rebellions.

See also Díaz, Adolfo; Zelaya, José Santos.

BIBLIOGRAPHY

Doctor General Benjamín F. Zeledón (Managua, 1980).

Gregorio Selser, *Sandino: General of the Free,* translated by Cedric Belfrage (1981).

Lester D. Langley, *The Banana Wars: United States Intervention in the Caribbean, 1898–1934* (1983).

John A. Booth, *The End and the Beginning: The Nicaraguan Revolution,* 2d ed. (1985), esp. p. 31.

Donald C. Hodges, *Intellectual Foundations of the Nicaraguan Revolution* (1986).

Additional Bibliography

Gobat, Michel. *Confronting the American Dream: Nicaragua under U.S. Imperial Rule.* Durham, NC: Duke University Press, 2005.

Selser, Gregorio. *La restauración conservadora y la gesta de Benjamín Zeledón: Nicaragua-USA, 1909–1916.* Managua, Nicaragua: Aldilà Editor, 2001.

SHANNON BELLAMY

ZEMPOALA. *See* Cempoala.

ZEMURRAY, SAMUEL (1877–1961).

Samuel Zemurray (*b.* 18 January 1877; *d.* 30 November 1961), Bessarabian immigrant who arrived impoverished in the United States in 1892 and amassed a $30 million fortune in the banana industry. From 1911, when he financed a revolution in Honduras in order to gain valuable concessions for his Cuyamel Fruit Company on the Honduran north coast, until his retirement as president of United Fruit Company in 1951, he was one of the most powerful North Americans in Central America.

Zemurray began modestly, selling overripe bananas he acquired from United Fruit to upcountry Alabama towns. Later, he acquired a steamship to ferry bananas from the north Honduran coast to Gulf coast ports. Cuyamel began as a small company of minor annoyance to United Fruit, but Zemurray (who recognized that knowledge of local conditions was critical in the industry) expanded his business rapidly, especially after the 1911 Honduran revolution. By the 1920s, Cuyamel became more and more a threat to United Fruit's interests, especially in the banana lands along the Honduran-Guatemalan border.

Zemurray anticipated that United would try to absorb Cuyamel, so he secretly began acquiring United stock. In 1929, he accepted United's offer of 300,000 shares of stock for his interest in Cuyamel. With a $30 million account in his ledger, he retired to an estate outside New Orleans and became involved in various philanthropic projects, among them the Middle American Institute at Tulane University. But when the worth of United stock fell to $10 a share during the Great Depression legend has it that Zemurray stormed into United offices, threw his shares on the table, and declared he was taking over. He became managing director of the company in 1933. Zemurray then went back to Central America, fought the Sigatoka disease that was devastating the banana plantations, and in a few years returned United to profitability. He became president of the company in 1938.

See also **Banana Industry; United States-Latin American Relations.**

BIBLIOGRAPHY

Thomas P. Mc Cann, *An American Company* (1976).

Thomas L. Karnes, *Tropical Enterprise* (1978).

Walter La Feber, *Inevitable Revolutions: The United States in Central America* (1983).

Additional Bibliography

Argueta, Mario. *Bananos y política: Samuel Zemurray y la Cuyamel Fruit Company en Honduras.* Tegucigalpa, Honduras: Editorial Universitaria, 1989.

Dosal, Paul J. *Doing Business with the Dictators: A Political History of United Fruit in Guatemala, 1899–1944.* Wilmington, DE: Scholarly Research Books, 1993.

Euraque, Darío A. *Reinterpreting the Banana Republic: Region and State in Honduras, 1870–1972.* Chapel Hill: University of North Carolina Press, 1996.

Langley, Lester D., and Thomas David Schoonover. *The Banana Men: American Mercenaries and Entrepreneurs in Central America, 1880–1930.* Lexington: University Press of Kentucky, 1995.

LESTER D. LANGLEY

ZENIL, NAHUM BERNABÉ (1947–).

Nahum Bernabé Zenil (b. 1 January 1947), Mexican painter. Zenil, a native of Chicontepec, Veracruz, graduated from the National Teachers School in 1964 and began to teach primary school. In 1972 he completed studies at the National School of Painting and Sculpture, then continued to teach and paint until the late 1980s, when he dedicated himself to painting full time. Zenil's mixed-media paintings, generally self-portraits done on paper, address social circumstances and traditions in contemporary Mexican society, such as sexual identity, religion, and the family. His paintings are highly personal and autobiographical. Zenil is much influenced by the work of Frida Kahlo and popular painting of the nineteenth century, including the traditional *ex-voto* and *retablo* formats. He often incorporates text into his compositions. Zenil's work is consistently imbued with a profound gay sensibility. His first important exhibitions were held at the Galería de Arte Mexicano, in Mexico City, in 1985. Since that time he has been exhibited and collected internationally.

See also **Art: The Twentieth Century.**

BIBLIOGRAPHY

Edward J. Sullivan, "Nahum Zenil's 'Auto-Iconography,'" in *Arts Magazine* 63 (November 1988): 86–91, and *Aspects of Contemporary Mexican Painting* (1990), esp. pp. 67–74.

Luis Carlos Emerich, *Nahum B. Zenil… presente* (1991).

Additional Bibliography

Bender, Daniel J. "In Search of Nahum B. Zenil." M.A. thesis, School of the Art Institute of Chicago, 1997.

Zenil, Nahum B., Edward J. Sullivan, and Clayton Kirking. *Nahum B. Zenil: Witness to the Self/Testigo Del Ser*. San Francisco: Mexican Museum, 1996.

CLAYTON C. KIRKING

ZENO GANDÍA, MANUEL (1855–1930).

Manuel Zeno Gandía (*b.* 10 January 1855; *d.* 30 January 1930), Puerto Rican writer and politician. Zeno Gandía was born in Arecibo, Puerto Rico, where he attended elementary school. He did undergraduate and graduate work in medicine in Barcelona and Madrid, respectively. During this time he met the Cuban José Martí, with whom he established a friendship that influenced him in literature and politics. Through his novels, newspaper articles, and poetry Zeno Gandía exposed the major social, economic, ethical, and political problems that afflicted Puerto Rico during the nineteenth and early twentieth centuries. In the political arena he fought for Puerto Rican independence from Spain and from the United States. In 1902 Zeno Gandía bought *La Correspondencia*, a newspaper in which he criticized public officials. Because of this criticism he was sued for libel by a U.S. representative, a case he won in the U.S. Supreme Court. In 1904 Zeno Gandía participated in the founding of the Partido de Unión de Puerto Rico, which remained dominant in Puerto Rican politics until the mid-1920s.

Zeno Gandía is considered by many to be Puerto Rico's most important novelist of the nineteenth century, because his works represent the first serious realization of the genre in his country. His novels *La charca* (1894), *Garduña* (1896), *El negocio* (1922), and *Redentores* (1925) were grouped together under the series title of *Crónicas de un mundo enfermo*. In *La charca*, his best-known novel, which richly portrays the rural nineteenth-century Puerto Rican, he expressed all of his theories on naturalism and determinism.

See also **Literature: Spanish America.**

BIBLIOGRAPHY

Luz María Umpierre, *Ideología y novela en Puerto Rico* (1983).

Additional Bibliography

Díaz, Luis Felipe. *Modernidad literaria puertorriqueña*. San Juan, Puerto Rico: Editorial Isla Negra: Editorial Cultural, 2005.

Sánchez de Silva, Arlyn. *La novelistica de Manuel Zeno Gandia*. San Juan, Puerto Rico: Instituto de Cultura Puertorriqueña, Programa de Publicaciones Y Grabaciones, 1996.

MAYRA FELICIANO

ZEPEDA, ERACLIO (1937–).

Eraclio Zepeda (*b.* 24 March 1937), Mexican author. Born in Chiapas, Zepeda was educated at the Universidad Veracruzana, where he also taught. Considered the premier writer and storyteller in Mexico, Zepeda concentrates mostly on the indigenous culture of Chiapas. In 1959, he gained national prominence with the publication of *Benzulul,* a book of indigenous stories. Most of his work is socially oriented, speaking of humanity's basic needs and its relationship to nature. *Asalto nocturno* (1973; Nocturnal Assault) won Mexico's national prize for the best short-story collection in 1974. Also a renowned poet and member of La Espiga Amotinada, Zepeda, with four friends, published the collective work *La espiga amotinada* (1960) and *Ocupación de la palabra* (1965). These anthologies collected the works of a generation of Mexican poets who grounded their poetry in the social reality of the country. Other members of La Espiga Amotinada were Juan Banuelos, Oscar Oliva, Jaime Augusto Shelley, and Jaime Labastida. As a political activist, actor, and popular television personality, Zepeda is a forceful and affirmative figure, having earned worldwide respect and recognition. Other major works are *Andando el tiempo* (1982; Time Marching On), *Relación de travesía* (1985; Cross-Street Story), and *Confrontaciones* (1985; Confrontations).

See also **Literature: Spanish America.**

BIBLIOGRAPHY

Joseph Sommers, "El ciclo de Chiapas: Nueva corriente literaria," *Cuadernos Americanos* 2 (1964): 246–261.

Barbara L. C. Brodman, *The Mexican Cult of Death in Myth and Literature* (1976), pp. 76–82.

Joseph Sommers, "Eraclio Zepeda y el oficio de narrar," in *La brújula en el bolsillo* (1982), pp. 14–25.

Jeanne C. Wallace, "Eracillo Zepeda," in *Dictionary of Mexican Literature,* edited by Eladio Cortés (1992).

Additional Bibliography

Cluff, Russell M. *Los resortes de la sorpresa: (Ensayos sobre el cuento mexicano del siglo XX).* Tlaxcala, México: Universidad Autónoma de Tlaxcala, 2003.

L'échelard-Le Duc, Marie-José. "Études libériques et latino-americaines Benzulul d'eraclio zepeda, la voix de l'indien chiapanéque." Ph.D. diss. Université de Rennes II, 1992.

JEANNE C. WALLACE

ZEPEDA Y ZEPEDA, JUAN DE JESÚS (1808–1885).

Juan de Jesús Zepeda y Zepeda (*b.* 20 November 1808; *d.* 20 April 1885), bishop of Comayagua, Honduras (1861–1885). Zepeda was born in San Antonio de Oriente and ordained a Franciscan priest in 1832. He became Guatemalan auxiliary bishop in 1859 and in 1861 was named bishop of Comayagua, where he soon distinguished himself as a friend of the needy and as a peacemaker. When Liberal President Marco Aurelio Soto initiated anticlerical legislation in 1879–1880, Zepeda, in poor health, complained but promised not to resist if the state provided funds to partly compensate for the loss of the tithe. Soto evidently complied, but when Luis Bográn Baraona became president in 1883, the church was treated more harshly. Financially weakened, it was unable to carry out even basic programs. Consequently, its role in Honduran society was reduced.

See also **Anticlericalism; Soto, Marco Aurelio.**

BIBLIOGRAPHY

Ernesto Fiallos, *Bosquejo biográfico del exmo. y. rmo. mons. Dr. Fray Juan de Jesús Zepeda y Zepeda* (1938).

José María Tojeira, *Panorama histórico de la iglesia en Honduras* (1986), pp. 138–152.

Additional Bibliography

Carías, Marcos. *La Iglesia Católica en Honduras, 1492–1975.* Tegucigalpa, Honduras: Editorial Guaymuras, 1991.

Flores Andino, Francisco A. *Presencia histórica franciscana en Honduras del siglo XVI al siglo XX.* Honduras: F.A. Flores Andino, 1992.

Sierra Fonseca, Rolando. *Iglesia y liberalismo en Honduras en el siglo XIX.* Tegucigalpa, Honduras: Centro de Publicaciones Obispado Choluteca, 1993.

EDWARD T. BRETT

ZIMMERMANN TELEGRAM.

In January 1917, as World War I remained stalemated, Germany decided to resume unrestricted submarine warfare, an action likely to cause the United States to enter the war on the side of the Allies. Seeking a means of immobilizing the United States, Germany seized on the U.S. preoccupation with Mexico.

Accordingly, German Foreign Minister Arthur Zimmermann sent the German minister to Mexico, Heinrich von Eckhardt, a wire for President Venustiano Carranza proposing that Mexico form an alliance with Germany against the United States, promising German support for Mexico to "reconquer the lost provinces of Texas, New Mexico, and Arizona," and that Japan be approached to join the alliance. The telegram was intercepted by British intelligence. Publication of the message in March caused outrage in the United States, helping to turn public opinion toward a declaration of war against Germany, which was issued 6 April 1917.

The furor regarding the German proposal obscured the fact that the Mexican Revolutionary Government rejected the idea. The event ultimately served to calm Mexican-American relations, as the United States shifted its focus toward Europe.

See also **Carranza, Venustiano; World War I.**

BIBLIOGRAPHY

Barbara W. Tuchman, *The Zimmerman Telegram* (1958).

P. Edward Haley, *Revolution and Intervention: The Diplomacy of Taft and Wilson with Mexico, 1910–1917* (1970).

Additional Bibliography

Katz, Friedrich. *The Secret War in Mexico: Europe, the United States, and the Mexican Revolution.* Chicago: University of Chicago Press, 1981.

Suárez Argüello, Ana Rosa. *Pragmatismo y principios: La relación conflictiva entre México y Estados Unidos, 1810–1942.* Mexico City: Instituto Mora, 1998.

KENNETH J. GRIEB

ZINNY, ANTONIO (1821–1890). The
historian, writer, and journalist Antonio Zinny, born in Gibraltar in 1821, came to Buenos Aires in 1842 and became a naturalized Argentine citizen. His principal works are of great importance to South American historiography: *Historia de los gobernadores de las provincias argentinas* (1879), *Índice de la Gaceta de Buenos Aires, desde 1810 a 1821* (1875), *Bibliografía histórica del Paraguay y Misiones* (1887), *La Gaceta Mercantil de Buenos Aires 1823–1852: Resumen de su contenido* (published posthumously in 1912), and the biographies of important Argentine politicians including Domingo Faustino Sarmiento (1811–1888), Juan Martín de Pueyrredón (1776–1850), and Ignacio Álvarez Thomas (1787–1857).

Zinny was dedicated to public education and was one of the founders of the Colegio Argentino, in the province of Corrientes. He also contributed to important national newspapers of the period, such as *La Tribuna* and *La Nación*. As a historian he carried out important research work, including the cataloging and synthesis of the dailies, *La Gaceta de Buenos Aires* (1810–1821) and *La Gaceta Mercantil* (1823–1852). On the political journalism of the Río de la Plata area in the postcolonial years, he also published *Efemeridografía argirometropolitana hasta la caída del gobierno de Rosas* (1869) and *Historia de la prensa periódica de la República Oriental del Uruguay, 1807–1852* (1883). Zinny died in Buenos Aires in 1890.

See also **Argentina: The Nineteenth Century; Pueyrredón, Juan Martín de; Sarmiento, Domingo Faustino.**

BIBLIOGRAPHY

Benítez, José Antonio. *Los Orígenes del Periodismo en Nuestra América.* Buenos Aires: Lumen, 2000.

Zinny, Antonio. *La Gaceta Mercantil de Buenos Aires, 1823–1852: Resumen de su contenido con relación á la parte americana y con especialidad á la historia de la República Argentina,* 3 vols. Buenos Aires, 1912.

Zinny, Antonio. *Estudios biográficos.* Buenos Aires: Hachette, 1958.

VICENTE PALERMO

ZIPA. *See* **Muisca.**

ZIPAQUIRÁ, CAPITULATIONS OF.
The high-water mark of the Comunero Revolt of New Granada was the gathering in May 1781 of a Comunero army, traditionally said to number 20,000 at Zipaquirá, about 30 miles from Bogotá. The authorities remaining in the capital, in the absence of the viceroy, who was at Cartagena, commissioned Archbishop Antonio Caballero y Góngora to negotiate, hoping above all that the revolutionary army could be prevented from entering the city. With regular forces concentrated on the coast, the archbishop felt compelled to grant most of the Comuneros' demands, including repeal of the new taxes that had triggered the uprising and reduction of others. Among the political concessions was the granting of preference to creoles over peninsular Spaniards in appointments to public office. These "capitulations" were ratified on 8 June by the *junta superior de tribunales* in Bogotá, whereupon the Comunero forces began to disperse. However, once the viceroy heard of the agreement, he formally repudiated it.

See also **Comunero Revolt (New Granada).**

BIBLIOGRAPHY

John Leddy Phelan, *The People and the King: The Comunero Revolution in Colombia, 1781* (1978), chaps. 12–14.

Mario Aguilera Peña, *Los comuneros: Guerra social y lucha anticolonial* (1985).

Additional Bibliography

Aguilera Peña, Mario. *La rebelión de los comuneros.* Bogotá: Editorial Panamericana, 1998.

Arciniegas, Germán. *Los comuneros.* Caracas: Biblioteca Ayacucho, 2002.

Caballero, Enrique and Alfredo Iriarte. *Incensio y pólvora: comuneros y procursores.* Bogotá: Amazonas Editores, 1993.

DAVID BUSHNELL

ZIPOLI, DOMENICO (1688–1726).
Domenico Zipoli (*b.* 16 or 17 October 1688; *d.* 2 January 1726), Italian organist and composer. Born in Prato, Tuscany, Zipoli commenced musical studies early. At the age of twenty-one, he moved to Naples to study with Alessandro Scarlatti. Later teachers included Lavinio Felice Vannucci and Bernardo Pasquini. Zipoli became choirmaster and

organist of the Church of the Jesuits in Rome in 1715. He joined the Society of Jesus in 1716, and the following year traveled to Argentina, where he became choirmaster and organist in the Cathedral of Córdoba. His fame as a composer was established in 1716 with the publication of the *Sonate d'intavolatura,* a collection of keyboard music, the first part for organ and the second for harpsichord. Not much survives of the music he composed while in Argentina, and for many years his contribution to Argentine music was primarily thought to consist of his having brought to it music in the style of Scarlatti and Pasquini. But in 1959, in the Sucre Cathedral archives, a copy made at Potosí in 1784 of one of his masses was discovered. In 1966, the compositions *Tantum Ergo* and *Letania* were found in Beni, Bolivia, by Samuel Claro Valdés. While remembered particularly for his harpsichord works, Zipoli composed sonatas and toccatas for various instruments. He died in Córdoba.

See also **Music: Art Music.**

BIBLIOGRAPHY

Nicolas Slonimsky, *Music of Latin America* (1945).

Francisco Curt Lange, "La música eclesiástica argentina en el período de la dominación hispánica," in *Revista de estudios musicales* 3 (December 1954).

Samuel Claro Valdés, "La música de las misiones jesuitas de Moxos," in *Revista musical chilena* 108 (July–September 1969).

J. P. Franze, "La obra completa para Órgano de Domenico Zipoli," in *Buenos Aires musical* 29, no. 46 (July 1974).

Samuel Claro Valdés, *Oyendo a Chile* (1978).

Gérard Béhague, *Music in Latin America: An Introduction* (1979).

Additional Bibliography

Szarán, Luis. *Domenico Zipoli: Una vida, un enigma.* Asunción: Fundación Paracuaria, 2005.

Zambrano, Jorge. *Una Semblanza de Domenico Zipoli.* Córdoba: Dirección General de Publicaciones, Universidad Nacional de Córdoba, 1996.

SERGIO BARROSO

ZORITA, ALONSO DE (1511–c. 1585).
Alonso de Zorita (Zurita; *b.* 1511/12; *d.* ca. 1585), judge of the Audiencia of Mexico (1556–1564). Zorita held various legal posts in the Caribbean

and South America before reaching New Spain and, after ten years there, returned to Spain. Zorita's early career experiences in the fringe areas influenced the direction he took in Mexico attacking the *encomienda* system and promoting the role of the regular clergy, particularly the Franciscans, in dealings with the indigenous peoples.

Zorita left writings on New Spain's indigenous cultures, Nahua government and tribute systems, the Spanish invasion and post-Conquest Christianization efforts, published partly in his *Breve y sumaria relación de los señores de la Nueva España.* Although portions of his writings are based on earlier (now lost) sources, making them especially valuable, controversy nevertheless exists regarding some of his interpretations of the meaning of terms such as *mayeque* and *calpulli* and his remarks about Nahua nobility and municipal officers.

See also **Audiencia; New Spain, Viceroyalty of.**

BIBLIOGRAPHY

The most recent biography is Ralph H. Vigil, *Alonso de Zorita: Royal Judge and Christian Humanist, 1512–1585* (1987). Skepticism about the reliability of some of Zorita's information comes out, for example, in James Lockhart, *The Nahuas After the Conquest* (1992), pp. 97, 111, 112, 506, 508.

Additional Bibliography

Frost, Elsa Cecilia. "Fray Andrés de Olmos en la *Relación* de Alonso de Zorita." *Revista de Indias* 51, no. 191 (Jan.–Apr. 1991): 169–178.

STEPHANIE WOOD

ZORRILLA DE SAN MARTÍN, JUAN
(1855–1931). Juan Zorrilla de San Martín (*b.* 28 December 1855; *d.* 3 November 1931), Uruguayan statesman and poet. Zorrilla de San Martín received his early education in Jesuit schools in Montevideo and in Santa Fe, Argentina. He received his law degree in 1877 from the university in Santiago de Chile. Returning to Montevideo in 1878, he took a position in the federal courts. In 1880, Zorrilla was appointed professor of aesthetics at the National University in Montevideo.

Zorrilla is best known as the author of the epic poem *Tabaré* (1888), an homage to the Charrúa Indians and an exaltation of the fusion of Hispanic and indigenous races. The post-romantic verses of *Tabaré* recite the story of Uruguay—its people, its civilization, its spirit, and its aspirations. A dynamic orator, Zorrilla was also one of the most revered public figures in Uruguay: a defender of his country's democratic institutions and the voice of Uruguay in its art and music, its heritage and traditions.

In 1878, Zorrilla founded *El bien público,* a Catholic periodical. In 1885, his opposition to President Máximo Santos forced him to resign his position as professor of aesthetics at the National University and take refuge in Argentina, where he joined other Uruguayans in unsuccessful efforts to overthrow Santos.

Zorrilla was elected to Congress by the National Party in 1886. In 1892 he went to Madrid as Uruguayan representative to celebrate the four-hundredth anniversary of Columbus's arrival in the New World, and in 1894 served as Uruguayan ambassador in Paris. In 1899, Zorrilla edited *El Bien,* the new name of the journal he had founded. In recognition of his many years of public service, the National University in 1899 conferred on Zorrilla the title of professor of international law.

Zorrilla's political views apparently clashed with the policies of the liberal government of José Batlle y Ordóñez during the years 1903–1904. Despite this opposition, Zorrilla was appointed treasurer of the Bank of the Republic and was reelected as a government delegate every three years thereafter until his death.

See also **Banking: Overview; Literature: Spanish America.**

BIBLIOGRAPHY

Rimaelvo A. Ardoino, *La prosa de Juan Zorrilla de San Martín* (1945).

Enrique Anderson Imbert, "La originalidad de Zorrilla de San Martín," in *Los grandes libros de Occidente y otros ensayos* (1957), pp. 121–163.

Domingo L. Bordoli, *Vida de Juan Zorrilla de San Martín* (1961).

Carlos A. Solé and Maria Isabel Abreu, *Latin American Writers,* vol. 1 (1989), pp. 327–331.

Additional Bibliography

Pickenhayn, Jorge Oscar. *El amplio mundo de Juan Zorrilla de San Martín: sus aportes en materia literaria (verso y prosa), filosófica, teatral, historiográfica, pictórica y musicológica.* Montevideo, Uruguay: Barreiro y Ramos Editores, 1992.

Zuccherino, Ricardo Miguel. *La tempestad y la quietud: historia de la relación entre Miguel de Unamuno y Juan Zorrilla de San Martín.* La Plata, Argentina: Fondo Editorial "Esto es Historia," 2002.

MYRON I. LICHTBLAU

ZUBIRÁN ANCHONDO, SALVADOR

(1898–1998). Salvador Zubirán Anchondo was a Mexican physician, educator, and nutritional expert. Born on December 23, 1898, as a 1923 graduate of the National University, Zubirán was one of an important generation of medical students. A disciple of Gastón Melo, he continued his medical studies at Harvard University, and in 1925 joined the medical faculty at the National University, where he taught for many years. He served as first head of the Child Welfare Department (1937), before becoming assistant secretary of health (1938–1943). Appointed rector of the National University in 1946, he resigned in 1948 after a violent student protest. Following his resignation, he directed programs in nutrition, and his efforts contributed substantially to Mexican knowledge in this field. He served as president of the Mexican Academy of Medicine (1947), and received Mexico's National Prize in Sciences (1968) and the Belisario Domínguez Medal of Honor (1986). He died on June 10, 1998.

See also **Medicine: The Modern Era.**

BIBLIOGRAPHY

Doctor Salvador Zubirán, 50 años de vida profesional (1973).

Additional Bibliography

Instituto Nacional de la Nutrición. *Salvador Zubirán: 1898–1998.* 7 vols. Mexico: Fundación Mexicana para la Salud, 1998.

Zubirán, Salvador. *Mi vida y mi lucha: Autobiografía.* Mexico: Fundación Mexicana para la Salud, 1996.

RODERIC AI CAMP

ZUBIRÍA, JOSÉ ANTONIO LAUREANO DE (c. 1780–1845). José Antonio Laureano de Zubiría (*b.* ca. 1780; *d.* after 1845), bishop of Durango, Mexico. Zubiría's pronouncements outlined the canonical justification for bringing the new Mexican church back under Episcopal

control and curbing aspects of folk piety that Catholic orthodoxy deemed harmful. Although Zubiría could not enforce his decrees, he laid the foundation for the reforms instituted by the first bishops of Santa Fe under American control.

Many of the criticisms that Zubiría leveled against the churches and Franciscan missions in New Mexico reflected the innovations and improvisations that New Mexicans had adopted since the 1760s, when the Spanish province found itself virtually isolated from the rest of Mexico by Comanche, Apache, and Ute raids. Symbolic of his view of New Mexican religious devotion, Zubiría criticized the crude pictures of the saints that some Franciscan missionaries had painted on animal hides because they had little access to religious art imported from Mexico. The combination of Episcopal disapproval and the rise of an indigenous style of Santos carved from pine wood and decorated with brightly colored tempera on a coat of gesso led to the loss of most hide paintings from the missions during the Mexican period. Zubiría described even the new devotional art as "ugly images."

Zubiría's denunciation of the Brotherhood of Penitentes during the 1833 visitation is one of the few descriptions of the confraternity during its formative period. He mentioned that the organization had existed "for a good number of years, but without any authorization or even the knowledge of the bishops." He ordered the clergy in New Mexico to forbid Penitente meetings and ritual, because of "the excesses of very indiscreet corporal punishment which they are accustomed to practice...even publicly."

Zubiría's condemnation of the Penitentes had little effect. The church failed in its attempt to exert control over the brotherhood until the reforms of 1851–1852 promulgated by Bishop Jean Baptiste Lamy, first bishop of Santa Fe under the jurisdiction of the United States.

See also **Missions: Spanish America; Penitentes.**

BIBLIOGRAPHY

Elizabeth Boyd, *Popular Arts of Colonial New Mexico* (1974).

Frances Leon Swadesh, *Los Primeros Pobladores: Hispanic Americans of the Ute Frontier* (1974).

Marc Simmons, *New Mexico: An Interpretive History* (1977).

David J. Weber, *The Mexican Frontier, 1821–1846: The American Southwest under Mexico* (1982).

Thomas J. Steele, S.J., and Rowena A. Rivera, *Penitente Self-Government: Brotherhoods and Councils, 1797–1947* (1985).

Additional Bibliography

Defouri, James H., and Thomas J. Steele. *Historical Sketch of the Catholic Church in New Mexico.* Las Cruces, NM: Yucca Tree Press, 2003.

Kessell, John L., and Rick Hendricks. *The Spanish Missions of New Mexico.* New York: Garland, 1991.

ROSS H. FRANK

ZUBIZARRETA, GERÓNIMO (1880–1952).

Gerónimo Zubizarreta (*b.* 9 October 1880; *d.* 14 May 1952), Paraguayan politician and university professor. Zubizarreta studied and later taught law at the National University in Asunción. After joining the Liberal Party in 1909, he occupied various positions in the party as well as in the Paraguayan Congress. Zubizarreta was highly respected for defending Paraguay's legal position before the Chaco War erupted between Paraguay and Bolivia in 1932. In 1937 he headed the Paraguayan delegation at the Buenos Aires Peace Conference but resigned in 1938 after losing in a power struggle with Paraguay's leader of the armed forces, General José Félix Estigarribia. He was elected president of the Liberal Party in 1946, but he was forced into exile the following year after his arrest under President Higínio Morínigo's regime. He returned to Paraguay in 1951 and remained president of his party until his death.

See also **Paraguay, Political Parties: Liberal Party.**

BIBLIOGRAPHY

Julio Cesar Chaves, "Géronimo Zubizarreta," in *Cien vida paraguayas* (1961), edited by Carlos Zubizarreta.

Leslie Rout, *Politics of the Chaco Peace Conference, 1935–39* (1970).

Additional Bibliography

Farcau, Bruce W. *The Chaco War: Bolivia and Paraguay, 1932–1935.* Westport, CT: Praeger, 1996.

Lewis, Paul H. *Political Parties and Generations in Paraguay's Liberal Era, 1869–1940.* Chapel Hill: University of North Carolina Press, 1993.

Lorini, Irma. *El nacionalismo en Bolivia de la pre y posguerra del Chaco (1910–1945)*. La Paz, Bolivia: Plural Editores, 2006.

MIGUEL A. GATTI

ZULEN, PEDRO S., AND DORA MAYER DE ZULEN.

Pedro S. Zulen (*b.* 1889; *d.* 1925) and Dora Mayer de Zulen (*b.* 1868; *d.* 1957), Peruvian intellectuals and leaders of the *indigenismo* movement. *Indigenismo* has been one of the most controversial aspects of social reform in modern Peru. Alive since the 1880s in the essays of writers like Ricardo Palma, Clorinda Matto De Turner, and Manuel González Prada, the movement rests on the idea that the culture of the indigenous Andean population is at the core of the country's culture and should receive its due recognition. Several strategies were developed in the early twentieth century to make this idea a reality. Some of the proponents of *indigenismo* worked directly in the highland center of Cuzco, where under the leadership of men like archaeologist Luis E. Valcárcel, the movement became intertwined with the drive to end the abuse of villagers at the hands of landlords. In Lima early-twentieth-century intellectuals, under the leadership of Pedro Zulen and Dora Mayer, sought to unify urban, sophisticated culture with their Andean roots. To do this they founded the Pro-Indigenous Association in 1909. In a weekly newsletter, *El Deber Pro-Indígena,* they fought for legal relief of Andean misery. Senator Joaquín Capelo and José Antonio Encinas later joined their legal struggle. Soon delegates of the Pro-Indigenous Association throughout the country began reporting in the press and in the association newsletter injustices committed against indigenous people. The association recruited lawyers to defend villagers, and to arouse public opinion it sponsored public debates. The Zulens hoped thus to prod the legislature into passing remedial legislation. After 1919 the government of President Augusto Leguía undermined the effectiveness of the association by absorbing its more important efforts into government programs. Laws, decrees, and resolutions reflecting the influence of the *indigenistas* were passed, but Leguía did not try to enforce them against the opposition of major highland landowners. Many highland villagers thereafter became more aware of their legal rights, and by the mid-1920s the *indigenista* movement had been absorbed into the revolutionary and reformist political movements taking shape in Peru.

See also Indigenismo; Indigenous Peoples; Leguía Augusto Bernardino.

BIBLIOGRAPHY

Eugenio Chang Rodríguez, *La literatura política de González Prada, Mariátegui, y Haya de la Torre* (1957).

Thomas M. Davies, Jr., *Indian Integration in Peru: A Half Century of Experience, 1900–1948* (1974).

José Tamayo Herrera, *Historia del indigenismo cuzqueño: Siglos xvi–xx* (1980).

Additional Bibliography

Castro Carpio, Augusto. *Filosofía y sociedad en el Perú*. Lima, Perú: Pontificia Universidad Católica del Perú, 2003.

Veres, Luis. *Periodismo y literatura de vanguardia en América Latina: el caso peruano*. Moncada, Valencia, Spain: Ajuntament de Valencia, 2003.

VINCENT PELOSO

ZULOAGA, FÉLIX MARÍA (1813–1898).

Félix María Zuloaga (*b.* 1813; *d.* 1898), Mexican military officer and president of Mexico (January 1858–January 1859). Born in Álamos, Sonora, Zuloaga was raised in Chihuahua. He studied for a time in Mexico City but returned to the north, where he began a military career by joining the civic militia of Chihuahua in 1834 and fighting the Apaches and Comanches. He then returned to Mexico City, where he passed the engineering exam in 1838 and received a commission as second lieutenant in an engineering battalion of the regular army. He fought against the separatists in Yucatán, and was raised to the rank of lieutenant colonel in 1841. During the war with the United States, Zuloaga directed the fortifications at Monterrey in 1846 and fought in defense of Mexico City in 1847. After the war he returned to Chihuahua, where he held posts in the city government before returning to the army in 1851. He served as president of the Council of War of the Plaza of Mexico under President Santa Anna in 1853. Zuloaga fought against the Revolution of Ayutla in 1854 and was raised to the rank of brigadier general before being taken prisoner by the liberals.

After President Ignacio Comonfort reintegrated him into the army, Zuloaga fought against a conservative rebellion in Puebla before supporting the Plan of Tacubaya in December 1857. The Plan of Tacubaya backed President Comonfort in the struggle between *puros* and *moderados,* and called for a new congress to write a new constitution "more in harmony with the will of the Nation." At first Comonfort supported the plan; then he organized against it and was deposed by General José de la Parra in January 1858. Benito Juárez, head of the supreme court and next in legal succession to the presidency, assumed that office with the support of the liberals. Zuloaga, however, was elected president by the conservative Council of Representatives of the Departments (22 January 1853). This political clash began the War of the Reform. By presidential decree, Zuloaga annulled the Ley Iglesias, the Ley Juárez, and the Ley Lerdo, and reinstated all government employees who had lost their jobs for failing to swear allegiance to the Constitution of 1857. For his part in the execution of Melchor Ocampo, Zuloaga was declared an outlaw by the liberals. He spent the years of the French Intervention in Cuba but returned to Mexico before his death.

See also **Comonfort, Ignacio; Ocampo, Melchor.**

BIBLIOGRAPHY

Walter V. Scholes, *Mexican Politics During the Juárez Regime, 1855–1872* (1957), pp. 23, 28–29; *Diccionario Porrúa de historia, biografía y geografía de México,* 5th ed. (1986).

Additional Bibliography

Fowler, Wil. *Mexico in the Age of Proposals, 1821–1853.* Westport, CT: Greenwood Press, 1998.

Rodríguez O, Jaime E. *The Divine Charter: Constitutionalism and Liberalism in Nineteenth-century Mexico.* Lanham, MD: Rowman & Littlefield, 2005.

Villegas Revueltas, Silvestre. *El liberalismo moderado en México, 1852–1864.* Mexico City: Universidad Nacional Autónoma de México, 1997.

D. F. STEVENS

ZUMÁRRAGA, JUAN DE (c. 1468–1548). Juan de Zumárraga (*b.* ca. 1468; *d.* 3 June 1548), first bishop (1528–1547) and archbishop (1547–1548) of Mexico. Fray Juan de Zumárraga was born in Durango, near Bilbao, Spain; his birthdate is unknown but he was said to have been over eighty at death. Impressed by Zumárraga's campaign against alleged Basque witches, Charles V appointed him bishop of Mexico City. Zumárraga arrived in Mexico in 1528 as bishop-elect and Protector of the Indians. Zumárraga went to Spain in 1532 to report to the emperor; he was consecrated as bishop there in 1534. In 1535 Zumárraga joined forces with Don Antonio de Mendoza, newly arrived first viceroy, to stabilize colonial rule and promote Indian education and Christianization. In 1536 they founded the Colegio de Santa Cruz, a Franciscan college for indigenous nobles. Zumárraga imported a printing press in 1536 and authored or sponsored a number of imprints, including Erasmian tracts. Zumárraga's thinking, typical of Spanish Franciscans, combined Renaissance humanism with mysticism and militant religious zeal. He conducted inquisitorial proceedings against Indians suspected of religious violations; the trials culminated with the 1539 burning at the stake of Don Carlos Mendoza Ometochtzin, native ruler of Texcoco. In 1547 Zumárraga was named archbishop of a new archdiocese comprising the bishoprics of México, Oaxaca, Michoacán, Tlaxcala, Guatemala, and Chiapas; he died soon after receiving the news.

See also **Catholic Church: The Colonial Period.**

BIBLIOGRAPHY

Joaquín García Icazbalceta, *Don Fray Juan de Zumárraga: Primer Obispo y Arzobispo de México* (1947).

Richard E. Greenleaf, *Zumárraga and the Mexican Inquisition, 1536–1543* (1962).

Robert Ricard, *The Spiritual Conquest of Mexico* (1966).

Additional Bibliography

Alejos-Grau, Carmen José. *Juan de Zumárraga y su regla cristiana breve (México 1547): autoría, fuentes y principales tesis teológicas.* Pamplona: Servicio de Publicaciones de la Universidad de Navarra, 1991.

Elizondo, Virgilio P. *Guadalupe, Mother of the New Creation.* Maryknoll, NY: Orbis Books, 1997.

Gutiérrez Zamora, Angel Camiro. *El origen del guadalupanism: Fue Montúfar, y no Zumárraga, el padre de la devoción a la Virgen de Guadalupe.* Mexico City: EDAMEX, 1996.

LOUISE M. BURKHART

ZUMAYA, MANUEL DE (c. 1678–1756).

Manuel de Zumaya (*b.* ca. 1678; *d.* between 12 March and 6 May 1756), Mexican composer and the first Mexican-born chapelmaster of the cathedral of Mexico City. Zumaya was a choirboy at the cathedral and became a pupil of the chapelmaster, the composer and organist Antonio Salazar. At sixteen he began lessons with the principal organist, José de Ydíaquez. Zumaya was ordained a priest in 1700 and a few years later was appointed one of three organists of the cathedral and polyphony teacher of the choirboys; he served as assistant to and substitute for Salazar. At Salazar's death in 1715, Zumaya was designated his successor as cathedral chapelmaster. To celebrate his twenty-four years at the cathedral, a new great organ was installed, considered the best of its kind in the Americas; its inauguration (15 August 1735) was commemorated with lavish festivities.

As a church composer Zumaya followed the traditional Spanish religious music style, but in some of his *villancicos* and in all his stage works he was strongly influenced by Italian opera. The music of the church at that time was not only for organ; strings and wind instruments accompanied the choirs with embellished melodic lines, strongly resembling operatic arias. In 1708 Zumaya had composed the music for *Don Rodrigo* [*El Rodrigo*], a play performed at the viceroyal palace; the manuscript, however, has been lost. The duke of Linares, the viceroy, made possible the performance of Zumaya's opera *La parténope* at the palace in May 1711. After Tomás de Torrejón y Velasco's *La púrpura de la rosa,* this opera was the second premiered in the New World and the first written by an American-born composer. In 1739 Zumaya moved to Oaxaca, where he became chapelmaster in 1745. He remained in that position until his death in Oaxaca.

See also **Music: Art Music.**

BIBLIOGRAPHY

Robert Stevenson, *Music in Mexico* (1952), and "Mexico City Cathedral Music, 1600–1750," *The Americas* 21 (1964): 130; *New Grove Dictionary of Music and Musicians,* vol. 20 (1980).

Additional Bibliography

Dean, Michael Noel. *Renaissance and Baroque Characteristics in Four Choral Villancicos of Manuel de Sumaya: Analysis and Performance Editions.* Ph.D. diss. Texas Tech University, 2002.

SUSANA SALGADO

ZUMBI (1655?–1695).

Zumbi (*b.* 1655?; *d.* 20 November 1695), organizer and leader of the free black republic (*quilombo*) of Palmares, in Alagoas state, northeastern Brazil. Little information is available concerning the early life of Zumbi and that which is known is subject to speculation. In 1685 he murdered his uncle Ganga Zumba, who had attempted to live in peace with the Portuguese, and proclaimed himself king of Palmares. He was responsible for the strengthening of a series of fortifications that made Palmares almost invincible to attackers. Zumbi's leadership proved effective in defeating a Portuguese expedition against the *quilombo* in 1686. When the forces of the *bandeirante* Domingos Jorge Velho attacked Palmares in 1691, Zumbi's ambushes and counterattacks devastated them. In 1692 attempts were initiated to surround the *quilombo,* but Zumbi's forces were able to hold out until 1694, when a Luso-Brazilian expedition backed by artillery and reinforcements was finally able to destroy Palmares. Zumbi was decapitated and his head displayed in public in order to prevent any further legends of his immortality, but tradition grew about a heroic suicide in which he threw himself off a cliff rather than surrender and submit to enslavement. The actions of Zumbi forced the Portuguese to change their military strategy with regard to Maroon communities; henceforth, special military units were given the task of finding and destroying potentially dangerous fugitive Maroon settlements. Zumbi is considered an African Brazilian hero; his date of death is commemorated each year.

See also **Maroons (Cimarrones); Palmares.**

BIBLIOGRAPHY

R. K. Kent, "Palmares: An African State in Brazil," in *Journal of African History* 6 (1965): 161–175.

Leda Maria De Albuquerque, *Zumbi dos Palmares* (1978).

Additional Bibliography

Gomes, Flávio dos Santos. *Palmares: Escravidão e liberdade no Atlântico Sul.* São Paulo: Contexto, 2005.

Lins, Audemário. *Zumbi: o rebelde herói negro.* Maceió: Edições Catavento, 2001.

MICHAEL L. JAMES

ZUM FELDE, ALBERTO (1889–1976).

Alberto Zum Felde (*b.* 1889; *d.* 1976), Uruguayan poet, literary critic, and essayist. Alberto Zum Felde was born in Bahía Blanca, Argentina, but his parents moved to Uruguay when he was a young child. He joined the intellectual circle headed by Roberto de las Carreras. His poetry was first published under a pseudonym in *La Razón* and *El Siglo*. In 1908 Zum Felde selected the name Aurelio del Hebrón as his pseudonym and his first book, *Domus aurea* (1908), a collection of sonnets and plays, was published under that name. These modernist sonnets and plays reflect both his talent and the influence that Nietzsche and Ibsen had on his writings.

With the publication of *El huanakauri* (1917), Zum Felde began to distance himself from modernist influences. The book, a didactic poem, argues for the autonomous cultural development of the Americas based upon tradition and historical reality. From 1919 until 1929, he worked as a literary critic for the afternoon edition of the newspaper *El Día* (later called *El Ideal*). He served as secretary, assistant director, and director (1940–1944) of the National Library. During the 1920s he also directed the literary magazine *La Pluma*. One of his notable books, *Proceso histórico del Uruguay* (1919) analyzes the sociopolitical evolution of the country. *Crítica de la literatura uruguaya* (1921) is a collection of weekly articles that were published in 1919–1920 in *El Día*. One of his most important books, *Proceso intelectual del Uruguay y crítica de su literatura* (1930), evaluates intellectual and literary production in the country beginning with the colonial period.

Zum Felde has been credited with the professionalization of literary studies in Uruguay. After his conversion to Catholicism, he published *Cristo y nosotros* (1959) and *Diálogo Cristo-Marx* (1971). Zum Felde was one of nine writers who founded the National Academy of Letters in 1943. In 1957 he won the National Literature Prize, and in 1968 he was awarded Uruguay's Grand Prize for Literature.

See also **Catholic Church: The Modern Period; Literature: Spanish America.**

BIBLIOGRAPHY

Francisco Aguilera and Georgette M. Dorn, *The Archive of Hispanic Literature on Tape* (1974), pp. 511–512.

Uruguay Cortazzo, *La hermeneutica de Alberto Zum Felde* (1983).

Additional Bibliography

Michelena, Alejandro Daniel. "Zum Felde, iniciador múltiple." *Hoy Es Historia* 10, no. 55 (January–February 1993): 14–20.

DANUSIA L. MESON

ZÚÑIGA, IGNACIO (?–?).

Ignacio Zúñiga, nineteenth-century frontier military officer and politician. Zúñiga rose in the colonial army to command a series of presidio garrisons on Mexico's northwestern frontier, beginning with that of Tucson in 1809. As senator and then deputy in the national congress in the late 1820s, he unsuccessfully opposed the division of the state of Occidente into Sonora and Sinaloa. His 1835 treatise (*Rápida ojeada*...) detailed the problems of Sonora and proposed measures to alleviate public insecurities and promote enterprise. He supported the federalist revolts of José de Urrea in 1837 and Santa Anna in 1841, and served as a federal deputy in 1842.

See also **Sonora; Urrea, José de.**

BIBLIOGRAPHY

Ignacio Zúñiga, *Rápida ojeada al Estado de Sonora, territorios de California y Arizona, 1835* (1835; repr. 1948).

Stuart F. Voss, *On the Periphery of Nineteenth Century Mexico: Sonora and Sinaloa, 1810–1877* (1982), pp. 87–91, 102–103.

Francisco R. Almada, *Diccionario de historia, geografía y biografía sonorenses* (1983), p. 746.

Additional Bibliography

Tinker Salas, Miguel. *In the Shadow of the Eagles: Sonora and the Transformation of the Border During the Porfiriato.* Berkeley: University of California Press, 1997.

STUART F. VOSS

ZÚÑIGA FIGUEROA, CARLOS (1884–1964).

Carlos Zúñiga Figueroa (*b.* 1884; *d.* 1964), Honduran neorealist painter. Zúñiga studied during the 1920s at the San Fernando Academy in Madrid, where he received wide acclaim. He returned to Honduras to become one of Central America's leading painters in the following decades. His work was exhibited widely in Central America and the United States. He specialized in realistic portraits of ordinary people, but he also painted many contemporary Honduran leaders of society and politics. His series of historical paintings of Honduras's independence leaders, especially his *Glorification of General Morazán,* received favorable recognition. Toward the end of his life he began to focus his work on those at the bottom of the society—vagabonds, beggars, the mentally ill, and the poor. Unfortunately, a great many of these paintings were destroyed in a 1959 fire.

See also **Art: The Twentieth Century.**

BIBLIOGRAPHY

J. Evaristo López and Longino Becerra, *Honduras: 40 pintores* (1989).

RALPH LEE WOODWARD JR.

ZUTUHIL. *See* **Tz'utujil.**

CHRONOLOGY

DATE	EVENT
c. 20000 BCE	Evidence emerges of human existence in the Americas, resulting from two waves of migration across the Bering strait.
c. 10500 BCE	The first settlement of people in the Americas emerges around Monte Verde in southern Chile.
c. 9000 BCE	Evidence of several human settlements in Latin America.
c. 8000 BCE	"Tepexpan Man" (who was a woman) is thought to have lived. The remains were unearthed in the 1940s in Tepexpan, just north of Mexico City, marking the earliest human remains discovered in Latin America.
c. 7500–7000 BCE	Climactic changes lead to drier conditions and many large animals become extinct. Experimentation with agriculture begins.
c. 5000 BCE	Primitive farmers practice rudimentary agriculture in Tehuacán, in the modern state of Puebla, Mexico.
c. 4000 BCE	Agriculture settlements develop in the Amazon region.
c. 3500 BCE	Llamas are domesticated in Peru.
c. 3000 BCE	Cotton is used for cloth.
c. 2000 BCE	Maize emerges as the staple of human sustenance in the region.
c. 2000–400 BCE	The Olmec civilization in Mexico develops hieroglyphic writing and calendars.
c. 1800 BCE	The first settlements of the Classic Maya civilization take root.
c. 1400–400 BCE	Chavín culture develops in South America.
c. 1150 BCE	The Olmec center of San Lorenzo, Veracruz (Mexico), flourishes as an urban center with public buildings and drainage systems.
c. 900 BCE	La Venta surpasses San Lorenzo as the epicenter of Olmec activity.
c. 900–500 BCE	The Chavín culture in central Peru dominates the Andean region.
c. 400 BCE	Olmec civilization declines.
c. 200 BCE	Teotihuacán emerges as the most vibrant culture in the Valley of Mexico.
c. 200 BCE–c. 700 CE	The Nazca lines are created in the Peruvian desert.
c. 100–900 CE	Huari, Moche, and Tiwanaku cultures develop in the Andes.
292	The Mayan metropolis Tikal is settled. Its population eventually grows to about fifty thousand. Tikal features six enormous pyramids, with the largest rising more than 230 feet.
c. 500–800	The Classic Maya civilization declines, marked by internal upheaval, warfare, and increased human sacrifice.
c. 600	Teotihuacán is burned and desecrated by its own inhabitants.

DATE	EVENT
c. 950	Toltec civilization emerges in Mexico.
c. 968	The Toltec capital of Tula is founded by Topiltzin-Quetzalcóatl. Tula serves as the most important city in the area between the fall of Teotihuacán and the rise of Tenochtitlán.
c. 987	Topiltzin-Quetzalcóatl and his followers depart from Cholula, sailing across the Gulf of Mexico to Mayan territory. Bearded and with a fair complexion, the deposed ruler speaks of returning from where the sun rose in the year of Ce Acatl (which recurred cyclically) to reclaim his throne.
c. 1000	Metallurgy is developed.
c. 1000–1250	The city of Chichén Itzá dominates the twilight of the Toltec civilization.
c. 1080–1156	Drought and famine ravages the Toltec civilization, leading to civil strife and warfare. The Toltec abandon Tula, spreading in various directions.
c. 1100–1474	The Chimu kingdom develops in northern Peru.
1111	Occupants of Aztlán leave their village to meander throughout the Valley of Mexico for over a century before coalescing around Chapultepec, forming what would become the Aztec Empire.
c. 1200	Manco Capac founds the Kingdom of Cuzco, marking the birth of the Inca civilization.
1325	Aztec settlers begin expanding the capacity of their small island, transforming it into Tenochtitlán.
1415–1460	Prince Henry the Navigator of Portugal encourages European exploration to find easier trade routes to Asia.
1438	Incan ruler Pachacuti begins a military expedition that would enlarge the realm of the Inca to include the whole of the Andes.
c. 1450	Natural disasters create famine, stunting Aztec growth.
1469	Isabella of Castille marries Ferdinand of Aragon, uniting the kingdoms of Spain.
1475–1476	The Inca conquer the Chimu after a decade of conflict.
1492	Christopher Columbus reaches the Caribbean islands. Though widely regarded as a pacific man, what he writes of his initial impressions is portentous: "They would make fine servants . . . with fifty men we could subjugate them all and make them do whatever we want."
	The Spanish Crown expels the Muslim Moors from Spain; the Reconquista heavily influences Spanish conquistadors.
1493	Columbus settles Hispaniola on his second voyage.
	The Crown establishes the encomienda system on Hispaniola.
1494	Portugal and Spain sign the Treaty of Tordesillas, divvying control of the discovered continent between the two European countries.
1496	The first Spanish city in the Americas, Santo Domingo, is founded on Hispaniola.
1498	Columbus reaches mainland South America on his third voyage.
	Portuguese explorer Vasco da Gama circumnavigates Africa en route to India.

DATE	EVENT
c. 1500–1532	Smallpox spreads into the Inca world. A civil war breaks out among the Inca. Atahualpa emerges victorious, though the Inca are weakened as a result of war and disease.
1500	Pedro Álvarez Cabral, a Portuguese navigator, lands on the coast of Brazil.
1502	The trans-Atlantic slave trade begins on a systematic basis, transporting Africans to the Americas.
	Motecuhzoma II begins his seventeen-year reign of the Aztec empire, marking the high point of Aztec civilization.
	Tenochtitlán has a population of between 150,000–200,000 people, making it one of the largest cities in the world.
1507	The first world map showing "America" is published.
1511	The first Spanish settlement is established in Cuba.
	The first audiencia in Spanish America is established on Hispaniola.
	Antonio de Montesinos, a Dominican friar who was part of the first wave of priests to visit the Americas, gives a sermon condemning the colonists treatment of indigenous populations.
	The Taino cacique (chief) Hatuey begins a guerrilla war against the Spanish on Hispaniola.
1512	Bartolomé de Las Casas arrives in the Americas.
	Prompted by Dominican entreaties, the Spanish Crown issues the Laws of Burgos, which seeks to regulate the encomienda system; the regulations are ignored.
1513	Juan Ponce de León claims Florida for Spain.
	Spanish explorer Vasco Núñez de Balboa views the Pacific Ocean from Panama.
	Balboa writes to King Ferdinand that in the settlement of Darien, on the Gulf of Urabá (Colombia), gold is more plentiful than food.
1517	Spanish forces under the command of Hernán Cortés arrive on the Yucatán Peninsula.
1519	Cortés encounters the Aztecs (during the year of Ce Acatl, which in Aztec lore was supposed to herald the return of Topiltzin-Quetzalcóatl). He capitalizes on the Aztecs' mistaken hospitality, building alliances with Aztec enemies and preparing for war.
	Charles I is crowned in Spain.
1520	Aztec ruler Motecuhzoma II dies in Spanish captivity.
	Portuguese explorer Ferdinand Magellan fails to establish a settlement near the Río de la Plata. He sails south, navigating the strait that bears his name.
1521	The Spanish destroy the Aztec empire, razing Tenochtitlán.
1524	Council of the Indies is formed to oversee Spanish colonies in the Americas.
	Twelve Franciscan friars arrive in Veracruz, Mexico, to begin the work of converting the indigenous people to Christianity.
1531	The Virgin of Guadalupe appears to an indigenous Mexican named Juan Diego outside of Mexico City.
1532	About 100 conquistadors under the charge of Francisco Pizarro encounter the Inca in Cajamarca. Despite being confronted by 6,000 Inca warriors Pizarro prevails and captures Atahualpa.

DATE	EVENT
1533	Pizarro kills Atahualpa.
	Pizarro invades Cuzco, the Inca capital.
1534	Pizarro's lieutenants defeat Atahualpa's remaining generals around Quito.
1535	Spanish authority is firmly established in New Spain (Mexico) with the creation of a viceroyalty.
	The first printing press in the Americas becomes operational in Mexico City.
	The Araucanian Indians successfully repel Spanish attempts to colonize Chile.
1536	Spanish settlement at Buenos Aires is attempted, but quickly abandoned because of the resistance of the indigenous population.
1537	In the papal bull SUBLIMUS DEUS Pope Paul III declares that indigenous Americans are human beings and have souls.
1537–1538	In the aftermath of Inca defeat Spanish loyalties fragment. Forces of the Pizarro family fight the clan of Diego de Almagro. They win, murdering Almagro.
1540–1542	Francisco Vasquez de Coronado discovers the Grand Canyon while exploring the area from the Gulf of California to Kansas.
1541	Spanish settlement of Chile begins; conquistador Pedro de Valdivia founds Santiago.
	Spanish conquistador Pedro de Mendoza establishes Asunción, in present-day Paraguay, the first permanent colony east of the Andes.
	Pizarro is assassinated by loyalists of Almagro.
	Francisco de Orellana navigates the Amazon River.
1542	Spain issues the "New Laws" to improve treatment of Indians.
	Las Casas is appointed Bishop of Chiapas. He urges improved treatment of Indians.
1545	Silver is discovered in Potosí (in what is now Bolivia).
1549	Tomé de Sousa founds the Brazilian capital at Salvador.
1550s–1560s	Spanish authority is consolidated in the Andes with the creation of a viceroy in Lima. Viceroy Francisco de Toledo begins an extensive pacification effort.
1551	The National University of San Marcos (Lima) and the University of Mexico are founded.
1553	Araucanians capture and kill Valdivia.
c. 1555	The *Popul Vuh* text is created, providing narratives and genealogies of the post-Classic Maya.
1556	Philip II becomes king of Spain.
1557	The Spanish treasury is unable to meet its debts.
1565	The city of Saint Augustine is founded in Florida.
	The Manila-Acapulco galleon trade begins, realizing the idea of sailing west to trade with Asia.

DATE	EVENT
1568	Jesuits initiate successful missions in northern Mexico and Paraguay.
1569	*La Araucana* is published by Spanish poet Alonso de Ercilla in three parts, beginning in this year (the latter parts are published in 1578 and 1589). Considered the greatest epic poem of its kind, it recounts the Spanish conquests of Chile.
1570–1571	Spanish Inquisition tribunals are set up in Mexico and Peru.
1572	English explorer Francis Drake begins stealing Spanish treasure.
	Viceroy Francisco de Toledo quells Tupac Amaru's rebellion and destroys the last Inca settlement at Vilcabamba.
1575	The Spanish treasury goes into default.
1580–1640	The Iberian Union is formed as the Portuguese and Spanish monarchies unite.
1588	The British defeat the Spanish Armada.
1596	The Spanish Crown goes into default, again.
1605, 1615	*Don Quixote* is published by Spanish author Miguel Cervantes in two parts.
1609–1610	Santa Fe is founded in New Mexico.
1618–1648	The Thirty Years' War involves the major European powers.
1621	The Dutch West India Company is chartered to monopolize trade to the colonies.
1630	The Netherlands claims a toehold in northeast Brazil, establishing a capital in Recife.
1636	A Dutch fleet under von Tromp destroys a Spanish fleet in the English channel.
1637–1639	Brazil's borders expand to include the entire Amazon basin.
1654	The Dutch surrender control of Brazilian territory to Portugal, relocating their sugar-growing expertise to the Caribbean.
1655	Britain captures the island of Jamaica.
1660–1671	Welsh buccaneer Henry Morgan's privateering raids climax with the sacking of Portobelo, Panama, and Panama City, which he burns to the ground.
c. 1680–1694	Mexican writer Sor Juana Inés de la Cruz composes poetry and fiction that explores issues of sexuality, love, and jealousy, greatly influencing later literature.
1680–1692	Spanish control of New Mexico is challenged by the Pueblo Rebellion.
1695	Gold is discovered in Brazil's south-central region of Minas Gerais.
1697	The Treaty of Ryswick gives part of Hispaniola to France.

DATE	EVENT
1700–1714	Charles II of Spain dies, slowly begetting a power struggle that would involve every European power. Philip V becomes king of Spain as the Bourbon dynasty replaces Hapsburg rule.
1719	The Viceroyalty of New Granada is established.
1721–1732	Popular uprisings known as comunero revolts break out against Spanish rule in Paraguay.
1729	The Treaty of Seville is brokered among Britain, France, and Spain. Britain retains rights to Gibraltar, but forfeits rights to trade with Spanish colonies.
1739–1748	The War of Jenkins's Ear pits Britain against Spain over commerce with the Caribbean islands and sea lanes.
1756–1763	The Seven Years' War results in the British acquisition of French territories in the Americas.
1762–1763	Havana is occupied by the British, enabling Cuban trade with Britain.
1763	Brazil's seat of government is moved from Salvador to Rio de Janeiro.
1767	King Charles III of Spain expels the Jesuits from Spanish America, expropriating their assets.
1769	Spanish settlements in California take hold.
1773	Earthquakes destroy Guatemala City.
1776–1783	The American Revolution leads to the creation of the United States of America.
1776	The Viceroyalty of Río de la Plata, comprising much of the area of modern-day Argentina, Bolivia, Paraguay, and Uruguay, is established.
1777	Portugal and Spain sign the Treaty of San Ildefonso, settling borders in the Río de la Plata region.
1779–1780	Smallpox ravages Mexico City, killing 20 percent of its inhabitants.
1780–1781	Tupac Amaru II foments an Inca rebellion.
1781	Comunero revolt erupts in Colombia.
1791–1804	Toussaint Louverture leads a slave revolt on Saint-Domingue (Haiti), eventually wresting independence of the island from France, ending slavery, and creating a second democracy in the Americas.
1795	The Treaty of Basel ends the War of the Pyrenees between France, Prussia, and Spain. Spain cedes two-thirds of Hispaniola to France.
1803	The United States purchases the Louisiana Territory from France for just over $23 million.
1805	British admiral Horatio Nelson defeats a combined French-Spanish armada at Trafalgar.
1806–1807	British attempts to invade Río de la Plata result in failure.
1807–1808	Napoleon invades the Iberian peninsula. The Portuguese court flees to Brazil.

DATE	EVENT
1808	Napoleon installs his brother, Joseph Bonaparte, as king of Spain.
1810	Miguel Hidalgo y Costillo issues the "Grito de Dolores," sparking the Mexican Wars of Independence.
	Simón Bolívar joins the independence movement in New Granada (Venezuela).
1811	Paraguay and Venezuela declare independence from Spain.
1812	The Constitution of Cádiz is promulgated.
	José de San Martín joins the revolutionary movement in Argentina.
1814	Napoleon is driven from the Iberian peninsula; Ferdinand VII of Spain reclaims his throne.
	José Francia is named Supreme Dictator of Paraguay, ruling until his death in 1840.
c. 1815–1860	The "Age of Manifest Destiny" dominates U.S. politics.
1816	Argentina's provinces declare independence from Spain.
1818	Forces under the command of San Martín and Bernardo O'Higgins defeat the Spanish in a series of battles, ensuring Chilean independence.
1819	The Adams-Onís Treaty cedes Spanish Florida to the United States for $5 million.
	Gran Colombia is formed, including Colombia, Ecuador, Panama, and Venezuela.
1820	The Office of the Holy Inquisition is abolished.
1821	Treaty of Córdoba grants Mexico independence from Spain.
1822	Pedro I, a member of the Portuguese royal family, breaks with the Portuguese court and declares Brazil's independence from Portugal.
	Bolívar and San Martín meet in Guayaquil to discuss the future of South America.
1823–1824	The United Provinces of Central America is formed.
1823	U.S. president James Monroe issues the Monroe Doctrine, cordoning off Latin America to European intervention.
1824	Bolivar's Lieutenant Antonio José de Sucre defeats Spanish forces at Ayacucho, liberating South America from Spanish rule.
1825	Bolivia declares independence.
1826	Simón Bolívar presides over a conference to foster pan-American unity, which yields few results.
1828	The Argentine-Brazil war produces the independent nation of Uruguay to serve as a buffer state.

DATE	EVENT
1829	Antonio López de Santa Anna crushes Spain's final attempt to reclaim Mexico in a battle near Tampico.
	Juan Manuel de Rosas becomes governor of Buenos Aires province, enjoying dictatorial powers.
	Andrés de Santa Cruz is elected president of Bolivia, beginning a decade of rule marked by stability and administrative reform.
	Gran Colombian forces defeat a Peruvian army at Tarqui, but the underlying boundary issue is not resolved.
	Vicente Guerrero, with the aid of Santa Anna, seizes power in Mexico, becoming the first Afro-descendent president of the country. He immediately orders the abolition of slavery in Mexico.
1830	Simón Bolívar, "El Libertador," dies of tuberculosis on December 17.
	Gran Colombia effectively dissolves, creating independent nations of Ecuador, Venezuela, and New Granada.
	Diego Portales spearheads Conservative rule in Chile after the Battle of Lircay.
1831	The Federal Pact is brokered in Argentina, creating a loose Argentine Confederation in which Buenos Aires determines foreign policy.
	Pedro I abdicates the throne in Brazil, naming his son as successor with a regency to govern until he reaches 18 years of age.
1833	Chile's constitution is enacted, lasting (with one brief interruption) until 1925.
	Britain seizes the Falklands Islands (Islas Malvinas).
1835	After a three-year campaign against the indigenous population in Argentina, Rosas returns to power.
	Vicente Rocafuerte is elected president of Ecuador, apparently forming a power-sharing alliance with Juan José Flores.
	Charles Darwin visits the Galápagos Islands; the trip informs his views on natural selection.
1836	Texas declares independence from Mexico, defeating the forces of Santa Anna. Defenders of the Alamo succumb to siege after thirteen days. Weeks later Santa Anna orders the execution of 365 prisoners-of-war at Goliad.
1836–1839	The War of the Confederation is fought between Chile and the Peru-Bolivian confederation, resulting in the dissolution of the confederation between Peru and Bolivia.
1837	Popular rebellion erupts in Guatemala, led by Rafael Carrera. The uprising enjoys massive support among the indigenous populations and spreads throughout Central America.
	Portales is assassinated in Chile.
1838–1839	Fructuoso Rivera and Manuel Oribe's attempts to politically outmaneuver one another in Uruguay precipitates civil war, creating the Blanco Party and the Colorado Party, which continue to dominate Uruguayan politics into the twenty-first century.
1838	Costa Rica and Honduras withdraw from the United Provinces of Central America.
1839	Flores is elected president of Ecuador.
1840s	The guano boom begins in Peru. The popular fertilizer sparks dramatic economic growth in the country over the next three decades.
1840	Carrera, effectively the ruler of Guatemala, installs friendly regimes in El Salvador and Honduras.
1841	After being asked by a parliamentary delegation to rule, Pedro II is crowned in Brazil at age fourteen.
	The Havana-Güines railroad is completed, the first in Latin America.

DATE	EVENT
1844	Santo Domingo declares independence from Haiti, forming the Dominican Republic.
	Carlos López is elected president of Paraguay by a national congress.
1845	Texas is annexed by the United States.
	Rocafuerte, with support of Ecuador's Catholic clergy, engineers a revolution against Flores's rule; Flores flees for Europe.
1846–1848	Mexico is defeated by the United States in the Mexican-American War, losing half of its territory in the Treaty of Guadalupe Hidalgo.
1846	New Granada (Colombia) and the United States sign the Bidlack Treaty granting the United States significant access rights to the Panamanian isthmus.
1847	Six military cadets die defending Mexico City's Chapultepec Castle against invading U.S. forces. They become known as *Los Niños Héroes* (the Boy Heroes).
1849–1874	Between 80,000–100,000 Chinese laborers arrive in Peru.
1850	The Clayton-Bulwer Treaty is signed between the United States and Britain, promising that neither country would seek exclusive control of any trans-isthmian canal that might be built.
1851	Rosas becomes Supreme Chief of the Argentina Confederation, essentially guaranteeing him dictatorship of the nation.
	Carrera assumes the presidency in Guatemala.
	Oribe surrenders to Brazil, turning his back on his political ally Rosas.
1852	Rosas is overthrown in Argentina.
1853	Argentina adopts a liberal and federalist constitution, which remains (with few substantive changes) in force today.
	The Gadsden Purchase provides Mexico $10 million in exchange for a swath of land that would make up parts of Arizona and New Mexico.
	Women are briefly offered the right to vote in Colombia, for the first time in the Americas.
1854	Plan of Ayutla promulgates a new constitution and return to republican principles in Mexico, starting the process known as "La Reforma."
	The Ostend Manifesto urges U.S. purchase of Cuba from Spain.
1855–1860	U.S. adventurer William Walker invades Nicaragua and rules for two years, before being overthrown and executed.
1855	Santa Anna is ousted; La Reforma cohorts take over the Mexican government.
	The Panama Railway opens, serving as an overland route from the Atlantic to the Pacific.
1856	El Salvador becomes an independent nation.
	Publicist José María Torres Caicedo coins the term "Latin America," which is quickly adopted by the French.
1861	Benito Juárez becomes the first democratically elected president of Mexico.
1862	Bartolomé Mitre becomes president of Argentina, marking the unification of Argentina and the incorporation of Buenos Aires province.
	Francisco López gains power in Paraguay after his father's death.

DATE	EVENT
1863	France invades Mexico, installing Maximilian I as emperor.
	Guatemalan forces drive Gerardo Barrios, a former ally of Carrera, from power in El Salvador and occupy San Salvador.
1864–1870	Argentina, Brazil, and Uruguay fight Paraguay in the War of the Triple Alliance. The war decimates Paraguay.
1865	The Dominican Republic becomes an independent nation.
1866	Peru declares war on Spain, allying itself with Chile, which is already warring with Spain; Bolivia and Ecuador also ally against Spain eventually.
	The Carrera era comes to a close with Carrera's death in Guatemala.
1867	Napoleon III withdraws French troops from Mexico; Maximilian I is promptly executed.
1868–1878	The Ten Years' War for Cuban independence is suppressed by the Spanish.
1868	Argentine jurist Carlos Calvo creates the doctrine bearing his name in an attempt to gain respect for the legal norm of nonintervention in Latin America.
1869	Paraguayan forces, many of whom are children, are defeated at the Battle of Acosta Ñu, the last major battle of the War of the Triple Alliance.
1870	Bartolomé Mitre founds the newspaper *La Nación* in Buenos Aires.
	Francisco López is killed at the Battle of Cerro Corá, marking the end of the War of the Triple Alliance.
	The Dominican Republic offers annexation to the United States, but the treaty fails in the Senate.
	Tomàs Guardia gains power in Costa Rica, quickly establishing a liberal dictatorship.
	Guzmàn Blanco ousts Conservative rule in Venezuela.
1871	Santiago Gonzàlez gains power in El Salvador, beginning an era of Liberal rule that lasts until 1944.
1873–1896	A global depression leads to tumbling commodity prices.
1874	U.S. entrepreneur Minor Cooper Keith begins banana cultivation in Costa Rica.
1876–1911	Porfirio Díaz seizes power in Mexico. His reign, known as the "Porfiriato," dominates Mexican politics for thirty-four years.
1876	The first trans-Atlantic shipment of refrigerated meat is made from France to Buenos Aires. This begins an era of rapid economic growth in Argentina.
1879–1883	Chile defeats Bolivia and Peru in the War of the Pacific, leaving Bolivia landlocked.
1879–1880	The subjugation of indigenous peoples in the Argentine pampas and Patagonia is completed.
1879	The Amazon rubber boom begins, transforming society and culture in Brazil and creating many large port cities.
1880–1893	The French begin to build a trans-isthmian canal across Panama.

DATE	EVENT
1883	The Treaty of Ancón attempts to settle boundary disputes between Chile and Peru after the conclusion of the War of the Pacific.
1886	Slavery is abolished in Cuba.
1888	Slavery is abolished in Brazil, quickly followed by an influx of European immigration.
	Rubén Darío publishes a book of poems titled Azul, establishing himself as the central figure of modernismo in Latin American literature.
1889	Brazil becomes an independent republic after Pedro II abdicates.
	First Pan-American Conference is hosted in Washington, D.C.
1891	Pope Leo XII issues the encyclical Rerum Novarum (Of New Things), seeking to promote social justice.
	Chile experiences a quick but bloody civil war in which the congressional faction usurps presidential power.
1895	José Martí launches a second drive for Cuban independence. He is killed at the Battle of Dos Ríos on May 19.
1898	The USS Maine mysteriously blows up in Havana harbor, sparking the Spanish-American War. The Treaty of Paris ends the war after 109 days, transferring Guam, the Philippines, and Puerto Rico to the United States.
1899–1902	Cuba becomes a U.S. protectorate.
	The Conservative and Liberal parties fight the War of the Thousand Days in Colombia. The civil war costs 100,000 lives.
1899	Argentina adopts the gold standard.
	A merger creates the United Fruit Company.
1900	José Enrique Rodó publishes his essay Ariel, which stokes resentment against the United States and promotes nationalist sentiments throughout Latin America.
1901	The Platt Amendment to the Cuban constitution permits the United States to intervene in Cuban affairs.
	Britain and the United States sign the Hay-Pauncefote Treaty, conferring British consent to U.S. construction of a canal across Central America.
1902	Cuba becomes independent, though the Platt Amendment remains in effect.
	Argentine foreign minister Luis Drago issues the Drago Doctrine, attempting to bolster the principle of nonintervention in the Americas.
1903	Panama declares independence from Colombia under the aegis of U.S. warships. Two weeks later the Hay-Bunau-Varilla Treaty is signed, finalizing plans for the Panama Canal.
	José Batlle y Ordóñez is elected president of Uruguay, igniting a brief civil war. In two terms he introduces free universal education, public pensions, comprehensive health care, and other measures that create what many scholars term the first modern welfare state.
1904	Theodore Roosevelt issues the Roosevelt Corollary to the Monroe Doctrine, positioning the United States to serve as the "international police power" in cases of "chronic wrongdoing" in Latin America.
	The United States begins construction of the Panama Canal.
	U.S. writer O. Henry coins the term "banana republic" in his book Cabbages and Kings.
1905	Mexico adopts the gold standard.

DATE	EVENT
1906	Delegations at the Third International Conference of American States meet at Rio de Janeiro, expressing their disapproval with U.S. "gunboat diplomacy."
	Brazil adopts the gold standard.
1908	Augusto Leguía is elected president in Peru, undertaking reforms to modernize Peru's economy.
1909	The U.S. military helps overthrow dictator General Jose Santos Zelaya in Nicaragua.
1910	Emiliano Zapata, allied with Francisco Madero, forms the Liberation Army of the South to help overthrow the Díaz regime in Mexico.
1911	Supporters of Madero, including Pancho Villa and Zapata, defeat Díaz at Cuidad Juárez, ending the Porfiriato.
	Francisco Madero is elected president of Mexico with overwhelming support.
1912–1933	The U.S. military intervenes in Nicaragua on numerous occasions.
1912	U.S. forces invade Cuba to suppress black protests against discrimination.
1913	Madero is assassinated in Mexico. Victoriano Huerta seizes power.
	The Argentine dance known as the tango, already popular in Europe, captivates New York City.
1914	The Panama Canal opens.
	Huerta resigns and is succeeded by Venustiano Carranza.
	The outbreak of World War I disrupts commercial ties between Latin America and Europe, damaging most Latin American economies.
1915	The United States invades the Mexican port of Veracruz.
1916–1924	U.S. forces occupy the Dominican Republic.
1916	Pancho Villa raids Columbus, New Mexico; the United States responds by sending an expeditionary force into northern Mexico to find Villa.
	Hipólito Irigoyen is elected president of Argentina. He quickly introduces a minimum wage.
	The Aluminum Company of America (Alcoa) begins mining bauxite in Suriname.
1917	A new constitution is adopted in Mexico, designed to ensure democracy and worker rights, as well as establishing a strict separation between church and state.
	Germany proposes a secret military pact with Mexico. The intercepted cable, known as the "Zimmermann telegram," provokes U.S. entry into World War I.
	The Jones Act extends U.S. citizenship to Puerto Ricans.
1919	Labor strikes and uprisings by anarchists lead to a "tragic week" of bloody repression in Argentina.
	Leguía launches a coup to guarantee a return to power in Peru; his second term is marked by a new liberal constitution in 1920 (which he himself largely ignores) and reform of the banking sector.
1920	Carranza is murdered; Mexico recedes into civil war.
1922–1924	José Clemente Orozco and Diego Rivera depict aspects of Mexican life in various murals throughout the country.

DATE	EVENT
1922	Modern Art Week is celebrated in São Paulo, Brazil, featuring avant-garde styles.
1923	Argentine writer Jorge Luis Borges publishes his first collection of poetry, *Fervor de Buenos Aires*.
	Chilean Pablo Neruda publishes his first collection of verse, *Crepusculario*.
1924	Peruvian exile Victor Raúl Haya de la Torre establishes the American Revolutionary Popular Alliance (APRA) party while in Mexico City.
1927–1933	Forces led by Augusto César Sandino wage a guerrilla war against U.S. forces in Nicaragua.
1929	The Great Depression strikes Latin America. For most countries in the region GDP contracts between 25–30 percent.
	The National Revolutionary Party is formed in Mexico. It is later renamed the Institutional Revolutionary Party (PRI).
1930	Revolution in Brazil enables Getúlio Vargas to seize power as head of a provisional government.
	Irigoyen is overthrown by the military in Argentina.
	General Rafael Trujillo seizes power in the Dominican Republic, establishing a personal dictatorship.
	The Smoot-Hawley Tariff Act increases U.S. barriers to trade, exacerbating the Great Depression.
	Uruguay defeats Argentina in the first World Cup.
1931–1934	In 1931 Latin American governments begin to default on their debts. Three years later, only Argentina, the Dominican Republic, and Haiti maintain normal servicing of their external debt.
1932–1935	Bolivia and Paraguay fight the Chaco War.
1932	World trade bottoms out at one-third the level of 1929.
1933	U.S. President Franklin Delano Roosevelt announces the Good Neighbor Policy.
	Fulgencio Batista seizes power in Cuba.
1934	The United States repeals the Platt Amendment and begins offering Cuba advantageous terms of trade.
	Sandino is assassinated by General Anastasio Somoza in Nicaragua.
1937	Vargas seizes power in Brazil, creating the Estado Novo, a fascist state.
	The Dominican military kills approximately 20,000 Haitians living along its western border.
1938	President Lázaro Cárdenas nationalizes Mexico's oil industry, sparking a massive parade in Mexico City.
1940	Exiled Soviet revolutionary Leon Trotsky is murdered in Mexico.
1941	Ecuador relinquishes some territory to Peru after a brief border war.
1942	The United States and Mexico institute the Bracero Program to bring Mexican agricultural laborers to the United States.
	Mexico declares war on Germany and Japan; Argentina and Chile refuse to break diplomatic relations with the Axis.
	Allied demand sparks a second rubber boom in Brazil.

DATE	EVENT
1943	A junta, including Juan Perón, seizes power in Argentina.
	Brazil joins the Allies in World War II.
1944	The Bretton Woods Conference in the United States creates the International Monetary Fund, the International Bank for Reconstruction and Development (World Bank), and the General Agreement on Trade and Tariffs (GATT).
	Argentina declares war on Germany weeks before the fall of Berlin.
	Batista loses the election in Cuba and is succeeded by Ramón Grau San Martín.
1945	Chilean poet Gabriela Mistral wins the Nobel Prize for Literature.
	Trade unions organize massive demonstrations in Buenos Aires, prompting Perón's release from jail and reinstallation as labor minister.
	Vargas resigns from office in Brazil.
1946	Juan Perón is elected president of Argentina with 54 percent of the vote.
1947	The Rio Treaty is brokered, containing a "hemispheric defense" doctrine stating that an attack against any country in Latin America constitutes an attack against all.
1948	The United States helps found the Organization of American States (OAS), aiming to promote regional cooperation.
	The United Nations Economic Commission for Latin America (ECLA) is formed.
	The assassination of Bogotá's mayor sparks riots, beginning a civil war in Colombia known as "La Violencia."
1949	A new constitution in Argentina enshrines Perón's principle of Justicialismo.
1950	Raúl Prebisch publishes an ECLA study describing Latin America's "dependent development" and advocating import substitution industrialization.
	Vargas becomes the democratically elected president of Brazil.
	Uruguay defeats Brazil for its second World Cup title.
1951	Puerto Ricans overwhelmingly vote for U.S. commonwealth status in a referendum.
1952	Batista seizes power again in Cuba.
	Eva Perón dies of cancer on July 26 at the age of thirty-three.
	Jacobo Arbenz Guzmán enacts agrarian reform aimed at expropriating and redistributing vast fallow lands in Guatemala.
	A popular uprising overthrows the military government in Bolivia, allowing President Victor Paz Estenssoro to return and enact sweeping social reforms.
1953	On July 26, Fidel Castro launches a failed attack against the Moncada barracks and is incarcerated by Batista.
	Petrobrás is created, gaining a monopoly on most sectors of the petroleum industry in Brazil.
	Peasant pressure produces Agrarian Reform Law in Bolivia, essentially removing peasants from slavery and awarding them small plots of land.

DATE	EVENT
1954	Arbenz is overthrown in Guatemala with U.S. financing and covert support.
	Vargas commits suicide amid high inflation, extensive corruption, and worker revolts in Brazil.
	General Alfredo Stroessner seizes power in Paraguay after a coup.
1955	A coup attempt in Argentina topples Perón, but thousands are killed. The Federal Constitution of 1853 is restored.
1956	Somoza is assassinated in Nicaragua and is succeeded by his son, Luis.
	Fidel Castro invades Cuba, beginning a guerrilla war against the Batista government.
	Juscelino Kubitschek is elected president of Brazil. He helps instigate rapid economic growth.
1957	François "Papa Doc" Duvalier gains power in Haiti.
1958	Conservatives and Liberals in Colombia agree on a power-sharing arrangement to end the civil war, which has killed between 200,000–300,000.
	Brazil, led by a seventeen-year-old soccer player named Pelé, wins the World Cup.
1959	Castro's forces take power in Cuba on January 1. Batista flees to the Dominican Republic.
1960	Castro nationalizes U.S. businesses in Cuba without compensation.
	President Eisenhower places a complete embargo on U.S. exports to Cuba.
	The capital of Brazil is moved from Rio de Janeiro to Brasília.
	Civil war starts in Guatemala.
	The Latin American Free Trade Association (LAFTA) is brokered to foster regional integration. The Central American Common Market (CACM) is also created.
	The Valdivia earthquake, considered the most powerful in history, damages the Chilean coast.
1961	The United States breaks off diplomatic relations with Cuba.
	U.S.-backed Cuban exiles launch the Bay of Pigs invasion, which is quickly quelled.
	Rafael Trujillo is assassinated on May 30.
	President John F. Kennedy introduces the Alliance for Progress, extending U.S. aid to foster economic development in Latin America.
	The Sandinista National Liberation Front (FSLN) is founded in Nicaragua.
1962	U.S. discovery of missile silos in Cuba prompts the Cuban Missile Crisis, nearly starting a war between the United States and Soviet Union.
	The OAS imposes sanctions on Cuba.
	Jamaica gains its independence from Britain.
	The United Farm Workers of America is founded in the United States by César Chávez and others.
	Brazil wins the World Cup, hosted by Chile.
1963	The Pan-American highway opens, linking the Americas from Alaska to Chile.

DATE	EVENT
1964	A coup brings a military junta to power in Brazil.
	Eduardo Frei is elected president in Chile. He initiates social reforms, but inflation grows.
	René Barrientos Ortuño seizes power in a military coup in Bolivia, ending a dozen years of MNR rule.
1965–1967	Fernando Henrique Cardoso and Enzo Faletto shape thought throughout Latin America by describing dependency theory.
1965	Fearing a communist takeover, U.S. forces invade the Dominican Republic.
	The left-wing National Liberation Army (ELN) and Maoist People's Liberation Army (EPL) are founded in Colombia.
1966	A military junta seizes power in Argentina.
	Revolutionary Armed Forces of Colombia (FARC) is founded.
1967	CIA-backed Bolivian forces capture and execute Ché Guevara on October 9.
	Anastasio Somoza Debayle gains power in Nicaragua.
	Guatemalan writer Miguel Ángel Asturias is awarded the Nobel Prize for Literature.
	Gabriel García Márquez publishes *One Hundred Years of Solitude*.
1968	Student demonstrations and riots in Mexico City result in Tlatelolco massacre days before the beginning of the Olympic Games there.
	General Omar Torrijos seizes power in Panama.
	Juan Velasco Alvarado launches a military coup in Peru; his reign is marked by populist land reforms and nationalizations.
1969	The brief but costly "Soccer War" is fought between El Salvador and Honduras.
1970	In Chile Salvador Allende becomes the world's first democratically elected socialist president.
	A magnitude 7.9 earthquake destroys several villages in Peru, killing more than 50,000.
	Brazil wins its third World Cup, hosted by Mexico.
1971	"Papa Doc" Duvalier dies. His son, "Baby Doc" Duvalier, takes power in Haiti.
	Pablo Neruda receives the Nobel Prize for Literature.
	Guerrilla movements emerge in El Salvador.
	Eduardo Galeano publishes *Open Veins of Latin America*.
1972	A massive earthquake destroys much of Managua, Nicaragua.
1973	Amidst hyperinflation in Chile, General Augusto Pinochet deposes Allende on September 11. Pinochet immediately begins killing his opponents.
	Armed forces seize power in Uruguay.
1973–1974	Perón regains power in Argentina before dying in office. His second wife, Isabel, takes over.
	Worldwide oil crisis quadruples the price of oil.
1974–1983	An Argentine military junta gains power and launches a "dirty war," killing or "disappearing" thousands of political opponents.

DATE	EVENT
1975	A U.S. Senate panel referred to as the "Church Committee" releases two reports documenting U.S. involvement in the overthrow of Allende and attempts to assassinate foreign leaders.
1976	Political and economic mismanagement prompts a military coup in Argentina.
	Cuba sends troops to fight in Angola.
	Activist Orlando Letelier is murdered by Chilean agents in Washington, D.C.
	A series of earthquakes kill more than 23,000 just north of Guatemala City.
1977	Newly elected U.S. president Jimmy Carter announces human rights will form the cornerstone of his foreign policy.
	Revised Panama Canal treaties grant Panamanian control of the canal by Dec. 31, 1999.
1978	Jim Jones leads his followers to mass suicide in Guyana.
	Argentina hosts, and wins, the World Cup amid controversy regarding the brutal nature of its military regime.
1979	Sandinistas overthrow the Somoza dynasty in Nicaragua.
	A second oil crisis impacts Latin America.
	Two hurricanes devastate the Dominican Republic.
1980–1981	Landless families begin establishing encampments in southern Brazil. Support of the Catholic Church and the fall of the military junta provide support to the movement, which grows into the Landless Workers' Movement.
1980	Fidel Castro allows Cubans to leave for the United States from Mariel harbor.
	Shining Path (Sendero Luminoso) begins terrorist attacks in Peru, marring the country's first presidential elections since 1963.
	Oscar Romero, the archbishop of San Salvador, is murdered by death squads.
	Recently elected president Hernán Siles is overthrown by the drug mafia in Bolivia; the "cocaine coup" ushers in an era of unprecedented corruption and brutality in the country.
1981	Omar Torrijos is killed in an airplane crash.
	The Salvadoran army murders over 900 civilians at El Mozote.
	U.S.-backed anti-Sandinista guerrillas begin civil war in Nicaragua.
1982	The Argentine military seizes British-owned Falklands Islands prompting a swift response by the British. Argentina loses the ensuing Falklands/Malvinas War.
	Mexico defaults on its foreign debt, signaling a "lost decade" of economic growth throughout Latin America.
	Gabriel García Márquez receives the Nobel Prize for Literature.
	Democracy returns to Bolivia with the congressional election of Hernán Siles.
1983	U.S. president Ronald Reagan asserts that U.S. national security is being threatened in Central America.
	U.S. troops invade Grenada in the wake of Maurice Bishop's assassination.
	Contadora meeting begins negotiations to bring stability to Central America.
	The U.S. Congress passes the Caribbean Basin Initiative (CBI), seeking to stimulate trade and closer integration with Caribbean nations and the United States.
	Raúl Alfonsín is elected president of Argentina, ending military rule.

DATE	EVENT
1984	The report *Never Again* (Nunca Más) is presented to President Alfonsín, cataloging the disappearance of over 9,000 people between 1976 and 1983.
1985	Democracy is restored in Brazil.
	Bolivia is paralyzed by hyperinflation. U.S. economist Jeff Sachs helps introduce "shock therapy."
	The Nevado de Ruiz volcano erupts in Colombia, killing 23,000.
	An earthquake measuring 8.1 on the Richter scale kills more than 9,000 and leaves more than 100,000 homeless in Mexico City.
1986	The International Court of Justice rules in favor of Nicaragua and against the United States regarding U.S. mines placed in Corinto Bay.
	The Iran-Contra Affair creates political upheaval in the United States.
	Indigenous groups in Ecuador create CODAIE, a pan-Indian organization.
	"Baby Doc" Duvalier is overthrown by a popular uprising in Haiti.
	A major earthquake kills more than 1,000 in San Salvador.
	U.S. President Ronald Reagan signs the Immigration Reform and Control Act making it illegal to knowingly hire illegal aliens, but also providing amnesty to aliens who had lived in the United States since 1982.
	Diego Maradona leads Argentina to World Cup victory.
1987	Oscar Arias presents a peace plan to warring parties in Central America. The plan brings peace in the region and the Nobel Peace Prize for Arias.
	An earthquake strikes east of Quito, killing more than 1,000.
1988	Carlos Salinas de Gortari is elected president in Mexico, undertaking privatization.
	Contras and Sandinistas sign cease-fire in Nicaragua.
1989	U.S. Marines invade Panama, deposing Panamanian strongman Manuel Noriega.
	Chilean voters oppose continued rule by Pinochet in a referendum.
	Patricio Aylwin is elected president of Chile with 55 percent of the vote.
	Stroessner is ousted by the military in Paraguay.
	The United States extends the Brady Plan to aid Latin American countries teetering near default.
	Brazil suspends its foreign debt payments.
	Drug kingpin Pablo Escobar orders the bombing of Avianca Flight 203 and a security building in Bogotá, as well as the assassination of Luis Carlos Galán, Colombia's leading presidential candidate.
1990	Newly elected President Collor de Melo introduces "shock therapy" to quell hyperinflation in Brazil.
	Alberto Fujimori is elected president of Peru.
	Violeta Barrios de Chamorro is elected president in Nicaragua, ending Sandinista rule.
	Jean-Bertrand Aristide is elected president of Haiti.
	Octavio Paz receives the Nobel Prize for Literature.
1991–1992	A coup returns power to the military in Haiti. Brutal repression results in some 3,000–5,000 deaths, with tens of thousands attempting to flee to the United States.

DATE	EVENT
1991	The collapse of the Soviet Union damages the Cuban economy, ushering in a "special period" of emergency measures.
	The Treaty of Asunción creates the Southern Common Market (Mercosur).
	The Rettig Report is provided to President Aylwin, cataloging atrocities under Pinochet's rule in Chile.
	A cholera outbreak spreads from Peru through much of Latin America.
1992	El Salvador's twelve-year civil war ends.
	Shining Path is incapacitated after the capture of its leader.
	Argentina introduces a new currency, the peso, pegged to the U.S. dollar.
	The Earth Summit convenes in Rio de Janeiro.
	With military support Fujimori commits a "self-coup" against his own government, empowering him to suspend the constitution, close Congress, and purge the judiciary.
	The Cuban Democracy Act passes Congress, stiffening the U.S. embargo against Cuba.
	Hugo Chávez leads a failed coup attempt in Venezuela.
	Indigenous activist Rigoberta Menchú receives the Nobel Peace Prize.
1993	Pablo Escobar is gunned down; the powerful Medellin Cartel quickly withers.
	Changes to Argentina's constitution allows President Carlos Saúl Menem to run for reelection.
1994–1995	The Mexican peso crisis is ignited by the sudden devaluation of the peso. The United States offers some $50 billion in assistance to stabilize the country.
1994	The North American Free Trade Agreement (NAFTA) comes into force.
	Zapatista guerrillas spark an uprising in the Chiapas state of Mexico in response to NAFTA.
	Two high-level assassinations of PRI party members fuel instabilities in Mexico.
	Facing U.S. invasion, the Haitian military junta relinquishes power to Aristide.
	Fernando Henrique Cardoso is elected president in Brazil.
	The Historical Clarification Commission begins investigating human rights abuses during Guatemala's civil war.
	An earthquake followed by mudslides kills more than 1,000 in rural Colombia.
	A terrorist attack on a Jewish cultural center kills 86 people in Buenos Aires.
	California voters pass Proposition 187, curbing social services to illegal aliens.
	Brazil beats Italy in a shootout to win the World Cup.
1995	Fujimori is re-elected in Peru.
1996	Guatemala's thirty-five-year civil war ends.
	Tupac Amaru guerrillas seize hostages in Peru.
	The Helms-Burton Act seeks to strengthen the U.S. embargo of Cuba.
1997	Mexico's PRI loses its majority in congress for the first time since 1929.
	Peruvian special forces free hostages held by Tupac Amaru rebels.

DATE	EVENT
1998–1999	Financial trouble spreads from Asia to Brazil. A massive outflow of capital is followed by the devaluation of the Brazilian currency, the real.
1998	Hurricane George ravages parts of the Caribbean.
	Hurricane Mitch devastates much of Central America, killing more than 11,000.
	Hugo Chávez is elected president of Venezuela.
	Ecuador and Peru agree to end their longstanding border dispute.
	Performances in Amsterdam and Carnegie Hall, as well as a documentary of the band, bring renewed attention to the Buena Vista Social Club and traditional Cuban music.
	Pinochet retires from his military post and is later detained in London on murder charges.
1999–2000	Turmoil over the case of Elián González highlights the tensions and dynamics of U.S.-Cuban relations.
1999	Panama takes over control of the Panama Canal.
	At least 938 are killed when an earthquake hits rural Colombia.
	The United States extends a multi-billion dollar aid package to Colombia via Plan Colombia in order to eradicate cocaine production.
2000	Opposition candidate Vicente Fox is elected president in Mexico, ending the PRI monopoly on presidential politics in Mexico.
	Fujimori resigns in the wake of a corruption scandal in Peru.
	Ecuador adopts the U.S. dollar to end an economic crisis.
	Ricardo Lagos is elected president of Chile.
	Pinochet is stripped of his immunity, but his ill-health keeps him from standing trial.
2001–2002	Argentina's economy goes into a tailspin. The government defaults on $155 billion in debt and floats its currency. Crisis spreads into the political realm, precipitating a quick succession of presidents.
2001	A series of earthquakes rips through El Salvador.
	The Peruvian Truth and Reconciliation Commission begins investigating human rights abuses during the 1980s and 1990s.
2002	Luiz Inacio Lula da Silva is elected president of Brazil on a leftist platform.
	Chávez is ousted from office by a military coup in Venezuela, but quickly regains power.
	Argentina's financial crisis spreads to Uruguay.
	Pinochet resigns from his post as senator for life.
	Brazil wins the World Cup.
2003	Néstor Kirchner is elected president of Argentina.

DATE	EVENT
2004	The World Bank forgives 80 percent of Nicaragua's debt. An agreement also enables Nicaragua to write off its debt to Russia from the Soviet era.
	Chávez wins a referendum on his rule in Venezuela.
	Martin Torrijos is elected president of Panama.
	Severe floods in Haiti and the Dominican Republic leave thousands dead.
	Violent uprisings topple Aristide in Haiti.
2005	Evo Morales becomes the first indigenous person elected president of Bolivia.
	A free trade agreement encompassing Central America and the Dominican Republic passes the U.S. Congress.
	Argentina scraps its amnesty law, clearing the way for human rights violators under military rule to be prosecuted.
2006	Felipe Calderon narrowly defeats Andres Manuel López Obrador in Mexico's presidential elections. López Obrador challenges the outcome with mass street protests.
	Chávez is elected to a third term in Venezuela with over 60 percent of the vote.
	U.S. President George W. Bush signs legislation to create a 700-mile fence along the Mexican border.
	Rafael Correa is elected president in Ecuador.
	Lula is re-elected in Brazil.
	Michelle Bachelet becomes the first woman to be elected president of Chile.
	Pinochet dies in Santiago at the age of ninety-one.
2007	Venezuela's National Assembly grants Chávez the power to rule by decree for eighteen months.
	Heavy floods wrack the Mexican state of Tabasco.
	U.N. troops try to rid sections of Haiti's capital of its extensive gang presence.
	Chávez suffers his first electoral defeat, on a referendum that would have vastly increased his powers.
	Cristina Fernandez de Kirchner, wife of Néstor, becomes the first woman elected president of Argentina.
	Brazil's state-owned oil conglomerate, Petrobrás, announces the discovery of oil deposits that could boost Brazil's reserves by over 40 percent.
2008	Hugo Chávez helps broker the release of two FARC captives in Colombia.

THEMATIC OUTLINE OF TOPICS

1. AGRICULTURE AND LIVESTOCK

Agriculture
Argentina, Organizations: Argentine Rural Society
Argentina, Organizations: Argentine Trade Promotion Institute (IAPI)
Bajío
Banana Industry
Baquiano
Beans
Bóia-Fria
Boston Fruit Company
Bota de Potro
Brazilnut Industry
Brazil, Organizations: Movimento Sem Terra
Brazilwood
Caballería
Campesino
Cashew Industry
Changador
Charro
Chicle Industry
Chiles
Chinampas
Cochineal
Coffee, Valorization of (Brazil)
Coffee Industry
Colombia, Organizations: National Federation of Coffee Growers
Colono
Cotton

Cuban American Sugar Company
Cuyamel Fruit Company
Debt Peonage
Domador
Ejidos
Engenho
Estancia
Finca
Fishing Industry
Frigoríficos
Fruit Industry
Fundo
Gaucho
Gaúcho
Guano Industry
Guaraná Industry
Hacienda
Henequen Industry
Hides Industry
Indigo
Ingenios
Irrigation
Jíbaro
Lavrador de Cana
Linseed
Livestock
Lumber Industry
Maize
Manioc
Mayorazgo
Meat Industry
Mesta
Mexico, Organizations: National Peasant Federation (CNC)

Peons
Peru, Organizations: National Agrarian Society
    (SNA)
Pescaperú
Plantations
Potato
Rice Industry
Rubber Industry
Saladero
Sayaña
Seringueiros
Soconusco
Soybeans
Spices and Herbs
Sugar Industry
Tapir
Tobacco Industry
Tobacco Monopoly
Vaqueiros
Vaquería
Vaquero
Whaling
Wheat
Wine Industry
Wool Industry
Yerba Maté
Yerba Mate Industry

2. ARCHAEOLOGY AND ARCHAEOLOGICAL SITES

Altar de Sacrificios
Altun Ha
Amazon Basin, Archaeology
Archaeology
Aspero
Atacames
Bonampak
Caballo Muerto
Cacaxtla
Cajamarca, Pre-Columbian
Calima
Caracol
Caral
Cara Sucia
Casas Grandes
Cerén
Cerro Narrío
Cerros

Chacmools
Chalcatzingo
Chan Chan
Chavín de Huántar
Chiapa de Corzo
Chichén Itzá
Cholula (Pre-Columbian)
Chotuna
Cihuatán
Cobá
Cochasquí
Comalcalco
Copán
Cotocollao
Cuicuilco
Dainzú
Dos Pilas
Edzná
El Baúl
El Mirador
El Paraíso
El Tajín
Gallinazo Group Site
Garagay
Goldwork, Pre-Columbian
Guangala
Ica
Ingapirca
Izapa
Jaina
Kaminaljuyú
Kotosh
La Centinela
Lagoa Santa
Lambityeco
Lapa Vermelha
La Quemada
La Venta
Machu Picchu
Malinalco
Marajoara
Mayapan
Mitla
Mixco Viejo
Moneda Palace
Monte Albán
Monte Alto
Ollantaytambo
Palenque
Pampa de las Llamas-Moxeke

Paracas
Paracas Peninsular Sites
Pedra Furada
Petexbatún
Piedras Negras, Guatemala
Precontact History: Emergence of Complex
　　　Society
Pucará
Puerto Hormiga
Puná Island
Quelepa
Quimbaya
Quirigua
Real Alto
Recuay
Río Azul
Sacsahuaman
Sambaqui
San Lorenzo
Santa Luisa
Santarém Culture
Sayil
Sechín Alto
Seibal
Sipán
Tahuantinsuyu
Tairona
Takalik Abaj
Taperinha
Tazumal
Templo Mayor
Tenochtitlán
Teotihuacán
Tikal
Tiwanaku
Tlapacoya
Tlatelolco
Tomebamba
Toniná
Topoxté
Túcume
Tula
Tulum
Uaxactún (Waxactun)
Utatlan
Uxmal
Valdivia Culture
Valdivia, Ecuador
Vilcabamba

Xochicalco
Yaxchilán
Zaachila
Zaculeu

3. ARTS AND LETTERS

Araucana, La
Architecture: Architecture to 1900
Architecture: Modern Architecture
Ariel
Art: Pre-Columbian Art of Mesoamerica
Art: Pre-Columbian Art of South America
Art: The Colonial Era
Art: The Nineteenth Century
Art: The Twentieth Century
Art: Folk Art
Auto, Auto Sacramental
Bachata
Baião
Ballet Folklorico de México
Banda de Pífanos
Bolero
Bossa Nova
Buena Vista Social Club
Bullfighting
Café Tacuba
Calypso
Canción Ranchera
Cantoria
Capoeira
Carimbó
Choro, Chorinho
Churrigueresque
Cielito
Cinema: From the Silent Film to 1990
Cinema: Since 1990
Cinema Novo
Ciranda
Côco
Compadrito
Concretism
Congada
Contemporáneos, Los
Cordel, Literature of the
Corrido
Cueca
Cumbia

Cuzco School of Painting
Diálogos das Grandezas do Brasil
Enlightenment, The
Forró
French Artistic Mission
Frevo
Gauchesca Literature
Grupo de CAYC
Grupo Madí and Asociación Arte Concreto-
      Invención
Guayaquil, Group of
Güegüence
Huayno
Indianismo
Indianismo, Spanish America
Instituto Politécnico Nacional
Instituto Tecnológico Autonómo de México
Instituto Tecnológico de Estudios Superiores
      de Monterrey
Jongo
Lambada
Letrados
Library of Congress, Hispanic Division
Literature: Brazil
Literature: Spanish America
Maculelê
Mambo
Maracatu
Mariachi
Marimba
Martín Fierro
Maxixe
Merengue
Milonga
Modern Art Week
Modernism, Brazil
Modinha
MPB: Música Popular Brasileira
Music: Art Music
Music: Popular Music and Dance
Music: Pre-Columbian Music of Mesoamerica
Music: Pre-Columbian Music of South
      America
Musical Instruments
National Institute of Anthropology and
      History
Nationhood and the Imagination
Ollantay
Payador
Photography: The Nineteenth Century

Photography: 1900-1990
Photography: Since 1990
Pombero
Quito School of Art
Quito School of Sculpture
Rabinal Achí
Rock Music
Science Fiction in Latin America
Son
Taller de Gráfica Popular (TGP)
Tango
Teatro Colón
Teatro Solís
Theater
Travel Literature
Tropicalismo

4. BATTLES

Acosta Ñu, Battle of
Alamo, Battle of the
Alhóndiga
Arada, Battle of
Arroyo Grande, Battle of
Ayacucho, Battle of
Baton Rouge, Battle of
Boyacá, Battle of
Buena Vista, Battle of
Caaguazú, Battle of
Cancha Rayada, Battle of
Carabobo, Battle of
Carpintería, Battle of
Caseros, Battle of
Celaya, Battles of
Cepeda, Battles of
Cerdo Gordo, Battle of
Cerro Corá, Battle of
Chacabuco, Battle of
Chalchuapa, Battle of
Chapultepec, Battle of
Coatepeque, Battle of
Conquest of the Desert
Cuautla, Siege of
Curupayty, Battle of
Ituzaingó, Battle of
Junín, Battle of
Lircay, Battle of
Maipú, Battle of

Mobile, Battle of
Nanawa, Battle of
Noche Triste
Papudo, Battle of
Paraguarí, Battle of
Pavón, Battle of
Pensacola, Battle of
Pichincha, Battle of
Pitiantuta, Battles of
Puebla, Battle and Siege of
Rancagua, Battle of
Riachuelo, Battle of the
San Jacinto, Battle of
San Lorenzo, Battle of
San Pascual, Battle of
Sumapaz, Republic of
Tacuarí, Battle of
Tuyutí, Battle of
Veracruz, Occupation of
Yrendagúe, Battle of
Yungay, Battle of
Zarumilla, Battle of

5. BUSINESS, COMMERCE, TRADE

American Atlantic and Pacific Ship Canal
    Company
Argentina, Organizations: American Industrial
    Society for Machinery (SIAM)
Argentina, Organizations: Yacimientos
    Petrolíferos Fiscales (YPF)
Arriero
Automobile Industry
Aviation
Backus and Johnston
Banco de México
Banking: Overview
Belgian Colonization Company
Bolivia, Organizations: Bolivian State
    Petroleum Corporation (YPFB)
Brazil, Organizations: National Bank for
    Economic Development (BNDE)
Buenaventura
Cacao Industry
Cámara Nacional de la Industria de la
    Transformación (CANACINTRA)
Caracas Company

Carrera del Paraguay
Cartavio
Casa de Contratación
Cementos Mexicanos
Cerro de Pasco Corporation
Chile, Organizations: Chilean Nitrate
    Company (COSACH)
Colombia, Organizations: National
    Association of Industrialists
Coltejer
Commercial Policy: Colonial Brazil
Commercial Policy: Colonial Spanish America
Compañía Guipuzcoana
Computer Industry
Confederación de Cámaras de Comercio,
    (CONCANACO)
Confederación Nacional de Instituciones
    Empresariales Privadas (CONFIEP)
Confederación Patronal de la República
    Mexicana (COPARMEX)
Consulado
Dutch West India Company
Eastern Coast of Central America Commercial
    and Agricultural Company
Ecopetrol
Eletrobrás
Factor
Factory Commissions, Brazil
Galeones
Gasohol Industry
Gibbs and Sons, Antony
Grace, W. R., and Company
Guatemala Company
Guayaquil, Shipbuilding Industry
Havana Company
Honduras Company
International Petroleum Company (IPC)
Iron and Steel Industry
Izabal
Junta do Comércio
Kosmos Line
La Brea y Pariñas
Manila Galleon
Maquiladoras
Mercosur
Nicaragua, Organizations: Maritime Canal
    Company of Nicaragua
Nuclear Industry
Nuclebrás
Obraje

6. CITIES AND URBANIZATION

Havana
Iquitos
Iximché
João Pessoa
Jonestown
Juazeiro do Norte
La Democracia
Laguna, Santa Catarina
La Paz
La Serena
León
Lépero
Lima
Luján
Maceió
Managua
Manaus
Maracaibo
Maranhão, Estado do
Mar del Plata
Matacapán
Mazatlán
Medellín
Mendoza
Mercedes
Mérida
Mexico City
Monterrey
Montevideo
Moquegua
Município, Município Neutro
Nacaome
Nacogdoches
Natal
Netzahualcóyotl
New Orleans
Nova Friburgo
Oaxaca (City)
Olinda
Oruro
Otavalo
Ouro Prêto
Pachuca
Panama City
Paraná, Argentina
Parián
Parral
Pasto
Paulistas, Paulistanos
Paysandú

Pensacola
Petrópolis
Pisco
Piura
Popayán
Port-au-Prince
Porteño
Pôrto Alegre
Porto Bello (Portobelo)
Pôrto Seguro
Potosí
Puebla (City)
Puerto Barrios
Punta Arenas
Punta del Este
Querétaro (City)
Quetzaltenango
Quito
Recife
Recoleta
Riobamba
Rio de Janeiro (City)
Riohacha
Rondônia
Rosario
Sacramento, Colônia del
Saint Augustine
Salta
Salvador
San Antonio
San Cristóbal de las Casas
San José, Costa Rica
San Juan, Argentina
San Juan, Puerto Rico
San Luis
San Luis Potosí
San Rafael
San Salvador
Santa Cruz
Santa Elena
Santa Fe, Argentina
Santa Fe, New Mexico
Santa Marta
Santarém
Santiago, Chile
Santiago de Cuba
Santiago de los Caballeros
Santo Domingo
São Luís
São Paulo (City)

São Vicente
Seven Cities of Cíbola
Socorro
Sosúa
Sucre
Tegucigalpa
Tehuacán
Temuco
Tepito
Teresina
Tetzcoco
Tlaxcala
Trinidad, Paraguay
Tumbes
Tunja
Ushuaia
Valdivia, Chile
Valparaíso
Vassouras
Veracruz, City of
Vila
Villa El Salvador
Villarrica
Villavicencio
Viña del Mar
Vitória
Xochimilco
Zacatecas

7. COMMUNICATIONS, JOURNALISM, MEDIA

Ahuizote, El
Amauta
Americas, The
Cartoons in Latin America
Día, El
Excélsior (Mexico City)
Gazeta de Guatemala
Gazeta de Lima
Gazetas
Handbook of Latin American Studies
Hispanic American Historical Review
Internet
Journalism
Journalism in Mexico
Marcha
Mercurio, El

Mercurio Peruano
Nación, La (Buenos Aires)
Prensa, La (de Nicaragua)
Radio and Television
Regeneración
Telenovelas

8. CONSTITUTIONS AND CONSTITUTIONALISM

Amparo, Writ of
Argentina, Constitutions
Bases Orgánicas
Bolivia, Constitutions: Overview
Bolivia, Constitutions: Constitución Vitalicia
Brazil, Constitutions
Brazil, Revolutions: Constitutionalist Revolt (São Paulo)
Central America, Constitution of 1824
Chile, Constitutions
Colombia, Constitutions: Overview
Colombia, Constitutions: Constitution of 1863
Costa Rica, Constitutions
Cuba, Constitutions
Cúcuta, Congress of
Dominican Republic, Constitutions
Ecuador, Constitutions
El Salvador, Constitutions
Guatemala, Constitutions
Haiti, Constitutions
Honduras, Constitutions
Mexico, Constitutions: Constitution of 1917
Mexico, Constitutions: Constitutions Prior to 1917
Nicaragua, Constitutions
Panama, Constitutions
Paraguay, Constitutions
Peru, Constitutions
Spain, Constitution of 1812
Tucumán Congress
Uruguay, Constitutions
Venezuela, Constitutions

9. COUNTRIES

Angola
Argentina: The Colonial Period
Argentina: The Nineteenth Century

Argentina: The Twentieth Century
Argentina, Geography
Argentine Confederation
Aruba
Bahamas, Commonwealth of the
Barbados
Belize
Bolivia: The Colonial Period
Bolivia: Since 1825
Brazil: The Colonial Era, 1500-1808
Brazil: 1808-1889
Brazil: Since 1889
Brazil, The Empire (First)
Brazil, The Empire (Second)
Brazil, Geography
Cape Verde Islands
Caribbean Antilles
Cayman Islands
Chile: Foundations Through Independence
Chile: The Nineteenth Century
Chile: The Twentieth Century
Chile, Geography
Colombia: From the Conquest through
    Independence
Colombia: Since Independence
Costa Rica
Costa Rica, Second Republic
Cuba: The Colonial Era (1492-1898)
Cuba: The Republic (1898-1959)
Cuba: Cuba since 1959
Cuba, Geography
Dominican Republic
Ecuador: Conquest Through Independence
Ecuador: Since 1830
Ecuador, Geography
El Salvador
French Guiana
Grenada
Guatemala
Guyana
Haiti
Honduras
Jamaica
Martinique and Guadeloupe
Mexican Liberal Agrarian Policies, Nineteenth-
    Century
Mexico: The Colonial Period
Mexico: 1810-1910
Mexico: Since 1910
Nicaragua
Panama

Paraguay: The Colonial Period
Paraguay: The Nineteenth Century
Paraguay: The Twentieth Century
Paraguay, Demography
Paraguay, Geography
Peru: From the Conquest Through
    Independence
Peru: Peru Since Independence
Puerto Rico, Geography
Saint Lucia
San Nicolás, Acuerdo de (1852)
Trinidad and Tobago
Uruguay: Before 1900
Uruguay: The Twentieth Century
Uruguay, Geography
Venezuela: The Colonial Era
Venezuela: Venezuela since 1830
Virgin Islands

10. CRIMES, TREASON, AND TERRORIST ACTS

Banditry
Barranca Yaco
Buccaneers and Privateers
Cangaceiro
Contraband (Colonial Spanish America)
Corruption
Death Squads
Drugs and Drug Trade
Gangs
Guatemala, Terrorist Organizations: Mano Blanca
Guatemala, Terrorist Organizations: Ojo por Ojo
Jagunço
Malones
Mara Salvatrucha, La
Mazorca
Piracy
Terrorism
Tonton Macoutes
Violencia, La

11. DEVELOPMENT

Brazil, Organizations: Development
    Superintendency of the Northeast
    (SUDENE)

Brazil, Organizations: National Institute of
Colonization and Agrarian Reform
Brazil, Organizations: Superintendency for the
Development of Amazonia (SUDAM)
Chile, Organizations: Development
Corporation (CORFO)
Dependency Theory
Economic Development
Globalization
Industrialization
Inter-American Foundation (IAF)
Operation Bootstrap

---

12. ECONOMY, FINANCE, BANKING

Agiotista
Avio
Banco Comercial y Agrícola (Ecuador)
Banco de Avío
Banco de la República (Colombia)
Banco de Londres y México
Banco de San Carlos (Potosí)
Banco de San Carlos (Spain)
Banco do Brasil
Banking: Since 1990
Bank Nationalization
Baring Brothers
Brazil, Economic Miracle (1968-1974)
Brazil, Organizations: National Housing Bank
(BNH)
Caribbean Common Market (CARIFTA and
CARICOM)
Chicago Boys
Chile, Organizations: Grupo Cruzat-Larraín
Class Structure in Modern Latin America
Coinage (Colonial Spanish America)
Colombia, Organizations: Colombian
Indigenist Institute
Conselho da Fazenda
Currency
Currency (Brazil)
Dance of the Millions
Economic Commission for Latin America and
the Caribbean (ECLAC)
Economic Integration
Encilhamento
Esquilaches

Foreign Debt
Foreign Investment
Foreign Trade
Free Trade Act
Guatemala, Economic Society of
Income Distribution
Inflation
Inter-American Development Bank (IDB)
International Monetary Fund (IMF)
Jecker Bonds
Mexico, Organizations: Nacional Financiera
(NAFIN)
Neoliberalism
Privatization
Public Sector and Taxation
Quinto Real
Real Hacienda
San Domingo Improvement Company
Service Sector
Welser, House of

---

13. EDUCATION AND CULTURAL INSTITUTIONS

Academia de la Lengua y Cultura Guaraní
Academia de San Carlos
Academia Literaria de Querétaro
Academias
Argentina, University Reform
Asociación de Mayo
Ateneo de la Juventud (Athenaeum of Youth)
Ateneo del Uruguay
Bacharéis
Bienal de São Paulo
Brazilian Academy of Letters
Brazil, Organizations: Advanced Institute of
Brazilian Studies (ISEB)
Brazil, Organizations: Getúlio Vargas
Foundation (FGV)
Brazil, Organizations: National Students
Union (UNE)
Casa de las Américas
Chile, Organizations: Federation of Chilean
Students (FECH)
Coimbra, University of
Colegio de México
Colegio Nacional de Buenos Aires
Colégios (Brazil)

Córdoba, University of
DiTella Foundation
Education: Overview
Education: Nonformal Education
Education: Pre-Columbian Education
Ethnic Studies
González Prada Popular Universities
Instituto Histórico e Geográfico Brasileiro
Latin American Studies Association
Libraries in Latin America
Literacy
Monserrat, Colegio de
National Autonomous University of Mexico
 (UNAM)
Pan-American Institute of Geography and
 History
Peru, Organizations: Institute of Peruvian
 Studies (IEP)
Rio Branco Institute
Samba Schools
San Carlos de Guatemala, University of
Sanjuanistas
San Marcos, University of
Sociology
Sur
Universidad Autónoma de Santo Domingo
Universidad Católica Madre y Maestra
Universidad Central de Venezuela
Universidade de Campinas
Universidade de São Paulo
Universities: Colonial Spanish America
Universities: The Modern Era
University of the West Indies

14. ENVIRONMENT AND CONSERVATION

Agreste
Amazon Region
Antarctica
Batán Grande
Brazilian Highlands
Brazil, Organizations: Brazilian Institute of the
 Environment and Renewable Natural
 Resources (IBAMA)
Cerrado
Chaco Region
Costa (Ecuador)

Costa (Peru)
Cuchumatanes
Darién
Dzibilchaltún
Earthquakes
Earth Summit, Rio de Janeiro (1992)
El Niño
Environmental Movements
Environment and Climate
Hurricanes
Lacandon Forest
Llanos (Colombia)
Llanos (Venezuela)
Sloth
Volcanoes
Xingu Reserve

15. EXPLORATION AND CONQUEST

Africa, Portuguese
America
Bent's Fort
Borderlands, The
Capitulations of Santa Fe
Cartography: Overview
Castile
Cempoala
Companies, Chartered
Conquistadores
Dutch in Colonial Brazil
El Dorado
Explorers and Exploration: Brazil
Explorers and Exploration: Spanish
 America
Fort Ross
French Colonization in Brazil
Hidalgo
Hispaniola
Lisbon Earthquake
Nueva Burdeos, Colony of
Portuguese Empire
Quivira
Requerimiento
Spanish Empire
Suriname and the Dutch in the Caribbean
Tayasal

16. FAMILY, LIFE CYCLE, DAILY LIFE

Aguardiente de Pisco
Alcoholic Beverages
Asado
Boleadoras
Carnival
Cerro del Cubilete
Chacra
Charqui
Charreada
Children
China Poblana
Chiripá
Churrasco
Compadrazgo
Compadresco
Cuisines
Día de muertos, Calaveras
Élite (Haiti)
Facón
Fado
Family
Fiestas
Food and Cookery
Hammock
Ñandutí
Pato
Samba
Sports
Tanga

17. FLORA AND FAUNA

Algarrobo
Amaranth
Caatinga
Ceibo
Cinchona
Condor
Forests
Hornero Bird
Iguana
Jaguar
Llama
Monkey
Ombú

Puma
Quebracho Colorado
Quetzal
Rhea

18. GENDER AND SEXUALITY

Abertura
Asociación Cristiana Femenina (YWCA)
Chile, Organizations: Movimiento Pro-Emancipación de la Mujer Chilena
Cuba, Organizations: Club Femenino
Cuba, Organizations: Federation of Cuban Women (FMC)
Dowry
Feminism and Feminist Organizations
Homosexuality and Bisexuality in Literature
Inter-American Congress of Women
Marriage and Divorce
Montepíos
Peru, Organizations: National Social Mobilization Support System (Sinamos)
Proyectistas
Regidor
Resguardo
Residencia
Sexuality: Gender and Sexuality
Sexuality: Same-sex Behavior in Latin America, Pre-Conquest to Independence
Sexuality: Same-sex Behavior in Latin America, Modern Period
Women
Women in Paraguay
Yungas

19. GEOGRAPHICAL FEATURES

Acaray River
Aconcagua
Altiplano
Amazon River
Andes
Angel Falls
Apurímac
Araguaia River
Arroyo Asencio

Seringal
Serra do Mar
Sesmaria
Sicán
Sierra (Ecuador)
Sierra Madre
Sierra Maestra
Sierra (Peru)
Sonora
Southern Cone
Swan Islands
Tacna
Tamaulipas
Tambor de Mina
Tapajós River
Tarapacá
Tarija
Tarma
Tebicuary River
Tehuantepec, Isthmus of
Tierra del Fuego
Tietê River
Titicaca, Lake
Tocantins River
Torreón
Tortuga Island
Trinidade Island
Urabá
Uruguay River
Uspallata Pass
Usumacinta River
Windward Islands
Xingu River

---

20. GOVERNMENT AND POLITICS

Acre
Acuerdo
Additional Act of 1834
Adelantado
Adelantado of the South Sea
Agrarian Reform
Alagoas
Alcabalas
Alcalde
Alcalde Mayor
Alguacil Mayor
Alianza Cívica

Almojarifazgo
Altepetl
Alves Branco Tariff
Amapá
Amazonas
Ancash
Angostura, Congress of
Anguilla
Antigua
Antioquia
Antofagasta
Aragon
Arbitristas
Arequipa
Argentina, Truth Commissions
Arizona
Artigas
Assembly of Notables
Audiencia
Avería
Ayacucho
Babylonian Captivity
Bahía
Barbuda
Bolivia, Organizations: Federation of Bolivian
        University Students
Brazil, Liberal Movements
Brazil, New Republic
Brazil, Populist Republic, 1945-1964
Brazil, The Regency
Brazil, Truth Commission
Brazil, Viceroys of
Caaguazú
Cacique, Caciquismo
Caledonia
Camarilla
Cambio 90-Nueva Mayoría (C90-NM)
Captaincy System
Captain-General: Brazil
Captain-General: Spanish America
Caribbean Sea, Commonwealth States
Cartagena Manifesto
Cartago
Carter Center
Casanare
Casa Rosada
Castilla del Oro
Caudillismo, Caudillo
Cédula
Censorship

Central America
Central America, Independence of
Central America, United Provinces of
Central American Parliament
Charcas, Audiencia of
Chile, Organizations: Society of Equality
Chile, Parliamentary Regime
Chile, Socialist Republic of 100 Days
Chile, Truth Commissions
Chilpancingo, Congress of
Chucuito
Científicos
Cisplatine Congress
Cisplatine Province
Cohen Plan
Comarca
Comisión Nacional de Derechos los Humanos
Commissions Regarding 1968 Massacres in
        Tlaltelolco
Communism
Composición
Concordancia
Contaduría
Continuismo
Coparticipación
Coronel, Coronelismo
Corregidor
Cortes, Portuguese
Cortes of Cádiz
Council of the Indies
Creelman Interview
Delegative Democracy
Democracy
Diretório dos Índios
Distensão
Donatários
Effective Suffrage, No Reelection
Encomienda
Erário Régio
Estado Novo
Estanco, Estanquero
Exaltados
Fascism
Federal Electoral Institute (IFE)
Federalism
Foraker Act
Gamonalismo
Gobernador
Golpe de estado (coup d'état)
Gran Colombia

Guadalupe, Convenio de
Guadalupes, Los
Guatemala, Audiencia of
Hemispheric Affairs
Herrerismo
Indian Policy, Brazil
Intendancy System
Itu, Convention of
Jacobinism
Jefe Político
Judiciary in Latin America, The
Junta: Brazil
Junta: Spanish America
Juntas Portuguesas
Junta Suprema de Caracas
Land Tenure, Brazil
Latifundia
Lautaro, Logia de
Liberalism
Marshals of Ayacucho
Media Anata
Mexico, Centralism
Mexico, Truth Commissions
Military Dictatorships: 1821-1945
Military Dictatorships: Since 1945
Minister of the Indies
Moderados (Mexico)
Moderative Power
Nationalism
New Granada, United Provinces
New Granada, Viceroyalty of
New Spain, Colonization of the Northern
        Frontier
New Spain, Viceroyalty of
Oidor
Oncenio
Ordenanza de Intendentes
Overseas Council (Portugal)
Papel Sellado
Paraguay, Organizations: Asociación Paraguaya
        del Indígena
Paraguay, Organizations: League of
        Independent Youth
Patria Chica
Pelucones
Peru, Truth Commissions
Pesquisa, Pesquisador
Plan of Tacubaya
Política dos Governadores
Pombaline Reforms

Porfiriato
Portugal, Restoration of 1640
Portuguese Overseas Administration
Presidentialism/Presidential Systems
Provedor Mor da Fazenda
Provincial Deputation
Provincias Internas
Pueblos de indios
Quito, Audiencia (Presidency) of
Recopilación de Leyes de las Indias
Relaciones Geográficas
Río de la Plata, Viceroyalty of
Ruralismo
San José Conference of 1906
Santo Domingo, Audiencia of
Sebastianismo
Senado da Câmara
Tarata (Calle Tarata)
Tribunal de Cuentas
Truth Commissions
Unicato
Unión de Armas
Unitario
Uruguay, Colegiado
Uruguay, Congress of 1825
Uruguay, Electoral System
Uruguay, Medidas Prontas de Seguridad
Uruguay, Organizations: Autonomous Entities
Uruguay, Plebiscites
Uruguay, Truth Commissions
Venezuela, Congresses of 1811, 1830, and
   1864
Viceroyalty, Viceroy
Visita, Visitador

21. HEALTH, MEDICINE, AND DISEASE

Acquired Immune Deficiency Syndrome
   (AIDS)
Butantã Institute
Curandero/Curandeiro
Diseases
Institute of Nutrition of Central America and
   Panama (INCAP)
Medicinal Plants
Medicine: Colonial Spanish America
Medicine: The Modern Era

Nutrition
Oswaldo Cruz Institute
Protomedicato
Public Health
Quinine
Tropicalista School of Medicine (Bahia)

22. IMMIGRATION/ EMIGRATION/MIGRATION

African-Brazilian Emigration to Africa
Atlantic Islands, Migrants from
Germans in Latin America
Hispanics in the United States
Mariel Boatlift
Middle Easterners
Migration and Migrations
Paraguay, Immigration
Portuguese in Latin America
Retirante
Taínos
Venezuela, Immigration

23. INDIGENOUS PEOPLES

Abipón Indians
Aché
Alakaluf
Anáhuac
Annals of the Cakchiquels
Apaches
Apalachee
Araucanians
Ayllu
Aymara
Azcapotzalco
Aztecs
Aztlán
Ball Game, Pre-Columbian
Becan
Brazil, Organizations: Indian Protection
   Service (SPI)
Brazil, Organizations: Indigenist Missionary
   Council (CIMI)
Brazil, Organizations: National Indian
   Foundation (FUNAI)

Brazil, Organizations: Union of Indigenous
    Nations (UNI)
Calpulli
Calusa
Cañari
Cannibalism
Caribs
Chancay
Chavín
Chichimecs
Chilam Balam
Chimú
Chincha Kingdom
Chiriguanos
Chorrera
Chumash Indians
Closed Corporate Peasant Community
    (CCPC)
Codices
Comanches
Comenchingones
Congregación
Cupisnique Culture
Diaguitas
Djuka
Flowery Wars
Forasteros
Fundo Legal
Gallinazo
Gê
Genízaro
Guarani Indians
Huaca
Huari
Huarpa
Huastecos
Huichols
Huitzilopochtli
Ica, Pre-Columbian
Incas, The
Indigenismo
Indigenous Organizations
Indigenous Peoples
Inti
Jama-Coaque
Jangada
Kaqchikel
K'iche'
Kikapoo
Lacandones

Las Vegas
Lenca
Mamacocha
Mamaquilla
Manteño
Mapuche
Marquesado del Valle de Oaxaca
Maximón
Maya, The
Mayan Ethnohistory
Mbayá Indians
Mesoamerica
Miskitos
Mitmaes
Mixtecs
Moche
Mocoví
Muisca
Nahuas
Nasca
Nasca Lines
Navajos
Nicarao
Nuclear America
Olmecs
Omaguaca
Orejones
Otomí
Pacification
Patagones
Payaguá Indians
Pehuenches
Pipiles
Pipiltín
Pochteca
Popol Vuh
Potiguar
Precontact History: Latin America in the
    Precontact Period
Precontact History: Mesoamerica
Precontact History: Amazonia
Precontact History: Andean Region
Precontact History: Southern Cone
Pueblo Indians
Querandíes
Quipu
Quitu
Repartimiento de Mercancías
República de Tule
Resgate

Saramaka
Selk'nams
Sertanista
Shuar
Sirionó
Tapuia
Tarascans
Tehuelches
Tequesta
Textiles, Indigenous
Timucua
Tiwanaku
Tlatoani
Toltecs
Toqui
Totonacs
Tupi-Guarani
Tupinambá
Tz'utujil
Vicús
Volador Dance
Yagul
Yamana
Yanaconas
Yanomami
Yaqui Indians
Zapotecs

24. INTERNATIONAL AFFAIRS

ABC Countries
African-Latin American Relations
Alliance for Progress
American Revolution, Influence of
Arab-Latin American Relations
Asylum
Atlantic Charter
Baltimore Incident
Bay of Pigs Invasion
Beagle Channel Dispute
Big Stick Policy
Bloqueo de 1902, El
Blue Book
Boundary Disputes: Overview
Boundary Disputes: Brazil
Bracero
British in Argentina
British-Latin American Relations

Bucareli Conferences
Calvo Doctrine
Caribbean Basin Initiative
Central American Common Market (CACM)
Central American Defense Council
	(CONDECA)
Central Intelligence Agency (CIA)
Chadbourne Plan
Chamizal Conflict
Chinese-Latin American Relations
Christie Affair
Clark Memorandum
Confederates in Brazil and Mexico
Contadora
Cuban Intervention in Africa
Cuban Missile Crisis
Dictators League
Dollar Diplomacy
Drago Doctrine
Dutch-Latin American Relations
Ecuador-Peru Boundary Disputes
Esquipulas II
Estrada Doctrine
Free Trade Area of the Americas (FTAA)
French Intervention (Mexico)
French-Latin American Relations
Frontiers in Latin America
Gadsden Purchase
German-Latin American Relations
Good Neighbor Policy
Gringo
Guantánamo Bay
Hickenlooper Amendment
Holy Alliance
Human Rights
Imperialism
Inter-American Democratic Charter, 2001
Inter-American Organizations
Inter-American System
International Congress of Americanists
Israeli-Latin American Relations
Japanese-Latin American Relations
Kissinger Commission
Latin American Free Trade Association
	(LAFTA)
Law of the Sea
League of Nations
Leticia Dispute
Lima Conference (1847-1848)
Line of Demarcation (1493)

Monroe Doctrine
National Endowment for Democracy (NED)
Niagara Falls Conference
No-Transfer Resolution
Organization of American States (OAS)
Organization of Central American States
 (ODECA)
Ostend Manifesto
Panama Canal, Flag Riots
Panama Canal Tolls Question
Panama Congress of 1826
Pan-American Conferences: Bogotá
 Conference (1948)
Pan-American Conferences: Buenos Aires
 Conference (1936)
Pan-American Conferences: Caracas
 Conference (1954)
Pan-American Conferences: Havana
 Conference (1928)
Pan-American Conferences: Havana Meeting
 (1940)
Pan-American Conferences: Mexico City
 Conference (1945)
Pan-American Conferences: Montevideo
 Conference (1933)
Pan-American Conferences: Panama Meeting
 (1939)
Pan-American Conferences: Punta del Este
 Meeting (1962)
Pan-American Conferences: Rio Conference
 (1942)
Pan-American Conferences: Rio Conference
 (1947)
Pan-American Conferences: Rio Conference
 (1954)
Pan-American Conferences: Washington
 Conference (1889)
Pan-Americanism
Peace Corps
Pershing Expedition
Peru-Bolivia Confederation
Platt Amendment
Portugal
Portuguese Trade and International Relations
Roosevelt Corollary
Russian-Latin American Relations
São Tomé
Service for Peace and Justice (SERPAJ)
Soviet-Latin American Relations
Spain

Spooner Act
Summit of the Americas
Tacna-Arica Dispute
Talambo Affair
Teller Amendment
Tiwinza
Tobar Doctrine
Travelers, Latin American
United Nations
United Provinces of the Río de la Plata
United States Agency for International
 Development
United States-Latin American Relations
United States-Mexico Border
Virginius Affair
Water Witch Incident
West Indies Federation
Wilson Plan
World Bank
Yataity Corá, Conference of

25. LABOR AND WORKERS' GROUPS

Anarchism and Anarchosyndicalism
Argentina, Organizations: Argentine Patriotic
 League (LPA)
Argentina, Organizations: Federation of
 Argentine Workers (FOA)
Argentina, Organizations: General Labor
 Confederation (CGT)
Argentina, Organizations: Liga Federal, Liga
 Litoral, Liga Unitaria
Bolivia, Organizations: Bolivian Workers
 Central (COB)
Bolivia, Organizations: Syndical Federation of
 Bolivian Mineworkers (FSTMB)
Brazil, Organizations: Brazilian Labor
 Confederation (COB)
Brazil, Organizations: Frente Agrária (FA)
Brazil, Organizations: General Labor
 Command (CGT)
Brazil, Organizations: Peasant Leagues
Brazil, Organizations: Superintendency of
 Agrarian Reform (SUPRA)
Brazil, Organizations: Union of Farmers and
 Agricultural Laborers of Brazil (ULTAB)
Casa del Obrero Mundial

Chile, Organizations: Federation of Chilean
Workers (FOCH)
Chile, Organizations: Sociedad Nacional de
Agricultura (SNA)
Chinese Labor (Peru)
Colombia, Great Banana Strike
Colombia, Organizations: Confederation of
Colombian Workers (CTC)
Colombia, Organizations: Unified Central of
Workers (CUT)
Colombia, Organizations: Union of
Colombian Workers (UTC)
Colombia, Organizations: Union Society of
Artisans
Confederación de Trabajadores de América
Latina (CTAL)
Cuba, Organizations: Federation of Cuban
Workers (CTC)
Debt Peonage
Domestic Service
Ecuador, Organizations: Ecuadorian
Confederation of Class-based
Organizations (CEDOC)
Ecuador, Organizations: Workers
Confederation of Ecuador (CTE)
Guayaquil, General Strike of 1922
Guilds (Gremios)
Inquilinaje
Labor Movements
Land Law of 1850 (Brazil)
Mandamiento
Mesa da Consciência e Ordens
Mexico, Organizations: Federation of Mexican
Labor (CTM)
Mexico, Organizations: Mexican Regional
Labor Confederation (CROM)
Mutirão
Naboría
Nambikwára
Paraguay, Organizations: Confederación
Paraguaya de Trabajadores (CPT)
Partido
Patronage
Peru, Organizations: Confederation of
Peruvian Workers (CTP)
Peru, Organizations: Confederation of
Workers of the Peruvian Revolution
(CTRP)
Peru, Organizations: General Confederation of
Peruvian Workers (CGTP)

Poqomam
Real Consulado de Caracas
Real Cuerpo de Minería
Repartimiento
Río Blanco Strike
Rubber Gatherers' Unions
Semana Trágica
Tupi
United Farm Workers Union
Uruguay, Organizations: Catholic Workers'
Circle
Uruguay, Organizations: National Workers
Convention
Uruguay, Organizations: Workers' Interunion
Plenary-National Workers' Assembly

26. LANGUAGES

Aymara (Language)
Guaraní (Language)
Huincas
Indigenous Languages
Kuna (Cuna)
Ladino
Lunfardo
Luso-Brazilian
Maloca
Mam
Mayan Alphabet and Orthography
Mayan Epigraphy
Nahuatl
Portuguese Language
Quechua
Soroche
Spanish Language
Tamoio

27. LAW AND COURTS

Acordada
Argentina, Civil Code
Argentina, Commercial Code
Audiencia de los Confines
Bogotá, Santa Fe de: The Audiencia
Brazil, Amnesty Act (1979)
Brazil, Civil Code
Brazil, Council of State

Brazil, Electoral Reform Legislation
Brazil, National Security Law
Brazil, Organizations: Brazilian Bar Association
  (OAB)
Brazil, Organizations: Superior Military
  Tribunal
Bumba-Meu-Boi
Burgos, Laws of
Carabineros de Chile
Caracas, Audiencia of
Casa da Suplicação
Central American Court of Justice
Consolidación, Law of
Criminal Justice
Degredado
Desembargadores
Emphyteusis, Law of
Free Birth Law
Fueros
Golden Law
Institutional Acts
Judicial Systems: Brazil
Judicial Systems: Spanish America
Juzgado General de Indios
Ley Iglesias
Ley Juárez
Ley Lerdo
Livingston Codes
New Laws of 1542
Ordenações do Reino
Ouvidores
Queirós Law
Relações
Sacristan, Question of the
Sáenz Peña Law
Siete Partidas

28. MINERALS AND MINING

Bandeiras
Bauxite Industry
Californios
Cananea
Centromín
Chuquicamata Mine
Colombia, Organizations: National School of
  Mines of Medellín
Comibol

Companhia Vale do Rio Doce
Copper Industry
Emboaba
Extractive Reserves
Garimpo
Gems and Gemstones
Gold Rushes, Brazil
Gran Minería
Huancavelica
La Oroya
Mining: Colonial Brazil
Mining: Colonial Spanish America
Mining: Modern
Monções
Muzo Emerald Concession
Nitrate Industry
Oruro
Potosí
Taxco
Tin Industry

29. POLITICAL PARTIES

Argentina, Political Parties: Antipersonalist
  Radical Civil Union
Argentina, Political Parties: Democratic Union
  (UD)
Argentina, Political Parties: Independent
  Socialist Party
Argentina, Political Parties: Intransigent
  Radicals
Argentina, Political Parties: Justicialist Party
Argentina, Political Parties: National
  Autonomist Party (PAN)
Argentina, Political Parties: Personalist Radical
  Civic Union
Argentina, Political Parties: Progressive
  Democratic Party
Argentina, Political Parties: Radical Party
  (UCR)
Argentina, Political Parties: Socialist Party
Argentina, Political Parties: Youth
  Organization of the Radical Party
  (FORJA)
Bolivia, Political Parties: Overview
Bolivia, Political Parties: Bolivian Communist
  Party (PCB)

30. PROTEST AND REFORM

Chalco Agrarian Rebellion of 1868
Chile, Organizations: Corporation of Agrarian
    Reform (CORA)
Chile, Organizations: Vicariate of Solidarity
Colombia, Organizations: Colombian Institute
    for Agrarian Reform (INCORA)
Colombia, Organizations: Democratic Society
    of Artisans
Conciliação
Cordobazo, El
Descamisados
Escoceses
Marcha de los Cuatro Suyos
March of the Empty Pots
Movimiento Chamula 1869
Movimiento de Maestros 1958
Movimiento Ferrocarrilero
Movimiento Jaramillista
Movimiento Sinarquista
Movimiento Vasconselista 1929-1930
New Australia
Panama, Community Action
Puros
Rebelión de San Martín Texmelucan, Puebla
    1879
Rebelión Sierra Gorda
Venezuela, Organizations: Federation of
    Students of Venezuela (FEV)
Venezuela, Organizations: Patriotic Society of
    Caracas
Vicos Project
Vieques Protests
Yaqui Rebellion, 1885-1898

31. REBELLIONS, REVOLUTIONS, PROTESTS

Acordada, Revolt of
Arenas Conspiracy
Atusparia Revolt
Balaiada
Bear Flag Revolt
Beckman Revolt
Belén Conspiracy
Bogotazo
Brazil, Independence Movements
Brazil, Revolutions: Communist Revolts
    of 1935

Brazil, Revolutions: Federalist Revolt of 1893
Brazil, Revolutions: Liberal Revolution of
    1842
Brazil, Revolutions: Revolts of 1923-1924
Brazil, Revolutions: Revolution of 1930
Brazil, Revolutions: Revolution of 1964
Cabanagem
Caramurus
Chayanta, Revolt of (1777-1781)
Chayanta, Revolt of (1927)
Chibata, Revolt of the
Chile, Revolutions: Revolution of 1891
Chile, Revolutions: Revolutions of 1851 and
    1859
Colombia, Revolutionary Movements:
    Revolutionary Armed Forces of
    Colombia (FARC)
Colombia, Revolutionary Movements: Army of
    National Liberation (ELN)
Colombia, Revolutionary Movements: Army of
    Popular Liberation (EPL)
Colombia, Revolutionary Movements: M-19
Colombia, Revolutionary Movements: United
    Self-Defense Forces of Colombia
    (AUC)
Comunero Revolt (New Granada)
Comunero Revolt (Paraguay, 1730-1735)
Confederation of the Equator
Congress of April 1813
Contestado Rebellion
Contras
Copacabana Fort, Revolt of
Cosiata, La (1826)
Cristero Rebellion
Cuartelazo
Cuba, Revolutions: Cuban Revolution
Cuba, Revolutions: Revolution of 1933
Cuba, Twenty Sixth of July Movement
Cuba, War of Independence
Decena Trágica
Dominican Revolt (1965)
Ecuador, Revolutions: Revolution of 1895
Ecuador, Revolutions: Revolution of 1925
Farroupilha Revolt
Fredonia, Republic of
Grito de Asencio
Grito de Lares
Grito de Yara
Guayaquil, Republic of
Guerrilla Movements

Haiti, Caco Revolts
Illapa
Inconfidência dos Alfaiates
Inconfidência Mineira
La Escalera, Conspiracy of
La Galgada
La Libertadora Revolution
Louisiana Revolt of 1768
Mambises
Matanza
Messianic Movements: Brazil
Mexico, Expulsion of the Spaniards
Mexico, Wars and Revolutions: Coup d'État of
    1808
Mexico, Wars and Revolutions: Mexican
    Revolution
Mexico, Wars and Revolutions: Revolt of 1832
Mexico, Wars and Revolutions: The Reform
Mexico, Organizations: Zapatista Army of
    National Liberation
Montonera
Montoneros
Movimiento Revolucionanrio Tupaj Katari de
    Liberación (MRTKL)
Movimiento Revolucionario Tupac Amaru
    (MRTA)
Muckers' Rebellion
New Jewel Movement
Pachamama
Panama, Tenants' Revolt
Patria Nueva
Patria Vieja
Pernambucan Revolution (1817)
Peru, Revolutionary Movements: Army of
    National Liberation (ELN)
Peru, Revolutionary Movements: Shining Path
Plan Inca
Plan of Agua Prieta
Plan of Ayala
Plan of Ayutla
Plan of Casa Mata
Plan of Guadalupe
Plan of Iguala
Plan of La Noria
Plan of San Luis Potosí
Plan of Tuxtepec
Praieira Revolt
Prestes Column
Pronunciamiento
Pueblo Rebellion

Pumacahua Rebellion
Quito Revolt of 1765
Quito Revolt of 1809
Ranqueles
Reforma Agraria, Revolution
Republiquetas
Revoltosos
Rumi Maqui Revolt
Sabinada Revolt
Santa Cruz, Fortaleza de
Semana Roja
State of Siege
Tenentismo
Texas Revolution
Tomochic Rebellion
Treinta y Tres (33) Orientales
Trinitaria, La
Tzendal Rebellion
Uruguay, National Liberation Movement
    (MLN-T)
Valladolid Conspiracy (1809)
Venezuela, Armed Forces of National
    Liberation (FALN)
Venezuela, Las Reformas Revolution
Watermelon Riot (Panama Riot)
Zipaquirá, Capitulations of

32. RELIGION AND PHILOSOPHY

African-Latin American Religions: Overview
African-Latin American Religions: Brazil
Aldeias
Anticlericalism
Arielismo
Augustinians
Batllismo
Benedictines
Bethlehemites
Black Legend, The
Bonfim, Nosso Senhor do
Brazil, Organizations: National Conference of
    Brazilian Bishops (CNBB)
Brazil, Organizations: Pastoral Land
    Commission (CPT)
Brotherhoods
Buddhism
Bulas Cuadragesimales
Bulas de Santa Cruzada

Candomblé
Capellanía
Capuchin Friars
Carmelites (Discalced)
Catholic Action
Catholic Church: The Colonial Period
Catholic Church: The Modern Period
Central American Mission (CAM)
Chalma
Chiquinquirá
Christian Base Communities
Christ of the Andes
Coatlicue
Cofradía
Colonialism
Concordat of 1887
Conference of Latin American Bishops
    (CELAM)
Diezmo
Doce, Los
Dominicans
El Señor de los Milagros
El Señor de los Temblores
Esquipulas
Franciscans
Guadalupe, Basilica of
Guadalupe, Virgin of
Inquisition, The: Brazil
Inquisition, The: Spanish America
Islam
Jesuits
Jews
Krausismo
Liberation Theology
Luján, Virgin of
Lwa
Maryknoll Order
Masonic Orders
Mennonites
Mennonites in Latin America
Mercedarians
Mesada Eclesiástica
Messianic Movements: Spanish America
Misericórdia, Santa Casa da
Missionaries of Charity
Missions: Brazil
Missions: Jesuit Missions (Reducciones)
Missions: Spanish America
Moravian Church
Nossa Senhora da Aparecida

Obras Pías
Orixás
Pachacamac
Padroado Real
Patronato Real
Penitentes
Philosophy: Overview
Philosophy: Feminist
Positivism
Positivist Church of Brazil
Protestantism
Protestantismo en México
Quetzalcoatl
Rastafarians
Religion in Mexico, Catholic Church and
    Beyond
Retablos and Ex-Votos
Salesians
Santería
Santo, Santa
Sinarquismo
Spiritism
Syncretism
Tezcatlipoca
Tlaloc
Umbanda
Viracocha
Vodun, Voodoo, Vaudun

33. SCIENCE AND TECHNOLOGY

Anthropology
Astronomy
Aztec Calendar Stone
Calendars, Pre-Columbian
Cartography: The Spanish Borderlands
Engineering
Humboldt Current
Science
Technology

34. SLAVERY

African-Brazilian Cultural and Political
    Organizations
African Brazilians, Color Terminology
Africans in Hispanic America

Agregado
Asians in Latin America
Asiento
Basques in Latin America
Caboclo
Capitão do Mato
Casa Grande
Caste and Class Structure in Colonial Spanish
        America
Castizo
Cholo
Creole
Entrada
Fazenda, Fazendeiro
Huasipungo
Macehualli
Mameluco
Manumission
Marginal, Marginalidade
Maroons (Cimarrones)
Mazombos
Mestizo
Mina
Mita
Négritude
Orientales
Palmares
Pardo
Parentela
Peninsular
Pocho
Population: Brazil
Population: Spanish America
Quilombo
Race and Ethnicity
Reinóis
Roto
Senzala
Sexagenarian Law
Slave Revolts: Brazil
Slave Revolts: Spanish America
Slavery: Brazil
Slavery: Spanish America
Slavery: Indian Slavery and Forced Labor
Slavery: Abolition
Slave Trade
Slave Trade, Abolition of: Brazil
Slave Trade, Abolition of: Spanish America
Venta de indios mayas a Cuba
Yoruba
Zambo

35. SOCIAL HISTORY

Argentina, Organizations: Sociedad de
        Beneficiencia
Confederación de Nacionalidades Indígenas
        del Ecuador (CONAIE)
Defensoría del Pueblo (Human Rights
        Ombudsman Office)
Feminist Congresses, First and Second, 1916,
        Yucatan
Instituto Nacional de las Mujeres
Instituto Nacional Indigenista
Katarismo
League of United Latin American Citizens
Movimiento Indígena Pachacutik
National Council of La Raza
Peons
Tigres del Norte, Los

36. STATES AND PROVINCES

Bahia
California
Chiapas
Clipperton Island
Coahuila
Colonia
Cubagua
Cundinamarca
Curaçao
Cuyo
Danish West Indies
Dominica
Durazno
El Cerrejón
Entre Ríos
Esmeraldas
Esperanza Colony
Espírito Santo
Falkland Islands (Malvinas)
Fernando de Noronha
Flores
Florida
Florida, East
Florida, Spanish West
Fortaleza
French West Indies
Goiás

Grenadines
Guale
Guanabara State
Guanacaste
Guerrero
Guiné, Guinea
Heredia
Huancavelica
Huancayo
Huánuco
Huaraz
Huasteca, The
Iguaçú
Independent Republics (Colombia)
Jalisco
Jujuy
Lambayeque
Llanquihue
Loreto
Los Altos
Louisiana
Magallanes
Maldonado
Maranhão
Mato Grosso
Mato Grosso do Sul
Maule
Mexico, Federal District
Mexico State
Michoacán
Minas Gerais
Misiones
Mizque
Mojos
Montaña
Montserrat
Morelos
Neuquén
New Mexico
Nueva Galicia
Nueva Vizcaya
Nuevo León
Nuevo Santander
Oaxaca (State)
Olancho
Osorno
Pará (Grão Pará)
Paraíba
Paraná, Brazil
Paraty

Pernambuco
Philippines
Piauí
Ponta Porã (Federal Territory)
Potosí
Providencia
Puebla (State)
Puerto Rico
Puno
Querétaro (State)
Regionalism
Rio de Janeiro (Province and State)
Rio Grande do Norte
Rio Grande do Sul
Roraima
Saint Christopher (Saint Kitts)
Saint Vincent
São Paulo, state of
Sergipe
Sonsonate
Texas
Tlaxilacalli
Tocantins
Trujillo
Tucumán
Veracruz (State)
Verapaz
Yucatán

37. TRAVEL, TRANSPORT, AND INFRASTRUCTURE

Casiquiare Canal
Desagüe
Electrification
Energy
Foreign Travelers in Latin America
Guayaquil-Quito Railway
Hamburg-America Line
Highways
International Railways of Central America
    (IRCA, FICA)
Itaipú Hydroelectric Project
Madeira-Mamoré Railroad
Pacific Mail Steamship Navigation Company
    (PMSS)
Panama Canal
Panama Railroad

Pan-American Highway
Railroads
Tela Railroad
Tourism
Transamazon Highway

---

38. TREATIES

Adams-Onís Treaty (1819)
Amapala, Treaties of (1895, 1907)
Amazon Pact (1978)
Ancón, Treaty of (1883)
Andean Pact
Argentina, Federalist Pacts (1831, 1852)
Avalos, Pact of (1820)
Basel, Treaty of (1795)
Bidlack Treaty (Treaty of New Granada, 1846)
Boiso-Lanza Pact (1973)
Bryan-Chamorro Treaty (1914)
Cateau-Cambrésis, Treaty of (1559)
Chinchulín, Pact of
Clayton-Bulwer Treaty (1850)
Córdoba, Treaty of (1821)
Dawson Agreement
Eisenhower-Remón Treaty (1955)
Fontainebleau, Treaty of (1807)
Gondra Treaty (1923)
Guadalupe Hidalgo, Treaty of (1848)
Hay-Bunau-Varilla Treaty (1903)
Hay-Herrán Treaty (1903)
Hay-Pauncefote Treaties (1901)
Hise-Selva Treaty (1849)
Hull-Alfaro Treaty (1936)
International Coffee Agreement
Knox-Castrillo Treaty (1911)
Lima, Treaty of (1929)
London, Treaty of (1604)
Madrid, Treaty of (1670)
Madrid, Treaty of (1750)
Marblehead Pact (1906)
May Pacts (1902)
McLane-Ocampo Treaty (1859)
Methuen, Treaty of (1703)
Naval Club, Pact of the
North American Free Trade Agreement
Ottawa Agreement (1932)
Pact of the Embassy

Panama Canal Treaties of 1977
Petrópolis, Treaty of (1903)
Rinconcito, Treaty of (1838)
Rio Treaty (1947)
Roca-Runciman Pact (1933)
Salomón-Lozano Treaty (1922)
San Ildefonso, Treaty of (1777)
San José de Flores, Pact of
San Nicolás, Pact of
Strangford Treaties (1810)
Taft Agreement (1904)
Tipitapa Agreements
Tordesillas, Treaty of (1494)
Uriarte-Bayarta Agreement
Washington Treaties of 1907 and 1923
Wyke-Aycinena Treaty (1859)
Zanjón, Pact of

---

39. WAR AND THE MILITARY

Acá Carayá Cavalry
Admirable Campaign
Afrancesado
Aguascalientes, Convention of
Argentina, Organizations: Argentine Civic Legion (LCA)
Argentina, Organizations: United Officers Group (GOU)
Armada del Mar del Sur
Armed Forces
Blandengues
Brazilian Expeditionary Force (FEB)
Brazil, National Security Doctrine
Brazil, Organizations: Escola Superior da Guerra (ESG)
Brazil, Organizations: National Guard
British Invasions, Río de la Plata
Canudos Campaign
Capitão Mor
Caribbean Legion
Caste War of Yucatán
Catalonian Volunteers
Catavi Massacre
Cayenne, Brazilian Invasion of
Center for Advanced Military Studies (CAEM)
Chaco War
Chile, War with Spain
Chincha Islands War
Cinco de Mayo

Círculo Militar
Cisplatine War
Citadelle La Ferrière
Colegio Militar (Argentina)
Coto War
Counterinsurgency
Dirty War
El Morro (Havana)
El Morro (San Juan)
Falklands/Malvinas War
Federalist War (1898–1899)
Federal War (Venezuela 1859–1863)
Filibustering
Fleet System: Colonial Brazil
Fleet System: Colonial Spanish America
Football War
Forts and Fortifications, Spanish America
Graf Spee
Granaderos a Caballo
Grito de Baire
Guarani War
Guayaquil Conference (1822)
Guerra Grande
Guerrilla Movements
Humaitá
La Ciudadela
Linha Dura
Maine, U.S.S., Sinking of the
Mexico, Wars and Revolutions: Mexican-
    American War
Mexico, Wars and Revolutions: War of
    Independence
Military Orders: Portugal
Military Orders: Spain

Military Question of the 1880s
Militias: Colonial Brazil
Militias: Colonial Spanish America
Mixtón War
National War
Niños Héroes
Paramilitaries in Latin America
Pastry War
Peru, Organizations: Civil Guard
Presidio
Rurales
Salvacionismo
San Patricio
Seven Years' War
Soldaderas
Sorbonne Group
Spanish-American War
Tecún-Umán
Ten Years' War (1868–1878)
Three Guarantees, Army of the
War of Four Days
War of Jenkins's Ear (1739–1748)
War of the Mascates
War of the Pacific
War of the Peru-Bolivia Confederation
War of the Spanish Succession
War of the Supremes
War of the Thousand Days
War of the Triple Alliance
Wars of Independence, South America
War to the Death
World War I
World War II
Zimmermann Telegram

TABLE OF BIOGRAPHICAL
SUBJECTS BY PROFESSION

Prado y Ugarteche, Javier
Prado y Ugarteche, Manuel
Prado y Ugarteche, Mariano Ignacio
Prat Echaurren, Jorge
Prebisch, Raúl
Pueyrredón, Carlos Alberto
Quijano, Carlos
Ramos Mejía, Ezequiel
Rengifo Cárdenas, Manuel
Ríos Morales, Juan Antonio
Robertson, John Parish, and William Parish
Robles, Marcos Aurelio
Rockefeller, Nelson Aldrich
Romero de Terreros, Pedro
Roy, Eugène
Ruffo Appel, Ernesto
Ruíz Tagle Portales, Francisco
Sacasa, Juan Batista
Sachs, Jeffrey
Samper Agudelo, Miguel
Sánchez de Lozada Bustamante, Gonzalo
Sánchez Navarro, Juan
Sancho de Hoz, Pedro
Santos, Sílvio
Sardaneta y Llorente, José Mariano de
Simonsen, Mário Henrique
Slim Helú, Carlos
Terrazas, Luis
Tornquist, Ernesto
Trejos Fernández, José Joaquín
Uribe Uribe, Rafael
Urquidi, Victor
Vaccaro Brothers
Velázquez Cárdenas de León, Joaquín
Vergara Echeverez, José Francisco
Vernet, Louis
Vesco, Robert Lee
Villanueva, Carlos Raúl
Yermo, Gabriel de
Zamorano, Agustín Juan Vicente
Zaracondegui, Julián de
Zavala, Lorenzo de
Zemurray, Samuel

---

2. CINEMA, THEATER, TELEVISION, SPORTS, AND RECREATION

Acevedo Hernández, Antonio
Alcoriza, Luis

Alou, Felipe Rojas
Álvarez Armellino, Gregorio Conrado
Amorim, Enrique
Amorim, Pedro
Aparicio, Luis
Arau, Alfonso
Armendáriz, Pedro
Arnaz, Desi
Arriví, Francisco
Arrufat, Antón
Barbosa-Lima, Carlos
Bauzá, Mário
Bayly Letts, Jaime
Bedoya, Alfonso
Beltrán, Lola
Bemberg, María Luisa
Boal, Augusto
Bozzo, Laura
Cabrera, Angel Leopoldo
Capablanca, José Raúl
Carew, Rod
Castro, Juan José
Cepeda, Orlando
Chateaubriand Bandeira de Melo, Francisco
    de Assis
Chico Anísio
Chocrón, Isaac
Clair, Janete
Clemente Walker, Roberto
Concepcion, Dave
Córdova, Arturo de
Cugat, Xavier
Del Rio, Dolores
Denevi, Marco
Dihigo, Martín
Fernández, Emilio "El Indio"
Ferrer, José
Figueroa, Gabriel
Galindo, Alejandro
Gambaro, Griselda
García, Sara
García Bernal, Gael
Garciaparra, Nomar
Garmendia, Salvador
Garrincha
Gavidia, Francisco Antonio
Giménez, Susana
Ginobili, Manu
Gómez-Cruz, Ernesto
González Iñárritu, Alejandro

Grande Otelo
Guerra, Ruy
Guevara Espinosa, Ana Gabriela
Guilmain, Ofelia
Gutiérrez Alea, Tomás
Hayek, Salma
Hayworth, Rita
Hermosillo, Jaime-Humberto
Infante, Pedro
Jodorowski, Alejandro
Jurado, Katy
Kreutzberger, Mario
Lamarque, Libertad
Leduc, Paul
López Tarso, Ignacio
Maradona, Diego Armando
Marichal, Juan
Marqués, René
Martinez, Dennis
Martinez, Pedro
Mauro, Humberto
Merello, Tita
Miñoso, Minnie
Miranda, Carmen
Monterroso, Augusto
Montoya, Juan Pablo
Nalé Roxlo, Conrado
Nava, Gregory
Negrete, Jorge
Novarro, Ramón
Ochoa Reyes, Lorena
Pardavé, Joaquín
Pelé
Perez, Tony
Perricholi, La
Pinal, Silvia
Platas Alvarez, Fernando Fabricio
Prado y Ugarteche, Mariano Ignacio
Quinn, Anthony
Resortes, Adalberto Martínez
Ripstein, Arturo
Rivera, Mariano
Rocha, Glauber Pedro de Andrade
Rojo, María
Sabatini, Gabriela
Salles, Walter
Sánchez, Florencio
Santos, Nelson Pereira dos
Santos, Sílvio
Saralegui, Cristina

Sarduy, Severo
Silva, Orlando
Skármeta, Antonio
Solanas, Fernando E.
Solas, Humberto
Soler, Andrés, Domingo, and Fernando
Sosa, Sammy
Steimberg, Alicia
Sumac, Yma
Tiant, Luis
Tin-Tan
Torre Nilsson, Leopoldo
Triana, José
Uslar Pietri, Arturo
Valdez, Luis
Valenzuela, Fernando
Valle, Rafael Heliodoro
Vélez, Lupe
Wolff, Egon
Xuxa
Zorrilla de San Martín, Juan

3. EDUCATION AND SCHOLARSHIP

Aceval, Benjamín
Acosta, Cecilio
Acosta, José de
Adem Chahín, José
Adem Chahín, Julián
Aguayo, Sergio
Alcorta, Diego
Alegre, Francisco Javier
Alemán Valdés, Miguel
Alfaro, Ricardo Joaquín
Alonso, Amado
Alva Ixtlilxóchitl, Fernando
Alvarado, Lisandro
Alvarado Tezozomoc, Don Hernando
Álvarez Armellino, Gregorio Conrado
Álvarez Gardeazábal, Gustavo
Amorim, Enrique
Amunátegui Aldunate, Miguel Luis
Anchieta, José de
Anderson Imbert, Enrique
Andreoni, João Antônio
Angelis, Pedro de
Anzaldúa, Gloria

Arboleda, Carlos
Argüello, Leonardo
Arosemena, Justo
Arzáns Orsúa y Vela, Bartolomé
Ávila, Julio Enrique
Ayala, Eligio
Ayala, Eusebio
Ayala, José de la Cruz
Ayora Cueva, Isidro
Azara, Félix de
Azevedo, Fernando de
Azevedo, Thales de
Bachiller y Morales, Antonio
Baldorioty de Castro, Ramón
Baptista, Mariano
Baquedano, Manuel
Baquíjano y Carrillo de Córdoba, José de
Baralt, Rafael María
Barbero, Andrés
Barnola, Pedro Pablo
Barreda, Gabino
Barrera, Isaac J.
Barrera Barrera, Eulalia Beatriz
Barreto de Menezes, Tobias, Jr.
Barros, João de
Barros Arana, Diego
Basadre, Jorge
Bassols, Narciso
Bellegarde, Luis Dantès
Bello, Andrés
Benítez, Jaime
Benítez Zenteno, Raúl
Benson, Nettie Lee
Bermejo, Ildefonso
Bernal y García Pimentel, Ignacio
Bingham, Hiram
Boggiani, Guido
Bolaños, Luis de
Bolton, Herbert Eugene
Borah, Woodrow
Borges, Jorge Luis
Box, Pelham Horton
Boxer, Charles Ralph
Bray, Arturo
Brenner, Anita
Bresser Pereira, Luiz Carlos
Brum, Baltasar
Bulnes Pinto, Gonzalo
Bunge, Alejandro
Bunge, Carlos Octavio

Bustamante y Rivero, José Luis
Caballero y Rodríguez, José Agustín
Cabrera, Lydia
Caillet-Bois, Ricardo
Calcaño, José Antonio
Caldera Rodríguez, Rafael
Calógeras, João Pandiá
Calvo, Carlos
Campos, Francisco Luiz da Silva
Campos, Roberto (de Oliveira)
Cañas, José Simeón
Cândido de Mello e Souza, Antônio
Cané, Miguel
Capelo, Joaquín
Capistrano de Abreu, João
Cárdenas, Víctor Hugo
Cardim, Frei Fernão
Cardoso, Felipe Santiago
Cardoso, Fernando Henrique
Cardozo, Ramón Indalecio
Caro, Miguel Antonio
Carrillo Flores, Antonio
Carrillo Flores, Nabor
Caso y Andrade, Alfonso
Caso y Andrade, Antonio
Castañeda, Francisco de Paula
Castillo, Jesús
Castillo Ledón, Amalia
Castro Madriz, José María
Centurión, Carlos R.
Cerezo Arévalo, Marco Vinicio
Cervantes, Vicente
Cevallos, Pedro Fermín
Charlot, Jean
Chávez Sánchez, Ignacio
Clavigero, Francisco Javier
Cline, Howard F.
Cobo, Bernabé
Coe, Michael
Coni, Emilio R.
Constant Botelho de Magalhães, Benjamin
Cordero Crespo, Luis
Cornejo, Mariano H.
Corona, Ramón
Correa de Azevedo, Luiz Heitor
Correoso, Buenaventura
Corvalán Lepe, Luis
Cosío Medina, José Gabriel
Cosío Villegas, Daniel
Coutinho, José Joaquim da Cunha de Azeredo

Couto, José Bernardo
Covarrubias, Miguel
Craige, John Houston
Cue Canovas, Agustín
Cuervo, Rufino José
Damas, Léon-Gontran
Da Matta, Roberto
de la Fuente, Juan Ramón
Delfim Neto, Antônio
Deustua, Alejandro O.
Dias, Antônio Gonçalves
Díaz de Guzmán, Ruy
Díaz Soto y Gama, Antonio
Di Tella, Torcuato
Dobles Segreda, Luis
Dobrizhoffer, Martín
Domínguez, Manuel
Drago, Luis María
Durão, José de Santa Rita
Elhuyar, Juan José de
Elhuyar y Zúbice, Fausto de
Encina, Francisco Antonio
Escalada, Asunción
Esquiú, Mamerto
Estimé, Dumarsais
Etchepareborda, Roberto
Facio Brenes, Rodrigo
Falcón, José
Faoro, Raymundo
Feijóo, Benito Jerónimo
Fernandes, Florestan
Fernández Artucio, Hugo
Fernández de Piedrahita, Lucas
Figueiredo, Afonso Celso de Assis
Figueroa Gajardo, Ana
Figueroa Larraín, Emiliano
Flores Galindo, Alberto C.
Francia, José Gaspar Rodríguez de
Freire, Paulo
Freyre, Gilberto (de Mello)
Frías, Antonio
Frigerio, Rogelio
Frondizi, Risieri
Fuentes, Manuel Atanasio
Fuenzalida Grandón, Alejandro
Fúrlong Cárdiff, Guillermo
Furtado, Celso
Galarza, Ernesto
Galdames, Luis Galdames
Galindo, Juan

Gallegos, Rómulo
Galván Rivera, Mariano
Gamio Martínez, Manuel
Gandavo, Pero de Magalhães
Garay, Blas
García, Genaro
García, Juan Agustín
García Canclini, Néstor
García de Castro, Lope
García Diego y Moreno, Francisco
García Icazbalceta, Joaquín
García Robles, Alfonso
García Salinas, Francisco
Garibay Kintana, Ángel María
Gavidia, Francisco Antonio
Gelly, Juan Andrés
Gibson, Charles
Gil Fortoul, José
Golbery do Couto e Silva
Gómez, Benigno
Gondra, Manuel
González, Joaquín Víctor
González, Juan Natalicio
González Casanova, Pablo
González Prada, Manuel
González Suárez, (Manuel María) Federico
González y González, Luís
Gorostiza, Manuel Eduardo de
Gorriti, Juan Ignacio de
Graef Fernández, Carlos
Grau San Martín, Ramón
Guaman Poma de Ayala, Felipe
Guerra y Sánchez, Ramiro
Guevara Arze, Walter
Gutiérrez, Juan María
Halperín-Donghi, Tulio
Handelmann, Gottfried Heinrich
Hanke, Lewis Ulysses
Haro Barraza, Guillermo
Henríquez Ureña, Max
Henríquez Ureña, Pedro
Henry the Navigator
Hernández Colón, Rafael
Herrera, Bartolomé
Holanda, Sérgio Buarque de
Hostos y Bonilla, Eugenio María de
Howard, Jennie Eliza
Ianni, Octavio
Ibarguren, Carlos
Incháustegui Cabral, Héctor
Ingenieros, José

Ivaldi, Humberto
Jaguaribe Gomes de Matos, Hélio
James, Cyril Lionel Robert
Jaramillo Alvarado, Pío
Jerez, Francisco de
Jijón y Caamaño, Jacinto
Jiménez Moreno, Wigberto
Jobet Búrquez, Julio César
Justo, Juan B.
Kemmerer, Edwin Walter
Knorosov, Yuri
Koellreutter, Hans Joachim
Konetzke, Richard
Korn, Alejandro
Kumate Rodríguez, Jesús
Labarca Hubertson, Amanda
Landívar, Rafael
Las Casas, Bartolomé de
Lastarria, José Victorino
León-Portilla, Miguel
Le Plongeon, Augustus
Léry, Jean de
Lescot, Élie
Letelier Madariaga, Valentín
Levene, Ricardo
Lewis, Roberto
Ley, Salvador
Lida, Raimundo
Liendo y Goicoechea, José Antonio
Lima, Alceu Amoroso
Lindo Zelaya, Juan
Liscano Velutini, Juan
Llorente y Lafuente, Anselmo
López, Vicente Fidel
López Michelsen, Alfonso
Lozano, Pedro
Luna Pizarro, Francisco Javier de
Luz y Caballero, José de la
Maldonado, Francisco Severo
Mansilla, Lucio Victorio
Margil de Jesús, Antonio
Marroquín, Francisco
Masferrer, Alberto
Massera, José Pedro
Matienzo, José Nicolás
Maza, Manuel Vicente de
Medina, José Toribio
Mejía del Valle y Llequerica, José Joaquín
Mello, Zélia Maria Cardoso de
Mendes, Gilberto

Méndez Montenegro, Julio César
Mendiburu, Manuel de
Mendieta y Montefur, Carlos
Meyer Cosío, Lorenzo
Millas Jiménez, Jorge
Mir, Pedro
Mitre, Bartolomé
Mogrovejo, Toribio Alfonso de
Molina Garmendia, Enrique
Monteiro, Tobias do Rêgo
Montemayor, Carlos
Montt Torres, Manuel
Moog, Clodomiro Vianna
Morales Carrión, Arturo
Mora Porrás, Juan Rafael
Moreau de Justo, Alicia
Moreno, Fulgencio
Moreno, Mariano
Morley, Sylvanus Griswold
Morse, Richard
Moscote, José Dolores
Moshinsky Borodiansksy, Marcos
Moziño, José Mariano
Munguía, Clemente de Jesús
Muñoz Camargo, Diego
Murra, John V.
Mutis, José Celestino
Nabuco de Araújo, Joaquim
Nascimento, Abdias do
Nimuendajú, Curt
Nóbrega, Manuel da
Novo, Salvador
Núñez Vargas, Benjamín
Nusdorffer, Bernardo
O'Donnell, Guillermo
O'Gorman, Edmundo
Oliveira, Willy Correia de
Oliveira Lima, Manuel de
Oliveira Vianna, Francisco José de
Oré, Luis Gerónimo de
Orozco y Berra, Manuel
Ortiz, Fernando
Otero Vertíz, Gustavo Adolfo
Oviedo y Valdés, Gonzalo Fernández
Pacheco, José Emilio
País, Frank
Palafox y Mendoza, Juan de
Pane, Ignacio Alberto
Pardo y Aliaga, Felipe

Paso y Troncoso, Francisco del
Paterson, William
Paz Soldán Family
Pease, Franklin
Peixoto, Júlio Afrânio
Peláez, Amelia
Pellicer Cámara, Carlos
Pena, Afonso Augusto Moreira
Peralta Azurdia, Enrique
Peralta Barnuevo y Rocha, Pedro de
Pérez Acosta, Juan Francisco
Pérez Aguirre, Luis
Pinheiro, José Feliciano Fernandes
Pinho, José Wanderley de Araújo
Popenoe, Frederick Wilson
Porras Barrenechea, Raúl
Prado, João Fernando de Almeida
Prado, Paulo
Prado da Silva Júnior, Caio
Prescott, William Hickling
Prieto Rodríguez, Sotero
Querino, Manoel Raimundo
Quesada, Ernesto
Quiroga, Vasco de
Rabasa, Emilio
Rama, Angel
Ramírez, José Fernando
Ramírez Vázquez, Pedro
Ramos, Artur
Ramos Mejía, José María
Ramos y Magaña, Samuel
Ravignani, Emilio
Rebouças, André
Restrepo, Carlos Eugenio
Reyes, Oscar Efrén
Reyes, Rafael
Reyes Ochoa, Alfonso
Ribeiro, Darcy
Ribera y Espinosa, Lázaro de
Riva Agüero y Osma, José de la
Rivarola, Rodolfo
Robertson, John Parish, and William Parish
Rocafuerte, Vicente
Rocha, Justiniano José da
Rocha, Manoel Ribeiro
Rocha Pita, Sebastião
Rodrigues, José Honório
Rodrigues, Raimundo Nina
Rodríguez, Richard
Rodríguez, Simón

Rodríguez Lara, Guillermo
Rodríguez Monegal, Emir
Roig de Leuchsenring, Emilio
Rojas, Arístides
Romay y Valdés Chacón, Tomás
Romero, Emilio
Romero, Sílvio
Romero Rubio, Manuel
Rosenblueth, Arturo Stearns
Ruiz de Montoya, Antonio
Saco, José Antonio
Sáenz, Moisés
Sagra, Ramón de la
Salvador, Vicente do
Samora, Julian
Sánchez, Luis Alberto
Sánchez, Prisciliano
Sánchez de Bustamante y Sirven, Antonio
Sánchez de Tagle, Francisco Manuel
Sandoval Vallarta, Manuel
Santamaría, Haydée
Sarmiento, Domingo Faustino
Schomburg, Arturo Alfonso
Sepp, Anton
Serrano, José
Sierra O'Reilly, Justo
Sigüenza y Góngora, Carlos de
Silva Herzog, Jesús
Silva Lisboa, José da
Simonsen, Mário Henrique
Simonsen, Roberto Cochrane
Sodré, Nelson Werneck
Solano, Francisco
Solórzano Pereira, Juan de
Soto Alfaro, Bernardo
Sousa, Gabriel Soares de
Sousa, Otávio Tarqüínio de
Southey, Robert
Squier, Ephraim George
Staden, Hans
Stefanich, Juan
Suárez, Marco Fidel
Taborga Pizarro, Miguel de los Santos
Tallet, José Zacarías
Tamayo, Franz
Tannenbaum, Frank
Taunay, Affonso d'Escragnolle
Tavares Bastos, Aureliano Cândido
Teixeira, Anisio Espinola

Tello, Julio César
Thayer Ojeda, Tomás
Thompson, Eric
Tobar Donoso, Julio
Toledo y Figueroa, Francisco de
Torres Bello, Diego de
Torres Bodet, Jaime
Torre y Huerta, Carlos de la
Trejos Fernández, José Joaquín
Tugwell, Rexford Guy
Unanue, Hipólito
Uribe Uribe, Rafael
Urquidi, Victor
Uruguai, Visconde do
Valdivia, Luis de
Valencia, Guillermo León
Valle, José Cecilio del
Valle, Rafael Heliodoro
Varela, José Pedro
Varela y Morales, Félix
Varnhagen, Francisco Adolfo de
Varona y Pera, Enrique José
Vasconcelos Calderón, José
Vaz Ferreira, Carlos
Velasco, Juan de
Velázquez Cárdenas de León, Joaquín
Vélez Sarsfield, Dalmacio
Vera Cruz, Alonso de la
Viana, Francisco José de Oliveira
Vieira, Antônio
Vigil, Francisco de Paula González
Villacorta Calderón, José Antonio
Villanueva, Carlos Raúl
Villarán, Manuel Vicente
Villoro, Luis
Vitoria, Francisco de
Wagley, Charles Walter
Weffort, Francisco Correia
Wilde, Eduardo
Ximénez, Francisco
Yáñez Santos Delgadillo, Agustín
Ynsfrán, Pablo Max
Zaldúa, Francisco Javier
Zárate, Agustín de
Zavala, Joaquín
Zavala, Silvio
Zayas y Alfonso, Alfredo
Zea Aguilar, Leopoldo
Zinny, Antonio

Zubirán Achondo, Salvador
Zubiría, José Antonio Laureano de
Zulen, Pedro S., [and] Dora Mayer de Zulen
Zum Felde, Alberto

4. EXPLORATION AND CONQUEST

Abreu, Diego de
Aguayo, Marqués de
Aguilar, Jerónimo de
Aguilar, Martín de
Aguirre, Lope de
Alarcón, Martín de
Alberni, Pedro de
Almagro, Diego de
Alvarado y Mesía, Pedro de
Álvarez de Pineda, Alonso
Ampíes, Juan de
Andagoya, Pascual de
Anza, Juan Bautista de
Arias de Saavedra, Hernando
Ávila, Pedro Arias de
Balboa, Vasco Núñez de
Bazaine, François Achille
Belalcázar, Sebastián de
Bingham, Hiram
Bodega y Quadra, Juan Francisco de la
Boggiani, Guido
Bonpland, Aimé Jacques
Borba Gato, Manuel de
Brasseur de Bourbourg, Charles Étienne
Cabeza de Vaca, Alvar Núñez
Cabot, Sebastian
Cabral, Pedro Álvares
Casa da Torre
Castellanos, Juan de
Catherwood, Frederick
Cavallón, Juan de
Columbus, Diego (d. 1515)
Columbus, Bartholomew
Columbus, Christopher
Coronado, Juan Vázquez de
Cortés, Hernán
Díaz del Castillo, Bernal
Elcano, Juan Sebastián de
Enciso, Martín Fernández de
Escandón, José de

Espejo, Antonio de
Esteban
Estrada, José Manuel
Fajardo, Francisco
Fawcett, Percy
Féderman, Nicolás
Fernández, Juan
Fernández de Córdoba, Diego
Frémont, John Charles
Galindo, Juan
Gama, Vasco da
Garay, Juan de
Garcés, Francisco Tomás Hermenegildo
García, Aleixo
Girón, Francisco Hernández
González Dávila, Gil
Gregory XIII, Pope
Grijalva, Juan de
Groussac, Paul
Guzmán, Nuño Beltrán de
Henry the Navigator
Heredia y Heredia, José M.
Hernández (Fernández) de Córdoba,
        Francisco
Humboldt, Alexander von
Hurtado de Mendoza, Andrés
Hurtado de Mendoza, García
Ibarra, Diego
Irala, Domingo Martínez de
Jiménez de Quesada, Gonzalo
Juan y Santacilia, Jorge
Kinney, Henry L.
Kino, Eusebio Francisco
La Salle, René-Robert Cavelier, Sieur de
Lasuén, Fermín Francisco de
León, Alonso de
Lepe, Diego de
López, Narciso
López de Legazpi y Gurruchátegui, Miguel
Losada, Diego de
Luna y Arellano, Tristán de
Luque, Hernando de
Magellan, Ferdinand
Malinche
Manso de Velasco, José Antonio
Martínez, Esteban José
Martyr, Peter
Meiggs, Henry
Melgares, Facundo
Mendoza, Pedro de

Menéndez de Avilés, Pedro
Montejo, Francisco de
Muñoz Camargo, Diego
Narváez, Pánfilo de
Nicuesa, Diego
Niño, Pedro Alonso
Niza, Marcos de
Ojeda, Alonso de
Olid, Cristóbal de
Oña, Pedro de
Oñate, Juan de
Orellana, Francisco de
Pardo, Juan
Pérez, Juan
Pérez de Tolosa, Juan
Pinzón, Martín Alonso
Pinzón, Vicente Yáñez
Pizarro, Francisco
Pizarro, Gonzalo
Pizarro, Hernando
Pizarro, Pedro
Ponce de León, Juan
Portolá, Gaspar de
Ramalho, João
Reyes, Rafael
Rivera, Pedro de
Rivera y Moncada, Fernando de
Robertson, John Parish, and William Parish
Rodríguez Cabrillo, Juan
Rodríguez Freile, Juan
Rondon, Cândido Mariano da Silva
Salgado, José
Sarmiento de Gamboa, Pedro
Sedeño, Antonio de
Serra, Junipero
Solís, Juan Díaz de
Soto, Hernando de
Sousa, Martim Afonso de
Staden, Hans
Talamantes, Melchor de
Tavares, Antônio Rapôso
Ulloa, Antonio de
Urdaneta, Andrés de
Ursúa, Pedro de
Valdivia, Pedro de
Vargas, Diego de
Vázquez de Ayllón, Lucas
Vázquez de Coronado, Francisco
Velásquez, Diego de
Vélez de Escalante, Silvestre

Vespucci, Amerigo
Vial, Pedro
Villagra, Francisco de
Villagrá, Gaspar Pérez de
Villarroel, Gaspar de
Villas Bôas Brothers
Vizcaíno, Sebastián

5. JOURNALISM

Acosta, José de
Alamán, Lucas
Alberdi, Juan Bautista
Alencar, José Martiniano de
Alzate y Ramírez, José Antonio de
Amaral, Antônio José Azevedo do
Andrade, Carlos Drummond de
Andreve, Guillermo
Andueza Palacio, Raimundo
Ângelo, Ivan
Antuñano, Estevan de
Arango y Parreño, Francisco de
Arboleda, Julio
Arciniegas, Germán
Arguedas, Alcides
Ayala, José de la Cruz
Aycinena Piñol, Juan José de
Azevedo, Fernando de
Báez, Cecilio
Baldorioty de Castro, Ramón
Barreda y Laos, Felipe
Barreiro, Antonio
Barrera, Isaac J.
Barrett, Rafael
Barros Arana, Diego
Barroso, Gustavo Dodt
Bayly Letts, Jaime
Beals, Carleton
Bedoya Reyes, Luis
Belaúnde, Víctor Andrés
Beltrán, Pedro
Bergaño y Villegas, Simón
Berges, José
Betances y Alacán, Ramón Emeterio
Betancourt, Rómulo
Betancourt Cisneros, Gaspar
Blanco, Andrés Eloy
Blanco Acevedo, Eduardo

Blanco Galdós, Hugo
Bocaiúva, Quintino
Bolaño, Roberto
Brandão, Ignácio de Loyola
Bravo, Mario
Bray, Arturo
Brenner, Anita
Bulnes, Francisco
Bustamante, Carlos María de
Bustamante y Rivero, José Luis
Cabrera Lobato, Luis
Callado, Antônio
Campbell, Federico
Capistrano de Abreu, João
Cárcano, Miguel Ángel
Cárcano, Ramón José
Caro, José Eusebio
Caro, Miguel Antonio
Caso y Andrade, Antonio
Castelli, Juan José
Castro Madriz, José María
Centurión, Carlos R.
Centurión, Juan Crisóstomo
Chamorro Cardenal, Pedro Joaquín
Chateaubriand Bandeira de Melo, Francisco de
    Assis
Coelho Neto, Henrique
Coll y Toste, Cayetano
Cooke, John William
Correoso, Buenaventura
Corvalán Lepe, Luis
Cosío Villegas, Daniel
Costa, Hipólito José da
Cos y Pérez, José María
Creydt, Oscar
Cuadra, Pablo Antonio
Cumplido, Ignacio
Cunha, Euclides da
Darío, Rubén
Dávila Espinoza, Carlos Guillermo
Debray, [Jules] Régis
Del Prado, Jorge
Deustua, Alejandro O.
Dickmann, Adolfo
Dickmann, Enrique
Dobles Segreda, Luis
Echeverría, Esteban
Egaña Fabres, Mariano
Escalante, Aníbal

Etchepareborda, Roberto
Faoro, Raymundo
Fernández Artucio, Hugo
Fernández Madrid, José
Fernández Retamar, Roberto
Figueiredo, Afonso Celso de Assis
Flores Magón, Ricardo
Fortuny, José Manuel
Francia, José Gaspar Rodríguez de
Frondizi, Risieri
Fuentes, Manuel Atanasio
Gainza Paz, Alberto
Gaitan, Jorge Eliécer
Galeano, Eduardo Hughes
Gálvez, Manuel
Gama, Luís
Garay, Blas
Garcilaso de la Vega, El Inca
Garvey, Marcus
Gelly, Juan Andrés
Ghioldi, Américo
Ghioldi, Rodolfo
Gil Fortoul, José
Girri, Alberto
Gómez, Eugenio
Gómez, Juan Gualberto
Gómez Carrillo, Enrique
Gómez Castro, Laureano
González, Florentino
González, Joaquín Víctor
González, Juan Natalicio
González Obregón, Luís
Gorostiza, Manuel Eduardo de
Groussac, Paul
Guardia, Ricardo Adolfo de la
Gutiérrez, Gustavo
Gutiérrez, José María
Gutiérrez Estrada, José María
Gutiérrez Nájera, Manuel
Guzmán, Antonio Leocadio
Guzmán, Martín Luis
Haya de la Torre, Víctor Raúl
Henríquez Ureña, Max
Henríquez Ureña, Pedro
Hernández, José
Herrera, Bartolomé
Herrera, Luis Alberto de
Herrera y Obes, Julio
Herzog, Vladimir
Hidalgo, Bartolomé

Hidalgo, Enrique Agustín
Hidalgo y Costilla, Miguel
Hildebrandt Perez Treviño, César
Holanda, Sérgio Buarque de
Humboldt, Alexander von
Ibarguren, Carlos
Iglesias Pantin, Santiago
Infante, José Miguel
Ingenieros, José
Irisarri y Larraín, Juan Bautista
James, Cyril Lionel Robert
Justo, Juan B.
Krauze, Enrique
Lacerda, Carlos Frederico Werneck de
Larrea, Juan
Las Casas, Bartolomé de
Lastarria, José Victorino
Leguizamón, Martiniano
Lida, Raimundo
Lima, Alceu Amoroso
Lima Barreto, Afonso Henriques de
Liscano Velutini, Juan
Lleras Restrepo, Carlos
Lombardo Toledano, Vicente
López Michelsen, Alfonso
López Pumarejo, Alfonso
López Trujillo, Alfonso
López Vallecillos, Italo
López y Fuentes, Gregorio
Lugones, Leopoldo
Luisi, Luisa
Luna Pizarro, Francisco Javier de
Machado, Gustavo
Machado de Assis, Joaquim Maria
Maldonado, Francisco Severo
Mallea, Eduardo
Mañach y Robato, Jorge
Mansilla, Lucio Victorio
Mariátegui, José Carlos
Marinho, Roberto
Martínez Estrada, Ezequiel
Masferrer, Alberto
Massera, José Pedro
Mastretta, Angeles
Matto de Turner, Clorinda
Mendieta y Montefur, Carlos
Mesa, Carlos
Meyer Cosío, Lorenzo
Mier Noriega y Guerra, José Servando
    Teresa de

Solórzano Pereira, Juan de
Sotomayor Valdés, Ramón
Sousa, Otávio Tarqüínio de
Souza, Márcio Gonçalves Bentes
Squier, Ephraim George
Stephens, John Lloyd
Talavera, Natalício
Tallet, José Zacarías
Távara y Andrade, Santiago
Timerman, Jacobo
Torre, Lisandro de la
Torres Bodet, Jaime
Traba, Marta
Tristan, Flora
Trotsky, Leon
Trujillo, Manuel
Turbay, Gabriel
Ugarte, Manuel
Ulate Blanco, Otilio
Urbina, Luis Gonzaga
Valencia, Guillermo León
Valle, Artistóbulo del
Valle, José Cecilio del
Varela, José Pedro
Varela y Morales, Félix
Vargas Llosa, Mario
Varona y Pera, Enrique José
Vasconcelos Calderón, José
Vedia y Mitre, Mariano
Veiga, Evaristo Ferreira da
Villarán, Manuel Vicente
Villaurrutia, Jacobo de
Villeda Morales, Ramón
Walker, William
Wyld Ospina, Carlos
Zabludovski, Abraham
Zabludovski, Jacobo
Zapata, Felipe
Zarco, Francisco
Zavala, Lorenzo de
Zavala, Silvio
Zayas y Alfonso, Alfredo
Zeballos, Estanislao
Zulen, Pedro S., [and] Dora Mayer de Zulen

6. LABOR AND LABOR RELATIONS

Abadía Méndez, Miguel
Aguirre Cerda, Pedro

Alem, Leandro N.
Allende Gossens, Salvador
Arcos, Santiago
Arismendi, Rodney
Arze, José Antonio
Bemberg, Otto
Bilbao Barquín, Francisco
Bravo, Mario
Bulnes Prieto, Manuel
Campa Salazar, Valentín
Cano, María de los Ángeles
Chonchol, Jacques
Collor, Lindolfo
Corral Verdugo, Ramón
Del Prado, Jorge
Eder, Santiago Martín
Fallas Sibaja, Carlos Luis
Flores Magón, Ricardo
Galarza, Ernesto
Ghioldi, Américo
Ghioldi, Rodolfo
Guevara, Ernesto "Che"
Iglesias Pantin, Santiago
Julião Arruda de Paula, Francisco
Justo, Juan B.
Lacerda, Maurício Pavia de
Lechín Oquendo, Juan
Lombardo Toledano, Vicente
López, Ambrosio
Machado, Gustavo
Mendes Filho, Francisco ("Chico") Alves
Molina Solís, Olegario
Monge Álvarez, Luis Alberto
Morones, Luis
Núñez Vargas, Benjamín
Pacheco da Silva, Osvaldo
Palacios, Alfredo L.
Pellacani, Dante
Peña, Lázaro
Prieto Figueroa, Luis Beltrán
Querino, Manoel Raimundo
Recabarren Serrano, Luis Emilio
Riani, Clodsmith
Roca, Blas
Romero Rosa, Ramón
Seoane, Manuel
Siles Zuazo, Hernán
Silva, Lindolfo
Silva, Luis Inácio Lula da
Torre, Lisandro de la

Trotsky, Leon
Velázquez Sánchez, Fidel

---

7. LAND OWNERSHIP

Abasolo, Mariano
Agramonte y Loynaz, Ignacio
Aguayo, Marqués de
Álzaga, Martín de
Arana, Felipe de
Arana, Julio César
Arango y Parreño, Francisco de
Argüello, Santiago
Aspíllaga Family
Austin, Moses
Austin, Stephen Fuller
Aycinena, Juan Fermín de
Carvajal, Luis de
Cedillo Martínez, Saturnino
Chiari, Rodolfo E.
Chiari Remón, Roberto Francisco
Cisneros Betancourt, Salvador
Cortés, Hernán
Cortés, Martín
de León, Martín
Dellepiane, Luis J.
Dieseldorff, Erwin Paul
Egaña Fabres, Mariano
Elías, Domingo
Figueres Ferrer, José
Galindo, Juan
Garay, Juan de
Gildemeister Family
Gómez, Juan Vicente
Guerra, Ramón
Güiraldes, Ricardo
Irala, Domingo Martínez de
Lacalle Herrera, Luis Alberto
Leguía, Augusto Bernardino
López de Quiroga, Antonio
López de Romaña, Eduardo
Machado y Morales, Gerardo
Madero, Francisco Indalecio
Miró Quesada Family
Mora, Fernando de la
Nicuesa, Diego
Orlich Bolmarcich, Francisco José
Paz Soldán Family

Pétion, Alexandre Sabès
Romero, Matías
Rosáins, Juan Nepomuceno
Ruíz Tagle Portales, Francisco
Salgado, José
Sousa, Gabriel Soares de
Terrazas, Luis
Toro Zambrano, Mateo de
Torre Tagle y Portocarrero, José Bernardo de
Uribe Uribe, Rafael
Vallejo, Mariano Guadalupe
Zaracondegui, Julián de

---

8. LITERATURE, BELLES LETTRES, AND PHILOSOPHY

Abadía Méndez, Miguel
Abbad y Lasierra, Íñigo
Abente y Lago, Victorino
Abril, Xavier
Acevedo Díaz, Eduardo Inés
Acevedo Hernández, Antonio
Acosta, Cecilio
Acosta, José de
Aguiar, Adonias
Aguilera Malta, Demetrio
Aguirre, Nataniel
Agustín, José
Agustini, Delmira
Alamán, Lucas
Albán, Laureano
Alberto, João
Alegre, Francisco Javier
Alegría, Ciro
Alegría, Claribel
Alegría, Fernando
Alencar, José Martiniano de
Alexis, Jacques Stéphen
Alfaro, Ricardo Joaquín
Allende, Isabel
Almafuerte
Almeida, José Américo de
Almeida, Manuel Antônio de
Almonte, Juan Nepomuceno
Alonso, Amado
Alonso, Manuel A.
Altamirano, Ignacio Manuel
Alurista

Alva Ixtlilxóchitl, Fernando

Alvarado, Lisandro

Alvarado, Salvador

Alvarado Tezozomoc, Hernando

Alvarez, Julia

Álvarez Gardeazábal, Gustavo

Álvarez Ponce de León, Griselda

Alzate y Ramírez, José Antonio de

Amado, Jorge

Ambrogi, Arturo

Amorim, Enrique

Anaya, Rudolfo

Anchieta, José de

Andagoya, Pascual de

Anderson Imbert, Enrique

Andrade, Carlos Drummond de

Andrade, Jorge

Andrade, Mário de

Andrade, Olegario Victor

Andrade, Oswald de

Andrade, Roberto

Andreve, Guillermo

Angel, Albalucía

Angelis, Pedro de

Ângelo, Ivan

Anzaldúa, Gloria

Appleyard, José Luis

Arboleda, Julio

Arciniegas, Germán

Arcos, Santiago

Arenas, Reinaldo

Arévalo Bermejo, Juan José

Arévalo Martínez, Rafael

Arguedas, Alcides

Arguedas, José María

Argüelles, Hugo

Argüello Mora, Manuel

Arias, Arturo

Arias Sánchez, Oscar

Aridjis, Homero

Arlt, Roberto

Arosemena, Justo

Arreola, Juan José

Arriví, Francisco

Arrufat, Antón

Ascasubi, Hilario

Assunção, Leilah

Asturias, Miguel Ángel

Ávila, Julio Enrique

Azar, Héctor

Azcárate y Lezama, Juan Francisco de

Azevedo, Aluísio

Azuela, Mariano

Bachiller y Morales, Antonio

Balbuena, Bernardo de

Ballagas y Cubeñas, Emilio

Balseiro, José Agustín

Bandeira, Manuel Carneiro de Souza

Baquerizo Moreno, Alfredo

Baralt, Rafael María

Barbosa, Domingos Caldas

Barnet, Miguel

Barnola, Pedro Pablo

Barreiro, Antonio

Barrera Barrera, Eulalia Beatriz

Barreto de Menezes, Tobias, Jr.

Barrios, Eduardo

Barroso, Gustavo Dodt

Basso Maglio, Vicente

Basurto, Luis

Batlle y Ordóñez, José

Batres Montúfar, José

Bedregal de Conitzer, Yolanda

Bélance, René

Bellegarde, Luis Dantès

Belli, Gioconda

Bello, Andrés

Beltrán, Washington

Benedetti, Mario

Benítez, Gregorio

Berenguer, Amanda

Berman, Sabina

Bermejo, Ildefonso

Bianco, José

Bilbao Barquín, Francisco

Bioy Casares, Adolfo

Blanco, Andrés Eloy

Blanco Fombona, Rufino

Blest Gana, Alberto

Boal, Augusto

Bolaño, Roberto

Bombal, María Luisa

Bonifaz Nuño, Rubén

Borge, Tomás

Borges, Jorge Luis

Borno, Joseph Louis E. Antoine François

Bosch Gaviño, Juan

Boullosa, Carmen

Brañas Guerra, César

Brandão, Ignácio de Loyola

Brannon de Samayoa Chinchilla, Carmen
Brasseur de Bourbourg, Charles Étienne
Brathwaite, Edward Kamau
Brenner, Anita
Brierre, Jean-Fernand
Brull, Mariano
Brunet, Marta
Bryce Echenique, Alfredo
Bulnes, Francisco
Burgos, Julia de
Bustamante, Carlos María de
Caballero Calderón, Eduardo
Caballero y Rodríguez, José Agustín
Cabeza de Vaca, Alvar Núñez
Cabezas Lacayo, Omar
Cabral, Manuel del
Cabrera, Lydia
Cabrera Infante, Guillermo
Cáceres, Esther de
Calcaño, José Antonio
Calderón de la Barca, Fanny
Callado, Antônio
Camacho Solís, Manuel
Cambaceres, Eugenio
Camille, Roussan
Camões, Luís Vaz de
Campbell, Federico
Campo, Estanislao del
Campobello, Nellie
Campos, Augusto de
Campos, Haroldo de
Campos, Julieta
Campos Cervera, Hérib
Canales, Nemesio Rosario
Cané, Miguel
Cantón, Wilberto
Capelo, Joaquín
Cardenal, Ernesto
Cardoza y Aragón, Luis
Caro, José Eusebio
Caro, Miguel Antonio
Carpentier, Alejo
Carranza Fernández, Eduardo
Carrasquilla, Tomás
Carrera Andrade, Jorge
Carrió de la Vandera, Alonso
Carrión, Alejandro
Carrión, Manuel Benjamín
Carvajal, Luis de
Casal, Julián del

Casanova y Estrada, Ricardo
Caso y Andrade, Antonio
Castellanos, Juan de
Castellanos, Rosario
Castillo, Ana
Castillo, Jesús
Castillo, Otto René
Castillo y Guevara, Francisca Josefa de la
    Concepción de
Castro Alves, Antônio de
Centurión, Roque Miranda
Cerruto, Óscar
Césaire, Aimé
Céspedes y Quesada, Carlos Manuel de
Charry Lara, Fernando
Chauvet, Marie Vieux
Chávez Sánchez, Ignacio
Chimalpahin
Chiriboga, Luz Argentina
Chocano, José Santos
Chumacero, Alí
Cieza de León, Pedro de
Cisneros, Sandra
Clavigero, Francisco Javier
Cobo, Bernabé
Coelho, Paulo
Coelho Neto, Henrique
Coicou, Massillon
Coll y Toste, Cayetano
Colmán, Narciso
Condé, Maryse
Constant Botelho de Magalhães, Benjamin
Coronel Urtecho, José
Correa, Julio Myzkowsky
Cortázar, Julio
Cortés, Hernán
Cosío Villegas, Daniel
Costa, Cláudio Manuel da
Couto, José Bernardo
Cruz e Sousa, João da
Cuadra, Pablo Antonio
Cuevas, Mariano
Cunha, Euclides da
Cunha Dotti, Juan
Dalton García, Roque
Danticat, Edwidge
Darío, Rubén
Debray, [Jules] Régis
Dellepiane, Luis J.
Denevi, Marco

Depestre, René
D'Escoto Brockmann, Miguel
Desnoes, Edmundo Pérez
Dias, Antônio Gonçalves
Dias Gomes, Alfredo
Díaz, José Pedro
Díaz Lozano, Argentina
Diego, Eliseo
Diego, José de
Donoso, José
Dragún, Osvaldo
Durán, Diego
Durand, Oswald
Durão, José de Santa Rita
Echeverría, Esteban
Edwards, Agustín
Edwards, Jorge
Edwards Bello, Joaquín
Eguren, José María
Elizondo, Salvador
Enciso, Martín Fernández de
Enríquez de Guzmán, Alonso
Ercilla y Zúñiga, Alonso de
Esquivel, Laura
Estrada, José Manuel
Facio Brenes, Rodrigo
Fallas Sibaja, Carlos Luis
Fariña Núñez, Eloy
Féderman, Nicolás
Feijóo, Benito Jerónimo
Fernandes, Millôr
Fernández de Lizardi, José Joaquín
Fernández Madrid, José
Fernández Retamar, Roberto
Ferré, Rosario
Figueiredo, Afonso Celso de Assis
Florit, Eugenio
Fortuny, José Manuel
Franco, Rafael
Freire, Paulo
Freyre, Gilberto (de Mello)
Frondizi, Risieri
Fuentes, Carlos
Fuentes y Guzmán, Francisco Antonio de
Funes, Gregorio
Gage, Thomas
Gaitán Durán, Jorge
Galeano, Eduardo Hughes
Galindo, Sergio
Gallego Otero, Laura

Gallegos, Rómulo
Galván, Manuel de Jesús
Gálvez, Manuel
Gama, José Basilio da
Gama, Luís
Gambaro, Griselda
Gamboa Iglesias, Federico
Gaos, José
García, Genaro
García del Río, Juan
García Icazbalceta, Joaquín
García Márquez, Gabriel
García Ortíz, Laureano
García Peláez, Francisco de Paula
Garcilaso de la Vega, El Inca
Garmendia, Salvador
Garro, Elena
Gatón Arce, Freddy
Gavidia, Francisco Antonio
Gerchunoff, Alberto
Girri, Alberto
Glantz, Margo
Glissant, Édouard
Goldemberg, Isaac
Gómez, Juan Carlos
Gómez Carrillo, Enrique
Gómez de Avellaneda y Arteaga, Gertrudis
Gonzaga, Tomás Antônio
González, Joaquín Víctor
González, Juan Natalicio
González, Juan Vicente
González Casanova, Pablo
González de Eslava, Fernán
Gonzalez de Fanning, Teresa
González León, Adriano
González Martínez, Enrique
González Prada, Manuel
Gorodischer, Angélica
Gorostiza, Manuel Eduardo de
Gorriti, Juana Manuela
Graça Aranha, José Pereira da
Grimard, Luc
Groussac, Paul
Guarnieri, Gianfrancesco
Gudiño Kieffer, Eduardo
Guerra y Sánchez, Ramiro
Guido, Beatriz
Guido y Spano, Carlos
Guillén, Nicolás
Güiraldes, Ricardo

Guirao, Ramón
Gutiérrez González, Gregorio
Gutiérrez Nájera, Manuel
Guzmán, Augusto
Guzmán, Enrique
Guzmán, Martín Luis
Haro Barraza, Guillermo
Heiremans, Luis Alberto
Henríquez Ureña, Max
Henríquez Ureña, Pedro
Heredia y Heredia, José M.
Hernández, Felisberto
Hernández, José
Hernández, Luisa Josefina
Herrera, Flavio
Herrera y Reissig, Julio
Herrera y Tordesillas, Antonio de
Hidalgo, Bartolomé
Hidalgo, Enrique Agustín
Hinojosa-Smith, Rolando
Hippolyte, Dominique
Holguín, Jorge
Hudson, William Henry
Huerta, David
Huidobro Fernández, Vicente
Humboldt, Alexander von
Ibáñez, Roberto
Ibáñez, Sara de
Ibarbourou, Juana de
Ibargüengoitia, Jorge
Icaza Coronel, Jorge
Iglesias, José María
Illescas, Carlos
Incháustegui Cabral, Héctor
Isaacs, Jorge
James, Cyril Lionel Robert
Jaramillo Levi, Enrique
Jesus, Carolina Maria de
Jodorowski, Alejandro
Juana Inés de la Cruz, Sor
Kincaid, Jamaica
Korn, Alejandro
Krauze, Enrique
Labrador Ruíz, Enrique
Laguerre, Enrique Arturo
Laleau, Léon
Lame, Manuel Quintín
Landa, Diego de
Landívar, Rafael
Larreta, Enrique Rodríguez

Las Casas, Bartolomé de
Leante, César
Leguizamón, Martiniano
Leñero, Vicente
Levinson, Luisa Mercedes
Lezama Lima, José
Lida, Raimundo
Liendo y Goicoechea, José Antonio
Lihn, Enrique
Lima, Alceu Amoroso
Lima, Jorge de
Lima Barreto, Afonso Henriques de
Lins, Osman da Costa
Lins do Rego, José
Liscano Velutini, Juan
Lispector, Clarice
Llorens Torres, Luis
López, Wilebaldo
López de Cogolludo, Diego
López Portillo, José
López Vallecillos, Italo
López Velarde, Ramón
López y Fuentes, Gregorio
Lorenzana y Buitrón, Francisco Antonio de
Loynaz, Dulce María
Lugones, Leopoldo
Luz y Caballero, José de la
Lynch, Benito
Lynch, Marta
Macedo, Joaquim Manuel de
Machado de Assis, Joaquim Maria
Magalhães, Domingos José Gonçalves de
Magaña, Sergio
Magdaleno, Mauricio
Maíz, Fidel
Mallea, Eduardo
Mañach y Robato, Jorge
Manzano, Juan Francisco
Marechal, Leopoldo
Marinello, Juan
Markham, Clements Robert
Mármol, José Pedro Crisólogo
Marqués, René
Marroquín, José Manuel
Martínez, Tomás Eloy
Martínez Estrada, Ezequiel
Martyr, Peter
Masferrer, Alberto
Massera, José Pedro
Mastretta, Angeles

Matos, Gregório de
Matto de Turner, Clorinda
Meireles, Cecília
Melo Franco, Afonso Arinos de
Melo Neto, João Cabral de
Méndez Ballester, Manuel
Méndez Pereira, Octavio
Mendoza, Jaime
Mera, Juan León
Milla y Vidaurre, José
Mir, Pedro
Miró, César
Mistral, Gabriela
Mitre, Bartolomé
Mohr, Nicholasa
Molina, Juan Ramón
Molina Bedoya, Felipe
Molinari, Ricardo E.
Montalvo, Juan
Monteiro Lobato, José Bento
Montemayor, Carlos
Monterroso, Augusto
Montúfar, Lorenzo
Morais, Vinícius de
Morales, Mario Roberto
Morales Carrión, Arturo
Morejón, Nancy
Moscote, José Dolores
Moshinsky Borodianksky, Marcos
Motecuhzoma II
Motolinía, Toribio de
Munguía, Clemente de Jesús
Muñoz Marín, Luis
Muñoz Rivera, Luis
Mutis, Alvaro
Naipaul, V. S.
Nalé Roxlo, Conrado
Naranjo, Carmen
Nascimento, Abdias do
Neruda, Pablo
Nervo, Amado
Nezahualcoyotl
Nieves y Bustamante, María
Novás Calvo, Lino
Novo, Salvador
Núñez Moledo, Rafael
Obaldía, María Olimpia de
Ocampo, Victoria
Odio, Eunice
O'Gorman, Edmundo

O'Leary, Daniel Florencio
Oliveira, Manuel Botelho de
Olmedo, José Joaquín de
Onetti, Juan Carlos
Oreamuno, Yolanda
Oribe, Emilio
Orozco, Olga
Orozco y Berra, Manuel
Orphée, Elvira
Ortiz, Fernando
Ortiz de Ayala, Simón Tadeo
Otero, Mariano
Ovando, Nicolás de
Oviedo y Valdés, Gonzalo Fernández
Pacheco, José Emilio
Padilla, Heberto
Palacios, Antonia
Palés Matos, Luis
Palma, Clemente
Palma, Ricardo
Palma Román, Angélica
Pani Arteaga, Alberto J.
Pardo y Aliaga, Felipe
Pareja Diezcanseco, Alfredo
Parra, Nicanor
Parra, Teresa de la
Paso, Fernando del
Paso y Troncoso, Francisco del
Paterson, William
Patrocínio, José do
Payno y Flores, Manuel
Paz, Octavio
Peixoto, Floriano Vieira
Pellicer Cámara, Carlos
Pena, Luís Carlos Martins
Peralta Barnuevo y Rocha, Pedro de
Perera, Víctor
Peri Rossi, Cristina
Phelps, Anthony
Picón Salas, Mariano
Piñera, Virgilio
Piñon, Nélida
Pita Rodríguez, Félix
Pitol, Sergio
Pizarnik, Alejandra
Plá, Josefina
Pompéia, Raúl
Poniatowska, Elena
Porras Barrenechea, Raúl
Portal, Magda

Pôrto Alegre, Manuel Araújo
Prado, Pedro
Prescott, William Hickling
Price-Mars, Jean
Prieto, Guillermo
Puga, María Luisa
Puig, Manuel
Puig Casauranc, José Manuel
Queiroz, Dinah Silveira de
Queiroz, Rachel de
Quintana Roo, Andrés
Quiroga, Horacio
Rabasa, Emilio
Rada, Manuel de Jesús
Ramírez, Ignacio
Ramírez, José Fernando
Ramírez Mercado, Sergio
Ramos, Graciliano
Ramos Arizpe, José Miguel
Ramos y Magaña, Samuel
Rangel, Alberto
Rego Monteiro, Vicente do
Restrepo, José Manuel
Revueltas, José
Reyes, Rafael
Reyes Ochoa, Alfonso
Ribeiro, João Ubaldo
Ribeyro, Julio Ramón
Riesco, Laura
Rio, João do
Riva Agüero y Osma, José de la
Riva Palacio, Vicente
Rivera, José Eustasio
Rivera, Pedro de
Roa Barcena, José María
Roa Bastos, Augusto
Rodó, José Enrique
Rodrigues, Nelson
Rodríguez-Alcalá, Hugo
Rodríguez Cerna, José
Rodríguez Freile, Juan
Rodríguez Juliá, Edgardo
Roig de Leuchsenring, Emilio
Rojas, Manuel
Rojas, Ricardo
Rokha, Pablo de
Rokha, Winétt de
Romay y Valdés Chacón, Tomás
Romero, Emilio
Romero, Francisco

Romero, José Luis
Romero, José Rubén
Romero, Matías
Romero, Sílvio
Romero Rosa, Ramón
Rosa, João Guimarães
Rosa, José María
Rosáins, Juan Nepomuceno
Roscio, Juan Germán
Rosenblueth, Arturo Stearns
Roumain, Jacques
Rubião, Murilo
Rueda, Manuel
Ruiz de Alarcón y Mendoza, Juan
Rulfo, Juan
Sabat Ercasty, Carlos
Sábato, Ernesto
Sáenz, Jaime
Saer, Juan José
Sagra, Ramón de la
Sahagún, Bernardino de
Sáinz, Gustavo
Salazar Arrué, Salvador Efraín (Salarrué)
Salazar Bondy, Sebastián
Salgado, Plinio
Samayoa Chinchilla, Carlos
Samper, José María
Sánchez, Luis Rafael
Sánchez, Prisciliano
Sánchez de Bustamante y Sirven, Antonio
Sánchez de Tagle, Francisco Manuel
Santa Cruz y Espejo, Francisco Javier
        Eugenio de
Santiago, Esmeralda
Sarduy, Severo
Sarmiento, Domingo Faustino
Sarmiento de Gamboa, Pedro
Sarney, José
Schwarz-Bart, Simone
Scliar, Moacyr
Shimose, Pedro
Sierra, Stella
Sierra Méndez, Justo
Sierra O'Reilly, Justo
Sigüenza y Góngora, Carlos de
Silva, Clara
Silva, José Antonio da
Skármeta, Antonio
Sologuren, Javier
Solórzano, Carlos

Solórzano Pereira, Juan de
Somers, Armonía
Soriano, Osvaldo
Souza, Márcio Gonçalves Bentes
Squier, Ephraim George
Stedman, John G.
Steimberg, Alicia
Stephens, John Lloyd
Storni, Alfonsina
Suárez, Marco Fidel
Suassuna, Ariano Vilar
Subero, Efraín
Tablada, José Juan
Talamantes, Melchor de
Talavera, Natalício
Tallet, José Zacarías
Tamayo, Franz
Taunay, Alfredo d'Escragnolle, Vicomte de
Távara y Andrade, Santiago
Telles, Lygia Fagundes
Tello, Julio César
Thiel, Bernardo Augusto
Tinajero Martínez de Allen, Eugenia
Toro, Fermín
Torres Bodet, Jaime
Torre y Huerta, Carlos de la
Traba, Marta
Triana, José
Tristan, Flora
Trotsky, Leon
Trujillo, Manuel
Umaña Bernal, José
Unanue, Hipólito
Urbina, Luis Gonzaga
Urzagasti, Jesús
Usigli, Rodolfo
Uslar Pietri, Arturo
Valdés, Gabriel de la Concepción
Valenzuela, Luisa
Valero, Roberto
Vallejo, César
Vallenilla Lanz, Laureano
Varela, Florencio
Vargas Llosa, Mario
Varona y Pera, Enrique José
Vasconcelos Calderón, José
Vásquez, Francisco de Asís
Vega, Aurelio de la
Vera Cruz, Alonso de la
Veríssimo, Érico

Vespucci, Amerigo
Vial, Pedro
Vieira, Antônio
Vigil, Francisco de Paula González
Vilariño, Idea
Villacorta Calderón, José Antonio
Villagrá, Gaspar Pérez de
Villarán, Manuel Vicente
Villaurrutia, Xavier
Villaverde, Cirilo
Villegas, Oscar
Villoro, Luis
Vitier, Cintio
Vizcaíno, Sebastián
Von Vacano, Arturo
Walcott, Derek
Ward, Henry George
Welles, Sumner
Wheelock Román, Jaime
Wiesse, María
Wyld Ospina, Carlos
Ximénez, Francisco
Yánez Cossío, Alicia
Yáñez Santos Delgadillo, Agustín
Ydígoras Fuentes, Miguel
Zaid, Gabriel
Zavala, Lorenzo de
Zavala, Silvio
Zayas y Alfonso, Alfredo
Zea Aguilar, Leopoldo
Zelaya, José Santos
Zeno Gandía, Manuel
Zepeda, Eraclio
Zorita, Alonso de

9. MILITARY

Abascal y Souza, José Fernando
Acevedo Díaz, Eduardo Inés
Achá, José María
Acosta, Tomás
Agramonte y Loynaz, Ignacio
Aguayo, Marqués de
Aguilar, Jerónimo de
Aguirre, Atanasio
Aguirre, Juan Francisco de
Alarcón, Martín de
Alberni, Pedro de

Albuquerque, Antônio Francisco de Paula
Aldama y González, Juan de
Alexander, Edward Porter
Alfaro Delgado, José Eloy
Allende, Ignacio
Almazán, Juan Andréu
Almonte, Juan Nepomuceno
Alonso, Mariano Roque
Alvarado, Lisandro
Alvarado, Salvador
Alvarado y Mesía, Pedro de
Álvarez, Juan
Álvarez Armellino, Gregorio Conrado
Álvarez Martínez, Gustavo
Amat y Junient, Manuel de
Ampíes, Juan de
Ampudia y Grimarest, Pedro de
Anaya, Pedro María de
Andrade, Gomes Freire de
Andresote
Ángeles, Felipe
Anza, Juan Bautista de
Anzoátegui, José Antonio
Aramburu, Pedro Eugenio
Arana, Francisco J.
Arana Osorio, Carlos
Arbenz Guzmán, Jacobo
Arenales, Juan Antonio Álvarez de
Argüello, Santiago
Arias, Desiderio
Arismendi, Juan Bautista
Arista, Mariano
Armijo, Manuel
Artigas, José Gervasio
Auchmuty, Samuel
Aury, Louis-Michel
Ávila, Pedro Arias de
Ávila Camacho, Manuel
Avilés, Gabriel
Axayacatl
Ayolas, Juan de
Azcuénaga, Miguel de
Balboa, Vasco Núñez de
Balcarce, Mariano
Baldomir, Alfredo
Ballivián, José
Balta, José
Banzer Suárez, Hugo
Barrientos Ortuño, René
Barrios, Justo Rufino

Batista y Zaldívar, Fulgencio
Bazaine, François Achille
Belgrano, Manuel
Belzu, Manuel Isidoro
Beresford, William Carr
Bermúdez, José Francisco
Bermúdez Varela, Enrique
Beruti, Antonio Luis
Bignone, Reynaldo
Blanco, José Félix
Blanco Encalada, Manuel
Blanco Galindo, Carlos
Bodega y Quadra, Juan Francisco de la
Bolaño, Roberto
Bolívar, Simón
Bolognesi, Francisco
Bordaberry, Juan María
Borge, Tomás
Bouchard, Hipólito
Bouterse, Desi
Boves, José Tomás
Boyer, Jean-Pierre
Bravo, Leonardo
Bravo, Nicolás
Brión, Luis
Brizuela, Francisco
Brown, William
Bunau-Varilla, Philippe Jean
Busch Becerra, Germán
Bustamante, Anastasio
Bustamante y Guerra, José
Bustos, Juan Bautista
Butler, Smedley Darlington
Caamaño Deñó, Francisco
Caamaño y Gómez Cornejo, José María
        Plácido
Caballero, Pedro Juan
Cabañas, José Trinidad
Cáceres, Andrés Avelino
Cajeme
Calfucurá
Calleja del Rey, Félix María, Conde de Calderon
Calles, Plutarco Elías
Camarena, Enrique
Campero, Narciso
Campos, Luis María
Campos, Manuel Jorge
Cañas, José María
Candioti, Francisco Antonio
Cárdenas del Río, Lázaro

Cardozo, Efraím
Carondelet, François-Louis Hector
Carrera, José Miguel
Carrera, José Rafael
Carrión, Jerónimo
Carvalho, Antônio de Albuquerque Coelho de
Castañeda Castro, Salvador
Castello Branco, Humberto de Alencar
Castilla, Ramón
Castillo Armas, Carlos
Castro, Julián
Castro Jijón, Ramón
Castro Ruz, Fidel
Castro Ruz, Raúl
Caupolicán
Cazneau, William Leslie
Cedillo Martínez, Saturnino
Cerna, Vicente
Chacón, Lázaro
Chamorro Vargas, Emiliano
Chávez, Hugo
Chávez, Mariano
Chirino, José Leonardo
Christmas, Lee
Christophe, Henri
Cienfuegos, Camilo
Cieza de León, Pedro de
Cipriani, Arthur Andrew
Cochrane, Lord Thomas Alexander
Codazzi, Agustín
Comandante Ramona
Comonfort, Ignacio
Constant Botelho de Magalhães, Benjamin
Córdoba, José María
Corona, Ramón
Coronado, Juan Vázquez de
Cortés, Martín
Cos, Martín Perfecto de
Costa e Silva, Artur da
Cos y Pérez, José María
Craige, John Houston
Crespo, Joaquín
Croix, Marqués de
Croix, Teodoro de
Crowder, Enoch Herbert
Cruz, Serapio
Cruz, Vicente
Cuauhtemoc
Cuitlahuac
d'Aubuisson, Roberto

Dávila, Miguel R.
Daza, Hilarión
Debray, [Jules] Régis
Degollado, Santos
Delgado Chalbaud, Carlos
Dessalines, Jean Jacques
Dias, Henrique
Dias Lopes, Isidoro
Díaz, Félix, Jr.
Díaz, José Eduvigis
Díaz, Porfirio
Díaz Vélez, Eustaquio Antonio
Di Tella, Torcuato
Dorrego, Manuel
Drake, Francis
Duarte, Juan Pablo
Duarte, Pedro
Dutra, Eurico Gaspar
Echeandía, José María de
Elizalde, Rufino de
Enríquez de Guzmán, Alonso
Enríquez Gallo, Alberto
Escobedo, Mariano
Estigarribia, Antonio de la Cruz
Estrada, José Dolores
Facio Segreda, Gonzalo
Fages, Pedro
Falcón, Juan Crisóstomo
Fallas Sibaja, Carlos Luis
Farrell, Edelmiro
Fawcett, Percy
Febres-Cordero Ribadeneyra, León
Fernández de Castro Andrade y Portugal,
    Pedro Antonio
Fernández (Hernández) de Córdoba,
    Francisco
Fernández Oreamuno, Próspero
Ferreira, Benigno
Ferrera, Francisco
Figueiredo, João Baptista de Oliveira
Figueroa, José
Filísola, Vicente
Flores, Juan José
Flores, Venancio
Fonseca, Hermes Rodrigues da
Fonseca, Manoel Deodoro da
Fonseca Amador, Carlos
Francia, José Gaspar Rodríguez de
Franco, Guillermo
Frémont, John Charles

Fuentes y Guzmán, Francisco Antonio de
Gaínza, Gabino
Galán, Luis Carlos
Galeana, Hermenegildo
Galtieri, Leopoldo Fortunato
Galvarino
Gálvez, Bernardo de
Gálvez, Matías de
Gama, Vasco da
Gamarra, Agustín
Gándara Enríquez, Marcos
Garay, Eugenio
Garcés, Francisco Tomás Hermenegildo
García, Calixto
García Conde, Pedro
García y González, Vicente
Garibay, Pedro
Garro, José de
Geffrard, Fabre Nicolas
Geisel, Ernesto
Gelly y Obes, Juan Andrés
Gestido, Oscar Daniel
Girón, Francisco Hernández
Goethals, George Washington
Golbery do Couto e Silva
Gomes, Eduardo
Gómez, José Miguel (d. 1805)
Gómez, José Miguel (d. 1921)
Gómez, Juan Vicente
Gómez Pedraza, Manuel
Gómez y Báez, Máximo
González, Manuel
González, Pablo
González Dávila, Gil
Gonzalez Garza, Roque
González Ortega, Jesús
Grau, Miguel
Grijalva, Juan de
Guardia Gutiérrez, Tomás
Guardiola, Santos
Güemes, Martín
Guerra, Ramón
Guerrero, Vicente
Guevara, Ernesto "Che"
Gutiérrez, Eulalio
Gutiérrez Brothers
Gutiérrez de Lara, José Bernardo
Guzmán, Nuño Beltrán de
Haro y Tamariz, Antonio de
Heredia Acosta, Alejandro

Hernández, José Manuel
Hernández Martínez, Maximiliano
Herrán, Pedro Alcántara
Herrera, Benjamín
Herrera, José Joaquín Antonio Florencio
Herrera, Tomás
Heureaux, Ulises
Holguín, Jorge
Houston, Sam
Huascar
Huerta, Victoriano
Huertas, Esteban
Ibáñez del Campo, Carlos
Ibarra, Juan Felipe
Iglesias, Miguel
Irala, Domingo Martínez de
Iturbide, Agustín de
Itzcoatl
Jara Corona, Heriberto
Jerez, Máximo
Jiménez de Quesada, Gonzalo
Julião, Carlos
Justo, José Agustín Pedro
Kearny, Stephen W.
Körner, Emil
Lamadrid, Gregorio Aráoz de
Lanusse, Alejandro Augustín
Laprida, Francisco Narciso de
Laredo Bru, Federico
Larrazábal Ugueto, Wolfgang
La Salle, René-Robert Cavelier, Sieur de
Las Heras, Juan Gregorio de
Lavalle, Juan Galo
Lavalleja, Juan Antonio
Leclerc, Charles Victor Emmanuel
Leighton Guzmán, Bernardo
Lemus, José María
León, Alonso de
Levingston, Roberto Marcelo
Leyva Solano, Gabriel
Lima e Silva, Luís Alves de
Linares, José María
Linares Alcántara, Francisco
Lindley López, Nicolás
Lisboa, Joaquim Marques
Lonardi, Eduardo
López, Enrique Solano
López, Estanislao
López, Francisco Solano
López, José Hilario

López, Narciso
López Arellano, Oswaldo
López Chavez, Julio
López Contreras, Eleázar
López Jordán, Ricardo
López y Fuentes, Gregorio
Lorenzo Troya, Victoriano
Lott, Henrique Batista Duffles Teixeira
Louverture, Toussaint
Lozada, Manuel
Luperón, Gregorio
Maceo, Antonio
MacGregor, Gregor
Machado, Gustavo
Machado y Morales, Gerardo
Madureira, Antônio de Sena
Magloire, Paul Eugène
Majano, Adolfo Arnoldo
Maldonado, Francisco Severo
Malespín, Francisco
Manco Capac
Mandu Ladino
Manning, Thomas Courtland
Mansilla, Lucio Victorio
Manso de Maldonado, Antonio
Manso de Velasco, José Antonio
Mar, José de la
Mariño, Santiago
Márquez, Leonardo
Martínez, Esteban José
Martínez, Juan José
Martínez, Tomás
Massera, Emilio Eduardo
Matamoros y Guridi, Mariano
Maurits, Johan
Médici, Emílio Garrastazú
Medina Angarita, Isaías
Mejía, Tomás
Mejía Victores, Oscar Humberto
Melgarejo, Mariano
Melgares, Facundo
Melo, Custódio José de
Melo, José María
Mendiburu, Manuel de
Mendieta y Montefur, Carlos
Menéndez de Avilés, Pedro
Menocal, Mario García
Merino Castro, José Toribio
Mier y Terán, Manuel
Mina y Larrea, Javier

Miramón, Miguel
Molina, Arturo Armando
Molina Enríquez, Andrés
Molony, Guy
Monagas, José Gregorio
Moncada, José María
Montalvo y Ambulodi Arriola y Casabente
        Valdespino, Francisco
Monteiro, Pedro Aurélio de Góis
Montes, César
Montes, Ismael
Montesinos, Vladimiro
Montt Álvarez, Jorge
Montúfar Montes de Oca, Lorenzo
Mora, Fernando de la
Morales, Agustín
Morales, Francisco Tomás
Morales Bermúdez Cerruti, Francisco
Morales Lemus, José
Mora Porrás, Juan Rafael
Morazán, Francisco
Morelos y Pavón, José María
Morgan, Henry
Morillo, Pablo
Mosquera, Tomás Cipriano de
Motecuhzoma I
Motecuhzoma II
Múgica, Francisco José
Muñoz, José Trinidad
Napoleon I
Nariño, Antonio
Narváez, Pánfilo de
Navarro Wolff, Antonio
Neve, Felipe de
Nezahualcoyotl
Nord, Pierre Alexis
Noriega Moreno, Manuel Antonio
Nufio, José Dolores
Núñez Vela, Blasco
O, Genovevo de la
Obando, José María
Obregón Salido, Álvaro
O'Donojú, Juan
Odría, Manuel Apolinario
Ogé, Jacques Vicente
O'Higgins, Ambrosio
O'Higgins, Bernardo
O'Leary, Daniel Florencio
O'Leary, Juan Emiliano
Olid, Cristóbal de

Olivares, Conde-Duque de
Onganía, Juan Carlos
Orbegoso, Luis José de
Ordóñez, José
O'Reilly y McDowell, Alejandro
Orlich Bolmarcich, Francisco José
Orozco, Pascual, Jr.
Ortega Saavedra, Daniel
Ortega Saavedra, Humberto
Ortiz de Zárate, Juan and Juana
Osório, Manuel Luís
Ospina, Pedro Nel
Ovando Candía, Alfredo
Páez, José Antonio
País, Frank
Palacio Fajardo, Manuel
Palafox y Mendoza, Juan de
Pando, José Manuel
Pardo, Juan
Paredes, Mariano
Paredes y Arrillaga, Mariano
Pastora Gómez, Edén
Patrocínio, José do
Pavón Aycinena, Manuel Francisco
Paz, José María
Paz García, Policarpo
Pedreira, Antonio S.
Peixoto, Floriano Vieira
Peñalosa Briceño, Diego Dionisio de
Peñaloza, Ángel Vicente
Peñaranda del Castillo, Enrique
Péralte, Charlemagne Masséna
Pereda, Setembrino Ezequiel
Pérez, Albino
Pérez, Juan
Pérez Godoy, Ricardo
Pérez Jiménez, Marcos
Perón, Juan Domingo
Pétion, Alexandre Sabès
Pinochet Ugarte, Augusto
Pizarro, José Alonso
Plaza Gutiérrez, Leonidas
Ponce de León, Juan
Popham, Home Riggs
Porter, David
Portolá, Gaspar de
Prado, Mariano Ignacio
Prat, Arturo
Prats González, Carlos
Prestes, Luís Carlos

Pueyrredón, Honorio
Pueyrredón, Juan Martín de
Ramírez, Francisco
Ramírez, Pedro Pablo
Ramírez Mercado, Sergio
Raousset-Boulbon, Gaston Raul de
Rayón, Ignacio
Reed, Walter
Reeve, Henry M.
Regalado, Tomás
Remón Cantera, José Antonio
Reyes Ogazón, Bernardo
Riaño y Bárcena, Juan Antonio
Ribas, José Félix
Ricchieri, Pablo
Riego y Núñez, Rafael del
Rigaud, André
Ríos Montt, José Efraín
Riquelme, Daniel
Riva Palacio, Vicente
Rivera, Pedro de
Rivera Carballo, Julio Adalberto
Rivera y Moncada, Fernando de
Robles, Francisco
Robles, Wenceslao
Roca, Julio Argentino
Rochambeau, Donatien Marie Joseph de
        Vimeur de
Rodríguez, Andrés
Rodríguez Cabrillo, Juan
Rodríguez Erdoiza, Manuel
Rodríguez Lara, Guillermo
Rodríguez Luján, Abelardo
Rodríguez Sandoval, Luis Arsenio
Rojas, Isaac
Rojas Pinilla, Gustavo
Rolón, Raimundo
Romero, Carlos Humberto
Romero Rubio, Manuel
Rosa, Ramón
Rosáins, Juan Nepomuceno
Ruíz, Henry
Ruíz de Apodaca, Juan, Conde de Venadito
Russell, John H.
Sá, Estácio de
Sá, Mem de
Sá e Benavides, Salvador Correia de
Salaverry, Felipe Santiago
Salazar, Matías
Saldanha da Gama, Luís Felipe de

Salgar, Eustorgio
Salnave, Sylvain
Sam, Tirésias Augustin Simon
Samanez Ocampo, David
Sánchez Cerro, Luis Manuel
Sánchez Hernández, Fidel
Sandino, Augusto César
San Martín, José Francisco de
Santa Anna, Antonio López de
Santa Cruz, Andrés de
Santamaría, Haydée
Santana, Pedro
Santander, Francisco de Paula
Sardá, José
Schick Gutiérrez, René
Scott, Winfield
Sebastian (Sebastião) of Portugal
Sedeño, Antonio de
Seguín, Juan Nepomuceno
Sodré, Nelson Werneck
Soldados de Cuera
Solís, Juan Díaz de
Somoza Debayle, Luis
Somoza García, Anastasio
Soto, Hernando de
Soto Alfaro, Bernardo
Soublette, Carlos
Soulouque, Faustin Élie
Sousa, Martim Afonso de
Sousa, Tomé de
Stedman, John G.
Stroessner, Alfredo
Sucre Alcalá, Antonio José de
Tavares, Antônio Rapôso
Távora, Juárez
Taylor, Zachary
Tejeda Olivares, Adalberto
Thomson Porto Mariño, Manuel Tomás
Tinoco Granados, Federico
Tornel y Mendívil, José María
Toro, David
Torres, Juan José
Torres, Luis Emeterio
Torre Tagle y Portocarrero, José Bernardo de
Torrijos Herrera, Omar
Trujillo, Julián
Trujillo Molina, Rafael Leónidas
Túpac Amaru
Túpac Catari (Julián Apaza)
Ubico y Castañeda, Jorge

Urbina, José María
Urdaneta, Andrés de
Urdaneta, Rafael
Ureta, Eloy G.
Urracá
Urrea, José de
Valdivia, Pedro de
Vallejo, Mariano Guadalupe
Varela, Felipe
Vargas, Diego de
Veintemilla, José Ignacio de
Veintemilla, Marietta de
Velasco, José María
Velasco Alvarado, Juan
Velásquez, Diego de
Venegas de Saavedra, Francisco Javier
Vernet, Louis
Vértiz y Salcedo, Juan José de
Vial, Pedro
Victoria, Guadalupe
Victoria, Manuel
Vidaurri, Santiago
Videla, Jorge Rafael
Viera, Feliciano
Villa, Francisco "Pancho"
Villagrá, Gaspar Pérez de
Villagrán, Julián and José María
        "El Chito"
Villarroel López, Gualberto
Villegaignon, Nicolas Durand de
Viola, Roberto Eduardo
Vivanco, Manuel Ignacio
Walker, William
Weyler y Nicolau, Valeriano
Williams Rebolledo, Juan
Wisner von Morgenstern, Franz
Wood, Leonard
Wooster, Charles Whiting
Ydígoras Fuentes, Miguel
Yegros, Fulgencio
Yon Sosa, Marco Antonio
Zamorano, Agustín Juan Vicente
Zapata, Emiliano
Zaragoza, Ignacio
Zavala, José Víctor
Zelaya, José Santos
Zeledón, Benjamín Francisco
Zuloaga, Félix María
Zumbi
Zúñiga, Ignacio

10. MONARCHS AND ROYALTY

Agüeybana II
Alvarado Xicotencatl, Leonor
Amélia, Empress
Atahualpa
Atahualpa (Juan Santos)
Axayacatl
Bonaparte, Joseph
Bragança, House of
Cajeme
Calfucurá
Charles I of Spain
Charles II of Spain
Charles III of Spain
Charles IV of Spain
Cuauhtemoc
Cuitlahuac
Dessalines, Jean Jacques
Ferdinand II of Aragon
Ferdinand VI of Spain
Ferdinand VII of Spain
Henry the Navigator
Huascar
Huayna Capac
Isabella I of Castile
Isabel, Princess of Brazil
Itzcoatl
Jijón y Caamaño, Jacinto
João I of Portugal
João II of Portugal
João III of Portugal
João IV of Portugal
João V of Portugal
João VI of Portugal
José I of Portugal
Leopoldina, Empress
Manco Capac
Manco Inca
Manuel I of Portugal
Maria I
Maria II
Maximilian
Montalvo y Ambulodi Arriola y Casabente
        Valdespino, Francisco
Motecuhzoma I
Motecuhzoma II
Napoleon I
Napoleon III
Nezahualcoyotl

Nezahualpilli
Pedro I of Brazil
Pedro II of Brazil
Philip II of Spain
Philip III of Spain
Philip IV of Spain
Philip V of Spain
Sebastian (Sebastião) of Portugal
Teresa Cristina
Túpac Amaru
Zumbi

11. MUSIC AND DANCE

Aguirre, Julián
Alcaraz, José Antonio
Aldana, José María
Allende-Sarón, Pedro Humberto
Alomía Robles, Daniel
Alves, Francisco
Amenábar, Juan
Aponte-Ledée, Rafael
Arau, Alfonso
Araujo, Juan de
Archila, Andrés
Ardévol, José
Arnaz, Desi
Arrau, Claudio León
Asuar, José Vicente
Barbosa-Lima, Carlos
Barroso, Ary
Bauzá, Mário
Becerra-Schmidt, Gustavo
Bellinati, Paulo
Beltrán, Lola
Bernal Jiménez, Miguel
Berutti, Arturo
Blanco, Juan
Boero, Felipe
Bolaños, César
Broqua, Alfonso
Brouwer, Leo
Buarque, Chico
Calcaño, José Antonio
Callado Junior, Joaquim Antônio da Silva
Campobello, Nellie
Campos-Parsi, Héctor
Carlos, Roberto

Carrilho, Altamiro
Carrillo, Julián [Antonio]
Cartola
Castellanos, Gonzalo
Castillo, Jesús
Castro, Ricardo
Cavour, Ernesto
Caymmi, Dorival
Ceruti, Roque
Cervantes Kawanagh, Ignacio
Cervetti, Sergio
Chacrinha
Chávez, Carlos
Cluzeau-Mortet, Luis (Ricardo)
Compay Segundo
Contreras, Gloria
Cordero, Roque
Correa de Azevedo, Luiz Heitor
Cotapos Baeza, Acario
Cruz, Celia
Cugat, Xavier
de Jesus, Clementina
Dianda, Hilda
Discépolo, Enrique Santos
Domingo, Plácido
Downs, Lila
Duprat, Rogério
Elizaga, José María
Enríquez, Manuel
Escobar, Luis Antonio
Estefan, Gloria
Fabini, [Felix] Eduardo
Feliciano, José
Fernandez, Oscar Lorenzo
Fernández Hidalgo, Gutierre
Ficher, Jacobo
Franco, Hernando
Gabriel, Juan
Gaito, Constantino
Galindo, Blas
Gallet, Luciano
Gandini, Gerardo
Gante, Pedro de
García, José Maurício Nunes
García Caturla, Alejandro
García Morillo, Roberto
Gardel, Carlos
Garrido-Lecca Seminario, Celso
Gil, Gilberto
Gilardi, Gilardo

Gilberto, João
Ginastera, Alberto Evaristo
Giribaldi, (Vicente) Tomás E.
Gismonti, Egberto
Goicuría y Cabrera, Domingo
Gomes, Antônio Carlos
Gonzaga, Francisca Hedwiges
Gonzaga, Luiz
González, Rodrigo
González Ávila, Jorge
Guarnieri, M[ozart] Camargo
Gutiérrez de Padilla, Juan
Gutiérrez y Espinosa, Felipe
Halffter, Rodolfo
Hayworth, Rita
Hernández, Amalia
Hernández Moncado, Eduardo
Holzmann, Rodolfo
Infante, José Miguel
Isamitt Alarcón, Carlos
Jara, Víctor
Jobim, Antônio Carlos "Tom"
Kagel, Mauricio Raúl
Koellreutter, Hans Joachim
Krieger, Edino
Lacerda, Osvaldo
Lamarque, Libertad
Lamarque Pons, Jaurés
Lanza, Alcides
Lara, Agustín
Lavista, Mario
Lecuona y Casado, Ernesto
Leng, Alfonso
Letelier Valdés, Miguel Francisco
Levy, Alexandre
Ley, Salvador
López Buchardo, Carlos
López Capillas, Francisco
Machito
Marley, Bob
Mastrogiovanni, Antonio
Mata, Eduardo
Mejía Godoy, Carlos
Mendes, Gilberto
Merello, Tita
Mignone, Francisco
Miranda, Carmen
Mojica, José de Jesús
Moncayo García, José Pablo
Morais, Vinícius de

Morales, Melesio
Moré, Beny
Nascimento, Milton
Nazareth, Ernesto
Negrete, Jorge
Nepomuceno, Alberto
Nobre, Marlos
Nunes, Clara
Oliveira, Willy Correia de
Orbón, Julián
Orejón y Aparicio, José de
Orrego-Salas, Juan Antonio
Ortega del Villar, Aniceto
Paniagua y Vasques, Cenobio
Paquita la del Barrio
Pardavé, Joaquín
Parra, Violeta
Pascoal, Hermeto
Pasta, Carlo Enrico
Paz, Juan Carlos
Peixe, César Guerra
Peralta, Angela
Pérez Prado, Dámaso
Piazzola, Astor
Pineda-Duque, Roberto
Pinilla, Enrique
Pixinguinha
Ponce, Manuel
Portugal, Marcos Antônio da Fonseca
Puente, Tito
Quintanar, Héctor
Regina, Elis
Revueltas, Silvestre
Reyes, Lucha
Rodriguez, Arsenio
Rodriguez, Tito
Rogatis, Pascual de
Roldán, Amadeo
Rosa, Noel
Rosas, Juventino
Sambucetti, Luís (Nicolás)
Sánchez, Cuco
Sandi, Luis
Santana, Carlos
Santoro, Claudio
Sarmientos de León, Jorge Alvaro
Sas, Andrés
Seaga, Edward
Selena
Sepp, Anton
Serebrier, José

Silva, Francisco Manuel da
Silva, Orlando
Sinhô
Sosa, Mercedes
Storm, Ricardo
Tauriello, Antonio
Torrejón y Velasco, Tomás de
Tosar, Héctor Alberto
Uribe Holguín, Guillermo
Valcárcel Arce, Edgar
Valencia, Antonio María
Vargas, Chavela
Vega, Aurelio de la
Veloso, Caetano
Villa-Lobos, Heitor
Viola, Paulinho da
White y Lafitta, José
Williams, Alberto
Yupanqui, Atahualpa
Zipoli, Domenico
Zumaya, Manuel de

12. OUTLAWRY

Alvarado Xicotencatl, Leonor
Bonnet, Stede
Bonny, Anne
Crabb, Henry A.
Drake, Francis
Hawkins, John
Kinney, Henry L.
Lampião
L'Olonnais, Francis
López, Narciso
Morgan, Henry
Prado y Ugarteche, Jorge
Raousset Boulbon, Gaston Raul de
Read, Mary
Salinas de Gortari, Raul
Sharp, Bartholomew
Walker, William
Wallace, Peter

13. POLITICAL LEADERS: COLONIAL ERA

Abalos, José de
Abascal y Souza, José Fernando

Acosta, Tomás
Alarcón, Martín de
Alberro, Francisco de
Alvarado y Mesía, Pedro de
Álvarez, Manuel
Alves Branco, Manuel
Álzaga, Martín de
Amar y Borbón, Antonio
Amat y Junient, Manuel de
Anchorena, Tomás Manuel de
Andrade, Gomes Freire de
Arenales, Juan Antonio Álvarez de
Arias de Saavedra, Hernando
Artigas, José Gervasio
Atahualpa (Juan Santos)
Ávila, Pedro Arias de
Avilés, Gabriel
Aycinena, Juan Fermín de
Aycinena Piñol, Juan José de
Ayolas, Juan de
Azara, Félix de
Azcárate y Lezama, Juan Francisco de
Balboa, Vasco Núñez de
Baldorioty de Castro, Ramón
Barros, João de
Bennett, Marshall
Bobadilla, Francisco de
Borja y Aragón, Francisco de
Boves, José Tomás
Bucareli y Ursúa, Antonio María
Bucareli y Ursúa, Francisco de Paula
Bustos, Juan Bautista
Caballero y Góngora, Antonio
Cabeza de Vaca, Alvar Núñez
Calchaquí, Juan
Calleja del Rey, Félix María
Camacho Roldán, Salvador
Cañedo, Juan de Dios
Caramurú
Cárdenas, Bernardino de
Carlota
Carondelet, François-Louis Hector
Carrera, José Miguel
Carvalho, Antônio de Albuquerque Coelho de
Caupolicán
Cavallón, Juan de
Cevallos, Pedro Antonio de
Cisneros, Baltasar Hidalgo de
Coelho, Jorge de Albuquerque
Coelho Pereira, Duarte

Columbus, Diego (d. 1515)
Columbus, Diego (d. 1526)
Columbus, Bartholomew
Coronado, Juan Vázquez de
Coutinho, José Joaquim da Cunha de Azeredo
Croix, Marqués de
Croix, Teodoro de
Cueva, Francisco de la
Cueva de Alvarado, Beatriz de la
Cueva Enríquez y Saavedra, Baltásar de la
Díaz Vélez, José Miguel
Domínguez, Miguel
Elío, Francisco Javier
Enríquez de Almansa, Martín
Eslava y Lazaga, Sebastián de
Esquiú, Mamerto
Fages, Pedro
Fagoaga y Lizaur, José María
Fernández de Cabrera Bobadilla Cerda y
        Mendoza, Luis Gerónimo
Fernández de Córdoba, Diego
Flores Maldonado Martínez y Bodquín,
        Manuel Antonio
Funes, Gregorio
Gaínza, Gabino
Gálvez, Bernardo de
Gálvez, José de
Gálvez, Matías de
Gama, Vasco da
Ganga Zumba
Garay, Francisco de
García de Castro, Lope
Garibay, Pedro
Garro, José de
Gasca, Pedro de la
Gelves, Marqués de
Gil de Taboada y Lemos, Francisco
Girón, Francisco Hernández
Godoy Cruz, Tomás
Güemes, Martín
Guirior, Manuel
Gutiérrez de Piñeres, Juan Francisco
Guzmán, Nuño Beltrán de
Herrera, Tomás
Huascar
Hurtado de Mendoza, Andrés
Hurtado de Mendoza, García
Iturrigaray, José de
Jáuregui, Agustín de
Kearny, Stephen W.

Ladrón de Guevara, Diego
Lamar, Mirabeau Buonaparte
Lasuén, Fermín Francisco de
Lavradio, Marquês do
León, Alonso de
López de Cerrato, Alonso
López de Cogolludo, Diego
Lorenzana y Buitrón, Francisco Antonio de
Luna y Arellano, Tristán de
Maldonado, Rodrigo de Arias
Manco Inca
Manrique de Zúñiga, Alvaro
Manso de Velasco, José Antonio
Marroquín, Francisco
Maurits, Johan
Mendinueta y Múzquiz, Pedro de
Mendoza, Antonio de
Mendoza Caamaño y Sotomayor, José
    Antonio de
Mendoza y Luna, Juan Manuel de
Messía de la Cerda, Pedro de
Mompox de Zayas, Fernando
Montejo, Francisco de
Mon y Velarde, Juan Antonio
Morgan, Henry
Morga Sánchez Garay y López, Antonio de
Morillo, Pablo
Moya de Contreras, Pedro
Muñoz Rivera, Luis
Namuncurá, Ceferino
Namuncurá, Manuel
Navarra y Rocaful, Melchor de
Navarro Wolff, Antonio
Neve, Felipe de
Núñez Vela, Blasco
O'Donojú, Juan
Ogé, Jacques Vicente
O'Higgins, Ambrosio
O'Higgins, Bernardo
O'Leary, Juan Emiliano
Olivares, Conde-Duque de
Oliveira, Manuel Botelho de
Oñate, Juan de
O'Reilly y McDowell, Alejandro
Ovando, Nicolás de
Palafox y Mendoza, Juan de
Palou, Francisco
Pardo Leal, Jaime
Parish, Woodbine
Paso, Juan José

Pedrosa y Guerrero, Antonio de la
Peñalosa Briceño, Diego Dionisio de
Pérez de Tolosa, Juan
Pizarro, Francisco
Pizarro, Gonzalo
Pizarro, José Alonso
Ponce de León, Juan
Porras, José Basilio
Portocarrero y Lasso de la Vega, Melchor
Portolá, Gaspar de
Primo de Verdad y Ramos, Francisco
Quiroga, Vasco de
Rada, Manuel de Jesús
Ramalho, João
Ramírez y Blanco, Alejandro
Ramos Arizpe, José Miguel
Revillagigedo, Conde de
Rochambeau, Donatien Marie Joseph de
    Vimeur de
Roldán, Francisco
Rondeau, José
Rosas, Juan Manuel de
Ruíz de Apodaca, Juan, Conde de Venadito
Sá, Mem de
Saco, José Antonio
Sá e Benavides, Salvador Correia de
Sarmiento de Sotomayor, García
Seguín, Juan José María Erasmo
Seguín, Juan Nepomuceno
Sobremonte, Rafael de
Solís Folch de Cardona, José
Sousa, Martim Afonso de
Sousa, Tomé de
Suárez, Inés de
Talamantes, Melchor de
Toledo y Figueroa, Francisco de
Toledo y Leyva, Pedro de
Torres y Portugal, Fernando de
Túpac Amaru
Túpac Amaru (José Gabriel Condorcanqui)
Urdaneta, Andrés de
Ursúa, Pedro de
Vaca de Castro, Cristóval
Valdivia, Pedro de
Velasco, Luis de
Velásquez, Diego de
Venegas de Saavedra, Francisco Javier
Vértiz y Salcedo, Juan José de
Viamonte, Juan José
Vicuña Larraín, Francisco Ramón

Vicuña Mackenna, Benjamin
Villalonga, Jorge
Villegaignon, Nicolas Durand de
Weyler y Nicolau, Valeriano
Yegros, Fulgencio
Yermo, Gabriel de
Zapata, Felipe
Zárate, Agustín de
Zorita, Alonso de
Zumbi

14. POLITICAL LEADERS: MODERN

Abadía Méndez, Miguel
Aceval, Benjamín
Acevedo Díaz, Eduardo Inés
Achá, José María
Acosta García, Julio
Adams, Grantley Herbert
Agüero Rocha, Fernando
Aguilar Vargas, Cándido
Aguirre, Atanasio
Aguirre Cerda, Pedro
Aguirre y Salinas, Osmín
Alamán, Lucas
Alambert, Zuleika
Alberdi, Juan Bautista
Alberto, João
Albizu Campos, Pedro
Albuquerque, Antônio Francisco de Paula
Alem, Leandro N.
Alemán Valdés, Miguel
Alencar, José Martiniano de
Alessandri Palma, Arturo
Alessandri Rodríguez, Jorge
Alexis, Jacques Stéphen
Alfaro, Ricardo Joaquín
Alfaro Delgado, José Eloy
Alfonsín, Raúl Ricardo
Allende Gossens, Salvador
Almazán, Juan Andréu
Almeida, José Américo de
Alonso, Mariano Roque
Alonso, Raúl
Alsina, Adolfo
Alsina, Valentín
Alsogaray, Álvaro

Alvarado, Salvador
Álvarez, Juan
Álvarez, Luis Héctor
Álvarez Ponce de León, Griselda
Alvear, Carlos María de
Alvear, Marcelo Torcuato de
Amador Guerrero, Manuel
Amézaga, Juan José de
Amunátegui Aldunate, Miguel Luis
Andrada, Antônio Carlos Ribeiro de and
      Martim Francisco Ribeiro de
Andrada, José Bonifácio de
Andrade, Olegario Victor
Andrade, Oswald de
Andueza Palacio, Raimundo
Aramburu, Pedro Eugenio
Arana, Felipe de
Arana, Francisco J.
Arana Osorio, Carlos
Aranha, Oswaldo
Araujo, Arturo
Arbenz Guzmán, Jacobo
Arce, Aniceto
Arce, Manuel José
Arce Castaño, Bayardo
Arévalo Bermejo, Juan José
Argüello, Leonardo
Arias, Desiderio
Arias Calderón, Ricardo
Arias Madrid, Arnulfo
Arias Madrid, Harmodio
Arias Sánchez, Oscar
Arismendi, Juan Bautista
Arista, Mariano
Aristide, Jean-Bertrand
Armijo, Manuel
Arosemena, Florencio Harmodio
Arosemena, Juan Demóstenes
Arosemena, Pablo
Arosemena Gómez, Otto
Arosemena Monroy, Carlos Julio
Arosemena Quinzada, Albacíades
Arron, Henck A. E.
Arroyo del Río, Carlos Alberto
Arteaga, Rosalía
Arze, José Antonio
Aspíllaga Family
Austin, Stephen Fuller
Avellaneda, Nicolás
Ávila Camacho, Manuel

Ayala, Eligio
Ayala, Eusebio
Aycinena, Mariano de
Aycinena, Pedro de
Aylwin Azócar, Patricio
Ayora Cueva, Isidro
Azcona Hoyo, José Simón
Bachelet, Michele
Báez, Buenaventura
Báez, Cecilio
Balaguer, Joaquín
Balbín, Ricardo
Baldomir, Alfredo
Ballivián, José
Balmaceda Fernández, José Manuel
Balta, José
Banzer Suárez, Hugo
Baquerizo Moreno, Alfredo
Barbosa, Francisco Villela
Barbosa y Alcalá, José Celso
Barco Vargas, Virgilio
Bareiro, Cándido
Barrientos Ortuño, René
Barrillas, Manuel Lisandro
Barrios, Gerardo
Barrios, Gonzalo
Barrios de Chamorro, Violeta
Barros, Adhemar de
Barroso, Gustavo Dodt
Barrow, Errol Walton
Barrundia, José Francisco
Barrundia, Juan
Batista, Cícero Romão
Batista y Zaldívar, Fulgencio
Batlle, Lorenzo
Batlle Berres, Luis Conrado
Batlle y Ordóñez, José
Bazaine, François Achille
Bedoya de Molina, Dolores
Bedoya Reyes, Luis
Béjar, Héctor
Belaúnde, Víctor Andrés
Belaúnde Terry, Fernando
Belgrano, Manuel
Bellegarde, Luis Dantès
Belzu, Manuel Isidoro
Bemberg, María Luisa
Benavides, Oscar Raimundo
Benítez, Jaime
Bernardes, Artur da Silva

Berreta, Tomás
Berrío, Pedro Justo
Berro, Carlos
Bertrand, Francisco
Betancourt, Rómulo
Betancur Cuartas, Belisario
Bignone, Reynaldo
Billinghurst, Guillermo Enrique
Bird, Vere Cornwall
Bishop, Maurice
Blanco Acevedo, Eduardo
Blanco Galindo, Carlos
Bocaiúva, Quintino
Bolívar, Simón
Bonifaz Ascasubi, Neptalí
Bonilla, Policarpo
Bonilla Chirinos, Manuel
Bordaberry, Juan María
Borge, Tomás
Borges de Medeiros, Antônio Augusto
Borja Cevallos, Rodrigo
Borno, Joseph Louis E. Antoine François
Borrero y Cortázar, Antonio
Bosch Gaviño, Juan
Bouterse, Desi
Boyer, Jean-Pierre
Bramuglia, Juan Atilio
Brás Pereira Gomes, Wenceslau
Bravo, Nicolás
Bray, Arturo
Brizola, Leonel
Brum, Baltasar
Bucaram, Abdalá
Bucaram Elmhalin, Asaad
Bulnes Prieto, Manuel
Bunau-Varilla, Philippe Jean
Busch Becerra, Germán
Bustamante, Anastasio
Bustamante, William Alexander
Bustamante y Rivero, José Luis
Caamaño Deñó, Francisco
Caamaño y Gómez Cornejo, José María
    Plácido
Caballero, Bernardino
Cabañas, José Trinidad
Cabañas, Lucio
Cáceres, Andrés Avelino
Cáceres, Ramón
Café Filho, João
Caldera Rodríguez, Rafael

Calderon, Sila María
Calderón Fournier, Rafael Ángel
Calderón Guardia, Rafael Ángel
Callejas Romero, Rafael Leonardo
Calles, Plutarco Elías
Calógeras, João Pandiá
Camacho Solís, Manuel
Campero, Narciso
Campisteguy, Juan
Campo, Rafael
Cámpora, Héctor José
Campos, Francisco Luiz da Silva
Campos, Roberto (de Oliveira)
Campos Sales, Manuel Ferraz de
Candamo, Manuel
Caneca, Frei Joaquím do Amor Divino
Cañedo, Francisco
Cañedo, Juan de Dios
Cantilo, José Luis
Capelo, Joaquín
Carazo Odio, Rodrigo
Cárcano, Ramón José
Cárdenas del Río, Lázaro
Cárdenas Solorzano, Cuauhtémoc
Cardoso, Fernando Henrique
Cardozo, Efraím
Carías Andino, Tiburcio
Carneiro de Campos, José Joaquim
Carranza, Venustiano
Carrera, José Rafael
Carrillo Colina, Braulio
Carrillo Puerto, Felipe
Carrión, Jerónimo
Carter, Jimmy
Cass, Lewis
Castañeda Castro, Salvador
Castelli, Juan José
Castello Branco, Humberto de Alencar
Castilhos, Júlio de
Castilla, Ramón
Castillo, Ramón
Castillo Armas, Carlos
Castillo Ledón, Amalia
Castro, Cipriano
Castro, Julián
Castro Madriz, José María
Castro Pozo, Hildebrando
Castro Ruz, Fidel
Castro Ruz, Raúl
Centurión, Carlos R.

Centurión, Juan Crisóstomo
Cerezo Arévalo, Marco Vinicio
Cerna, Vicente
Céspedes, Carlos Manuel de (the Elder)
Cevallos, Pedro Fermín
Chacón, Lázaro
Chamorro, Fruto
Chamorro Cardenal, Pedro Joaquín
Chamorro Vargas, Emiliano
Charles, Eugenia
Chaves, Federico
Chaves, Francisco C.
Chaves, Julio César
Chávez, Hugo
Chiari, Rodolfo E.
Chiari Remón, Roberto Francisco
Chibás, Eduardo
Christophe, Henri
Cisneros Betancourt, Salvador
Clouthier del Rincón, Manuel J.
Codovilla, Vittorio
Collor, Lindolfo
Collor de Mello, Fernando Affonso
Coll y Toste, Cayetano
Colosio Murrieta, Luis Donaldo
Colunje, Gil
Comonfort, Ignacio
Concha, José Vicente
Cooke, John William
Cordero Crespo, Luis
Córdova, Jorge
Córdova Rivera, Gonzalo S.
Corral Verdugo, Ramón
Cortés Castro, León
Costa e Silva, Artur da
Cotegipe, Barão de
Creel, Enrique Clay
Crespo, Joaquín
Cristiani, Alfredo
Cruz, Arturo
Cruz, Vicente
Cruz Ucles, Ramón Ernesto
Cuestas, Juan Lindolfo
Dantas, Manuel Pinto de Souza
Dartiguenave, Philippe-Sudré
d'Aubuisson, Roberto
Dávila, Miguel R.
Dávila Espinoza, Carlos Guillermo
Daza, Hilarión
Decoud, Hector Francisco

Decoud, José Segundo
de la Huerta, Adolfo
Delfim Neto, Antônio
Delgado, José Matías
Del Prado, Jorge
Derqui, Santiago
D'Escoto Brockmann, Miguel
Díaz, Adolfo
Díaz, Porfirio
Díaz Arosemena, Domingo
Díaz Ordaz, Gustavo
Dickmann, Enrique
Domínguez, Manuel
Dorrego, Manuel
Dorticós Torrado, Osvaldo
Duarte, Juan Pablo
Duarte Fuentes, José Napoleón
Dueñas, Francisco
Duhalde, Eduardo
Durán-Ballén, Sixto
Dutra, Eurico Gaspar
Duvalier, François
Duvalier, Jean-Claude
Echenique, José Rufino
Echeverría Álvarez, Luis
Echeverría Bianchi, José Antonio
Egaña Fabres, Mariano
Egaña Risco, Juan
Elías, Domingo
Emparán, Vicente
Endara, Guillermo
Enríquez Gallo, Alberto
Errázuriz Echaurren, Federico
Errázuriz Zañartu, Federico
Erro, Enrique
Escobar, Patricio
Espaillat, Ulises Francisco
Espinosa y Espinosa, (Juan) Javier
Esquivel, Manuel Amadeo
Estigarribia, José Félix
Estimé, Dumarsais
Estrada, José María (d. 1856)
Estrada Cabrera, Manuel
Estrada Palma, Tomás
Falcón, Juan Crisóstomo
Faoro, Raymundo
Farrell, Edelmiro
Feijó, Diogo Antônio
Fernandes, Florestan
Fernández Alonso, Sévero

Fernández Crespo, Daniel
Fernández Madrid, José
Fernández Oreamuno, Próspero
Fernández y Medina, Benjamín
Ferré Aguayo, Luis Antonio
Ferreira, Benigno
Ferreira Aldunate, Wilson
Ferrera, Francisco
Figueiredo, Jackson de
Figueiredo, João Baptista de Oliveira
Figueres Ferrer, José
Figueroa Alcorta, José
Filísola, Vicente
Flores, Juan José
Flores, Luis A.
Flores, Venancio
Flôres da Cunha, José Antônio
Flores Jijón, Antonio
Fonseca, Manoel Deodoro da
Fortuny, José Manuel
Fox Quesada, Vicente
Franco, Guillermo
Franco, Itamar Augusto Cautiero
Franco, Wellington Moreira
Frei Montalva, Eduardo
Freire Serrano, Ramón
Frei Ruiz-Tagle, Eduardo
Freyre, Gilberto (de Mello)
Frondizi, Arturo
Fujimori, Alberto Keinya
Gabeira, Fernando Nagle
Gairy, Eric
Gallegos, Rómulo
Galtieri, Leopoldo Fortunato
Galván, Manuel de Jesús
Gálvez, Juan Manuel
Gálvez, Mariano
Gamarra, Agustín
Gamarra, Francisca Zubiaga Bernales de (La
    Mariscala)
Garay, Blas
García Calderón, Francisco
García del Río, Juan
García Godoy, Héctor
García Granados, Miguel
García Meza, Luis
García Moreno, Gabriel
García Pérez, Alan
García Salinas, Francisco
Gaviria Trujillo, César Augusto

Geffrard, Fabre Nicolas
Geisel, Ernesto
Gestido, Oscar Daniel
Gill, Juan Bautista
Girón de León, Andrés de Jesús
Godoi, Juan Silvano
Goethals, George Washington
Golbery do Couto e Silva
Gomes, Eduardo
Gómez, Indalecio
Gómez, José Miguel (d. 1921)
Gómez, Juan Vicente
Gómez, Miguel Mariano
Gómez Castro, Laureano
Gómez Farías, Valentín
Gómez Hurtado, Alvaro
Gómez Morín, Manuel
Gómez Pedraza, Manuel
González, Manuel
González Flores, Alfredo
González Ortega, Jesús
González Videla, Gabriel
González Víquez, Cleto
Goulart, João Belchior Marques
Grau San Martín, Ramón
Grove Vallejo, Marmaduke
Guardia, Ricardo Adolfo de la
Guardia Gutiérrez, Tomás
Guardia Navarro, Ernesto de la
Guardiola, Santos
Gueiler Tejada, Lidia
Guerra, Ramón
Guerrero, Vicente
Guevara, Ernesto "Che"
Guevara Arze, Walter
Guggiari, José Patricio
Guido, José María
Guimarães, Ulysses Silveira
Gutiérrez, José María
Gutiérrez Borbúa, Lucio
Gutiérrez Brothers
Gutiérrez Garbín, Víctor Manuel
Gutiérrez Guerra, José
Guzmán, Enrique
Guzmán Blanco, Antonio Leocadio
Haya de la Torre, Víctor Raúl
Henríquez, Camilo
Henríquez y Carvajal, Francisco
Hernández, José Manuel
Hernández Colón, Rafael

Hernández Martínez, Maximiliano
Herrán, Pedro Alcántara
Herrera, Benjamín
Herrera, Carlos
Herrera, Dionisio de
Herrera, José Joaquín Antonio Florencio
Herrera, Luis Alberto de
Herrera Campins, Luis
Herrera y Obes, Julio
Hertzog Garaizabal, Enrique
Heureaux, Ulises
Holguín, Jorge
Houston, Sam
Huerta, Victoriano
Hurtado Larrea, Osvaldo
Hyppolite, Louis Modestin Florville
Ibáñez del Campo, Carlos
Ibarra, Juan Felipe
Iglesias, Miguel
Iglesias Castro, Rafael
Iglesias Pantin, Santiago
Illia, Arturo Umberto
Infante, José Miguel
Irigoyen, Bernardo de
Irigoyen, Hipólito
Irisarri, Antonio José de
Iturbide, Agustín de
Jagan, Janet
Jiménez, Enrique A.
Jiménez de Palacios, Aurora
Jiménez Oreamuno, Manuel de Jesús
Jiménez Oreamuno, Ricardo
Jovellanos, Salvador
Juárez, Benito
Juárez Celman, Miguel
Julião Arruda de Paula, Francisco
Justo, José Agustín Pedro
Kirchner, Néstor
Kubitschek, Márcia
Kubitschek de Oliveira, Juscelino
Labastida y Dávalos, Pelagio Antonio de
Lacalle Herrera, Luis Alberto
Lacerda, Carlos Frederico Werneck de
Lacerda, Maurício Pavia de
Lagos, Ricardo
Lanusse, Alejandro Augustín
Laredo Bru, Federico
Larrazábal Ugueto, Wolfgang
Larrea, Juan
La Serna, José de
Las Heras, Juan Gregorio de

Latorre, Lorenzo
Laugerud García, Eugenio Kjell
Lavalleja, Juan Antonio
Lechín Oquendo, Juan
Leconte, Michel Cincinnatus
Leguía, Augusto Bernardino
Lemus, José María
Lencinas, Carlos Wáshington
León de la Barra, Francisco
Leoni, Raúl
Lerdo de Tejada, Sebastián
Lescot, Élie
Lesseps, Ferdinand Marie, Vicomte de
Levingston, Roberto Marcelo
Linares, José María
Linares Alcántara, Francisco
Lindo Zelaya, Juan
Liniers y Bremond, Santiago de
Lleras, Lorenzo María
Lleras Camargo, Alberto
Lleras Restrepo, Carlos
Lombardo Toledano, Vicente
Lonardi, Eduardo
López, Carlos Antonio
López, Enrique Solano
López, Estanislao
López, Francisco Solano
López, José Hilario
López, Vicente Fidel
López Arellano, Oswaldo
López Contreras, Eleázar
López de Romaña, Eduardo
López Jordán, Ricardo
López Mateos, Adolfo
López Michelsen, Alfonso
López Obrador, Manuel Andrés
López Portillo, José
López Pumarejo, Alfonso
Louverture, Toussaint
Lozano Díaz, Julio
Lucas García, Fernando Romeo
Luís Pereira de Sousa, Washington
Luna Pizarro, Francisco Javier de
Luperón, Gregorio
Lusinchi, Jaime
Lutz, Bertha Maria Julia
Lynch, Elisa Alicia
Macas, Luis
Machado y Morales, Gerardo
Mac-Iver Rodríguez, Enrique

Madero, Francisco Indalecio
Madrazo, Carlos A.
Madrid Hurtado, Miguel de la
Magloire, Paul Eugène
Magoon, Charles Edward
Malespín, Francisco
Maluf, Paulo Salim
Manley, Norman Washington
Manning, Thomas Courtland
Mar, José de la
Mariátegui, José Carlos
Marighella, Carlos
Mariño, Santiago
Márquez, José Ignacio de
Marroquín, José Manuel
Martí, Agustín Farabundo
Martínez, Tomás
Mauá, Visconde de
Maza, Manuel Vicente de
Médici, Emílio Garrastazú
Medina, Hugo
Medina Angarita, Isaías
Mejía Victores, Oscar Humberto
Meléndez Chaverri, Carlos
Meléndez Family
Melgarejo, Mariano
Mella, Julio Antonio
Melo, José María
Menchú Tum, Rigoberta
Méndez Fleitas, Epifanio
Méndez Montenegro, Julio César
Méndez Montenegro, Mario
Méndez Pereira, Octavio
Mendieta, Salvador
Mendoza, Carlos Antonio
Menem, Carlos Saúl
Menocal, Mario García
Merino Castro, José Toribio
Mesa, Carlos
Michelina, Santos
Michelini, Zelmar
Miró Cardona, José
Miró Quesada Family
Molina, Arturo Armando
Molina, Marcelo
Molina, Pedro
Molina Ureña, José Rafael
Monagas, José Gregorio
Monagas, José Tadeo
Moncada, José María

Monge Álvarez, Luis Alberto
Monteagudo, Bernardo de
Monte Alegre, José da Costa Carvalho,
    Marquís de
Montealegre Fernández, José María
Monteiro, Pedro Aurélio de Góis
Montes, Ismael
Montt Torres, Manuel
Montúfar, Lorenzo
Mora Fernández, Juan
Morais Barros, Prudente José de
Morales, Agustín
Morales, Eusebio A.
Morales, Evo
Morales Bermúdez, Remigio
Morales Bermúdez Cerruti, Francisco
Mora Valverde, Manuel
Morazán, Francisco
Moreira da Costa Ribeiro, Delfim
Morelos y Pavón, José María
Moreno, Mariano
Morínigo, Higínio
Mosquera, Manuel José
Mosquera, Tomás Cipriano de
Mosquera y Arboleda, Joaquín
Muñoz Ledo Lazo de la Vega, Porfirio
Muñoz Marín, Luis
Murillo Toro, Manuel
Murtinho, Joaquim Duarte
Musa, Said
Nabuco de Araújo, Joaquim
Nardone, Benito
Nascimento, Abdias do
Neruda, Pablo
Neves, Tancredo de Almeida
Noboa Bejarano, Gustavo
Noboa y Arteta, Diego
Nord, Pierre Alexis
Noriega Moreno, Manuel Antonio
Núñez Moledo, Rafael
Núñez Vargas, Benjamín
Obando, José María
Obando y Bravo, Miguel
Obregón Salido, Álvaro
Odría, Manuel Apolinario
Oduber Quirós, Daniel
Olañeta y Güemes, José Joaquín Casimiro
Olaya Herrera, Enrique
Olmedo, José Joaquín de
Onganía, Juan Carlos

Orbegoso, Luis José de
Orellana, José María
Orfila, Alejandro
Oribe, Manuel
Ortega Saavedra, Daniel
Ortega Saavedra, Humberto
Ortiz, Roberto Marcelino
Ortiz Rubio, Pascual
Osório, Manuel Luís
Osorio, Oscar
Ospina, Pedro Nel
Ospina Pérez, Mariano
Ospina Rodríguez, Mariano
Ottoni, Teofilo Benedito
Ovando Candía, Alfredo
Pacheco, Gregorio
Pacheco Areco, Jorge
Pacheco da Silva, Osvaldo
Páez, Federico
Páez, José Antonio
Palacio, Alfredo
Palacio Fajardo, Manuel
Palacios, Alfredo L.
Palenque, Carlos
Pando, José Manuel
Paraná, Honôrio Hermeto Carneiro Leão,
    Marquês de
Pardo y Barreda, José
Pardo y Lavalle, Manuel
Paredes, Mariano
Paredes y Arrillaga, Mariano
Parra, Aquileo
Pascal-Trouillot, Ertha
Paso, Juan José
Passarinho, Jarbas Gonçalves
Pastora Gómez, Edén
Pastrana Borrero, Misael
Patrón Costas, Robustiano
Pavón Aycinena, Manuel Francisco
Paz, José María
Paz Baraona, Miguel
Paz Estenssoro, Víctor
Paz García, Policarpo
Paz Zamora, Jaime
Peçanha, Nilo Procópio
Pedreira, Antonio S.
Peixoto, Floriano Vieira
Peixoto, Júlio Afrânio
Pellacani, Dante

Pellegrini, Carlos
Pena, Afonso Augusto Moreira
Peña, Manuel Pedro de
Peña Gómez, José Francisco
Peñaloza, Ángel Vicente
Peñaranda del Castillo, Enrique
Peralta Azurdia, Enrique
Pereira, José Clemente
Pérez, Carlos Andrés
Pérez Jiménez, Marcos
Pérez Mascayano, José Joaquín
Pérez Salas, Francisco Antonio
Perón, Juan Domingo
Perón, María Estela Martínez de
Perón, María Eva Duarte de
Pessoa, Epitácio da Silva
Pessoa Cavalcanti de Albuquerque, João
Pétion, Alexandre Sabès
Pezet, Juan Antonio
Picado Michalski, Teodoro
Piérola, Nicolás de
Pindling, Lynden Oscar
Pinedo, Federico
Pinheiro, José Feliciano Fernandes
Pinheiro Machado, José Gomes
Pinho, José Wanderley de Araújo
Pinochet Ugarte, Augusto
Pino Suárez, José María
Pinto Díaz, Francisco Antonio
Pinto Garmendia, Aníbal
Plaza, Victorino de la
Plaza Gutiérrez, Leonidas
Plaza Lasso, Galo
Polk, James Knox
Ponce Enríquez, Camilo
Porras, Belisario
Portes Gil, Emilio
Posadas, Gervasio Antonio de
Prado, Mariano Ignacio
Prado y Ugarteche, Javier
Prado y Ugarteche, Manuel
Prat Echaurren, Jorge
Prestes, Luís Carlos
Prestes de Albuquerque, Julio
Price, George
Prieto, Guillermo
Prieto Figueroa, Luis Beltrán
Prío Socarrás, Carlos
Puente Uceda, Luis de la
Pueyrredón, Carlos Alberto

Pueyrredón, Honorio
Pueyrredón, Juan Martín de
Quadros, Jânio da Silva
Queirós Coutinho Matoso da Câmera,
    Eusébio de
Quiñones Molina, Alfonso
Quintana, Manuel
Quintana Roo, Andrés
Quiroga, Jorge
Quiroga, Juan Facundo
Quiroga Santa Cruz, Marcelo
Quispe, Felipe
Ramírez, Francisco
Ramírez, Pedro Pablo
Ramos Mejía, Ezequiel
Regalado, Tomás
Remón Cantera, José Antonio
Restrepo, Carlos Eugenio
Restrepo, José Manuel
Revueltas, José
Reyes, Rafael
Reyes Ogazón, Bernardo
Reyes Villa, Manfred
Reyna Barrios, José María
Riani, Clodsmith
Riesco Errázuriz, Germán
Rio Branco, Barão do
Rio Branco, Visconde do
Ríos Montt, José Efraín
Ríos Morales, Juan Antonio
Rivadavia, Bernardino
Rivarola, Cirilo Antonio
Rivas, Patricio
Rivera, Fructuoso
Rivera, Joaquín
Rivera Cabezas, Antonio
Rivera Carballo, Julio Adalberto
Rivera Maestre, Miguel
Rivera Paz, Mariano
Robles, Francisco
Robles, Marcos Aurelio
Robles Berlanga, Rosario
Roca, Julio Argentino
Roca Rodríguez, Vicente Ramón
Rocha, Dardo
Rocha, Justiniano José da
Rockefeller, Nelson Aldrich
Rodas Alvarado, Modesto
Rodrigues Alves, Francisco de Paula
Rodríguez, Andrés

Rodríguez, Carlos Rafael
Rodríguez Demorizi, Emilio
Rodríguez Lara, Guillermo
Rodríguez Luján, Abelardo
Rojas, Isaac
Rojas Paúl, Juan Pablo
Rojas Pinilla, Gustavo
Roldós Aguilera, Jaime
Romero, Carlos Humberto
Romero, Oscar Arnulfo
Romero Barceló, Carlos
Roosevelt, Franklin Delano
Roosevelt, Theodore
Rosa, Ramón
Rosas, Juan Manuel de
Roy, Eugène
Rúa, Fernando de la
Ruiz Cortines, Adolfo
Russell, John H.
Saavedra, Cornelio de
Saavedra Lamas, Carlos
Saavedra Mallea, Bautista
Sacasa, Juan Batista
Sáenz Peña, Luis
Sáenz Peña, Roque
Salamanca, Daniel
Salas, Manuel de
Salaverry, Felipe Santiago
Salazar, Matías
Salgado, Plinio
Salgar, Eustorgio
Salinas de Gortari, Carlos
Salnave, Sylvain
Salomon, Louis Étienne Lysius Félicité
Sam, Jean Vilbrun Guillaume
Sam, Tirésias Augustin Simon
Samanez Ocampo, David
Samper Agudelo, Miguel
Sanabria Martínez, Víctor M.
Sánchez, Luis Alberto
Sánchez Cerro, Luis Manuel
Sánchez de Lozada Bustamante, Gonzalo
Sánchez Hernández, Fidel
Sánchez Vilella, Roberto
Sandino, Augusto César
Sandoval, José León
Sanfuentes Andonaegui, Juan Luis
Sanguinetti, Julio María
Santa Anna, Antonio López de
Santa Cruz, Andrés de

Santa María González, Domingo
Santana, Pedro
Santos, Eduardo
São Vicente, José Antônio Pimenta Bueno,
    Marquês de
Saraiva, José Antônio
Saravia, Aparicio
Sarney, José
Schaerer, Eduardo
Schick Gutiérrez, René
Sendic, Raúl
Seoane, Manuel
Seregni, Líber
Serrano Elías, Jorge Antonio
Siles Zuazo, Hernán
Silva, Benedita da
Silva, Lindolfo
Silva, Luis Inácio Lula da
Silva Lisboa, José da
Simon, Antoine
Somoza Debayle, Anastasio
Somoza Debayle, Luis
Somoza García, Anastasio
Soto, Marco Aurelio
Soto Alfaro, Bernardo
Soublette, Carlos
Soulouque, Faustin Élie
Souza, Luiza Erundina de
Stefanich, Juan
Stein, Eduardo
Stroessner, Alfredo
Suárez, Marco Fidel
Suazo Córdova, Roberto
Sucre Alcalá, Antonio José de
Tajes, Máximo
Talavera, Manuel
Taunay, Affonso d'Escragnolle
Tavares Bastos, Aureliano Cândido
Taylor, Zachary
Tejada Sorzano, José Luis
Tejedor, Carlos
Terra, Gabriel
Thompson, George
Tocornal, Joaquín
Toledo, Alejandro
Tomic, Radomiro
Toro, David
Toro Zambrano, Mateo de
Torre, Lisandro de la
Torres, Juan José

Torres, Luis Emeterio
Torre Tagle y Portocarrero, José Bernardo de
Torrijos Herrera, Omar
Trejos Fernández, José Joaquín
Tronscoso de la Concha, Manuel de Jesús
Trujillo, Julián
Trujillo Molina, Rafael Leónidas
Turbay, Gabriel
Turbay Ayala, Julio César
Ubico y Castañeda, Jorge
Ugarte, Marcelino
Ulate Blanco, Otilio
Ungo, Guillermo Manuel
Urbina, José María
Urdaneta, Rafael
Ureta, Eloy G.
Uriburu, José Evaristo
Uriburu, José Félix
Urquiza, Justo José de
Urriolagoitía, Mamerto
Urrutia Lleó, Manuel
Uruguai, Visconde do
Valencia, Guillermo León
Valladares, Armando
Valle, José Cecilio del
Vallejo, Mariano Guadalupe
Vallenilla Lanz, Laureano
Varas de la Barra, Antonio
Varela, Felipe
Vargas, Getúlio Dornelles
Vargas, José María
Vargas Llosa, Mario
Vasconcelos, Bernardo Pereira de
Vásquez, Horacio
Veiga, Evaristo Ferreira da
Veintemilla, José Ignacio de
Veintemilla, Marietta de
Velasco, José Miguel de
Velasco Alvarado, Juan
Velasco Ibarra, José María
Velázquez Sánchez, Fidel
Victoria, Guadalupe
Victoria, Manuel
Videla, Jorge Rafael
Viera, Feliciano
Vieytes, Hipólito
Vigil, Donaciano
Villa, Francisco "Pancho"
Villagrán Kramer, Francisco
Villalba, Jóvito

Villarroel López, Gualberto
Villazón, Eliodoro
Villeda Morales, Ramón
Vincent, Sténio Joseph
Viola, Roberto Eduardo
Viteri y Ungo, Jorge
Vivanco, Manuel Ignacio
Volio Jiménez, Jorge
Weffort, Francisco Correia
Williams Calderón, Abraham
Williman, Claudio
Wilson, Woodrow
Wolfskill, William
Ydígoras Fuentes, Miguel
Ynsfrán, Edgar L.
Zaldúa, Francisco Javier
Zeballos, Estanislao
Zedillo Ponce de León, Ernesto
Zelaya, José Santos
Zubizarreta, Gerónimo
Zuloaga, Félix María
Zúñiga, Ignacio

15. PUBLIC ADMINISTRATION, CIVIL SERVICE, AND DIPLOMACY

Acosta García, Julio
Adams, Grantley Herbert
Aguilar Vargas, Cándido
Albán, Laureano
Alberdi, Juan Bautista
Alberto, João
Albuquerque, Antônio Francisco de Paula
Alcorta, Diego
Almonte, Juan Nepomuceno
Altamirano, Ignacio Manuel
Alves Branco, Manuel
Amador, Manuel E.
Anchorena, Tomás Manuel de
Andrade, Carlos Drummond de
Andrade, Gomes Freire de
Andueza Palacio, Raimundo
Angelis, Pedro de
Arana, Felipe de
Arana Osorio, Carlos
Arango y Parreño, Francisco de
Arciniegas, Germán

Arévalo Bermejo, Juan José
Arévalo Martínez, Rafael
Arguedas, Alcides
Argüello, Leonardo
Argüello, Santiago
Arias Sánchez, Oscar
Armijo, Manuel
Arosemena, Justo
Arriaga, Ponciano
Austin, Stephen Fuller
Azcuénaga, Miguel de
Balcarce, Mariano
Baptista, Mariano
Baquíjano y Carrillo de Córdoba, José de
Barbosa, Francisco Villela
Barbosa de Oliveira, Rui
Barreda y Laos, Felipe
Barreiro, Antonio
Barrios, Gonzalo
Barros, João de
Barrow, Errol Walton
Barrundia, José Francisco
Barrundia, Juan
Bassols, Narciso
Batres Juarros, Luis
Bedoya Reyes, Luis
Benítez, Jaime
Berges, José
Bernardes, Artur da Silva
Betancourt, Rómulo
Blaine, James Gillespie
Blanco, José Félix
Boal, Augusto
Bonifaz Ascasubi, Neptalí
Borba Gato, Manuel de
Borges, Jorge Luis
Borno, Joseph Louis E. Antoine François
Borrero y Cortázar, Antonio
Braden, Spruille
Caldera Rodríguez, Rafael
Calderón Fournier, Rafael Ángel
Calderón Guardia, Rafael Ángel
Callejas Romero, Rafael Leonardo
Calógeras, João Pandiá
Calvo, Carlos
Camarena, Enrique
Campero, Narciso
Campo, Rafael
Campomanes, Pedro Rodríguez, Conde de
Campos, Francisco Luiz da Silva

Campos, Roberto (de Oliveira)
Campos Sales, Manuel Ferraz de
Cañas, José Simeón
Cañedo, Juan de Dios
Canning, George
Carazo Odio, Rodrigo
Carbo y Noboa, Pedro José
Cárcano, Miguel Ángel
Cárcano, Miguel Ángel
Cárdenas, Víctor Hugo
Cárdenas Solorzano, Cuauhtémoc
Cardozo, Ramón Indalecio
Carneiro de Campos, José Joaquim
Caro, José Eusebio
Carondelet, François-Louis Hector
Carrillo Colina, Braulio
Carrillo Flores, Antonio
Carrillo Flores, Nabor
Carrió de la Vandera, Alonso
Carvalho, Antônio de Albuquerque Coelho de
Caso y Andrade, Alfonso
Castañeda Castro, Salvador
Castillo Ledón, Amalia
Castro Ruz, Raúl
Cazneau, William Leslie
Cedillo Martínez, Saturnino
Cevallos, Pedro Fermín
Chamorro Vargas, Emiliano
Chatfield, Frederick
Chávez, Mariano
Chonchol, Jacques
Christmas, Lee
Clay, Henry
Cobos, Francisco de los
Coelho, Jorge de Albuquerque
Coelho Pereira, Duarte
Collor, Lindolfo
Colombres, José Eusebio
Colosio Murrieta, Luis Donaldo
Colunje, Gil
Concha, José Vicente
Córdova Rivera, Gonzalo S.
Corona, Ramón
Cortés Castro, León
Costa, Hipólito José da
Cotegipe, Barão de
Coutinho, Rodrigo Domingos Antonio
      de Sousa
Couto, José Bernardo
Creel, Enrique Clay

Crowder, Enoch Herbert
Cruz, Arturo
Cue Canovas, Agustín
Damas, Léon-Gontran
Dantas, Manuel Pinto de Souza
de la Huerta, Adolfo
Delfim Neto, Antônio
Delgado Chalbaud, Carlos
D'Escoto Brockmann, Miguel
Díaz, Félix, Jr.
Díaz Vélez, José Miguel
Diegues, Carlos
DiTella, Guido
Dobles Segreda, Luis
Domínguez, Miguel
Dorticós Torrado, Osvaldo
Drago, Luis María
Dulles, Allen
Dulles, John Foster
Durán, Fray Narciso
Dutra, Eurico Gaspar
Echeandía, José María de
Echeverría Álvarez, Luis
Einaudi, Luigi R.
Elizalde, Rufino de
Emparán, Vicente
Encinas, José Antonio
Endara, Guillermo
Ensenada, Cenón de Somodevilla,
    Marqués de la
Escalante, Aníbal
Escobedo, Mariano
Estimé, Dumarsais
Fabela Alfaro, Isidro
Facio Brenes, Rodrigo
Facio Segreda, Gonzalo
Falcón, José
Feijó, Diogo Antônio
Fernández, Max
Fernández de Piedrahita, Lucas
Fernández Guardia, Ricardo
Ferré Aguayo, Luis Antonio
Ferrera, Francisco
Figueroa, José
Figueroa Larraín, Emiliano
Finlay, Carlos Juan
Flores Nano, Lourdes
Fonseca, Juan Rodríguez de
Forbes, John Murray
Forbes, William Cameron

Fuentes, Carlos
Fuentes, Manuel Atanasio
Galván Rivera, Mariano
Gálvez, José de
Gamboa Iglesias, Federico
Gamio Martínez, Manuel
García Calderón, Francisco
García Godoy, Héctor
García Ortíz, Laureano
García Robles, Alfonso
García Salinas, Francisco
Garrido Canabal, Tomás
Gastão d'Orléans
Gelly, Juan Andrés
Gelly y Obes, Juan Andrés
Goethals, George Washington
Gomes, Eduardo
Gómez, Indalecio
Gómez, José Valentín
Gómez, Juan Gualberto
Gómez, Miguel Mariano
Gómez Pedraza, Manuel
Gómez Segura, Marte Rodolfo
Gondra, Manuel
Gonzaga, Tomás Antônio
González, Abraham
González, Elián
González, Florentino
González, Manuel
Gonzalez Garza, Roque
González Ortega, Jesús
Gorostiza Acalá, José
Graef Fernández, Carlos
Groot, José Manuel
Guardia, Ricardo Adolfo de la
Guido y Spano, Carlos
Gutiérrez, Eulalio
Gutiérrez Estrada, José María
Gutiérrez Garbín, Víctor Manuel
Guzmán, Antonio Leocadio
Haro Barraza, Guillermo
Haro y Tamariz, Antonio de
Hawkins, John
Heredia Acosta, Alejandro
Hernández, José
Hernández Colón, Rafael
Herrán, Pedro Alcántara
Herrera Campins, Luis
Herrera Lane, Felipe
Hull, Cordell

Ibarra de Piedra, Rosario
Iglesias, José María
Itaboraí, Visconde de
Jagan, Cheddi
Jara Corona, Heriberto
Jaramillo Alvarado, Pío
Jiménez, Enrique A.
Juan y Santacilia, Jorge
Kissinger, Henry
Kubitschek, Márcia
Kubitschek de Oliveira, Juscelino
Kumate Rodríguez, Jesús
Larkin, Thomas
Larrazábal Ugueto, Wolfgang
Lavalle Urbina, María
Lavradio, Marquês do
Le Bretón, Tomás Alberto
Lencinas, Carlos Wáshington
León de la Barra, Francisco
Leoni, Raúl
Lerdo de Tejada, Miguel
Lerdo de Tejada, Sebastián
Lescot, Élie
Letelier del Solar, Orlando
Lewis, Roberto
Limantour, José Yves
Lisboa, Joaquim Marques
Lleras, Lorenzo María
Lleras Camargo, Alberto
Lleras Restrepo, Carlos
Lobo, Hélio
López, Vicente Fidel
López Arellano, Oswaldo
López Mateos, Adolfo
López Portillo, José
López Rega, José
Lott, Henrique Batista Duffles Teixeira
Lutzenberger, José
Machado de Assis, Joaquim Maria
Madrazo, Carlos A.
Madrazo, Roberto
Madrid Hurtado, Miguel de la
Magalhães, Domingos José Gonçalves de
Mahuad, Jamil
Maluf, Paulo Salim
Manley, Michael Norman
Mann, Thomas Clifton
Manso de Maldonado, Antonio
Mantilla, Manuel Florencio
Mariño, Santiago

Márquez, José Ignacio de
Martyr, Peter
Maurits, Johan
Médici, Emílio Garrastazú
Mello, Zélia Maria Cardoso de
Melo, Leopoldo
Melo e Castro, Martinho de
Melo Franco, Afonso Arinos de
Melo Franco, Afrânio de
Melo Neto, João Cabral de
Méndez Pereira, Octavio
Mendiburu, Manuel de
Mendieta, Salvador
Mendoza, Antonio de
Michelina, Santos
Mindlin, José Ephim
Miró Cardona, José
Mistral, Gabriela
Molina, Marcelo
Molina Bedoya, Felipe
Molina Enríquez, Andrés
Molinari, Diego Luis
Monge Álvarez, Luis Alberto
Monteagudo, Bernardo de
Monte Alegre, José da Costa Carvalho,
    Marquís de
Montealegre Fernández, José María
Monteiro, Pedro Aurélio de Góis
Monteiro, Tobias do Rêgo
Montt Torres, Manuel
Montúfar, Lorenzo
Montúfar Montes de Oca, Lorenzo
Moog, Clodomiro Vianna
Mora, José María Luis
Morales Carrión, Arturo
Morales Lemus, José
Mora Otero, José Antonio
Mora Valverde, Manuel
Moreno, Fulgencio
Morones, Luis
Morrow, Dwight Whitney
Mosquera, Tomás Cipriano de
Mosquera y Arboleda, Joaquín
Moya de Contreras, Pedro
Múgica, Francisco José
Muñoz Ledo Lazo de la Vega, Porfirio
Murillo Toro, Manuel
Murtinho, Joaquim Duarte
Nabuco de Araújo, Joaquim
Naón, Rómulo S.

Neves, Tancredo de Almeida
Ocampo, Melchor
Oduber Quirós, Daniel
Olaya Herrera, Enrique
Olivares, Conde-Duque de
Oliveira Lima, Manuel de
Oliveira Vianna, Francisco José de
Orfila, Washington Alejandro José Luis
Orozco y Berra, Manuel
Ortiz de Ayala, Simón Tadeo
Ortiz Mena, Antonio
Osório, Manuel Luís
Ospina, Pedro Nel
Ospina Pérez, Mariano
Otero, Mariano
Otero Vertíz, Gustavo Adolfo
Padilla Peñalosa, Ezequiel
Páez, Federico
Palacio Fajardo, Manuel
Paniagua, Valentín
Pani Arteaga, Alberto J.
Paraná, Honório Hermeto Carneiro Leão,
    Marquês de
Pareja Diezcanseco, Alfredo
Parra, Aquileo
Passarinho, Jarbas Gonçalves
Pastrana Borrero, Misael
Paterson, William
Patiño, José de
Patiño, Simón Iturri
Payno y Flores, Manuel
Paz, Octavio
Pearson, Weetman Dickinson
Peçanha, Nilo Procópio
Peixoto, Júlio Afrânio
Pellacani, Dante
Pellegrini, Carlos
Pellicer Cámara, Carlos
Pena, Afonso Augusto Moreira
Pena, Luís Carlos Martins
Peña Gómez, José Francisco
Peña y Peña, Manuel de la
Peralta Azurdia, Enrique
Pereda, Setembrino Ezequiel
Pereira, José Clemente
Pérez, Albino
Pérez, Carlos Andrés
Pérez de Cuéllar, Javier
Pérez Jiménez, Marcos
Pérez Mascayano, José Joaquín

Pessoa, Epitácio da Silva
Pessoa Cavalcanti de Albuquerque, João
Picado Michalski, Teodoro
Pinedo, Federico
Pinheiro, José Feliciano Fernandes
Pinho, José Wanderley de Araújo
Piñol y Sala, José
Plaza Gutiérrez, Leonidas
Plaza Lasso, Galo
Poinsett, Joel Roberts
Polay Campos, Víctor
Pombal, Marquês de (Sebastião José de
    Carvalho e Melo)
Porras, Belisario
Porter, David
Portes Gil, Emilio
Prado y Ugarteche, Mariano Ignacio
Prebisch, Raúl
Prieto Figueroa, Luis Beltrán
Puig Casauranc, José Manuel
Queirós Coutinho Matoso da Câmera,
    Eusébio de
Queiroz, Dinah Silveira de
Quesada, Vicente Gregorio
Quiñones Molina, Alfonso
Quintana Roo, Andrés
Rabasa, Emilio
Ramírez, Ignacio
Ramírez Vázquez, Pedro
Ramírez y Blanco, Alejandro
Ramos Arizpe, José Miguel
Ramos Mejía, Ezequiel
Ramos y Magaña, Samuel
Rayón, Ignacio
Reed, Walter
Rejón, Manuel Crescencio
Rengifo Cárdenas, Manuel
Reyes Heroles, Jesús
Reyes Ochoa, Alfonso
Reyes Ogazón, Bernardo
Ribeiro, Darcy
Rio Branco, Barão do
Rio Branco, Visconde do
Rivarola, Rodolfo
Robles, Marcos Aurelio
Roca, Blas
Roca Rodríguez, Vicente Ramón
Rockefeller, Nelson Aldrich
Rodney, Caesar Augustus
Rodríguez, Carlos Rafael

Rodríguez Demorizi, Emilio
Rodríguez Erdoiza, Manuel
Rodríguez Luján, Abelardo
Rodríguez Saá, Adolfo
Rojas Paúl, Juan Pablo
Rojas Urtuguren, José Antonio de
Romero, Matías
Romero Barceló, Carlos
Romero Rubio, Manuel
Rondon, Cândido Mariano da Silva
Roscio, Juan Germán
Rubí, Marqués de
Rubião, Murilo
Ruffo Appel, Ernesto
Ruiz Cortines, Adolfo
Ruiz de Alarcón y Mendoza, Juan
Sá, Mem de
Saavedra Lamas, Carlos
Sá e Benavides, Salvador Correia de
Sáenz, Moisés
Sáenz Garza, Aarón
Saldías, Adolfo
Salgar, Eustorgio
Salinas de Gortari, Carlos
Salinas de Gortari, Raúl
Sánchez, Prisciliano
Sánchez de Tagle, Francisco Manuel
Sánchez Hernández, Fidel
Sánchez Vilella, Roberto
Sandoval Vallarta, Manuel
Santamaría, Haydée
Santos, Eduardo
São Vicente, José Antônio Pimenta Bueno,
    Marquês de
Schaerer, Eduardo
Schick Gutiérrez, René
Scliar, Moacyr
Seaga, Edward
Seguín, Juan José María Erasmo
Sierra Méndez, Justo
Silva Herzog, Jesús
Simonsen, Mário Henrique
Sotomayor Valdés, Ramón
Soublette, Carlos
Sousa, Otávio Tarqüínio de
Stephens, John Lloyd
Taboada, Antonino
Távara y Andrade, Santiago
Teixeira, Anisio Espinola
Tinoco Granados, Federico

Tobar Donoso, Julio
Tocornal, Joaquín
Toro, Fermín
Torres, Luis Emeterio
Tronscoso de la Concha, Manuel de Jesús
Trujillo, Julián
Tugwell, Rexford Guy
Turbay, Gabriel
Ugarte, Manuel
Urbina, José María
Urbina, Luis Gonzaga
Urrea, José de
Urrutia Lleó, Manuel
Uruguai, Visconde do
Urvina Jado, Francisco
Valle, Artistóbulo del
Varas de la Barra, Antonio
Vargas, Getúlio Dornelles
Varnhagen, Francisco Adolfo de
Vazquez, Tabare
Vázquez de Ayllón, Lucas
Velasco, Luis de ("the Younger")
Velázquez Sánchez, Fidel
Vélez Sarsfield, Dalmacio
Vidaurri, Santiago
Vieira, Antônio
Villanueva, Carlos Raúl
Villas Bôas Brothers
Villaurrutia, Jacobo de
Villeda Morales, Ramón
Vincent, Sténio Joseph
Volio Jiménez, Jorge
Ward, Henry George
Washburn, Charles Ames
Welles, Sumner
Wheelock Román, Jaime
Wilde, Eduardo
Wilson, Henry Lane
Wood, Leonard
Yáñez Santos Delgadillo, Agustín
Ynsfrán, Pablo Max
Zaldúa, Francisco Javier
Zamora, Rubén
Zaragoza, Ignacio
Zarco, Francisco
Zavala, Joaquín
Zeballos, Estanislao
Zubirán Achondo, Salvador
Zubizarreta, Gerónimo

16. RELIGION

Abad y Queipo, Manuel
Abbad y Lasierra, Íñigo
Alegre, Francisco Javier
Alexander VI, Pope
Alva Ixtlilxóchitl, Fernando
Anchieta, José de
Andreoni, João Antônio
Antequera y Castro, José de
Aristide, Jean-Bertrand
Arns, Paulo Evaristo
Balbuena, Bernardo de
Batista, Cícero Romão
Bazán, Juan Gregorio
Beltrán, Luis
Beltrán, Luis (Saint)
Benavides, Alonso de
Bethancourt, Pedro de San José de
Blanco, José Félix
Boff, Leonardo
Bolaños, Luis de
Brasseur de Bourbourg, Charles Étienne
Caballero y Góngora, Antonio
Câmara, Hélder
Cañas, José Simeón
Caneca, Frei Joaquím do Amor Divino
Cardenal, Ernesto
Cárdenas, Bernardino de
Cardim, Frei Fernão
Carney, James "Guadalupe"
Casaldáliga, Pedro
Casanova y Estrada, Ricardo
Casáus y Torres, Ramón
Castañeda, Francisco de Paula
Castillo y Guevara, Francisca Josefa de la
    Concepción de
Claver, Pedro
Clavigero, Francisco Javier
Cobo, Bernabé
Conselheiro, Antônio
Cortés de Madariaga, José
Cos y Pérez, José María
Coutinho, José Joaquim da Cunha de Azeredo
Cuadra, Pablo Antonio
Cuevas, Mariano
Delgado, José Matías
Díaz de Guzmán, Ruy
Dobrizhoffer, Martín
Donovan, Jean

Durán, Diego
Durán, Fray Narciso
Durão, José de Santa Rita
Errázuriz Valdivieso, Crescente
Esquiú, Mamerto
Feijóo, Benito Jerónimo
Fernández de Piedrahita, Lucas
Figueiredo, Jackson de
Flores Nano, Lourdes
Fonseca, Juan Rodríguez de
Fresno Larraín, Juan Francisco
Frías, Antonio
Funes, Gregorio
Fúrlong Cárdiff, Guillermo
Gage, Thomas
Gallo Goyenechea, Pedro León
Gante, Pedro de
Garcés, Francisco Tomás Hermenegildo
García, Diego
García Diego y Moreno, Francisco
García Peláez, Francisco de Paula
Gasca, Pedro de la
Girón de León, Andrés de Jesús
Godoy, Manuel
Gómez, José Valentín
González de Santa Cruz, Roque
González Suárez, (Manuel María) Federico
Gorriti, Juan Ignacio de
Gregory XIII, Pope
Groot, José Manuel
Gutiérrez, Gustavo
Henríquez, Camilo
Herrán y Zaldúa, Antonio Saturnino
Herrera, Bartolomé
Hidalgo y Costilla, Miguel
Jerez, Francisco de
John Paul II, Pope
Juana Inés de la Cruz, Sor
Juan Diego
Kino, Eusebio Francisco
Labastida y Dávalos, Pelagio Antonio de
Landa, Diego de
Landázuri Ricketts, Juan
Landívar, Rafael
Lasuén, Fermín Francisco de
Leo XIII, Pope
Liendo y Goicoechea, José Antonio
Llorente y Lafuente, Anselmo
López de Cogolludo, Diego
López Trujillo, Alfonso

Lorenzana y Buitrón, Francisco Antonio de
Lozano, Pedro
Luque, Hernando de
Maldonado, Rodrigo de Arias
Margil de Jesús, Antonio
Marroquín, Francisco
Martínez, Antonio J.
Martyr, Peter
Matamoros y Guridi, Mariano
Melville, Thomas and Margarita
Menininha do Gantois, Mãe
Mier Noriega y Guerra, José Servando
　　Teresa de
Mogrovejo, Toribio Alfonso de
Montesinos, Antonio de
Mora, José María Luis
Mora y del Río, José
Morelos y Pavón, José María
Mosquera, Manuel José
Motolinía, Toribio de
Moya de Contreras, Pedro
Niza, Marcos de
Nóbrega, Manuel da
Nusdorffer, Bernardo
Obando y Bravo, Miguel
Oré, Luis Gerónimo de
Oro, Justo Santa María de
Palou, Francisco
Pérez Aguirre, Luis
Piñol y Aycinena, Bernardo
Pius IX, Pope
Porres, Martín de
Posadas Ocampo, Juan Jesús
Proaño Villalba, Leonidas Eduardo (Bishop)
Quiroga, Vasco de
Rada, Manuel de Jesús
Rivera Damas, Arturo
Rocha, Manoel Ribeiro
Romero, Oscar Arnulfo
Rosa de Lima
Rossell y Arellano, Mariano
Ruiz, Samuel
Ruiz de Montoya, Antonio
Sahagún, Bernardino de
Sales, Eugênio de Araújo
Salvador, Vicente do
Sanabria Martínez, Víctor M.
Sepp, Anton
Serra, Junipero
Serrano, José

Silva Henríquez, Raúl
Solano, Francisco
Solís Folch de Cardona, José
Subirana, Manuel de Jesús
Taborga Pizarro, Miguel de los Santos
Thiel, Bernardo Augusto
Torquemada, Juan de
Torres Bello, Diego de
Torres Restrepo, Camilo
Turcios Lima, Luis Agosto
Urrea, Teresa
Valdivia, Luis de
Varela y Morales, Félix
Vásquez, Francisco de Asís
Velasco, Juan de
Vélez de Escalante, Silvestre
Vera Cruz, Alonso de la
Vigil, Francisco de Paula González
Villarroel, Gaspar de
Viñes y Martorell, Benito
Viscardo y Guzmán, Juan Pablo
Viteri y Ungo, Jorge
Vitoria, Francisco de
Xavier, Francisco Cándido (Chico)
Ximénez, Francisco
Zepeda y Zepeda, Juan de Jesús
Zubiría, José Antonio Laureano de
Zumárraga, Juan de

17. REVOLUTIONARY LEADERSHIP

Abasolo, Mariano
Agramonte y Loynaz, Ignacio
Agüeybana II
Albizu Campos, Pedro
Aldama y González, Ignacio de
Aldama y González, Juan de
Alem, Leandro N.
Alfaro Delgado, José Eloy
Alfaro Siqueiros, David
Allende, Ignacio
Allende Gossens, Salvador
Andrade, Roberto
Andresote
Anzoátegui, José Antonio
Aramburu, Pedro Eugenio
Arce Castaño, Bayardo

Arcos, Santiago
Arias Madrid, Arnulfo
Arismendi, Juan Bautista
Arismendi, Rodney
Arron, Henck A. E.
Atahualpa (Juan Santos)
Ávila, Alonso de
Azcárate y Lezama, Juan Francisco de
Barrett, Rafael
Barrios, Gonzalo
Barrios, Justo Rufino
Barrow, Errol Walton
Barrundia, José Francisco
Bedoya de Molina, Dolores
Bello, Andrés
Berbeo, Juan Francisco
Bermúdez, José Francisco
Bertoni, Moisés
Bilbao Barquín, Francisco
Bishop, Maurice
Blanco Galdós, Hugo
Bobo, Rosalvo
Bolívar, Simón
Bouterse, Desi
Bravo, Leonardo
Brión, Luis
Burnham, Linden Forbes Sampson
Bustamante, William Alexander
Bustos, Juan Bautista
Caamaño Deñó, Francisco
Caballero, Pedro Juan
Cabañas, Lucio
Caldas, Francisco José de
Campos, Luis María
Campos, Manuel Jorge
Candioti, Francisco Antonio
Canek, Jacinto
Carlés, Manuel
Carranza, Venustiano
Castro, Julián
Castro Ruz, Fidel
Céspedes, Carlos Manuel de (the Elder)
Chibás, Eduardo
Chirino, José Leonardo
Cienfuegos, Camilo
Cisneros Betancourt, Salvador
Codovilla, Vittorio
Contreras Brothers
Cortés de Madariaga, José
Creydt, Oscar

Cruz, Serapio
de la Huerta, Adolfo
Delgado, José Matías
Dessalines, Jean Jacques
Dias Lopes, Isidoro
Díaz Soto y Gama, Antonio
Diegues, Carlos
Domínguez, Miguel
Dorticós Torrado, Osvaldo
Duarte, Juan Pablo
Dulles, Allen
Echeverría Bianchi, José Antonio
Erro, Enrique
Escalante, Aníbal
Estrada Palma, Tomás
Facio Segreda, Gonzalo
Falcón, Juan Crisóstomo
Febres-Cordero Ribadeneyra, León
Flores, Juan José
Flores Magón, Ricardo
Fonseca Amador, Carlos
Freire Serrano, Ramón
Gabeira, Fernando Nagle
Galeana, Hermenegildo
Gallo Goyenechea, Pedro León
Gálvez, Mariano
Gamarra, Agustín
Ganga Zumba
García, Calixto
García Granados, Miguel
Garibaldi, Giuseppe
Godoi, Juan Silvano
Godoy Cruz, Tomás
Gómez, Eugenio
Gómez, José Miguel (d. 1805)
Gómez, José Miguel (d. 1921)
Gómez, José Valentín
González, Abraham
González, Pablo
Gonzalez Garza, Roque
González Prada, Manuel
Grove Vallejo, Marmaduke
Guerrero, Vicente
Gutiérrez, Eulalio
Gutiérrez, Juan María
Gutiérrez Borbúa, Lucio
Gutiérrez Brothers
Gutiérrez de Lara, José Bernardo
Guzmán, Abimael
Guzmán, Martín Luis

Hernández, José Manuel
Herrera, Tomás
Hidalgo y Costilla, Miguel
Hostos y Bonilla, Eugenio María de
Houston, Sam
Ibarra de Piedra, Rosario
Jauretche, Arturo M.
Jobet Búrquez, Julio César
Laprida, Francisco Narciso de
Laredo Bru, Federico
La Serna, José de
Lautaro
Leyva Solano, Gabriel
López Chavez, Julio
López Trujillo, Alfonso
Louverture, Toussaint
Maceo, Antonio
Madero, Francisco Indalecio
Mandu Ladino
Manley, Norman Washington
Marighella, Carlos
Martí, Agustín Farabundo
Martínez, Juan José
Matamoros y Guridi, Mariano
Mayorga, Silvio
Mella, Julio Antonio
Mella, Ramón Matías
Melo, José María
Mina y Larrea, Javier
Miranda, Francisco de
Miró Cardona, José
Molina, Pedro
Molina Ureña, José Rafael
Monagas, José Gregorio
Monagas, José Tadeo
Monteagudo, Bernardo de
Montes, César
Montt Álvarez, Jorge
Montúfar y Larrea, Juan Pío de
Morínigo, Higínio
Múgica, Francisco José
Nariño, Antonio
Navarro Wolff, Antonio
Nufio, José Dolores
O, Genovevo de la
Obregón Salido, Álvaro
Olañeta, José Joaquín Casimiro y Güemes
Orozco, Pascual, Jr.
Ortega Saavedra, Daniel
Ortega Saavedra, Humberto

Ortiz de Ayala, Simón Tadeo
Ortiz de Domínguez, Josefa
Padilla Peñalosa, Ezequiel
Páez, José Antonio
País, Frank
Palacio, Alfredo
Pani Arteaga, Alberto J.
Pastora Gómez, Edén
Paz Estenssoro, Víctor
Peimbert, Margarita
Peña, Lázaro
Pérez Salas, Francisco Antonio
Piérola, Nicolás de
Pinto Díaz, Francisco Antonio
Portes Gil, Emilio
Prestes, Luís Carlos
Puente Uceda, Luis de la
Quispe, Felipe
Ramírez Mercado, Sergio
Rayón, Ignacio
Recabarren Serrano, Luis Emilio
Rejón, Manuel Crescencio
Ribas, José Félix
Riego y Núñez, Rafael del
Rigaud, André
Roscio, Juan Germán
Ruíz, Henry
Ruiz, Tomás
Ruiz Cortines, Adolfo
Saldías, Adolfo
Sandino, Augusto César
San Martín, José Francisco de
Santa Cruz y Espejo, Francisco Javier Eugenio de
Saravia, Aparicio
Sardaneta y Llorente, José Mariano de
Sendic, Raúl
Serdán, Aquiles
Seregni, Líber
Siles Zuazo, Hernán
Silva Xavier, Joaquim José da
Subcomandante Marcos
Sucre Alcalá, Antonio José de
Tejeda Olivares, Adalberto
Torres Restrepo, Camilo
Túpac Amaru (José Gabriel Condorcanqui)
Turcios Lima, Luis Agosto
Urracá
Urrea, José de
Urrutia Lleó, Manuel
Velasco Alvarado, Juan

Vicario Fernández, [María] Leona
Victoria, Guadalupe
Vidaurri, Santiago
Villa, Francisco "Pancho"
Villagrán, Julián and José María "El Chito"
Villagrán Kramer, Francisco
Wheelock Román, Jaime
Yon Sosa, Marco Antonio
Zapata, Emiliano
Zaragoza, Ignacio
Zárate Willka, Pablo
Zeledón, Benjamín Francisco

18. SCIENCE AND MEDICINE

Adem Chahín, José
Adem Chahín, Julián
Alcorta, Diego
Alexis, Jacques Stéphen
Alonso, Manuel A.
Alzate y Ramírez, José Antonio de
Amador Guerrero, Manuel
Ameghino, Florentino
Ávila, Julio Enrique
Azara, Félix de
Barbero, Andrés
Barbosa y Alcalá, José Celso
Bertoni, Moisés
Bunge, Alejandro
Bunge, Augusto
Caldas, Francisco José de
Calderón Guardia, Rafael Ángel
Carrillo Flores, Nabor
Cervantes, Vicente
Chagas, Carlos Ribeiro Justiniano
Codazzi, Agustín
Coni, Gabriela Laperrière de
Cordero Crespo, Luis
Cruz, Oswaldo Gonçalves
Dobrizhoffer, Martín
Duvalier, François
Elhuyar, Juan José de
Elhuyar y Zúbice, Fausto de
Finlay, Carlos Juan
Frías, Antonio
García, Diego
García Conde, Pedro
González de Santa Cruz, Roque
Graef Fernández, Carlos
Grau San Martín, Ramón

Hernández, Francisco
Houssay, Bernardo A.
Kubitschek de Oliveira, Juscelino
Kumate Rodríguez, Jesús
Leloir, Luis F.
Longinos Martínez, José
Magalhães, Domingos José Gonçalves de
Mejía del Valle y Llequerica, José Joaquín
Mendinueta y Múzquiz, Pedro de
Messía de la Cerda, Pedro de
Molina, Mario
Montealegre Fernández, José María
Moreau de Justo, Alicia
Moziño, José Mariano
Murtinho, Joaquim Duarte
Mutis, Alvaro
Niza, Marcos de
Nusdorffer, Bernardo
Peralta Barnuevo y Rocha, Pedro de
Péralte, Charlemagne Masséna
Popenoe, Frederick Wilson
Prieto Rodríguez, Sotero
Ramos, Artur
Ramos Mejía, José María
Rawson, Guillermo
Reed, Walter
Rodrigues, Raimundo Nina
Rojas, Arístides
Romero, Emilio
Rosenblueth, Arturo Stearns
Ruiz de Montoya, Antonio
Sabato, Jorge Alberto
Sandoval Vallarta, Manuel
Scliar, Moacyr
Torres Bello, Diego de
Torre y Huerta, Carlos de la
Unanue, Hipólito
Vargas, José María
Velasco Ibarra, José María
Velázquez Cárdenas de León, Joaquín
Viñes y Martorell, Benito
Wilde, Eduardo
Zamora, Rubén
Zubirán Achondo, Salvador

19. SOCIAL PROTEST AND REFORM

Abad y Queipo, Manuel
Aguayo, Sergio

Albizu Campos, Pedro
Alvarado, María Jesús
Arguedas, José María
Arismendi, Rodney
Arriaga, Ponciano
Arze, José Antonio
Atahualpa
Bachiller y Morales, Antonio
Barrios, Justo Rufino
Bassols, Narciso
Beals, Carleton
Benedetti, Mario
Betances y Alacán, Ramón Emeterio
Betancourt Cisneros, Gaspar
Bonilla, Policarpo
Bonilla Chirinos, Manuel
Bravo, Mario
Bustamante, William Alexander
Caballero y Rodríguez, José Agustín
Cabezas, Omar
Campa Salazar, Valentín
Caneca, Frei Joaquím do Amor Divino
Canek, Jacinto
Cárdenas, Víctor Hugo
Carlés, Manuel
Carrasco, Barbara
Carrillo Puerto, Felipe
Carter, Jimmy
Casaldáliga, Pedro
Castro Alves, Antônio de
Castro Pozo, Hildebrando
Castro Ruz, Fidel
Caupolicán
Chibás, Eduardo
Chonchol, Jacques
Cipriani, Arthur Andrew
Clouthier del Rincón, Manuel J.
Comandante Ramona
Coni, Emilio R.
Coni, Gabriela Laperrière de
Conselheiro, Antônio
Degollado, Santos
Díaz Soto y Gama, Antonio
Donovan, Jean
Escobedo, Mariano
Estrada Palma, Tomás
Fernández Oreamuno, Próspero
Figueres Ferrer, José
Fonseca Amador, Carlos
Frei Ruiz-Tagle, Eduardo

Fresno Larraín, Juan Francisco
Frugoni, Emilio
Gabeira, Fernando Nagle
Gaitan, Jorge Eliécer
Galán, Luis Carlos
Galeano, Eduardo Hughes
Gallo Goyenechea, Pedro León
Gama, Luís
Gamarra, Francisca Zubiaga Bernales de (La Mariscala)
García Granados, Miguel
Garrido Canabal, Tomás
Garvey, Marcus
Ghioldi, Américo
Ghioldi, Rodolfo
Gómez, Juan Gualberto
Gómez Farías, Valentín
Gomez Rojas, José Domingo
Gonzaga, Tomás Antônio
González, Pablo
González Víquez, Cleto
Gutiérrez Alea, Tomás
Gutiérrez Estrada, José María
Gutiérrez Garbín, Víctor Manuel
Guzmán, Antonio Leocadio
Haro y Tamariz, Antonio de
Haya de la Torre, Víctor Raúl
Hertzog Garaizabal, Enrique
Hirsch, Maurice von
Ibarra de Piedra, Rosario
Iglesias, José María
Jara, Víctor
Jauretche, Arturo M.
John Paul II, Pope
Juárez, Benito
Julião Arruda de Paula, Francisco
Kahlo, Frida
Labarca Hubertson, Amanda
Landázuri Ricketts, Juan
Lerdo de Tejada, Miguel
Letelier del Solar, Orlando
Leyva Solano, Gabriel
Lima Barreto, Afonso Henriques de
López, Ambrosio
López, José Hilario
López Pumarejo, Alfonso
Lozada, Manuel
Luisi, Luisa
Lutz, Bertha Maria Julia
Lutzenberger, José

Luz y Caballero, José de la
Madrazo, Carlos A.
Magoon, Charles Edward
Martí, Agustín Farabundo
Mas Canosa, Jorge
Medeiros da Fonseca, Romy Martins
Mejía, Tomás
Mejía del Valle y Llequerica, José Joaquín
Mejía Godoy, Carlos
Mella, Julio Antonio
Mier Noriega y Guerra, José Servando
    Teresa de
Miramón, Miguel
Mon y Velarde, Juan Antonio
Mora Valverde, Manuel
Moreau de Justo, Alicia
Moyano, María Elena
Muñoz Ledo Lazo de la Vega, Porfirio
Neruda, Pablo
O, Genovevo de la
Ocampo, Melchor
Orozco, José Clemente
Ortiz de Domínguez, Josefa
Osorio, Oscar
Palacio, Alfredo
Palacios, Alfredo L.
Paniagua, Valentín
Paso, Fernando del
Paz Estenssoro, Víctor
Peimbert, Margarita
Peña, Lázaro
Péralte, Charlemagne Masséna
Pérez Esquivel, Adolfo
Poblete Poblete de Espinoza, Olga
Portal, Magda
Primo de Verdad y Ramos, Francisco
Prío Socarrás, Carlos
Proaño Villalba, Leonidas Eduardo (Bishop)
Puente Uceda, Luis de la
Rebouças, André
Recabarren Serrano, Luis Emilio
Rejón, Manuel Crescencio
Revueltas, José
Riaño y Bárcena, Juan Antonio
Riego y Núñez, Rafael del
Rius
Rivera, Diego
Rodríguez de Velasco y Osorio Barba, María
    Ignacia
Romero, Oscar Arnulfo

Roumain, Jacques
Ruiz, Samuel
Ruiz, Tomás
Sábato, Ernesto
Sáenz de Thorne, Manuela
Salavarrieta, Policarpa
Sanabria Martínez, Víctor M.
Sánchez Cerro, Luis Manuel
Sardaneta y Llorente, José Mariano de
Seoane, Manuel
Sierra Méndez, Justo
Silva Henríquez, Raúl
Solas, Humberto
Subcomandante Marcos
Tejeda Olivares, Adalberto
Torres Restrepo, Camilo
Tristan, Flora
Ulate Blanco, Otilio
Urrea, Teresa
Valladares, Armando
Vallejo, César
Vandor, Augusto Timoteo
Vergara, Marta
Vicario Fernández, [María] Leona
Villalba, Jóvito
Viscardo y Guzmán, Juan Pablo
Volio Jiménez, Jorge
Wood, Leonard
Wyld Ospina, Carlos
Yon Sosa, Marco Antonio
Zamora, Rubén
Zapata, Emiliano
Zarco, Francisco
Zulen, Pedro S., [and] Dora Mayer de Zulen

20. TECHNOLOGY AND INVENTION

Adem Chahín, José
Alvear, Marcelo Torcuato de
Belly, Félix
Cisneros, Francisco Javier
Codazzi, Agustín
Elhuyar, Juan José de
Elhuyar y Zúbice, Fausto de
Enciso, Martín Fernández de
Escandón, Antonio

Goldemberg, Jose
Humboldt, Alexander von
Ivaldi, Humberto
Keith, Minor Cooper
Lesseps, Ferdinand Marie, Vicomte de
Magoon, Charles Edward
Matienzo, Benjamín
Pearson, Weetman Dickinson
Porras, Diego
Pueyrredón, Prilidiano
Ramírez Vázquez, Pedro
Riaño y Bárcena, Juan Antonio
Rivera Maestre, Miguel
Santos-Dumont, Alberto
Vergara Echeverez, José Francisco
Vieytes, Hipólito
Wheelwright, William
Whytehead, William Keld
Wisner von Morgenstern, Franz

21. VISUAL ARTS

Acosta León, Ángel
Aizenberg, Roberto
Aleijadinho
Alfaro Siqueiros, David
Almeida Júnior, José Ferraz de
Alonso, Raúl
Alvarado, Antonio
Álvarez Bravo, Lola
Álvarez Bravo, Manuel
Amador, Manuel E.
Amaral, Tarsila do
Americo de Figuereido e Melo, Pedro
Antúnez, Nemesio
Apolinar
Arango, Débora
Arboleda, Carlos
Arciniega, Claudio de
Arden Quin, Carmelo
Arrieta, José Agustín
Arrieta, Pedro de
Atl, Dr.
Baca Flor, Carlos
Balbás, Jerónimo de
Barradas, Rafael
Barragán Morfin, Luis
Basaldúa, Hector

Berni, Antonio
Bicalho Oswald, Henrique Carlos
Bigaud, Wilson
Blanes, Juan Manuel
Bonpland, Aimé Jacques
Borges, Jacobo
Botero, Fernando
Bravo, Claudio
Brecheret, Vítor
Burle Marx, Roberto
Bustos, Hermenegildo
Cabrera, Miguel
Camargo, Sergio de
Camnitzer, Luis
Campos, Augusto de
Cantú, Federico
Carballo, Aída
Cárdenas Arroyo, Santiago
Carrasco, Barbara
Carreño, Mario
Carrington, Leonora
Casasola, Agustín
Castro, José Gil de
Cavalcanti, Newton
Cerezo Arévalo, Marco Vinicio
Chambi, Martín
Charlot, Jean
Chávez Morado, José
Chong Neto, Manuel
Clark, Lygia
Clavé, Pelegrín
Codesido, Julia
Concha, Andrés de la
Cordero, Juan
Coronel, Pedro
Coronel, Rafael
Correa, Juan
Costa, Lúcio
Covarrubias, Miguel
Cruz Diez, Carlos
Cuaron, Alfonso
Cuevas, José Luis
Cúneo Perinetti, José
Darié, Sandu
Davidovsky, Mario
Debret, Jean-Baptiste
De Castro, Amilcar
DeFuentes, Fernando
Deira, Ernesto
Díaz, Gonzalo

di Cavalcanti, Emiliano
Diomede, Miguel
Dittborn, Eugenio
Duarte, Augusto Rodrigues
Dutary, Alberto
Echave Orio, Baltasar de
Eckhout, Albert
Egas, Camilo Alejandro
Egerton, Daniel Thomas
Ender, Thomas
Enríquez, Carlos
Espinosa, José María
Estrada, José María (d. ca. 1862)
Euceda, Maximiliano
Felguérez, Manuel
Fernandes, Millôr
Ferrer, Rafael
Ferrez, Marc
Fierro Rimac, Francisco
Figari, Pedro
Figueroa, Pedro José
Fonseca, Gonzalo
Fonseca e Silva, Valentim da
Fontana, Lucio
Forner, Raquel
Fredricks, Charles DeForest
Frisch, Albert
Gahona, Gabriel Vicente
Galán, Julio
Gamarra, José
Garay, Carlos
Garay, Epifanio
García Canclini, Néstor
Gay, Claudio
Gego
Gerzso, Gunther
Gil, Jerónimo Antonio
Gironella, Alberto
Goeritz, Mathias
Gómez, Benigno
González, Beatriz
González, Carlos
González Camarena, Jorge
González Goyri, Roberto
Grandjean de Montigny, Auguste Henri Victor
Grau, Enrique
Grilo, Sarah
Grippo, Víctor
Guayasamín, Oswaldo
Guerrero, Xavier

Guerrero y Torres, Francisco Antonio
Herrán, Saturnino
Herrerabarría, Adriano
Homar, Lorenzo
Hyppolite, Hector
Iturbide, Graciela
Izquierdo, María
Jaar, Alfredo
Jimeno y Planes, Rafael
Joaquim, Leandro
Juárez, José
Juárez, Luis
Julião, Carlos
Kahlo, Frida
Kosice, Gyula
Lam y Castilla, Wifredo
Landaluze, Víctor Patricio de
Laplante, Eduardo
Laso, Francisco
Leal, Fernando
Lewis, Roberto
Liautaud, Georges
Linares, Pedro
Linati, Claudio
López, Cándido
López de Arteaga, Sebastián
Lozza, Raúl
Macció, Rómulo
Mac Entyre, Eduardo
Malfatti, Anita Catarina
Marisol
Martorell, Antonio
Matta Echaurren, Roberto Sebastián Antonio
Meireles de Lima, Vítor
Melé, Juan N.
Mérida, Carlos
Minujin, Marta
Modotti, Tina
Mohr, Nicholasa
Montenegro y Nervo, Roberto
Montes de Oca, Confucio
Morales, Armando
Nebel, Carl
Niemeyer Soares Filho, Oscar
Noé, Luis Felipe
Obin, Philomé
Obregón, Alejandro
Obregón, José
O'Gorman, Juan
O'Higgins, Pablo

Oiticica, Hélio
Oliveira, Geraldo Teles de
Orozco, José Clemente
Otero, Alejandro
Pacheco, María Luisa
Pape, Lygia
Parra, Félix
Peláez, Amelia
Pereyns, Simon
Pettoruti, Emilio
Pingret, Édouard Henri Théophile
Pinto, Joaquín
Ponce de León, Fidelio
Porter, Liliana
Portinari, Cândido Torquato
Pôrto Alegre, Manuel Araújo
Portocarrero, René
Posada, José Guadalupe
Post, Frans Jansz
Prado, Vasco
Pueyrredón, Prilidiano
Quinn, Anthony
Quinquela Martín, Benito
Quirós, Cesáreo Bernaldo de
Ramírez Villamizar, Eduardo
Rego Monteiro, Vicente do
Reverón, Armando
Rius
Rivera, Diego
Rodríguez, Lorenzo
Rodríguez Juárez, Juan
Rojo, Vicente
Rueda, Manuel
Ruelas, Julio
Rugendas, Johann Moritz
Ruiz, Antonio
Sabogal, José
Salazar Arrué, Salvador Efraín (Salarrué)
Salgado, Sebastião
Santa María, Andrés de
Schendel, Mira
Segall, Lasar
Sigaud, Eugenio de Proença
Silva, José Antonio da
Sinclair, Alfredo
Sojo, Felipe
Soldi, Raúl
Soriano, Juan
Soto, Jesús Rafael
Szyszlo, Fernando de

Tábara, Enrique
Tamarón y Romeral, Pedro
Tamayo, Rufino
Toledo, Francisco
Tolsá, Manuel
Torres García, Joaquín
Tresguerras, Francisco Eduardo de
Trujillo, Guillermo
Tsuchiya, Tilsa
Ureña, Felipe
Uribe, Juan Camilo
Valladares, José Antonio do Prado
Varo, Remedios
Vásquez de Arce y Ceballos, Gregorio
Vega, Jorge Luis de la
Veiga Vale, José Joaquim da
Velasco, José María
Velásquez, José Antonio
Vilar, Manuel
Villalpando, Cristóbal de
Visconti, Eliseu d'Angelo
Vitalino Pereira dos Santos, Mestre
Weingärtner, Pedro
Xul Solar
Zachrisson, Julio
Zelaya Sierra, Pablo
Zenil, Nahum Bernabé
Zúñiga Figueroa, Carlos

22. WOMEN

Aguilar, Rosario Fiallos de
Agustini, Delmira
Alambert, Zuleika
Alegría, Claribel
Allende, Isabel
Alvarado, María Jesús
Alvarez, Julia
Álvarez Ponce de León, Griselda
Amaral, Tarsila do
Amélia, Empress
Angel, Albalucía
Anzaldúa, Gloria
Arango, Débora
Arteaga, Rosalía
Assunção, Leilah
Bachelet, Michele
Barrera Barrera, Eulalia Beatriz
Barrios de Chamorro, Violeta

Bedoya de Molina, Dolores
Bedregal de Conitzer, Yolanda
Belli, Gioconda
Beltrán, Lola
Beltrán, Manuela
Bemberg, María Luisa
Benson, Nettie Lee
Berenguer, Amanda
Berman, Sabina
Bombal, María Luisa
Bonny, Anne
Boullosa, Carmen
Bozzo, Laura
Brannon de Samayoa Chinchilla, Carmen
Brunet, Marta
Burgos, Julia de
Cabrera, Lydia
Cáceres, Esther de
Calderon, Sila María
Calderón de la Barca, Fanny
Campobello, Nellie
Campos, Julieta
Cano, María de los Ángeles
Carballo, Aída
Carrasco, Barbara
Carrington, Leonora
Castellanos, Rosario
Castillo, Ana
Charles, Eugenia
Chiriboga, Luz Argentina
Cisneros, Sandra
Clair, Janete
Clark, Lygia
Codesido, Julia
Comandante Ramona
Condé, Maryse
Coni, Gabriela Laperrière de
Cruz, Celia
Cueva de Álvarado, Beatriz de la
Danticat, Edwidge
de Jesus, Clementina
Del Rio, Dolores
Dianda, Hilda
Díaz Lozano, Argentina
Downs, Lila
Espín de Castro, Vilma
Esquivel, Laura
Estefan, Gloria
Félix, María
Ferré, Rosario

Figueroa Gajardo, Ana
Flores Nano, Lourdes
Gallego Otero, Laura
Gamarra, Francisca Zubiaga Bernales de (La Mariscala)
Gambaro, Griselda
García, Sara
Garro, Elena
Gego
Glantz, Margo
Gómez de Avellaneda y Arteaga, Gertrudis
Gonzaga, Francisca Hedwiges
González, Beatriz
Gonzalez de Fanning, Teresa
Gorodischer, Angélica
Gorriti, Juana Manuela
Grilo, Sarah
Gueiler Tejada, Lidia
Guevara Espinosa, Ana Gabriela
Guido, Beatriz
Hayworth, Rita
Hernández, Luisa Josefina
Howard, Jennie Eliza
Ibáñez, Sara de
Ibarbourou, Juana de
Isabella I of Castile
Isabel, Princess of Brazil
Iturbide, Graciela
Izquierdo, María
Jagan, Janet
Jesus, Carolina Maria de
Juana Inés de la Cruz, Sor
Kahlo, Frida
Kincaid, Jamaica
Kosice, Gyula
Kubitschek, Márcia
Labarca Hubertson, Amanda
Lavalle Urbina, María
Leopoldina, Empress
Levinson, Luisa Mercedes
Lispector, Clarice
Loynaz, Dulce Maria de
Luisi, Luisa
Luisi, Paulina
Lutz, Bertha Maria Julia
Lynch, Elisa Alicia
Lynch, Marta
Malfatti, Anita Catarina
Malinche
Maria I of Portugal

Maria II of Portugal (Maria da Gloria)
Marisol
Mastretta, Angeles
Matto de Turner, Clorinda
Medeiros da Fonseca, Romy Martins
Meireles, Cecília
Menchú Tum, Rigoberta
Menininha do Gantois, Mãe
Minujin, Marta
Miranda, Carmen
Mistral, Gabriela
Modotti, Tina
Mohr, Nicholasa
Morejón, Nancy
Moyano, María Elena
Naranjo, Carmen
Nieves y Bustamante, María
Obaldía, María Olimpia de
Ocampo, Victoria
Ochoa Reyes, Lorena
Odio, Eunice
O'Gorman, Camila
Oreamuno, Yolanda
Orozco, Olga
Orphée, Elvira
Ortiz de Domínguez, Josefa
Pacheco, Maria Cristina
Pacheco, María Luisa
Palacios, Antonia
Palma Román, Angélica
Pape, Lygia
Parra, Teresa de la
Parra, Violeta
Pascal-Trouillot, Ertha
Peimbert, Margarita
Peláez, Amelia
Peralta, Angela
Peri Rossi, Cristina
Perón, María Estela Martínez de
Perón, María Eva Duarte de
Perricholi, La
Piñon, Nélida
Pizarnik, Alejandra
Plá, Josefina
Poblete Poblete de Espinoza, Olga
Poniatowska, Elena
Portal, Magda
Porter, Liliana

Puga, María Luisa
Queiroz, Dinah Silveira de
Queiroz, Rachel de
Read, Mary
Regina, Elis
Riesco, Laura
Robles Berlanga, Rosario
Rodríguez de Velasco y Osorio Barba, María
      Ignacia
Rojo, María
Rokha, Winétt de
Román de Núñez, Soledad
Rosa de Lima
Rosas de Terrero, Manuela
Sáenz de Thorne, Manuela
Salavarrieta, Policarpa
Sánchez de Thompson, María
Sánchez Manduley, Celia
Santiago, Esmeralda
Santos, Marquesa de
Schendel, Mira
Selena
Sierra, Stella
Silva, Benedita da
Silva, Clara
Silva, Xica da
Somers, Armonía
Souza, Luiza Erundina de
Steimberg, Alicia
Storni, Alfonsina
Suárez, Inés de
Sumac, Yma
Tejeda, Leonor de
Telles, Lygia Fagundes
Teresa Cristina
Tinajero Martínez de Allen, Eugenia
Traba, Marta
Tsuchiya, Tilsa
Ureña de Henríquez, Salomé
Valenzuela, Luisa
Varo, Remedios
Vergara, Marta
Vicario Fernández, [María] Leona
Vilariño, Idea
Wiesse, María
Xuxa
Yáñez Cossío, Alicia

INDEX

This index is sorted alphabetically on a letter-by-letter basis. Page numbers are prefaced by volume numbers in bold. Page numbers themselves in boldface refer to the main entry on a subject. Page numbers in italics refer to illustrations, figures, and tables. Overviews of subjects and peoples and profiles of countries are listed as the first subhead below the main headings. Chronological subheadings under countries are placed at the top of the list of subheadings.

Academia Paulista de Letras (Brazil), **5**:677

Academias (Brazil), **1:9–10**

Academia Universitaria del Paraguay (poetry group), **1**:204

Academy of American Franciscan History (AAFH), **1**:162

Academy of Christian Humanism (Chile), **5**:851

Academy of Fine Arts (Caracas), **5**:528

Academy of Fine Arts (Rio de Janeiro), **3**:504

"Ação; reação; transação" (Rocha), **5**:581

Ação Integralista Brasileira (Brazil), **2**:48; **5**:676

Acapulco de Juaréz (Mexico), **1:10–11**, *11*; **6**:121

Acaray River, **1:11–12**

Accessory Transit Company, **3**:511; **4**:824; **5**:563; **6**:408

Accidentes (Puga), **5**:420

Acción (newspaper, Uruguay), **1**:515

Acción Communitaria (San Salvador), **2**:866

Acción Comunal (Panama). *See* Community Action (Panama)

Acción Democrática (AD, Venezuela). *See* Democratic Action (AD, Venezuela)

Acción Democrática Nacionalista (ADN, Bolivia). *See* Nationalist Democratic Action

Acción Nacional (Chile), **5**:338

Acción Nacional (Venezuela). *See* Social Christian Party (COPEI, Venezuela)

Acción Nacional Revolucionaria (Cuba), **5**:12

Acción popular (weekly, Ecuador), **6**:95

Accompong Maroon Festival, **4**:*382*

Accounting
  quipu system of, **5**:447
  real hacienda, **5**:502

Acento literary circle (Guatemala), **3**:787

Aceval, Benjamín, **1**:12

Aceval-Tamayo Treaty (1887), **1**:12

Acevedo, Eduardo, **1**:279

Acevedo Díaz, Eduardo Inés, **1:12–13**, 366; **3**:679

Acevedo Hernández, Antonio, **1**:13

Acevedo Vilá, Aníbal, **5**:416, 418

Achá, José María, **1:13–14**; **4**:460

Aché (Guayakí), **1**:14

Acheson, Dean, **1**:679

Achiote, **3**:314; **5**:925

Acindar Industria Argentina de Aceros (ACIN), **4**:395

Acolhua, **3**:887; **4**:820–821

Acoma (journal, Martinique), **3**:443

Ácoma, Battle of (1599), **6**:374

Aconcagua (Argentina), **1:14–15**

Acordada, **1:15**; **2**:654

Acordada, Revolt of (Mexico, 1828), **1:15**; **3**:578; **4**:512; **6**:510

Acosta, Cecilio, **1**:16

Acosta, José de, **1**:16; **4**:180, 882

Acosta, José Julián, **1**:4

Acosta, Tomás, **1:16–17**

Acosta García, Julio, **1**:17

Acosta León, Ángel, **1**:17

Acosta Ñu, Battle of (1869), **1:16–17**; **6**:456

Acquired immune deficiency syndrome (AIDS), **1:18–20**
  affected populations, **2**:826
  archdiocese of São Paulo and, **1**:323
  Belize, **1**:539
  Brazil, **1**:*18t*, 19–20
    free medication, **4**:452
  gay activism and, **5**:833–834
  medical ethics and, **4**:452
  public health and, **5**:391
  World Bank loans and, **6**:463

Acre (Brazil), **1:20–21**; **5**:546

Acta Final (Acta de Iguaçú, Brazil and Paraguay, 1966), **3**:884

Action for National Liberation (Brazil, ALN), **3**:581; **4**:376

Action Plan for Combating Social Exclusion Based on Race and Ethnicity, **3**:853

Act of Dominican Reconciliation (1965), **2**:843, 847

Acuerdo, **1:21**; **5**:577
  oidores and, **4**:886

Acuña, Cristóbal de, **3**:158

Acuña, Juan de, **5**:568

Adalid y Gamero, Manuel de, **4**:742

Adalma, Juan, **4**:509

Adam and Eve (Bigaud), **1**:576

Adams, Grantley Herbert, **1:21–22**; **6**:430

Adams, J. M. G. (Tom), **1**:22

Adams, John, **4**:591

Adams, John Quincy
  Latin America interventions, **6**:179
  Monroe Doctrine, **4**:665
  No-Transfer Resolution and, **4**:851

Adams-Onís Treaty (1819), **1:22**; **3**:249, 250, 699

Adán, Martín, **1**:149

Adán Buenosayres (Marechal), **4**:370

Additional Act of 1834 (Brazil), **1:22–23**
  education and, **2**:484
  independence and, **1**:701
  Interpretation of, **6**:283
  Moderados and, **1**:761
  município, município neutro, **4**:732
  Regency and, **1**:770
  Vasconcelos, Bernardo Pereira de, and, **6**:293

ADE. *See* Democratic Alliance (ADE, Ecuador)

Adelantado, **1**:23

Adelantado of the South Sea, **1:23–24**; **2**:746

Adelantos, **2**:756

Adem Chahín, José, **1**:24

Adem Chahín, Julián, **1**:24

Los adioses (Onetti), **4**:901

Administración Nacional de Electricidad (ANDE, Paraguay), **3**:884

Admirable Campaign (Venezuela), **1:24–25**, 605–606; **6**:321–322

Admiradoras de Juárez (Mexico), **4**:517

ADN. *See* Nationalist Democratic Action (Bolivia, ADN)

Adonias Filho. *See* Aguiar, Adonias

Adoption, **1**:278; **2**:318

Adrian VI, Pope, **2**:214; **4**:598

Adriatic (Macció), **4**:302

Adultery
  criminal justice and, **2**:656
  as divorce grounds, **4**:389

Advanced Institute of Brazilian Studies (ISEB), **1**:739; **5**:885

Advance y Alerta (journal), **3**:596

AES Corporation (United States), **3**:272

"An Aesthetic of Hunger" (Rocha), **2**:423–424

Afectos espirituales (Castillo y Guevara), **2**:197

Affirmative action policies, Brazil, **1**:41; **5**:474

Affranchis (Haiti), **3**:618, 619–620, 623

Afrancesado, **1:25–26**

Africa
  Brazil and, **1**:33
    Brazilian districts, **1**:32
    immigration of Afro-Brazilians, **1**:30
  cacao cultivation, **2**:19
  crusade against Muslims in, **5**:791
  Cuban intervention in, **1**:33, 318; **2**:691–694
  decolonization, **1**:32
  diaspora, **5**:777
  and Dutch West India Company, **2**:877, 881
  exports of tobacco to, **6**:91
  Garvey, Marcus, on, **3**:408
  Guevarra, Ernesto Che, in, **2**:684
  maize, **4**:331
  migrations, **4**:571–572, *572*, *572*
  mining skills, **4**:609
  musical instruments, **4**:757–758
  Spanish Empire in, **5**:923
  state corporations in, **5**:940
  sugar industry in, **5**:958

Apaches *(continued)*
 Comanches and, **2:**538
 Provincias Internas, **5:**383
 puma worship, **5:**423
 in Sonora, **5:**898
 Zacatecas and, **6:**496
Apachetas, **3:**749
La apacible locura (González
 Martínez), **3:**489
Apalachee, **1:202–203**
El apando (film), **5:**604
El apando (Revueltas), **5:**530
Aparicio, Luis, **1:203**
Aparicio, Timoteo, **1:**515; **4:**149;
 6:217
Apa River, **5:**77
El apartamento (Marqués),
 4:384
A parte do fogo (journal), **6:**152
Apasa, Julián. *See* Túpac Catari (Julián
 Apaza)
La Apassionata (Azar), **1:**422
Apatzingán, Constitution of (1814).
 See Mexico, constitutions
APC (Association for Progressive
 Communications), **2:**559
A pena e a lei (Suassuna), **5:**950
Apinayé, **3:**420
El apocalipsis de Antón (Von Vacano),
 2:145
Apolinar (Pablo Livinalli Santaella),
 1:203
Apollo and the Muses (Montenegro y
 Nervo), **4:**675
Apologética historia sumaria (Las
 Casas), **4:**142, 434
Aponte, José Antonio, **2:**670
Aponte conspiracy (Cuba), **5:**860, 861
Aponte-Ledée, Rafael, **1:203–204**
Apóstol, Alexander, **5:**232
Apparel industry
 Colombia, **1:**198
 El Salvador, **3:**95
Appleyard, José Luis, **1:204**
APRA. *See* Alianza Popular
 Revolucionaria (APRA, Peru)
Apu Inku Atawallpaman (Szyszlo),
 5:966
Apuntes (journal, Chile), **6:**73
Apuntes de historia militar (Perón),
 5:163
Apuntes de un lugareño (Romero),
 5:610
*Apuntes para la historia de las letras y
 instrucción publica de la isla de
 Cuba* (Bachillery y Morales),
 1:437
Apuntes sobre la condición de la mujer
 (García), **3:**384
Apurímac, **1:204**
Aquaculture, **2:**381; **3:**237, *238*

"Aquarela do Brasil" (song, Barroso),
 1:505
Aqueducts, **3:**876
Aquel mar sin fondo ni playa (Aguilar),
 1:65
El águila y la serpiente (Guzmán),
 3:609
Aquilera Malta, Demetrio, **3:**568
Aquinaldo puertorriqueño (Alonso),
 1:119
Aquinas, Thomas, **5:**223
Aquino, Anastasio, **2:**241; **3:**90
Aquí nos tocó vivir (Pacheco), **5:**4
Aquí pasan cosas raras (Valenzuela),
 6:269
Arab, Ricardo, **3:**547; **6:**233
Arab-Israeli war, refugees from, **4:**568
Arab-Latin American Bank, **1:**206
Arab-Latin American relations,
 1:205–207; **3:**880–881
Arab League, **1:**205
Arab–Pan-American congresses, **1:**205
Arab–Pan-American Federation of
 Arab Communities in Latin
 America, **1:**205
Aracaju (Brazil), **1:**207
Arada, Battle of (1851), **1:207–208;**
 2:242, 262, 662
Aragão, Renato, **2:**420
Aragon, **1:208**
Aragón, Luis, **5:**14
Aragona, Alonso de, **6:**157
Araguaia River, **1:208–209**
Aramayo family, **1:209–210,** 621;
 6:81
Aramburu, Pedro Eugenio, **1:**210
 execution by Montoneros, **1:**272;
 4:683, 902
 Lanusse, Alejandro, and, **4:**130
 Rojas, Isaac, and, **5:**601
Arana, Felipe de, **1:210–211**
Arana, Francisco Hernández, **1:**187
Arana, Francisco Javier, **1:211;** **3:**546
 assassination, **1:**218, 247; **2:**120;
 3:547
Arana, Gregorio, **1:**245; **4:**544
Arana, Julio César, **1:211–212**
Arana Osorio, Carlos, **1:**212;
 3:548–549; **4:**472; **6:**485
Arandía, Pedro Manuel de, **5:**221
Arango, Débora, **1:212**
Arango y Parreño, Francisco de,
 1:212–213; **2:**669
Aranguren, José María, **1:**68
Aranha, Graça, **4:**647
Aranha, Oswaldo, **1:213–214,** 775;
 4:466; **6:**45
Aranha de Vasconcelos, Luis,
 3:164–165
Aranjuez, Treaty of (1777), **3:**317
Arano, Hugo, **4:**453
Aráoz, Bernabé, **2:**526; **3:**780
Arau, Alfonso, **1:**214; **3:**142

La Araucana (Ercilla y Zúñiga),
 1:214; **2:**322; **3:**128; **4:**228
 on Galvarino, **3:**359
 reaction of García Hurtado De
 Mendoza to, **4:**899
Araucanians, **1:215–216**
 battles, **2:**228; **4:**150–151
 Chile
 Bío-Bío River, **1:**580
 under Santa María, Domingo,
 5:741
 Galvarino, **3:**359
 García de Castro, Lope, and, **3:**389
 hides industry, **3:**689
 homosexuality, **5:**827
 Huincas and, **3:**761
 Hurtado de Mendoza, García, and,
 3:771
 malones, **4:**339
 music, **3:**879–880
 Spanish war against, **2:**322; **6:**374
 See also Mapuche
El Araucano (gazette, Chile), **1:**548
El Arauco domado (Vega), **3:**771
Arauco domado (Oña), **3:**598; **4:**228,
 899
Araujo, Arturo, **1:216;** **3:**91
 Aguirre y Salinas, Osmín, and
 overthrow, **1:**70
 Martí, Agustín Farabundo, and,
 4:391
 Martínez, Maximiliano, and,
 3:673
 Masferrer, Alberto, and, **4:**406
 Matanza, **4:**412
Araujo, Juan de, **1:217;** **4:**744
Araújo Lima, Pedro de, Marquis of
 Olinda, **1:217–218,** 761, 770;
 6:293
Arawak (Campos-Parsi), **2:**63
Arawakan language, **2:**124
Arawak Indians
 in Aruba, **1:**367
 in the Bahamas, **1:**440
 Barbados, **1:**483
 and epidemic disease, **2:**824–825
 evolution of, **3:**824
 on *gamonalismo,* **3:**370–371
 Grenadines, **3:**510
 hurricanes, **3:**769
 Jamaica, **4:**9
 manioc, **4:**348
 messianic movement, **4:**497
 Saint Vincent, **5:**669
 Sedeño, Antonio de, attacked by,
 5:792
 smallpox and, **3:**825
 in Xingu Reserve, **6:**472, 473
Araya (film, Benacerraf), **2:**416
Arbeláez, Vincente, **5:**679

Arbenz Guzmán, Jacobo, **1:218–219**
  agrarian land reform, **1:**43
  assassination of Francisco Javier
      Arana, **1:**247
  Fortuny, José Manuel, and, **3:**295
  Gálvez, Juan Manuel, and, **3:**362
  Guatemalan Labor Party and, **3:**563
  Illescas, Carlos, and, **3:**787
  and John Foster Dulles, **2:**869
  in junta, **3:**546
  labor movement and, **3:**547
  Los Altos, **4:**276
  Montes, César, and, **4:**678
  overthrow, **2:**196
    CIA and, **2:**869; **4:**350
    United Fruit Company and,
        6:173–174
  rebellion of Carlos Castillo Armas
      against, **2:**195
  Revolutionary Action Party and,
      3:564
  rivalry with Francisco J. Arana, **1:**211
  Rossell, Mariano, and, **5:**630
  Russian-Latin American relations
      and, **5:**647
  socialism under, **3:**546
  sports used by, **5:**936
  United States' concern with, **2:**255
  Villagrán Kramer, Francisco, and,
      6:375
  Ydígoras, Miguel, and, **6:**484
Arbitristas, **1:219–220; 5:**384–385
Árbol adentro (Paz), **4:**235
Árbol de Diana (Pizarnik), **5:**258
El árbol del placer (Steimberg), **5:**944
Arboleda, Carlos, **1:**220; **4:**795
Arboleda, Julio, **1:**220
Arboleda, Sergio, **2:**501
Arbol viejo (Acevedo Hernández), **1:**13
Arbre d'or à deux têtes (opera, Alcaraz),
    1:85
Arcadia Ultramarina, **4:**220
Arcaño y sus Maravillas (band), **4:**342
Arce, Aniceto, **1:221**
Arce, Elia, **6:**73
Arce, Manuel José, **1:221–222**
  Aycinena, Mariano de, and, **1:**416
  Barrundia, Juan, deposed by, **1:**507
  Belgian Colonization Company and,
      1:535
  Filísola, Vicente, and, **3:**234
  in Guatemala, **3:**540
  Herrera, Dionisio de, and, **3:**677
  and José Matías Delgado, **2:**766
  Malespín, Francisco, and, **4:**334
  president of Central America, **2:**241,
      249; **3:**90; **6:**273
  Rivera, Antonio, and, **5:**569
  support of Central American
      independence in 1821, **2:**66

Arce Castaño, Bayardo, **1:222**, 653;
    4:831
Archaeoastronomy, **1:**377
Archaeological sites
  Argentina
    Pocitos, **5:**357
  Belize, **1:**538, 539–540; **4:**422
    Altun Ha, **1:**126–127, 539
    Caracol, **1:**335; **2:**94–95
    Cerros, **1:**335; **2:**266
  Bolivia
    Tiwanaku, **1:**339, 420–421; **2:**860;
        3:794; **5:**355, 401; **6:**86
  Brazil
    Lagoa Santa, **4:**118–119
    Lapa Vermelha, **4:**119, 132
    Pedra Furada, **5:**128
    sambaqui, **5:**691–692
    Taperinha, **5:**350–351; **6:**17
  Colombia
    Calima, **2:**37
    Cinto, **6:**6
    El Pital, **2:**37
    Mamorón, **6:**6
    Nahuanjue, **6:**6
    Pacific Coast, **2:**518–519
    Puerto Gaira, **6:**6
    Puerto Hormiga, **1:**227; **4:**323;
        5:353, 407–408
  Ecuador
    Cerro Narrío, **1:**335; **2:**265
    Cochasquí, **2:**464–465
    Cotocollao, **2:**642
    Ingapirca, **2:**712; **3:**838–839
    La Plata, **1:**443; **4:**134
    Loma Alta, **6:**265, 267
    Real Alto, **5:**498; **6:**265
    Tomebamba, **2:**712; **3:**796; **6:**101
    Valdivia, **1:**226; **5:**353; **6:**265,
        266–267
  El Salvador
    Cara Sucia, **2:**99–100
    Cerén, **1:**225; **2:**260–261
    Cihuatán, **2:**411–412
    Quelepa, **5:**433–434
    San Andrés, **5:**697–698
    Tazumal, **6:**27–28, 121
  fishing industry and, **3:**235
  Guatemala
    Altar de Sacrificios, **1:**124–125
    Arroyo de Piedra, **5:**207
    Bilbao, **2:**100
    Dos Pilas, **2:**853; **5:**207
    El Baúl, **3:**77
    El Mirador, **1:**335; **3:**85–86
    La Democracia, **4:**115–116
    Mixco Viejo, **4:**640
    Monte Alto, **4:**115–116, 672
    Petén, **4:**713

    Piedras Negras, **1:**224; **5:**235–236
    Quirigua, **1:**336; **5:**447–448
    Río Azul, **1:**335; **5:**544
    Seibal, **1:**125; **2:**853; **5:**794–795
    Takalik Abaj, **1:**335; **6:**7–8
    Tamarindito, **5:**207
    Topoxté, **6:**104–105
    Uaxactum, **1:**335; **6:**163
    Utatlán, **6:**256–257
    Zaculeu, **6:**497–498
    See also Tikal
  Honduras (*See* Copán)
  Jamaica, **4:**9
  Magdalena Valley, **4:**323
  Mexico
    Becan, **1:**526
    Bonampak, **1:***335*, 336, 644; **2:**306
    Cacaxtla, **2:**20; **5:**439
    Calakmul, **2:**27
    Casas Grandes, **2:**174, 315
    Chalcatzingo, **2:**278
    Chiapa de Corzo, **2:**306; **6:**103
    Chiapas state, **2:**306
    Cholula, **2:**396–397
    Cobá, **2:**461–462
    Comalcalco, **2:**537–538
    Cueva del Diablo, **6:**11
    Cuicuilco, **2:**718
    Dainzú, **2:**741
    Dzibilchaltún, **2:**885
    Edzná, **3:**71
    El Tajín, **1:**334; **3:**103; **6:**352
    La Conchita, **5:**740
    Lambityeco, **4:**124–125
    La Quemada, **4:**135
    La Venta, **1:**333; **4:**153, 896;
        5:345; **6:**353
    Macuilxóchitl, **2:**741
    Malinalco, **4:**336
    Matacapán, **4:**410–411
    Mayapan, **4:**424–425, 435–436;
        5:349
    Mitla, **4:**637; **6:**477
    Ollantaytambo, **1:**340; **4:**896; **5:**2
    Remojadas, **6:**353
    restorations by Felipe Carrillo
        Puerto, **2:**147
    San Lorenzo, **1:**333; **4:**896; **5:**345,
        719–720; **6:**353
    Santa Luisa, **5:**739–740
    Soconusco, **5:**884
    Tlacuachero, **4:**422
    Tlapacoya, **6:**88–89
    Toniná, **2:**306; **6:**103
    Tres Zapotes, **4:**896; **5:**345
    Tula, **1:**336; **4:**32; **6:**100, 150–151
    Tulum, **6:**151
    Uxmal, **1:**223, 336; **4:**173;
        6:257–258

Arroyo del Río, Carlos Alberto, **1:**332
  and Battle of Zarumilla, **6:**509
  and boundary dispute with Peru, **3:**56
  and Rio Protocol, **3:**59
Arroyo de Piedra (archaeological site,
  Guatemala), **5:**207
Arroyo Grande, Battle of (1842),
  1:332–333
Arrufat, Antón, **1:**333; **6:**71, 72
Arrupe, Pedro, **4:**40
Arruza, Carlos, **1:**806
Art, **1:**333–364
  colonial era, **1:**340–347
    in Brazil, **1:**345–346
    in Spanish America, **1:**341–345
  nineteenth century, **1:**347–355
    architecture, **1:**353–354
    graphic arts, **1:**353
    history painting, **1:**348–349
    portraiture, **1:**350
    religious art, **1:**349–350
    sculpture, **1:**349
  twentieth century, **1:**355–362
    modernism, **1:**356–358; **2:**815
    social realism, **1:**358
  Brazil
    Indianist, **2:**865
    Modern Art Week, **1:**710
    modernism, **2:**815
  Chile, **2:**806, 830
  clownist , **1:**491
  costumbrista, **3:**223–224
  French Artistic Mission, **2:**755; **3:**311
  Haiti, **3:**772
  homosexuality and, **5:**827
  Huichols, **3:**759
  indigenous influences, **5:**683
  kinetic art, **2:**51
  Kuna, **4:**96
  Marxist, **3:**387
  on mestizo, **4:**499, *499*
  Mexican American, **3:**706
  Mexico, **1:**347–348
  nationalism and, **4:**785
  Puerto Rico, **3:**732
  at San Agustín, **5:**696
  santo, santa in, **5:**751
  surrealism, **2:**873
  vibracionismo, **1:**491
  vraiment naïf, **1:**576
  See also art, pre-Columbian; folk art;
    indigenismo
Art, Aesthetics and the Ideal (Figari),
  3:226
Art, pre-Columbian
  Ica, **3:**782
  Inca, **3:**795
  Izapa, **3:**889–890
  jaguars in, **4:**4
  Jaina, **4:**6

Jama-Coaque, **4:**7–8
  Maya, **4:***422*
  Mesoamerica, **1:**333–337
    La Democracia, **4:**115–116
  Moche, **4:**644
  Nasca, **4:**776–777
  Nasca Lines, **4:**776–778
  Olmec, themes in, **4:**423
  Olmec style, **4:**897; **5:**345
  South America, **1:**337–340
  Southern Cone, **5:**357
Artado, Javier, **1:**238
Artaud, Antonin, **5:**258
Arteaga, Ignacio, **5:**7–8
Arteaga, Rosalía, **1:**364–365; **3:**48;
  6:453
Arte bocabulario de la lengua Guaraní
  (Ruíz de Montoya), **3:**533
*El arte colombiano en el siglo XX: Colección
  Bancafé* (González), **3:**478
Arte Concreto-Invención movement
  (Argentina), **1:**359
El arte de la fuga (Pitol), **4:**239
El arte de narrar (Saer), **5:**663
Arte poético del Mon. Boileau (Alegre),
  3:214
Arte Quiteño, **5:**457
Las artes plásticas en el Paraguay (Plá),
  5:264–265
Arteta, Pedro José, **2:**149
Arte Telescopio (Uribe), **6:**204
Arte y vocabulario de la lengua guaraní
  (Ruiz), **3:**533; **5:**643
*La articulación de las diferencias o el
  sindrome de Maximón* (Morales),
  4:696
Artigas (Ramírez), **1:**366
Artigas (Uruguay), **1:**365
Artigas, Gustavo, **5:**232
Artigas, José Gervasio, **1:**365–367
  Abipón in armies of, **1:**6
  in Argentine revolution, **6:**214–215
  Banda Oriental under, **1:**469
  in Blandengues, **1:**589
  Candioti, Francisco, and, **2:**69
  Congress of April 1813, **2:**575
  Díaz Vélez, José Miguel, and, **2:**814
  Dorrego, Manuel, and, **2:**852
  federalist opposition, **6:**148
  Funes, Gregorio, and, **3:**337
  gaucho army, **3:**415
  Hidalgo, Bartolomé, and, **3:**686
  Lavalleja, Juan, and, **4:**152
  and Liga Federal, **1:**290
  López, Estanislao, and, **4:**256
  and Pact of Avalos, **1:**404–405
  Pereda, Setembrino Ezequiel, on,
    5:150
  Rivera, Fructuoso, and, **5:**566
  Viamonte, Juan José, and, **6:**359
  and war of independence, **6:**420

Artime, Manuel, **1:**522
Artisans
  Chimú, **2:**383
  Colombia, **2:**499
  societies of, **2:**777
  See also Democratic Society of
    Artisans (Colombia); Union
    Society of Artisans (Colombia)
Arturo (review, Argentina), **1:**243;
  3:518
Arturo, la estrella más brillante
  (Arenas), **1:**244–245
Aruba, **1:**367–368
  profile, **1:**368
  autonomy, **5:**961
  map, **1:***367*
Arzáns Orsúa y Vela, Bartolomé,
  1:368–369
Arze, José Antonio, **1:**369, 636
  Federation of Bolivian University
    Students and, **1:**633
  in Party of the Revolutionary Left,
    1:623, 641
Arzú Irigoyen, Álvaro, **5:**945
  Guatemala City under, **3:**560
  neoliberalism of, **3:**552–553
Asado, **1:**369; **2:**720, *721*
El asalto (Arenas), **1:**245
Asalto nocturno (Zepeda), **6:**518
La asamblea constituyente (journal,
  Chile), **2:**376
Asamblea de poetas jóvenes de México
  (Zaid, ed.), **6:**498
Asambleas constituyentes argentina
  (Ravignani), **5:**496
As asas de um anjo (Alencar), **1:**100
*As aventuras de Nhô Quim ou
  impressões de uma viagem à Corte*
  (Agostini), **2:**164
Ascasubi, Hilario, **1:**369–370
  admired by Estanislao del Campo, **2:**55
  Borges, Jorge Luis, and, **1:**655
  gauchesca literature, **3:**414, 415
  Ibarra, Juan Felipe, assassination plot,
    3:780
Ascásubi, Manuel de, **4:**842
ASCO (Nausea, performance group)
  1:361
Ascone, Vicente, **4:**746; **5:**802
As conrarias (Andrade), **1:**178
Asensio, Manuel, **6:**308
Asentamientos, **2:**355
Asfalto-infierno (González León), **3:**489
Ashanti, **1:**34
As horas nuas (Telles), **6:**42
Asia
  imports from Argentina, **1:**267
  influence on folk art, **1:**363
  plantations labor from, **5:**272
  telenovelas in, **6:**41
  See also China; India

B

Baptista, Mariano, **1:440–481; 5:**3
  in Conservative Party, **1:**638
  in Constitutionalist Party, **1:**638
Baquedano, Manuel, **1:**481; **2:**378;
  6:413
Baquerizo Moreno, Alfredo,
  1:481–482
Baquiano (baqueano), **1:**482; **5:**22
Baquíjano y Carrillo de Córdoba, José
  de, **1:**482–483
  Enlightenment thought, **5:**179
  in *Mercurio Peruano,* **4:**488
Bar, Paul, **3:**73
Baraguá, Protest of, **6:**501
Barahona, Bernardino, **2:**376
Baralt, Rafael María, **1:**483
Barandal (magazine, Mexico),
  5:120
Baraona, Pablo, **2:**311
Barbachano, Miguel, **6:**349
Barba de Padilla, Sebastián, **2:**463
Barbados, **1:**483–484
  CARICOM, **2:**119
  ECLAC member, **3:**10
  foreign investment in, **3:**270
  HIV/AIDS, **1:***18t*
  hurricanes, **3:**769
  labor unrest, **2:**122
  OAS member, **4:**913
  universities, **6:**200
Barbados Labour Party (BLP), **1:**22,
  483–484, 506
Barbados Progressive League,
  1:483–484
Barbados Workers' Union (BWU),
  1:22
Barba Jacob, Porfirio, **3:**732
Barbalho Bezerra, Luis, **2:**876
Barbaret. *See* Bahía, Islas de
  (Honduras)
Barbero, Andrés, **1:**484
Barbie, Klaus, **3:**395
Barbosa, Domingos Caldas,
  1:484–485; **4:**291
Barbosa, Duarte, **4:**325
Barbosa, Francisco Villela, **1:**485
Barbosa, Rui, **3:**105
Barbosa de Araújo, Damião, **4:**745
Barbosa de Oliveira, Rui, **1:**485–486;
  3:366; **5:**139
  Bahia under, **1:**443
  in Brazilian republic, **1:**708
  constitution by, **1:**720
  economic policies, **1:**708–709
  electoral fraud against, **5:**128
  journalism by, **4:**44
Barbosa-Lima, Carlos, **1:**486–487,
  547
Barbosa Rodrigues, João, **3:**160
Barbosa y Alcalá, José Celso, **1:**487
Barbuda, **1:**487; **4:**913
  See also Antigua

Barbuda, Júlio, **4:**784
Barbudo, María Mercedes, **5:**414
Barcala, Washington, **1:**358
Barco Vargas, Virgilio, **1:**488; **3:**417
Bar Don Juan (Callado), **2:**38
Bareiro, Cándido, **1:**488; **2:**4, 760,
  866; **3:**437
Barillas, Manuel Lisandro, **3:**544
Bariloche (Argentina), **1:**488–489
Baring, Alexander, **5:**573
Baring Brothers, **1:**489; **5:**573, 661
Barlaeus, Caspar, **3:**9; **5:**325
Barletta, Leónidas, **6:**70
Barletta, Nicolás Ardito, **5:**28
Barnet, Miguel, **1:**490
Barnola, Pedro Pablo, **1:**490–491
Barone, Daniel, **2:**423
Baron Samdi, **4:**297
Baroque literature, **4:**228
Baroque painting, **5:**595
Barra, Pierrot, **1:**361
Barrabás y otros relatos (Uslar Pietri),
  6:255
Barracas (Buenos Aires, Argentina),
  1:491
Barradas, Francisca Víveros. *See* Paquita
  la del Barrio
Barradas, Isidro, **4:**544; **6:**11
Barradas, Rafael, **1:**491–492
Barragán, José Antonio, **4:**544
Barragan, Juan José, **1:**492
Barragán Morfin, Luis, **1:**238, 239,
  358, **492–493**
Barranca abajo (Sánchez), **4:**230;
  5:700; **6:**70
Barrancabermeja (Colombia), **1:**493
Barranca Yaco (Argentina), **1:**493
Barranquilla (Colombia), **1:**494;
  2:504
Barrantes Lingán, Alfonso, **5:**198
Barraqué, Jean, **3:**442
Las barras bravas (film), **4:**488
Barravento (film, Rocha), **2:**424
Barreda, Gabino, **1:**494–495
  anti-Darwinian approach of, **5:**782
  positivism, **4:**516; **5:**224, 324
Barreda y Laos, Felipe, **1:**495
Barreiro, Antonio, **1:**495–496
Barreiro, José Luis, **2:**562
Barreiro, José María, **1:**675
Barrera, Isaac J., **1:**496
Barrera, Juan de la, **4:**840
Barrera, Marco Antonio, **5:**931
Barrera Barrera, Eulalia Beatriz, **1:**496
Barrera Vásquez, Alfredo, **4:**434
Barreto, Juan, **2:**92
Barreto, Paulo. *See* Rio, João do
Barreto, Tobias, **5:**613
Barreto de Meneses, Francisco, **2:**877,
  878
Barreto de Menezes, Tobias, Jr.,
  1:496–497
Barrett, Rafael, **1:**167, 497
Barretto, Ray, **2:**661

Barricada (newspaper, Nicaragua),
  1:222; **4:**835
Barrientos, José Luís, **4:**391
Barrientos Ortuño, René, **1:**480,
  497–498; 5:123
  in Bolivian Communist Party, **1:**636
  military-peasant pact, **1:**624
  in Nationalist Revolutionary
    Movement, **1:**640
  overthrow of Víctor Paz Estenssoro,
    4:942
  tin industry, **6:**83
Barrillas, Manuel Lisandro, **1:**498
Barrio Boy (Galarza), **3:**349
Barrios, Agustín, **1:**498–499
Barrios, Eduardo, **1:**499; **4:**235
Barrios, Francisco, **5:**251
Barrios, Gerardo, **1:**500; **2:**66, 142;
  4:334–335, 860
  at Battle of Coatepeque, **2:**460
  Liberal Party (Central America), **4:**191
  in National War, **2:**56; **4:**787
  political rival of Francisco Dueñas,
    2:867
Barrios, Gonzalo, **1:**501
Barrios, Justo Rufino, **1:**501–502
  Casanova, Ricardo, and, **2:**173
  Central American unity, **2:**242, 278
  constitution under, **3:**562
  death at Chalchuapa, **3:**91
  economic policies, **3:**543–544
  Economic Society of Guatemala and,
    3:559
  Fernández, Próspero, campaign
    against, **3:**216
  García Granados, Miguel, and, **3:**391
  Guardia Gutiérrez, Tomás, and, **3:**536
  Jiménez Oreamuno, Ricardo, and,
    4:32
  Liberal Party (Central America),
    4:191, 192
  Los Altos, **4:**275–276
  Medina, José, and, **3:**735
  Montúfar, Lorenzo, and, **4:**687
  Presbyterian missions, **5:**378
  revolution of 1871, **2:**263
  Reyna Barrios, José, and, **5:**534
  Romero, Matías, and, **5:**611
  Rosa, Ramón, and, **5:**623
  Soto, Marco Aurelio, and, **5:**905,
    906
  Zavala, José Víctor, and, **6:**510
  Zylaya, José Santos, admirer of,
    6:515
Barrios Alta (Peru), **2:**753
Barrios de Chamorro, Violeta,
  1:502–503; **2:**582; **4:**830–831;
  6:434, 453
  election, **2:**245; **4:**926
  guerrilla movements and, **3:**582

Blogs, **3:**866; **4:**45

Blondeel van Cuelebrouck, Édouard, **1:**535

Blood and Sand (film), **3:**645

Bloque de Izquiera (Chile), **2:**374

Bloque de Obreros y Campesinos (BOC, Costa Rica), **3:**171

Bloqueo de 1902, El, **1:**591

Blue Book, **1:**591–592, 678–679

Bluefields (Nicaragua), **1:**592–593

Blue Water pact (1957), **6:**385

Blumenbach, Johann Friedrich, **5:**463

Boal, Augusto, **1:**593; **6:**71

Board of Information on Reforms in Cuba and Puerto Rico, **2:**672

Boari, Adam, **1:**354

Boas, Franz, **3:**321–322

Boat people from Haiti, **1:**387

Bobadilla, Francisco de, **1:**115, **593–594**

   arrest of the Columbus brothers, **2:**531, 534, 536

   Columbus, Christopher, and, **3:**206

   as *gobernador,* **3:**451

   investigation by Nicolás de Ovando, **4:**941

   in Mercedarians, **4:**485

Bobbitt, Lorena, **1:**793

Bobo, Rosalvo, **1:**594; **3:**632; **5:**689

Bocaiúva, Quintino, **1:**594

Boca molhada de paixão calada (Assunção), **1:**377

Bocas del tiempo (Galeano), **3:**351

La boda del poeta (Skármeta), **5:**857

Bodas de sangre (Castro), **2:**199

Bodegas, pulperos and, **5:**423

Bodega y Quadra, Juan Francisco de la, **1:**594–595; **4:**728; **5:**7, 8

Bodley Codex, **4:**641

Body painting of the Kuna, **4:**96

Boeck, Auguste de, **3:**169

Boerhaave, Hermann, **4:**448

Boero, Felipe, **1:**595; **4:**746; **6:**28

Boff, Leonardo, **1:**595–596

   John Paul II on, **4:**40

   liberation theology, **2:**222; **4:**193, *193,* 194

   Maryknoll publication of, **4:**404

Bogarín, Francisco Xavier, **6:**485

Boggiani, Guido, **1:**596

Boggs, Stanley H., **6:**28

Bogotá, Pact of (1948)

   Monroe Doctrine in, **4:**666

   Rio Treaty (1947) and, **5:**558

Bogotá, Santa Fe de (Colombia), **1:**596–599; **2:**489, *495;* **4:**774–775

   academy, **1:**348

   as Distrito Capital, **2:**725

   foundation, **2:**488

   gangs, **3:**377

   growth in twentieth century, **2:**435

under Jiménez de Quesada, Gonzalo, **4:**31

libraries, **4:**196

under Pedrosa y Guerrero, Antonio de la, **5:**132–133

population growth, **2:**504

real hacienda, **5:**501, 502

transportation, **6:**33

Bogotá, Santa Fe de: The Audiencia, **1:**599–600

Bogotazo (Colombia, 1948), **1:**600; **3:**346

Bográn Baraona, Luis, **3:**736; **5:**906; **6:**519

Bohemia (magazine, Cuba), **4:**343; **6:**10

Bohón, Juan, **4:**143

Bohorques, Pedro, **1:**251

Bóia-fria, **1:**601

Bois d'ébène (Roumain), **5:**631

Boiso-Lanza Pact (1973), **1:**601

Boland Amendment (U.S., 1984), **2:**592

Bolaño, Roberto, **1:**601–602; **4:**239

Bolaños, César, **1:**602–603; **4:**744

Bolaños, Enrique

   anticorruption campaign of, **4:**832

   interoceanic canal and, **4:**826

   neoliberalism under, **4:**831–832

   Sandinista National Liberation Front and, **4:**835

Bolaños, Francisco, **2:**716

Bolaños, Luis de, **1:**603; **3:**533

Boleadoras (bolas), **1:**603–604

Bolero music, **1:**604; **4:**160–161, 749; **5:**55

Boletín histórico de Puerto Rico (Coll y Toste, pub.), **2:**486

Bolívar, Simón, **1:**604–609, *605, 608;* **4:**229

   abolition of slavery by, **5:**871

   Admirable Campaign, **6:**202, 321–322

   Anzoátegui, José, and, **1:**201

   Arismendi, Juan, and, **1:**313

   Aury, Louis-Michel, and, **1:**400

   in Battle of Boyacá, **1:**675

   in Battle of Carabobo, **2:**89; **6:**318

   in Battle of Junín, **4:**64

   in Battle of Pichincha, **5:**234

   Bello, Andrés, and, **1:**548; **5:**722

   Beltrán, Luis, in, **1:**551

   Bermúdez, José Francisco, and, **1:**565

   Betancourt Cisneros, Gaspar, and, **1:**573

   Blanco, José Félix, and, **1:**586

   Bolivia constitution by, **1:**629–630, 631

   Bolivia named after, **1:**616

in Bolivian independence, **1:**615

Brión, Luis, and, **1:**781

on civic virtues, **4:**794

Cochabamba and, **2:**463

Colombian independence war, **2:**495

at Congress of Angostura, **1:**186

controls on the Church, **1:**192

Díaz Vélez, José Miguel, and, **2:**814

on federalism, **3:**192

Figueroa, Pedro José, portraits of, **3:**231

Flores, Juan José, and, **3:**241–242

foreign debt under, **3:**261

funerary honors, **6:**107

Funes, Gregorio, and, **3:**337

García del Río, Juan, and, **3:**389

García Márquez, Gabriel, on, **3:**392–393

González, Florentino, and, **3:**480

in Gran Colombia, **3:**503

Guayaquil Conference, **3:**569–570

Herrera, Tomás, and, **3:**679

Huaraz as base, **3:**752

on independence, **4:**792

Irish and British soldiers with, **4:**575

Jewish supporters of, **4:**25

in London, **6:**128

López, José, and, **4:**257

MacGregor, Gregor, and, **4:**305

Mar, José de la, and, **4:**362

on Margarita, **4:**371

Mariño, Santiago, and, **4:**378

in Masonic Orders, **4:**407

on Miranda, Francisco de, **4:**621

Morillo, Pablo, and, **4:**712

Mosquera y Arboleda, Joaquín, and, **4:**718

Nariño, Antonio, and, **4:**775

nationalism and, **4:**786

in New Granada, **4:**813

O'Higgins, Bernardo, and, **4:**885

oil industry under, **3:**864

O'Leary, Daniel, and, **4:**890

Olmedo, José Joaquín de, and, **4:**898

Orbegoso, Luis José de, and, **4:**903

Páez, José Antonio, and, **5:**11–12

Palacio Fajardo, Manuel, and, **5:**13

Panama Conference, **4:**655

in Panama Congress of 1826, **5:**36

and Patriotic Society of Caracas, **6:**342

Pellicer Cámara, Carlos, on, **5:**138

peninsulares targeted by, **5:**144

Peru constitution by, **5:**193

in Peruvian independence, **5:**180, 183

on Pétion, Alexandre Sabès, **5:**208

1828 plot against life of, **4:**935

president of Gran Colombia, **2:**711

race and ethnicity and, **5:**469

C

Cannon, Walter, **4**:451; **5**:629
Cano, Baldomero Sanín, **3**:397
Cano, María de los Ángeles, **2**:76, 504
Cañonero II (racehorse), **5**:934
Cansino, Eduardo, **3**:645
Cansino, Elisa, **3**:645
Cantaclaro (Gallegos), **3**:355
El cántaro fresco (Ibarbourou), **3**:777
Cántaros de chicha, **3**:749
*Cantata al Santísimo Sacramento
    "Mariposa de sus rayos"* (Orejón),
    4:909
Cantata del Chimborazo (Nobre),
    4:843
Cantata de Navidad (Orrego-Salas),
    4:923
Cantata para América Mágica
    (Ginastera), **3**:438
Cantata Sudamericana (Sosa), **5**:902
Cántico (magazine), **2**:294
Cantilo, José Luis, **2**:76–77
Cantinflas (Mario Moreno), **2**:77, 415
Canto (Ibáñez, Sara de), **3**:776
Canto (magazine), **4**:921
Canto a Artigas (Ibáñez, Sara de),
    3:776
Canto de chingolo (Cluzeau-Mortet),
    2:458
El canto errante (Darío), **4**:231
Canto general (Neruda), **4**:233, 808,
    809
Canto hermético (Berenguer), **1**:561
Cantomedia, **5**:748
Cantón, Wilberto, **2**:77–78
Canto nacional (Cardenal), **2**:104
Cantoni, Federico, **4**:912
Cantoral (Rokha), **5**:605
Cantoria, **2**:78
Cantos de Cifar (Cuadra), **4**:236
Cantos de la mañana (Agustini), **1**:71
Cantos del arado y de las hélices (Miró),
    4:622
Cantos del peregrino (Mármol), **4**:380
Cantos de vida y esperanza (Darío),
    2:748; **4**:231
*Cantos para soldados y sones para
    turistas* (Guillén), **3**:592
Cantos y encantamiento de la lluvia
    (Angel), **1**:183
Cantú, Federico, **2**:78–79
Cantú, Rolando, **5**:935
Canudos, religious community of,
    2:579
Canudos Campaign (1896–1897),
    2:79–80, 579; **4**:730
  account of (*See Os sertões* (Cunha))
  jagunços in, **4**:5
Cão, Diogo, **4**:34
Caos (Herrera), **3**:678
Capa, Robert, **5**:678
Capablanca, José Raúl, **2**:80; **5**:934
Capac hucha, **4**:134
Capanga. See jagunço

Capellanía, **2**:80–81, 217
Capelo, Joaquín, **2**:81; **6**:524
Caperton, William B., **1**:594
Cape Verde Islands, **1**:26; **2**:81–82
Capinam, José Carlos, **6**:139, 311
Capistrán, Miguel, **6**:383
Capistrán, René, **2**:213
Capistrano de Abreu, João, **2**:82
  and *Diálogos das Grandezas do Brasil*,
    2:800
  Prado, Paulo, influenced by, **5**:333
  romanticism, **4**:221
  on Salvador, Vicente do, **5**:688
Capitães de areia (Amado), **1**:144
A Capital (newspaper, Brazil), **4**:895
Capital, foreign
  and agro-export sectors, **1**:55
  Cali and, **2**:34
  and tin mining, **6**:82
A capital federal (Coelho Neto), **2**:473
Capital flight
  from Argentina, **1**:276
  from Venezuela, **6**:332, 334
Capitalism
  Black Legend and, **1**:584
  Brazil, National Security Doctrine
    and, **1**:735–736
  corporate, imperialism and,
    3:791–792
  dependency theory, **2**:792
  Fernandes, Florestan, on, **3**:208
  gender and, **5**:825
  John Paul II on, **4**:40
  Masferrer, Alberto, on, **4**:406
  mining under, **4**:614
  modernity and, **4**:583
  positivism and, **5**:323–324
  Prebisch, Raúl, on, **5**:339–340
  Sachs, Jeffrey, on, **5**:656
  slavery and, **5**:872
  social imperialism and, **3**:791–792
  Soviet Union on, **5**:913
  W. R. Grace and Company, **3**:500
Capitalismo periférico (Prebisch),
    5:340
Capitanía. *See* captaincy system
Capitanía de Alto y Bajo Isoso (CABI),
    2:274
El Capitán Kid (Garmendia), **3**:405
Capitão do mato, **2**:82
Capitão mor, **2**:83
Capitulations of Santa Fe (1492),
    2:83, 532; **3**:451; **5**:752
Capitulations of Zipaquirá. *See*
    Zipaquirá, Capitulations of (1781)
Un capítulo de historia internacional
    (Amézaga), **1**:163
*Capítulos de história colonial,
    1500–1800* (Capistrano), **2**:82
Capítulos que se olvidaron a Cervantes
    (Montalvo), **4**:667

*CAP-Música CAP-Popular Brasileira
    (MPB)*, **2**:58
Capoeira, **2**:83–85, *84*
  in Bahia, **1**:443
  frevo from, **3**:321
  marginality and, **4**:372
Capricho interiorano (Cordero), **2**:599
Captaincy system, **2**:85–86
  Brazil, **5**:550
  Venezuela, **6**:317
Captain-general, **2**:86–87
  Brazil, **2**:86
  Chile, **2**:324
  Spanish America, **2**:86–87
Captain Zero. *See* Pastora Gómez,
    Edén
Capuchin Friars, **2**:87–88; **3**:299
  ambulatory missions, **4**:628
  Brazil, **2**:217; **4**:627
  in French colonization, **3**:312
  Venezuela, **2**:723; **6**:317
Caraballo, Francisco, **2**:524
Carabantes, Francisco de, **6**:443
Carabineros de Chile, **2**:88–89
Carabobo, Battle of (1821), **2**:89–90;
    6:318, 422
  Arismendi, Juan, at, **1**:313
  Bermúdez, José Francisco, in, **1**:565
  Mariño, Santiago, in, **4**:378
  Torre, Miguel de la, and, **6**:109
Cara Capital (journal, Brazil), **2**:765
Caracas (Venezuela), **2**:90–92; **6**:315
  academy, **1**:348
  earthquake, **3**:1
  founding of, **4**:275
  growth in twentieth century, **2**:435
  under Guzmán Blanco, Antonio
    Leocadio, **3**:611
  population, **2**:*91t*
  race and ethnicity, **5**:468
  Real Consulado de Caracas, **5**:499
  Villanueva, Carlos, and architecture
    of, **6**:379
Caracas, Audiencia of, **2**:92–94;
    5:629; **6**:317
Caracas Battalion, **6**:317
Caracas Company (Compañía
    Guipuzcoana), **1**:510; **2**:90, 94,
    555–556; **6**:314, 316
  Abalos, José de, and, **1**:2
  early success, **2**:557
  establishment, **2**:92
  Free Trade Act in, **3**:306
  rebellion in Venezuela against, **1**:182
  slave revolt against, **5**:861
Caracas Convention (1954), **1**:384
  Monroe Doctrine in, **4**:666
Caracas Protocol (1969), **4**:148
Caracazo (1989), **2**:299, 784
Caracol (archaeological site, Belize),
    1:335; **2**:94–95

Catholic Church *(continued)*
  Quito, **5:**453
  religious art production in Quito,
    5:457
  state religion, **3:**51
  education, **3:**62
    Margil de Jesús, Antonio, **4:**371
    Molina Garmendia, Enrique, on,
      4:656
  El Salvador, **3:**94, 98
    under Barrios, Gerardo, **1:**500
  El Señor de Los Milagros, **3:**102
  El Señor de Los Temblores,
    3:102–103
  expulsion from Haiti, **2:**883
  family systems and, **3:**180
  fascism and, **3:**187
  Feminist Congresses on, **3:**205
  fiestas and, **3:**224–225
  French Intervention and, **3:**316
  Frente Agrária, **1:**743
  Fúrlong Cárdiff, Guillermo, on,
    3:337–338
  Gage, Thomas, on, **3:**342–343
  gender in, **5:**822, 823–824
  Goa, **3:**449
  Groot, José Manuel, on, **3:**516
  Guarani, **3:**531–532
  Guatemala, **5:**629–630
  on homosexuality, **5:**834
    among natives, **5:**831
  human rights and, **3:**764, 765
  impact of migrations on, **4:**574
  on independence movements, **4:**792
  Islam and, **3:**881
  under John Paul II, **4:**40
  journalism under, **4:**43
  land ownership by, **1:**51; **3:**789;
    5:374
    Mexican agrarian reform, **4:**501
  Law of Consolidation on, **4:**509
  libraries, **4:**195
  Lima, Alceu, in, **4:**202
  Lima, Jorge de, in, **4:**203
  on marriage, **4:**386, 387
  on Masonic Orders, **4:**407
  Maximilian and, **4:**419
  Maximón and, **4:**420
  Mbayá Indians on, **4:**439
  mesada eclesiástica, **4:**492–493
  Mexico, **5:**516–517, *517*, 518
    under Calles, Plutarco, **4:**524–525
    Carro del Cubilete symbol of,
      2:264
    Cristero Rebellion, **4:**523–524,
      524, 526
    Gómez Farías, Valentín, and, **3:**471
    González, Manuel, and, **3:**482

Labastida, Pelagio Antonio de,
  4:99–100
Ley Iglesias, **4:**514
Ley Juárez, **4:**514
Ley Lerdo (1856), **4:**184, 514
  Martínez, Antonio J., on, **4:**393
  Morrow, Dwight Whitney, and,
    4:715
  Movimiento Sinarquista, **4:**726
  National Action Party and,
    4:550–551
  normalization with, **4:**531
  Plan of Iguala, **5:**268
  Posadas Ocampo, Juan, **5:**323
  Protestantism and, **5:**380
  the Reform and, **4:**562
  in *sinarquismo*, **5:**854
  Zapatista Army of National
    Liberation and, **4:**564
on miracles, **4:**55
modernism, **4:**648
modernization, **3:**129
music, **3:**215–216; **4:**739
Nahuas under, **4:**766
Nahuatl language record keeping,
  4:767
nationalism and, **4:**795
New Mexico, **5:**142
Nicaragua, **4:**829
Núñez Vargas, Benjamin, and,
  4:861
padroado real, **5:**10
Paraguay
  under Báez, Cecilio, **1:**439
  under Francia, José, **3:**297–298
  government control of, **5:**64
  Guaraní language in, **3:**534
Pastoral Land Commission, **1:**750
patronage, **1:**349
patronato real, **5:**113–114
patron of Aleijadinho, **1:**97
Peru, **4:**128
  Herrera, Bartolomé, in, **3:**676
philosophy and, **5:**224
Pius IX, **5:**257
popular piety, **2:**221
poverty and, in Central America,
  2:244
Prado, Mariano Ignacio, on, **5:**333
Puerto Rico, **5:**413
Question of the Sacristan in,
  5:657–658
reinóis in, **5:**514
and religious drama, **6:**67
santo, santa in, **5:**751
Service for Peace and Justice,
  5:808–809
on slavery, **4:**502–503
slaves and, **1:**34; **5:**866

social justice movements, **3:**321
and Spanish monarchy, **2:**768
spiritism and, **5:**926–927
state religion, **2:**249; **5:**377
suffrage and, **2:**772
syncretism in, **5:**964–965
in Trinidad, **6:**135
in Tunja, **6:**153
Umbanda and, **6:**168
United Farm Workers Union and,
  6:172
universities, **6:**198
Uruguay, **6:**217, 221
  Christian Democratic Party, **6:**248
Venezuela, Guzmán Blanco, Antonio
  Leocadio, and, **3:**610; **6:**326
Virgin of Guadalupe and, **3:**520–521
Vodun and, **3:**627
See also Inquisition; liberation
  theology; religious orders; Second
  Vatican Council (1962–1965);
  Trent, Council of (1545)
Catholic Foreign Mission Society of
  America. *See* Maryknoll Order
Catholic Social Action, **4:**701
Catholic Union Party (Costa Rica),
  6:74
Catholic Workers' Circle (Uruguay),
  6:243
Las catilinarias (Montalvo), **4:**667
Catlett, Elizabeth, **6:**10
Catlin, Stanton, **1:**351
El catolicismo y la democracia
  (Estrada), **3:**150
Catriel, Juan José, **2:**577
Cattle, hunts for wild, **6:**279
Cattle industry. *See* Livestock
Caturla, Alejandro García. *See* García
  Caturla, Alejandro
Cauca (Colombia)
  Lame, Manuel, **4:**125
  Mosquera, Tomás Cipriano de, and,
    4:718
  race and ethnicity, **5:**469
Cauca River (Colombia), **2:**224–225
  gold mining, **2:**490
Cauca Valley (Colombia), **2:**225; **3:**62
Caucho trees, **5:**634, 635
Caudillismo, caudillo, **2:**226–228, 776
  Bolivia, **1:**635
    Melgarejo, Mariano, **4:**460–461
    Republiquetas in, **5:**522
  British-Latin American relations and,
    1:785
  Bustos, Juan Bautista, in, **1:**818–819
  in Ecuador, **3:**56–57
  Estrada Cabrera, Manuel, **3:**152
  Honduras, **3:**222
  La Libertadora Revolution, **4:**121
  Marshals of Ayacucho, **4:**390

Civil rights *(continued)*
  military question, **4**:320
  National Security Doctrine and,
    1:735–736
  under Pedro II, **1**:701–702
  Superior Military Tribunal and, **1**:753
Chile
  Constitution of 1925, **2**:351
  Liberla Party and, **2**:367
  Radical Party, **2**:373
Ecuador
  under Páez, Federico, **5**:10
  Plaza Gutiérrez, Leonidas, **5**:274
feminism and, **3**:201
Haiti, **4**:326
journalism and, **4**:43
Mexico, **4**:393, 561–562
National Council of La Raza, **4**:782
Nicaragua, **5**:894
Peru, **5**:192
privatization and, **5**:373
Uruguay, **5**:5; **6**:228–229
Civil society, democracy and, **2**:777
El Civismo (newspaper, Uruguay),
  Washington
  Beltrán in, **1**:552
Civit, Emilio, **6**:444
Clair, Janete, **2**:441–442
Clairborne, William, **4**:817
El clamor de los surcos (Méndez
  Ballester), **4**:470
Los clandestinos (Candanedo), **2**:68
Clara dos Anjos (Lima Barreto), **4**:204
Clarim da Alvorada (newspaper, São
  Paulo), **1**:28
Clarimundo (Barros), **1**:504
Clarín (newspaper, Argentina), **5**:479
Clarissa (Veríssimo), **6**:355
Clark, George Rogers, **3**:360
Clark, Joshua Reuben, **2**:443
  on Roosevelt Corollary, **4**:666
Clark, Lygia, **2**:442–443
  De Castro, Amilcar, and, **2**:759
  in Grupo Frente, **4**:887
  influence on Tunga, **6**:152
Clark, Mark, **1**:732
Clarke, John Henrik, **5**:777
Clarke, Maura, **4**:404
Clark Memorandum (1930), **2**:443
Clarkson, Thomas, **4**:881
Claro (film, Rocha), **5**:580
Claro Enigma (Andrade), **4**:223
Claro Valdès, Samuel, **6**:521
Clases, estado y nación en el Perú
  (Cotler), **5**:195
Class structure, colonial, **2**:179–184
  castas, **2**:180, *181*
  castizo, **2**:197
  Catholic Church and, **2**:218
  Chile, **2**:322–323
  Colombia, **2**:492, 499

criminal justice and, **2**:656
debt peonage and, **2**:756
domestic service, **2**:834–835
Ecuador, **3**:36, 38–39
Haiti, **2**:798
hidalgo, **3**:686
Nahua, **4**:302–303
peasants, **2**:*183*
peninsulares, **5**:144
political representation, José Joaquín
  Mejía del Valle y Llequerica on,
  4:457
race and ethnicity, **5**:467–468
roto, **5**:630
and War of the Mascates, **6**:410
zambo, **6**:499
See also mestizo
Class structure, modern, **2**:443–453
asylum and, **1**:385
carnival and, **2**:130
children and, **2**:317
Chile, **2**:337
  development of middle and
    working class, **2**:338
conflicts, women and, **6**:449
Costa Rica, **2**:632
  coffee elite, **2**:629–630
Cuba, **2**:685
as distinguished from caste, **2**:183
education and, **3**:63–64
Haiti, élite, **3**:83
heterogeneity in, **2**:451–452
lépero, **4**:173
Liberal Party (Central America), **4**:192
and politics in Ecuador, **3**:42
race and ethnicity and, **5**:467–468
refugees and, **1**:386
rural, **2**:446–447, *447*
urban, **2**:447–449
working class
  effect of neoliberalism on, **2**:448
  expansion, **2**:444
  textile industry and, **2**:644
Class structure, pre-Columbian,
  Chimú Empire, **2**:383
Claude, Sylvio, **3**:*628*
Claussell, Joaquín, **1**:355
Clavé, Pelegrín, **2**:453
  Obregón, José, student of, **4**:873
  and portraiture, **1**:350
Claver, Pedro (Saint), **2**:150, **453–454**
Claves, **4**:758
"Claves para una poesía plural"
  (Rueda), **5**:637
Clavigero, Francisco Javier, **2**:454;
  4:791
Clavileño (periodical, Cuba), **6**:396
  Brull, Mariano, in, **1**:790
  editor, Eliseo Diego, **2**:817
Clavis Prophetarum (Vieira), **6**:367

Clay, Henry, **2**:454–455
Clayton, John M., **2**:455; **3**:695
Clayton-Bulwer Treaty (1850), **1**:160;
  2:296, 455
  Belize under, **1**:541
  Gulf of Fonseca and, **3**:252
  Hay-Pauncefote Treaties and, **3**:644
  interoceanic canal, **4**:826
  Monroe Doctrine, **4**:665
  Mosquito Coast and, **4**:720
  Panama Canal and, **6**:179
  Squier, Ephraim, and, **5**:938
  Wyke-Aycinena Treaty and, **6**:469
Clean Air Initiative for Latin American
  Cities, **6**:464
Clemenceau, Georges, travel
  literature by, **3**:285
Clemens, Roger, **4**:394
Clement X, Pope, **1**:574
Clement XIV, Pope, **1**:574
Clemente Walker, Roberto,
  2:455–456; **3**:709, *710*; **5**:414
Clementina. *See* de Jesus, Clementina
"Clementina, cade vocé?" (album, de
  Jesus), **2**:763
Cleopatra (vessel), **4**:258
Clergy
  as patriots and heroes, **2**:219–220
  secular, **2**:216–217
    episcopal vacancies, **2**:220
  See also religious orders
CLETa (Mexico), **6**:71
Cleveland, Grover
  in boundary disputes, **1**:670
  on Guanacaste, **3**:525
Clifford, George, **5**:408
Clifford, James, **4**:804
Clima (magazine, Brazil), **2**:69
Climate. *See* environment and climate
Cline, Howard F., **2**:456; **4**:198
Clinton, Bill
  Cuban Americans and, **3**:715
  Free Trade Area of the Americas and,
    3:306
  Mexican rescue program of, **3**:266
Clipperton, John, **2**:456
Clipperton Island, **2**:456–457
Clitandre, Pierre, **1**:103
Closed Corporate Peasant Community
  (CCPC), **2**:457
Clothing
  bota de potro, **1**:661
  china poblana, **2**:385
  chiripá, **2**:393
  gaucho, **3**:414
  huipil, **6**:64–65
  tanga, **6**:15
Clouthier del Rincón, Manuel J.,
  1:135; **2**:457–458, 571
  Fox, Vicente, and, **3**:296
  in National Action Party, **4**:551

and MIR, **2**:550
outlawing of, **2**:340–341, 364, 550
in Popular Front, **2**:372
Recabarren, Luis, in, **5**:505
Communist Party (Costa Rica), **2**:31;
 3:178–179; **4**:700
Communist Party (Cuba), **2**:676, 688,
 702–703
 Batista, Fulgencio, in, **1**:514
 Castro, Fidel and, **2**:205
 Escalante, Aníbal, and, **3**:131
 Guillén, Nicolás, in, **3**:592, 593
 labor movements, **4**:105
 and Manuel Dorrego, **2**:853
 Mella, Julio Antonio, in, **4**:462
 part of Democratic Socialist
  Coalition, **2**:697
 Peña, Lázaro, in, **5**:139
 Roca, Blas, in, **5**:575–576
 Rodríguez, Carlos, in, **5**:590
 Santamaría, Haydée, in, **5**:741
Communist Party (Ecuador), and
 indigenismo, **3**:817
Communist Party (El Salvador), **3**:91
 alliance with FMLN, **2**:550
 Martí, Agustín Farabundo, in,
  4:390–391
Communist Party (Guatemala), **3**:295
 Guatemalan Labor Party and, **3**:563
 and Rebel Armed Forces (FAR),
  6:489
Communist Party (Haiti)
 Roumain, Jacques, founder of, **5**:631
Communist Party (Mexico), **4**:552
 Cabañas, Lucio, in, **2**:10
 Modotti, Tina, in, **4**:650
 in Movimiento de Maestros, **4**:724
Communist Party (Paraguay), **2**:653
Communist Party (PCP-Unidad, Peru),
 and Jorge Del Prado, **2**:767
Communist Party (Peru)
 Aprista Party and, **5**:200
 Army of National Liberation and,
  5:202
 Bustamante y Rivero, José, and,
  1:817
 Confederation of Workers of the
  Peruvian Revolution and, **5**:194
 founded, **5**:187
 Guzmán, Abimael, in, **3**:608
 Shining Path and, **5**:202
Communist Party (Spain), **2**:470
Communist Party (Uruguay), **6**:250
 Arismendi, Rodney, leader of, **1**:314
 Gómez, Eugenio, in, **3**:463
Communist Party (Venezuela),
 6:343–344
 and FALN, **6**:337
 founding, **6**:329, 343
 Larrazábal, Wolfgang, **4**:137

Machado, Gustavo, in, **4**:306
split and creation of Movement to
 Socialism, **6**:347
Communist Unión General de
 Trabajadores (UGT, Uruguay),
 6:243
Communist Vanguard Party
 (Argentina), **1**:301
Communist Workers Party (PGT,
 Guatemala), **3**:583
Community Action (Panama), **5**:36
 Arias Madrid, Arnulfo, and, **1**:309
 nationalism and, **5**:26
 overthrow of Florencio Arosemena,
  1:323
Community of Portuguese Language
 Countries, **5**:318
Como agua para Chocolate (Esquivel),
 3:142
Cómo agua para chocolate (film, Arau),
 1:214; **3**:142
Comodoro Rivadavia (Argentina),
 2:552
Como en la guerra (Valenzuela), **6**:269
Como e porque sou romancista
 (Alencar), **4**:221
Como era gostoso o meu francês (film,
 Santos), **2**:75, 424; **5**:756
Cómo estamos y qué debemos hacer
 (Mendieta), **4**:474
Comonfort, Ignacio, **2**:552–553
 Juárez, Benito, and, **4**:52–53
 Lerdo, Sebastián, and, **4**:175
 Ley Iglesias (Mexico, 1857), **4**:183
 Ley Juárez, **4**:514
 Ley Lerdo (Mexico, 1856), **4**:184
 Payno y Flores, Manuel, and,
  5:117–118
 Plan of Ayutla, **5**:266
 Plan of Tacubaya, **5**:269
 Zuloaga and, **6**:525
Como segurar seu casamento (Chico
 Anísio), **2**:315
Como todas las mañanas (Steimberg),
 5:944
Compadrazgo, **2**:553
 among Totonacs, **6**:120
 Panama, and Belisario Porras,
  Belisario, **5**:298
El compadre Mendoza (film, de
 Fuentes), **2**:761
Compadresco, **2**:554
Compadrito, **2**:554–555
Compagnie Aramayo des Mines de
 Bolivie, **1**:209
Compagnie des Indes, slave trade,
 5:875
Compagnie Nouvelle, **3**:644
Compagnie Nouvelle du Canal de
 Panama, **5**:24

Compagnie Universelle du Canal
 Interocéanique de Panama, **4**:177
Companhia América Fabril, **6**:61
Companhia da Guiné, **5**:875
Companhia Editora Nacional (Brazil),
 4:674
Companhia Geral de Pernambuco e
 Paraíba. *See* Pernambuco
 Company
Companhia Geral do Comércio, **3**:239
Companhia Geral do Grão Pará e
 Maranhão (Brazil). *See* Grão-Pará
 Company
Companhia Gráfico-Editora Monteiro
 Lobato, **4**:674
Companhia Paulista de Estradas de
 Ferro (railroad, Brazil), **5**:481
Companhia Siderúrgica Nacional
 (CSN, Brazil), **6**:402–403
 production by, **3**:873
Companhia Vale do Rio Doce
 (CVDR), **2**:555
 Brazil, **4**:365
 Itabira in, **3**:185
 production by, **3**:873
La Compañía church (Guanajuato),
 6:203
Compañía de Barcelona, **5**:409
Compañía de Zarzuela, **3**:381
Compañía Guipuzcoana. *See* Caracas
 Company
Compañia Industrial de Orizaba
 (CIDOSA), **6**:61
Compañía Industrial de San Ildefonse,
 6:61
Compañía Mate Larnjeira, **6**:486
Compañía Mexicana de Aviación
 (CMA), **1**:407
Compañía Minera de Oruro, **3**:729
Compañía Unida de Minas (United
 Mining Company), **1**:73
Companies, chartered, **2**:556–557
 fleet system, **3**:239
Company of Eleutherian Adventurers,
 1:440
Company of Grão-Pará e Maranhão.
 See Grão-Pará and Maranhão
 Company
Company of Pernambuco e Paraíba, **1**:697
Company of Scotland Trading to
 Africa and the Indies, **2**:32
Company of the Islands of America, **3**:319
"La Comparsa" (Lecuona), **4**:161
Compay Segundo (Francisco
 Repilado), **2**:557–558
 in Buena Vista Social Club, **1**:800
*Compendio clemental de historia del
 Paraguay* (Garay), **3**:380
Compère général soleil (Alexis), **1**:103
Complemento (journal), **1**:185
Composición, **2**:558; **3**:108

Composición de lugar (Berenguer),
1:561
Compradors, and imperialism, 3:792
Comprobaciones históricas (Fidel
López), 4:640
Compton, John, in United Workers
Party, 5:668
Computadores e Sistemas Brasileiros,
S.A. (COBRA), 2:558
Computer industry, 2:558–560;
6:32
"Com qué roupa?" (song, Rosa), 5:622
COMSUR (Bolivia), 5:704
Comte, Auguste
Barreda, Gabina, and, 1:494
influence, 1:25
on Brazilian republic, 1:708
on Cândido Rondon, 5:616
on João Capistrano, 2:82
Lastarria, José, and, 4:145
Mexico, 4:519
positivism based on, 5:224, 323,
759, 781
and Manuel Domínguez, 2:837
Positivist Church of Brazil, 5:325
Comte, Louis, 5:228
Comunero Revolt (New Granada,
1781), 2:494, 560–561; 4:814
Beltrán, Manuela, in, 1:551
Berbeo, Juan Francisco, in, 1:561
Capitulations of Zipaquirá, 6:520
Flores, Manuel Antonio, and, 3:246
Gálvez, José de, and, 3:361
Gutiérrez de Piñeres, Juan Francisco,
and, 3:601
militias, 4:601
resulting from tobacco monopoly,
6:93
in San Gil, 5:713
in Socorro, 5:884
Tunja and, 6:152
Comunero Revolt (Paraguay,
1730–1735), 2:561–562
Los comuneros (Briceño), 2:561
*Los comuneros: guerra social y lucha
anticolonial* (Aguilera Peña),
2:561
El comunismo de las misiones (Garay),
3:380
El Comunista (newspaper, Cuba),
2:702
Conaghan, Catherine, 3:57
CONAIE. *See* Confederación de
Nacionalidades Indígenas del
Ecuador
Conan Doyle, Arthur, 3:605
CONCAMIN (Mexico).
See Confederación de Cámaras
Industriales
CONCANACO. *See* Confederación de
Cámaras de Comercio

Conceição Vellozo, José Mariano de,
3:159; 5:781
Concentración de Fuerzas Populares
(Ecuador). *See* Concentration of
Popular Forces (CFP, Ecuador)
Concentración Nacional (Chile),
2:364
Concentration Camp (Segall), 5:793
Concentration of Popular Forces
(CFP, Ecuador), 3:58–59
Bucaram, Asaad, in, 1:793–794
Hurtado, Osvaldo, in, 3:771
repeal of formula of charismatic
cuadillo, 3:57
Roldós Aguilera, Jaime, in, 5:606
Concepción (Chile), 2:562–563
founded by Pedro de Valdivia, 1:215;
6:264
rebellion in 1851, 2:375
Concepción (Paraguay), 2:563–564
Concepcion, Dave, 2:563
Concepción Valdés, Gabriel de la,
4:358
Concepción Valdés, José de la, 4:669
Conceptismo, 4:220
Concertación de Partidos por el No
(Chile), 2:362
Concertación de Partidos por la
Democracia (Chile), 2:349, 362
Frei, Eduardo, in, 3:310
Concertante (Dianda), 2:801
Concha, Andrés de la, 2:564; 5:152
Concha, José Vicente, 2:564–565
Concha, Malaquías, 2:366
Concha, Manuel, 4:708
Concha War (Ecuador, 1913–1916),
3:136
Concha y Toro, Domingo, 6:444
Conchillos, Lope, 2:462
Conchos, 2:315; 5:100
Conciencia de Patria (CONDEPA,
Bolivia), 3:210
"Concierto de amor" y otros poemas
(Cáceres), 2:21
Concierto para piano (Pineda-Duque),
5:239
Conciliação, 2:565
Rio Branco, Visconde do, in, 5:547
Concón, Battle of (Chile, 1891),
2:378
Concordancia (Argentina,
1931–1943), 2:565–566
Justo, José Agustín Pedro, and, 4:67
organization by Miguel Ángel
Cárcano, 2:103
Saavedra Lamas, Carlos, in, 5:650
support by Radical antipersonalists,
1:269
Concordat of 1887 (Colombia),
2:502, 566

Concordat of Burgos (1512), on
patronato real, 5:113
Concordats, 2:220
Concreción (Paz), 5:120
Concretism, 2:566–567
Clark, Lygia, and, 2:442
concrete art movement, 4:887
concrete poetry, 2:58, 59
Soussandrade, 4:221
Concubinage, 4:388
Condarco, Álvarez, Andean passes
surveyed by, 5:724
Condé, Maryse, 2:568
Conde, Oscar, 4:291
Conde, Pedro, 5:723
CONDECA. *See* Central American
Defense Council
Conde d'Eu. *See* Gastão d'Orléans
Os condenados (Andrade), 1:180
La condesa sangrienta (Pizarnik),
5:259
Condor, 2:568–569
The Condor and the Cows (Isherwood),
3:285
Condoreiros (condor poets), 2:200
"El condor pasa" (song, Alomía
Robles), 2:569
Con el tambor de las islas (Rueda),
5:637
Confabulario (Arreola), 1:328; 4:238
Confabulario total (Arreola), 4:238
A confederação dos Tamojos
(Magalhães), 4:321
Confederacão dos Trabalhadores na
Agricultura (CONTAG, Brazil),
5:632–633
Confederação Operária Brasileira.
See Brazilian Labor Confederation
(COB)
Confederación de Cámaras de Comercio
(CONCANACO), 2:569
Sánchez Navarro, Juan, in, 5:707
Confederación de Cámaras Industriales
(CONCAMIN, Mexico), 2:49;
5:707
Confederación de la Producción y del
Comercio (CPC, Chile), 2:359
Confederación de las Asociaciones
Japonesas en la República
Mexicana, 4:13
Confederación de Nacionalidades
Indígenas del Ecuador
(CONAIE), 2:570; 3:599; 4:301
emergence, 3:48
indigenismo and, 3:817
protest against Sixto Durán-Ballén,
2:871
Confederación de Trabajadores de
América Latina (CTAL), 2:570

Conquistadores *(continued)*
  Féderman, Nicolás, **3**:194–195
  Fernández de Córdoba, Francisco, **3**:215
  goldwork looted by, **3**:460
  heterogeneous peoples conquered by, **4**:789
  homosexuality among, **5**:827
  Hurtado de Mendoza, García, **3**:771
  Jiménez de Quesada, Gonzalo, **4**:31
  Manco Inca and, **4**:345
  Martyr, Peter, on, **4**:403–404
  messianic movements and, **4**:497
  Motecuhzoma II and, **4**:722
  in Olancho, **4**:888
  territorial conflicts among, **5**:753
  women and, **6**:446–447
Conquistadores y pobladores (Meléndez), **4**:459
Conquista espiritual (Ruiz), **5**:643
Las conquistas de la higiene social (Bunge), **1**:810
Conrad, Joseph
  Hudson, William, and, **3**:757
  travel literature by, **3**:285
Consag, Fernando, **5**:571
Conscience of the Fatherland (CONDEPA, Bolivia), **1**:626
  Palenque, Carlos, in, **5**:17
Conscription, military, **1**:318
Consejo de Sesarrollo de las Nacionalidades y Pueblos de Ecuador (CONDEPE), **2**:65
Consejo Mixto de Obreros y Estudiantes (Paraguay), **2**:653
Consejo Nacional de Educación (Argentina), **5**:492
Consejo Nacional de Gobierno (Uruguay), **3**:212
Consejo Regional Indígena del Cauca (CRIC, Colombia), **3**:823
Conselheiro, Antônio, **2**:578–580
  jagunços and, **4**:5
  messanic community, **2**:79
  Morais Barros, Prudente José de, and, **4**:692
  sertão, sertanejo and, **5**:808
Conselho da Fazenda, **2**:580
  fleet system and, **3**:239
  in overseas administration, **5**:320
  Pombal, marquês de, and, **2**:580
  responsibilities taken over by Overseas Council, **4**:943
Conselho da India (1604–1614), **4**:943; **5**:319–320
Conselho Nacional de Economica (Brazil), **2**:882
Conselho Nacional do Café (Brazil), **1**:711

Conselho Nacional dos Seringueiros (CNS, Brazil), **5**:633
El Conservador (newspaper, Chile), **5**:907
Conservation International, **3**:124
Conservative parties, **2**:580–584, 775
  and anticlericalism, **1**:191–192
  in Central America, **2**:240
  era of conservative-liberal consensus, **2**:580–581
  race and ethnicity, **5**:469–470
Conservative Party (Argentina), **2**:364–365
  Cámpora, Hector, in, **2**:58
  electoral fraud, **1**:269
Conservative Party (Bolivia), **1**:637–638
  Arce, Aniceto, leader of, **1**:221
  Baptista, Mariano, in, **1**:481
  Federalist War, **3**:193–194
  Fernández Alonso, Sévero, in, **3**:211
  rise of, **1**:620
  Sucre, **5**:954
Conservative Party (Brazil), **1**:758
  founding of, **6**:293
  liberalism in, **1**:734
  Lima e Silva, Luís in, **4**:205
  Moderados and, **1**:761
  Paraná, Honôrio, and, **5**:87
  Pedro II and, **1**:701
  Praieira Revolt, **5**:337
  Queirós, Eusébio de, in, **5**:431
  trindade saquarema, **5**:431
  Uruguai, Visconde do, in, **6**:211
Conservative Party (Chile), **2**:326, 364–365, 581
  Baquedano, Manuel, in, **1**:481
  Lircay, Battle of (1830), **4**:214
  Montt Torres, Manuel, in, **4**:686
  Pelucones, **5**:138–139
  Pinto Díaz, Francisco, and, **5**:247–248
  Portales, Diego José, **5**:302
  in Question of the Sacristan, **5**:658
  schism in, **2**:330
Conservative Party (Colombia), **2**:519–520, 521, 581
  Abadía, Mighel, and, **1**:1
  Berrío, Pedro, in, **1**:568
  Caro, José, and, **2**:133
  Gómez Hurtado, Álvaro, in, **3**:471–472
  "historical" wing, **2**:564
  Holguín, Jorge, in, **3**:730
  regionalism and, **2**:500
  San Gil, **5**:713
  in Siete de Marzo, **5**:841
  Suárez, Marco Fidel, in, **5**:950
  Tunja and, **6**:153
Conservative Party (Ecuador), **3**:59

Conservative Party (Nicaragua), **2**:581, 582
  and Adolfo Díaz, **2**:804–805
  Agüero, Fernando, and, **1**:62
  Chamorro, Emiliano, leader of, **2**:283
  and Emiliano Chamorro, **2**:804–805
  Fonseca Amador, Carlos, in, **3**:254
  formation, **2**:281
  Genuines, **6**:509
  Granada in, **3**:501
  Martínez, Tomás, **4**:394
  Moncada, José, María, and, **4**:662
Conservative Party (Panama), **5**:24
Conservative Party (Venezuela), **2**:581; **6**:344
  in Federal War, **3**:194
  Páez, José Antonio, in, **5**:12
  Quintero, Ángel, in, **5**:446
Conservatorio (publication), **6**:300
Conservatorio López Buchardo, **4**:260
Conservatorio Nacional (Colombia), **6**:205
Conservatorio Nacional (Montevideo), **6**:119
Conservatorio Nacional de Música (Mexico), **4**:740
Conservatory and School of Fine Arts of Cali, **6**:267
Considerant, Victor, **5**:503
Consolidación, Law of (Spain), **2**:584
Conspiracy of the Ladder (Cuba, 1843). *See* La Escalera, Conspiracy of (Cuba, 1843)
Conspiracy of the Tailors. *See* Inconfidência dos Alfaiates (Brazil, 1798)
Constant Botelho de Magalhães, Benjamin, **2**:584–585
  Baca Flor, Carlos, and, **1**:435
El Constitucional (newspaper, Peru), **5**:124
Constituent Revolution (Chile), **3**:357–358
"The Constituents and the Federal Constituent Assembly of 1824" (Mendieta), **4**:473–474
Constitutional Amendments Law (Bolivia, 1994), **1**:631
"Constitutional Frameworks and Democratic Consolidation: Parliamentarism *versus* Presidentialism" (Stepan and Skach), **5**:360–361
Constitutionalist Liberal Party (Nicaragua), **4**:926
Constitutionalist Party (Bolivia), **1**:638
Constitutionalist Progressive Party (PCP, Mexico), **4**:315–316
Constitutionalist Revolution (Brazil, 1932)
  Bernardes, Artur, in, **1**:566
  Borges, Antônio, in, **1**:656

in Modern Art Week, **4**:647

Rocha, Glauber, and, **5**:580

Diccionario de autores latinoamericanos (Aira), **4**:240

Diccionario de construcción y régimen de la lengua castellana (Cuervo), **2**:714

Diccionario de Motul (Ciudad Real), **4**:434

Diccionario de Peruanismos (Paz Soldán), **5**:125

Diccionario de Venezolanismos, **1**:490–491

Diccionario histórico-biográfico del Perú (Mendiburu), **4**:473

Diccionario universal de historia y geografía, **2**:649; **4**:922

Dickmann, Adolfo, **2**:815–816

Dickmann, Enrique, **2**:816

Gerchunoff, Alberto, and, **3**:427

Justo, Juan B., and, **4**:68

Dickson, Alexander, **1**:518

El dictador y yo (Samayoa), **5**:690

La dictadura de O'Higgins (Amunátegui), **1**:167

La dictadura perpetua (Montalvo), **1**:181; **4**:667

on García Moreno, Gabriel, **3**:396

El Dictamen (newspaper, Veracruz), **4**:45

Dictators League (Central America), **2**:817; **6**:165

Dictionnaire, grammaire et chrestomathie de la langue maya (Bourbourg), **4**:427

Didade de Deus (film), **2**:420

Diego, Eliseo, **2**:817; **6**:396

Diego, Gerardo

Huidobro, Vicente, and, **3**:760

influence on Eduardo Carranza, **2**:138

Diego, José de, **2**:818

Diego, Juan, Virgin of Guadalupe appearance to, **3**:520–521

Diego Padró, José I. de, **5**:17

Diegues, Carlos, **2**:424, 818

on Silva, Xica da, **5**:850

Diéguez, Ileana, **6**:73

Dieguez, Manuel M., **2**:64

Diente del Parnaso (Valle y Caviedes), **4**:228

Diepalismo movement, **5**:17

Dieseldorff, Erwin Paul, **2**:819

Los Diez (avant-guarde group, Chile), **2**:641

Díez-Canedo, Enrique, **2**:482

Diezmo (tithe), **2**:820; **5**:446

Difícil trabajo: Antología 1926–1930 (Abril), **1**:7

La dignidad de los nadies (film, Solanas), **5**:886

Dihigo, Martín, **2**:820

Dilke, Christopher, **3**:523

Dillon, Luis N., **6**:253

Dilthey, Wilhelm, **4**:87

D'Indy, Vincent, **2**:199

Diné. *See* Navajos

Dingler, Charles, **1**:809

Diógenes: Anuario Crítico del Teatro Latinoamericano (journal, U.S.), **6**:73

Diomede, Miguel, **2**:821

El dios creador andino (Pease), **5**:127

Díos Moncada Vidal, Juan de, **6**:337

Dios Rodríguez, Juan de, **4**:932

Di Peso, Charles, **2**:174

Diplomacia paraguaya-boliviana (Moreno), **4**:709

Dirección General de Estadística, Encuestas y Censos (DGEEC, Paraguay), **5**:77

Dirección Nacional de Inteligencia (DINA, Chile), **4**:178

Direct private investment, **3**:268

See also foreign investment

Direito publico brazileiro e analyse da Constituição do Império (São Vicente), **5**:763

Diretório dos Índios (1757–1798), **2**:821

Dirty War (Argentina, 1976–1982), **2**:821–823, *822*

countercultures after, **3**:572

migration and, **3**:723

at University of Córdoba, **2**:604

Videla, Jorge Rafael, and, **6**:365

Viola, Roberto Eduardo, and, **6**:389

"Discepolín" (Discépolo), **2**:823

Discépolo, Enrique Santos, **2**:823

Discípulos del miedo (Wolff), **6**:445

Discourse on the Agriculture in Havana and Ways of Developing It (Arango), **1**:213

Discours sur le colonialisme (Césaire), **2**:269

The Discovery of Pulque (Obregón), **4**:873

Discovery of the Land (Portinari), **5**:307

Discovery of the New World (Portinari), **5**:307

"Discurso sobre a história da literatura do Brasil" (Magalhães), **4**:220, 321

Discurso sobre la constitución de la iglesia (Couto), **2**:649

Discursos políticos (Valle), **6**:272

Discursos selectos (Valle), **6**:272

Diseases, **2**:824–827, *825*

antibiotic resistant, **5**:391

cholera

Costa Rica, **2**:630

pandemics of, **2**:825

climate and, **4**:450

dengue fever, reemergence of, **5**:391

diabetes, nutrition and, **4**:866

endemic in Costa Rica lowlands, **2**:631

European epidemic

Brazil, **1**:688–689

death rates in, **3**:814, 825–826

Mayan, **4**:425

Mexico, **4**:504–505

missions, **4**:627

Mizque, **4**:643

Morelos, **4**:706

Nahuas killed by, **4**:766

population and, **5**:293

Florida, **3**:247

germ theory of, **5**:386

goiter, **3**:845; **4**:865

hypertension, **4**:866

impact of migrations on, **4**:573

mad cow disease, **6**:231

nutrition and, **4**:864, 865, 866

pellagra, **4**:331

polio, eradication of, **5**:390

public health and, **5**:385

Reed, Walter, study of, **5**:509

slavery and, **5**:868

slave trade and, **5**:877

sleeping sickness, **4**:451; **5**:782

soroche, **5**:902

syphilis, **5**:249

tuberculosis

and antibiotics, **2**:826

drug-resistant, **5**:391

typhoid fever, **5**:509

typhus, **2**:825

Virgin of Guadalupe and, **3**:521

See also acquired immune deficiency syndrome (AIDS); smallpox; yellow fever

Los Disidentes (artist group), **4**:937

Disla, Revnaldo, **6**:72

Dissertación sobre la naturaleza y límites de la autoridad eclesiástica (Couto), **2**:649

Distensão, **2**:827–828; **3**:684

Distinguished Woman with Her Negro Slave (Alban), **3**:*39*

Disturnell, John, **2**:163; **3**:342

DiTella, Guido, **2**:828

DiTella, Torcuato, **1**:285; **2**:828–829

DiTella Foundation, **2**:829–830

Ditos de figurinhos de brancos, negros dos usos do Rio e Serro do Frio (Julião), **4**:63

Dittborn, Eugenio, **1**:362; **2**:830; **5**:232

Diu, Portuguese Empire in, **3**:449

The Divider (Pape), **5**:54

La Divina Pastora (Gómez), **3**:464

Divination

codices on, **2**:470

Santería and, **5**:747

Empresa Colombiana de Petróleos.
See Ecopetrol
Empresa Petrolera Fiscal. See Petroleos
del Peru (Petroperu)
Empresas Eléctricas Asociadas (Peru),
5:336–337
1990 en América (television show,
Peru), **1**:521
Enamorada (film, Fernández), **3**:198,
209
En bas (Carrington), **2**:147
En busca de Klingsor (Volpi), **4**:239
Encantadas, Las. See Galápagos Islands
Encarnación (Paraguay), **3**:105
Encilhamento (Brazilian stock-market
boom), **2**:63; **3**:105–106; **4**:737
O encilhamento (Taunay), **3**:105; **6**:22
Encina, Francisco Antonio, **3**:106
Encina, Juan de la, **2**:482
Encinas, José Antonio, **3**:106–107;
6:524
Enciso, Martín Fernández de, **1**:452;
2:746; **3**:107; **4**:837; **5**:259
Encomenderos
in cacao industry, **2**:18
and cloth manufacture in Ecuador,
3:35
and domestic service, **2**:834–835
Maya in, **4**:425
military orders and, **4**:598
Mixtec, **4**:641
Mixtón War and, **4**:505–506, 642
Pueblo Rebellion against, **5**:405
rebellion by Pizarro, Gonzalo, **5**:261
La encomienda indiana (Zavala),
6:511
Encomiendas, **1**:50; **3**:107–109
in Amazon region, **1**:152
in Arequipa, **1**:246
Argentina, in Tucumán, **1**:250, 252
Belize, **1**:540
Beltrán, Luis, and, **1**:551
Bolivia, La Paz, **4**:132
Chile, **2**:323
cloth as tribute in, **6**:57
Colombia, **2**:489, 491
Columbus, Christopher, and, **5**:606
Cuba, **2**:667
definition, **3**:107
ethnic complexity and, **4**:789
family in, **3**:179–180
Gasca, Pedro, on, **3**:410
González de Santa Cruz, Roque, on,
3:486–487
hacienda and, **3**:613
Hurtado de Mendoza, Andrés, and,
3:770
imperialism and, **3**:789
indigenous rights and, **3**:825
Isabella I of Castille on, **3**:879

under Jiménez de Quesada, Gonzalo,
4:31
Las Casas, Bartolomé de, and,
4:140–142
Laws of Burgos and, **1**:813
Mexico, **4**:504
epidemics and, **4**:504–505
Parral, **5**:100
mining labor, **4**:610
New Laws of 1542, **1**:43; **4**:815;
6:305
Nueva Galicia, **4**:857
Núñez Vela, Blasco, and, **4**:862
Paraguay, **5**:60
Peru, **3**:770; **5**:171–172
Philippines, **5**:221–222
resistance by the Quimbaya, **5**:442
in Santo Domingo Audiencia, **5**:753
Venezuela, **5**:155–156; **6**:314
Zorita against, **6**:521
Encrucijada (Méndez Ballester), **4**:470
Encrucijada (Wolff), **6**:446
"Encuentro de Descendientes de
Indígenas Comechingones"
(1998), **2**:541
Encuentro Feminista Latinoamericano
y del Cariba conferences, **3**:203
Encuentro Matrimonial, **2**:223
Encuentro Progresista-Frente Amplio
(Progressive Encounter-Broad
Front, Uruguay), **6**:297
Encuentros, visiones y repasos (Orrego-
Salas), **4**:924
En cuerpo de camisa (Sánchez), **5**:702
La encyclopedia (journal), **6**:116
Encyclopedia of Wonders (Albán), **1**:76
Endara, Guillermo, **2**:245; **3**:109
Arias Calderón, Ricardo, running
mate, **1**:307
Noriega, Manuel Antonio, and, **5**:28
U.S. support of, **4**:847
En defensa de mi raza (Lame), **4**:125
Ender, Thomas, **1**:351; **3**:109–110
The End of Poverty (Sachs), **5**:656
En el fonfo (Orphée), **4**:923
En el país del silencio (Urzagasti), **6**:253
"En el Teocalli de Cholula" (Heredia y
Heredia), **4**:229
Energy, **3**:110–114
Argentina, **3**:112
Brazil, **3**:110, 112
Colombia, **3**:111
consumption, **3**:110–111
Goldemberg, José, and, **3**:457
Inter-American Development Bank
in, **3**:854
Mexico, **3**:110, 111, 112
Nacional Financiera, **4**:547
Peru, **5**:336–337
primary consumption (2004), **3**:*110t*

privatization, **5**:372, 374
production, **3**:111–113, *112t*
public sector, **5**:393
steel industry and, **3**:874
subsidies, **5**:394
Venezuela, **3**:111
See also electrification; gasohol
industry; hydroelectric power;
nuclear industry; petroleum
industry
La enfermedad de Centro América
(Mendieta), **4**:474
"O enfermeiro" (Machado de Assis),
4:307
En fin, la noche (Valero), **6**:270
Enfoques de Mujer (journal, Paraguay),
3:203
Engache, **2**:756
El engaño de las razas (Ortiz), **4**:928
Engel, Frédéric, **3**:87
O engenheiro (Melo Neto), **2**:567
Engenho central, **2**:642
Engenhos, **1**:51; **3**:114–115; **5**:863
Engineering, **3**:115–117; **5**:367–368
colonial, **3**:115–116
desagüe, **2**:794–795
pre-Columbian, **3**:115; **5**:351
England. See Britain
England, Edward, **5**:253
The English American (Gage),
3:342–343; **6**:130
English language
enclave in Costa Rica, **2**:631–632,
632
Hispanics in the United States, **3**:697
Spanish language influenced by,
5:924
English-Spanish Peace (1574), **2**:858
Engoroy. See Chorrera culture
En la calzada de Jesús del Monte
(Diego, Eliseo), **2**:817
En la ciudad y en las montañas (Arias),
1:306
En ladiestra de Dios Padre
(Carrasquilla), **4**:230
En las calles (Icaza Coronel), **3**:783
En las tierras de Potosí (Mendoza),
4:477
En la zona (Saer), **5**:663
Enlightenment, The, **3**:117–119
Abad y Queipo, Manuel, and, **1**:2
anticlericalism and, **1**:192
bacharéis and, **1**:436
on Black Legend, **1**:584
Bolívar, Simón, influenced by,
1:604
Brazil, **1**:698; **5**:781
Bucareli, Francisco, influenced by,
1:795
in Chile, **2**:324–325
economic focus in, **4**:508

F

Military Question of the 1880s,
4:598
Murtinho, Joaquim Duarte, and,
4:737
Peixoto, Floriano Vieira, and, 5:135
Fonseca, Rubem, 4:223
Fonseca Amador, Carlos, 1:653;
2:609; 3:254–255; 4:436, 927;
6:433
guerrilla tactics of, 3:582
in Sandinista National Liberation
Front, 4:828, 835
Fonseca e Silva, Valentim da, 3:255;
4:37
Fonseca Rosa, Luis da, 3:255
Fon speakers, 1:34
Fontainebleau, Treaty of (1762),
4:278
Fontainebleau, Treaty of (1807),
3:255–256
Fontainebleau Instructions (1862),
3:316
Fontana, Lucio, 2:50; 3:256
Fontanarrosa, Roberto, 2:165
Food and cookery, 3:256–258
beans, 1:524–525
chili peppers, 5:925
fiestas and, 3:225
gaúcho, 3:416
impact of migrations on, 4:584
influence of slave trade on, 1:32
maize, 4:331–332
manioc, 4:348
potatoes, 5:328
pre-Columbian
Andean, 5:353
Mesoamerica, 5:346
Olmec, 5:345
Southern Cone, 5:357
salt trade and, 5:684–685
in slave trade, 5:877
soybeans, 5:917
See also cuisines
Food processing
Argentina, 1:283
Canelones, Uruguay, 2:74
Tarma, Peru, 6:20
technologies in colonial period,
1:49
Food supplies
alhóndiga and, 1:107–108; 5:536
Amazon, Brazil, 1:752
Aztec famines, 4:721
Inca and, 1:47
potato famine, 5:327
public health and, 5:386
Sandinista Defense Committees and,
4:834
Semana Roja and, 5:797
technology and, 6:31

Football, 5:929–930, 935, 936
Garrincha, 3:406–407
Maradona, Diego Armando, 4:363
Pelé, 3:407; 5:136
See also World Cup
Football War (1969), 1:318; 3:93,
258–259
boundary disputes in, 1:667–668
effects in Honduras, 3:739
guerrilla tactics in, 3:583
impact of on foreign trade, 3:278
impact on CACM, 2:243, 251
Sánchez Hernández, Fidel, in, 5:706
Fora de forma (Rangel), 5:493
Foraker Act (U.S., 1900), 3:259
Barbosa, José, and, 1:487
government under, 5:411–412
Puerto Ricans and, 3:706
Foraker Amendment (U.S., 1899),
2:674
Forantes de Carranza, André, 2:10–11
Forasteros, 3:259–260
Forbes, John, and Company, 5:52
Forbes, John Murray, 3:260
Forbes, William Cameron, 3:260
Forbes Commission, 5:632
A força do destino (Piñon), 5:246
Le forçat (Hippolyte), 3:694
Ford, Gerald, 4:83; 5:583
Ford, Glenn, 3:645
Ford, Guillermo, 1:307
Ford, Henry, 1:153
Ford, Ita, 4:404
Ford, John, 3:230
Ford, Ford Madox, 3:757
Ford Foundation, 3:766
Ford Motor Company, 1:403
Foreign Assistance Act (U.S., 1962),
3:685
Foreign assistance in Central America,
2:242–243
Foreign debt, 3:260–266, 262, 263,
264, 265
Argentina
Martínez de Hoz, José Alfredo,
4:396
Uriburu, José Evaristo, and, 6:206
balance-of-payments crises
International Monetary Fund and,
3:863–864
banking crises and, 1:476–477,
477–478
Belize, 1:545
Brazil
independence and, 1:700
modern, 1:715–716
Cuba, Platt Amendment on, 5:273
globalization and, 3:445
Guatemala, 3:551–552
Honduras, 5:122
industrialization and, 3:834

inflation and, 3:836, 837
Mexico
under García Salinas, Francisco,
3:400
Juárez moratorium on payments,
4:514
Morrow, Dwight Whitney, and,
4:715
Payno y Flores, Manuel, and, 5:118
Porfiriato, 4:516
Peru
under Balta, José, 1:460
guano industry and, 3:529; 5:185
Uruguay, 6:232
Venezuela, 6:332
El Bloqueo de 1902, 1:591
Michelina, Santos, 4:565
Foreign interventions in Central
America, 2:242
See also French Intervention
(Mexico); United States
Foreign investment, 2:733;
3:266–273, 267, 268, 269, 271
in Argentina, 1:193, 262, 277;
5:480–481
Irigoyen, Hipólito, 3:871
Menem, Carlos Saúl, 4:479
Perón, Juan, 5:165
Roca, Julio, and, 5:576–577
in Bahamas, 5:238
banana industry and, 1:462–463
in Brazil
Geisel, Ernesto, 3:422
under Kubitschek, Juscelino, 1:713
Petrobrás, 5:208
British, 1:785; 5:480–481, 482, 483
in Argentina, 1:782
in Chile, 5:303
in Colombia, 2:504
Banco de la República, 1:465
in Costa Rica, 2:628
in Cuba
Castro, Raúl, and, 2:207
by United States, 2:675, 677
deforestation and, 3:288
dependency theory and, 2:792–793
French, 3:318
German, 3:427
in Guatemala
under Barrios, Justo Rufino, 1:502
Ydígoras, Miguel, and, 3:548
in Haiti
Magloire, Paul Eugène, and, 4:326
under Salomon, Louis, 5:683
industrialization and, 3:831, 832,
833
Inter-American Development Bank
and, 3:854

G

Gallinazo Group Site (archaeological site, Peru), **3:357**
Gallo, Pedro León, **2:**376
Gallo, Vincente C., **1:**293
Gallo Goyenechea, Pedro León, **3:357–358**
Gallon, Noel, **3:**149
Galtieri, Leopoldo Fortunato, **3:358**
  in Falklands/Malvinas War, **1:**274; **3:**177
  overthrow of Roberto Viola, **6:**389
Galton, Francis, **5:**464
Galván, Manuel de Jesús, **3:358–359,** 813
Galván Rivera, Mariano, **3:**359
Galvão, Eduardo, **6:**405
Galvão, Patricia, **3:**202
Galvarino, **3:359–360**
Gálvez, Bernardo de, **3:**360
  in Battle of Baton Rouge, **1:**518
  in Battle of Mobile, **4:**643
  in Battle of Pensacola, **2:**134; **5:**146
  cartography, **2:**162
  castle at Chapultepec, **2:**287
  Louisiana expeditions, **4:**800
  in Pensacola, **5:**146
  Provincias Internas, **5:**383–384
  West Florida captured by, **3:**248, 249
Galvez, imperador do Acre (Souza), **5:**913
Gálvez, José de, **2:**291; **3:**40, **360–362**
  Bourbon Reforms and, **1:**671–672
  Bucareli, Antonio, and, **1:**795
  economic policies, **5:**178, 179
  Espejo, Francisco, on, **5:**737
  Fages, Pedro, and, **3:**174
  Gálvez, Matías de, and, **3:**364
  intendancy system under, **3:**849
  occupation of California, **2:**35
  Portolá, Gaspar de, and, **5:**311
  Provincias Internas, **5:**383
  Real Cuerpo de Minería, **5:**500
  visita of New Spain, **2:**659; **4:**509; **6:**395
Gálvez, Juan Manuel, **3:**362, 738
Gálvez, Manuel, **3:362–363**
  on Gerchunoff, Alberto, **3:**427
  on Ibarbourou, Juana de, **3:**777
  on Irigoyen, Hipólito, **3:**869
  opposition to liberal policies of, **2:**241
Gálvez, Mariano, **3:363–364**
  Barrundia, José, and, **1:**507
  Bennet, Marshall, and, **1:**560
  colonization program, **3:**4
  García Peláez, Francisco, and, **3:**398
  liberalism under, **3:**541–542
  Livingston Codes, **4:**245
  Molina, Marcelo, and, **4:**654

  1837 revolt against, **2:**141
  Rivera Paz, Mariano, and, **5:**571
  social restructuring, **4:**702
Gálvez, Matías de, **3:364–365**
Gálvez, Pedro, **2:**192
Gálvez Durón, Juan Manuel, **2:**115
Gálvez Olaechea, Alberto, **4:**725
Gama, José Basilio da, **3:365–366;** **4:**220
Gama, Luís, **3:**366
Gama, Sebastián de la, **1:**512
Gama, Vasco da, **3:366–367**
  Cabral, Pedro Alvares, and, **1:**688
  Manuel I and, **4:**356
Gamarra (Peru), **2:**448–449
Gamarra, Agustín, **3:367–368**
  in Battle of Ingaví, **1:**457
  in Battle of Yungay, **6:**493
  Belzu, Manuel Isidoro, and, **1:**552
  Bolivia invaded by, **5:**736
  Huaraz as base, **3:**752
  in Marshals of Ayacucho, **4:**390
  Orbegoso, Luis José de, and, **4:**903
  Salaverry, Felipe Santiago, and, **5:**672
  Santa Cruz, Andrés de, and, **5:**735
  support by Ramón Castilla, **2:**191–192
  Vivanco, Manuel, and, **6:**398
Gamarra, Francisca Zubiaga Bernales de (La Mariscala), **3:**367, **368**
Gamarra, José, **3:**368
Gamarra, Juan Manuel
  in Battle of Paraguarí, **5:**59
  in Battle of Tacuarí, **6:**4
Gamba, Carlos Martínez, **4:**439
Gamba, Martínez, **3:**533–534
Gambaro, Griselda, **3:**369; **4:**236; **6:**71
Gamboa, Federico, **4:**322
Gamboa, Harry, Jr., **2:**139
Gamboa Iglesias, Federico, **3:369–370**
Gamelin, Maurice, **5:**900
Gamio, Lorenzo, **6:**477
Gamio, Manuel, **1:**224
Gamio Martínez, Manuel, **3:**370, 819
Gamonalismo, **3:370–371**
Gamow, George, **5:**785
Gañanes. See peons
Ganassi, Chip, **4:**684
Gándara Enríquez, Marcos, **3:371–372**
Gandavo, Pero de Magalhães, **3:**372
Gandini, Gerardo, **3:**372–373; **4:**747
  Aponte-Medée, Rafael, student of, **1:**204
  cofounder of Agrupació Música Viva, **6:**23
  and Hilda Dianda, **2:**801
  Mastrogiovanni, Antonio, and, **4:**410
  Valcárcel Arce, Edgar, student of, **6:**260

Ganga bruta (film, Mauro), **2:**415; **4:**419
Ganga Zumba, **3:373–374**
  Palmares rebellion, **5:**21
Ganga Zumba (film, Diegues), **2:**818
Gangs, **3:***374,* 374–378, *376*
  as bandits, **1:**473
  Belize, **1:**539
  El Salvador, **3:**95, 96
    Mara 18, **3:***96*
  Honduras, **3:**742
  Mara Salvatrucha, La (MS, MS-13), **4:**366
Ganja, Rastafarians, **5:**495
  See also marijuana
Gans, Richard, **5:**784
Gante, Pedro de, **1:**363; **3:**378
  in education, **4:**508
  The Twelve and, **3:**299
Gaona, Rodolfo, **1:**806
Gaos, José, **3:378–379**
Gaos, Joseph, **2:**482
Garagay (archaeological site, Peru), **3:379–380;** **5:**354
Garay, Blas, **3:**380
Garay, Carlos, **3:**380
Garay, Epifanio, **1:**350; **3:**380–381
Garay, Eugenio, **3:**381; **6:**490
Garay, Francisco de, **3:**382
  Álvarez de Pineda, Alonso, and, **1:**137
  in Nuevo Santander, **4:**859
  in Tamaulipas, **6:**11
Garay, Juan de, **3:**382
  Bolaños, Luis de, and, **1:**603
  Buenos Aires settled by, **1:**800
  Montevideo expedition, **4:**681
  Salado River discovered by, **5:**670
  Santa Fe pioneered by, **5:**738
Garay, Miguel de, **2:**562
Garcés, Francisco Tomás Hermenegildo, **3:382–383**
García, Alan, **6:**142
  APRA and, **5:**198
  Confederation of Peruvian Workers and, **5:**194
  Belaúnde, Fernando, and, **1:**532
  Petroleos del Peru, **5:**209
  Toledo, Alejandro, and, **6:**97
García, Albino, **6:**11
García, Aleixo, **3:**383
García, Antonio, **2:**513
García, Calixto, **2:**673; **3:383–384**
  Gómez y Báez, Máximo, and, **3:**474
  Menocal, Mario García, and, **4:**484
Garcia, Charly, **5:**902
García, Cuca, **3:**201
García, Diego, **3:**384
García, Don Jenaro, **3:**234
García, Fernando, **4:**745
García, Genaro, **3:384–385**

Guatemala *(continued)*
  League of Nations and, **4:**156
  liberalism, **4:**187–188, 188
  Liberal Party (Central America),
    4:191, 192
  Liberal Reforma, **1:**501, 507
  liberal revolution of 1871, **2:**263;
    3:391
  libraries, **4:**196
  Livingston Codes, **2:**241; **3:**363; **4:**245
  Longinos, José, in, **4:**253
  Los Altos, **4:**275–276
  mandamiento, **4:**345
  map, **3:***540*
  Marblehead Pact, **4:**367
  Mayan alphabet, **4:**426–427, 428
  Mayan artifacts, **4:**422
  Maya population, **4:**421
  Melville, Thomas and Margarita, in,
    4:467
  Mennonites, **4:**482
  migration from, **4:**587, 588
    refugees from, **1:**386–387
  missions, CAM, **2:**253
  Mita, **4:**636
  monetary unit, **5:**438
  montaña revolt, **4:**859–860
  national bird, **5:**438
  in National War, **4:**787–788
  OAS member, **4:**913
  ODECA, **4:**914
  Pact of Nacaome, **4:**764
  paramilitaries, **5:**86
  peasant revolt of 1837, **2:**241
  poverty, **3:**804, *804*
    absolute, **3:**805, 806
  Protocol of Tegucigalpa, **2:**252
  provisional junta in 1824-1825, **6:**273
  publishing, **3:**780
  race and ethnicity, **5:**473
  Regalado, Tomás, and, **5:**511
  regionalism, **5:**513
  relations with Soviet Union, **1:**247
  revolt of 1837, **2:**141
  Rinconcito, Treaty of (1838), **5:**543
  salt trade, **5:**685
  social-service expenditures, **5:**817
  Soviet relations with, **5:**914
  suffrage, female, **2:**779; **6:**450, *450t*
  Treaty of Economic Association,
    2:250
  truth commissions, **6:**146, 147
  United States intervention in, **6:**183
    U.S. counterinsurgency efforts in,
      2:646
  universities, **6:**194
  Vagrancy Law (1934), **6:**164
  World Bank loans, **6:**463, 464
  World War I, **6:**465

  See also archaeological sites;
    *individual cities, personalities,
    provinces, and topics*
Guatemala, Audiencia of, **1:**397;
  3:555–558
  Central America in, **2:**248
  Gracias in, **3:**500
  Soconusco in, **5:**884
Guatemala, constitutions, **3:562–563**
  Constitution of 1824, **1:**507
  constitution of 1986, **4:**74
  Constitution of the Republic, **1:**518;
    2:142
Guatemala, Economic Society of,
  3:558–559; 4:199; **5:**570
Guatemala: Las líneas de su mano
  (Cardoza), **2:**113
Guatemala: Nunca Más, **6:**147
Guatemala, political parties
  Christian Democratic Party (DCG),
    3:548, 549, 583; **6:**376
  Communist Party, **3:**563; **6:**489
  constitutions on, **3:**563
  Democratic Institutional Party
    (PID), **3:**548
  Democratic Vanguard, **3:**563
  Guatemalan Labor Party (PGT),
    3:295, 551, **563–564**, 564; **4:**678
  Guatemalan Republican Front
    (FRG), **3:**552, 554; **5:**557
  Liberal Party, **3:**560; **4:**911; **5:**534
  National Redemption Party,
    3:547–548
  National Renovation Party (FPL),
    3:564
  Partido Movimiento Social y Político
    Cambio Nacional, **3:**441
  Revolutionary Action Party (PAR),
    1:247; **3:**295, 548, **564–565**;
    4:472
  Revolutionary Unity Party (URD),
    6:375
  Unionist Party, **3:**152, 544, **565**,
    677; **4:**911
  See also National Guatemalan
    Revolutionary Unity (URNG)
Guatemala, terrorist organizations
  Mano Blanca, **1:**212; **3:**565–566
  Ojo por Ojo, **3:**566
*Guatemala: The Politics of Land
  Ownership* (Melville and Melville),
  4:467
Guatemala City, **2:**247; **3:559–561**
  in Audiencia of Guatemala, **3:**556
  maps by Rivera Maestre, Miguel,
    5:570–571
Guatemala Company, **3:561**
Guatemalan Americans, **3:**720,
  721–722

Guatemalan Labor Party (PGT),
  3:563–564
  Fortuny, José Manuel, in, **3:**295
  Montes, César, in, **4:**678
  National Guatemalan Revolutionary
    Unity and, **3:**564
  Ríos Montt, José Efraín, and, **3:**551
Guatemalan Organized National
  Anticommunist Movement, **2:**753
Guatemalan Railway Company, **5:**407
Guatemalan Republican Front (FRG)
  Arzú, Álvaro, and, **3:**552
  credibility of, **3:**554
  Ríos Montt, José, and, **5:**557
Guatemalan Union of Democratic
  Women, **3:**850–851
Guatemalan Union of Educational
  Workers (STEG), **3:**602
Guatimotzin (opera, Ortega), **2:**665;
  4:740, 924; **5:**148
Guayakí. *See* Aché
Guayaquil (Ecuador), **2:**624;
  3:566–568; 5:453
  cacao industry, **2:**18, 19
  meeting of Simón Bolívar and
    Agustín de san Martín, **6:**322
  shipbuilding, **3:**571
  unhealthiness of, **2:**433–434
  1819 uprising in, **5:**955
  1820 uprising in, **5:**578
Guayaquil, General Strike of 1922,
  3:568
Guayaquil, Group of, **3:568–569**
Guayaquil, Republic of, **3:**569
Guayaquil, Treaty of (1829), **3:**55
Guayaquil Conference (1822),
  3:569–570
Guayaquil-Quito Railway, **3:**570
Guayasamín, Oswaldo, **1:**358; **3:**572
Guaycurú, **4:**645
Guayule, **5:**634
Gubi Abaya (Gorriti), **1:**472
Gudin, Eugenio, **5:**45
Gudiño Kieffer, Eduardo, **3:572–573**
Guedes Penteado, Olivia, **4:**647
Güegüence, **3:**573
El Güegüense (El mcho-ratón) (play),
  6:68
Gueiler Tejada, Lidia, **3:**395, **573–574**
Güemes, Martín, **2:**184, 226; **3:**574
Guérin, Charles, **1:**508
Guerra, Christopher, **4:**840
Guerra, Critóbal, **3:**161
Guerra, François Javier, **2:**410, 769
Guerra, Juan Luis, **1:**436; **4:**753
Guerra, Ramiro, **2:**669, 676
Guerra, Ramón, **3:574–575**
Guerra, Ruy, **1:**792; **2:**418, 424;
  3:575
La Guerra Chiquita (1879–1880), **3:**712
Guerra de Castas. *See* Caste War of
  Yucatán (1847–1901)

Constitution of 1881, **6:**339
Crespo, Joaquín, and, **2:**653
Guerra, Ramón, and, **3:**575
Guzmanato, **6:**326
liberalism, **4:**190
Linares Alcántara, Francisco, and, **4:**207–208
migration and, **3:**719
Peña Gómez, José Francisco, and, **5:**141
Rojas, Pedro, and, **5:**602
Rojas Paúl, Juan, and, **5:**603
Salazar, Matías, and, **5:**673
Guzmán de Rojas, Cecilio, **1:**358
Pacheco, María Luisa, and, **5:**4
Guzmán Fernandez, Antonio, **2:**843
Guzmán Reynoso, Abimael, **3:**335
Guzmuri, Jaime, **2:**371

H

Haaker, Robert, **1:**235
La Habana Elegante (magazine), **2:**171
Habanera music, **4:**749–750
El Habanero (periodical, U.S.), **2:**671; **6:**283
Habderhalden, Rolf, **6:**73
Haberly, David, **1:**179
Los habitantes (Garmendia), **3:**405
El hablador (Vargas), **6:**289
Hacendados
hacienda and, **3:**615
justice and, **2:**655
Hacia un tercer cine (Liberation Film Group), **5:**886
Hacienda of Chimalpa (Velasco), **6:**303
Haciendas, **1:**50–51; **3:**613–616, *614*
architecture, **1:**492
Argentina, **1:**250
Bolivia, **1:**613
indigenous lands, **1:**621
La Paz, **4:**132
subversion of, **1:**623, 624
Sucre, **5:**954
Cali and, **2:**34
Chile, **2:**323
encomineda and, **3:**108
foreign debt and, **3:**262
henequen industry and, **3:**662
indigenismo and, **3:**816–817
Mexico
Bajío, **1:**448
Jalisco, **4:**6
peons in, **5:**147–148
Peru, **5:**188
sayaña and, **5:**773
See also fazenda, fazendeiro
Haddad, Astrid, **6:**73

Hadju, Étienne, **5:**334
Hadriana dans tous mes rêves (Depestre), **2:**794
Haeckel, Ernst, **1:**497; **5:**224
Haenke, Thadeus, **2:**463
Haenkes, Thaddeus, **3:**118
Hahn, Reynaldo, **4:**742
Hahner, June, **5:**317
Haigh, James, **1:**540
Haile Selassie, **2:**883; **5:**495
Hait, M. T., **3:**223
Haiti, **2:**116; **3:**616–632;
profile, **3:**806
colonial period, **3:**317, 616–618
from independence to political modernization, **3:**622–625
from U.S. occupation to Duvalier regimes, **3:**626–629
abolition of slavery in, **5:**870
bauxite industry, **1:**519
Bolívar, Simón, in, **1:**606
Caco Revolts, **3:**625, 632–633
Bobo, Rosalvo, in, **1:**594
CARICOM, **2:**119
carnival, **2:**132
Catholic Church, **2:**223
and Vodun, **6:**399
constitutions, **3:**633–634
Cuba and, **2:**684
Dominican Republic, **5:**743
Dominican Republic invaded by, **5:**871
early history, **3:**616–617, *620*
earthquakes, **3:**2
economic development under Soulouque, Faustin, **5:**908
emigration to Puerto Rico, **5:**409–410
exports, **3:**276, *277*
foreign debt, **3:**263
France and Haiti, colony of Saint-Domingue, **3:**317, 616–618
under Toussaint Louverture, **4:**280
French colonies in, **3:**317
French colony of Saint-Domingue, **3:**616–618
HIV/AIDS, **1:***18t,* 20
human rights, **3:**766
independence, **2:**797–978; **4:**784, 788
James, Cyril Lionel Robert, on, **4:**12
Jefferson, Thomas, on, **6:**179
Laleau, Léon, **4:**121
La Réforme, **4:**462
League of Nations and, **4:**156
Leclerc, Charles, in, **4:**159, 160
life expectancy, **5:**389
lwa in, **4:**296
map, **3:***617*
modernization attempts and foreign interference, **3:***624,* 625–626

mulatto elite, **3:**83, 148, 618; **4:**326
négritude in, **4:**804
OAS member, **4:**913
occupation of Dominican Republic, **2:**838
Orixás in, **4:**918
plantations, **5:**271
Port-au-Prince, **5:**304–305
poverty, **3:**806
public health, **5:**389
race and ethnicity, **5:**469, 473
refugees from, **1:**386–387, *387*
Revolution of 1946
Alexis, Jaques, and, **1:**103
and Estimé, Dumarsais, **2:**883
Santo Domingo occupied by, **1:**438
slave rebellions, **4:**11; **5:**859
slave trade, **4:**572
Standard Fruit and Steamship in, **5:**940
suffrage (female), **2:**779; **6:***450t*
transition and democracy, **3:**629–631, *630*
truth commission, **6:**146
tuberculosis in, **5:**391
United States and
Borno, Joseph, on, **1:**657–658
Butler, Smedley Darlington, in, **1:**819
Forbes, William Cameron, on, **3:**260
Geffrard, Fabre Nicolas, and, **3:**421
Grimard, Luc, and, **3:**513
Leconte, Michel, **4:**160
Lescott, Élie, **4:**176
occupation, **2:**833; **5:**632, 688–689; **6:**182
Russell, John H., in, **5:**646
Vincent, Sténio, **6:**440
Wilson, Woodrow, **6:**388
Vodun, **1:**35
Wilson Plan, **6:**440
and World War I, **6:**465
See also Hispaniola; Quisqueya; *individual cities, personalities, provinces, and topics*
Haiti, political parties
Liberal Party, **3:**625
Nationalist Party, **6:**388
National Party, **3:**625; **5:**682
Noiriste Party, **3:**148
Popular Socialist Party, **4:**367
Haitian Revolution (1791–1804), **3:**618–621
aftermath and significance, **3:**622
Cacos in, **3:**632
impact on Cuba, **2:**669
Rigaud, André, in, **5:**542–543

Irigoyen, Hipólito, opposition to, **3**:871

Roy, Eugène, and, **5**:632

Hope, Peace, and Liberty (Colombia), **2**:524

Hopi Indians

resistance to Christianity by, **5**:965

Treaty of Guadalupe Hidalgo and, **3**:522

Hopkins, Edward Augustus, **3**:745–746

Hopkins, Frederick Gowland, **4**:165

La Hora (newspaper, Costa Rica), **6**:166

La Hora (Sologuren), **5**:890

"Hora Azul" (radio program), **4**:136

La hora cera (Cardenal), **2**:104

A hora da estrala (film, Amaral), **2**:418

A hora da Estrela (Lispector), **4**:216

Hora de junio (Pellicer Cámara), **5**:138

"La hora del lobo" (column, Campbell), **2**:54

La hora de los hornos (film, Solanas and Getino), **2**:416; **5**:886

La Hora del Pueblo (Argentina), **1**:451

Horas de lucha (González Prada), **3**:491

Horas de sol (Rokha), **5**:605

Las horas doradas (Lugones), **4**:232

Horizon carré (Huidobro), **4**:233

Horizontes incendiados (Otero Vértiz), **4**:939

Horn, Cape, **3**:746

Horna, José, **6**:292

Horna, Kati, **6**:292

Hornberger, Nancy, **3**:822

Hornero bird, **3**:746

Horovitz, Salomón, **5**:783

Horses

in colonial period, **1**:48–49

impact on indigenous people, **3**:327

Mexico, **5**:436

racing, **5**:934

as symbol of European superiority, **2**:180

Uruguay, **6**:212–214

See also livestock

Las hortensias (Hernández), **3**:668

Hospicio Cabañas (Guadalajara, Mexico), **4**:920

Hostos, Eugenio Maria de, **2**:81

Hostos Review, **3**:457

Hostos y Bonilla, Eugenio María de, **3**:747–748; **4**:90, 230; **6**:203

indianismo, **3**:813

on *jíbaro*, **4**:29

positivism, **5**:324

on slavery, **5**:414

"Hot Baby of Hollywood." *See* Vélez, Lupe

Hot Pepper (film), **6**:310

House, Allen, **1**:202

A House for Mr. Biswas (Naipaul), **4**:768

The House of Mist (Bombal), **1**:643

House of the World Worker, **4**:714

The House on Mango Street (Cisneros), **2**:427

The House on the Lagoon (Ferré), **3**:219

Houses in the Rain (Silva), **5**:846

Housing

Argentina, **1**:269

Brazil

Buenos Aires, **1**:*803*, 804

National Housing Bank, **1**:748

Caracas, **6**:379

Chile, **2**:341

Costa Rica, **4**:919

favela, **3**:189–190

foreign investment and, **3**:271

maloca, **4**:338–339

Managua, **4**:343

Mexico City, **4**:539

Montevideo, **4**:681

mortgage banks in, **1**:475

Panama

government-subsidized public housing, **6**:117

Panama City, **5**:35

Paraguay, **5**:64

Port-au-Prince (Haiti), **5**:304

public, World Bank and, **6**:463

public health and, **5**:386

shortages of, family size and, **3**:181

Houssay, Bernardo A., **3**:748

Leloir, Luis, and, **4**:165

Nobel Prize to, **4**:451; **5**:783

Houston, Sam, **3**:748–749

in Battle of San Jacinto, **5**:715

Kinney, Henry, and, **4**:80

and Texas Revolution, **6**:57

Houston, Stephen, **5**:236

Howard, Jennie Eliza, **3**:749

Howe, Walter, **3**:81

Howell, Leonard P., **5**:495

How the García Girls Lost Their Accents (Alvarez), **1**:134

Hoy (newspaper, Ecuador), **4**:44–45

Hoy (periodical, Cuba), **2**:702; **3**:131; **5**:590

Hoyte, Desmond, **4**:2

Huaca, **3**:749–750

Huaca (Incan animistic spirits), **3**:797

Huaca de los Reyes (Caballo Merto), **2**:7

Huacaloma (archaeological site, Peru), **2**:25

Huairapamushcas (Icaza Coronel), **3**:783

Huamanga. *See* Ayacucho (Peru)

Huaman Poma, Felipe, **3**:*163*

El huanakauri (Zum Felde), **6**:527

Huancavelica (Peru), **3**:750–751

mercury mining, **4**:608

monopoly on, **4**:609

mita, **4**:636

mita abolition, **5**:178

Huancavilca culture. *See* Manteño culture

Huancayo (Peru), **3**:751; **4**:143

Huanchaca Company

Arce, Aniceto, sharholder of the, **1**:221

Campero, Narciso, and, **2**:54

Patiño, Simón Iturri, in, **5**:110

technology at, **5**:330

Huánuco (Peru), **3**:751–752

uprising of 1812, **6**:420

Huánuco Pampa (archaeological site, Peru), **4**:736

Huapango (Moncayo García), **4**:662

Huaraz (Peru), **1**:170; **3**:752

Huari (archaeological site, Peru), **3**:752–753

art, **1**:339

Inca growth from, **3**:794

Moche collapse and, **4**:644

quipu system of accounting, **5**:447

state expansion, **2**:26

Tiwanaku culture and, **6**:86–87

urbanization, **5**:355

Huaricoto, **4**:89

Huarpa culture, **3**:753–754

Huascar, **3**:754

Cañari and, **2**:65

Huayna Capac and, **3**:756

Spanish resisted by, **1**:609

war with Atahualpa, **1**:390; **3**:796; **5**:260

Huáscar (ironclad)

Grau, Miguel, and, **3**:506, 507

Prat, Arturo, and, **5**:338

Huasipungo, **3**:754–755

Huasipungo (Icaza), **3**:755, 783; **4**:235

Group of Guayaquil and, **3**:568

Los Huasos Quincheros (music group), **4**:752

Huasteca, The (Mexico), **3**:755; **5**:740

Huastecan people, **6**:11

Huastecos, **3**:755–756

Huaxtecs, **1**:334

Huayana Capac, **2**:65

Huaylas. *See* Ancash (Peru)

Huayna Capac, **3**:756

death, **5**:173

father of Atahualpa, **1**:390

Huascar and, **3**:754

Inca conquest, **5**:459

Inca empire under, **3**:795–796

and Quito, **5**:452

and Tomebamba, **6**:101

Huayno, **3**:756–757

Huazyacac. *See* Oaxaca (city, Mexico)

I

Joaseiro do Norte. *See* Juazeiro do Norte
Jobet Búrquez, Julio César, **4:**38
Jobim, Antônio Carlos "Tom,"
  4:38–39
  Barbosa-Lima, Carlos, and, **1:**486
  bossa nova by, **1:**659; **2:**625; **4:**751
  Gilberto, João, and, **3:**435
  Regina, Elis, and, **5:**512
Jocay, Manteño culture in, **4:**353
Jochamowitz, Alberto, **1:**235
Jockey Club, **4:**39
  in Bogotazo, **1:**600
  Cané, Miguel, on, **2:**72
Jodorowski, Alejandro, **4:**39–40
  Felguérez, Manuel, and, **3:**197
Joffré, Edgar "Yayo," **2:**229
Jofré, Juan de
  San Juan founded by, **5:**717
  in San Luis, **5:**720
John XXIII, Pope
  Benedictines under, **1:**557
  call for missionaries for Latin
    America, **2:**222
  Frente Agrária and, **1:**743
John, Patrick, **2:**289
John and Alfred Blyth (firm), **6:**435
John Carmichael Company, **1:**542
John Paul II, Pope, **4:**40–41
  Arns, Paulo, Evaristo, and,
    1:322–323
  on boundary disputes, **1:**667
  in Guatemala, **3:**554
  on Juan Diego, **4:**49
  Mexico and, **5:***517*
  Obando, Miguel, and, **4:**870
  on Proaño Villalba, Leonidas
    Eduardo, **5:**376
  Sales, Eugénio, and, **5:**675
  Salinas, Carlos, and, **5:**680
  on Serra, Junípero, **5:**805
  support of conservative clergy,
    2:223–224
Johnson, Andrew, **5:**689
Johnson, Earvin (Magic), **5:**931
Johnson, Lyndon B.
  Alliance for Progress, **1:**113
  on border disputes, **1:**668
  Cuban Americans and, **3:**713
  intervention in Dominican Revolt
    (1965), **1:**659; **2:**843, 847; **6:**183
  López Arellano, Oswaldo, and, **5:**584
  Mann, Thomas Clifton, and, **4:**350
  Mexican Americans and, **3:**704
  Panama Canal treaties, **5:**27
Johnson, Randy, **4:**392
Johnston, Harry Hamilton, **3:***624*
Johnston, J. Howard, **1:**438
Joint Endeavor for Welfare, Education,
  and Liberation (JEWEL), **4:**814
Joint-stock companies in colonial
  Brazil, **2:**543

Jol, Cornelis, **3:**9
Joliet, Louis, **3:**165, 318
Jolivet, André, **4:**179
Jonase, **5:**504
Jonassaint, Émile, **3:**634
Jonatás y Manuela (Chiriboga), **2:**391
Jones, James (Jim) Warren, **4:**41
Jones, Robert Trent, **5:**933
Jones Act (U.S., 1917)
  citizenship granted by, **5:**412
  Foraker Act mitigated by, **3:**259
  Muñoz Rivera, Luis, and, **4:**735
  Puerto Ricans, **3:**706–707
Jonestown, **4:**41
Jongo (musical form), **2:**763; **4:**41–42
Jongo da Serrinha (music group), **4:**42
Jopara, **1:**8
Jordan, Thomas, **5:**510
Jordán de Reina, Juan, **5:**145–146
Jorge; o, El jiho del pueblo (Nieves y
  Bustamante), **1:**246; **4:**838–839
Jorge Vera, Pedro, **3:**568
La Jornada (Mexico)
  González Casanova, Pablo, in, **3:**484
  Monsiváis, Carlos, in, **4:**667
O Jornal (newspaper, Rio de Janeiro),
  2:295
  Lima, Alceu, literary critic for, **4:**202
O Jornal (newspaper, São Paulo),
  3:730
O Jornal das Senhoras (Brazil), **3:**199
Jornal da Tarde (newspaper, Brazil),
  1:185
Jornal do Brasil (newspaper, Brazil),
  2:295, 776
  political power of, **4:**44
Jornal do Comercio (newspaper, Río de
  Janeiro), **5:**581
  Monteiro, Tobias do Rêgo, in, **4:**673
  Varela, Florencio, published in,
    6:281
Jornal do Commércio, a Notícia
  (newspaper), **1:**146
José, Juan, **5:**119
José, Salvador, **3:**385
*José Carlos Mariátegui: Etapas de su
  vida* (Wiesse), **6:**436
Josefa (mulata), **5:**467
José I of Portugal, **4:**42
  blood purity under, **4:**355
  Maria I and, **4:**372
  Pombaline Reforms, **5:**279–280
*José Luis Cuevas . . . Ilustrador de su
  tiempo* (film, Bolaños), **2:**716
José Martí Popular University, **2:**676
Joseph, Gilbert, on banditry, **1:**473
José Trigo (Paso), **5:**103
Journalism, **4:**42–45
  Argentina, **6:**369
    Buenos Aires, **4:**765
    unitarios and, **6:**172

Brazil, Carlos de Lacerda, and,
  4:113
Colombia
  Los Nuevos generation, **6:**167
Cuba, **4:**127
El Salvador, José Lemus, and, **4:**166
gazetas, **3:**419
Jewish, **4:**26–27
in Mexico, **4:**45–46
Naipaul, V. S., and, **4:**768
Peru, César Hildebrandt, in,
  3:693
Queiroz, Dinah, and, **5:**432
Queiroz, Rachel de, and, **5:**432
Journal of a Residence in Chile
  (Graham), **6:**131
*The Journal of Latin American
  Anthropology,* **1:**190
Journals
  on film, **2:**420
  on theater, **6:**73
Jovellanos, Gaspar de
  proyectista, **5:**385
Jovellanos, Salvador, **4:**46
  Ferreira, Benigno, and, **3:**220
  Gill, Juan Bautista, and, **3:**437–483
  Rivarola, Cirilo, and, **5:**562
Jovem Guarda (Brazil), **4:**728
"Jovem Guarda" (television show,
  Brazil), **2:**127
Los jóvenes (film, Alcoriza), **1:**90
Joven Generación Argentina. *See*
  Young Argentine Generation
Joyce, James, João Rosa, compared to,
  5:621
Juan, Jorge, **6:**130
  on corruption of *corregidores,* **5:**178
  and expedition of La Condamine,
    2:157
Juana Inés de la Cruz, Sor, **4:**46–49,
  228
  education of, **5:**824
  homosexuality in literature, **3:**733
  as lesbian, **5:**831
  plays by, **6:**67–68
  vindication of Creole by, **4:**790
  on women's rights, **5:**227
Juan Bobo (weekly), **4:**249
Juan Bobo y las fiestas (Campos-Parsi),
  2:63
Juan Cruz Varela (Gutiérrez), **3:**598
*Juan de la Rosa: Memorias del último
  soldado de la Independencia*
  (Aguirre), **1:**69
Juan Diego, **4:**49
Juan Fernández Islands, **4:**50
  discovery of, **3:**209
*Juan Manuel de Rosas: Su vida, su
  tiempo, su drama* (Ibarguren),
  3:779

Cuba, Narciso López and, **4:**258
Honduras, **3:**738–741
El Salvador, **2:**866
Peru, Ricardo Pérez Godoy and,
5:156
Spanish America, **4:**65
Junta, political (El Salvador), and José
Napoleón Duarte, **2:**866
Junta Conservadora de los Derechos de
Gernando VII (Venezuela),
6:321, 342
Junta Cubana de Renovación Nacional,
Fernando Ortiz, and, **4:**928
Junta de Beneficencia (Ecuador),
Carlos Arroyo del Río, member
of, **1:**332
Junta de Buenos Aires, Juan Gorriti in,
3:498
Junta de Gobierno (Peru), Franciso
Gil, in, **3:**436
Junta de hacienda, **1:**21
Junta de Historia Eclesiástica Argentina,
Guillermo Fúrlong Cárdiff in,
3:338
Junta de Mayo, Argentine revolution
and, **6:**214
Junta do Comércio, **4:**65–66
Junta Fundadora de la Segunda
República (Costa Rica), Otilio
Ulate, in, **6:**166
Junta Patriótica de Venezuela, Antonio
Guamán, and, **3:**608
Juntas (military)
Venezuela, **2:**767
and wars of independence,
6:418–419
Juntas de Buen Gobierno, **2:**308
Junta Seprema de Caracas, **2:**93
Juntas Portuguesas, **4:**66
Junta Suprema de Caracas, **4:**66
Cortés de Madariaga, José, in, **2:**620
Ribas, José, in, **5:**537
Roscio, Juan, in, **5:**629
La junto al río (Garro), **3:**407
"Jura" (samba, Sinhô), **5:**855
Jurado, Katy, **4:**66–67
Jury Tribunal (Brazil), **4:**58
*Justa defensa de la Academia Cubana
de literatura* (Saco), **5:**656
Justices of the peace (Brazil), **4:**58
La Justicia Humana (Orozco), **1:***357*
Justicialism, **1:**295–296
Cooke, John William, theoritician of,
2:594
Justicialista Liberation Front, Hector
José Cámpora, and, **2:**58
Justicialist Party (Argentina),
1:295–297
and Duhalde, Eduardo, **2:**868
and DiTella, Guido, **2:**828

Kirchner, Néstor, and, **5:**166
liberalism, **4:**190
Molinari, Diego Luís, in, **4:**657
Perón, Juan, and, **5:**162, 165
La Justicia Social (newspaper, Costa
Rica), **6:**402
La justicia social (Palacios), **5:**14
Justo, Agustín P., **4:**465
Justo, José Agustín Pedro, **4:**67
Cárcano, Miguel Ángel, and, **2:**103
Castillo, Ramón, under, **2:**195
and Círculo Militar, **2:**426
election, **2:**565
electoral fraud, **1:**269; **6:**206
Ortiz, Roberto, and, **4:**928
Perón, Juan, and, **5:**163
Pinedo, Federico, and, **5:**239
Saavedra Lamas, Carlos, and, **5:**650
Justo, Juan B., **4:**68
and Dickmann, Enrique, **2:**816
head of the Socialist Party, **1:**300
Moreau de Justo, Alicia, and, **4:**704
Just war doctrine, **4:**142
Juvenilia (Cané), **2:**72
Juvenilia (film), music for by Roberto,
García Morillo, **3:**396
Juventude Universitária Católica
(Catholic Youth Movement,
Brazil), **2:**213
and Carlos Diegues, **2:**818
Juventud Obrera Actólica (JOC;
Young Catholic Workers), **2:**213
Juventud Peronista. *See* Peronist
Youth
Juzgado de Bebidas Prohibidas, **1:**15
Juzgado de Capellanías, **2:**584
Juzgado General de Indios, **4:**69

K

Kaa-Iya National Park (Bolivia),
2:274
Kab'raqän, **4:**74
Kagel, Mauricio Raúl, **4:71–72,** 747
Kaggaba (Kágaba), **6:**6
Kahler, Mary Ellis, Library of
Congress, Hispanic Division,
4:198
Kahlo, Frida, **1:**358; **4:***72,* 72–73
depiction of Tehuantepec costumes,
6:36
Galán, Julio, influenced by, **3:**347
Hayek, Salma, portrayal of, **3:**643
influence on
Gorman, Juan, **4:**882
Zenil, Nahum Bernabé, **6:**517
machismo and, **5:**226
retablos and *ex-votos*, **5:**527

Rivera, Diego, and, **5:**565
tourism, **6:**121
Trotsky, Leon, and, **6:**140
Kaiser Bauxite, **1:**519, 520
Kaiwa, **6:**157
Kakchikel. *See* Kaqchikel
Kalenberg, Angel, on Joaquín Torres
García, **6:**114
Kalinago. *See* Garifuna
Kallawaya herbal healers, **4:**446
Kalpa Imperial (Gorodischer),
3:496
Kamchatka (film, Piñeyro), **2:**423
Kamiko, Venancio, messianic
movement, **4:**497
Kaminaljuyú (Maya site, Guatemala),
4:73–74
art, **1:**335
Tazumal compared to, **6:**28
ties with Tikal, **6:**79
Kanari. *See* Cañari
Kaqchikel, **4:74–75,** 425
conquest of, **5:**349
Iximché and, **3:**888
K'iche', **4:**78; **6:**257
Mixco Viejo, **4:**640
Pipiles warfare with, **5:**250
revolt suppressed by Pedro de
Alvarado, **1:**132
teaching of, **2:**175
Kaqchikel language, grammar and
dictionary by Cameron
Townsend, **2:**253
Karasch, Mary, **1:**37
Kardec, Allan, **6:**471
spiritism founded by, **5:**926–927
Kardecismo, **1:**36, 37
Karl Marx Studies Center (Argentina),
1:300
Karttunen, Frances, **4:**767
Kast, Miguel, **2:**311
Katari, Tupaj, **4:**75
indigenismo and, **3:**818
Kataris, resistance by, **3:**826
Katarismo, **4:**75
Cárdenas, Victor Hugo, partisan of,
2:105
Katarista Campesino Confederation,
4:75
Katarist indigenous movements,
Felipe Quispe and, **5:**452
Katz, Alex, student of Santiago
Cárdenas, **2:**106
Katz, Friedrich
on *científicos*, **2:**410
on Francisco "Pancho" Villa, **6:**371
Katz, Richard S., **2:**770
Kaweshkar. *See* Alakaluf
Kaweshrar. *See* Alakaluf
Kayapó, land rights, **3:**420, 421

Kosko (magazine, Peru), **2:**280; **5:**231
Kosmos Line, **4:88–89**
  Hamburg-America Line and, **3:**635
  Pacific Mail Steamship Navigation
    Company, **5:**7
Kosok, Paul, **4:**777
Kotosh (archaeological site, Peru),
  2:98; **3:**752; **4:89; 5:**354; **6:**43
Koufax, Sandy, **4:**394
Kraftwerk Union (KWU), **4:**854, 855
Kramer, Frederick, **6:**300
Krause, Karl Christian Friedrich,
  1:515; **2:**798; **3:**869; **4:**90
Krause, Martin, **1:**327
Krausismo, **4:89–90**
  influence on Hipólito Irigoyen,
    1:299
  influence on Marietta de Veintemilla,
    6:302
  positivism and, **5:**224
Krauze, Enrique, **3:**156; **4:90–91**
  on Venustiano Carranza, **2:**137
Krenak, Ailton, **1:**754
Krenek, Ernst, **2:**268, 599
Kreutzberger, Mario, **4:**91
Krieger, Armando, **4:**747
  and Agrupación Música Viva, **3:**372;
    6:23
  Dianda, Hilda, and, **2:**801
Krieger, Edino, **4:**91
Krieger Vasena, Adalberto, **4:**92
Kristal, Efraín, **3:**491
Kroeber, Alfred, **4:**777
Kronfuss, Juan, **1:**234, 240
Kröpfl, Francisco, **4:**410, 747
Kruel, Amaury, **1:**732
Kubitschek, Márcia, **4:**92
Kubitschek de Oliveira, Juscelino,
  4:92–95, *94*
  Advanced Institute of Brazilian
    Studies and, **1:**739
  Brasília built by, **1:**682
  corruption in awarding of public
    contracts, **2:**615
  in Development Superintendency of
    the Northeast, **1:**742
  economic policies, **1:**713
  Franco, Itamar, and, **3:**301–302
  Furtado, Celso, and, **3:**338
  Goulart, João, and, **3:**498
  laborism under, **1:**768
  Lacerda, Carlos de, and, **4:**113
  Lott, Henrique, and, **4:**276–277
  National Democratic Union of Brazil
    on, **1:**761
  Niemeyer Soares Filho, Oscar, and,
    4:837
  opposition by João Café Filho,
    2:23
  Prestes, Carlos Luís, and, **5:**363
  Rubião, Murilo, and, **5:**636

Stroessner, Alfredo, and, **5:**72
Kubler, George, **1:**364; **3:**433
Kufman, Terrence, **3:**820
Kuitca, Guillermo, **1:**362
Kukulcan, **4:**435
Kumate Rodríguez, Jesús, **4:95–96**
Kuna (Cuna), **4:96–97**
  in Chocó, **2:**394
  1925 rebellion, **2:**309
  rebellions by, **3:**826
  República de Tule, **5:**521
Kundt, Hans, **2:**275; **4:**770–771
Kupchik, Christian, **3:**286
Kupia-Kumi Pact (1971), **1:**63
Kuri-Aldana, Mario, **4:**741
Kuskov, Ivan, **3:**291
Kutzinski, Vera, **3:**593
"Kygua Verá" (Abente), **1:**5

L

Laañ, Diyi, **3:**518
Labarca, Amanda, **3:**200
Labarca Hubertson, Amanda, **4:**99
Labastida, Jaime, **6:**518
Labastida, José María, **1:**349
Labastida, Pelagio Antonio de,
  1:376; **4:**515
Labastida Ochoa, Francisco
  Fox, Vicente, and, **3:**296
  Maximilian and, **4:**419
Labastida y Dávalos, Pelagio Antonio
  de, **4:99–100**
Labasttida, Pelagio Antonio de,
  1:376
*El laberinto de fortuna: Un retrato
  en la geografía* (Uslar Pietri),
  6:255
Laberinto de Jerusalem, **3:**454
El laberinto de la soledad (Paz), **4:**235;
  5:121
El laberinto del fauno (film, Toro),
  2:420
Los laberintos insolados (Traba), **6:**123
"Lábios que beijei" (song, Silva),
  5:849
Labor
  in agriculture, **1:**55
  in Backus and Johnston, **1:**438
  Bolivia, Juan Lechín, in, **4:**159
  Brazil, **1:**711, 712, *712*
    Collor, Lindolfo, and, **2:**485
    under Getúlio Vargas, **6:**285, 286
    law, **4:**57
    legislation under Estado Novo,
      6:288
  Caribbean Commonwealth states
    after abolition, **2:**122
  Colombia, **2:**504

Cuba, Indian labor, **6:**307
debt peonage as form of labor
  mobilization, **2:**756–758
division of
  industrialization and, **3:**830
  Jesuit missions, **4:**630
  migration and, **4:**580
emergence of, in Guatemala, **3:**152
encomiendas and, **3:**107–108
feminism and, **3:**202
forced labor
  and Diretório dos Índios, **2:**821
  huasipungo, **3:**754–755
fruit industry, **3:**330
gangs and, **3:**374–378
globalization, **3:**445
hacienda and, **3:**614
henequen industry and, **3:**662
imperialism and, **3:**792
income distribution and, **3:**799,
  802–803, *803*
indigenous peoples in, **3:**825, 826
Manteño culture, **4:**354
mining, **4:**610–611
mobility
  and domestic service, **2:**835–836
  and wage income, **2:**758
multinational corporations, **3:**270
naboría, **4:**763
NAFTA and, **4:**849
Peru, **4:**800
privatization, **5:**373
Puerto Rico, **5:**413
railroads, **5:**482–483
repartimiento, **5:**520
rural, **3:**840
and seasonal need for, **2:**757
service sector, **5:**809, *810,* 812–813,
  816, 818
in state corporations, **5:**941
in textile industry, **6:**62
Vatican and, **6:**348
women and, **2:**449–450; **3:**181–182;
  6:449, 452
  cottage industries, **5:**824
  domestic service, **2:**835–836
  slow downs, **6:**449
Labor Courts (Brazil), **4:**57
Laborista Party (Argentina), **1:**295
Labor laws
  Brazil, **1:**326
  Costa Rica, **2:**634
  and domestic service, **2:**836
  Guatemala, **1:**247
  Labor Act (Danish West Indies,
    1849), **2:**744
  labor code in Ecuador, **3:**121
  under Rafael Ángel Calderón
    Guardia, **2:**31

La Cava, Gregory, Alejandro Galindo, and, 3:353
Lacayo, Antonio, on Chamorro, 4:831
Lace (*ñandutí*), 4:771
La Centinela (archaeological site, Peru), 2:387; 4:112–113
Lacerda, Carlos Frederico Werneck de, 4:113–114
　attempted murder of, 1:713
Lacerda, Maurício Pavia de, 4:114
Lacerda, Osvaldo, 4:114–115
　Guarnieri, M. Camargo, and, 3:539
Lachapelle, Jerome, 4:816
La Ciudadela (Mexico City), 4:115
La Colère, Jacques. *See* Alexis, Jacques Stéphen
Lacomba, José, 6:71
La Conchita (archaeological site, Mexico), 5:740
La Condamine, Charles Marie de, 3:118
　in Amazon region, 1:153
　commentary on colonial society, 6:130
　Juan y Santacilia, Jorge, and, 4:50–51
　Ulloa, Antonio de, and, 6:166–167
Lacondê language, 4:769
La Constancia Mexicana, 1:199
La Cumbe (archaeological site, Peru), 4:113
Ladder Conspiracy (Cuba). *See* La Escalesa, Conspiracy of
La Democracia (Guatemala), 4:115–116
Ladino, 1:445; 2:812; 4:116; 5:467
Ladrón de Guevara, Diego, 4:116–117
The Lady from Shanghai (film), 3:645
La Escalera, Conspiracy of (Cuba, 1843), 2:671; 4:117–118
　Luz y Caballero, José, and, 4:295
　slave revolt in, 5:860, 861
Laet, Johannes de, 3:9
Lafaye, Frederico, 4:693
Laferrère, Gregoria, 6:70
La firme (comic book), 2:164
La Florida, colony of, 6:298
Lafora, Gonzalo, 2:482
Lafora, Nicolás de, 2:162; 5:636
La France Antarctique, 6:386
La Galgada (archaeological site, Peru), 4:89, 118; 5:354
Lagar (Mistral), 4:232, 634, 635
Lagar II (Mistral), 4:635
Lagarrigue, Jorge, 5:324
Lagarrigue, Juan, 5:324
Lagarrigue, Luis, 5:324
Lagasca, Pedro de, 6:264
Lagoa da Canoa Município de Arapiraca (Pascoal), 5:102
Lagôa Santa (Brazil), 4:118–119
Lagos, Hilario, 1:123

Lagos, Marta, 2:784
Lagos, Ricardo, 2:362; 4:119–120
　election, 1:111
　Mapuche under, 4:359
　Moneda Palace, 4:663
　presidency, 2:349
　Socialist Party and, 2:375
　Truth Commission and, 2:800
Lagos, Richard, 2:364
Lagos de Moreno, 4:7
Laguardia Trías, Rolando, 3:172
Laguerre, Enrique Arturo, 4:120
Laguna, Santa Catarina (Brazil), 4:120
Laguna de Los Cerros
　architecture, 5:345
　Olmecs in, 4:896
Laino, Domingo, 5:83
Laissez-faire
　in foreign trade, 3:274
　imperialism and, 3:791–792
　liberalism and, 4:186
　Uribe Uribe, Rafael, on, 6:205
Lake Region (Chile), 4:247
Lake Texcoco (Mexico), 2:794
Laleau, Léon, 4:121
La Libertadora Revolution (Venezuela, 1901–1903), 4:121
La Luz, Romá de, 2:670
La Luz y Caballero, José de, 2:671, 699
Lam, Wilfredo, 1:358
Lamadrid, Gregorio Aráoz de, 4:121–122
　defeat of Juan Facundo Quiroga, 5:449
Lamar, Hortensia, 2:695
Lamar, Mirabeau Buonaparte, 4:122
Lamarque, Libertad, 4:122–123
Lamarque Pons, Jaurés, 4:123, 746
Lamartine, Lourenço, 5:258
Lamas, Andrés, 3:598
Lambada, 4:123–124
Lambayeque (Peru), 4:124
　Sicán culture and, 5:836
Lambityeco (archaeological site, Mexico), 4:124–125
Lame, Manuel Quintín, 4:125–126
Lamennais, Hugh-Félicité-Robert, 1:578
La Mesilla, Treaty of (1853), 1:316
Laming-Emperaire, Annette, 4:132
Lampião (Queiroz), 5:433
Lampião (Virgulino Ferreira da Silva), 4:126
Lamprecht, Karl, 5:437
Lamy, Jean Baptiste
　and Brotherhood of Penitentes, 6:523
　Martínez, Antonio J., and, 4:393
Lam y Castilla, Wifredo, 4:126–127
Lancaster, James, 2:472
Lanchas en la bahía (Rojas), 5:601
"Lanchitas" (Roa Bárcena), 5:572

Land
　Catholic Church and, 2:217–218; 4:630
　communal. *See* property rights
　See also land tenure
Landa, Diego de, 4:127
　Brasseur, Charles, on, 1:684
　Inquisition under, 3:842
　Mayan ethnohistory, 4:434
　on Mayapan, 4:435
　Relación de las cosas de Ycatán, 4:85
Land Act, Californios and, 2:37
Landaeta, Juan José, 4:741
Landaluze, Víctor Patricio de, 2:672; 4:127–128
　and *costumbrista* art, 1:352
　"Landa's alphabet," 4:84–85
Landázuri Ricketts, Juan, 2:222; 4:128
Land colonization in Argentine Chaco, 4:158
Landesio, Eugenio, 1:351–352
　Velasco, José María, student of, 6:302
Landholding patterns, changes due to export-led growth, 2:443
　tenancy
　　plantations, 5:272
　　Tucumán (Argentina), 1:250–251, 252
Landi, Antonio Giuseppe, 1:345; 3:159
Land in Anguish (film, Rocha), 5:580
Landívar, Rafael, 4:128–129
Land Law 200 of 1936 (Colombia), 4:270
Land Law of 1850 (Brazil), 1:702; 4:129
　on *sesmaria*, 5:820
Landless Workers Movement (MST, Brazil). *See* Movimento Sem Terra (MST, Brazil)
The Land Liberated (Rivera), 5:565
Landowski, Paul, 2:598
Land reform. *See* agrarian reform
Land rights
　Bolivia
　　Liberal Party on, 1:639
　　sayaña, 5:773
　Brazil, 5:329
　Colombia, *resguardo*, 5:523
　family in, 3:179–180
　Guatemala
　　Gálvez, Mariano, on, 3:363–364
　　Menchú Tum, Rigoberta, in, 4:468
　industrialization and, 3:831
　Mexican Americans, 3:700–701, 705
　race and ethnicity and, 5:470
Landrú (Juan Carlos Colombres), 2:165

López Cordero, Alfonso, and, **4:**828
López de Arteaga, Sebastián, **4:**262–263
Juárez, José, influenced by, **4:**54
López de Castro, Baltasar, **5:**754
López de Cerrato, Alonso, **4:**263
and Audiencia de los Confines, **1:**398
in Audiencia of Guatemala, **3:**556
enforcement of the new Laws, **1:**195
López de Cogolludo, Diego, **4:**263
Mayan ethnohistory, **4:**434
López de Gómara, Francisco
on Black Legend, **1:**583
on Cortés, **4:**790
on Guzmán, Nuño Beltrán de, **3:**610
López de Haro, González, **4:**393
López de Legazpi y Gurruchátegui, Miguel, **4:**263–264
Manila galleons, **4:**346
Philippines colonization, **5:**221
Urdaneta, Andrés de, and, **6:**202
López del Rosario, Andrés. *See* Andresote
López de Palacios Rubios, Juan, **5:**522
López de Quintana, Antonio, **2:**93
López de Quiroga, Antonio, **4:**264–265
Potosí, **5:**329
López de Romaña, Eduardo, **4:**265
López de Velasco, Juan, **5:**293
López de Villalobos, Ruy, **5:**221
López de Zúñiga y Velasco, Diego
García de Castro, Lope, and, **3:**388
Ortiz de Zárate, Juan, and, **4:**930
López Gutiérrez, Rafael, **3:**737–738
López Jordán, Ricardo, **4:**265–266
Campos, Luis, against, **2:**61
Hernández, José, and, **3:**670
punishment for assassination of Urquiza, **1:**122
Urquiza, Justo José de, and, **6:**207
López Mateos, Adolfo, **4:**266–267; **6:**294
Díaz Ordaz, Gustavo, in cabinet of, **2:**813
economic development, **4:**527, 528
elections of 1958, **1:**135
in Instituto Tecnológico Autónomo de Mexico, **3:**848
Yáñez, Agustín, speechwriter for, **6:**479
López Mazz, José, **5:**341
López Michelsen, Alfonso, **2:**506; **4:**267
López Obrador, Manuel Andrés, **4:**267–268
Democratic Revolutionary Party and, **4:**549
election, **2:**110, 308
Federal Electoral Institute and, **3:**192

Fox, Vicente, and, **3:**296
Madrazo, Roberto, and, **4:**318
parallel government, **4:**534
support by Manuel Camacho, **2:**48
López Portillo, José, **4:**268–269, 529–531
banks nationalized by, **1:**477, 479
foreign debt under, **3:**264
Madrid Hurtado, Miguel de la, and, **4:**319–320
Muñoz Ledo Lazo de la Vega, Porfirio, in, **4:**734
Solórzano, Carlos, and, **5:**891
López Pumarejo, Alfonso, **4:**269–270
Gómez Castro, Laureano, on, **3:**469
liberalism, **4:**190
Lleras Camargo, Alberto, and, **4:**48
Lleras Restrepo, Carlos, and, **4:**248
presidency, **2:**505, 520
Santos, Eduardo, and, **5:**755
López Rega, José, **4:**270–271
Valenzuela, Luisa, on, **6:**269
López Reyes, Walter, Roberto Suazo Córdova and, **5:**951
López Tarso, Ignacio, **4:**271
López Trujillo, Alfonso, **4:**271
López Vallecillos, Italo, **4:**272
López Velarde, Ramón, **4:**272
modernism, **4:**232
López y Fuentes, Gregorio, **4:**272–273
López y Planes, Vicente
Alsina, Valentín, and, **1:**123
resignation of, **5:**728
Urquiza, Justo José de, and, **6:**207
Loranzana, Francisco, Jacobo de Villaurrutia, and, **6:**383
Lord Executor Kitchener, **2:**47
Lord of Miracles (Lima), **2:**221
Lorena, Frederico de, **3:**247
Lorençana, Marcello, **4:**629
Lorenz, Max, **3:**800
Lorenzana, Manuel de, Luis de Bolaños and, **1:**603
Lorenzana y Buitrón, Francisco Antonio de, **4:**273
Lorenz curve, **3:**800, *800*
Lorenzo Fernández, Oscar, **4:**745
Lorenzo Troya, Victoriano, **4:**273–274
Loreto (Peru), **4:**274
Loronha, Fernão de, **2:**542; **4:**356
Lorscheider, Aloísio, **2:**223
in National Conference of Brazilian Bishops, **1:**747
Losada, Diego de, **4:**274–275
founding of Caracas, **2:**90
Los Altos (Guatemala), **4:**275–276
regionalism, **5:**513
Los Angeles Music Center Opera, **2:**837

Los Carpinteros (art collective, Cuba), **1:**361
Los Cayos expeditions (war of independence), **1:**201
Los Compadres, **2:**558
Los Compontes (Puerto Rico), **5:**410–411
Los de abajo (Azuela), **1:**433
Los Estados Unidos de Centro América. *See* Central America, United Provinces of
Los Guadalupes (Mexico), **5:**766
Los Jairas (folk ensemble), **2:**229
Los que se van (Aguilera Malta), **1:**65
The Lost World (Conan Doyle), **3:**605
Lothe, André, **1:**508, 567
Lott, Henrique Batista Duffles Teixeira, **2:**23; **4:**276–277
Louisiana, **4:**277–278
Apalachee in, **1:**202
Battle of Baton Rouge, **1:**518
ceded to France, **5:**923
Cuban Americans in, **3:**712
lwa in, **4:**296
under Navarro, Martín Antonio, **4:**800
New Orleans, **4:**816–817
O'Reilly, Alejandro, and, **4:**908
slave revolts in, **5:**860
System of Penal Law (Livingston), **4:**245
Louisiana Revolt of 1768, **4:**278–279
Louis XIV of France, **3:**317
Louis XVI of France, **3:**250; **5:**327, 899–900
Louis XVIII of France, **3:**207
Loukotka, Čestmír, **3:**820
Lourdes Santiago, María de, **5:**417
Louverture, Toussaint, **4:**279–281
abolition of slavery by, **5:**870
assessments of, **4:**280–281
Boyer, Jean-Pierre, and, **1:**676
Christophe, Henri, and, **2:**404
Dessalines, Jean Jacques, and, **2:**797
French settlers under, **3:**317
Haiti, **3:**620–621, 623
Leclerc, Charles, and, **4:**160
as military officer, **4:**279, *280*
Pétion, Alexandre Sabès, and, **5:**207
pre-revolutionary years, **4:**279
Rigaud, André, and, **5:**543
Rochambeau, Donatien de, and, **5:**582
as ruler, **4:**280
Sonthonax, Léger, and, **5:**900
Low, Edward, **5:**253
Lowie, Robert, **4:**839
Lowry, Malcolm, **4:**367
Loyalists (Dominican Republican), **2:**847
Loynaz, Dulce María de, **4:**281

M

Maler, Teobert
Le Plongeon, Augustus, and, **4:**174
in Piedras Negras, **5:**236
and Yaxchilán, **6:**483
Malê slave revolt (Brazil, 1835)
Muslim leaders of, **5:**859
in Salvador, **5:**687
Malespín, Francisco, **4:334–335**
Arce, Manuel Joseé, opposed to,
1:221
Ferrera, Francisco, and, **3:**222
in Nacaome battle, **4:**764
opposition by José Trinidad Cabañas,
2:9
Viteri, Jorge, and, **6:**396
Malfatti, Anita Catarina, **4:335–336**
in Modern Art Week, **4:**647
Monteiro Lobato, José, on, **4:**673
Malfatti, Paulistas Anita, **2:**815
Malgatti, Anita, **1:**147
Malharro, Martín A., **1:**354
La Malhora (Azuela), **4:**235
Malinalco (archaeological site,
Mexico), **4:336**
Malinalli. *See* Malinche
Malinche, **1:**64; **4:336–337,** *337;*
6:447
machismo and, **5:**227
Malinche Show (López), **4:**260
Malinchosmo, **4:**337
Malintzín. *See* Malinche
Malipiero, Riccardo, **6:**260
Mallarino, Manuel María
Bidlack Treaty and, **1:**575
Holguín, Jorge, and, **3:**730
Mallarmé, Stéphane, **5:**847
Mallea, Eduardo, **4:338**
Ocampo, Victoria, and, **4:**877
prose fiction, **4:**237
Sur and, **5:**960
El mal metafísico (Gálvez), **3:**427
Malnutrition
El Salvador, **2:**844; **3:**92
Mexico, **4:**869
Maloca, **4:338–339**
Malones (malocas) (raids), **2:**34; **4:**339
Malraux, André, **1:**683
Maltby, William, **1:**583
Maluf, Flávio, **4:**340
Maluf, Paulo Salim, **4:339–340**
Sarney, José, and, **5:**772
Malu mujer (telenovela), **3:**203
Malval, Robert, **3:**634
Mam, **4:340,** 425
in Maximón, **4:**420
Zaculeu capital of, **6:**497
Mamacocha (Inca sea goddess), **3:**797;
4:341
Mamaindê language, **4:**769
Mamalakis, Markos J., **3:**802, 804,
808, 809

Mama Ocllo, **4:**344
Mamaquilla (Inca goddess), **4:341**
"Mamá X" (Parra), **5:**99
Mambisas (Cuban female soldiers),
4:341–342; 6:449
Mambo, **4:342**
Cuba, **4:**750
by Pérez Prado, Dámaso, **5:**158
Puente, Tito, in, **5:**406
Rodriguez, Tito, **5:**592
son influence on, **5:**897
Mambo Devils (band), **5:**592
"Mambo Diablo" (recording, Puente),
5:406
"Mambo Number Five", **4:**342; **5:**158
Mamby, Juan Ethninius, **4:**341
Mamede, Jurandir, **1:**732
Mamelucos, **4:342; 5:**466–467
Mamita Yunai (Fallas Sibaja), **3:**178,
179
Mamorón (archaeological site,
Colombia), **6:**6
Man (González Camarena), **3:**484
Mañach, Jorge, **1:**357
Mañach y Robato, Jorge, **4:342–343**
Managua (Nicaragua), **4:343–344,** *829*
earthquake, **3:**1; **4:**828
influence of, **4:**825
population, **4:**822
Managua, Protocol of (1993), **3:**857
Managua, Treaty of (1860), **4:**824
Mañana de Reyes (Fabini), **3:**170
Mañana los guerreros (F. Algría), **1:**96
Manati hunting, **4:**825
Manaus (Brazil), **1:**149; **4:**344
and rubber boom, **1:**153
Mancera, Marqués de. *See* Toledo y
Leyva, Pedro de
Manchester Guardian (newspaper,
U.K.)
James, Cyril Lionel Robert, in, **4:**12
Manchete (photo magazine), **2:**759;
6:475
Mancinelli, Luigi, **6:**28
Manco Capac, **4:344–345**
founder of Cuzco, **2:**736
guerrilla movement of, **3:**583
origins of Inca from, **3:**794
Manco Inca, **4:345**
assassination, **6:**259
cooperation with conquistadors,
5:171
founding of Vilcabamba, **6:**371
Pizarro, Francisco, and, **5:**261
Pizarro, Hernando, and, **5:**262–263
Pizarro, Pedro, and, **5:**264
Mandamientos, **4:345–346**
forced wage labor, **2:**758
Mandorla, **4:**215
Mandragón, Manuel, **2:**759
Mandu Ladino, **4:**346
The Man-Eating Myth (Arens), **2:**75

Manet, Eduardo, **6:**72
Manfredo, Fernando, **5:**34
La manga (Scalabrini), **5:**774
Mangabeira, Otávio, **1:**443
Manganese
in Amazon region, **1:**154
Argentina, **2:**600
Brazil, **4:**605
Latin American production, **4:**614
Mangelsdorf, Paul, **4:**330
Mangue (Segall), **5:**793
Mangueira (Brazil), **5:**692
Mani, **4:**433
"El manicero" (song, Azpiazú), **4:**750
Manifestes (Huidobro), **3:**761
Manifesto a la República mejicana
(Figueroa), **6:**500
"Manifesto antropofágico" (Andrade),
1:147; **2:**75
influence on *tropocalismo,* **6:**139
"Manifesto Antropófago" (Andrade),
4:222
"Manifesto da poesia pau Brasil"
(Andrade), **1:**147
Manifesto de Montecristi (Martí),
2:709
Manifesto do fico (Pereira), **5:**151
Manifesto música nova
Mendes, Gilberto, and, **4:**469
Manifesto of Monte Christi, **3:**474
Manifesto regionalista de 1926
(Lins do Rego), **4:**212
*Manifiesto de José del Valle a la nación
guatemalteca* (Valle), **6:**273
Manigat, Leslie François, **3:**633
Manila (Philippines), **5:**321
Manila, Audiencia of, **1:**397
Manila Galleon, **4:346–347**
in Acapulco, **1:**10
arrival of first Chinese, **2:**389
and Asians in Latin America, **1:**370
built in the Philippines, **5:**221–222
Japanese trade and, **4:**13
Pérez, Juan, and, **5:**153
route for by Urdaneta, Andrés de,
6:202
Manini Ríos, Pedro, **6:**246
Manioc, **4:347–349**
Amazon region, **1:**151
Brazil, **5:**233
in cuisines, **2:**719
domestication, **1:**46
fazenda in, **3:**190
Manizales (Colombia), **1:**198
Manley, Michael Norman, **4:**349;
5:790
social justice under, **4:**11
Manley, Norman Washington,
4:349–350
Bustamante, William, and, **1:**816
Manley, Michael Norman, and, **4:**349
and West Indies Federation, **6:**431

Martorell, Antonio, **4:**403; **6:**73

Martyr, Peter, **4:**403–404
  hurricanes, **3:**769
  on manioc, **4:**348
The Martyr of Olaya (Castro), **1:**350

Marulanda Vléz, Manuel (Pedro
  Antonio Marín), **2:**525

Marxism
  Batllism compared with, **1:**518
  Bolivia, **1:**635
  Brazil, **1:**763
  Chile
    Movement of the Revolutionary
      Left, **2:**369
    Pinochet, Augusto, **5:**243, 244
  Dalton García, Roque, and, **2:**741
  and dependency theory, **2:**792–793
  Faoro, Raymundo, on, **3:**184
  Farabundo Martí National Liberation
    Front and, **3:**100
  fascism and, **3:**187
  Federation of Bolivian University
    Students and, **1:**633
  Flores Galindo, Alberto C., in, **3:**244
  Guatemala, **3:**547
  Gutiérrez, Gustavo, in, **3:**597
  Guzmán, Abimael, and, **3:**608
  on imperialism, **3:**790
  indigenism and, **4:**796
  James, Cyril Lionel Robert, on,
    4:12
  John Paul II on, **4:**40
  liberation theology and, **4:**193, 194
  Mariátegui, José Carlos, in, **4:**374
  Martí, José, in, **4:**402
  Molina Garmendia, Enrique, on,
    4:657
  neoliberalism and, **4:**806
  in Nicaragua, **4:**829
  Peru
    Shining Path, **2:**753; **5:**189,
      202–204
  philosophy of, **5:**225
  Prebisch, Raúl, on, **5:**340
  race and ethnicity and, **5:**473
  sociology of art, **3:**387
  Sodré, Nelson, in, **5:**885
  Sousa, Luiza, in, **5:**912
  state corporations in, **5:**940
  in universities, **6:**199
  Venezuela, **1:**571
La Mary (film), **3:**438

Maryknoll Order, **2:**222; **4:**404–405
  D'Escoto Brockmann, Miguel, and,
    2:795–796
  Melville, Thomas and Margarita, in,
    4:467
  murder of nuns in El Salvador,
    2:754, 852
El mar y tú (Burgos), **1:**813

MAS. *See* Movement to Socialism
  (Venezuela)

Más Afuera. *See* Juan Fernández Islands

Masagua, Battle of (1855), **2:**9

Más Allá (magazine, Argentina)
  science fiction in, **5:**787

Más a Tierra. *See* Juan Fernández Islands

Masato, **1:**86

Mas Canosa, Jorge, **4:**405

Máscara puertorriqueña (Arriví), **1:**330

Mascardi, Nicolás, **1:**489

Mascarenhas, Fernão de
  (count of Torre), **2:**875

Masferrer, Alberto, **3:**91; **4:**405–406
  in Generation of the 1930s, **1:**682
  mínimum vital program, **1:**216
  Salazar, Salvador, and, **5:**673

Masó, Bartolomé, **2:**270

Mason, Alden, **3:**820

Mason, John Y., **4:**936

Masonic Orders, **4:**406–408
  Allende, Salvador, and, **1:**110
  anticlericalism, **1:**193
  Brazil
    Inconfidéncia dos Alfaiates,
      3:810–811
    Bustamante, Anastasio, and, **1:**815
    Catholic Church on, **1:**703–704, 705
    Groot, José Manuel, in, **3:**516
    Guerrero, Vicente, and, **3:**578
    Mac-Iver Rodríguez, Enrique, in,
      4:311
  Mexico
    expulsion of the Spaniards, **4:**544
    Fagoaga, José María, in, **3:**174
    Gómez Pedraza, Manuel, and,
      3:472
    O'Donojú, Juan, and, **4:**879
    political parties based on, **4:**512
    Sánchez, Francisco Manuel, in,
      5:705
  Mora, José María Luis, in, **4:**690
  Poinsett, Joel Roberts, and, **5:**277
  Ramos, José, in, **5:**491
  Saldías, Adolfo, in, **5:**675
  Sandino, Augusto César, in, **5:**709
  Sanjuanistas and, **5:**718
  use of the lodges by Carlos Manuel
    de Céspedes, **2:**270
  See also Caballeros Orientales
    (Masonic lodge, Montevideo);
    escoceses (Scottish rite Masonic
    lodges); *yorkinos*

*The Massacre in the [Aztec] Main
  Temple* (Charlot), **2:**292

Massenet, Jules, **5:**693

Massera, Emilio Eduardo, **4:**408–409

Massera, José Pedro, **4:**409

Mass media
  and AIDS prevention, **1:**20
  migration and, **4:**580

Masson, Ernst, **5:**240

Masson, Nicolas, **3:**117

Mass transportation, **6:**32–33

Massú, Nicolás, **5:**932

Mastretta, Angeles, **4:**409

Mastrogiovanni, Antonio, **4:**409–410,
  746

Mata, Eduardo, **4:**410, 741
  Halffter, Rodolfo, teacher of, **3:**634
  Lavista, Mario, and, **4:**153

Mata, Filomeno, **4:**45

Matacapán (archaeological site,
  Mexico), **4:**410–411

"El matadero" (Echeverría), **1:**655;
  4:229

Mata Marinheiro riots (Brazil), **5:**337

Matamoros, Miguel, **4:**704

Matamoros y Guridi, Mariano,
  4:411–412
  Morelos y Pavón, José María, and,
    4:707
  portrait by José Obregón, **4:**873

La Matanza (El Salvador, 1930s),
  1:44; **3:**91; **4:**412
  influence on Claribel Algría, **1:**95

La Matanza de Cholula (Parra), **5:**98

Mataquito, Second Battle of (1557),
  4:150–151

Matarile (Subero), **5:**953

Matas, Julio, **6:**72

Match Ball (Skármeta), **5:**857

Le mât de cocagne (Depestre), **1:**103;
  2:794

Mateo Sagasta, Práxedes, **5:**411

Materia de testamento (Rojas), **4:**236

Materia prima (Berenguer), **1:**561

Maternidad, **5:**822

The Mathematician (Rivera), **5:**564

Mathew, William, **4:**684

Mathias, Georges, **6:**437

Matienzo, Benjamín, **4:**412–413

Matienzo, José Nicolás, **4:**413
  Rivarola, Rodolfo, and, **5:**563

Matienzo, Juan de, **1:**250

Matiz, F. J., **5:**781

Matlazáhuatl, **2:**825

Mato Grosso (Brazil), **4:**413–414
  gold rush, **3:**458
  missions, **4:**628

Mato Grosso do Sul (Brazil), **4:**414

Matos, Gregório de, **4:**414
  colonial literature, **4:**219–220

Matos, Huber, **2:**681

Matos, Manuel Antonio
  revolt against Cipriano Castro,
    2:198
  revolution by, **6:**327

El matrero (Boero), **1:**595; **4:**746

Matriarchy, **6:**36

Matta, Manuel Antonio
  in Baltimore Incident, **1:**461
  Gallo, Pedro, and, **3:**358

Matta, Roberto, **1:**358

Memorias de Ponce (Ferré), **3:**219

Memorias de Subdesarrollo (film, Gutiérrez Alea), **2:**416

Mémorias de um sargento de milícias (Almeida), **1:**116; **4:**221

Memorias de un abandero (Espinosa), **3:**138

Memorias de un autor teatral (Acevedo Hernández), **1:**13

Memorias de un caminante (Candanedo), **2:**68

Memorias de un cortesano (Balaguer), **1:**449

Memorias de un medico higienista (Coni), **2:**576

Memorias de un Sacristán (García), **3:**386

Memorias diarias de la guerra del Brasil (Albuquerque Coelho), **2:**472

Memórias do cárcere (film, Santos), **2:**424; **5:**756

Memórias do cárcere (Ramos), **5:**490–491

Memórias do Institute Oswaldo Cruz (journal), **4:**936

Memoria sobre el plebiscito tacneño (Edwards), **3:**70

Memoria sobre la vagancia (Saco), **5:**656

Memoria sobre ortografía americana (Sarmiento), **5:**768

Memorias o reminiscencias históricas sobre la guerra del Paraguay (Centurión), **2:**257–258

Memorias para la historia del antiguo reino de Guatemala (García Peláez), **3:**398

Memorias para la historia de la revolución de Centro-América (Montúfar), **4:**686

Memorias para la historia de Tejas (Filísola), **3:**234

Memórias póstumas de Brás Cubas (Machado), **4:**221, 307

Memórias sentimentais de João Miramar (Andrade), **1:**180

Memory of Silence (Commission for Historical Clarification, Guatemala), **6:**146

Mena, Cristóbal de, **4:**19

Mena, Juan de, **1:**189

Mena, Luis

Menchú Tum, Rigoberta, **1:**190; **3:***827;* **4:**78, *425,* **468–469;** **6:**454

   in Guatemalan civil war, **3:**553

   on *machismo,* **5:**227

   member of Catholic Action, **2:**213

   Nobel Peace Prize, **4:**426

   in peace accords, **3:**554

and repatriations of Guatemalan Indians, **1:**387

and Vieques Protests, **6:**368

Mencos, Martín Carlos de, **3:**780

Mendel, Gregor, **5:**464

Mendes, Chico

   nature reserve named for, **5:**806

   Rubber Gatherers' Unions and, **5:**633

Mendes, Gilberto, **4:**469

   Duprat, Rogério, and, **2:**870

   Koellreutter, Hans Joachim, and, **4:**86

   and Música Nova, **4:**893

Mendes da Rocha, Paulo, **1:**240; **4:**94

Mendes de Almeida, Cândido, **1:**739

Mendes Filho, Francisco Chico Alves, **3:**123, 166; **4:**469–470

Mendes Maciel, Antônio Vicente, **1:**709

Méndez, Casto, **2:**386

Mendez, Josue, **2:**420

Méndez, Leopoldo, **6:**10

Méndez, Ramón Ignacio, **6:**324

Méndez, Tomás, **2:**67

Méndez Ballester, Manuel, **4:**470–471

Méndez Fleitas, Epifanio, **4:**471

   Stroessner, Alfredo, and, **5:**71–73

Méndez Montenegro, Julio César, **4:**471–472

   Asturias, Miguel, and, **1:**380

   counterinsurgency campaign, **1:**212

   human rights under, **3:**548

   Mano Blanca and, **3:**565–566

   Peralta Azurdia, Enrique, and, **5:**149

   Turcios Lima, Luis, and, **6:**159

Méndez Montenegro, Mario, **4:**472–473

   assassination of, **3:**548

   and Esquilaches, **3:**140

   Méndez Montenegro, Julio César, and, **4:**472

Méndez Pereira, Octavio, **4:**473

Mendez v. *Westminster* (U.S., 1946), **3:**704

Mendiburu, Manuel de, **4:**473

Mendieta, Carlos, **2:**678

Mendieta, Salvador, **4:**473–474

   Central American unionist movement, **2:**242

Mendieta y Montefur, Carlos, **2:**688; **4:**474–475

Mendinueta y Múzquiz, Pedro de, **3:**167; **4:**475

Mendive, Manuel, **1:**361

Mendive, Rafael María, **4:**400

Mendívil, Hilario, **5:**527

Mendonça, Maisa, **5:**845

Mendonça Furtado, Diogo de, **1:**82

Mendoza (Argentina), **4:**475–476

   founding, **1:**250

Hurtado de Mendoza, García, namesake of, **3:**771

Lencinas, Carlos, in, **4:**167

railroads, **5:**482

Mendoza, Alonso de, **4:**132

Mendoza, Antonio de, **4:**476–477

   Alvarado, Pedro de, and, **1:**133

   land, standard size of *caballería and peonía,* **2:**3

   Las Casas, Bartolomé de, and, **4:**141

   in Mercedarians, **4:**486

   Mixtón War, **4:**642

   New Laws of 1542 and, **4:**815

   New Spain under, **4:**504, 819

   search for Seven Cities of Cíbola, **5:**820

   Vázquez de Coronado, Francisco, protégé of, **6:**298

   Zumárraga and, **6:**525

Mendoza, Carlos Antonio, **4:**477

   Porras, Belisario, and, **5:**298

Mendoza, Cristóbal, **6:**479

Mendoza, Diego, **6:**379

Mendoza, Francisco de, **1:**7; **3:**164

Mendoza, Jaime, **4:**477–478

Mendoza, Pedro de, **3:**162; **4:**478

   Abreu, Diego de, in expedition of, **1:**6

   Ayolas, Juan de, and, **1:**421

   Buenos Aires settled by, **1:**800

   founding of Buenos Aires, **1:**249

   García, Diego, and, **3:**384

   Irala, Domingo Martínez de, and, **3:**868

   Paraguay explorations, **5:**59

Mendoza Caamaño y Sotomayor, José Antonio de, **4:**478–479

Mendoza Ometochtzin, Carlos, **6:**525

Mendoza y Luna, Juan Manuel de, **4:**479

Menem, Carlos Saúl, **4:**82, 479–480, *480*

   Alsogaray, Álvaro, adviser to, **1:**124

   arab descent, **1:**205

   candidate of the Justicialist Party, **1:**206

   delegative democracy and, **2:**764

   and DiTella, Guido, **2:**828

   and Duhalde, Eduardo, **2:**868

   election, **1:**276

   fishing industry under, **3:**236–237

   general amnesty decree, **6:**389

   homosexuality under, **5:**828

   Islam and, **3:**881

   in Israel, **3:**883

   judiciary under, **4:**61

   Krieger, Adalberto, and, **4:**92

   and labor movement, **1:**289

Morínigo, Higínio, **4:712–713;**
   5:70–71
  Bray, Arturo, and, **1:687**
  Chaves, Federico, and, **2:297**
  Colorado Party and, **5:81**
  constitution under, **5:76**
  Franco, Rafael, and, **3:303**
  Stroessner, Alfredo, and, **5:948**
  Zubizarreta's arrest under, **6:523**
Morínigo, Marcos, **1:8**
Morisseau, Roland, **5:217**
Morley, Sylvanus Griswold, **1:224;**
   2:312; 4:713–714
Morlon de Menéndez, Pilar, **3:201**
Morlon y Menéndez, Pilar, **2:695**
"Le morne de Massabielle" (Condé),
  2:568
El Moro (Marroquín), **4:390**
Morocco, observer status in OAS, **1:205**
Morones, Luis, **4:546, 714–715**
  government patronage by, **4:524**
Morris, Craig, **4:736**
Morris, Mary, **6:131**
Morris, Robert, **4:1**
Morrow, Dwight Whitney, **4:715**
  and Cristero Rebellion, **2:657**
Morse, Richard, **4:715–716**
Morse, Wayne, **3:352**
Mors ex vita (Palma), **5:18**
Mortara, Giogio, **5:287**
Morte e vida severina (Melo Neto), **4:223**
  Buarque, Chico, music for, **1:792**
Mortgage banks, **1:475**
Mortorell, Alejandra, **4:403**
Morúa, Friar, **4:486**
Mosaddeq, Mohammed, **2:869**
El Mosaico (journal, Colombia), **2:810**
Mosaico group, **4:390**
Mosaic Web browser, **3:865–866**
Mosca, Enrique N., **1:294**
Moscas sobre el mármol (Heiremans),
  3:646
Mosconi, Enrique, **1:292**
Moscoso, Mireya, **3:109**
Moscoso, Oscar, **5:255–256**
Moscoso de Alvarado, Luis, **6:55**
Moscote, José Dolores, **4:716**
Moshinsky Borodianksky, Marcos,
  4:716–717
Mosquera, Manuel José, **4:717**
  Herrán, Antonio, and, **3:675**
Mosquera, Tomás Cipriano de,
  4:717–718
  abortive coup, **2:518**
  Arboleda, Julio, and, **1:220**
  Caro, José, and, **2:133**
  González, Florentino, and, **3:480**
  Herrán, Antonio, and, **3:675**
  Herrán, Pedro, and, **3:674**
  Herrera, Tomás, and, **3:679**
  liberalism, **2:500; 4:189**

López, Ambrosio, and, **4:253**
López, José, and, **4:257**
Melo, José María, and, **4:464**
Obando, José, and, **4:870**
opposition of Felipe Zapata, **6:504**
Salgar, Eustorgio, and, **5:679**
in Sante Fe de Bogotá, **1:597**
in Siete de Marzo, **5:841**
Trujillo, Julián, and, **6:142**
Mosquera-Galdiano Agreement
  (1823), **3:55**
Mosquera Narváez, Aurelio, **1:332**
Mosquera y Arboleda, Joaquín,
  4:718–719
Mosquera y Figueroa, Joaquín,
  and Audiencia of Caracas, **2:93**
Mosquitia, Kingdom of, **4:824**
Mosquito Coast, **4:719–721; 6:515**
  Guardiola, Santos, in, **3:537**
  MacGregor, Gregor, in, **4:305**
  Morazán, Francisco, and, **4:703**
Mosquitos. *See* Miskitos
Mota, Agostinho José da, **1:352**
Mota, Edson, **5:842**
Motecuhzoma I, **4:721–722**
  Atahualpa's capture and, **5:170–171**
  capture of, **5:260**
  meeting with Cortés, **4:503**
  Nezahualpilli's prediction to, **4:821**
  and Tlaxcala, **6:90**
Motecuhzoma II, **2:617; 4:722–723**
  Hernández, Francisco, and, **3:672**
  and Quetzalcoatl, **5:439**
Motecuhzoma Inhuicamina, **6:11**
Mothers of the Plaza de Mayo
  (Argentina), **2:823**
Motivos de Proteo (Rodó), **4:232;**
  5:585–586
Motivos de son (Guillén), **3:592; 4:234**
Motolinía, Toribio de, **4:723**
  edition by Edmundo O'Gorman,
  4:882
  and Los Doce, **2:832**
The Motorcycle Diaries (Che Guevara),
  6:129, 131
Motta Diniz, Francisca, **3:199**
The Mountain and Its Era (Borges),
  1:654
Mountain lion. *See* puma
Moura, Cristóvão de, **5:908**
Mourão Filho, Olímpio, **1:776; 2:478**
The Movement (exhibition),
  5:904–905
Movement for a People's Government
  (Uruguay), **4:565**
Movement for Assemblies of the
  People (MAP), **4:814**
Movement for Basic Education
  (MBE, Brazil), **5:555**

Movement for Integration and
  Development (Argentina)
  Frigerio, Rogelio, in, **3:324**
  Frondizi, Arturo, in, **3:326**
Movement for National Liberation
  (MLN, Venezuela).
  See Universidad Central de
  Venezuela
Movement for National Liberation
  (Puerto Rico), **3:710**
Movement for the Creation of the
  State of Tocantins, **6:96**
Movement for the Fifth Republic
  (MVR, Venezuela), **6:334,**
  346–347
Movement of 19 April (M-19)
  (Colombia), **2:524–525**
  under Barco Vargas, Virgilio, **1:488**
  Betancur Cuartas, Belisario, and, **1:573**
  Gaviria Trujillo, César Augusto, and,
  3:417
  Gómez Hurtado, Álvaro, kidnapped
  by, **3:472**
  Navarro Wolff in, **4:801**
  origin of name, **2:522**
Movement of Integration and
  Development (MID, Argentina),
  1:295; 3:325
Movement of National Unity (Chile,
  MUN), **2:368**
Movement of the Revolutionary Left
  (Bolivia, MIR), **1:639**
  and *callampas*, **2:39**
  in Democratic Popular Unity,
  1:638–639
  domination by, **1:635**
  guerrilla tactics of, **3:583**
  in Patriotic Agreement, **1:641–642**
  Paz Estenssoro, Víctor, and, **5:123**
  Paz Zamora, Jaime, in, **5:125**
  political influence, **1:624**
Movement of the Revolutionary Left
  (Chile, MIR), **2:369**
  Communist Party and, **2:550**
Movement of the Revolutionary Left
  (Peru, MIR), **5:199**
  Army of National Liberation and,
  5:202
  Puente Uceda, Luis de la, in,
  5:406–407
Movement of the Revolutionary Left
  (Venezuela, MIR), **6:331**
  and FALN, **6:337**
Movement to Socialism (Venezuela,
  MAS), **1:420; 6:332, 343, 347**
  in Coordinadora Democrática, **6:344**
  influence of Eurocommunism, **2:551**
  Morales, Evo, president of, **1:420**
  Palenque, Carlos, and, **5:17**
  support of Hugo Chávez, **6:346**

Murillo, Bartolomé, **1**:343
Murillo, Pedro Domingo, **1**:615
Murillo Toro, Manuel, **4**:**736**
  Berrío, Pedro, and, **1**:568
  as Gólgota, **3**:460
  Herrán, Antonio, and, **3**:675
  member of Radical Olympus, **2**:523
Murilo de Carvalho, José, **1**:707;
  2:778
"El muro" (Los Tigres del Norte),
  6:78–79
Muró, Antonio
  in Economic Society of Guatemala,
  3:559
  Goicoechea, José, and, **4**:199
Los muros vacíos (Azar), **1**:422
Murphy, Gerald, **3**:352
Murra, John V., **4**:**736–737**
  on Aymara, **1**:419
Murtinho, Joaquim Duarte, **4**:737
Musa, Said, **3**:143; **4**:**738–739**
  on Belize, **1**:536
  government of, **1**:544–545
  Price, George, and, **5**:365
Museo de Antigüedades e Historia
  Nacional (Mexico), **1**:73
Museo del Arte Costarricense
  Naranjo, Carmen, and, **4**:773
Museo del Oro (Bogotá), **1**:466
Museo de Pueblo Maya (Mexico),
  2:885
Museo Histórica Nacional (Peru), and,
  6:43
El Museo Mexicano (periodical),
  2:724
Museo Nacional de Antropología e
  Historia (Mexico), **1**:566
Museo Nacional de Antropología y
  Arqueología (Peru), **6**:43
Los museos abandonados (Peri Rossi),
  5:159
El museo vacio (Traba), **6**:122
Museu de Arte da Bahia, **6**:271
Museu de Arte de São Paulo, **2**:295
Museum of Modern Art (Bogotá),
  6:122
Museum of Modern Art of Latin
  America, **4**:303
Mushrooms, hallucinogetic, **2**:860
Music, **4**:**739–756**
  aboriginal, **1**:118
  African musical instruments, **1**:41
  Afrocubanismo, **3**:387–388
  Araucanian, **3**:879–880
  Argentina
    avant-garde, **2**:801
    tango, **2**:823
  art music, **4**:**739–747**
    Argentina, **4**:131
    Brazil, **4**:114–115, 801–802, 843
    Uruguay, **4**:123

bachata, **1**:436
baião, **1**:446–447
Ballet Folklórico de México, **1**:456
bolero, **1**:604
bossa nova, **1**:659–660
  Jobim, Antônio Carlos, and,
    4:38–39
  Brazil, **3**:290; **4**:745, 806–807
    jovem guarda movement, **2**:127
    Música Nova, **2**:870
    popular, **4**:751–752
    rock music, **5**:584
    Tropicália movement, **2**:870
    Villa-Lobos, Heitor, and, **6**:378
  calypso, **2**:47
  canción ranchera, **2**:67, 761
  cantoria, **2**:78
  choro, **2**:398
  concrete, **1**:586–587
  corridos, **2**:**613**
    Los Tigres del Norte and, **6**:78
  Cuba, **1**:800
  Cuban Americans in, **3**:712
  cueca, **2**:711–712
  cumbia, **2**:723–724
  danzón, **4**:750
  education
    Aguirre, Julián, and, **1**:68
    in Chile, **1**:112
  fado, **3**:173–174
  folk
    Brazil, **3**:476–477
    Yupanqui and, **6**:494
  gaúcho, **3**:416
  Guatemala, National Symphony
    Orchestra, **1**:229
  huayno, **3**:756–757
  impact of migrations on, **4**:584
  indianismo, **3**:813
  indigenous, **2**:194
  jongo, **4**:41–42
  lunfardo in, **4**:291
  mambo, **4**:342
  mariachi, **4**:373–374
  maroon, **4**:382
  maxixe, **4**:421
  modinha, **4**:649
  MPB: Música Popular Brasileira,
    4:728–729
  Música Novo, **2**:870
  nationalism and, **1**:112
  norteño, **2**:854
  nueva canción movement, **6**:494
    Sosa, Mercedes, in, **5**:902
  opera, **2**:836–837
  of Otavalans, **4**:937
  payador, **5**:116–117
  Peru, **3**:731

popular music and dance,
  4:**747–754**
  Argentina, **6**:14–15
  banda de pífanos, **1**:468–469
  Brazil, **4**:123–124, 860; **5**:688
  Nascimento, Milton, **4**:779–780
  huayno, **3**:756–757
  lambada, **4**:123–124
  Mexico, **4**:136, 803
  New Chilean Song, **4**:15
  pre-Columbian music of
    Mesoamerica, **4**:**754–755**
  Sas, Andrés, on, **5**:773
  pre-Columbian music of South
    America, **4**:**755–756**
  huayno, **3**:756–757
  Puerto Ricans in the United States,
    3:709, 711
  ranchera, **2**:854
  reggae, **5**:790
  roc en español, **2**:24
  rock nacional, **5**:902
  rupestre, **3**:483
  samba, **2**:763; **5**:690–691
  ska, **5**:790
  son, **5**:897
  son jarocho, **2**:854
  tango, **6**:15–16
  Tropicália movement, **2**:870
  tropicalismo, **3**:433–434; **6**:139
  See also mariachi
Música (Paz), **5**:120
Música ao longe (Veríssimo), **6**:355
Música de cámara (Ardévol), **1**:243
Música de Parnasso (Oliveira), **4**:893
Musical instruments, **4**:**757–758**
  Andean, **4**:749, 753
  banda de pífanos, **1**:468–469
  caña de millo, **2**:724
  carimbó, **2**:125
  charango, **2**:229
  gaita hembra, **2**:724
  marimba, **4**:376–377
  pre-Columbian, **4**:754–756
  Rodriguez, Arsenio, and, **5**:589
  Sepp, Anton, workshop, **5**:800–801
  teponazhuéhuetl (drum), **4**:754, 755
  teponaztli (drum), **4**:754, 755, 757
La música Maya-Quiché (Castillo),
  2:194
The Music and the Song (mural,
  Tamayo), **6**:13
Música Nova (musical group)
  Mendes, Gilberto, in, **4**:469
  Oliveira, Willy Correia de, in,
    4:893
  and Rogério Duprat, **2**:870
Música para pequeña orquesta
  (Ardévol), **1**:243

National Democratic Union of Brazil
(UDN) *(continued)*
Sarney, José, in, **5:**771–772
on Vargas, Getúlio, **1:**712
National Democratic Union Party
(Brazil), **6:**25
National Department of Drought-
Fighting Works (DNOCS, Brazil),
2:859
*National Directory of Latin
Americanists,* **4:**198
National Economic Development Bank
(Brazil), **2:**62
National Educational Workers Union
(Mexico), **4:**723–724
National Endowment for Democracy
(NED), **4:**782–783
International Republican Institute
and, **3:**865
National Falangist Party (Chile), **2:**370
Aylwin, Patricio, and, **1:**418
formation, **2:**339–340, 361
National Farm Labor Union, **3:**349
National Farmworkers Association.
See United Farm Workers Union
National Federation of Coffee Growers
(Colombia), **2:**476, 503, **515–516**
effect on agrarian reform, **2:**514
National Federation of Printing
Workers (Brazil), **5:**137
National Feminist Union, **3:**201
National Free University of Mexico,
5:281–282
National Front (Colombia,
1958–1974), **2:**506–508, 520, **522**
democracy survival during, **2:**782
Lleras Camargo, Alberto, **4:**48
return to civilian rule, **6:**390
Valenci, Guillermo, and, **6:**268
National Front (Ecuador), **2:**583
National Front for Struggle against
Repression, in, **3:**781
National Front of Organizations and
Citizens (FNOC, Mexico), **4:**550
National Guard (Brazil), **1:**747–748;
3:196
Praieira Revolt, **5:**337
Regency and, **1:**770
National Guard (Dominican
Republic), **2:**840
National Guard (Panama)
flag riots and, **5:**33
rise of, **5:**26
National Guatemalan Revolutionary
Unity (URNG), **2:**262; **3:**564
Guatemalan Labor Party and, **3:**563
guerrilla tactics of, **3:**583
Indian focus of, **3:**579
Ríos Montt, José Efraín, and, **3:**551;
5:557

National Housing Bank (BNH, Brazil),
1:748
National Hydrocarbons Agency
(Colombia), **3:**34
National Independence League
(Paraguay), **5:**943–944
National Independent Convention of
Anti-reelectionist Parties
(Mexico), **5:**247
National Independent Salon, **6:**204
National Indian Foundation (FUNAI,
Brazil), **1:**745, **748–749;**
3:814–815
pacification and, **5:**6
Rondon, Cândido, and, **5:**616
National Indigenous Congress
(Mexico, 1996), **2:**539
National Indigenous Institute
(Mexico), **2:**177
National Institute of Agrarian Reform
(INRA, Cuba), **2:**681
Guevara, Che, in, **3:**585–586
National Institute of Anthropology
and History (INAH, Mexico),
3:71, 103; **4:783–784**
excavations at Toniná, **6:**103
National Institute of Cinema
(Argentina), **2:**417
National Institute of Colonization and
Agrarian Reform (INCRA,
Brazil), **1:749–750**
National Institute of Fine Arts
(Mexico)
Chávez, Carlos, founding director,
2:298
Glantz, Margo, in, **3:**442
music department
Enríquez, Manuel, and, **3:**120
Opera de Cámara, **1:**85
National Institute of Industry and
Tourism (Cuba), **1:**17
National Institute of Vitiviniculture
(INV, Argentina), **6:**444
National Insurance Bank (Costa Rica),
2:633
National Intelligence Agency (SNI,
Brazil), **3:**228, 456
National Intelligence Service (SIN,
Peru)
Fujimori, Alberto, and, **5:**190
Nationalism, **4:783–787**
anti-globalization, **3:**445
architecture and, **1:**235
Argentina
Gálvez, Manuel, in, **3:**362–363
Ibarguren, Carlos, in, **3:**779
Illia, Arturo Umberto, in,
3:787–788
Jauretche, Arturo M., on, **4:**17–18
Scalabrini, Raúl, in, **5:**774–775

black, Jamaica, **4:**11
Bolivia, **5:**671
Brazil
Instituto Históricoe Geográfico
Brasileiro, **3:**846
Lima, Jorge de, and, **4:**203
music, **4:**570
Pôrto Alegre, Manuel, and, **5:**308
Silva Xavier, Joaquim, in, **5:**852
social organization and, **4:**5
British-Latin American relations and,
1:785
concept of national art, **1:**356
Cuba, **4:**402
Dominican Republic, **4:**462–463
El Salvador, **3:**88
fascism and, **3:**187–188
of Fidel Castro, **2:**203
food and cookery in, **3:**257
Freyre, Gilberto, on, **3:**322
Guyana, **4:**3
Haiti, **3:**626–627
Roumain, Jacques, and, **5:**631
highways and, **3:**692
immigration control and, **4:**568
imperialism and, **3:**790
Jacobinism, **4:**1–2
Japanese, **4:**14
medicine and, **4:**450–451
Mexico
Cuauhtemoc symbol of, **2:**665
cultural, **1:**456
in dance, **2:**649
Juárez, Benito, and, **4:**51, 53
Mier Noriega y Guerra, José
Servando Teresa de, and,
4:569
Virgin of Guadalupe in, **3:**521
music and, **2:**458, 599, **4:**570
Nicaragua
indigenous roots of national
culture, **2:**609
Sandino, Augusto, in, **5:**709–711
Panama
Community Action, **5:**36
constitutions and, **5:**37
Urracá in, **6:**208
Peru
Pardo y Lavalle, Manuel, in,
5:94
War of the Pacific in, **1:**642
service sector and, **5:**812–813
Southern Cone, **5:**911
sports in, **5:**936
Uruguay, **1:**13; **6:**218
Fernández Crespo, Daniel, in,
3:212
and music, **2:**458

New Historical School, **4**:657
New International Economic Order
  (NIEO)
  Group of 77 on, **6**:176
  Law of the Sea, **4**:155
New Interoceanic Canal Company
  Bunau-Varilla, Philippe, and, **1**:809
New Jewel Movement (Grenada),
  4:814–815
  Bishop, Maurice, in, **1**:581–582
  Gairy, Eric, in, **3**:345
  social class and, **3**:509
  Soviet influence in, **5**:914–915
New Laws of 1542, **4**:815
  in Audiencia of Guatemala,
    3:556
  in Audiencia of Santa Fe de Bogotá,
    1:599
  in Colombia, **2**:493
  creation of the Audiencia de los
    Confines, **1**:398
  Gasca, Pedro, and, **3**:410
  implementation by Luis de Velasco,
    6:305
  on indigenous slaves, **5**:860
  Las Casas, Bartolomé de, and,
    4:141
  López de Cerrato, Alonso, and,
    4:263
  Mendoza, Antonio de, and,
    4:476–477
  Núñez Vela, Blasco, and, **4**:862
  Peru
    under Núñez Vela, Blasco,
      5:171–172
  Pizarro, Gonzalo, and, **5**:262
  protection of Indian labor, **3**:108
  regulation of *encomiendas,* **3**:108
  on slavery of indigenous peoples,
    2:182
New Liberalism movement
  (Colombia), **3**:348
A New Map of Mexico (Arrowsmith),
  2:162
New Mexico, **4**:815–816
  Anglo-American incursions,
    1:321–322
  Benavides, Alonso de, in, **1**:554
  Catholic Church, **5**:142
  colonization, **4**:818
  Comanches allies to the New
    Mexicans, **2**:538
  exploration by Franciscans, **6**:311
  foundation by Juan de Oñate,
    4:899
  in Gadsden Purchase, **3**:342
  genízaro, **3**:426
  judicial system, **1**:495
  livestock, **4**:243
  Melgares, Facundo, in, **4**:461

  Mexican Americans in, **3**:701, 702
  Mexican-American War, **4**:513
  Penitentes, **5**:144–145
  under Pérez, Albino, **5**:152
  Pueblo Indians, **5**:404
  Pueblo Rebellion, **5**:404–405
  Rada, Manuel, in, **5**:476–477
  reconquest, **6**:284
  Revolution of 1837
    Vigil, Donaciano, in, **6**:369
  Santa Fe, **5**:739
  as Seven Cities of Cíbola, **5**:820
  in Treaty of Guadalupe Hidalgo,
    3:522
New National Party (NNP, Grenada),
  3:509–510
New Nicaragua Movement
  Fonseca Amador, Carlos, in, **3**:254
  Mayorga, Silvio, in, **4**:436
New Orleans, **4**:816–817
  Revolt of 1768, **4**:816
New Panama Canal Company, **5**:928
New Progressive Party (PNP, Puerto
  Rico)
  evolution of, **5**:416
  Ferré Aguayo, Luis Antonio, in,
    3:219
New Regulation of the Presidios
  (1772), **4**:765
New School of History (Argentina),
  2:24
New Seven Wonders of the World,
  2:312
New Space (Uruguay), **6**:248
New Spain, colonization of the
  northern frontier, **4**:817–819
  media anata, **4**:442
  Nueva Galicia, **4**:857
  Nuevo Santander, **4**:859
  Rubí, Marqués de, and, **5**:636
New Spain, Viceroyalty of,
  4:819–820
  Apodaca, Juan, and, **5**:642
  Carmelites in, **2**:128
  Central America in, **2**:248
  Franciscans in, **2**:832
  López de Arteaga, Sebastián, and,
    4:263
  Luna, Tristán de, in, **4**:290
  monasteries, **2**:215
  Relaciones Geográficas, **5**:515
  religion, **5**:516
  Revillagigedo, Conde de,
    5:528–529
  viceroyalty, **6**:361
  wine industry, **6**:442–443
The New Statesman (journal), **4**:768
New World, expression, **6**:358
New York and Honduras Rosario
  Mining Company, **3**:735–736

New York City
  Cuban Americans in, **3**:712
  Dominican Americans in, **3**:719
  Machito in, **4**:310
  Mexican Americans in, **3**:699
  Puerto Ricans in, **3**:699, 707, *708,*
    708–709
  Varela y Morales, Félix, in, **6**:283
New Yorker (magazine)
  Kincaid, Jamaica, at, **4**:79
  Timerman, Jacobo, and, **6**:80
New York Graphic Workshop, **2**:53
  Porter, Liliana, in, **5**:306
New York World, **4**:304
Nezahualcoyotl (ruler of Tetzcoco),
  4:820–821; **6**:55
  Alva Ixtlilxochitl on, **1**:128
  design of Chapultepec, **2**:287
  Itzcoatl alliance with, **3**:887–888
  legal code, **4**:502
  literature, **4**:226, *227*
Nezahualpilli, **4**:821
  and Tetzcoco, **6**:55
Nheengaiba tribe, **4**:364
Nhengatú (vulgar Tupi), promotion as
  national language by Pedro II,
  6:156
"Niágara" (Heredia y Heredia),
  3:667; **4**:229
Niagara Falls Conference (1914),
  4:821–822; **6**:352
  Rabasa, Emilio, representative to,
    5:461
Nican mopohua (Lasso de la Vega),
  3:521
Nicaragua, **4**:822–833
  profile, **4**:824
  Afro-Latinos, **1**:39
  agrarian reform
    in 1981, **6**:434
    in 1986, **6**:434
  Algeria and, **1**:206
  amparo, **1**:165
  Area of People's Property, **6**:434
  in Audiencia of Guatemala, **3**:555
  banana industry, **1**:462
  bank nationalization, **1**:480
  Bluefields, **1**:592
  Boliverian Alternative for the
    Americas (ALBA), **3**:659
  boundary disputes, **1**:102, 668;
    2:158
  and CACM, **2**:250
  CAFTA-DR, **3**:657–658
  canal proposals
    Batres Montúfar, José, and,
      1:519
    by Belly, Félix, **1**:548
    Bryan-Chamorro Treaty, **1**:791
    Squier, Ephraim, and, **5**:938

Los Niños Heroes (Mexico), **4**:513

Niños Héroes, **4:840**

Nippon Amazon Aluminum, **1**:520

Nispa ninchis/Decimos diciendo (Murra), **4**:736

Niterói: Revista Brasiliense (journal), **4**:220, 321

Nitrate industry, **4:840–841**

  Bolivia, **4**:840, 841

    after independence, **1**:619

  Chile, **2**:353; **4**:840, 841

    Antofagasta, **1**:198

    Balmaceda, José, in, **1**:458

    impact on economy, **2**:334–335

    Norte Grande, **4**:849

    private ownership of *salitreras,* **2**:334

    under Santa María, Domingo, **5**:741

    during World War I, **6**:465

  effect of technology on, **6**:31

  Peru

    Gibbs and Sons in, **3**:432

    guano industry and, **3**:529

    Morales Bermúdez, Remigio, and, **4**:697

    nationalization of, **1**:666

  W. R. Grace and Company, **3**:500

Nivaclé Indians, **4**:483

Nixon, Richard

  Alliance for Progress, **1**:113

  International Petroleum Company and, **3**:685, 864

  Kissinger, Henry, and, **4**:82–83

  Pinochet, Augusto, and, **5**:243

  reaffirmation on no Cuban invasion pledge, **2**:694

  Rockefeller, Nelson, and, **5**:583

Niza, Marcos de, **2**:215–216; **3**:163; **4:841–842**; **5**:458

  search for Seven Cities of Cíbola, **5**:820; **6**:298

Nobel Prizes

  Chemistry, **4**:165

    Leloir, Luis F., **4**:165, 451

  García Márquez, Gabriel, **3**:392

  García Robles, Alfonso, **3**:399

  Kissinger, Henry, **4**:83

  Literature

    Asturias, Miguel Ángel, **1**:379–380; **4**:237

    García Márquez, Gabriel, **4**:238

    Laguerre, Enrique, **4**:120

    Mistral, Gabriela, **3**:733; **4**:232, 634, *634*

    Neruda, Pablo, **4**:233

    Paz, Octavio, **4**:235; **5**:120

    Walcott, Derek, **6**:405–407

Medicine, **4**:451

Peace

  Arias Sánchez, Oscar, **1**:310; **2**:587, 637; **3**:141

  Carter, Jimmy, **2**:153

  Menchú, Rigoberta, **2**:213; **3**:553; **4**:426, 468; **6**:454

  Pérez Esquivel, Adolfo, **3**:765; **5**:156, 809

  Saavedra Lamas, Carlos, **5**:650

  Science, **4**:654

Noblat, Ricardo, **4**:45

Noboa, Álvaro, **3**:48, 50

Noboa Bejarano, Gustavo, **3**:49; **4:842**

  Mahuad, Jamil, and, **4**:327

Noboa y Arteta, Diego, **4:842–843**

Nobre, Carlos, **4**:745

Nobre, Marlos, **4:843**

Nóbrega, Manuel da, **2**:215, 480; **4:843–844**

  Anchieta, José de, and, **1**:171

  in Brazil, **1**:694

  Brazil mission of, **4**:20

  Sousa, Tomé de, and, **5**:910

Noche al raso (Roa Bárcena), **5**:572

La noche del aguafiestas (Arrufat), **1**:333

La Noche del Diez (television program), **4**:363

La noche de los asesinos (Triana), **4**:236; **6**:133

Noche de luna (Samudio), **5**:695

La noche de Tlatelolco (Poniatowska), **5**:283

La noche es virgen (Bayly), **1**:521

La noche oscura del Niño Avilés (Rodríguez Juliá), **5**:596

Las noches (Rueda), **5**:637

La noche transfigurada (Magaña), **4**:322

Noche Triste (30 June 1520), **2**:617; **4:844–845**

  Alvarado y Mesía, Pedro de, and, **1**:132

Nociones de derecho constitucional (Valle), **6**:272

Nocioni, Andrés, **5**:932

"Nocturno" (Silva), **4**:231

El nocturno a Rosario (Cantón), **2**:78

Nocturno de Bujara (Pitol), **5**:256

"Nocturno III" (Silva), **4**:847

Noé, Luis Felipe, **1**:359, 361; **4:845**

Noel, Carlos, **1**:234

Noel, Martín, **1**:240

Nó em Pingo D'Água (band), **1**:164

Nogales Treaty (1793), **4**:278

Nogueira, Eduardo Angelim, **2**:8–9

No habrá más penas ni olvido (Soriano), **5**:901

Noigandres (art group, Brazil), **2**:59

Noigandres (magazine, Brazil), **2**:567

Noirism, 2:883

Noiriste Party (Haiti), **3**:148

"Noite de almirante" (Machado de Assis), **4**:307

A noite de São João (musical, Alencar and Lobo), **1**:100

Nolasco, Peter, **4**:485

Nolasco Colón, Pedro, **4**:741

Noli Me Tangere (Rizal), **5**:222

Nomads of the seas. *See* Yamana (Yaghanes)

Nombre de Dios (Panama), **2**:858

Nombres y figuras (Pizarnik), **5**:258

No me agarrarán viva: La mujer salvadoreña en la lucha (Claribel Alegría and Flakoll), **1**:95

"No meio do caminho" (Andrade), **1**:176

No me preguntes cómo pasa el tiempo (Pacheco), **5**:3

Non-Aligned Movement, **1**:32, 205; **3**:882

  Argentina, **1**:275

  Panama, **6**:117

Nonetos (Villa-Lobos), **6**:378

Non-governmental organizations

  environmental movement and, **3**:122

  human rights, **3**:766

  indigenous organizations and, **3**:823

  indigenous peoples and, **3**:828

  and truth commissions, **6**:146

  women in, **6**:454

Nonintervention doctrine

  Calvo Doctrine and, **2**:46

  Inter-American System, **3**:859

Nonoalca, **6**:100

Non-Proliferation Treaty (NPT) (1968), **4**:854

Nootka Indians, **1**:79

Nootka Sound Conventions (1790), **5**:8

Nootka Sound expeditions, **4**:728

No pasó nada (Skármeta), **5**:857

Ñorairõ ñemomb'u Guérra Guasúro guare (Gamba), **3**:534

Nord, Pierre Alexis, **4:845–846**

Nordenflicht, Thaddeus von, **3**:118, 750

  mining mission, **5**:179

Nord-Sud (periodical, Paris), **3**:760, 761

Noriega Moreno, Manuel Antonio, **4:846–847**

  Bush, George H. W., and, **2**:245; **6**:184, *184*

  Carter, Jimmy, and, **2**:153–154

  driven from Panama City, **5**:35

  military dictatorship of, **4**:594

Noriega Moreno, Manuel Antonio
  (continued)
 military under, **5:**28
 opposition by Arnulfo Arias Madrid,
   1:309
 opposition by Ricardo Aras Calderón,
   1:307
Noriega y Guerra, Mier, **1:**816
"Norma Culta" project, **5:**924
Normal Institute for Girls (Montevideo,
   Uruguay), **4:**285–286
Noronha, Fernão de, **4:**847
 as administrator, **1:**691
 Fernando de Noronha discovered by,
   3:218
Norsk Hydro, **1:**520
El Norte (Nava), **4:**798
Norte Chico (Chile), **4:**847–848
 migrants to Antofagasta, **1:**198
 precontact society, **5:**343–344
Norte Chico (Peru), **4:**848
Norte Grande (Chile), **4:**848–849;
   6:18
Norteño (music)
 and Lila Downs, **2:**854
 Los Tigres del Norte and, **6:**78–79
Norte-Sul Railway (Brazil), **4:**365
North, John Thomas, **1:**458
North, Oliver, **2:**592
North American Free Trade Agreement
   (NAFTA), **4:**849–850
 agriculture and, **1:**58
 automobile industry and, **1:**404
 CANACINTRA and, **2:**49
 Caribbean and, **2:**117, 118
 debate over, **6:**185
 drug trafficking and, **6:**191
 effect on Puerto Rico, **4:**903
 environmental and labor impact of,
   3:272
 fascism and, **3:**189
 Federation of Mexican Labor and,
   4:545
 foreign investment in, **3:**271
 Free Trade Area of the Americas and,
   3:306
 globalization and, **3:**446
 hemispheric affairs, **3:**656, *657*,
   657–658
 impact of on foreign trade, **3:**278
 indigenous peoples and, **3:**826–827
 labor movements, **4:**107
 Latin American Free Trade
   Association (LAFTA) and, **4:**149
 maize in, **4:**331–332
 maquiladoras, **4:**360–361
 Mexico petroleum industry,
   5:213–214
 National Peasant Federation and,
   4:548

 protests against, **4:***532*
 Saint Lucia affected by, **5:**668
 Velázquez Sánchez, Fidel, and, **6:**310
North Atlantic Alliance, Rio Treaty
   (1947) and, **5:**558
Northeastern Brazil Integration
   Development Program
   (POLONOROESTE, Brazil),
   5:617
Northeastern Generation of 1930
 Lins do Rego, José, in, **4:**211
Northern Cemetery (Recoleta, Buenos
   Aires), **5:**506
Northern Railroad (Guatemala), **5:**407
Northwest Passage. *See* Strait of Anián
No se lo digas a nadie (Bayly), **1:**521
No sos vos, soy yo (film, Taratuto), **2:**421
Nosotros somos Dios (Cantón), **2:**78
Nossa Senhora da Aparecida, **4:**851
Nossa Senhora do Rosário (Our Lady
   of the Rosary) (brotherhood),
   1:28
"A nossa Vendéia" (Cunha), **2:**726
Nostalgia de la muerte (Villaurrutia),
   4:234
Nostromo (Conrad), **3:**285
Notas de viaje (Camacho Roldán),
   2:48
Nothing to Declare (Morris), **6:**131
Noticias de Hoy (periodical, Cuba),
   5:254
Noticias del imperio (Paso), **5:**103
Noticias secretas de America (Ulloa and
   Juan), **6:**167
 on corruption of *corregidores*, **5:**178
No-Transfer Resolution, **4:**851–852
La nouvelle ronde (periodical), **4:**367
Nouvelle Tendence group (Paris),
   2:662
Le nouvelliste (journal), **1:**530
Nova Arcádia club (Brazil), **1:**485
Novaes, Guiomar, **4:**647
Nova Friburgo (Brazil), **4:**852
Novais, Fernando, **5:**314
"No Vale la Pena" (Gabriel), **3:**342
Nova Mazagão (Brazil), **1:**395
Novarro, Ramón, **4:**852
Novás Calvo, Lino, **4:**852–853
Novas fábulas fabulosas (Fernandes),
   3:208
Novedades (newspaper, Mexico City),
   2:716
 Sánchez Navarro, Juan, in, **5:**707
La novela de Perón (Martínez), **4:**395
Novela negra con argentinos
   (Valenzuela), **6:**269
Novelle galanti (Casti), **1:**519
November 13 Revolutionary
   Movement (MR-13, Guatemala)
 formation of, **3:**583
 Montes, César, in, **4:**678
 Yon Sosa, Marco Antonio, in, **3:**548

Novenarios, **3:**135
El Noventa (Argentina), **3:**869
La Novia del hereje (opera, Rogatis),
   5:599
Novo, Salvador, **4:**853; **6:**70
 and group Ulises, **6:**383
 member of Los Contemporáneos,
   2:588
La nube (film, Solanas), **5:**886
La nube y el reloj (Cardoza), **2:**113
Nuclam, **4:**855, 856
Nuclear America, **4:**854
Nuclear Arms Treaty of Tlatelolco
   (1967)
 García Robles, Alfonso, and, **3:**399
Nuclear industry, **3:**112, 501;
   4:854–855; 6:31
 Argentina, **1:**283; **3:**116–117
 Sabato, Jorge Alberto, and, **5:**653
 arms, **6:**427
 Brazil, **3:***113*, 116; **4:**854, 855–856;
   6:31
 Geisel, Ernesto, **3:**422
 nuclear arms, **6:**427
 Chile, **6:**31
 Eletrobrás and, **3:**80
 García Robles, Alfonso, on, **3:**399
 Mexico, **3:**501
Nuclear physics, **4:**716–717; **5:**785
Nuclebrás, **4:855–856**
Nuclei, **4:**855, 856
Nuclemon, **4:**855, 856
Nuclen, **4:**855
Núcleo Bernardelli, **5:**842
Núcleos (Paz), **5:**120
Nuclep, **4:**855, 856
Nucon, **4:**855, 856
Nuestra América (Bunge), **1:**811
Nuestra Barrio (telenovela, United
   States), **3:**698
Nuestra comunidad indígena (Castro
   Pozo), **2:**202
Nuestra inferioridad económica
   (Encina), **3:**106
Nuestra razón (manifesto of
   Twenty-sixth of July Movement),
   2:706
Nuestra Señora de Guadalupe de
   Zacatecas, **4:**371
Nuestra Señora del Mar (Ballagas),
   1:455
Nuestra Señora del Rosario de Timbó,
   2:832
Nuestros hijos (Sánchez), **5:**700–701
Nueva Burdeos, Colony of, **4:**856
Nueva canción movement, **5:**902
Nueva corónica y buen gobierno
   (Guamán Poma de Ayala),
   4:790
Nueva Frontera (magazine,
   Colombia), **4:**249
 Galán, Luis Carlos, in, **3:**348

Odriista National Union (Peru), **4**:880
　Belaúnde Terry, Fernando, in, **1**:532
Oduber Quirós, Daniel, **2**:636;
　4:880–881
　Facio Segreda, Gonzalo, and, **3**:171
O Estado de São Paulo (newspaper,
　Brazil)
　Noblat blog in, **4**:45
　political power of, **4**:44
Oesterheld, Héctor, **2**:164
L'oeuvre (journal), **2**:478
O'Farrill, José Ricardo, **2**:671
O'Farrill, Rómulo, **1**:424
Office of Planning and Coordination
　to Prevent Drug Addiction and
　Fight Drug Trafficking
　(Argentina)
　created by Eduardo Duhalde, **2**:868
Offshore finances
　Cayman Islands (*See* Cayman Islands)
　Curaçao, **2**:729
El oficio de historiar (González y
　González), **3**:494
Oficio de Tinieblas (Castellanos),
　2:186; **4**:238
Ofrenda, **2**:799
Of the Ocean Isles (López de Palacios
　Rubios), **5**:522
Ogazón, Luis, **2**:298
Ogé, Jacques Vicente, **4**:881
　Haiti, **3**:618
Ogéron, Bertrand d', **3**:617; **6**:118
Oglethorpe, James, **5**:665
O'Gorman, Camila, **4**:881
O'Gorman, Charles, **6**:409
O'Gorman, Edmundo, **4**:882
O'Gorman, Juan, **1**:238, 358;
　4:882–883
Ogou, **4**:297
El ogro filantrópico (Paz), **5**:121
Ogum (Yoruba deity), **1**:36
O'Higgins, Ambrosio, **4**:883
　Chile declaration of independence
　　signed, **4**:417
　Salas, Manuel de, and, **5**:671
　and settlement of Osorno, **4**:934
O'Higgins, Bernardo, **2**:325, 327,
　328; **4**:883–886, *884*
　and Battle of Cancha Rayada, **2**:67
　Carrera, José, and, **2**:141
　Casro, José Gil de, on military
　　campaign of, **2**:198
　foreign debt under, **3**:261
　Freire, Ramón, and, **3**:309
　García del Río, Juan, and, **3**:389
　Henríquez, Camilo, and, **3**:663
　Infante, José Miguel, and, **3**:835
　Irisarri, Antonio José de, and, **3**:872
　in London, **6**:128
　in Masonic Orders, **4**:407
　Methodism, **5**:377

　in Patria Vieja, **5**:112
　Pérez Salas, Francisco Antonio, and,
　　5:159
　Prieto Vial, Joaquín, and, **5**:368
　Rancagua, Battle of (1814), **5**:493
　reforms under, **2**:326
　Rodríguez, Manuel, and, **5**:595
　San Martín, José Francisco de, and,
　　5:723, 724, 725
　support of Justo Santa María de Oro,
　　4:920
　and wars of independence, **2**:326;
　　4:884; **6**:421
O'Higgins, Pablo, **4**:886
　cofounder of Taller de Gráfica
　　Popular, **6**:10
O homem do pau-brasil (film,
　Andrade), **2**:424
O'Horan, Tomás, **6**:273
Oidor (judge of an audiencia),
　4:886–887
Oil industry. *See* petroleum industry
Oiticica, Hélio, **4**:887
　in Grupo Frente, **2**:442
　in neo-concrete group, **2**:442
　and *tropicalismo,* **6**:139, 311
Oito anos de Parlamento (Figueiredo),
　3:227
*Ojeada histórico-crítica sobre la poesía
　ecuatoriana* (Mera), **4**:484
Ojeada sobre Nuevo-México (Barreiro),
　1:495
Ojeda, Alonso de, **2**:150; **3**:107, 161;
　4:887–888
　in Cubagua, **2**:690
　discovery of Colombia, **2**:487
　Pizarro, Francisco, and, **5**:259
　San Sebastián founded by, **6**:200
　Vespucci, Amerigo, pilot for, **6**:358
Ojeda, Diego de, **2**:849
Ojeda Ríos, Filiberto, **5**:414
Ojo por Ojo (Eye for Eye, El
　Salvador), **2**:754
Ojo por Ojo (Guatemala), **3**:566
O Judeu (Antônio José da Silva), **6**:68
O.K. (Chocrón), **2**:395
Okon, Yoshua, **1**:361
Olancho (Honduras), **4**:888–889
　massacre of peasants, **2**:663
Olañeta, Pedro Antonio de
　Olañeta, José Joaquín, and, **4**:889
　Sucre Alcalá, Antonio José de, and,
　　5:955
Olañeta y Güemes, José Joaquín
　Casimiro, **4**:889
Olas (R. Ibáñez), **3**:775
Olavarriaga, Pedro José de, **2**:555
Olaya Herrera, Enrique, **4**:889
　Leticia Dispute, **4**:179
Olazábal, Manuel de, **5**:726
Old Lima (Peru), **4**:201

The Old Patagonia Express (Theroux),
　6:131
O'Leary, Daniel Florencio, **4**:890
O'Leary, Juan Emiliano, **4**:890–891
　González, Juan Natalicio, and, **3**:480
　on López, Francisco Solano, **5**:66
　and Manuel Domínguez, **2**:837
　Pane, Ignacio Alberto, and, **5**:50
Olid, Cristóbal de, **3**:162; **4**:891
　González Dávila, Gil, and, **3**:485
　and Hernan Cortés, **2**:618
　and Tarascans, **6**:19
Olímpica (Azar), **1**:422
Olinda (Brazil), **4**:892
Olinda, Marquess of
　See Araújo Lima, Pedro de, Marquis
　　of Olinda
Olinda Seminary (Brazil), **2**:484
Oliva, Oscar, **6**:518
Olivares, Conde-Duque de (Gaspar de
　Guamán y Pimental), **4**:892
　financial reforms, **5**:219
Olivares, José Trueba, **4**:726
Oliveira, Alberto de, **4**:222
Oliveira, Geraldo Teles de, **4**:892–893
Oliveira, Manuel Botelho de, **4**:893
　plays by, **6**:68
Oliveira, Willy Correia de, **4**:893–894
　Mendes, Gilberto, and, **4**:469
　and Rogério Dupret, **2**:870
Oliveira Lima, Flora de, suffrage and,
　3:200
Oliveira Lima, Manuel de, **4**:894
Oliveira Torres, João Camilo de,　in
　Coleção Documentos Brasileiros,
　5:909
Oliveira Vianna, Francisco José de,
　4:894–895
Olivencia, Tommy, **4**:750
Olivera, Héctor, **2**:417
Olive trees
　in colonial period, **1**:48
　Cuyo, **2**:736
　Peru, **5**:174
Los olividados (film), **1**:812
Olivos Pact (1994), **1**:106, 280
Ollantáy, **4**:895–896
　"discovery" by Antonio Valdez, **6**:69
　literature, **4**:227
Ollantay Academy of Dramatic Art,
　1:129
Ollantaytambo (archaeological site,
　Mexico), **1**:340; **4**:896; **5**:2
Ollantay Theater Magazine (U.S.),
　6:73
Ollonai, Francois L', **1**:797
Olmeca-Xicalanca culture, **2**:20
Olmecs, **4**:896–898
　archaeology and, **1**:224
　art, **1**:333–334
　Covarrubias, Miguel, research on,
　　2:649

liberalism under, **4**:806

Mapuche assimilated by, **4**:359

March of the Empty Pots, **4**:369

El Mercurio on, **4**:488

Merino Castro, José Toribio, and, **4**:491

migration and, **3**:723

military dictatorship of, **4**:593

Pahuenches under, **5**:133

PDC and, **2**:362

photography on, **5**:231

police force under, **2**:88

and political prisoners, **2**:752

Prats González, Carlos, and, **5**:339

presidency, **2**:346–348

privatization, **5**:371, 374

reversion of agrarian reform, **2**:359

Santiago opposition to, **5**:749

service sector under, **5**:816

Silva Henríquez, Raúl, and, **5**:850–851

sports used by, **5**:936

support for, **2**:*348*

Pinole, **2**:719

Piñol y Aycinena, Bernardo, **5**:245

Piñol y Sala, José, **5**:245–246

Pinome speakers in Tlaxcala, **6**:90

Piñon, Nélida, **5**:246

Pino Suárez, José María, **5**:246–247

death of, **4**:560

Madero, Francisco Indalecio, and, **4**:316

in Mexican Revolution, **4**:559

Pact of the Embassy and, **5**:9

Pinto, **2**:165

Pinto, Aníbal

Amunátegui, Miguel Luis, and, **1**:167

election, **6**:363

presidency, **2**:332–333

Radicals in cabinet of, **2**:373

supported by National Party, **2**:369

and War of the Pacific, **6**:411, 413

Pinto, Francisco Antonio

presidency, **2**:328

Vicuña Larraín, Francisco, and, **6**:362–363

Pinto, Godofredo, fixed election of, **3**:303

Pinto, Joaquín, **1**:352; **5**:247

Pinto, Matías, **1**:362

Pintó, Ramón, execution of, **2**:671

Pínto, Roquette, indigenous music collected by, **3**:210

Pinto Díaz, Francisco Antonio, **5**:247–248

Ruíz Tagle, Francisco, and, **5**:643

Pinto Garmendia, Aníbal, **5**:248

Pinto Díaz, Francisco, and, **5**:248

Pinto Revolt (Goa, 1787), Portuguese trade and, **5**:321

Pinto Santa Cruz, Anibal, **5**:248–249

Pinturas Aeropostales (Airmail Paintings), Eugenio Dittborn, **2**:830

Pinturas mejicanas 1800–1860 (Montenegro y Nervo), **4**:675

Las pinturas negras de Goya (García Morillo), **3**:396

La pinture nueva en Latinoamérica (Traba), **6**:122

Pinzón, Martín Alonso, **5**:249

on first voyage of Christopher Columbus, **2**:532–533

Pinzón, Vicente Yáñez, **3**:157, 161; **5**:249–250

Brazil claimed by, **1**:688

exploration of Amazon region, **1**:151, 155

Lepe, Diego de, and, **4**:172

Solís, Juan, and, **5**:889

Pioneers of New Education (Brazil), **6**:38

Pipelines

Argentina, **1**:283

Pipiles, **5**:250

Alvarado, Pedro de, and, **4**:74

El Salvador, **3**:88, 90

massacre of, **4**:412

Pipiltín, **5**:251

El Pipiolo (newspaper, Chile), **5**:251

Pipiolos, **5**:251

Piquera Cotolí, Manuel, **1**:235

Piqueteros, **5**:251–252

women in, **6**:452

Piquets (Haiti), **3**:624

Piquiza, Treaty of (1828), Bolivian constitution in, **1**:631

Piracy, **5**:252–254

attacks on Cartagena de Indias, **2**:150

Audiencia of Guatemala, **3**:557

Bahamas, **1**:441

Belize, **1**:540

by Bonnet, Stede, **1**:648

by Bonny, Anne, **1**:648–649

Brazil, **5**:803

British-Latin American relations and, **1**:784

by Brown, William, **1**:789

Dutch repelled by Sebastián Vizcaíno, **6**:398

fleet system and, **3**:239–241

Florida, **3**:248, 249

Fortaleza de Santa Cruz against, **5**:736

fortifications against, **3**:292–293

and Francis Drake, **2**:858

French, **3**:317

attack on Veracruz, **6**:350

Haiti, **3**:617

by Hawkins, John, **3**:641

Islas de Bahía, **1**:445–4

Mosquito Coast, **4**:719

Peru, **5**:175

Philippines, **5**:222

Porto Bello, **5**:309

Providencia, **5**:382

Puerto Rico, **5**:408, 409

by Read, Mary, **5**:497–498

in Saint Augustine, **5**:665

Saint Christopher, **5**:667

silver and, **4**:506

slave trade as, **5**:878–879

suppressed by Morgan, Henry, **4**:710

Swan Islands, **5**:964

O pirotécnico Zacarias (Rubião), **5**:637

O Pirralho (magazine), contributions of Oswald de Andrade, **1**:180

Pisagua (Arguedas), **1**:304

Pisco (brandy)

in Ica, **3**:781

as national beverage, **3**:257

Pisco (Peru), **5**:254

Piso, Willem, **3**:9, 159

Maurits, Johan, and, **4**:418

La pista de hielo (Bolaño), **1**:601

Pita Rodríguez, Félix, **5**:254–255

Pitiantuta, Battles of, **5**:68, 255–256

Pitol, Sergio, **4**:239; **5**:256

Pitt, William, and Albera Poyer scheme, **5**:333

Pitt, William, the Younger, andHaiti, **3**:619

Pittman, Philip, **2**:162

Piura (Peru), **5**:256–257

Pius VI, Pope, Francisco Antonio de Lorenzana and, **4**:273

Pius VII, Pope, Francisco Antonio de Lorenzana and, **4**:273

Pius IX, Pope, **5**:257

García Peláez, Francisco, and, **3**:398

and liberalism, **1**:192

Llorente, Anselmo, and, **4**:249–250

Maxmilian blessed by, **4**:419

Munguía, Clemente de Jesús, and, **4**:732

Pius X, Pope, Alfonso Figueiredo honored by, **3**:227

Pius XI, Pope

Catholic Action, **2**:212, 221

Christian Democratic movement and, **2**:581, 582

corporatism and, **3**:779

Pius XII, Pope

Baca Flor, Carlos, portrait of, **1**:435–436

call for missionaries for Latin America, **2**:222

Fresno, Juan Francisco, and, **3**:320

on Virgin of Guadalupe, **3**:521

Porteño, **2:**791; **5:305**

Porter, Charles, and Jesús de Galíndez, **3:**352

Porter, David, **5:305**

Porter, Liliana, **1:**362; **5:305–306**

Portes Gil, Emilio, **5:306–307**
    influenced by Plutarco Calles, **4:**525
    Padilla Peñalosa, Ezequiel, and, **5:**10
    and Tamaulipas, **6:**12

Portfolio investment, **3:**267, 268
    See also foreign investment

Portillo, Alfredo
    Arzú, Álvaro, and, **3:**552
    corruption under, **3:**553–554
    in Grupo de CAYC, **3:**517–518

Portinari, Cândido Torquato, **4:**93; **5:307**
    in Bienal de São Paulo, **1:**576
    mural painting, **1:**358
    nationalism of, **4:**785

Pôrto Alegre (Brazil), **5:307–308**
    Clube de Gravura, **5:**334

Pôrto Alegre, Manuel Araújo, **5:308–309**
    and history painting, **1:**349
    influenced by Debret, Jean-Baptiste, **3:**311
    Magalhães, Domingos, and, **4:**321
    romanticism, **4:**220–221

Porto Bello (Portobelo), **5:309**

Portobelo, fortification of, **3:**293

Portocarrero, René, **1:**359; **5:309–310**

Portocarrero y Lasso de la Vega, Melchor, **5:310**
    reforms by, **5:**176

Portolá, Gaspar de, **3:**165; **5:310–311**
    Fages, Pedro, and, **3:**174
    Rivera y Moncada, Fernando de, and, **5:**571
    Serra, Junípero, and, **5:**805

Pôrto Seguro (Brazil), **5:311**

Portrait of Fernando VII (Castol), **2:**198

Portraits of Flora (Portocarrero), **5:**310

Portraits of Lucy (Segall), **5:**793

Portraiture
    casta paintings, **1:**344
        Cabrera, Miguel, **2:**16
        De Espagnol y Mestiza: Castiza (Cabrera), **1:***345*
        Castro, José Gil de, **2:**198
        Cedeño, Juan **2:**233
        Coronel, Rafael, **2:**609
        Estrada, José María, **3:**151

Portugal, **5:311–313**
    in Africa, **1:**26–28
    Babylonian Captivity, **1:**435
    exports of tobacco to, **6:**91
    factors, **3:**172

Freyre, Gilberto, on, **3:**322–323

hammocks, **3:**636

House of Bragança, **1:**679–680

independence, **5:**219

Inquisition in, **3:**841

Junta do Comércio, **4:**65

Juntas Portuguesas, **4:**66

liberalism, **4:**186

Line of Demarcation (1493), **4:**210

Lisbon earthquake (1755), **4:**215

Luso-Brazilian, **4:**293

Maria I, **4:**372

Maria II, **4:**372–373

migration to, **4:**577

military orders, **4:**595–597

New State dictatorship and colonialism, **1:**27 1820
        revolution and elections in Brazil, **2:**771–772

spice trade, **5:**926

Strangford Treaties, **5:**947

Treaty of Fontainebleu on, **3:**255–256

Treaty of Madrid (1750), **4:**318

Treaty of Methuen, **4:**500

viradeira, **4:**372

War of Oranges, **5:**538
    and War of the Spanish Succession, **6:**415

Portugal, Diego de, **6:**115

Portugal, Marcos Antônio da Fonseca, **5:313**
    García, José Maurício Nunes, and, **3:**385

Portugal, Restoration of 1640, **5:313–314**

Portuguese Brazil and Dutch West India Company, **2:**881

Portuguese Empire, **5:314–315**
    Boxer, Charles Ralph, on, **1:**675
    Brazil, **5:**922–923
    Goa, **3:**448–449
    gold rushes, **3:**458
    Henry the Navigator in, **3:**665
    India, **3:**448–451
    under João I, **4:**33–34
    under João II, **4:**34
    under João III, **4:**34
    under João IV, **4:**35
    under João V, **4:**35
    under João VI, **4:**36
    under José I, **4:**42
    land distribution (*sesmaria*), **5:**819–820
    liberalism, **4:**186–187
    race and ethnicity, **5:**466
    salt trade, **5:**685
    São Tomé in, **5:**762
    under Sebastian of Portugal, **5:**791
    slave trade, **5:**873–874

slave trade, abolition of, **5:**878–879

Treaty of San Ildefonso on, **5:**714

Uruguay, **6:**214–215

Portuguese in Latin America, **5:315–317**
    Brazil, *reinóis,* **5:**514
    migrations, **4:***572,* 573
    rivalry with Dutch, **2:**880, 881

Portuguese language, **5:317–319**
    Luso-Brazilian and, **4:**293

Portuguese overseas administration, **5:319–320**

Portuguese trade and international relations, **5:320–322**

Porvenir (newspaper, Argentina), contributions of Alegario Andrade, **1:**179

POS. *See* Socialist Workers Party (POS, Chile)

Posada, José Guadalupe, **5:322**
    Charlot, Jean, on, **2:**292
    influence on José Clemente Orozco, **4:**920
    Linares, Pedro, and, **4:**207
    lithography, **1:**353
    retablos and *ex-votos,* **5:**527

Posada-Amador, Carlos, and Roberto Pineda-Duque, **5:**238

Posada Carriles, Luis, **6:**53

Posadas, Gervasio Antonio de, **5:322–323**
    San Martín, José Francisco de, and, **5:**723

Posadas, Manuel, student of Juan José Castro, **2:**199

Posadas Ocampo, Juan Jesús, **5:323**

Posdata (Paz), **5:**121

Posesión (Herrerabarría), **3:**680

Las posibilidades del odio (Puga), **5:**420

Positivism, **5:**224, **323–324**
    anticlericalism and, **1:**193
    Barreda y Laos, Felipe, in, **1:**495
    Brazil
        Republic, **1:**705, 708
        São Paulo (city), **5:**759–760
        Second Empire, **1:**728
    científicos and, **2:**409
    criticism by Miguel Taborga Pizarro, **6:**436
    Cuba, Enrique Varona and, **6:**293
    El Salvador under Gerardo Barrios, **1:**500
    Guatemala, and Justo Rufino Barrios, **1:**501
    Honduras, Ramón Rosa and, **5:**623
    influence, **1:**25
        on Benjamin Constant, **2:**584
        on education, **3:**63
        on José de Almeida, **1:**116
        on Júlio de Castilhos, **2:**191

Rain forests. *See* forests
Raízes do Brasil (Holanda), **3**:730
Raíz salvaje (Ibarbourou), **3**:777;
  4:232
"La raíz y la aurora" (Plá), **5**:264
Raleigh, Walter, in Orinoco region,
  4:917
Rama, Angel, **5**:483–484
  on Berenguer, Amanda, **1**:561
  Cândido, Antônio, and, **2**:69
  on Ibarbourou, Juana de, **3**:778
  in *Marcha*, **5**:441
  married to Marta Traba, **6**:123
Rama Indians, Nicaragua, **4**:822
Ramalho, Elba
  Gonzaga, Luiz, and, **3**:477
  in Música Popular Brasileira, **4**:729
Ramalho, João, **5**:484
Ramas, Ernesto, human rights
  violations and, **6**:233
Ramela, Carlos, in truth commissions,
  6:252
Ramérez, Ariel, **5**:902
Ramírez, Alejandro, Economic Society
  of Guatemala and, **3**:559
Ramírez, Alonso, travel to Asia, **5**:414
Ramírez, Ariel, neofolk music, **4**:752
Ramírez, Belkis, **1**:362
Ramírez, Carlo María
  in Ateneo del Uruguay, **1**:393
  and image of José Artigas, **1**:366
Ramírez, Francisco, **5**:485
  in Battle of Cepeda (1820), **2**:258
  López, Estanislao, and, **4**:256
Ramírez, Ignacio, **5**:485–486
  editor of *El Siglo XIX*, **2**:724
  Prieto, Guillermo, and, **5**:366
  as *puro*, **5**:428
Ramírez, José Fernando, **5**:486
  in Assembly of Notables, **1**:376
  as moderado, **4**:646
  Orozco, Manuel, and, **4**:922
Ramírez, María Elena, foundation of
  Mexican YWCA, **1**:373
Ramírez, Óscar, in Shining Path,
  3:584
Ramírez, Pedro Pablo, **5**:486–487
  Farrell, Edelmiro, and, **3**:185
  Perón, Juan, and, **5**:163
  president of the United Officers
    Group, **1**:292
Ramírez, Victor, **1**:236
Ramírez Chirinos, Edgardo, **1**:238
Ramírez de Fuenleal, Sebastián, in
  Santo Domingo Audiencia, **5**:753
Ramírez Mercado, Sergio, **4**:926;
  5:487
Ramírez Vázquez, Pedro, **5**:487–488
  Basilica of Guadalupe by, **3**:520
Ramírez Villamizar, Eduardo, **5**:488
  influence of, **3**:506

Ramírez y Blanco, Alejandro,
  5:488–489
  in Puerto Rico, **5**:410
Ramón, Domingo
  colonization of Texas, **6**:55
  livestock provided by Marqués de
    Aguayo, **1**:61
Ramos, Artur, **5**:489, 588
Ramos, Benito, **4**:439
Ramos, Graciliano, **1**:72; **5**:489–490
  modernism, **4**:648
  novel adaptation by Nelson Santos,
    5:756
Ramos, Lorenzo, **4**:439
Ramos, Nereu, **1**:713; **4**:276
Ramos Arizpe, José Miguel, **5**:491
  provincial deputation, **5**:382
  yorkinos and, **6**:489
Ramos-García, Luis, **6**:73
Ramos Mejía, Ezequiel, **5**:491–492
Ramos Mejía, José María, **5**:492, 563
Ramos-Perca, Roberto, **6**:72
Ramos y Magaña, Samuel, **3**:638;
  5:492–493, 533
Rancagua, Battle of (1814), **5**:493
  Patria Vieja ended by, **5**:112
Ranchera films, **4**:803
Ranchera music, **2**:854
  by Beltrán, Lola, **1**:550
  Mexico, **4**:749
  by Sánchez, Cuco, **5**:700
  by Víveros Barradas, Francisco, **5**:55
Rancherío (Cluzeau-Mortet), **2**:458
Ranching
  along Tebicuary River, **6**:29
  and *domador*, **2**:834
  Mexico, Coahuila, **2**:459
  Nicaragua, **2**:239
El rancho abandonado (Williams), **6**:437
Ranchos, **2**:91
Rangel, Alberto, **5**:493–494
Rangel, Nicolás, **2**:175; **6**:201
Rangel, Rafael, **6**:390
Rangel Arroyo, Enrique "Quique," **2**:24
Rangel Arroyo, José Alfredo "Joselo,"
  2:24
"Ran Kan Kan" (recording, Puente),
  5:406
Ranke, Leopold von, **3**:637
Ranney, Edward, **2**:280
Ranqueles, **5**:494
  alliance with Calfucurá, **2**:33
  Mansilla, Lucio Victorio, on, **4**:351
  Roca, Julio, campaign against, **5**:576
  salt trade, **5**:686
Raoul, Nicolás, **1**:221
Raousset-Boulbon, Gaston Raul de,
  3:233; **5**:494–495
Les rapaces (Chauvet), **2**:296
The Rape of the Mulattas (Enríquez),
  3:119
Rápida ojeada ... (Zúñiga), **6**:527

*Rápido tránsito (al ritmo de
  norteamérica)* (Coronel Urtecho),
  2:609
Rap music, **4**:753
Rapsodia campesina (Cordero), **2**:599
Rapsodia criolla (Aguirre), **1**:68
Raramuri, **2**:315
Rarezas (recording), **4**:342
Los Raros (Darío), **2**:748
Rastafarians, **5**:495
  Jamaica, **4**:11
  and marijuana, **2**:862
  Marley, Bob, **4**:380
  messianic movement, **4**:497
  négritude and, **4**:796
El rastro (Glantz), **3**:442
Las ratas (Bianco), **1**:575
Ratas, Ratones, Rateros (film,
  Cordero), **2**:421
Ratison, Truce of (1684), **1**:797
Rávago, Francisco de, **3**:206–207
Ravignani, Emilio, **5**:496
  Caillet Bois, Ricardo, disciple of, **2**:24
  Molinari, Diego Luís, and, **4**:657
Rawson (Argentina), **2**:405
Rawson, Arturo, **2**:426
Rawson, Elvira, **3**:201
Rawson, Guillermo, **5**:496–497
Raya, Antonio de la, **4**:907
Raynal, Guillaume-Thomas-François
  de, **3**:662
Raynaud, Georges
  Asturias, Miguel, student of, **1**:379
  translation of *Rabinal Achí*, **2**:113;
    5:461–462
Rayo, Faustino, **1**:181
Rayo, Omar, **1**:360
Rayón, Ignacio [López], **2**:382; **5**:497
  Cos y Pérez, José, and, **2**:641
  Jiménez, José Ignacio, and, **5**:134
  and Junta de Zitácuaro, **2**:382
  Los Guadalupes and, **3**:522
  Morelos y Pavón, José María, and,
    4:707
Rayuela (Cortázar), **2**:615, 616; **4**:238
La Raza: Forgotten Americans
  (Samora, ed.), **5**:694
La raza cósmica (Vasconcelos
  Calderón), **4**:232
Raza de bronce (Arguedas), **1**:303;
  4:235, 795
La raza de Caín (Reyles), **4**:230
La Raza Unida Party (LRUP, United
  States), **3**:705
Raznovich, Diana, **6**:72
La Razón (newspaper, Argentina), **6**:80
La Razón (newspaper, Bolivia), **1**:210
La Razón (newspaper, Uruguay)
  Acevedo Díaz, Eduardo, and, **1**:12
  Basso Maglio, Vicente, in, **1**:511
  Ibarbourou, Juana de, in, **3**:777
  Sabata Ercasty, Carlos, in, **5**:651

Reducciones *(continued)*
Torres Bello, Diego de, and, **6:**113
in Verapaz, **6:**354
War of the Seven Reductions, **3:**365
See also aldeias; congregación
Reduções. See aldeias
Reed (film, Leduc), **4:**161
Reed, John, **6:**131
Reed, Walter, **5:**509
Finlay, Carlos Juan, and, **2:**825; **3:**235
and Yellow Fever Commission, **2:**825
Reencuentro de personajes (Garro), **3:**407
Reeve, Henry M., **5:**509–510
"La refalosa" (Ascasubi), Jorge Luis Borges on, **1:**655
Refavela (album, Gil), **3:**434
Reflejos (Mastrogiovanni), **4:**410
Reflexión ciudadana (film, Solanas), **5:**886
Reflexiones: Acerca de un método seguro para preservar a los pueblos de las viruelas (Espejo), **5:**737
Reflexiones maquiavélicas (Shimose), **5:**835
Reflexiones sobre el nacionalismo musicl mexicano (Alcaraz), **1:**85
Reflexiones sobre la historia de Nicaragua (Coronel Urtecho), **2:**609
Reflexiones sobre la historia de Nicaragua: De la Colonia a la Independencia (Coronel Urtecho), **2:**609–610
Reflexiones sobre la ley del 10 de abril de 1834 (Toro), **6:**107
"Reflexiones sobre las causas morales de las convulsiones interiores de los nuevos estados americanos y examen de los medios eficaces para remerdiarlas" (Gorriti), **3:**498
Reflexiones sobre política económica: Apuntes desde la prisión (Sendic), **5:**799
Reflexiones sobre Rodó (Massera), **4:**409
Reforestation, **3:**288–289
Inter-American Development Bank and, **3:**855
La Reforma (newspaper, Montevideo)
Basso Maglio, Vicente, in, **1:**511
La Reforma (newspaper, Paraguay), **2:**257
Aceval, Benjamín, and, **1:**12
Reforma Agraria, Revolution, **5:**510
Reforma Liberal (Guatemala), under Vicente Cerna, **3:**542–543
Reforma Pacífica (newspaper, Argentina), contributions of Alegario Andrade, **1:**179
La reforma politica en Colombia (Núñez Moledo), **4:**861

La reforma universitaria (Benítez), **1:**558
La Réforme (Haiti), Ramón Matías Mella and, **4:**462
Reformist Party (Costa Rica), **2:**633; **6:**402
Reformist Party (Cuba), **2:**671
Reformist Party (Dominican Republic), Joaquín Balaguer in, **1:**449
Reform of the Criminal Procedure Code (Brazil, 1841), support by Pedro de Araújo Lima, **1:**217
Reforms, of Alberto Enríquez Gallo, **3:**121
Refrigeration and meat industry, **4:**440
Refugee Act (U.S., 1980)
Central Americans and, **3:**720
Cuban Americans and, **3:**715
Refugees, **1:**386–388
Central American, **3:**720–722
Chilean, **3:**722, 723
definition, **1:**387–388; **3:**720
Guatemalan, **3:**721–722
Peru, Shining Path and, **5:**204
Salvadoran, **3:**721–722
South American, **3:**722–723
See also asylum
Regalado, Tomás, **5:**510–511
Regalism and anticlericalism, **1:**191–192
La Regeneración (newspaper, Paraguay)
and Hector Francisco Decoud, **2:**760
edited by Jóse Segundo Decoud, **2:**760
Regeneración (Colombia), **2:**501
Regeneración (weekly newspaper, Mexico), **5:**511
Flores Magón, Ricardo, and, **3:**245
labor and, **4:**517
in Mexican Revolution, **4:**45
El Regenerador (Ecuador), Juan Montalvo in, **4:**667
Reggae music
Marley, Bob, **4:**378–379
reggaetón, **4:**753
Regidores, **2:**22; **5:**511–512
El regimen municipal (Torre), **6:**108
Regina (González de Fanning), **3:**486
Regina, Elis, **2:**231; **5:**512
in Música Popular Brasileira, **4:**729
Regional Conference of Ministers of Education (1979), literacy and, **4:**217
Regional Development period, **5:**358
Regional Electoral Tribunals (Brazil), **4:**57
Regional Electrical Intergration Commission, **3:**114

Regionalism, **5:512–514**
banking and, **1:**476
Bird, Vere Cornwall, in, **1:**581
Brazil, **1:**701
Lima, Jorge de, and, **4:**203
Recife, **5:**505
of colonial contraband, **2:**590
in Ecuador, **3:**42, 45
Freyre, Gilberto on, **3:**323
Lins do Rego, José, and, **4:**211–212
modernism, **4:**648–649
Rosa, João, and, **5:**621
Regional Labor Tribunals (Brazil), **4:**57
La región más transparente (Fuentes), **3:**331; **4:**238, 540
Región Oriental (Paraguay), **5:**78
Registros, **6:**410
Reglamento (Morelos y Pavón), **4:**708
Rego Monteiro, Vicente do, **4:**647; **5:514**
El regreso (Storm), **5:**945–946
Regreso de tres mundos (Picón Salas), **1:**313
Regresso (Brazil), **6:**293
Regulation and Instruction for the Presidios of New Spain, **5:**888
Regulation of Free Trade (1778), **1:**672
Regulation of Free Trade for the Caribbean Islands (1765), **3:**639
Regulations of Missions (1686), **4:**627
Reiche, Maria, **4:**777
Reichel Dolmatoff, Gerardo
and Colombian Indigenist Institute, **2:**513
Puerto Hormiga excavations, **5:**407
Reid, William, **3:**769
Reid Cabral, Donald, **2:**842, 844, 847; **4:**659
O rei fantasma (Coelho Neto), **2:**473
Reimer, Everett, **3:**66
Rein, Mercedes, **5:**441
Reina, Carlos Roberto, **3:**741
Reina Andrade, José María, **3:**545
Reinecke, Carl, **1:**570; **2:**144
Reinforcing Democracy in the Americas (conference, 1986), **2:**153
Reinhardt, Max, **1:**422
El reino de este mundo (Carpentier), **4:**237
Reinóis, **5:**514
Reinoso, Alonso, **2:**228
Rejón, Manuel Crescencio, **5:514–515**
as *puro,* **5:**428
and writ of Amparo, **1:**164
Relação sumária das cousas do Maranhão (Estácio da Silveira), **5:**688

Reyna Barrios, José María, **5:534–535**
  assassination of, **3:**151, 544
Reynolds Aluminum, **1:**520
Reza, Jorge de la, **5:**4
Rhea, **5:535**
Rhea (nandu), **6:**37
Rhet, William, **1:**648
Rhodakanaty, Plotino, **2:**279; **4:**261
Rhtymetron (Nobre), **4:**843
Riachuelo, Battle of the (1865),
  5:535–536; 6:416
Riani, Clodsmith, **5:536**
Riaño, Juan Antonio de, **4:**509
Riaño y Bárcena, Juan Antonio,
  5:536–537
  Alhóndiga of Guanajuato, Mexico,
    1:108
  Hidalgo, Miguel, and, **3:**688
Ribas, José Félix, **5:537**
Ribault, Jean, **5:**664
Ribeiro, Darcy, **1:**190; **5:537**
  on Indian extinction, **3:**814
  indianismo, **3:**813
Ribeiro, Diogo, **2:**161
Ribeiro, João Ubaldo, **5:537–538**
  in Pernambucan Revolution, **5:**160
Ribeiro, Joaquím, **5:**586
Ribeiro, León, **4:**746
Ribeiro, Martins, **4:**647
Ribera, Alonso de, **1:**533
Ribera, José Patricio de, **2:**93
Riberalta y otros poemas (Shimose),
  5:835
Ribera y Espinosa, Lázaro de, **5:538**
Ribero, Carlos, **1:**285
Ribeyro, Julio Ramón, **5:539**
Ricard, Robert, **4:**632
Ricardo, David, **3:**803
Ricardo, Jesús, **5:**511
Ricchieri, Pablo, **5:539–540**
Rice industry, **5:540–541**
  Argentina, **1:**282
    Corrientes, **2:**614
    Entre Ríos, **3:**122
  Brazil, **5:**540, *540*, 541
    Campo Grande, **2:**57
    Espírito Santo, **3:**139
    Maranhão, Estado do, **4:**366
    Santarém, **5:***540*
    São Luís, **5:**758–759
  Costa Rica, Guanacaste, **3:**526
  in cuisines, **2:**720
  Dominican Republic, Santiago de los
    Caballeros, **5:**751
  Ecuador, **5:**541
  El Salvador, **3:**92
  Mexico, Michoacán, **4:**566
  Peru
    Batán Grande, **1:**512
    Cajamarca, **2:**25
    Trujillo, **6:**142
  slavery in, **5:**863

Richa, José, **1:**762
Richard, Pablo, **4:**194
Richter, Ronald, **5:**785
Ricke, Jodoco, **5:**457
Rickey, Branch, **5:**930
Rico tipo (magazine, Argentina), **2:**165
Ried, Aquinas, **4:**744–745
Riego Revolt (1820), **2:**621; **5:**180, 920
Riego y Núñez, Rafael del, **5:541–542**
Riesco, Laura, **5:542**
Riesco Errázuriz, Germán, **5:542**
Rigaud, André, **3:**618, 620;
  5:542–543
  Dessalines, Jean-Jacques, and, **2:**797
  Louverture, Toussaint, and, **4:**279
Riggs, Francis, **1:**80
Riggs National Bank (Washington,
  D.C.), **5:**244
*Rigoberta Menchú and the Story of All
  Poor Guatemalans* (Stoll), **4:**468
Rigo es amor (film, Casals), **2:**172
Riley, John, **5:**728–729
Rilke, Rainer Maria, **6:**167
Rímac River (Peru), **5:**543
Rincón, César, **1:**806–807
Un rincón cerca del cielo (film), **5:**238
Rinconcito, Treaty of (1838), **5:543**
Rincón Rincón, Miguel, **4:**725
El río (Berenguer), **1:**561
Río, Andrés del, **5:**780
Rio, João do, **1:**146; **5:543–544**
Río Azul (archaeological site,
  Guatemala), **1:**335; **5:544–545**
Riobamba (Ecuador), **5:545**
Río Blanco Strike (1907), **5:545–546**
Rio Branco. *See* Roraima
Rio Branco, Barão do, **5:546–547**
  Acre and, **1:**21; **5:**588
  in boundary disputes, **1:**670
Rio Branco, José Maria da Silva
  Paranhos, Barão de, Zeballos's
  feud with, **6:**512
Rio Branco, Miguel, **5:**232
Rio Branco, Visconde do (José Maria
  de Silva Paranhos), **5:547–548**
  in abolition of slavery, **5:**763
  Rio Branco, Barão do, and, **5:**546
Rio Branco Institute (Brazil), **5:548**
Rio Branco Law. *See* Free Birth Law
  (Brazil)
Río Bravo Industrial Company, **1:**135
Rio Conference (1947). *See under* Pan-
  American conferences
Rio Declaration on Environment and
  Development, **3:**122
Rio de Janeiro (city, Brazil), **2:***434;*
  5:548–550
  architecture, **4:**37
    by Grandjean de Montigny, **3:**504
    Nossa Senhora da Glória do
      Outeiro, **1:**345, *346*
  blockade by British navy, **2:**402

  carnival, **2:**130–131
  colonial era, **5:**548
    founding, **5:**649
    population, **2:**433
    trade, **6:**123–124
  Communist rebellion of 1935, **2:**882
  favela, **3:**189–190
    São Sebastião Crusade and, **2:**49
  Fortaleza de Santa Cruz defense of,
    5:736
  French Artistic Mission, **3:**311
  gangs, **3:***374*
  gold rushes, **4:**607
  Great Mercenary Revolt, **4:**575
  HIV/AIDS, **1:**20
  under João VI, **4:**36
  Julião, Carlos, on, **4:**63
  literature, modernism, **4:**222–223
  missions, **4:**628
  município, município neutro, **4:**732
  national primacy, **5:**548–549
  Passeio Público, **3:**254
  Portuguese immigration, **5:**316, 317
  Portuguese language, **5:**318
  Relações, **5:**515
  royal family arrival, effect of, **6:**124
  under Sá e Benavides, Salvador, **5:**659
  samba schools, **5:**692–693
  slaves, **3:**458
    revolts, **5:**858, 859
  struggle against decline, **5:**549
  tobacco industry, **6:**92
  volleyball, **5:**932, *932*
  See also Carioca
Rio de Janeiro (Krieger), **4:**91
Rio de Janeiro (province and state,
  Brazil), **3:**525; **5:550–551**
Rio de Janeiro Treaty (1947), **4:**666
Río de la Plata, **5:551**
  Beresford, William Carr, and, **1:**562
  Blandengues, **1:**589
  Bonpland, Aimé Jacques, on, **1:**649
  boundary disputes, **1:**665–666
  Bourbon Reforms on, **1:**672
  British interest in, **6:**215
  British invasions, **1:**257, 425, 783;
    6:359
    Auchmuty, Samuel, in, **1:**396
  exploration
    by Cabot, Sebastian, **2:**14
    Irala, Domingo Martínez de, **3:**868
  Franciscans in, and Luis de Bolaños,
    1:603
  French intervention in, **3:**318
    ending, **1:**211
  Garay, Juan de, in, **3:**382
  García, Aleixo, expedition, **3:**383
  García, Diego, expedition, **3:**384
  gauchos, **3:**414

Rivas, Rafael Cordova, in Broad
Opposition Front, **4**:829
Rivas Mercado, Antonieta, member of
Los Contemporáneos, **2**:588
Rivas Mercafo, Antonieta, patron of
theater, **6**:70
Rivera, Diego, **1**:356; **5**:*564,* **564–565**
Beals, Carleton, on, **1**:524
and cubism, **1**:356
director of the Academia de San
Carlos, **1**:9
on Figueroa, Gabriel, **3**:230
Guerrero, Xavier, and, **3**:579
house designed by Juan O'Gorman,
4:882
influence on Juan O'Gorman, **4**:883
Kahlo, Frida, and, **4**:72
Modotti, Tina, and, **4**:650
Montenegro y Nervo, Roberto,
portrait of, **4**:676
nationalism and, **4**:785
O'Higgins, Pablo, sutiod assistant of,
4:885
retablos and *ex-votos,* **5**:527
in Syndicate of Revolutionary
Painters, **4**:920
tourism, **6**:121
as of the *tres grandes,* **1**:105
Trotsky, Leon, and, **6**:140
Rivera, Fructuoso, **2**:1; **5**:**565–566**
at Battle of Arroyo Grande, **1**:332
Blanco Party against, **6**:246
Colorado Party and, **6**:248–249
defeat at Battle of Carpintería,
2:135
in Farroupilha Revolt, **3**:186
Flores, Venancio, and, **3**:243
Garibaldi, Giuseppe, and, **3**:402
in Guerra Grande, **3**:576
Lavalleja, Juan, and, **4**:152
Oribe, Manuel, and, **4**:915
orientales under, **6**:215
Pereda, Setembrino Ezequiel, on,
5:150
and Treinta y tres Orientales, **6**:132
uprisings under, **6**:216
Urquiza, Justo José de, and, **6**:207
Rivera, Galvarino, **6**:412
Rivera, Ismael, **5**:414
Rivera, Joaquín, **3**:222; **5**:**566–567**
Rivera, José Eustasio, **4**:235; **5**:567
Rivera, Julio Adalberto, **3**:93, 101;
5:706
Rivera, Mariano, **5**:**568**
Rivera, Pedro de, **5**:**568–569**
Rivera, Ron, **5**:935
Rivera Cabezas, Antonio, **5**:569
Rivera Carballo, Julio Adalberto,
5:**569–570**
Rivera Damas, Arturo, **5**:570, 611

Rivera Maestre, Julián, **5**:570
Rivera Maestre, Miguel, **2**:158;
5:**570–571**
Rivera Paz, Mariano, **3**:542; **5**:543, 571
Rivera y Moncada, Fernando de,
5:**571–572**
in California, **4**:818
Yuma massacre of, **4**:811
Rivero, Agustín P., **5**:138
Rivero, Marcelo, **5**:300
Rivero y Ustariz, Mariano Eduardo,
6:128
Rivier, Jean, **6**:119
Rizal, José, **5**:222
Roa Bárcena, José María, **5**:572
Roa Bastos, Augusto, **2**:63; **4**:237;
5:**572–573**, 593
Road building, **1**:54
in Amazon region, **1**:154
Bolivia, Aniceto Arce and, **1**:221
Brazil, Rondônia, **5**:617
Costa Rica, **2**:629
El Salvador, Salvador Castañeda
Castro and, **2**:179
Guatemala, under Vicente Cerna,
2:262
See also highways
Roa Ramírez, Felipe, **2**:518
Roatán
British takeover, **2**:296
Garifuna, **2**:124
See also Bahía, Islas de (Honduras)
Roballo, Alba, **6**:228, 247
Robert-Fleury, Tony, **6**:428
Roberts, Bartholomew, **5**:253
Robertson, John Parish, **5**:**573–574**
Robertson, William Parish, **5**:**573–574**
Robertson, William Spence, **3**:696
Robinson, Jackie, **5**:930
Robinson Crusoe (Defoe), **4**:50
Robledo, Jorge de, **1**:197; **2**:411, 488
Robles, Francisco, **5**:574
Carrión, Jerónimo, vice president
under, **2**:149
Urbina, José María, and, **6**:201
use of force, **3**:42
Robles, Manuel, **4**:745
Robles, Marcos Aurelio, **2**:310; **5**:27,
574–575
Robles, Wenceslao, **5**:575
Robles Berlanga, Rosario, **5**:575
Roca, Blas, **2**:702; **5**:**575–576**
Roca, Julio Argentino, **5**:**576–578**
Araucanian resistance against, **4**:770
in art, **5**:*577*
Conquest of the Desert, **1**:261, 405;
2:577
González, Joaquín Véctor, and, **3**:480
Irigoyen, Bernardo de, and, **3**:868
Juárez Celman, Miguel, and, **4**:54
López Jordán, Ricardo, and, **4**:265
Mitre, Bartolomé, and, **4**:639

nationalization of the Sociedad de
Beneficiencia, **1**:291
in Neuquén, **4**:811
Pellegrini, Carlos, and, **5**:137
presidency, **1**:263
Quesada, Vicente, and, **5**:438
Ramos Mejía, Ezequiel, and, **5**:491
Roca-Runciman Pact (1933), **5**:579
Sáenz Peña, Luis, in, **5**:661
Sáenz Peña, Roque, and, **5**:662
Salesians with, **5**:676
Tornquist, Ernesto, financial adviser
to, **6**:106
Wilde, Eduardo, and, **6**:436
Rocafuerte, Vicente, **5**:578
Barrera, Isaac, on, **1**:496
Flores, Juan José, and, **3**:242
García Moreno, Gabriel, and, **3**:395
liberalism, **4**:189
in London, **6**:128
in Masonic Orders, **4**:407
Urbina, José María, and, **6**:201
use of force, **3**:42
Roca Rodríguez, Vicente Ramón,
5:**578–579**; **6**:201
Roca-Runciman Pact (1933), **1**:269;
4:940; **5**:579
Cárcano, Miguel Ángel, and, **2**:103
Jauretche, Arturo M., on, **4**:17
Justo, José Agustín Pedro, and, **4**:67
meat industry and, **1**:782; **4**:440
opposition by Lisandro de la Torre,
6:109
Rocha, Dardo, **5**:**579–580**
Rocha, Evaristo, **6**:271
Rocha, Glauber Pedro de Andrade,
2:416, 423–424, 818–819;
5:580, 756
Rocha, José Joaquim da, **1**:345
Rocha, Juan Eligio de la, **6**:68
Rocha, Justiniano José da, **5**:**580–581**
Rocha, Manoel Ribeiro, **5**:**581–582**
Rocha Dórea, Gumercindo, **5**:787
Rocha Lima, Henrique da, **4**:936
Rochambeau, Donatien Marie Joseph
de Vimeur de, **3**:621; **5**:582
Rocha Pita, Sebastião, **5**:**582–583**
Academia Brasílica dos Esquecidos
and, **1**:9
on nationalism, **4**:784
Roche, Paul, **6**:507
Rockefeller, Nelson Aldrich, **5**:583
Guayasamín, Oswaldo, and, **3**:572
Office of Inter-American Affairs, **6**:467
Rockefeller Foundation
Baquerizo Moreno, Alfredo, and,
1:482
disease control and, **2**:826; **5**:387
yellow fever eradication, **4**:451;
5:782–783

La sangre devota (López Velarde), **4**:232, 272

Sangre patricia (Díaz Rodríguez), **4**:232

Sanguily, Julio, **1**:42

Sanguinetti, Julio María, **1**:135, 136; **5**:713–714

constitution restored by, **6**:238

democracy under, **6**:229–231

Ferreira Aldunate, Wilson, and, **3**:221

Medina, Hugo, and, **4**:453

Pacheco Areco, Jorge, and, **5**:5

plebiscites under, **6**:245

truth commissions, **6**:252

San Ildefonso, Treaty of (1777), **1**:150; **2**:527; **5**:714–715

Brazil borders in, **5**:923

Colonia del Sacramento in, **5**:657

negotiations before, **1**:67

Río de la Plata, **5**:551

on Santa Catarina, **1**:698

San Inocencio, Victor García, **5**:417

Sanitation, **2**:434, 436; **4**:865

Buenos Aires, **1**:255; **2**:576

cholera and, **5**:390

medicine and, **4**:450

population and, **5**:296

public health and, **5**:385, 386

San Jacinto, Battle of (1836), **1**:75; **5**:715

Almonte, Juan N., at, **1**:118

Estrada, José Dolores, in, **3**:149

Seguín, Juan Nepomuceno, in, **5**:794

Sanjinés, Jorge, **2**:416, 417

San José (Costa Rica), **2**:145, 628; **5**:715–716

San José, Pact of (1969), **3**:766

San José Conference of 1906, **5**:716

San José de Flores, Pact of (1859), **1**:123; **4**:638; **5**:716–717

San José de los Naturales (Mexico City), **1**:363; **3**:378

San José del Parral (Mexico), **5**:100

San Juan (Argentina), **1**:250; **3**:1; **5**:717

San Juan (Puerto Rico), **5**:282, 718–719

fortification of, **3**:86, 292, 294

illegitimate births, **4**:388

redevelopment projects, **2**:29

Sanjuan, Pedro, **3**:387; **5**:605

San Juan del Norte. *See* Greytown (San Juan del Norte)

San Juan de Ulúa, **5**:717–718

attack on, **2**:858

fortification of, **3**:292, 293, 294; **6**:350

Hawkins, John, in, **3**:641

landing of Hernán Cortés, **6**:350

San Juan Hill, Battle of, **5**:*921*

Sanjuanistas, **5**:718

San Juan Parangaricutiro (Mexico), **5**:97

San Lorenzo (archaeological site, Mexico), **5**:719–720

iconography, **5**:345

Olmecs in, **1**:333; **4**:896; **6**:353

San Lorenzo, Battle of (1813), **3**:502; **5**:720

San Lorenzo del Escorial, Treaty of (1795), **5**:923

San Luis (Argentina), **1**:250; **5**:720–721

San Luis Potosí (Mexico), **5**:504, 721

San Marcos, University of (Peru), **5**:721–722

letrados, **4**:180

Mendoza Caamaño, José Antonio de, in, **4**:478

Sánchez, Luis, at, **5**:701

San Martín (Chilean ship), **6**:460

San Martín, Agustín de, **5**:234; **6**:322

San Martín, Cosme, **1**:435

San Martín, José Francisco de, **1**:258; **2**:*328*; **4**:792; **5**:*722*, 722–727

Alberdi, Juan Bautista, and, **1**:77

Arenales, Juan de, and, **1**:244

in Argentine independence, **5**:180

Balcarce, Mariano, and, **1**:454

and Battle of Cancha Rayada, **2**:67

Battle of Maipú, **4**:328

in Belgium, **6**:128

Belgrano, Manuel, and, **1**:536

Beruti, Antonio Luis, and, **1**:569

Bolívar, Simón, and, **1**:606–607

Bouchard, Hipólito, and, **1**:662

Castilla, Ramón, and, **2**:191

Cochrane, Thomas, and, **2**:466

Gamarra, Agustín, and, **3**:367

García del Río, Juan, and, **3**:389

Godoy Cruz, Tomás, and, **3**:453

granaderos a caballo under, **3**:502

Guayaquil Conference, **3**:569–570

Güemes, Martín, and, **3**:574

Guido, Tomás, and, **3**:590

La Serna, José de, and, **4**:143

Las Heras, Juan de, and, **4**:144

Lavalle, Juan, and, **4**:151

liberation of Chile, **2**:326

Logia de Lautaro founder, **4**:151

Luján, Virgin of, and, **4**:288

Mar, José de la, and, **4**:362

in Masonic Orders, **4**:407

Monteagudo, Bernardo de, and, **4**:670

O'Higgins, Bernardo, and, **4**:884

Orbegoso, Luis José de, and, **4**:903

Oro, Justo Santa María de, and, **4**:920

in Patria Nueva, **5**:111

in Peruvian independence, **5**:183

in Pisco, **5**:254

Pueyrredón, Juan, and, **5**:419

race and ethnicity and, **5**:469

in Republic of Guayaquil, **3**:569

Torre Tagle, José de, and, **6**:116

and war of independence, **6**:421, 422

San Miguel de Gualdape (colony), **3**:699; **6**:298

San Miguel de Piura, **5**:171

San Miguel de Tucumán (Argentina), **1**:249; **6**:148

San Nicolás, Pact of (1852), **4**:638; **5**:727–728

San Pascual, Battle of (1846), **5**:728

San Patricio, **5**:728–729

San Pedro cactus, **2**:861

San Rafael (Argentina), **5**:729

San Román, Miguel de, **2**:192; **4**:390

San Roque, Battle of (1829), **1**:818

San Salvador (El Salvador), **2**:247; **3**:91; **5**:729–730

Central American Federation capital, **4**:702

San Salvador (island). *See* Galápagos Islands

San Salvador, Convention of (1896), **1**:102

San Simón. *See* Maximón

Sansinena Company, **6**:106

Santa (Gamboa), **4**:322

Santa Ana Island. *See* Swan Islands

Santa Anna, Antonio López de, **5**:730–733

Banco de Avío dissolved by, **1**:465

Bases Orgánicas, **1**:509

in Battle of San Jacinto, **5**:715

border under, **6**:188

control of Veracruz, **6**:353

expulsion of the Spaniards, **4**:544

Gadsden Purchase and, **3**:342

Gómez Farías, Valentín, and, **3**:470–471

Gutiérrez Estrada, José María, and, **3**:602

Haro y Tamariz, Antonio de, and, **3**:639

Iglesias, José María, opposition to, **3**:783

Juárez, Benito, and, **4**:51–52

La Mesilla sold by, **4**:514

Lerdo, Miguel, and, **4**:174

liberalism, **4**:188

in Mexican-American War, **4**:556, 557

Battle of Buena Vista, **1**:799–800

Battle of Cerdo Gordo, **2**:260

military dependency, **2**:226

military dictatorship of, **4**:592

Miramón, Miguel, and, **4**:619

Sección Industria Amasadoras Mecánicas (S.I.A.M.), **2**:829
Sechín Alto (archaeological site, Peru), **5**:354, 792
Sechín Bajo (archaeological site, Peru), **5**:792
Secondary Students Union of Brazil (UBES), **1**:750
Second Congress for the Defense of Culture (Spain, 1937), **2**:134
Second Dutch West India Company, **2**:881
Second Hague Conference
  and Drago Doctrine, **2**:856
  and Luis María Drago, **2**:856
Second International Peace Conference (1907)
  Barbosa, Rui, in, **1**:486
  Batlle y Ordóñez, José, in, **1**:516
Second Vatican Council (1962–1965)
  Benedictines in, **1**:557
  Fresno, Juan Francisco, in, **3**:321
  Gutiérrez, Gustavo, in, **3**:597
  impact on Latin American Catholics, **2**:222
  implementation of doctrines through Christian base communisites, **2**:400
  liberation theology and, **4**:192, 193
  Maryknoll and, **4**:404
  Protestantism after, **5**:379
  Ruiz, Samuel, in, **5**:640
Secret Anticommunist Army (Guatemala), **2**:753
Secretariat of Foreign Relations (Mexico), **5**:487
Secret Ceremony (film, 1967), **2**:792
Secret societies, African, **1**:35
Secret societies, New Spain. *See* Caballeros Racionales, Sociedad de; Los Guadalupes
Sectoral income distribution, **3**:799, 804–805
Secuencial I (Mastrogiovanni), **4**:410
El secuestro del general (Aguilera Malta), **1**:65, 66
Secuestro Express (film, Jakobowicz), **2**:419
Secularization
  Argentina, **1**:262
    education, **3**:63
  art and, **1**:344
  Bolivia, **6**:3
    Wilde, Eduardo, and, **6**:436
  Chile, **2**:351
    under Domingo Santa María, **2**:334
    Errázuriz Zañartu, Federico, and, **3**:130
    under Federico Errázuriz, **2**:331
    Liberla Party and, **2**:367
  education and, **3**:62, 63

Mexico, **2**:44
missions in California, **2**:36
modern, **6**:453
Nicaragua, **6**:514
La seda mágica (Azar), **1**:422
Sedeño, Antonio de, **5**:792
Sedeño, Arévalo, **3**:301
Sedition, definition in Guatemalan law, **1**:247
"Seditionists," *revoltosos* and, **5**:529
Seelinger, Hélios, **1**:779
Se está haciendo tarde (final en laguna) (Agustín), **1**:70
Segall, Lasar, **1**:576; **5**:793
Segiliú, Bergoñer de. *See* Bergaño y Villegas, Simón
Segond, Pablo, **4**:816
Segovia, Andrés, **1**:486, 499
Seguín, Juan José María Erasmo, **5**:793–794
Seguín, Juan Nepomuceno, **5**:794
Seguir andando (film, Solanas), **5**:886
Segundo, Compay. *See* Compay Segundo (Francisco Repilado)
Segundo, Juan Luis
  liberation theology, **2**:222; **4**:23, 194
  Maryknoll publication of, **4**:404
Segundo Cuarteto (Ginastera), **3**:438
Segura, Pancho, **5**:932
Segura, Vicente, **5**:485
"Segura êle" (Lamartine), **5**:258
Se habla español (Fuguet and Paz Soldán, eds.), **4**:239
Seibal (archaeological site, Guatemala), **1**:125; **2**:853; **5**:794–795
Seine Laundresses (Santa María), **5**:740
Seineldin, Muhammad Alí, **3**:881
Seis ensayos en busca de nuestra expresión (Henríquez Ureña), **1**:313; **3**:664; **4**:233
Seís momentos de esperanza (Mir), **4**:618
Seixas, Raul, **2**:472
Selecta (magazine, Brazil), **1**:506
Selected Poetry (Melo Neto), **4**:467
Selected Poetry of Delmira Agustini: Poetics of Eros, **1**:71
Selena (film, Nava), **4**:798; **5**:795
Selena (Selena Quintanilla-Pérez), **5**:795
Selena Live! (album), **5**:795
Selenia (journal, Costa Rica), **2**:831
Seler, Eduard, **4**:493
Self-Portrait with Easel (Macció), **4**:302
Selkirk, Alexander, **4**:50; **6**:130
Selk'nams, **5**:795–796
  music, **4**:756
  Patagones and, **5**:107
  Yamana compared to, **6**:478
Sell, Barry D., **6**:68
Selva (Ecuador), **5**:796–797

Selva (Peru), **5**:797
Selva, Buenaventura, **3**:695
Selva, Salomón de la, **1**:682
Selva Alegre, Marqués de, **3**:41; **5**:456
Selva de pedra (telenovela), **2**:442
O selvagem (Magalhães), **3**:160
Selva Lacandona. *See* Lacandon Forest (Mexico)
La Semana (periodical, Puerto Rico), **2**:64
Semana (magazine, Guatemala), **6**:469
Semana da Pátria (Ribeiro), **5**:538
Semana de Arte Moderna. *See* Modern Art Week
La semana en colores (Garro), **3**:407
Semanario de Agricultura (newspaper, Argentina), **6**:368
Semanario de Agricultura, Industria y Comercio (newspaper, Argentina), **1**:255
El Semanario de Avisos y Conocimientos Útiles (newspaper, Paraguay), **1**:564; **4**:255; **6**:9
El Semanario del Nuevo Reino de Granada (newspaper, Santa Fe de Bogotá), **1**:597; **2**:28
Semanario Mundo Gráfico (weekly, Panama), **5**:837
Semanario Patriótico Americano (newspaper, Mexico), **5**:446
El Semanario Republicano (Chile), **3**:872
Semana Roja (Chile, 1905), **5**:797
Semana Trágica (Argentina, 1919), **2**:126; **5**:797–798
  Dellepiane, Luis J., **2**:767
  Jews in, **4**:26
  Patriotic League and, **1**:286
Semences (journal, Haiti), **5**:217
La semilla estéril (Tallet), **6**:10
Seminar on the Acquisition of Latin American Library Materials (SALALM), **1**:560; **4**:198
Seminoles, **4**:381
Semipublic services, **5**:392, 810, 811, 815
Semmel, Bernard, **3**:791
Sempreviva (Callado), **2**:38
Senado da câmara, **5**:798–799
Señales (Rojo), **5**:604
Las señales furtivas (González Martínez), **3**:489
Sendeño, Antonio, **4**:274
Sendero Luminoso. *See* Shining Path
Los senderos ocultos (González Martínez), **3**:489
Sendic, Raúl, **3**:582; **5**:799
Senghor, Léopold Sédar
  on Bélance, René, **1**:531
  Brierre, Jean-Fernand, and, **1**:781
  and Depestre, René, **2**:793
  négritude and, **4**:803

Temple of the Feathered Serpent,
  5:439
  ties with Tikal, **6**:79
  tourism, **6**:121
Tepanecs
  Azcapotzalco, capital city of, **1**:423
  conquest of Tetzcoco, **6**:55
  Itzcoatl's rebellion against, **3**:887
  under Nezahualcoyotl, **4**:820
  Otomí and, **4**:939
Tepatitlán, **4**:7
Tepatitlán, Battle of (1929), **2**:657
Tepeyac Institute (Ecuador), **5**:376
Tepito (Mexico City), **6**:50–51
Teque Indians, **3**:175
Tequesta, **6**:51
Tequila
  Guadalajara, **3**:519
  harvesting agave bulbs, **1**:*89*
  Jalisco, **4**:7
Tequitqui style, **1**:342
Teran, Tomas, **4**:38
Terán, Victor, **6**:505
Tercera Conferencia Internacional de la
  Alimentación (1939), **4**:865
Tercera residencia (Neruda), **4**:233,
  808
Teresa (telenovela, Mexico), **3**:643
Teresa Cristina (empress of Brazil),
  6:51–52
Teresa d'Avila, Saint, **2**:749
Teresa de Mier, Servando, **4**:605
Teresina (Brazil), **5**:763; **6**:52
Terezhina. *See* Teresina (Brazil)
Ternura (Mistral), **4**:634, 635
Terra, Gabriel, **6**:52
  Baldomir, Alfredo, and, **1**:454
  Battlism of, **1**:790
  Blanco Acevedo, Eduardo, and,
    1:587
  colegiado under, **6**:234–235
  Colorado Party and, **6**:249
  constitutions under, **6**:236–237
  Gómez, Eugenio, and, **3**:463
  Herrerismo and, **3**:683
  opposition of Enrique Amorim,
    1:164
  reforms by, **6**:225–226
Terra, Juan Pablo, **6**:248
Terra: Struggles of the Landless
  (Salgado), **5**:678
Terra de sol (Barroso), **1**:506
Terra em transe (film, Rocha), **2**:424;
  5:580
Terra Estrangeira (film, Salles),
  5:681–682
Terra Livre (journal, Brazil), **1**:753
Terra nostra (Fuentes), **2**:851; **3**:332
Terrazas, Bartolomeu de, **6**:443
Terrazas, Luis, **4**:559; **6**:52–53
Terrazas-Creel family, **2**:315
Terreiro do Gantois, **4**:481

Terrenos baldíos, land reform and, **4**:501
Terrero, Máximo, **5**:628
Terronistas (Guatemala), **4**:687
Terrorism, **6**:53–55
  Argentina, **4**:396
  Argentine Civic Legion and, **1**:286
  Bahamas tourism affected by, **1**:442
  Chile
    under Augusto Pinochet, **2**:346
    Movement of the Revolutionary
      Left and, **2**:369
  drug cartels and, **2**:863
  filmmakers victims of, **2**:416
  Guantánamo Bay, **3**:530
  Guatemala
    Lucas García, Fernando Romeo,
      and, **3**:550
    organizations in, **3**:565–566
  handling by military forces, **1**:320
  Islamic Jihad, **1**:206; **3**:883
  Jews and, **4**:28
  migration and, **4**:591
  politics of, women and, **6**:451
  state-sponsored
    Argentina, **2**:821–823
    and death squads, **2**:753–754
    Tarata (Calle tarata), **6**:19
    Tri-Border Area (Argentina, Brazil,
      and Paraguay), **1**:206; **6**:54
  by United Self-Defense Forces of
    Colombia, **2**:525
Terry, Clark, **5**:592
Tertulia Patriótica (Guatemala), **1**:507
Terzián, Alicia, **4**:747
Tesis andinista (Mendoza), **4**:477
Tesoro de la lengua guaraní (Ruiz),
  5:643
Testa, Clorindo, **3**:512, 517; **5**:507
Testa group (Brazil), **4**:648
Los testigos de afuera (Martínez), **4**:395
Testimonal theater, **6**:72–73
Testimonio (magazine, Peru), **3**:693
Testimonios sobre Mariana (Garro),
  3:407
Tetzcoco (Mexico), **6**:55
  history by Alva Ixtlilxochitl, **1**:128
  under Nezahualcoyotl, **4**:820–821
  under Nezahualpilli, **4**:821
  Triple Alliance and, **4**:502, 766
Texas, **6**:55–56
  Adams-Onís Treaty and, **1**:22
  boundaries
    disputes, **6**:187–191
    Talamantes, Melchor de, and, **6**:8
  Cass, Lewis, and annexation of,
    2:178
  colonization, **4**:817–818
    Anglo colony, **1**:402
    La Salle, René-Robert, Sieur de,
      and, **4**:139

  filibustering in, **4**:818
  Fredonian Rebellion, **3**:304
  Hispanics in, **3**:699
  League of United Latin American
    Citizens, **4**:157
  León, Alonso de, in, **4**:169
  livestock, **4**:243
  Mexican Americans in, **3**:701, 702,
    705
  Nacogdoches, **4**:765
  regionalism, **5**:513
  Seguín, Juan Nepomuceno, in,
    5:794
  Spanish influence in, **1**:75; **3**:700
  U.S. annexation of, **5**:515
  See also San Antonio
Texas, Republic of
  declaration of independence, **6**:56,
    57
  Kinney, Henry, and, **4**:80
  Lamar, Mirabeau, **4**:122
  Texas Constitution (1876), **3**:702
  Texas Rangers, Mexican Americans
    and, **3**:701
  Texas Revolution (1835–1836),
    4:512–513; **6**:56–57
    Filísola, Vicente, in, **3**:234
    Houston, Sam, in, **3**:748
    Lamar, Mirabeau, in, **4**:122
    Santa Anna and, **5**:732
    Seguín, Juan José, in, **5**:793
    Seguín, Juan Nepomuceno, in,
      5:794
  U.S. annexation and, **3**:700; **6**:179
  See also Alamo, Battle of the (1836);
    San Jacinto, Battle of (1836)
Texcoco. *See* Tetzcoco (Mexico)
Tex-Mex music, **5**:795
Textile industry, **6**:57–63
  colonial era, **6**:57–59
    as cottage industry, **3**:38; **5**:824
    Quito, **3**:35, 37
    Velasco, Luis de (the Younger) and,
      6:306
  modern textiles, **6**:59–63
    Argentina, **1**:283
      Godoy Cruz, Tomás, in, **3**:453
      impact of Bourbon economic
        reforms, **1**:250
    Belize, **1**:537, 544
    Brazil, **6**:61
      Alagoas, **1**:72
      Aracaji, **1**:207
      factory commissions, **3**:172–173
      Maceió, **4**:303
      Santa Catarina, **5**:733
      Teresina, **6**:52
    Chile, **6**:61
      Bío-Bío River, **1**:580

Villagrá, Gaspar Pérez de, **6:374–375**
Villagra, Pedro de, **4**:150; **6**:374
Villagrán, Francisco de. *See* Villagra,
  Francisco de
Villagrán, José, **6**:413
Villagrán, José María (El Chito)
  (Mexican insurgent), **6**:375
Villagrán, Julián, **6**:375
Villagrán Kramer, Francisco, **6:375–376**
Villa Jardin (band), **2**:24
Villalba, Jóvito, **6**:376
Villalba, Juan de, **1**:671; **4**:600; **5**:636
Villa-Lobos, Heitor, **6:376–378**, *377*
  Barbosa-Lima, Carlos, and, **1**:486
  and *choro*, **2**:39
  Fernandez, Oscar Lorenzo, on, **3**:210
  Jobim, António Carlos, inspired by,
    4:38
  Malfatti, Anita Catarina, and, **4**:335
  Mignone, Francisco, and, **4**:571
  in Modern Art Week, **4**:647
  modinhas, **4**:649
  monument to by Vasco Prado, **5**:334
  nationalism of, **4**:745, 785
  Nazareth, Ernesto, and, **4**:801
  Nepomuceno, Alberto, and, **4**:807
  travels to Europe, **1**:147
Villa-Lobos, Lucília Guimarães, **1**:147;
    4:335, 647
Villalobos, Marceto, **4**:371
Villalonga, Jorge, **2**:493; **4**:352;
    6:378–379
Villalpando, Alberto, **4**:744
Villalpando, Cristóbal de, **6**:379
Villamizar, Ramírez, **1**:359
Villaneuva, Gabino, **5**:651
Villanueva, Carlos Raúl, **6:379–380**
Villanueva, Patricia, **1**:361
Villarán, Manuel Vicente, **6**:380
Villarica (Chile), **6**:264
Villa Rica (Costa), **4**:220
Villarino, J., **4**:669
Villaroel, Gaspar de, **6:380–381**
Villa Rojas, Alfonso, **4**:434
Villarreal, Antonio J., **2**:814
Villarreal, Francisco, **6**:12
Villarrica (Paraguay), **6**:380
Villarroel López, Gualberto, **1**:623;
    3:729; **5**:123; **6:381–382**
  in Bolivian Communist Party, **1**:636
  Federation of Bolivian University
    Students and, **1**:633
  Syndical Federation of Bolivian
    Mineworkers and, **1**:634
Villasana, José María, **1**:71
Villas Bôas, Cláudio, **6:382**, 472, 473
Villas Bôas, Leonardo, **6**:382
Villas Bôas, Orlando, **6:382**, 472, 473
Villaurrutia, Jacobo de, **3**:174;
    6:382–383
  Economic Society of Guatemala and,
    3:559

Villaurrutia, Xavier, **4**:236; **6**:70,
    383–384
  edited by Alí Chumacero, **2**:406
  member of Los Contemporáneos,
    2:588
  vanguardism, **4**:234
Villaverde, Cirilo, **6**:384
Villavicencio (Colombia), **4**:246; **6**:384
Villazón, Eliodoro, **6:384–385**
Villeda Morales, Ramón, **3**:362,
    738–739; **4**:283; **5**:584; **6:385**,
    438
Villegaignon, Nicolas Durand de,
    1:695; **3**:312; **4**:176; **6**:386
Villegas, Juan de, **4**:274
Villegas, Micaela. *See* La Perricholi
Villegas, Oscar, **6**:72, **386–387**
Villena, Federico, **4**:742
Villoro, Juan, **4**:239–240
Villoro, Luis, **6**:387
Viña del Mar (Chile), **6**:387
Vinagre, Francisco, **2**:8
Vincencio de Ripperda, Juan María,
    4:765
Vincent, Sténio Joseph, **1**:546; **5**:366,
    632; **6:387–388**
A Vindication of the Rights of Women
    (Wollstonecraft), **3**:199
Viñes y Martorell, Benito, **3**:770;
    6:388–389
Vineyards. *See* wine industry
Viola, Paulinho da (Paulo César Batista
    de Faia), **4**:860; **5**:693; **6**:389
Viola, Roberto Eduardo, **3**:358;
    6:365, 389
Viola de Lereno (Barbosa), **1**:485
Violencia, La (Colombia), **2**:505–506,
    506, 520; **6:389–391**
  Angel, Albalucía, on, **1**:183
  Caballero Calderón, Eduardo, on, **2**:5
  and creation of the National Front,
    2:522
  Independent Republics and, **3**:812
  influence on Gustavo Álvarez
    Gardeazábal, **1**:137
  migration and, **3**:724
Viotti da Costa, Emilia, **1**:708
Viracocha (Inca god), **3**:797; **6**:87,
    391–392
  Chanca war under, **3**:794
  messianic movements, **4**:496
Viracocha Inca, overthrown by
    Pachacuti, **5**:2
La virgen de los sicarios (Vallejo), **4**:239
Virgen del Perdón (Pereyns),
    5:151–152
La virgen del Sol (Mera), **4**:484
Virginia (Montero), **4**:742
Virgin Islands, **6:392–393**
  profile, **6**:393
  British, **2**:117
  map, **6**:*392*

Virginius Affair, **6**:47–48, **393–394**
Virgin of Guadalupe. *See* Guadalupe,
    Virgin of
Virgin of Guadalupe (Ehcave), **3**:6
Virgin of Luján, **2**:221
Virgin of Quito, **5**:458
Virgin of Remedios, **3**:521
Virgin of the Rosary, shrine of, **2**:391
Viridiana (film), **5**:238
*Los virreyes españoles en América
    durante el gobierno de la casa de
    Austria* (Hanke, ed.), **3**:637
Viru Valley Project, **1**:226
Visão do paraíso (Holanda), **3**:730
Visca, María, **2**:458
Viscardo y Guzmán, Juan Pablo,
    4:791; **6**:394
Visconti, Eliseu d'Angelo, **1**:349, 355,
    576; **6:394–395**
Visión (magazine), **4**:48
Visión de Anáhuac (Reyes), **1**:313;
    4:232
*Visiones del siglo XX colombiano a
    través de sus protagonistas ya
    muertosas* (López Michelsen),
    4:267
Visita, visitador, **2**:291; **6:395**
  of Chucuito, **2**:405
  Council of the Indies and, **2**:645
  Gálvez, José de, and, **3**:360–361
  residencia and, **5**:524
  Rubí, Marqués de, **5**:636
  visita general by Francisco de Toledo,
    6:98
Visita de Jayanca (Gama), **1**:512
The Visit to the River Negro (Blanes),
    5:*577*
Viso, Antonio del, **2**:103
*Visoes: Maurício Albano e Rachel de
    Queiroz* (Queiroz), **5**:433
Vistas de México (Egerton), **3**:74
Vitale, Ida, **5**:483, 484
Vitalino Pereira dos Santos, Mestre,
    6:395–396
Viteri y Ungo, Jorge, **3**:398; **4**:334,
    335; **6**:396
Vitier, Cintio, **6:396–397**
Vitores, Francisco, **3**:39
Vitória (Brazil), **3**:139; **6**:397
Vitoria, Francisco de, **5**:223; **6**:350,
    397–398
VIVA (periodical, Peru), **3**:203
Viva Cuba (film, Cremata Malberti),
    2:421
¡Viva mi desgracia! (film), **3**:835
Vivanco, Manuel Ignacio, **1**:642;
    2:192; **3**:506; **6**:398
  in Marshals of Ayacucho, **4**:390
Vivanco, Moises, **5**:959
Vivanco-Pareja Treaty, **5**:217; **6**:8
Vivanco-Pareja Treaty (1865), **6**:398
Vivar para ver (Aridjis), **1**:312

Viva Zapata! (film), **5:**443
Víveros Barradas, Francisco.
  See Paquita la del Barrio
    (Francisca Víveros Barradas)
Vives, Francisco, **1:**22
Viviendo (Peri Rossi), **5:**159
El vivo al pollo (Arrufat), **1:**333
Vizcaíno, Sebastián, **1:**64; **6:**398–399
Vladimiroff, Pierre, **2:**592
Vlía (Gatón Arce), **3:**413
Vocabulario de la Lengua Aymara
    (Bertonio), **1:**429
Vocabularios (Velasco), **6:**304
Voces de primavera (film), **5:**524
Vodun (Voodoo, Vaudun), **1:**34, 35;
    6:399–400
  in art, **3:**772
  drums, **4:**758
  and François Duvalier, **2:**883
  Haiti, **3:**627; **5:**366
  lwa in, **4:**296–297
  Sonthonax, Léger, on, **5:**900
  under Soulouque, Faustin, **5:**908
*The Voice and the Guitar of Jose
    Feliciano* (album), **3:**197
Voice of Xtabay (album, Sumac), **5:**959
Volador dance, **6:**120, **400**
Volcanoes, **6:**400–402
  in Arequipa, **1:**246
  Ecuador, **5:**545
  Ilopango, **4:**423
  León (Nicaragua), **4:**169
  Martinique and Guadeloupe, **4:**398
  Montserrat, **4:**685
  Paricutín (Mexico), **5:**97
  Saint Vincent, **5:**669
  Sierra Madre, **4:**422
Volio Jiménez, Jorge, **2:**632–633;
    6:402
Volkswagen, **3:**832, *832*
Volleyball, **5:**929, 932, *932,* 937
Volontaires de la Sécurité Nationale
    (VSN, Haiti), **2:**883; **6:**103–104
  See also Tonton Macoutes
Volpi, Jorge, **4:**239
Volstead Act (U.S., 1919), **6:**190
Voltaire, **5:**801
Volta Redonda (Brazil), **6:**402–403
Vómonos patria a caminar (Castillo),
    2:194
Vônagre, Antônio, **2:**8
Von Liebig, Justus, **4:**440
Von Vacano, Arturo, **6:**403
Voodoo. *See* Vodun, Voodoo, Vaudun
La vorágine (Rivera), **4:**235; **5:**567
Voroganos, **2:**33
Vorwärts (German Socialist Club), **1:**300
Voting
  double simultaneous, **6:**223, 224
  Guatemala, **3:**545, *545*
  Hispanics in the United States,
    3:698–699, 704, 705, 717

secret ballot, **2:**775, 845
  Uruguay, **6:**231
  See also elections; suffrage
Voyage dans l'Amérique méridionale
    (Orbigny), **4:**904
Voyage pittoresque et historique au Brésil
    (Debret), **2:**755
La voz adolorida (Leñero), **4:**167
A Voz Adorável de Clara Nunes
    (album, Nunes), **4:**860
"La Voz Cultural de la Nación" (radio
    program, Paraguay), **2:**258
A Voz do Trabalhador (newspaper,
    Brazil), **1:**740
"Vozes d'áfrica" (Castro Alves), **2:**200
La voz que nos hablamos (Appleyard),
    1:204
Vrangel, F. P., **5:**913
"Vuela la Paloma" (song), **5:**592
El vuelo de la reina (Martínez), **4:**395
Vuelta (magazine, Mexico), **3:**85;
    5:121
Vuelta (periodical), **2:**60; **4:**90
La vuelta al nido (film, Torres Ríos),
    2:414
La vuelta completa (Saer), **5:**663
La vuelta de Martín Fierro
    (Hernández), **4:**229–230
Vueltas del citrillo (film, Casals), **2:**172
Vy'araity (literary group), **2:**62

W

W. K. Kellogg Foundation, **3:**844
Waddington, Andrucha, **2:**423
Wafer, Jam, **1:**36
Wafer, Lionel, **4:**96
Wagener, Zacharias, **4:**418
Wagley, Charles Walter, **5:**270; **6:**405
Waika. *See* Yanomami
Wailer, Bunny, **4:**380
Wailers (band), **4:**380
The Wake (Jara), **1:**352
Wakeham, Roberto, **1:**236
Walcott, Derek, **6:**405–407
Waldseemüller, Martin, **1:**158; **2:**155;
    6:358
Walker, Gilbert, **3:**87
Walker, Robert, **4:**720
Walker, William, **6:**407–408
  Barrios, Gerardo, and, **1:**500
  Estrada, José Dolores, resistance to,
    3:149
  filibustering expeditions, **3:**233;
    6:188
  Goicuría y Cabrera, Domingo, and,
    3:456
  Granada burned by, **3:**501
  Guardiola, Santos, and, **3:**537

Guatemala against, **3:**542
  in Honduras, **3:**735
  Jerez, Máximo, and, **4:**19–20
  liberalism, **4:**188
  Martínez, Tomás, and, **4:**394
  Mora, Juan Rafael, and, **2:**630;
    3:525; **4:**698–699
  Muñoz, José Trinidad, and, **4:**733
  in National War, **2:**281; **4:**787–788;
    6:510
  Nicaragua invasion, **2:**231, 384;
    4:824–825
  Paredes, Mariano, and, **5:**95
  Rivas, Patricio, and, **5:**563
  slavery reintroduced by, **6:**179
Walking Together with the People (Pérez
    Esquivel), **5:**156
Wallace (Willis), Peter, **1:**540;
    6:408–409
Wallerstein, Immanuel, **3:**788
Wal-Mart, **4:**107
Walsh, James E., **4:**404
Walsin-Esterhazy, C. F., **1:**809
Walter, Vernon A., **1:**732
Wandenkolk, Eduardo, **5:**674
Waorani, **4:**917
War and Peace (Portinari), **5:**307
*The War Between the United States and
    Mexico* (Nebel), **4:**803
Warchavchik, Gregori, **1:**239
Ward, Bernardo, **5:**385
Ward, Henry George, **5:**277; **6:**409
Ward, Thomas, **3:**491
Warhaftige Historia (Staden), **5:**939
Wari. *See* Huari (archaeological site,
    Peru)
Warihios, **2:**315
Wari-Kayan Necropolis (Paracas),
    5:57, 58
The War in Paraguay (Thompson),
    6:75
Warner, John, **5:**410
Warner, Thomas, **5:**667
Warner, William Lloyd, **2:**183
Warnes, Ignacio, **5:**522
War of 1812
  Florida and, **3:**249; **6:**179
  Porter, David, in, **5:**305
War of Four Days (1932), **1:**646;
    6:409–410
War of Independence (Argentina),
    4:121–122, **6:**420, 421
  Battle of San Lorenzo, **5:**720
  Belgrano, Manuel, in, **1:**535–536
  Forbes, John Murray, on, **3:**260
  Gorriti, Juan, in, **3:**498
  in Jujuy, **4:**62
  Moreno, Mariano, in, **4:**709
  Paz, José María, in, **5:**118–119
  Pueyrredón, Juan, in, **5:**419
  Saavedra, Cornelio de, in, **5:**650

X

Y